AMERICAN HISTORY

THE MODERN ERA SINCE 1865

AMERICAN HISTORY

THE MODERN ERA SINCE 1865

DONALD A. RITCHIE

McGraw-Hill

New York, New York   Columbus, Ohio   Mission Hills, California   Peoria, Illinois

Author

Donald A. Ritchie is Associate Historian of the United States Senate Historical Office. Dr. Ritchie received his doctorate in American history from the University of Maryland after service in the U.S. Marine Corps. He has taught American history at various levels, from high school to the university. He edits the Historical Series of the Senate Foreign Relations Committee and is the author of several books, including *Press Gallery: Congress and the Washington Correspondents,* which received the Organization of American Historians' Richard W. Leopold Prize. Dr. Ritchie has served as president of the Oral History Association and as a council member of the American Historical Association.

Glencoe/McGraw-Hill

A Division of The **McGraw·Hill** Companies

ISBN 0-02-822365-9 (Student Edition)
ISBN 0-02-822366-7 (Teacher's Wraparound Edition)

2 3 4 5 6 7 8 9 10 RRW/MC 02 01 00 99 98 97 96

Academic Consultants

Sarah Witham Bednarz
Visiting Assistant Professor
Texas A&M University
College Station, Texas

Barbara Anne Egypt
Bruce. R. Watkins Cultural Heritage Center
Kansas City, Missouri

Delbert A. Jurden
Instructor (retired)
Johnson County Community College
Overland Park, Kansas

Keith Ian Polakoff
Associate Vice President for Academic Affairs and
  Dean of Graduate Students
California State University, Long Beach
Long Beach, California

John F. Waukechon
Assistant Instructor
University of Texas
Austin, Texas

Teacher Reviewers

Rose Marie Floyd
Social Studies Teacher
Jefferson Davis High School
Montgomery, Alabama

Janice A. Hardeman
Department Chair, Social Studies
Ephrata High School
Ephrata, Pennsylvania

George W. Henry, Jr.
Teacher, Chair History
  Department
St. Mark's School
Salt Lake City, Utah

Marjorie B. Hollowell
Chairperson, Social Studies
  Department
John A. Holmes High School
Edenton, North Carolina

Alan Kaplan
Social Studies Educator
Huntington High School
Huntington, West Virginia

James LaMastus
Social Studies Teacher
North High School
Evansville, Indiana

Michael L. Manson, Ed.D.
Teacher of Social Studies
  (retired)
Townsend Harris High School
Flushing, New York

Todd Kent Meyer
History Teacher
Watertown Senior High School
Watertown, South Dakota

Susan P. Owens
Social Studies Teacher
K-12 Department Chair
Howard L. Goff Middle School
East Greenbush, New York

Simmie G. Plummer
History Teacher
Valley High School
Albuquerque, New Mexico

Irene Ramnarine
Secondary Social Studies
  Resource Teacher
Brevard County School Board
Melbourne, Florida

James M. Wolfe
History Teacher
Suitland University High School
Forestville, Maryland

Teacher's Wraparound Edition

Contents

◄ The first African American members of Congress are shown in this Currier and Ives print. The first African American senator, Hiram R. Revels, is at the far left.

CLASSROOM RESOURCES

General Douglas MacArthur

Boy Scouts of America
Handbook

Student Edition

Conestoga wagon ▼

Contents

▲ Revolutionary War drum

Cattle branding iron

1914 Mercer Runabout

Allies Day, by Childe Hassam, 1916 ▼

▲ Prohibition agent's badge

▲ Vietnam Veterans statue, Washington, D.C.

▼ 1986 *Challenger* Crew

Features
Cultural Kaleidoscope

Linking Past and Present

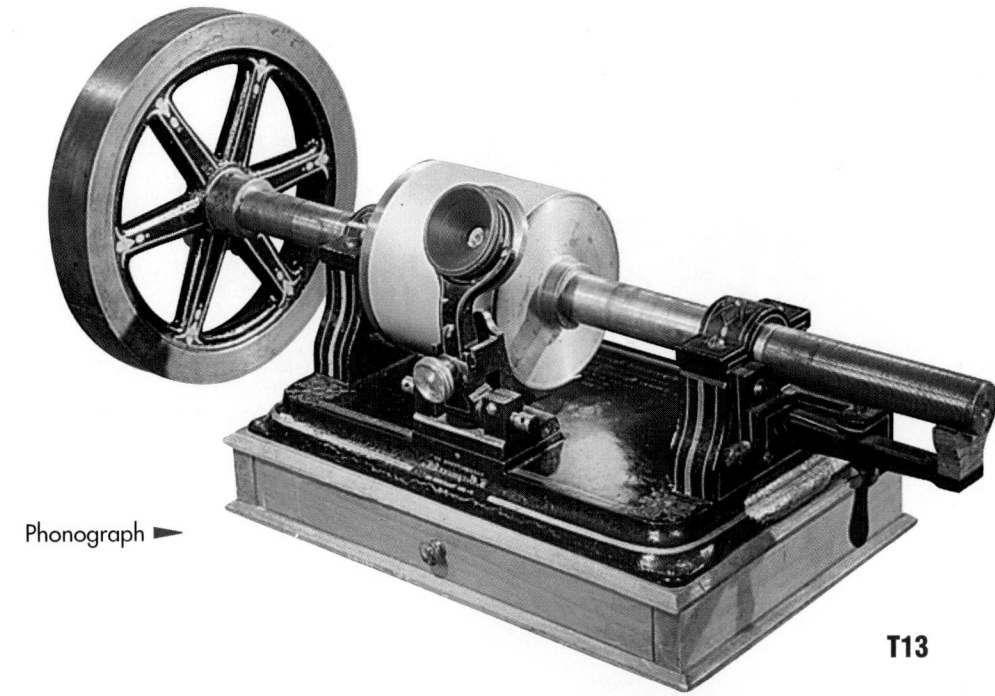

Compact discs and player

Phonograph ►

Features

History
AND

BUILDING SKILLS

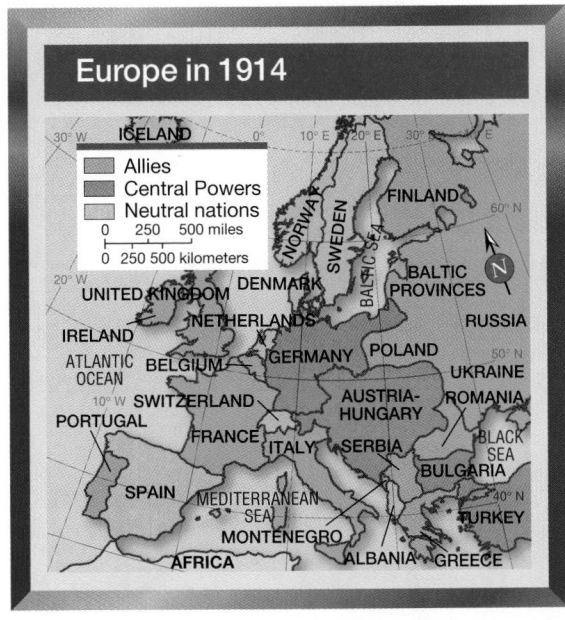

Europe in 1914

Allies
Central Powers
Neutral nations

0 250 500 miles
0 250 500 kilometers

ICELAND
NORWAY
SWEDEN
FINLAND
UNITED KINGDOM
DENMARK
BALTIC PROVINCES
IRELAND
NETHERLANDS
RUSSIA
ATLANTIC OCEAN
BELGIUM
GERMANY
POLAND
UKRAINE
PORTUGAL
SWITZERLAND
AUSTRIA-HUNGARY
ROMANIA
FRANCE
ITALY
SERBIA
BLACK SEA
BALTIC SEA
BULGARIA
SPAIN
MEDITERRANEAN SEA
TURKEY
MONTENEGRO
ALBANIA
GREECE
AFRICA

Features

Langston Hughes ➤

American Literary Heritage

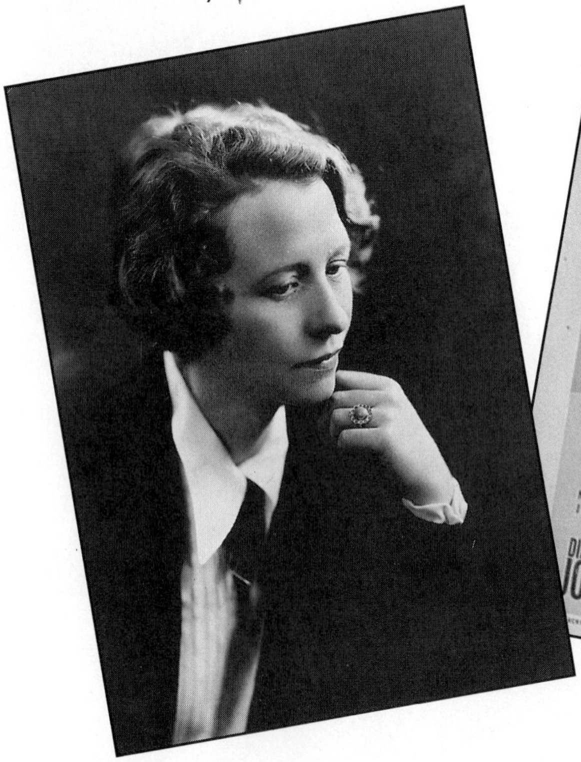

▼ Movie poster for
The Grapes of Wrath

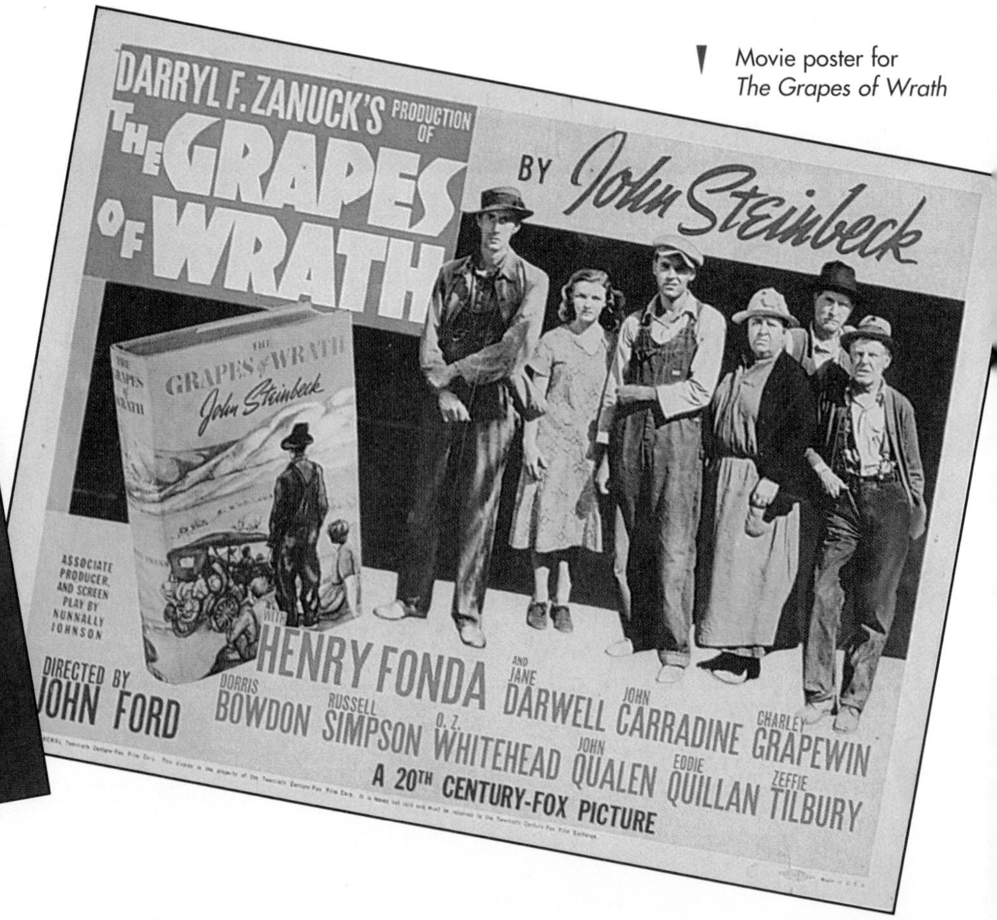

Edna St. Vincent Millay ▼

DARRYL F. ZANUCK'S PRODUCTION OF

THE GRAPES OF WRATH

BY *John Steinbeck*

THE
GRAPES OF
WRATH
John Steinbeck

ASSOCIATE
PRODUCER
AND SCREEN
PLAY BY
NUNNALLY
JOHNSON

DIRECTED BY
JOHN FORD

DORRIS
BOWDON

RUSSELL
SIMPSON

O. Z.
WHITEHEAD

HENRY FONDA

AND JANE
DARWELL

JOHN
CARRADINE

CHARLEY
GRAPEWIN

JOHN
QUALEN

EDDIE
QUILLAN

ZEFFIE
TILBURY

A 20TH CENTURY-FOX PICTURE

AMERICAN PORTRAITS

Eleanor Roosevelt
1884–1962 ►

Features

Maps

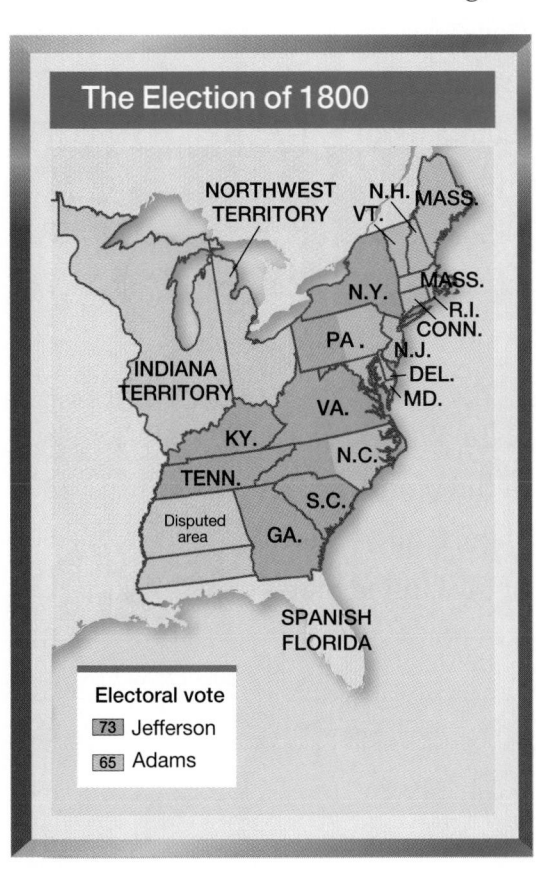

The Election of 1800

NORTHWEST TERRITORY
INDIANA TERRITORY
N.H.
VT.
MASS.
N.Y.
MASS.
R.I.
CONN.
PA.
N.J.
DEL.
MD.
VA.
KY.
N.C.
TENN.
S.C.
Disputed area
GA.
SPANISH FLORIDA

Electoral vote
73 Jefferson
65 Adams

Features

Maps continued

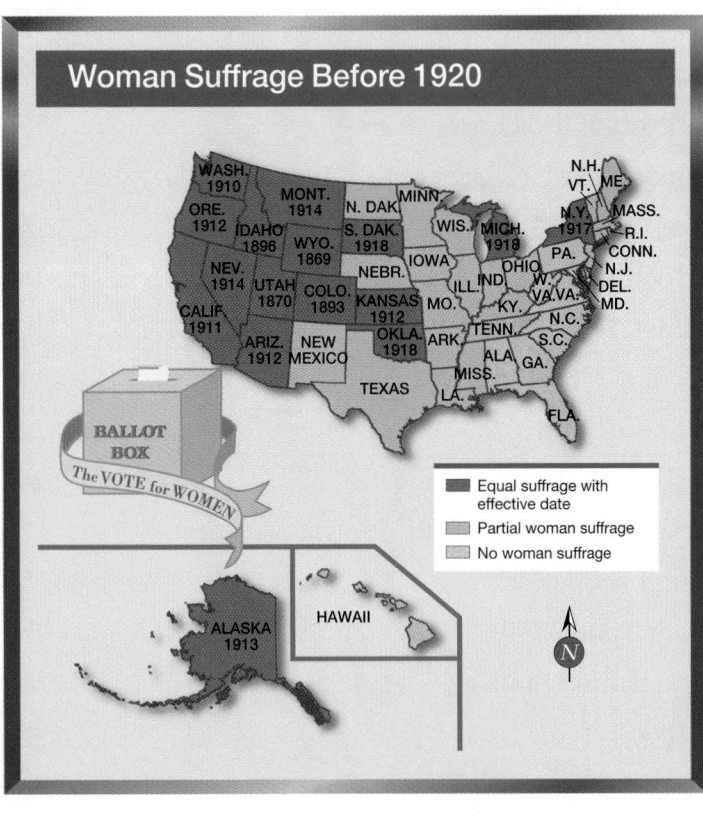

Charts, Graphs, and Tables

Scope and Sequence

Themes and Concepts	Chapter 1	Chapter 2	Chapter 3	Chapter 4	
American Democracy	Sec. 3	Sec. 1-4	Sec. 1,2	Sec. 1,3	
Civil Rights and Liberties	Sec. 3,4	Sec. 1-3	Sec. 1	Sec. 2-4	
Economic Development	Sec. 1,2,4	Sec. 3,4	Sec. 1	Sec. 1-3	
Geography and Environment	Sec. 1,2,4	Sec. 2,3	Sec. 2-4	Sec. 1,2	
Conflict and Cooperation	Sec. 2-4	Sec. 1-3	Sec. 1-4	Sec. 1,3-4	
Influence of Technology	Sec. 1		Sec. 3	Sec. 1,2,4	
The Individual and Family Life	Sec. 3,4	Sec. 1,3	Sec. 2	Sec. 2,4	
Ideas, Beliefs, and Institutions	Sec. 1,3,4	Sec. 2-4	Sec. 2	Sec. 2,4	
Cultural Diversity	Sec. 1,3	Sec. 2	Sec. 3	Sec. 2,3	
U.S. Role in World Affairs		Sec. 3	Sec. 2-4	Sec. 1	
Skills					
Social Studies Skills					
Critical Thinking Skills		Sec. 1	Sec. 3	Sec. 4	
Study and Writing Skills	Sec. 3				

Chapter 5	Chapter 6	Chapter 7	Chapter 8	Chapter 9
Sec. 1-4	Sec. 2,3	Sec. 1	Sec. 1,3	Sec. 2,4
Sec. 3-5	Sec. 1-3	Sec. 1,3	Sec. 3	Sec. 1-4
Sec. 1,2,4,5	Sec. 1-3	Sec. 2,3	Sec. 1-3	Sec. 1,3,4
Sec. 1-3,5	Sec. 2,3	Sec. 1-3	Sec. 1	Sec. 3,4
Sec. 1-6	Sec. 1,3	Sec. 1	Sec. 3	Sec. 1-3
Sec. 2,4	Sec. 3	Sec. 1,3	Sec. 1,2	Sec. 4
Sec. 1-3,5	Sec. 1,3	Sec. 1-3	Sec. 1,3	Sec. 1,3,4
Sec. 2,3,5,6	Sec. 1,3	Sec. 1	Sec. 3	Sec. 1-4
Sec. 2,3,5	Sec. 1-3	Sec. 1,3		Sec. 3
Sec. 1,4			Sec. 1,2	
		Sec. 1	Sec. 3	
Sec. 2	Sec. 2			
				Sec. 1

Scope and Sequence

Themes and Concepts	Chapter 10	Chapter 11	Chapter 12	Chapter 13	
American Democracy	Sec. 1-3	Sec. 1,2	Sec. 1,3,4	Sec. 2	
Civil Rights and Liberties	Sec. 2	Sec. 1,3	Sec. 3	Sec. 1,2	
Economic Development	Sec. 1,2	Sec. 1-2	Sec. 1-2	Sec. 1	
Geography and Environment	Sec. 1	Sec. 1-2	Sec. 1,3	Sec. 1,2	
Conflict and Cooperation	Sec. 1-3	Sec. 2,3	Sec. 2-4	Sec. 1,2	
Influence of Technology		Sec. 1		Sec. 2	
The Individual and Family Life	Sec. 3	Sec. 1,3	Sec. 3	Sec. 1,3	
Ideas, Beliefs, and Institutions	Sec. 2,3	Sec. 1,3	Sec. 1	Sec. 1-3	
Cultural Diversity	Sec. 3	Sec. 3	Sec. 3	Sec. 1,3	
U.S. Role in World Affairs			Sec. 1-4		
Skills					
Social Studies Skills	Sec. 1		Sec. 3		
Critical Thinking Skills		Sec. 3		Sec. 3	
Study and Writing Skills					

Chapter 14	Chapter 15	Chapter 16	Chapter 17	Chapter 18
Sec. 1-4	Sec. 1	Sec. 1,2	Sec. 1,3	Sec. 1
Sec. 1,4	Sec. 3	Sec. 1,3	Sec. 3	Sec. 3
Sec. 2,4	Sec. 3,4	Sec. 1,2	Sec. 1-3	Sec. 1-4
Sec. 1	Sec. 1,2,4	Sec. 1,2	Sec. 1	Sec. 2
Sec. 1	Sec. 1-4	Sec. 1,2	Sec. 2,3	Sec. 3
	Sec. 3	Sec. 2	Sec. 1	Sec. 4
Sec. 4	Sec. 3,4	Sec. 1-3	Sec. 1-3	Sec. 1
Sec. 1,3	Sec. 1,4	Sec. 1,3	Sec. 2,3	Sec. 2-4
Sec. 4	Sec. 2-4	Sec. 1,3	Sec. 2	Sec. 2,4
Sec. 4	Sec. 1-4	Sec. 1,2	Sec. 2	
	Sec. 1			
Sec. 3		Sec. 3		Sec. 3
			Sec. 2	

ASTRONAUT
JOHN GLENN

LIFE
MAKING OF
A BRAVE M

Scope and Sequence

Themes and Concepts	Chapter 19	Chapter 20	Chapter 21	Chapter 22	
American Democracy	Sec. 1	Sec. 3	Sec. 1	Sec. 1,3	
Civil Rights and Liberties	Sec. 1,3,4	Sec. 2	Sec. 1,2	Sec. 1-4	
Economic Development	Sec. 4	Sec. 3	Sec. 2,3	Sec. 1	
Geography and Environment	Sec. 2	Sec. 1,2	Sec. 2-4	Sec. 1-3	
Conflict and Cooperation	Sec. 2,3	Sec. 1-3	Sec. 2,4	Sec. 1-4	
Influence of Technology	Sec. 4	Sec. 3	Sec. 3		
The Individual and Family Life	Sec. 4	Sec. 3	Sec. 3	Sec. 1	
Ideas, Beliefs, and Institutions	Sec. 1	Sec. 1-3	Sec. 2,3	Sec. 1-4	
Cultural Diversity	Sec. 4	Sec. 3	Sec. 3	Sec. 1-4	
U.S. Role in World Affairs	Sec. 1-4	Sec. 1-3	Sec. 4		

Skills					
Social Studies Skills					
Critical Thinking Skills	Sec. 4	Sec. 1	Sec. 1	Sec. 2	
Study and Writing Skills					

Chapter 23	Chapter 24	Chapter 25	Chapter 26
Sec. 2-4	Sec. 1-4	Sec. 1-3	Sec. 1,3
Sec. 1,2	Sec. 1-4	Sec. 1,3	Sec. 2,3
Sec. 2	Sec. 1-3	Sec. 1-3	Sec. 1,3
Sec. 1,2	Sec. 1-3	Sec. 1,3	Sec. 2
Sec. 1-4	Sec. 1,4	Sec. 1,3	Sec. 1-3
Sec. 1,2	Sec. 2	Sec. 1,2	
Sec. 3	Sec. 2	Sec. 1,3	Sec. 2,3
Sec. 3	Sec. 1-3	Sec. 1,3	Sec. 2,3
Sec. 3	Sec. 2	Sec. 3	Sec. 2,3
Sec. 1,2,4	Sec. 1,2	Sec. 1-3	Sec. 2
Sec. 2		Sec. 2	Sec. 2
	Sec. 2		

Implementing Block Scheduling

IN recent years educators have looked for ways to improve instruction without increasing staff or stretching already tight budgets. Block scheduling has shown promising results in school districts throughout the nation where it has resulted in higher levels of student achievement using the same instructional and financial resources.

Scheduling

Traditionally, middle and high schools schedule six or seven 40- to 55-minute classes per day. These classes usually meet for 180 days per school year. For example, a school might assign students to 45-minute classes—one each for social studies, English, mathematics, science, physical education, and two electives. Each class meets for 45 minutes, five days per week.

Block scheduling differs from traditional scheduling in that fewer class sessions meet for large blocks of time over fewer days. Rather than schedule students for 4 separate classes of English, social studies, science, and mathematics, schools with block schedules assign students to a 195-minute class. Each quarter of the school year, the students study one of the four core subjects in-depth. For example, students study English for 195 minutes per day during the first quarter, social studies during the second quarter, mathematics during the third quarter, and science during the fourth quarter. The rest of the school day would be devoted to electives and other activities.

Advantages for Teachers

Teachers who have used block scheduling have reported several advantages. Many educators believe that teacher-student relationships are improved. In traditional scheduling, teachers may teach seven or eight classes a day with as many as five different preparations. They are expected to know and teach 150 or more students each day. With block scheduling, teachers have responsibility for a smaller number of students at one time—often two classes with 25 to 30 students in each class. With more time, teachers are able to focus their attention and other resources on meeting the individual needs of students.

Teachers can be more focused on what they are teaching. Block scheduling seems to result in changes in teaching approaches, classrooms that are more student-centered, improved teacher morale, and increased teacher effectiveness. Teachers feel free to venture away from discussion and lecture to use more productive models of teaching.

Many teachers find the block approach more time-efficient. Block scheduling cuts in half the time needed for introducing and closing classes. It also creates more opportunities for cooperative-teaching strategies, such as team teaching and interdisciplinary studies. Block scheduling also increases the number of nontraditional, activity-based courses that can be offered.

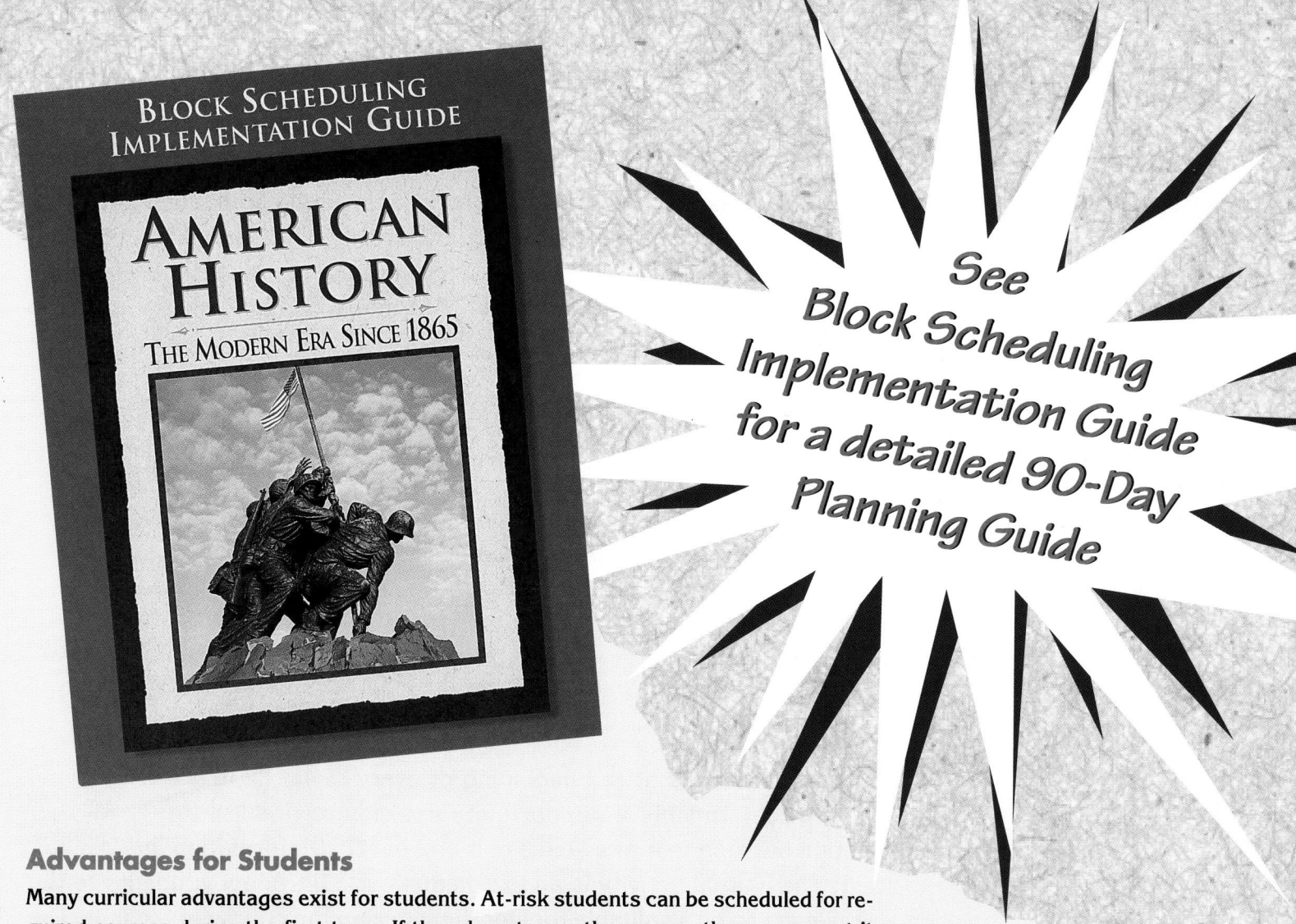

BLOCK SCHEDULING
IMPLEMENTATION GUIDE

AMERICAN
HISTORY
THE MODERN ERA SINCE 1865

See
Block Scheduling
Implementation Guide
for a detailed 90-Day
Planning Guide

Advantages for Students

Many curricular advantages exist for students. At-risk students can be scheduled for required courses during the first term. If they do not pass the course, they can repeat it during the second term. More accomplished students can move ahead more quickly and those students who develop a late interest in certain courses can take more of them. Gifted students, for example, might opt to take two core courses in a given quarter.

Modified Block Scheduling

Many school districts use a modified form of block scheduling that combines two core classes. Under this system, students might study social studies for 90 minutes each day for 90 days during the first semester. During the second semester, the same students would study science.

Many school districts that have adopted modified block scheduling assign students to English and social studies blocks in the first semester and science and mathematics blocks in the second semester. Such scheduling often encourages the English and social studies teachers and the science and mathematics teachers to institute team teaching or similar interdisciplinary approaches.

Implementation

The *Block Scheduling Implementation Guide* provides sample outlines for using this textbook for block scheduling in your classroom. For your convenience, the outlines provide suggestions for 45-day classes as well as 90-day classes.

Using Portfolios & Journals

Performance-based assessment as part of an overall approach to authentic assessment may include the keeping of portfolios and journals. Portfolios contain samples of student work collected over a period of time—often an entire grading period or even a semester. A primary component of a portfolio may be a history journal.

Portfolios

Having students maintain individual portfolios, or collections, of their work allows them to keep and review a variety of material. Portfolios might include samples of student writing, art, research, statistical analysis, and other work. Each unit of *American History: The Modern Era Since 1865* begins with a suggested **Portfolio Project** for students to complete.

Portfolio Project

Design a political cartoon that shows the contrasting sides of one of the divisive issues of this era; for example, Native American and settler, labor and big business, or political machine and reformer.

Journals

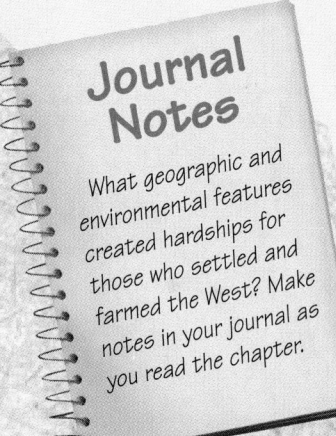

Journal Notes

What geographic and environmental features created hardships for those who settled and farmed the West? Make notes in your journal as you read the chapter.

Journal Notes, placed at the beginning of every chapter, provide students an opportunity not only to find information but also to make sense of it and put that information in context. The journal activity is an excellent way to introduce students to the material and can be a valuable tool for them during the course of the unit. The journal may be used in several ways—you may use the journal activity as a basis for class discussion or you may wish to give students other assignments to be completed in their journals. You may give students options in how they complete their journal assignments, or in the topics they choose.

Journals may also be used for students' reflections about what they are learning and how it affects them. If you wish, the journal may be used as an ongoing dialogue between teacher and student.

Using Your Journal

Compare and contrast the hardships for the settlers in the West with those faced by the colonists in the 1600s.

Writing About History

The **Journal Notes** and the follow-up writing activity, **Using Your Journal**, found in every Chapter Review may become an essential component of and addition to each student's portfolio.

T30

Expanding Cultural Perspectives in History

The study of history furnishes a wealth of material that can help students learn to appreciate the cultural diversity of the United States. By reading *American History: The Modern Era Since 1865*, students receive a broad view of the people and events that have contributed to the foundation of this country and the smooth operation of our system of democracy.

Diversity Expands and Grows

As immigration continues to make the United States a society with a wide variety of cultural perspectives, it is increasingly important for students to see peoples different from themselves as interesting neighbors who have different ideas, customs, and languages, but who also share many of the same values. By studying all aspects of our culturally diverse society, students gain a keen understanding of the roles that all Americans have played and continue to play in our government.

Cultural Perspectives in the Classroom

The following five points have been identified as some of the major goals of promoting culturally diverse education.

- Promoting the strength and value of cultural diversity
- Promoting human rights and respect for those who are different from oneself
- Promoting alternative life choices for people
- Promoting social justice and equal opportunity for all people
- Promoting equity in the distribution of power among groups

— from *Making Choices for Multicultural Education: Five Approaches to Race, Class, and Gender* by Sleeter, Grant. Columbus: Merrill Publishing, 1988.

Evaluating Learning with Performance Assessment

Defining Performance Assessment

In response to the growing demand for accountability in the classroom, many educators are advocating performance assessment, which measures student achievement in a more constructive and interactive manner than traditional tests do. In general, performance assessment includes performance-based activities and tests, and portfolios.

Performance Assessment Portfolios and Tests

The portfolio approach is often used with performance-based assessment. Portfolios contain samples of students' work collected over a period of time—an entire grading period or even a semester. Students often help choose which items will be included in their portfolios. Portfolios allow for assessing a broad range of skills. Students can see how much progress they are making by comparing the work that they have completed throughout the course.

Performance tests ask students to effectively and creatively apply the knowledge they have gained. These tests require the application of problem-solving skills rather than mere recall. Scoring involves rating students' performance on multiple factors, resulting in a descriptive profile of performance.

Performance Assessment Activities

Performance assessment activities provide "hands-on" approaches to learning concepts. Through the activities students are able to actually experience these concepts rather than just reading, writing, and listening about them. At the end of each activity, the student is assigned a performance task that checks understanding of the lesson's concepts.

Performance assessment tasks get students involved in constructing various types of products for diverse audiences. Performance assessment measures what you can do with what you know, not how much you know. Performance assessment tasks are based on what is most essential in the curriculum and what is interesting to a student.

More Like Playing Baseball Than Just Playing Catch

A baseball coach teaches and drills players and promotes appropriate attitudes. However, if the training stopped there, the players would never learn the game. They must *play* baseball. Similarly, teachers can present the information and skills of a discipline and quiz the students on the details, but students also must "play the game." Students need the opportunity to put the concepts, skills, and attitudes together. Performance assessment allows students to demonstrate how effectively they can put the pieces together in ways similar to how information is used in the larger world.

Looking at Authentic Use of Information

A common model of assessment is to teach the chapter, then stop and test the students. Performance assessment changes this pattern. The textbook becomes a resource for learning; it becomes a means to an end rather than the end in itself.

With performance assessment, students are engaged in tasks in which they are crafting products. The teacher is the coach who is guiding the students' work, providing models of excellent work, and giving feedback all along the way. Performance assessment tasks get students highly involved in meaningful learning.

The word *authentic* used with performance assessment means that the performance uses information, concepts, and skills in ways that people use them in the larger world.

Performance Assessment Requires Thinking Skills

Thinking skills provide the "verbs" that direct the action in performance assessment tasks. These include getting information, processing it, and using it to make a product. Thinking skills include those activities related to understanding the audience and crafting a product that fulfills a certain purpose for that audience. The assessment of the students' work should not only look at the final product, but should also assess the processes that lead to it.

Performance Assessment Makes Use of Different Learning Styles and Preferences

All learning styles are important and students should not use only the style in which they excel, but should also work on tasks that require other styles so that they can expand their competency. A variety of Performance Assessment tasks allows for these different styles. The student who prefers to write detailed, factual information pamphlets for peers should also be given the opportunity to become better at making persuasive posters for adult groups. Some performance tasks will dictate what the product is to be like. Other performance tasks will involve all students with the same information, but will allow them to choose the format, purpose, and audience for their product.

Performance Assessment Involves Cooperative Learning

Cooperative learning simulates how teamwork is used in a business environment. Effectively managed cooperative learning not only develops essential life-long interpersonal skills, it also gets the students to spend more time actively thinking. Performance assessment often uses a combination of individual and group cooperative learning. Group work may be used as the initial step to get students actively engaged and to allow for a diversity of ideas to emerge. Sometimes the whole project is done through group work and, in this case, individuals should have specific tasks for which they are accountable.

Performance Assessment in the *American History: The Modern Era Since 1865* Program

The *American History: The Modern Era Since 1865* program provides a variety of performance assessment suggestions and options. The **Teacher's Wraparound Edition** provides **Portfolio Project** suggestions at the beginning of each unit. **Performance Assessment Activities** are included on each Chapter Planning Guide. Additional performance assessment activities and rubrics are provided in the **Performance Assessment Strategies and Activities** booklet found in the **Teacher's Classroom Resources**.

Addressing Different Learning Styles

Your classroom undoubtedly contains students from a variety of backgrounds and with a variety of learning styles. In order to reach all of your students and make their learning experiences the most rewarding for their individual needs, *American History: The Modern Era Since 1865* provides a wealth of instructional approaches and strategies.

Visual Learners

Visual learners benefit most when they can carefully look at the material to be studied. In general, visual learners retain more information if they are able to visualize what they are learning. These types of learners benefit from laserdisc presentations as well as from CD-ROMs. Visual learners also benefit from reading the text and studying the accompanying visuals.

Auditory Learners

Auditory learners retain the most information when they hear what they are to learn. Oral instructions from the teacher are ideal ways to introduce these learners to new concepts. Technology also plays an essential role in helping these learners master the course content. For example, audiocassette transcripts of chapters or lessons provide these students with invaluable learning aids. These students also benefit from laserdisc and CD-ROM presentations because the soundtracks help them comprehend the information with a higher retention rate.

Kinesthetic Learners

Kinesthetic learners retain information more easily when they can actually perform basic tasks using the information. Individual or group projects in which they construct models, charts, or graphs are ideal.

Helping the At-Risk Student

Most educators today agree that the nation's schools are facing an epidemic of students who are at risk of failure. If their special needs are not met, these students usually drop out of school. Without a high-school education, these young people face a life of low wages and unfulfilling jobs. Occupying the lowest ranks of our society, these young people seldom have the opportunity to enjoy the advantages that most Americans take for granted.

Identifying At-Risk Students

It is difficult to define exactly what constitutes an at-risk student because being at risk is not linked to a single cause. Rather it is often linked to several environmental causes, such as limited English proficiency, poverty, low self-esteem, homelessness, substance abuse, or pregnancy. Whatever the causes, at-risk students share a common characteristic. They have extreme difficulty with learning and are almost always low achievers.

Teaching Methods

TIME-ON-TASK Current educational research has shown that certain teaching methods can make a difference with at-risk students and help to keep them from dropping out. One method is to maximize time-on-task. By doing so, teachers can help students overcome the outside stimuli that distract them from academic work.

HIGH EXPECTATIONS Another method is to establish high expectations and a school climate that supports learning. Expecting students to succeed will help them believe that they are capable of succeeding. Many schools actively involve parents in this process so that the expectations for success are not left inside the classroom after school is out. By including the parents in decision making, many teachers have found that the entire school community benefits.

POSITIVE FEEDBACK Because at-risk students have often failed in school, it is important to give them as much positive feedback as possible. Many teachers try to give this feedback at the end of each successfully completed assignment and regularly include award ceremonies for those students who are meeting expectations.

Incorporating Cooperative Learning In Your Classroom

Cooperative learning occupies a special place in the social studies curriculum because of its success in imparting the abilities needed to work effectively in a group. Such social studies skills are beneficial for all citizens living in a democracy. Research suggests that mixed ability grouping in learning activities leads to higher student achievement, especially for lower ability level students.

Defining Cooperative Learning

Cooperative learning requires students to work together – each with a specific task – to pursue a common goal. Because part of each student's evaluation is determined by the overall quality of the group's work, students help one another accomplish the group goal.

Cooperative learning requires careful structuring and monitoring by the teacher. Characteristics of cooperative learning include the following:

- Students work face-to-face in heterogeneous groups.
- The activity promotes a sense of positive interdependence.
- Each member of a group has individual accountability.
- The group has a common product or goal.

Role of the Teacher

Although successful Cooperative Learning groups may appear to work independently, this is no doubt due to the astute coaching of a good teacher. Groups may need the teacher's assistance at key moments during a project, such as agreeing on goals, establishing a structure of accountability, or evaluating their success. In particular, the teacher needs to assure that no one student in a group does most of the work.

Cooperative Learning in the *American History: The Modern Era Since 1865* Program

Throughout the *American History: The Modern Era Since 1865* program, students are asked to work together to address significant questions and resolve pertinent issues raised in their study. Activities require students to work together to analyze, synthesize, and apply lesson content. Many activities involve students in hands-on research and in presenting learning to others.

The **Student Edition** includes cooperative learning activities in each of the **Chapter Reviews.** They provide a variety of opportunities for students to work together on activities related to the chapter content.

The **Teacher's Wraparound Edition** contains both individual and cooperative learning activities. The cooperative learning suggestions, found in the bottom channel throughout the lessons, offer a variety of interesting, activity-based teaching ideas.

The **Teacher's Classroom Resources** includes a **Cooperative Learning Activities** booklet containing blackline master cooperative learning activities for each chapter. These activities reinforce learning and build management and interpersonal skills by requiring students to work together to acquire, organize, and present information.

Developing Critical Thinking

To learn about history in a way that prepares students to become thoughtful participants in our society, students must learn to think critically. They need to be able to evaluate and to question the meaning of what they see, read, and hear. The teacher plays a crucial role in this development by creating a classroom climate that actively encourages critical thinking. To help teach critical thinking, teachers may wish to refer to Benjamin Bloom's *Taxonomy of Cognitive Behavior.* Bloom's Taxonomy organizes cognitive learning into six hierarchical classes:

- Knowledge involves recalling, identifying, and defining.
- Comprehension includes describing, explaining, summarizing, and interpreting.
- Application entails applying, solving, and predicting.
- Analysis involves organizing, comparing, differentiating, relating, and inferring.
- Synthesis includes combining, producing, proposing, and hypothesizing.
- Evaluation entails appraising, judging, and deciding.

The Classroom Climate

The teacher can promote critical thinking in the classroom by asking questions that encourage students to analyze, synthesize, apply, and evaluate the information they hear and read daily. Sources for critical thinking activities or discussions range from the textbooks to newspaper and magazine stories and television news reports. Questions dealing with what happened, when it happened, or who was involved check the student's comprehension of facts. Questions that ask them to compare or explain events require that they dig deeper.

Critical Thinking in the *American History: The Modern Era Since 1865* Program

Critical thinking is taught, reviewed, and reinforced throughout the *American History: the Modern Era Since 1865* program. The **Student Edition** teaches the skills used in critical thinking, such as distinguishing between fact and opinion, determining cause and effect, and recognizing bias. Each of the skill pages provides opportunities for students to both learn and practice the skill being taught. Similar application of critical thinking is allowed for on Interdisciplinary Connections pages. Additional Critical Thinking practice is provided in each **Section Review, Chapter Review,** and **Unit Digest** especially in the areas of understanding themes and concepts, and identifying cause and effect.

The **Teacher's Wraparound Edition** includes additional critical thinking activities. These are found in the bottom channel throughout the lessons.

Plugging into the *inter*NET

THE INTERNET (or simply the Net) is the collective name for the connections among computers the world over. The Internet has been in existence for some time now, starting off as a military network and expanding throughout universities and, more recently, into the commercial realm.

Using the Internet

THINK of using the Internet as similar to using a telephone. If you know the name of the computer you want to contact, you can look up its number, have your computer dial it, and talk to it. You can reach a specific person, using E-mail, or you can join a conference call by subscribing to bulletin boards and list-servers; there are hundreds that relate to history alone.

World Wide Web

RECENTLY getting information through the Internet became much easier with the development of the **World Wide Web.** The Web is a part of the Internet—a very exciting region that contains pictures, sound, and video in addition to text. You can "browse" the Web using "browsers": programs such as *Netscape* and *Mosaic.*

Navigating the Web

THIS SOFTWARE can navigate the Web for you, meaning that you no longer have to know the number of the computer that you want. Many libraries now have electronic catalogues which allow you to search for information not only by the name of the author, but also by the name of the book, topic, keyword, and so on. Similarly, on the Web there are several ways to find what you want. You can go directly to the information address (its **URL,** or **Uniform Reference Locator**). Every photograph, map, diagram, and text file has one of these unique addresses.

Searches

FOR ALL SITES mentioned here, the URL follows in parentheses. You can use "search engines" which are a part of the program you are using to access the Web, or use another service such as Yahoo (http://www.yahoo.com/). These work just like the electronic catalogue in a library, except that when you have found the reference you want, you simply point and click and the information appears on your screen. Often it's faster to use a search than to type in the URL, especially if it is particularly long.

THE BEST PART of the Web is that you can print and copy everything you find. You don't have to have a computer connected to the Internet in your classroom to benefit. If you or your school has a single connection you can print materials for your class or save files for later use. You can even print directly onto overhead transparencies.

Printing and Saving

IF YOU ARE INTERESTED in joining one of the list-servers mentioned, you can see what is available by consulting *A Directory of Discussion Lists for Historians* (http://ukanaix.cc.ukans.edu/history/histlist.html). Already there is a wealth of Internet resources on-line for the history teacher to use. Internet Resources:

- The Library of Congress (http://lcweb.loc.gov/homepage/lchp.html) has documents from its collections on-line
- Vote Smart Web (http://www.vote-smart.org/) is a political database that includes lots of interest to historians
- There is and extensive and easy-to-use collection of major historical documents on-line from the University of Kansas (http://history.cc.ukans.edu/carrie/docs/docs_us.html), organized by time period
- Columbus and the Age of Discovery (http://www.millersv.edu/~columbus/) is a linked set of over 100 documents related to the "encounter of two worlds"
- Eighteenth Century Resources on the Net (http://www.english.upenn.edu/~jlynch/18th.html)
- The Smithsonian Institution (http://www.si.edu/) has an extensive Web site, including The Hall of Presidents (http://www.si.edu/organiza/museums/portgal/homepage/previews/pres.htm)
- The Bureau of the Census (http:/www.census.gov/) has some historical information available
- "From Revolution to Reconstruction" (http://grid.let.rug.nl/~welling/usa/) is an on-line American history textbook
- History of the U.S. Senate (http://www.senate.gov/history/history.html)
- Search the Constitution of the United States (http://lcweb2.loc.gov:8080/constquery.html); it is actually available in several different sites
- Everything there is to know about Old Glory (http://www.elk-grove.k12.il.us/usflag/)
- A history of money (http://www.ex.ac.uk/~RDavies/arian/northamerica.html)
- There is an on-line map collection with maps of just about everywhere at http://www.lib.utexas.edu/Libs/PCL/Map_collection/Map_collection.html

Possible Internet Connections

MANY SITES provide you with links to other sites, so you can travel the Internet world by pointing and clicking. Or you can visit several sites that are clearinghouses for information:

- American Studies Web from Yale University (http://pantheon.cis.yale.edu/~davidp/amstud.html)
- Armadillo from Rice University (http://chico.rice.edu/armadillo/about.hxml);
- ERIC Clearinghouse (http://www.cua.edu/www/eric_ae/home.html);
- Joint Education Initiative at Maryland (http://jei.umd.edu/)
- The TENET homepage (http://www.tenet.edu:80/)

A major university is always a good place to start browsing. Look one up at http://www.utexas.edu/world/univ

Linking Internet Sites

Glencoe's Internet Connection

GLENCOE is bringing the **Internet** connection to your classroom through practical **Internet Activities** provided at the beginning of each unit of the *American History: The Modern Era Since 1865* Teacher's Wraparound Edition. These activities give your students various **Internet** references and applications for using the **Internet** as they read and study each unit. Additional **Internet** sites can be located in the *Internet Yellow Pages,* Osborn **McGraw-Hill,** 1996.

Glencoe/McGraw-Hill's unique **Internet** connections are a source for extended information related to Unit and Chapter content. The sites referenced in Glencoe's **Internet** connections are not under the control of Glencoe and therefore Glencoe makes no representation concerning the content of these sites. We encourage teachers to preview these sites before students access them. **Internet** sites are sometimes under construction and may not always be available, sites may move, or sites may have been discontinued completely.

Publishing Your Own Material

YOU SHOULD also realize that more and more teachers and students are publishing in the **Internet** World Wide Web because it is so easy. For information about publishing, a good starting point is (http://www.utexas.edu/learn/).

Getting Connected

GETTING CONNECTED to the **Internet** is sometimes a problem, but school districts are establishing connections at a very rapid rate. Also, it is possible for you to join the **Internet** through a local university or by subscribing to a private provider such as CompuServe, America On-Line, or Microsoft Network. These providers let you use the Web for a monthly fee or at an hourly rate.

If you want to know more about the **Internet,** read "A Survey of the Internet", published in the July 1, 1995 issue of *The Economist,* which you can access on the World Wide Web (http://www.economist.com/).

Webbing the Social Studies

THE NATIONAL COUNCIL FOR THE SOCIAL STUDIES has provided information on using the **Internet** in Social Studies, in *Social Education,* February, 1996. The article "Webbing the Social Studies" provides helpful information on social studies-specific **Internet** sites and guidance on how the Web works.

Glencoe Brings Technology to Your Classroom

Advances in technology are continually being made, and these advances dramatically affect all aspects of the social studies. Social studies instruction should include an awareness of advances in technology. Wherever possible, discuss technology with your students as an ongoing part of the social studies courses.

Using Software with Limited Hardware

As with many other types of instructional tools, the more equipment available, the more flexibility your program can have. The ideal situation is to have one computer for each member of the class. You also might have access several times a week to a school computer lab. If either of these situations exists, you have unlimited opportunities for providing a wide range of computer activities. It is possible, however, to provide some computer activities with limited computer hardware.

- ONE COMPUTER FOR TWENTY-FIVE STUDENTS With one computer, three to five students can be accommodated in an average class period by rotating students at the computer. Rather than have each student complete a specific exercise, form teams of two or possibly three students and assign each a portion of the software for the chapter. All students can then gain some computer experience without taking an excessive amount of classroom time. The one-computer classroom is also ideal for demonstration using an electronic display device hooked up to a computer and an overhead projector. Remember that computerized student demonstrations of social studies concepts are excellent learning situations that develop not only content knowledge, but software and communication skills as well.

- THREE TO FIVE COMPUTERS FOR TWENTY-FIVE STUDENTS Three to five students can be accommodated at each computer in an average class period. All students should be able to complete review and reinforcement activities and become familiar with computers.

- SEVEN TO TEN COMPUTERS FOR TWENTY-FIVE STUDENTS Review and reinforcement programs can all be completed on an individual basis. With proper scheduling, students should have sufficient time to complete several computer activities without intruding on instructional time.

Multimedia

As a social studies teacher, you know that your students have varying learning styles. Some students are print-dominant learners; others are non-print-dominant learners. To help you accommodate these varying learning styles and to integrate listening, hands-on application, and more frequent stimulation and interactivity into the classroom, Glencoe offers a variety of multimedia programs, including software, laserdiscs, CD-ROMs, and audiocassettes.

Laserdiscs

If your school has a basic system consisting of a videodisc player and a television receiver, Glencoe laserdiscs provide an effective took for classroom presentations. Students can see the connection between concepts and the real world. Students are also given opportunities to apply what they have learned.

CD-Roms

CD-ROM programs provide large databases of information as well as sound and motion. A display panel allows for large-screen display.

Audiocassettes

Audiocassettes offer auditory learners opportunities for remediation and reinforcement of important text concepts while facilitating individually paced learning.

Computer Training for Teachers

You must have a general knowledge of computer operation, but you do not have to have a knowledge of internal hardware elements or programming languages. Resources exist in every school or district for help in using any troubleshooting equipment. These resources include other computer teachers, lab assistants, and technology supervisors. Remember that software hotlines are one of your best resources when using any type of software. Glencoe's SOFTWARE HOTLINE is 1-800-437-3715.

Chapter Resources

Chapter 1

Literature from the Period
Columbus, Christopher. *The Log of Christopher Columbus*. Translated by Robert H. Fuson. International Marine Publishing, 1987.

Franklin, Benjamin. *Poor Richard's Almanac*. Houghton Mifflin, 1986.

Nabakov, Peter, ed. *Native American Testimony: An Anthology of Indian and White Relations: First Encounter to Dispossession*. Crowell, 1978.

Readings for the Student
Boorstin, Daniel J. *The Americans: The Colonial Experience*. Random House, 1964.

Brandon, William. *Indians*. American Heritage, 1985.

Leon, George deLucenay. *Explorers of the Americas Before Columbus*. Franklin Watts, 1989.

Readings for the Teacher
Cardini, Franco. *Europe 1492: Portrait of a Continent Five Hundred Years Ago*. Facts on File, 1989.

Hawke, David Freeman. *Everyday Life in Early America*. Perennial Library, 1988.

Lang, James. *Conquest and Commerce: Spain and England in the Americas*. Academic Press, 1975.

Multimedia Resources
Decisions, Decisions: Colonization. Tom Snyder Productions. (Apple or IBM PC diskette)

Who Really Discovered America? Interact. (Simulation)

Chapter 2

Literature from the Period
Jefferson, Thomas. "The Declaration of Independence." 1776

Paine, Thomas. *Common Sense*. 1776

Wheatley, Phillis. "To His Excellency, General Washington." 1775

Readings for the Student
DePaux, Linda Grant. *Founding Mothers: Women in the Revolutionary Era*. Houghton Mifflin, 1975.

Kennedy, Caroline, and Ellen Alderman. *In Our Defense: The Bill of Rights in Action*. Morrow, 1991

Readings for the Teacher
Lipman, Jean, Elizabeth V. Warren, and Robert Bishop.

Young America: A Folk-Art History. Museum of American Folk-Art, 1987.

Norton, Mary Beth. *Liberty's Daughters: The Revolutionary Experiences of American Women, 1750-1800*. Scott, Foresman, 1980.

Wood, W. J. *Battles of the Revolutionary War, 1775-1781*. Algonquin, 1990.

Multimedia Resources
The Constitution as a Living Document. Close-Up Foundation. (VHS, 57 minutes)

Creating the U.S. Constitution. Educational Activities. (Apple diskette, backup, guide)

Revolution '76. Britannica Software. (Apple IIGS or IBM diskette)

Revolutionary Wars: Choosing Sides. Tom Snyder Productions. (Apple diskette)

To Keep Our Liberty. National Park Service. (VHS, 23 minutes)

Chapter 3

Literature from the Period
Jefferson, Thomas. "The Inaugural Address." March 4, 1801.

Madison, Dolley. "Letters." 1814.

Washington, George. "Farewell Address." 1796.

Readings for the Student
Farber, Doris and Harold. *The Birth of a Nation*. Scribner's, 1989.

Flexner, James T. *Washington: The Indispensable Man*. Mentor, 1979.

Musselman, Lloyd. *The Federalist Period, 1790-1800*. Glencoe, 1980.

Readings for the Teacher
Adams, Henry. *History of the United States of America During the Administrations of Thomas Jefferson and James Madison*. Library of America, 1986.

Hickey, Donald R. *The War of 1812: A Forgotten Conflict*. University of Illinois Press, 1990.

Miller, John C. *The Federalist Era 1789-1801*. Harper, 1960.

Multimedia Resources
America Moves West. Orange Cherry. (2 Apple diskettes, backups, guide)

George Washington and the Whiskey Rebellion. LCA. (film, 27 minutes)

On the Campaign Trail: Decisions, Decisions. Tom Snyder (Apple or IBM diskette, backup, guide, booklets)

U.S. Constitution Tutor. Micro Learn/Word Associates. (Apple or IBM diskette)

Chapter 4

Literature from the Period
De Tocqueville, Alexis. *Democracy in America, I*. 1835.

Irving, Washington. "The Legend of Sleepy Hollow." 1819-1820.

Thoreau, Henry David. "Civil Disobedience." 1849.

_____. *Walden*. 1854

Readings for the Student
Blockson, Charles L., *The Underground Railroad: First Person Narratives of Escapes to Freedom in the North*. Prentice Hall, 1987.

Germer, Lucie. "Dorothea Dix: Quiet Crusader." *Cobblestone*, Vol. 10, No. 6, June 1989.

Marsh, Carole. *Out of the Mouths of Slaves*. Gallopade, 1989.

Shank, William. *Towpaths to Tugboats: A History of American Canal Engineering*. American Canal and Transportation Center, 1982.

Readings for the Teacher
Brown, Richard D. *Modernization: The Transformation of American Life: 1600-1865*. Hill and Wang, 1976.

Cremin, Lawrence A. *American Education: The National Experience, 1783-1876*. Harper 1980.

Dangerfield, George. *The Awakening of American Nationalism: 1815-1828*. Harper, 1980.

Multimedia Resources
A Woman's Place. Time. (VHS, 25 minutes)

Industrializing America: A Game of American Industrial Development. Perfection Form. (Apple diskette, backup, guide)

Views of Vanishing Frontier. Metropolitan Museum of Art. (VHS, 27 minutes)

Women in History. Tom Snyder. (Apple or IBM diskette)

Chapter 5

Literature from the Period
Douglass, Frederick. *Narrative of the Life of Frederick Douglass: An American Slave*. 1845.

Lincoln, Abraham. "Emancipation Proclamation." 1863.

_____. "Gettysburg Address." 1863.

Stowe, Harriet Beecher. *Uncle Tom's Cabin*. 1852.

Readings for the Student
Carlson, Judy. *Harriet Tubman: Call to Freedom*. Fawcett, 1989.

Catton, Bruce. *The Civil War*. American Heritage, 1971.

Levine, I.E. *The Many Faces of Slavery*. Messner, 1975.

Readings for the Teacher
Catton, Bruce. *A Stillness at Appomattox*. Washington Square, 1970.

Foote, Shelby. *The Civil War*. Random House, 1958.

Ward, Geoffrey C., with Ric and Ken Burns. *The Civil War: An Illustrated History*. Knopf, 1990.

Multimedia Resources
America Moves West. Orange Cherry. (2 Apple diskettes, backups, guide)

The Civil War. Westport Media. (5 filmstrips)

Living American History Series. U.S. History II: 1840-1876. Prive Learning Systems (2 Apple diskettes, guide)

The Time Tunnel: American History Series I. Focus Media. (Apple or IBM diskette, backup, guide)

Chapter 6

Literature from the Period
Douglass, Frederick. "What the Black Man Wants." 1865.

Stevens, Thaddeus. "Speech in the U.S. House of Representatives." January 3, 1867.

Readings for the Student
Cook, Fred. *The Ku Klux Klan: America's Recurring Nightmare*. Messner, 1989.

Morris, Roy, Jr. "Master Fraud of the Century." *American History Illustrated*, Vol. 23, No. 7, November 1988.

Woodward, C. Vann. *The Strange Career of Jim Crow*. Oxford. 1974.

Readings for the Teacher

Foner, Eric. *Reconstruction: America's Unfinished Revolution.* Harper, 1988.

Sernett, Milton C., ed. *Afro-American Religious History: A Documentary Witness.* Duke University Press, 1985.

Stampp, Kenneth M. *The Era of Reconstruction, 1865-1877.* Random House, 1967.

Multimedia Resources

Frederick Douglass: An American Life. Your World Video. (VHS, 30 minutes)

Living American History Series. U.S. History II: 1840-1875. Priven Learning Systems (2 Apple diskettes, guide)

Rebuilding the American Nation, 1865-1890. Guidance Associates. (2 filmstrips)

Reconstruction. Dallas Community College. (VHS, 30 minutes)

Chapter 7

Literature from the Period

Chief Joseph. *Chief Joseph's Own Story.* Montana Council for Indian Education, 1983.

_____. "I Will Fight No More Forever." 1877.

Harte, Bret. "The Outcasts of Poker Flat." 1869.

Readings for the Student

Freedman , Russell. *Buffalo Hunt.* Holiday House, 1988.

Hoig, Stan. "The Great Oklahoma Land Rush of 1889." *American History Illustrated,* Vol. 24, No. 1, March 1989.

"Joseph, A Chief of the Nez Perce." *Cobblestone,* Vol. 2, No. 9, September 1990.

Readings for the Teacher

Dale, Edward E. *Frontier Ways: Sketches of Life in the Old West.* University of Texas, 1989.

Moyniham, Ruth B., et. al., eds *So Much to Be Done: Women Settlers on the Mining and Ranching Frontier.* University of Nebraska Press, 1990.

Schlissel, Lillian, et al. *Far From Home: Families of the Westward Journey.* Schocken, 1989.

Vine, Robert V. *Community on the American Frontier: Separate But Not Alone.* University of Oklahoma Press, 1980.

Multimedia Resources

Famous Women of the West. Multi Media Productions. (filmstrip, cassette, guide)

Nez Perce: Portrait of a People. National Park Service. (VHS, 23 minutes)

Vaquero: The Forgotten Cowboy. PBS (VHS, 60 minutes)

Chapter 8

Literature from the Period

Carnegie, Andrew. "Steel Manufacture in the United States in the Nineteenth Century." 1902.

Readings for the Student

Brown, Dee. *Hear That Lonesome Whistle Blow.* Holt, 1977.

"Entrepreneurs of the Past." *Cobblestone,* Vol. 10, No. 5, May 1989.

Jennings, Walter Wilson. *20 Giants of American Business.* Exposition Press, 1953.

Walker, Robert H. *Everyday Life in the Age of Enterprise: 1865-1900.* Putnam, 1967.

Wilson, Everett B. *America's Vanishing Folkways.* Barnes, 1965.

Readings for the Teacher

Higgs, Robert. *Competition and Coercion: Blacks in the American Economy, 1865-1914.* University of Chicago, 1980.

Livesay, Harold C. *Andrew Carnegie and the Rise of Big Business.* Little, Brown, 1975.

Takaki, Ronald. *Strangers From a Different Shore.* Little, Brown, 1989.

Multimedia Resources

Cartels and Cutthroats. Micro Center. (Apple diskette)

The Entrepreneurs: An American Adventure. Martin Sandler. (6 VHS, 5 hours)

Urbanization: The Growth of Cities. Tom Snyder. (Apple or IBM diskette)

Chapter 9

Literature from the Period

Bellamy, Francis. "Pledge of Allegiance." 1892.

Wheeler, Thomas C., ed. *The Immigrant Experience: The Anguish of Becoming American.* Penguin, 1972.

Readings for the Student

Oxford, Edward. "Hope, Tears, and Remembrance." *American History Illustrated,* Vol. 25, No. 4, September/October 1990.

Robbins, Peggy. "Alas Memphis." *American History Illustrated,* Vol. 26, No. 9, January 1982.

"The Working American." *American Heritage,* Vol. 31, No. 4, June/July 1980.

Readings for the Teacher

Higham, John. *Strangers in the Land: Patterns of American Nativism, 1860-1925.* Atheneum, 1963.

Numbers, R.L., and D.W. Amundsen, eds. *Caring and Curing: Historical Essays on Health, Medicine, and the Faith Traditions.* Macmillan, 1986.

Wetheimer, Barbara Meyer. *We Were There: The Story of Working Women in America.* Pantheon, 1977.

Multimedia Resources

The Immigrant Experience: The Long, Long Journey. LCA. (VHS, 30 minutes)

Immigration: Maintaining the Open Door. Tom Snyder. (Apple or IBM diskette)

The Inheritance. Harold Meyer Productions. (VHS, 45 minutes)

The Rise of the American Labor Movement: Toil and Struggle. Educational Enrichment. (2 color filmstrips)

Urbanization: The Growth of American Cities. Tom Snyder. (Apple or IBM diskettes)

Chapter 10

Literature from the Period

Anthony, Susan B. *History of Woman's Suffrage.* 1902.

Twain, Mark. *Life on the Mississippi.* 1975.

Readings for the Student

Tower, Samuel A. *Cartoons and Lampoons: The Art of Political Satire.* Messner, 1982.

Readings for the Teacher

Callow, Alexander B., Jr. *The Tweed Ring.* Oxford, 1966.

Dobson, John M. *Politics in the Gilded Age.* Praeger, 1972.

Multimedia Resources

The Abuse of Political Power. Guidance Associates.

Living American History Series. U.S. History III, 1876-1914. Priven Learning Systems. (2 Apple diskettes)

Women in American Life, 1880-1920. National Women's History Project. (VHS, 15 minutes)

Chapter 11

Literature from the Period

Addams, Jane. *Twenty Years at Hull House.* 1910.

Cather, Willa. *My Antonia.* 1918.

Readings for the Student

Meltzer, Milton. *Bread and Roses: The Struggle of American Labor, 1865-1915.* Facts on File. 1990.

Walker, Robert Harris. *Everyday Life in the Age of Enterprise 1865-1900.* Putnam, 1967.

Readings for the Teacher

Grob, Gerald N. *Workers and Utopia.* Quadrangle, 1961.

Wilson, Charles Morrow. *The Commoner: William Jennings Bryan.* Doubleday, 1970.

Multimedia Resources

Labor Movement: Beginnings and Growth in America. Coronet. (13 1/2 minutes)

Living American History Series. U.S. History III, 1876-1914. Priven Learning Systems. (2 Apple diskettes)

Progressives, Populists, and Reform in America. Guidance Associates. (VHS, 32 minutes)

Chapter 12

Literature from the Period

Crane, Stephen. "The Open Boat." 1897.

Roosevelt, Theodore. *Autobiography.* 1913.

Readings for the Student

Boorstin, Daniel J. *The Landmark History of the American People, Volume 2.* Random House, 1987.

O'Toole, G.J.A. *The Spanish War: An American Epic, 1898.* Norton, 1986.

Readings for the Teacher

Hutchison, William R. *Errand to the World: American Protestant Thought & Foreign Missions.* University of Chicago Press, 1987.

Chapter Resources

Milton, Joyce. *The Yellow Kids: Foreign Correspondents in the Heyday of Yellow Journalism.* Harper & Row, 1989.

Multimedia Resources

American Foreign Policy. Focus Media. (Apple diskette, backup, guide)

Becoming a Modern Nation. Video Knowledge. (VHS, 28 minutes)

Foreign Policy: The Burdens of World Power. Tom Snyder. (Apple or IBM diskette)

The Philippine-American War. Multi-Media Productions. (Filmstrip, cassette, guide)

The Spanish-American War. Multi-Media Productions. (sound filmstrip)

The Spanish-American War: The Dynamics of Change. Multi Media Productions. (VHS, 30 minutes)

Chapter 13

Literature from the Period

Sinclair, Upton. *The Jungle.* 1906.

Tarbell, Ida. *History of the Standard Oil Company.* 1904.

Readings for the Student

Marshall, Megan. "Three Sisters Who Showed the Way." *American Heritage,* Vol. 38, No. 6, September/October 1987.

Mitelman, Bonnie. "Rose Schneiderman and the Triangle Fire." *American History Illustrated.* Vol. 16, No. 4, July 1981.

Readings for the Teacher

Abell, Aaron I. ed. *American Catholic Thought on Social Questions.* Bobbs-Merrill, 1968.

Filler, Louis. *The Muckrackers.* Rev. ed. Pennsylvania State University, 1980.

Hopkins, C. Howard. *The Rise of the Social Gospel in American Protestantism, 1865-1895.* Yale University Press, 1967.

Multimedia Resources

The Cross of Gold - William Jennings Bryan and the Politics of Progressivism. Multi-Media Productions (sound filmstrip)

Progressives, Populists, and Reform in America. Guidance Associates (VHS, 32 minutes)

Chapter 14

Literature from the Period

Dreiser, Theodore. *The Financier.* 1912.

Du Bois, W.E.B. "Of the Meaning of Progress." 1903.

Readings for the Student

Dillon, Richard H. "The Most Unique and Majestic of Nature's Marvels." *American History Illustrated,* Vol. 25, No. 4, September/October 1990.

"Environmentalism." *Cobblestone,* Vol. 10, No. 8, August 1988.

Morris, Edmund. *The Rise of Theodore Roosevelt.* Ballantine Books, 1980.

Readings for the Teacher

Harbaugh, William H. *The Life and Times of Teddy Roosevelt.* Oxford University Press, 1975.

Link, Arthur S. *Woodrow Wilson: Revolution, War and Peace.* Harlan Davidson, 1979.

Multimedia Resources

The Federal Reserve System. Federal Reserve Board. (VHS, 30 minutes)

Focus 1900-1909. ABC Wide World of Learning. (color, 58 minutes)

Theodore Roosevelt - Cowboy in the White House. Centron (29 minutes)

Theodore Roosevelt: A Portrait of Power. Prentice-Hall Media. (color, sound filmstrip)

The Time Tunnel: American History Series 2. Focus Media. (Apple diskette, backup)

The U.S. Economic System. United Learning. (VHS, 75 minutes)

Chapter 15

Literature from the Period

Anderson, Sherwood. *Winesburg, Ohio.* 1919.

Norris, George. "Opposition to War." April 4, 1917.

Wilson, Woodrow. "Appeal for Neutrality." August 19, 1914.

_____. "Fourteen Points." January 8, 1918.

Readings for the Student

Carr, Stephen M. "Smidley Butler: Hero or Demagogue?" *American History Illustrated,* Vol. 15, No. 1, April 1980.

McGinty, Brian. "Alvin York." *American History Illustrated,* Vol. 21, No. 7, November 1986.

Readings for the Teacher

Coffman, Edward M. *The War to End All Wars.* University of Wisconsin Press, 1968.

Greenwald, Maurine W. *Women, War and Work.* Greenwood Press, 1980.

Lemann, Nicholas. *The Promised Land: The Great Black Migration and How it Changed America.* Knopf, 1991.

Multimedia Resources

Living American History Series. US History IV: 1915-1960. Priven Learning Systems. (2 Apple diskettes)

Mirror of America. National Archives. (VHS, 36 minutes)

The Ordeal of Woodrow Wilson. NBC. (VHS, 26 minutes)

The United States in World War I: Witness to History. Guidance Associates. (VHS, 15 minutes)

World War I: 1914-1918. Films for the Humanities. (VHS, 52 minutes)

Chapter 16

Literature from the Period

Fitzgerald, F. Scott. *The Great Gatsby.* 1925.

Hughes, Langston. *The Weary Blues.* 1926.

Lewis, Sinclair. *Babbit.* 1922.

Readings for the Student

"The Harlem Renaissance." Cobblestone, Vol. 12, No. 2, February 1991.

Lyons, Mary E. *Sorrow's Kitchen: The Life and Folklore of Zora Neale Hurston.* Charles Scribner's Sons, 1990.

Readings for the Teacher

Nash, Roderick. *The Nervous Generation: American Thought, 1917-1930.* Yale University Press, 1970.

Multimedia Resources

Cultural Contributions of Black Americans: A Literary Renaissance. SVE (color filmstrips)

Living American History Series. US History IV: 1915-1960. Priven Learning Systems. (2 Apple diskettes, guide).

The Spirit of St. Louis. Warners (VHS, 137 minutes)

Chapter 17

Literature from the Period

Hemingway, Ernest. *A Farewell to Arms.* 1929.

Hoover, Herbert. "Speech at New York City." October 22, 1928.

Readings for the Student

Meltzer, Milton. *Brother, Can You Spare a Dime? The Great Depression 1929-1933.* Mentor, 1977.

Scraff, Anne E. *The Great Depression and the New Deal: America's Economic Collapse and Recovery.* Watts, 1980.

Readings for the Teacher

Terkel, Studs. *Hard Times: An Oral History of the Depression.* Random House, 1980.

Multimedia Resources

Brother, Can You Spare a Dime? History in Action. Films for the Humanities. (VHS, 20 minutes)

Living American History Series. U.S. History IV: 1915-1960. Priven Learning Systems. (2 Apple diskettes, guide)

The 20's and 30's. Westport Media. (5 color filmstrips)

Chapter 18

Literature from the Period

Roosevelt, Franklin D. "First Inaugural Address." March 4, 1933.

Steinbeck, John. *The Grapes of Wrath.* 1939.

Readings for the Student

Dillon, Richard. "Spanning the Golden Gate." *American History Illustrated,* Vol. 22, No. 3, May 1987.

Oxford, Edward. "The Night of the Martians." *American History Illustrated,* Vol. 23, No. 6, October 1988.

Readings for the Teacher

McElvaine, Thomas Gordon. *The Great Depression.* TimeBooks, 1985.

Sternsher, Bernard, and Judith Sealander, eds. *Women of Valor: The Struggle Against the Great Depression as Told in Their Own Life Stories.* Ivan R. Dee, 1990.

Multimedia Resources

The Grapes of Wrath. 20th Century Fox. (VHS, 129 minutes)

The Great Depression: 1929-1933. Guidance Associates. (2 filmstrip programs)

Industrializing America: A Game of American Industrial Development. Perfection Form. (Apple diskette, backup, guide)

Chapter 19

Literature from the Period
Parker, Dorothy. "Soldiers of the Republic." 1938.

Roosevelt, Franklin D. "Radio Address." September 3, 1939.

Readings for the Student
Berenbaum, Michael. *The World Must Know: The History of the Holocaust as Told in the United States Holocaust Memorial Museum.* Little Brown, 1993.

Gregory, Ross. *America 1941: A Nation at the Crossroads.* The Free Press, 1989.

Readings for the Teacher
Davis, Daniel S. *Behind Barbed Wire: The Imprisonment of Japanese Americans During World War II.* Dutton, 1982.

Multimedia Resources
American Foreign Policy. Focus Media. (Apple diskette, backup, guide)

December 7th. National Archives. (VHS, 34 minutes)

Home Front, World War II. Multi-Media Productions. (2 filmstrips, cassette)

Chapter 20

Literature from the Period
Churchill, Winston, "Speech at Fulton, Missouri." March 5, 1946.

Williams, Tennessee. *The Glass Menagerie.* 1945.

Readings for the Student
Caute, David. *The Great Fear.* Simon and Schuster, 1978.

Ingalls, Robert. *Point of Order - A Profile of Senator Joe McCarthy.* Putnam, 1981.

Readings for the Teacher
Fried, Richard M. *Nightmare in Red: The McCarthy Era in Perspective.* Oxford, 1990.

Weisberger, Bernard A. *Cold War, Cold Peace: The United States and Russia since 1945.* American Heritage, 1985.

Multimedia Resources
America and the World Since World War II, 1945-1952: Volume 1. ABC (VHS, 52 minutes)

The Berlin Airlift. Prentice-Hall Media. (color, sound filmstrip)

Foreign Policy: The Burdens of World Power. Tom Snyder. (Apple or IBM diskette)

Chapter 21

Literature from the Period
Ellison, Ralph. *Invisible Man.* 1952.

Galbraith, John Kenneth. *The Affluent Society.* 1958.

Hansberry, Lorraine. *A Raisin in the Sun.* 1959.

Readings for the Student
Cheney, Glenn Alan. *Television in American Society.* Franklin Watts, 1983.

Divine, Robert. *Eisenhower and the Cold War.* Oxford University Press, 1981.

Readings for the Teacher
Girling, John L.S. *America and the Third World.* Routledge and Kegan, 1980.

Multimedia Resources
Balance of Power. Software Toolworks (Apple, IBM, and MAC diskettes, with guide)

The Cold War. Educational Environment. (VHS, 31 minutes)

Focus on the Fifties. ABC Wide World of Learning. (color film)

Chapter 22

Literature from the Period
Brown, et. al. v. Board of Education of Topeka, KA. et al. May 17, 1954.

Ellison, Ralph. *Shadow and Act.* Random House, 1964.

King, Jr., Martin Luther. "I Have a Dream." 1963.

Readings for the Student
Durham, Michael S. *Powerful Days: The Civil Rights Photography of Charles Moore.* Stewart, Tabori, and Chang, 1991.

Patterson, Lillie. *Martin Luther King, Jr. and the Freedom Movement.* Facts on File, 1989.

Readings for the Teacher
King, Jr., Martin Luther. *Stride Toward Freedom.* Harper, 1958.

Powledge, Fred. *Free at Last? The Civil Rights Movement and the People Who Made It.* Little, Brown, 1991.

Multimedia Resources
All the Unsung Heroes. American Heritage Group. (VHS, 30 minutes)

The Civil Rights Movement: Witness to History. Guidance Associates. (VHS, 15 minutes)

King. Filmways. (VHS, 24 minutes)

Chapter 23

Literature from the Period
Kennedy, John F. "Inaugural Address." January 20, 1963.

Readings for the Student
Oxford, Edward. "Destiny in Dallas." *American History Illustrated,* Vol. 23, No. 7y, November 1988.

Lawson, Don. *The United States in the Vietnam War.* Crowell, 1981.

Readings for the Teacher
Barnet, Richard J. *The Giants: Russia and America.* Touchstone, 1977.

Multimedia Resources
America and the World Since World War II, 1961-1975, Volume III. ABC News. (VHS, 52 minutes)

America and the World Since World War II, 1961-1975, Volume IX. ABC News. (VHS, 52 minutes)

The Cuban Missile Crisis. Prentice-Hall Media. (color sound filmstrip)

Chapter 24

Literature from the Period
Nixon, Richard M. "Farewell Address." August, 1974.

Readings for the Student
Cummings, Duane. *Conflict and Compromise: The 1960's and 1970's.* Glencoe, 1980.

"Energy: Powering Our Nation." *Cobblestone,* Vol. 2, No 10, October 1990.

Readings for the Teacher
Ambrose, Stephen E. *Nixon: The Triumph of a Politician.* Simon and Schuster, 1989.

Goodwin, Richard. *Remembering America: A Voice from the Sixties.* Little, Brown, 1988.

Manchester, William. *The Glory and the Dream.* Little, Brown, 1972.

Multimedia Resources
All the President's Men. Warner. (VHS, 135 minutes)

That Memorable Year: 1963. Media Access Corp. (VHS, 50 minutes)

Television: A Study of Media Ethics. Tom Snyder. (Apple or IBM diskette)

Watergate: Computer Version. Thomas Henderson. (Apple diskette)

Watergate Hearings: Summer of Judgment. WETA (VHS, 120 minutes)

Chapter 25

Literature from the Period
Bush, George. "The Liberation of Kuwait." January 16, 1991.

Wiesel, Elie. "Nobel Acceptance Speech." December 11, 1986.

Readings for the Student
Kennedy, Caroline, and Ellen Alderman. *In Our Defense: The Bill of Rights in Action.* William Morrow, 1991.

Readings for the Teacher
Blumenthal, Sidney. *Pledging Allegiance: The Last Campaign of the Cold War.* HarperCollins, 1990.

Friedman, Thomas L. *From Beirut to Jerusalem.* Doubleday, 1991.

Multimedia Resources
The Eagle and the Bear. Guidance Associates. (VHS 48 minutes)

The Budget Deficit: A Question of Balance. Tom Snyder. (Apple or IBM diskette)

Chapter 26

Readings for the Student
Hewett, Ed. A., and Victor H. Winston, eds. *Milestones in Glasnost and Perestroyka: Politics and People.* Brookings, 1991.

Hyde, Margaret O. *The Homeless: Profiling the Problem.* Enslow Publishers, 1989.

Parillo, Vincent N., ed. *Rethinking Today's Minorities.* Greenwood Press, 1991.

Readings for the Teacher
Dinnerstein, Leonard, et al. *Natives and Strangers: Blacks, Indians, and Immigrants in America.* Oxford University Press, 1990.

Takaki, Ronald. *A Different Mirror. A History of Multicultural America.* Little, Brown, 1993.

Multimedia Resources
COPE: A Simulation of Adapting to Change and Anticipating the Future. Interact. (Teaching time frame: 3 weeks)

Energy: The Key to Our Future. United Learning. (VHS, 60 minutes)

Spaceship Earth: Our Global Environment. WORLDLINK. (VHS, 25 minutes)

Classroom

Easy-to-use Reproducible Lesson Plans help you integrate these powerful resources into your daily lessons.

Resources

Review and Reinforcement

Name _____

Date _____

Class _____

Vocabulary Activity 23

A B C

The Vietnam Era 1954–1975

DIRECTIONS: Fill In the Blanks Use the following terms to complete the sentences below.

credibility gap	student deferment	escalation
teach-ins	shuttle diplomacy	

1. When President Johnson ordered American troops to engage in bombing and ground combat, he authorized _____ of the Vietnam War.

2. The Pentagon Papers contributed to the _____ by demonstrating that four presidents had deceived the public about Vietnam.

3. _____ allowed men to finish college before going to war.

4. Using _____, Secretary of State Henry Kissinger traveled between Israel and Egypt to negotiate for peace between the two countries.

5. On university campuses, students and teachers held _____ to examine and protest the war in Vietnam.

DIRECTIONS: Matching Match each term in Column A with its definition in Column B.

Column A

_____ 6. search-and-destroy strategy

_____ 7. war of national liberation

_____ 8. commune

_____ 9. détente

_____ 10. conscientious objector

_____ 11. summit

Column B

a. Community with shared living quarters, food, and work

b. Relaxation of tensions

c. Person whose religious beliefs do not allow him to fight in a war

d. Confrontation to free a nation from another country's control

e. Bombing of supply lines to force enemy troops into the open

f. Diplomatic meeting

DIRECTIONS: Exploring Roots The words **counter** and **reaction** both refer to someone or something moving in the opposite direction of something else. How does the idea of opposition relate to the following terms? Refer to a dictionary if necessary.

12. Counter culture _____

13. Reactionary government _____
_____
_____

Vocabulary Activities

American History: The Modern Era Since 1865

Guided Reading Activity 23-3

Protest and Reaction

DIRECTIONS: Recording Who, What, When, Where, Why, and How Use your textbook to identify key ideas in this section.

1. **How** did the Senate's educational hearings affect public opinion?

_____

_____

2. **Where** did America's antiwar movement flourish?

_____

3. **Why** did many people feel the draft was unfair?

_____

_____

4. **What** groups of men did not have to fight in the Vietnam War?

_____

5. **What** triggered the 1970 riots at Kent State University?

_____

6. **What** major European event was sparked by student protests?

_____

7. **How** did members of the counterculture behave differently than mainstream America?

_____

_____

8. **What** sparked the conservative backlash?

_____

9. **When** did Lyndon Johnson drop out of the 1968 presidential election?

_____

_____

10. **Who** assassinated Robert Kennedy and why?

_____

11. **What** event brought thousands of antiwar protesters to Chicago?

_____

12. **How** did the state of the Democratic party help Nixon win the 1968 presidential election?

_____

13. **What** plan did Nixon claim to have when running for President?

_____

14. **Where** did Independent candidate George Wallace find voter backing?

_____

_____

Guided Reading Activities These activities help students:

- read with a purpose
- master new material as they read
- prepare for quizzes and tests

Review and Reinforcement

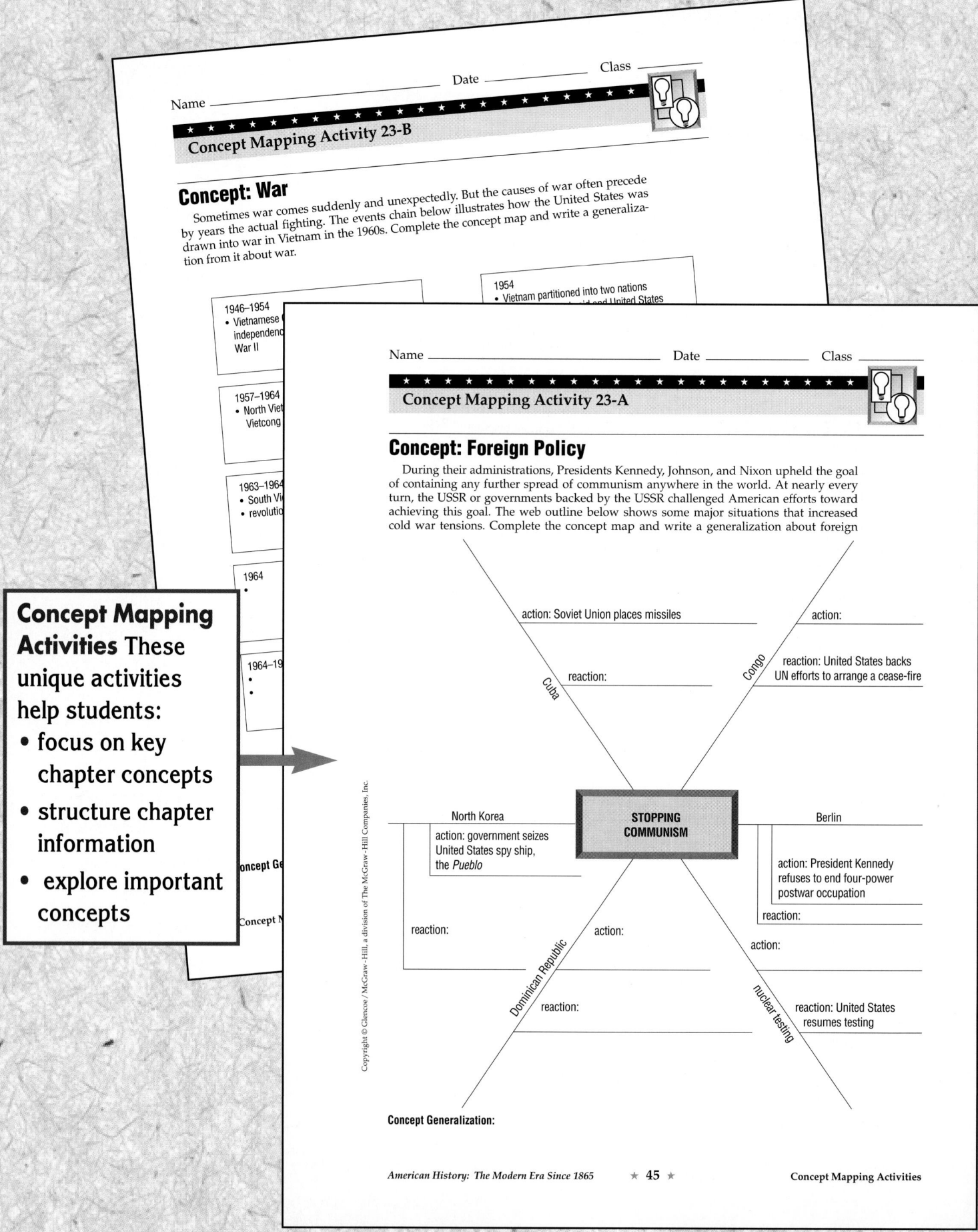

Concept Mapping Activities These unique activities help students:

- focus on key chapter concepts
- structure chapter information
- explore important concepts

Concept Mapping Activity 23-B

Concept: War

Sometimes war comes suddenly and unexpectedly. But the causes of war often precede by years the actual fighting. The events chain below illustrates how the United States was drawn into war in Vietnam in the 1960s. Complete the concept map and write a generalization from it about war.

1946–1954
- Vietnamese
  independenc
  War II

1957–1964
- North Viet
  Vietcong

1963–1964
- South Vi
- revolutio

1964
- •

1964–19
- •
- •

1954
- Vietnam partitioned into two nations

Concept Mapping Activity 23-A

Concept: Foreign Policy

During their administrations, Presidents Kennedy, Johnson, and Nixon upheld the goal of containing any further spread of communism anywhere in the world. At nearly every turn, the USSR or governments backed by the USSR challenged American efforts toward achieving this goal. The web outline below shows some major situations that increased cold war tensions. Complete the concept map and write a generalization about foreign

action: Soviet Union places missiles

action:

reaction: United States backs
UN efforts to arrange a cease-fire

Cuba

reaction:

Congo

STOPPING COMMUNISM

North Korea

action: government seizes
United States spy ship,
the *Pueblo*

reaction:

action:

Berlin

action: President Kennedy
refuses to end four-power
postwar occupation

reaction:

action:

Dominican Republic

reaction:

nuclear testing

reaction: United States
resumes testing

Concept Generalization:

American History: The Modern Era Since 1865   ★ **45** ★   Concept Mapping Activities

T50

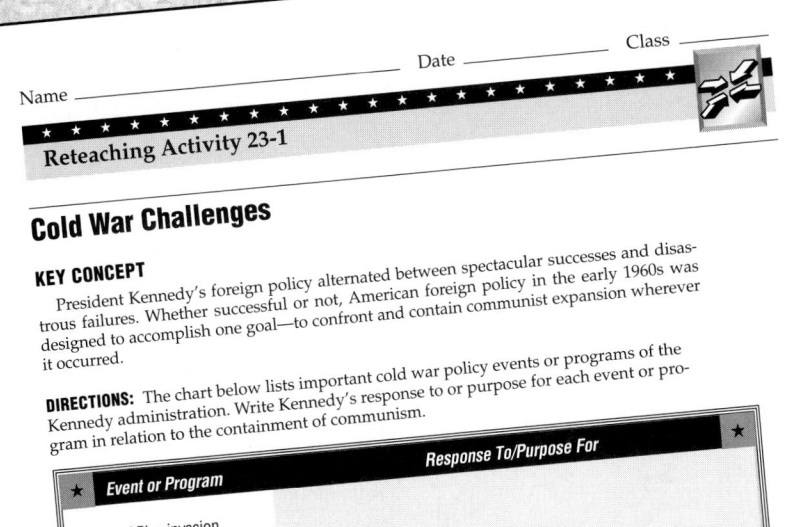

Name _____ Date _____ Class _____

★ ★ ★ ★ ★ ★ ★ ★ ★ ★ ★ ★ ★ ★ ★ ★ ★ ★ ★ ★

Reteaching Activity 23-1

Cold War Challenges

KEY CONCEPT

President Kennedy's foreign policy alternated between spectacular successes and disastrous failures. Whether successful or not, American foreign policy in the early 1960s was designed to accomplish one goal—to confront and contain communist expansion wherever it occurred.

DIRECTIONS: The chart below lists important cold war policy events or programs of the Kennedy administration. Write Kennedy's response to or purpose for each event or program in relation to the containment of communism.

★ Event or Program	Response To/Purpose For ★
1. Bay of Pigs invasion	

Name _____ Date _____ Class _____

★ ★

Activity 23-2

War in Vietnam

The United States became involved in the Vietnam War because its leaders viewed the countries of Southeast Asia as a row of dominoes, all likely to fall to communist takeover. America's long and complex involvement began with a request for military advice. By the time of U. S. withdrawal in 1975, more than 58,000 American soldiers were dead or missing in action.

★★
DIRECTIONS: Completion In the space provided, write the word or phrase from the box that best completes each sentence.

the Mekong Delta	Ho Chi Minh	Laos
the Gulf of Tonkin	Ngo Dinh Diem	Napalm
General William Westmoreland	the Tet offensive	Agent Orange

1. _____Ho Chi Minh_____ led a war against the non-communist government of South Vietnam in an effort to unite it with the North.

2. _____Ngo Dinh Diem_____ was a Catholic and a militant anti-communist who led the South Vietnamese government from 1954 to 1963.

3. An incident in _____the Gulf of Tonkin_____ was used as justification for the extension of the war in Vietnam.

4. During _____the Tet offensive_____ , the Viet Cong attacked military targets throughout South Vietnam, even in the capital of Saigon.

5. The individual in charge of America's military effort in South Vietnam was _____General William Westmoreland_____ .

6. _____Agent Orange_____ was a chemical herbicide used to kill vegetation and destroy crops in South Vietnam.

★★
DIRECTIONS: Essay Answer the question in the space provided below.

In your opinion, why would the Vietnam War have been very difficult to win?

Answers will vary but most students will point to the fact that the Vietnam War was a guerrilla war in which the enemy used ambushes, booby traps, and other acts of terrorism. Also, it was extremely difficult to identify the enemy. At home, Americans watched the increasing violence on television and became more and more unhappy with the mounting death toll and what seemed to be a lack of progress toward an end to the fighting.

_____

_____

_____

Skills Development

Chapter Skills Activities With these activities, you can:
- reinforce essential chapter skills
- help students master social studies, critical thinking, and writing skills

Name _____ Date _____ Class _____

★ ★ ★ ★ ★ ★ ★ ★ ★ ★ ★ ★ ★ ★ ★ ★ ★ ★ ★ ★

Chapter Skills Activity 23

Interpreting Military Maps

DIRECTIONS: **Essays** Study the map. Then answer the questions that follow.

1. During the Vietnam War, American troops divided the map of Vietnam into four tactical zones, as shown on the map. Using a ruler and the map key, state the approximate number of kilometers troops had to travel from Zone I to Zone III. Assume, for the purposes of this exercise, that the troops could pursue a direct route over land.

_____

_____

2. Look at the map shading for the concentrations of people in Vietnam. Write a statement describing the locations of the largest numbers of people.

_____

_____

3. In 1975, Communist offensives led to the fall of Vietnam. The Viet Cong troops moved south from the demilitarized zone into South Vietnam. Hue fell to the Viet Cong on March 26, Qui Nhon on April 1, Phan Thiet on April 3, and Saigon on April 30. Using a colored marker, draw the path of the Viet Cong forces through these cities.

4. Many innocent Vietnam civilians were killed as a result of guerrilla warfare during the Vietnam War. Explain how the locations of the main guerrilla actions affected the civilian death rate.

_____

_____

_____

_____

_____

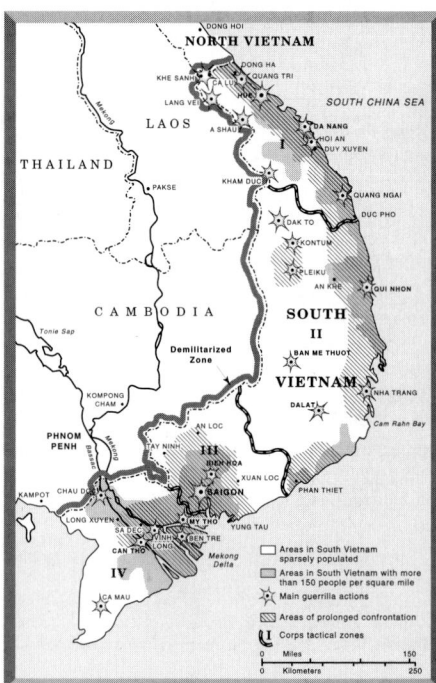

Name _____

Date _____ Class _____

DIRECTIONS: **Interpreting Points of View** As you read the following examples of statements made during the Vietnam War, look for words or phrases that suggest personal opinion. Identify which aspects of the topic the speaker has emphasized or excluded. Then answer the questions that follow.

A. By continuing the war in Vietnam, the United States is interfering in an internal struggle that we cannot win. Too many Americans are being sacrificed to protect a corrupt regime.

B. By preventing South Vietnam from becoming communist, we are helping to ensure peace and stability in Southeast Asia.

C. The young men who refused to be drafted should be pardoned because, although they broke the law, they were following their consciences by refusing to take part in an unjust war.

D. Because the enemy is able to hide among the friendly villagers, U.S. air and ground forces sent to Vietnam have maimed and killed large numbers of innocent Vietnamese citizens.

E. During the Tet offensive, the North Vietnamese soldiers struck with a fierce, bloody destructiveness against dozens of towns and military installations throughout South Vietnam. The attack was a treacherous and deceitful act of terror against the peaceful villages of the South.

1. Note below any words or phrases that appeal to emotional arguments. _____
_____
_____
_____
_____

2. Based on the context of the statements, at what point in the war were the speakers most likely expressing themselves? _____
_____

3. Indicate by letter which statements were probably made by people who were hawks during the Vietnam War. _____

4. Indicate by letter which statements were probably made by doves during the Vietnam War.

5. Compare the arguments of the speakers in statements A and B. Which one most likely matched the feelings of large numbers of the American public at the conclusion of the nation's involvement in Vietnam?
_____
_____
_____

Critical Thinking Skills Activities

These chapter activities:

- challenge students to apply knowledge in problem-solving situations
- develop higher-order thinking skills
- connect learned skills to the real world

T53

Enrichment and Extension

★ ★

Enrichment Activity 23 *(continued)*

the Organization of American States, to consider this threat to hemispheric security and to invoke articles six and eight of the Rio Treaty in support of all necessary action. . . . Our other allies around the world have also been alerted.

Sixth: Under the Charter of the United Nations, we are asking tonight that an emergency meeting of the Security Council be convoked without delay to take action against this latest Soviet threat to world peace. Our resolution will d __ __ for the prompt dismantling and withdrawal o __ __ off __ sive weapons in Cuba, under the sup __ __ __ UN observers, before the quarantine ca __ __ __ __

Seventh and finally: I call upon __ __ __ Khrushchev to halt and eliminate this __ __ __ reckless, and provocative threat to wo __ __ __ to stable relations between our two __ __ upon him further to abandon this co __ __ domination, and to join in an historic __ __ the perilous arms race and to transfo __ __ of man. He has an opportunity no __ __ world back from the abyss of destru __ __

1. **Making Generalizations** Place __ __ __ 1960s and describe your feeling __ __ in the speech makes you feel th __ __

---

ing to his government's own words that it had no need to station missiles outside its own territory, and withdrawing these weapons from Cuba—by refraining from any action which will widen or deepen the present crisis—and then by participating in a search for peaceful and permanent solutions. . . .

The path we have chosen for the present is full of hazards, as all paths are—but it is the one most consistent with our character and courage as a ___ ___ ___ ___ around the world.

Enrichment Activities These unique activities help you:

- expand chapter concepts
- stimulate critical thinking skills
- motivate students

★ ★

Enrichment Activity 23

The Cuban Missile Crisis

The foreign policy of the United States and of President John F. Kennedy received one of its sternest tests on October 22, 1962. On that day, the Cuban missile crisis threatened to engulf the United States, the Soviet Union, and much of the world in the worst of all types of conflicts, a nuclear war. To resolve the crisis, two nations, normally mortal enemies, had to find a way to cooperate.

DIRECTIONS: Imagine yourself sitting before the television set in the late afternoon of October 22, 1962. Your favorite program is interrupted by the sudden announcement that the President of the United States wishes to address the American people. Below is an excerpt of President Kennedy's speech on that day. Read it and respond to the items that follow.

This government, as promised, has maintained the closest surveillance of the Soviet military buildup on the island of Cuba. Within the past week, unmistakable evidence has established the fact that a series of offensive missile sites is now in preparation on that imprisoned island. The purpose of these bases can be none other than to provide a nuclear strike capability against the Western Hemisphere. . . .

The characteristics of these new missile sites indicate two distinct types of installations. Several of them include medium-range ballistic missiles, capable of carrying a nuclear warhead for a distance of more than a thousand nautical miles. Each of these missiles, in short, is capable of striking Washington, D.C., the Panama Canal, Cape Canaveral, Mexico City, or any other city in the southeastern part of the United States, in Central America, or in the Caribbean area.

Additional sites not yet completed appear to be designed for intermediate-range ballistic missiles—capable of traveling more than twice as far—and thus capable of striking most of the major cities in the Western Hemisphere, ranging as far north as Hudson Bay, Canada, and as far south as Lima, Peru. In addition, jet bombers, capable of carrying nuclear weapons, are now being uncrated and assembled in Cuba, while the necessary air bases are being prepared. . . .

Acting, therefore, in the defense of our own security and of the entire Western Hemisphere, and under the authority entrusted to me by the

Constitution as endorsed by the resolution of the Congress, I have directed that the following initial steps be taken immediately.

First: To halt this offensive buildup, a strict quarantine on all offensive military equipment under shipment to Cuba is being initiated. All ships of any kind bound for Cuba from whatever nation or port will, if found to contain cargoes of offensive weapons, be turned back. . . .

Second: I have directed the continued and increased close surveillance of Cuba and its military buildup. . . . Should these offensive military preparations continue, thus increasing the threat to the hemisphere, further action will be justified. I have directed the Armed Forces to prepare for any eventualities; and I trust that in the interest of both the Cuban people and the Soviet technicians at the sites, the hazards to all concerned of continuing this threat will be recognized.

Third: It shall be the policy of this nation to regard any nuclear missile launched from Cuba against any nation in the Western Hemisphere as an attack by the Soviet Union on the United States, requiring a full retaliatory response upon the Soviet Union.

Fourth: As a necessary military precaution, I have reinforced our base at Guantanamo, evacuated today the dependents of our personnel there, and ordered additional military units to be on a standby alert basis.

Fifth: We are calling tonight for an immediate meeting of the Organ of Consultation under

---

Name _____ Date _____ Class _____

★ ★

Linking Past and Present Activity 23 *(continued)*

EXAMINING THE PAST

DIRECTIONS: Recalling Information In the space provided, answer the questions below.

1. Why did the Air Force spray Agent Orange on Vietnam? _____

_____

2. In what ways were Americans exposed to the herbicide? _____

_____

3. What chemical by-products are associated with the manufacture of Agent Orange? _____

_____

4. What kinds of health problems have Americans experienced as a result of their exposure to Agent Orange? _____

5. Wh_____

_____ resulting from exposure to

_____

m? _____

Name _____ Date _____ Class _____

★ ★

Linking Past and Present Activity 23

The Curious Legacy of Agent Orange

THEN

In 1962, the U.S. Air Force launched a series of unusual bombing raids against South Vietnam and Laos. Low-flying planes sprayed streams of a liquid that drenched jungle foliage along roadsides and riverbanks. That liquid was Agent Orange, a chemical herbicide designed to end the successful guerrilla war being waged by the Viet Cong. Agent Orange was used to kill jungle vegetation so that North Vietnamese soldiers would have fewer places to hide from our troops. It was also used to destroy crops and food so that the guerrillas could not live off the land.

Throughout the 1960s and early 1970s, thousands of Americans were exposed to the chemical during its manufacture, its shipment overseas, and the time it was loaded aboard the planes for the spraying. Others served in ground areas that had been sprayed with the herbicide. Also exposed were thousands of Vietnamese troops and civilians.

Agent Orange got its name from the bright orange stripes painted on the steel drums in which it was shipped to Vietnam. When it was first used, the U.S. military did not believe it posed a threat to animals or humans. The herbicide belongs to a chemical family known as organo-halogen compounds. In the manufacturing process, by-products called dioxins are produced. These are among the most toxic synthetic substances on earth. Dioxins produce severe skin rashes, headaches, and intestinal disorders. They are also believed to cause cancer and birth defects. The U.S. government destroyed its remaining stocks of Agent Orange in 1977.

NOW

In recent years, American veterans exposed to Agent Orange while serving in Vietnam claim to have developed skin rashes, nerve disorders, cancer, and other long-term health disorders. A particularly poignant story concerns Elmo Zumwalt II, the commander-in-chief of naval forces in Vietnam. Zumwalt commanded a patrol boat in a region that had been treated with Agent Orange. Zumwalt developed two types of cancer and his son suffered from a birth defect that is believed to have resulted from his father's exposure to the herbicide.

A number of medical studies have investigated the connection between veterans' health disorders and exposure to Agent Orange. The results of these studies remain inconclusive. Although researchers have reported increased incidence of certain cancers and birth defects, they have failed to find a definite link between the herbicide and the illnesses. Some class action suits filed against the chemical companies that manufactured Agent Orange have resulted in cash settlements to people who claimed to be victims. Veterans' groups have urged further investigations into the effects of Agent Orange on ground troops and civilian personnel. In the meantime, these disorders remain part of the tragic and mysterious legacy of the Vietnam War.

Vietnamese troops and civilians have also developed similar maladies believed to be caused by Agent Orange. The vegetation in the country may take up to a century to fully recover from the use of this herbicide.

AC-123 SPRAYING DEFOLIANTS IN SOUTH VIETNAM

Linking Past and Present Activities

These engaging activities help students:

- see the relevancy of history in their lives
- compare past history to current events
- understand history's "big picture"

Enrichment and Extension

Name _____

Date _____ Class _____

★★★★★★★★★★★★★★★★★★★★★
Primary Source Reading

More than any election, more than any proud boasts, that simple fact reveals the truth. We have an ally in name only. We support a government without supporters. Without the effort of American arms that government would not last a day. . . .

And we are told that the war in Vietnam will settle the whole course of the future of Asia. But that is prayerful wish based on unsound hope, meant only to justify the enormous sacrifices we have already made. The truth is ~~~ umphed in China twenty ~~~ extended to Tibet. It los ~~~ Philippines, met disaster ~~~ still in K ~~~ nts in B ~~~ and it m ~~~

The outcome in each country depends and will depend on the intrinsic strength of the government, the particular circumstances of the country, and the particular character of the insurgent movement. The truth is that the war in Vietnam does not promise the end of all threats to Asia and ultimately to the United States; rather, if we proceed on our present course and follow our present policy, it promises only years and decades of further draining conflict on the mainland of Asia—conflict ~~~ finest military leaders have always ~~~ ~~~ nal tragedy. . . .

~~~-Times, Fe ~~~

~~~eading~~~
~~~to Sena~~~
~~~in a part~~~

~~~d Kenne~~~
~~~cy?~~~

CRITICAL THINK ~~~
3. Evaluating ~~~
progress of ~~~

American Histo ~~~

Primary and Secondary Source Readings These help students:

- experience first-hand accounts of history
- extend and enrich chapter content

Name _____ Date _____ Class _____

★★★★★★★★★★★★★★★★★★★★★★★★★
Primary Source Reading 23

The Reality of Vietnam

About the Selection As attorney general in the early 1960s, Robert Kennedy supported the Vietnam War. By 1968, however, he had emerged as a spokesperson for those wanting a peaceful resolution of the conflict. On February 8, 1968, shortly after the Vietcong's Tet Offensive, Kennedy—now a senator from New York—delivered a speech that was harshly critical of the Johnson administration's Vietnam policy. The speech propelled Kennedy into the race for the Democratic party's presidential nomination.

Guided Reading
1. Why did Kennedy oppose the war?
2. How did the South Vietnamese show their lack of enthusiasm for the war?

. . . But a short time ago we were serene in our reports and predictions of progress. In April, our commanding general told us that "the South Vietnamese are fighting now better than ever before . . . their record in combat . . . reveals an exceptional performance." In August, another general told us that "the really big battles of the Vietnam war are over . . . the enemy has been so badly pummeled he'll never give us trouble again." In December, we were told that we were winning "battle after battle," that "the secure proportion of the population has grown from about 45 percent to 65 percent and in the contested areas the tide continues to run with us."

That is what we were told, and what we were told at the highest possible level.

Those dreams are gone. The Viet Cong will probably withdraw from the cities, as they were forced to withdraw from the American Embassy. Thousands of them will be dead. But they will, nevertheless, have demonstrated that no part or person of South Vietnam is secure from their attacks: neither district capitals nor American bases, neither the peasant in his rice paddy nor our ambassadors nor the commanding general of our own great forces. . . .

. . . We will find no guide to the future in Vietnam unless we are bold enough to strip away the illusions and to confront the grim anguish, the reality of that battlefield which was once a nation called South Vietnam. . . . It is time for the truth.

We must, first of all, rid ourselves of the illusion that the events of the past two weeks represent some sort of victory. That is not so. . . .

Two Presidents and countless officials have told

us for seven years that although we can help the South Vietnamese, it is their war and they must win it; as Secretary of Defense McNamara told us last month, "We cannot provide the South Vietnamese with the will to survive as an independent nation . . . or with the ability and self-discipline a people must have to govern themselves. These qualities and attributes are essential contributions to the struggle only the South Vietnamese can supply." Yet this wise and certain counsel has gradually become an empty slogan, as mounting frustration has led us to transform the war into an American military effort.

The South Vietnamese Senate, with only one dissenting vote, refuses to draft eighteen- and nineteen-year-old South Vietnamese, with a member of the Assembly asking, "Why should Vietnamese boys be sent to die for Americans," while nineteen-year-old American boys fight to maintain the Senate and Assembly in Saigon. . . .

You cannot expect people to risk their lives and endure hardship unless they have a stake in their own society.

They must have a clear sense of identification with their own government, a belief they are participating in a cause worth fighting and dying for. Political and economic reform are not simply idealistic slogans or noble goals to be postponed until the end of the fighting. They are the principal weapons of battle. People will not fight—they will simply not fight—to line the pockets of generals or swell the bank accounts of the wealthy. They are far more likely to close their eyes and shut their doors in the face of their government—even as they did last week.

Name _____ Date _____ Class _____

★ ★

Geography in History Activity 23 *(continued)*

1. Look at the inset map, which shows the relative location of Vietnam and the United States. How might Vietnam's distance from the United States—about 8,000 miles across the Pacific Ocean—have affected the American war effort?

_____

_____

_____

2. Vietnam's coastline stretches more that 1,000 miles. How might such a long coastline have influenced American forces?

_____

_____

_____

3. The people of Southeast Asia have used rivers as transportation routes for thousands of years. American forces came to rely heavily on river transportation as well. Explain why rivers are "natural highways" in terrain like that of Vietnam.

_____

_____

Name _____ Date _____ Class _____

★ ★

Geography in History Activity 23

Vietnam: An Enormous Geographic Challenge

The American experience in Vietnam was colored largely by the geography of Vietnam. The country's jagged mountains and dense jungles make it among the most impenetrable on the globe. American forces were often frustrated in their attempts to deploy troops and equipment in such rugged terrain. Communist forces used it to their advantage, however, relying on the mountains and jungles as cover from American firepower. Many factors prevented the United States from achieving its objectives during the war, but Vietnam's rough physical features were among them.

The map below shows the mountains and jungles of Vietnam and Southeast Asia. Study the map. Then answer the questions that follow.

remely important to k this was so?

_____

he three cities shown

an Histor

Geography in History Activities

These engaging activities:

- show important role of geography in history
- develop students' geography skills
- demonstrate how geography affects daily life

American History: The Modern Era Since 1865   ★ **45** ★   **Geography in History Activities**

Enrichment and Extension

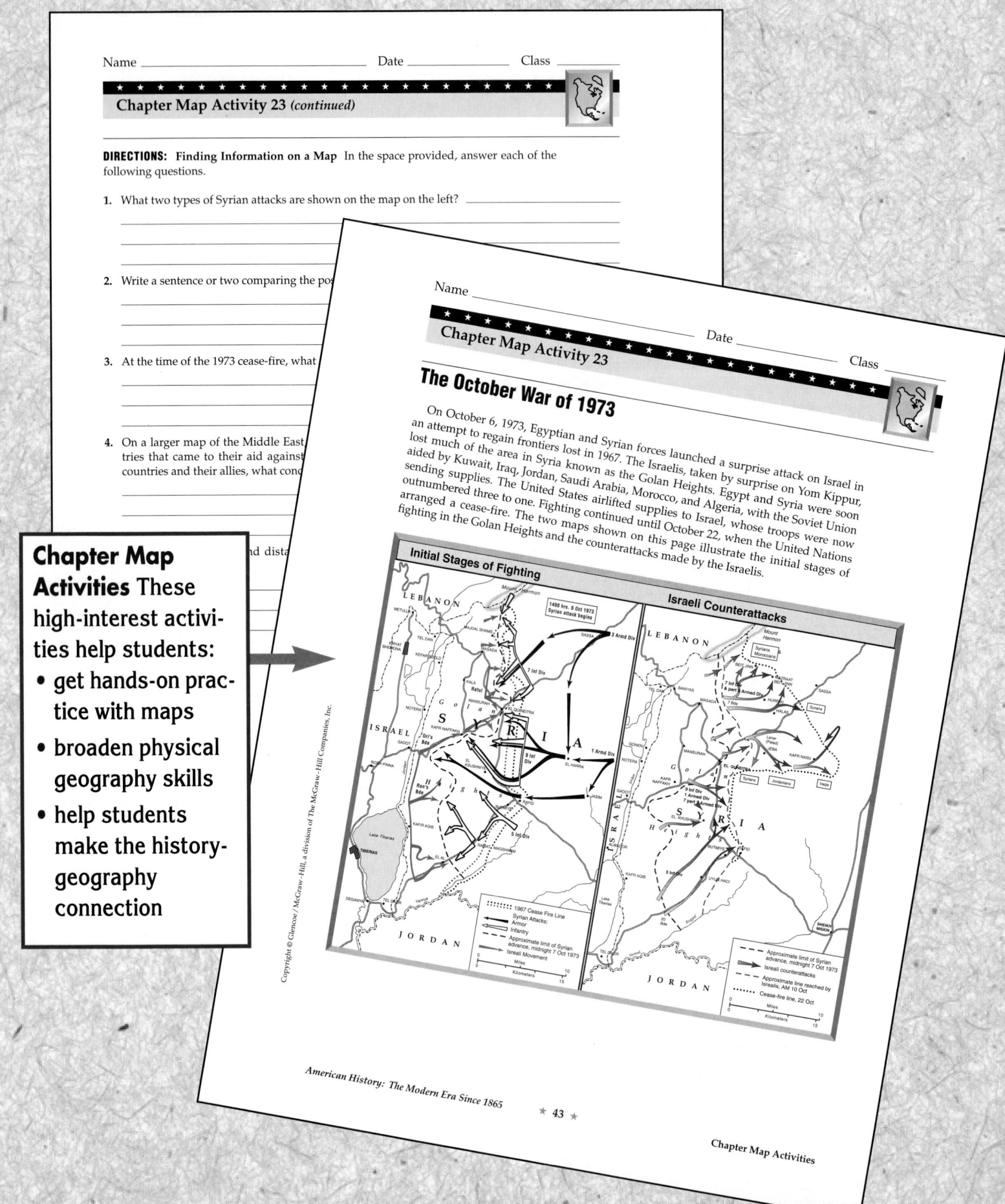

DIRECTIONS: **Finding Information on a Map** In the space provided, answer each of the following questions.

1. What two types of Syrian attacks are shown on the map on the left? _____
_____
_____

2. Write a sentence or two comparing the pos_____
_____
_____

3. At the time of the 1973 cease-fire, what _____
_____

4. On a larger map of the Middle East
tries that came to their aid against
countries and their allies, what con_____

_____ nd dista_____

Chapter Map Activities

These high-interest activities help students:

- get hands-on practice with maps
- broaden physical geography skills
- help students make the history-geography connection

The October War of 1973

On October 6, 1973, Egyptian and Syrian forces launched a surprise attack on Israel in an attempt to regain frontiers lost in 1967. The Israelis, taken by surprise on Yom Kippur, lost much of the area in Syria known as the Golan Heights. Egypt and Syria were soon aided by Kuwait, Iraq, Jordan, Saudi Arabia, Morocco, and Algeria, with the Soviet Union sending supplies. The United States airlifted supplies to Israel, whose troops were now outnumbered three to one. Fighting continued until October 22, when the United Nations arranged a cease-fire. The two maps shown on this page illustrate the initial stages of fighting in the Golan Heights and the counterattacks made by the Israelis.

T58

Name ———————————————————————— Date ——————— Class ———————

Cooperative Learning Activity 23

The Vietnam Era: Displaying the Unrest

GROUP PROJECT

The administrations of Presidents Kennedy, Johnson, and Nixon witnessed a period of national unrest. America's youth were protesting our involvement in the Vietnam War, as well as other "social injustices," by staging sit-ins and peace marches. President Kennedy, Martin Luther King, Jr., and Robert Kennedy were all assassinated. As a group, create a kiosk depicting the unrest of the 1960s. A kiosk is a three-dimensional advertising bulletin board.

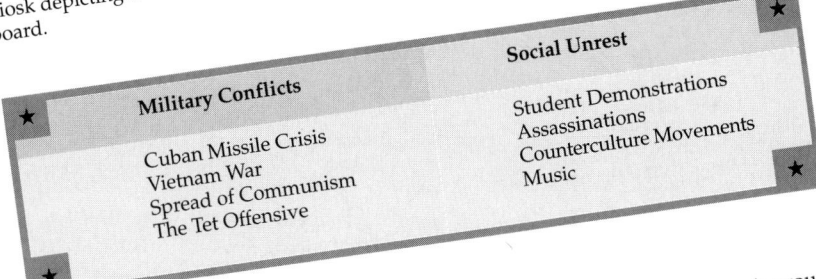

Military Conflicts

Cuban Missile Crisis
Vietnam War
Spread of Communism
The Tet Offensive

Social Unrest

Student Demonstrations
Assassinations
Counterculture Movements
Music

COOPERATIVE GROUP PROCESS

1. **Defining Tasks/Decision Making** Organize into four groups. Within each group, form two subgroups. Assign one subgroup Military Conflicts and the other Social Unrest. Have each subgroup select one topic from the appropriate list above.

2. **Individual Work** Research the topic you've selected, then collect magazine photos and/or create visual images of your own to represent your topic.

3. **Group Sharing/Decision Making** Group members assemble and share the visuals they have collected. After sharing, the group discusses how to execute its kiosk using the photos and samples and the sides of a 2 X 2' corrugated box. Select a group manager to direct completion of the kiosk: How many people will work on each side? How will the group display its information? Will you use any words or headings? How will you choose to represent any music that supports your topic?

4. **Analysis** Group members share their kiosks with the class. You may wish to stack the kiosks on top of each other to create a column. What common information did each group choose to represent?

GROUP PROCESS QUESTIONS

Did the group agree on the assignment of tasks?

How did the process help you learn new information?

Did members listen carefully to each other's contributions?

What conclusions can you draw about using this process to complete work?

Cooperative Learning Activities

★ 23 ★

Enrichment and Extension

Political Cartoons

These unique activities:

- present concepts in a high-interest format
- encourage class-room discussion
- explore how public opinion is formed

★ ★

Political Cartoon 25

Uproar Over Vietnam

No conflict since the Civil War so fiercely divided Americans as the Vietnam War. By the mid–1960s, American opinion was sharply divided. The two sides were known as "hawks," those who wanted to strongly pursue the war, and "doves," those who opposed American involvement in the war. This was the first war brought into millions of American homes by television, and it made the conflict more immediate to Americans.

Study the cartoon below, then answer the questions that follow.

The Strategists

Reprinted with permission, *Chicago Sun Times* © 1995

American History: The Modern Era Since 1865   ★ **49** ★

Political Cartoons

Name _____ Class _____ Date _____

SUPREME COURT CASE 22

BROWN V. BOARD OF EDUCATION OF TOPEKA, KANSAS (1954)

Background of the Case

Brown represents a collection of cases, all decided together. The cases had one common feature: African American children had been denied admission to segregated white public schools.

These cases reached the U.S. Supreme Court by way of appeals through lower courts, all of which had ruled in accordance with the decision in *Plessy* v. *Ferguson* (1896). The Plessy case determined that separate but equal facilities did not violate the Fourteenth Amendment's guarantee of "equal protection of the law."

An earlier case, *Sweatt* v. *Painter* (1950) had held that African Americans must be admitted to the previously segregated University of Texas Law School because no separate but equal facility existed in the state. In *Brown*, however, there were findings "that the Negro and white schools involved have been equalized or were being equalized. . . ."

Constitutional Issue

The *Brown* case was an explicit reappraisal of the question in *Plessy* v. *Ferguson*. Did separate but equal public facilities violate the equal protection clause of the Fourteenth Amendment?

The Court's Decision

Chief Justice Earl Warren wrote the Court's unanimous decision.

Justice Warren began by noting that attempts to determine the precise intent of the Fourteenth Amendment's original sponsors have proved inconclusive. Even more difficult was any effort to discover its relation to the issue of public schools, as so few were in existence when the Amendment took effect.

Warren explained that the Court's method of examination, then, was to "look to the effect of segregation itself on public education" in order to determine "if segregation in public schools deprives these plaintiffs of the equal protection of the law." Warren added, "In approaching this problem, we cannot turn the clock back to 1868 when the [Fourteenth] Amendment was adopted, or even to 1896 when *Plessy* v. *Ferguson* was written. We must consider public education in the light of its full development and its present place in American life throughout the Nation. . . . Only in this way can it be determined if segregation in public schools deprives these plaintiffs of the equal protection of the law."

Warren quoted a Kansas state court ruling, which held that "segregation with the sanction of law, therefore, has a tendency to retard the educational and mental development of Negro children and to deprive them of some of the benefits they would receive in a racially integrated school system." Likewise, the U. S. Supreme Court concluded that segregation of African American schoolchildren "generates a feeling of inferiority as to their status in the community that may affect their hearts and minds in a way unlikely ever to be undone."

Recognizing further the huge psychological impact of segregation, Warren quoted the finding of a lower court with which he agreed (even though that court did rule against the plaintiffs). That lower court stated the finding based on psychological authority that, "Segregation of white and colored children in public schools has a detrimental effect upon the colored children. The impact is greater when it has the sanction of the law; for the policy of separating the races is usually interpreted as denoting the inferiority of the Negro group. A sense of inferiority affects the motivation of a child to learn. Segregation with the sanction of law, therefore, has the tendency to [retard]

Copyright © by Glencoe/McGraw-Hill.

Enrichment and Extension

American History Flash Cards These unique, high-interest materials:

- use games and exercises to present history
- provide user-friendly information
- provoke classroom discussion

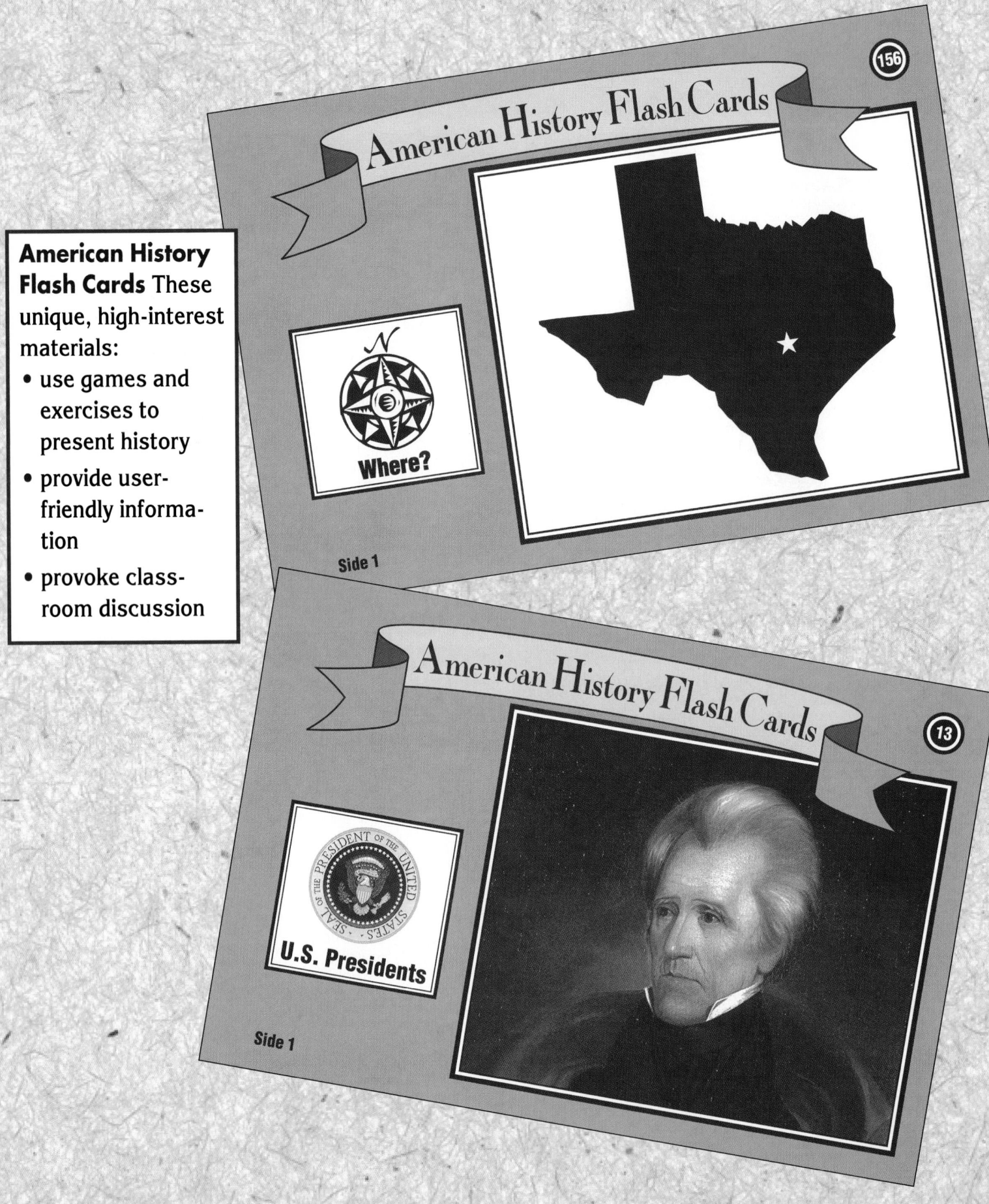

American History Flash Cards

156

Where?

Side 1

American History Flash Cards

13

SEAL OF THE PRESIDENT OF THE UNITED STATES

U.S. Presidents

Side 1

THE SPIRIT OF AMERICAN ART AND MUSIC

AMERICAN HISTORY

THE MODERN ERA SINCE 1865

The Spirit of American Art and Music

These unique activities and profiles:

- introduce important personalities in the arts
- make cross-curricular connections
- provoke classroom discussion

Assessment and Evaluation

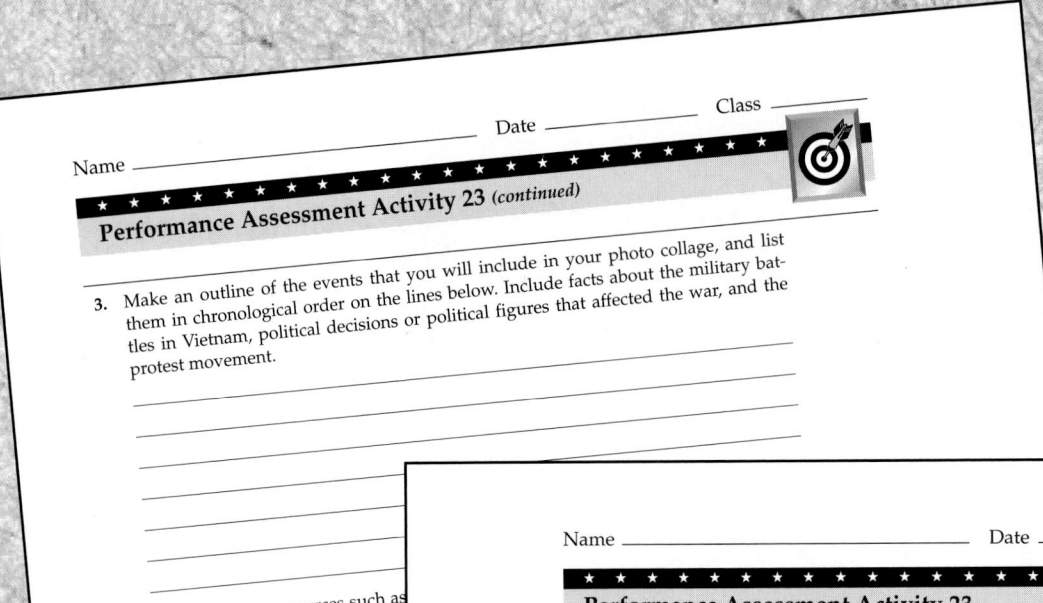

Performance Assessment Activity 23 (continued)

Name ——— Date ——— Class ———

3. Make an outline of the events that you will include in your photo collage, and list them in chronological order on the lines below. Include facts about the military battles in Vietnam, political decisions or political figures that affected the war, and the protest movement.

————————————————————————
————————————————————————
————————————————————————
————————————————————————

4. Consult primary sources such as ~~pho~~tographs that illustrate the even~~t~~ revise your outline to include ~~pho~~tographs.

5. Make photocopies of the photo~~graphs~~ the photographer or news serv~~ice~~ the approximate date the photo~~graph~~

6. Write captions or description~~s~~ date the photo was taken.

Performance Assessment Strategies and Activities

These comprehensive assessment strategies:

- meet alternative assessment needs
- save you preparation time
- include scoring rubrics

Name —————— Date ———— Class ———

Performance Assessment Activity 23

Vietnam on Display

BACKGROUND

The Gulf of Tonkin Resolution in 1964 gave President Johnson the authority to use force against aggression, which began the bombing of North Vietnam. What had been a civil war in Vietnam developed into a conflict between American forces that backed South Vietnam and communist forces that backed North Vietnam. As the war escalated and casualties mounted, the debate over the war became heated at home. The hawks supported American military involvement to prevent Asia from becoming communist. The doves objected to participating in another country's civil war, to being drafted into an undeclared war, and to the use of napalm and other defoliants. After the devastating Tet offensive in 1968, many Americans began to feel that it was impossible to win the war. Antiwar protests became widespread, including a nationwide demonstration in October 1969. Peace talks continued under President Nixon. To silence protesters, the President announced a policy of Vietnamization, which included pulling United States troops out of Vietnam; meanwhile, he ordered saturation bombing of North Vietnam and an invasion of Cambodia. In 1970, four student protesters were killed at Kent State University and two more at Jackson State University. Public outrage mounted after the release of *The Pentagon Papers* in 1971, which revealed how the government had attempted to deceive Congress and the public about the situation in Vietnam. Demonstrations continued until finally, in 1973, a cease-fire agreement was reached.

TASK

You are a historian who has been asked to create a photo essay to display in your local library. The subject of the photo essay is how Americans reacted to important military and political events in the Vietnam War. For your display, you will make photocopies of published photographs and arrange them chronologically to present a collage of the events of the war and the protests at home. You will include newspaper headlines, quotations or captions for each photograph, and the dates the photographs were taken.

AUDIENCE

Your audience is visitors to the library and your classmates.

PURPOSE

The purpose of this activity is to illustrate through pictures and captions how Americans reacted to the events of the Vietnam War. Planning your photo collage will give you experience in organizing visual material to tell a story.

PROCEDURE

1. Review information on the Vietnam era, the Vietnam War, the antiwar movement, student protests, and hawks and doves.

2. Conduct additional research to find out more about American involvement in the war and people's perceptions of the war.

Name _____ **Date** _____ **Class** _____

★ Score

Chapter 23 Test, Form A

The Vietnam Era

DIRECTIONS: Matching Match each item in Column A with the items in Column B.
Write the correct letters in the blanks. *(3 points each)*

Column A

_____ 1. military expansion, such as that in Vietnam

_____ 2. chemical defoliant used by the United States in Vietnam

_____ 3. North Vietnam's leader during the 1960s

_____ 4. secretary of state during Johnson's administration

_____ 5. American commander in Vietnam

_____ 6. "dove" candidate

Column B

A. Ngo Dinh Diem

B. Agent Orange

C. Dean Rusk

D. escalation

E. William Westmoreland

F. Alliance for Progress

G. Henry Kissinger

H. Ho Chi Minh

I. Nikita Khrushchev

J. Lyndon B. Johnson

K. Fulgencio Batista

L. Bay of Pigs

M. Vietcong

N. Hubert Humphrey

O. Richard M. Nixon

P. Eugene McCarthy

Q. Robert McNamara

that best

suspicions of

States would

ter and Unit Tests

Name _____ **Date** _____ **Class** _____

★ Q&A

Section Quiz 23-1

The Vietnam Era

DIRECTIONS: Matching Match each item in Column A with the items in Column B.
Write the correct letters in the blanks. *(10 points each)*

Column A

_____ 1. Caribbean nation that became center of international crisis in 1962

_____ 2. United States accused this nation of setting up missile bases in Cuba

_____ 3. city divided by communists

_____ 4. nation supported by the United States in the Middle East conflict of 1967

_____ 5. nation that seized a United States spy ship

Column B

A. Israel

B. Berlin

C. Soviet Union

D. Korea

E. Cuba

DIRECTIONS: Multiple Choice In the blank at the left, write the letter of the choice that best
completes the statement or answers the question. *(10 points each)*

_____ 6. The CIA believed an invasion of Cuba would succeed because
A. Castro was very weak militarily.
B. Castro had no support from any major power.
C. the invasion would involve elite units of the United States armed forces.
D. the invasion would touch off a popular uprising against Castro in Cuba.

_____ 7. When Kennedy refused to recognize East Germany, Kh
A. sealing off Berlin from the rest of Germany.
B. building a wall through Berlin.
C. calling for a summit meeting,
D. breaking the moratorium on testing nuclear weap

_____ 8. The Peace Corps was organized to help
A. prevent the spread of communism.
B. Americans build new colonies.
C. counter the power of rural politicians.
D. sell American goods in new markets.

_____ 9. When methods were developed to monitor nuclear t
the United States responded by
A. demanding that the Soviet Union dismantle its n
B. giving up its demands for on-site inspection.
C. resuming its own nucleartesting.
D. banning underground testing.

_____ 10. President Johnson sent Marines to the Dominican R
A. a communist takeover was imminent.
B. the United States should support reactionary g
C. Cuba was trying to take over the island nation.
D. he had to end the "credibility gap."

Section Quizzes

Glencoe/McGraw-Hill Companies, Inc.

TESTMAKER

AMERICAN HISTORY
THE MODERN ERA SINCE 1865

BANK

P/N G24221.28

Teacher Planning and Support

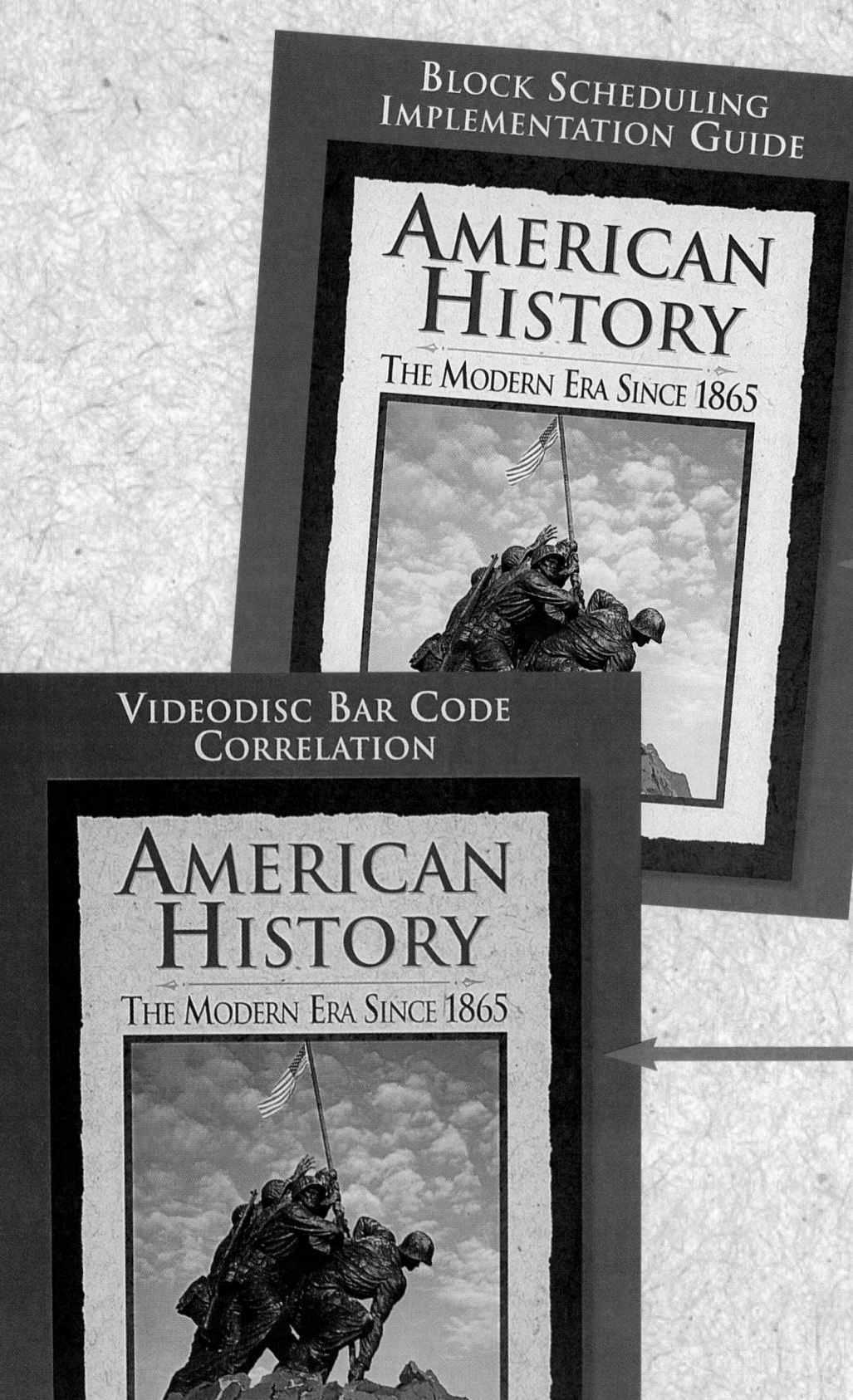

Block Scheduling Implementation Guide This helpful resource:
- gives tips for implementing block scheduling
- provides a complete course outline
- adapts to any teaching schedule

Videodisc Bar Code Correlation INCLUDES bar codes for National Geographic Society, Reuters, ABCNews InterActive™, and Glencoe videodiscs

Spanish Language Resources

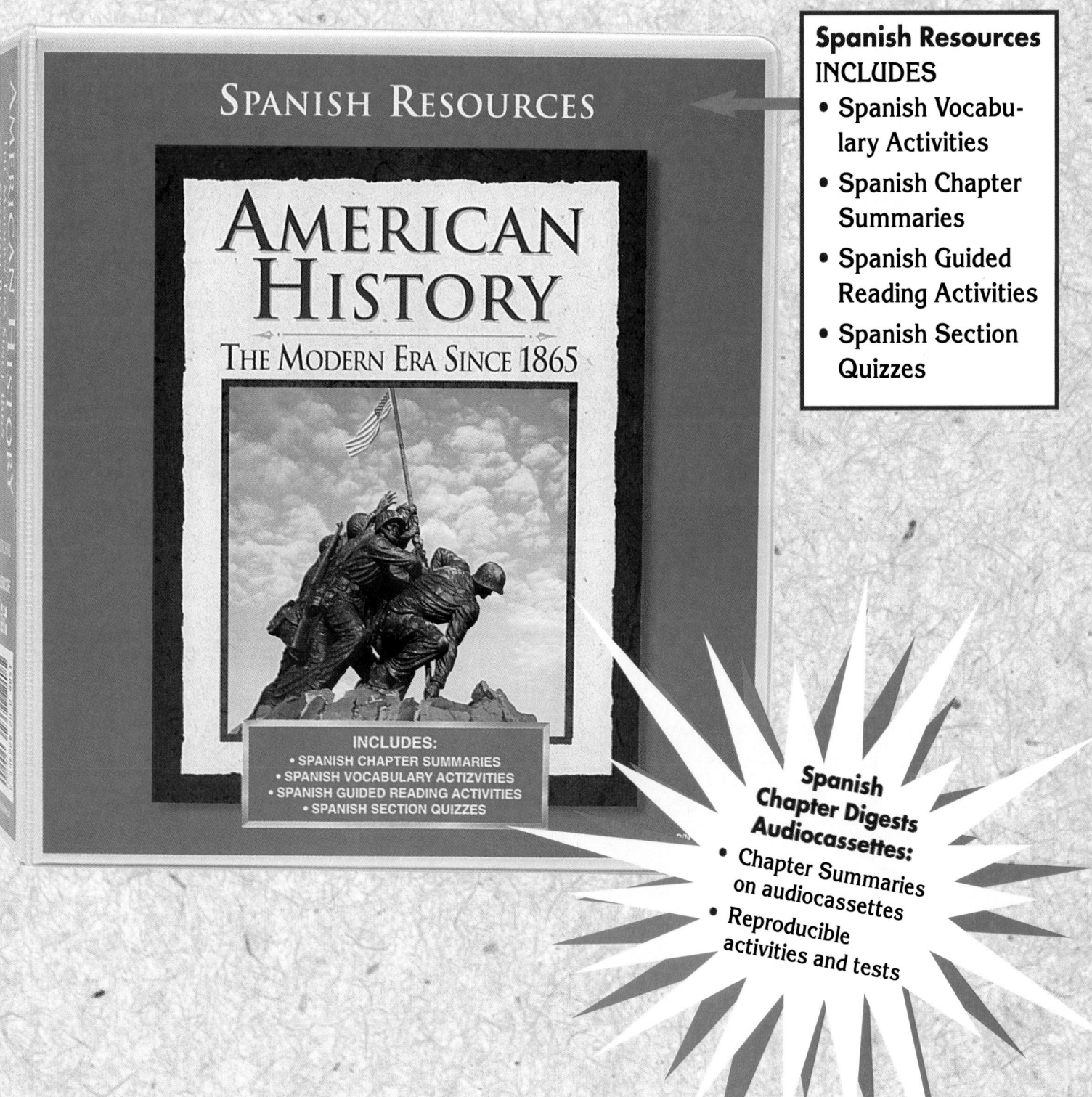

SPANISH RESOURCES

AMERICAN
HISTORY
THE MODERN ERA SINCE 1865

INCLUDES:
• SPANISH CHAPTER SUMMARIES
• SPANISH VOCABULARY ACTIZVITIES
• SPANISH GUIDED READING ACTIVITIES
• SPANISH SECTION QUIZZES

Spanish Resources
INCLUDES
• Spanish Vocabulary Activities
• Spanish Chapter Summaries
• Spanish Guided Reading Activities
• Spanish Section Quizzes

Spanish Chapter Digests Audiocassettes:
• Chapter Summaries on audiocassettes
• Reproducible activities and tests

Multimedia and Technology

In the Garden (1893)
Mary Cassatt
16

Day of the Fair (1963)
Andrew Wyeth
29

Forward (1967)
Jacob Lawrence
30

North Carolina Museum of Art, Raleigh. Purchased with funds from the state of North Carolina.

Museum Purchase.

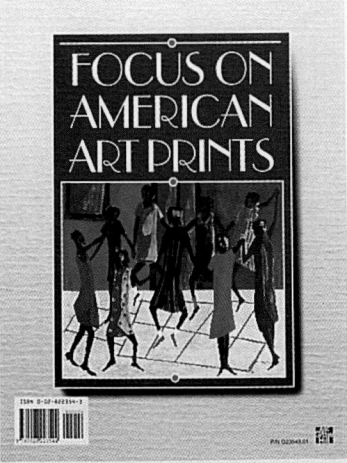

Fine Art Prints

GLENCOE

Focus on American Fine Art Prints This unique collection:
- includes 20 laminated fine art posters
- makes students aware of American cultural heritage

Multimedia and Technology

Also available in audiocassettes.

GLENCOE
American Music
★★★★★★★★★★★★★★★★★
Cultural Traditions

Includes:
Teacher's Guide • Student Activities
Compact Discs, Volume I and II

ISBN 0-02-823803-6

GLENCOE
McGraw-Hill
P/N G38036.01

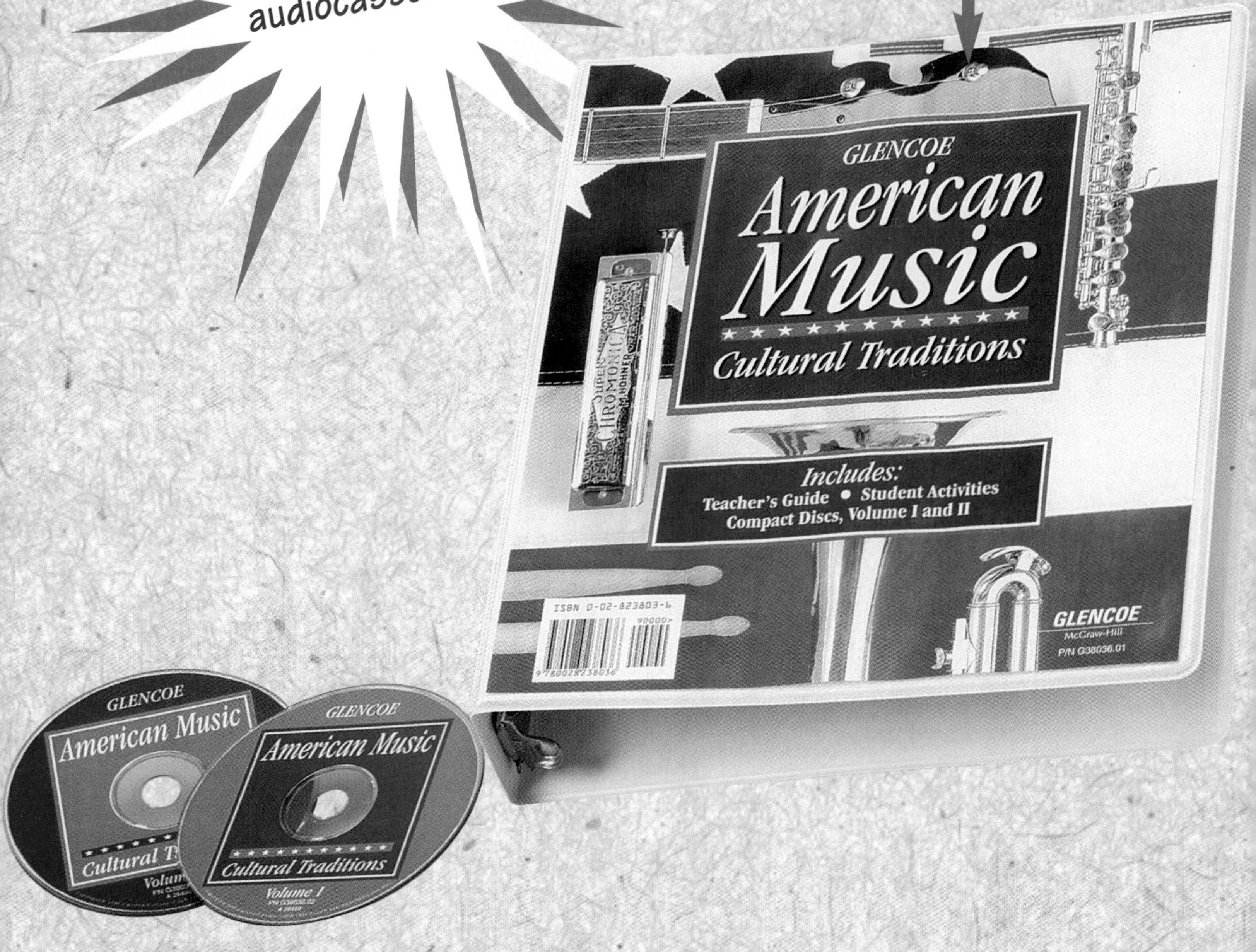

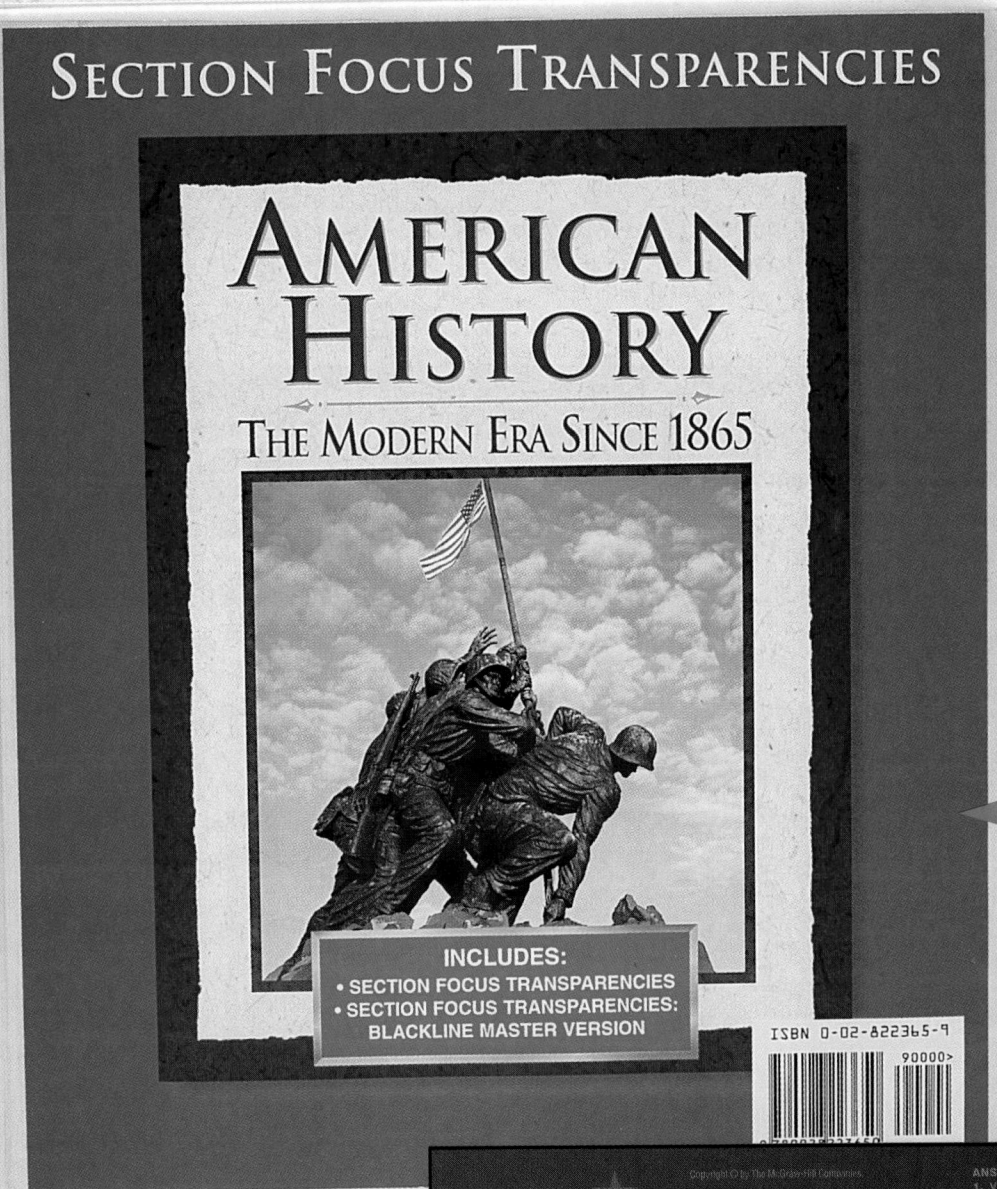

SECTION FOCUS TRANSPARENCIES

AMERICAN HISTORY
THE MODERN ERA SINCE 1865

INCLUDES:
- SECTION FOCUS TRANSPARENCIES
- SECTION FOCUS TRANSPARENCIES: BLACKLINE MASTER VERSION

ISBN 0-02-822365-9

Section Focus Transparencies

These thought-provoking transparencies:
- offer a variety of formats
- can be used as Bellringer activities
- help students focus on key concepts
- include blackline master versions

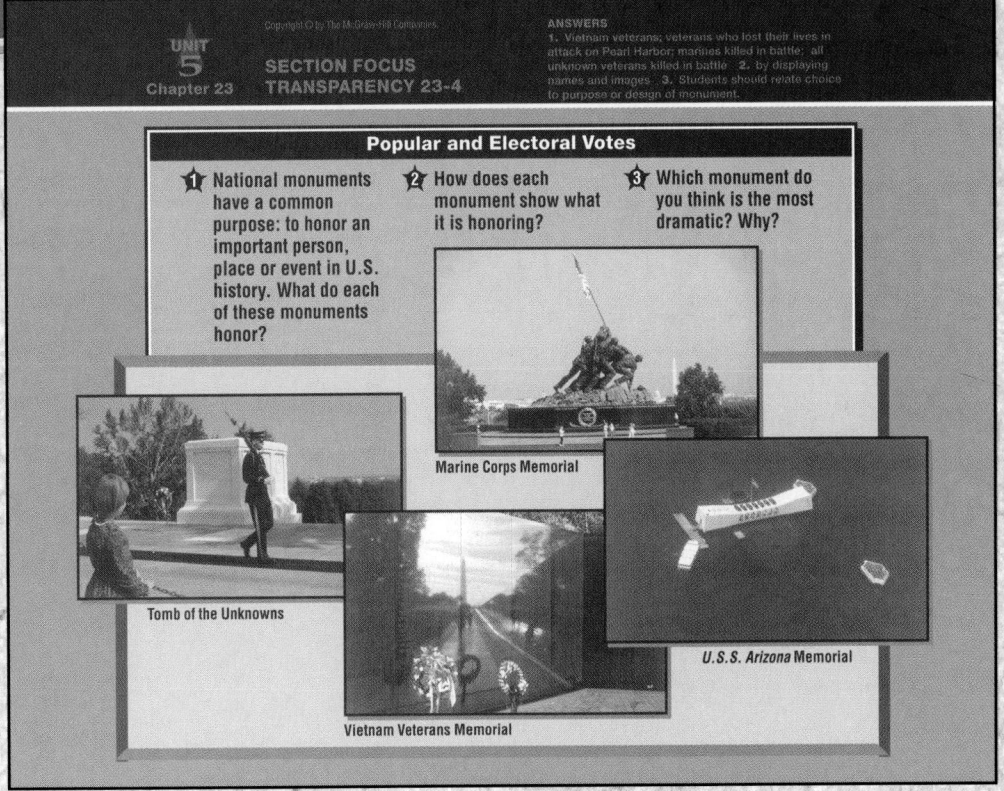

UNIT 5
Chapter 23

SECTION FOCUS
TRANSPARENCY 23-4

ANSWERS
1. Vietnam veterans; veterans who lost their lives in attack on Pearl Harbor; marines killed in battle; all unknown veterans killed in battle 2. by displaying names and images 3. Students should relate choice to purpose or design of monument.

Popular and Electoral Votes

1 National monuments have a common purpose: to honor an important person, place or event in U.S. history. What do each of these monuments honor?

2 How does each monument show what it is honoring?

3 Which monument do you think is the most dramatic? Why?

Marine Corps Memorial

Tomb of the Unknowns

Vietnam Veterans Memorial

U.S.S. Arizona Memorial

Multimedia and Technology

Teaching Transparencies
INCLUDES
- Chapter Concepts Transparencies
- Chapter Concepts Transparencies Strategies and Activities
- Map Transparencies
- Map Transparencies Strategies and Activities
- Skills Transparencies
- Skills Transparencies Strategies and Activities

TEACHING TRANSPARENCIES

AMERICAN HISTORY

THE MODERN ERA SINCE 1865

INCLUDES:
- CHAPTER CONCEPTS TRANSPARENCIES WITH STRATEGIES AND ACTIVITIES
- MAP TRANSPARENCIES WITH STRATEGIES AND ACTIVITIES
- SKILLS TRANSPARENCIES WITH STRATEGIES AND ACTIVITIES

P/N G23993.28

Chapter Concepts Transparencies

These high-interest transparencies:
- present images of chapter topics
- vividly reinforce key chapter concepts
- emphasize important historic themes

Includes exciting Strategies and Activities

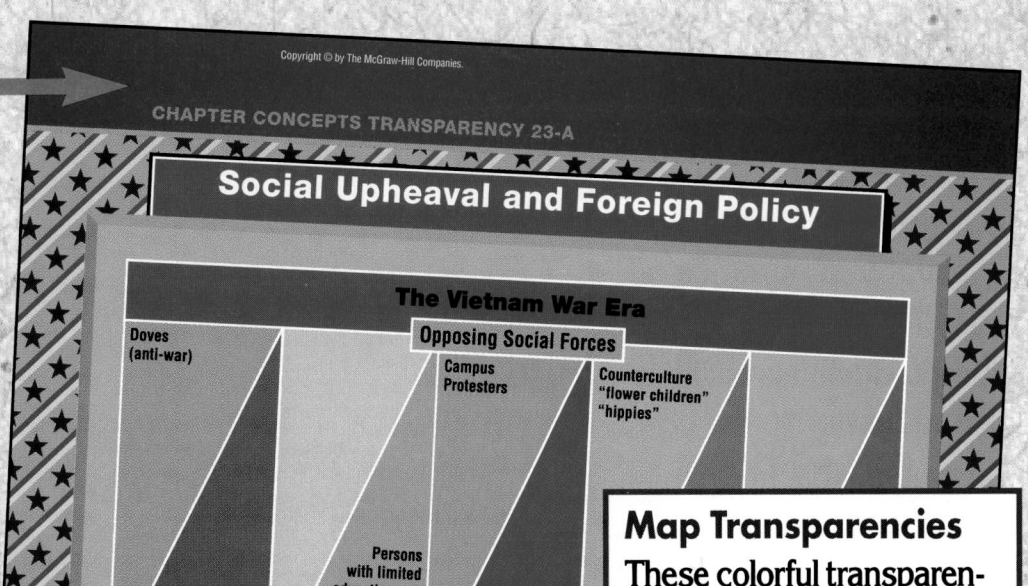

CHAPTER CONCEPTS TRANSPARENCY 23-A

Social Upheaval and Foreign Policy

The Vietnam War Era
Opposing Social Forces

Doves (anti-war)

Campus Protesters

Counterculture "flower children" "hippies"

Persons with limited education and low income—

Map Transparencies

These colorful transparencies:
- geographically present chapter information
- provide additional chapter maps
- allow student practice of geographic skills

Includes exciting Strategies and Activities

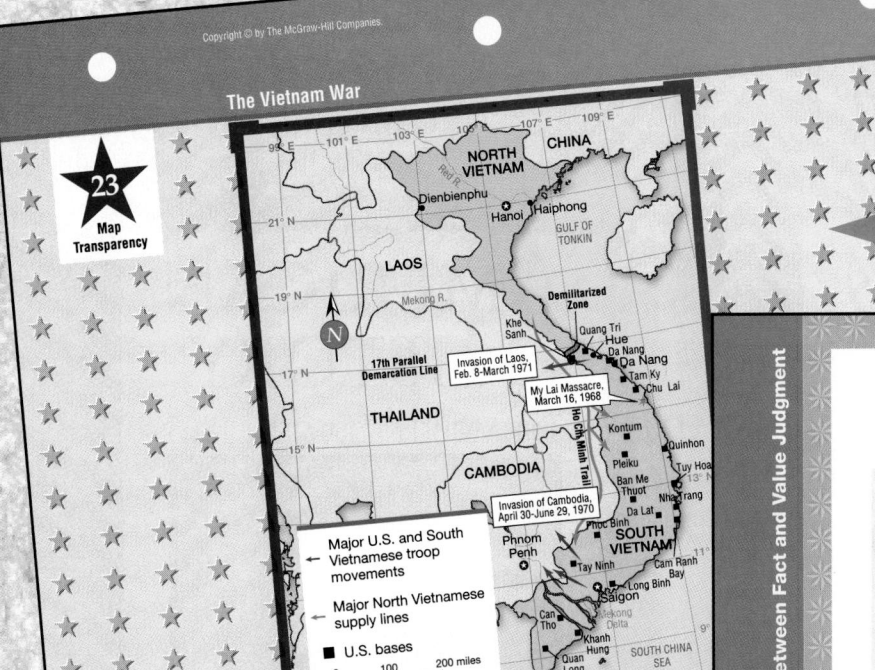

The Vietnam War

23 Map Transparency

Skills Transparencies

These thought-provoking transparencies:
- review and reinforce chapter skills
- visually present chapter material
- challenge students to apply knowledge

Includes exciting Strategies and Activities

Distinguishing Between Fact and Value Judgment

As the months wore on, peace did not seem any closer. The United States had three choices: go all out to win, get out, or hang in there.

The Strategists

ESCALATE! THERE IS NO SUBSTITUTE FOR VICTORY

REPENT ASIA IS NONE OF OUR BUSINESS

SKILLS TRANSPARENCY 23

Multimedia and Technology

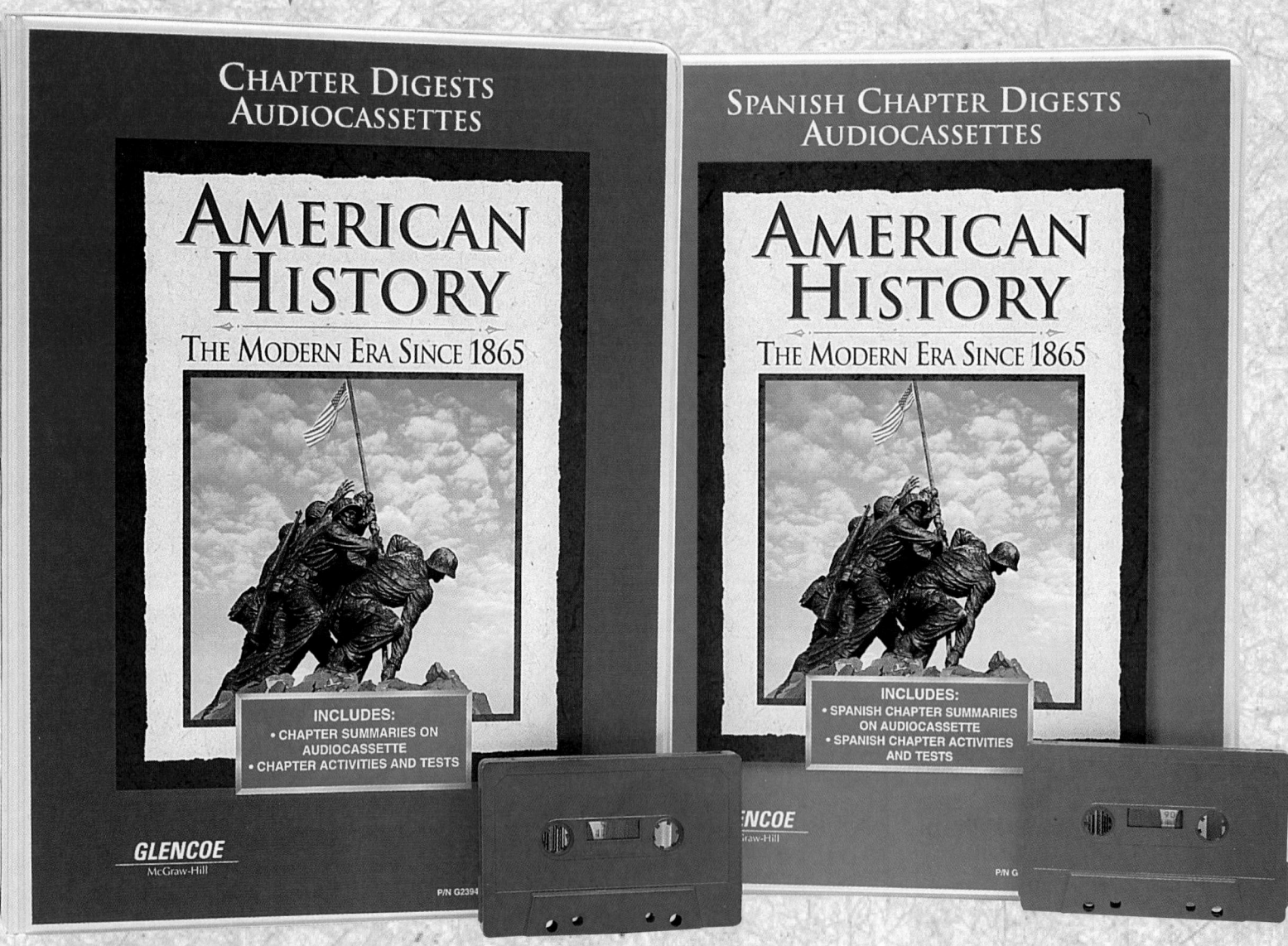

CHAPTER DIGESTS
AUDIOCASSETTES

AMERICAN HISTORY
THE MODERN ERA SINCE 1865

INCLUDES:
• CHAPTER SUMMARIES ON
AUDIOCASSETTE
• CHAPTER ACTIVITIES AND TESTS

GLENCOE
McGraw-Hill

P/N G2394

SPANISH CHAPTER DIGESTS
AUDIOCASSETTES

AMERICAN HISTORY
THE MODERN ERA SINCE 1865

INCLUDES:
• SPANISH CHAPTER SUMMARIES
ON AUDIOCASSETTE
• SPANISH CHAPTER ACTIVITIES
AND TESTS

GLENCOE
McGraw-Hill

P/N G

STUDENT SELF-TEST
& REVIEW SOFTWARE

AMERICAN
HISTORY

THE MODERN ERA SINCE 1865

INCLUDES:
• USER'S GUIDE
• SOFTWARE FOR DOS
  AND MAC

GLENCOE
McGraw-Hill

P/N G24140.28

Student Self-Test & Review Software

This comprehensive tool helps students:
• take responsibility for their learning
• pinpoint and correct their own mistakes
• review and reinforce chapter topics

Multimedia and Technology

Vocabulary PuzzleMaker This unique resource:

- reinforces all vocabulary terms
- lets you create puzzles to challenge students
- makes language lessons fun for students
- includes DOS and Macintosh software

VOCABULARY PUZZLEMAKER

AMERICAN HISTORY

THE MODERN ERA SINCE 1865

INCLUDES:
- USER'S GUIDE
- DOS SOFTWARE
- MACINTOSH SOFTWARE

GLENCOE
McGraw-Hill

ISBN 0-02-822365-9

90000>

9 780028 223650

P/N G24150.28

MindJogger Videoquiz
- Laser discs
- Teacher's Guide
- Answer cards

Also available in VHS

Multimedia and Technology

The American Indian CD-Roms
This exciting CD-ROM program:
- gives a unique view of Native American cultures
- offers geographic awareness of Native Americans' lifestyles

Landmark Documents in American History CD-Roms
This important primary resource includes:
- 1,000 full text resources
- 200 biographies
- 200 photographs and illustrations

NATIONAL GEOGRAPHIC SOCIETY

The prestigious National Geographic Society has teamed with Glencoe to provide your students with a variety of interactive videodiscs to extend and enrich the study of American history.

GTV: The American People: Fabric of a Nation This unique program:
- traces America's rich cultural heritage
- gives students insight into the people who built their nation

GTV: A Geographic Perspective on American History Exciting images provide students with:
- a geographic connection to history
- a unique look at events from colonial to modern times

Multimedia and Technology

NATIONAL GEOGRAPHIC SOCIETY

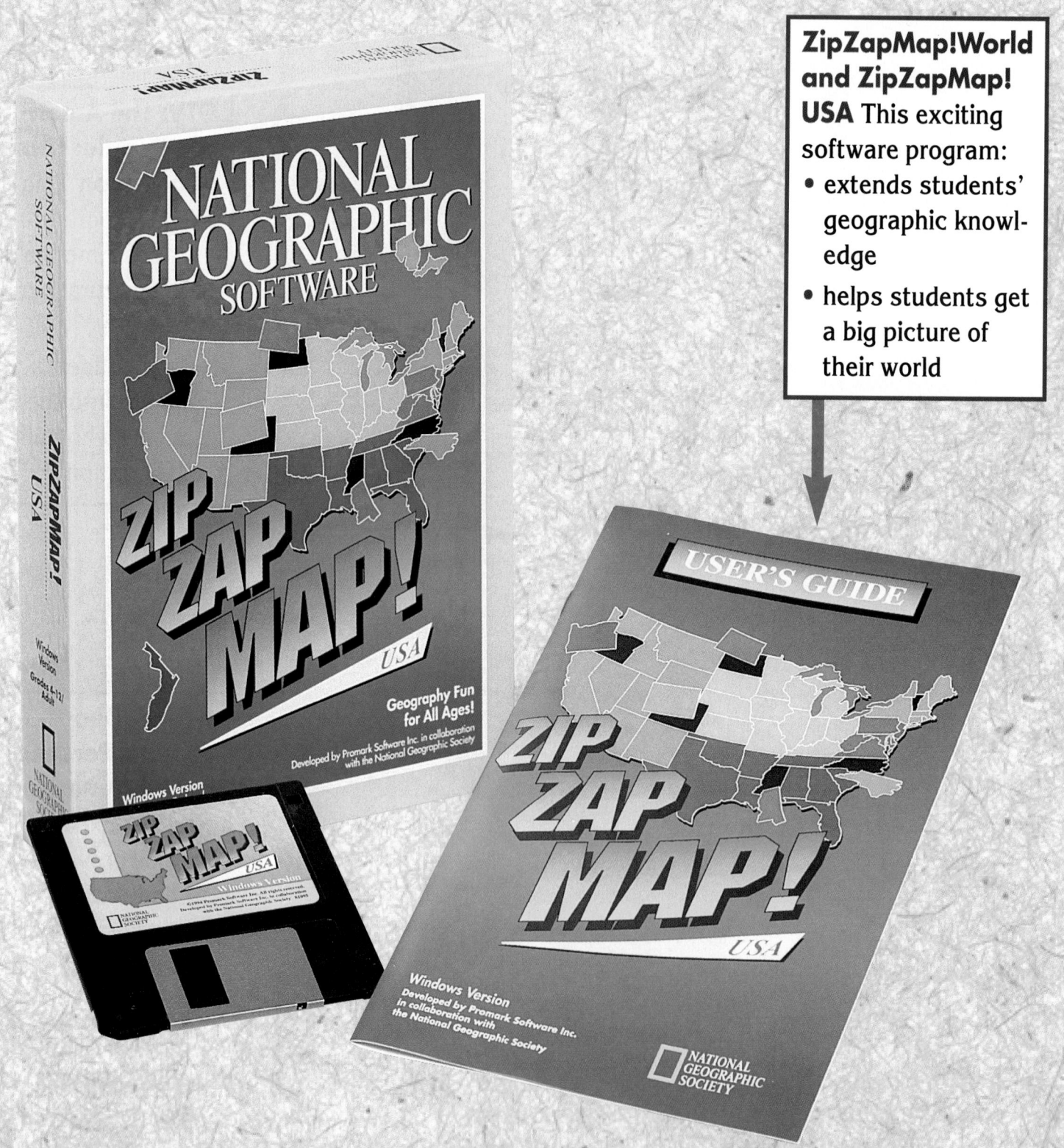

ZipZapMap!World and ZipZapMap! USA This exciting software program:
- extends students' geographic knowledge
- helps students get a big picture of their world

NATIONAL GEOGRAPHIC SOCIETY

**The Presidents:
A Picture History
of Our Nation**
Exciting historic
program:
- includes more
  than 1,400 full-
  screen, captioned
  photographs
- contains 33 video-
  clips of key
  historic events
- give students an
  in-depth look at
  U.S. Presidents

Multimedia and Technology

NATIONAL GEOGRAPHIC SOCIETY

NGS PictureShow: Native Americans, Part One NGS PictureShow: Native Americans, Part Two This unique program offers students:

- a unique look at Native American cultures
- an exciting view of the unfolding saga of Native American groups

ABCNEWS INTERACTIVE™

Each of the following ABCNews InterActive™ titles includes videodiscs, a guidebook, and an editorial framework.

Historic America Electronic Field Trips This unprecedented program allows:
- you to bring history alive in your classroom
- students an eye-witness visit to America's historic places
- expanded awareness of the relevancy of history

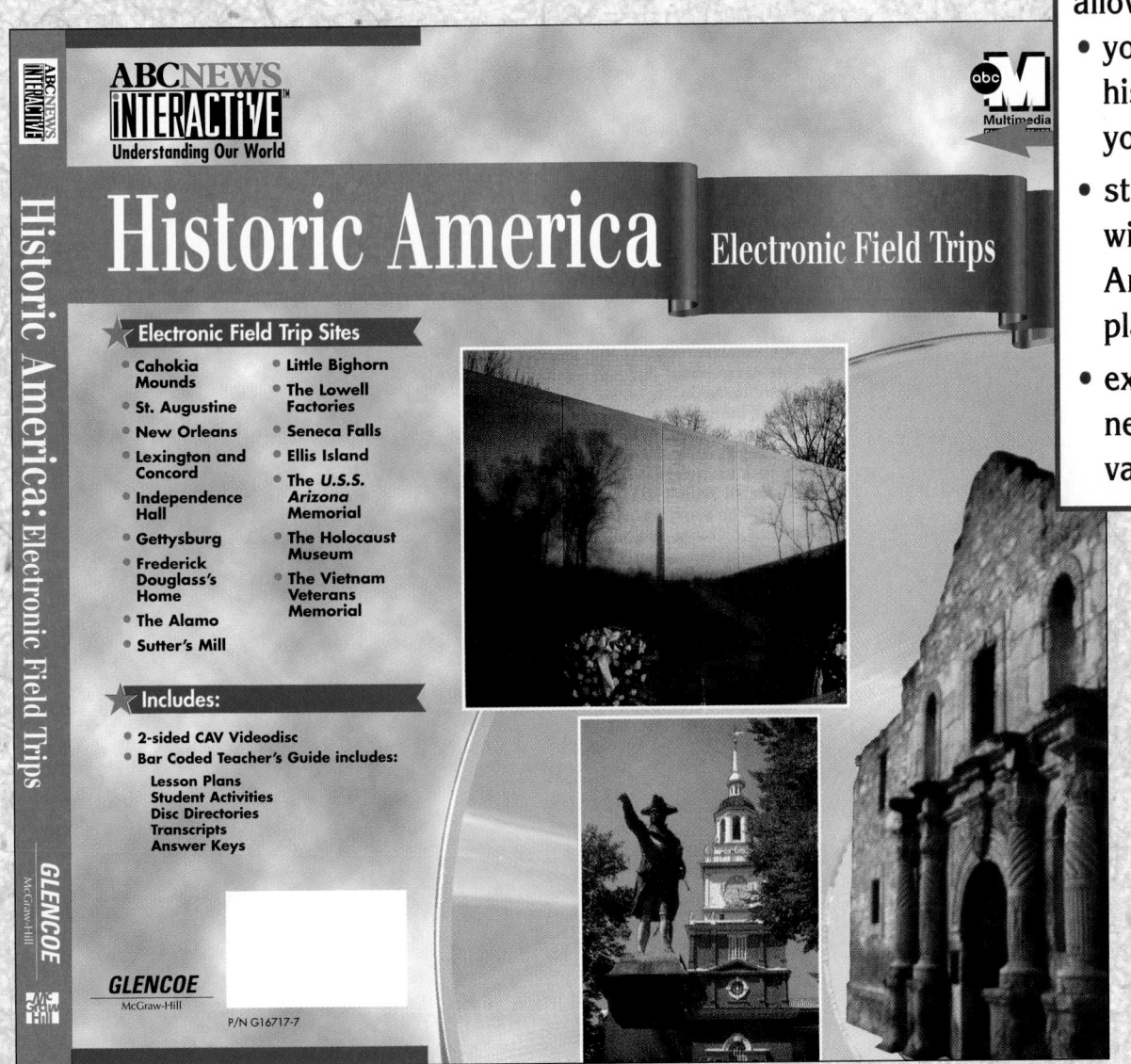

ABCNEWS INTERACTIVE™
Understanding Our World

abc M Multimedia

Historic America Electronic Field Trips

★ Electronic Field Trip Sites
- Cahokia Mounds
- St. Augustine
- New Orleans
- Lexington and Concord
- Independence Hall
- Gettysburg
- Frederick Douglass's Home
- The Alamo
- Sutter's Mill
- Little Bighorn
- The Lowell Factories
- Seneca Falls
- Ellis Island
- The *U.S.S. Arizona* Memorial
- The Holocaust Museum
- The Vietnam Veterans Memorial

★ Includes:
- 2-sided CAV Videodisc
- Bar Coded Teacher's Guide includes:
  Lesson Plans
  Student Activities
  Disc Directories
  Transcripts
  Answer Keys

GLENCOE
McGraw-Hill

P/N G16717-7

Historic America: Electronic Field Trips

GLENCOE
McGraw-Hill

Multimedia and Technology

Communism and the Cold War

This visual program:

- helps students understand historical rivalries between the United States and the former Soviet Union

- adds perspective to current events

ABCNEWS INTERACTIVE™

Powers of the President examines the constitutional role of the President as narrated by former President Jimmy Carter.

Powers of the Supreme Court reviews the Court's landmark decisions as narrated by Chief Justice of the United States William Rehnquist.

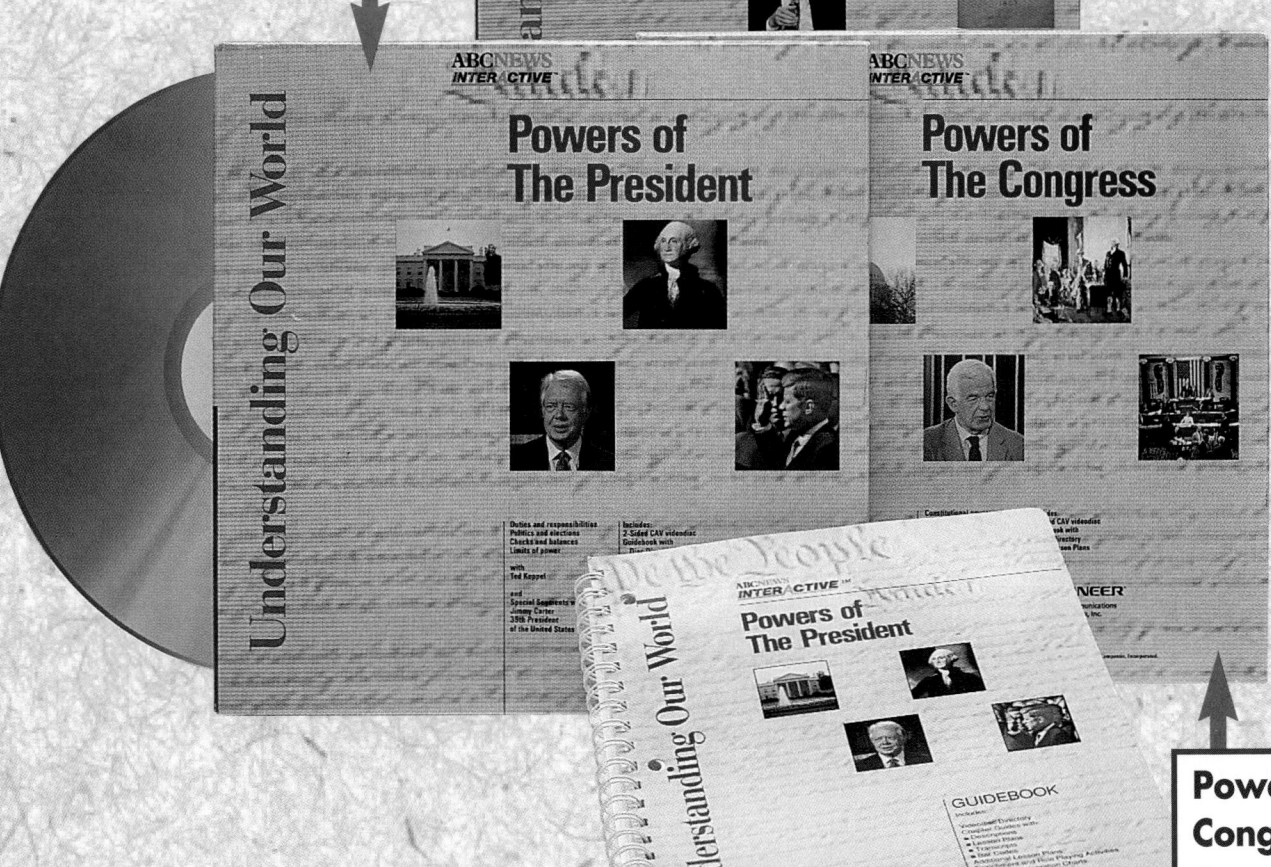

Powers of the Congress discusses the role Congress plays in governing as explained by former Speaker of the House Thomas Foley.

Multimedia and Technology

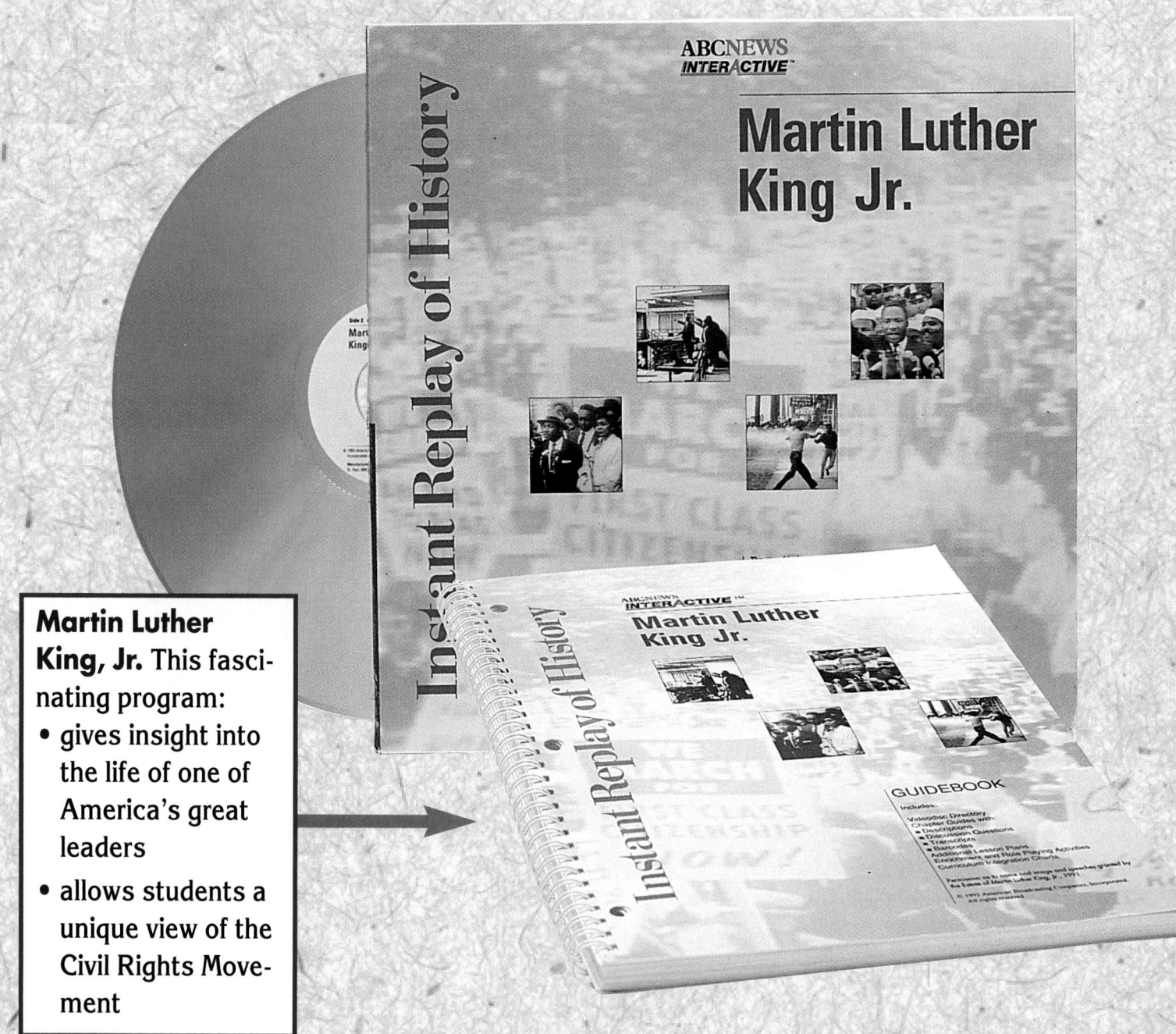

ABCNEWS INTERACTIVE™

Martin Luther King, Jr. This fascinating program:
- gives insight into the life of one of America's great leaders
- allows students a unique view of the Civil Rights Movement

Instant Replay of History

ABCNEWS INTERACTIVE™

Martin Luther King Jr.

GUIDEBOOK

ABCNEWS INTERACTIVE™

Lessons of War
This exciting program:
- takes a look at important events in conflicts from World War I to the Persian Gulf
- gives students front-row seats to war-time action

T87

Themes in American History

★ ★

*I*MAGINE a United States without computers, telephones, or automobiles, where women and most minorities cannot vote, a place where 8 of 10 people work on farms, and higher education is a privilege reserved for the fortunate few.

That we live today in a totally different country—yet one that is indeed still the United States—is no accident. What connects past generations and our own is an unbroken chain of events that shapes our lives. Every event in our personal lives has contributed to who we are today. So too have events throughout our nation's history created the American people of the 1990s. Like individual threads in a cloth, events by themselves may lack substance and seem insignificant. Seen together as part of the whole, however, events gain clarity and form.

To help make sense of countless events in history, historians use themes to organize events into meaningful patterns. Themes are recurrent threads, surfacing within an assortment of events, making up the substance of history's fabric—a rich design emblazoned with brilliant colors on the cloth of time.

American Democracy

Abraham Lincoln perhaps explained the meaning of democracy best when he called it "government of the people, by the people, for the people." Democracy at its best, according to many of our nation's leaders, is "among" the people, as exhibited by this "stump-speaking" politician of the mid-1800s, an era of frontier democracy championed by Andrew Jackson.

▲ *STUMP SPEAKING* by George Caleb Bingham, 1853–1854

Civil Rights and Liberties

The foundation of democracy is the right of every person to take part in government and to voice one's views on issues. Not all people in our nation's past have had this basic right. This lithograph illustrates when all African American men were granted suffrage in 1870 with the passage of the Fifteenth Amendment. Preservation of such civil rights and liberties for all citizens is how we guarantee that "we the people" control the government.

◀ MISSOURI'S COMMEMORATION OF THE FIFTEENTH AMENDMENT

Economic Development

The Preamble to the Constitution sets out the purposes of American government, one of which is to "promote the general welfare." Framers of the Constitution recognized that one of government's purposes must be to provide a climate in which citizens can better themselves economically. With few government restrictions, the nation's economy was built on the hard work of farmers and agricultural business.

▶ *CLASSIC LANDSCAPE*
by Charles Sheeler, 1931

Geography and Environment

The United States succeeded in part because of its rich natural resources and its vast open spaces. But in most regions of the nation, the natural landscape was transformed to accommodate ambitions that hard work could make dreams come true. The steel plow and the railroad helped Americans settle the West, but the unblemished environment of the Native American gave way to the demands of expansion.

◀ *MERCED RIVER, YOSEMITE*
by Albert Bierstadt, 1861

Conflict and Cooperation

It has been said that democracy is a poor form of government, but that no better form has been invented. President George Washington established the principle of placing the good of the nation above individual or sectional grievances in 1794, when he led troops against Pennsylvania farmers protesting a tax on whiskey. The conflict over, Washington pardoned the convicted leaders in the spirit of cooperation.

▶ *WASHINGTON RECEIVING THE WESTERN ARMY AT FORT CUMBERLAND, MARYLAND* by Frederick Kemmelmeyer, c. 1795

Influence of Technology

Americans have always been quick to embrace innovations—the country was settled and built by people who gave up old ways and sought new. Americans' lives are profoundly influenced by technology, the use of science and machines. Perhaps no machine has so shaped modern life as the automobile.

◀ FORD AUTOMOBILE, EARLY 1900s

The Individual and Family Life

Americans have a strong tradition of individual freedom sheltered by the protective core of the family unit. Families during the 1950s moved to suburban areas outside the central city to provide themselves with more living space and protection from the perceived dangers of the city. Our earliest experiences of freedom, which were limited by the rights of other individuals, come from interactions within our homes.

◀ Young suburban
family of the 1950s

Ideas, Beliefs, and Institutions

An important part of this nation's story is the origin and spread of social, religious, and educational ideas and values. The belief in fundamental rights lies at the heart of United States citizenship and enables people to worship as they wish, speak freely, and read and write what they choose. Along with the enjoyment of these rights, however, comes a responsibility to ensure their strength and endurance.

▶ ANNE HUTCHINSON PREACHING IN HER BOSTON HOME, from a painting by Howard Pyle

Cultural Diversity

American is not a pure nationality but a peculiar mosaic of ideals and ideas. People from around the world for generations have sung of this "land of the Pilgrims' pride, land where our fathers died" even though their ancestors arrived on these shores long after such events transpired. The public schools were the method by which those seeking a new future were transformed into Americans. These immigrant children in New York in the early 1900s pledged allegiance to a flag under which none had been born but which was justly theirs in every way.

◀ Students at a New York City school pledge allegiance, early 1900s.

U.S. Role in World Affairs

A nation composed of peoples from around the world—buying and selling goods around the world, with economic and military might felt across continents, displaying a form of government emulated in all four corners of the globe— cannot but play a leading role in world affairs. The American people have carried on a long tradition as champions of democracy.

▶ President Clinton addressing Jordan's parliament, 1994

Geography in History

★ ★

*G*EOGRAPHY—the study of Earth's surface and the processes that shape it, the relationship between people and their environments, and people and place connections—is an integral part of the web of history.

Indeed, all history happens somewhere. It is the task of geography to supply answers about where a place is, what it is like, how the people live there, how people from different places interact with one another, and how one place on Earth is like others on Earth.

The geography of a region not only includes its physical landscape, natural resources, and climate but also the people who have settled there and their distinctive way of life. The history of the American people—the countless events that make up who we are—is notably influenced by the interplay of our nation's geographic features.

Like historians, geographers use themes to help organize their study of geography into purposeful patterns. Organizing information by themes helps make sense of the vast amount of information we have learned about the myriad of distinctive places that make up the United States.

Location

A place's position on the earth's surface—its location—constitutes one of the five themes of geography. Location can be either absolute (one particular spot of ground) or relative (position as compared to some other place). *Location* answers the question "Where is that and why is its location significant?"

▶ The Southeast, by virtue of its location on the Atlantic Coast, was one of the first parts of North America settled by Europeans. Colonial Williamsburg recreates daily life as it unfolded in the Southeast three centuries ago.

◀ Los Angeles, California, one of the most densely populated urban areas in the United States, is located atop a network of active fault lines. Its Southwest location is a mixed blessing for Los Angeles—the city enjoys a Mediterranean climate, but it lives with the knowledge that earthquakes can strike at any time.

Place

A place's physical and human characteristics tell what is special about it and what makes it different from all others. Landforms, climate, and culture combine to make up the particular flavor of a particular place. *Place* answers the question "What is that place like?"

▶ Settlement of the Great Plains coincided with the development of machines for plowing, planting, and harvesting on a grand scale; the combination made the Midwest a supplier of meat and grain to the world.

◀ Rivers have had a tremendous impact on American history and life. The confluence of the Mississippi (left) and Ohio (right) rivers south of Cairo, Illinois, in the heart of the Midwest, imparts a special quality to land that is quite different from that found in the desert Southwest. Water is of paramount importance to both places—in the Midwest for its abundance, in the Southwest for its lack.

Human/Environment Interaction

The theme of human/environmental interaction describes how people use, affect, and are affected by their surroundings. Through such interaction, people change the environment in which they live. *Human/environment interaction* answers the question "How does the interaction of people within an environment affect their way of life?"

▶ *WHERE COTTON IS KING* by Konstantin Rodko, 1908 Warm climate, abundant rainfall, and rich soil combined to make large parts of the Southeast ideally suited for the cultivation of cotton. The use of slave labor for this industry set the stage for a confrontation between North and South that became this nation's bloodiest war.

◀ Fishing boats ply the coastal waters of the Northeast in search of such delicacies as lobster. The nutrient-rich waters of the Atlantic drew people to the sea. Yet centuries of fishing have reduced the ocean's bounty.

Movement

People interacting across the globe exemplifies interdependence, the need humans have to utilize skills and resources from around the earth. People travel, communicate, and trade goods, ideas, and information. *Movement* answers the question "How do the people in this place interact with peoples in other places?"

▲ Southwesterners who live along the border between the United States and Mexico can experience dramatic changes in culture and lifestyle by simply walking a few feet from one country to another. The movement of people between countries has political, social, and economic implications.

◄ *DANIEL BOONE ESCORTING SETTLERS THROUGH THE CUMBERLAND GAP* by George Caleb Bingham, 1851–1852

Regions

Regions is the ultimate theme of geography. Regions—how areas form and change—display unity through their characteristics, some physical, some human. The study of regions allows geographers to answer the question "How is this place like other places on the earth?"

◄ The Northeast, like other coastal regions around the world, used its natural advantages to become a center of fishing, shipping, and trade. Yankee clipper ships were the fastest merchant vessels in the world; in 1854 the *Flying Cloud* set a record of 89 days, 8 hours, between Boston and San Francisco.

► New England is known not only for its brilliant foliage but also for its charming countryside of small villages inhabited by descendants of early settlers whose motto was, "Use it up, wear it out, make it do."

Provide this cause-and-effect chart to students with the effects omitted. Assign students to complete the chart as they read the chapters in the unit.

Event
- Christopher Columbus's first voyage

Causes
- The growth of trade with Asia
- The rise of strong monarchs
- The growth of cities
- The Renaissance

Effects
- Competition for power among European nations
- Native Americans forced from their lands or enslaved
- European colonies in the Americas
- Africans enslaved

History AND ART

Drawings found on rocks and in caves reveal much about the earliest Americans. Similar drawings have been found in other parts of the world. Encourage students to find out about rock and cave paintings in Europe and Asia.

0:00 OUT OF TIME?

If time does not permit teaching the entire unit, use the Unit Digest on pages 132–133.

UNIT ONE
CREATING A NATION
PREHISTORY TO 1815

★★

CHAPTER 1	CHAPTER 2	CHAPTER 3
Exploration and Settlement Prehistory–1763	**A New Nation** 1750–1789	**Launching the Republic** 1789–1815

▲ ASTROLABE, ITALY, 1500s

History AND ART
Prehistoric Drawing
Baja California, Mexico

Native Americans came to the Western Hemisphere thousands of years ago. Artists have provided a glimpse of their way of life through cave and rock paintings.

2

Exploring Unit Themes

Geography and the Environment The Native American peoples created varied and distinct cultures as they adapted to the geography and environment where they settled.

The Individual and Family Life While a social hierarchy existed in Colonial America, it was far less rigid than in Europe. Success in the colonies required individual effort, so people with drive and ambition could rise to the top of American society. There was one exception—enslaved persons were held in bondage for life.

Beliefs, Ideas, and Institutions Scientific inquiry generated by the Renaissance led to an age of exploration and discovery. Many Europeans settled in the Americas because they wanted the freedom to worship as they pleased.

Setting the Scene

The Americas had long been inhabited by a rich variety of Native American cultures. Hundreds of years ago, however, other peoples—Europeans and enslaved Africans—set foot in what to them was a new world.

Themes

- Geography and the Environment
- The Individual and Family Life
- Beliefs, Ideas, and Institutions
- American Democracy
- Cultural Diversity

Key Events

- First Americans cross the Bering Strait
- Height of Mayan culture
- Norse seafarers land at Newfoundland
- Voyages of Columbus
- Spanish bring enslaved Africans to America
- Founding of English colonies
- Declaration of Independence
- Ratification of the Constitution
- Louisiana Purchase
- War of 1812

Major Issues

- The environment influences the development of Native American cultures and European colonies in the Americas.
- Patriot determinism, military skill, and French aid enable the colonies to win independence from Britain.
- Key compromises lead to the formation of a strong and democratic central government.

▼ GOLD PRESENTATION BOX, 1770S

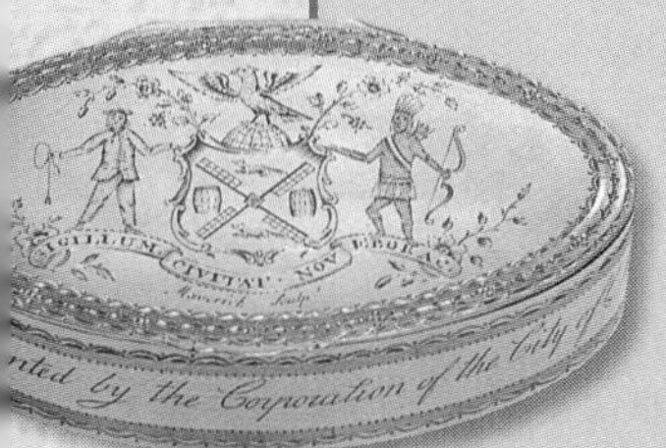

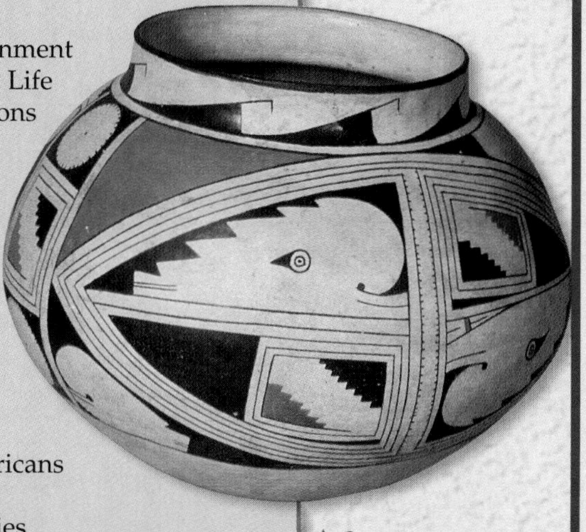

▲ SOUTHWESTERN POTTERY

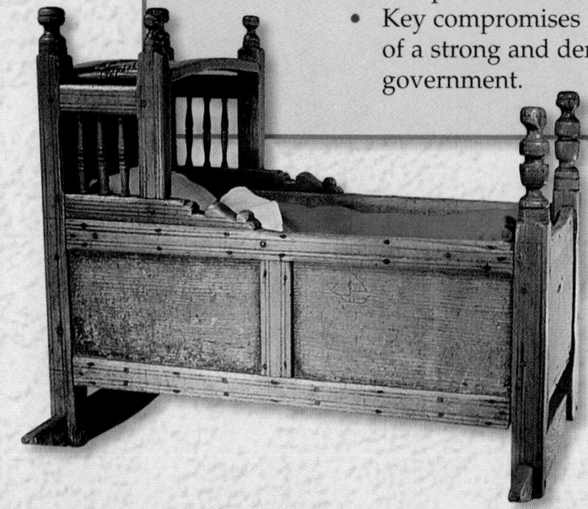

◄ EARLY AMERICAN FULLER CRADLE

Portfolio Project

Prepare a short report on a Native American culture in the United States today. Describe its peoples' occupations, living standards, and social life as well as traditional crafts, legends, and beliefs.

Portfolio Project

After students have completed the first draft of their report, ask each to edit a classmate's work.

History and the Humanities

American Music: Cultural Traditions: Native American Music "Rain Dance, Parts 1 & 2" by George Buck and George Green, leaders (1:13)
Early American Keyboard Music "Tunes from Colonial America & The President's March" by E. Power Biggs (3:40)

U.S. History & Art Transparency 4, *The Declaration of Independence* by John Trumbull

American Democracy Colonists claimed that Britain denied them their rights to representative self-government. After the war they formed a system of federal government containing checks and balances that would preclude future despotism.

Cultural Diversity The Europeans' interactions with many different groups of Native Americans and their adaptation to the new environment led to a new and unique American culture.
Examining Unit Themes Have students identify the various groups that settled in the Western Hemisphere.

FOCUS

Motivating Activity

Point out that the exchange of beliefs and knowledge among civilizations is called cultural diffusion. The peanut might serve as an illustration of this process. The Spanish first encountered the peanut in Hispaniola in the early 1500s. They later introduced the crop to their possessions in the Philippines and the Malay Archipelago. By the end of the century, it had spread to the Asian mainland. Today, the peanut is an important aspect of the cuisine of China, Thailand, and many other Southeast Asian countries. Ask students to suggest recent examples of cultural diffusion involving food. (*Most students will suggest that recent immigrants to the United States have introduced their cuisine to Americans.*) **L1**

TEACH

Guided Practice

Exploring the Time Line
Ask students to study the time line and note the European nations that explored or colonized the Americas. Then mention that the Russians, too, were interested in the Americas. During the 1700s, a Russian fleet regularly visited Monterey Bay in California to hunt the bay's sea otters. In 1812 they built a trading post and fort at Fort Ross. They sold it to John Sutter in 1841. **L1**

Global Perspectives

The World

	Prehistory		1600 A.D.	
Asia and Oceania	c. 4000 B.C. *Civilizations develop in Asia and Africa*	660 B.C. *Jimmu becomes first emperor of Japan*	1368 *Ming dynasty begins rule of China*	
Europe	509 B.C. *Romans set up a republic*		1400s *Age of Exploration begins*	
Africa	c. 1,750,000 B.C. *First groups of people appear in Africa*			1652 *Cape Town is founded*
South America			◀ 1400s *Inca and Aztec empires flourish*	
North and Central America			1492 *Columbus lands in the Americas*	1650 *Spanish introduce horses to the Plains people*

The United States

	Prehistory		1600 A.D.	
Pacific and Northwest	c. 1500 B.C. *People learn metalworking techniques*		1578 *Sir Francis Drake explores the California coast*	
Southeast			1607 *First permanent English settlement is formed at Jamestown*	
Midwest	▶ 200 B.C.–A.D. 400 *Hopewell culture reaches its zenith*			
Southwest		◀ 1050–1200 *Great Pueblo period flourishes*		
Atlantic Northeast			1620 *Pilgrims found Plymouth*	

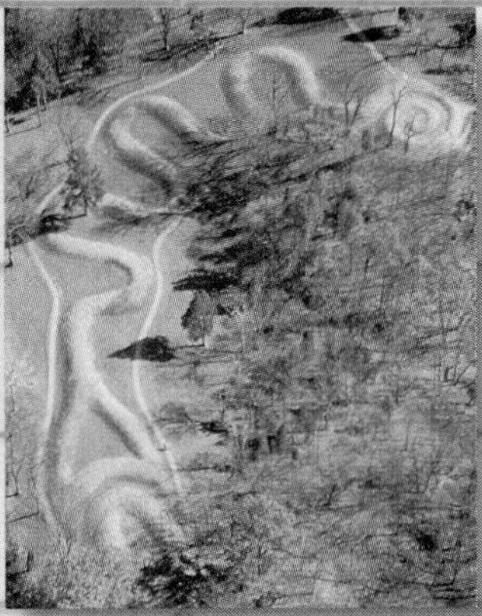

Cultural Perspectives

An American Language Native Americans have left an indelible mark on American English. Over 125 Algonquin words are in common use today. They include *chipmunk, skunk, moose, opossum, raccoon, caribou, hominy, pecan, squash, succotash,* and *terrapin.* Those words became a part of the language as a result of direct contacts between the English and Native Americans. Other words have entered the language through indirect contacts. From the Spanish, English-speaking colonists learned such Native American words as *coyote, mesquite, avocado, tomato,* and *barbecue.*

Native Americans have left an indelible mark on American life. Perhaps the most obvious sign of our country's Native American heritage is the hundreds of place names that dot the map. Some of these names offer a vivid physical description of the place. Chattanooga, for example, means "rock rising to a point," while Nantucket means "the far away place." Other names indicate what went on at the place. Milwaukee was the "gathering place by the river" and Kalamazoo was the "boiling pot."

1700 A.D.

1770 *Captain James Cook sails to Australia*

1800 A.D.

1800 | *Napoleon Bonaparte becomes ruler of France*

▼ 1660 *Several small kingdoms are established on the upper Niger*

◄ 1799 | *Rosetta Stone found in Egypt*

1693 *Gold rush begins in Brazil*

1791 *Toussaint Louverture leads slave revolt in Saint Domingue*

1697 *Jesuit missionaries enter California*

◄ 1793 | *Cotton gin invented*

1804 | *Lewis and Clark explore the Louisiana Territory*

1684 *LaSalle establishes Fort St. Louis*

1673 *Jacques Marquette and Louis Joliet explore the Upper Mississippi River for France*

1700 A.D.

▲ 1754 *French and Indian War begins*

1776 *Declaration of Independence signed*

1800 A.D.

UNIT 1 Creating a Nation: Prehistory to 1815   **5**

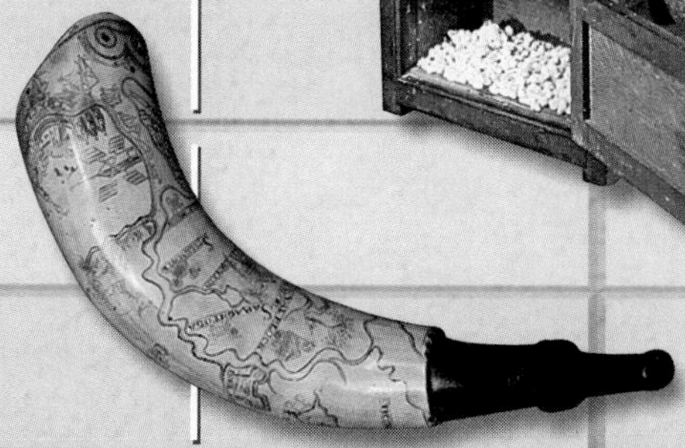

LESSON PLAN
Global Perspectives

Independent Practice

Linking World Events Direct students' attention to the time line entry on the founding of Plymouth. Then mention that 10 years before this event, there was a thriving Spanish colony in the Southwest, centered on what today is Santa Fe, New Mexico. Have students research and write a report on Spanish settlement in the Southwest prior to the establishment of English colonies in North America. **L2**

ASSESS
Studying the Time Line

1. What was happening in South America at about the time the Age of Exploration began? (*The Inca and Aztec empires were flourishing.*)

2. How many years after the Marquette-Joliet expedition did LaSalle establish Fort St. Louis? (*11 years*)

3. What event shown on the time line do you think was the most important for the development of the United States? Why? (*Answers will vary but may include the first permanent English settlements at Jamestown and Plymouth.*)

Cooperative Learning Activity

Researching Events Organize the class into five groups and assign one of the following continents to each: North America, South America, Africa, Asia, Europe. Ask groups to research what was happening in their assigned area at the time Columbus made his voyage of discovery. They should then write a brief narrative on their area for an imaginary radio broadcast titled "At This Time." Have groups select representatives to make their broadcasts. **L3**

Daily Lesson Objectives	Teacher Classroom Resources	Multimedia
SECTION 1 **World in Transition** **1 Day pp. 8–14** 1. Explain the origins of the first immigrants to the Americas and discuss the differences among the Native American cultures of the region. 2. Describe how European society changed as a result of the Crusades, the Renaissance and the Reformation.	Reproducible Lesson Plan 1-1 Concept Mapping Activities 1-A, 1-B Performance Assessment Activity 1 *Vocabulary Activity 1 *Guided Reading Activity 1-1 Linking Past and Present Activity 1 Enrichment Activity 1 Workbook Activity 1-1 Reteaching Activity 1-1 *Section Quiz 1-1	Section Focus Transparency 1-1 Chapter Concepts Transparencies 1-A, 1-B Vocabulary PuzzleMaker Testmaker MindJogger Videoquiz GTV: The American People: Fabric of a Nation Powers of the Congress The American Indian
SECTION 2 **European Explorations** **1 Day pp. 15–21** 1. Describe Spanish exploration, conquests, and settlement in the Americas. 2. Discuss English, French, and Dutch ventures in North America.	Reproducible Lesson Plan 1-2 *Guided Reading Activity 1-2 Cooperative Learning Activity 1 Workbook Activity 1-2 Reteaching Activity 1-2 *Section Quiz 1-2	Section Focus Transparency 1-2 Testmaker Historic America Electronic Field Trips GTV: The American People: Fabric of a Nation GTV: A Geographic Perspective on American History
SECTION 3 **The English Colonies** **1 Day pp. 23–27** 1. Examine the different kind of English colonies that were formed in America. 2. Discuss the ways in which American colonists differed from the British by 1750.	Reproducible Lesson Plan 1-3 *Guided Reading Activity 1-3 Chapter Skills Activity 1 Workbook Activity 1-3 Reteaching Activity 1-3 *Section Quiz 1-3	Section Focus Transparency 1-3 Skills Transparency 1 Testmaker GTV: A Geographic Perspective on American History GTV: The American People: Fabric of a Nation
SECTION 4 **Colonial Life** **1 Day pp. 29–35** 1. Describe social classes and roles. 2. Explain why religious toleration and freedom developed.	Reproducible Lesson Plan 1-4 *Guided Reading Activity 1-4 Critical Thinking Skills Activity 1 Reteaching Activity 1-4 *Section Quiz 1-4	Section Focus Transparency 1-4 Map Transparency Activity 1 GTV: A Geographic Perspective on American History GTV: The American People: Fabric of a Nation
CHAPTER REVIEW AND EVALUATION **1 Day**	Chapter 1 Test, Forms A and B Spanish Chapter 1 Summary Performance Assessment Activity 1	MindJogger Videoquiz Student Self-Test & Review Software *Chapter 1 Digest Audio-cassette Activity and Test

*Also available in Spanish

 `0:00` **OUT OF TIME?** If time does not permit teaching the entire chapter, use the Chapter 1 summary on pages 132–133 and the Chapter 1 audiocassette (English and Spanish) to point out the main ideas of the chapter.

A complete, 1-page lesson plan is provided for each section in the *Reproducible Lesson Plan* booklet.

Key to Ability Levels

Teaching strategies have been coded for varying learning styles and abilities.

L1 Basic activities for all students.

L2 Average activities for average to above-average students

L3 Challenging activities for above-average students

LEP Limited English Proficiency activities

Block Schedule

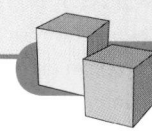

Block scheduling differs from traditional class scheduling in the amount of time allotted to each period. The extended time frame provided by block scheduling affords you the opportunity to implement a greater number of research-oriented and activity-intense projects to motivate and involve your students. Activities that are particularly suited to use within the block scheduling framework are identified throughout this unit by the following designation:

✔ *Performance Assessment Activity*

Broadsides and Brochures A broadside is a sizeable sheet of paper with print and art on one or both sides. A broadside often is a ballad or advertisement espousing a cause or position. Point out to students that promoters of the British colonies produced broadsides and brochures designed to entice people into becoming settlers. Organize students into groups of four or five to develop a broadside or brochure. Each group should select a specific colony and prepare an appropriate brochure illustrating the benefits that will accrue to those who settle there. Have each group present its broadside or brochure to the class. **L2**

POSSIBLE RUBRIC FEATURES

- Content Information
- Creativity
- Organization
- Written and Pictorial Communication Skills
- Collaborative Skills

☞ For additional activities, see Performance Assessment Strategies and Activities.

T E A C H E R ' S   C O R N E R

NATIONAL GEOGRAPHIC SOCIETY

INDEX TO NATIONAL GEOGRAPHIC MAGAZINE

The following articles may be used for research relating to this chapter:

- "The Timeless Vision of Teotihuacan," by George E. Stuart, December 1995.
- "Maya Masterpiece Revealed at Bonampak," by Mark Miller, February 1995.
- "Simon Bolivar: El Libertador," by Bryan Hodgson, March 1994.
- "Portugal's Sea Road to the East," by Merle Severy, November 1992.
- "Pizarro: Conqueror of the Inca," by John Hemming, February 1992.
- "Search for Columbus," by Eugene Lyon, January 1992.
- *1491: America Before Columbus,* (A Special Edition), October 1991.
- "The Battle To Save Our Past," by George E. Stuart, March 1989.
- "Exploring Our Forgotten Century: Between Columbus and Jamestown," by Joseph Judge, March 1988.
- "Searching for Columbus's Lost Colony: La Navidad," by Kathleen A. Deagan, November 1987.

NATIONAL GEOGRAPHIC SOCIETY PRODUCTS AVAILABLE FROM GLENCOE

To order the following products for use with this chapter, contact your local Glencoe sales representative or call Glencoe at 1-800-334-7344:

- *STV: World Geography* (Videodisc)
- *STV: North America* (Videodisc)
- *STV: Maya* (Videodisc)
- *ZipZapMap! USA* (Software)
- *GTV: A Geographic Perspective on American History* (Videodisc)
- *GTV: The American People: Fabric of a Nation* (Videodisc)
- *Native Americans, Part I* (CD-ROM)
- *Native Americans, Part II* (CD-ROM)
- *Native Americans: Eastern Woodlands and Plains* (Transparencies)
- *Native Americans: Southwest, Northwest Coast, Arctic* (Transparencies)

ADDITIONAL NATIONAL GEOGRAPHIC SOCIETY PRODUCTS

To order the following products for use with this chapter, call National Geographic Society at 1-800-368-2728:

- *Lost Kingdoms of the Maya* (Video)
- *Digging Up America's Past* (Filmstrip)
- *Great Explorers* (Filmstrip)
- *The Middle Ages* (Filmstrip)
- *The Renaissance* (Filmstrip)
- *Ancient Cities: A Geographic Perspective* (Filmstrip)
- *Ancient Civilizations* (Filmstrip)

BEGINNING THE CHAPTER

Recording Journal Notes

Tell students that a journal is a place where they can not only record their notes but also reflect on the ideas expressed in the chapter.

Linking Across
T I M E

Point out that the movement of people from Europe and Africa to North America in the 1600s and 1700s helped shape the character of colonial society. Today people coming from countries in Latin America and Asia are helping to shape American society.

Exploration and Settlement
Prehistory–1763

▼ ARROWHEAD, HAND-CHIPPED

Setting the Scene

Focus

The first people came to North America long before written history. Their descendants, known as Native Americans, developed unique cultures and civilizations in North America and South America. Then a series of events in Europe, Asia, and Africa opened the way to European exploration and settlement in the Americas. Thereafter, various nations—Spain, Portugal, France, England, and the Netherlands—sought to build a colonial empire.

Journal Notes

How do the accomplishments and ideas of a culture reflect values? Note important details about various cultures in your journal as you read the chapter.

Concepts to Understand

★ How different ways of life among the Native American societies created **cultural diversity**

★ What political, social, and economic **values and beliefs** the European colonists developed in America

Read to Discover . . .

★ who were the major Native American groups.

★ why European nations wanted to explore and colonize the Americas.

★ in what ways Americans differed from the British by 1750.

CULTURAL			
• c. 4500 B.C. *Writing develops*	• 900s *Chinese advance the art of printing*	• 1149 *University founded at Oxford, England*	
Prehistory–A.D. 500	**A.D. 900**	**1100**	
• 1000 B.C. *People inhabit present-day Peru and Ecuador*	• 900s *Mayan civilization begins to decline* • 900s *Feudalism spreads throughout western Europe*	• 1152 *Frederick I becomes Holy Roman Emperor*	
POLITICAL			

✚ EXTRA CREDIT PROJECT

Landscapes The world in the 1400s looked very different from the way it looks today. The eastern part of North America was covered by thick forests. Marshland stretched along much of Europe's Mediterranean coast and covered vast areas of northern Germany and Russia. Ask interested students to research the environment of each continent in the 1400s. Have students present their findings to the class in the form of a map. Encourage them to research when those environments began to change and the consequences of those changes. Ask them to discuss those findings as they explain their maps to their classmates. **L2**

Concept Mapping Activity

On the chalkboard, reproduce the following generalization and concepts map, and have students copy it in their notebooks.

> Continents separated by great oceans developed cultures in relative isolation until the age of exploration. New values and beliefs developed as peoples from several parts of the world migrated to the Americas.

Cultural Diversity	Values and Beliefs

To reinforce the two chapter concepts, use Concept Mapping Activities 1-A and 1-B and assign Chapter Concepts Transparency Activities 1-A and 1-B.

History AND ART

The pageantry of this painting contains no hint that Cabot's first voyage for England in 1496 ended in failure.

History AND ART

Cabot's Departure, 1497
by Ernest Board, 1906

English merchants persuaded their king to send John Cabot, an Italian navigator, to Asia by a northwest route. This painting, completed more than 400 years after the event, communicates a feeling of solemn pageantry.

◀ JAPANESE MILITARY EQUIPMENT

- **1300** *Cahokia is largest North American community*
- **1505** *Michaelangelo paints Sistine Chapel*
- **1740** *Great Awakening stimulates revivalist spirit*

1300	1500	1700

- **1337** *Hundred Years' War begins*
- **1570** *Iroquois form League of Five Nations*
- **1763** *Peace of Paris ends Seven Years' War*

NATIONAL GEOGRAPHIC SOCIETY

GTV: The American People: Fabric of a Nation

Side 1, Chapter 2
Frames 7362-11628
Title: *Kaleidoscope*
Subject: A look at the diversity of Native Americans

✓ Performance Assessment

African American Migration Have students research and report on the movement of African Americans from the South to the North known as the Great Migration. This massive exodus began during World War I when Northern industries needed workers to fill jobs left vacant by workers drafted into the armed forces. It was accelerated by the naval war, which all but stopped immigration from abroad.

Have students identify both "push" and "pull" factors for the Great Migration. Students may provide their findings in a written report accompanied by photographs, artwork, and graphs and tables. **L2**

FOCUS

Bellringer

Before taking roll, project Section Focus Transparency 1-1 or hand out Section Focus Transparency Activity 1-1. Have students answer the questions. Discuss student responses to the Section Focus Transparency questions.

Motivating Activity

Ask students what "World in Transition," the title of Section 1, indicates about the content of the section. (*Students might indicate that the section will deal with changes occurring in the world.*) Suggest that as they read the section, students look for events that illustrate these changes. **L1**

Vocabulary Precheck

Ask students to define each of the "Key Terms." Have a volunteer consult the dictionary for any unfamiliar words. **L1, LEP**

Use the Vocabulary PuzzleMaker for Chapter 1 to create a crossword puzzle. **L1**

Assign Vocabulary Activity 1.

SECTION 1

★★

World In Transition

Setting the Scene

Section Focus

By the 1400s, Native Americans had formed many rich and diverse cultures in the Americas. Meanwhile, contacts between Europe, Asia, and Africa stimulated trade, learning, and national rivalries. These developments soon affected the relatively isolated cultures of the Americas.

▶ **PAINTED CLAY IMAGE**

Objectives

After studying this section, you should be able to

★ explain the origins of the first immigrants to the Americas and discuss the differences among the Native American cultures of the region.

★ describe how European society changed as a result of the Crusades, the Renaissance, and the Reformation.

★ identify the leading empires of Asia and Africa.

Key Terms

confederation, feudalism, shogun, joint-stock company

---

efore the A.D. 1400s, people living in the Americas developed their ways of life isolated from other peoples of the world. Similarly, the people of other continents were unaware of America. Then the development of new ideas, technology, and trading links began moving the peoples of the Americas, Europe, Asia, and Africa toward interdependence.

■ The First Americans

Twenty thousand years ago, much of the water in today's oceans was frozen. Huge ice sheets covered much of present-day Canada and the northern United States. Scientists today believe that people from Asia walked across a "land bridge" that once connected Alaska and Asia. In small groups, they grad-

ually spread throughout North and South America, following great herds of game animals. Over time these people adapted to their environments. Their descendants became known as Native Americans.

In time Native Americans formed into many diverse groups based on language and customs. Despite their diversity, Native Americans had many similar ideas. For example, all Native Americans felt a close relationship to the land and their environment. They believed that all things, themselves included, were part of a universal spirit.

Native American Empires

Groups of Native Americans in present-day Mexico and South America gradually developed highly organized

---

Classroom Resources for SECTION 1

Blackline Masters:
- Reproducible Lesson Plan 1-1
- Vocabulary Activity 1
- Guided Reading Activity 1-1
- Linking Past and Present Activity 1

- Enrichment Activity 1
- Workbook Activity 1-1
- Reteaching Activity 1-1
- Section Quiz 1-1

Transparencies:
- Section Focus Transparency 1-1

Multimedia:
- Vocabulary PuzzleMaker
- Testmaker
- GTV: The American People: Fabric of a Nation
- Powers of the Congress
- The American Indian

and sophisticated societies. In western South America, the Inca ruled a large empire that stretched 3,000 miles (4,800 km) from present-day Colombia to the middle of Chile. A complex system of roads linked the various regions of the Inca Empire, and terraced hillside farms with complicated irrigation systems produced abundant food.

To the north, in the area called Mesoamerica—parts of the nations of Mexico, Guatemala, and Honduras—other powerful Native American civilizations arose. One of the earliest, the Olmec, developed large temple complexes and pyramids along the Gulf of Mexico. Farther south, in the Yucatán Peninsula, the Maya established city-states dominated by even larger pyramids. The Maya excelled in trade and mathematics. Mayan mathematicians invented the concept of zero and developed complicated calendars linked to the study of the stars.

Many other equally advanced groups emerged in Mesoamerica. The last was the Aztec. Their city, Tenochtitlán, is the site of modern Mexico City. By the late 1400s, Tenochtitlán had gold-adorned temples, floating gardens, and an enormous market.

Cultures North of Mexico

Native Americans living in the present-day southwestern United States and in the fertile Mississippi Valley traded with Mexico.

In these two areas, the population was only one-tenth that of Mexico and the Inca Empire. The way of life was also much different. Most people lived in small villages or bands.

In the Southwest, the Anasazi built large, multistory apartment-like buildings of adobe. Another southwestern group, the Hohokam, built large villages that had irrigation canals and temple mounds. During the 1300s, severe drought and climate change ended both cultures. The Hohokam did not survive, but the descendants of the Anasazi remain as the Pueblo people of New Mexico.

Around A.D. 900, in the Mississippi Valley, farmers and traders built great temple mounds and towns. Such cities as Cahokia (near present-day St. Louis) grew to great size, with hundreds of temple mounds. Another group of moundbuilders, the Hopewell culture, arose in the Ohio Valley about 200 B.C. and lasted about 700 years.

In other parts of North America, a variety of Native American groups flourished: the buffalo-hunters of the Great Plains, the rich fishing cultures of the Pacific Northwest, and the seed gatherers of California. In the Northeast, the Iroquois set up a **confederation,** or government made up of independent units, about A.D. 1580. The confederation worked to maintain peace between the various Iroquois nations. In the

▲ *MARKETPLACE OF TLATEOLCO* by Diego Rivera, 1920s Rivera's murals portray the culture and history of Mexico. Cities grew up around market centers, which drew great crowds of people. *What peoples developed complex road and irrigation systems?*

TEACH
Guided Practice

Summarizing Have students skim the subsection titled "The First Americans." Then ask them to write brief paragraphs about Native American cultures who lived in present-day Mexico, in South America, and in areas north of Mexico. For example: The Inca controlled western South America. Their culture was advanced, with a vast road and irrigation system. **L2**

Visualizing
 History Among the many accomplishments of early Native American empires was the Inca road system. Eventually, the Inca carved more than 14,000 miles of roads throughout the Andes. **Answer to Caption:** The Inca people of western South America

Facts on File

CD-ROM

The American Indian

Students can learn more about Native American life by selecting the category HISTORY from the main menu, and the subcategory INDIAN LIFESTYLES. Suggest students take notes on how the various Native American groups adapted to the environment.

Cooperative Learning Activity

Studying Native American Cultures Organize the class into groups of four or five. Assign each group one of the Native American cultures discussed in this section. Have group members brainstorm to come up with as much information as they can about their assigned culture. Then ask group members to work together to identify the most important points in the information they have gathered. Next, have each group write a sentence that summarizes these important points. Groups should select a representative to read their sentences to the rest of the class. **L2**

Map
Study *Using Maps*

Answers: Navajo, Hopi, Zuni, Pima, Papago, Pueblo, Comanche

Map Skills Practice

Have students determine which part of the Americas was settled last. Why did it take Native Americans so long to settle this area? (*The southernmost part of South America. It was the farthest point from the "land bridge" that connected the Americas to Asia.*)

Did You Know?

The large, multistory apartment-like adobe buildings built by the Anasazi contained elaborate ceremonial rooms. Early Spanish explorers called these houses *pueblos,* the Spanish word for "villages."

Food of the Times

According to the United Nations, the four staples of diets around the world are wheat, rice, maize, and potatoes. Two of the four—maize and potatoes—were developed by Native Americans.

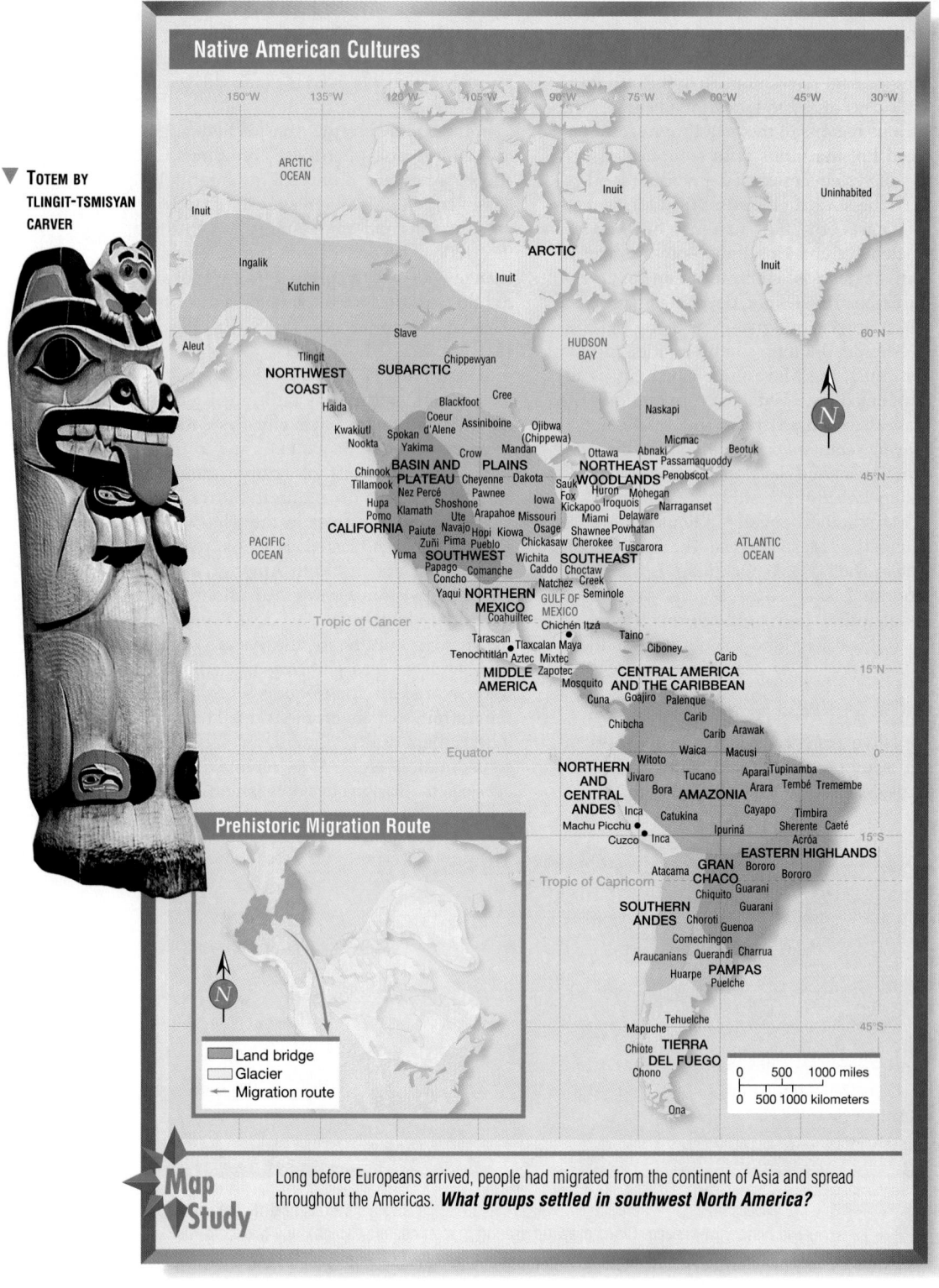

Native American Cultures

▼ TOTEM BY TLINGIT-TSMISYAN CARVER

Prehistoric Migration Route

- Land bridge
- Glacier
- ← Migration route

0   500   1000 miles
0   500 1000 kilometers

Map Study

Long before Europeans arrived, people had migrated from the continent of Asia and spread throughout the Americas. **What groups settled in southwest North America?**

Sidelight: Iroquois Society

Women yielded considerable power in many Native American societies north of Mexico. Among the Iroquois, for example, women owned the houses, fields, and crops, and descent was traced through the female line. While Iroquois women did not hold any leadership positions, it was their task to choose the leaders. Further, they decided whether or not a leader was effective. If after a number of warnings his performance did not improve, the women could demand that he be removed.

Southeast, the Creek, Cherokee, Choctaw, Seminole, and Chickasaw formed a confederation called the Five Civilized Tribes. This group later devised a written language and a dictionary, and practiced a loose-knit form of democracy.

■ A New Europe

Across the Atlantic Ocean, Europe entered a period known as the Middle Ages, which lasted from about A.D. 500 until about A.D. 1500. During the Middle Ages, central government in Europe was replaced by **feudalism,** a system in which powerful lords gave land to nobles in return for pledges of loyalty. The majority of Europe's people were peasants who worked on farmlands held by the nobles.

The Crusades

During the Middle Ages, the Roman Catholic Church, the western branch of Christianity, became a powerful force in Europe. From 1095 to about 1300, Church leaders asked Europeans to carry out a series of Crusades, or "holy wars," to recapture the "Holy Land" of Palestine from the Muslims, or people who follow the religion of Islam.

Although the Crusades were a failure, they had a major impact on western Europe. The Crusades helped break down feudalism. Contact with the East spurred a new demand in Europe for Asian luxury goods, such as spices and silk. European cities—especially Venice and Genoa in Italy—became more prosperous due to increased trading in the Mediterranean area.

Renaissance and Reformation

In Europe, a wealthy and educated middle class developed from an increase in commerce and the growth of cities. Prosperity, optimism, and an emphasis on human abilities led to a profound cultural awakening known as the Renaissance. Renaissance ideas and values began about 1350 in the city-states of northern Italy and spread to other parts of Europe. The Renaissance was

 **RELIGIOUS ART** Artists decorated books, crosses, and other items with religious images. Shrines in which sacred relics are kept, called reliquaries (shown above), were frequently made of gilded copper and decorated with precious stones. *What impact did the Crusades have on western Europe?*

a turning point in Europe's history. While the Middle Ages had emphasized faith and spiritual values, the Renaissance exalted human creativity and talent.

Religion was one area of European life in which traditional ways were challenged by these developments. In the early 1500s, the German monk and scholar Martin Luther attacked several church practices. In taking a stand against church authorities, Luther sparked what became known as the Protestant Reformation. A new form of Christianity—Protestantism—developed and grew throughout northern Europe. In other parts of Europe, most people remained loyal to the Roman Catholic Church.

Emerging Nations

During the 1400s, strong monarchs brought unity to the countries of England, France, Portugal, and Spain. All four lands had seaports on the Atlantic Ocean—soon to become a great avenue of trade and exploration.

Europeans, once isolated and bound by a rigid feudal system, were developing a spirit of curiosity and adventure. Unified monarchies and national rivalry led to competition for trade with Asia. The search for an all-water route to East Asia encouraged explorers to cross unknown oceans and seek new lands.

CURRICULUM CONNECTION

Science Leonardo da Vinci drew designs for machines and contraptions—the helicopter and the parachute, for example—that did not become a reality for hundreds of years.

Visualizing History Although the Crusaders did not intend to change life in Europe, their experiences had long-lasting effects. Perhaps the most important was that they brought home an assortment of luxury goods. Discuss with students how that one change led to many others.
Answer to Caption: helped break down feudalism, spurred a new demand in Europe for Asian luxury goods, made some European cities more prosperous due to increased trading in the Mediterranean area

Study Strategies The objectives given in the "Setting the Scene" feature provide a valuable tool for focusing reading on main ideas. Point out that the tasks required by the objectives are usually signaled in the first word. Some emphasize information collection ("List," "Identify"), while others call for description ("Describe," "Explain"), and still others ask students to compare and contrast. Ask students to look through each chapter objective and note the first word. Discuss the kinds of responses required. **LEP, L1**

■ Medieval Asia and Africa

Since ancient times, trade had linked the peoples of Europe, Asia, and Africa. Europe's share in foreign trade declined during much of the Middle Ages, but trade between Asia and Africa flourished.

The Influence of Islam

The most important influence in medieval Africa and Asia was the rise of the religion of Islam in the 600s. Inspired by the teachings of the prophet Muhammad, the prophet's followers spread Islam from the Arabian Peninsula through Southwest Asia to India and North Africa into Spain and the Mediterranean region.

As Islam spread, Muslims and Christians came into direct conflict. Contact between the groups, however, influenced trade and learning and brought new ideas. Muslim Arab scholars had made advances in medicine, astronomy, mathematics, and other sciences. From the Arabs, Europeans learned algebra and the system of Arabic numerals, which had come to Southwest Asia from India.

China

In the early 1200's the ancient empire of China was conquered by invading Mongols from central Asia. China prospered under Mongol rule. East-west trade revived, along with cultural exchanges among China, Europe, and Muslim Asia. European

▲ ILLUMINATED MANUSCRIPT, illustrated and handwritten document

traders, such as Marco Polo, returned with silk, spices, and important Chinese inventions, such as the compass, printing, and gunpowder. Polo's description of the luxury of the Chinese ruler's court stirred the imaginations of his European readers:

    ❝ *Inside, the walls and halls and chambers are all covered with gold and silver and decorated with pictures of dragons and birds and horsemen and various breeds of beasts and scenes of battle. . . . The hall is so vast that a meal might be served there for more than 6,000 men.* ❞

In 1294, the Chinese overthrew their Mongol rulers and set up the Ming Empire. Ming rulers at first encouraged trade, sending expeditions to India and East Africa. By the late 1400s, they ended China's contacts with the world. While the spirit of the Renaissance was transforming Europe, the mood in China was to preserve tradition against foreign influences. China would remain relatively isolated for centuries.

Japan

Like medieval Europe, Japan had a feudal society, based on bonds between landowning nobles and warriors who served them.

• •

Footnotes to History

Illuminated Manuscript Scholars of the Byzantine empire created an art form called the illuminated manuscript. These were books decorated with elaborate designs, beautiful lettering, and miniature paintings. The brilliantly colored paintings portrayed religious themes as well as scenes of Byzantine daily life. Adopted in western Europe, the art of illuminating manuscripts provided a vivid record of daily life between A.D. 300 and 1200.

Sidelight: The Salt Trade in West Africa

One of the most important commodities that changed hands in the trading centers of West Africa was common salt. The grasslands of the Western Sudan had no natural supplies of salt, and people from there were willing to part with sacks of gold—which they had in plentiful supply—pound for pound for blocks of the mineral. Salt was needed to preserve meat, which quickly spoiled in the hot climate. More importantly, it was a necessity of life. People lose some of their body salts when they sweat. A diet containing common salt helps replace those lost body salts.

Since the 1100s, the country had been led by **shoguns,** military dictators who had far more power than the Japanese emperor. By the late 1400s, the shogun's government had weakened, and local lords were almost constantly at war. Nonetheless, towns and trade prospered in medieval Japan.

African Trading Kingdoms

From ancient times, trade linked the continent of Africa with other cultures. The earliest African civilizations developed in northeastern Africa. From their base in the Nile River valley, Egyptians and, later, Kushites ruled extensive empires. A Christian African empire, Axum, arose during the Middle Ages in the area that is present-day Ethiopia.

Between A.D. 500 and 1500, three wealthy kingdoms—Ghana, Mali, and Songhai—developed one after the other in western Africa. The Muslim conquest of North Africa greatly increased trade, and Muslim culture spread throughout the area. East Africa, on the other hand, looked eastward, trading with Arabia, Persia, India, and China. In central and southern Africa, civil wars brought internal disorder to the Bantu-speaking nations. The resulting loss of power left little defense against Europeans who arrived in the 1500s.

■ Expansion of Europe

The Renaissance spirit of curiosity and adventure that swept over Europe helped launch the bold voyages of the Age of Exploration. Europeans wanted luxury goods and food-preserving spices from Asia. Western European merchants hoped to break the monopoly that Arab and Italian traders had on the overland routes to Asia. European monarchs desired to enrich their countries, and church leaders wanted to send missionaries overseas to spread Christianity.

Linking Past and Present

★★★★★★★★★★

African Art

In Africa, the arts are interwoven with many aspects of daily life. From ancient times to the present, Africans have used visual arts in many different forms and materials.

Then_____

Medieval Art

In ancient times, African artists and craftspeople created an extraordinary variety of art forms—from sculpted figures and masks to decorated cloth to the multi-rhythmic

music of traditional dances. Because of the forced migration of enslaved Africans to other parts of the world, these styles spread throughout the Americas, the Caribbean, and parts of Europe.

Now_____

A Heritage of Beauty

The influence of African masks, sculptures, and weavings can be seen in museums and in everyday life. Modern European artists such as Pablo Picasso drew inspiration from the abstract masks of the Yoruba of Nigeria. The bronze castings of the Benin are known around the world. So are the many types of textiles designed by Africans. Prized by many are Ghana's brightly colored *kente*

▲ **Yoruba Masks**

cloth, Nigeria's *adire* cloth, and East Africa's *kong* cloth—complete with a Swahili proverb on each piece.

Today there are thousands of artists in the towns and cities of Africa fashioning pots, carving wood masks, designing buildings, sculpting statues, and weaving and dyeing cloth.

★★★

▶ **Antelope figurine**

Classifying Information
Have students identify and list all the motives that prompted the Europeans to make voyages of exploration and discovery. Then ask students to think of classifications into which they might organize their lists. Provide the following examples: Geographic motives—location on the sea, better maps, more sophisticated navigational instruments; Economic motives—desire for financial gain, demand for luxury goods from Asia. **L2**

Did You Know?

Portugal was the first European nation to build an overseas colony organized around slave labor. The colony was Madeira, an island off the coast of Africa.

Linking Past and Present

Point out that traditional African music is reflected today in blues, jazz, and rock-'n'roll. Interested students might find examples of traditional African music and compare it to the rhythms and sounds of popular music today.

For additional practice, assign Linking Past and Present Activity 1.

Cooperative Learning Activity

Analyzing Point of View Organize students in groups of four or five. Ask one group to write a newscast for a Portuguese TV station describing the voyages of Bartholomeu Dias or Vasco da Gama. Ask other groups to describe the same event from an African, Asian, or Italian perspective. Discuss similarities and differences after each group has presented its version of the story. **L3**

ASSESS

Check Understanding

Assign Section 1 Review as homework or an in-class activity.

Evaluate

Assign Section Quiz 1-1 or use the Testmaker to create a customized quiz.

Reteach

Ask students to read the section. Test their retention of information by holding an oral quiz. Add an element of competition to the quiz by organizing the students into two teams.

Have students complete Reteaching Activity 1-1.

Enrich

Point out that Europeans knew little of the kingdoms of West Africa until the pilgrimage of the great Malian ruler, Mansa Musa, in the 1320s. Have students write a report on Mansa Musa's hajj to Makkah and the impact it had on North Africa. Ricky Rosenthal's *The Splendor That Was Africa* (1967) is a useful source of information for this report.

Assign Enrichment Activity 1

CLOSE

Have students construct a time line of the events and developments covered in Section 1. Suggest that they divide it into four sections: The Americas, Europe, Africa, and Asia.

Commerce and Technology

The great expense of ocean voyages made new ways of raising finances necessary. In England, France, and the Netherlands, the **joint-stock company** became a useful form for raising money. The company sold shares, called stock, to investors, thus providing money or capital for its venture.

No matter how well financed, long voyages could not have succeeded without better technology. By the 1400s, ship captains were using precise maps of the coasts of Europe and North Africa. From Arab sailors, Europeans learned to use improved navigational instruments, such as the compass, the astrolabe, and the quadrant—that allowed navigators to determine direction and distance. Ships were also built to new designs that made them faster and more seaworthy. The carrack had several masts and a rudder. Smaller but easier to handle was the Portuguese caravel, a double-rigged ship with both square and triangular sails.

The Pioneering Portuguese

Portugal was the first European country to search for a sea route to Asia. This small nation had a long Atlantic coast with good ports and a rich seafaring tradition.

In the early 1400s, Prince Henry, son of King John I of Portugal, brought together mapmakers, astronomers, and shipbuilders to plan voyages of exploration. He sent expeditions beyond the safety of the Mediterranean. One of Henry's plans was to have his ships sail around Africa and find a path to India. Expedition after expedition, the Portuguese inched their way down the west coast of Africa. By the time Prince Henry—known as "the Navigator"—died in 1460, his ships had reached just beyond the westernmost tip of Africa.

By this time, the Portuguese had established trading posts and sugar plantations on the West African coast. They acquired gold, ivory, pepper, palm oil, and slaves from African merchants. Using war captives as slaves had long been a practice throughout the world. The Portuguese used enslaved Africans as servants in Portugal or as laborers on their West African plantations.

Meanwhile, Portuguese navigators moved on to find a sea route to India. In 1487 and 1488, a Portuguese expedition led by Bartholomeu Dias rounded the southern tip of Africa. The area was soon named the "Cape of Good Hope" because it seemed to promise the existence of a new sea route to India. Ten years later, another Portuguese expedition led by Vasco da Gama rounded the Cape of Good Hope, sailed up the eastern coast of Africa, and crossed the Indian Ocean to Calicut on the coast of India. Da Gama finally returned home to Portugal in 1499. The sea route that he opened challenged other European nations to make their own explorations. In the following four centuries, western Europe's quest for wealth and empire would affect the lives of people on every continent.

Section 1 ★ Review

Checking for Understanding

1. **Identify** Inca, Iroquois, Crusades, Mali, Prince Henry, Vasco da Gama.

2. **Define** confederation, feudalism, shogun, joint-stock company.

3. **Summarize** the process by which the Americas were first settled.

4. **Analyze** the way in which the spread of Islam affected Europe, Asia, and Africa.

Critical Thinking

5. **Predicting Outcomes** How might European interest in exploration have increased as a result of the Crusades?

ACTIVITY

6. Select one of the Native American groups from the map on page 10 and research its way of life. Write a one-page paper that describes your findings.

Answers to Section 1 Review

1. Inca, 9; Iroquois, 9; Crusades, 11; Mali, 13; Prince Henry, 14; Vasco da Gama, 14
2. All vocabulary words are defined in the glossary.
3. Asians cross a "land bridge" between Siberia and Alaska, spread through Americas.
4. established empires in Africa and Asia; conquests of Holy Land prompted Crusades, brought Eastern goods and ideas back to Europe, fueled interest in exploration
5. Crusaders bring back goods, ideas, stories of sights, more people want goods and knowledge and to visit.
6. Students' papers should show evidence of research.

European Explorations

Setting the Scene

Section Focus

In their eagerness to find easier routes for trade in Asia, some Europeans had a new idea: instead of sailing south and east of Africa, they could sail west. This idea led to discoveries that brought drastic change to those who lived on the continents that lay between Europe and Asia.

▶ EXPLORER'S LOG BOOK

Objectives

After studying this section, you should be able to

★ describe Spanish exploration, conquests, and settlement in the Americas.

★ discuss English, French, and Dutch ventures in North America.

Key Terms

line of demarcation, conquistador, mestizo, *encomienda*, mercantilism, northwest passage

---

The first Europeans to arrive in the Americas were Norse seafarers from Scandinavia. Between A.D. 800 and 1100, the Norse established settlements in Iceland, Greenland, and along the coast of North America, which they called Vinland. Conflicts with Native Americans and lack of support from home, however, made the Norse settlements in Vinland unsuccessful. Not until the voyage of Christopher Columbus in 1492 did European exploration of the Americas begin in earnest.

■ Early Voyages

As a result of his studies and calculations, the Italian-born navigator Christopher Columbus came to believe that it would be easier to reach Asia by traveling west. He eagerly sought to lead such a voyage, and for years sought financial backing. Columbus finally persuaded King Ferdinand and Queen Isabella of Spain that his plan would bring them wealth, empire, and converts to the Catholic religion. The monarchs provided Columbus with three ships, the *Niña*, the *Pinta*, and the *Santa Maria.*

Voyages of Columbus

Columbus left Spain in August 1492 with 90 sailors. Two months later, after a difficult Atlantic voyage, Columbus went ashore onto a small island in the Bahamas (San Salvador) and claimed it for Spain. Believing he had reached the East Indies off the coast of Asia, he called the local people Indians. Columbus made three more voyages across the Atlantic. Despite his achievements, Columbus died in 1506 unaware that he had reached new continents in the Western Hemisphere.

CHAPTER 1 Exploration and Settlement: Prehistory–1763   **15**

LESSON PLAN
SECTION 2, 15–21

FOCUS

Bellringer

☞ Before taking roll, project Section Focus Transparency 1-2 or hand out Section Focus Transparency Activity 1-2. Have students answer the questions.

Motivating Activity

Ask students to imagine they have just signed on as crew for Christopher Columbus's "enterprise of the Indies." Then announce: Many people believe that if you sail westward, eventually you'll fall off the edge of the earth!

Point out that this was a widely accepted view in Columbus's day. Then ask: Given this belief, why would someone want to make such a voyage? **L2**

Vocabulary Precheck

Ask students to define each of the "Key Terms." Have a volunteer consult the dictionary for any unfamiliar words. **L1, LEP**

NATIONAL GEOGRAPHIC SOCIETY

GTV: The American People: Fabric of a Nation

Side 1, Chapter 3
Frames 11630-18740
Title: *Change of Scene*
Subject: Why Europeans sought a new home

Classroom Resources for SECTION 2

Blackline Masters:
☞ Reproducible Lesson Plan 1-2
☞ Guided Reading Activity 1-2
☞ Cooperative Learning Activity 1
☞ Workbook Activity 1-2
☞ Reteaching Activity 1-2
☞ Section Quiz 1-2

Transparencies:
☞ Section Focus Transparency 1-2
Multimedia:
▣ Testmaker
◉ GTV: The American People: Fabric of a Nation
◉ Historic America Electronic Field Trips
◉ GTV: A Geographic Perspective on American History

TEACH
Guided Practice

Analyzing Maps Provide students with atlases, and ask them to locate maps that show the world's ocean currents and prevailing winds. Then have them look at the Voyages of Exploration map on page 16. Ask them what currents and winds Columbus exploited on his first voyage to and from the Americas. (*To the Americas—Canary Current, North Equatorial Current, Northeast Trade Winds. From the Americas—Gulf Stream, Prevailing Westerlies.*) **L2**

◆Map ◆Study *Using Maps*

Answer: Pedro Cabral

Map Skills Practice

On the voyages of which explorers did England and Spain base their claims to the Americas? (*England— Cabot, Spain— Columbus*)

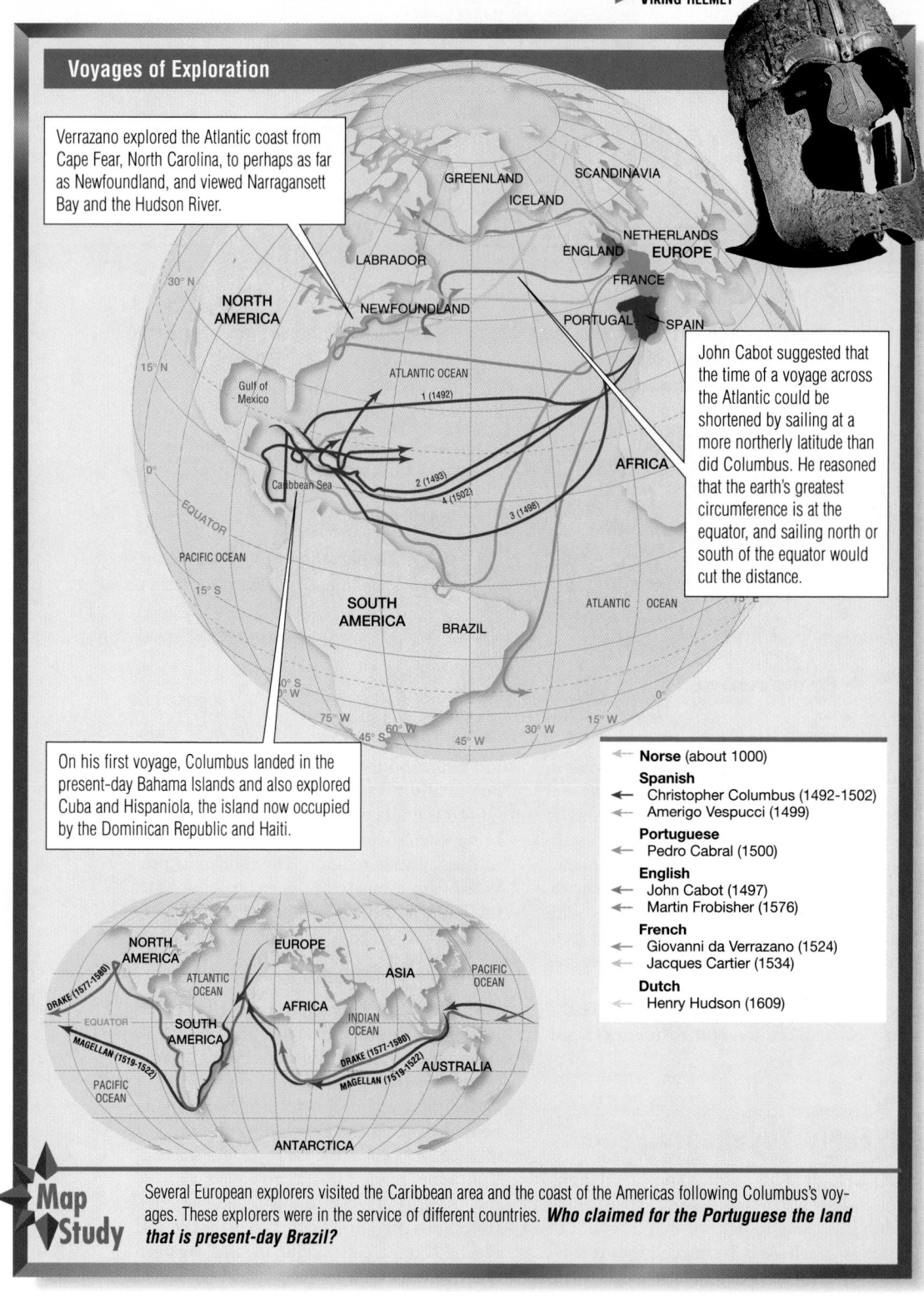

▶ VIKING HELMET

Voyages of Exploration

Verrazano explored the Atlantic coast from Cape Fear, North Carolina, to perhaps as far as Newfoundland, and viewed Narragansett Bay and the Hudson River.

John Cabot suggested that the time of a voyage across the Atlantic could be shortened by sailing at a more northerly latitude than did Columbus. He reasoned that the earth's greatest circumference is at the equator, and sailing north or south of the equator would cut the distance.

On his first voyage, Columbus landed in the present-day Bahama Islands and also explored Cuba and Hispaniola, the island now occupied by the Dominican Republic and Haiti.

GREENLAND • SCANDINAVIA • ICELAND • NETHERLANDS • ENGLAND • EUROPE • FRANCE • PORTUGAL • SPAIN • LABRADOR • NEWFOUNDLAND • NORTH AMERICA • ATLANTIC OCEAN • Gulf of Mexico • Caribbean Sea • AFRICA • EQUATOR • PACIFIC OCEAN • SOUTH AMERICA • BRAZIL • ATLANTIC OCEAN

1 (1492) • 2 (1493) • 4 (1502) • 3 (1498)

30° N • 15° N • 0° • 15° S • 75° W • 60° W • 45° W • 45° S • 30° W • 15° W • 0°

← **Norse** (about 1000)
Spanish
← Christopher Columbus (1492-1502)
← Amerigo Vespucci (1499)
Portuguese
← Pedro Cabral (1500)
English
← John Cabot (1497)
← Martin Frobisher (1576)
French
← Giovanni da Verrazano (1524)
← Jacques Cartier (1534)
Dutch
← Henry Hudson (1609)

NORTH AMERICA • EUROPE • ASIA • PACIFIC OCEAN • ATLANTIC OCEAN • AFRICA • INDIAN OCEAN • SOUTH AMERICA • AUSTRALIA • PACIFIC OCEAN • ANTARCTICA • EQUATOR

DRAKE (1577-1580) • MAGELLAN (1519-1522) • DRAKE (1577-1580) • MAGELLAN (1519-1522)

◆Map ◆Study

Several European explorers visited the Caribbean area and the coast of the Americas following Columbus's voyages. These explorers were in the service of different countries. ***Who claimed for the Portuguese the land that is present-day Brazil?***

16 UNIT 1 Creating a Nation: Prehistory to 1815

Critical Thinking Activity

Determining Relevance Point out that Columbus's voyages to the Americas had a major impact on the Americas and on Europe. Then ask students to complete the following sentences:

The greatest impact of Columbus's voyages on the Americas was . . .

The greatest impact of Columbus's voyages on Europe was . . .

Have students write brief paragraphs supporting their sentence completions. **L1, L2**

Division of the World

Columbus's exploration put Spain and Portugal in direct competition for trade and empire. In 1493, Pope Alexander VI convinced the two Catholic nations to divide any new overseas territories between them. He set a **line of demarcation,** an imaginary north-south line, west of the Azores, a group of islands in the North Atlantic about 800 miles off the coast of Portugal. The agreement gave Spain rights to all the non-Christian lands to the west of the line, and Portugal rights to all those to the east.

A New Land

In 1499, a Portuguese expedition led by the Italian-born navigator and explorer Amerigo Vespucci (veh•SPOO•chee) sailed along the coast of South America. Vespucci concluded that this land was a vast new continent. In 1504 Vespucci's sensational account was published, and he erroneously received credit for reaching the mainland of this land before Columbus. German mapmakers named the land "America," and the name stuck.

A Vast New Ocean

On expeditions into present-day Panama, the Spanish explorer Vasco Núñez de Balboa (VAHS•koh NOO•nyayth day bal•BOH•uh) was guided by local Native Americans to a vast body of water. Having climbed a peak alone to see the water first, Balboa in 1513 became the first European to see the eastern coast of the Pacific Ocean. It now appeared that the lands Columbus had reached were separated from Asia by this seemingly endless ocean.

Magellan's Voyage

Balboa's expedition revived hope of sailing west to reach Asia. Since only an isthmus, or strip of land, separated the oceans at Panama, it was thought that perhaps there was a strait, or narrow waterway, connecting the two bodies of water. Portuguese navigator Ferdinand Magellan believed he could find such a passage.

Magellan hoped to sail around the world to the Spice Islands, a center for the valuable spice trade located in present-day Indonesia. Spain's King Charles I agreed to finance Magellan, and in 1519 Magellan set sail with five ships. By October 1520, Magellan had reached the strait that now bears his name at the southern tip of South America.

The strait, with its fierce winds, was difficult to navigate. Because the ocean on the other side seemed so calm, Magellan called it the Pacific, meaning "peaceful." Magellan later died in April 1521 as the result of a local war in the Philippines. Only one of his ships, the *Victoria* carrying 18 survivors, finally reached Spain in 1522. These survivors and their ship were the first to circumnavigate the world.

■ Spain in America

After Columbus's voyages, Spanish **conquistadors** (kahn•KEES•tuh•dawrs), or conquerors, made their way to the Americas in hope of finding gold and silver. In the West Indies, the conquistadors enslaved the local Native Americans, forcing them to search for gold or to raise crops. Most of the Native Americans in the West Indies succumbed to such European diseases as smallpox and measles, from which they had no immunity. The Spaniards then began to abduct West Africans to work as slaves.

Cortés and Moctezuma

In 1519, the conquistador Hernán Cortés (kawr•TEHZ) led an expedition of 600 soldiers from the West Indies island of Cuba to the eastern shore of Mexico. The Spanish force had firearms and horses, both of which the local Native Americans had never seen. Believing that Cortés was a returning god, the Aztec emperor Moctezuma welcomed the Spaniards and lodged them in the Aztec capital of Tenochtitlán. Cortés wrote:

> The city itself is as big as Seville or Córdoba. . . . [it] has many squares where . . . markets are held continuously. . . .

FACT OR **FICTION?**

Magellan's expedition was a financial success.

FACT: On arriving in the Spice Islands, the survivors took on a cargo of cloves worth more than the whole cost of the voyage.

Did You Know?

Christopher Columbus never referred to himself as Columbus. Later in life he preferred to be called Cristóbal Colón.

NATIONAL GEOGRAPHIC SOCIETY

GTV: The American People: Fabric of a Nation

Side 1, Chapter 5
Frames 24070-28798
Title: *When Worlds Collide*
Subject: European and Native American encounters (1500s)

Special Needs Activity

Reading Disability Students with learning disabilities in reading should find that the organization, modified sentence constructions, and special features of this text facilitate their comprehension of the material. Because poor decoding (word attack) skills impede the reading process, it will be important for you to know the level at which each student has mastered these skills. Present each student with a list of 20 words from Section 2 to read aloud. Judge responses by both fluency (time) and power (correctness) criteria. **LEP**

Columbus made four trips to the Americas, each time bringing back to Europe plants and descriptions he claimed proved that the land he had found was part of Asia. An inedible West Indian nut, *nogal de pais*, Columbus insisted must be the coconut that Marco Polo described in his accounts of Cathay.
Answer to Caption: It put Spain and Portugal in direct competition for trade and empire.

Debate Have students debate the following statement:
The encomienda system was little more than slavery by another name. (*The basic pro argument might be that the system led to the large-scale exploitation of the Native American population. The basic con argument might be that, in theory, the system was established to protect the Native Americans.*) **L3**

Teaching American Portraits

Father Serra's missions were usually built a day's march from each other. Ask students why they think Father Serra followed this pattern. (*so that travelers would always have a place to rest after a long day's journey*) **L1**

There are ... many temples. ... Amongst these temples there is one ... whose great size and magnificence no human tongue could describe. ""

To ensure their safety, the Spaniards took Moctezuma captive. They also looted the city of gold and silver. Eight months later, when Moctezuma was killed by one of his subjects, the Aztec rose up against the Spaniards and forced them to retreat.

In 1521, Cortés returned to the Aztec capital, having amassed huge numbers of allies among local Native Americans dissatisfied with Aztec rule. After a long siege, the Spaniards destroyed Tenochtitlán whose splendor had so impressed them. Mexico City was built on its ruins, and the area's rich silver mines soon produced vast wealth.

Fall of the Inca

Another conquistador, Francisco Pizarro, set out to conquer the mighty and fabulously rich Inca Empire. In 1531 Pizarro sailed from Panama to present-day Peru with an army of only 180 soldiers. Reaching the Incan city of Cajamarca (KAH•

Visualizing
History

▲ COLUMBUS AND ISABELLA
Columbus believed Asia was accessible by traveling westward. Queen Isabella of Spain agreed to finance Columbus's explorations across the Atlantic. *What did Columbus's explorations mean for Spain?*

huh•MAHR•kuh), the Spaniards seized the Incan ruler, Atahualpa (AH•tah• WAHL•pah) and later executed him. Already weakened by civil war, the Inca Empire easily fell to the Spaniards.

Junípero Serra
1713–1784

★★★★AMERICAN PORTRAITS

Most Spanish conquests in the Americas were marked by a terrible slaughter of the local people. In contrast, a gentle priest established Spanish control in California by setting up a string of missions to care for and convert the Native Americans.

Born on an island off the Spanish coast, Junípero Serra became a Franciscan priest and professor of philosophy. Because he wanted to work as a missionary among Native Americans, in 1749 he left Spain to travel to Mexico.

At the age of 55, he was sent to take control of Upper California. He established a mission at San Diego, and later founded several missions stretching up the California coast to San Francisco. Taking as his motto "Always go forward and never turn back," Junípero Serra traveled by foot from mission to mission, making sure that Native Americans were not abused.

Cooperative Learning Activity

Role Playing Organize the students into pairs. Have one member of each pair play the role of a conquistador or explorer named in this section and the other member play the role of an interviewer. The interviewers should ask the interviewees about their life and travels in America. Have the pairs reverse roles and continue the interviews. When interviews have been completed, ask pairs who selected the same conquistador or explorer to compare the information they have gathered. **L2**

📁 Assign Cooperative Learning Activity 1.

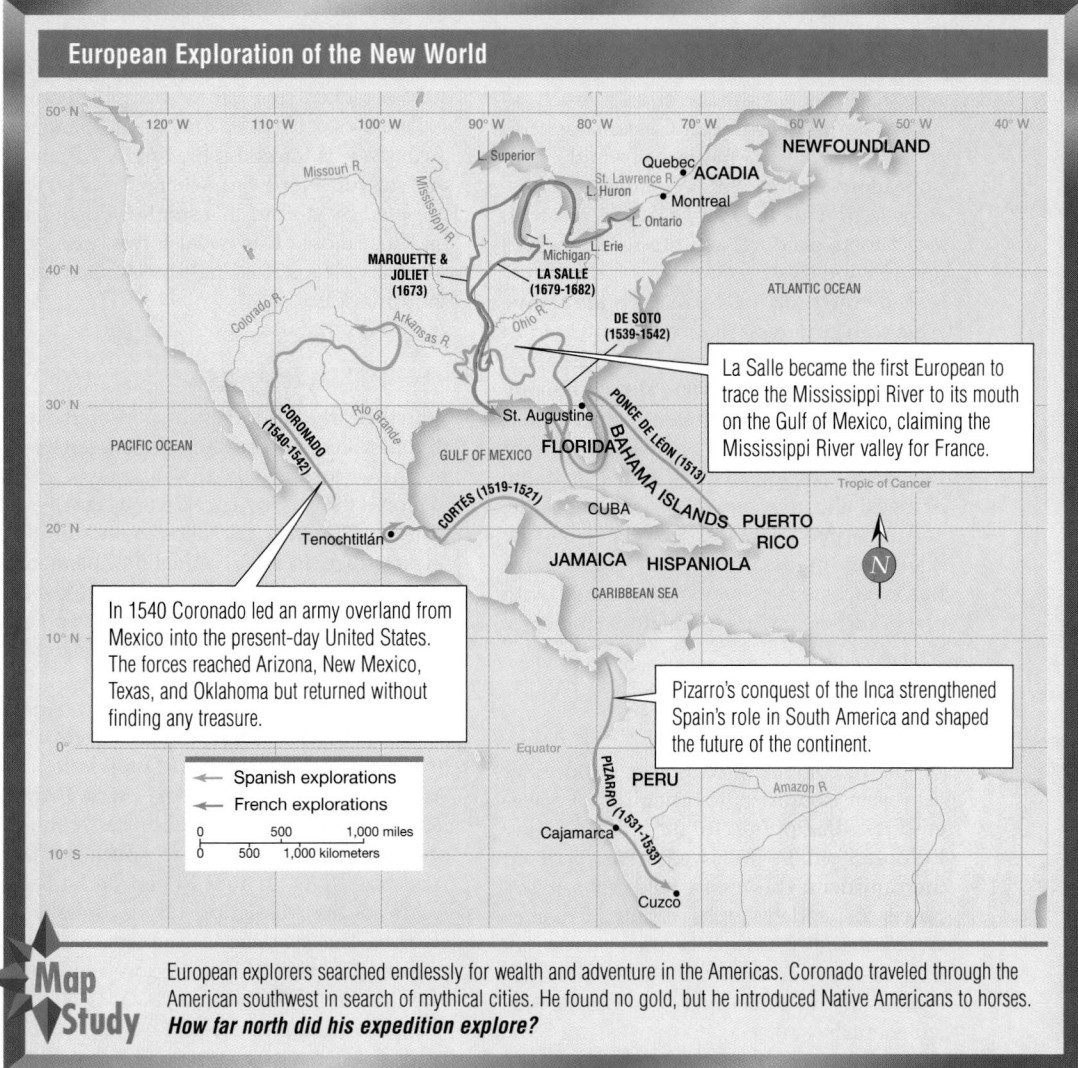

European Exploration of the New World

La Salle became the first European to trace the Mississippi River to its mouth on the Gulf of Mexico, claiming the Mississippi River valley for France.

In 1540 Coronado led an army overland from Mexico into the present-day United States. The forces reached Arizona, New Mexico, Texas, and Oklahoma but returned without finding any treasure.

Pizarro's conquest of the Inca strengthened Spain's role in South America and shaped the future of the continent.

→ Spanish explorations
→ French explorations

0   500   1,000 miles
0   500   1,000 kilometers

Map Study
European explorers searched endlessly for wealth and adventure in the Americas. Coronado traveled through the American southwest in search of mythical cities. He found no gold, but he introduced Native Americans to horses. *How far north did his expedition explore?*

ABCNEWS INTERACTIVE™

VIDEODISC

Historic America Electronic Field Trips

Side One, Chapter 4
Title: *St. Augustine*
Subject: Tour of America's first permanent European settlement
Ask: What factors helped this settlement survive? (*weather, location, abundant resources*)

Map Study *Using Maps*
Answer: Arkansas River valley
Map Skills Practice
Who explored the Mississippi River as far south as the Arkansas River? (*Marquette and Joliet*)

Food of the Times

European explorers encountered many new foods in the Americas. These included maize (corn); sweet potatoes; white potatoes; snap, kidney, and lima beans; peanuts; pumpkins; pineapples; chocolate; avocados; tomatoes; and turkeys.

Pizarro's conquest of the Inca Empire brought many Spanish settlers to Peru, where they mined silver and gold.

Colonial Life

Other Spanish conquistadors explored areas to the north, in the present-day southern and western United States. Because these northern lands appeared inhospitable, the Spanish considered them unsuitable for colonization. In other areas of the Americas, the Spaniards worked to strengthen their empire.

The people of Spain's American colonies formed a structured society, where position was determined predominately by birth. Spaniards born in Spain or in the Americas made up the highest social classes. **Mestizos** (meh•STEE•zohs), those born of Native American and Spanish parents, made up the next level of society. At the lowest levels were Native Americans, enslaved Africans, and people of mixed ancestry.

Through the *encomienda* system, the Spanish monarch rewarded conquistadors with land and the right to demand both labor and taxes from the Native Americans. The

Critical Thinking Activity

Analyzing a Point of View On the chalkboard, write the following quotation from *In the American Grain* by William Carlos Williams:
"Cortés was neither malicious, stupid nor blind, but a conqueror like other conquerors. . . . He was one among the rest."

Ask students to write a brief paper that answers the following questions: What point of view is being expressed? What evidence might be used in support of this view? What evidence might challenge it? Do you agree or disagree with the author? **L3**

Independent Practice

Working With Chronology
Have students use information from all three sections of Section 2 to construct a time line titled "Exploration in the Americas, 1492-1682." Suggest that students retain their time lines for review purposes. **L1, LEP**

Did You Know?

In Louisiana, two ethnic groups, both famous for their cuisine, boast French ancestry. The Cajuns descended from French settlers driven from Acadia in 1755. Creoles are a mix of early French and Spanish settlers.

NATIONAL GEOGRAPHIC SOCIETY

VIDEODISC

GTV: A Geographic Perspective on American History

Side 1, Chapter 4
Title: *Land of Opportunity*
Subject: Europeans gain a foothold in the Americas (1492-1603)

ASSESS

Check Understanding

Assign Section 2 Review as homework or an in-class activity.

Spanish colonists often treated the Native Americans cruelly, overworking them and using their forced labor to gain vast personal wealth. Roman Catholic priests, such as Father Bartolome de Las Casas, sought to protect the Native Americans from the conquistadors. Many clergy established missions to provide the Native Americans with work, food, clothing, a European education, and religious instruction.

The mingling of Spanish and Native American cultures produced a new kind of society in the Spanish colonies. Spanish became the major language, although many Native Americans continued to speak their original languages. The Spanish introduced European crops, such as wheat, alfalfa, oranges, and figs, as well as horses, cattle, and firearms. Likewise, products from the Americas made significant changes in Europe when the Spaniards returned with plants such as potatoes, tomatoes, and corn.

■ New Ventures

Spain's colonial success convinced other European countries to establish overseas empires. Beginning in the 1600s, many European nations followed a theory called **mercantilism.** This theory held that a state's power depended on its wealth. Colonies were especially valued because they were sources of raw materials and provided markets for the manufactured goods of the parent country.

English-Spanish Rivalry

In 1497, John Cabot explored the Atlantic shores of present-day Canada and claimed the land for England. But poor finances, religious conflict, and the threat of war with Spain kept the English from following up on Cabot's claims.

In the late 1500s, daring English sea captains, such as Francis Drake, cruised the shores of Spanish America, capturing treasure ships and looting towns. In 1588, seeking revenge for English attacks on Spanish ships and colonies, King Philip II of Spain sent a huge fleet of ships, known

as the Spanish Armada, to sail against the English fleet.

The outnumbered, but swift, English vessels attacked the slow, heavy Spanish galleons one by one. The badly damaged Armada was forced up the English Channel and into the North Sea, where it was further crippled by storms. In a single battle, Spain had lost most of its naval forces. The way was now cleared for English colonization in the Americas.

The French in America

In the early 1500s, French-sponsored expeditions sailed to North America in search of a **northwest passage.** In 1534, Jacques Cartier explored the St. Lawrence River as far as present-day Montreal, but failed to find the elusive passage. In 1608, Samuel de Champlain founded the first French settlement, Quebec, on the banks of the St. Lawrence River. Few French settlers, however, were attracted to this northern outpost.

French explorers soon ventured from present-day Canada south into the heartland of North America. In 1673 Louis Joliet, an American-born fur trader, and Father Jacques Marquette, a Catholic priest, canoed on the Mississippi as far south as the Arkansas River. In 1682 Robert de La Salle followed the Mississippi to its delta and claimed the vast lands drained by it for France. He named the region Louisiana after the French king Louis XIV.

France's colonies in North America eventually formed a long string of outposts from Canada to the Gulf of Mexico. Rather than encourage settlements and farms, the French directed their interests toward devel-

Footnotes to History

The Spanish Empire The Spanish empire in the Americas included more than one-half the continental United States. The oldest surviving building in the United States is the Spanish fort at St. Augustine, Florida. The city of Santa Fe was founded by the Spanish at about the same time the English Pilgrims were crossing the Atlantic on the *Mayflower.*

Cultural Perspectives

The French Presence During the 1500s the French tried to found colonies south of Canada. In 1562 French Huguenots set up a colony in present-day South Carolina, but it failed because of internal disagreements. In 1564 the French established Fort Caroline in Florida. The Spanish who viewed the Protestant French fort as a threat, attacked and drove out the French. Then Spain founded St. Augustine, Florida, in 1565.

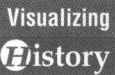

▲ NEW FRANCE The French explored and settled in a vast region that included the St. Lawrence River valley, the Great Lakes, and the Mississippi River valley. *Where did the French make settlements?*

The Dutch in America

The Netherlands, which had won its independence from Spain in the late 1500s, was also interested in exploration. In 1609, the Dutch funded an expedition by an English navigator, Henry Hudson. He reached New York Harbor and sailed up the river, which today bears his name, as far as present-day Albany, New York. The Dutch soon set up trading posts on Manhattan Island, which they named New Amsterdam, and along the Hudson River. A profitable fur trade was established with the Native Americans. The Dutch promised land to settlers in an attempt to populate the colony; however, few were interested. Because of poor leadership and weak government, the Dutch colony easily fell to the English in 1664.

◀ FUR TRADER

oping the fur trade. Beaver skins sent to France and made into hats were a particularly profitable item.

The French generally had better relations with Native Americans than did the Spanish. French trappers and traders known as *coureurs de bois*—"runners of the woods"—lived among the Native Americans and learned their ways. Without soldiers accompanying them, French missionaries bravely journeyed into the American wilderness to convert Native Americans to Catholicism.

Section 2 ★ Review

Checking for Understanding

1. **Identify** Americo Vespucci, Hernán Cortés, Moctezuma, Francisco Pizarro, Samuel de Champlain, Robert de La Salle.

2. **Define** line of demarcation, conquistador, mestizo, *encomienda*, mercantilism, northwest passage.

3. **Contrast** patterns of French settlement with colonization patterns of other European nations.

Critical Thinking

4. **Verifying Predictions** Spanish explorers introduced horses to Native Americans. Predict how the lives of the Plains peoples in North America might have been significantly altered by having horses.

ACTIVITY

5. Create a time line poster of important voyages of exploration during the 1500s.

Answers to Section 2 Review

1. Amerigo Vespucci, 17; Hernán Cortés, 17; Moctezuma, 17; Francisco Pizarro, 18; Samuel de Champlain, 20; Robert de la Salle, 20

2. All vocabulary words are defined in the Glossary.

3. did not establish large farming or mining settlements as did Spanish; French established small outposts and started fur trade; coexisted with most Native Americans.

4. Answers will vary, but predictions might include that they became mounted hunters and warriors, able to migrate more easily.

5. Posters will vary. Students should include a number of the significant voyages.

Visualizing History Point out that by 1670, some 60 years after the founding of Quebec, there were a little more than 8,000 French in New France. As a comparison, at that time the population of Boston was around 5,000.

Answer to Caption: Champlain founded Quebec, the first French settlement, on the banks of the St. Lawrence River. Eventually, France's colonial holdings included a string of outposts from Canada to the Gulf of Mexico.

Evaluate

☛ Assign Section Quiz 1-2 or use the Testmaker to create a customized quiz.

Reteach

☛ Have students complete Reteaching Activity 1-2.

Enrich

Have students write a report on the foods that the Spanish introduced to America.

CLOSE

Ask students to discuss the discoveries made by the explorers discussed in this chapter. Ask them to rank the discoveries in the order of importance.

CONNECTIONS

History
AND
ECONOMICS

History
AND
ECONOMICS

THE ARTS   GEOGRAPHY   SCIENCE   MATH

Stock Exchanges

The age of exploration brought sweeping changes to European society and to culture. Overseas trade and colonial ventures stimulated the European economy and helped it develop and grow. Business practices and banking practices soon became more sophisticated in order to facilitate profit from the flourishing world trade.

Launching an overseas trading venture was a major financial undertaking. Merchants in the sixteenth century reduced the risks of ocean trade by forming trading companies. Governments of western European states controlled the trade of their merchants and provided company charters that included the rights of stock ownership. Shares of stock allow the buyer a certain part of the future profits and assets of the company selling the stock. The person buying stock, therefore, becomes part owner of a company.

The early trading companies eventually led to the establishment of joint-stock companies such as the Dutch United East India Company, formed in the early 1600s. In order to sell large blocks of shares to investors, this company created a stock exchange in Amsterdam. The money raised became a permanent fund the company could draw money from when it initiated trading ventures.

In 1650 the English adopted the Dutch method of creating a permanent fund to finance trading enterprises. Before 1773, however, when English investors wanted to buy or sell shares of stock, they had to locate a broker to carry out their transactions. Then the London brokers founded the first English stock exchange. The first stock exchanges in the United States were organized in Philadelphia in 1791 and in New York City a year later.

▲ *THE MONEY CHANGER AND HIS WIFE* BY GUENTIN METYS, 1514

Not all the trading companies made money. England's Virginia Company was a costly failure, as were other European companies. By 1700, however, joint-stock companies had proved that free enterprise could raise the capital necessary for costly ventures, regardless of the risk.

Making the Economics Connection

1. Why did merchants form joint-stock companies?

2. What advantage did the Dutch United East India Company have over English companies in 1690?

ACTIVITY

3. Select three stocks that are listed on the New York Stock Exchange. Graph the performance of these stocks over a two-week period.

22

★★

The English Colonies

Setting the Scene

Section Focus

During the 1600s, England had naval power in the Atlantic, adequate finances for colonization, and a surplus population willing to settle overseas. For religious, political, or economic reasons, settlers from varied backgrounds began sailing to eastern North America. By the mid-1700s, a number of British colonies were flourishing along the Atlantic seaboard.

Objectives

After studying this section you should be able to

★ examine the different kind of English colonies that were formed in America.

★ discuss the ways in which American colonists differed from the British by 1750.

Key Terms

indentured servant, proprietor, congregation, commonwealth, constitution

◀ PINE TREE SHILLING, 1652

---

*I*n 1587, Sir Walter Raleigh, an English nobleman, tried to establish a permanent English colony on Roanoke Island near the coast of present-day North Carolina. He named the land "Virginia" in honor of the "Virgin Queen" Elizabeth I. This effort to build a colony failed because Spanish control of the sea delayed Raleigh's efforts to resupply the settlement until after England defeated the Spanish Armada in 1588. When English ships finally returned to Roanoke, they found none of the settlers. The fate of this "Lost Colony" remains a mystery.

■ The Southern Colonies

In 1606 King James I created the Virginia Company made up of merchants who had petitioned for permission to found colonies. Two parts of the company, the Virginia Company of London and the Virginia Company of Plymouth, were given exclusive settlement rights in North America.

Virginia

The London Company sent settlers to Virginia, where it was believed precious metals abounded. In the spring of 1607, the settlers founded Jamestown, named after King James I, a settlement 60 miles up the James River. Most of them were "gentlemen" who wanted to look for gold—not carpenters to build houses or farmers to raise crops for survival. The tragic result was that most of the 500 colonists who came in the first few years died. George Percy, one of the survivors, wrote of the sufferings at Jamestown:

❝ *Our men were destroyed with cruell diseases as Swellings, Flixes, Burning Fevers, and by*

CHAPTER 1 Exploration and Settlement: Prehistory–1763 **23**

LESSON PLAN
SECTION 3, 23–27

FOCUS
Bellringer

🎲 📁 Before taking roll, project Section Focus Transparency 1-3, or hand out Section Focus Transparency Activity 1-3. Have students answer the questions.

Motivating Activity

Ask students to imagine that they are about to make a long, hazardous journey to a new land of which they know nothing. Then ask: Why would you decide to make such a journey? What do you expect to find? Tell students that as they read this chapter they will discover how the first colonists answered these questions. **L1**

Vocabulary Precheck

Ask students to define each of the "Key Terms." Have a volunteer consult the dictionary for any unfamiliar words. **L1, LEP**

 VIDEODISC

GTV: A Geographic Perspective on American History

Side 1, Chapter 6
Title: *Hoping for the Best in America*
Subject: Trials and triumphs of English settlers (1607–1700)

Classroom Resources for SECTION 3

Blackline Masters:
- 📁 Reproducible Lesson Plan 1-3
- 📁 Guided Reading Activity 1-3
- 📁 Chapter Skills Activity 1
- 📁 Workbook Activity 1-3
- 📁 Reteaching Activity 1-3
- 📁 Section Quiz 1-3

Transparencies:
- 🎲 Section Focus Transparency 1-3
- 🎲 Skills Transparency 1

Multimedia
- 💿 Testmaker
- 💿 GTV: A Geographic Perspective on American History
- 💿 GTV: The American People: Fabric of a Nation

TEACH
Guided Practice

Demonstrating Reasoned Judgment Write the following statement on the chalkboard:

The desire for economic profit nearly destroyed Jamestown, yet it proved to be the colony's salvation.

Ask students to write a brief paragraph in support of the statement. (*Desire led settlers to search for gold rather than build houses and raise crops. As a result, colony almost failed. Desire to find cash crop to export to Britain led to development of tobacco. This ensured Jamestown's survival.*) **L2**

Map Study *Using Maps*

Answers: the English

Map Skills Practice

Ask students which immigrant group was predominant along the eastern side of the Appalachian Mountains in the Southern Colonies. (*Scotch-Irish*)

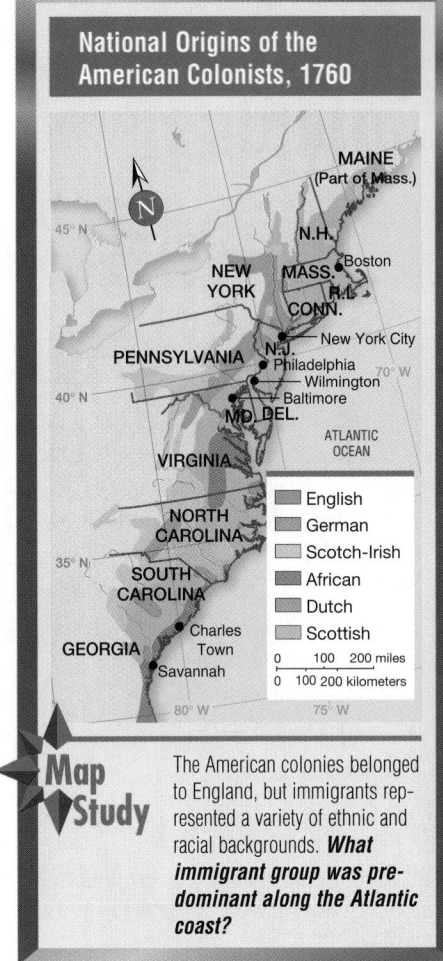

National Origins of the American Colonists, 1760

MAINE (Part of Mass.)
N.H.
NEW YORK
MASS.
Boston
R.I.
CONN.
New York City
PENNSYLVANIA
N.J.
Philadelphia
Wilmington
Baltimore
MD. DEL.
VIRGINIA
ATLANTIC OCEAN
NORTH CAROLINA
SOUTH CAROLINA
GEORGIA
Charles Town
Savannah

Legend:
- English
- German
- Scotch-Irish
- African
- Dutch
- Scottish

0   100   200 miles
0   100 200 kilometers

Map Study

The American colonies belonged to England, but immigrants represented a variety of ethnic and racial backgrounds. *What immigrant group was predominant along the Atlantic coast?*

warres, and some departed suddenly, but for the most part they died of mere famine. There were never Englishmen left in a forreigne Countrey in such miserie. . . .

By 1618, the company had expanded land sales, extended English law and rights to the colonists, and allowed settlers a representative assembly—the House of Burgesses. Soon after, new recruits, including various craftspeople, arrived in Virginia. Settlers, however, continued to die in large numbers from disease. Meanwhile the company

failed to realize any significant profits for its shareholders. In 1624, King James I dissolved the company and took control of the colony.

From nearby Native Americans, the settlers learned to grow corn, beans, squash, and tobacco, which soon became a profitable cash crop. Thousands of settlers streamed into Virginia, lured by the promise of free, abundant farmland. One source of workers for wealthy settlers were **indentured servants,** who worked for a set period of time to pay off their Atlantic passage and then were free to start their own farms.

In 1619 a Dutch warship brought 20 enslaved Africans to Jamestown. Virginians, desiring an additional source of labor for their tobacco fields, purchased the Africans. From 1600 to 1850, Europeans brought 15 million enslaved Africans to the Americas.

Maryland

In 1632 King Charles I gave his friend George Calvert, Lord Baltimore, a grant of land north of Virginia that became the colony of Maryland. The grant made Lord Baltimore **proprietor,** meaning that he had authority over the colony's government. Baltimore's son, Cecil Calvert, established Maryland as a refuge for Catholics. Protestants, however, soon outnumbered Catholics in Maryland. In 1649, the legislative assembly affirmed religious freedom to all Christian settlers by passing the Toleration Act, the first of its kind in America.

Carolina

Profits from tobacco in Virginia and Maryland lured settlers to Carolina, a proprietary colony located farther south along the Atlantic coast. In northern Carolina, subsistence farmers grew only enough to live on, while merchants exported tar, pitch, and turpentine from the area's pine forests. Southern Carolina, however, offered a better harbor and attracted more settlers. Charles Town—present-day Charleston—became a major port city in the South. Settlers in southern Carolina built large plantations to

Sidelight: Sports in the Colonies in the 1600s

The most popular spectator sports in the colonies during the 1600s were bull baiting, cockfighting, and horse racing. Bull baiting and cockfighting were open to people of all social classes, from the humblest farmhand to the wealthiest plantation owner. But horse racing was strictly for the gentry. One Chesapeake tailor, for example, was fined 100 pounds of tobacco for taking part in a race that was designated "for gentlemen only."

grow rice and indigo, a plant that produced a purple dye. In 1729, King George II made the two parts of Carolina separate royal colonies.

Georgia

Georgia, named after King George II, was the last of the 13 English colonies. Its wealthy proprietor, James Oglethorpe, planned Georgia as a refuge for debtors and a military outpost against the Spaniards in Florida. This plan did not succeed, however; and in 1752, Georgia became a royal colony.

■ New England

Unlike most of the southern colonies, New England was settled by people seeking a religious haven, not investors seeking a fortune. In England, Anglicans known as Puritans wanted to "purify" the Anglican Church of

▼ WILLIAM BRADFORD'S BIBLE

▲ *PILGRIMS GOING TO CHURCH* by George H. Boughton, 1867 Religion was important in Pilgrim life. **What evidence shown in this picture suggests that the settlers did not yet feel safe?**

its remaining Catholic practices. Another group, called Separatists, believed that it was better to separate themselves entirely from Anglicanism and to form their own church. Some Separatist "Pilgrims" settled in Holland to escape persecution by English authorities. Hoping to preserve their English language and culture, the Pilgrims finally decided to settle in America.

Plymouth

In 1619, the Pilgrims secured a grant of land in Virginia from the London Company. A year later, they and other passengers set sail from England on the *Mayflower*. The ship, however, accidentally landed far to the north of Virginia on the Massachusetts coast. Because they had no charter that applied to this area, the Pilgrims drew up the Mayflower Compact and established Plymouth Colony. The Compact stated that a government derives its just powers from the people who are governed.

The Pilgrims survived a difficult winter with the help of Native Americans, such as Squanto, who taught them about their new environment. The Pilgrims' deep sense of religious purpose also sustained the colony.

CHAPTER 1
SECTION 3

NATIONAL GEOGRAPHIC SOCIETY

 VIDEODISC

GTV: The American People: Fabric of a Nation

Side 1, Chapter 1

Title: *Living in the Promiseland*

Subject: America: people, promises, problems

Did You Know?

Most of the passengers aboard the *Mayflower* were not Pilgrims. Only 35 of the 101 passengers were members of the Separatist group that had settled in the Netherlands.

History AND ART

This painting's armed churchgoers suggest that the colonists felt more threatened during the first decades of the Plymouth colony than they actually were.
Answer to Caption: The men are armed.

Cooperative Learning Activity

Colonial Development Organize students in pairs; then write the following on the chalkboard: "The desire for religious freedom was the fundamental reason for the development of the New England colonies." Do you agree or disagree? Explain your answer.

Have the pairs of students consider and prepare a response to this question. Ask for volunteers to share their responses with the rest of the class. **L2, L3**

Independent Practice

Cultural Perspectives

The Dutch influence in American history can be seen in some of the place names in New Jersey and New York—Kinderhook and Hoboken, for example. Have students check atlases to locate and list 10 Dutch place names. **L1**

📂 Assign Guided Reading Activity 1-3.

FACT OR FICTION?

Descendants of the Dutch people who settled in eastern Pennsylvania in the 1700s are known as the Pennsylvania Dutch.

FICTION: The Pennsylvania Dutch are descendants of German, not Dutch, settlers. The confusion arose because the German word for "German" is *Deutsch*.

Food of the Times

Few colonists treated sugar casually. One observer notes that families kept their sugar loaves under lock and key. Popular and less costly substitutes were molasses, maple sugar, and honey.

▲ ANNE HUTCHINSON

Although Plymouth grew, it never became very large. It ran its own affairs until it became part of the larger Massachusetts Bay Colony in 1691.

Puritan Massachusetts

In 1629, prominent Puritans in England bought a trading company, changed its name to the Massachusetts Bay Company, and secured a charter directly from the king. Their plan was to built in Massachusetts a Christian society they believed would be a lighthouse for all the world. The first governor of Massachusetts, John Winthrop, made their intentions clear:

> ❝ We shall be as a city upon a hill. The eyes of all people are upon us. ❞

During the 1620s, thousands of Puritans escaping from religious persecution sailed for Massachusetts. Boston, the leading town, and its surrounding settlements flourished.

In Massachusetts, the Puritans set up churches governed by each **congregation,** or body of church members. They also transformed the Massachusetts Bay Company from a trading company into a **commonwealth,** a self-governing political unit, the first of its kind in America.

Dissent and Division

The Puritans who came to Massachusetts to worship as they pleased had no intention of granting the same freedom to those who were not Puritans. Roger Williams, a minister who disagreed with official Puritan views, preached that church and government should remain separate because involvement in political affairs would corrupt the church. He also asserted that the colonists had no right to settle on the land unless the land was purchased from the Native American people. Because of these views, Williams was banished from Massachusetts.

In 1644, Williams moved south and started the colony of Rhode Island on land purchased from the Native Americans. The new colony welcomed Jews as well as all Christians and guaranteed their religious freedom. In Rhode Island, church and state were completely separate, a principle that was to become an important part of America's political heritage.

Other dissenters fleeing Puritan persecution included Anne Hutchinson, who openly challenged Puritan interpretations of the Bible. She and her followers went to Rhode Island. Dissenters also founded colonies in New Hampshire and Connecticut. In 1639, the colony of Connecticut adopted the Fundamental Orders of Connecticut, the first written **constitution,** or plan of government, in America.

■ Middle Colonies

England's neglect of the American colonies between 1640 and 1660 enabled traditions of self-government to develop firmly in America. Colonial legislatures in New England and the South made their own laws, and local courts enforced them. The Middle Colonies also developed a degree of independence from England.

New York

In 1664 King Charles II granted his brother James, the Duke of York, the land west and south of New England, from the Connecticut River to the Delaware River. He did

Sidelight: The Puritan Ethic

The qualities that helped the settlers of the Massachusetts Bay Colony to succeed—discipline, industry, learning, and stubbornness—are usually referred to as the "Puritan ethic." Some historians have suggested that this ethic has become deeply embedded in the American character, emerging in varying forms at different historical periods. The "rugged individualism" of those who settled the West and the self-sacrifice of Americans during World War II, these historians argue, are but two aspects of the Puritan ethic.

this even though the territory had already been settled by the Dutch. In 1664, English warships captured the Dutch settlement of New Amsterdam and ended Dutch rule. The Duke of York did not hesitate to change the colony's name to New York.

Political affairs in New York were dominated by continual conflict between the royal governor and the elected representative assembly. Few settlers came at first because powerful landowners held much of the land. New York City provided a magnificent harbor, but the small population of the colony did not supply enough goods for export. Although Dutch customs remained strong, New York eventually had a varied population that included Dutch, Swedes, Native Americans, Africans, English, French, and people of other nationalities.

New Jersey

Shortly after the Duke of York received his grant of land in 1664, he started giving out parts of it to his friends. He gave New Jersey to two nobles who granted religious freedom and large land grants to settlers. By 1682, the colony had been sold to members of a religious group called the Society of Friends, or Quakers, who were seeking escape from persecution. In 1702, New Jersey finally became a royal colony under the authority of New York's governor.

Penn's Colonies

William Penn, the son of an English admiral, wanted to found a colony in America that would serve as a refuge for persecuted Quakers. In England, Quakers were considered religious radicals because they believed that paid clergy were unnecessary and that every person could know God's will through his or her own "inner light." Taking advantage of a debt that King Charles II owed his father, Penn asked the king for land in America. In 1681, Charles gave Penn authority over a vast area west of the Delaware River named "Penn's Woods," or Pennsylvania.

Arriving in Pennsylvania in 1682, Penn worked out a plan for a "city of brotherly love," Philadelphia. His promise of religious freedom and tolerance drew many settlers from Europe. Pennsylvania gave the right to vote to a large number of colonists. Penn also insisted that Native Americans be paid for their land. These measures meant rapid growth for the colony. By 1700 Philadelphia rivaled Boston and New York City as both a commercial and cultural center.

In 1682 William Penn bought the three counties south of Pennsylvania along the Atlantic coast from the Duke of York. These "lower counties," known as Delaware, had first been settled by the Dutch, then the Swedes, before the English captured them in 1664.

ASSESS

Check Understanding

Assign Section 3 Review as homework or an in-class activity.

Evaluate

Assign Section Quiz 1-3 or use the Testmaker to create a customized quiz.

Reteach

Ask students to identify the people who were important in the development of the Southern, New England, and Middle Colonies.

Have students complete Reteaching Activity 1-3.

Enrich

Ask students to complete the following sentence:
   William Penn's vision of America was different because....

CLOSE

Have students compare the reasons that the Middle Colonies were founded with the reasons that the Southern and New England Colonies were founded.

Section 3 ★ Review

Checking for Understanding

1. **Identify** Jamestown, Mayflower Compact, Roger Williams, Anne Hutchinson, William Penn.

2. **Define** indentured servant, proprietor, congregation, commonwealth, constitution.

3. **Explain** the factors that created hardships and initially limited the success of the Virginia colony.

4. **Discuss** the objectives of the Pilgrims and the Puritans in settling the Massachusetts Bay Colony.

Critical Thinking

5. **Analyzing Motives** Most New England colonies were settled by people escaping religious persecution. Which of these groups sought true religious freedom? How did they differ from the others?

ACTIVITY

6. Turn to the map on page 24. Which groups had settled in New Hampshire by 1760? What immigrant group had settled the farthest west?

CHAPTER 1 Exploration and Settlement: Prehistory–1763   **27**

Answers to SECTION 3 REVIEW

1. Jamestown, 23; Mayflower Compact, 25; Roger Williams, 26; Anne Hutchinson, 26; William Penn, 27
2. All vocabulary words are defined in the Glossary.
3. lack of skills among colonists and disinclination to work; disease
4. To escape religious persecution, freedom of worship for themselves only
5. Williams and his group. Others sought freedom to establish dominance of their own religion, while he sought universal religious freedom.
6. English and Scotch-Irish; Scotch-Irish

TEACH

Have students choose a document that they or their parents have filled out—for example, a tax form or a school or job application—and list the kinds of information one could learn about a person by reading it. (*Answers could include personal data, interests, job and educational background, and so on.*) Discuss students' responses. Ask: What information do such documents provide about our culture? Do they provide a definitive story or do they tell just part of the story? Point out that historians use documents to gain information about individuals and about society as a whole. **L2**

🗂 Project Skills Transparency 1 and have students complete Skills Transparency Activity 1.

🗂 Use Chapter Skills Activity 1 to reinforce students' understanding of the skill.

Did You Know?

Husbands in colonial society controlled the property of their wives. If a woman worked for money—for example, as a tavern keeper, printer, upholsterer, or silversmith—she was probably single or a widow carrying on her husband's business.

Interpreting Primary Sources

One often learns about the past by studying primary sources, or the original records of events made by people who witnessed them. Primary sources include letters, journals, legal documents, drawings, photographs, and artifacts. Historians have used documents, such as the following from the records of the Suffolk County Court in Massachusetts, to uncover information about life for women in the colonies. Read the excerpts, then answer the questions that follow.

▲ *Accused of Witchcraft* by Douglas Volk

Learning the Skill

Order abt Hitt (8 July, 1674)

In Answer to the request of Anne Hitt widdow . . . that Shee might have Liberty to dispose of & put to Sale some part of [her husband's] *Estate for the paiment of debts & Legacies & maintenance of her-selfe & Children: The Court Orders & Empowres the saide Anne Hitt (with the consent & advice) of those that are Sureties for her true Administracion upon the said Estate to dispose of & put to Sale the house & ground at Charlestown valued in the Inventory at L:170. Shee rendring an Account of Sd Sale unto the Court of this County.*

Walsebee's discharge (28 April, 1674)

The wife of David Walsebee of Brantery being presented for his Idleness and sottish carriage [drunken behavior]. *Upon hearing of the case The Court judge there is noe ground for the present-ment and so discharge her.*

Licenses (28 April, 1674)

Anne Puglice upon certificate from the Selectmen of Boston had her license renewed to distill & retail strong waters by small quantities for ye yeare ensuing; provided shee did not sell any of the inhabitants of the Town to drincke it in her house. . . . [O]n condicion that Anne Puglice should observe all the Laws . . .*

Practicing the Skill

1. When were the documents written?

2. What freedom was originally denied Anne Hitt that resulted in the court order?

3. What does the charge against the wife of David Walsebee indicate about the manners expected of women?

APPLYING THE SKILL

4. Why are these excerpts primary sources? What is the advantage of studying primary sources?

28

Answers to Practicing the Skill

1. in 1674
2. She did not own the property jointly with her husband. The court had to grant her the right to own and dispose of property.
3. The charge indicates that women could be arrested for looking idle or not carrying themselves properly. Also that people were brought to court for what we regard as moral rather than legal matters.
4. They are classified as primary sources because these are the original records of events that occurred in 1674. Primary sources are good indications of the way of life at a particular time.

★★★★★★★★★★★★★★★★★★★★★★★

Colonial Life

Setting the Scene

Section Focus

By the mid-1700s, colonial society differed from Britain in many ways. A diversity of people and new economic oppportunities helped to produce a society uniquely American. The history of social development in America is a story of progress for many. It is blemished by the enslavement of Africans and the eviction of Native Americans from their lands.

Objectives

After studying this section, you should be able to

★ describe social classes and the role of women, indentured servants, and African Americans.

★ discuss the relationship between English colonists and Native Americans.

★ explain why religious toleration and freedom developed during the colonial period.

Key Term

gentry

◀ SCRIMSHAW, CARVED ARTICLE MADE FROM WHALE IVORY

FOCUS

Bellringer

🔲 Before taking roll, project Section Focus Transparency 1-4 or hand out Section Focus Transparency Activity 1-4. Have students answer the questions.

Motivating Activity

Have students carefully read the following quotation from Benjamin Franklin's *Poor Richard's Almanac* (1775): "The day is short, the work great, the workmen lazy, the wages high, the master urgeth. Up then, and be doing." Then ask: What word would you use to characterize the life described in the quotation? Tough? Challenging? Boring? Rewarding? Give reasons for your choice. **L1**

Vocabulary Precheck

Ask students to define the "Key Term." Have a volunteer consult the dictionary for any unfamiliar words. **L1, LEP**

By European standards, the society of England during the 1600s and 1700s was remarkably mobile. An apprentice might become rich and marry his daughter to a noble. In turn, a noble's younger son, who inherited no property, might become an apprentice or hire himself out as a soldier. Like England, the colonies' social structure had many classes, but from the start it was more democratic.

■ Colonial Social Classes

In each of the 13 colonies, there was an upper class. In New England, merchants, shipowners, and the clergy composed this class. In the South and along the Hudson River in New York, great landowners imitated the country **gentry,** or upper class, of England. Early colonial laws permitted only upper-class men to wear silver but-

tons and upper-class women and girls to wear silk dresses. Social rank was indicated on marriage certificates and even on tombstones.

Near the bottom of society were indentured servants, bound by contract to work in the colonies in return for their passage to America. When the contract expired, the servant was free to work for wages. Because labor was scarce, wages in the colonies were two or three times those in England. Indentured servants could move up in society. For example, in the 1660s, 13 of 28 members of the Virginia House of Burgesses had come to the colony as indentured servants.

Quality of Life

For most people, life in colonial America was better than it had been in Europe. Still, many died within the first year because of hardships encountered during the ocean

CHAPTER 1 Exploration and Settlement: Prehistory–1763 **29**

Classroom Resources for SECTION 4

Blackline Masters:
- Reproducible Lesson Plan 1-4
- Guided Reading Activity 1-4
- Critical Thinking Skills Activity 1
- Writer's Guidebook Lessons 1-6
- Workbook Activity 1-4
- Geography in History Activity 1
- Chapter Map Activity 1

- Primary and Secondary Source Readings, pp. 1-2
- Reteaching Activity 1-4
- Section Quiz 1-4

Transparencies:
- Section Focus Transparency 1-4
- Map Transparency Activity 1

Multimedia:
- Testmaker
- GTV: A Geographic Perspective on American History
- GTV: The American People: Fabric of a Nation

Many families commissioned family portraits—sometimes done by untrained painters—to preserve accurate likenesses of family members for future generations, as well as to decorate their homes.
Answer to Caption: displays family's prosperity

NATIONAL GEOGRAPHIC SOCIETY

GTV: A Geographic Perspective on American History

Side 1, Chapter 9
Title: *Settling Down, Moving On*
Subject: Regional differences emerge in the colonies (1650–1750)

voyage. Frontier settlements faced conflict with Native Americans, starvation due to crop failures, disastrous fires, and epidemics of smallpox, dysentery, malaria, diphtheria, and yellow fever.

By the 1700s, conditions had improved, although epidemics continued to make life uncertain. There was widespread prosperity—a product of cheap land, a ready market for colonial exports, and hard work. Idleness was generally regarded as a sin like drunkenness or gluttony.

A Varied Population

By 1775 people of English origin accounted for just under half the population. The high birthrate—an average of seven births per woman in New England—and the long period of colonial history—1607 to 1776—meant that most of these children were born in the colonies. From about the time of the founding of Pennsylvania in 1681, people of different nationalities and religions—Scots, Irish Catholics, French Huguenots, Spanish Jews, and German Protestants—arrived in increasing numbers. Together with the Dutch in New York, these accounted for nearly one-third of the colonists.

▲ *The Mason Children: David, Joanna, and Abigail* Unknown Artist, c. 1670 Usually a person's place in colonial society was obvious from his or her appearance and dress. What can you conclude about the children's family from this painting?

Beginning in Virginia in 1619, the first enslaved Africans were brought by the Dutch from the West Indies. Africans, both enslaved and free, made up about 20 percent of the total population. The proportion of African Americans was highest in the southern colonies because slave labor proved profitable on rice and tobacco plantations. In South Carolina three out of four people were enslaved Africans.

■ Women in the Colonies

English colonial population grew rapidly because proportionately there were more women than in the Spanish and French colonies. The only respectable option for women at that time was thought to be marriage. As in all European societies of the time, women were denied higher education. Women generally married in their early twenties and had five or six children. Their principal task was rearing children, although most women died during the child-bearing years.

The second occupation for most women was farming. A farm could not carry on without the skills of women in making cloth, garments, candles, soap, and breadstuffs. A visitor to the North Carolina-Virginia border region in 1710 gave this description of a frontierswoman:

> ❝ . . . [S]he is a very civil woman and shows nothing of ruggedness or Immodesty in her carriage, yett she will carry a gunn in the woods and kill deer, turkeys, etc., shoot down wild cattle, catch and tye hoggs, knock down beeves with an axe. . . . ❞

In the South, plantation wives helped direct the workforce. When seafaring New England husbands left their wives, sometimes for years at a time, women were successful as merchants or storekeepers. Widespread home manufacturing allowed women to learn trades. Some women were printers, newspaper publishers, druggists, and doctors.

Cooperative Learning Activity

Life in the Americas Organize students into three or four groups. Have the groups work on developing a "theme" sentence that describes life in Colonial America. Suggest that they do this in three stages: brainstorming ideas, first draft, and final theme sentence. After all groups complete a stage, select a student to report on each group's progress. When all three stages have been completed, have all students work together to develop a class theme sentence. **L2, L3**

Slavery in the Colonies

At first it was not clear that enslaved Africans were to be treated differently from white indentured servants. Gradually legal distinctions were adopted. Indentured servants retained the rights of English people and the protection of the law. Africans were protected by no law or tradition. The South gave marriages between enslaved persons no legality, and children could be sold away from their mothers. Enslaved persons owned no property and had little legal protection against irresponsible or cruel slaveholders.

Slavery and Southern Plantations

Slave labor was adopted for the southern plantations, where the work was done in fields and easily overseen. Southern colonial laws declared Africans to be enslaved for life. It was illegal to teach Africans to read for fear that learning would spoil them for physical labor.

There were, in the South, slaveholders who disapproved of slavery but hesitated to act on their beliefs because free blacks faced serious discrimination. In addition, whites feared them as possible leaders of slave insurrections. Most southern colonies passed laws that made it difficult to give enslaved people their freedom.

Slavery in the North

In the North, slavery was less profitable and enslaved people less numerous. New England not only allowed, but required, people who were enslaved to marry; they could acquire property and testify in court. A slaveholder might punish a slave, but an owner who killed a slave could be charged with murder. A growing number of people argued that slavery was a moral wrong.

In Pennsylvania, Quakers and Mennonites, a German Protestant sect, denounced slavery. The number of free African Americans increased. In Jaffrey, New Hampshire, Amos Fortune bought other African Americans out of slavery and left money for the town school. But the northern colonies did not permit equality to free African Americans.

 **Visualizing History**

▲ **SLAVE TRADE** Trade that furnished Africans to markets was a horrible example of inhumanity. It has been estimated that about 30 percent of the enslaved Africans died crossing the Atlantic. *How were Africans treated in the northern colonies?*

cans. Custom usually kept them in menial positions, and the laws denied them the right to vote or hold office.

Native Americans

The first meetings between English settlers and Native Americans gave little evidence of the eventual destruction of the Native Americans' ways of life. A few colonial leaders, notably Roger Williams and William Penn, tried to treat them fairly, and some Protestant ministers regarded the Native Americans principally as souls to be converted to Christianity.

Land Ownership

The expansion of colonial farms became the principal cause of numerous conflicts. The colonists reasoned that since Native Americans did not have settled dwellings, but were on the move like "the foxes and wild beasts . . . so it is lawful now to take a land which none useth; and make use of it."

Some of the conflicts resulted from misunderstandings each culture had of the other's values. Europeans viewed land ownership as essential to progress.

Demonstrating Reasoned Judgment Organize students into two groups. Have one group work on a petition that Native Americans might have presented to the monarch complaining about their treatment at the hands of the colonists. Have the other group work on a petition from the colonists justifying their behavior toward the Native Americans. Have the groups present their petitions to the rest of the class. **L2**

Visualizing History The hundreds of thousands of Africans brought by force to the North American colonies came mainly from West Africa between the Senegal and Niger Rivers. They were of diverse ethnic backgrounds and spoke many different languages. **Answer to Caption:** treated as property; had very few legal rights; in some places could marry, own property, and testify in court

NATIONAL GEOGRAPHIC SOCIETY

 **VIDEODISC**

GTV: The American People: Fabric of a Nation

Side 1, Chapter 8
Frames: 37567-44838
Title: *The Journey*
Subject: Slavery in early America

Critical Thinking Activity

Making Comparisons Have students construct a table showing the similarities and differences between indentured service and enslavement in Colonial America. Then ask: What do you think is the most notable similarity and the most striking difference between these two forms of servitude? Have students write a few sentences explaining their choices. **L1, L2**

📁 Have students complete Critical Thinking Skill Activity 1.

Did You Know?

By 1775, the five largest religious groups in the colonies were the following: Congregationalist (575,000 members), Anglican (500,000), Presbyterian (410,000), Dutch Reformed (75,000), and German Lutheran (75,000).

Visualizing History Point out that even though freedom of religion was not yet a part of life in every state, the idea was beginning to take hold. **Answer to Caption:** religious revival in the mid-1600s

FACT or FICTION?

The leading textbook for young schoolchildren in the colonies combined lessons in religion and grammar.

FACT: The book, entitled *The New England Primer,* first appeared in 1688. The 1748 edition contained "Now I Lay Me Down to Sleep," then a newly published prayer.

Individual Native Americans did not own land, but jointly shared territory with all the members of the group. Native Americans viewed the land as a resource to be used and left unchanged. Those who sold or by treaty gave up lands did so without any authority, since no chief could dispose of land.

Colonists justified wars against Native Americans in many ways. Some Puritan ministers even claimed that Native Americans were children of the devil, so they could be killed in good conscience.

Weapons of Conquest

Individually, a colonist may not have been a match for a Native American who had learned the art of war in struggles over territory; but because of sheer numbers and weapons, the whites were destined to win. They also had grim allies in diseases such as smallpox. European diseases sometimes wiped out whole Native American communities that had not developed immunities. Of the estimated 120,000 Native Americans who had lived in the area occupied by the 13 colonies, perhaps only 20,000 survived. Most Native American nations, too small to resist,

simply disappeared as social units. The Iroquois were the only group that had the ability to protect its members from destruction.

■ The Colonial Mind

Although many came to America to worship as they pleased, they were not ready to grant others the same freedom. In New England and the Southern Colonies, a single official church was "established"—that is, supported by taxes. Massachusetts Puritans believed that religious toleration was a weakness inspired by the devil. Anyone who advocated it would suffer the consequences. While they expelled many like Roger Williams, they hanged Quakers on Boston Common. Anglican Virginia, on the other hand, expelled Puritan ministers from Massachusetts.

The Great Awakening

In the 1740s, the colonies experienced a religious revival called the Great Awakening. Some Puritan ministers in Massachusetts, concerned over declining religious

 **Visualizing History** ▲ RELIGION IN THE COLONIES In the 1600s and 1700s, most European countries had state religions. Persecution of religious dissenters was common, and many colonists who came to America sought the freedom to worship in their own way. Religion in the colonies was characterized by a growing tolerance. ***What was the Great Awakening?***

Critical Thinking Activity

Applying Principles Have students consider the ideas of Jean-Jacques Rousseau, a French philosopher, who blamed European society's evils on "the first man who, having enclosed a piece of ground, bethought himself of saying 'This is mine' . . . ." To this he added, "You are undone if you once forget that the fruits of the earth belong to us all, and the earth itself to nobody." Ask students to write a brief paragraph describing how Rousseau might have helped the colonists understand Native Americans. **L3**

▲ EDUCATION IN THE COLONIES Education was closely related to religion. The first colleges—William and Mary (above), Harvard, and Yale—were established mainly to train ministers. By the end of the colonial period, nine colleges had been founded, eight of them by churches. *How did formal education in the colonies differ from modern education?*

CURRICULUM CONNECTION

Literature Have students use Benjamin Franklin's *Poor Richard's Almanac* to locate and list five or ten sayings that are well-known American proverbs.

☞ Assign Guided Reading Activity 1-4.

Visualizing History Considering Colonial America was largely a rural, frontier society, the literacy rate—around 40 percent in 1700—was remarkable. In the New England colonies, where the churches put great store in their followers being able to read the Bible, the literacy rate stood at 70 percent. Since education for women was frowned upon—John Winthrop, for example, thought that it caused insanity—female literacy rates in New England were lower. **Answer to Caption:** Schools in the colonies were primitive, with few books, instruction given only two or three months a year, and most girls receiving little formal education.

fervor, began to preach sermons that warned of the impending dangers of hell. They were influenced by Jonathan Edwards, one of America's greatest colonial theologians.

As ministers took sides favoring or opposing the revivalists, new churches sprang up. The diversity of churches helped to make religious toleration even more essential. Other products of the revival were new colleges such as Princeton, Brown, Rutgers, and Dartmouth.

By the late 1700s, open religious persecution in the colonies was largely a thing of the past, although not all religious groups were equal before the law. Visitors from other countries were especially struck by the freedom granted Jews, who still suffered severe persecution in most European countries.

Colonial Education

The Puritans believed that citizens should learn enough English to read the Bible and understand the laws. The Massachusetts General School Act of 1647 stated two principles of education that remain today: local communities have a duty to set up schools, and this duty is enforced by law.

In the Middle Colonies, schooling was not as universal as in New England, but it was widespread. In the Southern Colonies,

formal education was generally limited to children of large landowners and professionals. Even where schools were desired, the widely separated plantations and farms of the South made them impractical.

By modern standards schools in the colonies were primitive. There were few books, and instruction was given only two or three months a year. Most girls received little formal education. Two-thirds of the women whose names appear on Massachusetts legal documents in the early 1700s could not write their signatures. Despite these shortcomings, no other region of equal size in the world had such a high proportion of the population that could read and write.

Religion was the principal force behind most institutions of higher learning in the colonies. The earliest colleges—Harvard, William and Mary, and Yale—were founded to train young men for the ministry.

The Enlightenment

By the mid-1700s, the college curriculum began to change, as interest in science and a demand for practical subjects arose. When King's College—later Columbia—opened in New York City in 1754, it announced that studies would include not only the traditional Latin, Greek, and Hebrew, but also:

Special Needs Activity

Inefficient Readers Scanning a passage before reading can help students develop a time frame for the events or ideas that are presented. Have students scan "The Colonial Mind" passages for time markers. Note that many paragraphs contain these markers. Examples are: "In the 1640s. . . ." (paragraph 2); "By the late 1700s. . . ." (paragraph 4); ". . . in the early 1700s" (paragraph 7); and "By the mid-1700s. . . ." (paragraph 9). **LEP, L1**

Independent Practice

Writing Editorials Ask students to write an editorial in support of Peter Zenger or an opinion article or editorial against the *Weekly Journal's* editor. Select a few students to read their editorials or articles to the rest of the class. Use these readings as the starting point for a discussion on the importance of freedom of the press. **L3**

👉 Use Writer's Guidebook Lessons 1-6.

Linking Across TIME

In 1735 John Peter Zenger faced charges of libel for printing a critical report about the royal governor of New York. The jury found Zenger not guilty. Freedom of the press was included in the Bill of Rights, ratified in 1791. In 1931 the Supreme Court expanded this right by declaring "prior restraint" laws against malicious or slanderous articles unconstitutional.

Visualizing History The Zenger case helped establish the right to publish criticisms of government.
Answer to Caption: found not guilty

> *Surveying and Navigation, Geography, History, Husbandry, Commerce, Government, the Knowledge of ALL Nature in the Heavens above us and in the Air, Water, and Earth Around us. . . .* ""

This interest in science originated in Europe, where it was known as the Enlightenment. English philosopher John Locke produced works that were widely read in America. In *An Essay Concerning Human Understanding,* Locke maintained that people could best gain knowledge of the universe by observing and by experimenting. This knowledge would guide them in developing a reasonable society. In the second of two *Treatises on Government,* Locke taught that people were born with certain natural rights to life, liberty, and property; that people formed governments to protect these rights; and that a government interfering with these might rightfully be overthrown. Many readily accepted the idea that government was the agent of the people, not their ruler.

■ The Press in America

In addition to schools and colleges, newspapers, almanacs, and books helped raise the level of public information. Because paper and type were expensive and the reading public in America small, most books came from Britain. But by 1750, there

• •

Footnotes to History

An American Style Imitating English ways was common in America at first. Slowly the colonists began to develop their own ways of doing things. Building styles were modified to suit local conditions. Cabinetmakers began to turn out excellent furniture of their own design. Silversmiths like Paul Revere put their own designs on their products. Colonists found ways of putting beauty into things they made for practical use, such as quilts and guns.

were 25 or 30 American newspapers, mostly 4 pages long, printed weekly. Printed on tough rag paper, these newspapers were passed from hand to hand at the local inn until often half the men in a village had read a single copy. European travelers in the colonies were amazed to find that political discussions in public inns were joined intelligently by everybody, from the college educated to stable help.

Colonial editors occasionally criticized British laws or officials. In 1735, John Peter Zenger of the *New York Weekly Journal* accused the royal governor of corruption. As a result, copies of the paper were publicly burned by the sheriff, and Zenger was brought to trial on a charge of libel. His lawyer, Andrew Hamilton, argued that the editor was not guilty since the charges were true and since free speech was a basic right of English people. As a result, Zenger was acquitted. At the time the case attracted little attention, but today it is regarded as a landmark in the development of the free press in America.

■ New Directions

By 1776 America was well on its way to establishing economic independence. Thirty percent of the ships in the British merchant marine were American, and most of these sailed from New England ports.

The Economy

New Englanders carried on a share of the African slave trade. They were the first to hunt whales in the Antarctic; in 1774, 360 whaling ships sailed from the island of Nantucket alone. While New England was a formidable competitor in trade, no colony offered much competition to the British in manufacturing. The American colonists usually obtained manufactured goods from Britain.

To pay for fine European goods, such as clothing, books, wine, and cutlery, the colonies had to trade staples that Europeans needed or to pay in gold or silver. Trade with the West Indies netted Spanish dollars,

---

Cooperative Learning Activity

The Zenger Trial Organize the class into groups of six or seven. Have each group work on a script for a "You Are There" broadcast on Peter Zenger's libel trial. Some members of each group might find more information about the trial. After the research is completed, students in each group should write a script. Remind students to answer who? what? when? where? why? and how? in writing the script. Once the groups have finished the script, have each group present the broadcast for the rest of the class. Have the class evaluate the broadcasts. **L2**

the common colonial currency. Later the new nation, the United States, would adopt the dollar instead of the British pound as its monetary unit. Gradually the colonies developed a culture distinctly different from that of Europe.

Stirrings of Independence

The degree of power exercised by British officials varied from colony to colony, but it was limited everywhere. In all colonies the voters elected their own legislature, and in charter colonies, their governor as well. In proprietary colonies the governor was appointed by the proprietor or by his heirs; in royal or crown colonies the governor was chosen by the king. The governor of a proprietary or crown colony had wide powers, such as a veto over the legislature and control of land grants.

Government at the town and county levels was run entirely by the colonists themselves. In New England, the important local unit was the township. Decisions were made at the town meeting, which most heads of families had a right to attend. The town meeting was the most direct form of democracy in the colonies. In the Southern and Middle colonies, local government was usually less democratic but, nevertheless, entirely independent of British control.

None of the colonies was so democratic as to allow full political rights to all men or to any women. Active citizenship and the right to vote and hold office were limited to

 ▲ FREEDOM OF THE PRESS John Peter Zenger, publisher of the *New York Weekly Journal*, was arrested and imprisoned for criticizing the governor of New York, and copies of the newspaper were burned. Andrew Hamilton, Zenger's lawyer, argued that the publisher had the right to speak and write the truth and to oppose arbitrary power. ***What was the outcome of the trial?***

adult white males owning property, who usually had to be members of the established church. In spite of these limitations, a higher proportion of people were involved in government than anywhere in the European world. This wide participation gave Americans training that was valuable when the colonies later became independent.

Section 4 ★ Review

Checking for Understanding

1. **Identify** Mennonites, the Great Awakening, John Locke.

2. **Define** gentry.

3. **Describe** the position of indentured servants, women, and African Americans in the colonies.

4. **Give** reasons for the development of religious freedom and toleration in the British colonies.

Critical Thinking

5. **Evaluating Cause and Effect** What factors contributed to social mobility in the colonies? What factors restricted it?

ACTIVITY

6. Analyze the illustrations in this section. Which illustration do you think best represents life in the colonies? Explain your answer in a paragraph.

Answers to SECTION 4 REVIEW

1. Mennonites, 31; the Great Awakening, 32; John Locke, 34
2. All vocabulary words are defined in the Glossary.
3. They possessed few rights, but white male indentured servants could acquire rights and status after being freed.
4. Some were founded for this purpose, diversity forced religious toleration, Great Awakening increased religious diversity, religious freedom attracted settlers
5. Economic success was a major factor in social mobility. Restrictions were stronger for women, African Americans.
6. Answers will vary, but students should provide valid reasons for their choices.

ASSESS

Check Understanding

Assign Section 4 Review as homework or an in-class activity.

Evaluate

☑ 🗁 Assign Section Quiz 1-4 or use the Testmaker to create a customized quiz.

Reteach

🗁 Have students complete Reteaching Activity 1-4.

🗁 Have students complete Workbook Activity 1-4.

Enrich

Point out that New England merchants, many of whom were opposed to slavery, took part in the African slave trade. Ask students to write a paragraph on whether or not they think our personal values and beliefs should direct all our actions.

🗁 Assign Geography in History Activity 1.

🗁 Assign Map Transparency Activity 1 and Chapter Map Activity 1.

CLOSE

Express the view that in colonial times, North America was truly a land of opportunity. Then ask students to discuss this statement based on what they have learned about the social, political, and cultural trends that developed in Colonial America.

Block Schedule

Team Teaching These selections can be presented in a team teaching context, in conjunction with English or Language Arts.

Historical Setting

The Iroquois originally comprised five warring nations—the Seneca, Oneida, Mohawk, Cayuga, Onondaga, and later the Tuscarara. When infighting became particularly vicious, Dekanawida emerged to promote peace and unity. In contrast, the Navajo believed humans should live harmoniously with nature and generally were peaceful.

Background

The literary device of repetition is used in the "Rain Chant" with the refrain "Comes the rain/ Comes the rain with me." This repetition stresses the oneness of nature (rain) and humans (me).

☞ Assign American Portraits 1: Dekanawida.

About the Oral Tradition

The excerpt from The Constitution of the Five Nations, unlike the Navajo "Song of the Rain Chant," is unique in that it possesses an originator. Dekanawida is a legendary figure. A prophet who preached peace, he managed at some time between 1575 and 1600 to convince the nations to unite.

Among the Native American groups with the richest oral literary traditions are the Iroquois and Navajo. During the 1500s a prophet named Dekanawida (dek•uhn• uh•WEE•duh) appeared among the Iroquois and urged them to lay down their weapons and join hands in the spirit of friendship and peace. His influence led to the formation of the Iroquois Confederation of the Five Nations. The Navajo expressed themselves in songlike chants and legends that provide a window on their ideals and beliefs.

Read to Discover

What values does Dekanawida stress in the Constitution of the Five Nations? Find examples of words or parts of lines that are repeated throughout the "Song of the Rain Chant." Why do you think these particular words are repeated?

Reader's Dictionary

confederacy	an alliance for mutual support or common action
lodgement	a place of rest or deposit

The Constitution of the Five Nations (excerpts)

I am Dekanawida and with the Five Nations confederate lords I plant the Tree of the Great Peace. I name the tree the Tree of the Great Long Leaves. Under the shade of this Tree of the Great Peace we spread the soft white feathery down of the globe thistle as seats for you . . . and your cousin lords.

We place . . . at the top of the Tree of the Long Leaves an eagle who is able to see afar. If he sees in the distance any evil approaching or any danger threatening he will at once warn the people of the confederacy. . . .

All lords of the Five Nations Confederacy must be honest in all things. . . . It shall be a serious wrong for anyone to lead a lord into trivial affairs, for the people must ever hold their lords high in estimation out of respect to their honorable positions. . . .

We now do crown you with the sacred emblem of the deer's antlers, the emblem of your lordship. You shall now become a mentor of the people of the Five Nations. The thickness of your skin shall be seven spans—which is to say that you shall be proof against anger, offensive actions and criticism. Your heart shall be filled with peace and good will and your mind filled with a yearning for the welfare of the people of the confederacy. With endless patience you shall carry out your duty and your firmness shall be tempered with tenderness for your people. Neither anger nor fury shall find lodgement in your mind and all your words and actions shall be marked with calm deliberation. . . .

Cultural Perspectives

To New Generations Point out that every culture has an oral tradition, which consists of stories, songs, and poems that have been passed from one generation to the next. Each generation adds new details and deletes those that no longer seem meaningful. As a result versions may vary greatly not only over time but also from place to place. Encourage students to collect folklore from various sources to make comparisons.

Navajo Song of the Rain Chant

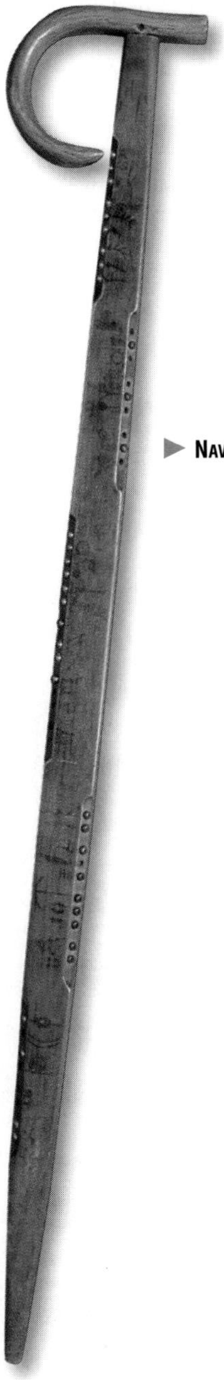

▶ Iroquois notched staff

Far as man can see,
Comes the rain,
Comes the rain with me.

From the Rain-Mount,
Rain-Mount far away,
Comes the rain,
Comes the rain with me.

O'er the corn,
O'er the corn, the tall corn,
Comes the rain,
Comes the rain with me.

'Mid the lightnings,
'Mid the lightning zigzag,
'Mid the lightning flashing
Comes the rain,
Comes the rain with me.

'Mid the swallows,
'Mid the swallows blue
Chirping glad together,
Comes the rain,
Comes the rain with me.

Through the pollen,
Through the pollen blest,
All in pollen hidden,
Comes the rain,
Comes the rain with me.

Far as man can see,
Comes the rain,
Comes the rain with me.

▶ Navajo rug

Responding to Literature

1. In the Iroquois Constitution, what is the function of the eagle that sits atop the Tree of the Long Leaves?
2. How does the Rain Chant reflect Navajo beliefs about nature?
3. In what ways are the qualities desired for Iroquois leaders similar to or different from those desired for today's leaders in the United States government?

ACTIVITY

4. Research information about one aspect of Iroquois or Navajo life. Subjects could include lifestyles, occupations, religious practices, or achievements. Present your information in a report to the other students.

INTEGRATING Language Arts

Developing Student Understanding

Explain that family histories often are shared in the oral tradition. Ask volunteers to share family stories. Then ask how the stories provide insight into certain periods of time. **L1**

Other Works of Native American Folklore

Because of the nature of the oral tradition, which was shared through word-of-mouth, it is difficult to identify other pieces of literature directly linked to this period. However, recent native American authors, such as Rosebud Yellow Robe, have retold and preserved in writing some myths and legends that have been handed down. Related works include *North American Indian Mythology* by Cottie Burland and *The Red Swan: Myths and Tales of the American Indians* edited by John Bierhorst.

History and the Humanities

American Literary Heritage, p. 1: *Native American Poetry.*

Primary and Secondary Source Readings, pp. 1–2: *The Origin of the Iroquois League.*

Answers to Responding to Literature

1. The eagle is a watchguard and warns the confederacy of approaching evil or danger.
2. Rain is a central part of nature and the cycle of growth. It comes from afar but is part of everything and covers everything.
3. Both are to be honest in all things and live in accordance with the laws. Both should strive to be leaders of peace and goodwill, whose concern is the welfare of the people.
4. Reports will vary, but should show evidence of research and valid rationale.

GLENCOE
TECHNOLOGY

VIDEODISC

Use the MindJogger Videoquiz to review students' knowledge.

MindJogger Videoquiz

Chapter 1
Disc 1, Side A

Available in VHS.

Using Key Vocabulary

Political—confederation, shogun, line of demarcation, conquistador, proprietor, commonwealth, constitution; Economic—joint-stock company, mercantilism, indentured servant, feudalism, encomienda, northwest passage; Religion and Culture—mestizo, gentry, congregation

Reviewing Facts

1. Leadership passes from feudal lords to national monarchs; middle class of merchants grows in towns.
2. Answers include China, Japan, Ghana, Mali, and Songhai. Areas provide source of gold, spices, silks, slaves, etc., and impetus for exploration.
3. Portuguese achievements included better maps and sea charts, the discovery of a route around Africa, and using the route to sail to India.
4. Columbus reached, but failed to recognize, new continent. He brought back gold and encour-

Using Vocabulary

Classify each of the terms listed below into one of the following categories: Political Structures and Systems, Economic Activity and Systems, Religion and Culture

confederation
shogun
joint-stock company
line of demarcation
conquistador
mestizo
mercantilism
indentured
  servant

feudalism
proprietor
commonwealth
constitution
gentry
encomienda
northwest
  passage
congregation

Reviewing Facts

1. **Discuss** the major changes in the political and social structure of Europe during the late Middle Ages.
2. **Identify** advanced cultures of Africa and Asia and the importance of their trade with Europe.
3. **Enumerate** the achievements of the Portuguese voyages of discovery.
4. **Summarize** Spanish exploration, exploitation, and colonization in America.
5. **Explain** the role economics played in the settlement of the British colonies.
6. **Analyze** why slavery became more prevalent in the South than in New England.

Understanding Concepts

Cultural Diversity

1. Compare the differences and similarities between each of the following sets of cultures: medieval European and medieval Japanese cultures; the West African trading kingdoms and the Aztec Empire.

Values and Beliefs

2. The colonists who left England to settle in America endured formidable hardships. List three reasons why different groups of colonists migrated to America in the face of these risks and hardships. How do their motives compare to the reasons people migrate today?
3. What role did religion play in the colonization of the Americas?
4. What values and beliefs were instrumental in establishing democratic institutions in the British colonies?

Critical Thinking

1. **Proposing Solutions** Imagine you are appointed to resolve disputes between Native Americans and European colonists who want farmland. Propose a fair plan for expansion. Remember that Native Americans did not own land.
2. **Analyzing Fine Art** Analyze the two paintings on this page and answer the questions that follow.

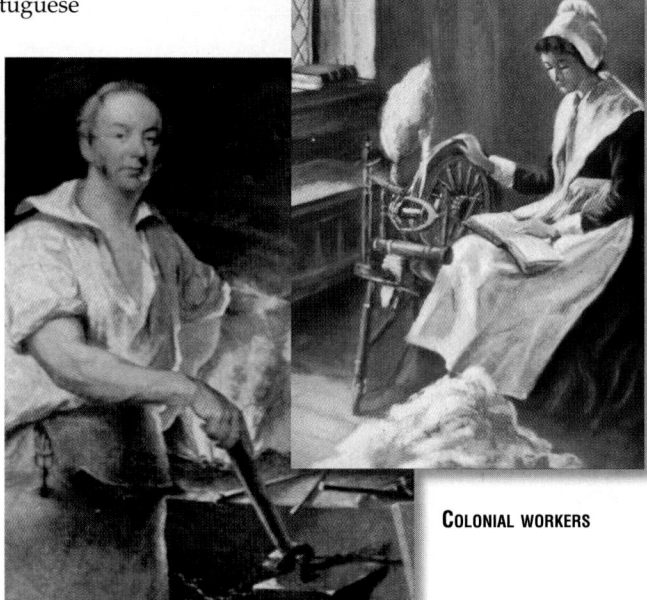

COLONIAL WORKERS

aged further ocean voyages west in hopes of finding Asia. Vespucci recognized South America as a new continent, renewing the search for a water route to Asia. Aztecs in Mexico and Incas in Peru conquered by Cortes and Pizarro, respectively.

Conquests brought many Spanish settlers to mine gold and silver using Native Americans as slave labor.
5. Economics motivated settlement by companies and determined lifestyle and values, for example, slavery.

6. Crops suited to it were labor intensive, making slavery profitable.

Understanding Concepts

1. Answers should include effects of feudalism, trade, and conquests.

a. What details in the paintings give you clues about the people's occupations?

b. What can you tell about town life in the British American colonies by looking at these paintings?

History and Geography

African Trading Kingdoms

Study the map of African trading kingdoms on this page. Then answer the questions that follow.

1. **Movement** In which direction would a trading party from Timbuktu travel to reach Ghat?

2. **Location** What city is the easternmost trade partner?

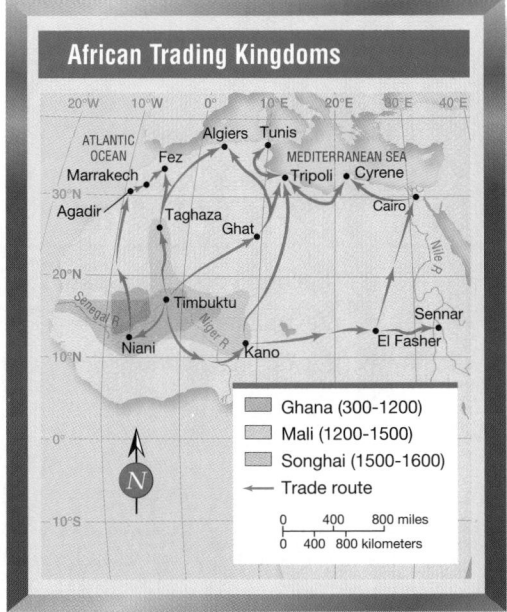

African Trading Kingdoms

Ghana (300–1200)
Mali (1200–1500)
Songhai (1500–1600)
← Trade route

0   400   800 miles
0 400 800 kilometers

Cooperative Learning — Interdisciplinary Activity: Cultural Studies

Working in a group with four members, study slavery around the world and throughout history. Assign each member one or more cultures or geo-

graphic areas to study. Report your findings and conduct a discussion comparing and contrasting slavery in other cultures with slavery in the British colonies.

Practicing Skills

Interpreting Primary Sources

Read the account below by an English settler who visited Native American towns during the 1580s. Then answer the questions that follow.

Their towns are small and few . . . a village may contain but ten or twelve houses—some perhaps as many as twenty. . . .

The houses are built of small poles . . . covered from top to bottom either with bark or with mats woven of long rushes. . . .

In one part of the country a . . . chief . . . may govern a single town, but in other parts the number of towns under one chief may vary to two, three, six, and even to eight or more.

1. How does the writer describe the size of the towns?

2. With what materials were the houses covered?

3. Would you describe the account as factual and objective or biased? Explain.

Writing ABOUT History — Using Your Journal

Compare the accomplishments and values of two different cultures. Write a paragraph explaining similarities and differences.

tures with those in the British colonies.

Practicing Skills

1. The towns were small, consisting of 10 to 20 houses.
2. bark and mats woven of long rushes
3. It is factual and objective. The account describes what the English settler saw, and does not give any opinions about it.

Writing ABOUT History — Using Your Journal

The ideas students present in their paragraphs will vary but should include specific similarities and differences. You might call on volunteers to read their paragraphs to the class and then have students contrast their varying views of the cultures they studied.

? Chapter Bonus Test Question

Ask students: Suppose it is 1730 and you are planning to settle in one of Britain's North American colonies. Briefly describe your social, economic, and political status. Which colony interests you most? For what reasons? (*Answers may vary but should include a discussion of how the character of a particular colony matches a potential settler's political, social, and religious beliefs.*)

2. Answers include religious freedom, profit, land.
3. Answers include established missions and migration to find religious freedom.
4. Answers include Enlightenment philosophy and tradition of self-government.

Critical Thinking

1. Answers should include equitable plans for each group.
2. a) the tools they are using
   b) Answers include: worked in solitude, people worked at home.

History and Geography

1. northeast
2. Sennar

Cooperative Learning

Group members should research slavery in other cultures. Discussions might compare conditions of enslaved people in other cul-

Daily Lesson Objectives	Teacher Classroom Resources	Multimedia
SECTION 1 **The Road to Revolution** **1 Day** pp. 42–47 1. Explain the causes and results of the French and Indian War. 2. Discuss the events that led the colonists to armed resistance to British control over the colonies.	Reproducible Lesson Plan 2-1 Concept Mapping Activities 2-A, 2-B Performance Assessment Activity 2 *Vocabulary Activity 2 Linking Past and Present Activity 2 Primary and Secondary Source Readings, pp. 3–4 Chapter Skills Activity 2 Reteaching Activity 2-1 *Section Quiz 2-1	Section Focus Transparency 2-1 Chapter Concepts Transparencies 2-A, 2-B Testmaker STV: North America Historic America Electronic Field Trips MindJogger Videoquiz
SECTION 2 **War for Independence** **1 Day** pp. 49–56 1. State what factors caused the American Revolution. 2. Explain why the Americans were able to win the war.	Reproducible Lesson Plan 2-2 *Guided Reading Activity 2-2 Critical Thinking Skills Activity 2 Chapter Map Activity 2 American Portrait 9 Reteaching Activity 2-2 *Section Quiz 2-2	Section Focus Transparency 2-2 Map Transparency 2 Testmaker GTV: A Geographic Perspective on American History Focus on Government Landmark Documents in American History
SECTION 3 **The Confederation** **1 Day** pp. 62–66 1. Explain political control under the Articles. 2. List the strengths and weaknesses of the Articles.	Reproducible Lesson Plan 2-3 *Guided Reading Activity 2-3 Geography in History Activity 2 Reteaching Activity 2-3 *Section Quiz 2-3	Section Focus Transparency 2-3 Testmaker Focus on Government Powers of the Congress
SECTION 4 **The Constitution** **1 Day** pp. 67–71 1. Explain the arguments for and against the new constitution. 2. Explain how the Constitution corrected the weaknesses of the Confederation government.	Reproducible Lesson Plan 2-4 *Guided Reading Activity 2-4 Critical Thinking Skills Activity 2 Cooperative Learning Activity 2 Enrichment Activity 2 Workbook Activity 2-4 Reteaching Activity 2-4 *Section Quiz 2-4	Section Focus Transparency 2-4 Testmaker Focus on Government
CHAPTER REVIEW AND EVALUATION **1 Day**	Chapter 2 Test, Forms A and B Spanish Chapter 2 Summary Performance Assessment Activity 2	MindJogger Videoquiz Student Self-Test & Review Software *Chapter 2 Digest Audiocassette Activity and Test

*Also available in Spanish

 OUT OF TIME? If time does not permit teaching the entire chapter, use the Chapter 2 summary on pages 132–133 and the Chapter 2 audiocassette (English and Spanish) to point out the main idea of the chapter.

A complete, 1-page lesson plan is provided for each section in the *Reproducible Lesson Plan* booklet.

Key to Ability Levels

Teaching strategies have been coded for varying learning styles and abilities.

L1 Basic activities for all students.

L2 Average activities for average to above-average students

L3 Challenging activities for above-average students

LEP Limited English Proficiency activities

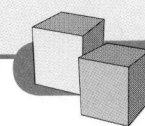

Block Schedule

Block scheduling differs from traditional class scheduling in the amount of time allotted to each period. The extended time frame provided by block scheduling affords you the opportunity to implement a greater number of research-oriented and activity-intense projects to motivate and involve your students. Activities that are particularly suited to use within the block scheduling framework are identified throughout this unit by the following designation:

✓ Performance Assessment Activity

Spreading the News Organize the class into groups. Assign each group one of the political events shown on the time line on pages 40–41. Examples include: French and Indian War begins (1754); Stamp Act passed (1765); Colonists dump tea in Boston Harbor (1773); Revolutionary War begins (1775); Declaration of Independence is signed (1776). Ask each group to prepare a TV news broadcast about the event. Have each group choose reporters to describe the event and news analysts to discuss its meaning. Invite each group to present its broadcast to the class.

POSSIBLE RUBRIC FEATURES

- Content
- Main Idea
- Creativity
- Clarity
- Visual and Written Communication Skills
- Organization
- Use of Maps and Illustrations

☞ For additional activities, see Performance Assessment Strategies and Activities.

TEACHER'S CORNER

NATIONAL GEOGRAPHIC SOCIETY

INDEX TO NATIONAL GEOGRAPHIC MAGAZINE

The following articles may be used for research relating to this chapter:

- "Two Revolutions," by Charles McCarry, July 1989.
- "Yorktown Shipwreck," by John D. Broadwater, June 1988.

NATIONAL GEOGRAPHIC SOCIETY PRODUCTS AVAILABLE FROM GLENCOE

To order the following products for use with this chapter, contact your local Glencoe sales representative or call Glencoe at 1-800-334-7344:

- *GTV: A Geographic Perspective on American History* (Videodisc)
- *GTV: The American People: Fabric of a Nation* (Videodisc)

ADDITIONAL NATIONAL GEOGRAPHIC SOCIETY PRODUCTS

To order the following products for use with this chapter, call National Geographic Society at 1-800-368-2728:

- *Our Living Constitution* (Filmstrip)
- *America: Colonization to Constitution* (Filmstrip)
- *The United States Congress* (Filmstrip)

- *Democratic Government Series,* "The United States." (Video)
- *Branches of Government Series* (Video)
- *Washington, D.C.* (Video)

CHAPTER 2
★★★

A New Nation
1750–1789

◄ EAGLE AND CROSSED FLAGS

Setting the Scene

Focus

Once the colonists' need for British protection ended, the road to independence was not far behind. The insurmountable breach between Britain and America led the thirteen colonies to issue a Declaration of Independence on July 4, 1776. Under General George Washington's leadership, the new United States fought a war for independence over six long years. During this period of experiment and uncertainty, American political leaders laid the foundations of a democratic government embodied in a new constitution.

Concepts to Understand

★ What steps the colonists took to secure and protect their **rights and freedom**

★ Why a strong central **authority** was needed to keep the new republic intact

Read to Discover . . .

★ what factors caused the American Revolution.

★ what important compromises made the Constitution possible.

Journal Notes

What contributions did women, African Americans, and Native Americans make to the American Revolution? Note details in your journal as you read the chapter.

CULTURAL			
• **1751** *Ben Franklin writes* Experiments on Electricity	• **1759** *Michael Hillegas of Philadelphia opens first music store in America*	• **1767** *Letters from a Farmer published by John Dickinson*	
1750	**1758**	**1766**	
• **1754** *French and Indian War begins*	• **1765** *Stamp Act passed*	• **1767** *Townshend Acts passed* • **1773** *Colonists dump tea in Boston Harbor*	

| POLITICAL |

✚ **EXTRA CREDIT PROJECT**

State Constitutions During the Revolution, the newly proclaimed states created their own constitutions. As more states were added to the growing nation, they too drew up constitutions. Suggest that interested students look up their state's constitution and outline its provisions. What rights does the state have? What are its responsibilities? Conduct a class discussion based on the students' findings. **L2**

History AND ART

The Signing of the Constitution
by Howard Chandler Christy, 1940

The delegates sign the final draft of the Constitution in Independence Hall. Despite mixed feelings regarding some aspects of the Constitution, most of those present were hopeful about the future.

◀ REVOLUTIONARY WAR DRUM

- **1775** *Quakers establish first antislavery society in the United States*

1774

- **1775** *Revolutionary War begins*
- **1776** *Declaration of Independence is signed*

- **1783** *Noah Webster publishes first spelling book*

1782

- **1783** *Treaty of Paris is signed*
- **1787** *Constitutional Convention is held*

- **1790** *Samuel Hopkins receives first United States patent*

1790

- **1790** *Congress hears first formal petition for abolition of slavery*

CHAPTER 2 A New Nation: 1750–1789 **41**

Concept Mapping Activity

On the chalkboard, reproduce the following generalization and concepts map, and have students copy it in their notebooks.

> Consensus on cherished political values leads to the formation of a new government

> Rights and Freedoms

> Authority

📁 To reinforce the two chapter concepts, use Concept Mapping Activities 2-A and 2-B.

📁 Assign Chapter Concepts Transparency Activities 2-A and 2-B.

History AND ART

Chandler's painting suggests the artist's admiration for Washington.

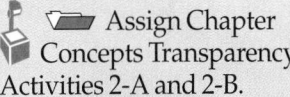

GLENCOE TECHNOLOGY

 VIDEODISC

The American History Videodisc

Side 1, Section C

Title: *The American Revolution and the Early Republic, 1765–1820*

Subject: Overview of American history from the background of the American Revolution to the early Republic

✔ **Performance Assessment**

Working With Time Lines Organize the students into three groups, and ask each to construct a large-scale time line on one of the following: the events leading up to the outbreak of war between Britain and the American colonies; the major events of the Revolutionary War; the major events of the postwar years up to the ratification of the Constitution. Ask each group to use at least two references in its research. When the groups complete their time lines, have each group present its time line to the class. Allow time for class discussion and feedback.

📁 Use Performance Assessment Activity 2 as an additional assessment technique.

SECTION 1

Bellringer

Before taking roll, project Section Focus Transparency 2-1 or hand out Section Focus Transparency Activity 2-1. Have students answer the questions. Discuss student responses.

Motivating Activity

Ask students to list possible reasons for conflict in North America between Britain and France. (*territorial, economic, political rivalry*) Ask them to speculate on how such a conflict might affect the colonists. Tell them that this section focuses on those questions. After they have read the section, ask them to compare their ideas with what actually happened. **L2**

Vocabulary Precheck

Ask students to define each of the "Key Terms." Have a volunteer consult the dictionary for any unfamiliar words. **L1, LEP**

Use the Vocabulary PuzzleMaker for Chapter 2 to create a crossword puzzle. **L1**

Assign Vocabulary Activity 2.

★★

The Road to Revolution

Setting the Scene

Section Focus

In settling North America, the colonists developed a sense that they were taking part in the birth of a new society, different from Europe, where men and women were able to better themselves. When Great Britain tried to impose controls on its American territories, the colonists vehemently expressed their dislike of British policies.

Objectives

After studying this section, you should be able to

★ explain the causes and results of the French and Indian War.

★ discuss the events that led the colonists to armed resistance to British control over the colonies.

Key Terms

salutary neglect, militia, direct tax, boycott, minutemen

◀ AMERICAN REVOLUTIONARY BANNER

During most of the colonial era, the British government followed a policy of **salutary neglect,** or non-interference, which allowed America's colonists to do as they wished. Britain, however, gradually tightened its control of the colonists' foreign trade in order to increase revenue. From the British point of view the colonies existed to supply raw materials and to provide markets for British goods.

■ New Policies

In 1651, the British Parliament passed a Navigation Act requiring all goods shipped between England and the colonies to be carried in ships built either in England or in the colonies. Then in 1660, it declared that specific colonial products—tobacco, cotton, indigo, and sugar—could be shipped only to Britain.

A number of other British laws also had a serious impact on the colonies. The Molasses Act of 1733 placed a heavy tax on the colonists' importation of sugar and molasses from the Spanish and French West Indies. The Woolen Act of 1699, the Hat Act of 1732, and the Iron Act of 1750 placed restrictions on colonial industries to keep them from competing with British industries. Benjamin Franklin's reaction to these laws was typical of the Americans' views:

❝ *A colonist cannot make a button, a horse shoe, nor a hobnail but some sooty iron monger or respectable buttonmaker of Britain shall bawl . . . that his honor's worship is . . . injured, cheated and robbed by the rascally Americans.* ❞

Classroom Resources for SECTION 1

Blackline Masters:
- Reproducible Lesson Plan 2-1
- Guided Reading Activity 2-1
- Vocabulary Activity 2
- Political Cartoons in American History Activity 3
- Writer's Guidebook Lessons 1-4

- Linking Past and Present Activity 2
- Primary and Secondary Source Readings, pp. 3–4
- Workbook Activity 2-1
- Chapter Skills Activity 2
- Reteaching Activity 2-1
- Section Quiz 2-1

Transparencies:
- Section Focus Transparency 2-1

Multimedia:
- Vocabulary PuzzleMaker
- Testmaker
- Historic America Electronic Field Trips
- STV: North America

The French and Indian War

While Britain passed trade laws for its colonies, a struggle for empire developed between Britain and France. Anglo-French wars fought between 1689 and 1713 brought areas of present-day Canada—Nova Scotia, Newfoundland, and Hudson's Bay Territory—under Britain. The French and Indian War, fought between 1754 and 1763, gave the British further opportunity to expand their territory in North America.

The Albany Plan

In 1754, at a meeting in Albany, New York between colonial delegates and representatives of the Iroquois, Benjamin Franklin proposed a union of the colonies with the power to levy taxes, raise troops, and regulate trade. The delegates adopted Franklin's plan, but the colonial and British governments feared a loss of power and rejected it. This lack of cooperation seriously handicapped the war effort against the French.

On the Battlefield

The final struggle between Britain and France for control of North America began in the Ohio Valley. There the French drove out English fur traders and in 1754 established Fort Duquesne (doo•KAYN). This move threatened the safety of both Virginia and Pennsylvania. A force of Virginia **militia**—a group of civilians trained as soldiers to fight in emergencies—under the command of a young officer named George Washington failed until 1758 in their attempt to seize the fort. One military disaster after another followed for the British. The British made an advance on Montreal by way of Lake George and Lake Champlain that met with utter failure. The British also failed to take the French fort of Louisbourg on Cape Breton Island, a key to the control of the mouth of the St. Lawrence River. These and other colonial defeats caused many Native Americans to switch their support from the British to the French.

The tide of battle shifted in Britain's favor when William Pitt became British minister of war in 1758. By giving aid to France's enemies in Europe, Pitt forced France to split its forces. Pitt also sent talented young officers to lead the campaigns in North America. After a series of victories, the British finally staged a showdown with the French at Quebec on the St. Lawrence River. British troops under Commander James Wolfe landed at night below Quebec and scaled a wooded cliff located under the guns of Quebec's fortress. On the Plains of Abraham at the top of the cliffs, the British soldiers forced French forces under Commander Louis Montcalm to surrender.

Treaty of Paris, 1763

Great Britain won its war with France—in America, Europe, and Asia. Under the Treaty of Paris of 1763, Great Britain gained the areas of Canada it did not already control and all the land east of the Mississippi River. From Spain, France's ally, Great Britain received Florida. Spain, in turn, obtained the Louisiana Territory from France. North America was now divided between Great Britain and Spain with the Mississippi River forming the boundary.

▲ GEORGE WASHINGTON AT FORT DUQUESNE, 1758

TEACH
Guided Practice

Debate Select students to debate the topic "Americans should buy only American-made goods." Then ask them to suggest what parallels exist between the "Buy American" campaign of recent years and British mercantile policies in the colonies. **L2**

Did You Know?

The present-day city of Pittsburgh, Pennsylvania, stands on the site of the old Fort Duquesne. When the British finally took the fort, they renamed it Fort Pitt.

 Have students complete Political Cartoons in American History Activity 3.

NATIONAL GEOGRAPHIC SOCIETY

 VIDEODISC

STV: North America

Side 1
Frames 00025-27602
Title: *The East*
Subject: Physical characteristics of the eastern region of North America

---

Cooperative Learning Activity

Analyzing Point of View Organize students into groups of three. One student is to be an interviewer; the second, a colonial farmer or manufacturer; the third, a British counterpart. The interviewer asks each of the other two in turn to respond to the various trade and navigation acts imposed by the British to control the American colonies. At the close of the activity, the interviewer should select one act and report to the class the two responses to it. **L2, L3**

Map Study   *Using Maps*

Answer: from Cape Breton Island through the Gulf of St. Lawrence and up the St. Lawrence River

Map Skills Practice

Ask students in which direction Murray traveled. *(southwest)*

ABCNEWS INTERACTIVE™

VIDEODISC

Historic America Electronic Field Trips

Side One, Chapter 6
Title: *Lexington/Concord*
Subject: Tour of the site
Ask: Why are Lexington and Concord significant places in American history? *(The Revolution began there.)*

■ Control and Protest

Victory in the French and Indian War brought Britain vast new territories—and new problems. Britain had to cope with a huge war debt and the handling of the recently acquired territory between the Appalachian and Allegheny mountains.

In 1763 Pontiac, chief of the Ottawa people, united several Native American groups into a fighting force against the British. He feared the further loss of Native American lands to the ever-advancing settlers of the British colonies. Pontiac's warriors captured a chain of British forts northwest of the Ohio River but failed to drive colonial settlers back across the Appalachian Mountains.

During Pontiac's Rebellion, the British government issued the Proclamation of 1763, which ended all settlement west of the Appalachian Mountains. Through the Proclamation, the British hoped to win the friendship of the Native Americans. But the colonists protested that the Proclamation deprived them of land for settlement.

Between 1764 and 1767, Parliament passed new taxes that shifted part of the burden of the war debt to the American colonies. The British felt that the colonists benefited from British protection and that it was only fair that they pay some of the cost of running the empire.

In 1764, Parliament enacted the Sugar Act. Although this law cut the rates of the Molasses Act of 1733, the British government had always winked at the colonists evading payment. The troubling thing about the Sugar Act was that the British intended to enforce it. Colonial merchants often evaded poorly enforced British revenue laws and smuggled foreign goods into the colonies. They realized that strict enforcement would wipe out their profits from the illegal trade with the Spanish and French West Indies.

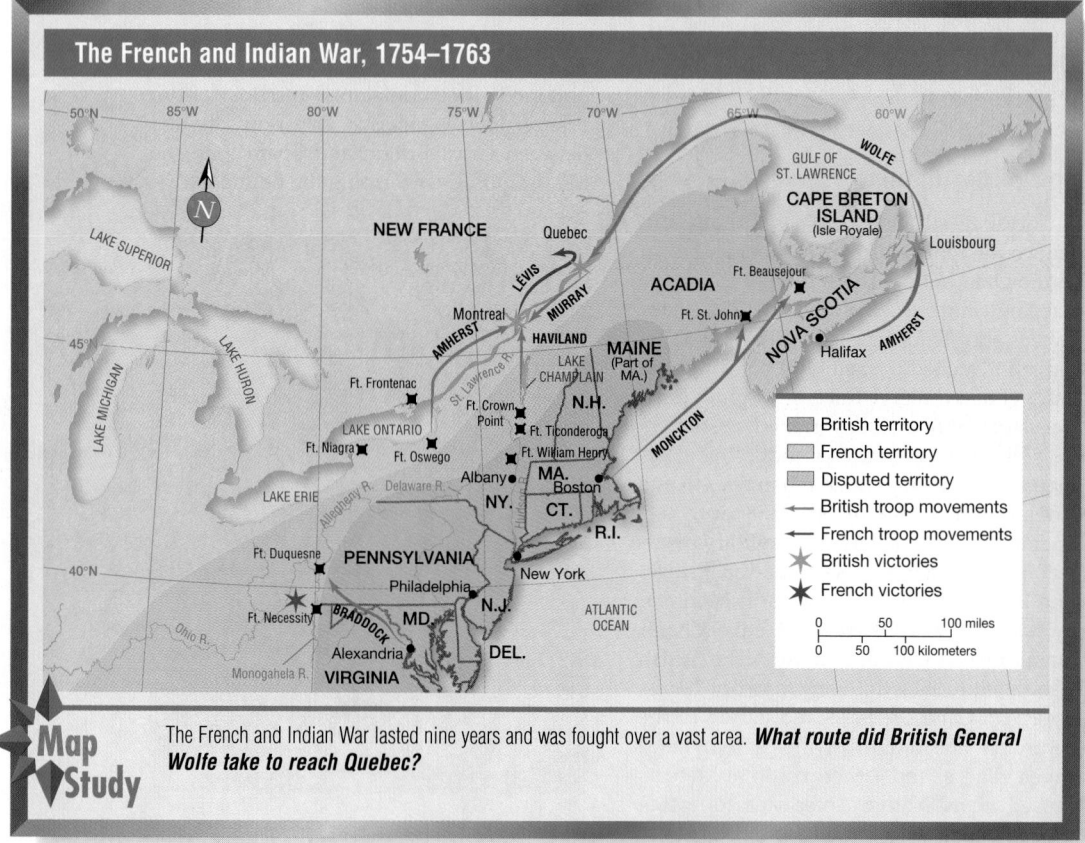

The French and Indian War, 1754–1763

▨	British territory
▨	French territory
▨	Disputed territory
←	British troop movements
←	French troop movements
★	British victories
✦	French victories

Map Study

The French and Indian War lasted nine years and was fought over a vast area. *What route did British General Wolfe take to reach Quebec?*

Special Needs Activity

Inefficient Readers Students whose reading skills are weak can greatly benefit from role-playing. Organize students into two groups. Have one group imagine they are members of the British government and the other group imagine they are American colonial leaders.

Have each group present its case on imposing taxes on the colonies, making certain the group provides arguments supporting its point of view. Discuss with students the possible outcomes if their views on taxation are adopted. **L1**

Lexington and Concord

Meanwhile, every colony organized military forces. Fighting between the Americans and the British soon broke out near Boston, which had been occupied in 1774 by a British army. Early on April 19, 1775, a detachment of 700 British soldiers was secretly sent to destroy the military supplies colonists had collected at Concord, 21 miles from Boston.

Learning of the soldiers' destination, the Boston Sons of Liberty took action. The organization sent Paul Revere and William Dawes, later joined by Samuel Prescott, to alert the **minutemen,** or militia members so named because they could be ready for battle on a minute's notice, in the towns and villages along the way. When the British reached the town of Lexington, about 70 armed minutemen awaited them. In the skirmish eight colonists were killed. The British force pushed on to the neighboring town of Concord and burned what little gunpowder the colonists had not used for themselves.

By the time the British began their march toward Boston, the countryside was swarming with minutemen, who fired at the redcoats from behind trees, buildings, and stone walls. Only a brigade sent out from Boston saved the British from annihilation. About 270 British and 100 Americans were killed or wounded at Concord.

Battle of Bunker Hill

In June 1775, the British discovered that American troops had occupied Breed's Hill, a peninsula overlooking Boston. The British commander made a frontal attack uphill. Because the range of a musket was scarcely more than 50 yards, the Americans were ordered to hold their fire until they could see the "whites of their enemies' eyes." After turning back two British attacks, the Americans ran out of ammunition. The Battle of Bunker Hill, as it came to be called, was a moral victory for the Americans because their untrained militia had stood up to professional troops.

Second Continental Congress

On May 10, 1775, a Second Continental Congress met in Philadelphia. The Congress assumed the powers of a central government and took steps to conduct the war that had, in fact, begun at Lexington. The Congress voted to ask the colonies for supplies and troops.

For commander in chief, Congress chose George Washington. It valued his experience and ability, but the fact that he was a Virginian was also important because it would keep the Southern and Middle colonies from thinking of the conflict as New England's war. Although it would be more than a year until independence was declared, the American Revolution had begun.

Section 1 ★ Review

Checking for Understanding

1. **Identify** Treaty of Paris, Pontiac, Proclamation of 1763, Stamp Act, Boston Tea Party, Second Continental Congress, George Washington.

2. **Define** salutary neglect, militia, direct tax, boycott, minutemen.

3. **State** two ways in which the interests of the British and the colonists differed.

4. **Explain** the purpose and significance of the two Continental Congresses.

Critical Thinking

4. **Supporting an Opinion**   Some historians place the cause of the Revolution on the series of tax laws passed after 1763. Others believe that the cause was a growing national consciousness of Americans. Point out the strengths of each theory.

ACTIVITY

5. Compose a series of American newspaper headlines that describe British actions and American reactions between 1763 and 1775.

ASSESS
Check Understanding
Assign Section 1 Review as homework or an in-class activity.

Evaluate
⟳ Assign Section Quiz 2-1 or use the Testmaker to create a customized quiz.

Reteach
Have students prepare an events-chain map of the events leading to the battles at Lexington and Concord, starting with the British Parliament voting to grant a British company sole control of the tea trade with America.

⟳ Have students complete Reteaching Activity 2-1.

Enrich
⟳ Assign Primary and Secondary Source Readings, pp. 3–4.

CLOSE
Have students trace the developments that brought the colonists to challenge British authority.

Answers to SECTION 1 REVIEW

1. Treaty of Paris, 43; Pontiac, 44; Proclamation of 1763, 44; Stamp Act, 45; Boston Tea Party, 46; Second Continental Congress, 47; George Washington, 47

2. All vocabulary terms are defined in the Glossary.

3. Colonists wanted unrestricted trade with other nations; Britain wanted to control trade for its own benefit. Britain wanted to expand its empire by gaining French territory; colonists were reluctant to fight Britain's wars.

4. Purpose was to protest British policies; significance was cooperation of all colonies.

5. Answers may include: tax laws created resentment and tried to subjugate colonies to British authority; growing national consciousness gave sense of being different from Britain and sharing common traits and ideals.

6. Newspaper headlines will vary but should focus on pertinent British actions and American reactions.

TEACH

Ask students to read the text explaining the steps involved in identifying and evaluating alternatives. Using their lists, have them write all the possible alternatives they can think of involving their decisions. Ask: Based on the steps you have read, did you make the best informed decision? **L2**

🖥️📁 Project Skills Transparency 2 and have students complete Skills Transparency Activity 2.

📁 Use Chapter Skills Activity 2 to reinforce students' understanding of the skill.

Did You Know?

Although he fought long and hard for independence, Samuel Adams refused to attend the convention held in 1787 to form a new Constitution. Adams feared a strong central government and was suspicious of many of the delegates' intentions.

Identifying Alternatives

In order to make an informed decision, you must identify the alternatives or the possible options in each situation. Almost any decision you make has alternatives, even if the choices are unpleasant.

Learning the Skill

Use the following steps to identify and evaluate alternatives:

- **State** the problem or decision to be made.
- **List** all the possible options you can think of.
- **Gather** information to evaluate the alternatives. Map out both positive and negative consequences of each alternative.

◀ **SAMUEL ADAMS**

Revolutionary leader and public official Samuel Adams early on took a firm position for independence. In 1765 he was elected to the Massachusetts House of Representatives, where he was linked with the colonists arousing public feeling against British measures. As one of the main spokespersons for this position, Adams agitated against the Stamp Act, the Townshend duties, and other measures imposed by Parliament.

Adams wrote many articles alerting Americans of Parliament's actions and helped organize the committees of correspondence in New England. A leading force behind the Boston Tea Party and a delegate to the Continental Congress, Adams was one of the first American leaders to call for immediate independence.

In 1772 Adams wrote *A List of Infringements and Violations of Rights,* detailing what he considered to be the wrongs committed by Great Britain against the colonists. Adams wrote to convince other colonists of his position:

> "We cannot help thinking, that an enumeration [list] of some of the most open infringements of our rights [by Great Britain], will by every candid person be judged sufficient to justify whatever measures have been already taken, or may be thought proper to be taken, in order to obtain a redress of the grievances under which we labour. . . ."

Practicing the Skill

1. What is the topic Adams is discussing?
2. What position does Adams advocate?
3. Identify at least two alternative viewpoints to Adams's position.
4. Following Adams's advice might lead to war with Great Britain. What are some possible consequences of the alternative positions you listed in question 3 above?

APPLYING THE SKILL

5. Suppose you have to decide whether to work after school, take part in an extracurricular activity, or use the time to study. Create a chart in which you list the alternatives and the pros and cons for each.

48

Answers to Practicing the Skill

1. wrongs Adams believed Britain committed
2. whatever Patriots did was justified
3. Responses will vary but examples may be that Britain did not commit any wrongs; patriots could decide to compromise; Britain could compromise.
4. Responses will vary depending on alternatives given. Answers should be reasonable and probable.
5. Charts will vary. Encourage students to list both positive and negative consequences of each alternative.

★★★

War for Independence

Setting the Scene

Section Focus

Even after the first skirmishes, the colonists still hoped to reconcile with the British crown. Events during the winter of 1775–1776, however, moved them toward separation. The writings of Thomas Paine, the king's inflexible attitude, and Britain's use of German mercenaries all pushed the colonies toward independence and a long conflict.

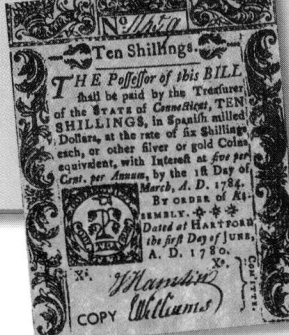

◀ CONTINENTAL MONEY

Objectives

After studying this section, you should be able to

★ state what factors caused the American Revolution.

★ explain why the Americans were able to win the war.

Key Terms

treason, propaganda, republic, Patriot, Loyalist, social contract, mercenary

---

After the bloodshed in Massachusetts, colonial leaders such as Patrick Henry of Virginia appealed for separation from Great Britain. Most colonists, however, were not ready for independence. They wanted the colonies to remain part of the British Empire but rule themselves through their legislatures.

■ Moving Toward Separation

The Second Continental Congress, which convened in Philadelphia in May 1775, sent a petition to the king that blamed all of the recent troubles on the king's ministers. The king, however, refused to accept the petition and charged the American leaders with **treason,** or attempting to overthrow the government.

Influential in swaying the colonists toward the idea of separation was Thomas Paine's *Common Sense,* which first appeared in January 1776. Paine, who had come to America from England in 1774, was a writer of revolutionary **propaganda,** or ideas spread deliberately to help a cause. Paine called upon Americans to proclaim their independence. He felt that they should not only break from Great Britain, but cast off kings altogether and form a **republic,** a government in which the highest power belongs to the citizens, who choose representatives to act for them.

Paine's stirring words divided Americans into **Patriots,** who favored separation, and **Loyalists,** who supported the king. Many Patriots hoped that independence would bring military aid from France and help replace lost British markets with new markets in other countries.

LESSON PLAN
SECTION 2, 49–56

FOCUS
Bellringer

📦 🗂 Before taking roll, project Section Focus Transparency 2-2 or hand out Section Focus Transparency Activity 2-2. Have students answer the questions.

Motivating Activity

Direct students to Jefferson's statement about equality from the Declaration of Independence on page 50. Ask them to write in their own words what this sentence means to them. **L2**

Vocabulary Precheck

Ask students to define each of the "Key Terms." Have a volunteer consult the dictionary for any unfamiliar words. **L1, LEP**

NATIONAL GEOGRAPHIC SOCIETY

GTV: A Geographic Perspective on American History

Side 1, Chapter 15
Title: *Laying Down the Law*
Subject: The rise of revolutionary feelings

Classroom Resources for SECTION 2

Blackline Masters:
🗂 Reproducible Lesson Plan 2-2
🗂 Guided Reading Activity 2-2
🗂 Critical Thinking Skills Activity 2
🗂 Chapter Map Activity 2

🗂 American Portrait 9
🗂 Workbook Activity 2-2
🗂 Reteaching Activity 2-2
🗂 Section Quiz 2-2

Transparencies:
📦 Section Focus Transparency 2-2
📦 Map Transparency 2
Multimedia:
⊙ Vocabulary PuzzleMaker
⊙ Testmaker

⦿ The American History Videodisc
⦿ GTV: A Geographic Perspective on American History
⦿ Focus on Government
⦿ Landmark Documents in American History

■ Declaration of Independence

The Continental Congress, sensing growing public support for independence, assigned five of its best thinkers to prepare a Declaration of Independence. The purpose of the Declaration was to justify the American cause, to state that the colonies were independent, and to express the new nation's principles.

Writing the Declaration

Thomas Jefferson, a young Virginian, was the principal author of the Declaration. Jefferson, like many other American leaders, knew and valued the works of John Locke and other European political thinkers. He incorporated many of their ideas into the Declaration.

Basic Rights

The Declaration of Independence stated that individuals have certain basic rights that cannot be taken away by any government. Like Locke, Jefferson believed that government is created by a **social contract,** or agreement between the rulers and those ruled. If a government loses the support of the people by taking away basic rights, the people have a right to change the government through rebellion. The beginning of the Declaration reads:

> ❝ *We hold these truths to be self-evident, that all men are created equal, that they are endowed by their Creator with certain unalienable Rights, that among these are Life, Liberty, and the pursuit of Happiness. That to secure these rights, Governments are instituted among Men, deriving their just powers from the consent of the governed; that whenever any Form of Government becomes destructive of these ends, it is the right of the People to alter or to abolish it.* ❞

The Declaration continued with a long list of the ways in which Great Britain and

 ▲ Independence Hall George Washington sat at this platform desk in Philadelphia's Independence Hall to preside over the Constitutional Convention. **What was the purpose of the Declaration of Independence?**

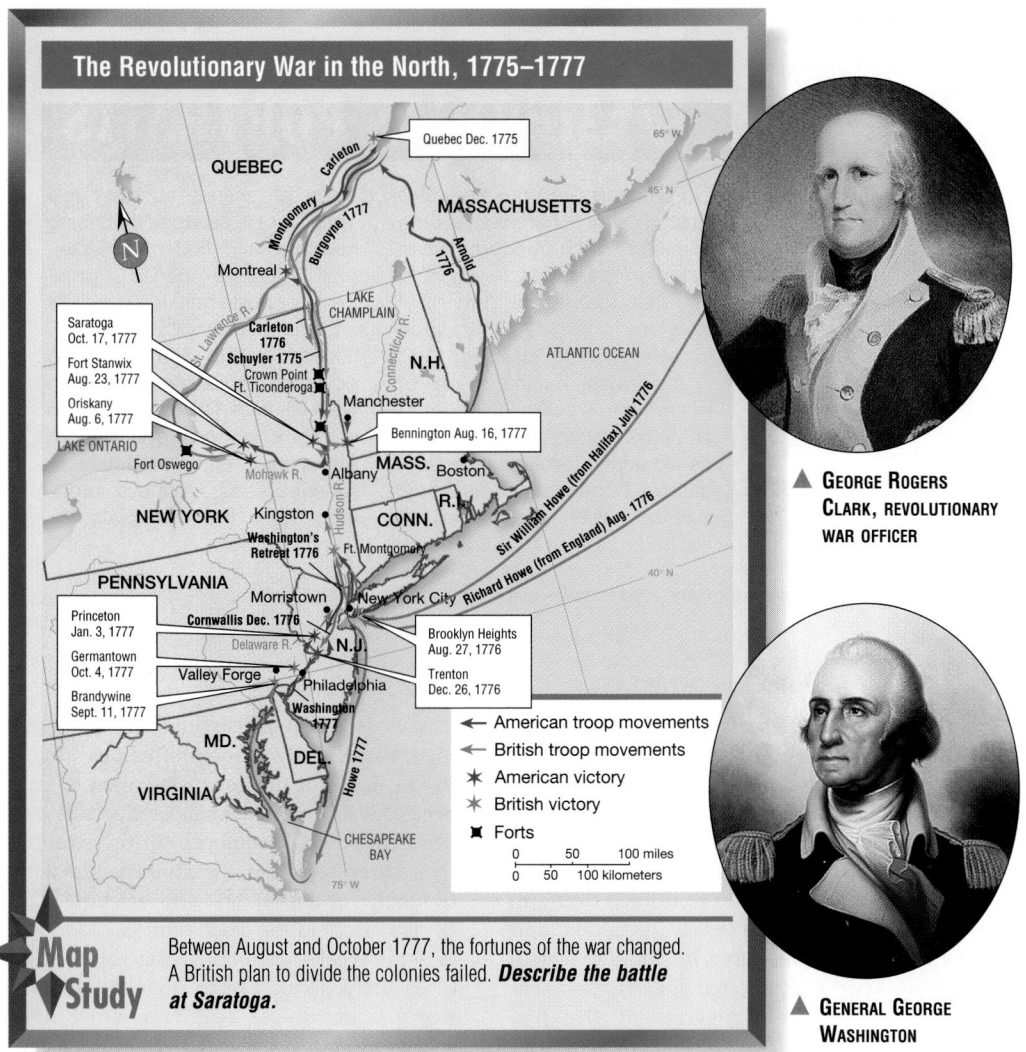

The Revolutionary War in the North, 1775–1777

Map labels: QUEBEC, Quebec Dec. 1775, Carleton, Burgoyne 1777, MASSACHUSETTS, Montgomery, Montreal, LAKE CHAMPLAIN, Arnold 1776, Saratoga Oct. 17, 1777, Fort Stanwix Aug. 23, 1777, Oriskany Aug. 6, 1777, Carleton 1776, Schuyler 1775, Crown Point, Ft. Ticonderoga, N.H., Manchester, ATLANTIC OCEAN, LAKE ONTARIO, Bennington Aug. 16, 1777, Fort Oswego, Mohawk R., Albany, MASS., Boston, NEW YORK, Kingston, CONN., R.I., Sir William Howe (from Halifax) July 1776, Washington's Retreat 1776, Ft. Montgomery, Richard Howe (from England) Aug. 1776, PENNSYLVANIA, Morristown, New York City, Princeton Jan. 3, 1777, Cornwallis Dec. 1776, Germantown Oct. 4, 1777, Delaware R., N.J., Valley Forge, Brandywine Sept. 11, 1777, Philadelphia, Washington 1777, MD., DEL., Howe 1777, VIRGINIA, CHESAPEAKE BAY

Legend:
← American troop movements
← British troop movements
✶ American victory
✶ British victory
■ Forts

0   50   100 miles
0 50   100 kilometers

▲ GEORGE ROGERS CLARK, REVOLUTIONARY WAR OFFICER

▲ GENERAL GEORGE WASHINGTON

Map Study Between August and October 1777, the fortunes of the war changed. A British plan to divide the colonies failed. ***Describe the battle at Saratoga.***

George III had abused their power and concludes that "these United Colonies are and of Right ought to be Free and Independent States."

Influence of the Declaration

On July 4, 1776, Congress adopted the Declaration of Independence, which became one of the world's most important political documents. Throughout the years, the American Declaration of Independence has inspired supporters of freedom in many parts of the world.

■ Fighting for Independence

The signing of the Declaration of Independence made war between Britain and the American colonies a certainty. Both the British and Americans had taken steps that made a peaceful reconciliation impossible. The only course that remained for the colonists was revolution. For American leaders, failure would mean disgrace and even death. As Benjamin Franklin said, "We must all hang together now, or assuredly we shall hang separately."

Class Discussion Ask students to read the quotations from the Declaration on page 50. Ask them to note the lines "that whenever any Form of Government becomes destructive of these ends, it is the right of the People to alter or to abolish it, ..." The British government would have considered this an act of treason. Americans considered it justified. Conduct a class discussion on situations in which students think the alteration or abolition of a government is justified. **L3**

Did You Know?

Against Thomas Jefferson's wishes, Congress deleted a scathing attack on the slave trade from the Declaration. This deletion was engineered by a coalition of Southern slave owners and Northern merchants whose ships transported slaves.

Map Study *Using Maps*

Answer: It was the turning point of the war, a decisive American victory.

Map Skills Practice
Who won the battles at Fort Stanwix, Oriskany, and Bennington? *(the Americans)*

Sidelight: The Fourth of July

While July 4 is celebrated as Independence Day, the process of declaring independence took close to six months. A formal resolution to separate from Britain was adopted by the Continental Congress on July 2, 1776. Two days later the Congress adopted the Declaration of Independence. The Declaration was proclaimed on July 8, and most of the delegates signed the document on August 2. However, it was January 19, 1777, before the Declaration and a complete list of its signatories were published.

GLENCOE
TECHNOLOGY

  VIDEODISC

The American History Videodisc

Side One, Section C
Frame 19970

Title: *The American Revolution and the Early Republic, 1765–1820*

Subject: Overview of American history from the background of the American Revolution to the Early Republic

Teaching American Portraits

At his death, the American government owed Haym Salomon about $650,000. Not all financiers of the Revolution were as unfortunate as Salomon, however. Robert Morris, for example, profited greatly from the war and died a wealthy man.

Ask students what criminal penalties, if any, there should be for making high profits from the misery of a war.

Food of the Times

A broth called Philadelphia Pepper Pot has been called the soup of the Revolution. It was invented for Washington's troops to give them a hot and filling food at Valley Forge. Made of peppercorns, tripe, and scraps, it saved many soldiers from starving.

Haym Salomon
1740(?)–1785

★★★★AMERICAN PORTRAITS

Forced to flee from his native Poland after championing the cause of Polish freedom, Haym Salomon went first to England and then to America. Arriving in New York in 1772, he soon joined the Patriot struggle.

A Jewish businessman of remarkable ability, Salomon acquired wealth, all of which he risked during the American Revolution. Twice arrested as a spy, Salomon was condemned to death for plotting to burn British ships at anchor outside New York City. He escaped by bribing his jailer and fled to Philadelphia. There he opened a prosperous private banking business and donated thousands of dollars for military supplies and government salaries. He also worked with Robert Morris to secure loans for the war effort. As a result of his devotion to America—and business problems after the war—Salomon died penniless.

Advantages and Disadvantages

The first battles of the American Revolution were concentrated in the states of New York and New Jersey. The British hoped to gain control of the middle states and separate New England from the southern states. Great Britain devised its plans from a position of military strength. Its troops were well led, well trained, and well equipped. Its navy, the most powerful in the world, controlled the Atlantic seacoast. The British government also had enough money to pay 30,000 German **mercenaries,** or hired soldiers, to fight with them. After decades of fighting around the world, the British forces were prepared for war.

The American colonists, on the other hand, had no navy, little battle experience, and lacked money, clothing, guns, ammunition, and food. Officers identified themselves with colored ribbon on their hats because they had no uniforms. The Americans, however, did find ways to match the seasoned British forces. Washington was a skillful general who mustered the support of the colonial forces. The Americans also found it easier to fight a war on familiar territory in defense of their homes.

Carrying Out the War

Volleys from British muskets scattered the colonial army in the first battles waged in the war. But the colonists began to surprise the British with their ability and tactics. They would ambush British troops, then disappear into the countryside with the help of neighbors and friends. The British also had the disadvantage of having to wait weeks or months for supplies to cross the Atlantic Ocean. In addition, the war was unpopular in Britain; and British soldiers found it difficult fighting in a war thousands of miles from home that they did not understand or even support.

The turning point of the war came in October 1777, with a decisive American victory against the British at Saratoga in New York. The French—anxious to strike back at the British—decided that the Americans were a good political risk and entered the war on the American side.

Before French military aid reached America, Washington's army had to endure the unusually harsh winter of 1777 and 1778 encamped at Valley Forge, Pennsylvania. The Prussian Baron Friedrich W.A. von Steuben and the French Marquis de Lafayette joined Washington at Valley

---

Special Needs Activity

Poor Learners Most students are familiar with the study system known as "SQ3R" (Survey, Question, Read, Recite, Review), but those with reading and learning problems often have difficulty surveying information. One task involved in surveying is predicting what kind of information will be given in a section of text. Ask students to consider whether the text under each subhead in this section will describe events or discuss concepts and ideas that shaped events. **L1**

Forge, bringing discipline and encouragement. By spring, the tattered army began to regain morale as new provisions arrived from France.

■ Difficult Choices

When the Declaration of Independence called the United States "one people," it expressed a hope rather than a fact. Only about one-third of the American people actively supported the war. Another third were indifferent to the Patriot cause. The rest were Loyalists who supported the British. The struggle between Patriots and the Loyalists was as bitter a struggle as the struggle between the rebels and the British. Patriots thought of the Loyalists as traitors to the American cause.

African Americans

From the beginning of the war, at Lexington, Concord, and Bunker Hill, African American soldiers fought for the American cause. Slaveholders were afraid to give guns to African Americans, however, whether enslaved or free. In November 1775, the Continental Congress ordered the discharge of all African American soldiers in the Continental Army and banned the enlistment of other African Americans.

When the British promised to free any enslaved person who joined their army, the Congress reversed its policy and allowed free African Americans to reenlist. Enslaved African Americans who were recruited into the army either won freedom from the start or at the end of their military service.

▲ *MOLLY PITCHER AT THE BATTLE OF MONMOUTH* by Dennis Malone Carter, 1854 Several women took an active part in the fighting. At the Battle of Monmouth, New Jersey, in 1778, Molly Pitcher takes her husband's place firing a cannon. ***In what other ways did women aid the American cause?***

CHAPTER 2 A New Nation: 1750–1789   **53**

Critical Thinking Activity

Making Predictions The American Revolution was fought for the ideals of freedom, yet many who participated were not free, either socially or politically. All women, African Americans, Native Americans, and poor white men were excluded from the political process. Have students predict how this problem might affect life in the new American nation by answering the following questions: What conflicts might develop? Who will be involved in these conflicts? How will these conflicts be resolved? **L2**

📁 To provide additional practice in critical thinking, assign Critical Thinking Activity 2.

Independent Practice

Creating Political Cartoons Have students draw cartoons of the figures of this period—Thomas Jefferson, George Washington, George III, a Patriot, a Loyalist, and so on. Suggest that students draw a caricature—an exaggeration of the subject's physical or behavioral characteristics. Encourage students to display their cartoons on the bulletin board. **L1**

📁 Assign Guided Reading Activity 2-2.

Did You Know?

The Continental currency issued by Congress was worth 40 paper dollars to 1 silver dollar. When Congress finally decided to stop issuing the money, people could turn in the paper money at one-fortieth of its value.

History AND ART

The battle at Monmouth, depicted here, was waged on July 4, 1778, and was the longest battle of the war.
Answer to Caption: They served as secret agents; raised money to equip troops; ran farms and businesses; accompanied the troops, serving as cooks, medics, launderers, and guides.

Map Study *Using Maps*

Answer: Washington: south overland from New York; De Grasse: north by sea from West Indies; Cornwallis: north from Carolinas, then east to Yorktown.

Map Skills Practice

What caused the British to lose control of the Atlantic? *(They were defeated by the French fleet.)*

📁 For additional practice in map skills, assign Chapter Map Activity 2.

NATIONAL GEOGRAPHIC SOCIETY

GTV: A Geographic Perspective on American History

Side 1, Chapter 17

Title: *The American Revolution*

Subject: The impact of geography and aid from France on the American Revolution

Native Americans

Some groups of Native Americans remained neutral, but many joined the British. They knew the Americans opposed the Proclamation Act of 1763, which reserved land west of the Appalachians for Native Americans. British agents encouraged the Native Americans to attack frontier settlements in Virginia, Georgia, the Carolinas, and the Northwest. These actions diverted many state militia from fighting against British troops.

In New York four nations of the Iroquois Confederation supported the British. General Washington sent troops against the Iroquois and broke their confederation. Many Native Americans—including almost all of the Mohawk—moved permanently to Canada.

Women

Many women actively supported the American cause. Women often served as secret agents supplying information about British positions and plans. They raised money to equip troops. They ran farms and businesses while their husbands were away at war. Women also accompanied the troops, serving as cooks, medics, laundresses, and guides. A few even fought in the ranks.

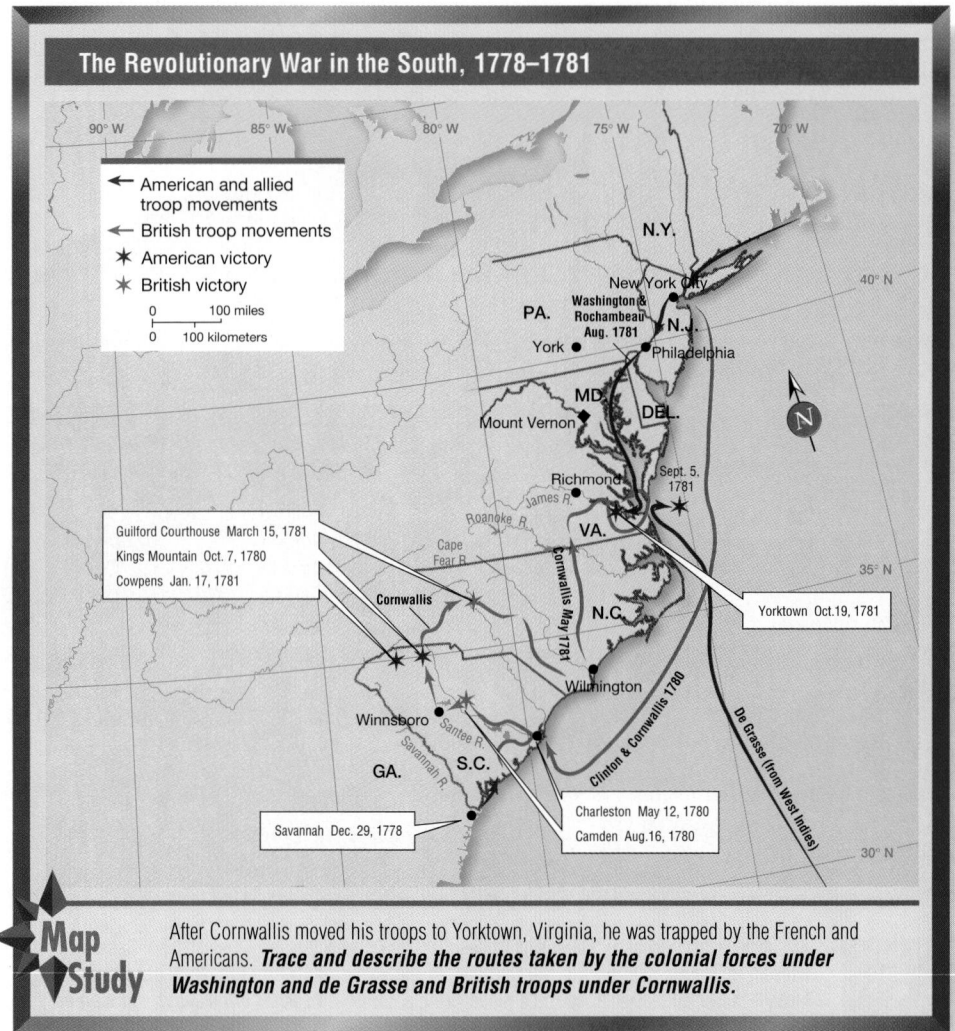

The Revolutionary War in the South, 1778–1781

- ← American and allied troop movements
- ← British troop movements
- ✶ American victory
- ✶ British victory

0   100 miles
0   100 kilometers

Guilford Courthouse March 15, 1781
Kings Mountain Oct. 7, 1780
Cowpens Jan. 17, 1781

Yorktown Oct.19, 1781

Charleston May 12, 1780
Camden Aug.16, 1780

Savannah Dec. 29, 1778

Map Study

After Cornwallis moved his troops to Yorktown, Virginia, he was trapped by the French and Americans. *Trace and describe the routes taken by the colonial forces under Washington and de Grasse and British troops under Cornwallis.*

Sidelight: Patriot Colonial Women

Colonial women asserted themselves as Patriots as best they could within the restrictive social and political framework of the time. In 1780, for example, women in Philadelphia, New Jersey, Maryland, and Virginia went from door to door collecting money for the troops. When General Washington denied their request that the money go straight to the soldiers, they refused to hand over the funds. Instead, they bought material, sewed shirts, and sent these directly to the troops.

Americans ship supplies up the Mississippi River. When Spain officially entered the war in 1779, Galvez's troops defeated the British at Baton Rouge, Natchez, and Pensacola. These battles forced the British to divert troops from their campaigns along the Atlantic coast.

Yorktown

In 1780 and 1781, the British suffered serious naval defeats at the hands of the French, causing them to lose control of the Atlantic. This made possible the capture of the principal British force in the south under Lord Cornwallis. In October 1781, with the aid of the French, the Americans defeated the British army. George Washington accepted the British surrender at Yorktown, Virginia.

Visualizing History

▲ WOMEN AND RIGHTS Abigail Adams was a crusader for women's rights, demonstrating the careful thought of educated women of this period. *To what group did the new state bills of rights reserve the full privileges of citizenship?*

Women who supported the Revolution expected to gain from its ideals of democracy and equality. However, the American Revolution did little to change the political rights of women. Although new state bills of rights declared that all people are equal, they reserved full privileges of citizenship for white males.

■ The War's End

Unable to capture Washington's army or to put down the rebellion in the north, the British turned their main military efforts to the south. For three years, beginning in 1778, British forces marched through Georgia, the Carolinas, and Virginia. Although successful at first, the British could not keep their conquests in the south because they could not win the loyalty of the inhabitants.

The Southwest

The British were also unsuccessful in the southwest. General Bernardo de Galvez, the governor of Spanish Louisiana, helped

★★★ AMERICA'S FLAGS ★★★

Flags of the Revolution The flag of the British Union flew over the English colonies in America, beginning with Jamestown, Virginia, in 1607 until the Revolution. The *Congress Colors* or *Grand Union* flag served as America's first national flag from 1775 to 1777. Its 13 stripes stood for the thirteen colonies. The crosses represented the British flag and symbolized the colonists' loyalty to Britain at that time.  After the Declaration of Independence, the British flag lost its meaning as a part of the United States flag. Thus the Continental Congress on June 14, 1777, designed the first Stars and Stripes. It determined that "the Flag of the United States be 13 stripes, alternate  red and white; that the Union be 13 stars, white in a blue field representing a new constellation."

★★★★★★★★★★★★★★★★★★★★★★★

Visualizing History Abigail Adams believed strongly in equal rights for women and African Americans at a time in history when such views were not well received. **Answer to Caption:** adult white males

FACT or FICTION?

At the Yorktown surrender, the British band played the tune "The World Turned Upside Down."

FICTION: The incident has never been verified. An eyewitness did report, however, that when a British officer offered his sword to French General Rochambeau instead of Washington, Lafayette was so angry at the insult that he asked the American band to play "Yankee Doodle" in derision of the British.

ASSESS

Check Understanding

Assign Section 2 Review as homework or an in-class activity.

Evaluate

🖰 📁 Assign Section Quiz 2-2 or use the Test-maker to create a customized quiz.

Reteach

📁 Have students complete Reteaching Activity 2-2.

Critical Thinking Activity

Summarizing Events Ask students to summarize the chain of events leading to the American victory at Yorktown, beginning with the move by Cornwallis and the British into Georgia, the Carolinas, and Virginia. Suggest that students present their summaries in flow-chart form. **L2**

Among Trumbull's best-known historical paintings are *The Battle of Bunker Hill* and *The Declaration of Independence*.
Answer to Caption: The British recognized America's independence and ceded to the new nation land from the Atlantic Ocean to the Mississippi River.

Enrich

Loyalists were generally treated harshly during the war. Suggest students find examples of Loyalist families who suffered at the hands of Patriots and write a story about what happened to them.

 Assign Map Transparency Activity 2.

CLOSE

Ask students to complete the following sentence:
Although the British captured most major colonial cities, they ultimately lost the war because . . . .
Have students justify their sentence completions in a class discussion.

▲ **SURRENDER OF LORD CORNWALLIS AT YORKTOWN** by John Trumbull, 1824 Surrounded by American and French forces, General Charles Cornwallis was forced to surrender. Although other skirmishes followed, the victory at Yorktown assured America's independence. *What were the terms of the treaty ending the war?*

The Treaty of Paris, 1783

The Treaty of Paris in 1783 acknowledged American independence and granted the new nation land from the Atlantic Ocean to the Mississippi River. Although several provisions of the treaty led to later disputes, it was a great diplomatic victory for the Americans. The United States gained an area that was four times the size of France and nearly ten times that of the British Isles.

Section 2 ★ Review

Checking for Understanding

1. **Identify** Thomas Paine, Patriot, Loyalist, Thomas Jefferson, Bernardo de Galvez, Yorktown.
2. **Define** treason, propaganda, republic, Patriots, Loyalists, social contract, mercenary.
3. **Name** three reasons for separating from Great Britain as described in *Common Sense*.
4. **Explain** the decisions facing African Americans and Native Americans during the Revolution.

Critical Thinking

5. **Analyzing Beliefs** The American Revolution has been described as a civil war as well as a rebellion. Analyze this theory based on the conflict between Loyalists and Patriots.

ACTIVITY

6. Imagine that you are living in the 1770s on the eve of the American Revolution. Record your observations and feelings about such events as the writing of the Declaration of Independence.

Answers to SECTION 2 REVIEW

1. Thomas Paine, 49; Patriot, 49; Loyalist, 49; Thomas Jefferson, 50; Bernardo De Galvez, 55; Yorktown, 55
2. All vocabulary words are defined in the Glossary.
3. to become independent, to cast off kings altogether, and to form a republic
4. African Americans had to decide which side would extend or guarantee their rights after the war. Native Americans had to determine whether joining the British would protect their land.
5. Answers will vary but should include that an equal number of Americans were Loyalists as were Patriots, each side had opposite views and allegiances, and each had intense feelings against the other.
6. Observations will vary. Encourage students to put themselves in the role of a person living in the 1770s.

The Revolutionary Pen

In the years leading up to the American Revolution, few colonists could claim to be professional writers. Yet Americans from every walk of life wrote on the topics of liberty, the nature of government, and law. By 1765 there were more than 20 newspapers in the colonies, publishing locally written poems, songs, and satires on the issues of the day as well as news from abroad and debates of colonial assemblies. Broadside ballads—emotionally charged story poems printed on a single sheet of paper that could be pasted on lampposts, nailed to trees, or slipped under doors for everyone to read—helped fuel colonists' passion for freedom.

◄ POET PHILLIS WHEATLEY

Such measures as the Sugar Act, the Stamp Act, the Quartering Act, and the Townshend Acts stirred even more colonists to write expressing their views. Poet Phillis Wheatley, who was born in Africa and taken as a slave to Massachusetts, wrote her first poem in 1766. It was to King George III when he repealed the Stamp Act:

And may each clime with equal gladness see
A monarch's smile can set his subjects free!

▲ TARRED AND FEATHERED TAX COLLECTOR, 1774 CARTOON

As relations between Great Britain and the colonies frayed, Thomas Paine made an impassioned appeal in his pamphlet *Common Sense:*
Everything that is right or natural pleads for separation. The blood of the slain, the weeping voice of nature cries, 'TIS TIME TO PART.
After reading Paine's pamphlet, thousands of colonists converted to the cause of independence and answered his call.

Making the Art Connection

1. What kinds of stories and features did newspapers of the period include?

2. What events influenced more colonists to express their views?

ACTIVITY

3. Think about something you believe in, some concern or issue you'd like others to view as you do. Write a broadside ballad that makes a convincing argument for believing as you do and build a case that will sway your reader to share your beliefs.

57

Motivating Activity

Ask students if they would risk their lives for an idea and, if so, for what idea. Remind them that the American Revolution involved great risks for the people who fought it. Ask what ideas were being fought for in the American Revolution. (*self-government, freedom, representation, equality*) **L1**

TEACH

Guided Practice

Paraphrasing Choose a student to read aloud the first paragraph under "Declaration of Natural Rights." Discuss some of the more difficult terms such as *self-evident* and *unalienable*. Assign students to write a paraphrase of the paragraph. **LEP, L1**

GLENCOE
TECHNOLOGY

VIDEODISC

Focus on Government

Side 1, Chapter 1

Title: *Electronic Field Trip to Independence Hall*

Subject: The role of Independence Hall in American History

The Declaration of Independence

*D*elegates at the Second Continental Congress faced an enormous task. The war against Great Britain had begun, but to many colonists the purpose for fighting was unclear. As sentiment increased for a complete break with Britain, Congress decided to act. A committee was appointed to prepare a document that declared the thirteen colonies free and independent from Britain. More important, the committee needed to explain why separation was the only fitting solution to long-standing disputes with Parliament and the British Crown. Thomas Jefferson was assigned to prepare a working draft of this document, which was then revised. It was officially adopted on July 4, 1776. More than any other action of the Congress, the Declaration of Independence served to make the American colonists one people.

★★★

> The printed text of the document shows the spelling and punctuation of the parchment original. To aid in comprehension, selected words and their definitions appear in the side margin, along with other explanatory notes.
>
> **impel** *force*
>
> **endowed** *provided*
>
> *People create governments to ensure that their natural rights are protected.*
>
> *If a government does not serve its purpose, the people have a right to abolish it. Then the people have the right and duty to create a new government that will safeguard their security.*
>
> **Despotism** *unlimited power*

In Congress, July 4, 1776. The unanimous Declaration of the thirteen united States of America,

Preamble

When in the Course of human events, it becomes necessary for one people to dissolve the political bands which have connected them with another, and to assume among the powers of the earth, the separate and equal station to which the Laws of Nature and Nature's God entitle them, a decent respect to the opinions of mankind requires that they should declare the causes which impel them to the separation.—

Declaration of Natural Rights

We hold these truths to be self-evident, that all men are created equal, that they are endowed by their Creator with certain unalienable Rights, that among these are Life, Liberty, and the pursuit of Happiness.—

That to secure these rights, Governments are instituted among Men, deriving their just powers from the consent of the governed,—

That whenever any Form of Government becomes destructive of these ends, it is the Right of the People to alter or to abolish it, and to institute new Government, laying its foundation on such principles and organizing its powers in such form, as to them shall seem most likely to effect their Safety and Happiness. Prudence, indeed, will dictate that Governments long established should not be changed for light and transient causes; and accordingly all experience hath shewn, that mankind are more disposed to suffer, while evils are sufferable, than to right themselves by abolishing the forms to which they are accustomed. But when a long train of abuses and usurpations, pursuing invariably the same Object evinces a design to reduce them under absolute Despotism, it is their right, it is their duty, to throw off such Government, and to provide new Guards for their future security.—

Sidelight: The Real Title of the Declaration of Independence

Strictly speaking, the title of this famous document is not the "Declaration of Independence" but rather "The Unanimous Declaration of the Thirteen United States of America." The original document does not bear that title, and it was not the act by which independence was declared. That had been done on July 2 when the Continental Congress adopted Richard Henry Lee's "Resolution of Independence."

★★★ ▲ *Declaration of Independence in Congress* by John Trumbull, 1824 ★★★★★★★★★★★★★★★★★★★★★★★★★

✍ **Analyzing Art** Assign U.S. History & Art Transparency 4, the painting of the Declaration of Independence. Point out that the calmness of the setting obscures the desperation of this step. In the eyes of the British government, each of these representatives was guilty of treason. For some time after, the names of the signers were kept secret, presumably to protect them from British reprisal.

Analyzing Information
Point out that the statements in the Declaration of Natural Rights voice some of the most important ideas of governments. Ask students to identify the important statements. (*Answers will vary but should include: All people are created equal; all people have certain basic rights; the purpose of government is to secure these rights; the power and sovereignty that governments have come from the people.*) **L2**

List of Grievances

Such has been the patient sufferance of these Colonies; and such is now the necessity which constrains them to alter their former Systems of Government. The history of the present King of Great Britain is a history of repeated injuries and usurpations, all having in direct object the establishment of an absolute Tyranny over these States. To prove this, let Facts be submitted to a candid world.—

He has refused his Assent to Laws, the most wholesome and necessary for the public good.—

He has forbidden his Governors to pass Laws of immediate and pressing importance, unless suspended in their operation till his Assent should be obtained; and when so suspended, he has utterly neglected to attend to them.—

He has refused to pass other Laws for the accommodation of large districts of people, unless those people would relinquish the right of Representation in the Legislature, a right inestimable to them and formidable to tyrants only.—

He has called together legislative bodies at places unusual, uncomfortable, and distant from the depository of their public Records, for the sole purpose of fatiguing them into compliance with his measures.—

He has dissolved Representative Houses repeatedly, for opposing with manly firmness his invasions on the rights of the people.—

He has refused for a long time, after such dissolutions, to cause others to be elected; whereby the Legislative powers, incapable of Annihilation, have returned to the People at large for their exercise; the State remaining in the meantime exposed to all the dangers of invasion from without, and convulsions within.—

He has endeavoured to prevent the population of these States; for

usurpations
unjust uses of power

Each paragraph lists alleged injustices of George III.

relinquish *give up*
inestimable *priceless*

Annihilation *destruction*

convulsions
violent disturbances

Cultural Perspectives

The Influence of the Declaration Once it was adopted, the Declaration of Independence exerted a wide influence. With its democratic principle that "all men are created equal," it stimulated humanitarianism movements in the United States and inspired leaders of the French Revolution and Latin American independence movements. For the short term, it led to increased foreign aid for the rebels' cause and paved the way for French intervention on their side. It also steeled Americans to carry on their struggle. Encourage students to find out more about the effects the Declaration of Independence had on peoples around the world.

Determining Cause and Effect
Ask students to think about the impact of the Declaration on the colonists. Have them list as many different effects as they can resulting from news that the Congress had issued the Declaration. (*Answers will vary but might include the following: The time for indecision was over. It forced Americans to decide whether they supported independence or the king. It rallied support and boosted morale. It also raised the conflict above the level of discontent over economic issues.*) **L2**

Independent Practice

Research Organize students into groups of four. Point out that the Declaration has been a force for change in the United States. People have used its words and its ideas to promote such measures as the abolition of slavery and equal rights for women. Have each group do research to find three examples in which an individual or a group used the words and ideas in the Declaration to promote change or reform. **L2**

Naturalization of Foreigners *process by which foreign-born persons become citizens*

tenure *term*

Refers to the British troops sent to the colonies after the French and Indian War.

Refers to the 1766 Declaratory Act.

quartering *lodging*

Refers to the 1774 Quebec Act.

render *make*

abdicated *given up*

perfidy *violation of trust*

insurrections *rebellions*

Petitioned for Redress *asked formally for a correction of wrongs*

---

that purpose obstructing the Laws for Naturalization of Foreigners; refusing to pass others to encourage their migrations hither, and raising the conditions of new Appropriations of Lands.—

He has obstructed the Administration of Justice, by refusing his Assent to Laws for establishing Judiciary powers.—

He has made Judges dependent on his Will alone, for the tenure of their offices, and the amount and payment of their salaries.—

He has erected a multitude of New Offices, and sent hither swarms of Officers to harass our people, and eat out their substance.—

He has kept among us, in times of peace, Standing Armies without the Consent of our legislatures.—

He has affected to render the Military independent of and superior to the Civil power.—

He has combined with others to subject us to a jurisdiction foreign to our constitution, and unacknowledged by our laws; giving his Assent to their Acts of pretended Legislation:—

For quartering large bodies of troops among us:—

For protecting them, by a mock Trial, from punishment for any Murders which they should commit on the Inhabitants of these States:—

For cutting off our Trade with all parts of the world:—

For imposing Taxes on us without our Consent:—

For depriving us in many cases, of the benefits of Trial by Jury:—

For transporting us beyond Seas to be tried for pretended offences:—

For abolishing the free System of English Laws in a neighbouring Province, establishing therein an Arbitrary government, and enlarging its Boundaries so as to render it at once an example and fit instrument for introducing the same absolute rule into these Colonies:—

For taking away our Charters, abolishing our most valuable Laws, and altering fundamentally the Forms of our Governments:—

For suspending our own Legislatures, and declaring themselves invested with power to legislate for us in all cases whatsoever.—

He has abdicated Government here, by declaring us out of his Protection and waging War against us.—

He has plundered our seas, ravaged our Coasts, burnt our towns, and destroyed the Lives of our people.—

He is at this time transporting large Armies of foreign Mercenaries to compleat the works of death, desolation and tyranny, already begun with circumstances of Cruelty & perfidy scarcely paralleled in the most barbarous ages, and totally unworthy the Head of a civilized nation.—

He has constrained our fellow Citizens taken Captive on the high Seas to bear Arms against their Country, to become the executioners of their friends and Brethren, or to fall themselves by their Hands.—

He has excited domestic insurrections amongst us, and has endeavoured to bring on the inhabitants of our frontiers, the merciless Indian Savages, whose known rule of warfare, is an undistinguished destruction of all ages, sexes and conditions.

In every stage of these Oppressions We have Petitioned for Redress in the most humble terms: Our repeated Petitions have been answered only by repeated injury. A Prince, whose character is thus marked by every act which may define a Tyrant, is unfit to be the ruler of a free people.

Critical Thinking Activity

Making Comparisons Have students read the Seneca Falls Declaration of 1848 on page 846 of this text. Compare and contrast the words expressed in this document with those in the Declaration of Independence. Then have students discuss why the writers of the Seneca Falls Declaration modeled their work on the Declaration of Independence. **L2, L3**

Nor have We been wanting in attentions to our British brethren. We have warned them from time to time of attempts by their legislature to extend an unwarrantable jurisdiction over us. We have reminded them of the circumstances of our emigration and settlement here. We have appealed to their native justice and magnanimity, and we have conjured them by the ties of our common kindred to disavow these usurpations, which would inevitably interrupt our connections and correspondence. They too have been deaf to the voice of justice and of consanguinity. We must, therefore, acquiesce in the necessity, which denounces our Separation, and hold them, as we hold the rest of mankind, Enemies in War, in Peace Friends.—

unwarrantable jurisdiction *unjustified authority*

consanguinity *originating from the same ancestor*

Resolution of Independence by the United States

We, therefore, the Representatives of the united States of America, in General Congress, Assembled, appealing to the Supreme Judge of the world for the rectitude of our intentions, do, in the Name, and by Authority of the good People of these Colonies, solemnly publish and declare, That these United Colonies are, and of Right ought to be Free and Independent States; that they are Absolved from all Allegiance to the British Crown, and that all political connection between them and the State of Great Britain, is and ought to be totally dissolved; and that as Free and Independent States, they have full Power to levy War, conclude Peace, contract Alliances, establish Commerce, and to do all other Acts and Things which Independent States may of right do.—

rectitude *rightness*

And for the support of this Declaration, with a firm reliance on the protection of divine Providence, we mutually pledge to each other our Lives, our Fortunes and our sacred Honour.

The signers, as representatives of the American people, declared the colonies independent from Great Britain. Most members signed the document on August 2, 1776.

John Hancock
    President from
    Massachusetts

Georgia
Button Gwinnett
Lyman Hall
George Walton

North Carolina
William Hooper
Joseph Hewes
John Penn

South Carolina
Edward Rutledge
Thomas Heyward, Jr.
Thomas Lynch, Jr.
Arthur Middleton

Maryland
Samuel Chase
William Paca
Thomas Stone
Charles Carroll
    of Carrollton

Virginia
George Wythe
Richard Henry Lee
Thomas Jefferson
Benjamin Harrison
Thomas Nelson Jr.
Francis Lightfoot Lee
Carter Braxton

Pennsylvania
Robert Morris
Benjamin Rush
Benjamin Franklin
John Morton
George Clymer
James Smith
George Taylor
James Wilson
George Ross

Delaware
Caesar Rodney
George Read
Thomas McKean

New York
William Floyd
Philip Livingston
Francis Lewis
Lewis Morris

New Jersey
Richard Stockton
John Witherspoon
Francis Hopkinson
John Hart
Abraham Clark

New Hampshire
Josiah Bartlett
William Whipple
Matthew Thornton

Massachusetts
Samuel Adams
John Adams
Robert Treat Paine
Elbridge Gerry

Rhode Island
Stephen Hopkins
William Ellery

Connecticut
Samuel Huntington
William Williams
Oliver Wolcott
Roger Sherman

The Declaration of Independence

Facts on File

CD-ROM

Landmark Documents in American History: The Declaration of Independence

Suggest that students write a one-page paper in answer to the question: Do you consider the truths that were listed by Thomas Jefferson in the Declaration of Independence to be self-evident? Explain.

Did You Know?

Roger Sherman was the only person who signed all of the four most important documents of the Revolution: the Articles of Association, the Declaration of Independence, the Articles of Confederation, and the Constitution.

Critical Thinking Activity

Identifying Central Issues On June 7, 1776, Richard Henry Lee submitted a resolution to the Continental Congress stating that "these United Colonies are, and of right ought to be, free and independent states." Ask: Why did the members of the Continental Congress believe it was necessary to also issue a longer declaration? (*More was required than a simple statement of withdrawal from the British Empire. It also required a statement of causes and principles.*) **L2**

FOCUS

Bellringer

  Before taking roll, project Section Focus Transparency 2-3 or hand out Section Focus Transparency Activity 2-3. Have students answer the questions.

Motivating Activity

Josiah Tucker, an English clergyman, claimed that once the British government was gone, "the Americans will have no center of union among them, and no common interests to pursue." Ask students if they think Tucker was accurate in his description of Americans in the 1780s. **L1**

Vocabulary Precheck

Ask students to define each of the "Key Terms." Have a volunteer consult the dictionary for any unfamiliar words. **L1, LEP**

GLENCOE TECHNOLOGY

⊙ **VIDEODISC**

Focus on Government

|||||||||||| |||||||||

Side 1, Chapter 2

Title: *Lecture Launcher, Government and Our Lives*

Subject: The role of government in providing goods and services

---

The Confederation

Setting the Scene

Section Focus

As the Revolution progressed, American leaders struggled to create a new government. Their first attempt—the Articles of Confederation—did not bring stability to the new nation. America continued to have problems with other nations. Constant bickering occurred among the states, and many groups in society were discontented.

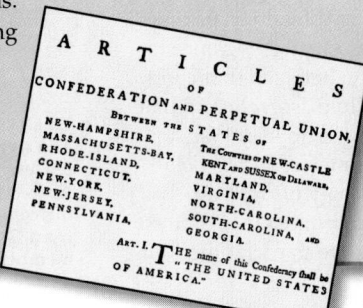

Objectives

After studying this section, you should be able to

★ explain how political control was allocated within the government under the Articles of Confederation.

★ list the strengths and weaknesses of the Articles of Confederation.

Key Terms

bicameral, veto, emancipation, confederation, unicameral, public land, speculator, depression

◀ THE ARTICLES OF CONFEDERATION

*A*s the fighting spread from Massachusetts in 1775, royal governors throughout the colonies watched their authority collapse. At first a few tried to organize Loyalist resistance, but eventually all royal governors abandoned their offices and fled. In May 1776, Congress urged the colonies to replace their colonial charters with new constitutions.

■ New State Governments

Most of the new state constitutions set up state governments similar to the colonial governments they replaced. All states except Pennsylvania and Georgia created **bicameral,** or two-house, legislatures. Members of each house represented geographic districts and, in nearly all the states, were directly elected by the voters.

Major changes were made in the executive branch, however. Many Americans had come to distrust strong executive power. So most state governors were elected to one-year terms by their legislatures and had no power to **veto,** or reject, bills passed.

For the most part, citizenship was restricted to white male property owners. However, because of the ideal of equality, many Americans began to question the institution of slavery. By 1804, every state north of Maryland had provided for the **emancipation,** or freeing, of enslaved African Americans.

In addition, many states upheld religious freedom by ending ties with established churches. In Virginia a bill for religious freedom written by Jefferson proclaimed that:

❝ *. . . [N]o man shall be compelled to frequent or support any religious worship, place, or ministry . . . nor shall otherwise*

Classroom Resources for SECTION 3

Blackline Masters:
- Reproducible Lesson Plan 2-3
- Guided Reading Activity 2-3
- Geography in History Activity 2
- Workbook Activity 2-3
- Reteaching Activity 2-3
- Section Quiz 2-3

Transparencies:
- Section Focus Transparency 2-3

Multimedia:
- Testmaker
- Focus on Government
- Powers of the Congress

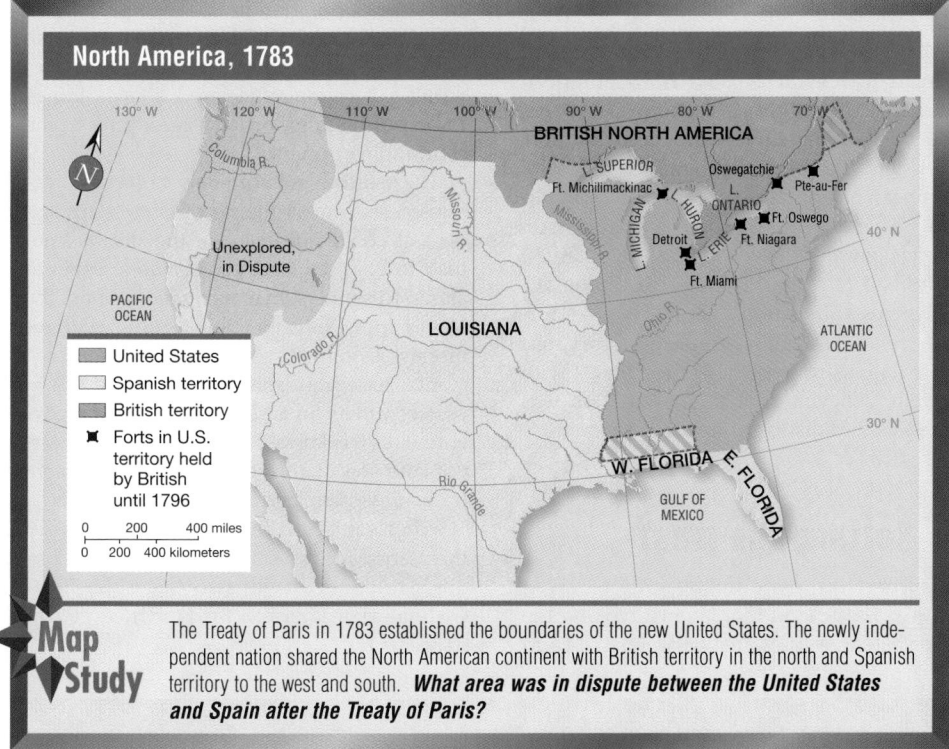

North America, 1783

BRITISH NORTH AMERICA

- United States
- Spanish territory
- British territory
- ✱ Forts in U.S. territory held by British until 1796

| 0 | 200 | 400 miles |
| 0 | 200 | 400 kilometers |

Map Study

The Treaty of Paris in 1783 established the boundaries of the new United States. The newly independent nation shared the North American continent with British territory in the north and Spanish territory to the west and south. *What area was in dispute between the United States and Spain after the Treaty of Paris?*

---

suffer on account of his religious opinions or belief, but that all men shall be free to profess, and by argument to maintain, their opinion in matters of religion. 🙹

Although states discriminated against their residents on the basis of race, sex, religion, and economic standing, most state constitutions included bills of rights that guaranteed trial by jury, freedom of the press, and other "unalienable rights."

■ The Articles of Confederation

America needed a workable central government that would unite the separate states. Instead, the states, reluctant to give up control, formed a **confederation,** a league of independent states, under an agreement called the Articles of Confederation. Congress completed the document in 1777, but not until 1781 did all the states approve it.

The Articles' Provisions

Governing authority was placed in a **unicameral,** or one-house, Congress in which each state had one vote. Congress could wage war and make treaties. It could raise an army and navy, borrow money, establish a postal system, and manage Native American affairs.

Despite these features, the national government under the Articles was too weak to operate effectively. There was not an executive branch to carry out laws, and no federal courts to interpret them. Executive power was divided among several congressional committees. Two important functions were denied to Congress—the power to tax and the power to regulate commerce. Unable to collect taxes, Congress had to depend on the generosity of the states for its income. Between 1781 and 1789, however, the states gave Congress only about one-sixth of the funds it requested. Without money or real power over the states, the Confederation Congress commanded so little respect that its members often did not bother to attend sessions.

CHAPTER 2 A New Nation: 1750–1789 **63**

TEACH
Guided Practice
Analyzing Evidence Have students skim the section to find evidence supporting or contradicting George Washington's view that the Articles of Confederation created a government that was "shadow without substance."

Have them collate their findings in a table with these column headings: Supporting Evidence and Contradicting Evidence. **L1**

Map Study *Using Maps*
Answer: The map indicates that an area between Georgia and Spanish Florida was in dispute.

Map Skills Practice
Have students note the lands owned by Spain and Britain on the North American continent. Ask how each might respond to a weak United States government. *(might encourage those nations to expand at the expense of the new nation)*

Special Needs Activity

Language Deficient Students with language-processing problems may more readily understand and retain new vocabulary if they look at word roots and origins. Write the words *bicameral, unicameral,* and *confederation* on the chalkboard. Ask students to think of words that have similar prefixes, such as *bicycle, bifocal, universe, unique, congregation,* and *converge.* Point out that these common prefixes give clues to the meanings of the words on the chalkboard. **L1**

Food of the Times

A French visitor to the United States was horrified at the meals Americans consumed. They were, he said, "calculated to injure the stomach, the teeth, and the health in general." For dinner, he went on, "they have boiled pastes under the name of puddings... all their sauces, even for roast beef, are melted butter." In fact, early Americans did not eat well-balanced meals. Settlers on the frontier ate mostly meat—wild turkey, duck, rabbit, deer, and bear meat.

Foreign Affairs

After independence, the United States wanted to remain isolated from European alliances. The country's economy, however, depended on trade with Europe. In addition, the United States had ongoing disputes with European nations about North American territory. Therefore, in spite of its wish to remain free of political involvement, the United States had to carry on trade and diplomatic exchanges with Europe. In many cases, foreign relations were complicated because other nations treated the United States with disdain, believing that the new nation was too weak and disunited to last very long.

■ Settling the West

During this period, the term *the West* referred to the land that lay just beyond the Appalachian Mountains. Between 1780 and 1790, the population in this area grew from about 2,000 to 100,000. In agreeing to the Articles of Confederation, eastern states with western lands declared their holdings to be **public land,** or land belonging to the central government.

The central government, however, was powerless to meet the needs of western settlers. It could not dislodge the British from their forts in the North or persuade Spain to allow westerners free navigation along the Mississippi River in the South. Without money, Congress could neither purchase Native American land nor provide troops to protect settlers. In addition to the central government's weakness, westerners resented eastern land **speculators,** or dealers, buying large tracts of western land from the government.

When settlers in Tennessee and Kentucky threatened to leave the United States, Congress responded with two laws: the Land Ordinance of 1785 and the Northwest Ordinance of 1787.

▲ *Daniel Boone Escorting Settlers Through the Cumberland Gap* by George Caleb Bingham, 1851–2 In many of his works, George Caleb Bingham depicts life along the Missouri and Mississippi Rivers. *What problems did western settlers face?*

Sidelight: Secession During the Revolutionary Era

Most people associate secession with the Civil War, but threats of secession abounded both during and after the Revolution. While the fighting raged, Ethan Allen schemed to make Vermont a province of Canada, although he may have been trying to force Congress to recognize Vermont as a separate state, rather than a territory of New York. At the same time, James Wilkinson, a Revolutionary officer working secretly for Spain, tried to annex Kentucky to Spain. Although these schemes came to nothing, they illustrate the deep divisions that existed in the Revolutionary era.

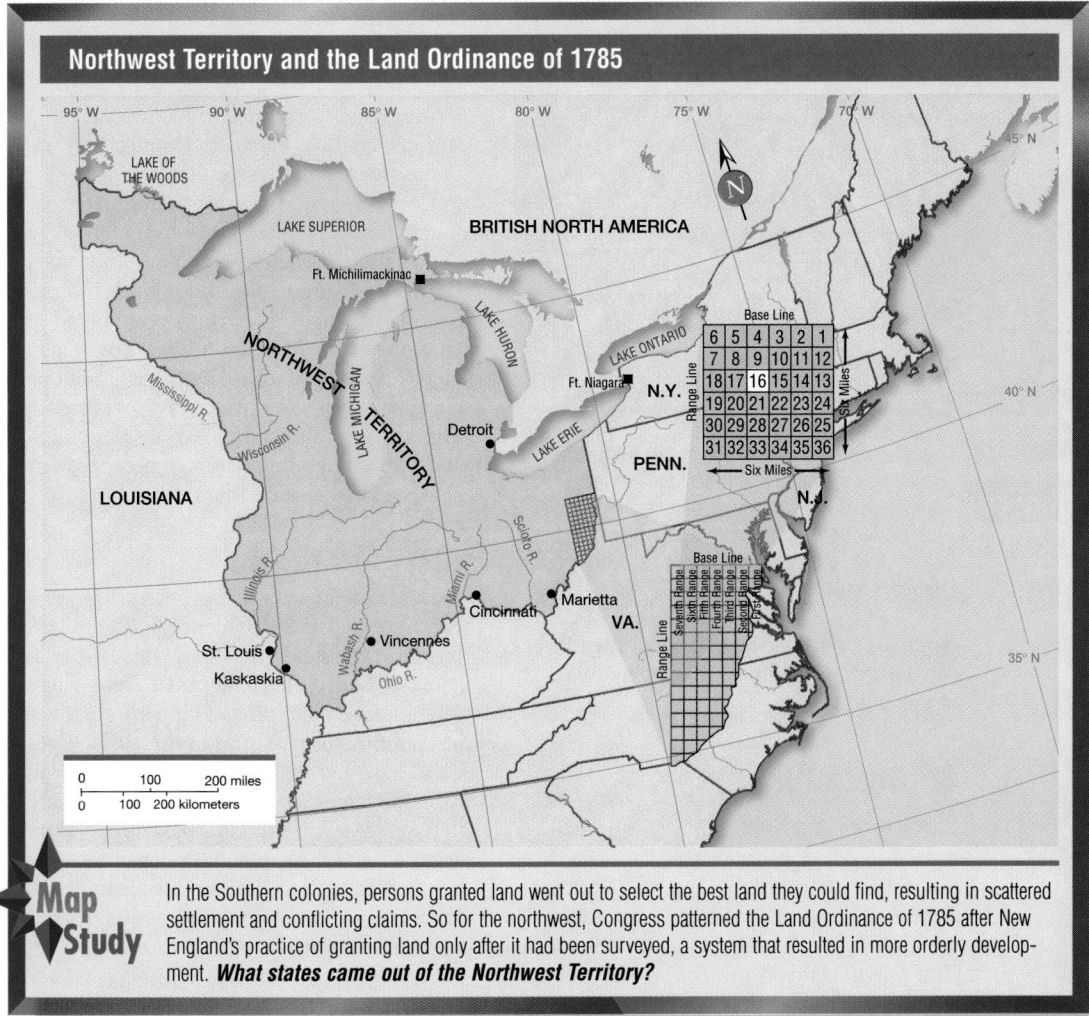

Northwest Territory and the Land Ordinance of 1785

Map Study

In the Southern colonies, persons granted land went out to select the best land they could find, resulting in scattered settlement and conflicting claims. So for the northwest, Congress patterned the Land Ordinance of 1785 after New England's practice of granting land only after it had been surveyed, a system that resulted in more orderly development. **What states came out of the Northwest Territory?**

Land Ordinance of 1785

The Land Ordinance of 1785 provided an orderly method for settling public land north of the Ohio River. The land would be surveyed and divided into townships six miles square. Every township was to contain 36 sections of one square mile, 640 acres each. Proceeds from the sale of Section 16 in each township had to be used to establish public schools. The land would sell for $1 per acre. To attract land speculators, the law required that buyers take at least one whole section. Speculators could divide their sections into smaller rectangular tracts and sell them to settlers at a profit.

Northwest Ordinance of 1787

To provide for a strong government, Congress passed the Northwest Ordinance of 1787. The region bounded by the Ohio River, the Great Lakes, and the Mississippi River was to be divided into three to five territories. Whenever 5,000 adult male citizens settled in a territory, they could set up a territorial government with an elected legislature.

The national government appointed and paid judges and a territorial governor. When the population of a territory reached 60,000, its people could organize as a state and apply for admission to the Union. The

---

Critical Thinking Activity

Supporting Generalizations Present this generalization to students: Despite the long struggle to break free of Britain, most Americans after the Revolutionary War continued to think of themselves either as individuals or as inhabitants of states, not as members of a nation. Ask students to list at least four facts that support this generalization, as well as any facts they have read or can think of that may offer a counterargument. **L3**

Independent Practice

Supporting an Opinion
Have students write a persuasive essay detailing their opinions of Daniel Shays's activities. Remind students that they need to include evidence to support their opinions. They may need to research the following topics: the conditions of debtors' prisons of the time, the kinds of people who sympathized with Shays, and how the weak Confederation contributed to Shays's Rebellion. **L3**

Assign Guided Reading Activity 2-3.

Map Study **Using Maps**
Answer: Illinois, Michigan, Indiana, Ohio, Wisconsin

Map Skills Practice
Give students a blank map of the Northwest Territory. Have them draw in the boundaries of the states that were part of the territory.

Assign Geography in History Activity 2.

ABCNEWS INTERACTIVE™

VIDEODISC
Powers of the Congress

Title: *Articles of Confederation*
Side 1, Chapter 4
Subject: Reading of the Preamble to the Articles of Confederation

65

 **Visualizing** **History** After his rebellion failed, Shays fled to Vermont. Later pardoned, he slipped from public view. He lived another 37 years, long enough to see most of his demands enacted by the state legislature. **Answer to Caption:** were being imprisoned or losing land because they could not pay debts

ASSESS

Check Understanding
Assign Section 3 Review as homework or an in-class activity.

Evaluate
Assign Section Quiz 2-3 or use the Testmaker to create a customized quiz.

Reteach
Have students complete Reteaching Activity 2-3.

Enrich
Suggest that students research life in the West and write an essay comparing their findings to the romantic view of the frontier held by many Americans.

CLOSE
Have students summarize this section by explaining why the new United States might have to form a government different from that created by the Articles of Confederation.

Visualizing **History** ▲ SHAYS'S REBELLION Some states printed so much paper money that it became virtually worthless. Jacobb Shattucks and Daniel Shays led the farmers' rebellion in western Massachusetts. *What grievances did these rebelling farmers have?*

Northwest Ordinance also guaranteed personal freedoms and prohibited slavery north of the Ohio River.

■ State Disputes

While the Confederation Congress was providing for stability in the West, the eastern states engaged in disputes with one another. These difficulties resulted from the postwar **depression**—or economic slowdown—and from the weak central government.

Boundary and Tax Disputes

Conflicts erupted as states engaged in boundary disputes. Parts of present-day Vermont were claimed by other states. A serious conflict between Connecticut and Pennsylvania almost resulted in war.

Congress was powerless to regulate commerce, so each state passed laws taxing goods from its neighbors. New York taxed firewood from Connecticut and cabbage from New Jersey. New Jersey retaliated by charging New Yorkers high fees for using a New Jersey lighthouse. Without a national currency, each state printed its own money. The notes' values differed from state to state, and they often were not accepted outside the state issuing them.

Shays's Rebellion

In Massachusetts, the economic situation became explosive. Unable to pay their debts, farmers in western Massachusetts were jailed or had property seized by the courts. These farmers felt the new government was just another form of tyranny. In late 1786 and early 1787, led by former Continental Army captain Daniel Shays, they closed the courts in two Massachusetts counties, stopped land seizures, and took over a local arsenal. Only through donations was Massachusetts able to raise a militia force to defeat Shays's ragtag band. Although defeated, the rebellion caused great alarm among people who believed in orderly government.

Section 3 ★ Review

Checking for Understanding

1. **Identify** Articles of Confederation, Confederation Congress.

2. **Define** bicameral, veto, emancipation, confederation, unicameral, public land, speculator, depression.

3. **Describe** the positive and negative features of the Articles of Confederation.

4. **Specify** the reasons for the rebellion led by Daniel Shays.

Critical Thinking

5. **Expressing Viewpoints** Imagine that you live in the new United States after the Revolution. Based on your sex, race, and religion, tell to what extent the Revolution has brought about equality for you.

ACTIVITY

6. Create a political cartoon that illustrates one of the weaknesses of the Articles of Confederation.

Answers to SECTION 3 REVIEW

1. Articles of Confederation, 63; Confederation Congress, 63
2. All vocabulary words are defined in the Glossary.
3. positive: central government with limited powers, equal voting power among the states. Negative: weakened central government, no executive branch, no federal courts, no power to tax or regulate commerce
4. Indebted farmers were jailed or had property seized by the courts.
5. Answers will vary depending on sex, race, and religion. Accept all reasonable statements.
6. Cartoons will vary but should illustrate student understanding of a weakness of the government.

★★★★★★★★★★★★★★★★★★★★★★★★★★★★

The Constitution

Setting the Scene

Section Focus

Some Americans became convinced that the Articles of Confederation were an inadequate framework for government. At a convention to address this problem, a new constitution was drawn up. Acceptance of the new government by the public, however, was not assured.

Objectives

After studying this section, you should be able to

★ explain the arguments for and against the new constitution.

★ explain how the Constitution corrected the weaknesses of the Confederation government.

Key Terms

ratification, federalism, amendment

▲ SURVEYOR'S TOOLS, EIGHTEENTH CENTURY

A fter the war, George Washington had retired to Mount Vernon, his Virginia estate on the Potomac River. But his concern about the nation's problems moved him to action once again. In 1785 he invited representatives of Virginia and Maryland to Mount Vernon to discuss their differences. The meeting's success inspired Maryland and Virginia to invite all the states to meet at Annapolis, Maryland, to discuss common problems.

When the Annapolis Convention met in September 1786, delegates from only five states were present, so they could do little. Included in this group, however, was Alexander Hamilton of New York, an outspoken supporter of a strong national government. Hamilton persuaded the delegates to propose another convention. Its purpose would be to regulate commerce and to propose measures making the national government more effective.

The Philadelphia Convention

Congress responded by calling a meeting of the states in Philadelphia, "for the sole and express purpose of revising the Articles of Confederation." The date set for the Convention was May 14, 1787, but it was May 24 before enough delegates arrived to do business. Eventually 12 of the 13 states were represented. Only Rhode Island was not represented.

Assembling the Delegates

The 55 delegates at the convention included many of the most able political leaders in the United States. More than half had sat in the Continental Congress and so had seen for themselves the unhappy consequences of a weak central government. Benjamin Franklin, the oldest delegate at 81,

CHAPTER 2 A New Nation: 1750–1789   **67**

LESSON PLAN
SECTION 4, 67–71

FOCUS
Bellringer

Before taking roll, project Section Focus Transparency 2-4 or hand out Section Focus Transparency Activity 2-4. Have students answer the questions.

Motivating Activity

Write the word *compromise* on the chalkboard and ask students to define it in their own words. Encourage students to look up the word in a dictionary and a thesaurus. Ask them to think of a time when they compromised. What did they give up? What did they gain? How did the agreement they finally reached differ from their initial idea? **L2**

Vocabulary Precheck

Ask students to define each of the "Key Terms." Have a volunteer consult the dictionary for any unfamiliar words. **L1, LEP**

Classroom Resources for SECTION 4

Blackline Masters:
- Reproducible Lesson Plan 2-4
- Guided Reading Activity 2-4
- Critical Thinking Skills Activity 2
- Cooperative Learning Activity 2

- Enrichment Activity 2
- Workbook Activity 2-4
- Reteaching Activity 2-4
- Section Quiz 2-4

Transparencies:
- Section Focus Transparency 2-4

Multimedia:
- Focus on Government
- Testmaker

TEACH
Guided Practice
Debating Have students act as the delegates to the Convention and argue the controversial issue of the executive branch. Volunteers should speak for each of the positions— group executive, individual executive, how chosen, and what length of term. Urge students to use historical events to buttress their positions, for example, fear of monarchy, distrust of common people, and so on. **L3**

Visualizing
History Jefferson's writings reflected careful reading and study. His enormous library later became the basis of the Library of Congress. Between 1785 and 1789, Jefferson shipped nearly 200 volumes to his good friend James Madison. These books—mostly works on political theory—had a profound impact on Madison's thinking about a new government for the United States.
Answer to Caption: a compromise dealing with representation in Congress

Visualizing History

▲ THE PHILADELPHIA CONVENTION Several important leaders of the Revolution did not attend the Philadelphia Convention. Thomas Jefferson (above) was serving as minister to France, and Massachusetts did not send Samuel Adams or John Hancock. Despite the absence of such notables, the gathering at Philadelphia brought together one of the greatest combinations of intelligence, knowledge, and ability in American history. *What was the "Great Compromise"?*

was in poor health and did not attend regularly. Washington was elected to preside over the proceedings, so, like Franklin, his participation in the discussions was limited. They were the best-known Americans of their time and their presence gave the convention great prestige.

The Virginia Plan

James Madison, a 36-year-old Virginian, was the first delegate to arrive at the convention, and he was the most prepared. He came to Philadelphia with a draft of a completely new framework of government. Virginia governor Edmund Randolph immediately presented Madison's proposal, known as the Virginia Plan. This document became the basis for discussion in the convention; it is the foundation for the Constitution of the United States.

■ Conflicting Plans

Almost all delegates at the convention agreed that the Articles were hopelessly weak, but there were two serious conflicts that proved difficult to resolve. Differences developed between large states and small states over representation in Congress and between northern and southern states over economic issues and the institution of slavery.

Representation

The dispute between large and small states nearly broke up the convention. The large states demanded that each state be represented by population in the bicameral Congress Madison had proposed. By what possible right, they asked, should Delaware's 59,000 people have equality with Virginia's 692,000? The small states insisted that they would never give up the equal power they enjoyed under the Articles of Confederation to be swallowed up by the large states. William Paterson of New Jersey presented an alternative proposal, known as the New Jersey Plan, which would have merely strengthened the Articles of Confederation.

Disagreement also arose over the structure of the new government. Large-state delegates generally favored Madison's plan for a national government with separate executive, legislative, and judicial branches and with the states subordinate to the national government. Most small-state delegates supported the New Jersey Plan, which continued the Confederation and left the states supreme.

For two weeks, bitter debate raged over these differences. The deadlock was finally broken when the delegates took a day off to celebrate the Fourth of July. During the recess, a committee worked out what became known as the "Great Compromise." According to this agreement, state representation in the lower house of Congress would be based on population; in the upper house each state would have an equal vote. The delegates' ability to resolve this dispute increased their confidence in compromise as the key to a successful convention.

Cultural Perspectives

The Iroquois and Unification The Iroquois leader Canassatego first suggested a federal model to unify the colonies as early as 1744. Some 43 years later, the Constitutional Convention incorporated elements of the League of the Iroquois—which had united six Native American nations—and its constitution, the Great Law of Peace. Encourage interested students to research the League of the Iroquois and report their findings to the class.

Economic Interests

A dispute arose between the commercial interests of the North and the plantation interests of the South. Southerners wanted to count slaves to determine representation to Congress but not for direct taxation. The North wanted to count slaves for taxation but not for representation. A "three-fifths compromise" established that five slaves would be equal to three free persons for both representation and taxation.

South Carolina and Georgia, afraid that a strong national government might act against slavery, insisted that the Constitution forbid interference with the slave trade. The delegates agreed that for 20 years the national government would not prevent the importation of slaves nor charge an import duty of more than ten dollars a head.

Compromises Yield a New Government

These compromises allowed the delegates to complete their two essential tasks: to give the national government more power and to provide a framework for a workable government. The delegates granted to the central government the powers it had needed most under the Articles of Confederation. The new government could levy and collect taxes, provided such taxes were "uniform throughout the United States." It could regulate commerce with foreign nations and between the states. Thus it could write and enforce commercial treaties that would increase foreign trade, and it could keep trade among the states free of barriers. It could also coin money and regulate its value, so there could be a national standard of money instead of state currency with different values.

The Executive Branch

Although the greatest disputes at the convention were over the structure and powers of the legislative branch, the delegates also disagreed about the executive branch. Everyone at the convention agreed on the need for an executive branch to operate the government, but some delegates favored a group executive, so that no one individual could become too powerful. The executive committees of the Confederation Congress had not worked out well, and Hamilton's proposal for a single executive chosen by Congress for life was too reminiscent of monarchy. In the final weeks of the convention, two more compromises were achieved. A single executive would serve a four-year term. This person would be chosen not directly by the people but indirectly by special electors named by the legislature of each state.

The Judicial Branch

As the long hot summer drew to a close, the exhausted delegates merely roughed out the framework of the judicial branch. In so doing, they created only a Supreme Court and empowered the new government to create "such inferior Courts as the Congress may from time to time ordain and establish."

Their work concluded, the delegates reviewed their efforts. No one was completely happy with the final plan, but most

Visualizing **History** ▲ JAMES MADISON As one of the delegates from Virginia, James Madison participated in the lengthy, often heated debates that created a foundation of government for the United States. *What other contributions did Madison make to the Constitution?*

 **CURRICULUM CONNECTION**

Technology Modern technology has helped preserve the Constitution. It is scanned by electronic scanners frequently to detect any minor changes in the ink or parchment. These periodic measurements enable curators to detect if any deterioration has taken place that is invisible to the human eye.

Visualizing **History** James Madison has been called the "master builder of the Constitution" because of his efforts to bring about compromise and his role in persuading fellow Virginians to accept the document. Discuss the skills required to help two sides reach a compromise. **Answer to Caption:** author of the Virginia Plan

GLENCOE TECHNOLOGY

 VIDEODISC

Focus on Government

Side 1, Chapter 3
Title: *Lecture Launcher: The Creation of the Federal Government*
Subject: How governmental standards develop and evolve

Cooperative Learning Activity

Analyzing Alternatives Have students imagine that they represent groups not included at the Constitutional Convention in Philadelphia (women, Native Americans, African Americans, men who did not own property). How might they react to the decisions made at the convention? Have students pair up and discuss their responses. Then ask students to share their findings with the class. **L2, L3**

📁 For additional practice, assign Cooperative Learning Activity 2.

Independent Practice
Recognizing Ideologies
have students paraphrase the formal language of the late 1700s by putting the Preamble to the Constitution in their own words.
L1

 Assign Guided Reading Activity 2-4.

Visualizing History The United States Constitution is the oldest written national constitution in the world. Its great influence on other constitutions comes from the fact that its endurance is remarkable. Although the original signers provided for change in the Constitution, they did not believe that its fundamental principles should be altered. This has not always been the case in other countries. For example, Mexico has had several constitutions since its independence in 1824. **Answer to Caption:** nine

ASSESS
Check Understanding
Assign Section 4 Review as homework or an in-class activity.

Evaluate
 Assign Section Quiz 2-4 or use the Testmaker to create a customized quiz.

Visualizing History

▲ CELEBRATION Ratification of the Constitution set off a wave of celebration. *How many states had to ratify the Constitution for it to become law?*

agreed it was a vast improvement on the Articles. Madison recorded the reaction of Benjamin Franklin:

> ❝ *Doctor Franklin, looking toward the President's chair, at the back of which a rising sun happened to be painted . . . "I have," said he, "often and often in the course of the Session . . . looked at that [sun] behind the President without being able to tell whether it was rising or setting; but now, at length I have the happiness to know it is a rising and not a setting Sun.* ❞

■ The Ratification Struggle

On September 17, 1787, after four months of work, the delegates to the Constitutional Convention gathered one last time to sign their work. Of the 55 who had come to Philadelphia that spring, 42 were still on hand, and all but 3 agreed to sign the document.

The Framers of the Constitution anticipated that **ratification,** or approval, of the document would be difficult. Rhode Island, which had boycotted the convention, certainly would not approve. So it seemed foolish to insist on the unanimous approval required to amend the Articles. Instead, the Constitution provided that "the ratification of nine States shall be sufficient for the establishment of this Constitution."

The Constitution Opposed

To get even nine states to ratify the Constitution was no small task. Some states objected to surrendering their power and independence to the national government. Nor were supporters of states' rights pleased that the new Constitution bypassed state governments in the ratification process. Ratification was to be decided by special conventions to be called in each state, a process implementing the idea expressed in the Declaration of Indepedence that governments "derive their just powers from the consent of the governed."

Even among the "governed," however, opposition was strong. Debtors and paper-money advocates were opposed to any plan forcing full payment of debts and restoring sound currency. There was certainly suspicion of a powerful central government. Why revolt from Great Britain, people asked, simply to fall under a new kind of tyranny? Popular leaders such as John Hancock, Samuel Adams, and Patrick Henry opposed it.

Support Organized

Those who favored the new plan of government called themselves "Federalists." They took this name to emphasize that the Constitution was based on the principle of **federalism,** a system in which power is divided between a central government and regional governments, and to remind Americans that the states would retain many of their powers. Of course, those who opposed the Constitution were "Federalists" too, because the league of states created by the Articles also was based on federalism. The real issue was whether the national govern-

---

Critical Thinking Activity

Analyzing Issues Delegates to the Constitutional Convention compromised on several issues. Ask students to research an issue currently being debated in Congress. Have them explain the issue and the positions of the opposing sides. Ask students to suggest ways that the two sides might come to an agreement. Discuss why compromise continues to be important to a democratic government. **L3**

 For additional practice in using critical thinking skills, assign Critical Thinking Skills Activity 2.

ment or state governments would be supreme. By taking the name "Federalists," however, the supporters of the Constitution caused their opponents to be tagged with the negative label "Anti-Federalists."

Although the two sides were almost equally divided, several factors worked against the Anti-Federalists. Their campaign was a negative one. They attacked almost everything about the Constitution and complained that it failed to protect basic liberties such as freedom of speech and religion. But the Anti-Federalists had nothing to offer in its place.

The Federalists, on the other hand, presented a definite program to meet the difficulties facing the nation. They promised that if the Constitution was ratified, **amendments,** or additions and changes, would be made to provide a Bill of Rights to protect the people.

The Federalists also made better use of communications. They were supported by most of the nation's newspapers. They presented their case more convincingly in sermons, pamphlets, and debates in state conventions.

The Federalists' campaign for ratification produced one of the finest pieces of political writing in the history of the world, *The Federalist*—a collection of 85 essays written by Hamilton, Madison, and John Jay. Originally published in the *New York Journal,* the essays explained in detail the importance of the Constitution to the success of the nation.

The Constitution Is Ratified

The Federalists succeeded in getting the Constitution ratified not merely because they were good speakers and writers, but because they were politically shrewd. In the states where strong opposition existed, the Federalists were able to outmaneuver their opponents.

In Pennsylvania, the Federalists called the election for the state's ratifying convention before the Anti-Federalists had an opportunity to organize. In Massachusetts, the Federalists used influential Anti-Federalist leader John Hancock to gain support for the Constitution. They suggested that if the Constitution were ratified, Hancock could be the first President of the United States.

In New York, two-thirds of the State Convention were Anti-Federalists. But the persuasiveness of John Jay and the news that 10 states had already ratified the Constitution convinced enough Anti-Federalists to change sides so that New York became the "eleventh pillar" of the new federal roof.

The vote in several key states—Massachusetts, Virginia, and New York—was extremely close. By July 1788, however, all the states except Rhode Island and North Carolina had ratified, and preparations were made to launch the new government without them.

Reteach
Ask each student to write ten interesting questions on this section's content. Use the questions to play Historical Pursuit.

📁 Have students complete Reteaching Activity 2-4.

📁 Assign Workbook Activity 2-4.

Enrich
Have students read selections from *The Federalist*. Ask them to prepare an oral report to the class on a specific essay. Students' reports should answer the following questions: When was it written? Which part of the Constitution did it speak to? What was the main idea?

📁 Assign Enrichment Activity 2.

CLOSE
Write the chapter concepts—political control, central authority—on the chalkboard. Ask students to give examples of how each concept is exemplified in the chapter content.

Section 4 ★ Review

Checking for Understanding
1. **Identify** Philadelphia Convention, Virginia Plan, Federalists, Anti-Federalists.

2. **Define** ratification, federalism, amendment.

3. **Detail** the key features of the Virginia and New Jersey Plans.

4. **Describe** the key compromises that were made in the Constitution concerning representation, slavery, and the executive branch.

5. **Distinguish** between the positions of the Federalists and the Anti-Federalists.

Critical Thinking
6. **Making Inferences** Why would it have been considered significant when people such as John Hancock, Samuel Adams, and Patrick Henry opposed the new Constitution?

ACTIVITY
7. Find photographs of buildings, people, or actions that illustrate the concept of a living Constitution. Write captions for each image that explain how illustrations represent this concept.

CHAPTER 2 A New Nation: 1750–1789 **71**

Answers to SECTION 4 REVIEW

1. Philadelphia Convention, 67; Virginia Plan, 68; Federalists, 70; Anti-Federalists, 71
2. All vocabulary words are defined in the Glossary.
3. The Virginia Plan called for a supreme national government with separate branches. The New Jersey Plan continued the Confederation and left the states supreme.
4. represented in lower house based on population; equal vote in upper house; five enslaved persons equal to three free persons for taxation and representation; single executive would serve a four-year term
5. Federalists favored constitutional government, Anti-Federalists attacked constitutional plan.
6. Their opposition could be interpreted as saying the Constitution betrayed the ideals of the Revolution.
7. Captions should indicate how they reflect the concept of a living Constitution.

Using Key Vocabulary

Sentences should indicate definitions.

Reviewing Facts

1. Answers may include: Stamp Act, quartering of soldiers, Stamp Act Congress, Boston Tea Party, Intolerable Acts, First Continental Congress, Lexington and Concord.
2. Stamp Act Congress—organized boycott; Sons and Daughters of Liberty—boycott
3. Both plans involved the multidirectional movement of forces, but the 1777 plan involved only land forces, whereas the 1780 plan involved land and naval forces.
4. raised money, ran farms and businesses, served as secret agents and soldiers
5. Answers include those relating to the weak central government, relations with foreign countries, trade, western territories, relations between the states.
6. representation, structure of the national

Using Vocabulary

Each of the following terms has a meaning that relates to government. Find the definition of each word and then write a sentence in which you give an example of its meaning.

> direct tax
> treason
> bicameral
> veto
> federalism
> amendment

Reviewing Facts

1. **Identify** the incidents that became turning points in the relationship between the American colonies and Britain.
2. **List** the organizations that came into being in the colonies to protest British tax laws and describe the ways in which the colonists defied those laws.
3. **Compare** the plan the British devised to win the Revolutionary War with that of the American and French, noting similarities and differences.
4. **Explain** the contributions and achievements made by women to the Revolutionary war effort.
5. **Describe** the problems faced by the United States under the Articles of Confederation.
6. **Identify** the disagreements that divided the delegates at the Constitutional Convention.
7. **Detail** why *The Federalist* helped win public support for the new Constitution.

Understanding Concepts

Civil Rights and Liberties

1. When the colonists refused to pay the taxes imposed by Parliament, the crown took measures to force obedience. List these measures and tell what effect they had on British-American relations.

2. Jefferson turned to natural rights and the contract theory of government when he was writing the Declaration of Independence. Explain why he used these particular concepts.

Authority

3. Propose possible reasons why a distrust of strong central authority after the Revolutionary War gradually gave way to its acceptance at the Constitutional Convention.

Critical Thinking

1. **Identifying Alternatives** Historians argue whether any war is inevitable. How could war between Britain and the American colonies have been avoided?
2. **Linking Past and Present** Detail the relationship you see between the theory of government as outlined in the Declaration of Independence and political changes that have occurred in eastern Europe in recent years.
3. **Analyzing Illustrations** Study the illustration on this page and answer the questions that follow.
   a. What two groups are shown in the painting?
   b. What are each of the two groups doing?

▲ **TRANSPORTING TOBACCO**

government, and its relation to the states, way in which enslaved persons were to be counted, slave trade, regulating commerce, executive
7. offered explanations why a strong, viable constitution was essential.

Understanding Concepts

1. Sugar Act—placed import duty on sugar; Stamp Act—placed duties on documents, wills, newspapers, and so on; Townshend Acts—placed import duties on tea, paper, glass, paint

2. Jefferson made use of these terms because others had employed them to justify overthrow of monarchy.
3. memory of British tyranny was receding and the new union required strong authority

c. Does the artist give the work a central focus?

d. What clues in the painting suggest a particular period of time or era? Explain.

History and Geography

Lexington and Concord

Study the information on the map. Then answer the questions that follow.

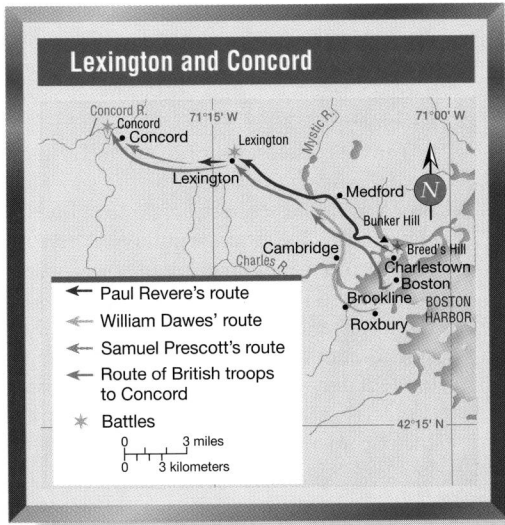

Lexington and Concord

← Paul Revere's route
← William Dawes' route
← Samuel Prescott's route
← Route of British troops to Concord
✳ Battles

1. **Movement** In which direction did the British troops move?

2. **Movement** Which of the Patriots reached Concord?

3. **Place** What battle sites are shown on the map?

4. **Location** Why was Boston an important strategic site for the Americans?

Cooperative Learning **Interdisciplinary Activity: Citizenship**

In order for people to operate effectively in a free society, individuals must give up some personal freedoms and agree to live by rules that operate in the best interests of all citizens. Work in a group of four on the following activity. Imagine that your group is being sent to the moon in order to establish a colony there. Together, write a constitution by which you agree to be governed while you are living on the moon. Decide which portions of the United States Constitution will work for your new situation and the changes that will need to be made to serve the best interests of your group.

Practicing Skills

Identifying Alternatives

Suppose you are an American colonist who has to decide whether to join the Sons or Daughters of Liberty.

1. What three questions might you ask about the organization?

2. What alternatives do you have besides joining?

3. What are the positive and negative consequences of each alternative?

4. Once you have made your decision, write an editorial expressing your viewpoint about joining the organization.

Writing ABOUT History

Using Your Journal

Review your notes on contributions made by women, African Americans, and Native Americans. What did these groups hope to gain by joining the fight for equality in the Revolutionary War? Write a paragraph explaining the outcomes.

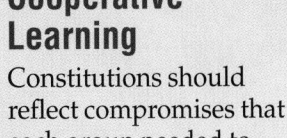

Cooperative Learning

Constitutions should reflect compromises that each group needed to make to arrive at a working Constitution.

Practicing Skills

1. Questions should be such that will gather information to evaluate the alternatives.

2. Answers include giving supplies or funds.

3. Students should demonstrate reasoned judgment in their responses.

4. Editorials should reflect that students have gathered information that evaluated their alternatives and enabled them to make an informed decision.

Writing ABOUT History *Using Your Journal*

Have students share their paragraphs and discuss their conclusions.

? *Chapter Bonus* Test Question

Ask students: During the Constitutional Convention, Benjamin Franklin observed a sun painted on the President's chair and wondered whether it was a rising or setting sun. As the convention ended, he was convinced it was a rising sun. Write a sentence explaining why. (*The Constitution established a government that would help the nation prosper.*)

Critical Thinking

1. Answers may include: Britain could have permitted colonies a say and prohibited direct taxes.

2. Answers include that since the authority of communist governments in Eastern Europe did not rest on consent of their citizens, the people rose against them and set up new governments.

3. **a.** slaveholders and enslaved workers
b. The slaveholders are overseeing the work of enslaved workers.
c. Yes, enslaved workers
d. The clothing suggests late 1700s and early 1800s.

History and Geography

1. generally northwest

2. Samuel Prescott

3. Lexington, Concord, and Breed's Hill

4. Answers include: it was a center of strong opposition to the British; its location on the coast.

Motivating Activity

Have students recall some of the aspects of self-government with which the American colonists had experimented. *(Possible responses: In the 1600s Mayflower Compact and organizations such as Virginia House of Burgesses had given colonists their first experience in self-government. Later, Stamp Act Congress of 1765, Committees of Correspondence [1722–1776], and Continental Congresses [1774–1775] were necessitated by colonists' growing dissatisfaction with English domination. Finally, Articles of Confederation and the U.S. Constitution took root, almost 170 years after the first colonial experiment in self-government.)*

Tell students that in this Constitution Handbook they will see how those early experiments shaped the American system of government. **L2**

Using Charts

Answer: the people

Chart Skills Practice

Ask students what the powers granted to the federal government have in common. *(regulate relations between the United States and other nations and relations among the states)*

Constitution Handbook

The entire system of federal government in the United States rests on a single document: the Constitution. It has served as the "supreme law of the land" for more than 200 years, making it the oldest written constitution in the world. Institutions that we take for granted—the Congress, the President, the Supreme Court—were created by the Constitution. Major governmental decisions that are made every day depend upon constitutional authority.

The authors of the Constitution created a strong central government. Article I, Section 8, which has been called the "heart of the Constitution," gave the new Congress various powers not possessed by the Confederation Congress, including the authority to levy taxes and regulate interstate commerce. The power to levy taxes enabled Congress to finance the federal government.

Through its authority over interstate commerce, Congress has enacted laws ranging from prohibitions against racial discrimination to regulations on consumer credit.

The "elastic clause" that appears in Article I, Section 8, says that Congress shall make all laws "necessary and proper" for putting into effect its enumerated powers. Determining what laws are necessary and proper has provided for ongoing debate and controversy over the years, beginning with the debate over the National Bank in 1790.

The Constitution reinforced the idea that the states were to remain sovereign in some matters. Through their authority in common law and criminal law, the state governments were left in control of local affairs. Their separate identities were protected, and their authority in matters not specifically given to the national government was limited only by the rights of the people within each state. The Tenth Amendment assured this basic protection of each state's sovereignty.

Another assurance of state and popular sovereignty is provided by the amending process. Because the Constitution and the states both derive their authority from the people, provisions for changing the Constitution depend upon the will of the people. This careful arrangement has resulted in only 27 amendments. The first 10 were added almost immediately—in 1791—as a Bill of Rights to protect against national government encroachments on individual freedom.

Division of Powers

EXCLUSIVE POWERS GRANTED TO THE FEDERAL GOVERNMENT	CONCURRENT POWERS SHARED BY THE FEDERAL AND STATE GOVERNMENTS	RESERVED POWERS SET ASIDE FOR THE STATES
•Regulate interstate and foreign commerce •Establish an army and navy •Declare war •Coin money •Establish postal system •Establish federal courts •Set standards for weights and measures •Regulate patents and copyrights •Admit new states •Establish laws of citizenship •Pass laws needed to carry out its powers	•Enforce the laws •Borrow money •Lay and collect taxes •Establish courts •Charter banks •Provide for the general welfare	•Regulate intrastate commerce •Conduct elections •Determine voting requirements •Establish local governments •Provide for public safety •Tenth Amendment reserves to the state governments all powers not granted to the federal government or prohibited by the Constitution

Chart Study

When the Constitution was written, the states reserved certain powers. The Constitution gave certain powers and rights to the national government. ***Who retains all other rights?***

Cooperative Learning Activity

Applying Ideas Have students work together to develop a set of five rules for use in the classroom. Offer the following as an example of the type of rule they should develop: During class discussion, students should not talk unless they raise their hands and are recognized by the teacher. Point out that the rules should be acceptable to a two-thirds majority of the class. Also, students should set up some system of adjusting the rules if they prove unworkable. After they have completed the task, ask them to discuss the most difficult problems they faced in establishing the rules. **L1, LEP**

The American System of Checks and Balances

Chart Study

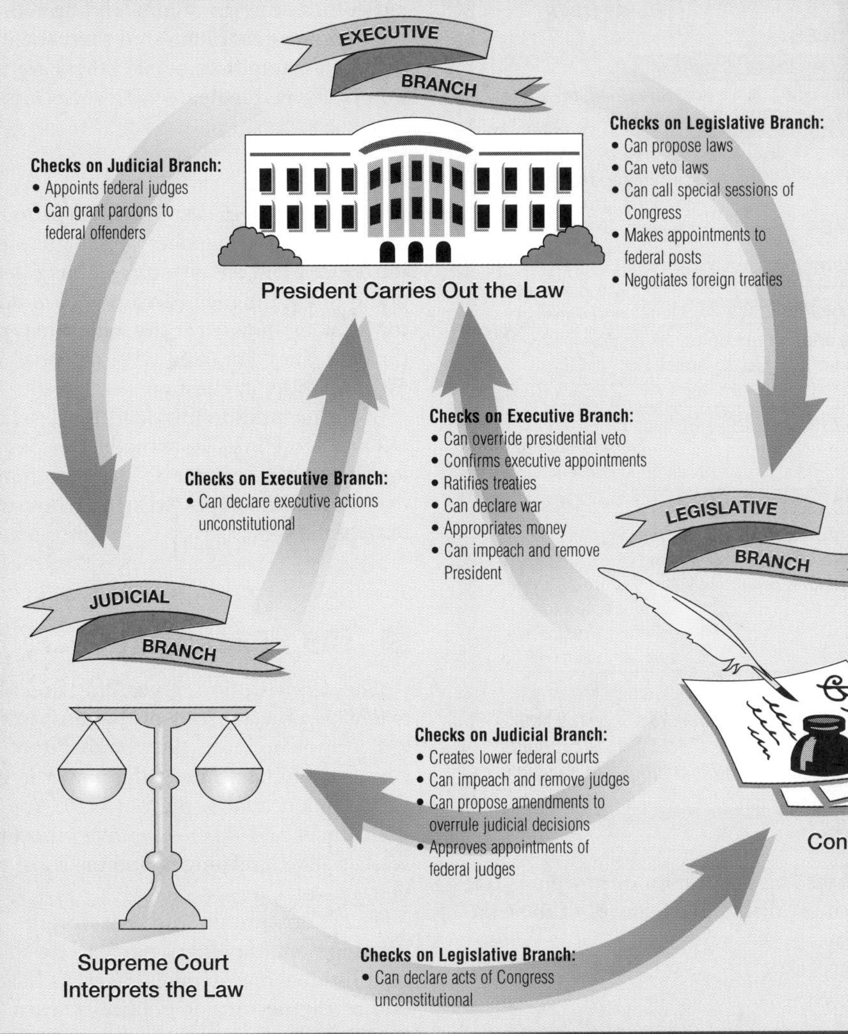

EXECUTIVE BRANCH

President Carries Out the Law

Checks on Judicial Branch:
• Appoints federal judges
• Can grant pardons to federal offenders

Checks on Legislative Branch:
• Can propose laws
• Can veto laws
• Can call special sessions of Congress
• Makes appointments to federal posts
• Negotiates foreign treaties

Checks on Executive Branch:
• Can declare executive actions unconstitutional

Checks on Executive Branch:
• Can override presidential veto
• Confirms executive appointments
• Ratifies treaties
• Can declare war
• Appropriates money
• Can impeach and remove President

JUDICIAL BRANCH

Supreme Court Interprets the Law

Checks on Judicial Branch:
• Creates lower federal courts
• Can impeach and remove judges
• Can propose amendments to overrule judicial decisions
• Approves appointments of federal judges

Checks on Legislative Branch:
• Can declare acts of Congress unconstitutional

LEGISLATIVE BRANCH

Congress Makes the Law

"You must first enable the government to control the governed," wrote Madison, "and in the next place, oblige it to control itself." The control Madison meant is found in the system of checks and balances in the Constitution. *How does the executive branch check the judicial branch?*

■ Congress

The Constitution provided different legislative powers for the Senate and House. The Senate approves treaties and presidential appointments and tries all **impeachment** cases of government officials formally accused of wrongdoing in office; the House originates all revenue bills, and has the power to impeach members of the executive and judicial branches. Legislation must pass both Houses before it can be sent to the President to be signed into law.

Most of the enumerated powers of Congress leave little room for interpretation. When the constitutional authority of Congress seems to conflict with the authority of the President, it is often because of a deliberate effort by the Constitutional Convention to limit the power of government. The framers of the Constitution chose to divide government powers among three separate

Constitution Handbook **75**

TEACH
Guided Practice
Analyzing Information

Point out how each house of Congress has powers denied the other. Then ask students to find newspaper or magazine articles that reflect the differences between these two branches of the legislature. Have them discuss which powers have been at the center of recent debates. **L1, LEP**

Using Charts

Answer: appoints federal judges, grants pardons to federal offenders

Chart Skills Practice

Ask students to explain how the legislative branch checks the judicial branch (*by creating lower federal courts, impeaching and removing judges, proposing amendments to overrule judicial decisions; approving appointment of judges*)

Facts on File

CD-ROM

Landmark Documents in American History: The Constitution

Suggest students prepare an outline of the Constitution in which they list each article and amendment and their topics. Students can keep the outline in their notebooks for future reference.

Critical Thinking Activity

Debate Have the class debate the merits of setting term limits for members of Congress. Supporters may wish to stress such advantages as limiting the powers of incumbency and seniority, whereas opponents may emphasize the advantages of experience. **L2**

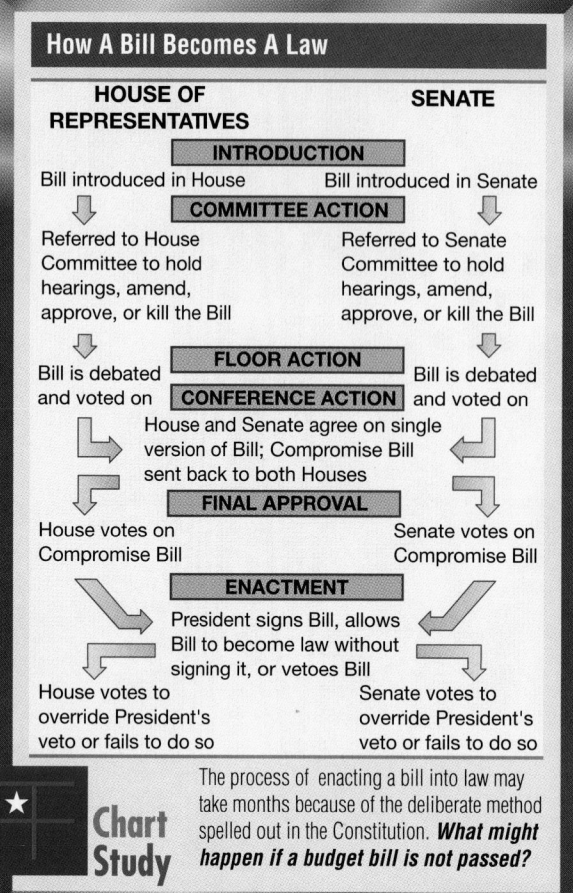

How A Bill Becomes A Law

HOUSE OF REPRESENTATIVES	SENATE
INTRODUCTION	
Bill introduced in House	Bill introduced in Senate
COMMITTEE ACTION	
Referred to House Committee to hold hearings, amend, approve, or kill the Bill	Referred to Senate Committee to hold hearings, amend, approve, or kill the Bill
FLOOR ACTION	
Bill is debated and voted on	Bill is debated and voted on
CONFERENCE ACTION	
House and Senate agree on single version of Bill; Compromise Bill sent back to both Houses	
FINAL APPROVAL	
House votes on Compromise Bill	Senate votes on Compromise Bill
ENACTMENT	
President signs Bill, allows Bill to become law without signing it, or vetoes Bill	
House votes to override President's veto or fails to do so	Senate votes to override President's veto or fails to do so

Chart Study The process of enacting a bill into law may take months because of the deliberate method spelled out in the Constitution. **What might happen if a budget bill is not passed?**

branches. This separation of powers is one of the most distinctive features of the Constitution.

Duties

The federal government is separated into legislative, executive, and judicial branches. These branches, described in the first three articles of the Constitution, are each given separate authority. Under this **separation of powers**, each branch exercises a check on the powers of the other two.

The Constitution describes the duties of the three branches, but it does not detail how those duties are to be carried out. To handle the heavy volume of legislation efficiently, both houses of Congress, from the very beginning, divided into committees.

These smaller units do most of the work of both houses. Each committee deals with particular problems, such as labor, banking, agriculture, foreign affairs, and armed services. Some committees are permanent, or standing committees, while others are temporary, formed to deal with a specific issue.

Legislation

Legislation begins with written proposals called bills. Any member of Congress may introduce a bill on any subject. Long before going to the full membership of each house for a vote, however, the bill must pass through the committee with responsibility for the subject in question.

The Constitution provided for a deliberate and sometimes slow method of passing legislation. One factor is the requirement that the legislation passed by both houses be exactly the same.

■ The Presidency

The Constitution gives the President extensive powers. Four of the most important are as follows: the command of the country's military forces; the power to conduct foreign affairs; the power to appoint the cabinet and other executive officers, as well as all federal judges; and the legislative veto power.

The Constitution did not foresee the development of political parties, one source of additional presidential power. As head of one of the two major political parties, the President can exert pressure for legislation and can give or withhold support for a senator's or representative's reelection.

Presidential power increases during crises involving actual or perceived danger from abroad. It is affected by the tendency of Congress to yield much of its power to the President for the duration of the crisis.

The President, who has access to a vast military and foreign service network, can control information that Congress receives. In addition, Congress, working as a whole or through committees, is inherently less capable of exercising decisive action quickly.

In domestic policy the Constitution clearly gives "the power of the purse" to Congress. Over time, the President has come to dominate many processes of allocating the government's money. The creation of the Bureau of the Budget in 1921 (now the Office of Management and Budget), whose director was appointed by the President, heralded the transfer of major budgetary power out of the hands of Congress.

■ The Courts

The judiciary is only briefly described in the Constitution. Article III provides that there shall be "one Supreme Court" and such lower courts as Congress may establish.

The Court System

The first Congress passed the Judiciary Act of 1789. This law set up the federal court system, the basics of which are still in place today. The federal judiciary may be envisioned as a three-tiered pyramid, with many district courts at the bottom, a smaller number of circuit courts in the middle, and one Supreme Court at the top.

Cases from a district court may be appealed, or taken for review, to the circuit court for the area in which the district court is located. Cases may be appealed to the Supreme Court, which currently consists of nine members: eight associate justices and one Chief Justice. Because the cases that reach them are so complex, the justices must decline to rule upon all but a small fraction of the cases they are asked to hear.

The main purpose of the federal judiciary is to provide a forum for disputes involving federal laws. The most important power of the federal courts, that of **judicial review**, is not stated in the Constitution. This is the power of the Court to decide whether a given law, federal or state, conflicts with the Constitution. If so, the law can be declared unconstitutional and ceases to have effect. This acts as a form of veto power over laws. If the Supreme Court rules a law unconstitutional, the Congress or the states may initiate an amendment to the Constitution.

The Court cannot rule on just any law, but only on those that come before it. In this sense its role is passive; it cannot take the initiative to correct problems that the justices see or hear about, but must wait for others to file lawsuits. The Court also must rely on the President to enforce its rulings.

Unlike Congress and the President, federal judges do not have to face reelection. The Constitution provides that they shall hold office "during good behavior"—which generally means for life or until they choose to resign—and that their salaries may not be reduced. The Framers wanted to protect federal judges from political pressures so they could rule fairly and wisely, without fear of popular hostility. A federal judge can be removed through the difficult process of impeachment by Congress.

■ A Living Document

When the Constitution reached its bicentennial year in 1989, it inspired interest in the significance of the document. Two broadly different views emerged. Some people saw the limitations and problems that the federal government faced and suggested a new constitutional convention to restructure the government to meet today's difficult challenges. Others emphasized the remarkable enduring quality of the Constitution and its basic principles that remain important today.

It is likely that if changes are to be made in basic principles of government, they will come by amendment or interpretation. Amendment, however, has historically been approached with caution. The founders wanted the Constitution to be safe from the passions of the public and political schemes.

The Constitution's adaptability to new circumstances has made it a lasting framework of government. It has permitted, perhaps even encouraged, debate over the proper role of each branch of government, or of government itself. Through the first two centuries of federal government, the Constitution has served to moderate change in government. It has also ably guarded those freedoms that we the people have entrusted it to preserve.

Independent Practice

Conducting an Opinion Poll
Point out that the Supreme Court has ruled that televising court proceedings does not necessarily deny defendants their right to a fair trial. Have the students conduct an opinion poll to determine whether class members favor or oppose television in the courtroom, and why. Post and discuss the results.
L1, LEP

FACT or FICTION?

The President must sign a constitutional amendment before it becomes law.

FICTION: An amendment becomes part of the Constitution on the date when the last state required to ratify it does so.

Did You Know?

The Constitution does not specify any requirements for a Supreme Court justice—not even a law degree. So far, however, all the justices have been lawyers, and the majority have served as judges.

Sidelight: English Common Law

The U.S. judicial system is based in large part on English common law. The latter began to develop in the 1100s, when the rulers of England tried to set up one system of justice for the entire country. The system relied not so much on laws as on decisions of judges. For example, any judge trying a case involving treason would look for precedents—judges' decisions in earlier, similar cases.

The Constitution of the United States

*T*he Constitution of the United States is truly a remarkable document. It was one of the first written constitutions in modern history. The Framers wanted to devise a plan for a strong central government that would unify the country, as well as preserve the ideals of the Declaration of Independence. The document they wrote created a representative legislature, the office of president, a system of courts, and a process for adding amendments. For over 200 years, the flexibility and strength of the Constitution has guided the nation's political leaders. The document has become a symbol of pride and a force for national unity. For easier study of the Constitution, those passages that have been set aside or changed by the adoption of amendments are printed in blue. Also included are explanatory notes that will help clarify the meaning of each article and section.

▲ THE CAPITOL, WASHINGTON, D.C.

Preamble

We, the people of the United States, in Order to form a more perfect Union, establish Justice, insure domestic Tranquility, provide for the common defence, promote the general Welfare, and secure the Blessings of Liberty to ourselves and our Posterity, do ordain and establish this Constitution for the United States of America.

Article I

Section 1

All legislative Powers herein granted shall be vested in a Congress of the United States, which shall consist of a Senate and House of Representatives.

Section 2

1. The House of Representatives shall be composed of Members chosen every second Year by the People of the several States, and the Electors in each State shall have the Qualifications requisite for Electors of the most numerous Branch of the State Legislature.

2. No Person shall be a Representative who shall not have attained to the Age of twenty-five Years, and been seven Years a Citizen of the United States, and who shall not, when elected, be an Inhabitant of that State in which he shall be chosen.

3. Representatives and direct Taxes shall be apportioned among the several states which may be included within this Union, according to the respective Numbers, which shall be determined by adding to the whole Number of free Persons, including those bound to Service for a Term of Years, and excluding Indians not taxed, three-fifths of all other Persons. The actual Enumeration shall be made within three Years after the first Meeting of the Congress of the United States, and within every subsequent Term of ten Years, in such Manner as they shall by Law direct. The Number of Representatives shall not exceed one for every thirty Thousand, but each state shall have at Least one Representative; and until such enumeration shall be made, the State of New Hampshire shall be entitled to chuse three; Massachusetts eight, Rhode Island and Providence Plantations one, Connecticut five, New York six, New Jersey four, Pennsylvania eight, Delaware one, Maryland six, Virginia ten; North Carolina five, South Carolina five, and Georgia three.

4. When vacancies happen in the Representation from any State, the Executive Authority thereof shall issue Writs of Election to fill such Vacancies.

5. The House of Representatives shall chuse their Speaker and other Officers; and shall have the sole Power of Impeachment.

The Preamble introduces the Constitution and sets forth the general purposes for which the government was established. The preamble also declares that the power of the government comes from the people.

The printed text of the document shows the spelling and punctuation of the parchment original.

Article I. The Legislative Branch

Section 1. Congress

The power to make laws is given to a Congress made up of two chambers to represent different interests: the Senate to represent the states; the House to be more responsive to the people's will.

Section 2. House of Representatives

1. Election and Term of Office

"Electors" means voters. Every two years the voters choose new Congress members to serve in the House of Representatives. The Constitution states that each state may specify who can vote. But the 15th, 19th, 24th, and 26th Amendments have established guidelines that all states must follow regarding the right to vote.

2. Qualifications

Representatives must be 25 years old, citizens of the United States for 7 years, and residents of the state they represent.

3. Division of Representatives Among the States

The number of representatives from each state is based on the size of the state's population. Each state is divided into congressional districts, with each district required to be equal in population. Each state is entitled to at least one representative. The number of representatives in the House was set at 435 in 1929. Since then, there has been a reapportionment of seats based on population shifts rather than on addition of seats.

Only three-fifths of a state's slave population was to be counted in determining the number of representatives elected by the state. Native Americans were not counted at all.

The "enumeration" referred to is the census, the population count taken every 10 years since 1790.

4. Vacancies

Vacancies in the House are filled through special elections called by the state's governor.

5. Officers

The speaker is the leader of the majority party in the House and is responsible for choosing the heads of various House committees. "Impeachment" means indictment, or bringing charges against an official.

FOCUS

Motivating Activity

Ask students to read the introduction to the Constitution known as the Preamble. Then ask them to read again the Declaration of Independence on pages 122–123.

Have students discuss the similarities and connections between the Declaration and the Preamble to the Constitution. *(The Constitution was written with the Declaration of Independence in mind. The connection comes out most strongly in the Preamble. Like the Declaration, the Preamble is concerned with liberty, and places responsibility for government in the hands of "We the People.")*

Explain that the Framers of the Constitution were concerned that states as well as individuals should receive fair representation in making the nation's laws. Article I shows how these concerns were finally resolved. **L2**

Did You Know?

Before Congress limited the size of the House of Representatives, it grew from 65 to 435 members. In the beginning, a state elected a representative for every 30,000 persons living there. If that rule were still in effect, the House today would have over 8,000 members!

Cooperative Learning Activity

Analyzing the Amendments Divide the class into four groups. Assign each one a section of Article I—2, 3, 4, or 9—that has been modified by amendment. Have each group explain how, why, and when the change was made. **L2**

Section 3. The Senate

1. Number of Members, Terms of Office, and Voting Procedure

Originally, senators were chosen by the state legislators of their own states. The 17th Amendment changed this, so that senators are now elected directly by the people. There are 100 senators, 2 from each state.

2. Staggered Elections; Vacancies

One-third of the Senate is elected every two years. The terms of the first Senate's membership was staggered: one group served two years, one four, and one six. All senators now serve a six-year term.

The 17th Amendment changed the method of filling vacancies in the Senate.

3. Qualifications

Qualifications for the Senate are more restrictive than those for the House. Senators must be at least 30 years old and they must have been citizens of the United States for at least 9 years. The Framers of the Constitution made the Senate a more elite body in order to produce a further check on the powers of the House of Representatives.

4. President of the Senate

The Vice President's only duty listed in the Constitution is to preside over the Senate. The only real power the Vice President has is to cast the deciding vote when there is a tie. However, modern Presidents have given their Vice Presidents new responsibilities.

5. Other Officers

The Senate selects its other officers, including a presiding officer (president pro tempore) who serves when the Vice President is absent or has become President of the United States.

6. Trial of Impeachments

When trying a case of impeachment brought by the House, the Senate convenes as a court. The Chief Justice of the Supreme Court acts as the presiding judge, and the Senate acts as the jury. A two-thirds vote of the members present is necessary to convict officials under impeachment charges.

7. Penalty for Conviction

If the Senate convicts an official, it may only remove the official from office and prevent that person from holding another federal position. However, the convicted official may still be tried for the same offense in a regular court of law.

Section 4. Elections and Meetings

1. Holding Elections

In 1842 Congress required members of the House to be elected from districts in states having more than one Representative rather than at large. In 1845 it set the first Tuesday after the first Monday in November as the day for selecting presidential electors.

2. Meetings

The 20th Amendment, ratified in 1933, has changed the date of the opening of the regular session of Congress to January 3.

Section 3

1. The Senate of the United States shall be composed of two Senators from each State, chosen by the Legislature thereof; for six Years; and each Senator shall have one Vote.

2. Immediately after they shall be assembled in Consequence of the first Election, they shall be divided as equally as may be into three Classes. The Seats of the Senators of the first Class shall be vacated at the Expiration of the second Year, of the second Class at the Expiration of the fourth Year, and of the third Class at the Expiration of the sixth Year, so that one-third may be chosen every second Year; and if Vacancies happen by Resignations, or otherwise, during the Recess of the Legislature of any State, the Executive thereof may make temporary Appointments until the next Meeting of the Legislature, which shall then fill such Vacancies.

3. No person shall be a Senator who shall not have attained the Age of thirty Years, and been nine Years a Citizen of the United States, and who shall not, when elected, be an Inhabitant of that State in which he shall be chosen.

4. The Vice President of the United States shall be President of the Senate, but shall have no vote, unless they be equally divided.

5. The Senate shall chuse their Officers, and also a President pro tempore, in the absence of the Vice-President or when he shall exercise the Office of the President of the United States.

6. The Senate shall have the sole Power to try all impeachments. When sitting for that purpose they shall be on Oath or Affirmation. When the President of the United States is tried, the Chief Justice shall preside: And no person shall be convicted without the Concurrence of two-thirds of the Members present.

7. Judgment in Cases of Impeachment shall not extend further than to removal from Office, and disqualification to hold and enjoy any Office of Honor, Trust or Profit under the United States: but the Party convicted shall nevertheless be liable and subject to Indictment, Trial, Judgment and Punishment, according to Law.

Section 4

1. The Times, Places, and Manner of holding Elections for Senators and Representatives, shall be prescribed in each state by the Legislature thereof; but the Congress may at any time by Law make or alter such Regulations, except as to the Places of Chusing Senators.

2. The Congress shall assemble at least once in every Year, and such Meeting shall be on the first Monday in December, unless they shall by Law appoint a different Day.

▲ THE WILL OF THE PEOPLE The idea of representative democracy works well when the legislature is responsive to the citizens. **Which chamber was not originally elected by the people?**

Section 5

1. Each House shall be the Judge of the Elections, Returns and Qualifications of its own Members, and a Majority of each shall constitute a Quorum to do Business; but a smaller Number may adjourn from day to day, and may be authorized to compel the Attendance of absent Members, in such Manner, and under such Penalties as each House may provide.

2. Each House may determine the Rules of its Proceedings, punish its Members for disorderly Behaviour, and, with the Concurrence of two-thirds, expel a Member.

3. Each House shall keep a Journal of its Proceedings, and from time to time publish the same, excepting such Parts as may in their Judgment require Secrecy; and the Yeas and Nays of the Members of either House on any question shall, at the desire of one-fifth of those Present, be entered on the Journal.

4. Neither House during the Session of Congress, shall, without the Consent of the other, adjourn for more than three days, nor to any other Place than that in which the two Houses shall be sitting.

Section 6

1. The Senators and Representatives shall receive a Compensation for their Services, to be ascertained by Law, and paid out of the Treasury of the United States. They shall in all Cases, except Treason, Felony and Breach of the Peace be privileged from Arrest during their attendance at the Session of their respective Houses, and in

Section 5. Organization and Rules of Procedure

1. Organization

Until 1969 Congress acted as the sole judge of qualifications of its own members. In that year, the Supreme Court ruled that Congress could not legally exclude victorious candidates who met all the requirements listed in Article I, Section 2.

A "quorum" is the minimum number of members that must be present for the House or Senate to conduct sessions. For a regular House session, a quorum consists of the majority of the House, or 218 of the 435 members.

2. Rules

Each house sets its own rules, can punish its members for disorderly behavior, and can expel a member by a two-thirds vote.

3. Journals

In addition to the journals, a complete official record of everything said on the floor, as well as the roll call votes on all bills or issues, is available in the *Congressional Record*, published daily by the Government Printing Office.

4. Adjournment

Neither house may adjourn for more than three days or move to another location without the approval of the other house.

Section 6. Privileges and Restrictions

1. Pay and Privileges

To strengthen the federal government, the Founders set congressional salaries to be paid by the United States Treasury rather than by members' respective states. Originally, members were paid $6 per day. Salaries for Senators and Representatives are $129,500.

The Constitution of the United States **81**

The Legislative Branch

Independent Practice

Creating a Chart Have students create a chart that categorizes the legislative powers of Congress. Instruct them to list the items under these categories: Monetary, Commerce, Regulatory, Judicial, War, Implied. **L1**

Visualizing History Point out that the Senate was originally intended to resemble the British House of Lords in its separation from popular control. **Answer to Caption:** the Senate

Did You Know?

When the first Congress was called to assemble in New York City, early in March 1789, there were not enough representatives or senators to form a quorum. Only after a month did enough members show up so that Congress could officially convene.

ABCNEWS INTERACTIVE™

VIDEODISC

Powers of the Congress

Side One, Chapter 38
Title: *Powers of the House and Senate*
Subject: Understand the powers of each house

Critical Thinking Activity

Demonstrating Reasoned Judgment Have students state the qualifications for serving in Congress as set forth in the Constitution. Then ask if they can think of any other qualifications that should be applied to members of Congress. For example, should lawmakers have certain legal or technical training? Why or why not? **L1, LEP**

81

The Legislative Branch

Making Comparisons In addition to the enumerated powers, Congress has certain implied powers that are not stated in the Constitution. Instead, they are based on the "necessary and proper" clause. This clause is also known as the "elastic clause." In it, Congress is granted the power to make any laws "necessary and proper" in carrying out its duties. Throughout American history, Supreme Court decisions have expanded the authority of Congress to act under this clause. Have students discuss the advantages and disadvantages of doing so. *(Possible answers: Because it is impossible to list all enumerated powers, the elastic clause provides the flexibility to address changing and unforeseen political and social conditions; the addition of powers might weaken the balance of powers between the branches.)* **L2**

The "immunity" privilege means members cannot be sued or be prosecuted for anything they say in Congress. They cannot be arrested while Congress is in session, except for treason, major crimes, or breaking the peace.

2. Restrictions

"Emoluments" means salaries. The purpose of this clause is to prevent members of Congress from passing laws that would benefit them personally. It also prevents the President from promising them jobs in other branches of the federal government.

Section 7. Passing Laws
1. Revenue Bills

"Revenue" is income raised by the government. The chief source of government revenue is taxes. All tax laws must originate in the House of Representatives. This insures that the branch of Congress which is elected by the people every two years has the major role in determining taxes. This clause does not prevent the Senate from amending tax bills.

2. How Bills Become Laws

A bill may become a law only by passing both houses of Congress and by being signed by the President. If the President disapproves, or vetoes, the bill, it is returned to the house where it originated, along with a written statement of the President's objections. If two-thirds of each house approves the bill after the President has vetoed it, it becomes law. In voting to override a President's veto, the votes of all members of Congress must be recorded in the journals or official records. If the President does not sign or veto a bill within 10 days (excluding Sundays), it becomes law. However, if Congress has adjourned during this 10-day period, the bill does not become law. This is known as a "pocket veto."

---

going to and returning from the same; and for any Speech or Debate in either House, they shall not be questioned in any other place.

2. No Senator or Representative shall, during the Time for which he was elected, be appointed to any civil Office under the Authority of the United States, which shall have been created, or the Emoluments whereof shall have been encreased, during such time; and no Person holding any Office under the United States, shall be a Member of either House during his continuance in Office.

Section 7

1. All Bills for raising Revenue shall originate in the House of Representatives; but the Senate may propose or concur with Amendments as on other bills.

2. Every Bill which shall have passed the House of Representatives and the Senate, shall, before it become a Law, be presented to the President of the United States; If he approve he shall sign it, but if not he shall return it, with his Objections, to that House in which it shall have originated, who shall enter the Objections at large on their Journal, and proceed to reconsider it. If after such Reconsideration two-thirds of that House shall agree to pass the bill, it shall be sent, together with the objections, to the other House, by which it shall likewise be reconsidered, and if approved by two-thirds of that House, it shall become a Law. But in all such Cases the Votes of both Houses shall be determined by Yeas and Nays, and the Names of the Persons voting for and against the Bill shall be entered on the Journal of each House respectively. If any Bill shall not be returned by the President within ten Days (Sundays excepted) after it shall have been presented to him, the Same shall be a Law, in like Manner as if he had signed it, unless the Congress by their Adjournment prevent its Return, in which Case it shall not be a Law.

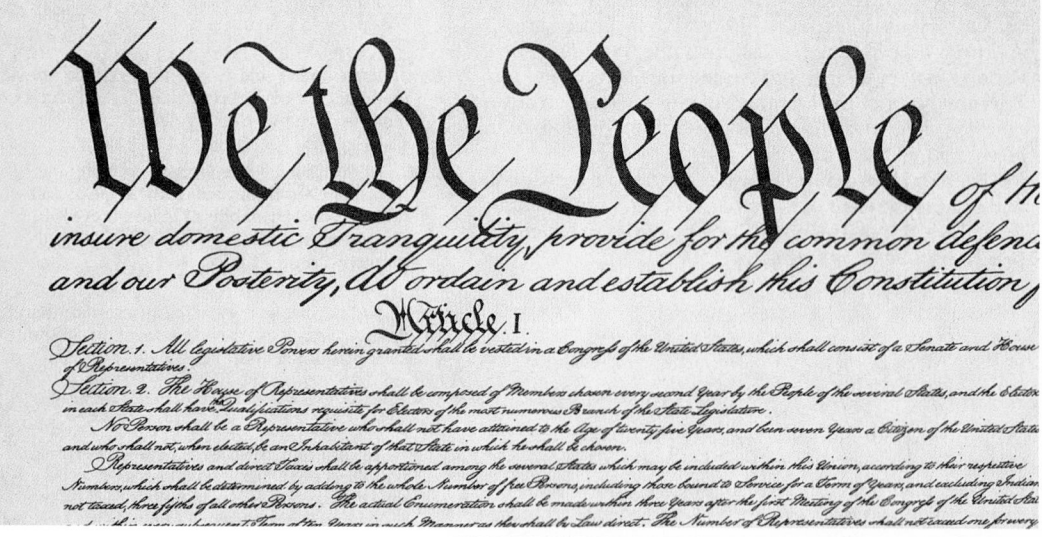

▲ **PREAMBLE OF THE CONSTITUTION**

Sidelight: The Capitol

The Capitol so familiar today—with the huge rotunda dome—was not completed until the 1860s. Today, each house of Congress meets in its own wing of the Capitol. Although many of the furnishings and works of art are the same as in the 1800s, signs of modern technology are everywhere. Roll call votes are counted electronically. In addition, members of both houses have access to computers and other information services. There are even underground tunnels with electric subways connecting many of the office buildings on Capitol Hill.

Visualizing
History

▲ THE WORK OF CONGRESS Although some of the work of the legislature is done on the floor of Congress, most of it is done outside the chambers by committees. Each member of Congress has a staff of legislative assistants and other aides who research issues, draft bills, and organize the member's office. *How does a resolution differ from a bill?*

Analyzing Information
Point out that because of the heavy volume of legislation, both houses of Congress have committees that do much of the work. Each committee deals with a particular issue, such as banking, foreign affairs, or natural resources. Ask students to bring in newspaper or magazine articles that deal with current congressional committees. In each case, ask them to indicate (1) whether the committee is standing or temporary and (2) who is the committee chair. **L2**

3. Every Order, Resolution, or Vote to which the Concurrence of the Senate and House of Representatives may be necessary (except on a question of Adjournment) shall be presented to the President of the United States; and before the Same shall take Effect, shall be approved by him, or, being disapproved by him, shall be repassed by two-thirds of the Senate and House of Representatives, according to the Rules and Limitations prescribed in the case of a Bill.

Section 8
The Congress shall have the Power
1. To lay and collect Taxes, Duties, Imposts and Excises, to pay the Debts and provide for the common Defence and general Welfare of the United States; but all Duties, Imposts and Excises shall be uniform throughout the United States;
2. To borrow money on the credit of the United States;
3. To regulate Commerce with foreign Nations, and among the several States, and with the Indian Tribes;
4. To establish an uniform Rule of Naturalization, and uniform Laws on the subject of Bankruptcies throughout the United States.
5. To coin Money, regulate the Value thereof, and of foreign Coin, and fix the Standard of Weights and Measures;
6. To provide for the Punishment of counterfeiting the Securities and current Coin of the United States;

3. Presidential Approval or Veto
The Framers included this paragraph to prevent Congress from passing joint resolutions instead of bills to avoid the possibility of a presidential veto. A bill is a draft of a proposed law, whereas a resolution is the legislature's formal expression of opinion or intent on a matter.

Section 8. Powers Granted to Congress
1. Revenue
This clause gives Congress the power to raise and spend revenue. Taxes must be levied at the same rate throughout the nation.
2. Borrowing
The federal government borrows money by issuing bonds.
3. Commerce
The exact meaning of "commerce" has caused controversy. The trend has been to expand its meaning and, consequently, the extent of Congress's powers.
4. Naturalization and Bankruptcy
"Naturalization" refers to the procedure by which a citizen of a foreign nation becomes a citizen of the United States.
5. Currency
Control over money is an exclusive federal power; the states are forbidden to issue currency.
6. Counterfeiting
"Counterfeiting" means illegally imitating or forging.

The Constitution of the United States   **83**

Did You Know?

Expertise can win committee members standing among their colleagues and enhance their committee roles. For example, Sam Nunn, the Democratic senator from Georgia, built a reputation for being very well prepared for Defense Committee meetings—so much so that Republican members often sought his advice.

Visualizing
History   Bills are discussed on the House and Senate floors only after they come out of committee hearings. Before debate begins, many important decisions have already been made.
Answer to Caption: A resolution expresses congressional opinion or intent; a bill is a draft of a proposed law.

Cooperative Learning Activity

Analyzing the Expressed Powers Organize the class into groups of five to consider one of the expressed powers of Congress—taxing and spending, regulating commerce, foreign policy and national defense, providing for nation's growth, and other powers. Have each group discuss why its power was delegated to Congress rather than to the executive branch. Have a reporter from each group summarize its conclusions for the class. **L2, L3**

Analyzing Information

Explain that the powers of Congress are great, but they are not unlimited. Congress has only those powers that are expressly granted to it by the Constitution. Some, such as the power to tax, are legislative powers. Others are described as non-legislative powers. Ask students to study Article I, Section 8, to identify some of Congress's non-legislative powers. *(Answers include conducting investigations; amending the Constitution; admitting new states; governing federal lands; choosing executive officials; impeaching officials; and giving advice and consent.)*
L1

Did You Know?

On many occasions when the United States has intervened militarily, Congress did not actually declare war. Among the so-called "undeclared wars" were the twentieth-century conflicts in Korea and Vietnam. Both wars were fought on the President's authority to support regimes against external aggression.

7. Post Office
In 1970 the United States Postal Service replaced the Post Office Department.

8. Copyrights and Patents
Under this provision, Congress has passed copyright and patent laws.

9. Courts
This provision allows Congress to establish a federal court system.

10. Piracy
Congress has the power to protect American ships on the high seas.

11. Declare War
While the Constitution gives Congress the right to declare war, the United States has sent troops into combat without a congressional declaration.

12. Army
This provision reveals the Framers' fears of a standing army.

13. Navy
This clause allows Congress to establish a navy.

14. Rules for Armed Forces
Congress may pass regulations that deal with military discipline.

15. Militia
The "militia" is now called the National Guard. It is organized by the states.

16. National Guard
Even though the National Guard is organized by the states, Congress has the authority to pass rules for governing its behavior.

17. Nation's Capital
This clause grants Congress the right to make laws for Washington, D.C.

18. Elastic Clause
This is the so-called "elastic clause" of the Constitution and one of its most important provisions. The "necessary and proper" laws must be related to one of the 17 enumerated powers.

Section 9. Powers Denied to the Federal Government.

1. Slave Trade
This paragraph contains the compromise the Framers reached regarding regulation of the slave trade in exchange for Congress's exclusive control over interstate commerce.

2. Habeas Corpus
Habeas corpus is a Latin term meaning "you may have the body." A writ of habeas corpus issued by a judge requires a law official to bring a prisoner to court and show cause for holding the prisoner. The writ may be suspended only during wartime.

3. Bills of Attainder
A "bill of attainder" is a bill that punishes a person without a jury trial. An "ex post facto" law is one that makes an act a crime after the act has been committed.

7. To establish Post Offices and post Roads;
8. To promote the Progress of Science and useful Arts, by securing for limited Times to Authors and Inventors the exclusive Right to their respective Writings and Discoveries;
9. To constitute Tribunals inferior to the Supreme Court;
10. To define and punish Piracies and Felonies committed on the high Seas, and Offenses against the Law of Nations.
11. To declare War, grant Letters of Marque and Reprisal, and make Rules concerning Captures on Land and Water;
12. To raise and support Armies, but no Appropriation of Money to that Use shall be for a longer Term than two Years;
13. To provide and maintain a Navy;
14. To make Rules for the Government and Regulation of the land and naval forces;
15. To provide for calling forth the Militia to execute the Laws of the Union, suppress Insurrections, and repel Invasions;
16. To provide for organizing, arming, and disciplining, the Militia, and for governing such Part of them as may be employed in the Service of the United States, reserving to the States respectively, the Appointment of the Officers, and the Authority of training the Militia according to the discipline prescribed by Congress;
17. To exercise exclusive Legislation in all Cases whatsoever, over such District (not exceeding ten Miles square) as may, by Cession of particular States, and the acceptance of Congress, become the Seat of Government of the United States, and to exercise like Authority over all Places purchased by the Consent of the Legislature of the State in which the Same shall be, for the Erection of Forts, Magazines, Arsenals, dock-Yards, and other needful Buildings;—And
18. To make all Laws which shall be necessary and proper for carrying into Execution the foregoing Powers, and all other Powers vested by this Constitution in the Government of the United States, or in any Department or Officer thereof.

Section 9

1. The Migration or Importation of such Persons as any of the States now existing shall think proper to admit, shall not be prohibited by the Congress prior to the Year one thousand eight hundred and eight, but a tax or duty may be imposed on such importation, not exceeding ten dollars for each Person.
2. The privilege of the Writ of Habeas Corpus shall not be suspended, unless when in Cases of Rebellion or Invasion the public Safety may require it.
3. No Bill of Attainder or ex post facto Law shall be passed.

Sidelight: Slavery

Although the first paragraph of Article I, Section 9 deals with the slave trade, note that the language of the Constitution does not use the term *slave*, but instead refers to "such persons." In fact, the word *slave* does not occur anywhere in the document. Elsewhere, enslaved people are referred to as "other persons" (Art. I, Sect. 2) and "person[s] held to service" (Art. IV, Sect. 2).

▲ INAUGURATION OF THE PRESIDENT The inauguration is held on January 20 following a presidential election. Generally held on the steps of the Capitol, the ceremony centers on swearing into office the new President. *What does Article II, Section 1, Clause 5 describe?*

Evaluating Issues Article I, Section 10 prohibits the states from signing a treaty with another country. Ask students to explain why the Framers did not want states to have this right. *(to make sure the nation acted as a unit; under the Articles of Confederation some states acted on their own, resulting in problems)* **L2**

Visualizing History Presidents are now inaugurated on January 20, but George Washington took the oath of office on April 30, 1789, following John Adams's inauguration as Vice President nine days earlier. Congress passed the first law outlining a procedure for administering oaths of office in June of that year. **Answer to Caption:** the qualifications for President

4. No capitation, or other direct, Tax shall be laid unless in Proportion to the Census or Enumeration herein before directed to be taken.

5. No Tax or Duty shall be laid on Articles exported from any State.

6. No Preference shall be given by any Regulation of Commerce or Revenue to the Ports of one State over those of another: nor shall Vessels bound to, or from, one State, be obliged to enter, clear, or pay Duties in another.

7. No Money shall be drawn from the Treasury, but in Consequence of Appropriations made by Law; and a regular Statement and Account of the Receipts and Expenditures of all public Money shall be published from time to time.

8. No Title of Nobility shall be granted by the United States:—And no Person holding any Office of Profit or Trust under them, shall, without the Consent of the Congress, accept of any present, Emolument, Office, or Title, of any kind whatever, from any King, Prince, or foreign State.

Section 10

1. No State shall enter into any Treaty, Alliance, or Confederation; grant Letters of Marque and Reprisal; coin Money; emit Bills of Credit; make any Thing but gold and silver Coin a Tender in Payment of Debts; pass any Bill of Attainder; ex post facto Law, or Law impairing the Obligation of Contracts, or grant any Title of Nobility.

4. Direct Taxes
The 16th Amendment allowed Congress to pass an income tax.

5. Tax on Exports
Congress may not tax goods that move from one state to another.

6. Uniformity of Treatment
This prohibition prevents Congress from favoring one state or region over another in the regulation of trade.

7. Appropriation Law
This clause protects against the misuse of funds. All of the President's expenditures must be made with the permission of Congress.

8. Titles of Nobility
This clause prevents the development of a nobility in the United States.

Section 10. Powers Denied to the States

1. Limitations on Power
The states are prohibited from conducting foreign affairs, carrying on a war, or controlling interstate and foreign commerce. States are also not allowed to pass laws that the federal government is prohibited from passing, such as enacting ex post facto laws or bills of attainder. These restrictions on the states were designed, in part, to prevent an overlapping in functions and authority with the federal government that could create conflict and chaos.

The Constitution of the United States   **85**

Sidelight: The Income Tax

Originally the Constitution did not allow Congress to levy direct taxes that were not divided equally among the states according to population. Thus, Congress could not raise money through income taxes because the income taxes would not be equally divided among the states. As the United States expanded and the amount of money required by government grew, this taxing limit became a serious problem. Congress found that it needed more sources of revenue. The Sixteenth Amendment, ratified in 1913, provided that income taxes could be collected without regard to a state's population.

FOCUS
Motivating Activity

Point out that one of the difficult questions facing the Framers was that of a chief executive. Clearly, a single leader with broad but limited powers was needed to carry on the daily business of government. Ask students: Why did the Framers set up an office of President with limited powers? (*Answers will vary but might include: Most delegates decided against having a king or any leader with uncontrolled powers; the people wanted an elected official who would work for the interests of a majority of the citizens.*) **L2**

Visualizing **H**istory Although Article II, Section 3 requires that the President report to Congress on the state of the Union, it does not require a speech. The President's annual State of the Union Address has, however, become a tradition. **Answer to Caption:** Article II, Sections 2 and 3

ABCNEWS
INTERACTIVE™

VIDEODISC

Powers of the President

Side One, Chapter 3
Title: *Constitution and the President*
Subject: Understand the basic duties of the President

---

2. Export and Import Taxes
This clause prevents states from levying duties on exports and imports. If states were permitted to tax imports and exports they could use their taxing power in a way that weakens or destroys Congress's power to control interstate and foreign commerce.

3. Duties, Armed Forces, War
This clause prohibits states from maintaining an army or navy and from going to war, except in cases where a state is directly attacked. It also forbids states from collecting fees from foreign vessels or from making treaties with other nations. All of these powers are reserved for the federal government.

Article II. The Executive Branch

Section 1. President and Vice President
1. Term of Office
The President is given power to enforce the laws passed by Congress. Both the President and the Vice President serve four-year terms. The 22nd Amendment limits the number of terms the President may serve to two.

2. Election
The Philadelphia Convention had trouble deciding how the President was to be chosen. The system finally agreed upon was indirect election by "electors" chosen for that purpose. The President and Vice President are not directly elected. Instead, the President and Vice President are elected by presidential electors from each state who form the electoral college. Each state has the number of presidential electors equal to the total number of its senators and representatives. State legislatures determine how the electors are chosen. Originally, the state legislatures chose the electors, but today they are nominated by political parties and elected by the voters. No senator, representative, or any other federal officeholder can serve as an elector.

---

2. No State shall, without the Consent of the Congress, lay any Imposts or Duties on Imports or Exports, except what may be absolutely necessary for executing its inspection Laws: and the net Produce of all Duties and Imposts, laid by any State on Imports and Exports, shall be for the Use of the Treasury of the United States; and all such Laws shall be subject to the Revision and Controul of the Congress.

3. No State shall, without the Consent of Congress, lay any duty on Tonnage, keep Troops, or Ships of War in time of Peace, enter into any Agreement or Compact with another State, or with a foreign Power, or engage in War, unless actually invaded, or in such imminent Danger as will not admit of delay.

Article II
Section 1

1. The executive Power shall be vested in a President of the United States of America. He shall hold his Office during the Term of four years, and together with the Vice-President chosen for the same Term, be elected, as follows:

2. Each State shall appoint, in such Manner as the Legislature thereof may direct, a Number of Electors, equal to the whole Number of Senators and Representatives to which the State may be entitled in the Congress: but no Senator or Representative, or Person holding an Office of Trust or Profit under the United States, shall be appointed an Elector.

Visualizing **H**istory

▲ STATE OF THE UNION Presidents use the annual State of the Union Address to outline yearly goals. *In which sections of the Constitution are the President's powers and duties defined?*

Sidelight: Presidential Term of Office

The Constitution originally did not limit the number of terms the chief executive could serve. George Washington served two terms and established a tradition that all Presidents followed until Franklin D. Roosevelt. Many people opposed Roosevelt's four terms in office.

This opposition eventually led to ratification of the Twenty-second Amendment in 1951, limiting the President to two terms. Since Roosevelt, however, only Eisenhower and Reagan have served two full terms.

3. The Electors shall meet in their respective States, and vote by Ballot for two Persons, of whom one at least shall not be an Inhabitant of the same State with themselves. And they shall make a List of all the Persons voted for and of the Number of Votes for each; which List they shall sign and certify, and transmit sealed to the Seat of the Government of the United States, directed to the President of the Senate. The President of the Senate shall, in the Presence of the Senate and House of Representatives, open all the Certificates, and the Votes shall then be counted. The Person having the greatest Number of Votes shall be the President, if such Number be a Majority of the whole Number of Electors appointed; and if there be more than one who have such Majority, and have an equal Number of Votes, then the House of Representatives shall immediately chuse by Ballot one of them for President; and if no Person have a Majority, then from the five highest on the List the said House shall in like Manner chuse the President. But in chusing the President, the Votes shall be taken by States, the Representation from each State having one Vote; a quorum for this Purpose shall consist of a Member or Members from two-thirds of the States, and a Majority of all the States shall be necessary to a Choice. In every Case, after the Choice of the President, the Person having the greatest Number of Votes of the Electors shall be the Vice-President. But if there should remain two or more who have equal votes, the Senate shall chuse from them by Ballot the Vice President.

4. The Congress may determine the Time of chusing the Electors, and the Day on which they shall give their Votes; which Day shall be the same throughout the United States.

5. No person except a natural born Citizen, or a Citizen of the United States, at the time of the Adoption of this Constitution, shall be eligible to the Office of President; neither shall any Person be eligible to that Office who shall not have attained to the Age of thirty-five years, and been fourteen Years a Resident within the United States.

6. In Case of the Removal of the President from Office, or of his Death, Resignation, or Inability to discharge the Powers and Duties of the said Office, the same shall devolve on the Vice-President, and the Congress may by Law provide for the Case of Removal, Death, Resignation or Inability, both of the President and Vice-President, declaring what Officer shall then act as President, and such Officer shall act accordingly, until the disability be removed, or a President shall be elected.

7. The President shall, at stated Times, receive for his Services a Compensation, which shall neither be encreased nor diminished during the Period for which he shall have been elected, and he shall not receive within that Period any other Emolument from the United States, or any of them.

8. Before he enter on the execution of his office, he shall take the following Oath or Affirmation "I do solemnly swear (or affirm) that I will faithfully execute the Office of President of the United States, and will to the best of my Ability, preserve, protect and defend the Constitution of the United States."

3. Former Method of Election

This clause describes the original method of electing the President and Vice President. According to this method, each elector voted for two candidates. The candidate with the most votes (as long as it was a majority) became President. The candidate with the second highest number of votes became Vice President. In the election of 1800, the two top candidates received the same number of votes, making it necessary for the House of Representatives to decide the election. To prevent such a situation from recurring, the 12th Amendment was added in 1804.

4. Date of Elections

Congress selects the date when the presidential electors are chosen and when they vote for President and Vice President. All electors must vote on the same day. The first Tuesday after the first Monday in November has been set as the date for presidential elections. Electors cast their votes on the Monday after the second Wednesday in December.

5. Qualifications

The President must be a citizen of the United States by birth, at least 35 years old, and a resident of the United States for 14 years. See Amendment 22.

6. Vacancies

If the President dies, resigns, is removed from office by impeachment, or is unable to carry out the duties of the office, the Vice President becomes President. (Amendment 25 deals with presidential disability.) If both the President and Vice President are unable to serve, Congress has the power to declare by law who acts as President. Congress set the line of succession in the Presidential Succession Act of 1947.

7. Salary

Originally, the President's salary was $25,000 per year. The President's current salary of $200,000 plus a $50,000 taxable expense account per year was enacted in 1969. The President also receives numerous fringe benefits including a $120,000 nontaxable allowance for travel and entertainment, and living accommodations in two residences—the White House and Camp David. However, the President cannot receive any other income from the United States Government or state governments while in office.

8. Oath of Office

The oath of office is generally administered by the chief justice, but can be administered by any official authorized to administer oaths. All Presidents-elect except Washington have been sworn into office by the chief justice. Only Vice Presidents John Tyler, Calvin Coolidge, and Lyndon Johnson in succeeding to the office have been sworn in by someone else.

TEACH
Guided Practice

Classifying Point out that Article II of the Constitution outlines the powers of the President. Their nature and extent have been shaped by the historical development of the office. Explain that these powers can be grouped under five headings— executive, legislative, diplomatic, military, and judicial. Although these powers are limited by the checks and balances of the other branches of government, the President can use them in a variety of formal and informal ways. Assign students to read Article II and find and classify the powers of the President under the appropriate headings. **L1**

FACT or FICTION?

Under the veto power, the President must veto the entire bill.

FACT: The President does not have a line-item veto as most state governors do.

Did You Know?

Some Presidents have used the veto sparingly, whereas others used it often. Franklin Roosevelt, for example, vetoed 635 pieces of legislation, only 9 of which were overridden. On the other hand, Richard Nixon vetoed 42 bills (5 overrides) and John F. Kennedy, 21 (no overrides).

Critical Thinking Activity

Determining Cause and Effect Write the following statement on the chalkboard:

"The increase in presidential power during this century has been largely related to crises, whether domestic or foreign."

Then ask: Do you think this is the true cause of the increase in presidential power? Why or why not? If not, what in your opinion did cause this increase? **L3**

Visualizing **History** ▲ THE PRESIDENT'S POWER As commander in chief of the United States armed forces, the President is the people's check on the power of the military. *What limits are placed on the President's power to make treaties?*

Section 2. Powers of the President

1. Military, Cabinet, Pardons

Mention of "the principal officer in each of the executive departments" is the only suggestion of the President's Cabinet to be found in the Constitution. The Cabinet is a purely advisory body, and its power depends on the President. Each Cabinet member is appointed by the President and must be confirmed by the Senate. This clause also makes the President, a civilian, the head of the armed services. This established the principle of civilian control of the military.

2. Treaties and Appointments

The President is the chief architect of American foreign policy. He or she is responsible for the conduct of foreign relations, or dealings with other countries. All treaties, however, require approval of two-thirds of the senators present. Most federal positions today are filled under the rules and regulations of the civil service system. Most presidential appointees serve at the pleasure of the President. Removal of an official by the President is not subject to congressional approval. But the power can be restricted by conditions set in creating the office.

3. Vacancies in Offices

The President can temporarily appoint officials to fill vacancies when the Senate is not in session.

Section 2

1. The President shall be Commander in Chief of the Army and Navy of the United States, and of the Militia of the several States, when called into the actual Service of the United States; he may require the Opinion, in writing, of the principal Officer in each of the executive Departments, upon any subject relating to the Duties of their respective Offices, and he shall have Power to Grant Reprieves and Pardons for Offences against the United States, except in Cases of Impeachment.

2. He shall have Power, by and with the Advice and Consent of the Senate, to make Treaties, provided two-thirds of the Senators present concur; and he shall nominate, and by and with the Advice and Consent of the Senate, shall appoint Ambassadors, other public Ministers and Consuls, Judges of the supreme Court, and all other Officers of the United States, whose Appointments are not herein otherwise provided for, and which shall be established by Law. But the Congress may by Law vest the Appointment of such inferior Officers, as they think proper, in the President alone, in the Courts of Law, or in the Heads of Departments.

3. The President shall have Power to fill up all Vacancies that may happen during the Recess of the Senate, by granting Commissions which shall expire at the End of their next Session.

Cultural Perspectives

The President's Cabinet Until the 1930s no President had selected a woman or a member of a minority to serve in the cabinet. Franklin D. Roosevelt appointed the first woman to serve in the cabinet. In 1933 he chose Frances T. Perkins to serve as secretary of labor. In 1966 Robert C. Weaver became the first African American appointed to the cabinet. Lyndon B. Johnson named him to head the newly created Department of Housing and Urban Development.

Section 3

He shall from time to time give to Congress Information of the State of the Union, and recommend to their Consideration such Measures as he shall judge necessary and expedient; he may, on extraordinary occasions, convene both Houses, or either of them, and in Case of Disagreement between them, with respect to the Time of Adjournment, he may adjourn them to such Time as he shall think proper; he shall receive Ambassadors and other public Ministers; he shall take Care that the Laws be faithfully executed, and shall Commission all the Officers of the United States.

Section 4

The President, Vice-President and all civil Officers of the United States, shall be removed from Office on Impeachment for, and Conviction of, Treason, Bribery, or other high Crimes and Misdemeanors.

Article III

Section 1

The Judicial Power of the United States, shall be vested in one supreme Court, and in such inferior Courts as the Congress may from time to time ordain and establish. The judges, both of the supreme and inferior Courts, shall hold their Offices during good Behaviour, and shall, at stated Times, receive for their Services, a Compensation, which shall not be diminished during their Continuance in Office.

Section 3. Duties of the President

Under this provision the President delivers annual State-of-the-Union messages. On occasion, Presidents have called Congress into special session to consider particular problems.

The President's duty to receive foreign diplomats also includes the power to ask a foreign country to withdraw its diplomatic officials from this country. This is called "breaking diplomatic relations" and often carries with it the implied threat of more drastic action, even war. The President likewise has the power of deciding whether or not to recognize foreign governments.

Section 4. Impeachment

This section states the reasons for which the President and Vice President may be impeached and removed from office. (See annotations of Article I, Section 3, Clauses 6 and 7.)

Article III. The Judicial Branch

Section 1. Federal Courts

The term *judicial* refers to courts. The Constitution set up only the Supreme Court but provided for the establishment of other federal courts. There are presently nine justices on the Supreme Court. Congress has created a system of federal district courts and courts of appeals, which review certain district court cases. Judges of these courts serve during "good behavior," which means that they usually serve for life or until they choose to retire.

Visualizing History

▲ THE SUPREME COURT Supreme Court proceedings are held in this room. The Constitution established the jurisdiction of the federal courts by defining the kinds of cases these courts may hear. **What is statute law?**

LESSON PLAN
The Judicial Branch

FOCUS
Motivating Activity

Ask students to consider the meaning of the phrase "respect for the law." Questions to address during the discussion might include: What is law? How can the law affect individuals and society? What is meant by the phrase "respect for the law"? Stress that the law is the foundation of representative democracy in the United States. **L2**

ABCNEWS INTERACTIVE™

 VIDEODISC

Powers of the Supreme Court

Side One, Chapter 3
Title: *Constitution and the Court*
Subject: Understand the separation of powers and checks and balances

Visualizing History The judiciary is only briefly described in the Constitution. The Judiciary Act of 1789 set up the federal court system. That system has been amended by later acts of Congress and by tradition.
Answer to Caption: laws passed by Congress

Critical Thinking Activity

Analyzing Ideas Show the film *Twelve Angry Men*. Before the jury takes its second vote on the case, stop the film. Divide the class into small groups. Have students in each group decide which juror they believe will be next to change his vote. Next, have students answer the question, If all jurors switched their votes, which juror would be the last to change his vote to not guilty? Have each group present its ideas. Complete the showing of the film. Conclude by leading a discussion in which students analyze the real outcome of the film. **L2**

TEACH

Guided Practice

Demonstrating Reasoned Judgment Point out that federal judges are appointed for life and can be removed only by their death, resignation, or impeachment. Have students discuss why the Framers decided to do this. *(Answers will vary but might include: The Framers wanted to free judges to make their best determinations without worrying that they might be punished for making unpopular decisions.)* **L2**

Independent Practice

Simulation Hold a mock trial in which students assume the roles of prosecuting and defense attorneys, members of the jury, witnesses, and a judge. The issue at stake could be an issue of local concern, an issue identified by earlier activities, or an issue resulting in a landmark Supreme Court decision. **L2**

Visualizing History Point out that until the late 1900s, all justices of the Supreme Court were white males. Discuss why the court has been slow to change. *(Justices are replaced only when they die or retire.)*

Answer to Caption: specified as "good behavior," meaning service for life or until retirement

Visualizing History ▲ JUSTICES OF THE SUPREME COURT Because we have judicial review, the Supreme Court is the official interpreter of the Constitution and has the final say in deciding what the Constitution means. *What is the term of office for a Supreme Court Justice?*

Section 2. Jurisdiction

1. General Jurisdiction

Use of the words *in law and equity* reflects the fact that American courts took over two kinds of traditional law from Great Britain. The basic law was the "common law," which was based on over five centuries of judicial decisions. "Equity" was a special branch of British law developed to handle cases where common law did not apply.

Federal courts deal mostly with "statute law," or laws passed by Congress, treaties, and cases involving the Constitution itself. "Admiralty and maritime jurisdiction" covers all sorts of cases involving ships and shipping on the high seas and on rivers, canals, and lakes.

2. The Supreme Court

When a court has "original jurisdiction" over certain kinds of cases, it means that the court has the authority to be the first court to hear a case. A court with "appellate jurisdiction" hears cases that have been appealed from lower courts. Most Supreme Court cases are heard on appeal from lower courts.

3. Jury Trials

Except in cases of impeachment, anyone accused of a crime has the right to a trial by jury. The trial must be held in the state where the crime was committed. Jury trial guarantees were strengthened in the 6th, 7th, 8th, and 9th Amendments.

90   The Constitution of the United States

Section 2

1. The judicial Power shall extend to all Cases, in Law and Equity, arising under this Constitution, the Laws of the United States, and treaties made, or which shall be made, under their Authority; to all Cases affecting ambassadors, other public ministers and consuls; to all cases of admiralty and maritime Jurisdiction; to Controversies to which the United States shall be a party; to Controversies between two or more states; between a State and Citizens of another State; between Citizens of different States; between Citizens of the same State claiming Lands under Grants of different States, and between a State, or the Citizens thereof, and foreign States, Citizens or Subjects.

2. In all Cases affecting Ambassadors, other public Ministers and Consuls, and those in which a State shall be Party, the supreme Court shall have original Jurisdiction. In all the other Cases before mentioned, the supreme Court shall have appellate Jurisdiction, both as to Law and Fact, with such Exceptions, and under such Regulations as the Congress shall make.

3. The trial of all Crimes, except in Cases of Impeachment, shall be by Jury; and such Trial shall be held in the State where the said Crimes shall have been committed; but when not committed within any State, the Trial shall be at such Place or Places as the Congress may by Law have directed.

Critical Thinking Activity

Predicting Outcomes Have students discuss the pros and cons of federal judges being elected instead of appointed. Have them include a discussion of the concept of "the tyranny of the majority" in their preparation. Then have them make a list of possible outcomes they foresee if the federal judiciary were to be subject to the electoral process. **L3**

Section 3

1. Treason against the United States, shall consist only in levying War against them, or in adhering to their Enemies, giving them Aid and Comfort. No Person shall be convicted of Treason unless on the Testimony of two Witnesses to the same overt Act, or on Confession in open Court.

2. The Congress shall have power to declare the Punishment of Treason, but no Attainder of Treason shall work Corruption of Blood, or Forfeiture except during the Life of the Person attainted.

Article IV

Section 1

Full Faith and Credit shall be given in each State to the public Acts, Records, and judicial Proceedings of every other State. And the Congress may by general Laws prescribe the Manner in which such Acts, Records, and Proceedings shall be proved, and the Effect thereof.

Section 2

1. The Citizens of each State shall be entitled to all Privileges and Immunities of Citizens in the several States.

2. A Person charged in any State with Treason, Felony, or other Crime, who shall flee from Justice, and be found in another State, shall on demand of the executive Authority of the State from which he fled, be delivered up, to be removed to the State having Jurisdiction of the crime.

3. No Person held to Service of Labour in one State, under the Laws thereof, escaping into another, shall, in Consequence of any Law or Regulation therein, be discharged from such Service or Labour, but shall be delivered up on Claim of the Party to whom such Service or Labour may be due.

Section 3

1. New States may be admitted by the Congress into this Union; but no new State shall be formed or erected within the Jurisdiction of any other State; nor any State be formed by the Junction of two or more States, or parts of States, without the Consent of the Legislatures of the States concerned as well as of the Congress.

2. The Congress shall have Power to dispose of and make all needful Rules and Regulations respecting the Territory of other Property belonging to the United States; and nothing in this Constitution shall be so construed as to Prejudice any Claims of the United States, or of any particular State.

Section 4

The United States shall guarantee to every State in this Union a Republican Form of Government, and shall protect each of them against Invasion; and on Application of the Legislature, or of the Executive (when the Legislature cannot be convened) against domestic Violence.

Section 3. Treason

1. Definition

Knowing that the charge of treason often had been used by monarchs to get rid of people who opposed them, the Framers of the Constitution defined treason carefully, requiring that at least two witnesses be present to testify in court that a treasonable act was committed.

2. Punishment

Congress is given the power to determine the punishment for treason. The children of a person convicted of treason may not be punished nor may the convicted person's property be taken away from the children. Convictions for treason have been relatively rare in the nation's history.

Article IV. Relations Among the States

Section 1. Official Acts

This provision insures that each state recognizes the laws, court decisions, and records of all other states. For example, a marriage license or corporation charter issued by one state must be accepted in other states.

Section 2. Mutual Duties of States

1. Privileges

The "privileges and immunities," or rights of citizens, guarantee each state's citizens equal treatment in all states.

2. Extradition

"Extradition" means that a person convicted of a crime or a person accused of a crime must be returned to the state where the crime was committed. Thus, a person cannot flee to another state hoping to escape the law.

3. Fugitive-Slave Clause

Formerly this clause meant that slaves could not become free persons by escaping to free states.

Section 3. New States and Territories

1. New States

Congress has the power to admit new states. It also determines the basic guidelines for applying for statehood. One state, Maine, was created within the original boundaries of another state (Massachusetts) with the consent of Congress and the state.

2. Territories

Congress has power over federal land. But neither in this clause nor anywhere else in the Constitution is the federal government explicitly empowered to acquire new territory.

Section 4. Federal Protection for States

This section allows the federal government to send troops into a state to guarantee law and order. The President may send in troops even without the consent of the state government involved.

FOCUS

Motivating Activity

Point out that one political scientist has called the supremacy clause—Article VI, Section 2—"the most important single provision of the Constitution." Ask students to think about why this might be so as they read Articles IV–VI and reflect on Articles I–III. (*This clause, by making it clear that the national Constitution and laws are supreme over state constitutions and laws, prevented what could have been devastating conflicts between Congress and the states.*) **L3**

TEACH

Guided Practice

Expressing Viewpoints

Have students discuss whether the amendment process should be simpler and why the Framers established this particular system. (*Answers will vary but might include: The Articles of Confederation had been too difficult to amend. Yet the Framers worried that if they made the Constitution too easy to amend, it would not be respected.*) **L2**

Sidelight: Articles IV–VII

The Articles of Confederation had concentrated power in the hands of the states. The Constitution reversed this by concentrating power at the federal level. If the new system was to be accepted, the states needed to know that their rights and the rights of their citizens would be protected. Article IV provides these guarantees. In Article V, the Framers provided a way to change the Constitution. Article VI established the Constitution as the supreme law over individuals and states. Finally, Article VII provides a system for ratifying the Constitution.

Article V. The Amending Process

There are now 27 Amendments to the Constitution. The Framers of the Constitution deliberately made it difficult to amend or change the Constitution. Two methods of proposing and ratifying amendments are provided for. A two-thirds majority is needed in Congress to propose an amendment, and at least three-fourths of the states (38 states) must accept the amendment before it can become law. No amendment has yet been proposed by a national convention called by the states, though in the 1980s a convention to propose an amendment requiring a balanced budget had been approved by 32 states.

Article VI. National Supremacy

1. Public Debts and Treaties

This section promised that all debts the colonies had incurred during the Revolution and under the Articles of Confederation would be honored by the new United States government.

2. The Supreme Law

The "supremacy clause" recognized the Constitution and federal laws as supreme when in conflict with those of the states. It was largely based on this clause that Chief Justice John Marshall wrote his historic decision in *McCulloch* v. *Maryland*. The 14th Amendment reinforced the supremacy of federal law over state laws.

3. Oaths of Office

This clause also declares that no religious test shall be required as a qualification for holding public office. This principle is also asserted in the First Amendment, which forbids Congress to set up an established church or to interfere with the religious freedom of Americans.

Article VII. Ratification of the Constitution

Unlike the Articles of Confederation, which required approval of all thirteen states for adoption, the Constitution required approval of only nine of thirteen states. Thirty-nine of the 55 delegates at the Constitutional Convention signed the Constitution. The Constitution went into effect in June 1788.

Article V

The Congress, whenever two-thirds of both Houses shall deem it necessary, shall propose Amendments to this Constitution, or, on the Application of the Legislatures of two-thirds of the several States, shall call a Convention for proposing Amendments, which, in either Case, shall be valid to all Intents and Purposes, as part of this Constitution, when ratified by the Legislatures of three-fourths of the several States, or by Conventions in three-fourths thereof, as the one or the other Mode of Ratification may be proposed by the Congress; Provided that no Amendment which may be made prior to the Year One thousand eight hundred and eight shall in any Manner affect the first and fourth clauses in the Ninth Section of the first Article; and that no State, without its Consent, shall be deprived of its equal Suffrage in the Senate.

Article VI

1. All Debts contracted and Engagements entered into, before the Adoption of this Constitution, shall be as valid against the United States under this Constitution as under the Confederation.

2. This Constitution, and the Laws of the United States which shall be made in Pursuance thereof; and all Treaties made, or which shall be made, under the Authority of the United States, shall be the supreme Law of the Land; and the Judges in every State shall be bound thereby, any Thing in the Constitution or Laws of any State to the Contrary notwithstanding.

3. The Senators and Representatives before mentioned, and the Members of the several State Legislatures, and all executive and judicial Officers, both of the United States and of the several States, shall be bound by Oath or Affirmation, to support this Constitution; but no religious Test shall ever be required as a Qualification to any Office or public Trust under the United States.

Article VII

The Ratification of the Conventions of nine States shall be sufficient for the Establishment of this Constitution between the States so ratifying the same.

Done in Convention, by the Unanimous Consent of the States present, the Seventeenth Day of September, in the Year of our Lord one thousand seven hundred and Eighty-seven, and of the Independence of the United States of America the Twelfth. In Witness whereof We have hereunto subscribed our Names.

Sidelight: Ratification

The first five states to ratify the Constitution—Delaware, Pennsylvania, New Jersey, Georgia, and Connecticut—did so quickly and by large majorities. Eleven states had ratified the Constitution by the time George Washington was inaugurated on April 30, 1789.

Signers
George Washington, **President and Deputy from Virginia**

New Hampshire
John Langdon
Nicholas Gilman

Massachusetts
Nathaniel Gorham
Rufus King

Connecticut
William Samuel Johnson
Roger Sherman

New York
Alexander Hamilton

New Jersey
William Livingston
David Brearley
William Paterson
Jonathan Dayton

Pennsylvania
Benjamin Franklin
Thomas Mifflin
Robert Morris
George Clymer
Thomas FitzSimons
Jared Ingersoll
James Wilson
Gouverneur Morris

Delaware
George Read
Gunning Bedford, Jr.
John Dickinson
Richard Bassett
Jacob Broom

Maryland
James McHenry
Daniel of St. Thomas Jenifer
Daniel Carroll

Virginia
John Blair
James Madison, Jr.

North Carolina
William Blount
Richard Dobbs Spaight
Hugh Williamson

South Carolina
John Rutledge
Charles Cotesworth Pinckney
Charles Pinckney
Pierce Butler

Georgia
William Few
Abraham Baldwin

Attest: William Jackson,
Secretary

Amendment I
Congress shall make no law respecting an establishment of religion, or prohibiting the free exercise thereof; or abridging the freedom of speech, or of the press; or the right of the people peaceably to assemble, and to petition the Government for a redress of grievances.

Amendment II
A well-regulated Militia, being necessary to the security of a free State, the right of the people to keep and bear Arms, shall not be infringed.

Amendment III
No soldier shall, in time of peace be quartered in any house, without the consent of the Owner, nor in time of war, but in a manner to be prescribed by law.

Amendment IV
The right of the people to be secure in their persons, houses, papers, and effects, against unreasonable searches and seizures, shall not be violated, and no Warrants shall issue, but upon probable cause, supported by Oath or affirmation, and particularly describing the place to be searched, and the persons or things to be seized.

Amendment 1.
Freedom of Religion, Speech, Press, and Assembly (1791)
The 1st Amendment protects the civil liberties of individuals in the United States. The 1st Amendment freedoms are not absolute, however. They are limited by the rights of other individuals.

Amendment 2.
Right to Bear Arms (1791)
The purpose of this amendment is to guarantee states the right to keep a militia.

Amendment 3.
Quartering Troops (1791)
This amendment is based on the principle that people have a right to privacy in their own homes. It also reflects the colonists' grievances against the British government before the Revolution. Britain had angered Americans by quartering (housing) troops in private homes.

Amendment 4.
Searches and Seizures (1791)
Like the 3rd Amendment, the 4th amendment reflects the colonists' desire to protect their privacy. Britain had used writs of assistance (general search warrants) to seek out smuggled goods. Americans wanted to make sure that such searches and seizures would be conducted only when a judge felt that there was "reasonable cause" to conduct them. The Supreme Court has ruled that evidence seized illegally without a search warrant may not be used in court.

The Constitution of the United States   **93**

Sidelight: The Bill of Rights

Critics felt the Constitution did not go far enough in protecting individual rights and liberties. To meet their objections, supporters of the Constitution promised to introduce a series of amendments listing these rights. On September 25, 1789, James Madison kept this promise by proposing 12 amendments to the Constitution. The 10 amendments that were adopted are known as the Bill of Rights. One of the two amendments that did not become part of the Constitution in 1789 eventually became the Twenty-seventh Amendment.

TEACH
Guided Practice
Analyzing Ideas

Ask students to give areas of concern they would like to see addressed by a Constitutional amendment. Write suggestions on the chalkboard and have the class discuss each in terms of the following questions: Why is an amendment needed? Might it be better to allow Congress to pass laws or the courts to establish precedents on this issue? What would be the best way to lobby for such an amendment? **L2**

Visualizing
ⓗistory Ask which amendment addresses bail and fines. *(the Eighth Amendment)*
Answer to Caption: Amendment VI

Did You Know?

One important requirement for a fair trial is that the judge must be impartial and disinterested. The Supreme Court has also held that a trial is unfair if it is dominated by a mob or if publicity has poisoned the jurors' minds.

Amendment 5.
Rights of Accused Persons (1791)

To bring a "presentment" or "indictment" means to formally charge a person with committing a crime. It is the function of a grand jury to see whether there is enough evidence to bring the accused person to trial. A person may not be tried more than once for the same crime (double jeopardy).

Members of the armed services are subject to military law. They may be tried in a court martial. In times of war or a natural disaster, civilians may also be put under martial law.

The 5th Amendment also guarantees that persons may not be forced in any criminal case to be a witness against themselves. That is, accused persons may refuse to answer questions on the ground that the answers might tend to incriminate them.

Amendment 6.
Right to Speedy, Fair Trial (1791)

The requirement of a "speedy" trial insures that an accused person will not be held in jail for a lengthy period as a means of punishing the accused without a trial. A "fair" trial means that the trial must be open to the public and that a jury must hear witnesses and evidence on both sides before deciding the guilt or innocence of a person charged with a crime. This amendment also provides that legal counsel must be provided to a defendant. In 1963, the Supreme Court ruled, in *Gideon v. Wainwright*, that if a defendant cannot afford a lawyer, the government must provide one to defend the accused person.

Amendment V

No person shall be held to answer for a capital, or otherwise infamous crime, unless on a presentment or indictment of a Grand Jury, except in cases arising in the land or naval forces, or in the Militia, when in actual service in time of War or public danger; nor shall any person be subject for the same offence to be twice put in jeopardy of life or limb; nor shall be compelled in any criminal case to be a witness against himself, nor be deprived of life, liberty, or property, without due process of law; nor shall private property be taken for public use, without just compensation.

Amendment VI

In all criminal prosecutions, the accused shall enjoy the right to a speedy and public trial, by an impartial jury of the State and district wherein the crime shall have been committed, which district shall have been previously ascertained by law, and to be informed of the nature and cause of the accusation; to be confronted with the witnesses against him; to have compulsory process for obtaining witnesses in his favor, and to have the Assistance of Counsel for his defence.

Visualizing
ⓗistory ▲ RIGHTS OF THE ACCUSED Several amendments protect the rights of the accused. While awaiting trial, a defendant may be released by posting bail, a procedure regulated by the Eighth Amendment. *Which amendment guarantees the right to a speedy and fair trial?*

Critical Thinking Activity

Analyzing Points of View Point out that there is disagreement about the amending process. Some people feel that it should be made easier, whereas others think that the process should remain complicated. Have students discuss the merits of each position, using specific amendments and/or proposed amendments to support their point of view. **L3**

Amendment VII

In suits at common law, where the value in controversy shall exceed twenty dollars, the right of trial by jury shall be preserved, and no fact tried by a jury, shall be otherwise reexamined in any Courts of the United States, than according to the rules of common law.

Amendment VIII

Excessive bail shall not be required, nor excessive fines imposed, nor cruel and unusual punishments inflicted.

Amendment IX

The enumeration in the Constitution, of certain rights, shall not be construed to deny or disparage others retained by the people.

Amendment X

The powers not delegated to the United States by the Constitution, nor prohibited by it to the States, are reserved to the States respectively, or to the people.

Amendment XI

The Judicial power of the United States shall not be construed to extend to any suit in law or equity, commenced or prosecuted against one of the United States by Citizens of another State, or by Citizens or Subjects of any Foreign State.

Amendment XII

The Electors shall meet in their respective States and vote by ballot for President and Vice-President, one of whom, at least, shall not be an inhabitant of the same State with themselves; they shall name in their ballots the person voted for as President, and in distinct ballots the person voted for as Vice-President, and they shall make distinct lists of all persons voted for as President, and of all persons voted for as Vice-President, and of the number of votes for each, which lists they shall sign and certify, and transmit sealed to the seat of the government of the United States, directed to the President of the Senate;—The President of the Senate shall, in the presence of the Senate and House of Representatives, open all the certificates and the votes shall then be counted;—The person having the greatest number of votes for President, shall be the President, if such number be a majority of the whole number of Electors appointed; and if no person have such majority, then from the persons having the highest numbers not exceeding three on the list of those voted for as President, the House of Representatives shall choose immediately, by ballot, the President. But

Amendment 7.
Civil Suits (1791)

"Common law" means the law established by previous court decisions. In civil cases where one person sues another for more than $20, a jury trial is provided for. But customarily, federal courts do not hear civil cases unless they involve a good deal more money.

Amendment 8.
Bail and Punishment (1791)

"Bail" is money that an accused person provides to the court as a guarantee that he or she will be present for a trial. This amendment insures that neither bail nor punishment for a crime shall be unreasonably severe.

Amendment 9.
Powers Reserved to the People (1791)

This amendment provides that the people's rights are not limited to those mentioned in the Constitution.

Amendment 10.
Powers Reserved to the States (1791)

This amendment protects the states and the people from an all-powerful federal government. It provides that the states or the people retain all powers except those denied them or those specifically granted to the federal government. This "reserved powers" provision is a check on the "necessary and proper" power of the federal government provided in the "elastic clause" in Article I, Section 8, Clause 18.

Amendment 11.
Suits Against States (1795)

This amendment provides that a lawsuit brought by a citizen of the United States or a foreign nation against a state must be tried in a state court, not in a federal court. This amendment was passed after the Supreme Court ruled that a federal court could try a lawsuit brought by citizens of South Carolina against a citizen of Georgia. This case, *Chisholm* v. *Georgia*, decided in 1793, was protected by many Americans, who insisted states would lose authority if they could be sued in federal courts.

Amendment 12.
Election of President and Vice President (1804)

This amendment changes the procedure for electing the President and Vice President as outlined in Article II, Section 1, Clause 3.

To prevent the recurrence of the election of 1800 whereby a candidate running for Vice President (Aaron Burr) could tie a candidate running for President (Thomas Jefferson) and thus force the election into the House of Representatives, the Twelfth Amendment specifies that the electors are to cast separate ballots for each office. The votes for each office are counted and listed separately. The results are signed, sealed, and sent to the president of the senate. At a joint session of Congress, the votes are

The Constitution of the United States **95**

THE AMENDMENTS

Independent Practice

Interpreting Primary Sources Have students discuss the meaning of Amendment IX. *(Not all the rights of the people have necessarily been listed in the Constitution.)* Ask why the Framers believed it was necessary to include this amendment. *(could not list all rights; made it clear that those listed were not the people's only rights)* **L2**

FACT or FICTION?

Freedom of speech, as guaranteed by the First Amendment, has limits.

FACT: Among other things, the amendment does not protect slander (a spoken lie meant to damage another person's reputation) or libel (slander that is published).

Did You Know?

The Framers regarded torture and such means of execution as beheading and drawing and quartering as "cruel and unusual punishments." More recently, opponents of the death penalty have argued that capital punishment as such is cruel and unusual; the Supreme Court has not upheld this view.

Sidelight: Due Process of Law

References to due process of law are found in the Fifth and Fourteenth Amendments. As a result of Supreme Court rulings, two kinds of due process have developed: procedural and substantive. Procedural due process requires that government use fair procedures in enforcing the law. Substantive due process requires that the laws under which government acts be fair.

counted. The candidate who receives the most votes, providing it is a majority, is elected President. Other changes include: (1) a reduction from five to the three highest candidates receiving votes among whom the House is to choose if no candidate receives a majority of the electoral votes, and (2) provision for the Senate to choose the Vice President from the two highest candidates if neither has received a majority of the electoral votes.

The Twelfth Amendment does place one restriction on electors. It prohibits electors from voting for two candidates (President and Vice President) from their home state.

Amendment 13.
Abolition of Slavery (1865)

This amendment was the final act in ending slavery in the United States. It also prohibits the binding of a person to perform a personal service due to debt. In addition to imprisonment for crime, the Supreme Court has held that the draft is not a violation of the amendment.

This amendment is the first adopted to be divided into sections. It is also the first to contain specifically a provision granting Congress power to enforce it by appropriate legislation.

Amendment 14.
Rights of Citizens (1868)

The clauses of this amendment were intended 1) to penalize southern states that refused to grant African Americans the vote, 2) to keep former Confederate leaders from serving in government, 3) to forbid payment of the Confederacy's debt by the federal government, and 4) to insure payment of the war debts owed the federal government.

Section 1. Citizenship Defined By granting citizenship to all persons born in the United States, this amendment granted citizenship to former slaves. The amendment also guaranteed "due process of law." By the 1950s, Supreme Court rulings used the due process clause to protect civil liberties. The last part of Section 1 establishes the doctrine that all citizens are entitled to equal protection of the laws. In 1954 the Supreme Court ruled, in *Brown* v. *Board of Education* of Topeka, that segregation in public schools was unconstitutional because it denied equal protection.

Section 2. Representation in Congress This section reduced the number of members a state had in the House of Representatives if it denied its citizens the right to vote. This section

in choosing the President, the votes shall be taken by states, the representation from each state having one vote; a quorum for this purpose shall consist of a member or members from two-thirds of the states, and a majority of all the states shall be necessary to a choice. And if the House of Representatives shall not choose a President whenever the right of choice shall devolve upon them, before the fourth day of March next following, then the Vice-President shall act as President, as in the case of the death or other constitutional disability of the President.—The person having the greatest number of votes as Vice-President, shall be the Vice-President, if such number be a majority of the whole number of Electors appointed, and if no person have a majority, then from the two highest numbers on the list, the Senate shall choose the Vice-President; a quorum for the purpose shall consist of two-thirds of the whole number of Senators, and a majority of the whole number shall be necessary to a choice. But no person constitutionally ineligible to the office of President shall be eligible to that of Vice-President of the United States.

Amendment XIII

Section 1
Neither slavery nor involuntary servitude, except as a punishment for crime whereof the party shall have been duly convicted, shall exist within the United States, or any place subject to their jurisdiction.

Section 2
Congress shall have power to enforce this article by appropriate legislation.

Amendment XIV

Section 1
All persons born or naturalized in the United States, and subject to the jurisdiction thereof, are citizens of the United States and of the State wherein they reside. No State shall make or enforce any law which shall abridge the privileges or immunities of citizens of the United States; nor shall any State deprive any person of life, liberty, or property, without due process of law, nor deny to any person within its jurisdiction the equal protection of the laws.

Section 2
Representatives shall be apportioned among the several States according to their respective numbers, counting the whole number of persons in each State, excluding Indians not taxed. But when the right to vote at any election for the choice of electors for President and Vice-President of the United States, Representatives in Congress, the Executive and Judicial officers of a

Cultural Perspectives

Rights and Reality Amendments 13, 14, and 15 represented attempts to use the Constitution to end slavery, extend citizenship to former enslaved persons, and guarantee African Americans the right to vote. Although the intent of these amendments was to prohibit racial discrimination, they failed to do so. For instance, literacy tests, poll taxes, and property taxes kept many African Americans from voting. In just 10 years (1896 to 1906), the number of African Americans registered to vote in Louisiana fell from 130,334 to 1,342.

Visualizing History ▲ POLITICAL PARTIES The Constitution did not provide for the existence of political parties, which today play a major role in the election of the President and Vice President. ***What restrictions does the Twelfth Amendment place on electors?***

Creating a Time Line Have students make a time line that includes each of the amendments, the year of ratification, and significant concurrent political, economic, and social events. After completing the activity, have students display and compare their time lines. **L2**

Visualizing History Not until the 1830s did political parties organize conventions to name their candidates for President and Vice President.
Answer to Caption: They must cast separate ballots for President and Vice President, one of whom must not come from their state.

Did You Know?

The Fourteenth Amendment's guarantee of equal protection of the law is the Constitution's first mention of equality.

State, or the members of the Legislature thereof, is denied to any of the male inhabitants of such State, being twenty-one years of age, and citizens of the United States, or in any way abridged, except for participation in rebellion, or other crime, the basis of representation therein shall be reduced in the proportion which the number of such male citizens shall bear to the whole number of male citizens twenty-one years of age in such State.

Section 3

No person shall be a Senator or Representative in Congress, or elector of President and Vice-President, or hold any office, civil or military, under the United States, or under any State, who, having previously taken an oath, as a member of Congress, or as an officer of the United States, or as a member of any State legislature, or as an executive or judicial officer of any State, to support the Constitution of the United States, shall have engaged in insurrection or rebellion against the same, or given aid or comfort to the enemies thereof. But Congress may by a vote of two-thirds of each House, remove such disability.

was not implemented, however. Later civil rights laws and the 24th Amendment guaranteed the vote to African Americans.

Section 3. Penalty for Engaging in Insurrection The leaders of the Confederacy were barred from state or federal offices unless Congress agreed to revoke this ban. By the end of Reconstruction all but a few Confederate leaders were allowed to return to public life.

The Constitution of the United States **97**

Sidelight: The Poll Tax

Explain that a poll tax is a special tax paid as a qualification for voting. After the Civil War, poll taxes were levied in many Southern states. Although taxes kept many low-income white males from voting, the major purpose of the poll tax was to keep African Americans from voting. Not until the 1960s did Congress take firm action to enforce the guarantee of the Fifteenth Amendment and end this kind of voter discrimination.

Section 4. Public Debt The public debt incurred by the federal government during the Civil War was valid and could not be questioned by the South. However, the debts of the Confederacy were declared to be illegal. And former slave owners could not collect compensation for the loss of their slaves.

Section 5. Enforcement Congress was empowered to pass civil rights bills to guarantee the provisions of the amendment.

Amendment 15.
The Right to Vote (1870)
Section 1. Suffrage for African Americans The 15th Amendment replaced Section 2 of the 14th Amendment in guaranteeing African Americans the right to vote, that is, the right of African Americans to vote was not to be left to the states. Yet, despite this prohibition, African Americans were denied the right to vote by many states by such means as poll taxes, literacy tests, and white primaries.
Section 2. Enforcement Congress was given the power to enforce this amendment. During the 1950s and 1960s, it passed successively stronger laws to end racial discrimination in voting rights.

Amendment 16.
Income Tax (1913)
The origins of this amendment went back to 1895, when the Supreme Court declared a federal income tax unconstitutional. To overcome this Supreme Court decision, this amendment authorized an income tax that was levied on a direct basis.

Amendment 17.
Direct Election of Senators (1913)
Section 1. Method of Election The right to elect senators was given directly to the people of each state. It replaced Article I, Section 3, Clause 1, which empowered state legislatures to elect senators. This amendment was designed not only to make the choice of senators more democratic but also to cut down on corruption and to improve state government.

Section 2. Vacancies A state must order an election to fill a senate vacancy. A state may empower its governor to appoint a person to fill a Senate seat if a vacancy occurs until an election can be held.

Section 4
The validity of the public debt of the United States incurred for payment of pensions and bounties for service, authorized by law, including debts in suppressing insurrections or rebellion, shall not be questioned. But neither the United States nor any State shall assume or pay any debt or obligation incurred in aid of insurrection or rebellion against the United States, or any claim for the loss or emancipation of any slave; but all such debts, obligations and claims shall be held illegal and void.

Section 5
The Congress shall have power to enforce, by appropriate legislation, the provisions of this article.

Amendment XV

Section 1
The right of citizens of the United States to vote shall not be denied or abridged by the United States or by any State on account of race, color, or previous condition of servitude.

Section 2
The Congress shall have power to enforce this article by appropriate legislation.

Amendment XVI

The Congress shall have power to lay and collect taxes on incomes, from whatever source derived, without apportionment among several States, and without regard to any census or enumeration.

Amendment XVII

Section 1
The Senate of the United States shall be composed of two Senators from each State, elected by the people thereof, for six years; and each Senator shall have one vote. The electors in each state shall have the qualifications requisite for electors of the most numerous branch of the state legislatures.

Section 2
When vacancies happen in the representation of any State in the Senate, the executive authority of such State shall issue writs of election to fill such vacancies: *Provided*, that the legislature of any State may empower the executive thereof to make temporary appointments until the people fill the vacancies by election as the legislature may direct.

98   The Constitution of the United States

Section 3

This amendment shall not be so construed as to affect the election or term of any Senator chosen before it becomes valid as part of the Constitution.

Amendment XVIII

Section 1

After one year from ratification of this article the manufacture, sale, or transportation of intoxicating liquors within, the importation thereof into, or the exportation thereof from the United States and all territory subject to the jurisdiction thereof for beverage purposes is hereby prohibited.

Section 2

The Congress and the several states shall have concurrent power to enforce this article by appropriate legislation.

Section 3

This article shall be inoperative unless it shall have been ratified as an amendment to the Constitution by the legislatures of the several States, as provided in the Constitution, within seven years from the date of the submission hereof to the states of the Congress.

Amendment XIX

Section 1

The right of citizens of the United States to vote shall not be denied or abridged by the United States or by any state on account of sex.

Section 2

Congress shall have power to enforce this article by appropriate legislation.

Amendment XX

Section 1

The terms of the President and Vice President shall end at noon on the 20th day of January, and the terms of the Senators and Representatives at noon on the 3rd day of January, of the years in which such terms would have ended if this article had not been ratified; and the terms of their successors shall then begin.

Section 3. Time in Effect This amendment was not to affect any senate election or temporary appointment until it was in effect.

Amendment 18.
Prohibition of Alcoholic Beverages (1919)

This amendment prohibited the production, sale, or transportation of alcoholic beverages in the United States. Prohibition proved to be difficult to enforce, especially in states with large urban populations. This amendment was later repealed by the 21st Amendment.

Amendment 19.
Women's Suffrage (1920)

This amendment, extending the vote to all qualified women in federal and state elections, was a landmark victory for the women's suffrage movement, which had worked to achieve this goal for many years. The women's movement had earlier gained full voting rights for women in four western states in the late nineteenth century.

Amendment 20.
"Lame-Duck" Amendment (1933)
Section 1. New Dates of Terms This amendment had two major purposes: (1) to shorten the time between the President's and Vice President's election and inauguration, and (2) to end "lame-duck" sessions of Congress.

When the Constitution first went into effect, transportation and communication were slow and uncertain. It often took many months after the election in November for the President and Vice President to travel to Washington, D.C., and prepare for their inauguration on March 4. This amendment ended this long wait for a new administration by fixing January 20 as inauguration day.

THE AMENDMENTS

Demonstrating Reasoned Judgment Tell students that at times our constitutional provisions protecting personal liberties have been sorely tested. One such test occurred during World War II. After the bombing of Pearl Harbor, more than 100,000 Japanese Americans, many of whom were citizens of the United States, were put into "detention camps." The United States government justified its action by claiming they were a security risk, even though there was no evidence of disloyalty. The Supreme Court upheld the action. Ask students if times of crisis, such as wartime, justify the suspension of personal liberties. **L2**

Did You Know?

Early in our history, women in one state— New Jersey—had the vote. The state's first constitution granted the suffrage to "any person" who met certain property qualifications. Many women took advantage of this provision to vote. The state legislature, however, took away this right from women in 1807.

Critical Thinking Activity

Making Comparisons Have students list advantages and disadvantages of the two-term limit for Presidents. Ask volunteers to present their list to the class and provide reasons for their choices. Finally, have students determine by vote whether or not they support presidential term limits. **L3**

Civil Disobedience

Tell students that before the passage of the Twenty-fourth Amendment, state and local governments could require people to pay a poll tax before being allowed to vote. This tax was often used to discriminate against voters with little money. Among those who opposed the poll tax was one of the nation's best writers and essayists, Henry David Thoreau.

In his "Essay on Civil Disobedience," Thoreau stressed that government can be a positive force in bettering society, but that the machinery of government at times appears unjust. When this happened, Thoreau believed a person had a right and a duty to take action. For Thoreau this meant not paying the poll tax and then using every public means to speak or write against it. The ideas expressed in "Civil Disobedience" became significant in the defense of minority rights in the twentieth century. Discuss with students the right to "disobey" government. Challenge them to determine when this tactic is appropriate. **L3**

Did You Know?

Although Prohibition caused many problems, it did succeed in reducing alcohol consumption, thus decreasing the number of alcohol-related deaths and accidents.

Section 2. Meeting Time of Congress "Lame-duck" sessions occurred every two years, after the November congressional election. That is, the Congress that held its session in December of an election year was not the newly elected Congress but the old Congress that had been elected two years earlier. This Congress continued to serve for several more months, usually until March of the next year. Often many of its members had failed to be re-elected and were called "lame-ducks." The 20th Amendment abolished this lame-duck session, and provided that the new Congress hold its first session soon after the November election, on January 3.

Section 3. Succession of President and Vice President This amendment provides that if the President-elect dies before taking office, the Vice President-elect becomes President. In the cases described, Congress will decide on a temporary President.

Section 4. Filling Presidential Vacancy If a presidential candidate dies while an election is being decided in the House, Congress may pass legislation to deal with the situation. Congress has similar power if this occurs when the Senate is deciding a vice-presidential election.

Section 5. Beginning the New Dates Sections 1 and 2 affected the Congress elected in 1934 and President Roosevelt, elected in 1936.

Section 6. Time Limit on Ratification The period for ratification by the states was limited to seven years.

Amendment 21.
Repeal of Prohibition Amendment (1933)
This amendment nullified the 18th Amendment. It is the only amendment ever passed to overturn an earlier amendment. It remained unlawful to transport alcoholic beverages into states that forbade their use. It is the only amendment ratified by special state conventions instead of state legislatures.

Section 2
The Congress shall assemble at least once in every year, and such meeting shall begin at noon on the 3rd day of January, unless they shall by law appoint a different day.

Section 3
If, at the time fixed for the beginning of the term of the President, the President elect shall have died, the Vice President elect shall become President. If a President shall not have been chosen before the time fixed for the beginning of his term, or if the President elect shall have failed to qualify, then the Vice President elect shall act as President until a President shall have qualified; and the Congress may by law provide for the case wherein neither a President elect nor a Vice President elect shall have qualified, declaring who shall then act as President, or the manner in which one who is to act shall be selected, and such person shall act accordingly until a President or Vice President shall have qualified.

Section 4
The Congress may by law provide for the case of the death of any of the persons from whom the House of Representatives may choose a President whenever the right of choice shall have devolved upon them, and for the case of the death of any of the persons from whom the Senate may choose a Vice President whenever the right of choice shall have devolved upon them.

Section 5
Sections 1 and 2 shall take effect on the 15th day of October following the ratification of this article.

Section 6
This article shall be inoperative unless it shall have been ratified as an amendment to the Constitution by the legislatures of three-fourths of the several States within seven years from the date of its submission.

Amendment XXI

Section 1
The eighteenth article of amendment to the Constitution of the United States is hereby repealed.

Section 2
The transportation or importation into any State, Territory, or possession of the United States for delivery or use therein of intoxicating liquors, in violation of the laws thereof, is hereby prohibited.

Section 3
This article shall be inoperative unless it shall have been ratified as an amendment to the Constitution by conventions in the several States, as provided in the Constitution, within seven years from the date of the submission hereof to the States by the Congress.

Critical Thinking Activity

Analyzing Ideas Have students debate the following topic:

"The principles of the Constitution have less and less impact on a government in which special-interest groups and their lobbies influence and control much of the legislation."

Have opposing sides present their arguments to the class. **L3**

Amendment XXII

Section 1

No person shall be elected to the office of the President more than twice, and no person who had held the office of President, or acted as President, for more than two years of a term to which some other person was elected President shall be elected to the office of the President more than once.

But this Article shall not apply to any person holding the office of President when this Article was proposed by the Congress, and shall not prevent any person who may be holding the office of President, or acting as President, during the term within which this Article becomes operative from holding the office of President or acting as President during the remainder of such term.

Section 2

This article shall be inoperative unless it shall have been ratified as an amendment to the Constitution by the legislatures of three-fourths of the several States within seven years from the date of its submission to the States by the Congress.

Amendment XXIII

Section 1

The District constituting the seat of Government of the United States shall appoint in such manner as the Congress may direct:

A number of electors of President and Vice President equal to the whole number of Senators and Representatives in Congress to which the District would be entitled if it were a State, but in no event more than the least populous State; they shall be in addition to those appointed by the States, but they shall be considered, for the purposes of the election of President and Vice President, to be electors appointed by a State; and they shall meet in the District and perform such duties as provided by the twelfth article of amendment.

Section 2

The Congress shall have power to enforce this article by appropriate legislation.

Amendment 22.
Limit on Presidential Terms (1951)

This amendment wrote into the Constitution a custom started by Washington, Jefferson, and Madison, whereby Presidents limited themselves to two terms in office. Although both Ulysses S. Grant and Theodore Roosevelt sought third terms, the two-term precedent was not broken until Franklin D. Roosevelt was elected to a third term in 1940 and then a fourth term in 1944. The passage of the 22nd amendment insures that no President is to be considered indispensable. It also provides that anyone who succeeds to the presidency and serves for more than two years of the term may not be elected more than one more time.

Amendment 23.
Presidential Electors for the District of Columbia (1961)

This amendment granted people living in the District of Columbia the right to vote in presidential elections. The District casts three electoral votes. The people of Washington, D.C., still are without representation in Congress.

Classifying Information
Write the headings that follow on the chalkboard:
- State-state and state-nation relations
- Executive branch
- Basic freedoms
- Extension of rights
- Congress and legislative procedures
- Military protection and rights
- Rights of the accused

Ask students to discuss what kinds of changes the amendments have produced. Have students review the amendments and categorize them according to the headings. *(Answers may vary slightly. The Twenty-third Amendment, for example, might be seen as either an extension of rights or a legislative procedure. Possible answers include: State-state [9, 10, 11]; Executive branch [12, 20, 22, 25]; Basic freedoms [1]; Extension of rights [13, 14, 15, 19, 26]; Procedures [16, 17, 23, 24]; Military [2, 3]; Rights: [5-8, 14])* **L3**

Did You Know?

During the 1960s the Supreme Court was dominated by Democratic appointees and made very broad interpretations in civil rights cases. In the 1990s a conservative-dominated Court made much narrower interpretations of civil rights issues.

Sidelight: The Twenty-fifth Amendment

When President Kennedy was assassinated in 1963, the need for a constitutional amendment dealing with presidential disability was obvious. Kennedy's successor, Lyndon B. Johnson, had once suffered a heart attack, and the two men in the line of succession after Johnson were both more than 70 years old. Congress passed the Twenty-fifth Amendment, which was submitted to the states in July 1965 and was ratified early in 1967.

THE AMENDMENTS

State Constitutions Each of the states has a state constitution. Have students discuss why it is necessary that states have a constitution although there is a national Constitution. *(The national Constitution is the supreme law of the land. On the state level, unless it is in conflict with national law, the state constitution is the supreme law of the state. State constitutions provide the basic framework for state governments themselves. State constitutions also establish systems of local government and a variety of state boards, agencies, and institutions as well as a revenue system for operation of the state government.)* **L3**

Did You Know?

The Twenty-seventh Amendment was proposed by James Madison and approved by Congress in 1798. It then went to the states for approval. It did not gain the approval of three-fourths of the states until May 7, 1992, when the Michigan Legislature approved it.

Amendment 24.
Abolition of the Poll Tax (1964)

A "poll tax" was a fee that persons were required to pay in order to vote in a number of Southern states. This amendment ended poll taxes as a requirement to vote in any presidential or congressional election. In 1966 the Supreme Court voided poll taxes in state elections as well.

Amendment 25.
Presidential Disability and Succession (1967)

Section 1. Replacing the President The Vice President becomes President if the President dies, resigns, or is removed from office.

Section 2. Replacing the Vice President The President is to appoint a new Vice President in case of a vacancy in that office, with the approval of the Congress.

The 25th Amendment is unusually precise and explicit because it was intended to solve a serious constitutional problem. Sixteen times in American history, before passage of this amendment, the office of Vice President was vacant, but fortunately in none of these cases did the President die or resign.

This amendment was used in 1973, when Vice President Spiro Agnew resigned from office after being charged with accepting bribes. President Nixon then appointed Gerald R. Ford as Vice President in accordance with the provisions of the 25th Amendment. A year later, President Richard Nixon resigned during the Watergate scandal, and Ford became President. President Ford then had to fill the Vice Presidency, which he had left vacant upon assuming the Presidency. He named Nelson A. Rockefeller as Vice President. Thus both the presidency and vice-presidency were held by men who had not been elected to their offices.

Section 3. Replacing the President With Consent If the President informs Congress, in writing, that he or she cannot carry out the duties of the office of President, the Vice President becomes Acting President.

Amendment XXIV

Section 1
The right of citizens of the United States to vote in any primary or other election for President or Vice President, for electors for President or Vice President, or for Senator or Representative in Congress, shall not be denied or abridged by the United States or any State by reason of failure to pay any poll tax or other tax.

Section 2
The Congress shall have power to enforce this article by appropriate legislation.

Amendment XXV

Section 1
In case of the removal of the President from office or his death or resignation, the Vice President shall become President.

Section 2
Whenever there is a vacancy in the office of the Vice President, the President shall nominate a Vice President who shall take the office upon confirmation by a majority vote of both houses of Congress.

Section 3
Whenever the President transmits to the President pro tempore of the Senate and the Speaker of the House of Representatives his written declaration that he is unable to discharge the powers and duties of his office, and until he transmits to them a written declaration to the contrary, such powers and duties shall be discharged by the Vice President as Acting President.

Section 4
Whenever the Vice President and a majority of either the principal officers of the executive departments or of such other body as Congress may by law provide, transmit to the President pro tempore of the Senate and the Speaker of the House of Representatives their written declaration that the President is unable to discharge the powers and duties of his office, the Vice President shall immediately assume the power and duties of the office of Acting President.

Thereafter, when the President transmits to the President pro tempore of the Senate and the Speaker of the House of Representatives his written declaration that no inability exists, he shall resume the powers and duties of his office unless the Vice President and a majority of either the principal officers of the executive departments or of such other body as Congress may by law provide, transmit within four days to the President pro tempore of the Senate and the Speaker of the House of Representa-

Critical Thinking Activity

Research Point out that compared to other written constitutions from around the world, the United States Constitution might be characterized as succinct. The average federal constitution has about 26,500 words, whereas the United States Constitution—with all its amendments—has less than 7,500 words. Have students research and write a brief report

comparing the United States Constitution with the constitutions of other nations. Suggest that they focus on such points as length, time in effective use, and political values espoused. Resource: *Written Constitutions: A Computerized Comparative Study* by Hene van Maarseveen and Ger van der Tang. **L3**

tives their written declaration that the President is unable to discharge the powers and duties of his office. Thereupon Congress shall decide the issue, assembling within forty-eight hours for that purpose if not in session. If the Congress within twenty-one days after receipt of the latter written declaration, or, if Congress is not in session, within twenty-one days after Congress is required to assemble, determines by two-thirds vote of both houses that the President is unable to discharge the powers and duties of his office, the Vice President shall continue to discharge the same as Acting President; otherwise, the President shall resume the power and duties of his office.

Amendment XXVI

Section 1

The right of citizens of the United States, who are eighteen years of age or older, to vote shall not be denied or abridged by the United States or by any State on account of age.

Section 2

The Congress shall have power to enforce this article by appropriate legislation.

Amendment XXVII

No law, varying the compensation for the services of Senators and Representatives, shall take effect, until an election of Representatives shall have intervened.

Section 4. Replacing the President Without Consent If the President is unable to carry out the duties of the office but is unable or unwilling to so notify Congress, the Cabinet and the Vice President are to inform Congress of this fact. The Vice President then becomes Acting President. The procedure by which the President may regain the office if he or she recovers is also spelled out in this amendment.

Amendment 26.
Eighteen-Year-Old Vote (1971)
This amendment made 18-year-olds eligible to vote in all federal, state, and local elections. Until then, the minimum age had been 21 in most states.

Amendment 27.
Restraint on Congressional Salaries (1992)
Any increase in the salaries of members of Congress will take effect in the subsequent session of Congress.

Did You Know?

The United States had had a disabled President several times in its history. In the 1880s James Garfield lingered 80 days in a coma before succumbing to an assassin's bullet. In this century Woodrow Wilson suffered a stroke that incapacitated him for the last several months of his presidency.

Visualizing History Point out to students that the amendment was passed during the Vietnam War. Many Americans argued that those old enough to fight were old enough to vote.
Answer to Caption: It lowered the minimum voting age from 21 to 18.

▲ VOTING RIGHTS The Twenty-sixth Amendment, ratified in 1971, extended the right and the responsibility of voting. *In what way did the amendment change voting eligibility?*

The Constitution of the United States **103**

Daily Lesson Objectives	Teacher Classroom Resources	Multimedia
SECTION 1 **Organizing the Government** **1 Day** pp. 106–109 1. List the precedents set by Washington as first President. 2. Discuss the key features of Hamilton's financial plan.	Reproducible Lesson Plan 3-1 *Guided Reading Activity 3-1 Concept Mapping Activities 3-A, 3-B Performance Assessment Activity 3 *Vocabulary Activity 3 Reteaching Activity 3-1 *Section Quiz 3-1	Section Focus Transparency 3-1 Chapter Concepts Transparencies 3-A, 3-B Vocabulary PuzzleMaker Testmaker MindJogger Videoquiz Powers of the President
SECTION 2 **The Federalist Era** **1 Day** pp. 111–116 1. Discuss the leaders and groups that opposed Hamilton's plan. 2. Describe the problems settlers faced during western expansion. 3. State how foreign affairs contributed to the growth of political parties.	Reproducible Lesson Plan 3-2 *Guided Reading Activity 3-2 Critical Thinking Skills Activity 3 American Portrait 13 Primary and Secondary Source Readings, pp. 5-6 Workbook Activity 3-2 Reteaching Activity 3-2 *Section Quiz 3-2	Section Focus Transparency 3-2 Testmaker Focus on Government The American History Videodisc
SECTION 3 **Age of Jefferson** **1 Day** pp. 117–122 1. Explain Thomas Jefferson's views on government. 2. Discuss the significance of the Louisiana Purchase. 3. Identify the problems that the United States faced in its attempt to remain neutral in the conflict between Great Britain and France.	Reproducible Lesson Plan 3-3 *Guided Reading Activity 3-3 Chapter Map Activity 3 Linking Past and Present Activity 3 American Portrait 15 Political Cartoons in American History Activity 10 Supreme Court Case Study 1 Chapter Skills Activity 3 Reteaching Activity 3-3 *Section Quiz 3-3	Section Focus Transparency 3-3 Skills Transparency 3 Testmaker Historic America Electronic Field Trips
SECTION 4 **The War of 1812** **1 Day** pp. 124–127 1. Describe the major campaigns of the War of 1812. 2. Summarize the results of the War of 1812 and the Treaty of Ghent.	Reproducible Lesson Plan 3-4 *Guided Reading Activity 3-4 Geography in History Activity 3 Workbook Activity 3-4 Enrichment Activity 3 Reteaching Activity 3-4 *Section Quiz 3-4	Section Focus Transparency 3-4 Map Transparency 3 Testmaker MindJogger Videoquiz
CHAPTER REVIEW AND EVALUATION **1 Day**	Chapter 3 Test, Forms A and B Spanish Chapter 3 Summary Performance Assessment Activity 3	MindJogger Videoquiz Student Self-Test & Review Software *Chapter 3 Digest Audiocassette Activity and Test

*Also available in Spanish

 0:00   **OUT OF TIME?** If time does not permit teaching the entire chapter, use the Chapter 3 Summary on pages 132–133 and the Chapter 3 audiocassette (English and Spanish) to point out the main ideas of the chapter.

A complete, 1-page lesson plan is provided for each section in the *Reproducible Lesson Plan* booklet.

Key to Ability Levels

Teaching strategies have been coded for varying learning styles and abilities.

L1 Basic activities for all students

L2 Average activities for average to above-average students

L3 Challenging activities for above-average students

LEP Limited English Proficiency activities

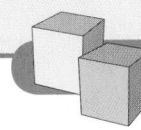

Block Schedule

Block scheduling differs from traditional class scheduling in the amount of time allotted to each period. The extended time frame provided by block scheduling affords you the opportunity to implement a greater number of research-oriented and activity-intense projects to motivate and involve your students. Activities that are particularly suited to use within the block scheduling frame work are identified throughout this unit by the following designation:

✓ Performance Assessment Activity

Comparing Political Administrations Ask students to work with a partner to identify similarities and differences between Washington's administration and Jefferson's. Encourage partners to develop a list of areas they might feature in their analysis: foreign policies, domestic policies, quality of political appointments, leadership style. Encourage students to find an appropriate way of sharing their findings with the class. Possibilities include charts and diagrams as well as oral and written reports.

POSSIBLE RUBRIC FEATURES

- Content
- Creativity
- Clarity
- Visual and Written Communication Skills
- Organization
- Use of Diagrams
- Cooperative Skills

📁 For additional activities, see Performance Assessment Strategies and Activities.

T E A C H E R ' S   C O R N E R

NATIONAL GEOGRAPHIC SOCIETY

INDEX TO NATIONAL GEOGRAPHIC MAGAZINE

The following articles may be used for research relating to this chapter:

- "L'Enfant's Washington," by Alice J. Hall, August 1991.
- "The Peales: America's First Family of Art," by Otto Friedrich, December 1990.
- "George Washington's Patowmack Canal," by Wilbur E. Garrett, June 1987.

NATIONAL GEOGRAPHIC SOCIETY PRODUCTS AVAILABLE FROM GLENCOE

To order the following products for use with this chapter, contact your local Glencoe sales representative or call Glencoe at 1-800-334-7344:

- *The Presidents: A Picture History of Our Nation* (CD-ROM)
- *GTV: A Geographic Perspective on American History* (Videodisc)
- *GTV: The American People: Fabric of a Nation* (Videodisc)

ADDITIONAL NATIONAL GEOGRAPHIC SOCIETY PRODUCTS

To order the following products for use with this chapter, call National Geographic Society at 1-800-368-2728:

- *The American Presidency* (Filmstrip)
- *Washington, D.C.* (Video)

BEGINNING THE CHAPTER

Recording Journal Notes

Before students read Chapter 3, ask them to list in their journals characteristics and beliefs elected officials ought to have. When students have completed reading the chapter, encourage them to see how closely early leaders matched the lists students prepared.

Point out that George Washington served two terms as President. That tradition of presidential term limits held for almost a century and a half.

CHAPTER 3
★★★★★★★★★★★★★★★★★★★★★★★★★★★★★★★★★★★★

Launching the Republic
1789–1815

▶ CHEROKEE BEADED SHOULDER BAG

Setting the Scene

Focus

With the ratification of the Constitution in 1789, a new national government set out to deal with the country's financial problems. As the United States developed politically, it faced new challenges in other ways. Between 1800 and 1815, the young republic doubled in size and found itself once more at war with Great Britain.

Concepts to Understand

★ How strong **leadership** brought stability to the new government

★ How **geographic expansion,** economic change, and conflict unified Americans and helped them form a national identity

Read to Discover . . .

★ some of the major issues faced by Presidents Washington and Adams during their terms of office.

★ the factors that caused the War of 1812.

Journal Notes

What were the personal characteristics and beliefs of the country's early leaders? Note details about them in your journal as you read the chapter.

CULTURAL	• **1789** *University of North Carolina founded*	• **1790** Columbia *is first American ship to circle globe*	• **1795** *Wooden-railed tramway built in Boston*
	1785	**1790**	**1795**
POLITICAL	• **1789** *George Washington is inaugurated*	• **1795** *Northwest Territory opens for settlement*	• **1797** *John Adams is inaugurated* • **1801** *Thomas Jefferson is inaugurated*

✚ EXTRA CREDIT PROJECT

The Bill of Rights Within six months of Washington's taking office, Congress had passed the first ten amendments to the Constitution, known collectively as the Bill of Rights. Then three-fourths of the states had to ratify those amendments. That process took more than two years. Ask interested students to work as a group to research the arguments used for and against approving the Bill of Rights. Have students present their findings to the class, listing the main points of each amendment and the arguments for and against it. **L2**

☆UNDER☆ ☆MY☆ ☆WINGS☆ ☆EVERY☆ ☆THING☆ ☆PROSPERS☆

◀ HOOKED RUG, 1790s

History AND ART

A View of New Orleans
by John L. Boqueta de Woiseri, 1803

This aquatint of New Orleans was painted in celebration of the purchase of the Louisiana Territory from France in 1803. The American eagle holds what some called a prophetic banner.

 1804 *San Gabriel Mission is site of first California orange grove*

 1807 *Inventor Robert Fulton perfects the steamboat* Clermont

1813 *Francis Scott Key writes "The Star-Spangled Banner"*

1800	1805	1810

1803 *Louisiana Purchase completed*
1807 *The* Chesapeake *is attacked*

1809 *Embargo Act is repealed*

1812 *War with Great Britain begins*
1815 *Treaty of Ghent ratified*

CHAPTER 3 Launching the Republic: 1789–1815 **105**

✔ Performance Assessment

Refer to the Performance Assessment Activity in the Planning Guide on page 104b. When the students have finished their analyses comparing Washington's and Jefferson's administrations, have each group present its analysis to the class. Allow time for class discussion and feedback.

🗁 Use Performance Assessment Activity 3 as an additional assessment technique.

CHAPTER 3 CONCEPTS

Concept Mapping Activity

Draw the concept map below on the chalkboard for students to copy. Have students underline the key words in the generalization and predict what topics will be covered in the chapter.

> Government affects political and economic values as it establishes the power of the growing nation

> Geographic Expansion

> Leadership

🗄 🗁 To reinforce the two chapter concepts, use Chapter Concept Mapping Activities 3-A and 3-B and assign Chapter Concepts Transparency Activities 3-A and 3-B.

History AND ART

This aquatint celebrates the purchase of the Louisiana Territory from France in 1803.

ABCNEWS INTERACTIVE™

💿 VIDEODISC

Powers of the President

Side One, Chapter 3
Title: *Constitution and the President*
Subject: The basic duties of the President, explained by President Jimmy Carter.

FOCUS

Bellringer

Before taking roll, project Section Focus Transparency 3-1 or hand out Section Focus Transparency Activity 3-1. Have students answer the questions.

Motivating Activity

Organize students into two groups. Have one group compile lists naming the areas of knowledge a President needs. *(Examples: politics, foreign policy, economics)* Have the other group list the qualities an effective leader should possess. *(Examples: intelligence, trustworthiness, sensitivity to people's needs)* Discuss why the first President of any new government would need outstanding skills. **L2**

Vocabulary Precheck

Ask students to define each of the "Key Terms." Have a volunteer consult the dictionary for any unfamiliar words. **L1, LEP**

Use the Vocabulary PuzzleMaker for Chapter 3 to create a crossword puzzle. **L1**

Assign Vocabulary Activity 3.

★★★

Organizing the Government

Setting the Scene

Section Focus

Although George Washington was reluctant to take the job of President, his reputation and stature were critical to the nation's success. His secretary of the treasury, Alexander Hamilton, brought financial stability to the new government.

◀ PRESIDENTIAL SEAL

Objectives

After studying this section, you should be able to

★ list the precedents set by Washington as first President.

★ discuss the key features of Hamilton's financial plan.

Key Terms

cabinet, protective tariff, revenue tariff, excise tax

George Washington accepted the presidency reluctantly. On the day he left for his inauguration, he wrote in his diary:

❝ *About ten o'clock I bade adieu to Mt. Vernon, to private life, and to domestic felicity, and with a mind oppressed with more anxious and painful sensations than I care to express, set out for New York.* ❞

When Washington reached New York, the nation's capital, on April 23, 1789, he was rowed across the Hudson River on a barge built especially for the occasion. Most of New York's residents lined the wharves and cheered as the barge neared shore. Seven days later, Washington took the oath of office and gave the first Inaugural Address. Throughout the land there was public rejoic-

ing for the man many believed to be the United States's greatest national asset.

■ Setting Precedents

Washington's background was as plantation manager and soldier. Because he lacked experience in government, he felt he was unprepared to be the chief executive. Although Washington doubted his own qualifications, many Americans regarded him with deep admiration. Such respect had its value to the new government. As a visible symbol of unity and power, Washington provided a focus for loyalty to the nation.

Washington as President

Washington proved to be a first-rate administrator. In the summer of 1789, Congress set up three executive departments: a

---

Classroom Resources for SECTION 1

Blackline Masters:
- Reproducible Lesson Plan 3-1
- Guided Reading Activity 3-1
- Vocabulary Activity 3
- Workbook Activity 3-1
- Reteaching Activity 3-1
- Section Quiz 3-1

Transparencies:
- Section Focus Transparency 3-1

Multimedia
- Vocabulary PuzzleMaker
- Testmaker
- Powers of the President

Department of State to take charge of foreign affairs, a Department of the Treasury to handle the nation's finances, and a Department of War to manage the military. Congress also created the position of attorney general to handle the government's legal matters. On important matters, Washington sought the advice of executive department heads, establishing what became known as the **cabinet,** a group of advisers to the President that continues to serve the same function today.

Creating a cabinet was only one of several precedents set by Washington in areas where the Constitution was silent or unclear. He determined that the Senate's approval power over presidential appointments did not extend to their removal from office. He took control of foreign affairs, limiting the Senate's role of advice and consent to ratifying or rejecting treaties only after they were made.

Although he headed the executive branch, Washington assumed leadership in legislative affairs as well. In written messages to Congress, Washington urged passage of laws he believed were in the public interest. With such encouragement, Congress almost invariably followed his lead. Later Presidents would follow suit and become what some have called "chief legislator."

The First Congress

Congress—both Senate and House of Representatives—met for the first time in April 1789. The Senate was a small, quiet, and formal body consisting of two members from each state elected by their state legislature. Senators dressed in powdered wigs, lace, and velvet. For its first five years, the Senate conducted its business in private. Not until 1794 was a gallery built for the public and the press.

▲ *THE WASHINGTON FAMILY* by Edward Savage, c. 1798 When Washington took the oath of office on April 30, 1789, the machinery of government did not exist. There were no federal laws, no federal courts, and no federal law-enforcement officials. *What was Washington's background before he became President?*

TEACH
Guided Practice
Making Comparisons
Have students work with groups of three to four people to create charts that compare major differences in the function of the House and the Senate in the 1790s and today. **L2, L3**

Discuss the changes in functions of the House and the Senate and the reasons for the changes in sizes of both bodies. **L2, L3**

History AND ART

Savage painted George and Martha Washington and their two grandchildren after Martha's daughter died in the 1770s. The map represents their vast landholdings, and the African American symbolizes the enslaved people who worked their estates.
Answer to Caption: as plantation manager and soldier

Did You Know?

Congress voted George Washington a yearly salary of $25,000. At the time the average skilled artisan earned about $300 a year. Unskilled laborers earned about $160 a year.

Special Needs Activity

Attention Deficiency Many students have difficulty paying attention in class. For some students inattention is related to an attention deficit hyperactivity disorder (the name given by psychologists). Severe inattention problems call for special interventions in the classroom.

One popular intervention is to give a time limit for a task. Ask students to read the text "Washington as President," a section of approximately 200 words. Give students five minutes to read (enough time for average readers). Did the time limit help them pay attention? Discuss. **L1**

Independent Practice

Research and Writing

Write the following on the chalkboard:

Historians consider Alexander Hamilton a brilliant secretary of the treasury but a failure as a politician.

Have students research information about Alexander Hamilton. Then ask them to write several paragraphs citing evidence to explain whether they agree or disagree with this assessment. **L3**

📁 Assign Guided Reading Activity 3-1.

History AND ART

The half dime was the first coin struck by the U.S. government in July 1792. Dunsmore captures the inspection of the coins, the portrait on which—emblematic of Liberty—may have been modeled by Martha Washington.
Answer to Caption: debts owed to foreign governments and individual Americans to fight the Revolutionary War

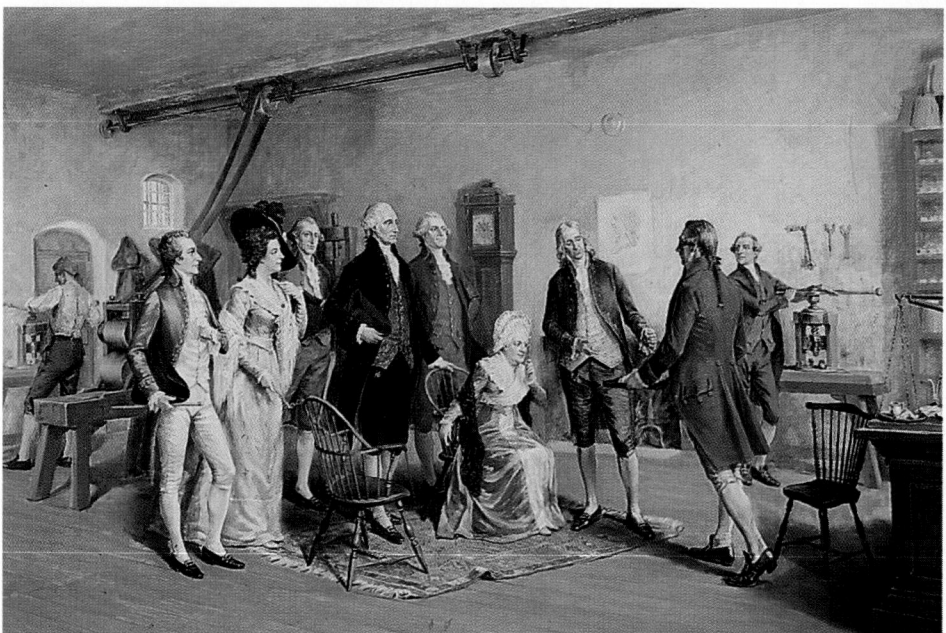

▲ *THE INSPECTION OF THE FIRST U.S. COINS* by John W. Dunsmore, 1914 The half disme [dime] was the first coin struck by the United States government in July 1792. ***What debts did the new nation owe?***

The House was more informal. Elected by the people, the House welcomed the public and the press from the beginning. Debate was loud, and members often wore their hats inside the chamber. The House took the lead in legislative matters, especially in dealing with the nation's troubled finances.

Creation of the Judiciary

Congress also turned its attention to the judicial branch and passed the Judiciary Act of 1789, setting up the Supreme Court and lower courts. President Washington quickly named the first Supreme Court justices, deliberately choosing three from Northern and three from Southern states.

The Bill of Rights

Although a majority in both the Senate and the House had supported ratification of the Constitution, the Anti-Federalist minority insisted that Congress quickly provide the Bill of Rights promised during the ratifi-

cation campaign. In September 1789, after much debate, Congress proposed 12 amendments. Of these, 10 were ratified by the states and added to the Constitution in 1791. The Bill of Rights protected personal liberties, such as freedom of religion, freedom of speech, and trial by jury. It also protected the rights of the individual states.

■ Hamilton's Program

To pay for the country's expenses, Congress in 1789 passed a tariff, or tax on imports. Representatives from New England and the South at first wanted a **protective tariff**—a high tax on imports to protect their products from foreign competition. They finally agreed to a **revenue tariff,** a low tax on imports designed to provide income for the government rather than protection for private businesses.

Most of the money raised by the tariff was needed to pay off the national debt. The Continental Congress had borrowed money from foreign governments and individual

Critical Thinking Activity

Analyzing Viewpoints Organize the class into two groups, and have them conduct an informal debate. Ask one group to attack Hamilton's economic plan for the elimination of the national debt, and have the other group defend the plan. As students prepare, have them take the following questions into consideration:

1. What group(s) and section(s) would be helped by the plan? Hurt by the plan?
2. What other viable solutions could have been used? **L3**

Americans to fight the Revolutionary War. The new government now wanted to honor these debts as well as make payments to the soldiers who had fought in the conflict.

The debate over national finances in 1790 and 1791 was dominated by 33-year-old Alexander Hamilton, the secretary of the treasury. Hamilton presented Congress with a financial plan that reflected his belief in a strong government that favored the wealthy classes and fulfilled its financial obligations.

In dealing with debts owed to foreigners and individual Americans, Hamilton called for the national government to pay its creditors in full. In doing so, he argued, the United States would tell its citizens and the world that it was a strong, independent nation whose promises were good. Congress responded by repaying foreign governments by 1796. It also enacted legislation to pay back American creditors.

Hamilton also proposed that the federal government pay the debts accumulated by individual states since the Revolution. The states had fought for the entire nation, he stated, so the cost of their help during the Revolution should be assumed by the national government. Most Southern states, however, had already paid their debts in full and did not want their taxes used to pay the debts of Northern states. A compromise, however, was finally worked out. The Southerners would back the federal govern-

ment's assumption of state debts. In return, the nation's capital would eventually move to a new federal city on the Potomac River between Maryland and Virginia.

To help the government with its expenses, Hamilton favored an excise tax in addition to the tariff. An **excise tax** is a tax paid by the manufacturer of a product and passed on to those who buy the product. In 1791, Congress enacted the first excise tax—on whiskey.

A key element of Hamilton's proposals was that the federal government establish a national bank. The bank would be a place for the federal government to deposit its tax receipts, as well as a place where tax revenues and private deposits could be used for large loans to government and to businesses.

Most important, the proposed bank would issue paper money backed by gold and silver in the bank's vaults. The public could have confidence in this currency because it could be exchanged for coins on demand.

On the whole, Hamilton's plan had immediate success in restoring the credit of the United States. Most of his proposals had been enacted by Congress; however, the debate over many of them—especially the national bank—became bitter and divisive.

▲ MEMORIAL TANKARD

Section 1 ★ Review

Checking for Understanding

1. **Identify** Department of Treasury, Judiciary Act of 1789.

2. **Define** cabinet, protective tariff, revenue tariff, excise tax.

3. **Describe** some of the precedents set by Washington that are still practiced by Presidents today.

4. **Explain** the purpose and function of the national bank.

Critical Thinking

5. **Evaluating Performance** Given his lack of experience in government and politics, explain why Washington was able to head a new framework of government.

ACTIVITY

6. How would life be different without the Bill of Rights? Develop a chart that lists events that happen in your life and the way these events would be different without your basic rights.

ASSESS
Check Understanding
Assign Section 1 Review as homework or an in-class activity.

Evaluate
Assign Section Quiz 3-1 or use the Test-maker to create a customized quiz.

Reteach
Have students write three statements about George Washington based on facts and three statements expressing opinions about the First Congress and about Hamilton's program.

Have students complete Reteaching Activity 3-1.

Enrich
Have students write newspaper headlines and brief editorials that reflect the conflicts created by Hamilton's national bank.

CLOSE
Have students speculate how government in the United States might have been different had Washington made different decisions.

Answers to SECTION 1 REVIEW

1. Department of Treasury, 107; Judiciary Act of 1789, 108
2. All vocabulary words are defined in the Glossary.
3. established a cabinet, limited Senate's power to only ratify or reject but not make treaties
4. A depository for federal tax receipts and private deposits to be used for loans to government and businesses; would issue paper

currency backed by the bank's gold and silver.
5. Answers will vary but may include that he had no political preconceptions or biases based on previous government experience, an open mind, and no attachments to the previous Confederation government.
6. Charts should include examples of ways that the Bill of Rights is reflected in daily events.

TEACH

Demonstrating Reasoned Judgment Ask students why L'Enfant's plan for the capital proved to be a success. (*The capital is accessible and has provided a logical arrangement for key structures.*)

CURRICULUM CONNECTION

Architecture Because of disagreements with government planners and massive cost overruns, L'Enfant was dismissed in 1792 and his plans for the national capital were shelved. Some 100 years later, his original designs were readopted as guidelines for all future developments in the city

Did You Know?

French-born American engineer Pierre Charles L'Enfant completed the plan for the capital city of Washington in 1791, but Congress paid him only $3,800 of the $95,500 he thought was due to him. L'Enfant died in poverty.

Planning Washington, D.C.

By using inspiration, imagination, and his skill in geometry, engineer Pierre Charles L'Enfant created the design for a national capital unlike any other. When L'Enfant, who fought in the Revolution, heard that Congress was planning a new national capital, he quickly offered his services. President Washington hired L'Enfant, and the President himself negotiated purchase from the farmers who owned the land where the capital was to rise.

▲ WASHINGTON, D.C., TODAY

▲ THE CAPITOL, 1824

Although L'Enfant's design was soon modified, his basic plan allowed a spacious, modern city to develop. He envisioned a rationally laid-out metropolis that would embody the new nation's republican ideals, with wide boulevards connecting the branches of government, national monuments, parks, and entry gates.

L'Enfant began by choosing the spots for the Capitol and President's house. The Congress building became the central point in a square

grid of streets occupying the terrain between the Potomac and Anacostia rivers. The grid was slashed by avenues that radiated from the capitol hill like spokes on a wheel. These avenues provided a direct route to different parts of the city. At strategic spots, L'Enfant's unique blend of topography and geometric symmetry called for circular intersections to join three or more avenues.

Making the Math Connection

1. What geometric forms did L'Enfant use in planning the design of Washington, D.C.?

2. What are the advantages of locating a capital in a planned city? What might be some disadvantages?

3. What kinds of geometric shapes are used in the design of modern government buildings?

ACTIVITY

4. Make a map of your community. Include a compass rose, a scale, and a map legend that explains the symbols used on the map. Points of interest should include neighborhood stores, parks, community centers, or medical centers. Indicate any important geographic features.

Answers to Making the Connection

1. squares, circles, angles, triangles, rectangles
2. the ability to site important buildings and monuments for best effect and to create an over-all sense of order and dignity
3. Answers will vary but may include rectangles and circles.
4. Maps will vary but should include the map elements requested.

★★★

The Federalist Era

Setting the Scene

Section Focus

Hamilton's proposals created a sound basis for the nation's finances. The plan, however, rekindled a national debate over the amount of power exercised by the national government. The growing controversy eventually resulted in the formation of the nation's first political parties.

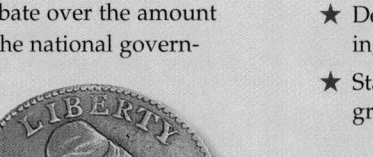

Objectives

★ Discuss the leaders and groups that opposed Hamilton's plan.

★ Describe the problems settlers faced during western expansion.

★ State how foreign affairs contributed to the growth of political parties.

Key Terms

enumerated power, implied power, nullification

◄ AMERICAN COINS, 1795-1796

*D*espite its merits, Alexander Hamilton's program encountered a good deal of opposition. Much of the opposition was led by Thomas Jefferson, Washington's secretary of state. These tensions between Hamilton and Jefferson involved a personal struggle for power in Washington's cabinet. In addition, their conflict also reflected larger differences in the vision each man had for the nation's future.

■ A Question of Power

Alexander Hamilton was a self-made man who called democracy "poison" and characterized the general public as selfish, unreasonable, and violent. He believed that a powerful central government was neces-

sary to keep law and order. Also, he wanted to reduce the power of the states.

Thomas Jefferson, born to wealth and social position, believed that if people were given the opportunity, they would be decent and reasonable. A defender of liberty, Jefferson believed in a minimum of government and favored power at the local level. Because Jefferson could not block Hamilton in the executive branch, the conflict between the two men was played out in Congress, where Jefferson's ally, James Madison, represented Virginia.

When Congress debated the bill to establish a national bank, Madison attacked it on constitutional grounds. Congress had no right to set up a bank, he argued, because it was not among the **enumerated powers,** or powers mentioned specifically

---

Classroom Resources for SECTION 2

Blackline Masters:
- 🗂 Reproducible Lesson Plan 3-2
- 🗂 Guided Reading Activity 3-2
- 🗂 Critical Thinking Skills Activity 3
- 🗂 American Portrait 13
- 🗂 Primary and Secondary Source Readings, pp. 5-6
- 🗂 Reteaching Activity 3-2
- 🗂 Section Quiz 3-2

Transparencies:
- 🖐 Section Focus Transparency 3-2

Multimedia
- 📺 Testmaker
- 💿 Focus on Government
- 💿 The American History Videodisc

LESSON PLAN
SECTION 2, 111–116

FOCUS
Bellringer

🖐 🗂 Before taking roll, project Section Focus Transparency 3-2 or hand out Section Focus Transparency Activity 3-2. Have students answer the questions.

Motivating Activity

Ask students to discuss how they would feel if they had no choice in their everyday lives—they could buy only one style of clothes for example. Explain that in a democratic society, people are theoretically able to make choices that affect their lives. Then write "Republican Party" and "Democratic Party" on the chalkboard. Ask students why people like to have a choice in voting for either party. (*represent different points of view and different platforms*) **L1**

Vocabulary Precheck

Ask students to define each of the "Key Terms." Have a volunteer consult the dictionary for any unfamiliar words. **L1, LEP**

GLENCOE
TECHNOLOGY

 VIDEODISC

Focus on Government

Side 1, Chapter 5
Title: *Lecture Launcher, The Federal System*
Subject: Relationship among Federal, state, and local governments

TEACH
Guided Practice
Analyzing Arguments
Divide the chalkboard into two sections. Label one section "Arguments for a National Bank," and label the other one "Arguments Against a National Bank." Have students volunteer to provide the information for each heading. (*Examples—For: Government could use it for borrowing and collecting taxes; it would promote interstate business. Against: Federal government has no right to establish such a bank since it is not provided for in the Constitution.*) Hold a discussion on the need for such a bank. Tell students that today's Federal Reserve Bank fulfills some of the same functions as Hamilton's National Bank. **L2**

Map Study *Using Maps*

Answer: near Fort Miami and the Maumee River

Map Skills Practice
Ask students in which general direction Wayne and St. Clair traveled in their campaigns against the Native Americans. (*north*)

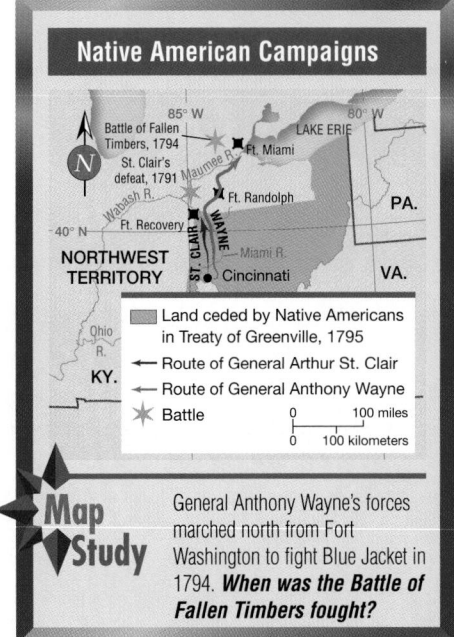

Native American Campaigns

Battle of Fallen Timbers, 1794
St. Clair's defeat, 1791
Ft. Recovery
Ft. Miami
LAKE ERIE
Ft. Randolph
PA.
Miami R.
Cincinnati
VA.
NORTHWEST TERRITORY
Ohio R.
KY.

☐ Land ceded by Native Americans in Treaty of Greenville, 1795
← Route of General Arthur St. Clair
← Route of General Anthony Wayne
✶ Battle

0   100 miles
0   100 kilometers

Map Study General Anthony Wayne's forces marched north from Fort Washington to fight Blue Jacket in 1794. **When was the Battle of Fallen Timbers fought?**

in the Constitution. Nor was it an **implied power,** a power that, while not directly stated in the Constitution, is suggested and does allow Congress to exercise its stated powers. If the federal government established a national bank, he feared there would be no limits to federal power.

Despite Madison's arguments, Congress passed the Bank Bill. Washington, however, hesitated to sign the bill, realizing that any action he took would set an important precedent. Instead, he asked Attorney General Edmund Randolph and Secretary of State Jefferson for written opinions on the constitutionality of a national bank. Each opposed it on the basis of Madison's argument that it was an overextension of federal power.

Washington passed these opinions on to Hamilton, who wrote a reply that convinced the President to sign the bill. In a classic statement of implied powers, Hamilton argued that because the bank's functions were among the powers given Congress, the Constitution gave Congress the right to choose any legal means to carry out those functions. In 1791 the Bank of the United States was established.

■ Problems in the West
While Americans debated the powers of the federal government, the nation faced continuing concerns about the western territories. The most immediate cause for alarm was conflict over land between western settlers and Native American nations.

Treaties and Settlement
South of the Ohio River, treaties were signed with the Cherokee in 1791 and the Chickamauga in 1794—and the Creek asked for federal government protection from settlers. The influx of settlers continued, however; and population increases enabled Kentucky and Tennessee to join the Union as states in the 1790s.

Northwest Conflicts
In November 1791, Native Americans in the Northwest Territory defeated United States regular troops and militia led by General Arthur St. Clair. The Native Americans demanded that all settlers north of the Ohio River leave the territory. Washington turned to Anthony Wayne, known for his military skills in the Revolutionary War. In August 1794, Wayne's force defeated Native Americans under Shawnee Chief Blue Jacket at the Battle of Fallen Timbers. A year later, in the Treaty of Greenville, the Native Americans agreed to surrender most of present-day Ohio.

The Whiskey Rebellion
Another western uprising occurred among farmers who opposed Hamilton's excise tax on whiskey. Because of the high cost of transportation, many farmers distilled their grain into whiskey and sold it or used it in place of scarce currency. Antitax sentiment drove farmers in western Pennsylvania to refuse to pay the tax and to attack revenue officers. Known as the Whiskey Rebellion, this revolt was put down by a strong federal government.

Sidelight: The French Revolution

After the American Revolution, the French sought major changes in their own nation. In many ways French society of the late 1700s was feudal. By law, people belonged to one of three classes, or estates. A person's social status, political rights, and economic privileges were determined by which estate he or she belonged to. Many people in all of the estates were dissatisfied with their positions because of unequal privileges. This and the heavy burden of taxation placed on the poor were major causes of the French Revolution.

Foreign Affairs Under Washington

Shortly after Washington was inaugurated in 1789, the French Revolution flared in Europe. Americans sympathized with the French revolutionaries because they were demanding the same rights Americans had won a few years earlier. Cheers for France, however, were often joined with damnation of Britain. Not only was the memory of the American Revolution still strong, but there was resentment because of the British refusal to give up the fur posts and to stop arming Native Americans in the Northwest.

America's European Problems

When Britain and France went to war in 1793, Washington issued a Proclamation of Neutrality that declared the United States would not help either side. Washington's administration opposed French efforts to gain American public support for France in this war. The British also tested America's neutral stance by forbidding neutral ships to trade with France. British warships seized hundreds of American vessels and seized their cargo, a clear violation of international law. These attacks, plus British support of Native Americans in the Northwest, pushed Congress to the brink of war. Washington, however, sought peace and sent John Jay, chief justice of the United States, as a special envoy to Great Britain.

Treaties With Britain and Spain

Britain and the United States were important trading partners, so they both sought a treaty. In the Jay Treaty of 1794, the British, however, gave fewer concessions than they received. They agreed to abandon the fur posts in the Northwest but gave no promise to stop arming Native Americans or to respect American neutral rights on the high seas. Because of its unpopularity in the United States, the Jay Treaty was only narrowly ratified by the Senate.

The United States also worked to improve relations with Spain. In the Pinckney Treaty, completed in 1795, the Americans won free navigation of the Mississippi River and the right to deposit goods at New Orleans without paying taxes. The United States also gained Spain's recognition of the United States's southern boundary at the 31st parallel and western boundary at the Mississippi.

Rise of Political Parties

Washington had wanted to retire to private life after his first term as President. He consented to run for a second term only after prominent politicians, including both Jefferson and Hamilton, urged him to do so as a patriotic duty. In 1792, as in 1789, he received no opposition in the electoral college. Washington's second term, however, was filled with political turmoil. Washington continued to favor Hamilton over Jefferson, and Jefferson finally resigned from the cabinet in 1793. Washington was harshly criticized by Jefferson's supporters.

▲ GLASSWARE HONORING PRESIDENT WASHINGTON

Farewell Address

Feeling that the government had been safely launched, Washington decided not to seek a third term in 1796, setting a precedent that was followed until 1940 when President Franklin Roosevelt ran for a third term.

In his Farewell Address, Washington warned the nation against political parties and entanglement in the affairs of other countries:

> ❝ Let me warn you in the most solemn manner against the baneful effects of the spirit of party generally. . . . This spirit, unfortunately, is inseparable from our nature, having its root in the strongest passions of the human mind. . . .

Cooperative Learning Activity

Teaching Key Concepts To review the problems in the West, group students into teams of three, and appoint a team leader for each group. Assign the two other team members in each group one of the following topics: the Native Americans and their defeat at the Battle of Fallen Timbers or the Whiskey Rebellion. Allow team members 15 minutes to study and summarize the key concepts of their topics and teach them to the members of their teams. Have team leaders make outlines of the key concepts that each group member teaches. **L1, L2**

Independent Practice

Constructing a Flow Chart
Have students construct vertical flow charts to show the causes, events, and effects of the Jay and Pinckney treaties. **L2**

📁 Assign Guided Reading Activity 2-2.

Did You Know?

In 1796, for the first time in the United States an election was held in which the winning candidate for President represented one party and the Vice President another.

Food of the Times

European settlers brought the custom of making ice cream to the United States in the late 1700s. (The dish was invented in Paris.) Ice cream did not become popular with Americans until Thomas Jefferson, George Washington, and James Madison served it to their guests.

So, likewise, a passionate attachment of one nation for another produces a variety of evils. . . .

The great rule of conduct for us in regard to foreign nations is, in extending our commercial relations, to have with them as little political connection as possible. So far as we have already formed engagements let them be fulfilled with perfect good faith. Here let us stop. 🙶🙶

The Farewell Address charted a sensible course for the young nation. When Washington left office, however, the Federalist party lost its only candidate with significant nationwide appeal.

Republicans and Federalists

Washington's first administration had no permanent divisions based on politics or causes. Jefferson's resignation from the cabinet, however, signaled a formal split in the ranks of the nation's political leadership. It led to the beginnings of America's two-party political system.

After resigning, Jefferson openly allied with James Madison to form what they called the "Republican" interest. They chose this name to suggest they were defending freedom and self-government from the anti-democratic influence of Hamilton. Republicans advocated limiting the power of the central government in favor of the states and the individual. Their strength was among Southern planters, subsistence farmers of the backcountry, and "mechanics" such as carpenters and shoemakers.

Hamilton's supporters took the name "Federalists," the label used by supporters of the Constitution during the ratification campaign. This maneuver was intended to imply that the Republicans did not support the Constitution. Reflecting Hamilton's distrust of the people, the Federalists hoped to put the direction of government into the hands of the "rich, well-born, and able." Many of them were creditors, merchants, and bondholders.

Election of 1796

When Washington decided not to run for President in 1796, the Federalists selected Vice President John Adams to run. The Republicans countered with Thomas Jefferson. Because the Framers of the Constitution had not anticipated political parties, the nation's first presidential election involving parties was a confusing contest. The Constitution provided that each elector cast two votes, and the candidate receiving the largest number would become President; the runner-up, Vice President. The result was that Adams won an electoral victory of only three votes, and Thomas Jefferson came in second. Thus a Federalist President was elected with a Republican Vice President.

■ Adams in Office

John Adams had spent most of his life in public service. An early leader of the revolutionary movement in Massachusetts, he was

★★★ AMERICA'S FLAGS ★★★

The First Flag Legend holds that Philadelphia seamstress Betsy Ross stitched the first Stars and Stripes. Historical records do not support this account, however. The popular "Betsy Ross flag," which arranged the 13 stars in a circle, did not appear until the early 1790s. Its creator is unknown.

The Second Flag The Stars and Stripes gained two more stars and two more stripes when Kentucky and Vermont  joined the Union in 1794. Captain Samuel C. Reid realized that the flag would become too large if a stripe were added for every new state. He suggested to Congress that the stripes remain at 13—for the original 13 colonies—and that a star be added for each new state admitted to the Union.

★★★★★★★★★★★★★★★★★★★★★★★★

Critical Thinking Activity

Analyzing Viewpoints In his "Farewell Address," George Washington wrote: "'Tis our true policy to steer clear of permanent alliances, with any portion of the foreign world. . . . There can be no greater error than to expect or calculate upon real favors from nation to nation." Ask students to write a paragraph analyzing why Washington thought the United States should avoid permanent foreign alliances and why he thought the nation would be able to avoid such alliances. **L2**

📁 For additional practice, assign Critical Thinking Skills Activity 3.

★★★★★ AMERICAN PORTRAITS ★★★★★

Born into a free family in Maryland, Benjamin Banneker was largely self-educated. When his father died, Banneker sold the family farm and devoted the rest of his life to mathematics and natural science.

Banneker's skill in mathematics prompted Thomas Jefferson to secure him a job surveying the land for the new national capital at Washington, D.C. Legend has it that when the French architect Pierre L'Enfant quit the project and took his detailed maps with him, Banneker reproduced L'Enfant's plans from memory.

Later, Banneker wrote and published a most successful almanac. His picture on the cover proclaimed it as the work of an African American. Banneker's efforts and his achievements brought attention to racial injustice in a land not yet willing to grant him rights of citizenship.

Benjamin Banneker
1731–1806

a prominent member of the First and Second Continental Congresses. After the Revolutionary War, he became the nation's first minister to Great Britain. Under Washington, Adams served two terms as Vice President.

Relations With France

French disappointment over American neutrality turned to hostility after the Jay Treaty. Immediately after taking office, Adams sent envoys to France to negotiate a treaty. When government agents in Paris offered a bribe, the American envoys refused and broke off negotiations. Because reports labeled the agents as X, Y, and Z, this scandal became known as the XYZ affair, and it produced an outburst of American public anger against France.

An undeclared naval war with France strengthened the federal government, made the Federalists popular, and discredited the pro-French Republicans. By the end of his presidency, however, Adams restored peace with the French. Most Federalists opposed the President's action.

Anti-Republican Legislation

In addition to their stand against Adams, many Federalists decided to act against prominent Republicans whom they believed were actively in league with France. In 1798, the Federalist majority in Congress pushed laws through Congress designed to hurt the Republican party. One of these measures, the Sedition Act, tried to muzzle

Visualizing History ▲ ADAMS IN OFFICE John Adams's influence in the Constitutional Convention helped to produce the strong office of the President. *As President, Adams faced opposition from what political party?*

Cooperative Learning Activity

Analyzing Topics Organize students into groups of four or five. Give each group the topic "John Adams as President." Using one piece of paper per group, have each person take a turn writing a statement about Adams's presidency. Have each group critique and change statements that do not relate to the topic. Then have each group share its statements with the class. Discuss any missing information. **L1, LEP**

📁 For additional practice in cooperative learning, assign Cooperative Learning Activity 3.

Biography Have students write a one-page biography of President John Adams. Ask them to describe his successes and failures as President. **L2**

📁 Assign American Portrait 13: Abigail Adams.

Teaching American Portraits

Besides being a mathematician, surveyor, and scientist, Benjamin Banneker was a farmer and a publisher of a well-known yearly almanac. He is known for accurately predicting an eclipse. Ask: Why do you think people considered Banneker an amazing person? (*Sample answer: It is amazing that someone who was largely self-educated became so accomplished.*) **L1**

Visualizing History Twenty-one years before becoming President, John Adams had successfully pushed the Declaration of Independence through Congress. He also helped negotiate the 1783 peace treaty that had ended the Revolutionary War. **Answer to Caption:** the Republicans

ASSESS
Check Understanding

Assign Section 2 Review as homework or an in-class activity.

Visualizing History Under the Sedition Act, Representative Matthew Lyon of Vermont was fined $1,000 and put in jail for four months for publishing criticism of President John Adams. **Answer to Caption:** This law made it a crime to speak or publish anything false or malicious against the government or government officials.

Evaluate

☞ Assign Section Quiz 3-2 or use the Testmaker to create a customized quiz.

Reteach

☞ Have students complete Reteaching Activity 3-2.

Enrich

☞ Assign Primary and Secondary Source Readings, pp. 5-6.

CLOSE

Point out that John Adams was not a popular President. Ask students to tell why he was a successful President even though he was unpopular.

▲ FIST FIGHT IN CONGRESS The difficulties of the new nation were portrayed in the cartoons of the day. Republican Matthew Lyon and Federalist Roger Griswold brawled in Congress. **What was the Sedition Act?**

the Republican press by making it a crime to speak or publish anything false or malicious against the federal government or any of its officers.

Instead of weakening the Republicans, the laws enabled the Republicans to broaden their support. Republicans were horrified by these attacks on freedom of speech and press. In 1798 and 1799, the Republican legislatures of Kentucky and Virginia passed resolutions denouncing the Sedition Act as unconstitutional. The Kentucky Resolutions presented the theory of **nullification.** According to this theory, a state had the right to disobey any act of the federal government that exceeded the powers granted by the Constitution. Other states denounced this nullification theory as threatening to the Union. If a state could nullify any federal law it considered unconstitutional, the power of the federal government would cease.

Section 2 ★ Review

Checking for Understanding

1. **Identify** Fallen Timbers, Whiskey Rebellion, Jay Treaty, Pinckney Treaty, XYZ affair, Kentucky and Virginia Resolutions.

2. **Define** enumerated power, implied power, nullification.

3. **Show** how Great Britain's actions against the United States nearly resulted in war.

4. **List** the main differences between the Republicans and the Federalists.

Critical Thinking

5. **Evaluating Ideas** List what you consider to be the strengths and weaknesses of having political parties. Use your list to write a paragraph explaining why you favor or oppose parties.

ACTIVITY

6. Select one American political party, either a major party or a third party. Create a time line poster showing major events in the party's history.

Answers to SECTION 2 REVIEW

1. Fallen Timbers, 112; Whiskey Rebellion, 112; Jay Treaty, 113; Pinckney Treaty, 113; XYZ affair, 115; Kentucky and Virginia Resolutions, 116
2. All vocabulary words are defined in the Glossary.
3. British restrictions on neutral trade with France hit the United States especially hard; British seizures of American ships and cargoes violated international law.
4. Republicans advocated limited authority for central government and catered to people of ordinary means. Federalists advocated strong authority for central government and catered to people of privilege, wealth.
5. Strengths—provide choices of possible action, monitor opposition party members; Weaknesses—sometimes place party loyalty above public concern, force compromises resulting in unsatisfactory laws.
6. Time lines should show evidence of student research.

★★★★★★★★★★★★★★★★★★★★★★★★★★★★★★★

Age of Jefferson

Setting the Scene

Section Focus

The election of 1800 brought the Republican party to power under Thomas Jefferson. A new democratic spirit took hold of the nation. During Jefferson's term, the United States experienced rapid expansion as well as the challenge of war.

▲ THOMAS JEFFERSON

Objectives

After studying this section, you should be able to

★ explain Thomas Jefferson's views on government.

★ discuss the significance of the Louisiana Purchase.

★ identify the problems that the United States faced in its attempt to remain neutral in the conflict between Great Britain and France.

Key Terms

laissez-faire, judicial review, expedition, impressment

FOCUS

Bellringer

Before taking roll, project Section Focus Transparency 3-3 or hand out Section Focus Transparency Activity 3-3. Have students answer the questions.

Motivating Activity

Present this scenario to students:

You are the captain of an American ship. Your ship, loaded with goods, is in the Strait of Gibraltar. Pirates in the narrow strait will prey on your ship unless you pay a ransom. What are your options? (*to pay or not to pay*) What will you do? Why?

Tell students that in this section they will read about ways in which the United States tried to maintain its freedom of the seas. **L1**

Vocabulary Precheck

Ask students to define each of the "Key Terms." Have a volunteer consult the dictionary for any unfamiliar words. **L1, LEP**

As the presidential election of 1800 approached, the Federalists selected John Adams and Charles Pinckney as their candidates; the Republicans, Jefferson and Aaron Burr. The Republicans won the election, but *which* Republican candidate became President? There was no doubt that the party had intended Jefferson as President and Burr as Vice President. Unlike today's election practices, however, candidates in 1800 were not designated as the candidate for President or the candidate for Vice President.

Because every Republican elector had two votes and voted separately for both Jefferson and Burr, each candidate received 73 electoral votes. When there is no majority, the Constitution stipulated that the House of Representatives selects the President. Some Federalists schemed to deny Jefferson the

presidency and elect Burr—and came close to doing so. The House was so evenly divided that it took 6 days and 36 ballots. The deadlock was broken after a group of Federalists led by Hamilton supported Jefferson.

The Federalists were unhappy at losing the presidency, but they accepted their losses and surrendered control of the federal government. This marked the first time in modern history that the political control of a country had been transferred through a democratic election.

■ Jefferson and Government

Jefferson was the first President to be inaugurated in the new capital city of Washington, D.C. He brought both a political and

---

Classroom Resources for SECTION 3

Blackline Masters:
- Reproducible Lesson Plan 3-3
- Guided Reading Activity 3-3
- Chapter Map Activity 3
- Linking Past and Present Activity 3
- American Portrait 15

- Political Cartoons in American History Activity 10
- Supreme Court Case Study 1
- Chapter Skills Activity 3
- Workbook Activity 3-3
- Reteaching Activity 3-3
- Section Quiz 3-3

Transparencies:
- Section Focus Transparency 3-3
- Skills Transparency 3

Multimedia:
- Testmaker
- Historic America Electronic Field Trips

TEACH

Guided Practice

Supporting a Viewpoint

Provide this statement: Jefferson justified the acquisition of the Louisiana Territory on the grounds that it was part of the President's implied powers to protect the nation.

Ask students whether they think Jefferson's justification was valid. Have them write several sentences supporting their answers. (*Most will answer yes. It provided unhindered access to Mississippi River and port of New Orleans; eliminated France as a potential threat to the United States.*) **L2**

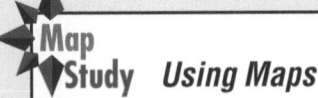

Map Study   *Using Maps*

Answers: Pennsylvania, North Carolina, Maryland

Map Skills Practice
Which candidate won Tennessee's electoral votes? (*Jefferson*)

📁 For additional map practice, assign Chapter Map Activity 3.

FACT or FICTION?
President Thomas Jefferson paid France about $18.12 per square mile of land for the Louisiana Purchase.

FACT: The total cost was $15 million for about 828,000 square miles of land.

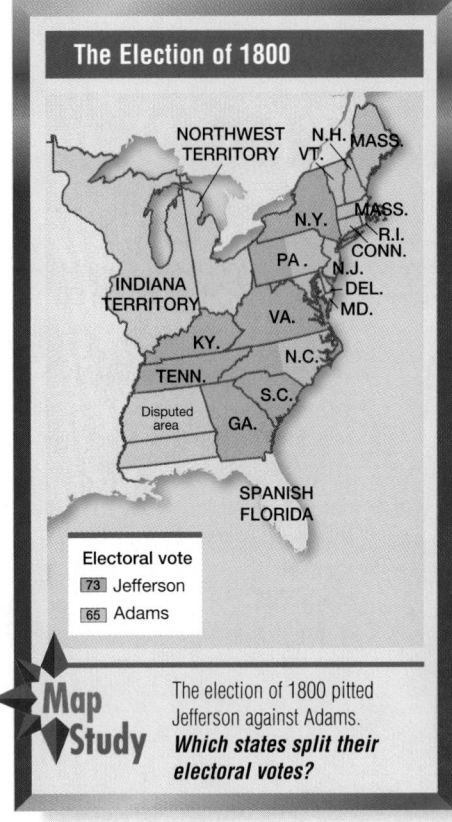

The Election of 1800

NORTHWEST TERRITORY

N.H. VT. MASS.

N.Y. MASS. R.I. CONN.

PA. N.J. DEL. MD.

INDIANA TERRITORY

VA.

KY.

N.C.

TENN.

Disputed area

S.C.

GA.

SPANISH FLORIDA

Electoral vote
73 Jefferson
65 Adams

Map Study
The election of 1800 pitted Jefferson against Adams. **Which states split their electoral votes?**

philosophical change to the presidency. In contrast to Hamilton's idea that the government should actively promote banking, commerce, and industry, Jefferson advocated a "hands-off" policy called **laissez-faire,** meaning generally, "let people do as they choose." A government should not control the way people do business or farm but should keep its role to restraining people from injuring each other and allowing them to be "free to regulate their own pursuits."

Judicial Review

Just before leaving office, John Adams had signed the Judiciary Act of 1801, creating a number of new federal judgeships. These judgeships and their staffs were all filled by loyal Federalists. Jefferson was able to get the Republican Congress to repeal the Judiciary Act. This eliminated the last-minute judgeships, or "midnight appointments," as Jefferson called them. He instructed Secretary of State James Madison not to deliver the official letters of appointment. As a result, William Marbury, one of those appointed by Adams, sued Madison before the Supreme Court. Marbury asked the Court to issue a writ of mandamus, or written order, to Madison.

The result was a landmark decision. The Supreme Court ruled against Marbury on the grounds that the Judiciary Act of 1789, which gave the Court power to issue writs of mandamus, was illegal, since the power was not specifically mentioned in the Constitution. The Supreme Court had ruled that it did not have power in this case.

Chief Justice John Marshall also argued that since the courts exist to enforce the law, and since the Constitution is "the supreme law of the land," it is for federal judges to decide, when cases come before them, if laws passed by Congress are constitutional.

The strong and forceful logic with which Marshall showed that the federal courts had the power of **judicial review** over acts of Congress was stamped deeply into people's minds. The great power of the federal judiciary, and especially of the Supreme Court to carry out judicial review, became as much a fact as the President's veto.

■ Looking Westward

In 1800, Spain handed over Louisiana, including New Orleans, to France. This development was of great concern to the United States. The French ruler, Napoleon Bonaparte, had conquered much of Europe and planned to create a new French empire in North America.

The Louisiana Purchase

Jefferson was especially alarmed at the prospect of New Orleans being in French hands. The city was a major trade center for the United States, especially as a market for Western goods. Jefferson feared that the French might close New Orleans to American trade, thus blocking the development of the American West. He took steps to offer France $10 million for New Orleans and West Florida.

118   UNIT 1 Creating a Nation: Prehistory to 1815

Cooperative Learning Activity

Comparing Government Philosophies Place students into groups of four and give each student a number from one to four. Have groups compare and contrast Hamilton's and Jefferson's beliefs about government. At various points in students' discussions, call upon number one students and ask them to report on their group's progress. Continue this procedure at varying intervals until all students have responded. **L1, L2** 📦

American dollars, however, did not influence Napoleon as much as the loss of Saint Domingue (Haiti), one of France's most valuable colonies. Under the leadership of a remarkable general, Pierre Toussaint Louverture, the people of Saint Domingue successfully resisted French forces and won their independence. Abandoning his American ambitions, Napoleon in 1803 agreed to sell the entire Louisiana Territory to the United States for $15 million—about 4 cents an acre.

Jefferson was torn between a desire to significantly extend the nation's boundaries and concern over whether the government could legally acquire such a vast foreign territory. Finally, he decided to ask the Senate to ratify the treaty; and the Senate gave its consent. New England Federalists opposed the Louisiana Purchase, fearing that westward expansion would weaken their region's influence in national affairs. Jefferson, however, justified the acquisition on the grounds that it was part of the President's implied powers to protect the nation.

The Louisiana Purchase doubled the size of the United States and opened the way for westward expansion by removing the threat of French interference.

Lewis and Clark

Very little was known about the area west of the Mississippi, and it excited Jefferson's curiosity. He sent an **expedition,** a journey with a specific purpose, led by two officers in the United States Army—Meriwether Lewis and William Clark—up the Missouri River to explore the new territory. The expedition left St. Louis in May 1804. It returned more than two years later, having surmounted hardships that ranged from "ticks and musquiters" to near starvation and floods.

Among the members of the expedition was York, an enslaved person. York's skills in hunting and fishing made him a valuable member of the expedition. Sacajawea (SA•kuh•juh•WEE•uh), a Shoshone woman, and her French-Canadian husband

ABCNEWS INTERACTIVE™

VIDEODISC

Historic America Electronic Field Trips

Side One, Chapter 5
Title: *New Orleans*
Subject: Study of American city of many peoples and cultures
Ask: What people have had the most influence over the culture and customs of the city's people? (*The French*)
See ABCNews Inter-active™ Historic America Electronic Field Trips Guidebook for complete lesson plan.

Linking Past and Present

★★★★★★★★★★ ★★★★★★★★★★★★★★★★★★

Keeping Time

The first portable watches were used in Europe. Guards on watch wore timepieces on straps around their necks or hanging from a belt as they made their rounds. Soon, the name was shortened to watch.

Then

Early Innovations

Many early timepieces ran erratically. By the start of the 1800s, however, craft workers

had developed most of the devices found in modern mechanical timepieces. The pendulum, balance spring, and escape lever vastly improved the accuracy of clocks. Watches became more popular when designers crafted easy-to-carry pocket watches that displayed a minute hand as well as an hour hand.

Now

New Styles, New Functions

The twentieth century brought a wave of innovation. Electric clocks, developed in the mid-1800s, were in many homes by the 1920s. Quartz-based clocks were introduced during the 1930s, and researchers perfected

the first atomic clock in the 1940s. Digital clocks became fashionable in the 1970s, especially as wrist watches. In the 1980s, researchers linked the chip—a complex electronic circuit etched onto a tiny piece of silicon—into clock mechanisms. Watches with electronic chips can save information and function as electronic calculators as well as show the time.

◄ **BOX CLOCK, c. 1815**

▶ **DIGITAL WATCH**

Sidelight: John Marshall and Thomas Jefferson

Thomas Jefferson and John Marshall held two different views of government. Marshall believed that the Constitution established a government of law, not of people. In his view, no one ought to be above the law; therefore, it was the duty of the Court "to say what the law is." It was the duty of the American people and their elected officials, including the President, to

obey the law. To Jefferson and his followers, such ideas were undemocratic. They believed that elections registered the wishes of the people, and elected officials had a duty to carry out those wishes. The Supreme Court, an appointed institution, had no right to interfere with the will of the people.

Linking Past and Present

Point out that wrist-watches did not come into vogue until the late 1800s, and then only for women. Wrist watches became a popular item for men during World War I after soldiers realized that wristwatches were more convenient than pocket watches.

Ask students to speculate why knowing the time has become more important in the last half of this century than in previous years. (*Students might compare the pace of life in the early 1800s with the pace of life today.*)

📁 For additional practice, assign Linking Past and Present Activity 3.

Independent Practice

Evaluating Foreign Policy

Ask students to write a speech to be given to Congress that argues why the United States should or should not go to war in 1812. Select students to present their speeches to the rest of the class. After the speeches have been made, have the class vote on whether or not to go to war. **L3**

📁 Assign Guided Reading Activity 3-3.

📁 Have students complete the reading and activity on Sacajawea in American Portraits.

Map Study — *Using Maps*

Answer: Fort Clatsop on the Pacific

Map Skills Practice
Ask students which area was disputed by the United States and Spain. *(area west of Orleans Territory in what is now Texas)*

---

later joined the party as interpreters and guides. Her role was important because Lewis and Clark wanted to build peaceful relations with the Native Americans living in the newly acquired territory.

The Lewis and Clark expedition added to the knowledge of the huge, new area. It also helped the United States lay claim to the region between the Rocky Mountains and the Pacific Ocean known as Oregon. Within a few years, fur traders based in St. Louis were traveling to and settling in the Rockies, and by 1812 there were about 70,000 people living in the southern part of the Louisiana Territory.

Conflict With Native Americans

During Jefferson's administration, settlers, hunters, and land speculators continued to move westward. By persuasion, force, and fraud, Native Americans were forced to hand over more and more land. In 15 treaties negotiated with United States officials, they gave up nearly all of present-day Indiana and Illinois.

During these difficult times, a remarkable leader named Tecumseh (tuh•KUHM•suh) became chief of the Shawnee. He wanted to unite all the peoples of the Mississippi Valley into a great federation to protect themselves against the white intruders. In 1811, William Henry Harrison, governor of the Indiana Territory, launched a war against Tecumseh's followers, knowing that the great leader had journeyed south to persuade Native American communities to join the confederation. Harrison became a national hero after leading American troops in battle at Tippecanoe near present-day West Lafayette, Indiana. Tecumseh's death in 1813 destroyed the

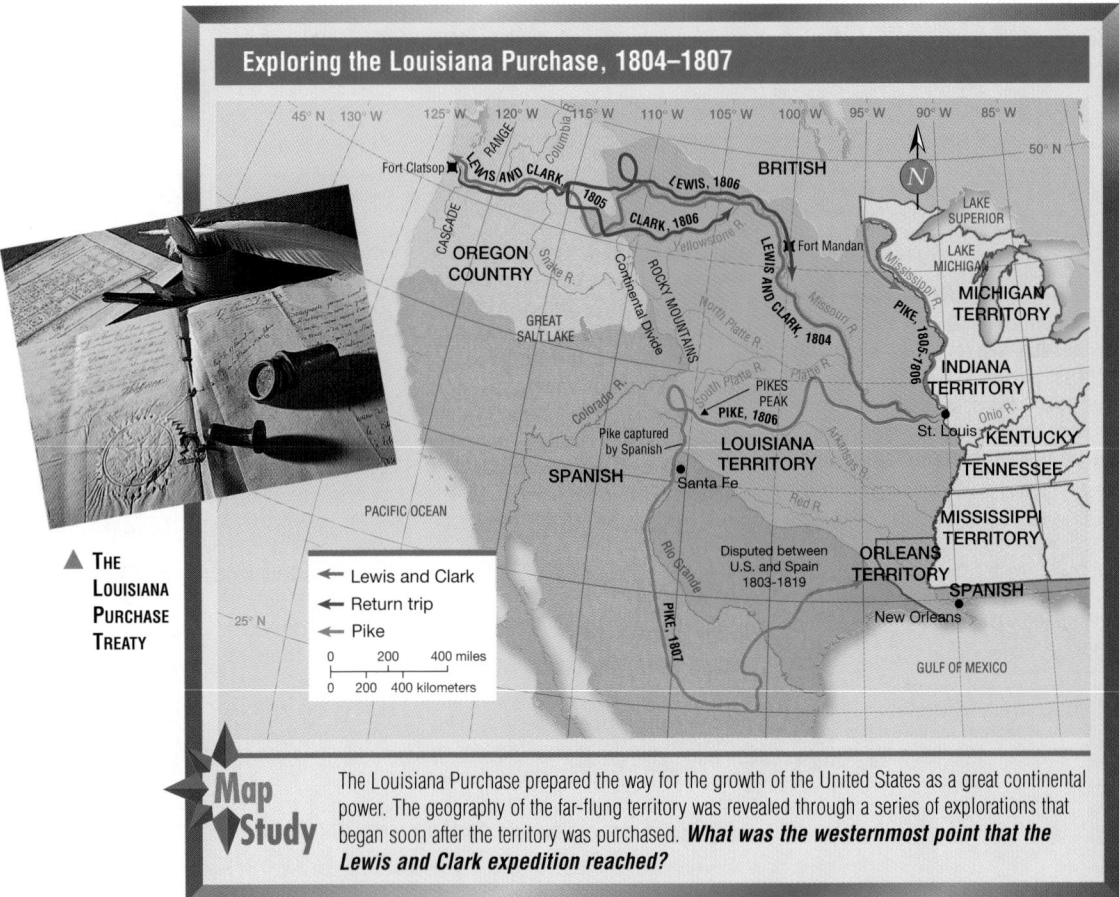

Exploring the Louisiana Purchase, 1804–1807

▲ THE LOUISIANA PURCHASE TREATY

Legend:
← Lewis and Clark
← Return trip
← Pike

0 200 400 miles
0 200 400 kilometers

Map Study The Louisiana Purchase prepared the way for the growth of the United States as a great continental power. The geography of the far-flung territory was revealed through a series of explorations that began soon after the territory was purchased. *What was the westernmost point that the Lewis and Clark expedition reached?*

Cultural Perspectives

The People of the Louisiana Territory French people from eastern Canada moved to the bayou region of Spanish-controlled Louisiana after the British took over Canada in 1763. Their descendants are called Cajuns (originally Acadians). By 1800 most of the population of Louisiana (by then French-controlled) lived on the lower banks of the Mississippi. The majority were Creoles (descendants of Spanish and French settlers) and African Americans, both enslaved and free. The area north of the Orleans Territory was populated by the Osage, Pawnee, Apache, and Dakota.

dream of a Native American confederation. Afterward, several Native American nations made peace with Harrison.

■ Foreign Affairs

Jefferson hoped that "nature and a wide ocean" would keep the United States entirely isolated from European rivalries. "Peace," he wrote to an English friend, "is our passion." Most of Jefferson's second term, however, was spent trying to maintain American neutrality. In 1803 Great Britain and France had once again gone to war. The United States was an important source of supply to both sides. Each side tried to limit what it saw as aid to the enemy and, in doing so, violated American freedom of the seas.

Even more distressing than the attempt to cut off the United States trade was the British practice of taking sailors from American ships. British sailors frequently deserted and signed on with American vessels, where the conditions and pay were better. To combat this problem, Britain claimed the right to stop American ships, search for former British subjects, and force them back into service. Americans resented this form of kidnapping known as **impressment.**

Embargo Act

Jefferson reasoned that both Britain and France were so dependent upon American goods that if the United States cut off trade with them, they would stop violating the nation's neutral rights. With the President's urging, Congress passed the Embargo Act in December 1807, forbidding United States ships to sail for foreign ports.

• •

Footnotes to History

Pike's Travels   Other Americans also made exploratory trips westward. While Lewis and Clark were in the Northwest, Zebulon Pike was exploring the upper Mississippi River and the Southwest. Pikes Peak in the Rocky Mountains was named after him. Pike believed that the Great Plains were uninhabitable, predicting they would become "as celebrated as the sandy deserts of Africa."

▲ TECUMSEH Shawnee chief Tecumseh was a bold and imaginative leader along the frontiers of the Northwest. *What did Tecumseh hope to achieve by establishing a confederation?*

The Embargo Act caused some suffering in Britain, hurt France very little, but was disastrous for the United States. American merchants bitterly resented the law and engaged in smuggling and in secret runs to European ports.

Drifting Into War

After two terms, Jefferson was glad to retire to Monticello, his home near Charlottesville, Virginia. He used his influence to secure the nomination of his close friend and secretary of state, James Madison. In the election of 1808, Madison easily defeated the Federalist candidate, Charles Pinckney.

Before Jefferson left office in March 1809, Congress repealed the unpopular Embargo Act and replaced it with two other measures: the Non-Intercourse Act and later Macon's Bill No. 2. These measures were less harmful to American trade than the Embargo Act, but they were no more successful in forcing France and Britain to respect the rights of the United States.

Although neither Britain nor the United States really wanted war, their actions steered them in that direction. In May 1811,

Linking Across TIME

The plight of the sailors thrown into unemployment by the embargo prompted a 13-year-old Massachusetts boy to write a poem in 1808.

The writer, William Cullen Bryant, went on to become one of America's leading poets and newspaper editors. He was editor of the *New York Evening Post* from 1829 until his death in 1878.

Visualizing History The Native American hope of a vast confederation organized to protect their lands from American settlers was crushed when Tecumseh was killed in 1813. He died while serving as a brigadier general, leading Native Americans who supported the British during the War of 1812. **Answer to Caption:** protection of Native Americans from white settlers

▭ Assign Political Cartoons in American History Activity 10.

ASSESS

Check Understanding
Assign Section 3 Review as homework or an in-class activity.

Special Needs Activity

Learning Disability Students with learning disabilities in reading or with other reading comprehension problems seldom use good self-appraisal and self-management skills while they read. Encourage these skills by making students aware of the need for these unconscious activities. As students read "Foreign Affairs" in Section 3, tell them to be aware of processes they use to help them understand the material. Have them note the number of times they reread phrases or sentences. Explain that rereading is important for understanding. **LEP**

Visualizing History People opposed to the war refused to lend money to support it, and the government was forced to pay high interest to obtain the money it needed. **Answer to Caption:** members of Congress who led the call for war against Britain

Evaluate

Assign Section Quiz 3-3 or use the Testmaker to create a customized quiz.

Reteach

Have students complete Reteaching Activity 3-3.

Enrich

Assign Supreme Court Case Study 1.

CLOSE

Some historians consider Jefferson's purchase of the Louisiana Territory his greatest accomplishment. Ask students if they agree with this assessment.

Visualizing History

▲ THE APPROACH OF WAR The United States was not well prepared for war. The British Royal Navy vastly outnumbered the United States Navy. *Who were the war hawks?*

an American ship attacked a British warship. Americans saw it as revenge for earlier British attacks on American shipping.

Some young members of Congress, most of them Republicans from the West and the South, called for war. Among the leaders were Henry Clay of Kentucky, Felix Grundy of Tennessee, and John C. Calhoun of South Carolina. Hunger for land heightened this war fever. Westerners wanted to take Canada, while Southerners were eager for Spanish Florida.

Alone, the "war hawks" did not have enough votes in Congress to pass a declaration of war. More Americans became angry over seizure of American sailors and ships, and pressure to fight increased. Finally, Congress decided that the United States must accept the risks of war rather than be pushed around.

Section 3 ★ Review

Checking for Understanding

1. **Identify** Aaron Burr, Judiciary Act of 1801, *Marbury* v. *Madison*, John Marshall, Louisiana Purchase, Lewis and Clark, Tecumseh, Embargo Act.

2. **Define** laissez-faire, judicial review, expedition, impressment.

3. **State** the significance of the Supreme Court's decision in *Marbury* v. *Madison*.

4. **Specify** Jefferson's reasons for making the Louisiana Purchase.

Critical Thinking

5. **Analyzing Events** There were a number of opposing influences leading to war. Explain the American sectional interests to be served by war with the British.

ACTIVITY

6. Study the map on page 120. List the present-day states through which the Lewis and Clark and the Pike expeditions traveled. Then calculate the number of miles the expeditions traveled.

Answers to SECTION 3 REVIEW

1. Aaron Burr, 117; Judiciary Act of 1801, 118; *Marbury* v. *Madison,* 118; John Marshall, 118; Louisiana Purchase, 119; Lewis and Clark, 119; Tecumseh, 120; Embargo Act, 121
2. All vocabulary words are defined in the Glossary.
3. It established the power of judicial review over acts of Congress.
4. wanted to extend the boundaries westward and rid the U.S. of foreign interference

5. The embargo affected New England, impressment affected all sections, and British incitement of Native Americans inhibited frontier expansion.
6. Lewis and Clark expedition—through Missouri, Iowa, South Dakota, North Dakota, Montana, Idaho, and Washington; about 4,000 miles. Pike expedition—Minnesota, Illinois, Missouri, Iowa, Nebraska, Kansas, Colorado, New Mexico, Texas; about 4,000 miles.

BUILDING SKILLS
Critical Thinking Skills

Identifying Central Issues

Historical dates, events, and names are easier to understand and remember when they are connected to a central issue. Central issues are the main ideas found in historical material. Identifying central issues allows you to grasp the whole picture or story. The details then become more easily understood.

Learning the Skill

To identify central issues, follow these steps:

- **Read** the material and ask, "What is the purpose of this material?"
- **Recognize** the most forceful statements in the material.
- **Identify** any details that support a larger idea or issue.
- **Identify** the central issue or main idea.
- **Read** the following letter that Eliza Southgate wrote to a male cousin in 1801. Then answer the questions that follow.

But every human being who has contemplated human nature on a large scale will certainly justify me when I declare that the inequality of privilege between the sexes is very sensibly felt by us females, and in no instance is it greater than in the liberty of choosing a partner in marriage; true, we have the liberty of refusing those we don't like, but not of selecting those we do. This is undoubtedly as it should be. . . .

I never was of opinion that the pursuits of the sexes ought to be the same; on the contrary, I believe it would be destructive to happiness, there would a degree of rivalry exist[;] each should have a separate sphere of action—in such a case there could be no clashing unless one or the other should leap their respective bounds. Yet to cultivate the qualities with which we are endowed can never be called infringing the prerogatives of man. . . .

▲ MOTHER AND DAUGHTER, 1790s

The cultivation of the power we possess, I have ever thought a privilege (or I may say duty) that belonged to the human species, and not man's exclusive prerogative. Far from destroying the harmony that ought to subsist, it would fix it on a foundation that would not totter at every jar. Women would be under the same degree of subordination that they now are; enlighten and expand their minds, and they would perceive the necessity of such a regulation to preserve the order and happiness of society. . . .

Practicing the Skill

1. What is the purpose of Eliza's letter?
2. What points are stated most forcefully?
3. What details are provided that support a larger issue or idea?
4. State the central issue or issues of this letter.

APPLYING THE SKILL

5. Write a letter to Eliza in which you explain why you agree or disagree with her position.

123

Answers to Practicing the Skill

1. to make sense of the contradictory doctrines of female subordination and sexual equality
2. that if women and men pursue the same activities they will become rivals
3. that women and men should have a separate sphere of action, that pursuing the same sphere would lead to unhappiness, that both women and men should cultivate the qualities that they possess
4. Answers will vary but should basically state that competition between men and women creates unhappiness in male-female relationships.
5. Letters will vary but may include: agree, because losers in any competition are jealous of winners; disagree, because competition fosters respect between men and women.

FOCUS

Bellringer

Before taking roll, project Section Focus Transparency 3-4 or hand out Section Focus Transparency Activity 3-4. Have students answer the questions.

Motivating Activity

Have students read the information in "Section Focus" and list Madison's grievances against Britain. *(impressment, blockades, inciting Native American uprisings, and rejecting diplomatic efforts)* Ask students to vote for or against war with Britain. Count and record the number of doves and the number of hawks in the class. Explain that people who are in favor of peace are often called doves, which are symbols of peace. Those in favor of war are called hawks, which are predatory, aggressive birds. Then ask: Why did you vote for or against the war? **L1**

Vocabulary Precheck

Ask students to define each of the "Key Terms." Have a volunteer consult the dictionary for any unfamiliar words. **L1, LEP**

★★★★★★★★★★★★★★★★★★★★★★★★★★★★★★★★

The War of 1812

Setting the Scene

Section Focus

President Madison listed a number of grievances against Great Britain in his war message. Among the President's concerns were impressment, blockades, inciting Native American uprisings, and rejecting diplomatic efforts. Yet the war that some hailed as the "Second War for American Independence" was not a popular one, especially in New England. The fighting ended in 1814 with the Treaty of Ghent, but it did not settle the issues that had caused the war.

Objectives

After studying this section, you should be able to

★ describe the major campaigns of the War of 1812.

★ summarize the results of the War of 1812 and the Treaty of Ghent.

Key Terms

frigate, privateer

► **AMERICAN MILITIA COAT, WORN DURING WAR OF 1812**

On June 23, 1812, the British government ended its interference in neutral trade with Europe. British harvests had been poor, and the British desperately needed grain from the United States. The British move, however, came too late. The United States had declared war against Great Britain four days earlier.

■ The War in Canada

American military leaders believed that an attack on Canada would be an easy way to get back at the British. Canada was sparsely populated, and French Canadians were lukewarm toward their British rulers. The narrow strip of settlement along the St. Lawrence River and north of Lake Ontario was close to the United States and open to attack. Montreal, the strategic center of Canada, was only 30 miles (48 m) from New York State.

Lack of Preparation

The conquest of Canada stalled, however, because the military forces of the United States were unprepared. The regular army, numbering about 6,000 soldiers, was scattered throughout the frontier posts. The top commanders, veterans of the Revolution, were too old for warfare. There was no single commanding general and no overall strategy.

To compensate for the small size of the army, Madison called on the states to furnish militia. Some New England governors

Classroom Resources for SECTION 4

Blackline Masters:
- Reproducible Lesson Plan 3-4
- Guided Reading Activity 3-4
- Geography in History Activity 3
- Workbook Activity 3-4
- Enrichment Activity 3
- Reteaching Activity 3-4
- Section Quiz 3-4

Transparencies:
- Section Focus Transparency 3-4
- Map Transparency 3

Multimedia:
- MindJogger Videoquiz
- Testmaker

Visualizing History

▲ WAR ON THE SEAS On August 19, 1812, the United States frigate *Constitution* decisively defeated the British warship *Guerriere*. **Why was it surprising that American ships were victorious in many early battles?**

refused to supply any troops because they were opposed to "Mr. Madison's War." Members of New York's militia refused to cross the Niagara River into Canada because they had enlisted only to defend their state from invasion.

Failures and Successes

The lack of preparation was evident when small but ably led Canadian forces took Detroit and two forts on Lake Michigan. An American attack across the Niagara River was turned back.

In 1813 matters improved at the western end of the war zone. Commodore Oliver Hazard Perry, having built a small fleet, won a brilliant victory over a British squadron and established American control of Lake Erie. Perry's victory made possible an invasion of Canada by way of Detroit. Kentucky volunteers under William Henry Harrison advanced into Canada and defeated a British army at the Battle of the Thames, about 60 miles northeast of Detroit. In the East, however, attempted invasions of Canada from Sackett Harbor and Lake Champlain failed.

With the defeat of France in 1814, the British were free to strike hard at the United States. In late summer a powerful British army advanced southward from Montreal to invade New York. Blocking its way was an American army stationed at Lake Champlain. Although outnumbered nearly 3 to 1, American forces drove back the attacks, and the British retreated to Montreal. The northern border of the United States was safe.

• •

Footnotes to History

Step Lightly Sailors usually fought barefooted, a tactic attackers manipulated to their advantage. Cannons fired glass fragments and rusty nails at the enemy ship's deck. The *Constitution* used this tactic in its battle with the British ship *Guerriere*.

CURRICULUM CONNECTION

Geography Have students work with a partner to list the places where the War of 1812 was fought. *(Places should include the following: along the border of Canada; on Lake Michigan and Lake Erie; near Lake Champlain; in Toronto, Detroit, Washington, D.C., Baltimore; near New Orleans)* Have students locate these places on the map on page 126. **L1, LEP**

🗁 Assign Geography in History Activity 3.

Visualizing History Of the 2,260 American battle deaths during the War of 1812, there were 265 people killed while serving in the navy.
Answer to Caption: The British navy had long been regarded as invincible.

Special Needs Activity

Specialized Learners Ask students who learn best by reading to research one of the maritime battles of the War of 1812, such as the engagement between HMS *Shannon* and USS *Chesapeake* off Boston. Have students who prefer visual or hands-on learning experiences draw a detailed picture of a battleship of the period. Have students who undertook research projects read them to the class, and ask students who made drawings to display them on the bulletin board. **LEP, L1**

CHAPTER 3
SECTION 4

Independent Practice

Military History Have students write a brief summary describing the major campaigns of the War of 1812. **L2**

📂 Assign Guided Reading Activity 3-4.

Map Study   *Using Maps*

Answers: Mississippi Territory

Map Skills Practice
Ask students to identify the sites of British victories in the War of 1812. (*Frenchtown, Lundy's Lane, Washington, D.C.*)

🖹 For additional map practice, assign Map Transparency Activity 3.

Did You Know?

During the War of 1812, a meatpacker named Samuel Adams shipped beef to the Army with "U.S." stamped on the shipments. The initials stood for United States, but those who opposed the war said the initials stood for "Uncle Sam." Curiously, today, "Uncle Sam" is a symbol of national pride.

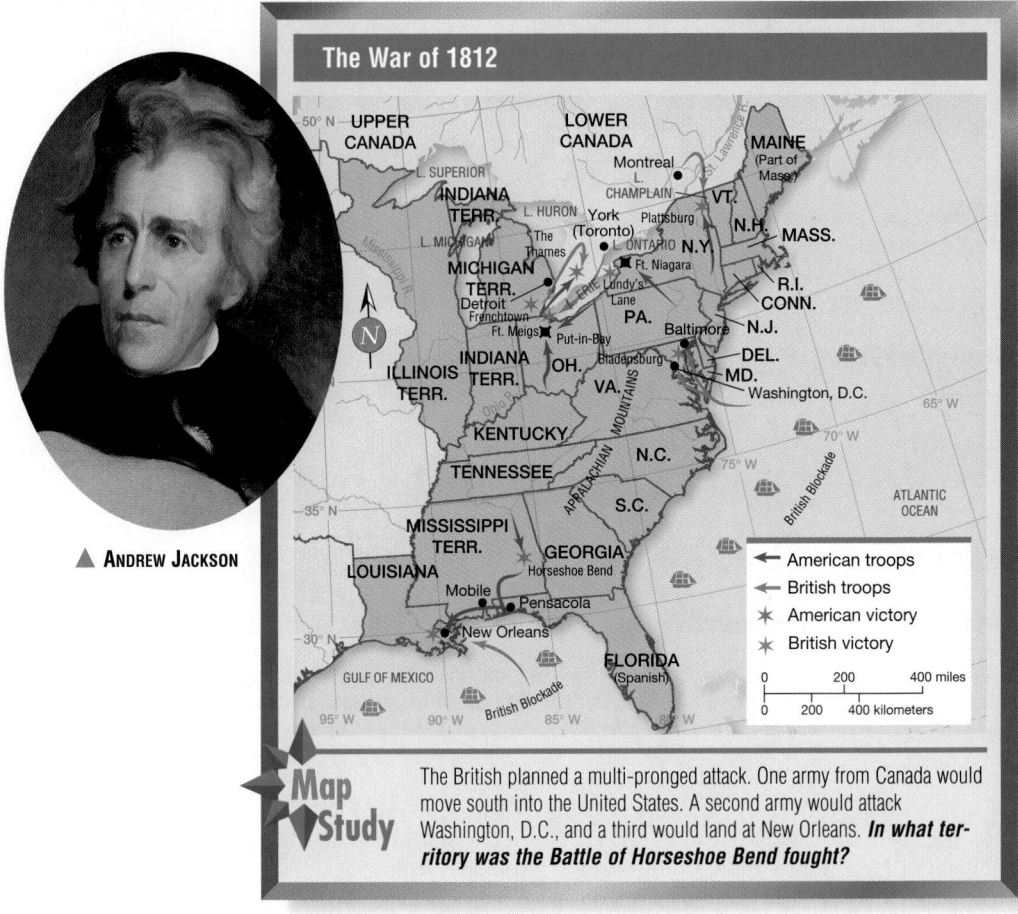

▲ ANDREW JACKSON

Map Study The British planned a multi-pronged attack. One army from Canada would move south into the United States. A second army would attack Washington, D.C., and a third would land at New Orleans. *In what territory was the Battle of Horseshoe Bend fought?*

■ The British Offensive

In 1814 the British sent two other expeditions into the United States—one to attack Washington, D.C., and Baltimore, the other to take New Orleans.

Washington, D.C., and Baltimore

In August, a British army landed at Chesapeake Bay and marched into Washington, D.C. To retaliate against the American burning of York (now Toronto) in 1813, the British destroyed the Capitol and the White House. From Washington the British proceeded to Baltimore but were turned back by the forces guarding the city. During the bombardment of Fort McHenry in Baltimore harbor, Francis Scott Key wrote "The Star-Spangled Banner."

New Orleans

Unable to take Baltimore, the British army joined forces with the expedition attempting to capture New Orleans. Awaiting the British there was an American force under the command of Andrew Jackson of Tennessee. Jackson's army of regular soldiers and militia included two battalions of free African American volunteers. The British, advancing in the open, were no match for Jackson's soldiers, who were sheltered behind a barricade of cotton bales. The Battle of New Orleans was the greatest American victory of the war, but it was a useless slaughter. News traveled slowly in those days, and it was learned only after the battle that a peace treaty had been signed in Europe two weeks earlier.

126   UNIT 1 Creating a Nation: Prehistory to 1815

Cooperative Learning Activity

Teaching Key Concepts Have students form groups of three to review events of the War of 1812. Assign each member one of the following topics: the reasons for going to war with Britain, the main land battles, and the main sea battles. Set a time limit for students to study, summarize, and teach the key facts of their topics to the other members of the group. **L1, L2** 📂

The War of 1812 (map labels)

UPPER CANADA · LOWER CANADA · MAINE (Part of Mass.) · Montreal · L. CHAMPLAIN · VT. · N.H. · MASS. · L. SUPERIOR · INDIANA TERR. · L. HURON · York (Toronto) · Plattsburg · L. ONTARIO · N.Y. · The Thames · Lundy's Lane · Ft. Niagara · R.I. · CONN. · MICHIGAN TERR. · Detroit · Frenchtown · Ft. Meigs · PA. · Baltimore · N.J. · DEL. · Put-in-Bay · OH. · Bladensburg · MD. · ILLINOIS TERR. · INDIANA TERR. · VA. · Washington, D.C. · KENTUCKY · APPALACHIAN MOUNTAINS · N.C. · TENNESSEE · S.C. · MISSISSIPPI TERR. · GEORGIA · Horseshoe Bend · LOUISIANA · Mobile · Pensacola · New Orleans · FLORIDA (Spanish) · GULF OF MEXICO · British Blockade · ATLANTIC OCEAN

Legend:
← American troops
← British troops
✳ American victory
✳ British victory

0   200   400 miles
0   200   400 kilometers

126

The War at Sea

At the beginning of the war, the small navy of the United States appeared to be no match for the British fleet. During John Adams's term in office, however, half a dozen excellent **frigates**—medium-sized warships—had been built. These frigates had more firepower than any European ships of the same size and were speedy enough to escape from larger warships.

When war broke out, the frigates put to sea and within a few months had won a series of victories in battles with British vessels. On August 19, 1812, the U.S.S. *Constitution* decisively defeated the British ship *Guerriere* in the North Atlantic. British cannonballs bouncing off the solid planking of the *Constitution* provided the ship with its nickname, "Old Ironsides." Other American ships did equally well. In October the frigate *United States* destroyed the H.M.S. *Macedonian* in combat near the Canary Islands.

In addition to the frigates, the United States sent to sea more than 500 **privateers,** or armed private ships licensed to attack enemy shipping. The privateers captured more than 1,300 British vessels, some within sight of Britain.

As the war went on, however, American victories at sea grew fewer and fewer. With its superior numbers, the British fleet blockaded the entire Atlantic coast from Boston to Savannah. United States trade with other countries ceased, and the United States navy, bottled up in port, could not repeat its early successes.

The War's End

As the war dragged on, opposition grew, especially in New England. Public meetings were held to protest the conflict. Above all, they foresaw that the war would be damaging to their economies:

66 *About three-fourths of our townsmen depend on the sea for the means of subsistence for themselves and their families. By the recent declaration of war more than one-half of that proportion is liable to fall into the hands of the enemy. . . . We feel therefore most strongly incumbent. . . . to seek a speedy termination of the present war.* 99

In December 1814, delegates from New England met in secret at Hartford, Connecticut. The Hartford Convention did not insist that New England leave the Union, but it did demand seven constitutional amendments to increase the region's political power. The end of the war, however, undercut the purpose and work of the Convention.

The Treaty of Ghent ended the War of 1812, but it did not contain a word about neutral rights or impressment. Not a square mile of territory changed hands. The United States and Great Britain simply agreed to stop fighting, to restore the old boundaries, and to put other problems off for future settlement. Signed on Christmas Eve, 1814, the treaty was unanimously ratified by the Senate in February 1815.

Section 4 ★ Review

Checking for Understanding

1. **Identify** Oliver Hazard Perry, Andrew Jackson, Battle of New Orleans, Hartford Convention, Treaty of Ghent.
2. **Define** frigate, privateer.
3. **Explain** why American troops failed to capture Canada.

Critical Thinking

4. **Analyzing Cause and Effect** Why was the Hartford Convention unsuccessful?

ACTIVITY

5. Create a one-paragraph news bulletin about the Battle of New Orleans.

Answers to SECTION 4 REVIEW

1. Oliver Hazard Perry, 125; Andrew Jackson, 126; Battle of New Orleans, 126; Hartford Convention, 127; Treaty of Ghent, 127
2. All vocabulary words are defined in the glossary.
3. military forces unprepared, regular army scattered, commanders too old for warfare, no single commanding general or overall plan
4. The end of the war undercut the purpose and work of the Convention.
5. News bulletins will vary but should include how and where the battle was fought and its outcome.

ASSESS

Check Understanding
Assign Section 4 Review as homework or an in-class activity.

Evaluate
⬛ 🗂 Assign Section Quiz 3-4 or use the Testmaker to create a customized quiz.

Reteach
Ask students to write a paragraph about the War of 1812. The paragraph should explain why the war was fought, how and where it was fought, and its outcome.

🗂 Have students complete Reteaching Activity 3-4.

🗂 Assign Workbook Activity 3-4.

Enrich
Ask students to write a one-page essay on why economic power is more effective than military power. In addition to using the War of 1812 as an example, have students use examples from recent history.

🗂 Assign Enrichment Activity 3.

CLOSE
Hold a discussion on what the Americans gained by fighting the War of 1812. (*confidence, self-respect, and new strength as a nation*)

127

Using Vocabulary

Sentences will vary but might include the *cabinet, revenue tariff,* and *judicial review* as having a unifying effect and *protective tariff, excise tax, enumerated power, implied power,* and *nullification* as having a divisive effect.

Reviewing Facts

1. established a cabinet, paid off foreign debt, assumed state debts, established a national bank, made treaties, suppressed the Whiskey Rebellion
2. National debt was addressed by repaying foreign governments and by the Funding Bill; state debts were paid by the federal government; lack of a national currency was addressed by establishing a national bank.
3. opposition to Hamilton's program; Hamilton's and Jefferson's opposing views; political criticism against Washington; split between pro-French and pro-British feelings
4. Hamilton's views: gov-

128

Using Vocabulary

For each term below, write a sentence explaining why it had either a unifying effect or a divisive effect on the new government.

cabinet	enumerated power
protective tariff	implied power
revenue tariff	nullification
excise tax	judicial review

Reviewing Facts

1. **List** the actions taken during Washington's presidency that reflected the Federalist principle of strong central government authority.
2. **Identify** the economic problems facing the nation in 1789, and tell how Hamilton's financial program addressed those problems.
3. **Outline** the causes that gradually led to the development of political parties.
4. **Compare** the views of Thomas Jefferson and Alexander Hamilton on the role of government and society.
5. **Explain** why *Marbury* v. *Madison* was a great victory for the Federalists and the judiciary.
6. **Describe** the military accomplishments of Andrew Jackson between 1813 and 1815.

Understanding Concepts

Leadership

1. Characterize the leadership style that George Washington exercised as President.
2. Describe the kind of leadership the Federalists provided in relation to the kind provided in the Confederation government.

Geographic Expansion

1. When Jefferson doubled the size of the United States through the Louisiana Purchase, many people believed it was God's will that the United States should extend from sea to sea. Explain why Americans held this belief.

---

2. American expansion also occurred through the cession of Native American lands. Discuss how William Henry Harrison handled the conflict with the Native Americans.

Critical Thinking

1. **Drawing Conclusions** Washington was the first of several generals who later became President. Why do people think a good general will make a good President?
2. **Cause and Effect** What effects did the Louisiana Purchase have on the United States politically and economically?
3. **Analyzing Results** Explain why neither side won or lost under the terms of the Treaty of Ghent.
4. **Analyzing Illustrations** Study the illustration below and answer the questions.
   a. Who are the central figures in the picture?
   b. What is happening?
   c. Does the artist express a point of view in this illustration?

▲ **IMPRESSMENT OF AMERICAN SAILORS**

---

ernment should support industry and trade; strong central government, weak state legislatures; Jefferson's views: government should promote farming and small businesses; common people should have greater government role; strong state, weak central government.

5. Marshall carried out the Federalist principles and established judicial review.
6. Andrew Jackson defeated a superior British force in New Orleans in 1815.

Understanding Concepts

1. He was a good leader, his style elicited confidence,

and he selected capable officials.
2. Federalists provided more decisive leadership.
3. Many Americans believed that God had allowed them to come through the War of 1812 and wanted them to continue that success.
4. Harrison put down the dream of a Native American confederation.

History and Geography

The Barbary States

During the late 1700s and early 1800s, American ships were virtually driven from the Mediterranean Sea by the Barbary Coast States of Tripoli, Morocco, Algiers, and Tunis. These nations patrolled the Mediterranean, raiding the ships of nations that refused to pay them tribute, or protection money. The piracy ended when an American fleet of ships under Stephen Decatur, joined by warships of European nations, put an end to the practice. Study the map of the Barbary States and answer the questions.

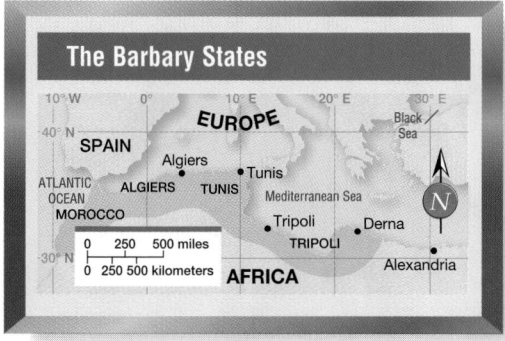

The Barbary States

1. **Location** In between approximately what lines of longitude do the Barbary States fall?
2. **Movement** In which direction would a traveler from Tunis go to reach Tripoli?
3. **Place** What major city shown on the map is not part of the Barbary States?

Cooperative Learning Interdisciplinary Activity: Economics

You and four class members will portray a banker and the following persons asking for a loan: (1) a New England manufacturer wanting to build a furniture factory, (2) a Western farmer wanting to buy 100 acres of land, (3) a Southern plantation owner wanting to acquire more land and enslaved persons, (4) a land speculator wanting to buy a million acres

of land in the West. Each team member should portray a different person. After interviews are finished, decide together whether and why each of the loans should be granted or denied.

Practicing Skills

Identifying Central Issues

Read the following excerpt from a speech by Senator Daniel Webster that he made at the beginning of the War of 1812. Then answer the questions that follow.

The nation is not yet in a temper to submit to conscription. The people have too fresh and strong a feeling of the blessings of civil liberty to be willing thus to surrender it. You may talk to them as much as you please, of the victory, and the glory to be obtained in the enemy's provinces; they will hold those objects in light estimation if the means be a forced military service.

1. What is Webster's purpose?
2. What points does he state most forcefully?
3. What details are provided that support a larger issue or idea?
4. What is the central issue of this passage?

Writing ABOUT History Using Your Journal

Compare the details you have noted about the character and beliefs of early leaders with those of two political leaders of today.

Cooperative Learning

Hold a class discussion to decide whether the loans should be granted or denied, and elicit reasons for students' decisions.

Practicing Skills

1. to explain why Americans would be opposed to forced military service
2. The nation is not in the right mood for conscription.
3. Americans are enjoying their freedom too much to give it up for forced military service.
4. Americans would reject the idea of a draft.

Writing ABOUT History Using Your Journal

The ideas students present in their comparisons will vary depending upon the political leaders they selected. Entries should show evidence of student research.

Chapter Bonus Test Question

Ask students: Was any one person indispensable to the existence of the United States during the nation's formative years? Give reasons to support your answer. (*Students who do select an individual should provide logical arguments for their choice. Those students who note that no one individual was essential should provide valid argumentation to support their position.*)

Critical Thinking

1. Generals are considered leaders, are used to exercising authority, and frequently command great respect.
2. The Louisiana Purchase opened the way for settlers to move westward and stretched the interpretation of the Constitution.
3. The terms did not address neutral rights or impressment and did not change any land boundaries.
4. **a.** Two British soldiers and an American sailor
   b. The British soldiers are taking the sailor prisoner.
   c. The illustration can be considered pro-American; the British officer is imperious while the American sailor can do nothing.

History and Geography

1. 10 W and 25 E
2. southeast
3. Alexandria

Making Connections
History and Economics

Work in colonial times—when each family unit was largely self-sufficient—was very different from what it is today. Children were responsible for many chores, such as taking care of younger children and tending animals. Women handled many jobs later thought of as men's work. Some also worked alongside their husbands in the fields.

More About . . .
Eating

In colonial times most family members ate out of a single, common wooden bowl that was placed in the middle of the table. Forks were rare. Most people used a knife to spear their food. They also ate with their hands. That is why colonial households were well supplied with napkins.

Cultural Kaleidoscope

Colonial Life

In The Kitchen

When Europeans first settled in America, they found no great treasures of gold or rare spices. From Native American peoples, however, they did gain something more vital for survival—plentiful foods and methods of cultivation. For early colonists, Indian corn, or maize, was the main food staple. Gradually, the colonists came to appreciate other native foods.

► Children performed chores to help prepare the day's meals. In many colonial households, children had no place at the table. They stood to eat and were not allowed to speak.

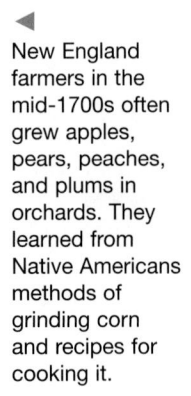

◄ New England farmers in the mid-1700s often grew apples, pears, peaches, and plums in orchards. They learned from Native Americans methods of grinding corn and recipes for cooking it.

130

Cooperative Learning Activity

Favorite Foods Organize the class into several small groups. Ask each to research a basic colonial food, such as hominy, game birds, rabbit, dried fruits, pumpkins, and cider. The groups should report to the class on how each food was obtained and prepared. As a class project, the groups may want to join efforts to prepare a typical colonial meal. **L1**

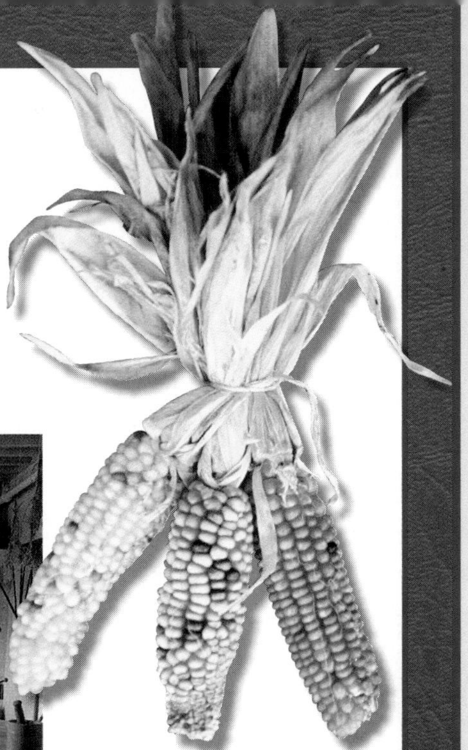

▶ During the summer, maize was eaten green, but colonists usually allowed it to ripen and then ground it into cornmeal. Sometimes it was hulled and eaten whole as hominy.

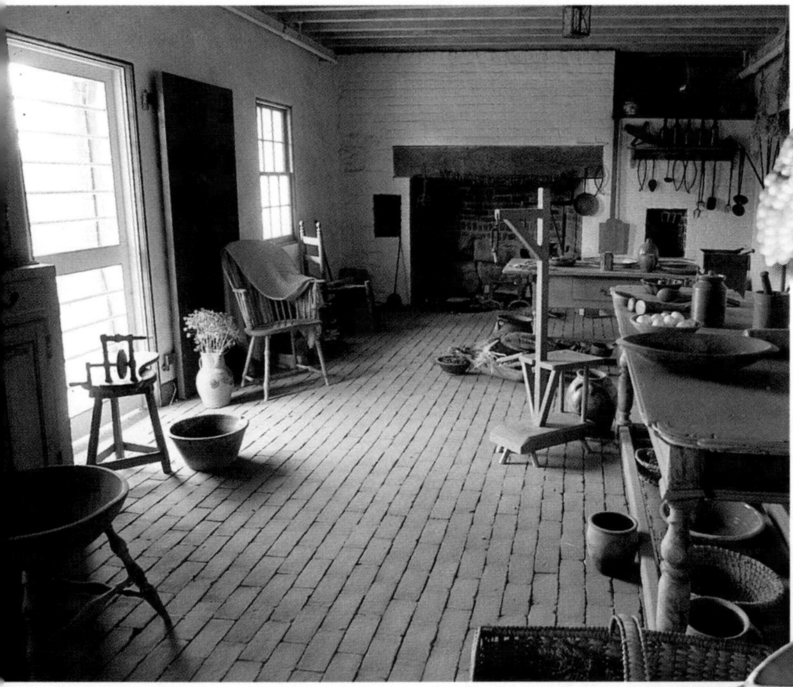

▲ Cooking in the early 1700s was done over an open fire, and utensils for cooking necessarily had long handles. Metal was usually reserved for cooking tools. Utensils that today are made of metal, ceramic, or plastic were made of wood.

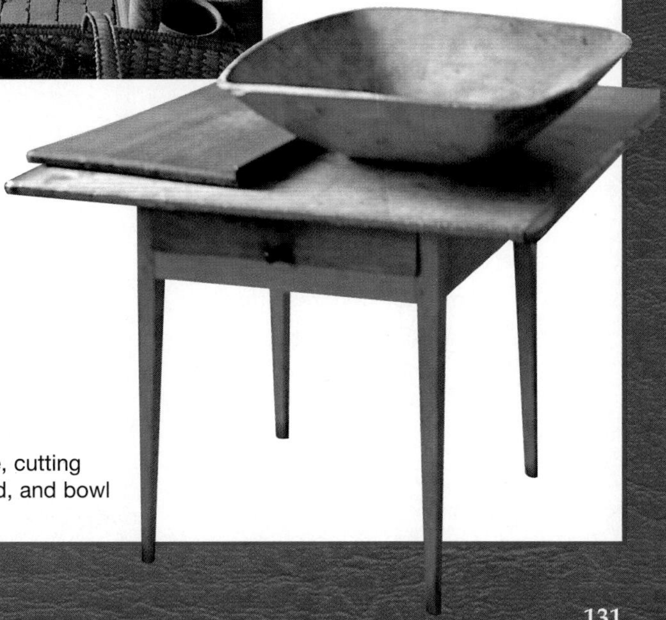

▶ Table, cutting board, and bowl

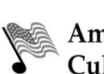

Cultural Kaleidoscope

Portfolio Project

Ask students to collect pictures of their favorite foods. For each one, the student should determine whether it would have been available to settlers in the English colonies of North America.

History and the Humanities

American Music: Cultural Traditions: Early New England Psalmody "Ainsworth Psalm 100" and "Standish" by Gregg Smith Singers (0:22; 1:02)

U.S. History & Art Transparency 9. *Shooting for the Beef* by George Caleb Bingham (1850).

The Historian's Craft

Although the colonial diet was limited in many ways, it was of better quality than that of the European diet. Historians believe that this is the main reason colonists lived longer. While life expectancy for a European in the late 1600s was about 40 years, that of an American colonist was closer to 60. Because there was no census at this time, historians use tax records, church records, and registrations for the militia to arrive at their population estimates.

UNIT ONE DIGEST

Exploring Unit Themes

The Unit Digest may be used to teach unit coverage when time is limited, to review unit content, or to relate the content of one unit to that of another.

■ Chapter 1

Ask students: Making profits was the force behind early entrepreneurs' efforts. Is this still their goal?

■ Chapter 2

Have students research paintings on the Revolutionary War and ask them to write a paragraph on their findings.

■ Chapter 3

Ask: Do you think political parties are helpful or harmful to government? Why?

Causes and Effects

Ask students to select one of the events under "Causes" from the chart "The Move Toward Independence" on page 132. Assign the students to write a paper explaining how Americans responded to that particular event.

Chapter 1

Exploration and Settlement

The first Americans traveled across a land bridge connecting Siberia and Alaska and spread throughout the Americas. These Native American civilizations developed highly organized societies.

In other parts of the world, a new age of discovery and exploration dawned. After a period of decline, Europe developed under strong monarchs and a wealthy middle class who profited from the growth of trade, cities, and a spirit of inquiry. In Asia and Africa, empires expanded their territories, and ancient trade routes linked civilizations from China to Europe.

By the 1400s, Europeans had developed the technology, financing, and attitudes necessary to begin overseas voyages of exploration. Exploration led to empire building. Portugal, Spain, France, England, and the Netherlands conquered lands in Asia, Africa, and the Americas for European settlement and control.

In the 1600s and early 1700s, the English founded settlements along the Atlantic coast of North America. England largely left the colonies to govern themselves. Religious diversity eventually made religious toleration necessary. With a thriving export and trade economy, many people moved up in class.

Women could not vote, but they were full partners in running farms and sometimes businesses. Enslaved persons became property with no legal protection in the South. Native Americans suffered from battles with colonists over land and from epidemics of European diseases.

The Move Toward Independence

CAUSES

- 1763 Treaty of Paris ends French and Indian War
- 1764 Parliament passes Sugar Act
- 1765 Stamp Act is passed
- 1767 Townshend Acts are passed
- 1770 Boston Massacre takes place
- 1774 Parliament passes Intolerable Acts

• Declaring Independence

EFFECTS

- 1765 Stamp Act Congress meets
- 1773 Colonists carry out Boston Tea Party
- 1774 First Continental Congress meets
- 1775 Fighting occurs at Lexington and Concord

Chapter 2

A New Nation

Britain emerged victorious from the French and Indian War to become the dominant European power in North America. Britain's victory, however, brought a huge war debt and the problem of administering newly acquired territories. The British government levied new taxes on the colonists and issued the Proclamation Act of 1763 that banned all settlement west of the Appalachians. In protesting Britain's tightening controls, the colonists discovered a sense of unity and patriotism.

British refusal to compromise pushed the colonists toward the Declaration of Independence (1776), which formally notified the world that the

Cooperative Learning Activity

Revolutionary Writing Remind students that during the American Revolution various patriotic groups penned American slogans, poems, and songs in support of the cause. Organize the class into groups of five. Ask groups to compose a slogan, poem, or song on one of the following: the Boston Tea Party, the Declaration of Independence, the Louisiana Purchase, or the War of 1812. Encourage students to find or create illustrations for their compositions. Have each group select a representative to read its work to the class. **L1**

colonies were "free and independent States." During the War for Independence, the Americans—with only a volunteer army—carried out a long struggle against a larger British military force. The struggle was eased when France allied itself with the American cause following a major victory over British forces at Saratoga. In 1781, the British finally surrendered at Yorktown, Virginia.

With independence, the colonies developed a plan—the Articles of Confederation—to unite them. Under the Articles, the national government was weak and had difficulty collecting taxes, enforcing laws, and mediating disputes between the states. Because of these problems, a bold group of leaders met and drafted a new plan of government—the Constitution—during the summer of 1787. The Constitution created a powerful two-house Congress, a strong chief executive, and a national judicial system.

Chapter 3

Launching the Republic

As the nation's first President, George Washington set several precedents—creating a cabinet, directing foreign affairs, and serving as "chief legislator." His secretary of the treasury, Alexander Hamilton, carried out a financial policy that restored the credit of the United States. Hamilton's program met with bitter opposition from people who believed that the federal government should not wield such power. These disagreements eventually led to the formation of the nation's first political parties: the Federalists and the Republicans.

Under Washington, the defeat of Native Americans in the Northwest opened the way for continued Western settlement. Overseas, the United States adopted a policy of neutrality. To keep the peace, however, it agreed to treaties with Britain and Spain.

John Adams, who succeeded Washington as the nation's leader, faced a difficult term in office. Adams's tenure was marked by the XYZ affair, an undeclared war with France, and anti-Republican legislation that ultimately hurt Adams's Federalist party.

Republican Thomas Jefferson favored a decreased role for the federal government in national affairs. However, much of the earlier Federalist legislation remained in effect. In addition, the Federalist Chief Justice John Marshall of the Supreme Court established the principle of judicial review.

A major event during Jefferson's presidency was the Louisiana Purchase, which doubled the size of the United States by extending its boundaries west of the Mississippi. Despite the threat of foreign attacks on American ships, Jefferson tried to remain neutral in foreign affairs. Under James Madison, Jefferson's successor, the United States became embroiled in an unpopular war with Britain, which finally ended in 1814 with the Treaty of Ghent.

Understanding Unit Themes

1. **Geography and the Environment** How did the location of Asian centers of trade relative to Europe lead to colonies in the Americas?

2. **Beliefs, Ideas, and Institutions** What roles did religion play in motivating European voyages of exploration and in colonizing America?

3. **Cultural Diversity** What role did cultural diversity play in colonization?

4. **Conflict and Cooperation** How did the conflicting interests of the British and Americans lead to the Revolutionary War?

5. **American Democracy** What beliefs held by Thomas Jefferson furthered democracy?

 Student Self-Test Software allows students to test their understanding of historical concepts.

🎧 Have students listen to the Chapter Digests on the audiocassettes

Use the Testmaker to create a customized test.

GLENCOE TECHNOLOGY

 **VIDEODISC**

Use the MindJogger videodiscs to review students' knowledge.

MindJogger Videoquiz

Chapter 1
Disc 1, Side A

Chapter 2
Disc 1, Side A

Chapter 3
Disc 1, Side A

📼 Available in VHS.

Flashcards

Use American History Flashcards to reinforce students' knowledge of places and events in American history.

Answers to Understanding Unit Themes

1. Innovations allowed longer, faster, and safer voyages, and eventually made the exploration and colonizing of the Americas possible.

2. Crusades whetted appetites for Eastern goods; Church wanted to spread Christianity; dissenters wanted freedom.

3. Native Americans and Europeans clashed over cultural differences such as those relating to religion, wealth, exploitation of peoples and resources, and slavery.

4. Britain wanted to legislate for the colonies, which wanted to make their own laws. British wanted to regulate American trade, but colonists wanted freedom to pursue their own economic interests. Britain wanted military control over colonies, which colonists opposed.

5. Jefferson's belief in people's ability to govern themselves and his belief that people were the source of the government's power

BEGINNING THE UNIT

Present this cause-and-effect chart to students with the effects omitted. Assign them to complete the chart as they read the chapters in the unit.

Event
- Civil War

Causes
- Growth of slavery
- Growth in antislavery sentiment
- Dependence on cotton
- Growth of belief in states' rights

Effects
- Abolition of slavery
- Preservation of the United States
- Primacy of the national government
- Deaths of about 620,000 Americans
- Extension of civil rights to African Americans

History AND ART

Henry Ossawa Tanner (1859–1937) studied at the Philadelphia Academy of Fine Arts. He painted this picture in 1893 in Paris.

0:00 OUT OF TIME?

If time does not permit teaching the entire unit, use the Unit Digest on pages 234–235.

134

UNIT TWO
FORGING A NATION
1815–1877

★★★

CHAPTER 4	CHAPTER 5	CHAPTER 6
Toward a Democracy 1815–1850	The Civil War Era 1820–1865	Reconstruction 1865–1877

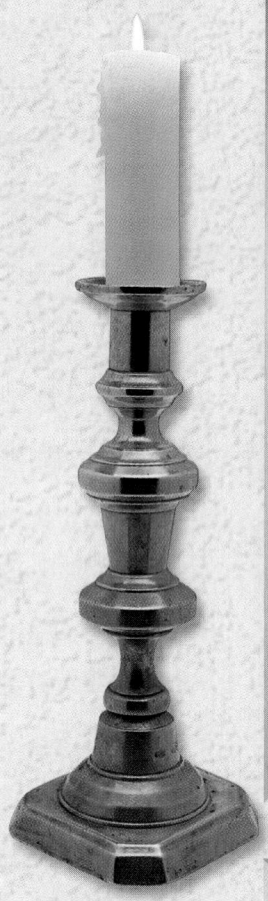

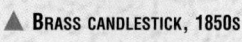
▲ BRASS CANDLESTICK, 1850S

History AND ART

The Banjo Lesson
by Henry Tanner, 1893

American artist Henry Ossawa Tanner produced a number of realistic studies of American life. After he moved to Europe in the early 1900s, he found another source of inspiration—the Bible.

134

Exploring Unit Themes

American Democracy Such reforms as national nominating conventions and the direct election of presidential electors increased voter participation in the political process. Women, African Americans, and native Americans, however, benefited little from these changes.

Civil Rights and Liberties The Freedmen's Bureau was established to assist African Americans in their transition from slavery to freedom. Congress also passed three amendments to protect African American rights.

Economic Development The Industrial Revolution brought changes throughout the United States.

Geography and Environment Acquisitions of new territory helped the United States grow rapidly in the first half of the nineteenth century.

Setting the Scene

The slavery issue dominated American life during the first half of the nineteenth century. Compromise had worked in the past, but a growing antislavery movement would not let the moral shame of slavery die.

Themes

- American Democracy
- Civil Rights and Liberties
- Economic Development
- Geography and Environment
- Beliefs, Ideas, and Institutions
- Conflict and Cooperation

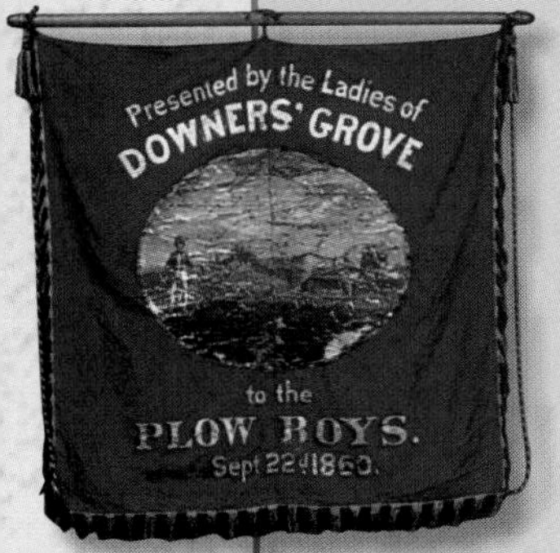

Key Events

- Monroe Doctrine
- Missouri Compromise
- Native American removal
- Seneca Falls Convention
- War with Mexico
- Compromise of 1850
- Confederate States formed
- War Between the States
- Surrender of General Lee
- Assassination of Lincoln
- Radical Reconstruction
- Compromise of 1877

Major Issues

- Distinct sections—North, South, and West—cooperate and compete for economic development.
- A belief in Manifest Destiny results in war with Mexico.
- Section differences strain the Union and lead to war.
- Reconstruction of the South left many problems unsolved, including the place of African Americans in American society.

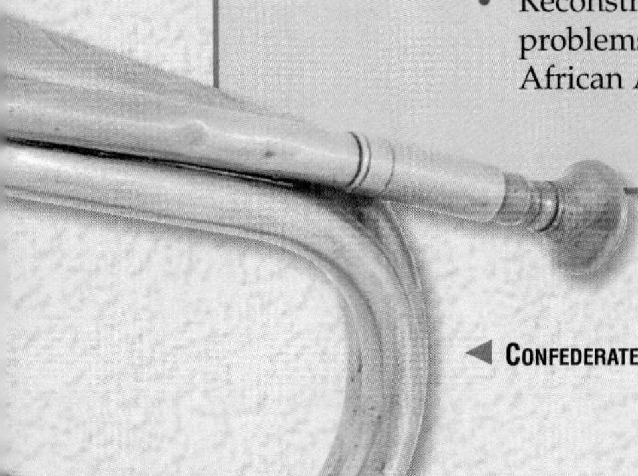

▲ HONORARY BANNER, 1860

◀ CONFEDERATE BUGLE

▲ UNION SOLDIER

Portfolio Project

Use the library to locate sources about one of the important individuals, events, or developments discussed in this unit. Organize information about these sources to create an efficient reference guide for someone interested in writing an in-depth study of the subject.

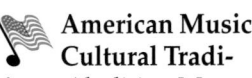

interNET CONNECTIONS

For more in-depth study of Unit 2, you or your students may use the Internet to research individual topics. The following list details some of the wealth of information available on the era. **The American Civil War Homepage:** http://cobweb.utcc.utk.edu/~hoemann/warweb.html

Portfolio Project

To help students get started, suggest they organize their sources into categories such as primary sources and secondary sources.

History and the Humanities

U.S. History & Art Transparency 11: *A Rainy Day in Camp* by Winslow Homer

American Music: Cultural Traditions: Abolition Movement "Get Off the Track!" by The Hutchinson Family Singers (2:46) Civil War "Bonnie Blue Flag" by the First Brigade Band (1:18); "Glory! Glory! Glory! Hallelujah!" by the Princely Players (1:35)

Beliefs, Ideas, and Institutions In the mid-1800s reformers attempted to increase economic and educational opportunities and improve the moral tone of society in general.
Conflict and Cooperation For almost 40 years, political compromises provided a temporary solution to the issue of slavery. In the 1860s compromises failed, and the country plunged into a bloody civil war.
Examining Unit Themes Ask students to select one of the themes and jot down notes dealing with it as they read this unit. Upon completion of the unit, students should write one paragraph summarizing the theme.

Global Perspectives

★★★★★ ★★★

FOCUS
Motivating Activity

Point out to students that the early and mid-1800s were a period of transition and conflict around the world. In the Western Hemisphere, revolutions against colonial rule took place throughout Latin America. In Europe revolution overturned monarchies and established republics. Tell students that the years between 1828 and 1840 have been referred to as the Age of Revolution. Ask what recent examples they can suggest of similar change and conflict in the world. *(Responses may include the fall of communism in the former Soviet Union and the nations of Eastern Europe; the establishment of majority rule in South Africa and ethnic conflicts in the former nation of Yugoslavia.)* **L1**

TEACH
Guided Practice
Exploring the Time Line

On the chalkboard draw a chart with two vertical columns, one headed The World and the other The United States, and two horizontal columns headed Conflict and Cooperation, respectively. Direct students to study the time line and then enter appropriate events from the time line onto the chart. *(Examples: World, Conflict—Opium War; Cooperation—Pan-Americanism; U.S., Conflict—Trail of Tears; Cooperation—Erie Canal completed)* **L1**

The World

	1820		1840
Asia and Oceania	**1819** *Thomas Raffles obtains Singapore for Britain*		**1839** *Britain and China battle in First Opium War*
Europe	**1815** *Napoleon defeated at Waterloo*		**1837** *Victoria becomes Queen of Great Britain*
Africa			**1835** *Boer farmers start the "Great Trek"* **1847** *Liberia becomes an independent republ.*
South America	**1821** *Peru becomes independent of Spain*	**1824** *Simón Bolívar frees Peru and Bolivia from Spanish rule*	
North and Central America		**1823** *Monroe Doctrine proclaimed* **1826** *Pan-Americanism gets under way at Panama*	**1840** *Act of Union unites Upper and Lower Canada*

The United States

		1820		1840
Pacific and Northwest		**1821** *California becomes a Mexican province*	**1830** *Fur traders open the Oregon Trail*	
Southeast	**1819** *Florida is purchased from Spain*			**1831** *Cyrus McCormick invents the reaper*
Midwest				**1838** *Cherokee endure the "Trail of Tears"*
Southwest			**1836** *Battle of the Alamo fought*	**1845** *Texas annexed*
Atlantic Northeast		**1825** *Erie Canal completed*		**1839** *Charles Goodyear makes first vulcanized rubber*

1820   1840

136   UNIT 2 Forging a Nation: 1815–1877

Cultural Perspectives

Immigration The first massive wave of nineteenth-century European immigration occurred between 1845 and 1860 as the U.S. economy improved after a deep economic depression. More than 2.6 million immigrants arrived, most of them Roman Catholics. The Irish made up the largest ethnic group. Many were fleeing the disastrous Irish potato famine of the late 1840s. The Germans, the second-largest group, were fleeing for economic and political reasons, particularly the repression that followed the failed revolutions of 1848.

Linking Across TIME

African Americans have made major contributions to our country's music. Gospel, an exuberant and joyous celebration of faith through music, grew out of the religious services held by enslaved African Americans. Blues, which grew out of work songs and chants, had a strong impact on the pioneers of rock 'n roll. Jazz, which some people consider the only new art form to be developed in the twentieth century, was influenced by both gospel and the blues.

1853 Commodore Matthew Perry arrives in Japan

1860

1880

▶ **1848** Nationalist revolutions occur throughout Europe

1881 French seize Tunis

◀ **1861** Benito Juárez becomes President of Mexico

1867 Dominion of Canada formed

1848 Gold discovered in California

1867 Alaska purchased from Russia

1877 Nez Perce War fought

▼ **1861** Civil War begins

1872 Yellowstone National Park created

1875 Black Hills open to gold seekers

1848 United States acquires Mexican cession

1852 Uncle Tom's Cabin published

1860

1880

UNIT 2 Forging a Nation: 1815–1877 **137**

LESSON PLAN
Global Perspectives

Independent Practice

Linking World Events A French observer of events in the United States in the early nineteenth century was Alexis de Tocqueville. His book *Democracy in America* had a tremendous influence on the leaders of revolutions that swept through Europe in the mid-1800s. Ask students to research European revolutions of the period and create a time line of these revolutions. **L2**

ASSESS
Studying the Time Line

1. What two efforts at unity took place between 1820 and 1850? (*Pan-Americanism and Act of Union in Canada*)
2. What event revolutionized American transportation? (*completion of Erie Canal*)
3. Which world event and which United States event had the greatest impact on U.S. history? Explain your answers. (*Answers will vary. Sample answers: World—Commodore Perry's arrival in Japan, established United States influence in Asia; United States—discovery of gold in California, brought expansion of slavery to political forefront.*)

Cooperative Learning Activity

Creating Illustrations Organize students into small groups and tell them their task is to design a T-shirt that might have been sold in conjunction with one of the events mentioned in the time line. Have half the groups select world events and the other half United States events. Suggest that their designs include illustrations and some form of slogan. Display the finished designs on the bulletin board. **L2**

137

Daily Lesson Objectives	Teacher Classroom Resources	Multimedia
SECTION 1 **The Era of Good Feelings** **1 Day** pp. 140–146 1. List events that showed a spirit of nationalism. 2. Explain how the Supreme Court increased the national government's power.	Reproducible Lesson Plan 4-1 Chapter Concept Mapping Activities 4-A, 4-B * Guided Reading Activity 4-1 Cooperative Learning Activity 4 Chapter Map Activity 4 Reteaching Activity 4-1 * Section Quiz 4-1	Section Focus Transparency 4-1 Chapter Map Transparency 4 Chapter Concepts Transparencies 4-A, 4-B Testmaker GTV: A Geographic Perspective on American History The American History Videodisc MindJogger Videoquiz
SECTION 2 **Growth of Sectionalism** **1 Day** pp. 147–152 1. Discuss the impact of the Industrial Revolution on American life. 2. Explain how industrialization contributed to wider acceptance of slavery in the South. 3. Identify four areas of sectional conflict.	Reproducible Lesson Plan 4-2 * Vocabulary Activity 4 Geography in History Activity 4 * Guided Reading Activity 4-2 Critical Thinking Skills Activity 4 Workbook Activity 4-2 Reteaching Activity 4-2 * Section Quiz 4-2	Section Focus Transparency 4-2 Vocabulary PuzzleMaker Software Testmaker American Music: Cultural Traditions
SECTION 3 **Age of Jackson** **1 Day** pp. 154–159 1. Summarize the political career of Andrew Jackson. 2. List three democratic changes that developed during this period.	Reproducible Lesson Plan 4-3 * Guided Reading Activity 4-3 Workbook Activity 4-3 Reteaching Activity 4-3 * Section Quiz 4-3	Section Focus Transparency 4-3 Testmaker GTV: The American People: Fabric of a Nation Powers of the President Focus on Government The American Indian
SECTION 4 **The Spirit of Reform** **1 Day** pp. 160–164 1. Identify social reform movements that were widespread during the early 1800s. 2. Discuss the new values and beliefs that influenced educators, artists, and writers.	Reproducible Lesson Plan 4-4 * Guided Reading Activity 4-4 Linking Past and Present Activity 4 Reteaching Activity 4-4 Enrichment Activity 4 * Section Quiz 4-4	Section Focus Transparency 4-4 Skills Transparency 4 Testmaker Historic America Electronic Field Trips Focus on Government
CHAPTER REVIEW AND EVALUATION **1 Day**	Chapter 4 Test, Forms A and B Spanish Chapter 4 Summary Performance Assessment Activity 4	MindJogger Videoquiz Student Self-Test & Review Software * Chapter 4 Digest Audiocassettes Activity and Test

*Also available in Spanish

 **OUT OF TIME?** If time does not permit teaching the entire chapter, use the Chapter 4 Summary on pages 234–235 and the Chapter 4 audiocassette (English and Spanish) to point out the main ideas of the chapter.

A complete, 1-page lesson plan is provided for each section in the *Reproducible Lesson Plan* booklet.

Key to Ability Levels

Teaching strategies have been coded for varying learning styles and abilities.

L1 Basic activities for all students

L2 Average activities for average to above-average students

L3 Challenging activities for above-average students

LEP Limited English Proficiency activities

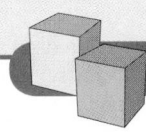

Block Schedule

Block scheduling differs from traditional class scheduling in the amount of time allotted to each period. The extended time frame provided by block scheduling afford you the opportunity to implement a greater number of research-oriented and activity-intense projects to motivate and involve your students. Activities that are particularly suited to use within the block scheduling framework are identified throughout this unit by the following designation:

✓ Performance Assessment Activity

Reporting Changes As the United States grew and expanded, so did its transportation network. Ask students to work alone or in small groups to research and report on one form of transportation (railroads, stagecoach service, canals, rivers). Excellent resources include the following: *Towpaths to Tugboats: A History of American Canal Engineering* by William Shank and *Modernization: The Transformation of American Life: 1600–1865* by Richard D. Brown. You may also wish to have students view the videodisc *Getting Up to Speed* (National Geographic Society GTV: A Geographic Perspective on American History). Encourage them to use maps, graphs, and other illustrations in their reports. As students present their findings, discuss the importance of transportation and how it linked the regions of the nation together. **L2**

POSSIBLE RUBRIC FEATURES

* Content
* Written and Visual Communication Skills
* Organization
* Interdependence of Geography and Economics

📁 For additional activities, see Performance Assessment

TEACHER'S CORNER

NATIONAL GEOGRAPHIC SOCIETY

INDEX TO NATIONAL GEOGRAPHIC MAGAZINE

The following articles may be used for research relating to this chapter:

* "Philadelphia's African Americans," by Roland L. Freeman, August 1990.
* "The Cherokee", by Geoffrey Norman, May 1995.
* "The Cruelest Commerce: African Slave Trade," by Colin Palmer, September 1992.
* "Erie Canal: Living Link to Our Past," by Joel L. Swerdlow, November 1990.
* "I Dream a World: America's Black Women," by Brian Lanker, August 1989.
* "The Underground Railroad," by Charles L. Blockson, July 1984.

NATIONAL GEOGRAPHIC SOCIETY PRODUCTS AVAILABLE FROM GLENCOE

To order the following products for use with this chapter, contact your local Glencoe sales representative or call Glencoe at 1-800-334-7344:

* *The Presidents: A Picture History of Our Nation* (CD-ROM)
* *GTV: A Geographic Perspective on American History* (Videodisc)
* *GTV: The American People: Fabric of a Nation* (Videodisc)
* *Native Americans, Part I* (CD-ROM)
* *Native Americans: Eastern Woodlands and Plains* (Transparencies)

ADDITIONAL NATIONAL GEOGRAPHIC SOCIETY PRODUCTS

To order the following products for use with this chapter, call National Geographic Society at 1-800-368-2728:

* *The American Presidency* (Filmstrip)

CHAPTER 4
★★★

Toward a Democracy
1815–1850

► CORNHUSK DOLL

Setting the Scene

Focus

The years after the War of 1812 until 1850 were a time of national optimism and the growth of democracy and the economy. Confident of their future, Americans experimented with social reform movements aimed at bettering society. At the same time, a strong sectional rivalry was developing. Each region wanted to further its own economic and political interests.

Concepts to Understand

★ What political, economic, and social factors affected national and regional feelings and **American democracy**

★ How **economic change** brought about the Industrial Revolution and changes in the workplace

Read to Discover . . .

★ how each section viewed the major issues faced by the nation.

★ in what ways Andrew Jackson was a symbol of his times.

★ how the spirit of reform affected various groups in American society.

Journal Notes

How did different regions respond to the idea of protective tariffs? Note details about how they responded in your journal as you read the chapter.

CULTURAL			
● **1816** *African Methodist Episcopal Church organized*	● **1821** *Emma Willard founds Troy Female Seminary*	● **1827** *First African American newspaper,* Freedom's Journal, *begins publication*	
1815	**1821**	**1827**	
● **1820** *Missouri Compromise reached*	● **1823** *Monroe Doctrine proclaimed*	● **1828** *Andrew Jackson elected President*	
POLITICAL			

✚ EXTRA CREDIT PROJECT

Comparing Presidents Point out to students that Andrew Jackson was the first President from a Western state. Suggest that interested students research the lives of the six preceding Presidents as well as that of Andrew Jackson. Have them compare Jackson with the other Presidents. Ask students to present their findings in a report and to draw conclusions about Jackson's election and the expansion of democracy in the early nineteenth century. **L2**

On the chalkboard, reproduce the following generalization and concepts map, and have students copy it in their notebooks.

As the nation grew, differences in economic activities and needs increased sectionalism. At the same time, democracy emerged as the leading force in American political life.

American Democracy

Economic Change

📁 To reinforce the two chapter concepts, assign Chapter Concept Mapping Activities 4-A and 4-B.

History AND ART

Winslow Homer's painting offers an idyllic view of early New England factory life.

◀ AKAN DRUM

History AND ART

Morning Bell
by Winslow Homer, 1866

After the Civil War, Winslow Homer often painted scenes of everyday life. Homer's painting *Morning Bell* depicts young women going to work in a New England textile mill.

NATIONAL GEOGRAPHIC SOCIETY

 VIDEODISC

GTV: A Geographic Perspective on American History

Side 2, Chapter 9
Title: *Getting Up to Speed*
Subject: Transportation and a growing nation (1825–1850)

- **1833** *National Temperance movement founded*
- **1836** *Bank of the United States charter expires*

- **1844** *First telegraph message sent*
- **1840** *Whigs nominate Harrison*

- **1846** *Smithsonian Institution founded*
- **1848** *First presidential election to be held on the same day in all states*

| 1833 | 1839 | 1845 |

✔ **Performance Assessment**

Refer to the Performance Assessment Activity in the Planning Guide on page 138b. When the students have finished their report about changes in transportation, have them present their reports to the class. Allow time for class discussion and feedback.

📁 Use Performance Assessment Activity 4 as an additional assessment technique.

FOCUS

Bellringer

Before taking roll, project Section Focus Transparency 4-1 or hand out Section Focus Transparency Activity 4-1. Have students answer the questions.

Motivating Activity

Have students list their school's symbols. (*examples: school colors; school uniforms for sports or other activities; school emblem and motto*) Ask why these symbols are important to students. (*They make students feel special, provide a feeling of belonging, and help create pride in attending a school.*) Then ask and discuss: What are some examples of national symbols that create in Americans feelings of belonging? (*examples: national flag, national anthem*) Point out that this section deals with the spirit of nationalism as a powerful force in the development of the United States. **L1**

Vocabulary Precheck

Ask students to define each of the "Key Terms." Have a volunteer consult the dictionary for any unfamiliar words. **L1, LEP**

★★★

The Era of Good Feelings

Setting the Scene

Section Focus

After the War of 1812, a powerful spirit of nationalism swept through American life. Both manufacturers and farmers produced more and more goods for sale. A transportation network began to crisscross the country, stimulating the movement of people and products. In foreign affairs, the United States worked to establish peace along its borders and to expand them where possible.

◀ NATIONAL ROAD MILE MARKER

Objectives

After studying this section, you should be able to

★ list events that showed a spirit of nationalism.

★ explain how the Supreme Court increased the national government's power.

Key Terms

nationalism, internal improvement, turnpike, toll, ultimatum

Nationalism is a feeling of intense loyalty and devotion to one's country. It is a spirit that unifies into one nation diverse groups that share a geographic area. Nationalism can be demonstrated by people's actions, illustrated by such symbols as a flag, and expressed in a nation's art, literature, and music. In the United States, the spirit of nationalism increased significantly after the War of 1812. In 1816, James Monroe, a Virginia Republican, was elected President over New York Federalist Rufus King.

On a national goodwill tour, the new President promoted a spirit of unity everywhere he went. His warm reception by cheering crowds in Boston caused a local Federalist newspaper to proclaim that an "Era of Good Feelings" had begun. By 1820 the Federalists, discredited by their anti-war position during the War of 1812, had vanished from national politics, and President Monroe was reelected without opposition.

■ Nationalist Legislation

The new American nationalism was revealed in legislation as well as in politics. The War of 1812 had clearly demonstrated that Jefferson's ideal of a central government with strictly limited functions could not meet the needs of a nation in crisis. After the war, a Republican-controlled Congress passed a series of laws that seemed as though they had been written by Federalists.

The American System

Henry Clay of Kentucky and John C. Calhoun of South Carolina proposed an ambitious program called the "American System" based on a protective tariff and **internal improvements**—roads, canals, and other transportation needs. Clay and Calhoun also wanted to reinstate the national bank. Congress had refused to renew the charter of the First Bank in 1811 with disastrous results.

140 UNIT 2 Forging a Nation: 1815–1877

Classroom Resources for SECTION 1

Blackline Masters:
- Reproducible Lesson Plan 4-1
- Guided Reading Activity 4-1
- Cooperative Learning Activity 4
- Chapter Map Activity 4
- Outline Map Resource Book, pp. 8-9

- Primary and Secondary Source Readings, p. 7
- Workbook Activity 4-1
- Reteaching Activity 4-1
- Section Quiz 4-1

Transparencies:
- Section Focus Transparency 4-1
- Chapter Map Transparency 4

Multimedia:
- Testmaker
- GTV: A Geographic Perspective on American History
- The American History Videodisc

The notes of the Bank had been accepted everywhere as a national currency. State bank notes were generally accepted only in the locality where they were issued. Without a national bank, the federal government also had a difficult time borrowing money during the War of 1812. Clay and Calhoun argued that a national bank would create a national currency and encourage economic growth. They hoped that this nationalistic program would bring prosperity to all sections of the country and, to the nation, economic independence from the rest of the world.

A Second Bank

In 1816 Congress passed a bill to establish a second Bank of the United States that could issue currency and regulate state banks. Congress also responded with the Tariff of 1816. Unlike earlier revenue tariffs, which had provided income for the federal government, this tariff protected American manufacturers from foreign competition by placing high taxes on imports.

■ Supreme Court Nationalism

Nationalism also was demonstrated in a series of Supreme Court decisions by Chief Justice John Marshall. Between 1819 and 1824, Marshall ruled in three important Court cases that strengthened the power of the federal government over the states. Although opposed by defenders of states' rights, Marshall's decisions made the Constitution flexible enough to meet the nation's changing needs.

Implied Powers

In the landmark case *McCulloch* v. *Maryland* (1819), Marshall stated that the federal government possessed implied powers— that is, powers not specifically stated in the Constitution. In this instance, the Court ruled that Congress had the power to create the second Bank of the United States and that an attempt by Maryland to tax the bank

was unconstitutional. *McCulloch* v. *Maryland* established the superiority of federal power over state power in case of conflict.

Contract and Property Rights

In *Dartmouth College* v. *Woodward* (1819), the Court set out to protect contracts and property rights from state power. It was responding to efforts by New Hampshire to change the charter of Dartmouth College and make the private school a state institution. In the decision, Marshall noted that "the state legislatures were forbidden 'to pass any law impairing the obligation of contracts,' that is, of contracts respecting property." A college charter is a contract, he said, and a state had no right to interfere. Thus, the attempt to seize this private college was unconstitutional.

Interstate Commerce

In *Gibbons* v. *Ogden* (1824), the Court overturned a New York law that hindered out-of-state commercial steamboats from doing business in New York waters. Marshall

★★★ AMERICA'S FLAGS ★★★

The Flag of 1818 By 1818 the number of the states in the Union had reached 20. In April, President Monroe signed into law a bill that determined the basic design of the flag. Each newly admitted state would add a star to the field of blue—on the Fourth of July following the state's year of entry. The 13 stripes symbolizing the original states remained unchanged.

The Great Star Flag Congress did not stipulate how the stars should be arranged, so flagmakers used various designs. One  design had four rows of five stars each. The *Great Star Flag* placed the stars in the form of a five-pointed star.

★★★★★★★★★★★★★★★★★★★★★★★

TEACH
Guided Practice
Evaluating Technology
Ask each student to select either the period before the War of 1812 or the period from 1812 to 1840 and write a brief evaluation of the means of transportation in terms of safety, ease, and speed of moving people and products. *(before 1812: horse and wagon—difficult and slow; flatboat or keelboat—faster, cheaper than land transportation but could only float downstream; 1812–1840: National Road, turnpikes, and state roads—most not surfaced, muddy in spring; steamboats—high-risk, but much faster and more efficient; canals—superior to roads; railroads—best means of transportation, initially slow to take hold)*
L2

Did You Know?

People in the early 1800s could be imprisoned if they were unable to pay their debts. An 1817 New York law prevented people who owed less than $25 from being put into debtor's prison. Kentucky, in 1821, was the first state to abolish imprisonment for debt.

Cooperative Learning Activity

Analyzing Landmark Supreme Court Decisions
Have students discuss in groups of four the precedent-setting cases of the Marshall Court that are covered in detail in this section and in the chart on page 142. Assign numbers and the following tasks to individual students in each group: (1) to present the opposing sides of a case, (2) to analyze the issue, (3) to state the outcome, and (4) to speculate on the effect the outcome would have on future cases. Tell students that you will call on them by number and that they are to carry out their assigned task for the class. **L1, L2**

CURRICULUM CONNECTION

Political Science Write the word *doctrine* on the chalkboard. Invite volunteers to define it. *(possible answer: position statement)* Then have students discuss why the Monroe Doctrine is not an agreement but a declaration or policy statement. **L3**

Using Charts

Answer: It stated that the federal government possessed implied powers.

Chart Skills Practice

Which case reviewed by the Supreme Court resulted in a decision giving the Court the power to declare federal and state laws unconstitutional? *(Marbury v. Madison)*

NATIONAL GEOGRAPHIC SOCIETY

VIDEODISC

GTV: A Geographic Perspective on American History

Side 2, Chapter 11

Title: *Going to Extremes: The Far West*

Subject: Settlement in the Far West (1820–1850)

declared that the New York legislature had overstepped its power, because the Constitution gave the federal government control over interstate commerce. By establishing national power over interstate commerce, Marshall's opinion opened the way for easy trade between the states and national economic growth. It also provided the federal government with the constitutional basis for many of the broad and sweeping powers it exercises today.

■ Tying the Nation Together

After the War of 1812, the United States began to develop transportation systems. By the mid-1800s, roads, canals, steamboats, and railroads had created a truly national economy. People could now buy goods pro-

duced in distant places. Information joined the flow of products as mail became deliverable throughout the nation. With the mail came newspapers, which brought national issues to the attention of the most remote rural communities.

Roads

In general, states or private businesses undertook improvements in overland transportation. State-chartered private companies constructed hundreds of miles of **turnpikes,** roads that were barricaded at intervals by poles that stopped travelers until they paid a **toll,** or fee. In the West, highways usually were constructed by the states themselves, at times with federal aid. From the sale of western lands, the federal government funded the National Road,

The Marshall Court and the National Interest

Case and Year	Issue and Decision
Marbury v. *Madison* (1803)	Declared an act of Congress unconstitutional. Court given power of judicial review and power to declare congressional and state legislation unconstitutional.
Fletcher v. *Peck* (Yazoo land fraud case, 1810)	Declared sanctity of contracts. Gave Supreme Court right to overturn state laws that ran counter to specific provisions of Constitution.
Martin v. *Hunter's Lessee* (1816)	Gave Supreme Court right to reverse decisions of state courts.
Trustees of Dartmouth College v. *Woodward* (1819)	Reaffirmed sanctity of contracts. Protected banks and corporations with state charters from meddling by state legislators.
Sturges v. *Crowninshield* (1819)	Tested constitutionality of state bankruptcy laws. Court determined that in absence of federal regulation, states were free to legislate.
McCulloch v. *Maryland* (1819)	Challenged constitutionality of Bank of the United States. Court said "implied powers" enabled Congress to enact any legislation within letter and spirit of Constitution.
Cohens v. *Virginia* (1821)	Tested constitutionality of Judiciary Act of 1789. Court said states gave up some sovereignty in ratifying Constitution, so state courts must accept federal jurisdiction.
Gibbons v. *Ogden* (1824)	Invalidated a state monopoly. Court gave Congress right to regulate interstate commerce, a decision of great importance for national development.

Source: *The Guide to American Law*, vol. 7 (1984).

Chart Study Chief Justice John Marshall dominated the Supreme Court until his death in 1835. The Marshall Court handed down a series of decisions that increased federal power over state governments. ***What was significant about the McCulloch decision?***

Special Needs Activity

Reading Disability Students with reading problems often have difficulty finding main ideas in sections of text. Explain that charts often collect main ideas and state them in concise form. Have students turn to the chart titled "The Marshall Court and the National Interest" on

this page. Note that three of the cases presented in the chart are described in detail in the text. Read about the cases in the text and have students find one or two sentences that give the main ideas of the case. Have students check to see if this information is in the chart. **LEP, L1**

★★★★★★★★★★★ AMERICAN PORTRAITS

Henry Clay
1777–1852

Virginia-born and raised, Henry Clay moved to Kentucky, a state that kept him in Congress—and in the forefront of national politics—for nearly 50 years.

A fierce political rivalry soon developed between Clay and another Westerner, Andrew Jackson of Tennessee. The two first clashed in 1819 when Clay blasted Jackson's Florida invasion. The election of 1824 made them bitter enemies. Ignoring instructions from Kentucky to back Jackson for President, Clay supported John Quincy Adams, who appointed Clay secretary of state. Jackson's revenge came when he defeated Clay in the presidential election of 1832. Clay sought the presidency three more times before retiring. In 1849, however, he returned to Congress and put together a compromise between North and South that helped delay the Civil War.

which began in Cumberland, Maryland, and eventually reached Vandalia, Illinois. Great Conestoga wagons drawn by oxen or teams of 4, 6, or 8 horses moved westward along this route.

By 1840, roads crisscrossed the country, but they did not provide satisfactory transportation. David Stevenson described a journey by stagecoach along a typical route of the time in his book *Sketch of the Civil Engineering of North America*, published in 1838:

❝ *Sometimes our way lay for miles through extensive marshes, which we crossed by corduroy roads [roads having logs laid sideways across the roadbed]. . . . At others the coach stuck fast in mud, from which it could be extricated only by the combined efforts of the coachman and passengers; and at one place we traveled. . . . through a forest flooded with water, which stood to a height of several feet. . . . The distance of the route from Pittsburgh to Erie is 128 miles, which was accomplished* in forty-six hours . . . although the conveyance by which I traveled carried the mail, and stopped only for breakfast, dinner, and tea, but there was considerable delay by the coach being once upset and several times 'mired.'* ❞

Steamboats

Bulky goods, such as farm crops or manufactured goods, could not be quickly or profitably moved long distances by land. Far more important to commerce were America's inland waterways.

In 1807, Robert Fulton's steamboat, the *Clermont,* made its first voyages on the Hudson River from New York City to Albany. By demonstrating the usefulness of two-way river travel, Fulton launched the steamboat era. By 1850, nearly 800 steamboats regularly traveled the Mississippi River and its tributaries. Steamboats proved their ability to carry passengers and goods quickly and efficiently, but risks were high. The average life of a river steamboat was three to six years—not surprising considering the dangers presented by ice, bursting boilers, collisions, fires, and sandbars.

CHAPTER 4 Toward a Democracy: 1815–1850 **143**

CHAPTER 4
SECTION 1

Independent Practice

🗀 Assign Guided Reading Activity 4-1.

Analyzing Geographic Change Have students name some cities located on major transportation routes in 1840, as shown on the map on page 144. *(examples: Canals—New York, Buffalo; Mississippi River—St. Louis, New Orleans)* Have students use atlases to determine the approximate size of these cities today.

Teaching American Portraits

In 1819 Clay wanted Congress to pass a report condemning Jackson for his decision to execute two British citizens caught aiding the Spanish and the Seminole in Florida. Congress did not support Clay's report.

Ask students how the competition between Jackson and Clay for the presidency affected their relationship as national policy makers. *(intensified policy disagreements between them)* **L1**

Cooperative Learning Activity

Studying America's Transportation Organize students into groups of five. Assign each group one of these topics to discuss: railroads, canals, and roads and turnpikes. Give each student a set of colored chips and each group a container to place the chips into and a one-minute timer. Explain that when a student wishes to participate in the discussion, he or she must give up a chip and place it in the container. Tell students that they must spend all their chips in 15 minutes and that 1 minute is the longest a person can talk. **L1, L2**

🗀 For additional practice in cooperative learning, assign Cooperative Learning Activity 4.

Map Study *Using Maps*

Answer: east on Forbes Road to Philadelphia and north to New York City

Map Skills Practice

Which is the western-most canal? *(the Illinois and Michigan)*

📁 For additional map practice, assign Chapter Map Activity 4.

GLENCOE
TECHNOLOGY

💿 **VIDEODISC**

The American History Videodisc

Side One, Section D
Title: *Expansion, Development, Sectionalism, and Division, 1820-1860*

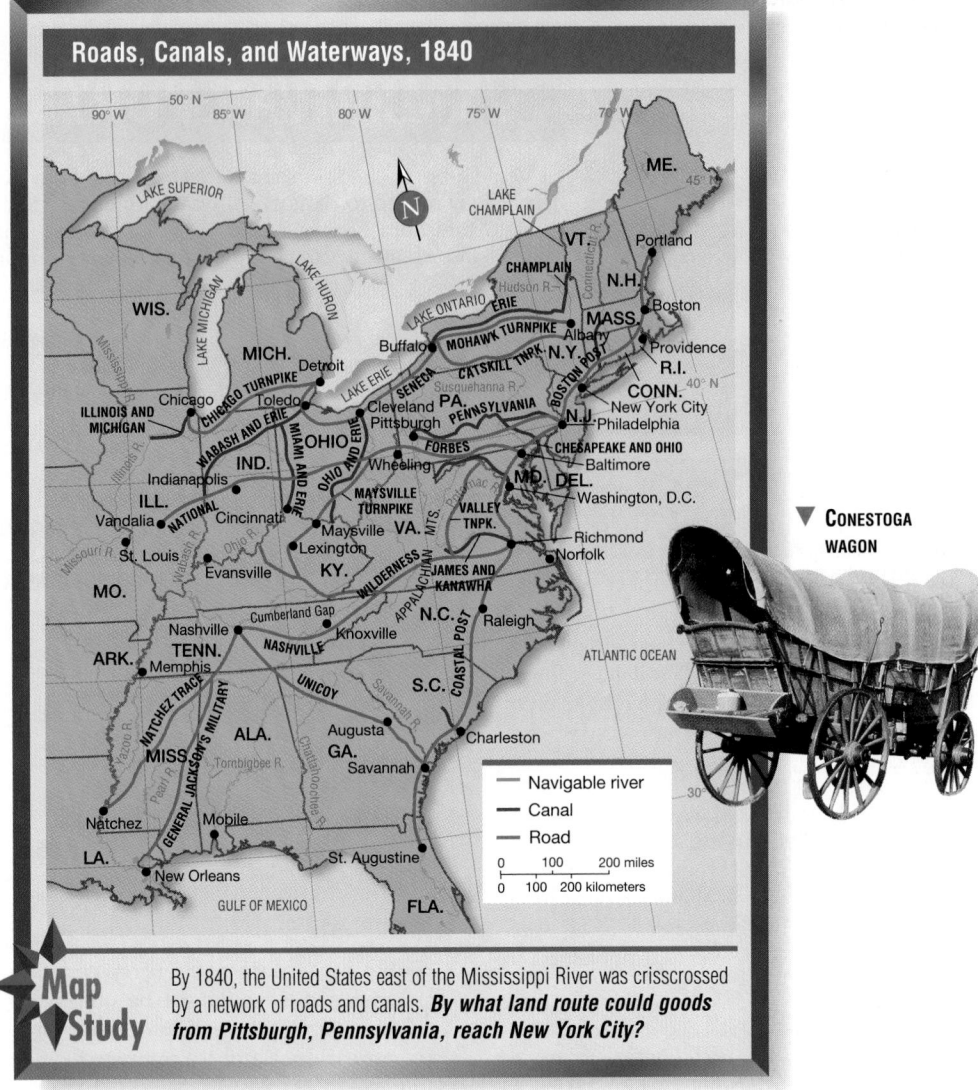

Roads, Canals, and Waterways, 1840

Navigable river
Canal
Road

0   100   200 miles
0   100   200 kilometers

▼ **CONESTOGA WAGON**

Map Study

By 1840, the United States east of the Mississippi River was crisscrossed by a network of roads and canals. **By what land route could goods from Pittsburgh, Pennsylvania, reach New York City?**

Canals

For moving heavy goods, the thousands of miles of canals built during the first part of the 1800s were far more efficient than even the best roads. Most canals bypassed rapids and falls in rivers or linked natural waterways. The Erie Canal, completed in 1825, ran from Albany on the Hudson River to Buffalo on Lake Erie. The canal lowered the cost of moving goods and reduced travel time from 20 days to 6. It quickly made New York City the great port in America and brought prosperity to rural areas upstate. The success of the Erie Canal encouraged other states, such as Pennsylvania, Ohio, and Indiana, to invest in canals.

Railroads

Railroads proved the most practical of all internal improvements. They were faster than roads and waterways and were passable in almost all weather. Nevertheless, railroads were slow to take hold, many because of opposition from state governments, which had heavy investments in roads and canals. Not until the second half

Sidelight: Settlement of the West

The transportation revolution helped to open the West. Since Congress followed an open land policy, farmers bought land cheaply in the 1800s—for between $1.25 and $2 an acre. Squatters, settlers intruding on public land, cleared and cultivated the land. Congressional legislation provided penalties, but they were never enforced, since the nation benefited from squatters' work. In 1841 Congress passed the Pre-Emption Act, allowing squatters to lay claim to their cultivated lands. They could buy it at $1.25 an acre or sell their preemption rights to the highest bidder.

of the 1800s would railroads dominate the nation's transportation systems.

■ Foreign Affairs

Domestic growth was accompanied by the search for peace abroad. Although the Treaty of Ghent had ended the War of 1812, bitter feelings remained between the United States and the two European powers who were allies in the war: Great Britain and Spain.

Easing of Tensions

Because of their strong trading ties, the United States and Great Britain recognized they had nothing to gain by continuing hostilities. Between 1815 and 1817, they worked out several of their disputes peacefully. The Rush-Bagot Agreement of 1817 removed all warships from the Great Lakes except for a few small vessels to control smuggling. The

Convention of 1818 settled the United States-Canadian boundary at the forty-ninth parallel from the Lake of the Woods in Minnesota to the Rocky Mountains. Beyond the Rockies, the treaty provided "joint occupation" of the disputed Oregon Territory for 10 years.

The United States also reached agreement with Spain over Spanish Florida. American forces led by Andrew Jackson, in pursuit of Seminoles and Creeks who were battling Georgia settlers, had seized two Spanish settlements in Florida. President Monroe, at the urging of Secretary of State John Quincy Adams, issued an **ultimatum,** a demand that would have serious consequences if ignored, likely a resort to force. The Spanish were told either to govern Florida effectively or surrender it to the United States. Occupied with problems in its Latin American empire, Spain ceded Florida to the United States in the Adams-Onís Treaty of 1819. The treaty also set the boundary between the Louisiana Purchase lands and the Texas

 ▲ *ON THE RIVER* by George Catlin Steamboats and canal boats speeded the movement of people and the transportation of goods. ***How did New York City benefit from the Erie Canal?***

CHAPTER 4 Toward a Democracy: 1815–1850 **145**

Cultural Perspectives

The Seminole Some of the Native Americans of the Creek people moved south from Georgia beginning about 1750. They were joined by runaway enslaved Native Americans and African Americans. By 1775 the group began calling itself by the Creek word *Seminole,* meaning "separatist" or "runaway." The United States wanted to recapture escaped enslaved people, prevent the fleeing of more, and eventually obtain Seminole lands.

Creating Maps Have students work in pairs of pairs. Provide two outline maps showing the boundaries in North America after the War of 1812 to each pair of pairs. Have one pair work together to indicate with colored pencils on one map the United States and its territories, the undisputed and disputed borders, and the disputed areas. Have the second set of pairs create a map showing the change in boundaries precipitated by the Rush-Bagot Agreement and the Adams-Onis Treaty. **L2**

📁 Provide maps on pages 8 and 9 from the Social Studies Outline Map Resource Book to complete the activity.

📦 Assign Map Transparency Activity 4.

History AND ART

George Catlin (1796–1872) painted this Mississippi riverboat scene. He is famous for his hundreds of paintings of Native American peoples. Catlin wished to record their traditional ways of life before they were gone forever.
Answer to Caption: By connecting the Hudson River to the Great Lakes, the canal made the city a great commercial center.

ASSESS

Check Understanding
Assign Section 1 Review as homework or an in-class activity.

Evaluate
Assign Section Quiz 4-1 or use the Testmaker to create a customized quiz.

Reteach
Have students complete Reteaching Activity 4-1.

Enrich
Have students research the political changes that were taking place in South America during the Era of Good Feelings in the United States.

Assign Primary and Secondary Source Readings, p. 7.

CLOSE
Have students discuss why they think historians do not consider James Monroe an outstanding President.

▲ THE MONROE DOCTRINE President Monroe consulted his cabinet before issuing the Monroe Doctrine. *What warning did the Doctrine contain?*

territory. The boundary was set at the western bank of the Sabine, Red, and Arkansas rivers to the Continental Divide. From there, the line followed the forty-second parallel west to the Pacific Ocean.

The Monroe Doctrine

In 1800, the United States was the only independent country in the Americas. European powers, such as Great Britain, France, the Netherlands, Portugal, and particularly Spain, ruled the rest of the hemisphere. Over the next two decades, however, many Latin American colonies revolted against Spain and declared their independence.

In the early 1820s, Spain gave signs of trying to regain its colonial empire. In 1823, Great Britain suggested to the United States that the two nations oppose intervention in Latin America by any power and that neither nation would acquire any part of Latin America for itself.

At that time, the Monroe administration was wrestling with another foreign-policy concern. Russia already claimed Alaska and was making aggressive moves on the Pacific coast. Reflecting the strong nationalism of the period, Monroe and Adams decided that the United States would act on its own, without consulting the British. In an address to Congress late in 1823, President Monroe set forth the policy that is now called the Monroe Doctrine. He declared that the Americas "are henceforth not to be considered as subjects for future colonization by any European powers" and that "we should consider any attempt on their part to extend their system to any portion of this hemisphere as dangerous to our peace and safety."

Throughout the 1800s, the European powers made few interventions in the Americas; however, it was the British navy, not the Monroe Doctrine, that made them back down. The significance of the Monroe Doctrine is in later events. Its bold warnings gained meaning only when the United States became a major sea power—a development that took nearly a century. Nor did the Monroe Doctrine restrict the nationalism, expansion, and intervention of the United States itself over the next 150 years.

Section 1 ★ Review

Checking for Understanding

1. **Identify** American System, John Marshall, *Marbury* v. *Madison*, Erie Canal, Rush-Bagot Agreement, Monroe Doctrine.

2. **Define** nationalism, internal improvement, turnpike, toll, ultimatum.

3. **List** two ways in which the Republicans adopted a Federalist point of view of government after 1812.

4. **Describe** the chain of events that formed the background to the Monroe Doctrine.

Critical Thinking Activity

5. **Linking Past and Present** Roads, canals, and railroads were early transportation links between East and West. What major links tie different sections of the country together today?

ACTIVITY

6. Trace a route from Savannah, Georgia, to Indianapolis, Indiana, using the roads, canals, and waterways shown on the map on page 144. List the cities you will pass through on your journey.

Answers to SECTION 1 REVIEW

1. American System, 140; John Marshall, 141; *Marbury* v. *Madison*, 142; Erie Canal, 144; Rush-Bagot Agreement, 145; Monroe Doctrine, 146
2. All vocabulary words are defined in the Glossary.
3. saw need for national currency and hence national bank, saw need to protect industry and business

4. Many Latin American colonies revolted against Spain. Spain gave signs of trying to regain its colonial empire. The United States was sympathetic to Latin America's quest for independence.
5. Answers will vary but may include television, radio, printed materials, cars, computers, fax, telephones, and airlines.
6. Cities in journal entries will vary.

Growth of Sectionalism

Setting the Scene

Section Focus

While a spirit of nationalism spread throughout the United States, a strong sectional rivalry was also developing. Issues such as land policy, the tariff, internal improvements, and slavery were favored or opposed by different regions. At times sectional differences grew bitter enough to threaten national unity.

Objectives

After studying this section, you should be able to

★ discuss the impact of the Industrial Revolution on American life.

★ explain how industrialization contributed to wider acceptance of slavery in the South.

★ identify four areas of sectional conflict.

Key Terms

textile, closed shop, cotton gin, favorite son

◀ COTTON GIN

The late 1700s and early 1800s brought developments that would change life in all regions of the United States. With newly developed machines, goods could be produced more quickly and efficiently than ever before. The growth of industry—mainly in the North—brought new challenges that tested the resolve of the young nation.

■ The North

The Industrial Revolution spread from Great Britain to the United States during the late 1700s. In 1790, English-born businessman Samuel Slater opened America's first **textile,** or woven fabric, mill in Pawtucket, Rhode Island. More than 20 years later, the trade embargo against England in the War of 1812 gave a significant boost to the development of industry in northern areas of the United States.

Growth of Industry

New England became an early center of industry for a variety of reasons. The region boasted many swift-flowing streams, an abundant source of waterpower. New England's shippers were seeking additional opportunities in which to invest their profits. After the 1820s, European immigration to the region provided a large labor force. By 1840, 800 cotton mills and 500 woolen mills in New England employed nearly 50,000 workers. Shipping continued to thrive, and many small factories in the region were turning out such products as shoes, clocks, carriages, and paper.

Manufacturing also took hold in the Middle Atlantic states—Pennsylvania, New Jersey, and New York. Although textile mills thrived in this region, the area was better known for its coal and iron ore resources. Improved roads and the expansion of the

FOCUS
Bellringer

Before taking roll, project Section Focus Transparency 4-2 or hand out Section Focus Transparency Activity 4-2. Have students answer the questions.

Motivating Activity

Read to students these statements by a French observer of life in the United States in the early 1800s: "No people in the world has made such progress in trade and manufacturing...." "[The farmer] brings land into tillage in order to sell it again...." "...inhabitants of the North arrive... and settle in the parts where the cotton plant and the sugar cane grow." Ask students to which sections of the nation these statements apply. (*North, West, South*) Tell students that as they read Section 2 they will discover how accurate an observer Alexis de Tocqueville was. **L2**

Vocabulary Precheck

Ask students to define each of the "Key Terms." Have a volunteer consult the dictionary for any unfamiliar words. **L1, LEP**

Use the Vocabulary PuzzleMaker for Chapter 4 to create a crossword puzzle. **L1**

Assign Vocabulary Activity 4.

Classroom Resources for SECTION 2

Blackline Masters:
- Reproducible Lesson Plan 4-2
- Vocabulary Activity 4
- Geography in History Activity 4
- Guided Reading Activity 4-2
- Critical Thinking Skills Activity 4
- Reteaching Activity 4-2
- Section Quiz 4-2

Transparencies:
- Section Focus Transparency 4-2

Multimedia:
- Testmaker
- American Music: Cultural Traditions
- Vocabulary PuzzleMaker

TEACH
Guided Practice

CURRICULUM CONNECTION

Geography Introduce the term *fall line* and locate the line on a U.S. map. Explain that this imaginary line marks the boundary between the coastal lowlands and the Piedmont at a higher elevation. Eastward-flowing rivers fall over the edge of the Piedmont onto the coastal plains at the fall line. Many of the first factories in the North were located along this line.

📁 For additional practice, assign Geography in History Activity 4.

Visualizing History Point out that many New England towns sprang up around factories such as this one. **Answer to Caption:** cotton textiles, shoes, clocks, carriages, paper

▲ RISE OF AMERICAN FACTORIES As the Industrial Revolution spread, factories sprang up in many cities and towns in New England. *What types of products did these new factories produce?*

nation's railway systems opened markets in other regions, and increased the demand for machinery.

Social Changes

In the early 1800s, the North was still a region where families lived and worked together at farming, crafts, and home-based businesses. The Industrial Revolution, however, was gradually transforming the region to one in which people lived mostly in cities and earned their livings by working in factories. Industrialization created two new classes of people—the industrial capitalists who built and owned the factories and the industrial laborers who worked in them.

The Labor Movement

As machines replaced hand tools, jobs for skilled craftsworkers became scarcer, and many such workers were reduced to performing unskilled labor. In an effort to improve working conditions, workers organized into labor unions. In the United States, the first labor unions were formed by skilled craftspeople, such as carpenters, shoemakers, and printers. These unions, found in all major Northeastern cities, demanded higher wages, shorter hours, and the **closed shop**—a place of employment open only to union members.

Unskilled factory workers were less successful in forming unions. Strikes could be easily broken by employers who simply hired recent European immigrants to fill vacant factory positions. Incentive to organize was low, too, among textile workers, many of whom were young women from poor farms. By the early 1820s, however, some women had organized unions and were carrying out strikes to protest working conditions.

During the 1830s, an economic depression and widespread unemployment caused the collapse of many unions. In spite of setbacks, organized labor did secure some permanent gains during this period.

Special Needs Activity

Reading Disability Students with poor reading skills often learn best by having new procedures modeled for them several times. Many reading comprehension strategies require students to restate what they have read. Explain to students that you are going to model a restating strategy for a sentence. Have students turn to the heading "The Labor Movement" and read the first sentence in the third paragraph. Demonstrate restating: "Many unions broke apart during the 1830s because the economy was poor and many people were unemployed." **L1, LEP**

For example, several states limited the workday to 10 hours and placed restrictions on child labor.

■ The South

As textile mills produced cheaper goods for a worldwide market, the demand increased for raw cotton from the Southern states. To produce more cotton, Southern planters turned to the cotton gin, an invention developed in 1793 by a Northerner named Eli Whitney. The **cotton gin,** a machine that efficiently and cheaply cleaned the seeds from cotton fibers, made cotton increasingly profitable throughout the South.

Plantation Slavery

The invention of the cotton gin also strengthened the hold of slavery on the region. The planting, hoeing, picking, and ginning of cotton all required manual labor, and enslaved persons provided a fairly cheap source. Because the growing and harvesting of cotton continued throughout much of the year in the Deep South, there were no long periods of idleness. Thus, slave labor suddenly became profitable for cotton growers.

Cotton Is King

"Cotton is king" was a common Southern phrase that accurately reflected the importance of cotton to the South's economy. Because the South had few factories, cotton continued to be sent out of the region for manufacture. As the demand for raw cotton increased, and as constant replanting depleted soil fertility, the "cotton kingdom" moved westward into fertile areas of Mississippi, Alabama, and Arkansas.

Mathematics Write the following information on the chalkboard: Before the invention of the cotton gin, an enslaved person spent one full day cleaning one pound of cotton. With a small gin a worker could clean ten pounds of cotton in a day. A large gin, tended by several workers and turned by a horse, could clean 50 pounds a day and a water-powered gin, 1,000 pounds. In 1790 cotton sold for 40 cents a pound. Have students calculate the increase in a day's profits from using each type of gin rather than hand-picking. *(by hand: 40-cents, small gin: $4, horse-drawn $20; water powered $400; gin could boost profits as much as 1000 percent.)* **L1**

▲ Eli whitney

Visualizing History

▲ THE PLANTATION SYSTEM The invention of the cotton gin by Eli Whitney helped make cotton the most important Southern agricultural product. Bountiful cotton harvests, particularly in the newer growing regions of Alabama and Mississippi, were the basis of the South's increasing prosperity. The cultivation of cotton, however, required intensive hand labor. *What tasks in cotton production did enslaved people perform?*

Visualizing History Eli Whitney never made much money from his cotton gin. It was so easy to build that few planters bothered to buy one.
Answer to Caption: planted, hoed, picked cotton in the fields, operated cotton gin

---

Cultural Perspectives

Music of the Times One of the most popular composers of the times was Stephen Foster, famous for his songs idealizing the South. Foster used African American melodies to create lively songs. He wrote mostly for the popular minstrel shows, which incorporated the songs, dances, and instruments of African Americans. In the cities, opera was beginning to be popular. European musicians, mostly German immigrants, delighted audiences with band concerts. Other European performers, such as the singer Jenny Lind, the "Swedish Nightingale," toured the country and drew huge crowds.

Class Structure

The profound influence of cotton on the South was reflected in the class structure of Southern society. At the top were a few wealthy planters, who enslaved 50 to 200 or more people and cultivated the best land. Below these rich owners was a larger class of less wealthy planters who owned medium-sized farms and usually had fewer than 20 enslaved persons. Then there were the owners of small farms, who made up a large majority of Southern farmers and owned either a few enslaved persons or none at all. Near the bottom of the social scale was a class of impoverished white people, who were usually illiterate and obtained food by hunting or farming the exhausted soils for which cotton planters had no use. Seen as lowest on this cotton-created scale were the African Americans. All but a few were enslaved, and nearly all performed heavy labor or menial tasks.

■ The West

Hostilities between settlers and Native Americans had limited settlement of the West until the end of the War of 1812. That war resulted in the breakup of Tecumseh's league and put an end to British support of the northern nations. Following the defeat of the Sauk (SAWK) leader, Chief Black Hawk, in 1832, the Native Americans were driven west of the Mississippi.

Perhaps the greatest lure of the Northwest was vast, fertile, and inexpensive land. Farmers poured in from northern and southern parts of the United States and from Europe. To meet farmers' needs for markets, merchandise, and transportation, merchants, storekeepers, and other suppliers gathered in towns, such as Cincinnati and Louisville, where cargo was transferred.

■ Sectional Rivalry

Because the regions were so different in geography, it is not surprising that Americans in these regions had different concerns and reacted differently to important issues.

Public Lands

One of the issues tackled by the country was public land policy. Western frontier farmers favored cheap land, rapid settlement, and the right of people to settle on whatever unoccupied acres they could find.

▶ IRON LADLES

Visualizing History ▲ THE TARIFF QUESTION Generally, Northeastern manufacturers and laborers favored protective tariffs while Southerners did not. **Why did the people of the Northwest support tariffs?**

Critical Thinking Activity

Interpreting Ideas Review with the class the concepts of specialization and interdependence. Then write this statement on the chalkboard:

"By the Jacksonian era economic specialization made the regions at once more different and more dependent on one another."

Have students identify the seeming contradiction in this statement (*sections more different and more dependent*) and write a paragraph explaining it, noting sectional economic differences and how they contributed to interdependence. (*growth of northern textile mills provided market for Southern cotton*) **L3**

📂 For additional practice in critical thinking, assign Critical Thinking Skill Activity 4.

Eastern manufacturers, on the other hand, opposed such policies for fear the West would draw off their labor supply. Eastern farmers believed that cheap Western lands would result in unfair competition.

Southerners were divided on this issue. Plantation owners wanted public lands opened for sale, but opposed people taking whatever unoccupied land they could find because these people might claim the best lands.

Protective Tariffs

Another controversial issue was protective tariffs. Northeastern manufacturers and laborers wanted protective tariffs to ensure that their factories could compete successfully with foreign manufacturers. Southerners, whose economy rested mainly on agriculture, opposed high tariffs because they would have to pay more for imported manufactured goods. Surprisingly, the Northwest, a farming region, was the section most completely in favor of protection. This was because many Northwesterners thought that high tariffs would provide revenue for new roads and canals and would increase urban markets for farm products.

Slavery

Among all the issues, the spread of slavery into Western territories raised feverish emotion. Because cotton production demanded the movement of plantations onto new lands and the plantation system depended on slave labor, Southerners insisted that they be allowed to take their enslaved workers with them anywhere except the free states. In the North and West, which were not economically dependent on slave labor, there was an increasing conviction that slavery was morally wrong. While allowing Southern states to maintain slavery where it already existed, Northerners did not want it extended to the territories. To Southerners, this meant that no new slave states could be formed, and the political power of the South would decrease.

■ The Missouri Compromise

The question of slavery's expansion became politically controversial in 1819 when Missouri applied for admission to the Union as a slave state. As soon as the bill reached the floor of Congress, Representative James Tallmadge of New York presented an amendment that stated, in part:

> 66 . . . That the further introduction of slavery or involuntary servitude be prohibited . . . and that all children of slaves, born within [Missouri] shall be free. . . . 99

The Tallmadge Amendment would gradually end slavery in an area where it already existed. A new twist to the debate was introduced when Maine petitioned to be separated from Massachusetts and admitted to the Union as a free state. At this time slave and nonslave states were evenly represented in the Senate, although the North's population gave it a majority in the House.

The Missouri Compromise, 1820

Missouri Compromise Line (36°30′N) — MISSOURI

Free states
Free territories
Slave states
Slave territories
Non-United States territory

0 200 400 miles
0 200 400 kilometers

Map Study The Missouri Compromise was an attempt to resolve the question of slavery in the Western territories. **How many slave states are shown?**

CURRICULUM CONNECTION

Language Arts Tell students that Thomas Jefferson, in 1820, wrote to a friend that the issue of Missouri's joining the Union "like a firebell in the night, awakened and filled me with terror. I consider it at once as the knell of the Union." Note that the statement contains a *simile*—a direct comparison between two objects or ideas that uses the word *like* or *as*. Ask students what objects or ideas are compared. *(issue of Missouri and firebell)* How is the issue like a firebell? *(warns or frightens the listener)* **L2**

Map Study *Using Maps*

Answer: 12

Map Skills Practice
How does the map help explain why the Missouri Compromise is seen as a postponement of the slavery issue? *(A vast region south of the parallel had potential for American expansion and settlement. Its future would test the compromise.)*

Sidelight: History and Politics

For his part in helping John Quincy Adams win the 1824 election, Clay earned the nickname "President Maker." His support for the Missouri Compromise of 1820 led to his nickname "The Great Pacificator," and his efforts to avert civil war in 1850 gave him his most famous title, the "Great Compromiser." Clay's name is famous for another reason as well. The first nationally newsworthy message sent by telegraph concerned Henry Clay. In May 1844, the wires tapped out the message that Clay had won the nomination for President.

ASSESS

Check Understanding

Assign Section 2 Review as homework or an in-class activity.

Evaluate

Assign Section Quiz 4-2 or use the Testmaker to create a customized quiz.

Reteach

Have students complete Reteaching Activity 4-2.

Enrich

Have students write a brief paragraph on how industrialism encouraged sectionalism and how it also promoted nationalism.

CLOSE

Ask students to give examples of how sectional conflicts were "products of the country's growth."

152

To maintain this balance of slave and non-slave states, a compromise was reached: Missouri and Maine would be admitted together. In the unsettled parts of the Louisiana Purchase, however, slavery would be forbidden north of the parallel 36°30′, a line running west from the southern boundary of Missouri. The South agreed to this arrangement because of a widely held belief that the region west of the Mississippi was unfit for human settlement. When Southerners realized that this region was not "a great American desert," they began to demand changes in the Missouri Compromise.

■ Election of 1824

The election of 1824 reflected the growing sectionalism in American politics. In that election four Democratic-Republican candidates—John Quincy Adams, Henry Clay, William H. Crawford, and Andrew Jackson—ran for President. Each candidate was also a **favorite son**—a candidate supported by the political leaders from their own state and region. Each of the candidates was identified with regional interests; Jackson was the only one who showed strength ouside his own region, carrying Pennsylvania and New Jersey as well as most of the South and West. Although Jackson won a plurality (the largest number but less than half) of the popular vote, he failed to receive a majority of the electoral votes. Therefore, the House of Representatives had to choose

▲ JOHN QUINCY ADAMS By the time of his election in 1824, John Quincy Adams was already an established figure in American political life. **Why was Adams's presidency not a successful one?**

the President from among the top three vote-getters. Clay was eliminated because he had placed fourth. He then threw his support to Adams, who was elected in February 1825.

When Adams named Clay secretary of state, Jackson's powerful supporters in Congress charged that the two men had made a "corrupt bargain." The denials of Adams and Clay, however, failed to remove suspicion. Jackson's supporters were determined that Adams's presidency should not succeed, and the President's ambitious federal programs received little support in Congress. The stage was set for Adams's defeat in the presidential election of 1828.

Section 2 ★ Review

Checking for Understanding

1. **Identify** Samuel Slater, Eli Whitney, John Quincy Adams.

2. **Define** textile, closed shop, cotton gin, favorite son.

3. **Explain** the importance of cotton to the South and its effect on the region's way of life.

4. **Describe** the effects of the Industrial Revolution on the economy and lifestyles of the North.

Critical Thinking Activity

5. **Recognizing Relationships** What geographic features favored industrial growth in the Northeast over the other regions?

ACTIVITY

6. Imagine you are a settler who is traveling to the Western frontier in the 1820s. List the 10 most essential items you would take with you.

Answers to SECTION 2 REVIEW

1. Samuel Slater, 147; Eli Whitney, 149; John Quincy Adams, 152
2. All vocabulary words are defined in the Glossary.
3. Cotton became the section's most important crop and export, entrenching the plantation system and the resulting class structure.
4. Economic—rapid growth to textile and iron industries, increased manufacturing, and improved transportation. Lifestyles—Many moved to the city to labor in factories, where they worked long hours.
5. Many swift-flowing streams provided an abundant source of waterpower, abundance of coal and iron resources.
6. Lists should be based on rational choices.

▲ *Cotton pickers* by Ethel Magafan

Songs of Slavery

Enslaved African Americans used music to help endure long, tedious hours of forced labor and to relax when they were released from chores. Although slaveholders forbade enslaved Africans from playing horns or drums, for fear that these could be used to send messages about planned rebellions, they were permitted to sing.

One kind of African American music that developed in the early 1800s was the spiritual. Sung in a lively style with strong rhythms and rich harmonies, the spirituals usually express themes of redemption from sin and from slavery and of a better life waiting in the future. Well-known spirituals include "Jacob's Ladder" and "Many a Thousand Gone."

The repertoire of songs African Americans sang was much more extensive than the slaveholders knew. It was not uncommon for African Americans to slip out of their quarters at night for secret meetings. In these secret gatherings, they poked fun at the slaveholders by telling folktales and singing songs such as "They Give Us the Husk."

They Give Us the Husk
We raise the wheat,
They give us the corn;
We bake the bread,
They give us the crust;
We sift the meal,
They give us the husk;
We peel the meat,
They give us the skin;
And that's the way
They take us in.

Making the Art Connection

1. Identify the "we" and "they" in this song.

2. What response might enslaved persons make to the idea that the slaveholders cared for them? Why do you think this is the case?

ACTIVITY

3. Do people still write and sing songs to give one another courage and hope in desperate situations? Name one such song, and tell its message in your own words.

153

Answers to Making the Connection

1. we: enslaved Africans; they: slaveholders
2. Answers will vary. Students might note that enslaved people would disagree. They get the leftovers slaveholders do not want.
3. Songs will vary but students should describe the message.

TEACH

One of the few ways African Americans who were enslaved could express their creativity and feelings was through music. Their songs were also a form of protest.

Food of the Times

What today we call "soul food" comes from the kinds of food that African Americans created from the meager rations they received or could grow on plantations.

Did You Know?

African Americans also passed on folktales that reminded them of their homeland. Many tales described their ancestors or enslaved people who had outwitted their owners. Tales about animals often featured weaker creatures who got the best of stronger animals. One such series of tales is that of the clever Brer Rabbit who always outsmarted the fox.

History and the Humanities

American Music: Cultural Traditions: African Music "Yarum Praise Songs" by the Fra-Fra Tribesmen (2:56); Slave Shout "Kneebone Bend" by the McIntosh County Shouters (2:38)

FOCUS

Bellringer

 Before taking roll, project Section Focus Transparency 4-3 or hand out Section Focus Transparency Activity 4-3. Have students answer the questions.

Motivating Activity

Write the following on the chalkboard:

You are cordially invited to President Jackson's Inauguration at the Capitol Steps on March 4, 1828. White House Reception to follow. Attire: Informal. No RSVP needed.

Tell students that on the day of Jackson's inauguration, thousands of his supporters overran the White House as though they had received just such an invitation. **L1**

Vocabulary Precheck

Ask students to define each of the "Key Terms." Have a volunteer consult the dictionary for any unfamiliar words. **L1, LEP**

 VIDEODISC

Powers of the President

Side One, Chapter 11
Title: *The Election Campaign*
Subject: The traditions of American presidential campaigns

Age of Jackson

Setting the Scene

Section Focus

Andrew Jackson's victory in the election of 1828 symbolized the growth of popular democracy. Although a Westerner, Jackson fought sectionalism by insisting on the supremacy of federal laws over the states. He also fought economic injustice and social inequality. Jackson's political movement resulted in the formation of the Democratic party.

Objectives

After studying this section, you should be able to

★ summarize the political career of Andrew Jackson.

★ list three democratic changes that developed during this period.

Key Terms

spoils system, pocket veto

◀ ANDREW JACKSON'S DUELING PISTOLS

*D*uring Adams's administration, the differences among the Jeffersonian Republicans had led to a split in party ranks. The group supporting Adams, known as National Republicans, wanted a strong role for the federal government in funding national projects. In opposition were the Jacksonians, soon to call themselves Democratic Republicans, or Democrats, who favored a less powerful federal government and stressed their ties to the common people.

■ Jacksonian Democracy

The party split made the presidential campaign of 1828 one of the bitterest in American history. In the end, Andrew Jackson won a sweeping victory—178 electoral votes to 83 for Adams. Jackson won every Southern and Western state and carried Pennsylvania and New York. For the first time, a candidate from the region west of the Appalachians was elected President. Jackson's victory was a major indication of the growing political power of the West.

The election of 1828 was also significant in that a large number of new voters participated. This turnout was partly because many states had lowered or eliminated property ownership as a voting qualification. Jackson appealed to many of the new voters, who believed that he defended the interests of the "common man." Although he was a dignified country gentleman, Jackson was born in a log cabin on the North Carolina frontier. His lowly beginnings made him a symbol of the growing power of democracy.

Classroom Resources for SECTION 3

Blackline Masters:
- Reproducible Lesson Plan 4-3
- Guided Reading Activity 4-3
- Workbook Activity 4-3
- Reteaching Activity 4-3
- Section Quiz 4-3

Transparencies:
- Section Focus Transparency 4-3

Multimedia:
- Testmaker
- GTV: The American People: Fabric of a Nation
- Powers of the President
- Focus on Government
- The American Indian

The People's Government

During Jackson's presidency, new voters made increasing demands on the government and learned the power of political organization. National issues became as much topics of conversation as local issues had always been. As national parties built stronger state and local ties, they began to rely upon a growing number of professional or career politicians. These changes helped to extend the **spoils system,** the practice of appointing people to government positions on the basis of party loyalty and party service.

Jackson actively influenced the rise of the new political system. He became the first President to oust large numbers of government employees in order to appoint his followers to office. Jackson often sought advice from several sources. As President, he had a group of personal friends, called by his enemies the "Kitchen Cabinet." This group advised him on all major decisions. He also increased presidential power by using the veto more than all previous Presidents. He was also one of the first Presidents to use the **pocket veto,** killing a bill by taking no action on it and waiting for Congress to adjourn.

Democracy made many advances under Jackson's presidency, but not all Americans shared in its benefits. In many states, women won the right to control property, but they did not yet have the right to vote. Native Americans and African Americans also did not achieve equal rights or freedom.

The "Trail of Tears"

In 1830, Jackson's supporters in Congress passed an act that called for moving the Native Americans in the East to lands west of the Mississippi River. One of the most

▲ *Stump Speaking* by George Caleb Bingham, 1854–1855 Bingham's series of election paintings expresses faith in the democratic process. For nearly five years, the artist devoted his talent to illustrating the human aspect of the political process. ***What was significant about voter turnout in the election of 1828?***

Cultural Perspectives

Jackson and Minorities Jacksonian democracy did not benefit all Americans. Even when the courts sided with Native Americans, President Andrew Jackson refused to enforce the rulings. African Americans also lost ground. Southern states severely limited their mobility, rights, and opportunities. Free African Americans in the South could not vote, bear arms, buy liquor, speak in public, form organizations, or testify against whites in court. African Americans in the North were only marginally better off.

CHAPTER 4
SECTION 3

TEACH
Guided Practice
Analyzing Viewpoints

Discuss with students Jackson's policy towards Native Americans, specifically the Cherokee. Have students write a dialogue between a Jackson supporter and a Cherokee leader in which each gives his or her view of Jackson and Jacksonian democracy. **L3**

History AND ART

Point out that George Caleb Bingham drew most of his subjects from everyday life. Discuss how this painting reflects the spirit of the times as Americans entered the Age of Jackson.
Answer to Caption: A large number of new voters participated.

FACT or FICTION?

Andrew Jackson was the first man of ordinary means to become President.

FICTION: By the 1820s Jackson was a wealthy planter who held many enslaved persons.

Facts on File

 CD-ROM

The American Indian

Students can learn more about the Trail of Tears by selecting the categories HISTORY and TRIBES from the main menu.

Map Study — Using Maps

Answers: Cherokee, Creek, Chickasaw, Choctaw

Map Skills Practice
Have students locate and identify on the map the area to which Native Americans were forced to move.

Linking Across TIME

The state of Oklahoma entered the Union in 1907. It was created from the Indian and Oklahoma territories. The state seal displays a large circle in whose center is a five-pointed star. Within the points of the star are five symbols, one for each seal of the "Five Civilized Tribes."

NATIONAL GEOGRAPHIC SOCIETY

 VIDEODISC

GTV: The American People: Fabric of a Nation

Side 2, Chapter 2
Frames 6248-14277
Title: *Between Worlds*
Subject: For Native Americans, a shrinking realm

---

powerful groups—the Cherokee—resisted this policy, and Jackson sent in the army. Forced to move from their homes to what is now Arkansas and Oklahoma, an estimated 4,000 Cherokee died of starvation, disease, or exposure on the march that became known as the "Trail of Tears."

By 1840, the United States government had moved all eastern Native Americans to western lands. The only exception was the Seminoles of Florida, some of whom settled deep in the Everglades after years of fighting American forces. Most citizens supported the harsh removal policy; only a few political and religious leaders raised their voices in protest.

"The Great Silence"

In the 1830s the cotton culture in the South had firmly established the institution of slavery, and criticism of the system became increasingly unacceptable to many people. In the South, those who spoke out against slavery risked physical harm. In the North, African Americans were free, but they were generally second-class citizens.

The debates of the 1820s leading to the Missouri Compromise had shown the slavery issue to be so explosive that a policy called "the great silence" began, and discussion of slavery as a national issue temporarily faded.

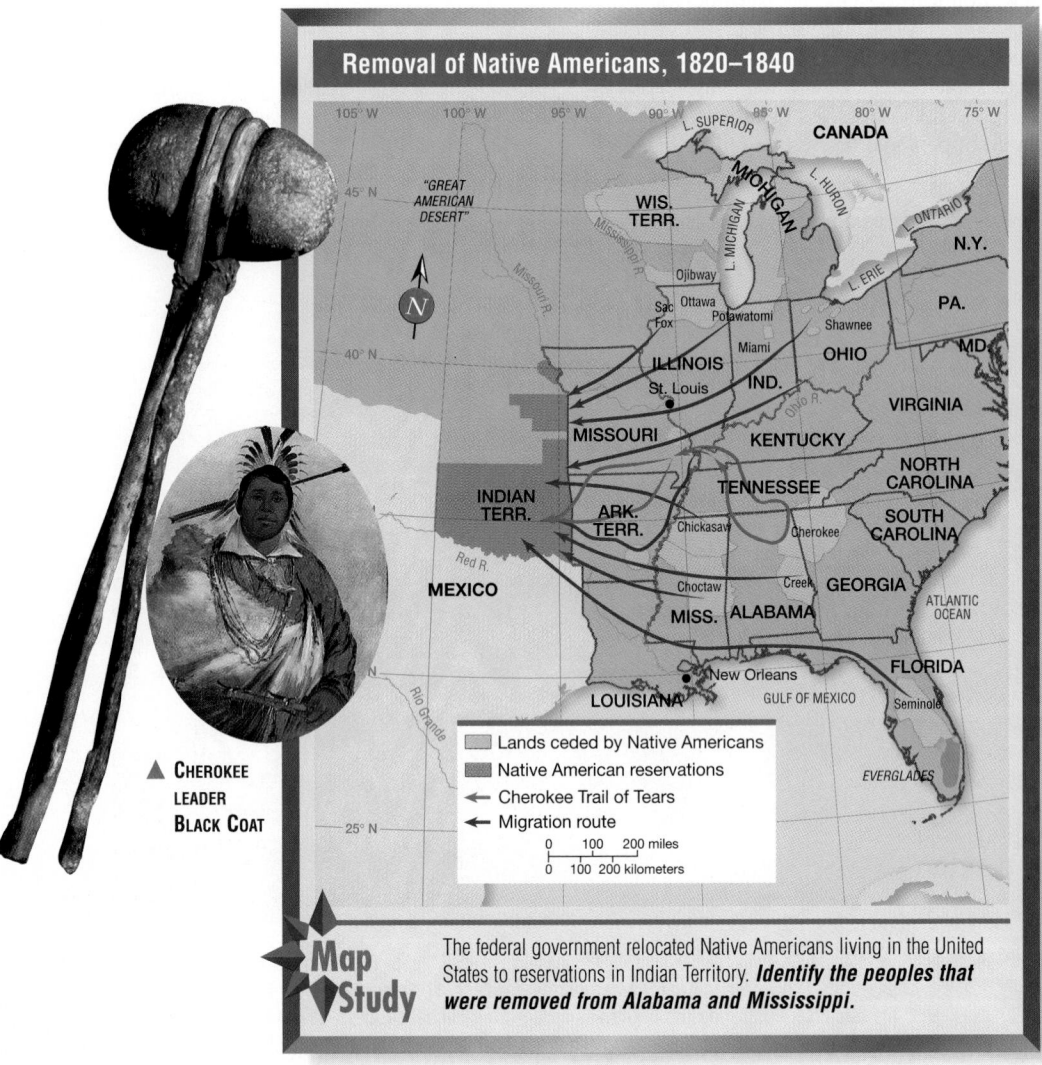

Removal of Native Americans, 1820–1840

▲ CHEROKEE LEADER BLACK COAT

Lands ceded by Native Americans
Native American reservations
← Cherokee Trail of Tears
← Migration route
0   100   200 miles
0 100 200 kilometers

Map Study
The federal government relocated Native Americans living in the United States to reservations in Indian Territory. *Identify the peoples that were removed from Alabama and Mississippi.*

Cooperative Learning Activity

Jacksonian Policies Organize the class into groups of four or five. Tell students they will be called on to make reaction statements. Have each group appoint a recorder to write these phrases on separate sheets of paper: spoils system, Jackson Native American removal policy, and Jacksonian democracy. Each person in a group takes a turn writing a phrase or sentence expressing his or her reaction to each term. Then ask each group to choose a writer/editor. This person's job is to use the written reactions to create three one-paragraph reaction statements that reflect his or her group's reactions to these phrases. **L2**

History AND ART

▲ *TRAIL OF TEARS* by Robert Lindneux Native Americans who were forced from their land traveled west in the 1830s. **Why did the Cherokee call the forced march from their land the "Trail of Tears"?**

■ Political Controversies

During his term of office, Jackson made bold decisions on such issues as internal improvements, tariffs, and banking. Although a strong nationalist, Jackson opposed federal aid for roads. His stand, which dismayed Westerners and pleased Southerners, demonstrated his belief in a strict interpretation of the Constitution.

Tariff of 1828

Tariffs became a major issue during Jackson's presidency. Early in 1828, Congress had passed a law that increased tariff rates on foreign manufactured goods. This tariff aroused deep resentment in the South, especially in South Carolina where the cotton economy was depressed. South Carolina, however, held back from acting against the tariff because John C. Calhoun, the state's leading politician, was Andrew Jackson's running mate.

Calhoun anonymously wrote *The South Carolina Exposition*, in which he claimed that the Tariff of 1828 made the South a servant of Northern industrialists. He declared that a state could nullify, or reject, any law passed by Congress which the state believed had violated the Constitution.

Some supporters of nullification hoped to get Jackson on their side. They invited him to a dinner celebrating Jefferson's birthday on April 13, 1830. Jackson stood up to make a toast, raised his glass, looked at Calhoun, and solemnly said: "Our Federal Union: it must be preserved." Jackson's statement left no doubt that he would oppose nullification. Calhoun, pale and trembling, responded, "Our Union, next to liberty, the most dear."

The Nullification Crisis

In 1832, Congress passed another high-tariff act. South Carolina declared the tariff law "null, void, and no law." It threatened to secede, or leave the Union, if the government tried to collect duties in the state. In response, Jackson issued a proclamation in which he pointed out that nullification meant disunion and disunion meant treason. South Carolina's Senator Robert Y. Hayne resigned from the Senate to become governor of South Carolina, and Calhoun resigned the vice presidency to lead the fight in the Senate.

Upon Jackson's demand, Congress passed a force bill allowing him to use the armed forces to collect tariffs. At the same time, Senator Henry Clay of Kentucky pushed through a compromise tariff bill that provided for a gradual scaling down of

---

CHAPTER 4
SECTION 3

Independent Practice
Making Comparisons
Have students research recent government policies toward Native Americans. Ask students to write two or three paragraphs comparing these policies with those of the Jacksonian period. How do they differ? Are there any similarities? L2

📁 Assign Guided Reading Activity 4-3.

📁 Assign Workbook Activity 4-3.

History AND ART

Although created a century after the event, John Lindneaux's painting captures the defeat and sadness of the Cherokee people. **Answer to Caption:** Thousands died on the march from hunger, disease, and exposure.

GLENCOE
TECHNOLOGY

VIDEODISC

Focus on Government

Side 1, Chapter 5
Title: *Lecture Launcher, The Federal System*
Subject: Relationship among Federal, state, and local governments

---

Critical Thinking Activity

Evaluating Evidence To find out how popular or unpopular Andrew Jackson was, suggest that students research the public opinion of the time. They will find evidence in contemporary political cartoons, voting records, newspaper articles, journal or diary entries, letters, and so on. When students have completed their research, have them present their findings to the class and draw conclusions about Jackson's popularity from the evidence. **L3**

Food of the Times

In criticizing the elegant dinner parties given by President Van Buren, one Whig implied that they were un-American, saying that Whigs were contented with "hog and hominy." Hominy was a mainstay of the diet of ordinary people, especially in the South and West. It is made from corn and could be baked, fried, or boiled.

tariffs. Thus Congress removed South Carolina's grievance about the tariff while denying its right to nullify a federal law. Jackson agreed to the compromise, but recognized that the issue of nullification had not been settled once and for all.

■ Jackson and the Bank

While the question of nullification was dividing the nation, Jackson was engaged in a dramatic struggle with the second Bank of the United States. Jackson believed that the Bank's vast powers threatened democratic government and distrusted its links with his political opponents.

A Campaign Issue

Jackson's opponents tried to make the Bank an issue in the election campaign of 1832. Henry Clay, Jackson's likely challenger for the presidency, introduced a bill to give the Bank a new charter even though the old one would not run out until 1836. Clay hoped to embarrass Jackson by forcing him either to sign a bill he disliked or to veto it. He did not believe that Jackson could defend a veto in the presidential campaign.

Disregarding controversy, Jackson proceeded to veto the bill after its passage by Congress. His veto message to Congress showed little knowledge of banking but great understanding of why many people disliked the Bank of the United States. Jackson wrote that the Bank favored the rich against the common people and that it was an overextension of federal power. The Constitution, he stated, nowhere explicitly granted the federal government the right to establish a central bank.

Destruction of the Bank

Winning an overwhelming victory in the 1832 election, Jackson took his triumph as a directive from the people to destroy the power of the Bank at once. In spite of initial opposition in his cabinet, Jackson had the government's deposits removed from the Bank and placed in strong state banks. In response, the Bank's president, Nicholas Biddle, called in loans and stopped lending. Biddle's move created such a scarcity of credit that hundreds of businesspeople were driven into bankruptcy and scores of banks failed. Factories closed down and workers were laid off.

After much public pressure, Biddle finally started extending easy credit to state banks. With money once again plentiful, the administration and Congress stimulated an economic boom by selling millions of acres of public lands and issuing surplus funds to the states for internal improvement projects. Worried by the free spending, reckless investments, and resulting inflation, Jackson then ordered that all payments for public lands be made in silver or gold. This drastic reversal of policy virtually stopped land sales, eliminated easy credit, and set the stage for a severe panic and depression in 1837.

Visualizing **H**istory ▲ MARTIN VAN BUREN Jackson used his influence to have Vice President Martin Van Buren nominated for President in 1836. *What economic woes struck the nation soon after Van Buren took office?*

Sidelight: Van Buren's Nicknames

Martin Van Buren had several nicknames, one of which was "Little Van," because he was 5 feet, 6 inches tall. Other nicknames were based on his character and personality. Because he was a master at political wheeling and dealing, he earned the titles "Red Fox" and "Little Magician." One of his magician's tricks was to outmaneuver John C. Calhoun for the vice presidency, thus leaving himself in line as Jackson's successor.

Rise and Fall of the Whigs

The fight over the second Bank of the United States divided the nation. National Republicans and others opposed to Jackson's policies formed the Whig party. The Whigs, however, were so divided that they could not agree on a single candidate for President in 1836. They ended up nominating three candidates, hoping to divide the electoral college vote and throw the election into the Whig-controlled House of Representatives. Jackson's continuing popularity was enough to give the Democrats the election. Jackson's handpicked successor, Vice President Martin Van Buren, won 170 electoral votes against a combined total of 124 votes for all his Whig opponents.

Van Buren

Van Buren had hardly taken office when the country was hit by the Panic of 1837, one of the most severe depressions in history. Many people out of work turned to the government for help, but Van Buren refused all public aid. He believed in the laissez-faire idea that government should play the smallest possible role in American life. His only major legislative effort was to get the federal government entirely out of banking. Van Buren succeeded in having Congress approve an independent treasury system in which government funds in gold and silver would be stored in vaults throughout the country.

Harrison and Tyler

In 1840, the Democrats nominated Van Buren for reelection in spite of his unpopularity. The Whigs named the military hero of the Battle of Tippecanoe, General William Henry Harrison, for President, and chose former Senator John Tyler of Virginia as his running mate. Using the slogan, "Tippecanoe and Tyler too," Harrison stressed his colorful military career and portrayed himself as a simple frontiersman, although he had been born to wealth. Van Buren, on the other hand, was characterized as an aristocrat who had no concern for the people left without jobs by the depression. The result of the campaign was a decisive victory for Harrison—234 electoral votes to 60— although the popular vote was close.

▲ GENERAL WILLIAM HENRY HARRISON

After only a month in office, however, President Harrison died of pneumonia. John Tyler became the first Vice President to become President by the death of the incumbent. Having been placed on the Whig ticket simply to attract Southern support, Tyler favored states' rights and was opposed to most Whig programs that stressed a strong national government. As a result, he lost the support of leading Whigs, such as Henry Clay and Daniel Webster. Divided, without a program or leadership, the Whigs lost heavily in the congressional elections of 1842, and John Tyler became a President without a party.

Section 3 ★ Review

Checking for Understanding

1. **Identify** National Republicans, Democratic Republicans, "Trail of Tears," Whigs.

2. **Define** spoils system, pocket veto.

3. **Summarize** the political changes that took place in the United States during the Jacksonian period.

4. **Describe** the role the Bank of the United States played in the election of 1832.

Critical Thinking Activity

5. **Inferring Values** At a celebration, President Andrew Jackson and Vice President John Calhoun exchanged toasts to the Union. In your own words, restate their implied messages.

ACTIVITY

6. Create campaign slogans for the presidential election in 1840 for the Whig and the Democratic candidates.

ASSESS

Check Understanding
Assign Section 3 Review as homework or an in-class activity.

Evaluate
Assign Section Quiz 4-3 or use the Testmaker to create a customized quiz.

Reteach
Ask students to explain how the controversy over the Tariff of 1828 and the Bank of the United States contributed to sectional conflict during the 1830s.

Have students complete Reteaching Activity 4-3.

Enrich
Have students write brief biographical sketches of Chief Sequoyah of the Cherokee, Osceola of the Seminole, and Black Hawk of the Sac and Fox. Sketches might indicate how these leaders resisted Native American removal and what effect that resistance had.

CLOSE
Refer students to the section title "Age of Jackson." Have students write a paragraph describing the economic policies established by Jackson and the political issues he faced.

FOCUS

Bellringer

Before taking roll, project Section Focus Transparency 4-4 or hand out Section Focus Transparency Activity 4-4. Have students answer the questions.

Motivating Activity

Write on the chalkboard the following statement by New England philosopher Ralph Waldo Emerson: "What is man born for but to be a Reformer, a Re-maker of what man has made, a renouncer...."

Discuss the quotation, asking students to describe Emerson's idea of a reformer. How is it like their own views of a reformer? How does it differ? Tell students that in Section 4, they will learn how reformers attempted to remake American society politically and socially **L2**.

📁 Assign American Literary Heritage, pp. 16–17: *Self-Reliance*.

Vocabulary Precheck

Ask students to define each of the "Key Terms." Have a volunteer consult the dictionary for any unfamiliar words. **L1, LEP**

★★★★★★★★★★★★★★★★★★★★★★★★★★★★★★★★★★★★★★★

The Spirit of Reform

Setting the Scene

Section Focus

American reformers during the early 1800s worked selflessly to create a more perfect society. Many reformers were religiously motivated, while others traced their reform spirit to ideas in the Declaration of Independence. In either case, the noble goal of achieving a just American society would serve as a model for the rest of the world.

Objectives

After studying this section, you should be able to

★ identify social reform movements that were widespread during the early 1800s.

★ discuss the new values and beliefs that influenced educators, artists, and writers.

Key Terms

abolitionist, socialism

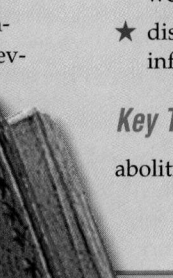

◄ MINIATURE BOOKS OF THE 1830s

---

*D*uring the early 1800s, many Americans began examining their society on the basis of ideas in the Declaration of Independence. In search of a better, more democratic world, they formed organizations to persuade others to their ways of thinking.

■ Advances in Education

In the 1820s and 1830s, as more Americans gained the right to vote, the need for free public education grew. In addition, it became necessary to educate the increasing number of immigrants who came to the United States in the mid-1800s. Democracy demanded an informed educated electorate, a goal not easy to achieve.

Free Public Education

In Massachusetts, the educator Horace Mann expanded public education in the late 1830s. As a result of Mann's efforts, Massachusetts quickly became the model for all other Northern states. By 1850, in spite of some initial resistance from taxpayers, most Northern states provided tuition-free elementary education.

Adult Education

While opportunities for formal higher education were limited for most people, there was a move toward adult education for the common person. Tax-supported libraries and privately supported learning societies began to take hold in many areas.

160   UNIT 2 Forging a Nation: 1815–1877

Classroom Resources for SECTION 4

Blackline Masters:
📁 Reproducible Lesson Plan 4-4
📁 American Literary Heritage, pp. 16-17
📁 Guided Reading Activity 4-4
📁 Linking Past and Present Activity 4

📁 Reteaching Activity 4-4
📁 Workbook Activity 4-4
📁 Enrichment Activity 4
📁 Chapter Skills Activity 4
📁 Section Quiz 4-4

Transparencies:
🗄 Section Focus Transparency 4-4
🗄 Skills Transparency 4

Multimedia:
💿 Testmaker
💿 Historic America Electronic Field Trips
💿 Focus on Government

Interest in training teachers helped the cause of education for women. Although many men feared that higher education for women would disrupt home life, feminist leaders, such as Emma Willard, Catharine Beecher, and Mary Lyon, argued that chemistry could be used in cooking and math in household finance. Oberlin College in Ohio, the first coeducational school, saw its first female students graduate in 1841.

Oberlin College and Bowdoin College in Maine were the first institutions to allow African Americans to attend as students. Because African American men and women were generally barred from educational opportunities, there were fewer than 15 African American college students in the United States before 1840.

■ Struggle for Rights

During the Jacksonian period, many reformers called for action on such issues as care for the mentally ill, women's rights, and abolition of slavery. Their persistent efforts eventually awakened the United States to many of the needs of more than one-half of the population.

Treating Mental Illness

In the early 1840s, the reformer Dorothea Dix began visiting prisons, where she found many mentally ill persons who were being treated as criminals. Dix's findings led Massachusetts to pass a law establishing asylums where mental illness could be treated as a disease rather than as a crime. Largely as a result of Dix's influence, 20 more states founded insane asylums.

Women's Rights

In the early 1800s, women were considered "second-class citizens" in many ways. They could not vote and had no legal right to manage the affairs of their own children. They received less pay for work than men did. Almost all institutions of higher learning and most professional careers were closed to women.

Frustrated by limits on their actions, female reformers began a campaign for women's rights. In 1848 Lucretia Mott and Elizabeth Cady Stanton organized the Seneca Falls Convention. This gathering of female reformers drew up a "Declaration of Sentiments and Resolutions" that echoed the words of the Declaration of Independence:

> **We hold these truths to be self-evident: that all men and women are created equal; that they are endowed by their Creator with certain inalienable rights; that among these are life, liberty, and the pursuit of happiness. . . .**

Most politicians were either indifferent or hostile to the issue of women's rights. Women did, however, gain relief from some of their worst legal handicaps. For example, many states passed laws permitting women to retain and manage their own property.

■ Antislavery Crusade

A glaring violation of democratic principles in the United States was African American slavery. It is not surprising, then, that the upsurge of democratic feeling in the Jacksonian period made the freeing of enslaved persons the dominant reform effort.

Abolitionists

Religious groups, such as the Quakers and the Baptists, had been the first to oppose slavery in the late 1700s. As slavery strengthened its hold over the South in the early 1800s, the voices of **abolitionists,** or those persons in favor of doing away with slavery, grew louder. Many abolitionists, such as the Massachusetts journalist William Lloyd Garrison, demanded immediate freedom for enslaved African Americans without compensation for slaveholders. They were willing to see the Union divided if necessary in order to rid the free states of the shame of being tied to the slave states.

TEACH
Guided Practice

Biography Ask students to choose the name in each pair below that best completes the sentence.
1. (**Dorothea Dix,** Horace Mann) worked for better treatment of the mentally ill.
2. The most famous African American abolitionist and publisher of *The North Star* was (William Lloyd Garrison, **Frederick Douglass**).
3. Along with Elizabeth Cady Stanton, (Emma Willard, **Lucretia Mott**) helped organize the Seneca Falls women's rights convention. **L1, LEP**

ABCNEWS
INTERACTIVE™

  VIDEODISC

Historic America Electronic Field Trips

Side Two, Chapter 6
Title: *Seneca Falls*
Subject: Commemoration of nation's first public political meeting dealing with women's rights
Ask: Who were the leaders of the Seneca Falls Convention? *(Elizabeth Cady Stanton and Lucretia Mott)*

Cooperative Learning Activity

Formulating Opinions Organize students into groups. Invite each group to write on a sheet of paper the following question raised by opponents of public schools: "Why should I be taxed to educate other people's children?" Ask each group to circulate the paper among the members, with each member providing a response to the question. Continue circulating the paper until all group members have given at least two responses. Then have each group select a writer/editor to summarize and compile the group's arguments into an opinion statement or a letter to the editor to be read aloud to the class. **L2**

Independent Practice

 Assign Guided Reading Activity 4-4.

CURRICULUM CONNECTION

Music Have students research the lyrics of the folk song "Follow the Drinking Gourd." This song, in which the drinking gourd represents the Big Dipper constellation, helped some enslaved people going north on the Underground Railroad remember their route. **L2**

Linking Past and Present

Point out to students that in the 1800s many people died from infection after surgical procedures because of the lack of sterile conditions. Discuss with students modern medical procedures that are available today.

 For additional practice, assign Linking Past and Present Activity 4.

Linking Past and Present

Surgical Tools

Early medicine depended a great deal on superstition and folklore. The doctors had only the most basic surgical tools.

Then_____

Basic Instruments

Early surgical instruments were simple. At best, a physician might carry in his saddlebag a set of amputating instruments, a trephine used to cut out sections of bone, and some crooked and straight needles. Some early physicians carried a scalpel or incision knife and a pair of forceps. Many physicians in the early 1800s had little training in surgical procedures.

Now_____

New Tools, New Methods

Modern technology has moved the practice of surgery forward. Clamps are used to close off blood vessels. Retractors hold back folds of skin. Lasers are used to make precise cuts in body tissues where using a scalpel would be impractical.

Infection during surgery was once a great danger. With the aseptic method of surgery, infection-causing germs are eliminated by cleaning and sterilizing all equipment used in the operating room.

▲ MODERN SURGICAL TOOLS

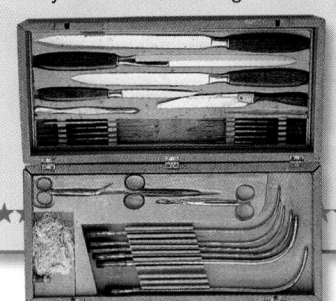

◄ MEDICAL SURGEON'S KIT, 1800S

The Underground Railroad

Another abolitionist leader who favored political action was Frederick Douglass. Self-educated and formerly enslaved, Douglass edited an abolitionist paper, *The North Star.* The title was meant to remind people of the Underground Railroad. This secret abolitionist organization, which had hiding places, or stations, throughout the Northern states and even into Canada, brought enslaved people out of the South. Moving at night, agents of the Underground Railroad, such as Harriet Tubman, had only Polaris, the fixed star in the northern skies, to guide them as they led enslaved people to freedom.

Southern Reactions

Southern slaveholders feared the influence of abolitionist ideas among enslaved African Americans. In 1831, Nat Turner, an African American preacher and enslaved person, led a rebellion in Virginia to free the slaves. Although unsuccessful, the revolt spread panic throughout the South, effectively ending the antislavery movement in the region.

As Southern hostility to abolition grew stronger, many Southerners demanded the suppression of abolitionist material as a condition for remaining in the Union. In 1836, under Southern pressure, the House of Representatives passed a "gag rule" providing that all abolitionist petitions should be shelved without debate. No prominent politician wanted to endanger the Union by attacking slavery where it was protected by law.

■ Arts and Sciences

During the 1830s and 1840s, many Americans wanted to prove that their culture was truly independent of Europe. This period saw many achievements by American writers, artists, and scientists.

American writers during the second quarter of the 1800s wanted Americans to feel proud of their country's heritage. James Fenimore Cooper's novels gloried in the drama of Native Americans and pioneers on the New York frontier. Nathaniel Hawthorne unfolded the Puritan history of New England in his

162 UNIT 2 Forging a Nation: 1815–1877

Sidelight: Slave Rebellion

At least three large-scale slave revolts took place in the period before the Civil War. In 1800 Gabriel Prosser organized a slave army and tried to take Richmond, Virginia. In 1822 Denmark Vesey attempted to seize Charleston, South Carolina. In 1831 Nat Turner led a rebellion that killed about 60 whites. Many small-scale uprisings and individual acts of resistance went unreported.

novels and short stories. In *Moby Dick,* Herman Melville used his experience as a sailor to write a fascinating account of whaling that symbolized the human struggle itself.

American poets, too, turned from European to American subjects. Henry Wadsworth Longfellow immortalized the Native American hero Hiawatha. John Greenleaf Whittier in "Snow-Bound" described winter on a New England farm. Edgar Allen Poe wrote of the terrors that lurk in the world of the imagination.

Many American writers took an active part in reform movements. Whittier and Longfel-

low joined the crusade against slavery, as did poet James Russell Lowell and poet and novelist Lydia Maria Child. Henry David Thoreau himself spent a night in jail rather than pay taxes to support the Mexican War.

American painters and sculptors used European styles to portray the American scene. A group of landscape painters in the East was known as the Hudson River School. Their romantic paintings of the Catskill Mountains and Hudson River became highly prized. In architecture, Americans favored the "Federalist" and "Greek Revival" styles modeled on the classical buildings of ancient Greece and Rome.

Men and women in the United States also won fame in the field of science. The astronomer Maria Mitchell discovered a new comet and several groups of distant stars.

Matthew Maury, a naval officer, developed the science of oceanography with his studies of the ocean bottom. Dr. Crawford

▶ **Frederick Douglass**

Visualizing
History

▲ **Moving Toward Freedom** Before the Civil War, thousands of enslaved people fled hundreds of miles and endangered their lives to reach the first station on the Underground Railroad. Frederick Douglass (inset) spoke on behalf of the emancipation of women as well as of enslaved people. **Why was Polaris important?**

Cultural Perspectives

Writers and Democracy The works of writers such as Cooper, Hawthorne, and Longfellow glorified the American past, idealizing the wilderness and the frontier. At the same time, the poet Walt Whitman captured the hopefulness and idealism of the early years of the nineteenth century. Sometimes called the "poet of democracy," Whitman passionately believed in democracy. His poetry expresses the virtues of ordinary people and everyday life. Whitman was also unique in that he wrote of the vitality of the nation's growing cities, largely ignored by his contemporaries.

Food of the Times

Sylvester Graham was an eighteenth-century vegetarian who traveled the country preaching dietary reform. Spurning meat, processed flour, and alcohol, Graham insisted that a healthy diet consisted of vegetables, fresh fruit, and whole wheat bread. (The graham cracker is named for him.)

Visualizing
History Tell students that a "station" such as this farm provided only a temporary refuge for escaped slaves. For most, the end of their journey was along the border between the United States and Canada. A great many escapees crossed the border into Canada, where they could not be retaken into slavery. **Answer to Caption:** The star helped to guide the people on their route.

GLENCOE
TECHNOLOGY

 Videodisc

Focus on Government

Side 3, Chapter 60
Title: *Speaking Out, Moving Toward Democracy*
Subject: Concept of and participation in a democracy

ASSESS
Check Understanding
Assign Section 4 Review as homework or an in-class activity.

Evaluate
Assign Section Quiz 4-4 or use the Testmaker to create a customized quiz.

Reteach
Have students complete Reteaching Activity 4-4.

Assign Workbook Activity 4-4.

Enrich
Use Enrichment Activity 4.

CLOSE
Henry David Thoreau once observed that some people do not keep in step with their companions because they "march to the beat of a different drummer." Have students note the "different drummers" in this section from those with more traditional ideas.

W. Long and Dr. W.T.G. Morton were the first physicians to use ether as an anesthetic during surgery.

■ Building a New World

During the early 1800s, new social, philosophical, and religious movements developed at this time that had a remarkable impact in transforming many areas of American society.

From Europe came a new idea—**socialism.** Socialists believed that business competition and individual ownership of property caused poverty and inequality. They proposed to substitute cooperation for competition and common ownership for individual ownership. Early followers of the idea started small, voluntary communities where their ideas could be put into practice. Among these communities were New Harmony, Indiana, and Brook Farm, Massachusetts.

A great ferment in American religious life occurred in the first half of the 1800s. New religious groups arose, including some that practiced community living. Among these were the Church of Jesus Christ of Latter-day Saints, or the Mormon Church, and the Shakers.

In New England, new religious movements took separate paths from the region's Puritan heritage. The Unitarians rejected the doctrine of the Trinity and stressed the oneness of God and the perfectibility of human nature. The Transcendentalists emphasized the relationship between human beings and nature as well as the importance of the human conscience. They attracted writers, such as Margaret Fuller, Ralph Waldo Emerson, and Henry David Thoreau.

Protestantism experienced a renewal, a "Second Great Awakening." Throughout the country, beginning in New England and spreading westward, the growth of Protestant denominations was marked by great revival meetings, the building of new churches, and the founding of colleges and universities.

In cities a similar stirring of religious activity arose in the Catholic churches. In Boston and New York, for example, the Roman Catholic Church provided not only places of worship for Catholic European immigrants, but also schools, orphanages, and charitable organizations.

Among many Protestant groups the temperance movement developed in an effort to ban the use of alcohol. Temperance leaders wanted to do away with social evils, poverty, and crime that were often brought on by heavy drinking. In addition to trying to persuade people not to drink, temperance societies demanded laws to put an end to the sale of liquor. In 1851, Maine passed the first state prohibition law, an example followed by about a dozen states.

Section 4 ★ Review

Checking for Understanding
1. **Identify** Horace Mann, Dorothea Dix, Seneca Falls Declaration, William Lloyd Garrison, Frederick Douglass, Harriet Tubman, Hudson River School, Transcendentalism, Second Great Awakening.
2. **Define** abolitionist, socialism.
3. **Describe** the contributions of three key individuals to the antislavery movement.
4. **List** four prominent American writers of the 1800s.

Critical Thinking Activity
5. **Analyzing Reform**   The reform movements of the 1800s were initiated to extend rights and freedom of choice. What movement was an exception? What laws exist today that have similar goals to those of this movement?

ACTIVITY
6. Select a community issue you might want to research, such as landfills or recycling. Visit your library and find at least three resources for your topic.

Answers to SECTION 4 REVIEW
1. Horace Mann, 160; Dorothea Dix, 161; Seneca Falls Declaration, 161; William Lloyd Garrison, 161; Frederick Douglass, 162; Harriet Tubman, 162; Hudson River School, 163; Transcendentalism, 164; Second Great Awakening, 164
2. All vocabulary words are defined in the Glossary.
3. Possible answers include: Garrison—abolitionist, journal-ist; Douglass—editor, antislavery newspaper; Tubman—liberated many enslaved people.
4. Responses include: Cooper, Hawthorne, Melville, Longfellow, Whittier, Poe, Lowell, Child, Thoreau.
5. temperance movement; laws controlling drug use and sale
6. Students should use appropriate resources for their topic.

BUILDING SKILLS
Critical Thinking Skills

Making Comparisons

Imagine that your young sister cannot decide between joining the debate team or playing basketball. She has limited free time, so she asks you to help her compare the two. You tell her that you cannot because that is "like comparing apples and oranges." Your friend hears this conversation and comes in to tell you that you can indeed compare the debate team to basketball.

▲ THE COUNTRY SCHOOL BY WINSLOW HOMER

Learning the Skill

To compare means to examine in order to identify similarities and differences. You can compare any two things. To be an accurate comparison, however, you must note at least one similarity and one difference.

In the example cited above, there are obvious differences between debating and basketball, yet there are at least two similarities. Both are group activities, and both are competitive in the nature in which points are scored. This means that a comparison is possible.

No matter what you are comparing, there are steps that can help in making effective comparisons. They are:

• examine the information and take notes
• classify the information
• identify similarities and differences
• draw conclusions based on the comparisons you made

Read the two passages on this page. Then answer the questions that follow.

Passage A

. . . *Give them a little spelling, a little ciphering* [mathematics], *and a little handwriting, with a liberal sprinkling of the rod, and they'll have more* than their fathers had before them. Did Tippecanoe Harrison graduate from a seminary? Did Old Hickory Jackson know any Latin or Greek?

Passage B

Free public education is the mechanism by which democracy can be preserved. Horace Mann noted that education was the "great equalizer" and the "balance wheel of the social machinery." To Mann and his followers, education was the only way to "counterwork this tendency to the domination of capital and the servility of labor." A well-rounded education provides our citizens the means to better themselves.

Practicing the Skill

1. What is the topic of these passages?

2. In what ways are the passages similar? In what ways are they different?

3. What conclusions can you draw about the beliefs of the two writers?

APPLYING THE SKILL

4. Examine the sections on the women's rights movement and the antislavery crusade on pages 161–162. Create a chart that shows their similarities and differences.

165

GLENCOE
TECHNOLOGY

VIDEODISC

Use the MindJogger Videoquiz to review students' knowledge.

MindJogger Videoquiz

Chapter 4
Disc 1, Side A

Available in VHS.

Reviewing Facts

1. by ruling in favor of implied powers and by broadly defining interstate commerce
2. westward movement, movement of goods, and travel
3. vote extended; politicians sought support of ordinary people
4. Native Americans and African Americans regarded as second-class citizens; women were judged inferior to men
5. North developed factory system; South expanded agriculture; Northwest developed with lure of fertile lands and improved transportation.
6. Answers include land use policy, tariffs, slavery, internal improvements.
7. lack of security, low pay, long hours, and poor working conditions
8. Cotton was the single most important crop and the nation's greatest export.
9. Missouri Compromise
10. free schools, training

Using Vocabulary

Use each vocabulary term in a sentence about the growth of sectional conflict.

nationalism   cotton gin
internal improvement   closed shop
protective tariff   spoils system
turnpike   abolitionist

Reviewing Facts

1. **Explain** how the federal judiciary strengthened nationalism in key decisions between 1819 and 1824.
2. **Summarize** the changes that resulted from internal improvements in transportation.
3. **Identify** the important democratic changes that developed during the Jackson era.
4. **Identify** the groups that did not benefit from democracy under Jackson and why.
5. **Compare** the effects of the Industrial Revolution on different sections.
6. **List** four issues on which the sections had major differences.
7. **Describe** the problems workers faced during the 1830s.
8. **Explain** why "cotton was king" in the South.
9. **Name** the plan that temporarily resolved sectional conflict over slavery.
10. **Summarize** advances in American education in the early 1800s.

Understanding Concepts

1. What political and democratic changes aided Andrew Jackson's election victory in 1828?
2. What reasons can you give for why both the abolitionist and temperance movements began among religious groups?
3. The Underground Railroad was run by decent people who broke the law. Under the law these people were technically stealing property. What

values did they consider to be above the law? Do you think breaking the law is ever justified under certain circumstances? Explain.

Economic Change

4. What were some of the abuses of the free enterprise system that factory workers experienced? In what way did the government and citizens address these abuses?
5. Describe how trade unions in the 1820s and 1830s might have changed the free enterprise system.
6. In what ways did the Industrial Revolution divide the nation?

Critical Thinking

1. **Making Global Comparisons** Slavery was abolished in Great Britain, France, and Latin America before it was abolished in the United States. What economic and political differences probably accounted for this?
2. **Analyzing Fine Art** Study the painting on this page by artist James Hamilton entitled *Scene on the Hudson*. Then answer the questions that follow.

▲ *SCENE ON THE HUDSON* BY JAMES HAMILTON

Understanding Concepts

1. extension of vote, influence of common people, West
2. Both movements required people to whom moral values were more important than economic interest.
3. Some students may note

when laws are immoral, they should be broken.
4. underpaid, long hours, and unsafe conditions
5. By demanding higher wages and a shorter working day, workers were seeking to regulate a free enterprise system driven by supply and demand.

6. Each section needed different things, which led to sectional conflicts.

Critical Thinking

1. In the United States, enlightenment and spirit of reform was outweighed by the economic interests.

a. What captured your attention when you first looked at this painting?

b. What kind of mood is suggested by this painting?

c. Does Hamilton's painting stir any memories of your own past experiences when in a forest or near the sea?

d. What is your personal response to this painting?

3. **Making Judgments** Why would President Monroe want to issue the Monroe Doctrine independently of Great Britain? Was it possible for the United States during the Monroe administration to enforce this policy? Explain your reasoning.

4. **Evaluating Policy** Argue for or against the spoils system.

5. **Analyzing Evidence** What evidence can you find that at the beginning of the 1800s, European art and literature was considered superior to American art and literature?

6. **Linking Past and Present** Today the law requires all students to attend school until a certain age. During the 1800s, high school attendance was voluntary. Why might a democratic society prefer compulsory education to voluntary attendance?

History and Geography

The Nation and the Industrial Revolution

The Industrial Revolution affected each region of the country differently due to its physical characteristics. The North was rocky and mountainous with a short growing season, abundant moving water, and coal deposits. The South was lush and fertile with warm temperatures and a long growing season. The West had abundant fertile land but was distant from markets and separated from the rest of the country by rugged terrain.

1. **Human/Environment Interaction** How did the physical characteristics explain the economies that developed in each region?

2. **Human/Environment Interaction** How did workers and settlers adapt to their environment?

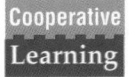 **Cooperative Learning** Interdisciplinary Activity: Government

Working in pairs, research the history of the government's and settlers' dealings with Black Hawk's nation. Imagine it is 1832 and Black Hawk has returned with his followers to reclaim Iowa lands that farmers now hold. You and your partner have been appointed by Jackson to recommend a solution. Agree on a fair plan and present it to your class.

Practicing Skills

Making Comparisons

Examine the paintings of the mill on page 139 and the factory on page 148. Then answer the questions that follow.

1. In what ways are the scenes the artists present similar? In what ways are the scenes different?

2. What mood or feeling is communicated in each work?

3. Compare the techniques of the artists. Which style of art do you prefer? Explain.

Writing ABOUT History Using Your Journal

Controversy still exists over tariffs and other legislation to protect American industry from foreign competition. In a paragraph, discuss how such measures affect American consumers and workers.

owners lived in luxury while enslaved people lived under deplorable conditions. Settlers in the West developed town centers, although most of them lived far from neighbors.

Cooperative Learning

Encourage students to work together to come to a consensus for a fair plan.

Practicing Skills

1. Both scenes show a factory; different perspectives

2. Page 139 depicts a tranquil scene, whereas the picture on page 148 shows a more stark scene.

3. The artist on page 139 uses a gentler technique, using subtler tones. The artist on page 148 uses brighter colors to achieve a more realistic look. Preferences will vary.

Writing ABOUT History Using Your Journal

Responses should reflect an understanding that consumers will pay higher prices for manufactured goods.

? Chapter Bonus Test Question

Ask: What did Americans gain and lose because of the rapid growth of the nation in the early nineteenth century? *(Gains include: prosperity, linking of sections, growth. Losses include: sectional antagonism, growth of slavery.)*

---

2. a. Answers include the water or sky.
   b. a tranquil mood
   c. Memories will vary.
   d. Responses will vary.

3. He did not want to appear to be tagging along on Britain's coattails; lack of a strong navy would have prevented its enforcement.

4. Answers include: make the President too powerful; allows newcomers an opportunity; provides a cooperative working relationship.

5. Few recognized achievements

6. A democratic society demands an informed, educated electorate.

History and Geography

1. Water and coal allowed rapid development of manufacturing in the North. Conditions favored cotton production in the South and agriculture in the West.

2. Northern workers left farms to move to the city. In the South, plantation

Daily Lesson Objectives	Teacher Classroom Resources	Multimedia
SECTION 1 **1 Day** pp. 170–175 **Manifest Destiny** 1. Describe western settlement. 2. Explain how Texas became part of the United States.	Reproducible Lesson Plan 5-1 Chapter Concept Mapping Activities 5-A, 5-B Critical Thinking Skills Activity 5 *Section Quiz 5-1	Section Focus Transparency 5-1 Historic America Electronic Field Trips GTV: The American People: Fabric of a Nation
SECTION 2 **1 Day** pp. 176–180 **Compromise and Growth** 1. Describe the debates on the question of slavery. 2. Explain how immigration affected economic growth.	Reproducible Lesson Plan 5-2 *Vocabulary Activity 5 Guided Reading Activity 5-2 Reteaching Activity 5-2 *Section Quiz 5-2	Section Focus Transparency 5-2 Vocabulary PuzzleMaker STV: North America Focus on Government
SECTION 3 **1 Day** pp. 182–187 **The Approaching Conflict** 1. Explain key political events. 2. List the political events that led to secession.	Reproducible Lesson Plan 5-3 Political Cartoons in American History Activity 5 Supreme Court Case Study 4 *Section Quiz 5-3	Section Focus Transparency 5-3 GTV: The American People: Fabric of a Nation The Presidents: A Picture History of Our Nation
SECTION 4 **1 Day** pp. 190–196 **The Civil War** 1. Explain war strategies. 2. Identify major battles of the Civil War.	Reproducible Lesson Plan 5-4 *Guided Reading Activity 5-4 Reteaching Activity 5-4 Section Quiz 5-4	Section Focus Transparency 5-4 GTV: A Geographic Perspective on American History Historic America Electronic Field Trips
SECTION 5 **1 Day** pp. 197–201 **Behind the Lines** 1. Discuss behind-the-lines activity during the war. 2. Explain the wartime roles played by civilians.	Reproducible Lesson Plan 5-5 Chapter Skills Activity 5 Reteaching Activity 5-5 Workbook Activity 5-5 *Section Quiz 5-5	Section Focus Transparency 5-5 Skills Transparency 5 Powers of the Supreme Court American Music: Cultural Traditions
SECTION 6 **1 Day** pp. 203–207 **Ending the War** 1. Explain changes in military strategy. 2. Discuss the election of 1864.	Reproducible Lesson Plan 5-6 *Guided Reading Activity 5-6 Enrichment Activity 5 Reteaching Activity 5-6 *Section Quiz 5-6	Section Focus Transparency 5-6 Testmaker Lessons of War
CHAPTER REVIEW AND EVALUATION **1 Day**	Chapter 5 Test, Forms A and B Spanish Chapter 5 Summary Performance Assessment Activity 5	MindJogger Videoquiz Student Self-Test & Review *Chapter 5 Digest Audiocassette

*Also available in Spanish

 OUT OF TIME? If time does not permit teaching the entire chapter, use the Chapter 5 Summary on pages 234–235 and the Chapter 5 audiocassette (English and Spanish) to point out the main ideas of the chapter.

A complete, 1-page lesson plan is provided for each section in the *Reproducible Lesson Plan* booklet.

Key to Ability Levels

Teaching strategies have been coded for varying learning styles and abilities.

L1 Basic activities for all students

L2 Average activities for average to above-average students

L3 Challenging activities for above-average students

LEP Limited English Proficiency activities

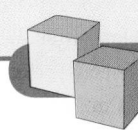

Block Schedule

Block scheduling differs from traditional class scheduling in the amount of time allotted to each period. The extended time frame provided by block scheduling affords you the opportunity to implement a greater number of research-oriented and activity-intense projects to motivate and involve your students. Activities that are particularly suited to use within the block scheduling framework are identified throughout this unit by the following designation:

✓ Performance Assessment Activity

Political Highlights Assign students to one of three groups representing section divisions in the United States and its territories between 1848 and 1860: the North, the South, and the West. Ask each group to develop 10 cleverly worded and easy-to-remember slogans that encapsulate its section's political beliefs and goals. Make sure that the groups write their slogan on separate sheets of paper. As a prelude, you might ask students to identify slogans from other periods of American history. Draw the slogans randomly from a box and ask the class to identify the region each represents.

POSSIBLE RUBRIC FEATURES

- Content Information
- Summary Skills
- Creativity
- Clarity
- Written Communication Skills
- Cooperative Learning Skills

👉 For additional activities, see Performance Assessment Strategies and Activities.

TEACHER'S CORNER

NATIONAL GEOGRAPHIC SOCIETY

INDEX TO NATIONAL GEOGRAPHIC MAGAZINE

The following articles may be used for research relating to this chapter:

- "America's Poet: Walt Whitman," by Joel L. Swerdlow, December 1994.
- "C.S.S. Alabama," by Max Guerout, December 1994.
- "The Cruelest Commerce: African Slave Trade," by Colin Palmer, September 1992.
- "Life and Death on the Oregon Trail: The Itch to Move West," by Boyd Gibbons, August 1986.

NATIONAL GEOGRAPHIC SOCIETY PRODUCTS AVAILABLE FROM GLENCOE

To order the following products for use with this chapter, contact your local Glencoe sales representative or call Glencoe at 1-800-334-7344:

- *The Presidents: A Picture History of Our Nation* (CD-ROM)
- *GTV: A Geographic Perspective on American History* (Videodisc)
- *GTV: The American People: Fabric of a Nation* (Videodisc)

ADDITIONAL NATIONAL GEOGRAPHIC SOCIETY PRODUCTS

To order the following products for use with this chapter, call National Geographic Society at 1-800-368-2728:

- *Building a Nation: The Story of Immigration* (Filmstrip)
- *Immigration: The Triumph of Hope* (Video)
- *The Civil War* (Filmstrip)

CHAPTER 5
★★

BEGINNING THE CHAPTER

GLENCOE TECHNOLOGY

VIDEODISC

Use the Chapter 5 MindJogger Videoquiz to preview the content of this chapter.

MindJogger Videoquiz

Chapter 5
Disc 1, Side A

 Available in VHS.

Recording Journal Notes

Tell students to read the chapter and record events that contributed to the Union's division. Upon completing the chapter, ask them to rank in importance the events leading to war.

In 1850 the United States was not a nation as we know it today. Tensions between the states divided the nation into three separate regions. Fierce differences of opinion, geographic diversity, economic inequalities, and slavery contributed to this sectionalism.

The Civil War Era
1820–1865

▶ COTTON CARDING PADDLES

Setting the Scene

Focus

During the mid-1800s, the United States used war and diplomacy to significantly expand its western territory. By 1850 thousands of settlers moved into this area to create new homes. Meanwhile, sectional divisions—especially concerning slavery—threatened the existence of the Union. Compromise at first seemed to work in holding the country together. With the election of an anti-slavery President in 1860, however, the South believed it had no choice but to leave the Union.

Concepts to Understand

★ How expansion was influenced by **geography and environment**
★ How political **conflict** over slavery and the nature of the Union led to secession

Read to Discover . . .

★ the causes and results of the Mexican War.
★ the events that led seven Southern states to secede from the Union.

Journal Notes

What contributed to division of the Union? As you read the chapter, record the events, decisions, acts, and other activities that answer the question.

CULTURAL			
	• **1819** *University of Virginia founded*	• **1820** *Nation's population reaches 10 million*	• **1830** *Church of Jesus Christ of Latter-day Saints organized*
	1810	**1820**	**1830**
POLITICAL	• **1818** *National Road reaches Wheeling*	• **1821** *Moses Austin receives land grant in Texas*	• **1836** *Texas wins independence*

✚ EXTRA CREDIT PROJECT

Presidential Powers President Lincoln was the first U.S. President to expand presidential war powers. Without consulting Congress, Lincoln spent millions of dollars enlarging the army and navy. Ask interested students to conduct research to find examples of U.S. Presidents sending armed forces into conflict without a declaration of war from the Congress and discover what law Congress passed in 1973 to remedy that problem. Have students present their findings to the rest of the class. **L2**

Concept Mapping Activity

On the chalkboard, reproduce the following generalization and concepts map, and have students copy it in their notebooks.

Growing sectional tensions lead to differences that cannot be resolved by compromise. The Civil War challenges the survival of the nation.

Geography and Environment

Conflict

  Assign Chapter Concepts Transparency Activities 5-A and 5-B.

History AND ART

View of Harpers Ferry
by Ferdinand Richardt, 1858

Danish artist Ferdinand Richardt captured a serene view of Harpers Ferry, Virginia—the location of the armory targeted for assault by abolitionist John Brown in 1859.

▲ FLAG OF THE REPUBLIC OF TEXAS

History AND ART

In 1859 Harpers Ferry was a town of about 2,000 people. Located on Virginia's border with Maryland, the town was bounded on the south by the Shenandoah River and on the north by the Potomac.

- **1846** *Elias Howe patents sewing machine*
- **1852** *Harriet Beecher Stowe's* Uncle Tom's Cabin *published*
- **1861** *First transcontinental telegraph message sent*

1840	1850	1860

- **1846** *Mexican War begins*
- **1850** *Compromise of 1850 passed*
- **1854** *Kansas-Nebraska Act passed*
- **1860** *South Carolina secedes from the Union*
- **1865** *Civil War ends*

CHAPTER 5 The Civil War Era: 1820–1865   **169**

NATIONAL GEOGRAPHIC SOCIETY

 VIDEODISC

GTV: A Geographic Perspective on American History

Side 2, Chapter 15
Title: *The Gathering Storm*
Subject: Conflict and compromise before the Civil War (1850–1860)

✓ **Performance Assessment**

Refer to the Performance Assessment Activity in the Planning Guide on page 168b. When the students have finished their slogans that encapsulate the political beliefs of the nation's three sections, have each group present their slogans to the class. Allow time for class discussion and feedback.

Use Performance Assessment Activity 5 as an additional assessment technique.

★★★★★★★★★★★★★★★★★★★★★★★★★★★★★★★★

Manifest Destiny

FOCUS

Bellringer

Before taking roll, project Section Focus Transparency 5-1 or hand out Section Focus Transparency Activity 5-1. Have students answer the questions. Discuss student responses.

Motivating Activity

Present the following description to students:

Imagine that it is 1849. You have just trekked through a Navajo canyon searching for a wagon route. As you search the canyon, you come across a lost cliff dwelling of the ancient Anasazi people.

Ask: What do you think the early settlers who traveled through the Southwest felt? *(a tremendous pride in the new lands they were settling)* As they read this section, ask students to keep in mind that the southwest boundary of the United States would be drawn on the basis of the nation's territorial claims. **L2**

Vocabulary Precheck

Ask students to define each of the "Key Terms." Have a volunteer consult the dictionary for any unfamiliar words. **L1, LEP**

Setting the Scene

Section Focus

"Manifest Destiny"—the drive to expand the boundaries of the United States across North America—became a single-minded goal for many Americans. From the 1820s to the 1840s, the American flag followed settlers westward to Texas, Oregon, and Utah. In the late 1840s, war with Mexico nearly completed this transcontinental expansion with the United States acquisition of California and New Mexico.

Objectives

After studying this section, you should be able to

★ describe American settlement of Oregon and Utah.

★ explain how Texas became part of the United States.

★ contrast the United States's short-term and long-range goals in the war with Mexico.

★ list the terms of the Treaty of Guadalupe Hidalgo.

Key Terms

dark horse, joint resolution

▲ THE PRAIRIE HUNTER

Manifest Destiny developed from America's restless pioneer spirit that continually sought the settlement of new lands. Expanding the United States to the Pacific, however, meant taking land claimed or settled by other peoples. The United States, with limited military power, had to weigh carefully the possibility of hostilities with Native Americans on the plains, with Great Britain in Oregon, and with Mexico in Texas and in other territories of the Far West.

■ The Thirst for New Lands

The Oregon Territory extended from the Pacific Ocean to the Rocky Mountains, bordering Russian Alaska to the north and California to the south. Four countries— the United States, Great Britain, Spain, and Russia—had originally claimed Oregon. By 1824, however, only the Americans and the British were left to compete for the vast Pacific Northwest territory.

Oregon

In the mid-1830s, American missionaries settled the Oregon Territory to convert Native Americans to Christianity. Their glowing reports of the land's fertility eventually brought a number of American pioneers, most of whom came by covered wagon over the Oregon Trail. By 1845, 5,000 Americans were living south of the Columbia River and demanding that their government take full possession of the Oregon Territory.

Classroom Resources for SECTION 1

Blackline Masters:
- Reproducible Lesson Plan 5-1
- Guided Reading Activity 5-1
- Performance Assessment Activity 5
- Chapter Map Activity 5

- Critical Thinking Skills Activity 5
- Workbook Activity 5-1
- Reteaching Activity 5-1
- Section Quiz 5-1

Transparencies:
- Section Focus Transparency 5-1

Multimedia:
- Testmaker
- Historic America Electronic Field Trips
- MindJogger Videoquiz

Utah

Another group of settlers moved west, not to expand United States territory but to escape from it. The Mormon Church and its founder Joseph Smith were forced to move several times to flee persecution. Many people resented the new religion because of its communal organization and Smith's teaching that a man could have more than one wife. After Smith's death at the hands of a mob, Brigham Young, the new leader, led the Mormons from Illinois—their latest place of settlement—to an isolated haven in territory that belonged to Mexico.

The move took place in 1847. The Mormons soon established flourishing settlements near the Great Salt Lake in Utah. They developed an advanced system for controlling the water supply in the semiarid regions of the Far West. Around Salt Lake City, irrigation transformed the desert into a garden spot.

Texas

Texas—a vast, ill-defined area extending southwest from Louisiana to the Rio Grande and west to the foothills of the Rocky Mountains—belonged to Mexico. The original Spanish settlements in Texas were limited to a few hundred people and a dozen missions.

When Mexico broke away from Spain in 1821, its government sought migrants to come and develop Texas. In 1822 Stephen F. Austin, an American settler, took over a grant of land that the Spanish government had given his father. Mexican officials welcomed Austin and other Americans, provided they became Roman Catholics and accepted Mexican law.

Austin's settlement proved so successful that by 1830 Texas had attracted almost 30,000 Americans. In that year Mexico passed a law restricting further immigration because it was concerned about developments in Texas. Americans, knowing

▲ *Spirit of the Frontier* by John Gast, 1872 Driven by a sense of Manifest Destiny, Americans moved west. By 1848 the United States stretched unchallenged from sea to sea. *What role did Stephen Austin play in extending American settlement?*

TEACH
Guided Practice

Role Playing Have students dramatize a scene in which they have to respond to their parents' questions about why they have chosen to make the long journey across the Oregon Trail. Students acting as parents should ask: Why have you decided to leave? How much money do you have? How will you make the long journey? What will you take with you? What will you do when you arrive in Oregon? **L2**

History AND ART

Brooklyn-based painter John Gast created this work based on the specifications of a publicist who used it to promote a travel guide. **Answer to Caption:** He extended settlement into Texas.

Did You Know?

Fairly prosperous Americans found it easier to afford to move west. The trip cost from $700 to $1,500. Land cost from $1.25 to $10 an acre. Clearing the land and tools cost $100 to $400. Building a log cabin cost as much as $50.

Critical Thinking Activity

Expressing Point of View Ask students to write a sentence expressing the point of view on the United States expansion westward of each of the following: a young American settler migrating to Oregon, a frontiersman living in the Rocky Mountains, a Native American living on the Great Plains, a Mexican citizen farming in Texas, and a British shipowner operating off the Oregon coast. Have volunteers read their sentences aloud to the class. **L1, L2**

VIDEODISC

Historic America Electronic Field Trips

Side One, Chapter 10
Title: *The Alamo*

Subject: Tour of the legendary battle site

Ask: What effect did the heroic efforts by the defenders at the Alamo have on the war? *(provided time for Houston to raise forces; rallied others to cause)*

See ABCNews Interactive™ Historic America Electronic Field Trips Guidebook for complete lesson plan.

Food of the Times

In the summer, most people lived on barreled salt pork and beef because fresh meat spoiled in the heat. By the 1840s rich people used boxes filled with cut ice to keep their fresh meat, butter, and milk from spoiling.

Map Study *Using Maps*

Answer: San Jacinto

Map Skills Practice

Ask: Which river is farther south, the Nueces or the Rio Grande? *(Rio Grande)*

For additional map practice, assign Chapter Map Activity 5.

---

that Mexico's law against slavery was not strictly enforced in Texas, had brought thousands of enslaved people. In addition, they had failed to become Catholics, and the flood of settlers now outnumbered local Mexicans 10 to 1.

■ Texas Independence

When the Mexicans abolished local rights, rebellion broke out in Texas. In 1835, Mexico's president General Antonio Santa Anna marched an army north to subdue the rebels. In February 1836, 2,000 Mexican troops besieged 188 Texans in the Alamo, a mission station in San Antonio. After two

▲ **GENERAL SAM HOUSTON**

weeks of resistance, the defenders of the Alamo were defeated.

The Mexican army pursued Sam Houston, the military leader of the Texans, and his troops toward the United States border. Then at San Jacinto (SAN juh•SIHN•tuh) Creek, Houston's forces turned and attacked. Crying "Remember the Alamo!" they surprised and defeated the Mexican troops. A captured Santa Anna signed a treaty recognizing the independence of Texas but renounced it as soon as he was free.

In 1836 Texas declared itself the Lone Star Republic and immediately sought admission to the United States. The United States government, however, refused to annex Texas because of Northern opposition to adding more slave territory to the Union and fears that admission of Texas would bring war with Mexico.

■ Election of 1844

As the presidential election of 1844 approached, the issue of territorial expansion took center stage. Former President Van Buren, a Democrat, and Henry Clay, a Whig, were expected to be the rival candidates. Then the unexpected happened: Van

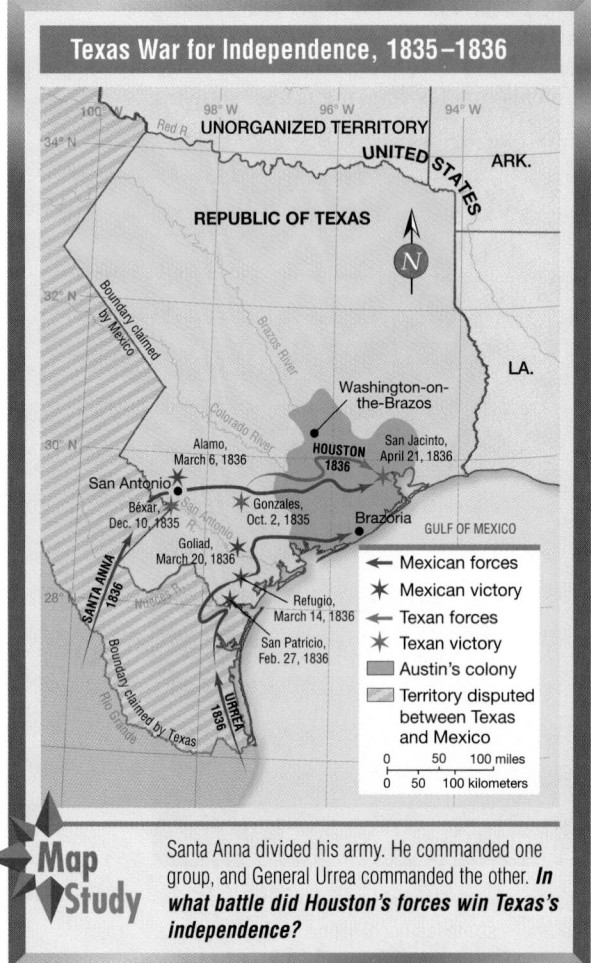

Texas War for Independence, 1835–1836

UNORGANIZED TERRITORY
UNITED STATES
ARK.
REPUBLIC OF TEXAS
Boundary claimed by Mexico
Red R.
Brazos River
Colorado River
Washington-on-the-Brazos
LA.
Alamo, March 6, 1836
HOUSTON 1836
San Jacinto, April 21, 1836
San Antonio
Béxar, Dec. 10, 1835
Gonzales, Oct. 2, 1835
Brazoria
GULF OF MEXICO
Goliad, March 20, 1836
SANTA ANNA 1836
Refugio, March 14, 1836
San Patricio, Feb. 27, 1836
Boundary claimed by Texas
Rio Grande
URREA 1836
Nueces R.
N

← Mexican forces
✳ Mexican victory
← Texan forces
✳ Texan victory
⬛ Austin's colony
▨ Territory disputed between Texas and Mexico

0   50   100 miles
0   50   100 kilometers

Map Study

Santa Anna divided his army. He commanded one group, and General Urrea commanded the other. *In what battle did Houston's forces win Texas's independence?*

Sidelight: Mapping the West

By the 1840s a team of government explorers had conducted scientific explorations of the West. One of these, Colonel John C. Frémont of the United States Corps of Topographical Engineers, described the Salt Lake Valley in such glowing terms—"still and solitary grandeur"—that Brigham Young moved his

Mormons from Illinois to the deserts of Utah. During the Mexican War, United States Army explorers accompanied American cavalry. Their journeys resulted in the first detailed maps of the Southwest and a great regional survey of the geology, flora, fauna, and Native American peoples of the region.

Buren failed to receive the Democratic nomination. A group of Southerners who wanted Texas and Westerners who wanted Oregon nominated the first **dark horse,** or unexpected candidate, in the history of the presidency—James K. Polk of Tennessee.

Support for Expansion

Polk backed the annexation of both Oregon and Texas. Regarding Oregon, the Democrats' pro-expansion enthusiasm was dramatized by the campaign slogan "Fifty-four forty or fight!" (The parallel 54°40' was the southern boundary of Alaska.) To counter this unexpected challenge, the Whigs had only Henry Clay's popularity. Although Clay had earlier opposed the admission of Texas, he issued a cautious statement accepting annexation if war could be avoided. Clay's hedging did not work, and Polk won the 1844 election by a slim margin.

Texas Statehood

President Tyler, who was still in office, asserted that Polk's victory was a mandate for the admission of Texas to the Union. He asked Congress to admit Texas by a **joint resolution** that would require only a simple majority, instead of a treaty that required a vote of two-thirds of the Senate.

In February 1845, both houses of Congress, by narrow majorities, passed the joint resolution. In December 1845, the Lone Star Republic became the twenty-eighth state. The boundary between Mexico and Texas remained undetermined, and the Mexican government threatened war.

■ Division of Oregon

The risk of war with Mexico put pressure on the United States to settle the Oregon question. It was one thing to shout, "Fifty-four forty or fight!" in an election campaign. It was quite another to take on Great Britain, the greatest sea power in the world, and prepare to fight Mexico.

Great Britain, however, was concerned about the large number of American settlers

in Oregon who seemed willing to fight. Rather than losing all of the territory, the British were willing to relinquish the southern half. In 1846, Polk, now President, submitted to the Senate a British proposal to divide Oregon along the 49th parallel. In spite of the objections of Westerners, who accused the President of backing down on his demand for all of Oregon, the Senate approved the treaty, which was signed on June 15, 1846.

■ War With Mexico

The spark that finally ignited war between Mexico and the United States resulted from a dispute over the southern boundary of Texas. Mexico claimed it was the Nueces River, while the United States said it was the Rio Grande 130 miles to the south. Failing to reach a diplomatic settlement with Mexico, Polk ordered General Zachary Taylor to move his troops south to the Rio Grande. Taylor's troops were, in effect, looking for trouble, waiting for an incident justifying retaliation.

War Begins

Late in April 1846, Mexican soldiers crossed the Rio Grande and attacked a small group of United States cavalry. At Polk's urging, Congress declared war by overwhelming majorities in both houses. Although attacking Polk for starting the war, the Whigs in Congress supported it by voting for supplies and troops.

Many Americans, however, refused to support a war of aggression against a weaker neighbor. Even American soldiers had their doubts about the legitimacy of the war. In 1846 Colonel Ethan Allen Hitchcock wrote:

> ❝ *I have said from the first that the United States are the aggressors. . . . We have not one particle of right to be here. It looks as if the government sent a small force on purpose to bring on a war, so as to have a pretext for taking California and as*

Independent Practice

 Assign Guided Reading Activity 5-1.

 Assign Workbook Activity 5-1.

Did You Know?

Ex-President Van Buren was expected to be the Democratic candidate in the 1844 presidential election. Texas's annexation, with its threat of disunion over slavery, alarmed him so much that he wrote a letter to the press opposing it. Van Buren then failed to receive the Democratic nomination.

NATIONAL GEOGRAPHIC SOCIETY

 VIDEODISC

GTV: The American People: Fabric of a Nation

Side 2, Chapter 6
Frames 31267-36347
Title: *No Place Like Home*
Subject: The turbulent history of Texas

Cooperative Learning Activity

Reaching a Consensus To review the issues of conflict between Mexico and the United States, organize the class into groups of four. Have two students in each group research the Mexican view that the United States was provoking a war by encroaching on Mexican territory in California and Texas. Have the other two students research points made by Polk's administration that it had tried to negotiate with the Mexican government. Following the sharing of information from both sides, have each group come to a consensus on which side provoked the Mexican War and why. **L3**

Map Study *Using Maps*

Answer: Feb. 1847

Map Skills Practice

Ask: What is the southernmost city in which fighting occurred? (*Mexico City*)

Did You Know?

President Polk was the first President to inform Congress that war existed before Congress formally declared war.

ABCNEWS INTERACTIVE™

Historic America Electronic Field Trips

Side One, Chapter 11
Title: *Sutter's Mill*

Subject: Site of 1848 California gold strike

Ask: What effect did the discovery of gold have on California settlers? (*led to enormous population growth*)

See ABCNews Interactive™ Historic America Electronic Field Trips Guidebook for complete lesson plan.

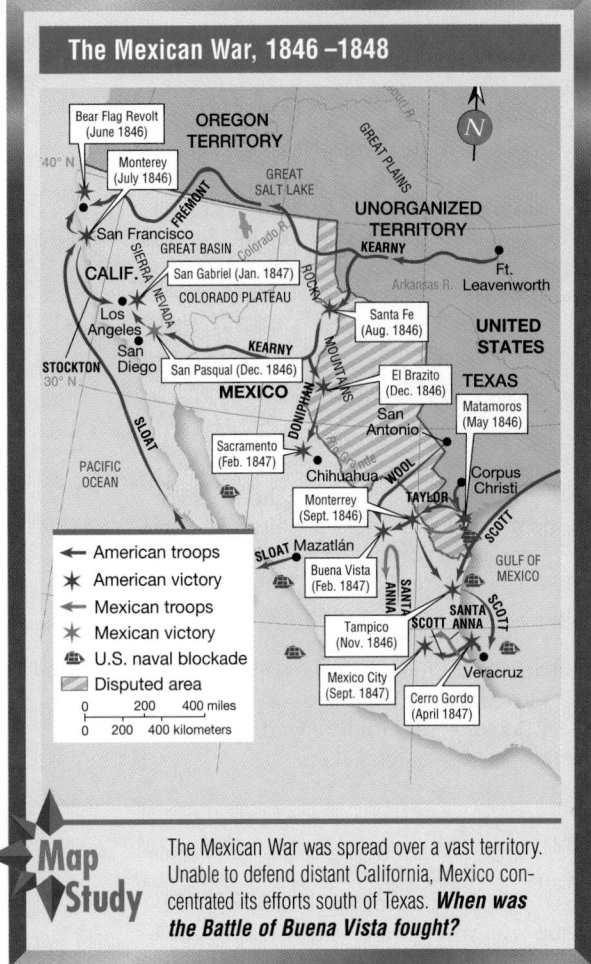

The Mexican War, 1846–1848

← American troops
✶ American victory
← Mexican troops
✶ Mexican victory
⚓ U.S. naval blockade
▨ Disputed area

0   200   400 miles
0   200   400 kilometers

Map Study
The Mexican War was spread over a vast territory. Unable to defend distant California, Mexico concentrated its efforts south of Texas. **When was the Battle of Buena Vista fought?**

much of this country as it chooses, for, whatever becomes of this army, there is no doubt of a war between the United States and Mexico.... My heart is not in this business ... but, as a military man, I am bound to execute orders. "

Polk's War Strategy

President Polk planned the military campaigns of the Mexican War as a three-part strategy. First, General Taylor and his troops invaded northern Mexico. By February 1847, they had penetrated nearly 300 miles into the country and won the Battle of Buena Vista.

As the second part of the strategy, a force under General Stephen Kearney took Santa Fe and marched to California, where they helped an American naval force defeat the Mexicans in Los Angeles. A local revolt in northern California, assisted by Americans, had already shaken off Mexican rule. Thus California came under United States control, and fighting in the West ended.

When Mexico still refused to make peace, Polk launched the third part of his war strategy, sending General Winfield Scott to conquer Mexico City. With a force of 10,000, Scott sailed south and landed at Veracruz. In September 1847, after six months of difficult fighting, he occupied the capital.

Treaty of Guadalupe Hidalgo

Working to the Americans' advantage was the disorganization of the Mexican government. After the capture of Mexico City, some months passed before a Mexican government could be organized to sign a peace treaty. Meanwhile, advocates of Manifest Destiny urged that the United States annex all of Mexico.

In February 1848, before the movement for total annexation had proceeded very far, a peace treaty was signed at Guadalupe Hidalgo, outside Mexico City. In spite of Polk's dissatisfaction with the agreement, he submitted the treaty to the Senate. After a round of expansionist arguments by those favoring annexation of all of Mexico, the Senate finally voted 38 to 14 in favor of the treaty.

Under the agreement, the United States gained full title to Texas (with the Rio Grande as the boundary). The United States also gained California and all of what was then called New Mexico. The nation paid $15 million outright for New Mexico and California and agree to pay some of the Mexican debt. Mexico lost only 1 percent of its population but half of its territory.

Critical Thinking Activity

Making Predictions Organize students into pairs. Ask each pair to predict what could have happened in American history if James K. Polk had not been elected President in 1844. Would the war with Mexico have occurred? Why or why not? What effect would this have had on the United States acquisition of California and New Mexico? How about the establishment of our political boundaries? Ask students to write their predictions in a short statement. Discuss student answers. **L2, L3**

📁 For additional practice in critical thinking, assign Critical Thinking Skill Activity 5.

 Visualizing History

▲ ENTERING MEXICO CITY After six months of difficult fighting, General Winfield Scott forced his way into Mexico City. Scott's troops included young military officers Ulysses S. Grant and Robert E. Lee. **Why did some of the troops oppose the war?**

Further Expansion

In 1853, the United States completed expansion across the continent with the Gadsden Purchase for $10 million. This land provided a route were the land elevation was low enough to built a railroad across the southern part of the country to California.

Once the United States gained control of large areas of the West, Americans began moving into these regions in greater and greater numbers. In 1848, gold was discovered in California at Sutter's mill near Sacramento. Stories of instant riches led to a gold rush from the eastern United States and Europe.

In addition to gold, the acquisition of California gave the United States valuable ports from which to launch its Pacific trade. Along with the European powers, Americans secured trading privileges in China. By 1850, American clipper ships carried most of the Chinese tea exported to Europe. In 1854, a small United States fleet under Commodore Matthew C. Perry also persuaded isolationist Japan to open trade with the outside world.

Section 1 ★ Review

Checking for Understanding

1. **Identify** Manifest Destiny, Sam Houston, Treaty of Guadalupe Hidalgo, Matthew C. Perry.

2. **Define** dark horse, joint resolution.

3. **List** three rivals to American settlers for Western lands.

4. **Discuss** the results of the presidential election of 1844 and cite Polk's position on Texas annexation.

Critical Thinking

5. **Evaluating an Action** Imagine you are a newspaper editor in the mid-1840s. Write your opinion on whether the United States's actions to wage war against Mexico were justified.

ACTIVITY

6. Suppose you are a farmer wishing to settle in Texas in the early 1820s. Write a letter to Stephen F. Austin asking three questions about his colony.

ASSESS

Check Understanding

Assign Section 1 Review as homework or an in-class activity.

Evaluate

☞ Assign Section Quiz 5-1 or use the Test-maker to create a customized quiz.

Reteach

☞ Have students complete Reteaching Activity 5-1.

Enrich

Have students research minorities who fought in the Mexican War

CLOSE

Discuss the extent to which diplomatic negotiations should take place before people risk their lives in a war.

Answers to SECTION 1 REVIEW

1. Manifest Destiny, 170; Sam Houston, 172; Treaty of Guadalupe Hidalgo, 174; Matthew C. Perry, 175
2. All vocabulary words are defined in the Glossary.
3. Answers include Native Americans, Mexico, and Britain.
4. Polk, who supported annexation of Texas and Oregon, won the election.
5. *Yes:* because Mexico was seeking revenge for Texas and was the first to attack. *No:* Polk provoked the war in order to acquire California.
6. Students' questions should express valid concerns.

FOCUS

Bellringer

 Before taking roll, project Section Focus Transparency 5-2 or hand out Section Focus transparency Activity 5-2. Have students answer the questions. Discuss student responses.

Motivating Activity

Present the following: Town Meeting to Be Held!

All citizens are invited to attend a meeting this Sunday to discuss our urgent need for a state constitution to support California's admission as a free state.

Ask: What reasons would you have for voting for or against slavery? **L1**

Vocabulary Precheck

Ask students to define each of the "Key Terms." Have a volunteer consult the dictionary for any unfamiliar words. **L1, LEP**

Use the Vocabulary PuzzleMaker Software to create a crossword puzzle. **L1**

Assign Vocabulary Activity 5.

176

★★★

Compromise and Growth

▶ CANNED FOODS AND MEDICINE, MID-1800s

Setting the Scene

Section Focus

The acquisition of New Mexico and California brought into the open the slavery issue. It became clear that some decision had to be made regarding the legality of slavery in these new areas. In spite of the growing political crisis, the 1850s was a time of remarkable national prosperity. Every major economic interest—cotton planting, wheat farming, manufacturing, and transportation—was booming. The huge gold strike in California paid for imports; the flood of gold expanded United States currency. Also, increasing numbers of immigrants began arriving.

Objectives

After studying this section, you should be able to

★ explain why California's application for admission to the Union incited heated debates on the question of slavery.

★ explain how invention and increased immigration affected the economic growth of the United States.

Key Term

popular sovereignty

---

*E*ven before the war with Mexico had ended, growing antislavery sentiment in the North led the House of Representatives, with its Northern majority, to pass the Wilmot Proviso. This bill provided that all territory acquired from Mexico should be closed to slavery.

The Wilmot Proviso was defeated in the Senate, where the North and South were equally represented. Many Southern senators argued that Congress had no constitutional power to forbid slavery in the territories. If the representatives did outlaw slavery there, they would be denying slaveholders their rights as citizens.

■ Election of 1848

There seemed to be no way of reconciling these opposing views on the issues of slavery in the new territories. When the Polk administration ended in 1849, no steps had been taken to provide for civil government in New Mexico and California.

Democrats and Whigs

In the presidential election of 1848, both Northerners and Southerners took precautions to play down discussion of slavery. The Democrats, although controlled by their Southern wing, nominated a Northern senator, Lewis Cass of Michigan. Cass supported a compromise solution known as **popular sovereignty,** whereby voters within the territories would decide whether slavery would be permitted inside their borders. The Whigs, whose principal stronghold was in the North, nominated Zachary Taylor from Louisiana, a slaveholder himself. The Whigs avoided the issue of slavery by focusing on Taylor's military successes in the Mexican War.

Classroom Resources for SECTION 2

The Free-Soil Party

Efforts to keep slavery out of the campaign failed, however. A third party emerged when various antislavery groups united with many Whigs and Democrats to form the Free-Soil party. Although the Free-Soil presidential candidate Martin Van Buren gained no electoral votes, he kept Cass from gaining New York's 36 electoral votes. This gave the election to Taylor with 163 electoral votes—exactly 36 more than Cass had.

■ The California Question

The issue of slavery in the new territories intensified after gold was discovered in California in 1848. By the end of 1849, an estimated 95,000 "forty-niners" from all over the world had settled in northern California.

Application for Statehood

With this tremendous growth in population came an urgent need to make California a state. In 1849, the newly established territorial government applied for admission to the Union as a free state in which slavery was forbidden. California's application for statehood touched off a long bitter debate. Admission of California would tip the balance of power in the Senate in favor of the free states, already in the majority in the House. If California were admitted as a free state, Southern leaders warned, their states would leave the Union.

Compromise of 1850

To deal with this alarming situation, Henry Clay, who had been in retirement since his defeat in the presidential election of 1844, successfully ran for reelection as senator. The Whig senator from Kentucky, a master of negotiation, proceeded to arrange his great compromise to save the Union. Clay's compromise was a series of measures intended to satisfy Northern and Southern demands. The principal provisions favoring the North were that California would be

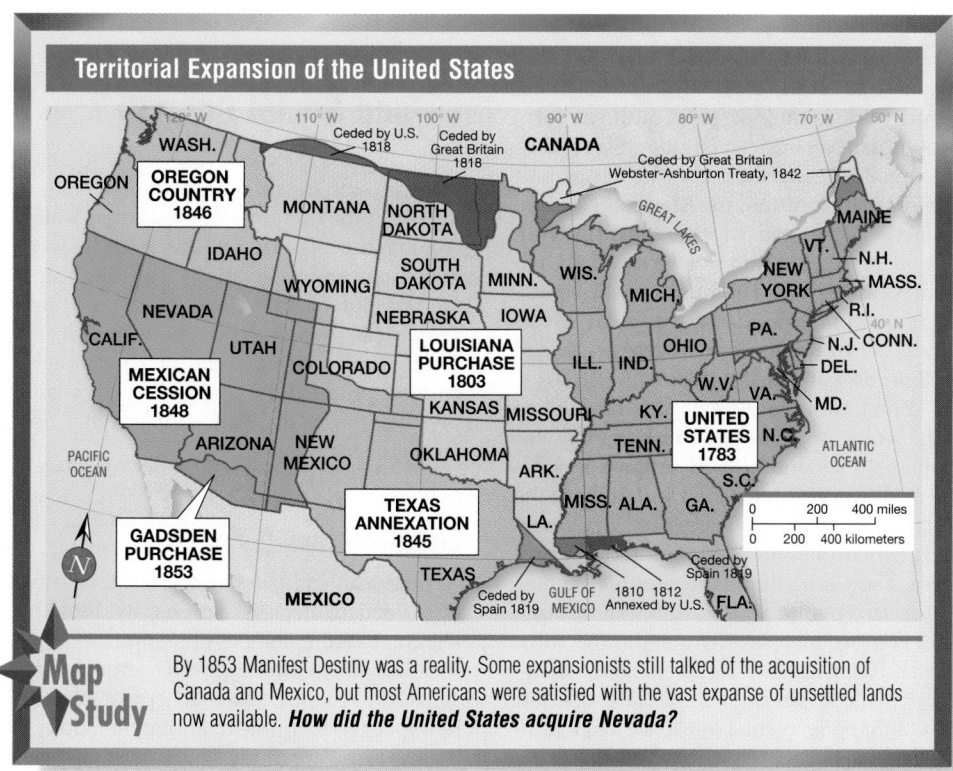

Territorial Expansion of the United States

Map Study By 1853 Manifest Destiny was a reality. Some expansionists still talked of the acquisition of Canada and Mexico, but most Americans were satisfied with the vast expanse of unsettled lands now available. *How did the United States acquire Nevada?*

TEACH
Guided Practice

Summarizing In a brief paragraph, have students explain each provision of the Compromise of 1850 in their own words as if they were teaching it to someone else. **L2**

Did You Know?

The debates over Clay's proposals were so important that the dying Senator Calhoun insisted on attending so he could protect Southern rights. He was so weak that a friend read his speech for him. Daniel Webster urged compromise in an emotional speech in which he spoke "not as a Massachusetts man, nor as a northern man, but as an American."

Map Study *Using Maps*

Answer: through the Mexican Cession

Map Skills Practice
Ask: What land was the last to be added to the contiguous part of the United States? *(the Gadsden Purchase in 1853)*

📁 Assign Geography in History Activity 5.

Special Needs Activity

Attention Deficiency Many students have difficulty paying attention in class. For some students inattention is related to an attention deficit hyperactivity disorder (the name given by psychologists). Severe inattention problems call for special intervention in the classroom.

One popular intervention is to give a time limit for a task. Ask students to read the text "The Election of 1848," a section of approximately 200 words. Give students five minutes to read (enough time for average readers). Did the time limit help them pay attention? Discuss. **LEP, L1**

Visualizing  **History** It cost New York State $7 million to build the 363-mile-long Erie Canal.
Answer to Caption: Answers include steamboats, telegraph, canals, and railroads.

Independent Practice

Using Visual Evidence
Have students find pictures that illustrate advances in transportation, communications, manufacturing, and agriculture in the mid-1800s. Below each picture have them write important information such as the date it was invented, the inventor, and how it changed life in the United States. **L1**

📁 Assign Guided Reading Activity 5-2.

 VIDEODISC

STV: North America

Side 3
Frames 0020-22832
Title: *The Rocky Mountains* (in its entirety)
Subject: Geological history, region, and climate of the Rocky Mountains.

Visualizing History ▲ COMMUNICATIONS AND TRANSPORTATION Westward expansion created an urgent need for better connections between locations. A canal boom was ushered in with the completion of the Erie Canal. *What innovations helped improve communications?*

admitted as a free state and that the slave trade—but not slavery—be forbidden in the District of Columbia. The South, in turn, would gain a stronger Fugitive Slave Law, designed to suppress the Underground Railroad. In addition, the Mexican Cession, gained at the end of the Mexican War, would be divided into two territories, Utah and New Mexico. The question of slavery there would be decided by popular sovereignty when the territories were organized with territorial legislatures.

At first, Clay's proposals failed to receive sufficient support to pass. President Taylor opposed Clay and offered proposals of his own. However, Taylor died suddenly in the summer of 1850. His successor, Vice President Millard Fillmore, favored the compromise. The young Illinois senator Stephen A. Douglas, a Democrat, skillfully put through the compromise as five separate bills, which Fillmore duly signed. The Compromise of 1850 averted immediate disaster but, unhappily, turned out to be just a temporary truce.

■ Economic and Social Growth

During the 20 years from 1840 to 1860, rapid growth became the dominant characteristic of the economy of the United States. Among the reasons for this growth were inventions and innovations, sufficient capital to build factories, and a class of businesspeople willing to start new enterprises. Other factors included an increase in agricultural productivity, a growing labor supply, and the increase in railroads that tied farms to factories.

Inventions and Industries

American industry grew partly because of a flood of new inventions. By 1861 the telegraph had made possible rapid communication throughout the continent and across the Atlantic. The rotary press allowed newspapers to publish far larger editions than ever before. Some inventions, such as

Cooperative Learning Activity

Popular Sovereignty To discuss the doctrine of popular sovereignty, organize students into groups of three or four. Have each group explain why Northern Democrats left their party in 1848 and joined the Free-Soil party. Students should note events leading up to the split in the party. Have each group conclude by preparing a statement explaining how popular sovereignty affected the election. Have them share their statements with the class. Then discuss their conclusions. For accountability, number the members of each group, and call upon students at random. **L2** 📦

the sewing machine, vulcanized rubber, and the steam engine, had the greatest impact on Northern industries.

Textile factories, powered by more efficient steam engines, increased in size as several operations were combined under a single roof. Techniques invented and developed by Eli Whitney and Simeon North for making interchangeable parts and breaking down manufacturing into simple operations now were applied in the mass production of clocks, watches, and farm machinery.

Advances in Agriculture

In spite of industrial advances, two-thirds of the nation's people in 1850 were still engaged in agriculture. Inventions, innovations, and government policies allowed agricultural productivity to keep pace with the nation's fast-growing industries.

The Midwest with its fertile plains attracted farmers from the northeastern United States and from Europe. Public lands there could be purchased for as little as 25 cents an acre. The development of a steel plow with replaceable parts enabled farmers to cut through tree roots in recently cleared forestland and to turn the tough sod of the prairies. With the new plows, farmers could plant more land than they could harvest. To solve this problem, Cyrus McCormick, a Virginia blacksmith, developed a mechanical "reaper," or grain harvester. These inventions were accompanied by still others: a mechanical drill to plant grain, the threshing machine, and the horsedrawn hay rake.

Although the West benefited more from these inventions than did the South, which still depended on slave labor, the Southern economy also improved. Increased demand for raw cotton by an efficient British textile

Using Graphs

Answer: 1851 and 1854

Graph Skills Practice
When did immigration from Ireland first reach 50,000? *(early 1840s)*

Linking Across TIME

A 21-year old German immigrant arrived in San Francisco in 1850 to sell dry goods to gold-rush miners. He saw the need for durable trousers. At first Levi Strauss made trousers out of tent canvas. Then he tried brown denim. Later he used blue denim with copper rivets to strengthen the pockets. The trousers became one of the nation's most famous products—known as dungarees, Levis, or blue jeans.

NATIONAL GEOGRAPHIC SOCIETY

 VIDEODISC

STV: North America

Side 4
Frames 00004-33724
Title: *The Western Dry Lands* (in its entirety)
Subject: Physical characteristics of subregions of the Western Dry Lands

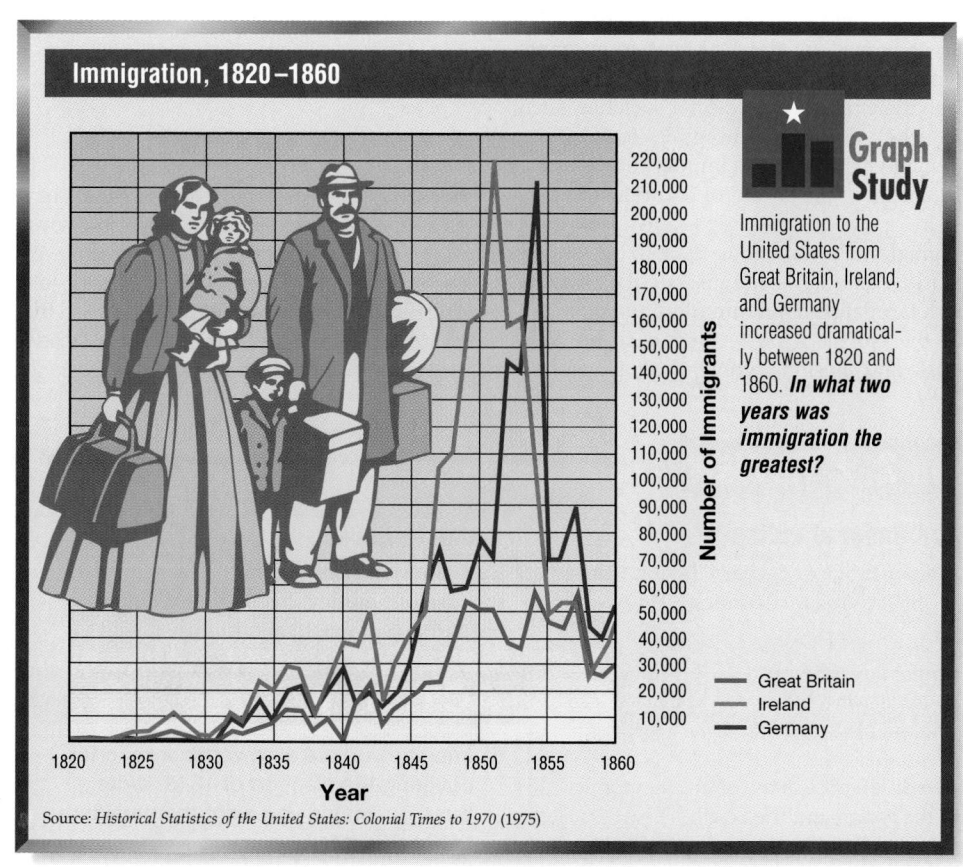

Immigration, 1820–1860

Graph Study

Immigration to the United States from Great Britain, Ireland, and Germany increased dramatically between 1820 and 1860. *In what two years was immigration the greatest?*

Number of Immigrants

— Great Britain
— Ireland
— Germany

Year

Source: *Historical Statistics of the United States: Colonial Times to 1970* (1975)

Critical Thinking Activity

Summarizing Tell students that many historians link the growth of slavery in the South to Eli Whitney's invention of the cotton gin. Have students work in small groups to analyze the economic factors that would have made this possible. Have them discuss how the cotton gin stimulated the South's economy and indirectly contributed to the institution of slavery. Ask groups to summarize their ideas in short statements and present them to the class. Discuss students' answers. **L1**

ASSESS

Check Understanding

Assign Section 2 Review as homework or an in-class activity.

Evaluate

☞ Assign Section Quiz 5-2 or use the Test-maker to create a customized quiz.

Reteach

On the chalkboard write the six factors that spurred economic growth (Inventions, Available Capital, Businesspeople, Increased Agricultural Production, Growing Labor Supply). Discuss how each contributed to growth.

☞ Have students complete Reteaching Activity 5-2.

☞ Assign Workbook Activity 5-2.

Enrich

Ask students to research secret societies such as the "Know-Nothings," mentioned on page 180.

CLOSE

In 1850 Daniel Webster told the U.S. Senate: "I can now sleep of nights. We have gone through the most important crisis that has occurred since the founding of the government, and whatever party may prevail, hereafter the Union stands firm." Ask: Do you think Webster's prediction was realistic for the time?

industry brought prosperity to the Deep South. By 1860 seven-eighths of the world's supply of cotton came from the United States, and raw cotton comprised three-fifths of the nation's exports.

Increased Immigration

During the second quarter of the 1800s, a great migration from Europe to America began. Between 1840 and 1860, an average of more than 200,000 immigrants reached American shores each year. The reasons for this migration were both political and economic. Thousands of English, Irish, Scandinavian, and Dutch farmers and workers made the often perilous voyage to escape poverty and starvation. Others, like German thinkers and writers, came to avoid political persecution. By 1860, about one out of every eight Americans was foreign-born.

Some established Americans resented immigrants with their different languages, religions, and customs. Such bigotry was accompanied by the fear that immigrants would bring new and radical political ideas into the United States. Secret societies, such as the "Know-Nothings," formed to demand restrictions on immigration and the extension of the period of naturalization.

In spite of hardships and prejudice, immigrants continued to flock to the United States. Although some migrated West to its rich farmlands, many immigrants remained in the Northern port cities, such as New York and Boston, where their ships had

▲ "KNOW-NOTHING" SONG SHEET COVER

docked. One reason for this was that they had little money to continue their journeys. Also, the South already had a source of cheap labor—enslaved African Americans. The result was that immigrants supplied the North's growing industries with a steady stream of low-paid workers.

Section 2 ★ Review

Checking for Understanding

1. **Identify** Wilmot Proviso, Zachary Taylor, Compromise of 1850, Cyrus McCormick, "Know-Nothings."

2. **Define** popular sovereignty.

3. **List** four provisions of the Compromise of 1850.

4. **Identify** two differences between the economic systems of the North and the South.

Critical Thinking

5. **Evaluating Policies** Explain why acceptance of the idea of popular sovereignty would have been unacceptable to abolitionists.

ACTIVITY

6. Imagine you are a newspaper reporter covering the election of 1848. Write three questions you want the presidential candidates to answer.

Answers to SECTION 2 REVIEW

1. Wilmot Proviso, 176; Zachary Taylor, 176; Compromise of 1850, 177-178; Cyrus McCormick, 179; "Know-Nothings," 180
2. All vocabulary words are defined in the Glossary.
3. admitted California as free state, forbade slave trade in District of Columbia, stricter Fugitive Slave Law, Mexico Cession divided into two territories, in which slavery to be decided by popular sovereignty
4. North was industrial, used immigrant labor. South was agricultural, used slave labor.
5. Abolitionists demanded immediate emancipation.
6. Students' questions should focus on significant issues of the day.

CONNECTIONS
History AND ECONOMICS

Industrial Innovation

"What is the North," asked a Southern writer during the 1850s, "but a conglomeration [group] of greasy mechanics, filthy operatives, small-fisted farmers, and moonstruck theorists?" Southerners may have looked scornfully at manufacturing in the North, but Europeans were fascinated by "Yankee notions" like machine-made clocks and buckets, canned food, and handguns with revolving chambers. These products were the result of Yankee ingenuity and the machine and tool industry, which mass-produced interchangeable parts.

The British called this industry "the American system of manufacturing," but "the Northeastern American system" would have been more accurate. More than half of America's 140,000 factories were concentrated between New York and Massachusetts, and they were the country's largest and most productive. The South had 20,000 factories, but they were small and concentrated on processing local products like cotton or tobacco rather than manufacturing.

In 1820 most manufacturing was done in homes or small shops. After 1820, however, the factory system began to take over. In factories the total process of manufacturing took place at one location. The need for a single location was due to the new sources of power—water and steam. The first factories used waterpower and were built in rural areas along rivers and streams.

Improved transportation and communication increased the importance of Northern cities as centers of trade. As city merchants grew wealthier, they sought investments that would further increase their business. Much of their capital, or investment money, went into new manufacturing industries.

▲ CRYSTAL PALACE, INDUSTRIAL EXHIBITION IN LONDON, 1851

Connecticut inventor Eli Whitney started the use of interchangeable parts. These were identical machine parts that could be quickly put together to make a complete product. Because all the parts were alike, they could be manufactured with less skilled labor, and they made machine repair easier.

Making the Economics Connection

1. Where did most manufacturing take place during this era?

2. What factors increased the growth of centers of trade?

3. How might the level of industrialization affect the ability of the North and the South to wage war?

ACTIVITY

4. Research specific developments that influenced economic growth during this period. Include these innovations in a chart using the following headings: Industry, Agriculture, and Transportation.

181

TEACH

Ask students to analyze the effects of differences in development between North and South. *(Answers will vary but might include: The difference in development between the North and South created fierce differences of opinion and economic inequalities.)*
L2

CURRICULUM CONNECTION

Economics Between 1850 and 1860, the number of nonfarm workers increased by an astounding 55 percent. By 1860 about 4 out of every 10 workers no longer worked on farms.

FACT or FICTION?

In the 1840s and 1850s, the average American factory workers worked about eight hours a day, six days a week.

FICTION: In 1840 the average daily hours of work for factory workers was 11.4 hours, six days a week. In the late 1840s and early 1850s, laws in the North and in California attempted to limit work hours to 10 hours a day.

Answers to Making the Connection

1. in the North
2. improved transportation and communication
3. Northern armies would be better supplied and equipped owing to manufacturing capability.
4. Charts will vary but should indicate how particular innovations influenced economic growth.

★★

The Approaching Conflict

FOCUS

Bellringer

Before taking roll, project Section Focus Transparency 5-3 or hand out Section Focus Transparency Activity 5-3. Have students answer the questions. Discuss student responses.

Motivating Activity

Present the following advertisement to students:

Wanted: Dedicated individual to work for abolitionist organization. Long hours (14–16 hours a day) and low pay ($35 weekly). Must enjoy public speaking and be dedicated to abolishing slavery.

Ask: Would you apply for this job? Why or why not? *(Dedicated students might apply for this well-meaning position.)* **L2**

Vocabulary Precheck

Ask students to define each of the "Key Terms." Have a volunteer consult the dictionary for any unfamiliar words. **L1, LEP**

Setting the Scene

Section Focus

The 1850s found the South feeling increasingly isolated—isolated from the industrial boom of the North and from the new technologies that were transforming agriculture in the West, and isolated by its support of the slavery system. Both the North and the South watched with dread as the events surrounding the election of 1860 led toward the dissolution of the Union.

Objectives

After studying this section, you should be able to

★ discuss how most Southerners viewed and defended the institution of slavery.

★ explain the significance of the Kansas-Nebraska Act and the *Dred Scott* decision.

★ list the political events that led to the secession of seven Southern states.

Key Terms

platform, secession

◀ LINCOLN CAMPAIGN TORCH

Southern legislatures made it increasingly difficult for slaveholders to emancipate their enslaved men and women. Some states decreed that free African Americans must either go somewhere else or be sold back into slavery. All African Americans, enslaved or free, had to carry identification passes when away from their homes. At night, patrols equipped with dogs and guns watched for runaways.

■ The South and Slavery

Although slavery was common in the South, the majority of people were not slaveholders. In addition, the bondage of African Americans assumed many different forms.

Some enslaved African Americans worked as house servants or were hired out to work in urban businesses. Most, however, worked on plantations and lived lives marked by hard labor, cruel discipline, and isolation. Marriages between enslaved persons were not legally recognized. Families could be broken up by sale. It was against the law to teach enslaved persons to read, although some white Southerners broke that law.

To support the system, many Southerners developed an elaborate defense of slavery. Southerners argued that slavery was necessary to provide an adequate labor supply and was "a positive good" because all the enslaved person's material needs were provided. Finally, defenders of slavery tried to use arguments from science and the Bible to show that slavery was acceptable.

182   UNIT 2 Forging a Nation: 1815–1877

Classroom Resources for SECTION 3

Blackline Masters:
- Reproducible Lesson Plan 5-3
- Guided Reading Activity 5-3
- American Portraits 24, 28
- Political Cartoons in American History Activity 5

- Supreme Court Case Study 4
- Workbook Activity 5-3
- Reteaching Activity 5-3
- Section Quiz 5-3

Transparencies:
- Section Focus Transparency 5-3

Multimedia:
- Testmaker
- GTV: The American People: Fabric of a Nation
- GTV: A Geographic Perspective on American History
- The Presidents: A Picture History of Our Nation

The Rift Widens

For a few years it looked as though the Compromise of 1850 might provide a permanent solution to the slavery controversy. In the North, however, opposition to the stringent Fugitive Slave Law included in the Compromise of 1850 increased. Under this law, the word of a slaveholder, or even one who claimed to be, was taken as conclusive proof of identity of the runaway. A suspected runaway (who might in fact be a free person) had no right to testify on his or her own behalf. Any citizen might be required to join in pursuit of a runaway.

To fight this injustice, most free state legislatures passed personal liberty laws that nullified the Fugitive Slave Law by forbidding state officials to assist in the capture of runaways. Antislavery feeling in the North was also heightened by Harriet Beecher Stowe's *Uncle Tom's Cabin*, a novel portraying slavery at its worst. The book sold 300,000 copies in 1852, its first year of publication.

Kansas-Nebraska Act

In 1854, the political truce over slavery ended with the passage of the Kansas-Nebraska Act. Senator Stephen A. Douglas proposed the act to encourage the rapid settlement of the trans-Missouri region and the building of a transcontinental railroad with terminals at St. Louis and Chicago.

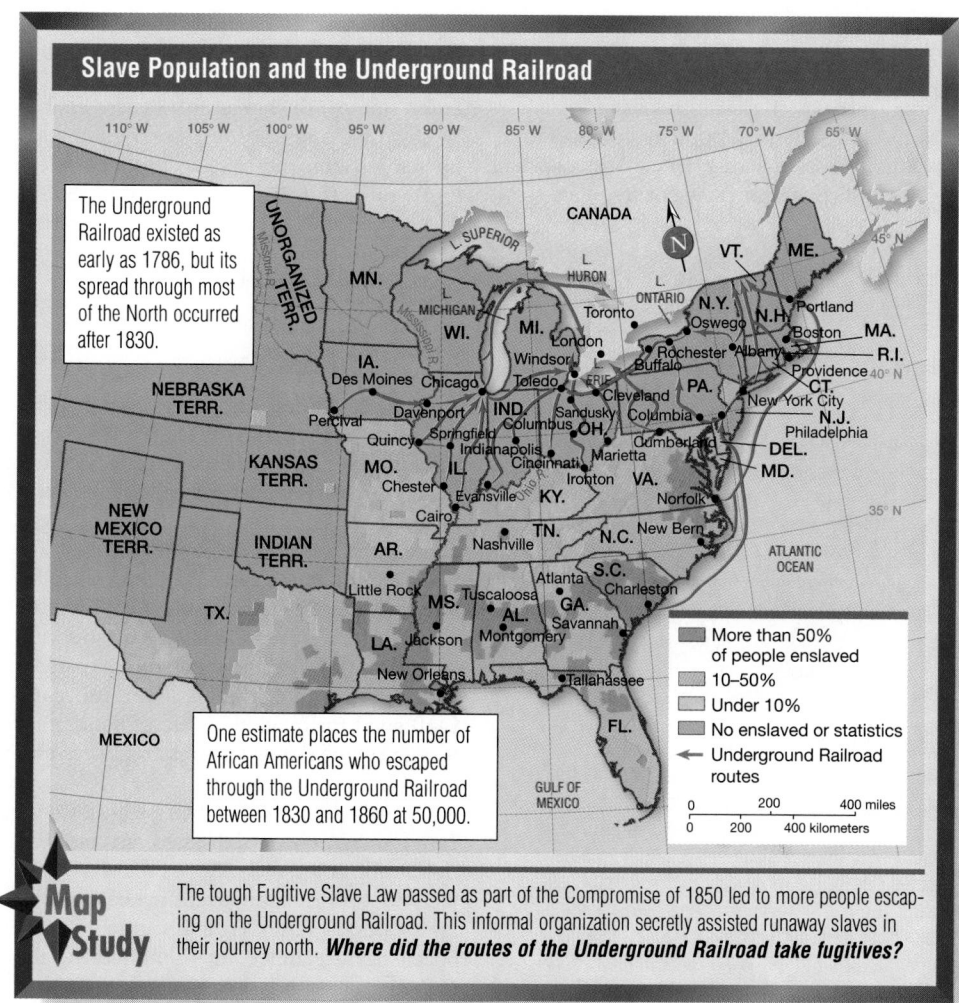

Slave Population and the Underground Railroad

The Underground Railroad existed as early as 1786, but its spread through most of the North occurred after 1830.

One estimate places the number of African Americans who escaped through the Underground Railroad between 1830 and 1860 at 50,000.

- More than 50% of people enslaved
- 10–50%
- Under 10%
- No enslaved or statistics
- ← Underground Railroad routes

0   200   400 miles
0   200   400 kilometers

Map Study The tough Fugitive Slave Law passed as part of the Compromise of 1850 led to more people escaping on the Underground Railroad. This informal organization secretly assisted runaway slaves in their journey north. **Where did the routes of the Underground Railroad take fugitives?**

TEACH
Guided Practice
Making a Concept Map
Have students make an Events-Chain concept map listing the steps that led to secession. *(Suggested sequence: 1857—Dred Scott decision, 1859—John Brown's raid, 1860—Lincoln elected.)* Ask: What common characteristics did all of the events have? **L3**

Did You Know?
According to the 1850 Fugitive Slave Law, anyone convicted of helping an enslaved person escape could be fined $1,000 and sentenced to jail. Bystanders could be deputized and forced to help search for anyone who had escaped from slavery. If they refused to help, they too could be fined $1,000—at a time when yearly wages averaged about $300 to $400.

Map Study *Using Maps*
Answer: into Northern states and from there into Canada

Map Skills Practice
Ask: How did people trying to escape from slavery get from Charleston, South Carolina, to Canada? *(sailed along the coast, then went overland)*

Cooperative Learning Activity

Analyzing the Dred Scott Decision To review the *Dred Scott* decision, organize students into groups of four. Have each student present one aspect of the event to the rest of the group. Among possible choices are President Buchanan's reasons for not deciding on the issue, the reasons for the Supreme Court's decision, and Northern and Southern reactions. To conclude, have each group draw up a hypothesis stating what might have happened had Northerners not challenged the Court's decision. **L1, L2**

Assign Supreme Court Case Study 4, *Dred Scott* v. *Milligan* (1857).

Visualizing History Slaveholders offered $40,000 for Harriet Tubman's capture. After the Civil War began, she worked as a nurse and as a Union spy. **Answer to Caption:** *Uncle Tom's Cabin* by Harriet Beecher Stowe

📁 Assign American Portraits 24 and 28: Sojourner Truth and Harriet Beecher Stowe.

Did You Know?

In the early 1850s, Indiana, Iowa, and Illinois bordered slave states. All three had laws that banned African Americans, whether free or enslaved, from entering their states.

📁 Assign Political Cartoons in American History Activity 5.

NATIONAL GEOGRAPHIC SOCIETY

VIDEODISC

GTV: A Geographic Perspective on American History

Side 2, Chapter 13
Title: *One Nation, Still?*
Subject: Regional differences deepen (1850–1860)

The act, however, opened intersectional controversy. It provided that the trans-Missouri region be divided into two new territories, Nebraska and Kansas. The question of whether or not slavery would exist in the new territories was to be decided by popular sovereignty. This part of the act negated the Missouri Compromise, because both territories lay above latitude 36°30'. A clause specifically repealing the Missouri ban on slavery north of that line was added.

The Kansas-Nebraska Act was criticized. The repeal of the Missouri Compromise was denounced in the North. The South continued to demand that the North recognize the rights of slaveholders in the territories of the United States.

Bleeding Kansas

Settlers started at once to move into the Kansas Territory. Because the slavery issue was to be decided by popular vote, a race developed to see whether the majority of settlers would come from slave or free states.

Visualizing History ▲ **HARRIET TUBMAN** Underground Railroad "agents" not only helped runaway enslaved people after they had come North but risked their lives to go into slave states and help others escape. One of the most successful agents was Harriet Tubman. After making her own escape, she returned to the South again and again, freeing more than 300 others. *What book helped raise antislavery feelings in the North?*

A bloody struggle between the proslavery and antislavery factions assumed the proportions of a civil war. The violence in "Bleeding Kansas" reached its peak on the eve of the presidential election of 1856.

Election of 1856

After the passage of the Kansas-Nebraska Act, the Whig party broke up over the slavery issue. To fill the void, a new party—the Republicans—appeared. In their **platform,** or statement of beliefs, the Republicans upheld the principle of "free soil," or keeping slavery out of the territories. Strongly organized in every northern state, the Republican party nominated General John C. Frémont.

Meanwhile, the Democrats dodged the slavery issue. To balance Southerners' dominance of the party, they nominated a Northerner, James Buchanan of Pennsylvania. With only a minority of the popular vote, Buchanan won the election with 174 electoral votes. The Democrats swept the South and gained enough votes to win, while the Republican Frémont won two-thirds of the electoral votes of the free states.

The *Dred Scott* Decision

In his Inaugural Address in March 1857, President Buchanan suggested that the controversy over slavery in the territories be left to the Supreme Court, which had recently heard a case on this question and was expected to render a decision soon.

Dred Scott was an enslaved man taken by a former master from the state of Missouri into territory closed to slavery by the Missouri Compromise and then brought back to Missouri again. For more than 10 years, Scott sued for freedom on the grounds that residence in a free territory released him from slavery.

On March 6, 1857, Chief Justice Roger Taney (TAW•nee) delivered an opinion upholding completely the Southern point of view that Scott had no right to sue in a federal court. Taney ruled against Scott because, he claimed, the founders of the United States did not intend for African

---

Critical Thinking Activity

Analyzing Consequences Ask students to answer the following question: Passage of the Kansas-Nebraska Act of 1854 had what important consequence for the history of American political parties? Have students write their answers in three paragraphs. Discuss student answers.

(The Republican party was formed. Because antislavery Northerners were shocked by the passage of the act, many broke away from the Whig party and formed the Republican party to keep slavery out of all the territories.) **L3**

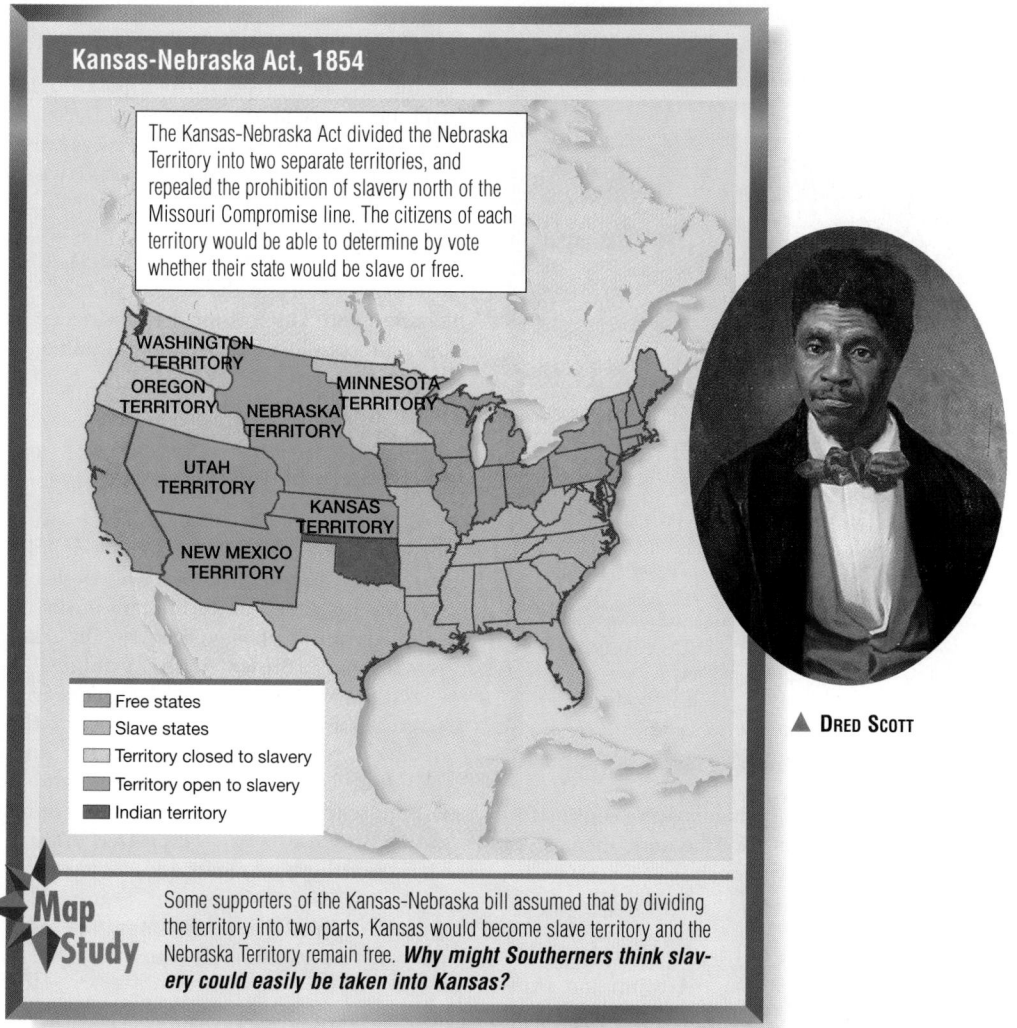

Kansas-Nebraska Act, 1854

The Kansas-Nebraska Act divided the Nebraska Territory into two separate territories, and repealed the prohibition of slavery north of the Missouri Compromise line. The citizens of each territory would be able to determine by vote whether their state would be slave or free.

WASHINGTON TERRITORY
OREGON TERRITORY
MINNESOTA TERRITORY
NEBRASKA TERRITORY
UTAH TERRITORY
KANSAS TERRITORY
NEW MEXICO TERRITORY

- Free states
- Slave states
- Territory closed to slavery
- Territory open to slavery
- Indian territory

▲ DRED SCOTT

Map Study Some supporters of the Kansas-Nebraska bill assumed that by dividing the territory into two parts, Kansas would become slave territory and the Nebraska Territory remain free. **Why might Southerners think slavery could easily be taken into Kansas?**

Americans to be citizens. The Missouri Compromise ban on slavery north of the 36°30′ line, the Court said, was unconstitutional because Congress had no right to ban slavery in the territories.

Instead of settling the slavery dispute, the *Dred Scott* decision made it more bitter. Many Northerners, especially Republicans, flatly opposed the decision. If the decision stood, the Republican party might as well go out of existence, because its basic principle—free soil—had been declared unconstitutional. Southerners, on the other hand, called on the North to obey the decision as the price of the South's remaining in the Union.

Lincoln and Douglas

The *Dred Scott* decision left the nation in a state of almost hopeless confusion about the principle of popular sovereignty. Did the decision forbid the people of a territory to decide whether or not they wanted slavery?

Stephen A. Douglas and Abraham Lincoln were rival candidates in the Illinois senatorial election in 1858. Douglas, a defender of popular sovereignty, was the most prominent Democrat in Congress and hoped to be elected President in 1860. Lincoln, on the other hand, had served only a single term in the House of Representatives. Although Lincoln was not an abolitionist,

CHAPTER 5 The Civil War Era: 1820–1865 **185**

Independent Practice

 Assign Guided Reading Activity 5-3.

Categorizing Using the headings of the subsections as a guide, have students list the major events described in Section 3. **L1**

Map Study *Using Maps*

Answer: The agricultural frontier of the nation moved farther and farther west. Kansas is directly west of Missouri, a slave state.

Map Skills Practice
Ask students to compare the map on page 177 with the map on this page. Ask: What territories were organized from the Mexican Cession? *(Utah and New Mexico territories)*

 NATIONAL GEOGRAPHIC SOCIETY

 **VIDEODISC**

GTV: The American People: Fabric of a Nation

Side 2, Chapter 7
Frames 36349-44369

Title: *Justice is Blind*

Subject: *Dred Scott* decision and the growing national division over slavery

Cooperative Learning Activity

The Lincoln-Douglas Debates To research the Lincoln-Douglas debates, organize the class into groups of four. Have two members from each group research and summarize the position Senator Douglas took in his debate with Lincoln and the other two members research and summarize Lincoln's position. Have each pair combine their ideas into a single page. Groups should present their ideas to the class in the form of a television news special. Tell students to be creative in the format they choose for their news presentation. **L2, L3**

185

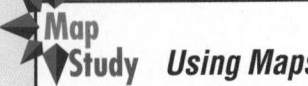

Map Study *Using Maps*

Answer: Missouri (also received three of New Jersey's seven electoral votes)

Map Skills Practice
Ask: What percentage of the popular vote did Lincoln receive? *(almost 40 percent)*

Did You Know?

Abraham Lincoln was famous for his good sense of humor. When someone asked him if he had consulted his cabinet about a particular decision, Lincoln replied, "I never consult my cabinet, they all disagree too much."

📁 Assign Primary and Secondary Source Readings, pp. 8–9: *The Lincoln-Douglas Debates.*

NATIONAL GEOGRAPHIC SOCIETY

VIDEODISC

GTV: A Geographic Perspective on American History

Side 2, Chapter 15
Title: *The Gathering Storm*
Subject: Conflict and compromise before the Civil War (1850–1860)

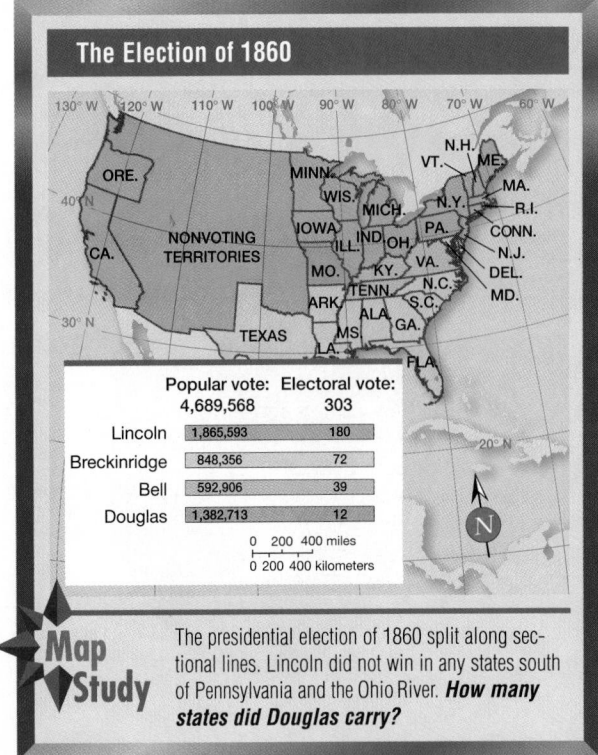

The Election of 1860

	Popular vote:	Electoral vote:
	4,689,568	303
Lincoln	1,865,593	180
Breckinridge	848,356	72
Bell	592,906	39
Douglas	1,382,713	12

0   200   400 miles
0   200   400 kilometers

Map Study The presidential election of 1860 split along sectional lines. Lincoln did not win in any states south of Pennsylvania and the Ohio River. **How many states did Douglas carry?**

he believed that if slavery were confined to its existing area, Southerners themselves might eventually abolish it.

Debates

During the campaign Lincoln and Douglas debated the issues. Douglas attempted to show that Republicans in general—and Lincoln, in particular—were abolitionists in disguise, bent on destroying the Union. During their debate at Freeport, Illinois, Lincoln asked Douglas if the people of a territory could exclude slavery. Douglas was trapped. If he answered "Yes," he would appear to support popular sovereignty, thereby opposing the *Dred Scott* decision. A "yes" answer would improve his chances for reelection as senator, but cost him Southern support for the 1860 presidency. A "no" answer would make it seem as if he had abandoned popular sovereignty, on which he had based his political career. This answer would be welcomed by the South but could cost him the senatorial election.

Freeport Doctrine

To solve this dilemma, Douglas formulated the so-called Freeport Doctrine. Douglas said he accepted the *Dred Scott* decision; however, a territory might effectively discourage slavery if it failed to pass laws to keep enslaved persons under control. By admitting that a territory could practically nullify the *Dred Scott* decision, Douglas won a narrow victory in the senatorial race but lost Southern support for the presidency in 1860. Lincoln lost the election but gained a national reputation.

■ John Brown's Raid

Tensions over the issue of slavery were further heightened by the actions of John Brown, a fiery abolitionist who believed that his mission was to liberate enslaved people and punish slaveholders. On October 16, 1859, Brown, with 21 followers, seized the federal arsenal at Harpers Ferry, Virginia, intending to free and arm the enslaved men and women of the surrounding countryside. The siege ended with the capture and trial of Brown. Found guilty, Brown was hanged on December 2. Many Northerners regarded him as a martyr to the cause of freedom. Southerners regarded Brown's punishment as just. They feared nothing so much as a slave revolt.

■ The Election of 1860

As the election of 1860 approached, Democrats split over the issue of slavery in the territories. A Northern wing of the party nominated Douglas for the presidency and backed popular sovereignty; a Southern wing nominated John C. Breckinridge of Kentucky and supported the *Dred Scott* decision. The Constitutional Union party, composed of former Southern Whigs, nominated John Bell of Tennessee and attempted to avoid the slavery issue.

With such division among their opponents, the door to the presidency stood open to the Republicans. They held that

---

Critical Thinking Activity

Analyzing Effects Organize students into pairs to analyze the effects of the growth of slavery. Tell them that in 1790 there were 698,000 slaves in the entire United States. By 1860 there were 3,954,000 slaves in the South. Ask each pair to list reasons why political compromise over the slavery question would have been easier right after the American Revolution than during the 1850s. Discuss student answers. *(Slavery had spread throughout the South by the 1850s, and the economy of the South depended on slavery. A better political climate for compromise existed after the Revolution.)* **L2**

slavery should be left undisturbed where it existed, but that it should be excluded from the territories. They denounced John Brown's raid and also called for a protective tariff, free homesteads for settlers, and federal funds for internal improvements, including a railroad to the Pacific. Abraham Lincoln, the Republican candidate for President, gained a majority in the electoral college and carried nearly every free state. Breckinridge carried the Deep South, and Bell and Douglas divided the border states.

■ The South Secedes

The Republican victory caused great alarm in the Deep South. Many Southerners felt that they had no other recourse but to leave the Union. They believed that Lincoln's election meant abolition and rebellion by those who were enslaved. Mississippi senator Albert Gallatin Brown told a Southern audience:

❝ *The North is accumulating power, and it means to use that power [for emancipation]. . . . When that is done, no pen can describe, no tongue can depict, no pencil can point the horrors that will overspread this country. . . . Disunion is a fearful thing, but emancipation is worse.* ❞

■ The Confederacy

Between Lincoln's election in November 1860 and his inaugural in March 1861, seven states of the Deep South (South Carolina, Mississippi, Florida, Alabama, Georgia, Louisiana, and Texas) voted for **secession**—withdrawal from the Union. They drafted a constitution for their new alliance—the Confederate States of America—and called on the other slave states to join them.

When Lincoln reached Washington, D.C., in late February 1861, eight slave states remained in the Union. Although most Northerners believed that states did not have the right to leave the Union, few at first wished to fight to force them back in. In his Inaugural Address, Lincoln pleaded that the North and South be "not enemies, but friends" and said that "there need be no bloodshed or violence." Sadly, these hopes were soon dashed.

▲ REPUBLICAN CAMPAIGN POSTER

 CD-ROM

The Presidents: A Picture History of Our Nation
Have students view "Abraham Lincoln" and use the information to write a brief biography to include in their portfolios.

ASSESS

Check Understanding
Assign Section 3 Review as homework or an in-class activity.

Evaluate
Assign Section Quiz 5-3 or use the Test-maker to create a customized test.

Reteach
Have students complete Reteaching Activity 5-3.
Assign Workbook Activity 5-3.

Enrich
Have interested students illustrate the phrase "bleeding Kansas" in an editorial cartoon.

CLOSE

Discuss with students the views Southerners had on secession.

Section 3 ★ Review

Checking for Understanding
1. **Identify** Harriet Beecher Stowe, James Buchanan, Republican party, Dred Scott, Abraham Lincoln, John Brown, Confederate States of America.
2. **Define** platform, secession.
3. **Distinguish** Northern and Southern reactions to the passage of the Kansas-Nebraska Act.
4. **Identify** the viewpoints demonstrated during the Lincoln-Douglas debates.

Critical Thinking
5. **Analyzing Choices** Compile a list of events, other than the election of Lincoln, that might have led to secession.

ACTIVITY
6. Create a bar graph that shows the electoral votes for the presidential candidates in the 1860 election. Write a caption that explains the election results.

Answers to SECTION 3 REVIEW

1. Harriet Beecher Stowe, 183; James Buchanan, 184; Republican party, 184; Dred Scott, 184; Abraham Lincoln, 185; John Brown, 186; Confederate States of America, 187
2. All vocabulary words are defined in the Glossary.
3. Southerners were happy with popular sovereignty clause, but Northerners viewed it as a repeal of the Missouri Compromise.
4. Douglas championed policy of popular sovereignty. Lincoln defended Compromise of 1850.
5. Answers will vary but may include growing abolitionist movement, John Brown's raid, isolation of South from the rest of country
6. Bar graphs will vary. Students should include explanatory captions.

American Literary Heritage

Historical Setting

By 1860 there were about 4 million enslaved African Americans in the United States. When the Civil War commenced, enslaved people made up more than one-third of the South's population.

Background

Spirituals provided a way for African Americans to create unity and to protest the actions of their oppressors. The songs were often sung as work songs. Passed down through the oral tradition, spirituals helped to form an African American culture.

About the Oral Tradition

As with much of the literature derived from the oral tradition, the spirituals have no known authors or originators. Folk songs were produced primarily in cultures in which formal education was limited. Perhaps the spirituals were the results of collaborations among various authors. No one can be certain. Subsequent generations were responsible for preserving in writing some of these songs.

▼ CUMBERLAND LANDING, VIRGINIA, 1862

The struggles that tore the nation apart at mid-century were reflected in much of the period's writing. Spirituals—songs of salvation—provided the African Americans who wrote and chanted them not only with a measure of solace in bleak times but with a means for communicating secretly among themselves under their masters' watchful eye.

Read to Discover

How did spirituals reflect the views of Christianity held by enslaved persons? In what ways did spirituals contribute to a unique African American culture?

Reader's Dictionary

drinking gourd	long-handled utensil; in the poem, it symbolizes the Big Dipper, which points to the North Star
smite	to strike
bondage	slavery

Follow the Drinking Gourd

When the sun comes back and the first quail calls,
Follow the drinking gourd,
For the old man is a-waiting for to carry you to freedom
If you follow the drinking gourd.

Follow the drinking gourd,
Follow the drinking gourd,

For the old man is a-waiting for to carry you to freedom
If you follow the drinking gourd.

The river bank will make a very good road,
The dead trees show you the way,
Left foot, peg foot traveling on
Follow the drinking gourd,
The river ends between two hills

Follow the drinking gourd,
There's another river on the other side,
Follow the drinking gourd,
Where the little river meets the great big river,
Follow the drinking gourd,
For the old man is a-waiting for to carry you to freedom
If you follow the drinking gourd.

Cultural Perspectives

The Origin of African American Spirituals

Historians of music have tried to trace the history of African American spirituals. Much of the imagery is drawn from the Hebrew Scriptures and the New Testament. African traditions are evident in the vocal style, polyrhythmic accompaniment, choral singing, and the call-and-response pattern. Many historians also believe there is a relationship between African American spirituals and hymns popular among rural white Southerners in the late eighteenth century, especially those sung at religious revival camp meetings.

Go Down, Moses

When Israel was in Egypt land,
Let my people go!
Oppressed so hard they could not stand,
Let my people go!

Chorus

Go down, Moses,
Way down in Egypt land
Tell ole Pharaoh,
Let my people go!
Thus say the Lord, bold Moses said,
Let my people go!
If not I'll smite your first-born dead,
Let my people go!
No more shall they in bondage toil,
Let my people go!
Let them come out with Egypt's spoil,
Let my people go!

Swing Low, Sweet Chariot

Swing low, sweet chariot,
Coming for to carry me home,
Swing low, sweet chariot,
Coming to carry me home.
I looked over Jordan and what did I see
Coming for to carry me home,
A band of angels coming after me,
Coming to carry me home.
If you get there before I do,
Coming for to carry me home,
Tell all my friends I'm coming too,
Coming to carry me home.
Swing low, sweet chariot,
Coming for to carry me home,
Swing low, sweet chariot,
Coming to carry me home.

▲ MUSIC ON THE PLANTATION

Responding to Literature

1. What is the message from one enslaved person to another in "Follow the Drinking Gourd"?

2. Which spiritual equates the plight of the African Americans with that of another group? Which group?

3. Describe the mood of the spirituals.

ACTIVITY

4. Prepare a table with the headings "Word or Phrase" and "Symbolizes." Under the first heading, list the following: *drinking gourd, old man, chariot,* and *home.* Under the second heading, write your ideas on what these words and phrases represent in these spirituals.

Developing Student Understanding

Explain that the selections show how enslaved African Americans struggled to achieve a sense of unity and culture during a grim era.

Other Works of African American Folklore

Spirituals were a combination of gospel songs that slaves heard their Christian masters singing and traditional African music. Most spirituals appear in four-part harmony. A collection of spirituals is *The Book of American Negro Spirituals* by James Weldon Johnson and J. Rosamond Johnson. African American author Virginia Hamilton, a Newbery medalist, has published a collection of African American folklore, *The People Could Fly: American Black Folktales.*

History and the Humanities

Excerpts from the following works of the period are included in Glencoe's United States History Enrichment Series: **American Literary Heritage,** pp. 21–25: *Life and Times of Frederick Douglass; Uncle Tom's Cabin* by Harriet Beecher Stowe; *Leaves of Grass* by Walt Whitman

Answers to Responding to Literature

1. The directions are possible instructions on escape routes.
2. "Go Down, Moses"; the Hebrews of ancient Egypt
3. Answers may vary. Appropriate responses should be words like *plaintive, angry, hopeful,* *resigned,* and *religious.*
4. Symbols will vary. Possible responses: *drinking gourd* —the Big Dipper; *old man* —God; *chariot* —the means to get to freedom; *home* —place of freedom.

189

Bellringer

 Before taking roll, project Section Focus Transparency 5-4 or hand out Section Focus Transparency Activity 5-4. Have students answer the questions. Discuss student responses.

Motivating Activity

Present the following announcement to students:

Wanted—Soldiers to fight for the Union! Sharpshooters needed for the 9th Regiment of Boston. Volunteer! Sign up today.

Discuss with students whether they would enlist and why or why not. **L1**

Vocabulary Precheck

Ask students to define each of the "Key Terms." Have a volunteer consult the dictionary for any unfamiliar words. **L1, LEP**

ABCNEWS INTERACTIVE™

VIDEODISC

Lessons of War

Side 1, Chapter 3
Frames 2861-8612

Title: *What Does War Mean?*

Subject: Various definitions and images of war are offered

The Civil War

Setting the Scene

Section Focus

With the Confederate attack on Fort Sumter, war became the solution to the long-standing differences between the North and the South. The goal of the South was to defend its independence. The goal of the North was to restore the Union by force. Each side was determined to do what was necessary to win a quick victory. Neither could predict the terrible cost of the long war that was to come.

Objectives

After studying this section, you should be able to

★ explain the strategies of the North and the South.

★ identify and explain the significance of major battles of the war.

Key Terms

conscription, blockade

▶ **UNION RECRUITMENT POSTER, 1861**

The Civil War began on April 12, 1861, when Southern troops fired on Fort Sumter, a federally controlled military post in the harbor of Charleston, South Carolina. Both sides prepared for battle after the Fort Sumter clash. In the North, Lincoln requested 75,000 volunteers for 90 days to suppress the rebellion and preserve the Union; more responded than could be equipped or trained. In the South, four more states—Virginia, Arkansas, North Carolina, and Tennessee—left the Union and joined the Confederacy.

■ Strategies and Advantages

The Civil War was fought across the continent from southern Pennsylvania in the Northeast to New Mexico in the Southwest.

Almost 3 million soldiers wore the uniforms of the Union or the Confederacy. Countless other men and women supported these troops—on the farms, in the factories, on the battlefields, and behind the lines.

In many ways, the Civil War was the "last of the old wars and the first of the new." Still prominent were muzzle-loading rifles, horse cavalry, and chivalrous respect for the enemy. New were the use of railroads, the telegraph, ironclad ships, and observation balloons. The Civil War also saw the introduction of **conscription,** or the drafting of men for military service. It became the world's first major "total war" in which civilians as well as soldiers were directly affected.

The South's Leaders

The South had the better army, especially during the early years of the war. Because of a strong military tradition, many Confederate

190   UNIT 2 Forging a Nation: 1815–1877

Classroom Resources for SECTION 4

Blackline Masters:
- Reproducible Lesson Plan 5-4
- Guided Reading Activity 5-4
- The Spirit of American Art and Music, pp. 13–14
- Outline Map Resource Book, p. 9
- Workbook Activity 5-4
- Reteaching Activity 5-4
- Section Quiz 5-4

Transparencies:
- Section Focus Transparency 5-4
- U.S. History & Art Transparency 11

Multimedia:
- Lessons of War
- GTV: A Geographic Perspective on American History
- Historic America Electronic Field Trips

officers had attended the United States Military Academy at West Point in New York. Most of the top officers in the United States Army resigned their commissions to fight for the Confederacy, among them Robert E. Lee. After his native Virginia seceded, Lee decided that he could not "raise my hand against my relatives, my children, my home." He rejected Lincoln's offer to lead the Union armies and took command of Confederate forces in Virginia.

Northern and Southern Strategies

The Union's military strategy was simple: **blockade,** or close off, Confederate ports and ruin its economy; invade the South and split it into thirds at the Mississippi River and through Tennessee and Georgia; and capture the Confederate capital at Richmond, Virginia. Southern strategy was even simpler. Southerners would be fighting for their independence on familiar terrain. To win, the South did not have to do anything except hold out against enemy attacks.

Differences in Resources

The North was superior to the South in nearly every resource. The Union had most of the country's factories, railroads, banks, minerals, grain crops, and meat. The Confederacy had less than one-half as many people as the North, and more than one-third of these were enslaved persons. The Confederacy was open to attack along its land borders and its extensive coastline. In addition, with its stress on states' rights, the Confederate central government had difficulty getting needed troops and taxes from member states. In short, the South was ill-equipped to wage war, even in its own defense.

▲ *SUNSET AT FORT SUMTER* by Conrad Wise Chapman, 1864 Chapman produced some of the most brilliant paintings associated with the Civil War. This work displays the artist's use of strong light and shade contrasts. Chapman, an enlisted soldier, was 22 years old when he painted this scene. ***When did the bombardment begin?***

Special Needs Activity

Learning Disability Students with learning disabilities in reading or with other reading comprehension problems seldom use good self-appraisal and self-management skills while they read. Encourage these skills by making students aware of the need for these unconscious activities. As students read "Strategies and Advantages" in Section 4, tell them to be aware of processes they use to help them understand the material. Have them note the number of times they reread phrases or sentences. Explain that rereading is important for understanding. **L1**

TEACH
Guided Practice
Making Generalizations
Ask students to list the strengths and weaknesses of the North and the South and to make a generalization about each side's chances of winning the war. (*North: Strengths — larger population, larger transportation network, more agricultural and industrial resources; South: Strengths — fighting for independence, fighting on home soil, stronger military tradition.*) **L2**

Have students discuss what possible advantages Lincoln gained by forcing the South to make the first move in the war.
Answer to Caption:
April 12, 1861

 NATIONAL GEOGRAPHIC SOCIETY

 **VIDEODISC**

GTV: A Geographic Perspective on American History

Side 2, Chapter 16
Title: *The Civil War*
Subject: Summary of the Civil War and how geography played a role in the outcome (1861–1865)

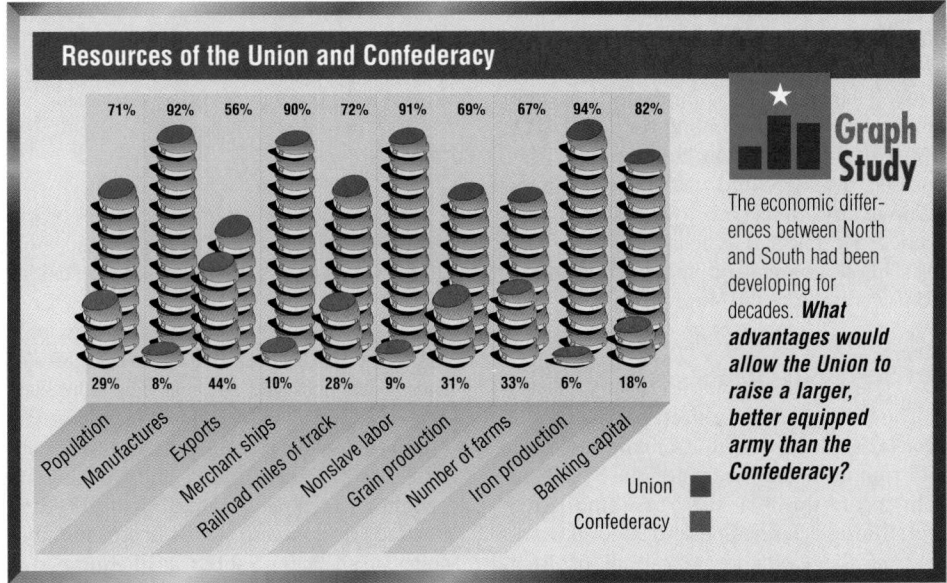

Resources of the Union and Confederacy

Population 71% / 29%; Manufactures 92% / 8%; Exports 56% / 44%; Merchant ships 90% / 10%; Railroad miles of track 72% / 28%; Nonslave labor 91% / 9%; Grain production 69% / 31%; Number of farms 67% / 33%; Iron production 94% / 6%; Banking capital 82% / 18%

Union ■ Confederacy ■

Graph Study

The economic differences between North and South had been developing for decades. *What advantages would allow the Union to raise a larger, better equipped army than the Confederacy?*

Wartime Diplomacy

The principal task of Union diplomacy during the Civil War was to prevent European nations from supporting the Confederacy. The British and French governments, in particular, were openly sympathetic to Southern independence.

The South expected Britain's aid because British textile mills used Southern cotton. To prevent Britain and the South from developing closer commercial ties, President Lincoln ordered the blockade of Southern ports. The South did not let the blockade go unchallenged. The Confederates built an ironclad—a floating fort with slanted sides of iron plates from a wooden frigate originally called the *Merrimac,* but renamed the *Virginia.* The Confederates unleashed the *Virginia* on the Union fleet in Norfolk Harbor. Union officials hurriedly built their own ironclad, the *Monitor.* The battle on March 9, 1862, was the first ever between ironclad warships. Neither ship was able to inflict much damage on the other, but the *Monitor* did keep the *Virginia* from destroying the rest of the Union fleet.

Unable to break the blockade militarily, Southern leaders tried diplomacy. They arranged for British shipyards to build and outfit Confederate warships to prey on Northern shipping. These vessels, however, could not break the Union blockade, nor could Britain's need for cotton. Increased cotton production by Britain's colonies in Egypt and India replaced the loss of Southern cotton and ended the Confederacy's best hope for European support.

■ The War in the East

The first major area of land warfare lay east of the Appalachians and centered on the region surrounding the two capitals, Washington, D.C., and Richmond, Virginia. On June 21, 1861, the Union army invaded Virginia to capture Richmond. About 30 miles from Washington, D.C., 30,000 Northern troops met a smaller Confederate force near a stream called Bull Run. Expecting victory and a quick end to the war, members of Congress and Washington civilians came along to picnic and watch the battle. What they saw was a confusing clash of two untrained armies. Union troops fought well at first, but the Confederates proved better organized. Using the railroad and the telegraph, Confederate officers were able to quickly supply reinforcements.

Sidelight: Military History

Estimates of the effectiveness of the Union blockade show that in general the blockade was a failure until the end of the war. Historians estimate that between 1861 and 1865 only one in every six blockade runners was captured. As a result, half the Southern cotton crop made it through the Union blockade after 1862. By comparison, records show that the British blockade of the United States during the War of 1812 was far more effective in stopping trade.

Together, panic-stricken Union soldiers and civilians fled back to Washington. Indeed, Northern predictions of a quick war could have come true. "Give me 10,000 fresh troops, and I will be in Washington tomorrow," Confederate General Thomas "Stonewall" Jackson said after Bull Run. Jefferson Davis, the Confederate president, however, insisted on a defensive war, and the Union was saved.

After the Northern disaster at Bull Run, Lincoln replaced General Irvin McDowell with General George McClellan, who trained and reorganized the Union army. But in 1862 the Confederates turned back McClellan in several confrontations throughout Virginia.

Antietam

Confederate military success, however, did not extend onto Northern soil. Lee planned to attack Washington, D.C., from the north and destroy Northern morale. In September 1862, his 45,000 troops slipped into Maryland; and Lee split his army into two forces. McClellan, who was to protect Washington by keeping between Lee and the capital, frantically chased after his enemy.

Discovering Lee's plans, General McClellan attacked Lee on September 17, 1862, at Antietam (An•TEE•tuhm) Creek near Sharpsburg, Maryland. In the bloodiest single day of the war, McClellan forced Lee to retreat back into Virginia. The Confederates suffered more than 11,000 casualties. McClellan lost even more, and his army was too damaged to pursue Lee and finish him.

Gettysburg

The following summer, Lee's army defeated Union forces at Chancellorsville. This victory encouraged Lee to head north

▲ *BATTLE OF GETTYSBURG* Lithograph by L. Frang and Company The location of the Battle of Gettysburg was a matter of chance. Commanding officers did not decide on it, but some detached units clashed on the northern side of the town, and then Meade quickly concentrated his army there. **What was the result of the battle?**

Did You Know?

Although Northerners usually referred to a battle by the closest stream or river, such as Bull Run, Southerners named battles after the nearest settlement, such as Manassas.

History AND ART

Have students discuss whether a noble purpose is needed for Americans to fight hard. Are practical goals not enough? Review the goals in previous wars; allude to goals in later wars. **Answer to Caption:** Union troops forced Lee's army to retreat.

Did You Know?

The Civil War was the first war to be documented by photographs. Mathew Brady and other photographers carried their bulky cameras to camps and battlefields, leaving us a record of the war.

Assign The Spirit of American Art and Music, p. 13, Mathew Brady.

Cooperative Learning Activity

Analyzing Strengths and Weaknesses Organize the class into groups of four or five students. Have each group hold a roundtable discussion on the strengths and weaknesses of the North and of the South and how their strategies compensated for or took advantage of these strengths and weaknesses. Students should summarize their conclusions. A recorder for each group should write the summaries and present them to the class. **L1, L2**

Independent Practice

Constructing a Map

Using the maps in this section and an outline map provided in the Teacher's Classroom Resources, ask students to trace or draw a map showing the location and dates of the major Civil War battles. **L1, LEP**

 Use Outline Map Resource Book, p. 9.

 Assign Guided Reading Activity 5-4.

Map Study *Using Maps*

Answer: Gettysburg

Map Skills Practice

How far is Washington, D.C., from Richmond, Virginia? *(about 100 miles)*

ABCNEWS INTERACTIVE™

VIDEODISC

Historic America Electronic Field Trips

Side One, Chapter 8

Title: *Gettysburg Battlefield*

Subject: Tour of site of 1863 Civil War battle

Ask: What was the significance of Gettysburg? *(blocked Lee's efforts to invade North; major defeat for Confederacy in one of the most critical battles of the war)*

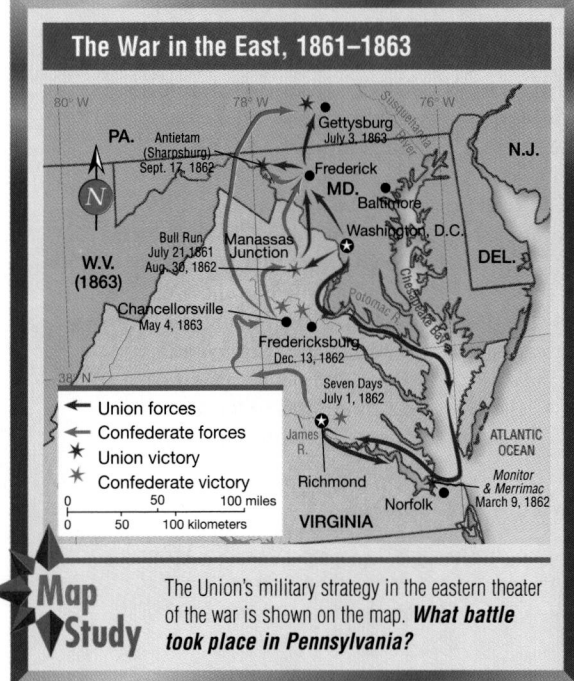

The War in the East, 1861–1863

- ← Union forces
- ← Confederate forces
- ★ Union victory
- ✴ Confederate victory

0   50   100 miles
0   50   100 kilometers

Map Study The Union's military strategy in the eastern theater of the war is shown on the map. **What battle took place in Pennsylvania?**

The Gettysburg Address

Although both sides suffered heavy casualties at Gettysburg, it was a devastating loss of life from which the sparsely populated South could not recover. On November 19, 1863, President Lincoln visited Gettysburg to dedicate the battlefield cemetery and to honor the soldiers buried there. In this Gettysburg address, the President promised that "these dead shall not have died in vain."

■ The War in the West

The second area of land warfare centered in the west, around the Mississippi River and its tributaries. In many ways, the west was critical to victory. If Union armies gained control of the Mississippi River, the Confederacy would lose its western food supplies.

The Union advance began in 1862 when General Ulysses S. Grant attacked Confederate positions at Fort Henry and Fort Donelson on the Kentucky-Tennessee border. When the Confederate commander at Fort Donelson tried to negotiate, Grant's reply created his reputation as a tough, no-nonsense soldier: "No terms except unconditional and immediate surrender can be accepted."

The fall of Fort Donelson, with about 13,000 Confederate prisoners, opened the way for a Union advance south toward a railroad center at Corinth, Mississippi. From there Grant planned to move west along the railroad to capture Memphis, Tennessee, on the Mississippi River.

Shiloh

The Union advance was slowed in April 1862 by the bloody, two-day battle of Shiloh on the Tennessee-Mississippi border. Grant's forces were surprised by the Confederates under General Albert Sidney Johnston. The Union army escaped disaster only when reinforcements arrived and Johnston was killed. Grant lost 13,000 of his 63,000 troops, and Confederate casualties numbered 11,000 of 40,000. Impressed by the determination of his enemy, Grant later wrote that after Shiloh, "I gave up all idea of saving the Union except by complete conquest."

into Pennsylvania. He was shadowed, however, by a Union army under General George G. Meade. An accidental clash between small units at Gettysburg developed into a bloody battle that marked the turning point of the war. As both armies gathered to do battle, Union troops took up positions on the crest of a low ridge. It became the Confederates' task to dislodge them from this high ground. Desperate Confederate attacks—concluding on July 3 in a gallant but suicidal charge across an open field by General George Pickett's troops—were all but repulsed. After 3 days of fighting, Union casualties were more than 23,000. More than 28,000 Confederate soldiers were killed or wounded. "Do not let the enemy escape," Lincoln wired the victorious Meade.

On July 4, Lee retreated into Virginia. Once again, the Union army failed to pursue him. "Our army held the war in the hollow of its hand," a frustrated Lincoln said. "We had only to stretch forth our hands and they were ours. And nothing I could say or do could make the army move."

Critical Thinking Activity

Analyzing Decisions When war appeared inevitable, President Lincoln asked Robert E. Lee to command the Union troops. Lee decided to defend his homeland of Virginia rather than lead the Union forces. To analyze Lee's decision, have students discuss the pros and cons of fighting for the Union. Pros: Lee was neither pro-secession nor pro-slavery, would have more resources, West Point education. Cons: attachment to the Southern culture and to his home in Virginia, would have to fight his friends and neighbors. **L2**

New Orleans

Meanwhile, Flag Officer David Farragut was ordered to capture New Orleans. To reach the city his warships had to move upriver from the Gulf of Mexico past 2 Confederate forts. After failing to destroy the forts, Farragut decided to pass under cover of darkness. As the maneuver began, the moon rose and Confederate forces opened fire. After a 90-minute battle, 20 of the 24 Union ships made it past the forts, and New Orleans surrendered without firing a shot.

By the end of 1862, Union armies occupied all of western Tennessee and were probing south into Mississippi. Other Union forces were advancing north from New Orleans. Only the strongly fortified city of Vicksburg blocked Union control of the river and success of the Union's western strategy.

Vicksburg and Chattanooga

After five attempts to capture Vicksburg failed, Grant began a daring campaign. After marching his army down the west bank of the Mississippi, below Vicksburg, he started inland. The Confederate commander at Vicksburg, thinking Grant was trying to trick him into the field, stayed behind his fortifications.

Moving quickly, Union forces reached Jackson, the capital of Mississippi, almost without opposition. Then Grant turned and fought his way back west to the outskirts of Vicksburg. In 17 days his troops marched 180 miles and won 5 battles against larger forces. Then he laid siege to Vicksburg.

With its citizens starving, Vicksburg finally surrendered on July 4. As a result of the Union capture of Vicksburg and other Mississippi River ports, Texas and Arkansas—the South's leading food producers—were cut off from the rest of the Confederacy.

Union forces then attempted to cut the Confederacy again—through eastern Tennessee and Georgia. The key was Chattanooga, a rail center on the Tennessee-Georgia border. In September 1863, a Union army under General William Rosecrans was

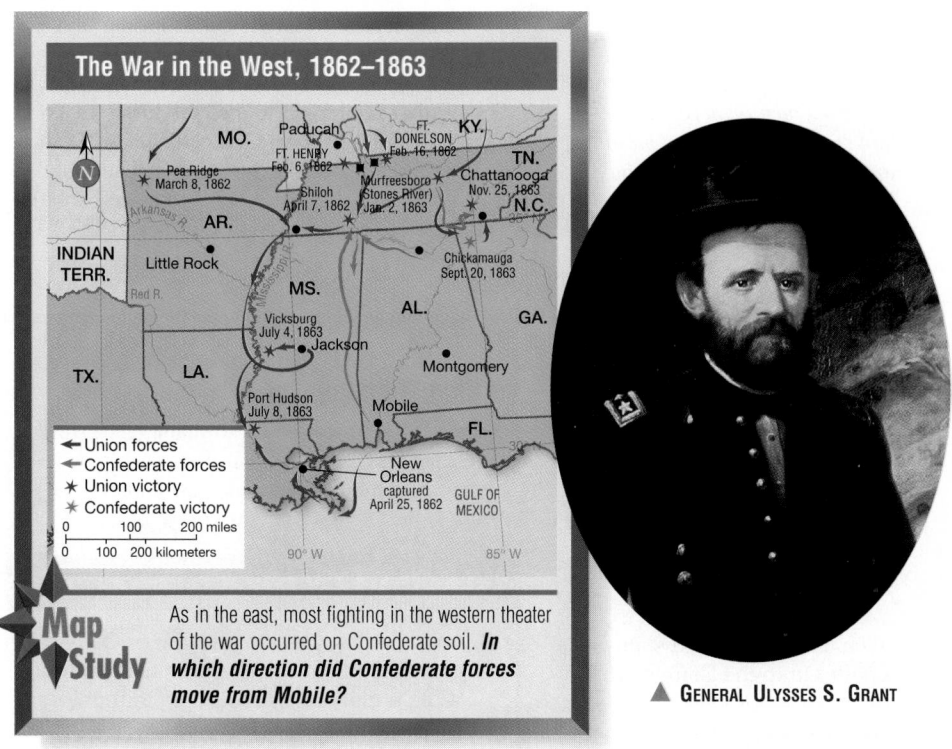

The War in the West, 1862–1863

MO. Paducah
Pea Ridge
March 8, 1862
FT. HENRY
Feb. 6, 1862
FT. DONELSON
Feb. 16, 1862
KY.
Shiloh
April 7, 1862
Murfreesboro
(Stones River)
Jan. 2, 1863
TN.
Chattanooga
Nov. 25, 1863
N.C.
AR.
Chickamauga
Sept. 20, 1863
INDIAN TERR.
Little Rock
MS.
AL.
GA.
Vicksburg
July 4, 1863
Jackson
Montgomery
TX.
LA.
Port Hudson
July 8, 1863
Mobile
FL.
New Orleans
captured
April 25, 1862
GULF OF MEXICO

← Union forces
← Confederate forces
★ Union victory
✴ Confederate victory
0   100   200 miles
0 100 200 kilometers

Map Study As in the east, most fighting in the western theater of the war occurred on Confederate soil. *In which direction did Confederate forces move from Mobile?*

▲ GENERAL ULYSSES S. GRANT

Map Study *Using Maps*

Answer: North

Map Skills Practice

Ask: What southernmost city on the Mississippi River controls the movement of ships from the Gulf of Mexico northward up the river? (*New Orleans*)

For additional map practice, assign Map Transparency Activity 5.

Did You Know?

More soldiers died from sickness during the Civil War than from bullets. Improper food and sanitation caused diarrhea, dysentery, measles, smallpox, typhoid, gangrene, and chicken pox, killing more than 400,000 of the 618,000 who died.

Assign U.S. History & Art Transparency Activity 11, *A Rainy Day in Camp*, by Winslow Homer.

ASSESS

Check Understanding

Assign Section 4 Review as homework or an in-class activity.

Sidelight: Weapons of War

Weapons of war have become more efficient, distant, and impersonal since the time of the American Revolution. During the Revolution, colonists carried smooth-bore muskets. During the Civil War, soldiers used the rifled musket, railroad mines, land mines, and telescopic sites for the first time. The United States government issued a total of 240 military patents. Weapons such as mines made war more impersonal. Modern weapons such as guided missiles have continued this trend.

History AND ART

▲ *OVERLOOKING CHATTANOOGA* by James Walker The Battle of Chattanooga was one of the few battles in which Confederate forces outnumbered Union troops, 70,000 to 56,000. At first, Confederate troops forced their foes to retreat to the city. ***What was the significance of the Battle of Chattanooga?***

badly defeated by Confederate General Braxton Bragg at the Battle of Chickamauga in northwest Georgia. A Union officer described his army's retreat:

> *The march was a melancholy one. All along the road for miles, wounded men were lying. They had crawled or hobbled slowly away from the fury of the battle, become exhausted, and lain down by the roadside to die.*

Rosecrans retreated to Chattanooga, where the Confederates attacked. The Union forces were saved when Grant arrived with reinforcements in late October and drove Confederate forces from the heights around the city. By the end of 1863, only four states—Georgia, South Carolina, North Carolina, and Virginia—remained to be subdued. In early 1864, Lincoln gave General William T. Sherman command in the west and summoned Grant to accomplish what none of his other generals could do—crush Robert E. Lee.

Section 4 ★ Review

Checking for Understanding

1. **Identify** Confederacy, Fort Sumter, Robert E. Lee, Bull Run, George McClellan, Gettysburg, Ulysses S. Grant, Vicksburg.

2. **Define** conscription, blockade

3. **Summarize** the advantages of the North and the South.

4. **Discuss** the Battle of Gettysburg and state why the battle was significant to the Union and Confederacy.

Critical Thinking

5. **Making Inferences** Bull Run changed people's perception of the war. From this reaction, what can you infer about the way people on both sides viewed the war before Bull Run?

ACTIVITY

6. Imagine that you are a Union or Confederate soldier at the Battle of Gettysburg. Write a diary entry recording that day's events and your emotions.

★★★★★★★★★★★★★★★★★★★★★★★★★★★★

Behind the Lines

Setting the Scene

Section Focus

Financial, agricultural, and industrial resources played a major role in determining which side would win the war. People, however, were the most important resource. The war provided opportunities for African Americans and women to make additional contributions to their nation's vital interests.

Objectives

After studying this section, you should be able to

★ discuss behind-the-lines activity in the North and South.

★ explain the wartime roles played by women, African Americans, and Native Americans.

Key Terms

bounty, greenback, martial law, habeas corpus

◀ POWDER HORN

The Civil War was the largest war ever fought on the North American continent. Of the 1.5 million Southern white males of fighting age, about 900,000 served in the Confederate armies. Of 4 million such males in the North, about half fought in the war. In addition, more than 200,000 African Americans fought and served in the Union military, and thousands more performed manual labor.

• •

Footnotes to History

The First Income Tax The North financed much of its war effort through taxes. Included was the nation's first income tax, passed in 1861. Individuals earning between $800 and $5,000 paid 5 percent; those with incomes between $5,001 and $10,000 paid 7.5 percent; and those with incomes above $10,000 paid 10 percent.

More Americans were killed in this war than in any other conflict in the history of the United States. Even in the early battles, the losses were shockingly high. As the war dragged on, the Union suffered terrible casualties but grew stronger. Confederate losses, however, gradually weakened the South's will to fight.

■ Wartime Government Powers

In a long war fought on a vast scale, victors are decided as much by government policies behind the lines as on the battlefield. Both the Union and Confederate governments exerted greatly increased powers in order to raise and supply the armies, finance the war, and suppress antiwar opinion.

CHAPTER 5 The Civil War Era: 1820–1865 **197**

LESSON PLAN
SECTION 5, 197–201

FOCUS

Bellringer

Before taking roll, project Section Focus Transparency 5-5 or hand out Section Focus Transparency Activity 5-5. Have students answer the questions. Discuss student responses.

Motivating Activity

Present the following advertisement to students:

Wanted: Volunteers to help out a refreshment saloon for the city of Philadelphia to welcome battle-bound units. Volunteers will dispense free meals and clothing to soldiers. Staff should expect to serve at least 100,000 soldiers over a period of three to four days. Join us for the Union Cause! Sign up at 312 No. Elm Street.

Ask: What benefit did the above action have on soldiers? (*boosted morale and provided needed meals and clothing*) **L2**

Vocabulary Precheck

Ask students to define each of the "Key Terms." Have a volunteer consult the dictionary for any unfamiliar words. **L1, LEP**

Classroom Resources for SECTION 5

Blackline Masters:
📁 Reproducible Lesson Plan 5-5
📁 Guided Reading Activity 5-5
📁 Supreme Court Case Study 5
📁 Writer's Guidebook Lessons 2-6

📁 Chapter Skills Activity 5
📁 American Portrait 29
📁 Workbook Activity 5-5
📁 Reteaching Activity 5-5
📁 Section Quiz 5-5

Transparencies:
📁 Section Focus Transparency 5-5
📁 Skills Transparency 5

Multimedia:
💿 Testmaker
💿 Powers of the Supreme Court
🎵 American Music: Cultural Traditions

TEACH
Guided Practice

Drawing a Political Cartoon Have students illustrate the phrase "a rich man's war and a poor man's fight" by drawing a political cartoon showing the drafting of men for military service. Have students present their cartoons in class. Then ask: How would you feel about being drafted in time of war? Discuss students' answers. Tell them that during the Vietnam crisis men avoided the draft. **L1**

📁 Assign Supreme Court Case Study 5, *Ex Parte Milligan* (1866).

Did You Know?

The Draft Riot of 1863 began in New York City with the drawing of names for those who had to serve in the Union army. Wealthy residential areas were looted by mobs, made up mainly of recent immigrants from Ireland.

FACT or FICTION?

Everyone in the South solidly supported the Confederacy's cause.

FICTION: There was much resistance to the Confederate cause from Southern Unionists. By 1863 two-fifths of the army had deserted.

Raising the Armies

At first, both North and South relied on volunteers and Lincoln's original 90-day volunteers were replaced by 3-year enlistments. But mounting casualties reduced enthusiasm for the war, and enlistments decreased. As the South's economy collapsed, and the scarcity of clothing and medicine was matched by shortages of food and shelter, Confederate desertions increased. Many Confederate soldiers saw no disgrace in going home to aid their suffering families.

The Draft

Both North and South were forced to draft men for military service. In April 1862, the South began drafting men aged 18 to 35 and later raised the upper age limit to 50. In March 1863, the United States Congress created a military draft in the North.

Draft laws were incomplete and discriminatory. A draftee could avoid service by hiring a substitute, and a Union draftee could buy his way out by paying the government $300. Such provisions aroused criticism that it was "a rich man's war and a poor man's fight."

▲ PRESIDENT ABRAHAM LINCOLN

In the South, some state governors helped their citizens evade the draft. In the North, opposition to conscription led to riots in New York City in July 1863. A resident reported that for four days:

> ❝ . . . there were dreadful scenes enacted in the city. The police were successfully opposed; many were killed, many houses were gutted and burned: the . . . asylum was burned and all the furniture was carried off by women. . . . ❞

To those who enlisted, the North paid a **bounty,** or lump sum of money, of as much as $1,500 for a single 3-year enlistment. This led to the practice of "bounty jumping," whereby a man would enlist, collect his bounty and then desert, only to reenlist somewhere else.

Supplies

The Confederacy faced an uphill struggle to carry out its war effort. The Confederate government encouraged factories to supply troops with arms and ammunition, but the South lacked the industrial capacity to provide other necessities. The South had depended upon the North for, as one observer noted, "everything from a hairpin to a toothpick, and from a cradle to a coffin." As the war dragged on, shortages for the civilian population as well as the Confederacy's armies became commonplace.

The South ran out of almost everything. Shortages in feed for animals and salt for curing meant that little meat was available. Fish and fowl disappeared from meals as tackle and ammunition were used up. Shortages in food were matched by shortages in clothing, medicine, and even shelter.

The North, on the other hand, had a strong industrial base, but the efforts of the Union government to supply its troops were hindered by overcharging and corruption. Army contractors sometimes supplied shoddy clothing, rotten meat, and defective shoes. The productivity of Northern factories was

Sidelight: Baseball

Baseball is said to have originated in a seventeenth-century English game called rounder played by the American colonists. Baseball spread during the Civil War largely because Union soldiers played it for recreation between battles. Confederate prisoners and other troops watched the game and learned it. Before long, people around the country were playing baseball.

★★★ AMERICA'S FLAGS ★★★

The Confederate Battle Flag During the battle of Bull Run (Manassas), soldiers had difficulty distinguishing between the Confederate and Union flags. As a result, Southern soldiers began carrying a new battle flag. It had stars for 11 states and for secession governments in Kentucky and Missouri.

The Seventeenth Flag of the Union came into being with the addition of the 35th star for the admittance of West Virginia into the Union. Like all the Union flags of the Civil War, it retained stars for the seceded Southern states.

★★★★★★★★★★★★★★★★★★★★★★★★

so great, though, that in spite of the graft, Union armies were better equipped than their enemy.

Financing the War

The North was also far more successful than the South in financing the war. About one-fourth of the $4 billion the North needed came from taxation, and the rest from borrowing and issuing paper money. The Union government printed a large amount of currency, but not to the point where it became worthless. It issued $400 million worth of **greenbacks,** paper money that was not backed by gold or silver, but whose value rose and fell with the success of Union armies in the field.

The Confederacy was less able to finance the war than was the North. The South had intended to obtain money by selling cotton to Europe, but the Union blockade prevented this. To raise money, the Confederacy enacted an income tax and demanded 10 percent of all crops produced. Above all, it raised money by simply printing more of it. The Confederate government was able to operate only by forcing its citizens to accept its worthless currency in exchange for supplies.

Civil Rights

Opposition to the war existed from the very beginning in both North and South. President Lincoln and President Davis each suppressed antiwar opinion by curtailing the civil rights of citizens. In parts of their territories, the two leaders declared **martial law,** a form of military rule that includes suspending constitutional guarantees of civil rights. They also put aside the right of **habeas corpus,** which requires that persons who are arrested be brought to court to show why they should be held. Lincoln, in particular, agonized over his decisions to deny citizens their civil rights. He believed, though, that the survival of the nation during an emergency overrode the Constitution.

■ The Emancipation Proclamation

When the Civil War began, there was not universal support in the North for a war to free enslaved persons. In many areas of the North there was open hostility to African Americans, and laws that limited their rights. Slavery still existed in Washington, D.C., and in five states that remained in the Union.

Lincoln, himself, declared that his goal in the war was "to save the Union . . . not either to save or to destroy slavery." While believing that slavery was a moral wrong, Lincoln recognized the constitutional guarantees for slavery and only opposed slavery's extension into the territories.

Pressure Mounts

As time passed, however, Lincoln came under increasing pressure to turn the war into a crusade against slavery. The abolitionists and a group of antislavery legislators in Congress known as Radical Republicans demanded that Southern slaveholders be punished for the war by loss of their property. As the number of battlefield casualties grew, Northerners increasingly began to feel that such bloodshed was justified only if it destroyed slavery. In addition,

CHAPTER 5 The Civil War Era: 1820–1865   **199**

CHAPTER 5
SECTION 5

ABCNEWS INTERACTIVE™

 VIDEODISC

Powers of the Supreme Court

Side One, Chapter 20
Title: *Amendment 13 (1865): Abolition of Slavery*
Subject: Historical paintings and illustrations on the Emancipation Proclamation

 **CURRICULUM CONNECTION**

Music The two songs that many people identify with the Civil War, "Dixie" and "The Battle Hymn of the Republic," ironically were each borrowed from the other side. Dan Emmett, the son of an Ohio abolitionist, wrote "Dixie" as a Northern minstrel tune. Julia Ward Howe wrote the words to "The Battle Hymn" to the melody of a Southern camp-meeting hymn.

History and the Humanities

📁 **American Portrait 29:** Julia Ward Howe.

🎵 **American Music: Cultural Traditions:** Abolition Movement "Get Off the Track!" by the Hutchinson Family Singers (2:48)

Critical Thinking Activity at bottom
Critical Thinking Activity

Analyzing Change Before the 1860s the majority of women working outside their homes or farms were employed as household servants and public school teachers. During the war, however, women performed many of the tasks previously done by men. After the war many women returned to their traditional roles. Why were the changes in women's status so short-lived? *(Answers will vary. Men and women alike were comfortable with the status quo. Many believed they benefited from the status quo. Cultural roles are difficult to change.)* **L2**

Independent Practice

Writing an Essay Have students research and write a two-page report on the Sand Creek massacre of Cheyenne and Arapaho in 1864. Have students include possible reasons why the relationship between the Native Americans and the federal government deteriorated during the Civil War. **L2**

📁 Assign Writer's Guidebook Lessons 2-6.

📁 Assign Guided Reading Activity 5-5.

Teaching American Portraits

Tell students that Clara Barton was called the "Angel of the Battlefield" because she led search parties to look for the wounded. Once a bullet went through her sleeve and killed the patient she was attending. Discuss the contributions of women during the war.

Did You Know?

Elizabeth Blackwell and Clara Barton helped improve conditions in military hospitals. Blackwell, the first female medical graduate in the United States, had received an M.D. from the Geneva (New York) Medical College in 1849.

AMERICAN PORTRAITS

Clara Barton
1821–1912

Clara Barton grew up loving sports and intended to make teaching her career. After 18 years in education, however, she went to work for the U.S. Patent Office. She was in the nation's capital when the guns of the Civil War started blazing.

Though lacking medical training, Clara Barton left her desk job to care for sick and wounded Union soldiers. Traveling to the sites of some of the worst carnage of the war, she even ventured deep into the Confederacy to assist federal forces laying siege to Charleston. She regularly risked her life by passing through the front lines to deliver supplies and nurse the wounded.

After the war—before she founded the American Red Cross in 1877—Clara Barton worked to identify thousands of soldiers who had perished at the Andersonville prison camp in Georgia.

Britain talked of mediating a settlement of the war. Lincoln realized that public opinion in Europe—and in Britain especially—was strongly opposed to slavery, and that no European government would defend the South in a war to end slavery.

Liberty Proclaimed

After Lee's defeat at Antietam in 1862, Lincoln announced that he would free enslaved people in the Confederate states on January 1, 1863. The Emancipation Proclamation, however, did not immediately free anyone, because it applied only to the areas held by the enemy. The Proclamation, however, turned the war into a moral crusade and aroused a new spirit in the North and among enslaved people themselves. As news of the Proclamation spread through the Confederacy, whenever Northern armies occupied Southern territory, thousands of African Americans poured into Union lines.

Slavery in areas where the Emancipation Proclamation did not apply remained a problem, however. About 800,000 enslaved persons lived in the slaveholding border states—Delaware, Maryland, Kentucky, and Missouri—that had remained in the Union. In addition, there were many more in areas of the South that the Union already had conquered. For these areas, Lincoln called for compensated emancipation—setting the enslaved free, but paying the slaveholders. Congress, however, adopted this idea only for the District of Columbia, which had about 3,000 enslaved people. Elsewhere, slavery was ended by the Thirteenth Amendment to the Constitution, ratified in 1865.

African American Soldiers

In the early years of the war, President Lincoln resisted appeals to enlist African Americans in the Union armies because he feared that such a policy would be resented in the border states. After the Emancipation Proclamation, the policy was changed. Nearly 200,000 African Americans enlisted for military service, and an additional 150,000 served in the quartermaster and engineering corps. African American soldiers were commanded by white officers, were paid less, and were segregated from white troops, who often resented them. Many African American regiments distinguished themselves in combat, however, and 23 soldiers won the Congressional Medal of Honor during the war.

Until the very end of the war, the South refused to accept African Americans for military service. Confederate armies, however,

Cooperative Learning Activity

Popular Culture Organize students into groups of four or five to research the popular culture of 1861–1865. Among the possible choices are art (Winslow Homer), patriotic prints (Currier and Ives), battle or religious hymns ("Dixie" and the "Cumberland Gap"), or patriotic literature (Edward Everett Hale and John Greenleaf Whittier). Have the groups present their individual reports to the class. Encourage them to use illustrations, recordings, and primary source readings. **L3**

often used enslaved persons to dig fortifications, cook, drive wagons, and perform other labor.

Native Americans and the War

The war also dramatically affected Native Americans. The South acted quickly to gain support, sending commissioners to the Indian Territory to sign treaties. The Cherokee even fought on the Confederate side.

In 1864, the Union sent troops to restore its authority over the Native Americans. Federal victories over forces in Arkansas and in the Indian Territory showed the Native Americans the weakness of their Confederate allies. The North then renegotiated treaties with their nations and took land away from those who had fought for the Confederacy.

■ Women Behind the Lines

The demands the war placed on civilian populations created new roles for women. In both the North and the South, many women for the first time worked as government clerks and factory workers. Some women accompanied the armies in the field, cooking, sewing, and washing.

On Farms and Factories

Southern women were required to run plantations. On smaller farms, women plowed fields and handled other chores.

Southern households became miniature factories, with spinning wheels and looms turning out clothing for the Confederacy.

In the North

Although most Northern women did not suffer from invading armies, they also were deeply affected by the war. In the North, the mechanical reaper and the sulky plow—where the operator rode on top of the plow itself rather than pushed it from behind—allowed women to take the place of husbands and sons. Industry's need for labor opened other opportunities in Northern factories. Many women needed such work to support their families.

On the Battlefield

Nurses were exposed to the worst horrors of war. Dorothea Dix became superintendent of female nurses in the Union army and in this position fought corruption and prejudice against her sex. Even more effective in widening the role of women in hospitals was Clara Barton, who later founded the American Red Cross.

Women also played a large part in America's first great private relief organization—the United States Sanitary Commission. This organization collected millions of dollars for projects to improve the living conditions of Union soldiers. It is little wonder that after the Civil War there was a renewed demand for woman suffrage.

Section 5 ★ Review

Checking for Understanding

1. **Identify** Radical Republicans, Clara Barton, Dorothea Dix.

2. **Define** bounty, greenback, martial law, habeas corpus.

3. **State** what factors caused Lincoln to change his war goals to include freeing enslaved persons.

4. **List** the contributions made by African Americans to the war effort on both sides.

Critical Thinking

5. **Cause and Effect**   The war provided women opportunities that were not open to them before. What effect do you think this had on their views about their status in society?

ACTIVITY

6. Create a recruitment poster calling for soldiers to enlist in either the Union or the Confederate army.

Answers to SECTION 5 REVIEW

1. Radical Republicans, 199; Clara Barton, 200; Dorothea Dix, 201
2. All vocabulary words are defined in the Glossary.
3. Answers include: pressure from abolitionists and Radical Republicans; need to justify battlefield casualties; threat of British intervention on behalf of the South.
4. served in military and support services; forced to support Confederate armies in various ways
5. spurred women to seek equality
6. Posters should reflect student creativity and appropriate copy for the era.

ASSESS
Check Understanding

Assign Section 5 Review as homework or an in-class activity.

Evaluate

🔲 🗀 Assign Section Quiz 5-5 or use the Testmaker to create a customized quiz.

Reteach

Ask students to list three sectors of the economy that welcomed women during the Civil War and to explain the jobs women held. Discuss students' answers. *(industry: factory workers; nursing: replaced men in caring for sick and wounded; agriculture: ran plantations and plowed fields)*

🗀 Have students complete Reteaching Activity 5-5.
🗀 Assign Workbook Activity 5-5.

Enrich

Have students write a biographical sketch describing the wartime contributions made by an important minority figure.

CLOSE

Summarize the section. Then discuss with students the effect of having Confederate money that did not have adequate backing of the people of the South during the Civil War.

BUILDING SKILLS
Social Studies Skills

TEACH

Ask: Why is it more difficult to analyze pictures than is at first apparent? Point out that sometimes the photographer's or artist's motivation in making the picture may not be obvious. A supposedly objective historical painting might, in fact, convey a political message. A supposedly candid photo may be computer-enhanced (or carefully composed, as were some Civil War photos in which the photographers rearranged bodies to influence viewers.)

CURRICULUM CONNECTION

Economics Both the Union and the Confederacy raised taxes and borrowed to help pay war expenses. They also printed large amounts of paper money. Dollar U.S. "greenbacks" decreased in value to 39 cents by 1864. Some Confederate treasury notes were worth only 1.6 cents by early 1865.

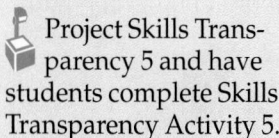 Project Skills Transparency 5 and have students complete Skills Transparency Activity 5.

Use Chapter Skills Activity 5 to reinforce students' understanding of the skill.

Analyzing Illustrations

▲ COMPANY E, 4TH U.S. INFANTRY

The photographs and illustrations that appear throughout this book contain special information. They aid in your understanding of each chapter. The pictures identify the focus of the material, and they make the book more interesting.

Learning the Skill

Look carefully at each picture to analyze its content. The steps you can take to analyze the picture are simple.

1. Look at the picture to get a general sense of what the subject is about. The picture could give useful evidence about aspects of daily life.
2. Read the caption that goes with each picture or group of pictures.
3. Decide if the picture is a drawing, a painting, or a photograph. (There will be no photographs before the middle of the 1800s when photography was developed.)
4. Decide, if possible, whether a drawing or a painting was done by someone who lived at the time or someone who lived at a later time.
5. Decide whether a drawing is a posed portrait or an unposed photograph.

6. Consider the main theme and the general message of the picture.
7. Identify the main focus of the picture or the illustration.
8. Consider how the figures in the picture support the main theme.
9. Consider how the use of color or lack of color supports the theme of the picture.
10. Decide why you think the picture is used at its location in the book.

Practicing the Skill

1. When was this photograph taken? How do you know?
2. All of the figures in the picture are African American soldiers. What does this tell you about the makeup of the Union army?
3. Study the expressions and the postures of the soldiers. What information does this give you?

APPLYING THE SKILL

4. Create a collage of Civil War paintings and photographs. Write a caption that identifies each illustration's main theme.

202

Answers to Practicing the Skill

1. during the Civil War era; soldiers are wearing Union uniforms
2. Answers will vary, but students should note that the forces are segregated.
3. Answers will vary. Most students will note

that the expressions are serious or grave and typical of soldiers.
4. Paintings, photographs, and captions will vary. Captions should focus on relevant themes.

202

Ending the War

Setting the Scene

Section Focus

In March 1864, it became Ulysses S. Grant's turn to face the brilliant Confederate general, Robert E. Lee. Lincoln brought Grant east and gave him command of all Union forces. At last the President found a commander who could win the war. The President, however, would not live to see the war's end.

Objectives

After studying this section, you should be able to

★ explain the changes in Union military strategy after Grant took command.

★ discuss the issues in the election of 1864.

Key Term

forage

◀ CONFEDERATE ARMY HAT

General Grant determined that to win the war he would utilize the Union's biggest advantages over the South—its overwhelming superiority in population and in production capacity. To end the South's ability to fight, he would not only defeat Confederate armies, but would destroy them. To end the South's will to fight, he would engage in "total war"—war against civilians and resources as well as against armies.

■ Grant in the East

Moving south into Virginia, in May and June 1864, Grant's force of 120,000 engaged the Confederate army of 60,000 almost continuously. At the Battle of the Wilderness, Lee stopped Grant in a forest where the fighting was so heavy that the woods caught fire, trapping the wounded in the flames and burning them to death. But instead of retreating after a defeat, as previous Union commanders had done, Grant

kept advancing. He attacked Lee at Spotsylvania in a bloody battle that one soldier called "the most terrible twenty-four hours of our service in the war." In early June, Grant attacked Lee again, at Cold Harbor, where he ordered suicidal charges against fortified Confederate positions.

In less than a month, Union forces had suffered casualties greater in number than Lee's entire army. A Union officer protested that "our men have, in many instances, been foolishly and wantonly sacrificed." Grant knew that he could replace his losses while his enemy could not, and he promised "to fight it out along this line if it takes all summer."

In mid-June Lee retreated to Petersburg, south of Richmond, where Grant surrounded the Confederates and their capital and laid siege to the city. In July Lee attempted to break the siege by instructing General Jubal Early to move through Virginia's Shenandoah River valley to threaten Washington, D.C. Grant dispatched the Union cavalry under General Philip Sheridan to

CHAPTER 5 The Civil War Era: 1820–1865   **203**

Classroom Resources for SECTION 6

Blackline Masters:
- 📁 Reproducible Lesson Plan 5-6
- 📁 Guided Reading Activity 5-6
- 📁 Linking Past and Present Activity 5
- 📁 Enrichment Activity 5
- 📁 Reteaching Activity 5-6
- 📁 Workbook Activity 5-6
- 📁 Section Quiz 5-6

Transparencies:
- 🖊 Section Focus Transparency 5-6

Multimedia:
- 💿 Testmaker
- 💿 Lessons of War

LESSON PLAN
SECTION 6, 203–207

FOCUS
Bellringer

📁 Before taking roll, project Section Focus Transparency 5-6 or hand out Section Focus Transparency Activity 5-6. Have students answer the questions. Discuss student responses.

Motivating Activity

Tell students that changes in Union military strategy in 1864 raised the price of the war in terms of human lives. Have students list relevant facts from the section to support this generalization. (*Over the short period of a month, Union forces suffered great casualties. Spotsylvania was one of the bloodiest battles of the war.*) List student responses on the chalkboard and discuss them. As they read the section, tell students to keep in mind the costs of war. **L2**

Vocabulary Precheck

Ask students to define each of the "Key Terms." Have a volunteer consult the dictionary for any unfamiliar words. **L1, LEP**

VIDEODISC

Lessons of War

Side 1, Chapter 4
Frames 8662-11204
Title: *Why Soldiers Fight*
Subject: Discussion and images of what motivates soldiers to fight

TEACH
Guided Practice

Critical Thinking Have students reread "Sherman's March." Discuss Sherman's methods and whether they were extreme. Have students write three paragraphs explaining why civilian guarantees broke down during the Civil War. **L3**

Visualizing **H**istory The city of Richmond is actively dedicated to preserving its rich history. Civil War monuments may be seen in many areas, such as the Richmond National Battlefield Park, which contains sites of seven sieges against the Confederate capital. Meadow Farm, an 1850s living history museum, presents authentic reenactments of major Civil War battles. The Museum of the Confederacy boasts the world's largest collection of Civil War artifacts.
Answer to Caption: to destroy its productive capacity and to bring the horrors of war to the civilian population

Did You Know?

When Sherman entered Savannah he wired President Lincoln: "I beg to present you, as a Christmas gift, the city of Savannah, with 150 heavy guns, plenty of ammunition, and 25,000 bales of cotton."

---

drive the Confederates from the area and told him "nothing should be left to invite the enemy to return." He ordered Sheridan to make the valley "a barren waste." By March 1865, Sheridan had carried out his orders so well, he reported to Grant, that a crow flying across the valley would have to carry its food. Meanwhile, Grant continued his siege of Richmond.

■ Sherman's March

In May 1864, as Grant invaded Virginia, he ordered General William T. Sherman and his 100,000 troops posted in Chattanooga, Tennessee, to engage and destroy the Confederate army in the west. The Confederates were forced to retreat toward Atlanta, Georgia, which Sherman captured in September and occupied until November, when he ordered the city evacuated and destroyed. City officials begged that Atlanta be spared, but Sherman replied:

◀ HISTORIC DISTRICT, RICHMOND TODAY

Visualizing **H**istory

▲ DESTRUCTION IN THE SOUTH By April 1865 many major cities of the Confederacy, including Atlanta and the capital city of Richmond (above), had felt the full force of war. **Why did Sherman burn Atlanta?**

"You might as well appeal against the thunderstorm as against these terrible hardships of war. They are inevitable, and the only way the people of Atlanta can hope once more to live in peace and quiet at home, is to stop the war...."

To divide the South a second time, Sherman adopted Grant's tactics before Vicksburg—strike into enemy territory and **forage,** or live off the land. His army marched southeast and for a month carved a path of destruction 60 miles wide through one of the richest agricultural regions of the South. Sherman reached the Atlantic coast at Savannah, Georgia, and reported to Grant that he had destroyed $100 million worth of property in Georgia—$20 million in military damage and "the remainder is simply waste and destruction."

As he entered Savannah on December 20, 1864, Sherman learned that five days before, outside Nashville, Tennessee, General George Thomas had destroyed the Confederates' western army. The war in the west was over. In February 1865, Sherman left Savannah and marched north through the Carolinas, destroying everything in his path and planning to link up with Grant at Richmond.

■ The Election of 1864

Throughout the war, federal, state, and city elections continued to be held in the North, but the war divided both major parties into War Democrats and Peace Democrats, Radical Republicans and Conservative Republicans. In the presidential election of 1864, the Republican party temporarily changed its name to the Union party to attract Democrats who supported the war.

The Unionists renominated Lincoln for President and chose a War Democrat for Vice President, Andrew Johnson, military governor of Tennessee. The Democrats nominated George McClellan, the popular general whom Lincoln had twice removed from command. But the Democrats drew up a peace platform that branded the war a fail-

Sidelight: Sherman's Legacy

When Sherman marched through Georgia, the weather was warm and dry, allowing his army and cannons to move easily across the countryside. The Confederates hoped in vain for rain to mire the roads and slow the advance. Because of the destruction Sherman caused, his name lives on in the South. During the 1988 Democratic National Convention in Atlanta, a barbecue was held for Ohio delegates. One Atlanta resident is said to have commented, "I never thought I would see the day that I would be lighting a fire in Atlanta for a bunch of people from Sherman's home state."

Linking Past and Present

Mess Call

Feeding the troops has always been a problem of warfare. Various means have been tried to provide soldiers nourishment efficiently.

Then

Pork and Hardtack

One of the more unpleasant features of life in the Civil War was the food. Neither the Confederacy nor the Union enlisted cooks and no training was available to those who received the mess assignment.

When in quarters, a company would receive a government issue of flour, pork, beans, potatoes, and coffee. Initially, six or eight recruits would form a mess team and take turns cooking.

On the march, rations typically consisted of dried salt pork, hardtack (a saltless hard biscuit made from flour), and coffee. Southern soldiers usually went without coffee, and cornmeal was substituted for hardtack. Veteran soldiers found fresh hardtack palatable enough. With age, however, it could become infested with weevils. Some soldiers thought it better to eat it in the dark. Soldiers from both armies frequently supplemented meager rations by stealing crops and livestock from nearby farms.

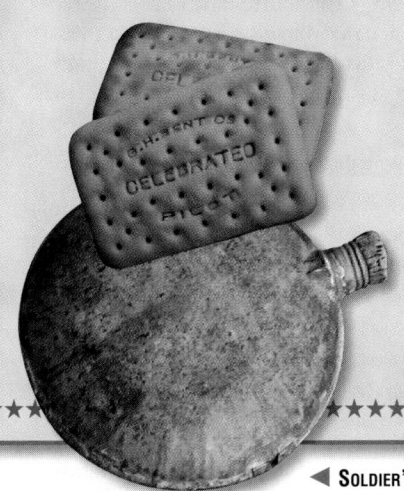

◀ SOLDIER'S CANTEEN

Now

Prepackaged Meals

Rations for the modern soldier are far different. Combat rations, popularly known as C-rations, were first developed in 1940. They consisted of 6 cans of food—3 meat units and 3 carbohydrate units—as well as a powdered drink.

MREs, or Meals Ready to Eat, were distributed to soldiers during the Persian Gulf War. MREs consist of prepackaged foods in airtight containers that are pasteurized by irradiation. Soldiers in combat areas can add hot water to these dehydrated foods to make them edible.

---

ure and called for the immediate restoration of the Union.

Lincoln's chances for victory largely depended on the fortunes of the Union armies in the field. In mid-1864 the war was going badly, and Lincoln was certain that he would be defeated. But Sherman's capture of Atlanta in September, coupled with McClellan's refusal to support his party's platform, gave Lincoln the victory. The voters had decided that "it was not best to swap horses while crossing the river," Lincoln said.

In his second Inaugural Address in March 1865, Lincoln reviewed the causes of the war and hoped for a peace without bitterness. Both sides "read the same Bible and pray to the same God," he noted, so "let us judge not that we be not judged." It may be, Lincoln said, that the war was divine vengeance on both North and South for two centuries of wrong to African American people.

Lincoln concluded his short address by extending charity to the defeated South. He directed his generals to offer the Confederate armies the most liberal terms of surrender and asked Northerners:

> 66 *With malice toward none, with charity for all . . . let us strive on to finish the work we are in, to bind up the nation's wounds, . . . to do all which may achieve and cherish a just and lasting peace among ourselves and with all nations.* 99

In the four years since the untried prairie lawyer delivered his first Inaugural

---

Cooperative Learning Activity

Your Community and the Civil War Organize students into groups of three or four. Have students research the role played by their community during the Civil War. Each student should choose one specific topic to research. Possible topics include support for the Union or Confederacy, Underground Railroad, or supplying the troops. Students might choose to narrow their topics to focus on the African American, white, ethnic, or Native American communities. Encourage students to use the resources of local historical societies, museums, chambers of commerce, and public libraries.

L2

FACT OR FICTION?

Life in prison camps was dangerous because of the conditions and disease.

FACT: After the war, federal government figures showed more than 26,000 fatalities among the 220,000 Confederate prisoners held in the North and more than 22,000 among the 126,000 Union captives in the South.

Linking Past and Present

Discuss with students other situations in which people might eat prepackaged foods. (*Situations might include astronauts in space and hikers and campers in remote areas.*) Find out if any students have eaten prepackaged foods and if so, why. Have them describe their experience.

For additional practice, assign Linking Past and Present Activity 5.

Food of the Times

Union and Confederate soldiers were issued hardtack, or "Army bread." This unpopular food staple was a quarter-inch thick cracker made of unleavened flour.

Independent Practice

Visualizing
Ⓗistory Lee wore his best uniform at Appomattox. Grant's was disheveled and spattered with mud. Nevertheless, the two men, so different in many ways, possessed mutual respect for one another.
Answer to Caption:
Lincoln wanted lenient treatment for the defeated South, and Grant's surrender terms were in that spirit.

Address, his stock had risen. In spite of violent attacks in Congress and in the press, Lincoln inspired affection and trust, as shown by the nicknames "Uncle Abe" and "Father Abraham." Many people had begun to appreciate the ability and strength of character hidden behind Lincoln's homely exterior. One of these was the novelist Nathaniel Hawthorne, who wrote about the President:

“ *There is no describing the lengthy awkwardness nor the uncouthness of his movement; and yet it seemed as if I had been in the habit of seeing him daily, and had shaken hands with him a thousand times in some village street . . . If put to guess his calling and livelihood, I should have taken him for a country schoolmaster as soon as anything else . . . [Yet, I like his appearance] . . . and, for my small share in the matter, would* as [soon] have Uncle Abe for a ruler as any man whom it would have been practicable to put in his place. ”

■ The Final Days

While Lincoln was delivering his second Inaugural Address in March 1865, Grant was pressing in on Richmond and Sherman was marching through the Carolinas. Aware that the situation was hopeless, General Lee advised President Davis that he could no longer defend Richmond. The Confederate government fled south, and Lee's army finally evacuated the city. By April 4, 1865, President Lincoln was able to walk through the streets of the former Confederate capital.

Lee Surrenders

Just days later, Grant's forces cut off Lee's troops as they attempted to unite with other Confederate armies. Grant urged Lee

Visualizing
Ⓗistory
▲ LEE (RIGHT) SURRENDERS TO GRANT AT APPOMATTOX COURT HOUSE Grant ordered Union troops not to celebrate. "The war is over," he said, "the rebels are our countrymen again." *How did Grant's surrender terms compare with Lincoln's attitude toward the South?*

Critical Thinking Activity

Making Comparisons Compare life in the agricultural South with life in the industrial North during the Civil War. Compare clothes, houses, food, types and availability of jobs. *(South: living conditions deteriorated, lack of clothing and mater- ial, lack of workers to plant and harvest crops, cotton crop shifted to food crops, little industry; North: living conditions improved, food and clothes available, industry prospered, jobs increased)* **L2**

to surrender in order to prevent "further effusion of blood." On April 9, 1865, the two men met at Appomattox Court House in central Virginia. Grant offered Lee generous terms: Southern soldiers could go home if they pledged not to fight again. The officers would keep their pistols and the men their horses.

When Lee's army came to lay down their arms, Union troops saluted each division as it appeared. As the Confederate forces marched before them, the Union troops watched silently, with "not a cheer, nor a word, nor whisper of vainglory," one Union officer described it, "but an awed stillness rather, a breath-holding, as if it were the passing of the dead."

Defying orders from President Davis, by June, all other Confederate generals also surrendered. The long, bitter struggle that split the nation finally came to an end.

Lincoln Is Assassinated

President Lincoln did not live to see the end of the war, however. On April 14, 1865, just five days after Lee's surrender, Lincoln was assassinated by John Wilkes Booth, a fanatical Confederate sympathizer. Booth's deed was a tragedy for both North and South, for it removed the one person best equipped to "bind up the nation's wounds." A Richmond newspaper called Lincoln's death "the heaviest blow which has ever fallen upon the people of the South." A young

Southern woman confided to her diary, "The most terrible part of the war is now to come."

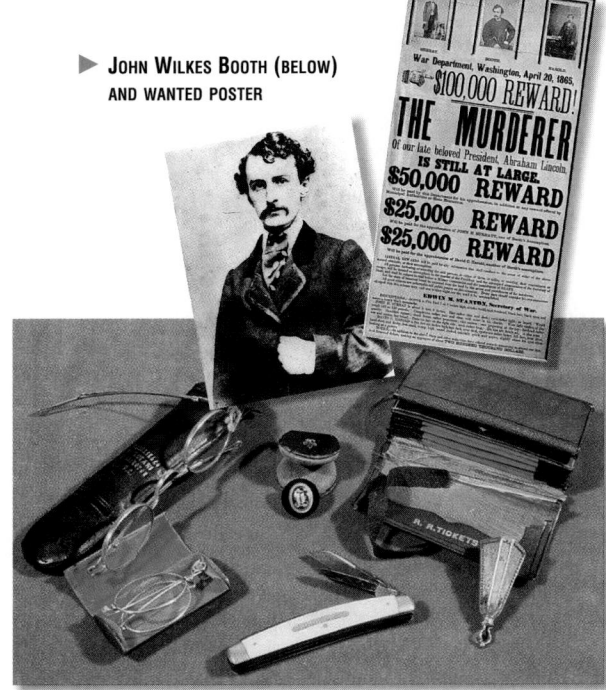

► JOHN WILKES BOOTH (BELOW) AND WANTED POSTER

 ▲ President Lincoln was shot and killed while attending a play at Ford's Theater in Washington, D.C. An eyewitness later recalled that the theater was filled with "the shouts, groans, curses, smashing of seats, screams, and cries of terror." The items shown below the wanted poster and Booth's photo are the contents of Lincoln's pockets the day he died. **Why did many Southerners as well as Northerners mourn the loss of the President?**

Section 6 ★ Review

Checking for Understanding

1. **Identify** William T. Sherman, Andrew Johnson, Appomattox, John Wilkes Booth.

2. **Define** forage.

3. **Explain** the strategy that Grant adopted to defeat the Confederacy.

4. **Examine** how the tactics used by Union generals Philip Sheridan and William Sherman broadened the scope of the war beyond purely military engagements.

Critical Thinking

5. **Analyzing a Quotation** To explain his reelection, Lincoln stated, "It was not best to swap horses while crossing the river." Explain the meaning of Lincoln's quotation and how it applied to him.

ACTIVITY

6. Write a one-paragraph news bulletin describing Lee's surrender to Grant at Appomattox.

CHAPTER 5 The Civil War Era: 1820–1865 **207**

Answers to SECTION 6 REVIEW

1. William T. Sherman, 204; Andrew Johnson, 204; Appomattox, 207; John Wilkes Booth, 207
2. All vocabulary words are defined in the Glossary.
3. used the North's superior numbers and suffered large battlefield casualties to wear down Confederacy
4. included destruction of land, property, and

crops—civilian targets aimed at destroying resources and morale
5. People prefer not to choose an unknown or untested alternative. In Lincoln's case, voters preferred not to change leaders in a time of crisis.
6. News bulletins should depict drama of the event.

ASSESS

Check Understanding
Assign Section 6 Review as homework or an in-class activity.

Evaluate
Assign Section Quiz 5-6 or use the Testmaker to create a customized quiz.

Visualizing History Booth was killed during his capture. **Answer to Caption:** Lincoln's Reconstruction plans were not vindictive.

Reteach
Refer students to the quotation from Abraham Lincoln's second inauguration, on page 205. Discuss how Grant upheld Lincoln's ideas when he asked for Lee's surrender.

Have students complete Reteaching Activity 5-6.

Enrich
Assign Enrichment Activity 5.

CLOSE
Refer students to the chapter concepts. Ask them to recall relevant facts in the chapter that addressed each concept. Discuss students' responses and list them on the chalkboard.

GLENCOE
TECHNOLOGY

VIDEODISC

Use the MindJogger Videoquiz to review students' knowledge.

MindJogger Videoquiz

Chapter 5
Disc 1, Side A

Available in VHS.

Using Vocabulary
Captions should indicate the meaning of the terms.

Reviewing Facts
1. Agrarian: farm western lands. Commercial: use West Coast ports for trade with China
2. Answers include the Battle of the Alamo and the capture of Santa Anna by Houston.
3. The war was precipitated by border clashes, but was the result of Polk's wish to annex California.
4. To please the South: stricter Fugitive Slave Law, popular sovereignty for Utah and New Mexico. To please the North: California admitted as a free state, ending of the slave trade in District of Columbia.
5. Negating clauses of the Missouri Compromise enraged Northerners and conflict broke out as proslavery and antislavery settlers raced into Kansas.
6. to escape poverty and starvation, to avoid political persecution, to gain employment

Using Vocabulary

Photography was first used extensively to record history during the American Civil War. Regard each of the terms below as captions for a pictorial history of the Civil War era. After each term, describe a photograph that would explain the concept or identify the term.

platform   martial law
secession   bounty
conscription   forage

Reviewing the Facts

1. **Specify** both agrarian and commercial reasons that promoted Manifest Destiny.
2. **Name** two important events in the Texas independence movement.
3. **Explain** the reasons for the war between the United States and Mexico.
4. **Classify** the provisions of the Compromise of 1850 into those that appealed to Southern states and those that appealed to Northern states.
5. **Explain** why the Kansas-Nebraska Act resulted in renewed fighting between slavery and antislavery forces.
6. **State** three reasons why large numbers of immigrants came to the United States between 1830 and 1860.
7. **Summarize** the *Dred Scott* decision.
8. **Relate** the issue of popular sovereignty to the Lincoln-Douglas debates.
9. **List** two Southern military advantages and two Northern military advantages at the beginning of the Civil War.
10. **Summarize** the effects the Emancipation Proclamation had on the war.

Understanding Concepts

Geography and Environment

1. Geography often plays a role in defining a nation's borders. Explain the role of geography

in supporting the belief that it was "natural" for the United States to expand westward to the Pacific Ocean.

Conflict

2. How did President Lincoln violate constitutional rights during the Civil War? Explain your reasoning.
3. How did attitudes about the war change after the Battle of Bull Run?

Economic Diversity

4. Explain how economic diversity might have affected Northern and Southern views on slavery. Include in your answer differences between the Northern and Southern economies.

Critical Thinking

1. **Linking Past and Present** The issues of slavery and popular sovereignty divided Americans in the 1850s. What are some issues today that divide Americans? What distinguishes a divisive issue from one that can be solved through compromise?
2. **Analyzing Fine Art** Study the painting on this page entitled *October, 1867* by John Whetton Ehninger and answer the questions that follow.
   a. What does the painting tell you about these individuals and the period in which they lived?
   b. What is your emotional reaction to the painting?

▲ *OCTOBER, 1867* BY JOHN WHETTON EHNINGER

7. Scott was not a citizen and could not bring suit in court. As property, slaves could be taken into the territories.
8. Douglas argued for popular sovereignty to decide whether slavery could be extended into the territories. Lincoln wanted to

confine slavery to the areas where it already existed.
9. Southern: superior military leadership, familiarity with the terrain. Northern: superior industrial production, more people.
10. For the first time, the war was now being fought over human rights.

Understanding Concepts

1. The Pacific Ocean is the "natural" western boundary of the United States.
2. He violated rights of free speech, press, assembly, and habeas corpus.
3. Americans on both sides realized that the war

3. **Evaluating Causes** List five factors that affected the military ability of both the Northern and Southern armies. Rank the items according to their importance in determining the outcome of the Civil War.

History and Geography

The Civil War, 1864–1865

Study the map of the final campaigns of the Civil War. Then answer the questions that follow.

1. **Movement** In which direction did Union forces move after the occupation of Atlanta?

2. **Location** In what state is Appomattox located?

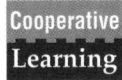 **Cooperative Learning** ## Interdisciplinary Activity: Political Science

Was President Polk a shrewd and visionary leader who expanded the power and borders of the United States, or was he a bully who took what he wanted without regard for other people's rights? You and a partner will evaluate Polk's presidency to answer this question. One of you will be a Polk supporter and the other an opponent. First, work together to compile a list of Polk's achievements. Then work separately and write an evaluation of each action according to your role of supporter or opponent. When you have finished writing, exchange and discuss each other's evaluations. Then present your findings to the class.

Practicing Skills

Analyzing Illustrations

Study the illustration of Harpers Ferry on page 169. Then answer the questions that follow.

1. Is the illustration a drawing, a painting, or a photograph?

2. In addition to the houses, what other kind of buildings can you identify in the village?

3. What colors dominate in this illustration?

4. What mood or feeling is communicated in this illustration?

5. What do you think the artist is trying to express?

The Final Campaigns, 1864–1865

 **Writing ABOUT History**

Using Your Journal

Considering the many things that contributed to the division of the Union, write a paragraph stating your opinion as to whether secession of the slave states could have been avoided.

Practicing Skills

1. painting
2. Possible answers include: church, factory.
3. Students might note green (for the trees and grasslands) or blue (water and sky).
4. a tranquil mood
5. Answers include peacefulness ; show the area in a positive light.

Writing ABOUT History **Using Your Journal**

Opinions will vary but should include specific details supporting students' viewpoints. Invite volunteers to read their paragraphs to the class, and have the class discuss major points.

? ***Chapter Bonus*** **Test Question**

Ask students: Which of the following Americans contributed the most to fulfilling the nation's dreams of "Manifest Destiny"? Give at least one reason for your answer.
Winfield Scott
Zachary Taylor
John C. Frémont
(Answers should be supported with at least one fact.)

would be long and bloody.
4. Students should relate how regional economic strengths and weaknesses affected views.

Critical Thinking

1. Extremely divisive issues are usually emotional and are perceived as either morally right or wrong.

2. **a.** They were self-sufficient and met the challenge of the land.
b. Answers may include respect for their hard work and cooperative spirit.
3. Answers include: wealth, industrial production, military leadership, size of population, support agricultural production.

History and Geography

1. southeast toward Savannah
2. Virginia

Cooperative Learning

Urge students to make a comprehensive list of accomplishments.

Daily Lesson Objectives	Teacher Classroom Resources	Multimedia
SECTION 1 **After Slavery** **1 Day**　pp. 212–216 1. Explain the changes in Southern society that occurred after the Civil War. 2. Discuss the changes that freedom brought to African American families.	Reproducible Lesson Plan 6-1 Concept Mapping Activities 6-A, 6-B *Guided Reading Activity 6-1 *Vocabulary Activity 6 Primary and Secondary Source Readings, pp. 10-11 Workbook Activity 6-1 Reteaching Activity 6-1 *Section Quiz 6-1	Section Focus Transparency 6-1 Chapter Concepts Transparencies 6-A, 6-B Vocabulary PuzzleMaker Testmaker GTV: A Geographic Perspective on American History GTV: The American People: Fabric of a Nation MindJogger Videoquiz
SECTION 2 **Reconstructing the South** **1 Day**　pp. 217–223 1. Compare the Lincoln and Johnson plans for Reconstruction with the plans of the Radical Republicans. 2. Explain how the black codes and the return of former Confederates to power affected Reconstruction.	Reproducible Lesson Plan 6-2 *Guided Reading Activity 6-2 Linking Past and Present Activity 6 Political Cartoons Activity 6 Chapter Map Activity 6 Geography in History Activity 6 Chapter Skills Activity 6 American Portrait 38 Workbook Activity 6-2 Reteaching Activity 6-2 *Section Quiz 6-2	Section Focus Transparency 6-2 Map Transparency 6 Skills Transparency 6 Testmaker GTV: The American People: Fabric of a Nation Powers of the Supreme Court Powers of the Congress The Presidents: A Picture History of Our Nation
SECTION 3 **Restoring Southern Power** **1 Day**　pp. 225–228 1. Describe Southern resistance to Reconstruction. 2. Discuss political and economic change in the South after Reconstruction.	Reproducible Lesson Plan 6-3 *Guided Reading Activity 6-3 Cooperative Learning Activity 6 Critical Thinking Skills Activity 6 Enrichment Activity 6 Workbook Activity 6-3 Reteaching Activity 6-3 *Section Quiz 6-3	Section Focus Transparency 6-3 Testmaker GTV: The American People: Fabric of a Nation Powers of the Congress The Presidents: A Picture History of Our Nation
CHAPTER REVIEW AND EVALUATION **1 Day**	Chapter 6 Test, Forms A and B Spanish Chapter 6 Summary Performance Assessment Activity 6	MindJogger Videoquiz Student Self-Test & Review Software *Chapter 6 Audiocassette Activity and Test

*Also available in Spanish

 OUT OF TIME? If time does not permit teaching the entire chapter, use the Chapter 6 Summary on pages 234–235 and the Chapter 6 audiocassette (English and Spanish) to point out the main ideas of the chapter.

A complete, 1-page lesson plan is provided for each section in the *Reproducible Lesson Plan* booklet.

Key to Ability Levels

Teaching strategies have been coded for varying learning styles and abilities.

L1 Basic activities for all students

L2 Average activities for average to above-average students

L3 Challenging activities for above-average students

LEP Limited English Proficiency activities

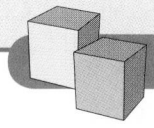

Block Schedule

Block scheduling differs from traditional class scheduling in the amount of time allotted to each period. The extended time frame provided by block scheduling affords you the opportunity to implement a greater number of research-oriented and activity-intense projects to motivate and involve your students. Activities that are particularly suited to use within the block scheduling framework are identified throughout this unit by the following designation:

✓ Performance Assessment Activity

Analyzing the State of Education Organize students into groups of four or five and assign each a different state in existence in 1870. Tell students that by 1870 about 43 percent of children between the ages of 5 and 17 were enrolled in an elementary or secondary school. Ask each group to research the status and quality of elementary education in their assigned state from 1865 to 1876. Have the groups create a checklist at the beginning of the activity. Among the items to consider are number of students, number of teachers, course offerings, and facilities. Ask each group to prepare a poster highlighting its findings. As a class, use the information on the posters to assess the education in the United States in the years after the Civil War.

POSSIBLE RUBRIC FEATURES
- Content
- Research Skills
- Organization
- Creativity
- Written and Visual Communication Skills
- Collaborative Skills

📁 For additional activities, see Performance Assessment Strategies and Activities.

TEACHER'S CORNER

NATIONAL GEOGRAPHIC SOCIETY

NATIONAL GEOGRAPHIC SOCIETY PRODUCTS AVAILABLE FROM GLENCOE

To order the following products for use with this chapter, contact your local Glencoe sales representative or call Glencoe at 1-800-334-7344:

- *The Presidents: A Picture History of Our Nation* (CD-ROM)
- *GTV: A Geographic Perspective on American History* (Videodisc)
- *GTV: The American People: Fabric of a Nation* (Videodisc)

ADDITIONAL NATIONAL GEOGRAPHIC SOCIETY PRODUCTS

To order the following products for use with this chapter, call National Geographic Society at 1-800-368-2728:

- *The Civil War* (Filmstrip)
- *The Westward Movement* (Filmstrip)
- *The American Presidency* (Filmstrip)

CHAPTER 6
★★★★★★★★★★★★★★★★★★★★★★★★★★★★★★★★★★

Reconstruction
1865–1877

► ELECTION CAMPAIGN
RIBBON, 1868

Recording Journal Notes
As students record the events that inhibited racial equality during Reconstruction, ask them to draw parallels and contrasts with events from the mid-1960s to the present.

One outcome of the Civil War was the rise of independent African American churches. By 1870, four—the Colored Primitive Baptist Church, the Colored Methodist Episcopal Church, the African Methodist Episcopal Church, and the Zion Church—had been formed.

Setting the Scene

Focus

Confederate war veterans who returned home after the war found their land devastated. African Americans quickly discovered that freedom did not mean equality. The first order of business for the federal government, however, was to readmit the Southern states to the Union. This proved difficult because white Southerners were bitter and Radical Republicans in Congress worked to keep their party in power.

Concepts to Understand

★ Why **adaptation** to new social conditions was necessary for newly freed men and women and white planters

★ How different groups sought to exercise **power and authority** during the Reconstruction era

Read to Discover . . .

★ why Reconstruction policies differed.

★ what the Compromise of 1877 established.

Journal Notes

As you read the chapter, note how racial equality was inhibited during Reconstruction. Write your findings in your journal.

CULTURAL

• **1866** *Fisk School, later Fisk University, founded in Nashville, Tennessee*

• **1871** *P. T. Barnum opens circus in Brooklyn, New York*

1865	1869

• **1868** *President Johnson impeached by House; Senate fails to convict him*

• **1869** *Federal government completes Great Western Survey*

POLITICAL

✚ EXTRA CREDIT PROJECT

Equality Under the Law The Fourteenth Amendment (1868) protected citizens from being deprived of their rights as citizens. The Fifteenth Amendment (1870) protected voting rights. Both were ratified during Reconstruction. Ask interested students to research specific protections in each amendment. Have students prepare and present charts comparing these with the provisions of the Civil Rights Act of 1964 and the Voting Rights Act of 1965. **L2**

Concept Mapping Activity

On the chalkboard, reproduce the following generalization and concept map. Have students copy it in their notebooks.

Northerners and Southerners move to rebuild the nation.

Adaptation

Power and Authority

📁 To reinforce the two chapter concepts, use Concept Mapping Activities 6-A and 6-B.

🗳 Assign Chapter Concepts Transparency Activities 6-A and 6-B.

History AND ART

Dog Swap
by R.N. Brooke

Artist R.N. Brooke skillfully captured the details of daily life during Reconstruction.

◀ TOY WHEELED HORSE, LATE 1800s

History AND ART

Richard Norris Brooke (1847–1920) was born in Virginia, studied at the Pennsylvania Academy of Fine Arts, and served as a U.S. consul in France in the mid-1870s.

NATIONAL GEOGRAPHIC SOCIETY

VIDEODISC

GTV: The American People: Fabric of a Nation

Side 2, Chapter 8
Frames 44371-49059
Title: *The Dream, Deferred*
Subject: Equal rights

- **1876** *Alexander Graham Bell transmits message on telephone*
- **1879** *The Church of Christ, Scientist, chartered*

1873	1877

- **1873** *New York Stock Exchange closes for 10 days after economic panic begins*
- **1877** *Compromise of 1877 completed*
- **1881** *Kansas passes a prohibition law*

✔ **Performance Assessment**

Reconstruction Policy Organize students into groups of three. Have them imagine they are federal officials touring the South immediately after the Civil War. Ask them to report on geographic conditions; the changing social status of white planters, merchants, poor whites, African Americans; and the changes in labor. Then they should make recommendations to the President for a harsher or more lenient Reconstruction policy. Have groups share their reports with the class. **L3** 📦

After Slavery

FOCUS

Bellringer

🖐 🗁 Before taking roll, project Section Focus Transparency 6-1 or hand out Section Focus Transparency Activity 6-1. Have students answer the questions. Discuss student answers.

Motivating Activity

Present the following letter to students:

July 15, 1867
You, my friends,
  A generous enemy will forgive us for taking a minute to remember what will fade from our memories . . . a lingering look on our Southern homes as they existed before the red hand of war made them desolate.
  Mary Lenox, Columbus, GA

Ask: What do you think this Southern writer was feeling at this moment? *(deep sadness for the loss of life as it had been)* Tell students that during Reconstruction many Southern writers romanticized life in the pre–Civil War South. As they read have them note the changes that would take place in Southern society. **L2**

Vocabulary Precheck

Ask students to define each of the "Key Terms." **L1, LEP**

💿 Use the Vocabulary PuzzleMaker for Chapter 6 to create a crossword puzzle.

🗁 Assign Vocabulary Activity 6.

212

Setting the Scene

Section Focus

The Civil War saved the Union but shook the nation to its roots. The fall of the Confederacy toppled the planter aristocracy that had ruled the South. Also gone was slavery, the labor system that was the basis of Southern society. The end of slavery, however, did not solve the problems that the newly freed African Americans were to face.

Objectives

After studying this section, you should be able to

★ explain the changes in Southern society that occurred after the Civil War.

★ discuss the changes that freedom brought to African American families.

Key Terms

tenant farmer, sharecropper

◀ BADGE WORN BY FREED AFRICAN AMERICANS

𝒲hen Confederate veterans— tired, ragged, and hungry— went home at the end of the Civil War, they returned to a ravaged land. Large areas of land had been systematically laid to waste by the armies of Sherman and Sheridan. One Mississippi woman remembered her father's homecoming after the war:

❝ *He had come home to a house stripped of every article of furniture. The plantation was stripped of the means of cultivating any but a small portion of it. A few mules and one cow made up the stock. . . . He owned nothing that could be turned into money without great sacrifice but five bales of cotton.* ❞

The wreckage stretched from South Carolina's Atlantic coast in the east to Tennessee in the west and from Virginia's Shenandoah Valley in the north through Georgia in the south. It was not only the land that was in ruin, however. Economically, politically, and socially, the South was in total disarray. Confederate money was worthless, and Southern banks were ruined. Government at every level had all but disappeared. There were no courts, no judges, no sheriffs, and no police— no law or authority except when groups of people took matters into their own hands. The war also left the South's transportation system in complete disorder. Roads were impassable, bridges had been destroyed or had washed away, and railroad tracks had been rendered unusable. For planters, the greatest economic blow was the loss of their enslaved workers, an investment worth more than $2 billion. When the workers were freed, the plantation system collapsed.

212   UNIT 2 Forging a Nation: 1815–1877

Classroom Resources for SECTION 1

Blackline Masters:
🗁 Reproducible Lesson Plan 6-1
🗁 Guided Reading Activity 6-1
🗁 Vocabulary Activity 6
🗁 Primary and Secondary Source Readings, pp. 10–11
🗁 Workbook Activity 6-1
🗁 Reteaching Activity 6-1
🗁 Section Quiz 6-1

Transparencies:
🖐 Section Focus Transparency 6-1

Multimedia:
💿 Vocabulary PuzzleMaker
💿 Testmaker
💿 GTV: A Geographic Perspective on American History

New Ways of Life

The devastation of war affected all levels of Southern society. For landowners it meant that their old way of life had been swept away.

The Plight of the Landowners

After his regiment surrendered at Appomattox, the planter Harry Hammond said he had "a pipe, some tobacco, and literally nothing else." Although Hammond owned a large plantation, he could find no one who could afford to buy his land when he put it up for sale. Hammond was saved from total ruin when most of the 300 African Americans on the plantation agreed to stay and work the land. In return for their labor, Hammond provided his formerly enslaved workers with housing, firewood, weekly food allotments, every other Saturday off, and $15 a year in cash after the crops were harvested. Hammond also agreed to provide the loan of a mule and a plow so that the workers could grow their own crops.

Not every planter was so fortunate. Southerners who had invested heavily in Confederate currency and bonds were wiped out financially when Confederate funds became worthless after the war. Many lost their land because of taxes or other debts they could not pay. Some sold their acres to anyone who could pay the outrageously low prices for which Southern farms and plantations were advertised in Northern newspapers. On other plantations and on small farms throughout the South, war widows struggled to hold on to their property and keep it producing.

★★★ AMERICA'S FLAGS ★★★

The 37-Star Flag By 1866 Nebraskans had ratified their state's constitution in accordance with the U.S. Constitution, and the state was admitted into the Union on March 1, 1867.

The Plight of Workers

Poor African Americans and whites realized that social and economic status in the South was tied to the land, but few had money to buy land, even at such low prices. So some became **tenant farmers,** farming land that they rented. The landowners usually received a part of the crop as rent. Some landowners provided the farming tools, seeds, and supplies in order to receive an even larger portion of the crop. Even tenant farming, however, was beyond the means of many poor Southerners, and more often they became **sharecroppers,** persons who worked the owner's land—sometimes using the owner's tools, animals, and seed—and received a share of the crops in return.

Although these arrangements seemed a solution that would provide a living for both workers and landowners, the system contained serious defects. For example, debt-ridden landowners wanted to get the highest possible return, so they pressured tenants to grow only cotton or tobacco, cash crops that paid the most. To prevent depletion of the soil, however, tenants should have planted a variety of crops, including food crops.

Tenants, black and white alike, usually had to buy seed, fertilizer, work animals, and food on credit, at interest rates as high as 40 percent. Thus, no matter how hard they worked, many tenants fell deeply into debt and remained trapped on the land until they paid those debts—no freer to leave than enslaved workers had been. The system often put poor farmers into debt from which they were unable to escape. Nevertheless, the tenant system expanded during these years. As late as 1907, a federal investigator estimated that one-third of the farms in the Cotton Belt depended on the labor of tenants tied to the land by their debts. Years later a former enslaved person recalled the frustration that many African Americans felt about the system:

> ❝ *Lincoln got praise for freeing us, but did he do it? He gave us freedom without giving us any chance to live to ourselves and we still had to depend on the*

TEACH

Guided Practice

Analyzing Principles Ask: Why was the principle of equal citizenship in the Emancipation Proclamation difficult to put into effect during Reconstruction? Discuss their answers. Then ask them to write a paragraph explaining whether equal citizenship is a reality today. **L3**

NATIONAL GEOGRAPHIC SOCIETY

VIDEODISC

GTV: A Geographic Perspective on American History

Side 3, Chapter 1
Title: *The State of the Union*
Subject: A look at the nation's status on its 100th birthday (1865–1890)

Special Needs Activity

Learning Disability One type of learning disability results in inefficient auditory processing. Students with this problem may look like they are not paying attention. Actually, however, they get "lost" in the confusion of language unless certain classroom modifications are made. To help students listen effectively, cue them when you are coming to an important point. For example, during the class discussion about tenancy, sharecropping, and the Freedmen's Bureau, use some key words like "the definition of," "the main point," and "the most important." **L1, LEP**

AMERICAN PORTRAITS

Frederick Douglass
1817–1895

Born enslaved, Frederick Douglass escaped (after one failed attempt) in 1838 and quickly emerged as a leading abolitionist. During the Civil War, he prodded President Lincoln to free African Americans, and he helped organize them to fight for freedom.

After Lincoln was assassinated, Douglass strongly opposed the Reconstruction program of President Johnson. Instead he backed the Radical Republican plan. He used his oratorical ability to insist on full equality for African Americans in all parts of the nation, and he was a vigorous backer of the Fourteenth Amendment. He was particularly outspoken in support of the Fifteenth Amendment, guaranteeing African American men the right to vote. To Douglass, being able to vote meant that African Americans would not only be full citizens but would also have a weapon to protect their rights.

southern white man for work, food, clothing, and he held us through our necessity and want in a state of servitude but little better than slavery. 99

From Slavery to Freedom

Even before the end of the war, some slaveholders noticed a change in the attitude of African Americans as they sensed freedom close at hand. Other planters were stunned, however, when enslaved workers they thought were content left without a word to try to reach the Union lines.

Freedom strengthened African American family ties. Families that had been separated were now reunited. Newspapers carried advertisements from African Americans seeking information about missing relatives:

66 *$200 reward. During the year 1849, Thomas Sample carried away from this city, as his slaves, our daughter Polly, and son, Geo. Washington, to the State of Mississippi, and subsequently to Texas. . . . We will give $100 each for them, to*

any person who assist them, or either of them, to get to Nashville, or get word to us of their whereabouts, if they are alive. 99

Freed men and women, many of whom had only first names, now went about choosing family names. Some chose the name of an ancestor or the name of a hero, like Lincoln. Some adopted their former slaveholder's family name, but many African Americans rejected such an idea. "That's my old rebel master's title," said one young man, "and I don't see any use in being called for him."

Leaving the Plantation

Newly freed workers who remained on the plantations as paid laborers usually refused to live in their old quarters. They objected to the common areas for cooking and washing and sought the privacy of separate cabins. For others, freedom meant leaving the plantation and their former masters and starting a new life. Some settled on the Great Plains and farmed land of their own. Others headed for large cities, hoping to find jobs there.

Cooperative Learning Activity

Social Changes in the South To review the changes in Southern society that occurred after the Civil War, organize students into three groups. Assign each group to represent a segment of Southern society: planters, African American sharecroppers, or poor white farmers and tenant farmers. Have each group review the material about their assigned topic in Section 1. Then have them develop a short play, a dialogue, a radio show, a graphic, or another creative presentation to illustrate social changes in the South. Each group should be prepared to answer questions after their presentation. **L1, L2** 📦

The Freedmen's Bureau

At the close of the war, Congress had created within the War Department a Bureau of Refugees, Freedmen, and Abandoned Lands, which became popularly known as the Freedmen's Bureau. Led by General O. Howard, the Bureau at first gave food and clothing to all families in the war-ravaged South. Its primary mission, however, was to help African Americans adjust to their new freedom. In addition, the Bureau provided medical help and founded 45 hospitals in 14 states.

Education

The Bureau was especially active in the field of education. Sponsored by the Freedmen's Bureau and the American Missionary Association, hundreds of Northern school teachers went South after the war. Many were young women who had been active in the antislavery and women's rights movements, who now dedicated themselves to educating the newly freed African Americans. The teachers frequently found their students just as dedicated to getting an education. One African American teacher from Philadelphia who taught school in Georgia noted that many of her students worked in the fields in the morning and came to class "after their hard toil in the hot sun, as bright and as anxious to learn as ever." At the end of the day, these same classrooms were filled with adults, equally hungry for the education that had been denied to them. The Freedmen's Bureau also worked to establish colleges to train African American teachers, contributing to the founding of Howard University, Hampton Institute, Fisk University, and other colleges for African Americans.

Jobs

In addition, the Freedmen's Bureau tried to find jobs for formerly enslaved workers. It encouraged them to sign labor contracts with planters to provide work in return for wages or a share of the crops. Because most formerly enslaved men and women could neither read nor write, Bureau agents tried to prevent them from being cheated in these contracts, but the Bureau never had enough agents to do this job fully.

Visualizing History

▲ FREEDMEN'S BUREAU SCHOOL The Freedmen's Bureau set up hundreds of schools in the South for African American children and adults. *In what other ways did the Bureau help African Americans adjust to a new life?*

Linking Across TIME

Founded in 1867 by the Freedmen's Bureau, Howard University now consists of 18 schools and 12 research institutes. Not only do the university's libraries hold the finest collection of materials on African American life in the United States, but the institution also has one of the very few laser chemistry laboratories in the eastern part of the country.

Visualizing History

The U.S. Bureau of Refugees, Freedmen, and Abandoned Lands (known as the Freedmen's Bureau) gave more than 21 million rations to impoverished Southerners— white and black. **Answer to Caption:** providing food, clothing, shelter, and medical help

Did You Know?

During Reconstruction thousands of people were able to attend college because of the Morrill Act of 1862. The national government gave each state 30,000 acres of federal land for each member of Congress from that state. States sold the land and used the profits to set up agricultural and other colleges.

Critical Thinking Activity

Assessing Outcomes Imagine that you are a Confederate soldier returning home in 1865. Before the war you were a blacksmith employed on a plantation outside Richmond, Virginia. Describe your home before and after the war, and explain how you are going to support yourself, your wife, and your two children. What will you use for money? (*Answers will vary but should include descriptions of a desolate area and should mention problems such as the lack of employment opportunities, schools, and transportation.*) **L1**

 **Visualizing History**

▲ **A RESETTLEMENT PLAN** After the Civil War, federal commissioners resettled a portion of the freed African Americans on abandoned and confiscated southern land, including the Sea Islands (shown above). *Why were the new tenants forced from the land?*

Land

The dream of most freed men and women was to own land. During the war Union troops had seized large amounts of land from Southern planters, and Congress decided to distribute some of this land to formerly enslaved workers. On the Sea Islands of South Carolina, the Freedmen's Bureau was permitted to sell or lease confiscated land in parcels of up to 40 acres. Many newly freed African American families hoped that 40 acres and a mule would help them start their lives anew. However, when President Andrew Johnson decided to pardon Confederates, he restored their property rights. If their land had been distributed to African Americans, it was returned to its former owners.

General Howard went to the Sea Islands to tell African American farmers that their land was being returned to pardoned Confederates. He urged them to sign labor contracts to work on the land they briefly had owned. Most of the farmers refused to sign contracts, and a large number refused to give up their land. They were evicted against their will—some at bayonet point—by Union troops.

Section 1 ★ Review

Checking for Understanding

1. **Identify** Freedmen's Bureau.
2. **Define** tenant farmer, sharecropper.
3. **List** three drawbacks to tenant farming.
4. **Describe** three changes in family life for African Americans after the war.
5. **Describe** the efforts made by the Freedmen's Bureau in the field of education and labor.
6. **Explain** efforts to provide land to the newly freed African Americans and the outcome of these efforts.

Critical Thinking

7. **Assessing Outcomes** Imagine that you are a newly freed worker living in the South. Write a short account of how freedom affects your life.

ACTIVITY

8. Many freed African Americans placed newspaper advertisements to locate members of their families who had been sold. Write such an ad of at least 50 words that includes pertinent details.

★★★

Reconstructing the South

Setting the Scene

Section Focus

Northern leaders varied in their opinions of the best way to deal with the defeated South. President Lincoln had contended that the task was to restore the nation quickly and without bitterness. Others, however, felt that the South should be punished.

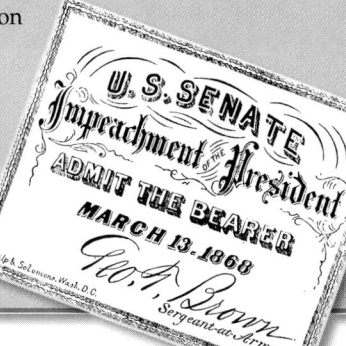

◀ TICKET TO IMPEACHMENT TRIAL

Objectives

After studying this section, you should be able to

★ compare the Lincoln and Johnson plans for Reconstruction with the plans of the Radical Republicans.

★ explain how the black codes and the return of former Confederates to power affected Reconstruction.

Key Terms

amnesty, mandate, disenfranchise, impeach

Reconstruction did involve much more than merely rebuilding and repairing the war damage inflicted on the South. It also meant restructuring Southern society by granting rights to formerly enslaved persons and restoring the nation by readmitting Southern states to the Union.

■ Presidential Reconstruction

Before the end of the war, Congress and President Lincoln struggled with, and frequently clashed over, Reconstruction policies and programs.

Some believed that the South should be punished. President Lincoln argued that the task before the country was to restore the Union.

Lincoln's Plan

Before the war ended, Lincoln began to plan for the peace that would follow the war. Because his primary goal was to restore the Union as quickly as possible, the President favored a generous policy. Except for a few high-ranking Confederate officials, he offered **amnesty,** or pardon, to all Southerners who pledged an oath of loyalty to the United States. Lincoln proposed that when 10 percent of a state's voters in the 1860 presidential election had taken this oath, Congress would readmit the state to the Union.

Lincoln's plan did not address the plight of the newly freed African Americans. Although Lincoln strongly supported the Thirteenth Amendment, for a long time he personally had favored colonization of free African Americans in Africa and the Caribbean. He was willing, though, to let the

CHAPTER 6 Reconstruction: 1865–1877   **217**

LESSON PLAN
SECTION 2, 217–223

FOCUS
Bellringer

🔲 📁 Before taking roll, project Section Focus Transparency 6-2 or hand out Section Focus Transparency Activity 6-2. Have students answer the questions. Discuss student responses.

Motivating Activity

Present the following information to students:

In 1867 and 1868, voters elected delegates to state constitutional conventions in the South. The constitutions they wrote provided for state governments that allowed homesteading so poor people could obtain land and offered help to small farmers deep in debt.

Ask: What might have been your attitude toward the new state government if you had been a plantation owner before the war? **L2**

Vocabulary Precheck

Ask students to define each of the "Key Terms." Have a volunteer consult the dictionary for any unfamiliar words. **L1, LEP**

Classroom Resources for SECTION 2

Blackline Masters:
📁 Reproducible Lesson Plan
📁 Guided Reading Activity 6-2
📁 Linking Past and Present Activity 6
📁 Political Cartoons Activity 6
📁 Chapter Map Activity 6
📁 Geography in History Activity 6

📁 Chapter Skills Activity 6
📁 American Portrait 38
📁 Reteaching Activity 6-2
📁 Workbook Activity 6-2
📁 Section Quiz 6-2

Transparencies:
📁 Section Focus Transparency 6-2
📁 Map Transparency 6
📁 Skills Transparency 6

Multimedia:
🔲 Testmaker
🔘 GTV: The American People: Fabric of a Nation
🔘 Powers of the Supreme Court
🔘 Powers of the Congress
🔘 The Presidents: A Picture History of Our Nation

Guided Practice

Making Comparisons To compare the plans for Reconstruction, have students work in pairs or small groups to create a three-column chart. Ask them to write Lincoln, Johnson, and Radical Republicans across the top of their paper and Federal Government, Readmission to the Union, and Racial Policy down the left side. Have students work together to complete their charts.

Then hold a discussion on the details of each plan. Ask: Which plan seems the fairest as far as civil rights and political freedom are concerned? Why? Which plan allows the least amount of democracy as embodied in the U.S. Constitution? Why? **L1**

Visualizing Point out
Ⓗistory that the
Civil Rights Act of 1866 was the first federal law to define citizenship and to protect civil rights in the states.
Answer to Caption: grant citizenship rights to African Americans and provide means for federal government to intervene to protect these rights

South handle the matter. The President urged, however, that African Americans who could read and write and those who had served in the Union army be allowed to vote.

The Radical Republicans' Plan

Resistance to Lincoln's plan surfaced at once from his Radical Republican opponents in Congress. The Radicals' alternative to Lincoln's plan came in the Wade-Davis Bill of 1864. This legislation proposed putting the South under military rule and required a majority of a state's electorate to take the loyalty oath as a condition for the state's readmission. Lincoln killed this bill with a pocket veto—he let the session of Congress expire without signing the legislation. However, when the states of Arkansas, Tennessee, and Louisiana met the conditions of Lincoln's plan, Congress refused to readmit them to the Union. The President then realized that a peace based on "malice toward none and charity for all" was not possible, and he began to negotiate with Radical congressional leaders. At this critical point, Lincoln was assassinated.

Johnson's Program

Andrew Johnson, who succeeded to the presidency, attempted to carry out Lincoln's Reconstruction policies. He was hampered in this effort because, as an unelected President, he had little popular following. In addition, as a former Democrat, he could not command the support of the Republican majority in Congress, and as a Tennessean and former slaveholder, he offended the Radicals. If these handicaps were not enough, he was viewed by his critics as being self-righteous, hot-tempered, stubborn, and crude.

In the summer of 1865, with Congress in recess, Johnson began to implement his Reconstruction program. His conditions for readmission were that each Southern state abolish slavery, repeal its ordinance of secession, and repudiate its war debts. When Congress returned in December, every state except Texas had followed Johnson's formula and asked to return to the Union. The Radicals, however, expressed alarm because the leniency of Johnson's plan allowed the return of traditional leadership in each of

▼ CARPETBAG

Visualizing
Ⓗistory ▲ CONGRESSIONAL ACTION Controlled by the Radical Republicans, the Joint Committee on Reconstruction maintained the authority of Congress over Reconstruction. *What was the goal of the Civil Rights Bill of 1866?*

Cooperative Learning Activity

Reconstruction Policy Organize the class into groups of six students each. Have students work in pairs, with each pair representing one of the following points of view: Johnson's moderate Reconstruction policy, the Republicans' radical Reconstruction policy, and a Southern Democrat's reactionary Reconstruction policy.

Students should prepare a short defense of their policy. To stimulate discussion, ask: Should the South be left alone to manage its own affairs? Have the groups make their presentations to the class in the form of a television panel discussion. **L2**

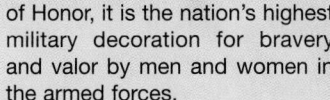
Honoring the Nation's Military Heroes

Since the beginning of history, heads of state have awarded decorations and medals to individuals for bravery or merit during times of war. Until the Civil War, the United States did not have any permanent national military decorations or medals.

Then____

The Medal of Honor

Congress authorized the first permanent U.S. military medal—the Medal of Honor—during the Civil War. Often called the Congressional Medal of Honor, it is the nation's highest military decoration for bravery and valor by men and women in the armed forces.

Campaign medals, also known as war service medals, have been awarded to all ranks of the military for service in every war fought by the United States from the Civil War to the present. The U.S. War Department authorized the Army Civil War Campaign Medal in 1907—42 years after the conflict ended.

Since the inception of the Medal of Honor, more than 3,400 have been awarded. Recipients receive $200 per month for life and a right to burial at Arlington National Cemetery. Nearly one-half of the Congressional Medals of Honor have been awarded to soldiers who fought in the Civil War.

Now____

Military Decorations and Medals

During the twentieth century, the United States has instituted other awards, including the Silver and Bronze stars, dating from World Wars I and II respectively, and the Distinguished Service Medal of the army, navy, and air force.

NATIONAL DEFENSE AWARDS FOR THOSE PARTICIPATING IN ARMED SERVICE ENGAGEMENTS

these states, and Southern voters elected former Confederate officials to power. As a result, Congress refused to seat members from the Southern states.

White Men and Black Codes

The Radicals were also concerned about the status of African Americans in the South. Like Lincoln, President Johnson believed that this was a state matter and that federal jurisdiction stopped with the abolition of slavery. Consequently, the new Southern state governments endorsed the principle stated by the governor of Mississippi, "Ours is and ever shall be a government of white men."

The new Southern state legislatures passed a series of laws known as "black codes" that severely limited the rights of African Americans and made it plain that African Americans were still to have a subordinate status in the South. State governments made few provisions for African Americans' schools.

In no Southern state were African Americans permitted to vote, testify against whites, handle weapons, or serve on juries. In some states, all African Americans were required by law to have steady work. Those who did not were arrested as vagrants and their labor sold to the highest bidder. Some states permitted African Americans to work only as farmers and servants and denied them many of the rights enjoyed by whites.

The North Responds

Northerners were outraged by the black codes, and even Johnson's supporters were alarmed by the actions of the Southern states. Their fears proved well founded. Events in the South increasingly led moderate Northerners to support the Radicals in Congress against the President.

CHAPTER 6 Reconstruction: 1865–1877   **219**

Cultural Perspectives

Civil War Film Motion pictures have created powerful popular images of the antebellum South and Reconstruction. In 1915 the silent film *Birth of a Nation* retold the story of the Civil War and the Ku Klux Klan from a reactionary white Southern viewpoint. The film, considered a technological breakthrough, was boycotted by those protesting against its racism. *Gone With the Wind*, a four-hour dramatization of Margaret Mitchell's book, opened to popular acclaim in Atlanta, Georgia, in 1939. The four-hour film told the story of how two Southern women survived in a war-ravaged South. Historians have criticized its presentation of stereotypes of African Americans and carpetbaggers.

Independent Practice

📁 Assign Guided Reading Activity 6-2.

📁 Assign Workbook Activity 6-2

Food of the Times

Americans in the 1860s and 1870s ate potatoes with almost every meal. Southerners preferred sweet potatoes; Northerners ate white potatoes, also known as Irish potatoes. Until the mid-1860s Americans ate their potatoes boiled, roasted, baked, or fried. Then cooks began preparing potatoes in a new way: french-fried.

 VIDEODISC

Powers of the Supreme Court

Side One, Chapter 21
Title: *Amendment 14 (1868): Civil Rights*
Subject: An introduction to the beginnings of the Montgomery, Alabama, bus boycott

---

In 1865, House and Senate leaders created a Joint Committee on Reconstruction to set congressional policy for restoring the Union. The Joint Committee proposed bills providing economic aid for African Americans and protection of their civil rights. Congress passed these bills, but President Johnson vetoed each one. Finally, in April 1866, Congress passed the Civil Rights Bill, which granted citizenship to African Americans and gave the federal government the power to intervene to protect the rights of freed men and women. When Johnson also vetoed this bill, Congress overrode his veto.

The Fourteenth Amendment

Fearing that the Civil Rights Act might be overturned in court, however, Congress passed the Fourteenth Amendment to the Constitution in June 1866. The amendment defined citizenship to include African Americans and required that no state deny any person "the equal protection of the laws." In addition, the amendment barred many Confederate political leaders from holding public office and prohibited any state from paying Confederate war debts.

President Johnson attacked the Fourteenth Amendment and campaigned against its ratification. As the 1866 congressional elections neared, it was clear that they would reveal whether the President or Congress would control the direction of Reconstruction.

The November election provided an overwhelming victory for the Radicals, who gained control of both the House and Senate. They now had the strength to override any presidential veto and could claim that they had been given a **mandate,** or command, from the public to enact their own Reconstruction program.

■ Radical Reconstruction

Now firmly in control, the Radical Republicans began implementing their policies for Reconstruction.

One goal was to sweep away the new state governments in the South and to replace them with military rule. Other goals

were to ensure that former Confederate leaders would have no role in governing the South and that the freed African Americans' right to vote was protected.

Reconstruction Plans

Radical plans were inspired by self-interest as well as by concern for the freed African Americans and a desire to punish the South. The Radicals expected that African Americans would express their gratitude for freedom by voting Republican. Radical plans also were supported by Northern business leaders, who feared that a Congress controlled by Democrats might lower tariffs or destroy the newly established national banking system.

Many Radicals genuinely cared about the plight of the freed men and women, of course. They had been abolitionists and had pushed Lincoln into making emancipation a goal of the war. They believed in a right to equality and that government must rest on the consent of the governed. Senator Henry Wilson of Massachusetts summarized their position by saying:

❝ *[Congress] must see to it that the man made free by the Constitution is a freeman indeed; that he can go where he pleases, work when and for whom he pleases . . . go into the schools and educate himself and his children; that the rights and guarantees of the common law are his, and that he walks the earth proud and erect in the conscious dignity of a free man.* ❞

Reconstruction Legislation

In March 1867, Congress passed a Reconstruction Act that abolished the South's new state governments and put them under military rule. Except for Tennessee, the former Confederacy was divided into five military districts, each under command of a Union general. To be restored to the Union, each of the states was required to hold a

---

Critical Thinking Activity

Making Inferences Lincoln believed that the Southern states had never legally seceded. Lincoln also believed that he could set the terms for restoring the rights of Southerners. Ask: On what did Lincoln base these beliefs? (*Answers will vary. In responding to the first point, students* *should mention that the Constitution had no provision for secession. In responding to the second point, students should remember that the Constitution gives the President the power to pardon individuals. Since individuals had rebelled, Lincoln could pardon them and restore their rights.*) **L2, L3**

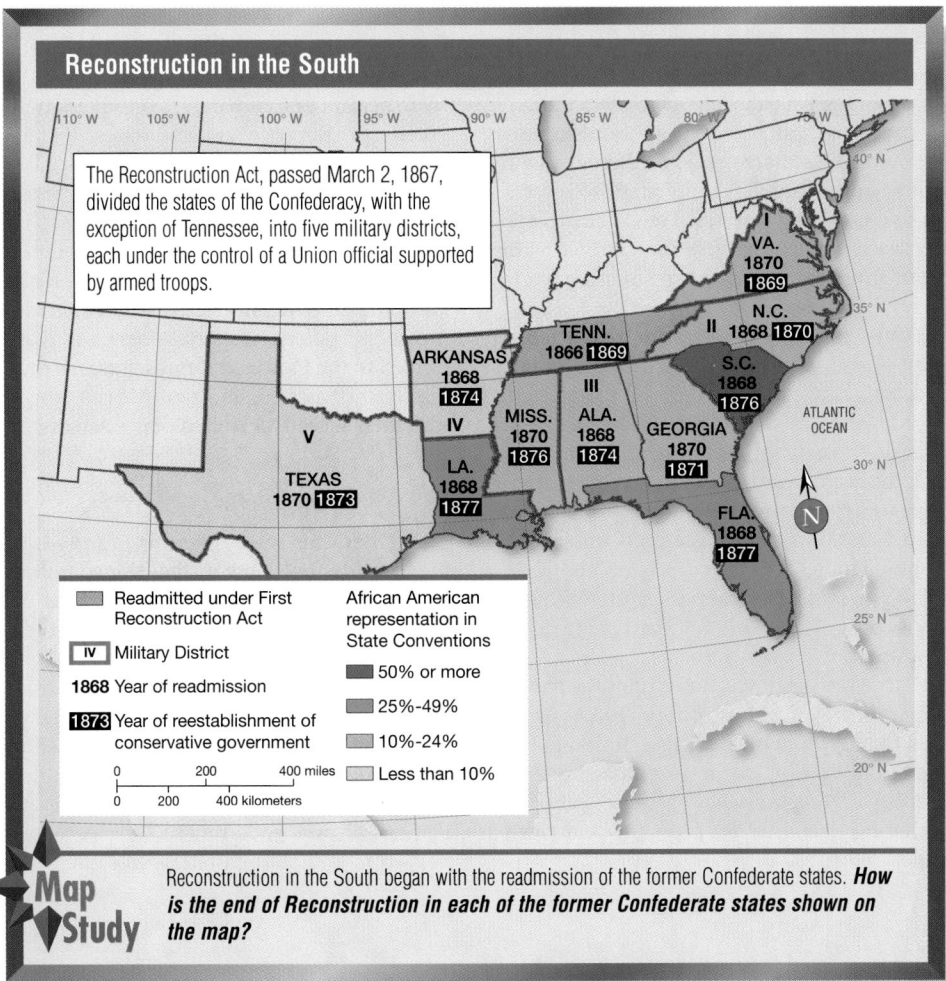

Reconstruction in the South

The Reconstruction Act, passed March 2, 1867, divided the states of the Confederacy, with the exception of Tennessee, into five military districts, each under the control of a Union official supported by armed troops.

VA. 1870 [1869]
N.C. 1868 [1870]
TENN. 1866 [1869]
ARKANSAS 1868 [1874]
S.C. 1868 [1876]
III
IV
MISS. 1870 [1876]
ALA. 1868 [1874]
GEORGIA 1870 [1871]
V
LA. 1868 [1877]
TEXAS 1870 [1873]
FLA. 1868 [1877]
ATLANTIC OCEAN

Legend:
- Readmitted under First Reconstruction Act
- [IV] Military District
- **1868** Year of readmission
- [1873] Year of reestablishment of conservative government

African American representation in State Conventions
- 50% or more
- 25%–49%
- 10%–24%
- Less than 10%

0   200   400 miles
0   200   400 kilometers

Map Study Reconstruction in the South began with the readmission of the former Confederate states. *How is the end of Reconstruction in each of the former Confederate states shown on the map?*

constitutional convention with delegates elected by all adult males and to frame a state constitution that gave African Americans the right to vote. If the voters ratified the constitution, a state government could be elected. Finally, if Congress approved the constitution, if the state legislature ratified the Fourteenth Amendment, and if the amendment became a part of the Constitution, then the state would be readmitted to the Union. By 1868 Louisiana, Alabama, Arkansas, Florida, North Carolina, and South Carolina had met these requirements and regained statehood.

In 1869 Congress protected African American suffrage by passing the Fifteenth Amendment to the Constitution, providing that the right to vote "shall not be denied . . . on account of race, color, or previous condition of servitude." Congress required that states not yet complying with the Reconstruction Act—Virginia, Georgia, Mississippi, and Texas—ratify the Fifteenth Amendment as a further condition for readmission to the Union.

■ Carpetbag Government

By 1870 each of the 10 states under military rule had been readmitted to the Union. However, Radical Reconstruction had **disenfranchised**—or taken the right to vote from—many former Confederates. In addi-

CHAPTER 6 Reconstruction: 1865–1877   **221**

★**Map Study** *Using Maps*
Answer: The year is indicated under the state's name.

Map Skills Practice
Ask: What state was the first to be readmitted to the Union? *(Tennessee)*

For additional map practice, use Map Transparency Activity 6 or Chapter Map Activity 6.

CURRICULUM CONNECTION

Language Arts *Carpetbaggers* were named for the luggage that they brought with them from the North. The word was connected to greedy, unprincipled people even before Reconstruction. In Britain crooked bankers often stashed their loot in carpetbags. So, over time, *carpetbagger* came to mean any kind of embezzler.

Scalawag comes from a term used by western ranchers to describe skinny, useless cattle. The word's origin is unknown, but one suggestion is that it comes from the Latin *scurra vagas*, which means "wandering buffoon."

Assign Geography in History Activity 6.

Project Skills Transparency 6 and have students complete Skills Transparency Activity 6.

Critical Thinking Activity

Making Decisions If you had been a member of the House of Representatives in 1868, would you have voted for or against impeaching President Johnson? Explain the reasons for your choice. *(Students' answers should show an understanding of the issues involved such as the political climate of the time and the Tenure of Office Act.)* Tell students that after leaving the presidency, Johnson ran for election to the Senate three times. The third time he succeeded; and when he entered the Senate chamber, he received a standing ovation. **L1, L2**

tion, many other Southern white men boycotted elections. As a result, government in the Southern states was left to two small groups. One was a group of white Southern Union sympathizers whom Southerners nicknamed "scalawags." Northerners who came South—called "carpetbaggers"—comprised the other group. They gained this derogatory name because they arrived with all their belongings in cheap suitcases made of carpet fabric.

Some carpetbaggers were respectable, honest, and sincerely devoted to the public interest. However, enough of them were greedy and self-seeking so as to give the phrase "carpetbag governments" a reputation for graft, fraud, and waste. One carpetbag governor admitted to accepting more than $40,000 in bribes. Railroad franchises, public lands, and government contracts went to white Northerners and Northern businesses. As a result, Southern state debts rose sharply.

Carpetbag rule was not without achievement, however. Most public funds were spent honestly to encourage rebuilding and industrial development. Carpetbag governments also established public schools, including facilities for African American children.

Many Southern whites despised carpetbag governments. African American voters, however, saw the carpetbag governments as their best hope, and they overwhelmingly voted for Republican candidates. At the height of Radical Reconstruction, 700,000 African Americans could vote in the South compared to 625,000 whites. Even so, no African Americans were elected governors, and only in South Carolina did a state legislature have a majority of African American members. Fifteen African Americans were elected to the House of Representatives during Reconstruction, and two African American men served as United States senators.

The Radicals in Power

The Radicals were determined to reduce the presidential power that Lincoln had assumed during the Civil War and to remove Johnson as an obstacle to their plans. In March 1867, Congress passed the Army Appropriation Act, which severely limited the President's power as commander in chief. Accompanying this legislation was the Tenure of Office Act, which required Senate approval for the President to remove any government official whose appointment had required its consent.

Visualizing History ▲ MEMBERS OF CONGRESS The first African American members of Congress are shown in this Currier and Ives print. The first African American senator, Hiram R. Revels, is at the far left. *What were the major achievements of Southern governments during this period?*

Sidelight: Women's Occupations

While the Civil War gave women a chance to show their skills, few opportunities opened up for them in the postwar years. For example, in 1870 only 5 of the United States' 40,736 lawyers, 67 of 43,874 ministers, and 525 of 62,383 doctors were women. Further, none of these women professionals received salaries approaching those of their male counterparts. In 1870 most of the 1.9 million American women who worked outside the home were farm workers or household servants.

Challenging the Tenure Law

The Radicals knew that President Johnson wanted to remove Edwin Stanton, Lincoln's secretary of war, who remained in Johnson's cabinet but who openly sided with the Radicals. Characteristically, Johnson ignored these warnings. He continued trying to block Radical Reconstruction. Johnson also removed commanders in the Southern military districts who supported the Radicals and, while Congress was in recess, he fired Stanton.

To replace Stanton, Johnson appointed General Grant, but when the Senate reconvened it rejected Grant's nomination, and Grant resigned in favor of Stanton. Outraged, Johnson fired Stanton again—on February 21, 1868—this time replacing him with General Lorenzo Thomas. In answer, Stanton barricaded himself inside his office and refused to leave.

Johnson Impeached

The Radicals came to Stanton's support. Three days later, the House of Representatives voted to **impeach**, or charge, Johnson with "high crimes and misdemeanors" in office. As provided in the Constitution, the President was tried by the Senate. A two-thirds majority vote was needed for a conviction.

For more than two months amid intense public excitement, the Senate debated the President's fate. Radical members of the House, led by Thaddeus Stevens, presented the case against Johnson. Johnson's lawyers argued that Lincoln, not Johnson, had appointed Stanton to the Cabinet and, therefore, that the Tenure of Office Act did not apply.

On May 16, 1868, the Senate voted 35 to 19 to find Johnson guilty, just 1 vote short of conviction. Seven Republican senators were not able to find honest evidence that Johnson was guilty. Under tremendous political pressure, they refused to give in to partisan politics. Although Johnson remained in office for the last few months of his term, he was powerless to challenge the Radicals' policies.

The 1868 Election

The Radical Republicans sought a candidate in the 1868 presidential election who could sweep the country and keep them in power. They chose General Grant. The Democrats nominated Horatio Seymour, former governor of New York, and their platform condemned Radical Republican actions.

Although Grant won easily, by a vote of 214 to 80 in the electoral college, a small shift in the popular vote in key states would have given Seymour the election. Grant won because he was supported by the carpetbag governments of the South and because three Southern states had not yet been readmitted.

Section 2 ★ Review

Checking for Understanding

1. **Identify** Radical Republicans, Andrew Johnson, Fourteenth Amendment, Fifteenth Amendment, Tenure of Office Act.

2. **Define** amnesty, mandate, disenfranchise, impeach.

3. **List** two objections the Radicals had to Lincoln's Reconstruction plans.

4. **Explain** the purpose of the black codes.

Critical Thinking

5. **Determining Cause and Effect** How do congressional elections during a President's term of office act as a barometer of presidential policies and popularity? Give specific examples.

ACTIVITY

6. Create a time line that shows important political events during the Reconstruction era.

CHAPTER 6
SECTION 2

ASSESS
Check Understanding
Assign Section 2 Review as homework or an in-class activity.

Evaluate
 Assign Section Quiz 6-2 or use the Testmaker to create a customized quiz.

Reteach
Have students complete Reteaching Activity 6-2.

Enrich
Have students illustrate the Fifteenth Amendment by drawing a political cartoon.

CLOSE
What problems did Lincoln foresee in reconstructing the Union? Ask: Had Lincoln lived, what might have been the outcome of Reconstruction?

NATIONAL GEOGRAPHIC SOCIETY

CD-ROM

The Presidents: A Picture History of Our Nation

Suggest students view "Andrew Johnson" to discover details of his life after he left the presidency.

Answers to SECTION 2 REVIEW

1. Radical Republicans, 218; Andrew Johnson, 218; Fourteenth Amendment, 220; Fifteenth Amendment, 221; Tenure of Office Act, 222

2. All vocabulary words are defined in the Glossary.

3. Southerners could not be trusted; state governments should not be based on the Ten Percent Plan.

4. The purpose was to subordinate African Americans by reducing and restricting their rights.

5. In midterm congressional elections, voters can show approval or objection to the President by voting for or against members of the President's political party.

6. Time lines should list major events and occurrences.

223

TEACH

Remind students that making predictions is different from guessing and that often very accurate predictions can be made if one takes into account both past and present conditions and information.

Go through the exercise using the Fourteenth Amendment. Ask: Where does the information come from? How does the information help you make an accurate prediction? Was your prediction correct?

 Use Chapter Skills Activity 6 to reinforce students' understanding of the skill.

CURRICULUM CONNECTION

Civics Under the Reconstruction Act, each former Confederate state had to set up a government that guaranteed African American men the right to vote. If the state did not do so, it could not be fully restored to the Union. By 1868 most Southern states had complied. Not until the Fifteenth Amendment was ratified in 1870 did African American men gain suffrage in many Northern states.

Making Predictions

A *prediction* is a foretelling of something before it happens. When you predict something, you are stating what you believe will happen in the future. Good predictions are based on present conditions as well as what has happened in the past.

Learning the Skill

Asking the questions that follow can help you predict the possible results of any historical event:

a. What related conditions existed prior to the event being studied?

b. What caused these conditions?

c. What was the event supposed to accomplish?

d. Based on the answers to these questions, what is your prediction about what will happen as a result of the event?

Note how the questions have been applied in predicting the results of the passage of the Fourteenth Amendment:

a. What related conditions existed prior to the passing of the Fourteenth Amendment?

- African Americans were considered by many to be inferior to whites.
- African Americans were denied rights guaranteed to whites.
- Many people spoke out against the institution of slavery.

b. What caused these conditions?

- the belief of many people that African Americans were inferior
- the belief by many that African Americans should be considered equal

c. What was the amendment supposed to accomplish?

- All persons born and naturalized in the United States would have all the rights due them under the Constitution.

d. Predict what will happen as a result of the passage of the Fourteenth Amendment.

- Passage will cause conflict, unrest, and confusion.

▲ FREED AFRICAN AMERICANS CAST THEIR FIRST BALLOTS

- Equality for African Americans will have to come gradually.

Practicing the Skill

1. Apply the four questions and make a prediction about the success of Lincoln's plan for Reconstruction had he lived to carry out his program.

2. Knowing that Grant's popular vote margin in the election of 1868 was slim, what prediction can you make about Grant's support in Congress?

APPLYING THE SKILL

3. Choose a headline from an article in a current news magazine or a newspaper about an important event that is still unfolding. Make one or more predictions concerning what may happen next. On what basis did you make your predictions? How confident are you of your predictions?

224

Answers to Practicing the Skill

1. Answers will vary. Possible answers include: **a.** The entire way of life in the Confederacy was shattered. **b.** The fighting that occurred there during the war brought on the devastation. **c.** Lincoln's plan was supposed to quickly restore the Union by adopting a generous policy toward the Confederate states. **d.** If Lincoln had lived to carry out his plan, there would have been an easier transition and less divisiveness.

2. Answers will vary, but might include that Grant would encounter problems getting the support of Congress.

3. Predictions will vary, but students should explain the basis of their predictions.

★★★

Restoring Southern Power

Setting the Scene

Section Focus

Reconstruction allowed the South to begin rebuilding its economy but proved to be of only temporary help to African American Southerners. As political and civil rights were restored to former Confederates, they were increasingly denied to African Americans.

Objectives

After studying this section, you should be able to

★ describe Southern resistance to Reconstruction.

★ discuss political and economic change in the South after Reconstruction.

Key Term

segregation

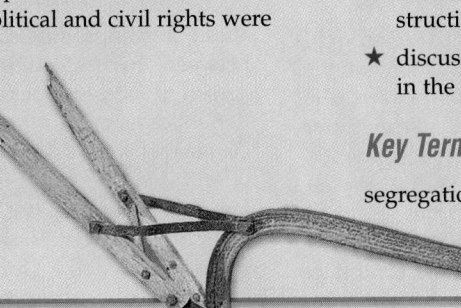

◄ PLOW USED BY SHARECROPPER, 1860s

*U*nable to strike openly at the federal government, opponents of Reconstruction organized secret resistance societies. The largest of these groups was the Ku Klux Klan. Started in Tennessee in 1866, the Klan spread throughout the former Confederacy. Hooded, white-robed Klan members rode in bands at night and threatened carpetbaggers, teachers in African American schools, and African Americans themselves. Using beatings, murder, and other violence to back up their threats, Klansmen broke up Republican meetings, tried to drive Freedmen's Bureau officials out of their communities, and tried to keep freed African Americans from voting.

Although by 1872 it had been greatly suppressed by federal troops, the Klan and similar organizations contributed to the establishment of Southern governments opposed to the Radicals. Democrats, often called "Redeemers," gained control of one

Southern state after another, until by 1876 only South Carolina, Florida, and Louisiana did not have governments controlled by white Democrats, many of whom were former Confederates.

One reason for these Democratic successes in the South was that Northerners were becoming weary of Radical Reconstruction. In 1872 a group called the Liberal Republicans, including several prominent Republican leaders, opposed the Radicals and refused to support Grant for reelection because they considered him unfit for the presidency. The Liberal Republicans joined with the Democrats to nominate newspaper publisher Horace Greeley for President. Although Grant won reelection, the Radicals' power was weakened, and Grant's administration loosened its controls over the South. As fewer troops were sent to protect African American voters during Southern elections, white political power was restored.

LESSON PLAN
SECTION 3, 225–228

FOCUS
Bellringer

Before taking roll, project Section Focus Transparency 6-3 or hand out Section Focus Transparency Activity 6-3. Have students answer the questions. Discuss student responses.

Motivating Activity

Ask: What do you think was the most important gain made by African Americans during Reconstruction? (*Answers will vary and may include education, citizenship, right to vote.*) **L1**

Vocabulary Precheck

Ask students to define each of the "Key Terms." **L1, LEP**

NATIONAL GEOGRAPHIC SOCIETY

 VIDEODISC

GTV: The American People: Fabric of a Nation

Side 3, Chapter 7
Frames 37462-43422
Title: *Enter the Klan*
Subject: Prejudice and intolerance in America

Classroom Resources for SECTION 3

Blackline Masters:
- Reproducible Lesson Plan 6-3
- Guided Reading Activity 6-3
- Cooperative Learning Activity 6
- Critical Thinking Skills Activity 6

- Enrichment Activity 6
- Workbook Activity 6-3
- Reteaching Activity 6-3
- Section Quiz 6-3

Transparencies:
- Section Focus Transparency 6-3

Multimedia:
- Testmaker
- GTV: The American People: Fabric of a Nation
- Powers of the Congress
- The Presidents: A Picture History of Our Nation

TEACH
Guided Practice

Economics Refer students to the graph "Agricultural Production in the South, 1850–1900" on page 455. Ask: After 1870 what general trend occurred? Why? *(Tobacco, corn, and cotton almost doubled because they were cash crops.)* How would this affect agricultural prices in the 1890s? *(Prices would fall.)* To conclude have students write a short paragraph explaining the effects of economic growth on the New South. **L2**

Did You Know?

Best-selling books during Reconstruction included Mary Mapes Dodge's *Hans Brinker and His Silver Skates* (1865), Horatio Alger's *Ragged Dick* (1867), Louisa May Alcott's *Little Women* (1868) and *Little Men* (1871), and Mark Twain's *Innocents Abroad* (1869), *Roughing It* (1872), and *Tom Sawyer* (1876).

ABCNEWS
INTERACTIVE™

 VIDEODISC

Powers of the Congress

Side 1, Chapter 41
Title: *Choosing a President*
Subject: The Constitutional mechanics of electing a President in the Electoral College

■ The Compromise of 1877

The presidential election of 1876 brought the end of Radical Reconstruction. In the campaign the Republicans "waved the bloody shirt," or attempted to stir up bitter memories of the war. Democrats countered by attacking the excesses of Radical Reconstruction and the corruption they claimed was rampant in the Grant administration.

On Election Day, Democratic candidate Samuel J. Tilden, governor of New York, polled 250,000 more popular votes than the Republican Rutherford B. Hayes, Ohio's governor. Tilden was a vote short of a majority in the electoral college, but 20 electoral votes were disputed. One of these electoral votes was from Oregon, and it was challenged on a technicality. The other 19 involved disputed results from the 3 Southern states still under carpetbag rule—Florida, South Carolina, and Louisiana—where charges of massive voting fraud flew.

Electoral Commission

Republicans complained that Democrats had prevented African Americans from voting, and Democrats accused Republicans of using federal troops to raise its vote totals. These 3 states each filed 2 sets of election returns, 1 for Tilden and another for Hayes.

Because the Constitution did not provide for settling such a dispute, Congress appointed a commission of 5 members each from the House, the Senate, and the Supreme Court to settle the matter. Tilden needed only 1 of the disputed electoral

votes to become President, but Hayes needed all of them. Voting strictly along party lines, the commission awarded all 20 disputed electoral votes to Hayes. Congress accepted the verdict on March 2, 1877, 2 days before the inauguration.

Reaching an Agreement

The Democrats were outraged at the commission's decisions, and they were determined not to be defrauded. There were threats of civil war and talk of blocking Hayes's inauguration. The Republicans were just as determined to keep control of the presidency, and they began to talk about a compromise. After negotiations between party leaders, the Democrats agreed to accept the election results and the Republicans agreed to several demands. Democrats were assured that a Southerner would become postmaster general, an important position because of the many federal jobs it controlled. Republicans also promised federal funds for internal improvements in the South. Most important, Republicans agreed to withdraw the remaining federal troops from the South. Without soldiers to protect them, the three remaining carpetbag governments collapsed and Reconstruction officially came to an end.

■ After Reconstruction

In many ways, the South after Reconstruction was similar to the South before the Civil War. As white Southern Democrats returned to power, African Americans lost many of their civil rights.

• •
Footnotes to History

Popular Vote Three times in American history—in the elections of John Quincy Adams in 1824, Rutherford B. Hayes in 1876, and Benjamin Harrison in 1888—the candidate who lost the popular vote won the election.

Cooperative Learning Activity

Events of Reconstruction Organize the class into small groups, each of which should develop an exhibit to illustrate Reconstruction. Groups may focus on an important person; an important event such as the impeachment of President Johnson; the culture of the period such as hair and clothing styles, songs, and available reading material; or an important idea such as what people expected of a Reconstruction policy. Exhibits should include illustrations, short written descriptions, and primary sources. **L1, LEP**

Assign Cooperative Learning Activity 6.

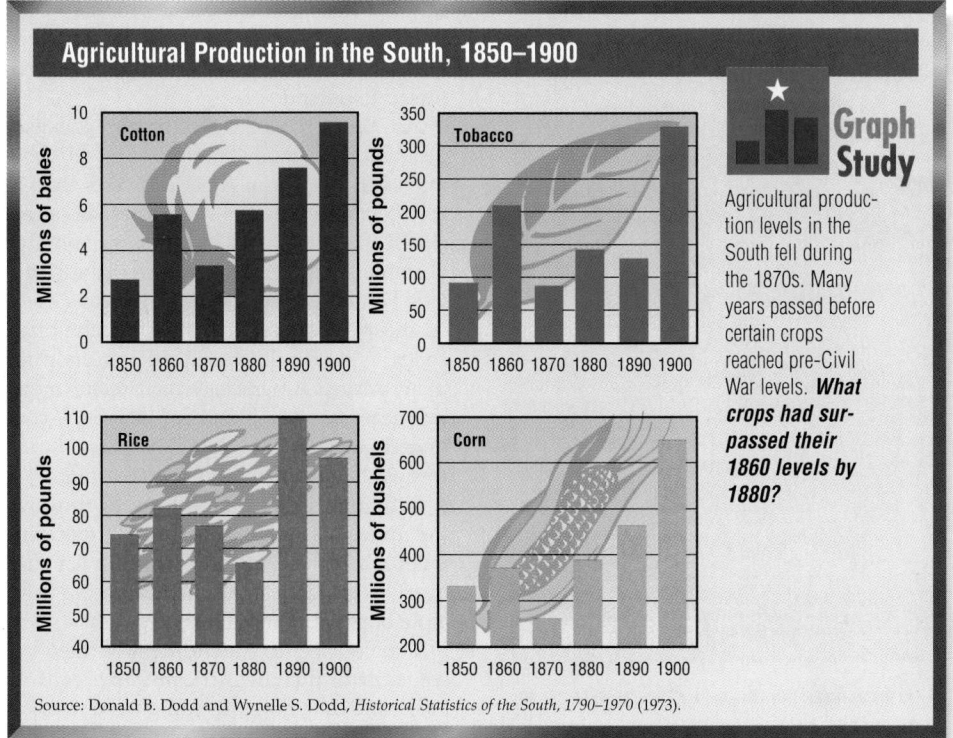

Agricultural Production in the South, 1850–1900

Cotton — Millions of bales (0–10), 1850 1860 1870 1880 1890 1900

Tobacco — Millions of pounds (0–350), 1850 1860 1870 1880 1890 1900

Rice — Millions of pounds (40–110), 1850 1860 1870 1880 1890 1900

Corn — Millions of bushels (200–700), 1850 1860 1870 1880 1890 1900

 Graph Study

Agricultural production levels in the South fell during the 1870s. Many years passed before certain crops reached pre-Civil War levels. *What crops had surpassed their 1860 levels by 1880?*

Source: Donald B. Dodd and Wynelle S. Dodd, *Historical Statistics of the South, 1790–1970* (1973).

Independent Practice

Identifying Point of View
Have students write a brief essay about citizenship from the point of view of one of these: a Northern black factory worker, a Northern white factory worker, a Southern white small farm owner, or a Southern black sharecropper. Ask students to utilize the redefinition of citizenship after the Civil War. **L2, L3**

 Assign Guided Reading Activity 6-3.

Using Graphs

Answers: cotton and corn

Graph Skills Practice
Ask: When did rice surpass its 1860 level? *(1890)*

NATIONAL GEOGRAPHIC SOCIETY

 CD-ROM

The Presidents: A Picture History of Our Nation
Suggest students view "Rutherford B. Hayes" and use the information to write a brief biography to include in their portfolios.

Segregation

For years, in the North as well as the South, **segregation,** or the practice of separating people on the basis of race, had been an accepted way of life. Even before the Civil War, custom in the North had separated African American and white travelers on railroads, coaches, and steamboats and in hotels. Such segregation also existed in Northern schools, churches, hospitals, and cemeteries. After Reconstruction, however, the South began to pass "Jim Crow" laws, which legally segregated blacks from whites in daily life.

Where possible, African Americans protested segregation. These protests helped to integrate the streetcar lines of Washington, D.C.; Richmond, Virginia; and Charleston, South Carolina. In 1875 Congress passed a Civil Rights Act requiring that all people have equal access to public places and transportation facilities. In 1883, however, the Supreme Court ruled that the act was unconstitutional, and by the 1890s Jim Crow laws were common throughout the South.

The "New South"

Despite the South's return to white supremacy, by the late 1870s there was increasing talk of a "New South." An alliance between powerful white Southerners and Northern financiers brought about the economic rebuilding of the South. Northern capital helped to build railroads, and by 1890 the South had twice the railroad mileage that it had had in 1860.

Better transportation encouraged the industrialization of the South. A growing iron and steel industry developed around Birmingham, Alabama, and in North Carolina tobacco processing became big business. Cotton mills appeared in countless small towns throughout the South. Nevertheless, far from populous Northern markets and paying high freight rates, Southern industries faced serious problems. To compete, Southern factory owners generally paid lower wages than did factories in the North.

With these developments in transportation and industry and with the spread of

CHAPTER 6 Reconstruction: 1865–1877   **227**

Critical Thinking Activity

Assessing Outcomes The issues of Reconstruction are as old as the American Republic. The enforcement of the rights of citizens and the problems of economic and racial justice were the central themes in this period. Have these issues been solved in our contemporary society? *(no)* What Reconstruction issues still exist? *(inequalities of economic and racial justice)* **L1, LEP**

For additional practice in using critical thinking skills, assign Critical Thinking Skills Activity 6.

ISAAC and ROSA, Emancipated Slave Children, From the Free Schools of Louisiana, Photographed by KIMBALL, 477 Broadway, N.Y. Entered according to Act of Congress, in the year 1863 by GEO. H. HANKS, in the Clerk's Office of the U. S. for the Sou. Dist. of N.Y.

▲ AFRICAN AMERICAN CHILDREN ATTENDING FREE SCHOOL

sharecropping in agriculture, the South's economy gradually revived. By 1900 Southern industrial production was four times what it had been in 1860.

Few Gains for African Americans

In many ways, Reconstruction aided the South. However, it also caused much bitterness in that region, helping to create the "Solid South"—a voting bloc dominated by the Democrats that did not break up for a century. Reconstruction also provided only limited and temporary help to Southern African Americans, whose rights it professed to defend.

As time passed, abolitionist idealism declined, and many Radicals proved more interested in African American votes than in the welfare of African Americans. Congress closed the Freedmen's Bureau after only five years, and it made no long-range plans to provide what the freed African Americans needed most—land and education. As the black codes revealed, without federal protection, for many African Americans emancipation merely meant a new kind of slavery—continued attachment to the white power structure as sharecroppers and tenant farmers.

Although immediate efforts to improve the lives of Southern African Americans failed, the Fourteenth and Fifteenth Amendments wrote into the Constitution the principle of equality for all people.

The Fourteenth Amendment defined citizenship to include African Americans. It also said that no state could take away a citizen's life, liberty, or property without due process of law, and that every citizen was entitled to equal protection of the laws. The Fifteenth Amendment stated that the right to vote "shall not be denied . . . on account of race, color, or previous condition of servitude."

For many years these amendments remained almost a dead letter, but in the 1900s they provided the legal basis and, in part, the inspiration for movements to obtain for African Americans their full rights as citizens.

Section 3 ★ Review

Checking for Understanding

1. **Identify** Ku Klux Klan, Compromise of 1877, "Solid South."
2. **Define** segregation.
3. **Describe** the strategies and tactics used by the Ku Klux Klan.
4. **Explain** two important concessions that were made in the Compromise of 1877 and the effects on Reconstruction.

Critical Thinking

5. **Distinguishing Fact from Opinion** Describe the images of the South created by motion pictures and novels. What facts from the era refute these images?

ACTIVITY

6. Create a display of photographs or drawings that illustrate the Fourteenth and Fifteenth Amendments.

Answers to SECTION 3 REVIEW

1. Ku Klux Klan, 225; Compromise of 1877, 226; "Solid South," 228
2. All vocabulary words are defined in the Glossary.
3. disguise, nighttime raids, whippings, murder, disruption of meetings, intimidation
4. withdrawal of federal troops, restoration of white-dominated Southern state governments
5. "Uncle Remus" stories portrayed an idyllic time on the plantation. Many African Americans tried to escape to seek a free, independent life.
6. Student selections should indicate an understanding of the amendments.

▲ FOUNDRY, BIRMINGHAM, ALABAMA, 1887

Growth of Southern Manufacturing

Many factors pushed the postwar South toward industrialization. Most important, however, was the surplus labor supply. Widows, orphans, and displaced formerly enslaved workers needed work, and agriculture could not employ them all. This meant there was a large pool of cheap labor. In addition, Northerners and Europeans invested capital in fledgling Southern industries, as did a number of Southerners themselves.

Two industries that made spectacular advances in the postwar South were textiles and tobacco processing. Cotton mills sprang up in the major cotton-growing areas of the South. By 1900 there were 400 mills in operation. The postwar demand for a new product—cigarettes—and the invention of the cigarette-rolling machine in 1880 were the catalysts that fueled the development of the tobacco-processing industry.

▶ SEWING MACHINE, MID-1800S

Other industries based on agriculture or minerals also developed, such as steel manufacturing and making cottonseed oil. Still, despite gains in industrialization, the South remained primarily rural and agricultural until the industrial advances of the mid-twentieth century.

Making the Economics Connection

1. What factors led to the development of industry in the postwar South?
2. What Southern cities of the 1900s are noted as industrial centers?

ACTIVITY

3. Create a table that lists innovations during your lifetime and describes their effects on the economy.

TEACH

In the late 1870s Southern male workers who worked in the coal mines, iron and steel foundries, and cotton mills earned from $1.25 to $1.50 a day. Women and children earned much less but had to work for the family to survive.

Did You Know?

Most foreign investment in the United States in the 1860s and 1870s came from Britain. British investors put a lot of their money into the new American railroads.

FACT OR FICTION?

By the 1870s half of all females who worked outside their homes or farms were household servants.

FACT: In towns and cities the percentage was even greater.

Answers to Making the Connection

1. A large pool of cheap labor existed. Also, Northerners and Europeans, as well as Southerners, invested capital in fledgling Southern industry.
2. Answers will vary but may include Atlanta, Georgia, and Baltimore, Maryland.
3. Student choices will vary but should include valid explanations of effects.

Using Vocabulary
Look for student creativity in formulating their categories.

Reviewing Facts
1. Laborers could not afford to purchase farms. Landowners could not afford to pay wages.
2. supplied food, clothing, and medicine; provided education; found employment
3. Both sides disagreed over: which branch of government should carry out Reconstruction, amnesty for former Confederates, requirements for readmission, political status of African Americans.
4. African Americans were not permitted to vote, testify against whites, handle weapons, or serve on juries.
5. to institute military rule, to ensure that former Confederate leaders would have no role in governing the South, and to ensure that the freed African Americans' right to vote was protected

---

Using Vocabulary

Create a classification system that demonstrates how these words below are related. First, write *Reconstruction* as your main heading. Under the main heading create several smaller categories. Challenge yourself to see how many different classifications you can devise.

tenant farmer	sharecropper
segregation	black codes
amnesty	carpetbagger
mandate	disenfranchise
impeach	

Reviewing Facts

1. **Cite** two reasons why tenant farming and sharecropping were used in the South.
2. **List** three services provided by the Freedmen's Bureau.
3. **Specify** two differences between the Reconstruction plans of Presidents Lincoln and Johnson and those of the Radical Republicans.
4. **Explain** how black codes prevented African Americans from achieving equality.
5. **List** three motives of the Radical Republicans in Congress.
6. **Name** three sectors of the Southern economy that improved after the Civil War.
7. **List** the long-term successes and failures of the Reconstruction era for Southern African Americans.

Understanding Concepts

Adaptation

1. Explain how tenant farming and sharecropping were a means for Southern landowners to adjust to new conditions after the Civil War.
2. Explain why freedom did not automatically lead to equality for African Americans after the Civil War.

Power and Authority

3. What are the significant reasons that explain how the power of the Radical Republicans first grew and later diminished?
4. What factors led to the rise of the Ku Klux Klan? What feelings and beliefs did the Ku Klux Klan appeal to among Southerners?

Critical Thinking

1. **Identifying Central Issues** The 1860s were a time of radical change. Summarize the string of events that caused so much political and social turbulence during the 1860s.
2. **Analyzing Fine Art** Study the painting on this page, entitled *A Visit from the Old Mistress* by Winslow Homer, and answer the questions that follow.
   a. Identify the two main figures.
   b. How does the artist contrast these figures?
   c. What idea do you think the artist is expressing?

3. **Making Comparisons** During Reconstruction, white Americans knew very little about the African continent. Africa at this time had hundreds of different ethnic groups, each with its own language and customs. How did Americans' ignorance about African culture affect their attitudes toward African Americans?

---

6. transportation, industry, and agriculture
7. successes: passage of the Fourteenth and Fifteenth amendments; failures: no real protection of African American civil rights

Understanding Concepts

1. The tenant-farming system gave them a source of workers who did not have to be paid directly.
2. partly because of the passage of the "black codes"

3. Their power grew as a result of their perception of Southern arrogance and their lack of respect for Johnson. Their power diminished when they failed to convict Johnson.
4. offered means of resistance; it appealed to the Southerners' opposition to the new changes.

4. Drawing Conclusions Do you think Lincoln would have suffered the same fate as Johnson had he lived?

5. Analyzing Alternatives If you had been in the Senate, would you have voted for or against conviction of President Johnson? Explain.

6. Recognizing Bias Study the following statements and decide which ones show evidence of emotional bias and which ones show an attempt to be objective. Explain your choices. Include a list of words in the statements that carry an emotional content.

   a. "The real human tragedy is the upward striving of downtrodden men, the groping for light among people born in darkness. . . ." (W.E.B. DuBois on Reconstruction)

   b. "If the question was, Is Andrew Johnson a fit person for President? I should answer, no; but it is not a party question, nor upon Andrew Johnson's deeds and acts, except so far as they are made to appear in the record, that I am to decide." (Senator Lyman Trumbell on Johnson's impeachment)

History and Geography

Reconstruction in the South

Study the map on Reconstruction on page 221. Then answer the questions that follow.

1. Region What two geographic divisions of the South are shown on the map?

2. Place Which state had the largest number of African American members in its convention? Which state had the smallest?

3. Place Which military district was composed of only one state? Which military district shown on the map was composed of three states?

Cooperative Learning **Interdisciplinary Activity: Government**

You belong to a group analyzing Reconstruction policies. Each member of your group will assume one of these roles: a Southern landowner, a Northern carpetbagger, and an African American sharecropper. Your goal is to write two Reconstruction laws that are acceptable to all. Write one law on voting rights for African Americans and a second law on the treatment of former Confederate soldiers.

Practicing Skills

Making Predictions

Suppose developments during the mid-1800s had turned out differently. What consequences might such developments have had for later history? Study the following fictitious events. For each event, make a prediction about its consequences and explain the reasons for your prediction.

1. Congress debates the Compromise of 1850 but is unable to reach agreement on the issue of slavery in the territories.

2. Congress impeaches President Andrew Johnson and removes him from office.

3. The Supreme Court rules that Congress overstepped its bounds in creating the Freedmen's Bureau.

4. Democrats refuse to accept the Compromise of 1877 and contend that Samuel Tilden should be President.

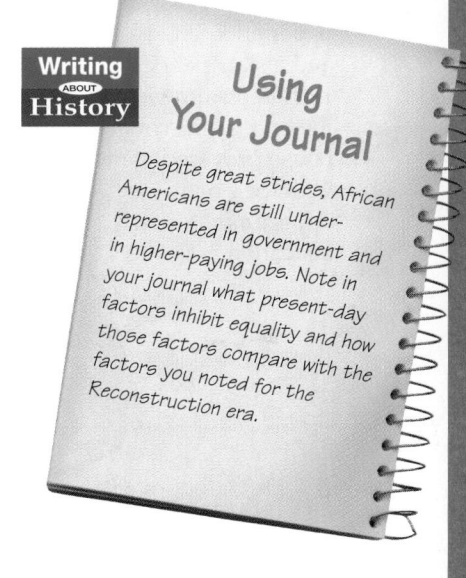

Writing ABOUT History
Using Your Journal

Despite great strides, African Americans are still underrepresented in government and in higher-paying jobs. Note in your journal what present-day factors inhibit equality and how those factors compare with the factors you noted for the Reconstruction era.

Cooperative Learning

Suggestions should display understanding of the political and social environment of the era.

Practicing Skills

1. Sample prediction: The failure to achieve compromise will intensify sectional conflict.
2. Sample prediction: Presidential power is weakened at the expense of congressional power.
3. Sample predictions: Freed African Americans make no gains in education.
4. Sample predictions: Another civil war breaks out.

Writing ABOUT History
Using Your Journal

Ask for volunteers to present their comparisons, and have the class discuss the factors.

❓ Chapter Bonus Test Question

Ask students: The Fifteenth Amendment guarantees that citizens shall not be denied, on account of race, the right to vote. In one or two paragraphs, explain why Congress saw the need to pass this amendment and why the states ratified it.

Critical Thinking

1. Answers include war, changes in status.
2. **a.** white female former slaveholder and African American woman
   b. They confront each other uneasily; the white woman is well-dressed and the black woman poorly clothed.
   c. that the Civil War created great change
3. Lack of knowledge about African culture probably increased bias.
4. Students should give reasons for their conclusions.
5. Students should indicate whether they believe Johnson violated the Tenure of Office Act.
6. Emotional bias is shown in **a.**

History and Geography

1. Student classifications will vary.
2. largest—South Carolina; smallest—Arkansas and Texas
3. District I; District III

Cultural Kaleidoscope

Education

The One-Room Schoolhouse

Until education became widespread, many children learned to read and write in one-room schoolhouses. The backbone of the curriculum was the three R's—reading, writing, and arithmetic. Children of all ages learned mostly by rote—one group recited while the rest studied their lessons. Students today might view the one-room schoolhouse as primitive. Chalkboards and maps were rare, and students, lacking even paper and pen, used a slate and a slate pencil. Despite its drawbacks, the one-room schoolhouse provided many with their only opportunity for an education.

▲ Many American leaders saw in public schools a means of promoting national spirit.

▼ The hornbook for learning the alphabet was still in use during the 1800s in many schoolhouses.

232

Cooperative Learning Activity

American Educators Divide the class into five groups. Assign each a notable figure in American education: Horace Mann, Henry Barnard, Emma Willard, Prudence Crandall, Catharine Beecher (or others of your own choosing). Ask each group to research its educator and then report its findings to the class. **L2**

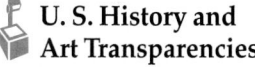

The drive for public education had several causes. Americans fervently believed that the United States should be a land of equal opportunity, a land where people "start from a humble origin and can attain to the most elevated positions." To deny a child education was to close the door of opportunity.

◄ Eventually adopted in 37 states, the *McGuffey's Readers* gave thousands of schoolchildren a shared background of popular culture and helped to mold the literary tastes of the reading public.

▲ More and more schools provided desks in the 1800s. Earlier, students sat on backless wooden benches. The teacher's desk was often on a raised platform.

◄ Even where there was a will to establish schools, the widely separated homesteads in rural areas made large schools impractical. The one-room schoolhouse filled a vital need.

233

The Historian's Craft

Many complex issues are associated with education in the United States today, among them student performance, the curriculum, school financing, teacher training, discipline, bilingualism, and segregation. Almost all of these concerns have their roots in the past, and educational historians use many kinds of evidence to analyze that history. In studying teacher training, for example, they may explore the development of normal schools, school-district records, and the experiences of individual teachers.

UNIT TWO
DIGEST

Exploring Unit Themes

The Unit Digest may be used to teach unit coverage when time is limited, to review unit content, or to relate the content of one unit to that of another.

■ Chapter 4

Have students list factors that bound the nation together and factors that tended to pull the nation apart. Ask which factors were strongest and why.

■ Chapter 5

Read the following statement by Shelby Foote: "The Civil War defined us as what we are and it opened us to being what we became.... It was the crossroads of our being...." Then ask students to discuss whether the Civil War made us what we are as Americans.

Causes and Effects

Ask students to use the information in the chart to write an imaginary article for a magazine describing the reasons for the Civil War and the results of the war. *(Articles will vary but should reflect the connections between the causes and the effects.)*

Chapter 4

Toward a Democracy

After the War of 1812, a spirit of nationalism swept the United States. Roads, canals, and railroads began to cross the landscape, a new national bank stimulated the economy, and tariffs protected American manufacturers from foreign goods. In foreign affairs, an assertive United States proclaimed the Monroe Doctrine in an effort to close the Western Hemisphere to further European colonization.

The Industrial Revolution brought changes to all sections of the country. In the North, goods became cheaper and more widely available, and workers formed labor unions to improve their lives. In the South, the cotton gin strengthened the importance of both cotton and slavery to the region's economy. The Northwest saw an influx of settlers and the growth of towns.

The period from the 1820s to the 1850s was a time of reform. During the administration of Andrew Jackson, the power of the presidency increased, the American definition of democracy broadened, and the people began to expect more from their political system.

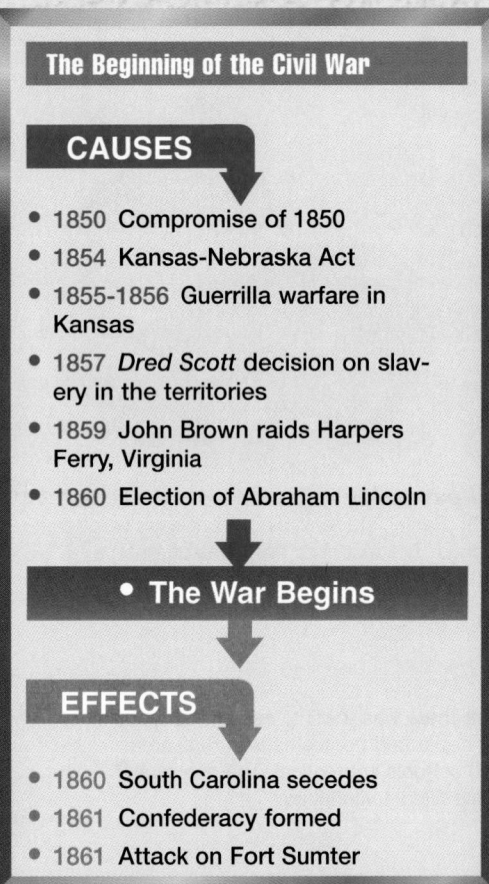

The Beginning of the Civil War

CAUSES

- 1850 Compromise of 1850
- 1854 Kansas-Nebraska Act
- 1855-1856 Guerrilla warfare in Kansas
- 1857 *Dred Scott* decision on slavery in the territories
- 1859 John Brown raids Harpers Ferry, Virginia
- 1860 Election of Abraham Lincoln

• The War Begins

EFFECTS

- 1860 South Carolina secedes
- 1861 Confederacy formed
- 1861 Attack on Fort Sumter

Chapter 5

The Civil War Era

During the second quarter of the 1800s, the United States expanded into new western territories. War between the United States and Mexico ended in 1848 with the United States receiving full title to Texas, California, and what was then New Mexico territory. The question of allowing slavery in the new territories, however, threatened national unity. The Compromise of 1850, which admitted California as a free state and allowed voters in the other territories to decide for or against slavery, temporarily dampened heated sectional debate.

In the election of 1860, slavery was the key issue, with the Republican candidate, Lincoln, victorious. Most of the Southern states, who viewed Lincoln as an abolitionist, seceded from the Union.

In the Civil War, the North drew upon advantages in manufacturing, population, transportation, and wealth, while the South relied on superior generals. Southern armies at first outmaneuvered Union forces in the east, but they were unsuccessful in invading the North. In the west, Union armies eventually gained control, and Grant's capture of Vicksburg and Sherman's march to the Atlantic coast both divided Southern territory.

Cooperative Learning Activity

Analyzing Warfare Point out that the Civil War is often characterized as "the first modern war." Organize students into three groups, and assign each group one of the following topics: military technology, military tactics, the home front. Ask the groups to use resources in the school and public libraries to find information about their topics that would support or refute the above characterization. Have the groups present their findings to the rest of the class. **L1**

Ask students to discuss this statement:
The North won the war, but the South won the peace.

 Student Self-Test Software allows students to test their understanding of historical concepts in this unit.

∩ Have students listen to the Chapter Digests on the audiocassettes.

Use the Testmaker to create a customized test for Unit 2.

GLENCOE TECHNOLOGY

VIDEODISC

Use the MindJogger Videoquiz to review students' knowledge.

MindJogger Videoquiz

 **Chapter 4**
Disc 1, Side A

 **Chapter 5**
Disc 1, Side A

 **Chapter 6**
Disc 1, Side A

 Available in VHS.

Flashcards

Use American History Flashcards to reinforce students' knowledge of places and events in American history.

Lincoln's issuing of the Emancipation Proclamation in 1862 transformed the war from a conflict fought solely to defend the Union into a moral crusade to end slavery. Shortly after Lincoln was reelected, Lee surrendered. But the President's assassination just five days later weakened any chances for a peaceful reconciliation between North and South.

Chapter 6

Reconstruction

The Civil War left the South's land, government, and transportation system in disarray. African Americans and whites set out to rebuild the South. Economically and politically, however, African Americans were thwarted by segregation and "black codes."

The Radical Republicans' version of Reconstruction, advocating voting rights for African Americans and harsh treatment of former Confederates, was set in motion when the Radicals gained control of Congress. Reconstruction governments were often handicapped by corruption. Eventually, white Southerners regained control of Southern state governments. Although Reconstruction was only partially effective for African Americans, a degree of cooperation was achieved between the North and the South.

Understanding Unit Themes

1. **American Democracy** What important democratic changes began to develop during the period of the Industrial Revolution?

2. **Geography and Environment** As settlers poured into the country's expanded Western lands, what effects did they have on the American environment?

3. **Economic Development** How did the Industrial Revolution lead to changes in the American economy, its lifestyle, and its values?

4. **Ideas, Beliefs, and Institutions** How did changes in religious philosophy relate to the growing leadership of religious groups in social reform?

5. **Conflict and Cooperation** How did sectional interests over economic issues develop into conflicts and division within the United States?

6. **Civil Rights and Liberties** Compare the legal and social status of African Americans before and after the Civil War.

UNIT 2 Forging a Nation: 1815–1877   **235**

Answers to Understanding Unit Themes

1. extension of voting rights, political influence of the common person, education reforms
2. changed the environment and used other natural resources
3. Lifestyles changed, creating new classes.
4. The focus of religious philosophy changed from preparing for the hereafter to improving the lives of the people.
5. Some described the union as a contract of the states. Nationalists contended the Union was an entity of the people.
6. Emancipation created little change.

BEGINNING THE UNIT

Provide this cause-and-effect chart to students with the effects omitted. Assign students to complete the chart as they read the chapters in the unit.

Event
- United States becomes industrialized.

Causes
- Abundant natural resources and labor
- Standardization and consolidation of railroads
- New forms of business organization

Effects
- Rapid settlement of the Great Plains
- Removal of buffalo and Native Americans from the plains
- American Federation of Labor formed.
- Populist party formed.

History AND ART

The first gold rush was in California in 1849. When the gold boom there ended in 1852, miners moved eastward to the Rocky Mountains. The first big gold strike there came in 1859 near Pikes Peak in what is now Colorado.

0:00 OUT OF TIME?

If time does not permit teaching the entire unit, use the Unit Digest on pages 362–363.

UNIT THREE
NEW HORIZONS
1860–1900

★★

CHAPTER 7	CHAPTER 8	CHAPTER 9	CHAPTER 10	CHAPTER 11
Into the West 1860–1900	The Rise of Industry 1860–1900	An Urban Society 1860–1900	The Gilded Age 1865–1900	Politics and Protest 1865–1900

History AND ART

Miners in the Sierra
by Charles Nahl and Frederick August Wenderoth, 1851–1852

An abundance and variety of natural resources were utilized for industrial production.

▲ HORATIO ALGER COVER

Exploring Unit Themes

Geography and the Environment As the West opened up, vast stores of natural resources became available. Newcomers set up farms in the central plains area, extracted minerals from the mountains, and grazed sheep and cattle on the western plains. However, lack of trees and water and climate variations created problems for western settlers.

Conflict and Cooperation As settlers moved westward, they laid claim to Native American hunting grounds and decimated the buffalo. The Native Americans fought to stay on their lands, but most ended up on government reservations. As the railroads spread across the country, so did their economic power. As a result, farmers united and called for needed reform.

Setting the Scene

This was an age of optimism, coupled with a belief in the certainty of human progress. As pioneers continued to spread across the continent and immigrants flocked to industrial centers, Americans adapted to the rapidly changing environment in which they found themselves.

Themes

- Geography and Environment
- Conflict and Cooperation
- Influence of Technology
- Cultural Diversity

Key Events

- First transcontinental railroad
- Interstate Commerce Act
- Civil service reform
- American Federation of Labor formed
- Sherman Antitrust Act
- Battle at Wounded Knee
- Populist party formed
- Pullman strike

Major Issues

- Transcontinental railroads allow the rapid settlement of the Great Plains.
- A wealth of natural resources and abundant labor makes the United States a major industrial power.
- The swift growth of industry creates a demand for new labor unions.
- The alliance between government and big business leads to widespread political corruption.
- Agrarian unrest promotes new political movements that seek to regulate commerce.

▲ EARLY PHONOGRAPH

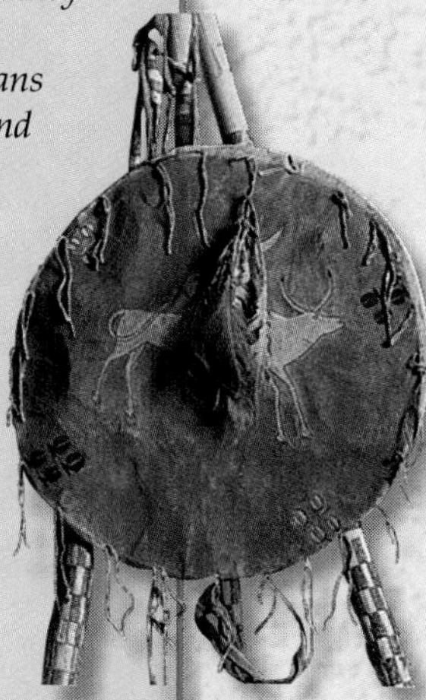

▲ CHEYENNE SHIELD OF PAINTED BUFFALO HIDE

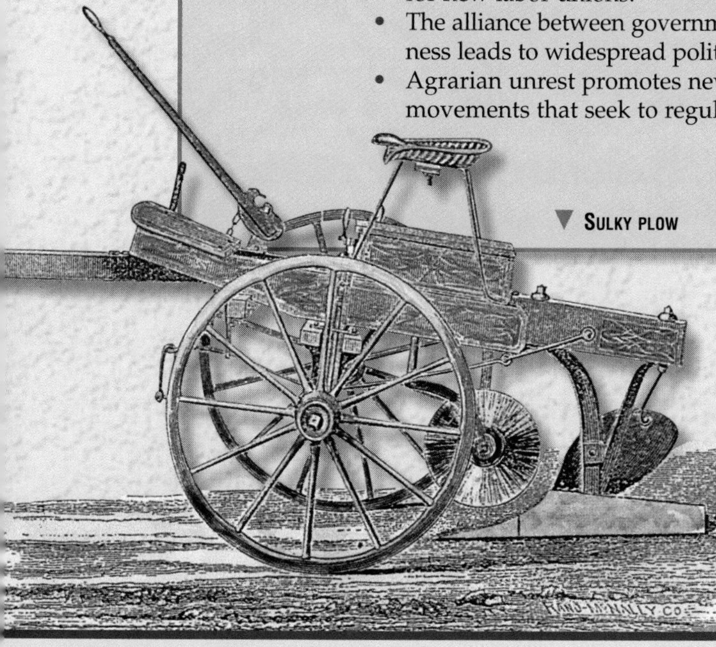

▼ SULKY PLOW

Portfolio Project

Design a political cartoon that shows the contrasting sides of one of the divisive issues of this era: for example, Native American and settler, labor and big business, or political machine and reformer.

INTRODUCING
UNIT 3

interNET CONNECTIONS

For more in-depth study of Unit 3, you or your students may use the Internet to research individual topics.

Wild West: The Home Page:
http://www.cs.umu.se/~dphln/wildwest/

How the Other Half Lives:
http://www.cis.yale.edu/amstud/inforev/riis/title.html

Portfolio Project

Ask students to share their cartoons with the class. Have the class identify the issue referred to by each cartoon and discuss differing views.

History and the Humanities

♫ **American Music: Cultural Traditions:** Western Settlement: "Little Old Sod Shanty" by Jimmy Denoon (2:12)

🎨 **U.S. History & Art Transparencies 13, 15,** *Chief Joseph* by Edward S. Curtis; *Let Us Prey* by Thomas Nast.

📖 **Focus on American Art Prints 11,** *The Gulf Stream* by Winslow Homer.

Influence of Technology Improved processes and transportation made available to items that once were considered luxuries. Other developments, such as electricity and the telephone, helped to spur industrial growth.

Cultural Diversity Until the late 1800s, the vast majority of immigrants came from northern Europe. After this time, "new immigrants"—people from southern and eastern Europe and China—came in large numbers.

Examining the Themes Tell students that during the period covered by this unit, the United States experienced a great surge in economic growth. Have students trace the development of economic growth in the United States and speculate about its benefits and disadvantages.

Global Perspectives

FOCUS
Motivating Activity

Refer students to the entry on the opening of Ellis Island in the United States section of the time line. Then point out that a refurbished Ellis Island was opened as a museum in 1990. This opening, an observer said, was a powerful reminder to "Americans of where they came from and for what their nation stood."

Have students discuss what this statement means. Close the discussion by telling students that during the time period covered by Unit 3, millions of people from all over the world immigrated to the United States. **L1**

TEACH
Guided Practice

Exploring the Time Line
The Native Americans' struggle to hold back the advance of settlement from the United States was not unique. The Maoris of New Zealand, for example, were engaged in a similar struggle with British settlers. Like their American counterparts, the Maoris felt that their only course of action was to fight. And like Native Americans, by the 1890s the Maoris had been forced from their ancestral lands on to bleak and desolate reservations. **L1**

The World

	1860		1875
Asia and Oceania			
Europe		◀ **1870** *Germany unifies under Bismarck*	
Africa	**1867** *Diamond fields discovered in South Africa*		
South America	**1861** *Gabriel Moreno becomes president of Ecuador*		
North and Central America			

The United States

	1860		1875
Pacific and Northwest		**1869** *First transcontinental rail route is completed*	▲ **1876** *Sioux nation defeats Custer at Little Bighorn*
Southeast		**1870** *H. R. Revels of Mississippi becomes the first African American in Congress*	
Midwest			
Southwest	**1860** *The Pony Express is established*		
Atlantic Northeast	1860		◀ **1878** *First electric light company is established* 1875

238   UNIT 3 New Horizons: 1860–1900

Cultural Perspectives

The Immigrants' Plight From 1882 on, immigration from China was severely limited. Later Congress also sharply curtailed immigration from Japan and other parts of East Asia. Those restrictions were not removed until the 1940s. The few East Asians who were able to enter the nation between 1910 and 1940 passed through an immigration center at Angel Island in San Francisco Bay. There inspectors studied their papers and questioned the immigrants for inconsistencies in their stories in hope of finding grounds for denying them entry. The questioning could drag on for weeks, and in some cases even months and years. During this time, the immigrants were prisoners on the island. Today Angel Island is a California state park.

Linking Across TIME

There has been a Jewish presence in North America for hundreds of years. Jews tended to gravitate to areas where they met little prejudice—Rhode Island, Pennsylvania, and South Carolina, for example. By the mid-1700s the largest concentration of Jews was found in South Carolina's major city, Charleston. The Jewish population in the United States remained relatively small until the late 1800s, when there was an influx of Jews from central and eastern Europe. Today, the United States has the largest Jewish population in the world.

1890 ▼ **1894** *Sino-Japanese War begins* **1900** *Boxer rebellion begins* 1905

1882 *Germany, Austria, and Italy form the Triple Alliance*

▼ **1899** *Boer War starts*

1895 *Cubans revolt against Spanish rule*

▲ **1884** *First steel-skeleton construction is begun, making it possible to build skyscrapers*

AMERICA
M. CAMMARATA ARKANGE
LO NIAGARA FALLS
N 510 20 STRETT N Y
AMERICA

▲ **1892** *Ellis Island becomes a receiving station for immigrants*

1890 1905

Independent Practice

Linking World Events Point out that the struggle for unification in Italy left the country politically unstable. This instability led to the emigration of some 5 million Italians to the Americas. Ask students to research the impact of nationalism in other European countries on immigration to the United States. **L2**

ASSESS
Studying the Time Line

1. What political-first occurred in the United States at about the same time Bismarck unified Germany? *(The first African American was elected to Congress.)*
2. What major transportation development occurred in 1869? *(The first transcontinental railroad route was completed.)*

Cooperative Learning Activity

Transcontinental Rail Routes Point out that in 1885, some 16 years after the completion of the United States transcontinental rail route, a rail route across Canada was opened. Divide the class into two groups. Have one group construct a large-scale map of the United States route and the other construct a large-scale map of the Canadian route. Suggest that the groups include illustrations, captions, and a detailed key on their maps. Display the maps and then lead the class in a discussion on the similarities and differences between the two routes. **L2**

Daily Lesson Objectives	Teacher Classroom Resources	Multimedia
SECTION 1 **People of the Plains** **1 Day** pp. 242–248 1. Describe the Plains peoples' way of life. 2. Give three reasons the Plains peoples' way of life came to an end.	Reproducible Lesson Plan 7-1 *Guided Reading Activity 7-1 Concept Mapping Activities 7-A, 7-B *Vocabulary Activity 7 Linking Past and Present Activity 7 Geography in History Activity 7 Primary and Secondary Source Readings, pp. 13–14 Chapter Skills Activity 7 Workbook Activity 7-1 Reteaching Activity 7-1 *Section Quiz 7-1	Section Focus Transparency 7-1 Chapter Concepts Transparencies 7-A, 7-B Vocabulary PuzzleMaker Testmaker Skills Transparency 7 GTV: A Geographic Perspective on American History GTV: The American People: Fabric of a Nation Historic America Electronic Field Trips MindJogger Videoquiz
SECTION 2 **Ranching and Mining** **1 Day** pp. 249–255 1. Explain the role of the environment in the rise and fall of the long drive. 2. Identify the realities behind the myths of the Old West.	Reproducible Lesson Plan 7-2 *Guided Reading Activity 7-2 Cooperative Learning Activity 7 Chapter Map Activity 7 The Spirit of American Art and Music, p. 25 Workbook Activity 7-2 Reteaching Activity 7-2 *Section Quiz 7-2	Section Focus Transparency 7-2 Map Transparency 7 Testmaker GTV: The American People: Fabric of a Nation
SECTION 3 **Farming Moves West** **1 Day** pp. 256–261 1. List three factors that made farming the Plains possible. 2. Summarize the problems faced by Plains farmers.	Reproducible Lesson Plan 7-3 *Guided Reading Activity 7-3 Critical Thinking Skills Activity 7 Workbook Activity 7-3 Enrichment Activity 7 Reteaching Activity 7-3 *Section Quiz 7-3	Section Focus Transparency 7-3 Testmaker MindJogger Videoquiz GTV: A Geographic Perspective on American History
CHAPTER REVIEW AND EVALUATION **1 Day**	Chapter 7 Test, Forms A and B Spanish Chapter 7 Summary Performance Assessment Activity 7	MindJogger Videoquiz Student Self-Test & Review Software *Chapter 7 Digest Audiocassette Activity and Test

*Also available in Spanish

 OUT OF TIME? If time does not permit teaching the entire chapter, use the Chapter 7 Summary on pages 362–363 and the Chapter 7 audiocassette (English and Spanish) to point out the main ideas of the chapter.

A complete, 1-page lesson plan is provided for each section in the *Reproducible Lesson Plan* booklet.

Key to Ability Levels

Teaching strategies have been coded for varying learning styles and abilities.

L1 Basic activities for all students

L2 Average activities for average to above-average students

L3 Challenging activities for above-average students

LEP Limited English Proficiency activities

Block Schedule

Block scheduling differs from traditional class scheduling in the amount of time allotted to each period. The extended time frame provided by block scheduling affords you the opportunity to implement a greater number of research-oriented and activity-intense projects to motivate and involve your students. Activities that are particularly suited to use within the block scheduling framework are identified throughout this unit by the following designation:

✔ Performance Assessment Activity

Picturing the West Have students work in small groups to create a poster that shows life in the West in the late 1800s. Encourage each group to depict the West from a particular point of view. For example, one group might show how the West looked to Native Americans; another might describe it from a farmer's point of view; and still another might focus on the way in which miners viewed the region. Outstanding resources for this activity include *American Indian Warrior Chiefs* by Jason Hook, *Frontier Ways: Sketches of Life in the Old West* by Edward E. Dale, and *So Much to Be Done: Women Settlers on the Mining and Ranching Frontier* by Ruth B. Moyniham. After each group has completed its poster, discuss similarities and differences in points of view.

POSSIBLE RUBRIC FEATURES

- Content Information
- Main Idea
- Creativity
- Clarity
- Visual and Written Communication Skills
- Collaborative Skills

☞ For additional activities, see Performance Assessment Strategies and Activities.

TEACHER'S CORNER

NATIONAL GEOGRAPHIC SOCIETY

INDEX TO NATIONAL GEOGRAPHIC MAGAZINE

The following articles may be used for research relating to this chapter:

- "Buffalo: Back Home on the Range," by Bryan Hodgson, November 1994.
- "John Wesley Powell," by Peter Miller, April 1994.
- "Federal Lands," by Richard Conniff, February 1994.
- "Wide Open Wyoming," by Thomas J. Abercrombie, January 1993.
- "The American Prairie: Roots of the Sky," by Douglas H. Chadwick, October 1993.
- "Geronimo," by David Roberts, October 1992.
- "Along the Santa Fe Trail," by Rowe Findley, March 1991.
- "The Life and Times of William Henry Jackson," by Rowe Findley, February 1989.
- "Remington, the Man and the Myth," by Louise E. Levathes, August 1988.
- "Life and Death on the Oregon Trail: The Itch to Move West," by Boyd Gibbons, August 1986.

NATIONAL GEOGRAPHIC SOCIETY PRODUCTS AVAILABLE FROM GLENCOE

To order the following products for use with this chapter, contact your local Glencoe sales representative or call Glencoe at 1-800-334-7344:

- *The Presidents: A Picture History of Our Nation* (CD-ROM)
- *GTV: A Geographic Perspective on American History* (Videodisc)
- *GTV: The American People: Fabric of a Nation* (Videodisc)
- *STV: North America* (Videodisc)
- *Native Americans, Part I & Part II* (CD-ROM)
- *Native Americans: Eastern Woodlands and Plains* (Transparencies)
- *Native Americans: Southwest, Northwest, Arctic* (Transparencies)

ADDITIONAL NATIONAL GEOGRAPHIC SOCIETY PRODUCTS

To order the following products for use with this chapter, call National Geographic Society at 1-800-368-2728:

- *The Westward Movement* (Filmstrip)
- *People of America's Western Frontier* (Filmstrip)

GLENCOE TECHNOLOGY

VIDEODISC

Use the Chapter 7 MindJogger Videoquiz to preview the content of this chapter.

MindJogger Videoquiz

Chapter 7
Disc 1, Side B

 Available in VHS.

Recording Journal Notes
To help students get started, suggest that they categorize their findings under two headings: Geographic Features and Environmental Features.

Linking Across TIME

A number of plains states' names are of Native American origin. Among them are *Dakota*, meaning "allies"; *Kansas*, meaning "south wind people"; and *Nebraska*, meaning "flat water."

CHAPTER 7
★★★

Into the West
1860–1900

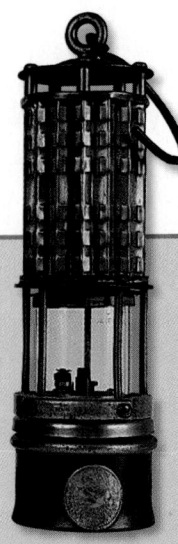

Setting the Scene

Focus

The settlement of the Far West frontier was filled with hardships and tragedy as well as adventure. For Native Americans, the slaughter of the buffalo and gradual expansion of white settlement meant the end of their way of life. For miners, ranchers, and farmers, life on the Great Plains meant long hours of work, a harsh climate, and isolation.

▲ LANTERN, LATE 1800S

Concepts to Understand

★ How **conflict** between the Plains peoples and settlers led to the destruction of Native American society

★ Why national **expansion** developed in the Great Plains region

Read to Discover . . .

★ the role of the railroads in the settlement of the Great Plains.

★ how life on the Great Plains measured up to settlers' expectations.

CULTURAL

● **1866** *First major "long drive" moves Texas longhorns to Missouri*

● **1872** *Yellowstone National Park is created in Wyoming Territory*

1860	1870

● **1862** *Homestead Act passes*

● **1869** *First transcontinental railroad is constructed*

POLITICAL

✚ **EXTRA CREDIT PROJECT**

Railroad Building Ask interested students to research aspects of the building of the transcontinental railroad. Some might focus on the physical obstacles work crews had to overcome. Others might find out about the Chinese, the Irish, and others who laid the tracks across the nation. Still other students might focus on the entrepreneurs who owned the Central Pacific and the Union Pacific railroads, the race across the West between the two companies, or the role the federal government played in the building of the railroad. Have students share their written reports by organizing them into a book. **L2**

Concept Mapping Activity

On the chalkboard, reproduce the following generalization and concepts map, and have students copy it in their notebooks.

People from the United States moved west because of unlimited opportunity but had to fight for survival in a harsh environment.

| Expansion | Conflict |

To reinforce the two chapter concepts, use Concept Mapping Activities 7-A and 7-B.

 Assign Chapter Concepts Transparency Activities 7-A, 7-B.

History
AND
ART

Ask a volunteer to look up the definition of *patriarch*. Have students discuss the meaning of the title.

 NATIONAL GEOGRAPHIC SOCIETY

VIDEODISC

GTV: A Geographic Perspective on American History

Side 3, Chapter 3
Title: *A World of Change*
Subject: Settlement on the Great Plains
See GTV Guide for complete lesson plan.

History
AND
ART

Last Stand of the Patriarch
by Henry Francis Farny, 1905

With the movement of white settlers to the West, Native American life began to change.

◄ SIOUX ORNAMENT WITH QUILLWORK AND FEATHERS

- **1883** *"Buffalo Bill" Cody opens his first wild west show*
- **1884** *United States government prohibits Native American Sun Dance*

| 1880 | 1890 |

- **1895** The Red Badge of Courage *published*
- **1890** *Census Department declares the frontier closed*

CHAPTER 7 Into the West: 1860–1900   **241**

✓ **Performance Assessment**

Research and Writing Organize the class into four research and study groups. Assign each group one of the following topics: cattle ranchers, miners, farmers, or Native Americans in the late 1800s. Ask the groups to prepare a research report on their topic to be presented to the class. Each report should list at least one primary source document, one secondary source document, and two historians' viewpoints. Have group representatives share their sources and findings with the rest of the class.

Use Performance Assessment Activity 7 as an additional assessment technique.

FOCUS

Bellringer

Before taking roll, project Section Focus Transparency 7-1 or hand out Section Focus Transparency Activity 7-1. Have students answer the questions.

Motivating Activity

Have students study the illustration of the buffalo hunt on page 243. Ask: Who participated in the hunt? (*difficult to say, but probably men*) Did this hunt take place before or after the coming of the Europeans? Why? (*probably before, since the hunters are not using horses*) Tell students that in this section they will learn why the buffalo was a major focus of the Plains peoples' way of life. **L1**

Vocabulary Precheck

Ask students to define each of the "Key Terms." Have a volunteer consult the dictionary for any unfamiliar words. **L1, LEP**

Use the Vocabulary PuzzleMaker for Chapter 7 to create a crossword puzzle. **L1**

Assign Vocabulary Activity 7.

★★★★★★★★★★★★★★★★★★★★★★★★★★★★★★★★★★★★★★

People of the Plains

Setting the Scene

Section Focus

The steady push of settlement across North America skipped over a thousand miles of treeless expanse before resuming again at the Pacific Coast. For a few years the United States government reserved most of the vast interior of the country to Native Americans because it believed these "Great Plains" to be too dry for farming. When settlers began to infringe on these territories, they met determined resistance from the Plains peoples.

Objectives

After studying this section, you should be able to

★ describe the Plains peoples' way of life.

★ give three reasons the Plains peoples' way of life came to an end.

Key Term

nomadic

▶ **OMAHA HIDE WAR SHIRT**

The United States government had assigned Major Stephen H. Long the exploration of the region beyond the Mississippi River in 1820. In his report, Long used the term "Great American Desert" to describe the territory—a term that soon appeared on nearly all the maps of the West. Believing the land to be completely desolate, many settlers who ventured to California and Oregon completely avoided it, choosing to travel by clipper ship around Cape Horn at the tip of South America.

■ A Nomadic Life

The territory that early European explorers believed to be a desert was home to countless species of wildlife. Hundreds of millions of jackrabbits and prairie dogs, millions of wolves and coyotes, and an estimated 12 to 15 million American bison—usually called buffalo—roamed the Great Plains.

The region was also home to many different Native American nations. Some, like the Omaha and the Osage nations, lived in communities as farmers and hunters. Most of the Native Americans, however, including the Sioux [SOO], the Comanche [kuh•MAN•chee], and the Blackfeet, were **nomadic** peoples. They roamed vast distances, following their main source of food: the great herds of buffalo that lived on the plains.

For generations the nomadic peoples of the plains had only dogs to haul their possessions as they traveled from one hunting area to another. In the 1600s, horses, either

242   UNIT 3 New Horizons: 1860–1900

Classroom Resources for SECTION 1

Blackline Masters:
- Reproducible Lesson Plan
- Guided Reading Activity 7-1
- Vocabulary Activity 7
- Linking Past and Present Activity 7
- Geography in History Activity 7

- Primary and Secondary Source Readings, pp. 13–14
- Chapter Skills Activity 7
- Workbook Activity 7-1
- Reteaching Activity 7-1
- Section Quiz

Transparencies:
- Section Focus Transparency 7-1
- Skills Transparency Activity 7

Multimedia:
- Vocabulary PuzzleMaker
- Testmaker
- GTV: A Geographic Perspective on American History

- GTV: The American People: Fabric of a Nation
- Historic America Electronic Field Trip

traded or stolen from Spanish settlers in the Southwest, changed the Plains peoples' way of life. By the mid-1750s, almost every Plains people rode on horseback. Horses became a vital part of their social, economic, and political life. The Comanche were perhaps the best riders, but the Sioux, Cheyenne [shy•AN], Pawnee, Blackfoot, and Crow nations were nearly as skilled. In the deserts of the region that are the present-day states of Arizona and New Mexico, the Apache [uh•PA•chee] and Navajo [NA•vuh•hoh] captured horses to sell to northern peoples.

The horse made the Plains people much more effective hunters than they had been on foot. It became easier to follow the buffalo, which provided the main source of food, skins for clothing and shelter, and bones for tools. The buffalo hunt not only yielded life's necessities, it also provided sport, ritual, worship, and training for war. Fighting from horseback, Native American warriors were better able to resist the encroachments of settlers and railroads.

■ Railroads Open the West

A Dakota newspaper editor wrote, "Without the railroad it would have required a century to accomplish what has been done in five years." What was "accomplished" was the killing of nearly all the buffalo and other prairie life, obstruction of the Plains peoples' way of life, and removal of any surviving peoples to reservations.

First Transcontinental Railroad

Railroad building in the West began at a furious pace during the Civil War. The most dramatic achievement was the completion of the first transcontinental line in 1869. Discussion of this project started when gold was discovered in California in 1848.

During the 1850s at least 10 routes were surveyed, and the Gadsden Purchase was acquired from Mexico principally because the Gila River valley provided the easiest route across the western plateau. Congress wanted to finance this gigantic project, but

▼ APACHE LEADER

▲ PLAINS LIFE Native Americans faced many hardships on the plains. *How did the extinction of the buffalo affect the Plains peoples' way of life?*

CHAPTER 7 Into the West: 1860–1900   **243**

Sidelight: The Horse

Spanish settlers first introduced the horse to the Native Americans. The Spanish used horses at their missions, and it was there that the Native Americans learned why the animal was useful. Not having a name for the horse they called it "mystery dog" or "mystery elk." In 1680 a revolt among Native Americans in the Southwest so terrified the Spanish that they fled the territory, releasing their horses into the wild. In the wilderness the horse quickly multiplied and, within a short time, became an important part of Native American life on the Great Plains.

TEACH
Guided Practice
Making Connections
Divide students into groups of three. Have each group list the ways in which the horse changed the Native Americans' way of life. *(improved transportation; made hunting buffalo easier)* Discuss the lists, and then have each student write one paragraph explaining how the cultures of the Plains peoples were related to the buffalo and the horse. **L1, LEP**

Visualizing Ⓗistory Buffalo hunting methods included donning buffalo skins and luring the animals over a cliff, or in winter driving the buffalo into deep snow, where they were much easier to approach and kill. **Answer to Caption:** eliminated their main source of food and other necessities of life

Linking Across TIME

In the nineteenth century, the United States negotiated hundreds of treaties with various Native American nations. These treaties were usually enforced very selectively, if at all. In the last half of the twentieth century, many Native American groups have gone to court seeking to address these grievances.

Independent Practice

Independent Practice

Study and Writing Have students research and write short papers on the religious beliefs of the Plains peoples. **L2**

 Assign Guided Reading Activity 7-1.

Using Graphs

Answer: 1880–1890

Graph Skills Practice

Have students determine by how much the Native American population declined between 1850 and 1900. *(about 160,000)*

NATIONAL GEOGRAPHIC SOCIETY

 **VIDEODISC**

GTV: A Geographic Perspective on American History

Side 3, Chapter 3

Title: *A World of Change*

Subject: Settlement on the Great Plains

See GTV Guide for complete lesson plan.

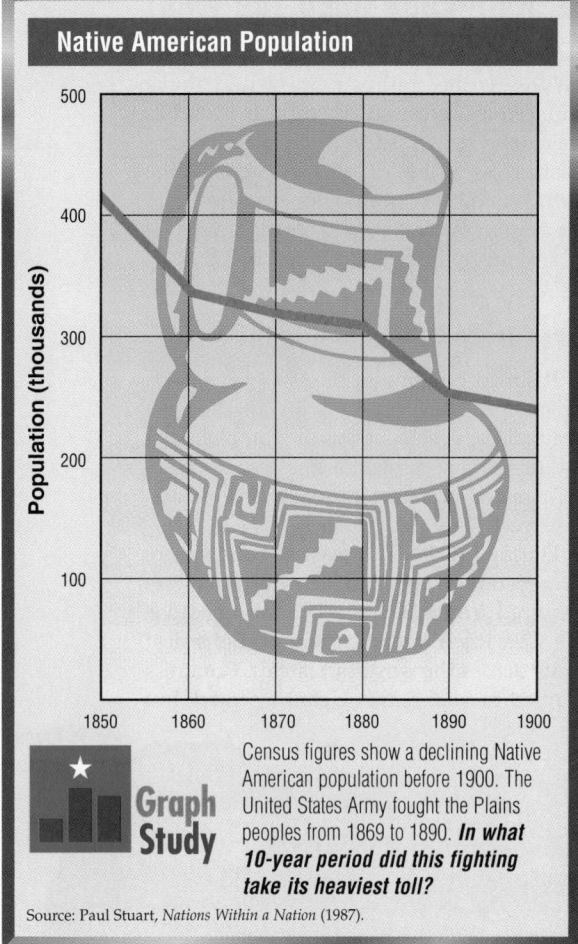

Native American Population

Population (thousands)

Census figures show a declining Native American population before 1900. The United States Army fought the Plains peoples from 1869 to 1890. *In what 10-year period did this fighting take its heaviest toll?*

Source: Paul Stuart, *Nations Within a Nation* (1987).

Construction proceeded rapidly as the 2 lines raced to get more government money and land. At the height of the competition, the Union Pacific builders employed 10,000 workers. Irish immigrant crews working for the Union Pacific and Chinese immigrants working for the Central Pacific sometimes laid as much as 10 miles of track a day—a remarkable feat because the digging and grading were done by hand. The Central Pacific had a difficult time in the Sierra Nevada ranges with snow that sometimes collected in drifts 60 feet deep. Its heavy equipment was carried from the East 19,000 miles around Cape Horn to California by a fleet of 30 ships.

On May 10, 1869, the "wedding of the rails" took place at Promontory Point, Utah. The whole country celebrated as a transcontinental telegraph reported the blow of a silver sledgehammer driving a golden spike to complete the railroad. A magnetic ball dropped from a pole on the top of the Capitol in Washington, D.C.; in Chicago a seven-mile procession paraded through the streets; in small towns citizens rang church bells.

Other Railroads

The first transcontinental line was soon followed by others—the Northern Pacific; the Atchison, Topeka and Santa Fe; the Southern Pacific; and the Great Northern. Like other big businesses, the railroads needed people of ability, imagination, and drive. The greatest of the Western builders was James J. Hill, a small, short-tempered, red-bearded man of enthusiasm and energy. Beginning in 1879, Hill built the Great Northern, connecting the state of Minnesota and the Washington Territory, without government help. By encouraging settlement as soon as the rails were laid, Hill ensured that his line would have customers. He offered free transportation from Eastern ports, credit, farm machinery, and even free advice on how to improve crops. Hill's careful construction of the Great Northern kept maintenance costs down and enabled him to charge lower rates. As a result, his railroad became the leading carrier in the Northwest.

sectional rivalry caused delays. The South preferred that the eastern terminal be located at New Orleans; the North argued for St. Louis or Chicago. In 1862, with Southern representation temporarily withdrawn from Congress, the government passed an act to encourage the building of a Pacific Railroad.

The Union Pacific Company was to build west from Omaha, while the Central Pacific Company was to run lines east from Sacramento. The federal government loaned money to both companies at the rate of $16,000, $32,000, or $48,000 per mile, according to the terrain. Each company also received land grants along the right-of-way averaging 640 acres per mile.

Cooperative Learning Activity

Writing a Proposal Organize the class into small groups. For each group provide a map showing the location of the various Native American nations. Have students compare that map with the one on page 250 that shows railroad lines. Then ask them to decide what conflicts could have been predicted before the railroads were built. Ask each student to write a creative proposal of how to avoid conflict. Have the group provide constructive suggestions on how to improve the content of the proposal. Finally ask the groups to present their proposals to the class. **L3**

Believing passionately in the life of the farmers on the plains, Hill wanted to promote maximum settlement. He expressed the idea that

> *Population without the Prairie is a mob, and the Prairie without Population is a desert.*

Killing of Buffalo

The railroads played a major role in the extermination of the buffalo. Though buffalo had formerly ranged eastward as far as Pennsylvania and the Carolinas, their natural habitat was the Great Plains, where they migrated north and south with the seasons. The Union Pacific Railroad effectively cut the huge herds in half. At first buffalo hunting supplied meat for railroad workers, but later it became "sport" for city vacationers to shoot the animals from train windows. In 1871 it was discovered that buffalo leather could be sold at a profit. Professional hunters

killed millions for their hides. Trainloads of bones were shipped east to make fertilizer or charcoal. By 1886 only a few hundred buffalo were left, deep in the Canadian woods.

■ Plains Wars

To protect their lands and to stop the waste of the buffalo, Plains people had to fight. For two and one-half centuries they had maintained their way of life against Spanish, English, French, and American invaders. The last battles against overwhelming forces proved futile. The military effort to remove Native Americans from the plains was relentless, with the United States spending an estimated million dollars for each adult male Native American killed.

Taking of Native American Land

The first concentrated fighting broke out in Colorado just after the Civil War started in the East. Government officials tried to

CHAPTER 7
SECTION 1

Linking Past and Present

Point out to students that the Indian Health Service (IHS) administers the major federal health programs for Native Americans. Since this organization became responsible for the health care of Native Americans in the mid-1950s, their health has improved. However, Native Americans still continue to be sicker than other Americans. Native Americans are geographically more isolated than the general U.S. population and have less access to health care. In addition, many elderly Native Americans avoid seeking health care because of language and cultural barriers.

📂 For additional practice, assign Linking Past and Present Activity 7.

NATIONAL GEOGRAPHIC SOCIETY

💿 **VIDEODISC**

GTV: The American People: Fabric of a Nation

Side 2, Chapter 2
Title: *Between Worlds*
Subject: For Native Americans, a shrinking realm

Linking Past and Present

Native American Survival

Millions of Native Americans lived in the Americas when Columbus arrived. Scattered across the North American continent were hundreds of different groups.

Then

A Shrinking Population

The well-being and longevity of the Native Americans experienced a steady decline with the arrival of the Europeans. The Europeans carried

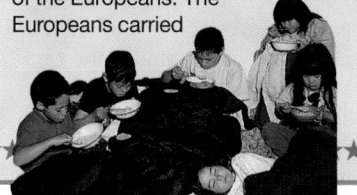

diseases such as smallpox and measles, for which the Native Americans had no immunity. The Native American population in the United States reached its low point in 1890. By the end of the 1800s, many tribes had been extinguished.

Now

Toward Well-Being

Recent history shows a strong reversal of many measures of decline. Life expectancy for Native Americans has increased to 72 years—a jump of more than 10 years from 1970 levels. Native Americans are now a rapidly growing minority group. The number of American Indian, Inuit, and Aleut peoples has surpassed

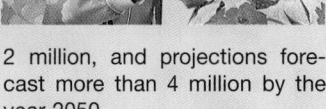

2 million, and projections forecast more than 4 million by the year 2050.

Campaigns at both the government and grassroots levels have brought results. The Indian Health Service provides both curative and preventive services to more than 1 million Native Americans residing in counties within or near reservations in 33 states. Leaders such as Cecilia Fire Thunder of the Oglala Sioux and Susie Yellowtail of the Crow have worked to promote wellness programs for Native Americans.

Critical Thinking Activity

Synthesizing Information In 1879 Chief Joseph of the Nez Percés, in an appeal to President Rutherford B. Hayes, said:

"Let me be a free man—free to travel, free to stop, free to work, free to trade where I choose, free to choose my own teachers, free to follow the religion of my father, free to think and talk

and act for myself—and I will obey every law or submit to the penalty."

Ask: Which of these requests are guaranteed in the Bill of Rights? *(all)* How were these rights denied to Native Americans? *(had to live on reservations)* **L2**

History AND ART

▲ *THE OUTLIER* by Frederic Remington, 1909
Artist Frederic Remington captured dramatic and compelling images of the vanishing Western frontier. **Why did the Dawes Act fail?**

[oh•GLA•lah] Sioux became enraged at the territorial government's plans to build a road through their sacred lands. Led by Red Cloud, they successfully resisted for several years. In the end, however, the Sioux lost their land to miners searching for gold in the Black Hills.

Efforts Toward Peace

After the bloody war with the Sioux, humanitarians in the East called for a change of government policies. The United States divided responsibility for the Native Americans between the Department of the Interior and the War Department. The Department of the Interior first was to placate Native Americans with gifts and to establish reservations; the War Department was to make war on those who resisted.

In 1867 the federal government sent a peace commission to meet with representatives of several nations, including the Comanche, Kiowa [KY•uh•WAW], Cheyenne, and Arapaho. This effort to end the constant warfare produced agreements that stipulated that the Native Americans were to live on two major reservations on the Great Plains, one in Oklahoma and one in the Dakota Territory. Not all nations were involved, however, so conflicts between Native Americans and the army continued.

Hostilities Resume

With the discovery of gold in the Dakota Territory in 1874, miners flooded into Sioux and Cheyenne lands. Two years later the Sioux, led by Chiefs Sitting Bull and Crazy Horse, attacked the miners and settlers. The conflict came to a climax in June 1876 at the Little Bighorn River, where a large group of Cheyenne and Sioux were camped. General George Custer attacked, but the Native Americans killed Custer and all of his troops at the Battle of the Little Bighorn. The Sioux victory meant only a brief reprieve. In 1881 they surrendered for a final time to the United States Army.

The final clash occurred at Wounded Knee, South Dakota, in December of 1890, where more than 190 unarmed Native

force the Arapaho and Cheyenne from an area that had been granted to them "forever" 10 years earlier. Warfare continued for 3 years until Black Kettle, the Cheyenne chief, was trapped at Sand Creek in eastern Colorado by Colonel John Chivington. The militia ignored Black Kettle's repeated attempts to surrender and killed men, women, and children.

In 1862 the Santee Sioux of Minnesota attacked a group of settlers who had moved into their hunting lands. After the militia defeated them, the Sioux were forced to move to reservations in the Dakota Territory. A short time later, the Oglala

Sidelight: The Ghost Dance

Early in 1889 a Paiute leader named Wovoka began to preach that a messiah was coming who would drive the whites out of North America and return the Native Americans to their former glory. To hasten the messiah's arrival, Wovoka said, the Native Americans must perform a ritual called the Ghost Dance. Native Americans all over the West quickly began to follow Wovoka's advice. American military authorities, believing the Ghost Dance was more a declaration of war than a ritual, dispatched troops to put a stop to it. At Wounded Knee in December 1890, the troops did just that.

Americans were killed. With this tragic encounter, the wars came to an end.

Although Plains nations fought hundreds of battles from 1860 to 1890, their cause was doomed because they were dependent on the buffalo for food, clothing, fuel, and shelter. When the herds were wiped out, resistance became impossible. In spite of some victories and heroic deeds, such as the 1,500-mile march of the Nez Perce (NEHZ PUHRS) under Chief Joseph in 1877 to avoid capture, the result was inevitable. Chief Joseph's speech at his surrender summarized the hopelessness of the cause:

❝ *Our chiefs are killed. . . . The little children are freezing to death. My people . . . have no blankets, no food. . . . Hear me, my chiefs; I am tired; my heart is sick and sad. From where the sun now stands, I will fight no more forever.* ❞

The Dawes Act

In 1887, three years before Wounded Knee, Congress passed the Dawes Act, which broke up Native American nations, even on the reservations. The Dawes Act gave each family 160 acres to cultivate. After a probation period of 25 years, Native Americans would be granted ownership of the land and United States citizenship.

The Dawes Act was the result of humanitarian opposition to the United States Army's extermination policy. In 1881 Helen Hunt Jackson had written *A Century of Dishonor,* a book that criticized the government policy toward Native Americans. Unfortunately, the new legislation did more harm than good. Plains peoples were nomads whose way of life was based on the buffalo hunt. They did not understand legal technicalities of land ownership, knew little about farming, and were demoralized by reservation life. Between 1887 and 1943, Native Americans lost to real estate speculators and dishonest government agents an estimated 86 million acres of the 138 million acres that had been set aside for them.

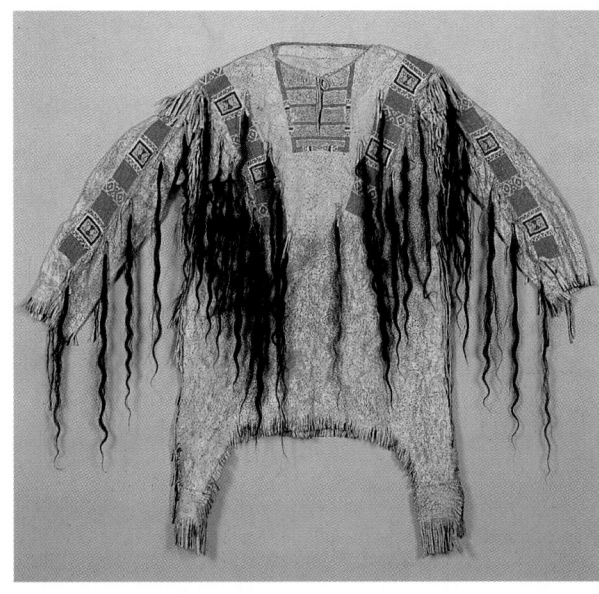

▲ PLAINS BEADED AND FRINGED HIDE SHIRT

Section 1 ★ Review

Checking for Understanding

1. **Identify** Sioux, Promontory Point, James J. Hill, Sitting Bull, Little Bighorn, Wounded Knee.
2. **Define** nomadic.
3. **Explain** how the expansion of the railroads benefited some people at the expense of others.
4. **Enumerate** the events that eventually brought an end to the Plains peoples' way of life.

Critical Thinking

5. **Formulating Hypotheses** Why did the United States government fight wars against Plains peoples in spite of the human costs?

ACTIVITY

6. Research the Sioux people during the late 1800s and create a Sioux pictorial time line.

Answers to Section 1 Review

1. Sioux, 242; Promontory Point, 244; James J. Hill, 244; Sitting Bull, 474; Little Bighorn, 246; Wounded Knee, 247
2. All vocabulary words are defined in the Glossary.
3. gave settlers access to the interior; destroyed Plains peoples' way of life
4. building of railroad, influx of settlers, slaughter of buffalo, discovery of gold and silver, wars
5. Nomadic nations extended over a vast area. Actions of settlers, railroads, and government were bound to cause conflict.
6. Time lines should include the important events of the Sioux people.

ASSESS
Check Understanding
Assign Section 1 Review as homework or an in-class activity.

Evaluate
🔘 📁 Assign Section Quiz 7-1 or use Testmaker to create a customized quiz.

Reteach
Have students write a summary statement explaining why the destruction of the Plains peoples' way of life was inevitable.

📁 Have students complete Reteaching Activity 7-1.

Enrich
Have students research life on reservations today. Suggest that they include information on the problems Native Americans face there and what economic successes they have achieved.

📁 Assign Geography in History Activity 7.

📁 Assign Primary and Secondary Source Reading, pp. 13–14: "The Native American Question" by Carl Schurz.

CLOSE
Divide students into five groups: farmers, railroad owners, miners, hunters and trappers, and Native Americans. Have each group give reasons why it has a right to land in the West.

BUILDING SKILLS
Social Studies Skills

TEACH

Relate weather maps to the map shown. How are the two maps alike? (*Both show how different kinds of data are related.*) Why are the title and key crucial to using the map accurately? (*These parts tell what data are provided, how the data are separated, and the time the data represent.*)

Discuss the conclusions students could make with this map. What can you say about climates of the United States? (*There are huge areas of similar climates and pockets of certain other kinds of climates.*) What similarities do some regions have? (*Sample: Both desert and steppe regions are dry.*) Of what historical significance would this map be? (*Based on the date, one could speculate about economic prosperity, agricultural potential, and possible population centers.*) **L2**

Project Skills Transparency 7 and have students complete Skills Transparency Activity 7.

Use Chapter Skills Activity 7 to reinforce students' understanding of the skill.

Did You Know?

The Mojave is the largest desert within the United States. Covering 15,000 square miles (24,135 square kilometers) in southern California, it receives only 5 inches of rain per year.

Interpreting Climate Maps

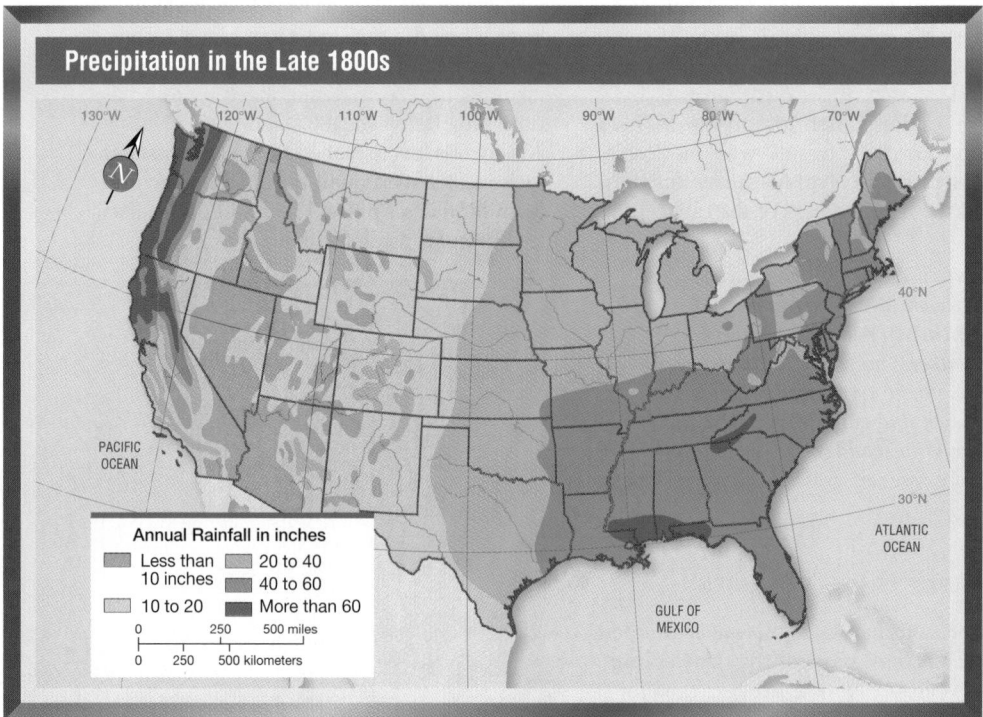

Precipitation in the Late 1800s

Annual Rainfall in inches
- Less than 10 inches
- 10 to 20
- 20 to 40
- 40 to 60
- More than 60

Climate plays an important role in determining the way of life in any geographic region. It affects what plants and animals thrive in the region. It also affects how people work, dress, and eat.

Learning the Skill

Climate maps may show differences in precipitation, temperature, or both. Steps to follow in reading a climate map include:

- **Read** the map title to identify the climatic factors that are shown on the map.
- **Study** the legend to identify the meaning of the colors or symbols on the map.
- **Use** the colors or symbols shown in the key to interpret the information on the map.
- **Draw** conclusions about the climate similarities and differences among regions.

Practicing the Skill

1. What information is shown?

2. Compare the eastern and western halves of the nation. Which section generally received more rain?

3. How much precipitation could a Wisconsin farmer expect?

APPLYING THE SKILL

4. Create a table that lists these three climate headings: Mild, rainy winters and hot, dry summers; Cool or cold temperatures year-round; and Hot summers and cold winters with little rain. Under each heading, predict how that particular climate might affect the economy, recreation, dress, food, and housing.

248

Answers to Practicing the Skill

1. the amount of rainfall in inches that fell over all of the United States during the late 1800s
2. the eastern half
3. 20 to 40 inches

4. Tables will vary. Students should provide cogent predictions on how the climate affects each of the factors.

★★★★★★★★★★★★★★★★★★★★★★★★★★★★★★★★★★★

Ranching and Mining

Setting the Scene

Section Focus

The "Old West" that inspired romantic tales for over a century is based on the realities of cattle ranching and mining. Removal of buffalo and Native Americans from the plains and the opening of Eastern markets by the railroad introduced the great days of the cattle ranchers. Discoveries of more gold and silver in mountains of the West lured thousands of fortune seekers to the mining towns.

◄ NAT LOVE

Objectives

After studying this section, you should be able to

★ explain the role of the environment in the rise and fall of the long drive.

★ identify the realities behind the myths of the Old West.

Key Terms

maverick, long drive, vigilance committee, vaudeville, "Western"

The open-range cattle industry started in Spanish Texas. The Spanish brought the techniques of herding on horseback, roping, and the roundup to the Americas. From the Spanish, too, came the distinctive dress and equipment of the cowhand. The cattle in Texas were mainly Spanish in origin, although some were brought by American and French settlers to Texas when it was part of Mexico. The Great Plains, with its vast open grasslands, was well suited for raising cattle. Faced with such an opportunity, ranchers rapidly moved into the last frontier.

■ The Cattle Kingdom

After the Texas Revolution in 1836, **mavericks,** or unbranded cattle, multiplied on the open range. An estimated 330,000 head of cattle in 1850 grew to between 3 and 4 million head by 1860. There were so many that they could be bought for as little as $3 or $4 a head in Texas.

Cattle Drives

After the Civil War, opportunity developed for great profit in the cattle industry as growing cities of the North provided huge

CHAPTER 7 Into the West: 1860–1900   **249**

Classroom Resources for SECTION 2

Blackline Masters:
- Reproducible Lesson Plan 7-2
- Guided Reading Activity 7-2
- Cooperative Learning Activity 7
- Chapter Map Activity 7
- Workbook Activity 7-2
- Reteaching Activity 7-2
- Section Quiz 7-2

Transparencies:
- Section Focus Transparency 7-2
- Map Transparency 7

Multimedia:
- Testmaker
- GTV: The American People: Fabric of a Nation

LESSON PLAN
SECTION 2, 249–253

FOCUS

Bellringer

🔲 Before taking roll, project Section Focus Transparency 7-2 or hand out Section Focus Transparency Activity 7-2. Have students answer the questions.

Motivating Activity

Write the following quotation on the chalkboard:

"There's gold from the grass roots down, but there's more gold from the grass roots up."

Students should quickly gather what "gold from the grass roots down" means. Have them speculate what "gold from the grass roots up" might refer to. (cattle) Then ask: Why might there be "more gold from the grass roots up"? (Gold must be mined, may be hard to find, may be in limited supply. Huge herds of cattle could be grazed across the extensive plains.) **L2**

Vocabulary Precheck

Ask students to define each of the "Key Terms." Have a volunteer consult the dictionary for any unfamiliar words. **L1, LEP**

Did You Know?

Many African Americans worked as cowhands. Some were brought to the West as slaves to herd cattle. Others headed west after emancipation in search of a better life. Unlike African Americans in other occupations, they experienced little discrimination.

TEACH
Guided Practice
Forming Generalizations
Have students formulate generalizations on the impact of supply and demand on the boom and bust in the Texas cattle industry. *(Example: Because of a large supply of cattle and a huge demand for meat, profits in the cattle industry increased. Profits decreased when there was supply of meat greater than demand for it.)* Discuss students' generalizations. **L2**

 Assign Guided Reading Activity 7-2.

Map Study   *Using Maps*

Answer: gold and silver

Map Skills Practice

Ask students to determine which state held the most extensive mining area. *(California)*

 For additional map practice, use Map Transparency Activity 7 or Chapter Map Activity 7.

Did You Know?

Nearly one out of three cowhands were either Mexican or African American.

---

markets for meat. There were, however, no direct railroad lines from Texas to the North. The result was the **long drive.** As the spring of 1866 turned the grasslands green, cowhands drove herds of steers to railroad shipping centers in Missouri and Kansas. The routes of the long drives became known as trails—such as the Chisholm Trail from near San Antonio to Abilene, a station on the Kansas Pacific Railroad.

A single herd might number 2,500 and be attended by 8 to 10 cowhands, a trail boss, and wranglers to care for the horses. The life of a cowhand on the trail demanded discipline, endurance, and courage, but it paid well to those who survived. More than 30,000 cowhands may have ridden the trails

to deliver cattle from Texas to the North. Several thousand of these were African Americans, free to earn their first wages after the Civil War.

Life in the cattle towns was exciting, but many cowhands told exaggerated tales of daring that multiplied as dime novels—books of stories that sold for a dime—spread the myths of the "Wild West" in Eastern towns and cities. A typical tale was *The Life and Adventures of Nat Love: Better Known in the Cattle Country as "Deadwood Dick"—By Himself.* Love was an authentic African American cowboy whose story became part of the romance of the West.

For the investor, the profits obtained from a successful cattle drive were enormous.

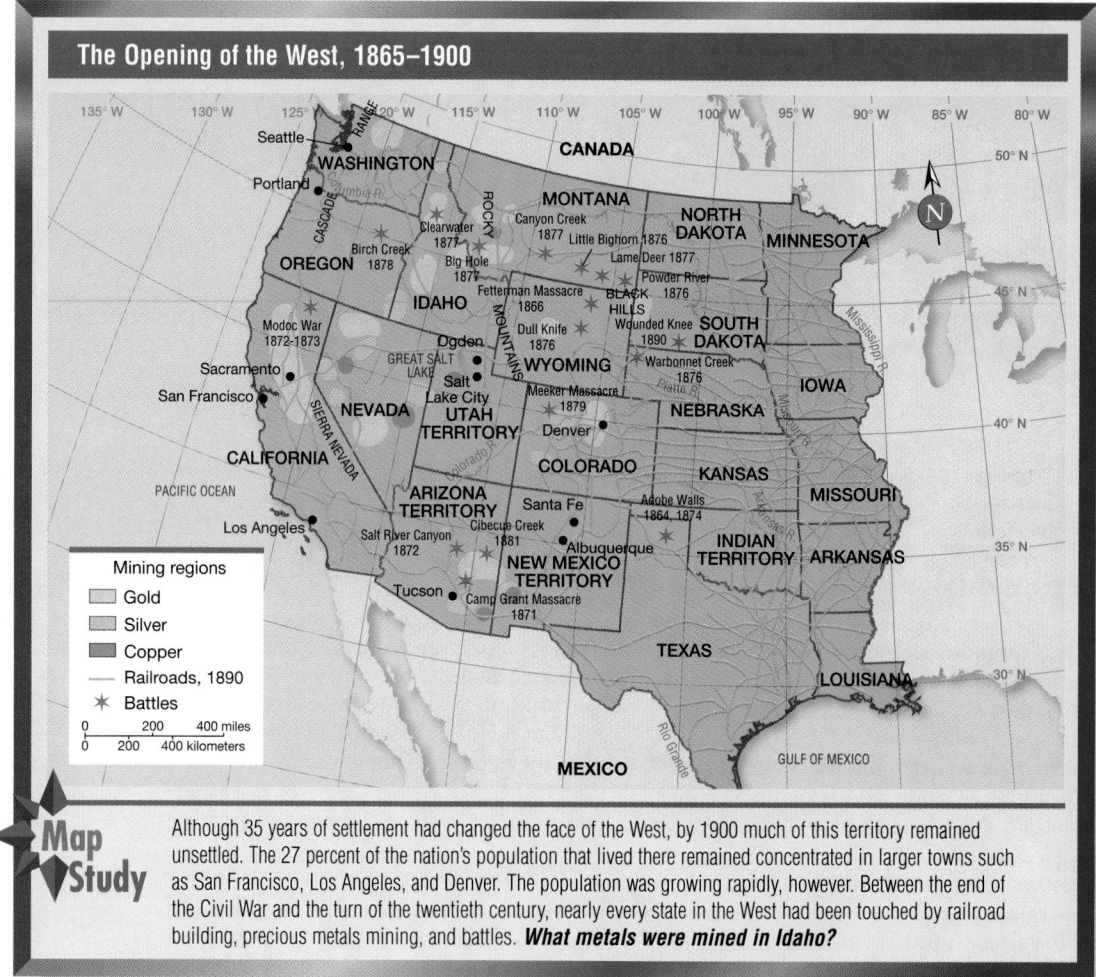

The Opening of the West, 1865–1900

Mining regions
- Gold
- Silver
- Copper
- Railroads, 1890
- * Battles

Map Study

Although 35 years of settlement had changed the face of the West, by 1900 much of this territory remained unsettled. The 27 percent of the nation's population that lived there remained concentrated in larger towns such as San Francisco, Los Angeles, and Denver. The population was growing rapidly, however. Between the end of the Civil War and the turn of the twentieth century, nearly every state in the West had been touched by railroad building, precious metals mining, and battles. *What metals were mined in Idaho?*

Special Needs Activity

Language Disability Help students with poor language development by structuring a response to the question about the myths and realities of the "Old West" presented in the section objectives. Tell students to use the skimming skills they learned earlier to find a single sentence that signals the shift from myth to reality. Refer them to the sentence "The romance of the Wild West conceals some of the truth," which begins the last paragraph on page 481. Discuss the sentence's role in marking the transition. **L1**

As the buffalo were cleared from the plains, the Cattle Kingdom expanded northward until, by 1885, it covered an area half as large as Europe, extending from Texas to Montana.

Decline of the Cattle Industry

Although offering vast profits, the industry was beset by difficulties. Steers could go blind from drought, drown in flash floods, die in stampedes, or get infected by the dreaded Texas fever. They might be stolen by rustlers or shot by angry homesteaders trying to protect their crops. The open-range cattle industry collapsed even more rapidly than it had risen. Too many animals were put on the ranges, and overgrazing resulted. Overproduction drove prices down. Sheepherders and homesteaders competed with the cattle ranchers for land.

Nature helped to end the long drives. The cold winter of 1885 and 1886 was followed by a summer so dry that the grass withered and streams disappeared. In the winter of 1886–1887, terrible blizzards covered the ground with snow so deep that the cattle could not paw down to grass. Next came an unprecedented cold spell, with temperatures ranging as low as –60°F. "When spring finally came," wrote historian Ray Allen Billington,

> ... cattlemen saw a sight they spent the rest of their lives trying to forget. Carcass piled upon carcass in every ravine, gaunt skeletons staggering about on frozen feet, trees stripped bare of their bark. ...

The cattle industry survived this terrible blow, but the day of the open range was over.

. . . .

Footnotes to History

A Growing Industry Some cattle ranches in the West were enormous, covering more land than Massachusetts and Vermont together. On these ranches, hundreds of thousands of cattle were raised for far-off markets. A newborn calf, which cost $5 when it was born, could be sold for $45 to $60 as an adult steer.

■ The Mining Frontier

The discovery of gold in California was just the beginning of prospecting in the West. Inspired fortune seekers moved to California.

Mining and Mining Towns

From California the fortune seekers spread east into the Great Basin and Rocky Mountain regions. A gold strike in Colorado in 1858 set off a stampede to the region the next year.

> The first breath of spring started the hordes westward. Steamboats crowded to the rails poured throngs of immigrants ashore at every Missouri River town. ... All through April, May, and June they left the jumping-off places in a regular parade of Conestoga wagons, hand carts, men on horseback, men on foot—each with "Pikes Peak or Bust" crudely pinned on their packs and wagon canvas. ... By the end of June more than 100,000 "fifty-niners" were in the Pikes Peak country.

The Colorado strike was followed by many other finds: gold in the Black Hills of South Dakota, copper in Montana, and silver in many places. The Comstock Lode at Virginia City, Nevada, yielded about $300 million worth of silver ore between 1859 and 1877. These discoveries attracted swarms of fortune seekers, and new mining towns appeared overnight.

The discovery of precious metals brought thousands of miners into a single area, giving rise first to makeshift camps and later to towns and cities. People from a variety of backgrounds mingled in these places. A study of one Western camp revealed that the population consisted of 37 from China, 35 from Great Britain, 29 from Mexico, 24 from other nations, and 81 from other parts of the United States. In addition, other newcomers, including a substantial number of women, set up businesses to serve the miners.

Independent Practice

Studying National Resources Divide the class into three groups—cattle ranchers, miners, and homesteaders. Have each group list on the chalkboard the ways in which they contributed to the destruction of natural resources. Have the class discuss the long-term effects of the actions of these three groups. **L3**

Did You Know?

The Comstock Lode was discovered by Henry T.P. Comstock but not in the way he claimed. Comstock rode past two prospectors hard at work. Noticing that they had found some gold, he informed them that they were working on his ground. His partners eventually discovered that the land taken by Comstock was rich in gold.

NATIONAL GEOGRAPHIC SOCIETY

VIDEODISC

GTV: The American People: Fabric of a Nation

Side 2, Chapter 5
Title: *Close-up U.S.A.*
Subject: The Gold Rush, microcosm of the West
See GTV Guide for complete lesson plan.

Cooperative Learning Activity

Locating Cattle Trails Have students work in pairs to create maps of cattle trails. Ask them to research in a historical atlas the names and locations of the main cattle trails from Texas to the various railroads and the names of the major railroad towns to which the cattle were driven. Have students indicate and label on an outline map of the United States the cattle trails, the important railroad towns, and the railroads. Tell them to make a map key for their map. Have the pairs exchange maps and correct or add to them. **L2**

☞ Assign Cooperative Learning Activity 7.

Teaching American Portraits

Charles Russell's wife, Nancy Cooper, contributed greatly to his success. As his sales agent, she worked tirelessly to bring his paintings to the notice of the American public. Ask students to discuss why they think Russell's work became so popular.

Food of the Times

The last great gold rush occurred in 1896 in the Klondike region of Canada's Yukon Territory. Because of its remoteness, there were often shortages of food for the miners. Salt sold for its weight in gold. Although no one starved, there were numerous cases of scurvy among the miners, whose diets rarely varied from flapjacks and beans.

Did You Know?

Some cattle ranches in the West were enormous, covering more land than Massachusetts and Vermont combined.

Despite differences in background, all of the miners shared one goal: an unbending desire to mine that lucky strike that would bring them wealth. After the minerals in one area were exhausted, miners would leave town, and a once-lively center of trade and commerce would become a deserted ghost town almost overnight. While the wealth lasted, however, mining communities could be spirited—as well as dangerous—places. One observer described one such mining town in this way:

> This human hive, numbering at least 10,000 people, was the product of 90 days. Into it were crowded all the elements of a rough and active civilization. . . . [F]illed with gambling tables and gamblers, and the miner who was bold enough to enter one of them with his day's earnings in his pocket seldom left until thoroughly fleeced. . . . Not a day or night passed which did not yield its full fruition of fights, quarrels, wounds or murders. . . . Street fights were frequent . . . and everyone was on his guard against a random shot.

Human life was cheap in these communities of tents and crude dwellings, with their rows of saloons and gambling houses. There was a vital need for law enforcement agencies to settle disputes over mining claims and to punish or prevent crime. Self-appointed volunteers called **vigilance committees** sometimes provided law and order. Other times mass meetings drew up their own rules and elected their own officials.

Soon the different communities of a region such as Colorado or Nevada would band together and demand territorial status or statehood. Usually the actual grant of statehood came after the arrival of homesteaders and miners, because cattle raisers were too nomadic to provide stable government.

The "Wild West"

The "Wild West" captured the imagination of Americans immediately. Dime novels and popular ballads spread the adventures of Wild Bill Hickok, Billy the Kid, and Jesse James. A Wild West Show became part of Barnum and Bailey's circus; and Annie Oakley, the sharpshooter, appeared on **vaudeville**, or live variety show, stages everywhere. The Wild West period lasted

Charles M. Russell
1864–1926

AMERICAN PORTRAITS

Born in St. Louis, Charles Russell much preferred to watch the fur traders and men who worked along the Mississippi River than to attend school.

In 1880, at the age of 16, Russell set out for Montana to work as a cowhand and to observe Native American life. He began to paint life as he saw it, creating realistic scenes of the untamed West. Among Russell's favorite subjects were cowhands riding

bucking broncos, Native Americans hunting buffalo, and outlaws holding up stagecoaches.

Little realizing the value of his paintings, he often gave them away. By the early 1890s, however, Russell was able to stop cowpunching and devote himself solely to art. By 1920 Russell's portrayals of "cowboys and Indians" commanded high prices, and he was recognized as one of the finest artists of the American West.

Critical Thinking Activity

Analyzing Quotations Write on the chalkboard the following quotation, taken from *Land Grab* by John Upton Terrell:

"The Cattle Barons were despots and tyrants who held their domains not by legal right but by force of arms and criminal violence. The enormous region of the so-called Cattle Kingdom did not produce many cows."

Ask students to study the quotation and identify the words that are "loaded," that is, that indicate that the author is trying to sway the reader to accept his opinion. (*despots, tyrants, criminal violence, so-called Cattle Kingdom*) **L3**

MINING TOWNS The discovery of gold in Colorado and silver in Nevada started a rush to the West. Thousands flocked into "boom towns" like Creede, Colorado, to strike it rich. *How many "fifty-niners" went to Pikes Peak country?*

Visualizing
History Other boom-
towns of the West in-
cluded Helena, Mon-
tana; Virginia City,
Nevada; Deadwood,
South Dakota; and
Leadville, Colorado.
Answer to Caption:
more than 100,000

little more than 30 years, yet its fascination has continued in storybooks and comics, Western songs and costumes, and **"West-erns"**—movies produced by Hollywood and shown at movie theaters or on television.

The romance of the Wild West conceals some of the truth. The conquest of the plains and the Rockies by the invading cattle ranchers, miners, and homesteaders destroyed natural resources, wildlife, and human beings. Charles Marion Russell, a frontier artist, gave this sobering message in a speech to "forward-looking citizens" in Helena, Montana:

> *I have been called a pioneer. . . . [A] pioneer is a man who comes to a virgin country, traps off all the fur, kills off all the wild meat, cuts down all the trees, grazes off all the grass, plows the roots up, and strings ten million miles of wire. A pioneer destroys things and calls it civilization. I wish to God this country was just like it was when I first saw it and that none of you folks were here at all.*

ASSESS

Check Understanding
Assign Section 2 Review as homework or an in-class activity.

Evaluate
Assign Section Quiz 7-2 or use the Test-maker to create a customized quiz.

Reteach
Have students complete Reteaching Activity 7-2.

Enrich
Have students research the conflict among cattle ranchers, sheepherders, and farmers. Ask students to write a few paragraphs suggesting ways in which this conflict might have been resolved without violence.

Section 2 ★ Review

Checking for Understanding

1. **Identify** Chisholm Trail, Nat Love, Cattle Kingdom, Comstock Lode, Annie Oakley.

2. **Define** maverick, long drive, vigilance committee, vaudeville, "Western."

3. **Summarize** the rise and fall of the open-range cattle industry.

4. **Examine** the realities of everyday life that inspired the romanticized myths and legends of the "Old West."

Critical Thinking

5. **Predicting Outcomes** Had the open-range system continued, what conflicts could have developed as the farmers settled the plains?

ACTIVITY

6. Find paintings by such artists as Frederic Remington, Charles Russell, or George Catlin. Write a paragraph on one of these artists answering the question: Is the artist's style realistic or romantic?

CLOSE

Refer students to the quotation by Charles Marion Russell on page 253. Ask them to discuss the reasons why people have not made greater efforts to prevent the destruction of the environment.

CHAPTER 7 Into the West: 1860–1900 **253**

Answers to SECTION 2 REVIEW

1. Chisholm Trail, 250; Nat Love, 250; Cattle Kingdom, 251; Comstock Lode, 251; Annie Oakley, 252
2. All vocabulary words are defined in the Glossary.
3. Rise: Abundant inexpensive cattle on open range and growing markets for meat in Northern cities led to profitable cattle drives; Fall: Too many cattle caused overgrazing; overproduction drove prices down.

4. distinctive dress; tools of trade such as horses and guns; skills such as horse handling, roping, shooting, driving cattle; ever-present dangers; violent quarrels
5. Answers will vary but may include that conflicts with cattle ranchers would have developed because farmers and townspeople would have eventually fenced off areas of range.
6. Answers will vary, but students should give reasons for their opinions.

American Literary Heritage

Historical Setting

In the second half of the nineteenth century, an unfortunate series of events led to widespread cynicism in the United States. These years proved to be an era of rampant political corruption. The American perspective was altered drastically in light of these events.

Background

Realism was a reaction against romanticism and transcendentalism. Realism dispensed with the idealized notions of the transcendentalists and scrutinized the individual under the harsh light of reality. The "warts and all" method of writing sought to reveal the truth in what the writer observed.

About the Author

Mark Twain was the pen name of Samuel Clemens (1835–1910). He worked as a journeyman printer and piloted a riverboat before embarking on a prolific career as a writer, lecturer, and journalist. Clemens is credited with changing the tone of American literature, writing in a relaxed, humorous, colloquial fashion that struck a responsive chord in his readers and in subsequent authors who emulated him.

The Civil War shattered the illusions of many Americans, including writers. They had little use for the idealism of antebellum books. This postwar generation of writers depicted events and characters in the hard, cold light of reality. One master of the new realism was Mark Twain.

Read to Discover

In this excerpt, Mark Twain applies a light touch to his account of a journey to Carson City with two miners. As you read, determine what the author is implying about human nature.

Reader's Dictionary

circussing	creating frenzied activity and confusion
stealthy	deliberate and secret
sinister	evil

Roughing It (excerpts)

The snow lay so deep on the ground that there was no sign of a road perceptible, and the snowfall was so thick that we could not see more than a hundred yards ahead, else we could have guided our course by the mountain ranges. The case looked dubious, but Ollendorff said his instinct was as sensitive as any compass, and that he could "strike a beeline" for Carson City and never diverge from it. . . . For half an hour we poked along warily enough, but at the end of that time we came upon a fresh trail, and Ollendorff shouted proudly:

"I knew I was as dead certain as a compass, boys! Here we are, right in somebody's tracks that will hunt the way for us without any trouble. Let's hurry up and join company with the party."

So we put the horses into as much of a trot as the deep snow would allow, and before long it was evident that we were gaining on our predecessors, for the tracks grew more distinct. We hurried along and at the end of an hour the tracks looked still newer and fresher—but what surprised us was, that the number of travelers in advance of us seemed to steadily increase. We wondered how so large a party came to be traveling at such a time and in such a solitude. . . . Presently [Ballou] stopped his horse and said:

"Boys, these are our own tracks, and we've actually been circussing round and round in a circle for more

▲ COLORADO GHOST TOWN

Cultural Perspectives

Failed Treaties Lured by Native American legends of gold in the Black Hills, prospectors flocked to the Dakotas. However, the 6,000-square-mile (9,654-square-kilometer) region belonged to the Teton Sioux according to a treaty that recognized the area as their sacred place. The United States government offered the Sioux $6 million for the land. When negotiations failed, the government stopped protecting the Sioux's treaty rights, and prospectors overran the region.

than two hours, out here in the blind desert! By George this is perfectly hydraulic!". . .

All agreed that a campfire was what would come nearest to saving us, now, and so we set about building it. We could find no matches. . . . This was distressing, but it paled before a greater horror—the horses were gone! I had been appointed to hold the bridles, but in my absorbing anxiety . . . I had unconsciously dropped them and the released animals had walked off in the storm. . . .

We were miserable enough, before; we felt still more forlorn, now. . . . At this critical moment Mr. Ballou fished four matches from the rubbish of an overlooked pocket. . . . when Mr. Ballou prepared to light the first match, there was an amount of interest centered upon him that pages of writing could not describe. The match burned hopefully a moment, and then went out. It could not have carried more regret with it if it had been a human life. The next match simply flashed and died. The wind puffed the third one out just as it was on the imminent verge of success. We gathered together closer than ever . . . as Mr. Ballou scratched our last hope on his leg. It lit, burned blue and sickly, and then budded into a robust flame. Shading it with his hands, the old gentleman bent gradually down and every heart went with him. . . . The flame touched the sticks at last, took gradual hold upon them . . . held its breath five heartbreaking seconds, then gave a sort of human gasp and went out.

Nobody said a word for several minutes. It was a solemn sort of silence; even the wind put on a stealthy, sinister quiet, and made no more noise than the falling flakes of snow. . . .

Then [next morning] came a white upheaval at my side, and a voice said, with bitterness: "Will some gentleman be so good as to kick me behind?" It was Ballou—at least it was a tousled snow image in a sitting posture, with Ballou's voice.

I rose up, and there in the gray dawn, not fifteen steps from us, were the frame buildings of a stage station and under a shed stood our still saddled and bridled horses!

▼ IDEALIZED SCENE OF MINING CAMP

Responding to Literature

1. Were the men in *Roughing It* experienced Western travelers? Explain.

2. Why does the narrator find the group's situation humiliating?

3. How does Twain's tone in this selection contribute to its humor?

ACTIVITY

4. Mark Twain is referred to as a realist. A realist is often described as one who views the world as it is, while an idealist views the world as it should be. Name historical and political figures and categorize them as realists or idealists. Write your opinion about which type of person makes a better leader.

Developing Student Understanding

Explain that the United States "grew up" during the nineteenth century. It lost its innocence, and this was reflected in its literature.

Explain that Twain leaves the unhappy band in the snow, without a fire, and expecting to die. Ask: Instead of death, what did the men experience? *(They realized that they were in front of a stage station and that their horses were there.)* Ask: Why didn't the men realize this before? *(As Twain states in the opening passage, the men "could not see more than a hundred yards ahead.")* L2

Other Works of the Author

Mark Twain is perhaps best known for his celebrations of boyhood recollections along the Mississippi River, *Tom Sawyer* (1876) and *Huckleberry Finn* (1885). In 1889 he wrote *A Connecticut Yankee in King Arthur's Court*, a social satire.

History and the Humanities

The Spirit of American Art and Music, p. 25, William Henry Jackson

Answers to RESPONDING TO LITERATURE

1. No; they did not know how to track in the snow, keep their horses nearby, or light a fire in the storm.

2. They were afraid they would freeze to death; yet they were only steps from a town.

3. Twain's light tone adds to the humor.

4. Political and historical figures will vary. Students should categorize each as being a realist or idealist. Students should explain why they feel one type of person makes a better leader than the other type.

★★

Farming Moves West

Setting the Scene

Section Focus

For years the Great Plains resisted settlement. The main reason for farmers' unwillingness to venture into the plains was the totally new environment. Three forces worked to overcome the farmers' hesitation: new agricultural technology, westward expansion of the railroads, and European immigration.

Objectives

After studying this section, you should be able to

★ list three factors that made farming the plains possible.

★ summarize the problems faced by plains farmers.

Key Terms

meridian, commodity

◀ McCORMICK HARVESTING MACHINE

*I*n 1862 Congress passed the Homestead Act, enabling a head of a family to acquire a 160-acre farm for $10. To ensure that the land went to actual settlers, the act required that the owner must reside on or cultivate the land for 5 years. The act was passed as a result of nearly half a century of agitation by Western farmers and Eastern laborers.

■ Farming the Great Plains

The Homestead Act did not work out as planned. Through fraud, speculators rather than actual settlers gained possession of much land. The law required that a would-be homesteader put up a home and cultivate the land. Speculators paid relatives or employees to lay down a few logs as a

"foundation" and scatter a few grains of corn. After five years they collected title to a large tract. A more important reason for the ineffectiveness of the Homestead Act was that much of the most desirable land near the railroad lines was usually controlled by the railroad companies themselves.

Technology

Before the plains could be settled, farmers had to be convinced that they could overcome the disadvantages of the dry environment. In the East a farmer could get water from a stream or by digging a well 10 to 20 feet deep. In the plains few streams ran year-round, and underground water was 30 to 300 feet down. The American farmer had always depended on trees for fuel, buildings, and fences. On the plains, trees were found only in the bottomlands near rivers.

Some of the difficulties of farming the plains were overcome by technology from the Industrial Revolution. Cheap iron and steel made possible the iron-encased, drilled well and the cast-iron windmill. Joseph Glidden sold his first barbed wire in 1874, making up for the lack of wooden fence rails.

Improved agricultural machinery cut the cost of raising crops. The reaper, in general use by 1865, was followed by the mechanical binder, which tied the grain into sheaves as fast as it was cut. By the 1880s, 2 people and a team of horses could harvest and bind 20 acres of wheat a day. The steam-driven threshing machine also came into general use. In addition to solving technical problems, the Industrial Revolution created a vast new urban population and expanded the market for food, both in America and Europe.

Railroads

The ineffectiveness of the Homestead Act provided Westerners with a grievance but did not interfere with settlement. Although railroads sometimes discouraged the acqui-sition of free land, they actively promoted the sale of their own. They did not charge high prices because they wanted settlers to get the land into production. In fact, the most important factor in promoting settlement was the railroad.

Land-grant railroads had "Bureaus of Immigration" to persuade farmers to settle along their lines. They maintained offices in the principal European cities and agents in Eastern seaports to meet immigrants as they left the boat. Steamship companies and Western states advertised the region as so healthy that it cured all known diseases. The industrious person could expect to become wealthy; an $8,000 investment, it was claimed, might soon result in a steady income of $11,000 per year—an enormous sum considering that a 160-acre farm was homesteaded for $10. The West was pictured as a place where unmarried women would easily find husbands. "When a daughter of the East is once beyond the Missouri," said one railroad advertisement, "she rarely recrosses it except on a bridal tour."

▲ LIVING ON THE PLAINS Lack of trees on the Great Plains forced homesteaders to build homes from materials other than wood. One of the most common was sod cut from the grassy turf. *What were the environmental realities that farmers on the plains faced?*

Sidelight: Sod Houses

The idea for the sod house probably came from English turf houses and earth-covered Native American lodges. To build a sod house, pioneers chose an area of prairie where grassroots were firmly enmeshed and intertwined. Using a special plow, they cut the turf into blocks. They laid these giant grass blocks like bricks and filled the cracks with loose dirt. Space was left for windows and a door. These accessories were bought from stores or ordered through mail-order catalogs. A sod house took about a week to build and usually lasted for 10 years.

TEACH
Guided Practice
Identifying Central Issues
Write the following topics on the chalkboard:
    Attracting Settlers From the East; Obtaining Land; Settling the Land; Working the Land; Transportation

Divide the class into five groups, and assign one of the topics to each group. Have each group list the problems and solutions associated with its topic. (*Example for Attracting Settlers: Problems—too few farmers from Eastern states who want to settle; potential settlers have no start-up money. Solutions—railroads advertise in Europe and Eastern seaports; settlers given free land.*) L2

Visualizing History In *The Little House on the Prairie,* Laura Ingalls Wilder describes the construction of a sod house. An interested student might find the passage and read it aloud to the rest of the class.
Answer to Caption: hot summers, cold winters with blizzards, prairie fires; grasshopper plagues; and drought

Did You Know?

The walls of a sod house were 3 to 4 feet (0.9 to 1.2 meters) thick, making these structures impervious to the high prairie winds.

Independent Practice

Creating Advertisements

Have students create advertisements that would entice European farmers to emigrate to the Great Plains region, sell Great Plains farm products, or sell railroad transportation to or from the Great Plains region. Tell them that in their brochures they can include charts, graphs, or any other graphic devices to pitch the region, product, or service. Have students present their advertisements to the class. **L2**

🗀 Assign Guided Reading Activity 7-3.

Visualizing
Ⓗistory In the late 1880s, the open range for cattle ranchers was near its end. Large herds of cattle, fenced in by barbed wire, could no longer roam freely across the plains. Then in the winter of 1886–1887, blizzards blanketed the region. Only about 10 percent of the cattle on the open range survived.
Answer to Caption: agricultural machinery, like the plow and reaper; windmills for water; fencing

Visualizing
Ⓗistory

▲ **BARBED WIRE** The introduction of barbed wire, perfected in 1874, was a blessing for farmers. Previously farmers had made do with earth embankments and hedges to keep cattle out of their crops. *What equipment and materials were needed to farm on the plains?*

To offset the myth of the "Great American Desert," a new myth was created. Some "experts" said that rainfall on the Great Plains would increase with the planting of trees or with simple cultivation; a Nebraska promoter summed it up in the catchy epigram, "Rain follows the plow."

As the plains were opened, the production of wheat—centering in Minnesota, the Dakotas, Kansas, and Nebraska—quadrupled. Wisconsin, too far from the market to send fresh dairy products, used its surplus milk for cheese production. Near every great city, truck gardens provided supplies of fresh vegetables.

■ Sod House Reality

The life of a Great Plains farmer seldom approached the railroad agents' glowing reports and prophecies. The realities of the

∙ ∙
Footnotes to History

Fencing Costs In 1871 the cost of fencing a 160-acre homestead on the Great Plains, with wood brought in from Wisconsin, was estimated at $1,000. The homestead itself would have cost $20 in land-office fees.

weather, economic conditions, and other hardships combined to make life on the plains difficult.

Weather

The climate that was supposed to cure all known diseases turned out to be severe. In the summer the temperature might go over 100°F for days at a time. In winter there were periods of extreme cold, and terrible blizzards drove the snow through every chink in doors and windows. Families could be stranded in sod houses for many days.

Prairie fires were a constant danger in the spring and fall. Sometimes grasshoppers appeared in huge numbers and destroyed the crops.

Worst of all disasters was drought. The normal rainfall of the plains region was markedly less than that of the wooded East, dropping from about 30 to 40 inches per year along the 98th **meridian**, or line of longitude, to 10 inches just east of the Rockies.

The greatest push westward into the Great Plains took place in the early 1880s, during a cycle of wet years that offered false promises of abundant crops. In the late 1880s, drought returned to drive thousands back east in despair. In spite of all the difficulties, most settlers managed to adjust to

Critical Thinking Activity

Constructing a Plan Have students work in groups to plan the building of an 1860s prairie town. Tell them to consider the following in preparing their plan: what buildings to build and where to locate them, what building materials to use, what energy sources to use, the kinds of landscaping to use, and so on. Ask students to draw pictorial maps of their town and label the buildings. Then have them write a short report explaining the planning choices they made. **L2**

🗀 For additional practice in using critical thinking skills, assign Critical Thinking Skills Activity 7.

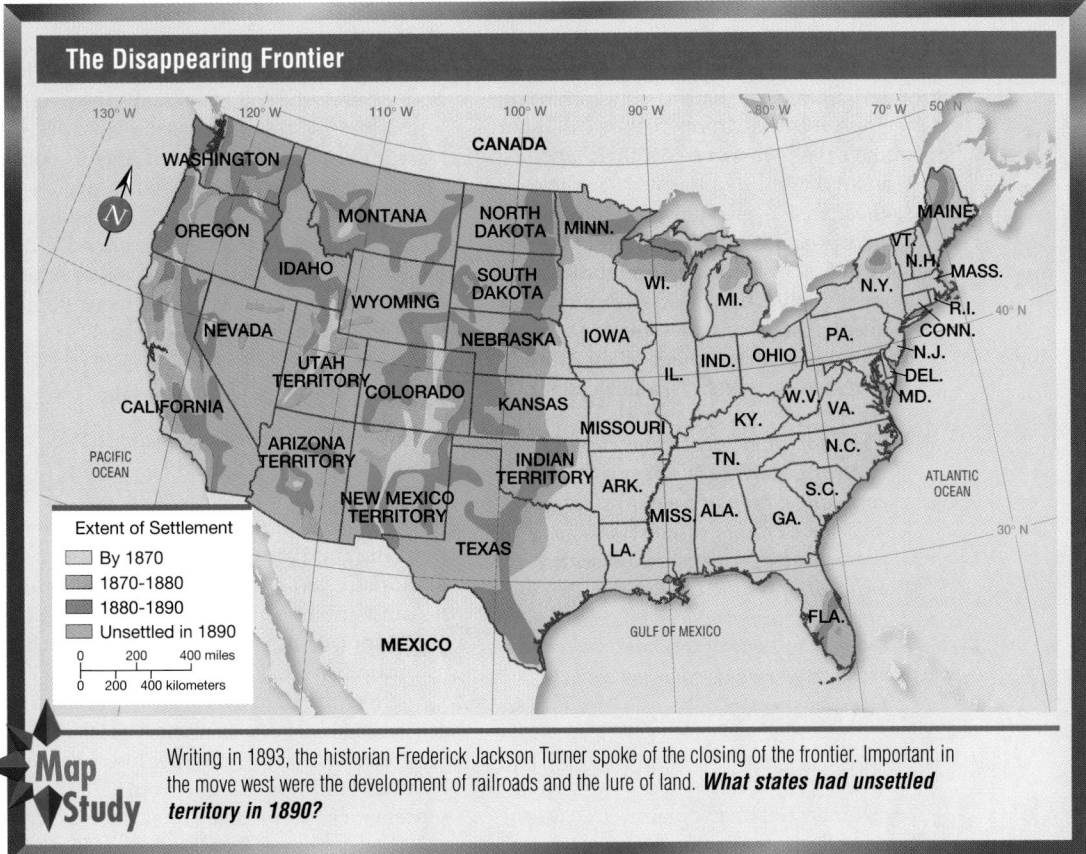

The Disappearing Frontier

CANADA

WASHINGTON
OREGON
MONTANA
NORTH DAKOTA
MINN.
IDAHO
WYOMING
SOUTH DAKOTA
WI.
MI.
MAINE
VT.
N.H.
MASS.
N.Y.
R.I.
CONN.
NEVADA
NEBRASKA
IOWA
PA.
N.J.
UTAH TERRITORY
COLORADO
IND.
OHIO
DEL.
MD.
CALIFORNIA
IL.
W.V.
VA.
KANSAS
MISSOURI
KY.
ARIZONA TERRITORY
INDIAN TERRITORY
N.C.
NEW MEXICO TERRITORY
TN.
ARK.
S.C.
TEXAS
MISS. ALA.
GA.
LA.
FLA.

PACIFIC OCEAN
ATLANTIC OCEAN
MEXICO
GULF OF MEXICO

Extent of Settlement
- By 1870
- 1870-1880
- 1880-1890
- Unsettled in 1890

0   200   400 miles
0 200 400 kilometers

Map Study Writing in 1893, the historian Frederick Jackson Turner spoke of the closing of the frontier. Important in the move west were the development of railroads and the lure of land. ***What states had unsettled territory in 1890?***

NATIONAL GEOGRAPHIC SOCIETY

 VIDEODISC

GTV: A Geographic Perspective on American History

Side 3, Chapter 3
Title: *A World of Change*
Subject: Settlement on the Great Plains

Map Study *Using Maps*

Answers: Maine, Florida, Minnesota, Nebraska, Texas, Nevada, California, Oregon, Kansas, Colorado, North Dakota, South Dakota, Montana, Washington, Idaho, and Wyoming

Map Skills Practice
Ask students why they think the Census Bureau declared the frontier closed after 1890. (*Settlement was so extensive that a true frontier line was unrecognizable.*)

---

their physical environment. Water from deep wells enabled them to plant gardens and trees around their homes. Railroads brought lumber and brick for houses to replace sod huts and coal to replace cornstalks or hay as fuel.

Economics

Plains farmers faced a second problem at least as frustrating as the weather. They were in the grip of economic forces beyond their control. Formerly, out of necessity as subsistence farmers, they had produced almost everything they needed. The independent farmer was admired in literature and melodramas, especially when contrasted with unhappy factory hands, the idle rich, or "city slickers." With the opening of great urban markets, however, farmers tended to specialize. Some farmers grew a single

cash crop, such as wheat or corn; others might specialize in dairy production or cattle raising. Their incomes went up, but so did their expenses. Large-scale farming required a great deal of agricultural machinery. The need to buy clothing and food made farmers less independent.

A farmer's prosperity, perhaps even the ownership of the farm, might depend on the unpredictable price of grain in an international market. Farmers also became dependent on the railroad, which carried their crops to market, on the commission merchant who marketed it, and on the owners of grain elevators who stored it. Farmers who raised hogs or beef cattle were in a similar situation; they had little bargaining power and were forced to take whatever the meat packers paid.

Farming on the plains demanded large investments of money to drill wells, put up windmills, enclose fields in barbed wire, and

Did You Know?

In 1890 about 250,000 women were running their own ranches and farms in the West. Besides gaining property rights, these women were the first to win the right to vote. The first seven states to grant women suffrage were in the West.

CHAPTER 7 Into the West: 1860–1900   **259**

Sidelight: The "Sooner" State

On April 22, 1889, over 60,000 settlers waited impatiently on the borders of the Oklahoma Territory. At noon a bugle call sent thousands in wagons, on horses, on bicycles, and on foot racing across the prairie to stake out their

homestead on the most desirable land. A few people, however, had sneaked in before the bugle call. Other settlers disparagingly called them "sooners." To this day Oklahoma is known as the "Sooner State."

ASSESS

Check Understanding

Assign Section 3 Review as homework or an in-class activity.

Evaluate

⬦ 🗁 Assign Section Quiz 7-3 or use the Testmaker to create a customized quiz.

Reteach

🗁 Have students complete Reteaching Activity 7-3.

🗁 Assign Workbook Activity 7-3.

Enrich

Ask students to read first-person accounts of frontier life, such as *Little House on the Prairie* by Laura Ingalls Wilder or *My Ántonia* by Willa Cather, *Pioneer Women: Voices From the Kansas Frontier* by Joanna L. Stratton, or novels by O.E. Rolvaag. Have them write a book report for presentation to the class.

🗁 Have students complete Enrichment Activity 7.

CLOSE

Have students name some factors that contributed to making the Great Plains "the breadbasket of the world."

buy machinery. Because few farmers could pay with cash, they had to borrow by mortgaging their land. Then, to pay interest on the mortgages, they had to concentrate on cash crops. If prices dropped, they could not meet their payments and lost their land. By 1900 about one-third of the farms in the corn and wheat areas were cultivated by tenants.

Not surprisingly, farmers protested. Even though they supplied the **commodities,** or economic goods, that paid for European investments, the wealth they created seemed to be siphoned off to others. Their attitude was expressed by a Nebraska newspaper:

> 66 *There are three great crops raised in Nebraska. One is a crop of corn, one a crop of freight rates, and one a crop of interest. One is produced by farmers, who sweat and toil, from the land. The other two are produced by men who sit in their offices and behind their bank counters and farm the farmers.* 99

The Plains Women

For women, life on the plains often meant solitude and drudgery. "Born and scrubbed, suffered and died," is the epitaph given a woman in one of Hamlin Garland's poems. Yet the settlement of the West owed much to the endless toil of frontier women.

Women have written some of the best accounts of plains life, such as *Cimarron* by Edna Ferber and *My Antonia* by Willa Cather. While not minimizing the sufferings, these novels reveal how much easier life became after the sod house days were past.

In *My Antonia* Cather mentioned a prominent building in Black Hawk, Nebraska, a new brick high school. As soon as farm communities had the funds, they established churches and schools. The Morrill Act helped states to establish universities. These were open to women as well as men; women had gained a new position of equality.

Declining Status of Farmers

Farmers, however, were losing status. For years they had been held up as the most admirable and the happiest of people. By the 1880s power and prestige had shifted from the rural areas to the cities. "Captains of industry" won the admiration of the public, and urban America regarded country people not as the backbone of the nation but as unsophisticated and backward.

In 1890 the Census Bureau reported that settlement had been so rapid "that there can hardly be said to be a frontier line." In reality, much land was still unoccupied, and new settlement continued at a brisk pace into the twentieth century, but the news that the frontier was closing encouraged prophets of doom, who saw the end of an era. They believed that the existence of unoccupied land at the frontier had provided a "safety-valve of social discontent," the idea that Americans could always make a fresh start.

Section 3 ★ Review

Checking for Understanding

1. **Identify** the Homestead Act, the Morrill Act, Hamlin Garland, Willa Cather.
2. **Define** meridian, commodity.
3. **Describe** the changes that made the West profitable for farmers.
4. **List** the problems the environment created for farmers on the plains.
5. **Explain** the role of the railroads in settling the Great Plains.

Critical Thinking

6. **Understanding Cause and Effect** What geographic features of the Great Plains created needs for new agricultural technology? How did technology answer these needs?

ACTIVITY

7. Create a pictorial display that shows the three machines and tools from the late 1800s you consider most essential for farming the Great Plains.

Answers to SECTION 3 REVIEW

1. Homestead Act, 256; Morrill Act, 260; Hamlin Garland, 260; Willa Cather, 260
2. All vocabulary words are defined in the Glossary.
3. Homestead Act, new farm machinery, growing urban population, railroads
4. little standing water and rainfall, few trees, hot summers, cold winters, blizzards, fires, grasshoppers, drought
5. Railroads sold land grants near their lines at affordable prices, persuaded farmers and immigrants to come West, and promoted the West in advertisements.
6. dryness and lack of trees; wells and windmills, barbed wire
7. Machines and tools for display will vary.

The Great American Desert

To Americans accustomed to well-watered, timbered lands east of the Mississippi River, the Great Plains seemed a vast and forbidding desert. The 100th meridian marked the line west of which annual rainfall was less than 20 inches. Farther west the annual rainfall was even less. Aquifers—strata of water-bearing rock—lay much farther below the surface than they did in the East, making hand-dug wells impractical.

The general aridity of the Great Plains region had caused explorers to label the area a desert. Major Stephen Long, leading an army expedition to explore the Great Plains in 1820, stated that ". . . it is almost wholly unfit for cultivation. . . . The scarcity of wood and water, almost uniformly prevalent, will prove an insuperable obstacle in the way of settling the country." Long prepared a map, labeled the region the Great American Desert, and influenced Americans' perception of the plains for decades.

Almost every map published between 1820 and 1860 used Long's label. Americans' misconception about the plains delayed settlement until new technology—drilling machines and the windmill—tapped deep aquifers. Until the water runs out, technology has conquered geography.

▲ THE CHRISMAN SISTERS AT THEIR NEBRASKA HOMESTEAD

▲ NEBRASKA WHEAT FIELD

Making the Geography Connection

1. The absence of which resources led people to think of the Great Plains as a desert?

2. In what ways could settlers adapt to the environment?

3. How might the "mining" of aquifers affect people on the Great Plains today?

ACTIVITY

4. Create a cartoon that illustrates in a humorous way one aspect of life on the Great Plains.

261

TEACH

The label *Great American Desert* was being widely used in newspapers and geography texts by the mid-1830s. So firm was the belief in the existence of a desert that some people imported camels for use in the West.

Did You Know?

Since water was scarce, some farmers used the "dry farming" method. Steel-tipped plows cut through the dry, hard-baked surface to reach the moist soil underneath. The moisture would rise through the plowed soil to the plants' roots. Farmers then packed down the topsoil to keep the moisture from rising to the surface and evaporating.

FACT or FICTION?

The Great Plains region has been labeled both "America's Breadbasket" and the "Dust Bowl."

FACT: After farmers covered the plains with wheat fields, the region became known as "America's Breadbasket." In the 1930s the plains suffered a drought, and winds blew away the dry soil. The plains were once again renamed, this time as the "Dust Bowl."

Answers to Making the Connection

1. trees and water
2. They dug wells and used windmills to get water; sod was used to build houses, for example.
3. As underground water supplies are diminished, both urban and rural people have to conserve water. Farmers must grow crops that need less water and must use more efficient irrigation methods.
4. Cartoons will vary but should focus on a relevant aspect of life during the era.

GLENCOE
TECHNOLOGY

 **VIDEODISC**

Use the MindJogger Videoquiz to review students' knowledge.

MindJogger Videoquiz

Chapter 7
Disc 1, Side B

Available in VHS.

Using Vocabulary

Explanations will vary but should include the relationship of the term to the opening of the West.

Reviewing Facts

1. They ranged over vast areas following and hunting the buffalo.
2. encroachment of settlers, building of railroads, slaughter of buffalo, conflicts with settlers and military
3. abundant inexpensive land, precious metals, availability of cattle and open range, opportunities for profit
4. Open-range cattle industry consisted of cowhands driving cattle over unclaimed land to railroad centers. It was replaced by a system that raised cattle on fenced-in ranches.
5. technology, barbed wire fences, machinery that made farming more efficient
6. long journeys, severe climate, harsh environment, drought, conflicts with Native Americans, primitive living conditions, solitude, drudgery, hard work

262

Using Vocabulary

Explain why each of these terms is used in a chapter about opening the West.

nomadic

long drive

"Western"

commodity

maverick

vigilance committees

meridian

vaudeville

Reviewing Facts

1. **Describe** the lives of the nomadic Plains peoples.
2. **Give** reasons why the Plains peoples' way of life came to an end.
3. **List** the factors that drew settlers to the West.
4. **Contrast** the open-range cattle industry with the system that replaced it.
5. **Specify** the changes that made farming attractive on the Great Plains.
6. **Discuss** the hardships faced in settling the Old West.

Understanding Concepts

Conflict

1. Explain the conflicts between Native Americans and settlers. What groups today might oppose unrestrained development and fencing of wilderness areas?
2. Conflict on the plains was not confined to wars with Native Americans. Open-range cattle ranchers often came into conflict with sheepherders and homesteaders. How might the interests of an open-range cattle industry conflict with those of other settlers?

Expansion

3. During the 1700s and early 1800s, most expansion took place east of the Mississippi. What changes and developments accelerated expansion west of the Mississippi?
4. What part did railroads play in the westward expansion?

Critical Thinking

1. **Recognizing Effects** How did the railroads benefit from encouraging farmers and immigrants to settle near their rail lines?
2. **Analyzing Art** Study the rendering on this page of a Kiowa calendar. Unique among Native Americans on the plains was the Kiowas' practice of recording time by painting pictures and symbols on animal hides. Winters on these historical calendars were recorded by black bars, which represented plants without leaves. Summers were recorded by a drawing of the sun-dance medicine lodge. On long winter nights, the painted hides were used to recite the group's history, keeping alive its memories.

   a. Why is the calendar important to the Kiowa?
   b. List other ways in which an artist might represent the seasons.

▲ KIOWA CALENDAR

3. **Assessing Change** How did the change from a nomadic to a reservation lifestyle affect Native Americans?
4. **Correcting Stereotypes** Imagine that you have been asked to direct the making of a Western film. What ideas would you recommend to correct some false notions about the Old West?
5. **Understanding Cause and Effect** What was the intention of the Dawes Act? What were its consequences for Native Americans?

Understanding Concepts

1. Native Americans depended on the buffalo and access to expansive territory; settlers owned and fenced off land, contributed to slaughter of the buffalo. Environmental groups, people who want to keep rural areas unspoiled, those who enjoy public access to wilderness areas.
2. Cattle industry needed large areas of open land accessible to cattle. Settlers wanted to fence in farms and protect crops.
3. Answers include demand for land and food, discovery of precious metals, new technology to farm the plains, and transcontinental railroads.
4. Railroads made moving, building, farming, and provisioning easier.

6. Point of View In the 1870s, railroads greatly improved travel by shortening travel time and smoothing the ride. Nevertheless, people who ventured on long journeys by train faced difficulties. Crossing the plains was still an adventure because the area was sparsely settled and government was just beginning to establish control and order. Write a day's entry in the diary of a 17-year-old traveling west by rail in 1870. Include details about the geographic features, the hardships, and the traveler's reactions.

History and Geography

Westward Movement

In the 1800s settlers moved west and established farms, towns, and cattle ranches. Settlement and development accelerated rapidly after the building of the railroads.

1. **Movement** What geographic features attracted people to move west?

2. **Human/Environment Interaction** Why did the building of the railroad accelerate the movement of people to the West?

Cooperative Learning — Interdisciplinary Activity: Dramatic Arts

In groups of 4–5 students, research the details of life during the days of the open-range cattle industry. Divide the research assignments so that each group member is responsible for reporting on a different aspect of life during this period.

Two good sources that provide an accurate account of life during the days of the open-range cattle industry are *Cowboys of the Wild West* by Russell Freedman and *The Day of the Cattleman* by Earnest Staples Osgood. Your teacher may have other suggestions.

After each group has completed its research and written notes, your group should create two dramatizations of an event during a roundup or a long drive. Remember that the long drive usually culminated in a railroad town such as Abilene, Dodge City, or Sedalia, where cowhands sold their cattle to buyers from the larger cities.

Shape the first dramatization to depict the event as it may have been shown in a Western. The second dramatization should present it as it might have happened in real life. Each dramatization should last from four to six minutes. Create both realistic and romanticized characters and dialogue. After rehearsing, present your dramatizations to the class.

Practicing Skills

Interpreting Climate Maps

Find a precipitation map of the United States in your local newspaper or in a national magazine. Use the map to answer the questions that follow.

1. What data is shown on the map?

2. Does the map include a legend? What categories are included?

3. What does the map predict about the area where you live?

Writing ABOUT History — Using Your Journal

Compare and contrast the hardships for the settlers in the West with those faced by the colonists in the 1600s.

free transportation from the East, credit for farm machinery, and free advice on how to improve crops.

Cooperative Learning

The event as shown in the Western would be a romanticized depiction, while the dramatization that presents the event as it really happened would be a realistic depiction.

Practicing Skills

1. Students should correctly identify the data.
2. Answers will vary but should include the categories shown in the map's legend.
3. Students should provide valid predictions.

Writing ABOUT History — Using Your Journal

Both experienced long journeys, harsh environment, conflicts with Native Americans, solitude, and hard work.

❓ Chapter Bonus Test Question

Ask students: Choose one of the events below, and explain how it contributed to changes in the West in the late 1800s.
• Homestead Act (*encouraged settlement on the plains*)
• Dawes Act (*broke up Native American nations*)

Critical Thinking

1. Railroads profited by charging people to ride West; by selling land that had been granted the railroads free of charge; by charging farmers to ship their crops.
2. a) It is a record of the group's history. b) Answers include pictures of a task that is specific to a particular season.
3. The change restricted their movements and sense of space and freedom.
4. Answers include not depicting all Native Americans as savages or hostile, not depicting all settlers as noble and patriotic.
5. to provide land and citizenship; changed way of life
6. Entries should impart adventure and the writer's reactions.

History and Geography

1. farm land and minerals for mining
2. Railroad companies offered

Daily Lesson Objectives	Teacher Classroom Resources	Multimedia
SECTION 1 **Industrialism Takes Hold** **1 Day** pp. 266–272 1. Identify and explain the factors that encouraged industrial growth. 2. Discuss the railroad's role in the growth of industry.	Reproducible Lesson Plan 8-1 Concept Mapping Activities 8-A, 8-B *Vocabulary Activity 8 *Guided Reading Activity 8-1 Chapter Map Activity 8 Linking Past and Present Activity 8 Workbook Activity 8-1 Reteaching Activity 8-1 *Section Quiz 8-1	Section Focus Transparency 8-1 Chapter Concepts Transparencies 8-A, 8-B Map Transparency 8 Vocabulary Puzzlemaker Testmaker GTV: A Geographic Perspective on American History Historic America Electronic Field Trips MindJogger Videoquiz
SECTION 2 **Growth of Big Business** **1 Day** pp. 274–277 1. Discuss the methods big business used to become successful. 2. Explain why incorporation encouraged business growth.	Reproducible Lesson Plan 8-2 *Guided Reading Activity 8-2 Cooperative Learning Activity 8 Primary and Secondary Source Readings, pp. 16–17 Workbook Activity 8-2 Reteaching Activity 8-2 *Section Quiz 8-2	Section Focus Transparency 8-2 Testmaker Powers of the Congress
SECTION 3 **Captains of Industry** **1 Day** pp. 278–284 1. Compare the methods used by Carnegie and Rockefeller to achieve success. 2. Explain social Darwinism.	Reproducible Lesson Plan 8-3 *Guided Reading Activity 8-3 Outline Map Resource Book, p. 39 Critical Thinking Skills Activity 8 Enrichment Activity 8 Geography in History Activity 8 Chapter Skills Activity 8 Workbook Activity 8-3 Reteaching Activity 8-3 *Section Quiz 8-3	Section Focus Transparency 8-3 Skills Transparency 8 Testmaker GTV: The American People: Fabric of a Nation
CHAPTER REVIEW AND EVALUATION **1 Day**	Chapter 8 Test, Forms A and B Spanish Chapter 8 Summary Performance Assessment Activity 8	MindJogger Videoquiz Student Self-Test & Review Software *Chapter 8 Digest Audiocassette Activity and Test

*Also available in Spanish

 0:00 **OUT OF TIME?** If time does not permit teaching the entire chapter, use the Chapter 8 Summary on pages 362–363 and the Chapter 8 audiocassette (English and Spanish) to point out the main ideas of the chapter.

A complete, 1-page lesson plan is provided for each section in the *Reproducible Lesson Plan* booklet.

Key to Ability Levels

Teaching strategies have been coded for varying learning styles and abilities.

L1   Basic activities for all students

L2   Average activities for average to above-average students

L3   Challenging activities for above-average students

LEP   Limited English Proficiency activities

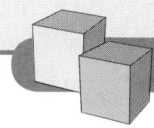

Block Schedule

Block scheduling differs from traditional class scheduling in the amount of time allotted to each period. The extended timeframe provided by block scheduling affords you the opportunity to implement a greater number of research-oriented and activity-intense projects to motivate and involve your students. Activities that are particularly suited to use within the block scheduling framework are identified throughout this unit by the following designation:

✓ Performance Assessment Activity

Managing a Business Working in small groups, have students imagine that they are entrepreneurs who want to start a medium- sized business in the late 1800s. Ask them to decide what type of business they wish to establish, how they might finance the day-to-day operation without investing personal capital (sell shares to investors), and how they would run the company. Who would manage the company? Have groups also plan for a vertical combination to take place within a few years. Ask a spokesperson from each group to present its plan to the class. Discuss the viability of each venture.

POSSIBLE RUBRIC FEATURES:
- Content Information
- Organization
- Creativity
- Clarity
- Oral Communication Skills
- Collaborative Skills

   For additional activities, see Performance Assessment Strategies and Activities.

T E A C H E R ' S   C O R N E R

NATIONAL GEOGRAPHIC SOCIETY

INDEX TO NATIONAL GEOGRAPHIC MAGAZINE

The following articles may be used for research relating to this chapter:

- "Alexander Graham Bell," by Robert V. Bruce, September 1988.

NATIONAL GEOGRAPHIC SOCIETY PRODUCTS AVAILABLE FROM GLENCOE

To order the following products for use with this chapter, contact your local Glencoe sales representative or call Glencoe at 1-800-334-7344:

- *The Presidents: A Picture History of Our Nation* (CD-ROM)
- *GTV: A Geographic Perspective on American History* (Videodisc)
- *GTV: The American People: Fabric of a Nation* (Videodisc)

ADDITIONAL NATIONAL GEOGRAPHIC SOCIETY PRODUCTS

To order the following products for use with this chapter, call National Geographic Society at 1-800-368-2728:

- *The United States as a World Power: From the 1890s to the 1970s* (Filmstrip)

BEGINNING THE CHAPTER

GLENCOE TECHNOLOGY

 VIDEODISC

Use the Chapter 8 MindJogger Videoquiz to preview the content of this chapter.

MindJogger Videoquiz

Chapter 8
Disc 1, Side B

 Available in VHS.

Recording Journal Notes
As students record information about Carnegie and Rockefeller, encourage them to write thoughts about their contributions.

Linking Across TIME

Until the early 1800s, most businesses in the United States were operated as sole proprietorships and partnerships. A few merchants began to experiment with business organization. One of the most successful was the corporation. It allowed businesses to accumulate large amounts of capital by selling stock. By the late 1800s, corporations were dominating the American economy.

CHAPTER 8
★★★

The Rise of Industry
1860–1900

▼ HAMMER USED BY OIL FIELD WORKERS

Setting the Scene

Focus

The United States developed into a great industrial power in the latter decades of the nineteenth century. By the year 1900, United States industrial production was the strongest in the world. This remarkable growth was the result of many different factors—cheap labor, abundant raw materials, new technology—but also of new forms of business organization.

Concepts to Understand

★ Why business leaders believed that **individual initiative** benefited all of society

★ How **government restriction** and other forces affected economic development

Read to Discover . . .

★ what factors caused American industry to grow so rapidly.

★ how Andrew Carnegie and John D. Rockefeller were able to become industrial giants.

Journal Notes

When you read about Rockefeller and Carnegie, look for instances when they gave away some of their wealth. Note these instances in your journal.

CULTURAL
- **1869** *Mark Twain publishes Innocents Abroad*
- **1879** *Thomas Edison invents the first practical electric light*

1860	1870

POLITICAL
- **1865** *Civil War ends*
- **1873** *Panic of 1873 strikes*

➕ EXTRA CREDIT PROJECT

Studying Inventions Have interested students research a modern-day invention of their choice (computer, laser, optic fiber). Ask them to prepare a talk with accompanying visuals in which they present information about the invention and the inventor. Their talks should also include information on how the invention has changed people's lives. **L2**

Concept Mapping Activity

On the chalkboard, reproduce the following generalization and concepts map, and have students copy it in their notebooks.

New industries emerge as a result of new opportunities, ambitious individuals, vast natural resources, and technological change.

Government Restriction

Individual Initiative

To reinforce the two chapter concepts, use Concept Mapping Activities 8-A and 8-B.

 Assign Chapter Concepts Transparency Activities 8-A, 8-B.

History AND ART

Factory Chimneys
by Maximillian Luce, 1896

Mass production—production of large quantities of goods at low cost—was the heart of the new industrial system.

◀ INVENTOR THOMAS ALVA EDISON

History AND ART

Factory Chimneys by Maximillian Luce captures the brisk growth of industry.

NATIONAL GEOGRAPHIC SOCIETY

 VIDEODISC

GTV: A Geographic Perspective on American History

Side 3, Chapter 8
Title: *The March of Industry*
Subject: Growth of American industry

• **1882** *Standard Oil Trust formed*

• **1893** *First successful gasoline-powered car operated*

| 1880 | 1890 |

• **1884** *Congress establishes the Federal Bureau of Labor*

• **1893** *Colorado grants women the right to vote*

✓ Performance Assessment

 Chinese Americans More than 10,000 Chinese workers helped to build the first transcontinental railroad. Others went on to become the main builders of the Southern Pacific and Northwest Pacific railroads. Chinese workers were also instrumental in turning California's San Joaquin and Sacramento River valleys from swampland into farmland. Despite these and other contributions, Chinese had few rights in the United States. Have students research what led Congress to pass the Chinese Exclusion Act. Students might also research the effects of the act on Chinese already living in the United States. Encourage students to share their findings in the form of art, photographs, graphs, and tables. **L2**

FOCUS

Bellringer

 Before taking roll, project Section Focus Transparency 8-1 or hand out Section Focus Transparency Activity 8-1. Have students answer the questions.

Motivating Activity

Ask students to imagine that they will be choosing modern inventions—machines, processes, materials, medicinal drugs, and so on—to exhibit at a technical fair in the year 2000. Discuss what inventions might be included in such a fair.

Vocabulary Precheck

Ask students to define each of the "Key Terms." Have a volunteer consult the dictionary for any unfamiliar words. **L1, LEP**

 Use the Vocabulary PuzzleMaker for Chapter 8 to create a crossword puzzle. **L1**

Assign Vocabulary Activity 8.

NATIONAL GEOGRAPHIC SOCIETY

VIDEODISC

GTV: A Geographic Perspective on American History

Side 3, Chapter 8
Title: *The March of Industry*
Subject: Growth of American Industry

★★★

Industrialization Takes Hold

Setting the Scene

Section Focus

The tremendous industrial growth that occurred in the United States after the Civil War resulted from foundations that had been laid over the previous half-century. Agriculture flourished in the South and Midwest, and manufacturing increased in the Northeast. A transportation network spread people, products, and information across the nation. Yet greater growth was ahead.

Objectives

After studying this section, you should be able to

★ identify and explain the factors that encouraged industrial growth.

★ discuss the railroad's role in the growth of industry.

Key Terms

entrepreneur, economies of scale

◄ CASH REGISTER, 1878

*U*nlike the South, the North emerged virtually undamaged by the Civil War, its railroads and factories intact. Furthermore, the war and Reconstruction eliminated Southern planters as rivals to Northern industrialists for political power, allowing industrial growth to proceed at an even greater pace. Although interrupted by depressions from 1873 to 1878, 1882 to 1884, and 1893 to 1896, America's industrial production doubled every 12 to 14 years. By the 1880s the United States had overtaken Great Britain as the world's industrial leader.

■ Resources

The change from a primarily agricultural society to an industrial one was possible because the United States had the means necessary for a changing and growing economy.

Among these were an abundance and variety of natural resources and large numbers of workers to turn raw materials into goods.

A Wealth of Natural Resources

Before the war, natural resources such as coal, iron ore, and petroleum had scarcely been touched. By the 1860s, however, methods for extracting and utilizing these resources were well developed.

As a result, the amount of coal mined in the United States more than doubled in every decade between 1840 and 1890. By the 1870s, vast deposits throughout the Appalachians from Pennsylvania to Alabama were being mined. Completion of the Soo Canal between Lake Superior and Lake Huron in 1855 allowed ships to move iron ore mined in Michigan and Wisconsin to iron and steel mills on the lower Great Lakes.

Classroom Resources for SECTION 1

Blackline Masters:
- Reproducible Lesson Plan 8-1
- Vocabulary Activity 8
- Guided Reading Activity 8-1
- Linking Past and Present Activity 8
- Workbook Activity 8-1
- Reteaching Activity 8-1
- Section Quiz 8-1

Transparencies:
- Section Focus Transparency 8-1

Multimedia:
- Vocabulary Puzzlemaker
- Historic America Electronic Field Trips
- GTV: A Geographic Perspective on American History

The American oil industry got its start in 1859 in western Pennsylvania when the first successful well was drilled. By 1900 oil fields extended as far west as Texas. Production had risen from 2,000 barrels per year in 1859 to 64 million barrels per year in 1900.

A Growing Labor Force

The human resources available to American industry were as important as the mineral resources. European capitalists sometimes had difficulty recruiting labor for new industries. Children of working-class families often were raised to follow traditional occupations, and in the European countryside peasants frequently were reluctant to leave their home villages. In the United States, however, labor was more mobile. Workers came to new jobs in cities the way pioneers moved to new lands.

Between 1860 and 1890, America's population more than doubled, rising from 31 million to nearly 75 million. The flood of immigration that had begun in the 1840s continued, contributing to this growth. Pulled by opportunities in America—and pushed out by the lack of them at home—14 million immigrants arrived between 1860 and 1900, more than twice the number of the previous 40 years. Many of these immigrants were adult males eager to find employment. These newcomers enlarged the labor pools that accumulated wherever jobs were available, and that helped keep industrial wages low.

■ Public Policies and Private Investment

American industry developed within a free enterprise system. Americans embraced a philosophy of laissez-faire, which comes

· ·

Footnotes to History

Wages Working-class incomes varied greatly during the late 1800s. For example, in 1889 a carpenter earned $680 annually, a laborer, $380, and a young woman in a silk mill, only $130.

from the French phrase meaning "let alone." As a result, American industries developed with few government restraints. In fact, some government policies actually encouraged industrialization. **Entrepreneurs,** or business organizers, sought and received special favors from Congress. Liberal immigration laws ensured a steady supply of cheap labor. High protective tariffs encouraged American industries and raised manufacturers' profits by keeping out foreign goods. The federal government sold public lands containing vast mineral resources for a small proportion of their true value and assumed about one-third of the cost of building Western railroads. It gave railroads grants of money totaling more than $700 million and gave them public lands throughout the West equaling the size of Texas.

While European entrepreneurs often retired when they acquired enough money to buy their way into the upper class, Americans regarded moneymaking itself as a worthwhile goal. "Such opportunities for making money," wrote Thomas Mellon, a Pittsburgh judge who later became a banker, "never existed before in all my former experience."

The money to be made in American manufacturing and transportation attracted private investors. The savings of New Englanders—accumulated from the West Indies and China trade, from clippers and whalers, from textile mills and shoe manu-

▼ OFFICE SECRETARY IN THE LATE 1800S

TEACH
Guided Practice

Categorizing Draw a hierarchical flowchart. In the top box, write "Industrial Development in the United States." Draw six boxes in a horizontal line below the top box, and attach them to the top box with arrows. Ask students to fill in the six boxes with the main factors that encouraged industrial growth. (*transportation, resources, science and technology, government, private investments, markets*) Discuss their flowcharts. Challenge them to suggest ways of showing graphically the interdependence of each of the factors. (*Sample answer: overlapping circles*) **L1, L2**

◿ Assign Guided Reading Activity 8-1.

Did You Know?

To supplement their income, many families rented rooms and provided meals to boarders. In 1890, 44,000 families reported that they shared housing with one or more boarders. By 1900 the figure had almost doubled.

Special Needs Activity

Writing Disability Many students with writing disabilities have difficulty organizing answers to questions that require written responses. Although they have usually studied "topic" or "lead" sentences, they often do not know how to form one independently. Read just the headings in this section aloud. Then, as a group have students write a topic sentence related to the increase in industrialization after the Civil War. For the Section Focus, for example, students may write "There were several factors that affected the growth of industry after the Civil War." **LEP, L1**

factures—helped build hundreds of factories and thousands of miles of railroad track. An equally important source of private capital was Europe, especially Great Britain. By 1900 British investors owned $2.5 billion in American railroad securities—more than twice the national debt of the United States.

■ Science and Technology

A flood of important inventions helped increase America's productive capacity and improved the network of transportation and communications that was vital to the nation's industrial growth. As American universities extended their activities beyond teaching, they became important centers of scientific research.

The Typewriter and the Telephone

The American public knew little of the university professors who extended the boundaries of science. People were greatly impressed, however, with inventors such as C. Latham Sholes, a Wisconsin printer whose idea for a typewriter in 1868 revolutionized business communications.

Equally inventive was Alexander Graham Bell, an immigrant from Scotland. Bell's profession was teaching deaf children to speak. He applied his speech training to developing the principles upon which the telephone is based. In 1876 he sent the first telephone communication to his laboratory assistant in the next room: "Mr. Watson, come here; I want you."

A year later he demonstrated the commercial value of his invention by sitting in Boston and talking with Watson in New York City—and the Bell Telephone Company was founded. By 1886 more than 250,000 phones were in use, mostly in businesses. This rapid growth created jobs for thousands of women as switchboard operators. By 1900 telephone rates had been lowered, and telephones increasingly began to appear in American homes.

Edison's Contributions

Perhaps even more famous than Bell was Thomas Alva Edison, who has been erroneously credited with inventing the electric light and moving pictures. Edison actually made few original discoveries. Instead, he was a great innovator who put the inventions of others to practical use. For example, Edison's redesign of Sholes's typewriter

▲ CANDLESTICK TELEPHONE, 1890s

Visualizing
History

▲ OFFICE WORK Among new opportunities for women living in the big cities were positions as secretaries, stenographers, and switchboard operators. Many women were able to find employment and earn a living. ***What innovations helped create new jobs?***

Cooperative Learning Activity

Starting a Business Organize students into groups of four. Each group will be entrepreneurs in the industrial climate of the late 1800s. Have each group decide what product or service it wants to provide. Assign each student in each group one of the following research topics: what human and mineral resources they need to use in their business, which of the newest scientific methods and inventions they plan to use, how they want to ship their product or sell their service, and what public policies and private investment practices they plan to follow. Have the group as a whole review and revise each other's work. **L2**

The Camera

For centuries scientists and inventors experimented with recording images in a lasting way. A French inventor produced the world's first photograph—a blurry farmyard view—by coating a metal plate with a light-sensitive chemical.

Then

Pictures for the Masses

Although the first true camera was not developed until 1826, improvements followed rapidly. Scientific and technical discoveries

Let the Children Kodak

For after all the home pictures are what count. We all enjoy the personal pictures that tell of our travels and our vacations—but the intimate home pictures of the children and by the children—those are the pictures that are most cherished as the years go by.

And with a Kodak or a Brownie it's all very simple. The youngsters, even from their kindergarten days, have no trouble in mastering the Brownie or one of the smaller Kodaks. Every step in picture making has been made easy and inexpensive by the Kodak system. Brownie cameras at one to twelve dollars, and Kodaks from five dollars up, offer a wide variety to suit all pockets and purposes.

EASTMAN KODAK COMPANY,
ROCHESTER, N.Y., *The Kodak City.*

aided in reducing the exposure time to 1/25 of a second by the 1870s. The development of negative film and specialized lenses also proved beneficial. Yet because photography required competent understanding of scientific and chemical processes, few Americans other than professional photographers owned cameras.

In 1888 George Eastman introduced the Kodak box camera, the first camera designed for amateur use. Lightweight and easy to operate, the Kodak put photography into the hands of millions.

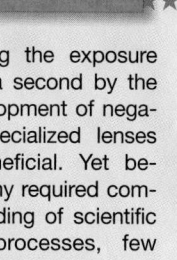

▲ MODERN CAMERA, 120 MM HASSELBLAD

Now

The Photographic Revolution

Photography progressed rapidly during the 1900s. Significant technical advances include color film, instant cameras, and the flash synchronization system. Today, a person can take a picture simply by pressing a button. An instant camera can produce a photo in about 15 seconds.

◀ TURN-OF-THE-CENTURY ADVERTISEMENT

permitted people to type faster than they could write. His improvement of Bell's telephone allowed voices to be transmitted longer distances. His work on improving the telegraph led to one of his few actual inventions, the phonograph.

The incandescent electric light had been demonstrated in Britain in 1840. But it was Edison who, in 1879, developed cheap methods of supplying power and wire, as well as filaments that lasted more than just a few minutes. The incandescent bulb lighted America's cities and made industrial production possible 24 hours a day.

The Canning Industry

During the Civil War, soldiers in the Union army had received some rations in cans, an innovation that demonstrated the value of canned food. After the war the canning industry improved its methods, and by 1900 machines had been designed to make, fill, and seal cans. A large variety of canned foods began to appear on the shelves of the nation's stores.

Textiles, Clothing, and Shoes

America's textile industry had long depended on machines to turn fibers into cloth. In 1893 the invention of the Northrup automatic loom led to the manufacture of cloth at an even faster rate. Bobbins, which had previously been changed by hand while the loom was stopped, were now changed automatically without stopping the loom.

Great changes also occurred in the clothing industry. Standard sizes, developed from measurements taken of Union soldiers during the Civil War, were used in the manufacture of ready-made clothes. The use of power-driven sewing machines and cloth cutters moved the clothing business from small tailor shops to large factories.

Similar changes took place in the shoe-making industry. New processes and inventions made **economies of scale** possible. In other words, large factories could mass-produce shoes more cheaply and efficiently than smaller companies. These factories could also pass these savings on to their

CHAPTER 8 The Rise of Industry: 1860–1900   **269**

Sidelight: Computers

The U.S. population for the 1890 census was tabulated on machines invented by Herman Hollerith. These tabulating machines eventually brought about the "Computer Age." Hollerith was visiting a friend's home where he met her father, head of the Vital Statistics Department for the 1880 census. The father

suggested that a machine using notched cards could take over the chore of counting census figures by hand. Hollerith devised a machine to electrically "read" or sort these cards. Since the machines were twice as fast as the hand method, Hollerith was given a contract.

Did You Know?

In the late 1800s, railroads became the nation's largest industry, surpassing all others as a buyer of iron, steel, and coal, and the nation's largest employer. By 1910 there were 1.7 million railroad workers. They expanded the size of the market for products, facilitated the acquisition of raw materials, and transported the labor pool to places where jobs existed.

Map Study *Using Maps*

Answer: They expanded the size of the market for products, facilitated the acquisition of raw materials, and transported the labor pool to places where jobs existed.

Map Skills Practice

Ask students to trace the Union Pacific Railroad route westward from Omaha to Promontory Point. Have them list the states the route crosses. (*Nebraska, Wyoming, Utah*)

 For additional map practice, use Map Transparency Activity 8 and Chapter Map Activity 8.

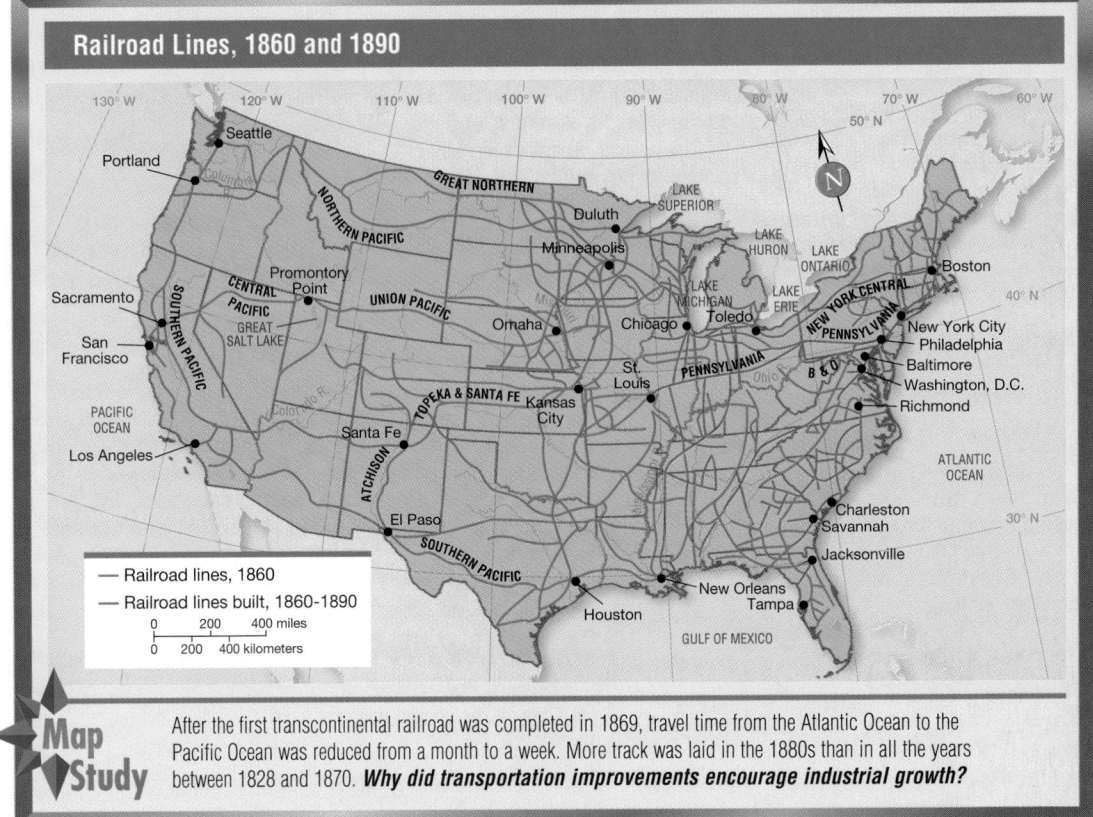

Railroad Lines, 1860 and 1890

— Railroad lines, 1860
— Railroad lines built, 1860-1890

0   200   400 miles
0 200 400 kilometers

Map Study After the first transcontinental railroad was completed in 1869, travel time from the Atlantic Ocean to the Pacific Ocean was reduced from a month to a week. More track was laid in the 1880s than in all the years between 1828 and 1870. **Why did transportation improvements encourage industrial growth?**

customers in the form of lower prices. By the turn of the century, local cobblers had nearly disappeared.

Steel, Oil, and Trains

Industrial growth was tied to advances in specific industries. The Bessemer process revolutionized American steelmaking in the 1870s. As steel was increasingly used for products such as machines, rails, and building beams, industry in general began to expand. The boom in the oil industry, along with the development of oil-lubricated machine tools—metal lathes, punches, and drill presses used to make other machines—brought tremendous growth in industrial capability.

New technology also stimulated the growth of the railroad industry. The Bessemer process was a factor in the expansion of railroad operations. This process allowed the railroad companies to replace iron rails with steel, which held up better and was able to carry heavier loads.

Another innovation was the Westinghouse air brake. The brake allowed the cars and locomotives to stop simultaneously—another factor making longer trains and heavier loads possible. Kerosene lamps, and later electric lights, provided better headlights for nighttime travel.

■ Railroad Building

Perhaps no other single factor was more responsible for the growth of industry in the United States than the expansion of the nation's railroads. At the end of the Civil War, there were 35,000 miles of railroad track in the United States. The tracks were of various gauges, or widths between the two rails.

Cultural Perspectives

Inventions of the 1800s Many of the inventions and ideas that helped industry to expand in the United States in the late 1800s were the work of immigrants. For example, Ottmar Mergenthaler, a German immigrant, invented the linotype machine in 1884. The machine made it possible to cast a "line of type" for a printing press in a few seconds. It sharply reduced the cost of print-ing books, magazines, and newspapers. Jan Matzeliger, an immigrant of African descent from Dutch Guiana, invented a machine that attached the uppers of a shoe to the soles as efficiently as workers could by hand. Patented in 1883, his revolutionary machine cut the cost of a pair of shoes in half.

Standardization and Consolidation

By the mid-1870s the amount of track had doubled, and by 1890 it had more than doubled again. In 1900 passenger and freight trains steamed along almost 200,000 miles of rails. By then track also was laid according to a standard gauge—4 feet, 8½ inches wide—so that freight could move from line to line without having to be unloaded from one car and reloaded onto another. This standardized railroad network bound all sections of the country into one market and one nation. Trains could carry bulky products long distances quickly and cheaply, making it possible for businesses to sell their goods across the continent. In 1860 railroads carried less than half as much freight as inland waterways. By 1890 railroads carried five times as much.

Railroads were not only the biggest shippers of industrial products; they were also American industry's best customers. In the mid-1880s, for example, rails were the single most important product of American steel companies. In addition, construction and operation of railroads required huge amounts of coal to power locomotives, lumber for ties and cars, iron for bridges, and petroleum products to lubricate moving parts.

Consolidating of smaller lines in the Midwest, East, and South was as important to development as the building of railroads spanning the West. Railroad building in the East was intended to promote specific cities or to serve local needs. As a result, hundreds of unconnected small lines, with tracks of varying gauges, were in use. The South had more than 400 railroads averaging less than 40 miles each. The challenge facing Eastern capitalists was to create a single rail system from this maze of small companies.

Railroad consolidation proceeded rapidly from the end of the Civil War to the turn of the century. By 1890 the Pennsylvania Railroad was a consolidation of 73 smaller companies with more than 5,000 miles of track. The Southern Pacific Railway had pieced together companies with 8,500 miles of lines. Eventually most rail traffic was controlled by 7 giant systems with terminals in major cities and scores of branches reaching into the countryside.

Linking Across TIME

Rising fuel costs and ecological concerns have revived interest in trains, especially for mass transit. Commuter rail lines can carry 70 times as many people as highways, yet cost one-tenth as much to build and use only 1 percent of the fuel.

History AND ART

Railroads brought eastern tourists to places that were once remote and inaccessible, places like the Grand Tetons in Wyoming. The Chicago, Burlington, and Quincy railroads, for example, conducted escorted tour groups. **Answer to Caption:** faster, cheaper, and more efficient

▲ *ACROSS THE CONTINENT* by Currier and Ives, 1868 Currier and Ives produced America's most popular and successful prints of the 1800s. *Why did rail transport surpass water transport in the late 1800s?*

Sidelight: Trunks and Carpetbags

Since most traveling in the late 1800s was done by railroad or ship, various sizes of trunks were used to transport personal belongings. One could pack an entire wardrobe in the Saratoga trunk. The more affluent had trunks made of deer hide and pigskin, while the less fortunate used wooden trunks with hinges and locks. For hand luggage people carried cases made of cardboard or carpetbags made from a piece of old carpet. For hats and collars, people carried a bandbox, which was a container made of wood or cardboard.

ASSESS

Check Understanding

Assign Section 1 Review as homework or an in-class activity.

Evaluate

⊙ 🗁 Assign Section Quiz 8-1 or use the Testmaker to create a customized quiz.

Reteach

Write these terms on the chalkboard: *expansion, consolidation, standardization.* Have students use these terms to write a paragraph about the development of the railroad.

🗁 Have students complete Reteaching Activity 8-1.

Enrich

Have students research one of the following subjects: the development of the steam locomotive in the United States, custom Pullman cars, or the architecture of railroad terminals.

CLOSE

Refer to the quotation in this section by Charles Francis Adams, Jr., on corruption in the railroad industry. Have students give their opinions on whether a *laissez-faire* attitude toward business regulation breeds corruption and why.

Getting a "Share of the Business"

In gaining and using such power, many railroad builders became tough, ruthless, and unethical competitors who amassed fortunes in the course of their activities. Railroad consolidator Jay Gould sold small lines that he owned to large railroads that he controlled at prices far above the small railroads' actual worth. When railroad builder Collis Huntington remarked, "It takes money to fix things," he meant bribing government officials, not repairing equipment! In describing his industry, railroad executive Charles Francis Adams, Jr., observed:

> ❝ *Honesty and good faith are scarcely regarded. Certainly they are not tolerated at all if they interfere with a man's getting his "share of the business." Gradually this demoralizing spirit of low cunning has pervaded the entire system. Its moral tone is deplorably low. . . .* ❞

Cornelius Vanderbilt

One of the most successful railroad consolidators was Cornelius Vanderbilt, who built the New York Central system. By the mid-1850s, he had built the largest steamboat fleet in America. Yet Vanderbilt saw that the future of transportation was in railroads. So at age 73 he merged 3 short New York railroads he had purchased to form the New York Central, which ran from New York City to Buffalo. Within 4 years Vanderbilt extended his control over lines all the way to Chicago. In addition to bringing many lines under one management, Vanderbilt made great improvements in service. He was one of the first to use the Westinghouse air brake and the very first to lay a four-track main line—two tracks for freight and two for passenger traffic.

Benefits

Vanderbilt, like other railroad tycoons, was a combination of shrewd speculator, ruthless competitor, and visionary. Yet Vanderbilt and other railroad entrepreneurs provided great benefits, too. Standard-gauge track was universally accepted, and standard time zones were established to simplify scheduling.

The big systems were able to improve equipment, to shift cars from one section of the country to another according to seasonal needs, and to speed long-distance transportation. They made railroad operation so much more efficient that the average rate per mile for a ton of freight dropped from 2 cents in 1860 to less than 1 cent in 1900. The railroad executives also showed entrepreneurs how to operate large companies across great distances.

Section 1 ★ Review

Checking for Understanding

1. **Identify** Alexander Graham Bell, Thomas Alva Edison, Cornelius Vanderbilt.

2. **Define** entrepreneur, economies of scale.

3. **List** reasons for the growth of industry in the United States.

4. **Describe** how specific technology accelerated the growth of industry.

5. **Explain** the contribution of the railroad in the growth of industry.

Critical Thinking

6. **Applying Ideas** One writer noted that "This standardized railroad network bound all sections of the country into one market and one nation." Explain what the writer meant.

ACTIVITY

7. Research a modern-day invention, such as the computer, laser, or optic fiber. Create a visual display that presents information about how the invention has changed people's lives.

272   UNIT 3 New Horizons: 1860–1900

Answers to SECTION 1 REVIEW

1. Alexander Graham Bell, 268; Thomas Alva Edison, 269; Cornelius Vanderbilt, 272
2. All vocabulary words are defined in the Glossary.
3. abundant resources, available labor, immigration, government policies, investment, advances in technology and transportation
4. Typewriter and telephone improved communications, electric lighting allowed industrial production at night; power-driven machines created large clothing and shoe factories.
5. Railroads created a national market; carried industrial products long distances quickly and cheaply; and served as a market.
6. Standardization promotes efficiency and quicker turnaround.
7. Displays will vary, but students should provide valid explanations.

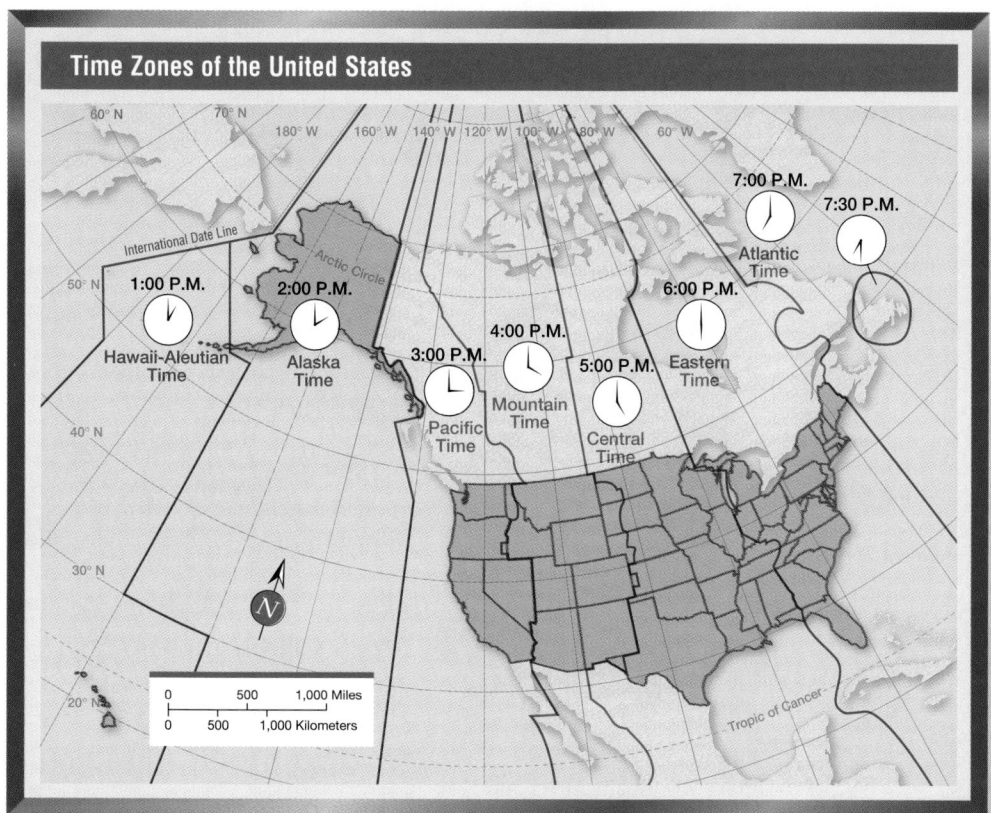

Time Zones of the United States

Standard Time Zones

Throughout most of the nineteenth century, few Americans could agree on the time of day because every community determined its own time by the position of the sun. Railways, however, required a single standard of time for scheduling and routing. In 1883 American and Canadian railroads established standardized time zones.

In 1884 delegates from 27 nations met in Washington, D.C., and divided the earth into 24 time zones. The base time zone was established with the Prime Meridian (0° longitude) as its midpoint. Since the Prime Meridian ran through Greenwich in Britain, the time in the base zone became known as Greenwich time.

Making the Geography Connection

1. Why did standardized time zones become necessary in the 1800s?

2. If you traveled from Detroit, Michigan, to Tucson, Arizona, what time zones would you cross?

ACTIVITY

3. If it is 6 A.M. in Omaha, Nebraska, what time is it in Jacksonville, Florida; Butte, Montana; and Anchorage, Alaska? Put your answers in the form of a table or a visual display.

TEACH

Have students refer to the time zone map on this page and locate the time zone in which they live. Ask them to locate the International Date Line, and ask them if they traveled east across the Date Line, what the present day would be. **L1**

Did You Know?

Opponents of standard time called local time "God's time" because it was based on the laws of nature—the sun's position in the sky—rather than on human criteria. They referred to standard time as "railroad time," and blocked attempts to create time zones. Not until 1918 was Congress able to pass a law that standardized time zones.

273

Answers to Making the Connection

1. Railroads and the need for standardized time for scheduling and routing, especially in countries covering a large area, led to the establishment of standardized time zones.

2. Central and Mountain

3. Jacksonville—5 A.M.; Butte—4 A.M.; Anchorage—3 A.M.

★★★

Growth of Big Business

FOCUS

Bellringer

 Before taking roll, project Section Focus Transparency 8-2 or hand out Section Focus Transparency Activity 8-2. Have students answer the questions.

Motivating Activity

Tell students that in this section they will read about how consolidation in business encouraged economic growth.

Ask students to define *consolidation*. Discuss their definitions. (*the process of uniting or merging something*)

Vocabulary Precheck

Ask students to define each of the "Key Terms." Have a volunteer consult the dictionary for any unfamiliar words. **L1, LEP**

ABCNEWS INTERACTIVE™

VIDEODISC

Powers of the Congress

Side Two, Chapter 10
Title: *Capitalism*
Subject: Exploration of what it means to live in a capitalist society

Setting the Scene

Section Focus

As railroads gave industrialists access to raw materials and markets, great opportunities developed for business expansion. The result was "Big Business." By 1900 gigantic companies owned scores of plants, sold products nationwide, and had hundreds of millions of dollars in capital and credit behind them.

◀ COVER OF HORATIO ALGER NOVEL

Objectives

After studying this section, you should be able to

★ discuss the methods big business used to become successful.

★ explain why incorporation encouraged business growth.

Key Terms

corporation, holding company, trust, horizontal integration, vertical integration

he railroads were America's first "Big Business." Founding a major railroad consumed larger sums of money than any previous American enterprise. The investment required was so great that no one individual could make it. Instead, a large railroad line was organized as a **corporation**—a company formed by a group of investors who each receive a share of ownership in proportion to the amount they invested. Investors also enjoyed the protection of limited liability: they risked only the amount of their investment, even if the corporation went bankrupt and could not pay its bills.

The expansion of the railroads, along with other improvements in transportation and communication, created the mass market. No longer were manufacturers limited to local or regional sales. The mass market made mass production practical.

■ Benefits of Big Business

Corporate structure allowed entrepreneurs in many industries to raise the money they needed to launch or expand companies as opportunities arose. Big business enjoyed many advantages.

Efficiency in Production and Labor

Large companies could manufacture enough products to meet the demands of a national market. They produced better products at lower cost than their smaller competitors through the economies of scale that resulted from using the newest processes and combining operations formerly performed by separate companies. High salaries were offered in order to get expert managers. At the same time, they increased efficiency by establishing separate departments for specialized functions such as purchasing, production, research, distribution, and sales.

274 UNIT 3 New Horizons: 1860–1900

Classroom Resources for SECTION 2

Blackline Masters:
- Reproducible Lesson Plan 8-2
- Guided Reading Activity 8-2
- Cooperative Learning Activity 8
- Workbook Activity 8-2
- Primary and Secondary Source Readings, pp. 16–17
- Reteaching Activity 8-2
- Section Quiz 8-2

Transparencies:
- Section Focus Transparency 8-2

Multimedia:
- Testmaker
- Powers of the Congress

In conducting their operations, big companies organized work to gain maximum production from their employees. A steel company engineer, Frederick W. Taylor, developed a system to study and time workers and to make changes so their jobs could be performed more efficiently. Such studies even included counting the steps a worker took in moving from one place to another on the job and determining what size shovels were best for shoveling coal, rice, and iron ore!

The Big Business of Meatpacking

The advantages of big business were shown dramatically by the development of large meatpacking companies. In the past, fresh meat had been slaughtered locally, and every town had at least one slaughterhouse. When the refrigerated railroad car made it possible to ship fresh meat over long distances, huge companies such as Swift and Armour appeared, selling their products throughout the country. The big packers were so highly organized and efficient that they could sell meat at a loss and make their profit from the rest of the carcass. Chicago humorist Finley Peter Dunne, writing under the name of the fictional Irish saloon keeper "Mr. Dooley," hardly exaggerated about Armour when he noted:

> " *A cow goes lowin' softly into Armour's an' comes out glue, gelatin, fertylizer, celooloid, joolry, sofy cushions, hair restorer, washin' sody, soap, lithrachoor an' bed springs so quick that while aft she's still cow, for'ard she may be anything fr'm buttons to pannyma hats.* "

Big Business

Because of their efficiency, organization, and size, large businesses were frequently in a position to take advantage of their competitors and sometimes of the public. Big companies could demand volume discounts from shippers. They could sell their products in an area at a loss until local competitors were forced to shut down or sell out. If a large company succeeded in getting a monopoly in its industry, it could raise consumer prices and pay less to suppliers of raw materials.

Big business in the late nineteenth century resulted from the vision of people who recognized great opportunities for wealth and were willing to take risks to get it. The companies they organized—American Tobacco, General Electric, and United

AMERICAN PORTRAITS

Gustavus Swift
1839–1903

At the age of 16, Gustavus Swift borrowed $25, bought a cow, slaughtered it, and sold the beef at a $10 profit. From that point on, Swift devoted his life to making money from meat.

Swift first opened several butcher shops. With a talent for buying only the best cattle, he next moved to Chicago—capital of the cattle market—and went into business shipping livestock by rail to Eastern cities. He soon realized, however, that he could make more money butchering the cattle in Chicago and shipping the meat.

At first, to prevent spoilage, Swift could ship only during winter months. But then he hired an engineer who developed a refrigerated railroad car that made it possible to ship year-round. As hungry workers swelled the size of Eastern cities, Swift & Co. made great profits by shipping huge quantities of meat to feed them.

Critical Thinking Activity

Analyzing Quotations Write the following quotation from the Rev. Russell H. Conwell's sermon "Acres of Diamonds" on the chalkboard:

"It is cruel to slander the rich because they have been successful . . . . They are not scoundrels because they have gotten money. They have gone into great enterprises that have enriched the nation and the nation has enriched them."

Have students write a paragraph giving their opinions on whether or not Rev. Conwell's defense is justified in regard to entrepreneurs in the late nineteenth century. Tell students to back up their opinions with facts. **L2, L3**

TEACH
Guided Practice
Linking Past and Present
Ask students to list some of the nineteenth-century business practices entrepreneurs engaged in that would today be punishable by fines or imprisonment. (*forcing competitors out of business through unfair business practices, evading the law, bribing officials, destroying labor unions, devastating the environment*) Discuss students' lists, and have them speculate why people allowed entrepreneurs to get away with such abuses. **L1, LEP**

Teaching American Portraits
Gustavus Swift was preoccupied with increasing profits. In order to detect wasted motion, waste in materials, and identify potential trouble spots, Swift often observed the workers on the packinghouse floor. Through systematic organization of work he increased productivity. Ask students how they feel when someone watches them work.

Food of the Times

By 1900 H.J. Heinz's company was the nation's largest food processor. The company manufactured more than two hundred food products, including such items as baked beans and tomato ketchup. Those inexpensive canned goods added variety to the diet of city families.

 **Visualizing History**

▲ **MARKETING GOODS** Mass production of consumer goods, such as hats, combined with transportation improvements inspired entrepreneurs to print merchandise catalogs and open mail-order stores. *Why were big businesses able to sell for less than local companies?*

Fruit, among them—came to dominate their industries and sold products not just nationwide but to the entire world.

Business Tactics

In attaining success, however, many entrepreneurs showed few scruples in driving competitors out of business. Their tactics included evading the law, bribing officials, destroying labor unions, and devastating the environment. Some entrepreneurs commonly sold products at below their cost until local businesses were forced to close down or sell out.

Mixed Feelings Toward Big Business

The American public, therefore, had mixed feelings about big business and its leaders. Americans worried about the corrupting influence of wealth and power. Yet others admitted that they benefited from big business's efficiency, its lower prices, and the jobs it created. Historian Vernon L. Parrington said of the entrepreneurs:

66 *These new Americans were primitive souls, ruthless, predatory,*

capable, single-minded men; rogues and rascals often, but never feeble, never hindered by petty scruples, never given to puling [whimpering] or whining. . . . Analyze the most talked-of men of the age and one is likely to find a splendid audacity coupled with immense wastefulness. A note of tough-minded-ness marks them. . . . They fought their way encased in rhinoceros hides. 99

Rags to Riches

Success in business became a best-selling theme in popular fiction. Horatio Alger became wealthy himself when he wrote novels like *Mark the Match Boy, Tattered Tom,* and more than 100 others—all "rags-to-riches" stories of young men who became successful in business because of hard work and lucky breaks.

■ The Role of Corporations

American law allowed the formation of business corporations, and conditions in the United States encouraged their existence.

276 UNIT 3 New Horizons: 1860–1900

As a business form, the corporation offered a number of advantages over a partnership or a sole proprietorship. The corporation had a permanence that lasted beyond the lives of its owners or stockholders. That meant company managers could confidently plan far into the future.

Kinds of Companies

By selling stocks and bonds, a corporation could raise the capital, or investment money, for its operations. Small amounts of capital from many individual investors could be pooled into the huge sums needed to start or expand a large company. In that way no one investor would have to take a big financial risk. To reduce risk even more, investors could spread it out by purchasing stock in several corporations. One specialized form of corporation, the **holding company,** became very popular. Holding companies manufactured no products and had no customers. They existed only to own stock in other corporations. Through holding companies, wealthy capitalists could own controlling interests in many businesses.

Other companies were organized into trusts. A **trust** was formed when several companies gave control of their operations to a single board of trustees. The shareholders of each individual company continued to own it and keep its profits, but management of all companies in the trust was in the same hands. Through holding companies and trusts, entrepreneurs formed the huge business combinations that dominated the late nineteenth century. Some combinations were able to restrict or prevent competition among their members.

Ways to Combine Companies

Business consolidation—combining companies into one unit—took various forms. Sometimes companies were consolidated by **horizontal integration,** in which several firms engaged in the same kind of business were joined together. If a horizontal combination became large enough, it could achieve a monopoly of that industry.

Companies also were consolidated by **vertical integration,** which joined businesses engaged in different but related activities. A vertical combination, for example, might include under the same ownership individual companies that provided raw materials, transported those raw materials to factories, manufactured a product from those raw materials, and distributed and sold the finished product.

A horizontal combination, once established, was able to expand vertically because of the control its size gave it over both suppliers and distributors. Similarly, a vertical combination could become so efficient that it expanded horizontally by buying its competitors, forcing them into trusts, or driving them out of business.

Section 2 ★ Review

Checking for Understanding

1. **Identify** Frederick W. Taylor, Horatio Alger.

2. **Define** corporation, holding company, trust, horizontal integration, vertical integration.

3. **Describe** the practices that made big business successful, but at the same time open to criticism from many Americans.

4. **List** the various ways businesses can be organized. Discuss the advantages of each type of organization.

Critical Thinking

5. **Evaluating Change**   How might the shift to the prevalence of big business work to the advantage or disadvantage of a consumer?

ACTIVITY

6. Keep track of all the purchases you make for one week. List the name of the businesses that sold them to you. Indicate whether you think each business is small, medium, or large.

Answers to SECTION 2 REVIEW

1. Frederick W. Taylor, 275; Horatio Alger, 276
2. All vocabulary words are defined in the Glossary.
3. Successful: produced greater volume, better products, at lower cost; used newest processes; combined operations; hired expert managers; departmentalized; created jobs. Objectionable: demanded discounts and
   forced smaller competitors out of business
4. corporations, holding companies, trusts, horizontal or vertical combinations
5. Answers will vary but might include the following: advantage—lower prices; disadvantage—monopolistic price gouging
6. Answers will vary. Students should provide valid reasoning for their conclusions.

ASSESS
Check Understanding
Assign Section 2 Review as homework or an in-class activity.

Evaluate
Assign the Section 2 Quiz or use the Testmaker to create a customized quiz.

Reteach
Pair students; have one partner list methods big business used in the 1800s to become successful, and the other list reasons incorporation encouraged business growth.

Have students complete Reteaching Activity 8-2.

Enrich
Have students read stories by Horatio Alger and then write their own rags-to-riches story using an Alger story as a model. Ask them to create an imaginative plot but to make the setting and the references historically accurate.

Assign Primary and Secondary Source Readings, pp. 16–17.

CLOSE
John D. Rockefeller claimed that consolidation protected businesses from "wasteful conditions." He insisted that "individualism has gone, never to return." Ask students if they agree. Have them give facts and arguments in support of their point of view.

FOCUS

Bellringer

Before taking roll, project Section Focus Transparency 8-3 or hand out Section Focus Transparency Activity 8-3. Have students answer the questions.

Motivating Activity

Have students list ways in which oil is used today. (*gasoline for cars, ships, airplanes; oil for heating homes; to generate electricity; to manufacture chemicals to produce cloth and paint*) Have students explain why a rise in oil prices today might have a serious impact on America's economy.

Vocabulary Precheck

Ask students to define each of the "Key Terms." Have a volunteer consult the dictionary for any unfamiliar words. **L1, LEP**

★★

Captains of Industry

Setting the Scene

Section Focus

The oil and steel industries were each dominated by a man as ruthless as he was efficient. Rising from poverty to attain great wealth and power, John D. Rockefeller and Andrew Carnegie represented to many the American Dream.

Objectives

After studying this section, you should be able to

★ compare the methods used by Carnegie and Rockefeller to achieve success.

★ explain social Darwinism.

Key Terms

rebate, social Darwinism, philanthropy

◄ COVER OF *McCLURE'S MAGAZINE*

*A*lthough giant combinations arose to control the beef, flour, whiskey, tobacco, lead, and sugar industries, as well as many others, by 1900 the American economy ran on oil, and its backbone was steel. No industrialists exemplified the principles of doing "big business" in late-nineteenth-century America more than the entrepreneurs who dominated these two basic industries—John D. Rockefeller in oil and Andrew Carnegie in steel.

■ Rockefeller and the Standard Oil Trust

The most successful example of horizontal consolidation was the Standard Oil Trust, which gained a near monopoly of oil refineries and pipelines. The guiding genius behind Standard Oil was John D. Rockefeller, who during his 98 years, from 1839 to 1937, amassed what was at the time the world's largest fortune—almost $1 billion.

The Early Years

Rockefeller went to work at age 16 as a bookkeeper in a wholesale commission and produce company in Cleveland, Ohio. Dominated by the idea that he was "bound to be rich," he saved $800 in 3 years on a salary of $15 per week. At 19 he left his job and opened his own commission house. In only 4 years he increased his capital to about $100,000. Then in 1862, at age 23, he put all his money into a new and growing industry—petroleum refining.

Until the 1850s, petroleum, then called "rock oil," had been used only as a patent medicine. In 1855 scientists discovered that petroleum, when refined into kerosene, gave

278   UNIT 3 New Horizons: 1860–1900

---

better light than whale oil in lamps and made a much better lubricant than animal fat.

The first oil well, drilled in 1859, set off a stampede to western Pennsylvania much like the California gold rush of 1849. Land values jumped from a few dollars an acre to hundreds of dollars a square foot, new towns appeared overnight, and the demand for kerosene spread worldwide. In spite of the Civil War, the petroleum industry grew so fast that by 1865 oil products had risen to fourth place among American exports.

Drilling for oil was always a big gamble, and Rockefeller realized oil refining was a safer investment. The entire oil business was highly disorganized, however. Fortunes were made and lost overnight as the price of oil fluctuated wildly. Rockefeller believed such unstable conditions resulted from competition among thousands of small producers and hundreds of small refiners.

Standard Oil Becomes a Giant

By 1870 Rockefeller's firm, the Standard Oil Company of Ohio, was the largest of 26 refineries in Cleveland, processing 2 or 3 percent of the crude oil produced in the United States. Over the next 9 years, Rockefeller gained control of more than 90 percent of the nation's refining business and brought order to a chaotic industry. But to achieve stability and efficiency in the oil business, Rockefeller used methods so shrewdly brutal that when they were revealed he became one of the most hated men in America.

One of Standard Oil's major weapons was the **rebate,** or discount, on freight charges. In 1872 the company offered to give certain railroads all its shipping business if those railroads secretly agreed to charge Standard Oil 25 to 50 percent less than they charged its competitors. In return for its business, these railroads also promised to tell Rockefeller the destinations of all his competitors' shipments. This information gave him valuable insights into his rivals' business dealings. These secret arrangements gave Standard Oil such an advantage over other Cleveland refineries that within 3 months all but 5 were forced

to sell out to Rockefeller. Once it controlled oil refining in Cleveland, Standard Oil moved rapidly toward a nationwide monopoly by allying with the strongest companies throughout the industry. In 1880 a committee of the New York legislature reported on the extent of Standard Oil's domination of the oil business:

> 66 *It owns and controls the pipe lines of the producing regions that connect with the railroads. It controls both ends of these roads. It ships 95 percent of all oil. . . . It dictates terms and rates to the railroads. It has bought out and frozen out refiners all over the country. By means of the superior facilities for transportation which it thus possessed, it could overbid [its competitors for crude oil] in the producing regions and undersell [its competitors] in the markets of the world.* 99

 ▲ **JOHN D. ROCKEFELLER** Although he was ruthless in business dealings, John D. Rockefeller always carried dimes in his pockets to give to small children he encountered on the street. *What change did Rockefeller bring to the oil industry?*

Guided Practice

 **CURRICULUM CONNECTION**

Economics Write the following on the chalkboard:

Date	Price per Barrel
1858	$30
1861	$1.35
1864	$14
1870	$2.70

Ask students to study the swings in oil prices and hypothesize why such wide swings were unsettling to the oil producers, oil refiners, oil towns, and oil users. (*Making a reasonable profit was not predictable, creating planning problems for producers and refiners. Towns were in boom or bust cycles. Users could not predict outlay for oil.*) **L2**

Did You Know?

Not all of the nineteenth-century business tycoons were comfortable with their wealth. J.P. Morgan, for example, spent almost 20 years giving money away.

Visualizing **History** During his 98 years, from 1839 to 1937, John D. Rockefeller amassed what was at the time the world's largest fortune—almost $1 billion.

Answer to Caption: stability, efficiency, consolidation

Sidelight: The Oil Industry

Much like Standard Oil, the Organization of Petroleum Exporting Countries (OPEC) tries to maintain stability in the oil industry to ensure profits. Since 1970 OPEC has controlled approximately one-third to one-half of the world's oil supply. In 1994 member nations included Algeria, Gabon, Indonesia, Iran, Iraq, Kuwait, Libya, Nigeria, Qatar, Saudi Arabia, United Arab Emirates, and Venezuela.

Independent Practice

Making a Map Provide Outline Map 39 from the Glencoe Social Studies Outline Map Resource Book. Ask students to label the areas where oil fields are located. Have them also investigate what percentage of oil the United States buys from other countries and what percentage is produced domestically. **LEP, L1**

Did You Know?

When he retired in 1897, John D. Rockefeller, Sr., dedicated the remainder of his life to philanthropic work. He gave over $35 million to the University of Chicago and also established the General Education Board. Through this board, established for the promotion of education throughout the United States, Rockefeller gave over $60 million for medical research, $78 million to colleges and universities, $18 million for African American education, and $18 million for other educational purposes. Before his death in 1937, Rockefeller had given away over $520 million.

Visualizing
History Point out that important muckrakers of the period included Charles E. Russell who wrote on the beef trust and Ray Stannard Baker on railroads.
Answer to Caption: Standard Oil.

Visualizing
History

▲ IDA TARBELL Ida Tarbell was one of several American writers who played a major part in exposing social problems. *What company did Tarbell target in her series of articles for McClure's Magazine?*

By a secret agreement that became known as the Standard Oil Trust, Rockefeller moved in 1882 to consolidate his control of the oil industry further by combining 40 companies under a single management. Once in control of most of the refining and transportation of oil in the United States, Standard Oil expanded vertically. It gained control of oil fields to have an independent supply source, and it marketed natural gas. At the other end of the production process, Standard Oil moved into the distribution of petroleum products, both in the United States and overseas. Eventually Standard Oil controlled a fleet of oceangoing tankers and door-to-door delivery wagons in Europe. It even manufactured and sold cooking stoves to increase the demand for kerosene!

Following Standard Oil's Lead

Standard Oil's spectacular success led others to establish horizontal combinations of companies in industries as varied as whiskey, bituminous coal, and rope. The

purpose of these combinations was mainly to prevent overproduction and to keep prices up. Yet it was difficult to control an entire industry and to keep new firms out of the market. Such efforts to obtain monopolies were greatly resented by small business people and consumers. Vertical combinations, on the other hand, were not monopolistic. The savings that resulted from the economies they brought to production were passed on to consumers in lower prices. Vertical combination thus became a common form of business organization.

Business Tactics Exposed

Although Rockefeller's rivals in the oil industry were painfully aware of his ruthless methods, it was an investigative journalist who exposed them to the public. This courageous woman was Ida Tarbell.

In 1903, in a series of brilliant articles in *McClure's Magazine,* Tarbell revealed Rockefeller's secret deals and his high-pressure tactics. She explained how companies controlled by Standard Oil continued to do business under their former names. She documented how, to conceal his control of these companies, Rockefeller appointed "dummy directors," who were sometimes employees such as errand-runners or secretaries.

Rockefeller, a devout churchgoer and Sunday school teacher, did not think that his actions were wrong. He pointed out that what he had done to destroy his competitors had not been illegal when he first did it. Rebates, for example, were granted by railroads to big shippers in many other industries. When buying out his competitors, Rockefeller offered to pay them in either cash or Standard Oil stock, advising them to take the stock. Those who took his advice became rich.

Much of Rockefeller's advantage over competitors came from his passion for efficiency and his hatred of waste. Standard Oil continuously improved its product. The company had few labor troubles because it paid its workers well. It tried to protect their jobs in times of depression and was one of the first companies to pay old-age pensions.

Critical Thinking Activity

Analyzing Quotations Write the following quotation from *Early Days of Oil* by P.H. Giddens on the chalkboard:

"Wells are sinking in every direction and strangers are flocking in from all parts of the country . . . every son of Pennsylvania should

rejoice in the good Providence that has enriched the state . . . with rivers of oil."

Have students read the quotation and write a paragraph comparing the excitement created by the discovery of oil in Pennsylvania with the excitement of the gold strike in California. **L3**

Andrew Carnegie, Master of Steel

The most remarkable example of the creation of a vertical combination was the giant steel corporation built by Andrew Carnegie.

Coming to Pittsburgh from Scotland at the age of 13, Carnegie went to work in a cotton factory where he earned $1.20 for working a 72-hour week. He saw an opportunity to grow with the railroad, however, and in 1853 he went to work as a clerk and telegraph operator for the Pennsylvania Railroad. His ability, energy, and ambition were so great that at age 23 he became superintendent of the railroad's western division.

Looking to the Future

While working for the railroad, Carnegie wisely invested his earnings in iron companies. As the railroads grew, Carnegie foresaw his opportunity for personal success in the increasing demand for rails, bridges, and locomotives. By age 30, when he left the railroad to manage an iron bridge company, his investments were producing an annual income of nearly $50,000.

After seven years making iron bridges, Carnegie again looked at the future and saw it was in steel. In 1873 he formed a group of investors to build the largest and most modern steel mill in the world near Pittsburgh. Carnegie was the first person in the United States to use two new ways of making steel—the Bessemer process and the open-hearth process. These processes enabled him to produce steel so cheaply that it could now be used for rails and construction girders, as well as for cutlery and precision machines.

Another Giant Is Born

Almost overnight Carnegie changed the character of the industry. Previously iron and steel had been manufactured at hundreds of small furnaces all over the country. But Bessemer converters and open-hearth furnaces required heavy investments of capital and huge amounts of coke and ore to keep them going. Small companies were soon forced out of business by big ones.

In less than 20 years, Carnegie was the greatest steelmaker in the world. One reason for his phenomenal success was that he took the guesswork out of making steel by getting the best technical and scientific experts he could find. Carnegie liked to boast that he "was smart enough to surround himself with men far cleverer than himself." For example, his managers were able to determine almost to the penny what it cost to produce a ton of steel. With this knowledge, Carnegie could set prices below his competitors and still make a profit. His chemists found uses for by-products previously considered to be industrial waste, and they discovered how to use low-grade ores.

▲ *THE STEEL MILL* by Maximillian Luce, 1895
Although the growth of the oil industry after the Civil War was phenomenal, the steel industry achieved even greater growth. *What benefits did the success of these industries bring to the nation?*

Cases in the 1990s involving unethical business practices such as those of Michael Milken, Ivan Boesky, and Dennis Levine—Wall Street millionaires—have stirred business schools to offer business ethics courses in their MBA programs. The Harvard Business School received a $30 million gift from alumnus John S. R. Shad, head of the bankrupt investment firm Drexel Burnham Lambert, that he targeted for a business ethics curriculum.

History AND ART

Between 1866 and 1876, the production of American steel jumped from 20,000 to 600,000 tons; by 1897 it had skyrocketed to more than 7 million tons.
Answer to Caption: Their efficiency in production brought more goods and lower prices to consumers.

Did You Know?

In 1802 Pittsburgh was described by a French traveler as a town of 40 to 50 acres with 400 homes. In 1890 a team of British ironworkers noted that Pittsburgh had 21 blast furnaces, 40 iron foundries, 15,000 coke ovens, and 33 rolling mills.

Cooperative Learning Activity

Oil Products Divide the class into small groups, and provide each group with a large piece of paper. Have group members work together to research how such by-products of oil as kerosene, paint, or paraffin are processed. Ask students to show the process on a poster, using explanatory labels. **L1**

Visualizing History Captains of industry like Rockefeller and Carnegie believed that competition in industry was wasteful. They argued that consolidated companies were more efficient than many, small, competing companies in the same industry. **Answer to Caption:** His railroad job made him realize the importance of these products.

FACT or FICTION?

Andrew Carnegie, like other wealthy people, had the deep conviction that if individuals worked hard in the United States, saved their earnings, and invested prudently, they would become wealthy in no time at all.

FICTION: Immigrant workers had little opportunity to amass wealth because they had neither political nor social connections. They were given no lands, other than homesteads, and received no grants from the government as the railroad builders had. Actually, some of the later immigrants were denied entry into schools and jobs and also into better neighborhoods.

In his constant effort to be more efficient, Carnegie combined all of the processes required for making steel into one great vertical combination. In addition to blast furnaces and steel mills, the Carnegie Steel Company controlled rich iron ore deposits near Lake Superior, fleets of ships to carry the ore over the Great Lakes, a railroad to carry the ore from the Lake Erie region to Pittsburgh, coal mines in Pennsylvania to fire the blast furnaces, and factories for producing finished steel products such as wire.

Crushing Labor and Gobbling the Competition

Seeking out the ablest people in the industry, Carnegie bought their loyalty by making them partners. Equally alert for ability inside his companies, he rapidly promoted exceptional employees. Common laborers in his mills fared less well, however, as he drove wages down and hours up. In 1892, with his partner, Henry C. Frick, he crushed the steelworkers' union, so that the 12-hour day remained standard for many years.

During the three major depressions of the late 1800s, while other steel companies closed down, Carnegie expanded. He rebuilt his factories to be even more efficient and acquired his weakened competitors.

■ Social Darwinism and the Industrialists

Andrew Carnegie was making $25 million a year at a time when there was no income tax. His workers, on the other hand, earned $8 or $9 a week. He made steel so cheaply and competed so mercilessly that remaining steel companies faced bankruptcy. Carnegie and most other great industrialists found justification for these actions and their consequences in a philosophy known as **social Darwinism,** which applied the biological theories of naturalist Charles Darwin to human society.

Darwin believed that in nature a competition exists in which only the fittest—the strongest, most clever, most efficient—

plants and animals survive. The weak individuals die out, and each species thereby remains strong and healthy. Philosophers such as Yale professor William Graham Sumner argued that this competition also operated in human society, and that industrialists like Rockefeller and Carnegie had succeeded because of their rare talents. "The millionaires are a product of natural selection," Sumner wrote. "They get high wages and live in luxury, but the bargain is a good one for society." Not surprisingly, Andrew Carnegie and John D. Rockefeller both believed wholeheartedly in the philosophy of social Darwinism. Carnegie called it a method better than elections for selecting leaders. "By a process of pitiless testing we discover who are the strong and who are the weak," he wrote. "To the strong we give power in the form of the autocratic control of industry and of wealth." Rockefeller told his Sunday school class that his business practices merely demonstrated "the survival of the fittest . . . a law of nature and a law of God."

Visualizing History ▲ **ANDREW CARNEGIE** If any entrepreneur symbolized the rags-to-riches legend, it was Andrew Carnegie. The son of poor immigrants, Carnegie built a company that by 1900 was making one-fourth of the nation's steel and serving a world market. *What caused Carnegie to believe the future was in iron and steel?*

Critical Thinking Activity

Analyzing Quotations Write on the chalkboard the following quotation attributed to Andrew Carnegie:

"Those who are most successful in the acquisition of property and who acquire it to such an enormous extent are the very men who are able to control it, to invest it, and to handle it in the way most useful to society."

Ask students to study the quotation and explain why the sentiment expressed in it was acceptable in the late 1800s but not today. **L2**

📁 For additional practice in using critical thinking skills, assign Critical Thinking Skills Activity 8.

▲ *THE SITWELL FAMILY* by John Singer Sargent Wealthy families lived in elegant homes staffed by scores of servants. While some of the wealthy were given to showy displays, others used their wealth and position to help others. ***What is philanthropy?***

But for Carnegie the achievement of great power and wealth was not enough. He looked beyond success to question whether those who profited from society owed anything to it in return.

Writing in the *North American Review* in 1889, Carnegie maintained that a wealthy person should:

> " . . . [C]onsider all surplus revenues which come to him simply as trust funds, which he is called upon to administer . . . in a manner which, in his judgment, is best calculated to produce the most beneficial results for the community . . . becoming the mere agent and trustee for his poorer brethren, bringing to their service his superior wisdom, experience, and ability to administer, doing for them better than they would or could do for themselves. "

Carnegie practiced what he preached. In 1901 he sold his steel properties to the newly formed United States Steel Corporation for $250 million and withdrew from business to devote the rest of his life to **philanthropy** (fuh•LANT•thruh•PEE), or actions benefiting society. By the time he died in 1919, he had donated $350 million—mostly to building public libraries, improving education, and promoting research. Rockefeller also returned much of his fortune to society in gifts that totaled more than $500 million.

Sherman Antitrust Act

In 1881 *The Atlantic Monthly* published an article entitled "The Story of a Great Monopoly," by Henry Demarest Lloyd, telling how the Standard Oil Company had monopolized the oil-refining business. The article caused such a sensation that the magazine had to print three times as many copies as usual. Throughout the next decade, as it was revealed that many industries were in danger

History
AND
ART
The homes of the wealthy contained much bric-a-brac, knickknacks, and trinkets of every type. Most of these objects had little or no function and merely graced the table or shelves because people felt that space should be filled up. Many of the items were very ornate and indisputably inane. For example, lamps were held up by figures of winged nymphs or cupids, teapots of superb china did not pour, and clocks often came in the belly of a figure.
Answer to Caption: actions benefiting society

NATIONAL
GEOGRAPHIC
SOCIETY

 VIDEODISC

GTV: The American People: Fabric of a Nation

Side 3, Chapter 2
Frames: 5993-12565
Title: *Going to Town!*
Subject: Migration to cities

Cultural Perspectives

Immigrating The immigrants who crossed the ocean to come to the United States in the 1800s left their homeland for a variety of reasons. Many Germans came to avoid compulsory military service; many Jews came to escape pogroms in Russia; crop failures brought Italians; and many people came to find religious freedom or just out of a sense of adventure. Most immigrants came in steerage, where conditions were crowded and filthy. The trip took up to 10 days and was unpleasant at best and dangerous in bad weather. On disembarking from the ship, immigrants had to cope with a new language, new customs, and a new land.

ASSESS

Check Understanding

Assign Section 3 Review as homework or an in-class activity.

Evaluate

Assign the Section 3 Quiz or use the Testmaker to create a customized quiz.

Reteach

Have students complete Reteaching Activity 8-3.

Assign Workbook Activity 8-3.

Enrich

Have students complete Enrichment Activity 8.

Assign Geography in History Activity 8.

CLOSE

Ask students to name some present-day abuses in business. Have them compare the abuses with those of the 1800s. Discuss the need for ethics in business.

of being monopolized, demands for federal regulation came from many groups—small businesses, farmers, consumers, laborers, and even some big businesses.

Even officials of the great corporations began to have concerns about growing public cries for reform. Henry O. Havemeyer, head of the American Sugar Refining Company, which controlled a trust producing more than 90 percent of the nation's sugar, urged that manufacturers of products in general use should submit to some federal regulation.

In the election of 1888, both the Democratic and the Republican political parties promised action. Then in 1890, with only one dissenting vote, Congress passed the Sherman Antitrust Act. The Sherman Act wrote into federal law a traditional principle of English common law. This is the idea that private monopolies and artificial restrictions on trade were wrong. In the words of the act:

> *Every contract, combination, in the form of trust or otherwise, or conspiracy, in restraint of trade or commerce among the several states or with foreign nations, is hereby declared to be illegal."*

The Sherman Act had little effect on preventing business consolidation. It was not strictly enforced and was so loosely worded that its meaning was doubtful. Did the law mean, for example, that all mergers were unlawful, that all business transactions

must be open and public, that any contract that permitted one company to take business from another was illegal?

Under the Constitution, the answers to such questions are left to the federal courts, which in the 1890s were probably more favorable to business interests than at any other time in the history of the United States. In *United States* v. *E. C. Knight Company,* the Supreme Court in 1895 agreed that the American Sugar Refining Company was a trust and that it enjoyed a near monopoly in the manufacture of sugar. The Court ruled, however, that the company's activities did not violate the Sherman Act because manufacturing was not interstate commerce.

The Supreme Court's decision in the *United States* v. *E.C. Knight Company* case was followed by one of the greatest periods of business consolidation in American history. In 1890 there had been 24 trusts worth a total of $436 million. In 1900 there were 183 huge combinations with a total worth of more than $3 billion. At the same time, big business simply turned away from trusts and toward holding companies in creating combinations.

In spite of its early failures, the Sherman Act was an important law. It signaled to large corporations to be more aware of how their activities looked to the public. As a result, corporate image and public relations became important business concerns. Later regulation of big business and industry would depend on additional legislation, on the interpretations of future courts, and on attitudes in the executive branch about enforcement.

Section 3 ★ Review

Checking for Understanding

1. **Identify** John D. Rockefeller, Standard Oil, Ida Tarbell, Andrew Carnegie, Sherman Antitrust Act.

2. **Define** rebate, social Darwinism, philanthropy.

3. **Compare** the methods used by Rockefeller and Carnegie to build their industrial empires.

4. **Explain** why the Sherman Antitrust Act failed to control big business.

Critical Thinking

5. **Judging Actions**   Would the United States have been better off without industrial giants such as John D. Rockefeller? Explain.

ACTIVITY

6. Write a one-page editorial in which you argue that government regulation either helps or hinders economic activity and the public welfare.

Answers to SECTION 3 REVIEW

1. John D. Rockefeller, 278; Standard Oil, 278; Ida Tarbell, 280; Andrew Carnegie, 281; Sherman Antitrust Act, 284
2. All vocabulary words are defined in the Glossary.
3. keen foresight, manipulated competition and prices, built industrial monopolies
4. not strictly enforced; too vague; interpreted

by federal courts favorable to business
5. positive effects—making goods available, lowering prices, providing jobs, improving the economy; negative effects—greed, materialism, unethical practices
6. Editorials will vary, but students should provide valid reasoning to support their view.

BUILDING SKILLS
Social Studies Skills

Reading Line Graphs

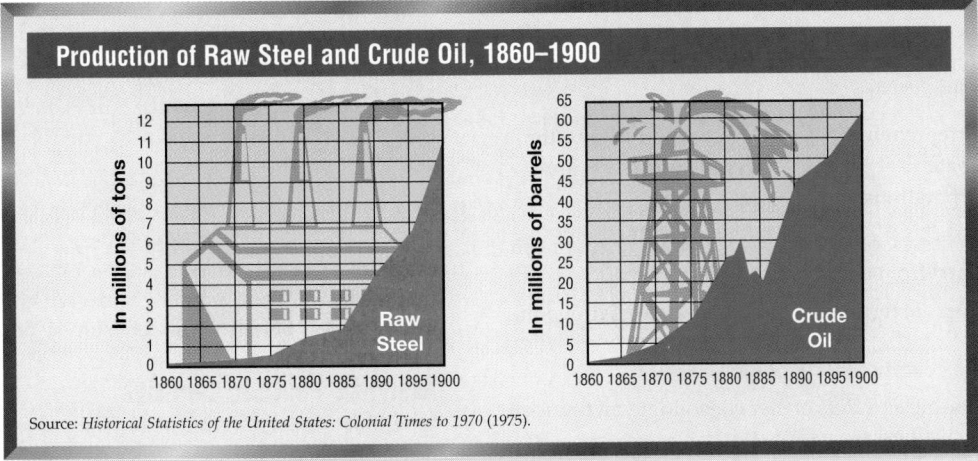

Production of Raw Steel and Crude Oil, 1860–1900

In millions of tons — Raw Steel

In millions of barrels — Crude Oil

Source: *Historical Statistics of the United States: Colonial Times to 1970* (1975).

When historical information involves numbers and statistics, it often is presented on a graph. Graphic data can be presented in the form of circle graphs, bar graphs, or line graphs.

Learning the Skill

Graphs are a good way to present data in a form that readers can grasp easily and quickly. Each type of graph has a different way to display information. Bar graphs show data in relation to a fixed scale, which is good for comparing items to each other. Circle graphs show a given item as a percentage of the whole. These graphs can be used to illustrate reports and presentations. Line graphs show data moving through a fixed period in time, which is good for showing trends and making predictions.

A line graph charts information about two variables. Line graphs typically show how one variable, depicted on the vertical axis, changes over time. Time, the second variable—whether minutes, hours, days, or years—is recorded on the horizontal axis.

To maximize the information you obtain from a line graph, follow this procedure:
- **Read** the title to get a general idea of what the graph shows.

- **Examine** the labels. Labels define the two variables and explain what the lines and/or points on the graph represent. Labels also specify the units of measurement.
- **Analyze** the graph. Look for increases, decreases, and sudden shifts. Analyze the *amount* and the *rate* of change.
- **Draw** conclusions or generalizations from the statistics presented on the graph. What trends or patterns appear?

Practicing the Skill

1. What is measured on these graphs? Over what time period?
2. Explain why the statistics are shown on two different graphs.
3. What generalizations can be made about steel and oil production between 1860 and 1875?

APPLYING THE SKILL

4. Keep track of the time you spend on homework each day over a one-week period. Chart the information on a line graph.

285

Ask students what the two graphs show. Tell them that although the growth of the oil industry after the Civil War was phenomenal, the growth of the steel industry, which started later, was nearly 30 times greater. Discuss the benefits the success of these industries brought to the nation. **L1**

Project Skills Transparency 8 and have students complete Skills Transparency Activity 8.

Use Chapter Skills Activity 8 to reinforce students' understanding of the skill.

Did You Know?

In 1898, although Carnegie Steel's output had risen threefold over the previous few years, the number of workers needed to produce the steel had decreased by 400. The use of electricity to drive automatic machinery was largely responsible for the decline in the workforce.

Answers to Practicing the Skill

1. the amount of raw steel and crude oil produced; between 1860 and 1900
2. It would be difficult to read the data if both were on the same graph because the measurements used are different.
3. There was relatively little growth in steel production between 1860 and 1875. There was steady growth in oil production from 1860 to 1875.
4. Line graphs will vary.

GLENCOE
TECHNOLOGY

VIDEODISC

Use the MindJogger Videoquiz to review students' knowledge.

MindJogger Videoquiz

Chapter 8
Disc 1, Side B

Available in VHS.

Using Vocabulary

1. corporations
2. entrepreneurs
3. horizontal integration; vertical integration

Reviewing Facts

1. abundant resources; available labor; immigration; favorable government policies; protective tariffs; private and foreign investment; advances in technology, communications, and transportation
2. unifier, distributor, carrier, customer
3. production volume, efficient organization and use of labor, best equipment, combined operations, expert management
4. individual ownership, partnership, corporation, holding company, trust, horizontal combination, vertical combination
5. built large businesses in areas critical to industry and the economy; forced competitors out; manipulated prices; disregarded the law
6. prohibited combining

286

Using Vocabulary

Use the listed vocabulary words to complete the sentences that follow. You will use all but one of the words. Write an original sentence using the remaining word.

entrepreneurs	horizontal integration
rebate	vertical integration
corporations	

1. Businesses organized as _____ can raise capital from a number of investors.

2. When governments practice laissez-faire policies, _____ can run businesses with very little government regulation.

3. Carnegie and Rockefeller consolidated a number of businesses using both _____ and _____ .

Reviewing Facts

1. **Enumerate** the factors that boosted industrial growth in the United States.

2. **State** the roles played by the railroad in the growth of American industry.

3. **Identify** the strategies that big business used to become successful.

4. **List** all the types of business organizations, big and small, that companies could form.

5. **Summarize** the common elements in the strategies of Rockefeller, Carnegie, and Vanderbilt.

6. **Describe** the provisions of the Sherman Antitrust Act and its effects.

7. **Cite** at least three industries that big business controlled during this era.

Understanding Concepts

Individual Initiative

1. Cite examples of individuals and how they used their initiative to shape industrial growth.

2. In what ways did Vanderbilt's individual initiative benefit others?

Government Restriction

3. Would a social Darwinist support or oppose laissez-faire government policies? Explain why.

4. Lack of government restriction benefited some businesses and hurt others. Which types of businesses benefited, and which might have been more successful with some protection?

Critical Thinking

1. **Judging Effects** Discuss how a big company manufacturing products high in both quantity and quality benefits the consumer and the company.

2. **Analyzing Political Cartoons** Study the cartoon that appears on this page. Then answer the questions that follow.

   a. What figures are shown?

   b. Who or what does the octopus symbolize?

   c. What does the cartoon suggest about big business?

   d. What title would you give this cartoon?

3. **Analyzing Cause and Effect** Why do you think the United States developed economically at a faster rate than most other countries?

4. **Drawing Conclusions** Do you think that it is still possible today to go from "rags to riches"? Explain your answer.

---

or conspiring to restrict trade; it had little impact at first

7. railroads, meatpacking, oil, steel, flour, whiskey, tobacco, lead, sugar

Understanding Concepts

1. Rockefeller offered to give all his business to a railroad in exchange for a rebate and information on his competitors. Carnegie utilized the newest steelmaking processes.

2. His consolidated railroad line acted as a trade link and provided an example of the benefits of consolidation.

3. would support them because policies would not interfere with economic competition, thus allowing the most able to rise

4. Entrepreneurs who developed big businesses benefited. Those who were driven out by monopolies and ruthless practices

5. **Demonstrating Reasoned Judgment** Do the doctrines of laissez-faire and social Darwinism have any following today? Explain.

6. **Making Comparisons** How did the benefits of industrialization compare to the problems it raised?

Writing a Report

Cause and Effect

Imagine you are a nineteenth-century writer who hopes to publish a collection of true rags-to-riches stories. Write a brief biography of a nineteenth-century captain of industry who began with little and built an industrial empire. Choose an entrepreneur from this chapter, or conduct research about another from the same period.

History and Geography

The Nation Industrializes

The period from the end of the Civil War to 1900 was an era of unmatched economic growth in the United States. Although agriculture was important, the key to this growth was industrialization.

1. **Human/Environment Interaction** What natural resources helped industry in the United States grow?

2. **Human/Environment Interaction** How did technology help to develop the resources of production?

Cooperative Learning — Interdisciplinary Activity: Economics

Meet in groups of four to discuss how to get capital to start a business. To begin with, you need to prepare a business plan. Your plan should describe your product or service and explain why the product or service is needed, how you plan to make or provide it, how your business will be run, what resources you need, and how you plan to use the capital. Write your plan, then present it to the class. Ask the class if it would finance the business outlined in your plan.

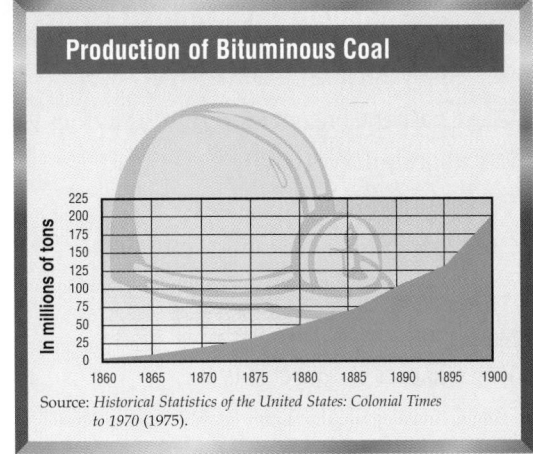

Production of Bituminous Coal

In millions of tons

Source: *Historical Statistics of the United States: Colonial Times to 1970* (1975).

Practicing Skills

Reading Line Graphs

Study the graph on this page, then answer the questions that follow.

1. What is measured on this line graph?

2. What period of time does the graph cover?

3. When did production surpass 100 million tons?

4. Does the graph show any decreases over time?

Writing About History

Using Your Journal

Read over your notes about Rockefeller and Carnegie. Do you think that people who make enormous amounts of money have an obligation to donate some of it to society? Can you think of any modern-day "Rockefellers" and "Carnegies"? Organize your thoughts into a paragraph in your journal.

Writing a Report

Students should show evidence of research.

History and Geography

1. coal, iron ore, petroleum

2. use of the Bessemer process helped to develop the steel industry; new methods in oil drilling helped to develop the oil industry; the development of the oil and steel industry contributed to the growth of the railroad industry

Cooperative Learning

Encourage students to prepare detailed plans.

Practicing Skills

1. bituminous coal production
2. 1860 to 1900
3. 1890
4. no

Writing About History

Using Your Journal

The ideas students present may include references to present-day movie and television personalities, athletes, musicians, and well-known businesspeople.

? Chapter Bonus Test Question

John D. Rockefeller told his Sunday school classes that his business practices demonstrated "survival of the fittest." What example might he give to support that point of view? (*Students are likely to refer to the way he forced out competitors to create a monopoly.*)

---

could have benefited from protective legislation.

Critical Thinking

1. Products made in large supply kept prices low. Well-made products satisfied consumers. Low prices and customer satisfaction won consumer loyalty to a company's products.

2. **a.** a tentacled monster and various other implements and edifices
   b. Standard Oil
   c. It is a monster.
   d. Student selections should show an understanding of the cartoon's content.

3. Answers include natural resources, government policy, innovation, entrepreneurs.

4. Students should support their opinion with valid rationale.

5. Students should support their opinion with valid rationale.

6. Students should provide examples of benefits as well as problems.

Daily Lesson Objectives	Teacher Classroom Resources	Multimedia
SECTION 1 **The Workers' Plight** **1 Day** pp. 290–294 1. Describe the conditions under which people worked during the late 1800s. 2. Explain the obstacles faced by labor unions during this period.	Reproducible Lesson Plan 9-1 Chapter Concept Mapping Activities 9-A, 9-B *Vocabulary Activity 9 *Guided Reading Activity 9-1 Cooperative Learning Activity 9 Reteaching Activity 9-1 Enrichment Activity 9 Chapter Map Activity 9 Chapter Skills Activity 9 *Section Quiz 9-1	Section Focus Transparency 9-1 Chapter Concepts Transparencies 9-A, 9-B Map Transparency Activity 9 Skills Transparency 9 Vocabulary PuzzleMaker Testmaker MindJogger Videoquiz GTV: The American People: Fabric of a Nation
SECTION 2 **The Rise of New Unions** **1 Day** pp. 296–299 1. Identify two of the strongest labor unions of the late 1800s. 2. Evaluate the gains labor unions achieved during this period.	Reproducible Lesson Plan 9-2 *Guided Reading Activity 9-2 Primary and Secondary Source Readings, pp. 19–20 American Portraits 36–37 Workbook Activity 9-2 Reteaching Activity 9-2 *Section Quiz 9-2	Section Focus Transparency 9-2 Testmaker GTV: A Geographic Perspective on American History
SECTION 3 **Patterns of Immigration** **1 Day** pp. 300–304 1. Identify the reasons that immigrants came to the United States. 2. Distinguish between the "old" and the "new" immigration.	Reproducible Lesson Plan 9-3 *Guided Reading Activity 9-3 Linking Past and Present Activity 9 Geography in History Activity 9 Workbook Activity 9-3 Reteaching Activity 9-3 *Section Quiz 9-3	Section Focus Transparency 9-3 Testmaker GTV: A Geographic Perspective of American History GTV: The American People: Fabric of a Nation
SECTION 4 **City Life and Problems** **1 Day** pp. 305–310 1. Identify the factors that led to the growth of cities during the late 1800s. 2. List the problems resulting from an increase in the urban population.	Reproducible Lesson Plan 9-4 *Guided Reading Activity 9-4 Critical Thinking Skills Activity 9 Workbook Activity 9-4 Reteaching Activity 9-4 *Section Quiz 9-4	Section Focus Transparency 9-4 Testmaker GTV: The American People: Fabric of a Nation GTV: A Geographic Perspective on American History
CHAPTER REVIEW AND EVALUATION **1 Day**	Chapter 9 Test, Forms A and B Spanish Chapter 9 Summary Performance Assessment Activity 9	MindJogger Videoquiz Student Self-Test & Review Software *Chapter 9 Audiocassette Activity and Test

*Also available in Spanish

 OUT OF TIME? If time does not permit teaching the entire chapter, use the Chapter 9 Summary on pages 362–363 and the Chapter 9 audiocassette (English and Spanish) to point out the main ideas of the chapter.

A complete, 1-page lesson plan is provided for each section in the *Reproducible Lesson Plan* booklet.

Key to Ability Levels

Teaching strategies have been coded for varying learning styles and abilities.

L1 Basic activities for all students

L2 Average activities for average to above-average students

L3 Challenging activities for above-average students

LEP Limited English Proficiency activities

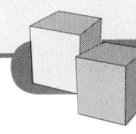

Block Schedule

Block scheduling differs from traditional class scheduling in the amount of time allotted to each period. The extended time frame provided by block scheduling affords you the opportunity to implement a greater number of research-oriented and activity-intense projects to motivate and involve your students. Activities that are particularly suited to use within the block scheduling framework are identified throughout this unit by the following designation:

✓ Performance Assessment Activity

Recognizing Differing Points of View Organize students into small groups. One member of each group should represent one of the following: worker, union leader, employer, government official, and a journalist. Give students time to research how their character would respond to the right of workers to strike. Be sure they gather evidence to support that position. Then ask each group to debate the topic. Encourage students to seek allies within their group. Have a spokesperson from each group summarize the outcome of its discussion. Which position prevailed? For what reasons?

POSSIBLE RUBRIC FEATURES

- Content Information
- Research Skills
- Organization
- Collaborative Skills
- Oral Communication Skills
- Creativity

☞ For additional activities, see Performance Assessment Strategies and Activities.

TEACHER'S CORNER

NATIONAL GEOGRAPHIC SOCIETY

INDEX TO NATIONAL GEOGRAPHIC MAGAZINE

The following articles may be used for research relating to this chapter:

- "Central Park: Oasis in the City," by Joel L. Swerdlow, May 1993.
- "Miami," by Charles E. Cobb, Jr., January 1992.
- "Chicago: Welcome to the Neighborhood," by Richard Conniff, May 1991.
- "Broadway, Street of Dreams," by Rick Gore, September 1990.
- "Immigration Today: New York's New Immigrants," by Alice J. Hall, September 1990.

- "New Life for Ellis Island," by Alice J. Hall, September 1990.
- "Philadelphia's African Americans: A Celebration of Life," by Roland L. Freeman, August 1990.
- "Growing Up in East Harlem," by Jere Van Dyk, May 1990.
- "Skyscrapers," by William S. Ellis, February 1989.

NATIONAL GEOGRAPHIC SOCIETY PRODUCTS AVAILABLE FROM GLENCOE

To order the following products for use with this chapter, contact your local Glencoe sales representative or call Glencoe at 1-800-334-7344:

- *The Presidents: A Picture History of Our Nation* (CD-ROM)
- *GTV: A Geographic Perspective on American History* (Videodisc)

- *GTV: The American People: Fabric of a Nation* (Videodisc)

ADDITIONAL NATIONAL GEOGRAPHIC SOCIETY PRODUCTS

To order the following products for use with this chapter, call National Geographic Society at 1-800-368-2728:

- *The United States as a World Power: From the 1890s to the 1970s* (Filmstrip)
- *Building a Nation: The Story of Immigration* (Filmstrip)

- *Immigration: The Triumph of Hope* (Video)

GLENCOE TECHNOLOGY

 VIDEODISC

Use the Chapter 9 MindJogger Videoquiz to preview the content of this chapter.

MindJogger Videoquiz

Chapter 9
Disc 1, Side B

 Available in VHS.

Recording Journal Notes
To get students started, have them categorize the obstacles under such heads as Working Conditions, Family Life, City Life, Social Life.

Linking Across TIME

By the late 1800s, the way people worked had changed drastically because of industrialization. Today, major changes are again shaping the ways people work. These changes are brought about by new communications networks: computers, telephones, and satellite links.

CHAPTER 9
★★★

An Urban Society
1860–1900

▶ UNION SYMBOL

Setting the Scene

Focus

One factor supporting industrialization in the late nineteenth century was the abundant labor supply. For workers, poor pay and working conditions led to a renewed interest in labor unions. Efforts by unions such as the Knights of Labor to improve conditions, however, were only modestly successful. The union movement was also influenced by the influx of millions of immigrants. These new arrivals crowded into America's cities and brought with them the cultural heritage of their old world.

Concepts to Understand

★ How **unity** among workers led to the growth of unions

★ How **conflict** between workers and employees resulted in unrest

Read to Discover . . .

★ the difficulties experienced by labor unions in the late 1800s.

★ the major factors behind the migration to American cities.

Journal Notes

What were some of the major obstacles facing immigrants coming to the United States in the late 1800s? Note examples as you read the chapter.

CULTURAL		
• **1868** *Immigration drops to 130,000*		• **1876** *Central Park opens in New York City*

| | 1860 | 1870 |

POLITICAL		
• **1867** *Great Western Surveys begin*		• **1872** *Victoria Claflin Woodhull, first woman presidential candidate, is nominated*

✚ EXTRA CREDIT PROJECT

Labor Leaders Ask interested students to find out more about Terence Powderly, Samuel Gompers, or some other union leader of the period. What prompted that individual to form a union? What were his or her goals? What values guided the methods used to achieve those goals? What contribution did that individual make to American life? Invite students who prepared reports to share their information with the class by participating in a panel discussion entitled "Early Labor Leaders—Successes and Failures."

Concept Mapping Activity

On the chalkboard, reproduce the following generalization and concepts map, and have students copy it in their notebooks.

Workers in growing numbers accepted the idea of forming unions. The union movement was stymied by the resistance of big corporations.

Unity	Conflict

To reinforce the two chapter concepts, use Chapter Concept Mapping Activities 9-A and 9-B.

Use Chapter Concepts Transparency Activities 9-A, 9-B.

History AND ART

Hester Street
by George Luks, 1905

Hester Street in New York City—part of a Jewish immigrant neighborhood—was filled with vitality and color.

◀ FAMILY AT ELLIS ISLAND, EARLY 1900S

History AND ART

Hester Street in New York City—part of a Jewish immigrant neighborhood—was filled with vitality and color as shown by artist George Luks.

NATIONAL GEOGRAPHIC SOCIETY

 VIDEODISC

GTV: The American People: Fabric of a Nation

Side 3, Chapter 2
Frames 5993-12565
Title: *Going to Town!*
Subject: Migration to cities

- **1883** *Brooklyn Bridge in New York City is completed*

1880

- **1886** *Haymarket Square riot takes place in Chicago*

- **1893** *Columbian Exposition opens in Chicago*

1890

- **1892** *Steelworkers' strike put down at the Homestead mill*
- **1894** *Pullman strike ends*

CHAPTER 9 An Urban Society: 1860–1900   **289**

✔ Performance Assessment

Immigrants and Assimilation Write the terms *Old Immigrants* and *New Immigrants* on the chalkboard. Have students list differences between the two groups, focusing on countries of origin, reasons for emigrating, social and economic status. Point out that despite the rhetoric of the period, the "new Americans" were as skilled and as well-educated as most Americans of their day. Ask students to research answers to the following questions. Why did many people focus on the ways the newcomers differed from other Americans rather than on similarities? What does the term *assimilate* mean? Was assimilation a reasonable goal then? Is it a reasonable goal for immigrants today? Why or why not? **L2**

FOCUS

Bellringer

🔲 Before taking roll, project Section Focus Transparency 9-1 or hand out Section Focus Transparency Activity 9-1. Discuss student answers.

Motivating Activity

Present the following:
"Last year [1892], I made only 4.5% profit and this year it will be less than 4%. I am entitled to make more money than that. My workers will have to take a pay cut."
George Pullman

Ask students whether they think Pullman was justified in asking his workers to take a cut in pay and, if so, why? Examine the hardships that pay cuts create for workers. **L1**

Vocabulary Precheck

List this section's "Key Terms" on the chalkboard. Have students develop questions for which each term is an answer. **LEP**

🔲 Use the Vocabulary PuzzleMaker for Chapter 9 to create a crossword puzzle. **L1**

🔲 Assign Vocabulary Activity 9.

★★★

The Workers' Plight

Setting the Scene

Section Focus

The new industrial age brought many problems for workers, who toiled long hours for low wages. In an attempt to improve working conditions, workers began to organize. In spite of rapid growth after the Civil War, unions encountered many difficulties.

▲ COAL MINER'S HELMET

Objectives

After studying this section, you should be able to
★ describe the conditions under which people worked during the late 1800s.
★ explain the obstacles faced by labor unions during this period.

Key Terms

real wages, company town, scrip, business cycle, blacklist, lockout, scab, collective bargaining

W ith the growth of industry, the number of factory workers rose from about 900,000 in 1860 to more than 3.2 million in 1890. Industrialization affected various aspects of workers' lives—where they worked and lived, the size of the workforce, and the nature of work itself. Many workers were forced to make the transition from skilled to semiskilled or unskilled labor. The experience and skill of such artisans as carpenters, silversmiths, and furniture makers no longer gave them any advantage over the unskilled. It took little training to tend a machine.

■ Problems

With machines taking the place of human skills, work became monotonous. Workers concentrated on highly specific, repetitive tasks and could take little pride in the fruits of their labor. As factories increased the efficiency of production, more and more people worked for fewer and fewer employers. The workers began to feel like "cogs in a wheel." Machines were designed to work at a given pace, and the workers were forced to try and keep up.

Unfair Conditions of Employment

Low wages and long hours posed additional burdens for industrial workers. Workdays of 10 to 14 hours were common. Although **real wages**—wages adjusted for inflation—rose more than 10 percent between 1870 and 1900, the average income remained inadequate. Most industrial workers earned between $400 and $500 a year during the 1890s; $600 was the minimum annual income needed to maintain a decent standard of living.

290   UNIT 3 New Horizons: 1860–1900

▲ ELEMENTARY SCHOOL, EARLY 1900s

Visualizing History

In 1893, Josiah Strong, a minister, described the conditions under which children worked: A few years ago a skilled workman could make up to three dozen pairs of sleeve buttons per day. Now, by the aid of the most improved machinery, a boy can make up 9,000 pairs or 250 times as many. . . . Now the boy, who does as much as 250 men could then, receives less than 90 cents for it.
Answer to Caption: Many families needed the money their children earned; laws were worded in such a way that evading them was easy.

Project Skills Transparency 9 and have students complete Skills Transparencies Activity 9.

Visualizing History

▲ CHILD LABOR Children were often employed in small, makeshift factories in which workers were hired on a piecework basis. *How were state labor laws evaded?*

In some industries workers were required to live in **company towns,** built and run by the companies. The best known was the town of Pullman, Illinois, where every citizen worked for the Pullman Palace Car Company. The usual practice was for companies to deduct money from the workers' pay for rent and advances to the company store as well as medical and fuel fees. Some companies paid their workers in **scrip,** or company money, that could be redeemed only at the company store. This store usually charged higher prices than did stores in other towns, and many workers remained in constant debt.

Health and Safety Hazards

Factory work was unhealthful as well as dangerous. Miners breathed coal dust all day. Factory workers breathed sawdust, stone dust, cotton dust, or toxic fumes. Heavy machines, grouped together on shop and mill floors for the sake of efficiency, caused an appallingly high injury rate among workers. An 1884 government report described working conditions for women in a small factory in Boston:

❝ *The work is dangerous . . . [they] are liable to get their fingers jammed under the bench, or caught in the die when it comes down to press the parts of the buttons together. A man (although not a surgeon) is provided to dress wounds three times for each individual without charge; afterwards, the person injured must pay all expenses. There are 35 machines in use, and accidents are of very frequent occurrence.* ❞

Child Labor

Children, some as young as six, were regularly employed as factory workers. Throughout the 1800s there were some efforts to restrict child labor, but state laws were usually worded in such a way that they could be easily evaded both by employers and by parents who needed the income. In 1885 in New Jersey, there were 340,000 children of school age. About 90,000

CHAPTER 9 An Urban Society: 1860–1900   **291**

Sidelight: Home Alone

At the turn of the century, many parents working 12 hours or longer a day often had to leave young children home all alone or in the care of older children. Some parents unable to care for their children abandoned them. Reporter Jacob Riis, an immigrant from Denmark, described how one little boy had been found with this note: "Take care of Johnny, for God's sake. I cannot." According to Riis, by 1889 the Children's Aid Society had taken in about 300,000 children who had been outcast, homeless, or orphaned.

of them did not attend school; most worked full-time jobs. Industrial work was neither less difficult nor less dangerous for children than it was for adults. As a Pennsylvania newspaper, the *Luzerne Union,* reported in January 1876:

❝ *During the past week, nearly one boy a day has been killed, and the public has become so familiar with these calamities that no attention is given them after the first announcement through a newspaper or friend.* ❞

Job Insecurity

Always looming was the threat of pay cuts or layoffs. Workers were vulnerable to the **business cycle**—a recurring sequence of change in business activity. Beginning with a period of prosperity, business activity declines until a low point, or depression, is reached. A period of recovery follows when business conditions become more active. A period of prosperity is again reached. The cycle is then repeated.

In the late 1800s, business went through many such cycles. During slack periods employers kept their costs down by reduc-

Visualizing
ⓗistory

▲ ORGANIZING THE WORKERS Union leaders hoped to improve conditions for workers, such as these immigrants working at home. *What were the difficulties that unions encountered in organizing immigrants?*

ing wages or laying off workers. Millions of people lost their jobs or had their wages slashed during the depressions of 1873, 1882, and 1893. Workers looked to labor unions for protection.

■ The Revival of Labor Unions

The growth of labor unions during the early 1800s had been halting and sporadic, but conditions during the Civil War spurred the revival of unionism. With hundreds of thousands of workers not available while serving in the army, unions were in a strong position to demand better pay. During the war the number of local unions rose dramatically. To strengthen local unions, labor also began to organize on a national scale.

Problems With Organizing

Labor unions faced serious difficulties in organizing because of the mobility and diversity of the American labor force. Workers who did not "stay hitched," but moved from job to job were difficult to organize. The constant influx of large numbers of immigrants—averaging more than one-third of a million a year between 1870 and 1900—also presented a problem. Differences in language, religion, and customs among the immigrants made it hard to unite them into an effective union.

Another problem was that different labor leaders had different goals. Some leaders envisioned uniting all workers into one large union in order to promote widespread reforms. Others believed that unions should be organized by particular crafts or industries and work only for short-term benefits.

Unions also faced strong opposition from employers. Workers were often required to take oaths swearing they would not join a union. If found to have been involved in union activity, a worker would be fired and often could not get another job because of **blacklists,** or records of "troublemakers" kept by employers. Once blacklisted, a laborer could get a job only by changing residence, trade, or even name. Another way employers

 RAILWAY STRIKE The railway strike of 1877 resulted in one of the most violent upheavals in the history of American labor. *How did the strike start?*

Visualizing **H**istory

retaliated against union organizing in a workplace was the **lockout**—whereby the factory was shut down—or by firing union members and hiring **scabs,** or replacement workers. In any lockout or strike, the odds favored employers. Few unions had enough money to support their members through the long period of unemployment caused by a strike.

Problems With Public Image

Labor unions also had to fight public opinion. Many Americans viewed fixing wages and hours by **collective bargaining**—negotiation between an employer and a labor union—as violating the right of an individual to deal personally with the employer. Only infrequently did public opinion condemn employers when labor disputes resulted in violence. This happened during the Homestead lockout in 1892 when the Carnegie Steel Company hired a private army of 300 Pinkerton detectives armed with repeating rifles. Generally, however, labor unions were held responsible when disorder occurred.

Another problem for unions was that law enforcement agencies usually sided with the employers. Employers suffered no penalties for lockouts and blacklists. Union strikes and boycotts, on the other hand, were judged to be "conspiracies in restraint of trade" for which labor leaders might be jailed or fined. Contracts between employers and unions were not usually enforceable by law. When violence occurred, or was even threatened, the police—and sometimes armed troops—were sent to the aid of employers.

■ Railroad Strike of 1877

Despite these obstacles labor unions survived—sometimes just barely. Membership in the union fluctuated according to business conditions. Following the depression of 1873, 5,000 businesses closed, causing widespread unemployment and homelessness.

Union membership dropped from more than 300,000 to 50,000. Three million workers were unemployed. At this time there were no unemployment or relief benefits available from either the state or federal government. Tramps and hobos roamed the countryside; workers' rallies to demand relief were stopped or suppressed by mounted police.

CHAPTER 9 An Urban Society: 1860–1900 **293**

Did You Know?

Almost one hundred years after the railroad strike of 1877, another group of transportation workers, air traffic controllers, went on strike demanding higher wages and fewer working hours.

CURRICULUM CONNECTION

Language Arts Railroads and locomotives have achieved a special place in American literature, song, and folklore. Emily Dickinson and Walt Whitman could not resist writing about the mighty locomotive. Folk songs like "I've Been Working on the Railroad" paid tribute to the building of the road. "Chattanooga Choo-Choo" and "The Atchison, Topeka, and the Santa Fe" were popular tunes that celebrated the railroads themselves. Jelly Roll Morton, the man who supposedly invented jazz, traces the first blues he heard in his mind to the sound of southern railway trains.

Critical Thinking Activity

Identifying Problems Present the following description by Sadie Frowne from *Plain Folk: The Life Stories of Undistinguished Americans,* and ask students to suggest changes that they think are needed in the condition of the sweatshop.

"The [sewing] machines [are loud and] go like mad all day, because the faster you work the more money you get. Sometimes in my haste I get my finger caught and the needle goes right through it . . . . I bind the finger up . . . and go on working. We all have accidents like that . . . . Sometimes a finger has to come off."
L3

ASSESS

Check Understanding

Assign Section 1 Review as homework or an in-class activity.

Evaluate

Assign Section 9-1 Quiz or use the Testmaker to create a customized quiz.

Reteach

Have students complete Reteaching Activity 9-1.

Assign Workbook Activity 9-1.

Enrich

Have students complete Enrichment Activity 9.

Assign Chapter 9 Map Transparency Activities and Chapter 9 Map Activity.

CLOSE

Hold a discussion with students on child labor laws today.

Labor Responds to Wage Cuts

The hard times of the 1870s reached a climax in the railroad strike of 1877, which shook the nation as no labor conflict in its history had done before. After years of prosperity, railroad companies were hit hard by economic woes. They turned to drastic measures to cut their losses. Some railways cut workers' pay as much as 35 percent. Workdays were lengthened up to 15 and sometimes even 18 hours. Companies discontinued the "free ride" policy that had allowed workers to travel free to and from their jobs. These measures made railway workers bitter and angry.

In 1877 wages were cut another 10 percent by the Pennsylvania Railroad and then by the Baltimore and Ohio (B & O) line. Workers threatened to walk off the job if nothing was done. Management refused to budge, certain that replacements for the strikers could be found. On July 16 about 40 B & O workers held a work stoppage. The trains rolled anyway, but down the line at Martinsburg, West Virginia, the firemen, those who tend the furnace and supply it with fuel, abandoned the trains. Strikers soon took over the town. The governor of West Virginia, at the urging of a B & O vice president, sent two companies of state militia to Martinsburg. It took federal troops, however, to regain control of the town.

The scene at Martinsburg was only the beginning. Troops and workers clashed in the streets of Pittsburgh, Buffalo, San Francisco, and Toledo. In late July, 20 persons were killed in Philadelphia, and, in another Pennsylvania city, Reading, 11 were killed. At the height of the strike, more than one-half of the freight on the nation's 76,000 miles of track had stopped running. Although the clashes were usually spontaneous, newspapers viewed them collectively as

> " *. . . an insurrection, a revolution, an attempt of Communists and vagabonds to coerce society and endeavor to undermine American institutions.* "

Management Gains a Costly Victory

In several cities order was restored only after President Rutherford B. Hayes had sent in federal troops. Hayes himself, however, was troubled. He felt railroad officials had brought on the crisis by their own ruthless actions. The President confided in his diary, "Shall the railroads govern the country or shall the people govern the railroads?"

When the railroad strike was over, more than 100 persons were dead, 1,000 had been jailed, and 100,000 workers had gone on strike. In addition there was such fear of violent revolution that state militia were reorganized. National Guard armories were built in many large cities as fortresses, where troops could hold out against strikers if necessary. Union leaders learned from the strike that they were not united or strong enough to defeat the powerful combination of business and government.

Section 1 ★ Review

Checking for Understanding

1. **Identify** 1877 railroad strike.
2. **Define** real wages, company town, scrip, business cycle, blacklist, lockout, scab, collective bargaining.
3. **Discuss** the hardships facing industrial workers during the late 1800s.
4. **Give** examples of problems unions faced once they were organized.

Critical Thinking

5. **Weighing Options** Imagine that you are an industrial worker in 1870. List the advantages and disadvantages of joining a union.

ACTIVITY

6. Imagine you are a reporter assigned to cover the railroad strike of 1877. Write an article describing the scene of the strike as you arrive.

Answers to SECTION 1 REVIEW

1. 1877 railroad strike, 293
2. All vocabulary words are defined in the Glossary.
3. monotony, low wages, long hours, unhealthful conditions, unemployment
4. lockouts, hiring of strikebreakers, negative siding of law enforcement agencies with employers

5. Answers will vary. Advantages: union will fight for better wages, hours, and conditions; will help during hard times. Disadvantages: poor public opinion about unions, risk employer sanctions such as blacklisting and lockouts.
6. Articles should contain vivid details and depict the drama of the strike.

BUILDING SKILLS
Study and Writing Skills

Summarizing

Imagine that you have received an expensive camera for your birthday. The instructions are complicated with at least 12 pages describing how to adjust the camera for certain shots. The more you read, the more confused you become. Finally, you discover a *summary* of the main steps, and your confusion disappears.

Learning the Skill

Summarizing is the process of recapping main ideas by bringing together the major points and excluding the minor ones. A summary does not use examples except to clarify main ideas or concepts that may be new to you or to your audience. Knowing how to summarize is a useful skill for you when you have to answer essay questions, take notes, and write research papers.

Read the following material carefully. Then answer the questions that follow.

During the late 1800s, the United States, like other modernized nations, was experiencing societal changes brought on by the shift from an agriculture-based economy to one based on industrial production. American life up to this time had been based on a rugged self-determinism, a belief that one should take care of one's self and family. This was largely done through owning and farming land.

To encourage settlement in the frontier, Congress passed laws that provided land to settlers who would cultivate it and pay a fee. Farmers moved west in greater and greater numbers. More land was occupied and improved in the closing years of the 1800s than had been occupied and improved during the first 250 years of American history.

The growth of industry lured many people to the cities and into jobs that required a new set of values. In new industrial centers, such as Pittsburgh and Chicago, there was work available for thousands. People in the industrial labor force faced

▲ Moving assembly line, Highland Park, Michigan

profound changes in their lives. Often a man did not so much work for his family as he did for his boss. Further, working conditions and pay were often a source of discontent.

Long hours were another burden to workers. During the late 1800s, 65- and 70-hour workweeks were common. Labor unions began to organize, and although their intent was to lend support to exploited employees, it often made workers feel they were helpless to take care of themselves.

Practicing the Skill

1. Locate and list in order of appearance the main ideas expressed in the material.

2. Summarize the text by rewriting the main ideas in your own words.

APPLYING THE SKILL

3. Reread the material under the heading "Railroad Strike of 1877" on page 293. Then, following the guidelines suggested in the example, list the main ideas of the material and write a short summary of the material presented.

295

FOCUS

Bellringer

Before taking roll, project Section Focus Transparency 9-2 or hand out Section Focus Transparency Activity 9-2. Have students answer the questions.

Motivating Activity

Write the following job description on the chalkboard:

Wanted: Woman to make linings for caps. Hours 8 A.M. to 6 P.M. Pay is 3½ cents to 10 cents a dozen . . . . Earn an average of $5 a week. Must provide your own machine, which costs $45.

Ask students what they would find objectionable about this job if they had to take it. (*low pay, number of working hours per day, having to buy one's own machine*) Discuss why women took these jobs in the late 1800s. (*It was difficult to make a living, especially for immigrant women who did not speak English well.*) Point out that this description was for a job that Rose Schneiderman had around the turn of the century. When her bosses kept reducing women's pay, she left the sweatshop to organize women workers. **L2**

Vocabulary Precheck

Call on students to read aloud the definitions of the key terms from the Glossary. Then have volunteers use each term in a sentence. **LEP**

The Rise of New Unions

Setting the Scene

Section Focus

Individually, workers were powerless to change hazardous working conditions, low pay, and long hours. When little was done to improve their lot, workers in growing numbers came to accept the idea of forming new, better-organized unions.

Objectives

After studying this section, you should be able to

★ identify two of the strongest labor unions of the late 1800s.

★ evaluate the gains labor unions achieved during this period.

Key Terms

arbitration, industrial union, injunction

▲ JUDGE'S GAVEL

s industrialization was an urban phenomenon, so too were unions. Those states with the highest percentage of workers in industry had the greatest urban populations. It was in these industrial areas of the North and the Midwest that a score of new labor organizations were established in the late 1860s.

■ The Knights of Labor and the AFL Unions

By far the most influential labor organization was the Noble Order of the Knights of Labor. Founded in 1869, the Knights of Labor attempted to bring all laboring people—skilled and unskilled, black and white, men and women, white-collar and blue-collar—into one big union.

The Desire for Widespread Reform

Terence V. Powderly, an immigrant and a former railway switchtender, led the Knights of Labor after 1879. An eloquent speaker and a tireless organizer, Powderly believed a single, powerful union was the best means of gaining concessions from employers for better working conditions.

Powderly persuaded the Knights to support equal pay for women, temperance, abolition of child labor and, above all, establishment of cooperatively owned industrial plants. A man of peace, he opposed strikes and wished to submit labor disputes to **arbitration**—a process whereby an impartial third party helps workers and management reach an agreement.

Membership in the Knights grew rapidly in the early 1880s—especially after the striking Knights won the dispute against Jay Gould's Wabash Railway. Membership in

296 UNIT 3 New Horizons: 1860–1900

Classroom Resources for SECTION 2

Blackline Masters:
- Reproducible Lesson Plan 9-2
- Guided Reading Activity 9-2
- Primary and Secondary Source Readings, pp. 19–20
- American Portraits 37-38
- Workbook Activity 9-2
- Reteaching Activity 9-2
- Section Quiz 9-2

Transparencies:
- Section Focus Transparency 9-2

Multimedia:
- Testmaker
- GTV: A Geographic Perspective on American History

the Knights soared from 100,000 in 1885 to 700,000 in less than a year. Some newspapers feared that Powderly would become stronger than the President.

The Knights of Labor, however, were soon swamped with troubles. The union had wasted its funds in unsuccessful attempts to set up cooperative businesses. Moreover, the effort to unite different kinds of labor into one big union had failed. Workers in different crafts and industries often had little in common with one another and little interest in working for the same goals.

Haymarket Square Riot

The decline of the Knights was hastened by the Haymarket Square riot in Chicago on May 4, 1886. This event followed a peaceful meeting of some 3,000 workers who gathered together to protest the shooting of striking McCormick Harvester Company workers by the police. As the meeting was breaking up, someone threw a bomb into a group of police officers. Seven persons were killed and more than 60 were injured. Although the identity of the bomb-thrower was never established, 8 anarchist leaders were arrested and found guilty of taking part in the crime. Four were later executed for murder. Although the Knights of Labor could in no way be held responsible for the Haymarket affair, it became identified with radicals and violence. From then on the Knights of Labor declined rapidly.

Foundation of the AFL

In 1886, the year the Knights began to decline, the American Federation of Labor (AFL) was organized. In its principles as well as its structure, the AFL differed greatly from the Knights. While the Knights had accepted a large number of unskilled workers, the AFL accepted only skilled workers. This policy indicated the reluctance of the

Visualizing History

▲ TROUBLE AT THE HAYMARKET On the night of May 4, 1886, a crowd gathered in Chicago's Haymarket Square to protest police violence. As the meeting was breaking up, a bomb was thrown into a group of police and the police fired into the crowd. *What effect did the Haymarket affair have on the labor movement?*

TEACH
Guided Practice
Making Value Judgments
Have students list some of the antiunion activities of the federal government in Chicago in 1893. *(sending in federal troops to guard mail trains, using an injunction to end the strike, imprisoning Debs without a trial)* Discuss whether the federal government had a right to interfere in the 1893 Pullman strike. **L2**

📁 Assign Guided Reading Activity 9-2.

Visualizing History After the Haymarket Affair, membership in the Knights of Labor declined from 729,677 on July 1, 1886, to 259,518 two years later. **Answer to Caption:** It led to the decline of the Knights and the identification of the labor movement with anarchy and violence.

NATIONAL GEOGRAPHIC SOCIETY

 VIDEODISC
GTV: A Geographic Perspective on American History

Side 3, Chapter 5
Title: *Making a Mark*
Subject: The impact of immigration (1870–1910)

Cooperative Learning Activity

Union Organizing Divide students into two groups. Ask one group to be the employers and decide what they would tell their employees to keep them from joining a union. Ask the other group to be union organizers and decide what they would tell workers about the advantages of joining a union. Have several students from each group present their arguments.

Discuss the long-range economic and social effects of U.S. unions. **L1, LEP** 📦

AFL to accept women, African Americans, and immigrants—the majority of whom were unskilled—into their union. Also, the AFL organized workers into separate unions, each covering a particular craft.

Each union managed its own affairs with only occasional help from the national organization. The AFL's fees were relatively high, in order to restrict membership, build up strike funds, and provide benefits to members and their families in cases of sickness, unemployment, or death.

The AFL might never have enjoyed the success it did were it not for Samuel Gompers, its president for 37 years. Born in London, Gompers adapted some ideas of British trade unions, the best established in the world. Gompers, who prided himself on being practical, was interested only in day-to-day gains of AFL members—higher wages, shorter hours, and benefits for disabled workers.

So effective was the organization and leadership of the AFL that when hard times hit again in 1893, its member unions not only survived but thrived. Between 1890 and 1900, when other labor organizations lost members, AFL membership rose from 190,000 to 500,000.

■ The Pullman Strike

To address the needs of unskilled and semiskilled labor—and yet avoid the "one big union" approach—a new type of labor organization developed. This was the **industrial union**, in which all classes of workers in a single industry are joined together. Among those who saw the advantages of an industrial union was Eugene V. Debs, an officer of the Brotherhood of Locomotive Firemen, one of several railway unions. He felt that the separation of railway workers into different unions weakened their power. Conductors and engineers, the "aristocracy of labor," looked down on less skilled and lower paid workers, and the unskilled had no organization at all. Debs, therefore, started a new organization in 1893—the American Railway Union. This union included all types of railroad workers—from conductors, firemen, and engineers to telegraph opera-

tors and station clerks. By 1894 the American Railway Union was powerful enough to force James J. Hill, the owner of the Great Northern Railway, to restore wage cuts.

Protest Leads to Walkout

Hardly had the Great Northern strike ended than the Pullman strike began in Pullman, Illinois, the company town built by George M. Pullman for his workers. Losing profit because of a reduced demand for its railroad cars, the Pullman Palace Car Company laid off two-thirds of its employees and cut the wages of the rest. It did not, however, reduce either the dividends it paid to stockholders or the rents charged to workers in the town. When a delegation of workers met with Pullman to protest the pay cuts, they were fired. At noon the following day, 10,000 Pullman workers walked off the job.

The American Railway Union took up the Pullman workers' cause. Debs's first move was to propose that the dispute be referred to arbitration. Pullman, however, replied, "There is nothing to arbitrate." Realizing that negotiating with Pullman was futile, the union called for members to refuse to work

▲ RIDING IN LUXURY—THE PULLMAN CAR

Cooperative Learning Activity

Labor Negotiations Organize students into groups of four. Have each group write a skit and role-play the prestrike negotiations of a company representative, two union workers, and a union representative. The dialogue should reflect the attitudes of the characters and should include the vocabulary in the section. Each group member should write the dialogue for his or her character. Have several groups present their skits. **L2** 📦

on any train that included a Pullman car. Railway workers answered the union's call. Within 5 days 100,000 railroad workers had walked off the job. Railway traffic west of Chicago was almost paralyzed. Debs warned his followers not to interfere with the mail and appealed to them to be "orderly and law-abiding." A few mail trains were delayed, but there were few disturbances.

Federal Intervention Turns the Tide

Quickly, President Grover Cleveland stepped in. Over protests by the mayor of Chicago and the governor of Illinois, President Cleveland sent federal troops to guard mail trains. Immediately, rioting broke out as angry mobs, sympathetic to the strikers, taunted the soldiers. Members of the American Railway Union kept out of trouble but nevertheless received the blame. Even before the troops had arrived, the federal government obtained an **injunction,** or court order, forbidding the union to continue the strike. Debs refused to obey the injunction and was imprisoned.

Without Debs's leadership, the Pullman strike collapsed and with it the American Railway Union. From that point on, employers used the injunction as a means of breaking up strikes.

Although labor unions lost more disputes than they won, and most workers remained unorganized (only 4 percent of American workers belonged to unions in 1900), workers made some gains in the late 1800s. Fed-

Visualizing History ▲ LABOR LEADER The only major labor union to endure into the 1900s was the American Federation of Labor, or AFL. It was founded in 1886 by an immigrant cigar maker named Samuel Gompers. *What were the goals of the AFL?*

eral and state legislation reflected the growing political influence of labor. Wages began to increase slowly, and the workday was shortened. Moreover, nearly every state passed laws regulating working conditions and requiring minimum standards of health and safety.

Section 2 ★ Review

Checking for Understanding

1. **Identify** Knights of Labor, American Federation of Labor, Terence V. Powderly, Samuel Gompers, Eugene Debs.

2. **Define** arbitration, industrial union, injunction.

3. **Summarize** the difficulties faced by the Knights of Labor and the American Railway Union.

4. **Examine** the achievements of labor unions during the late 1800s.

Critical Thinking

5. **Supporting an Opinion** Do you agree with Debs that an industrial union was more powerful than separate unions of craft workers? Why or why not?

ACTIVITY

6. Create a collage of the American labor force from newspapers, magazines, and other media pictures of people at work.

Answers to Section 2 Review

1. Knights of Labor, 296; American Federation of Labor, 297; Terence V. Powderly, 296; Samuel Gompers, 298; Eugene Debs, 298
2. All vocabulary words are defined in the Glossary.
3. confrontations with law enforcement agencies, violence

4. wage increases, shorter hours, health and safety standards
5. Supporters may say an industrial union wields more power within a particular industry. Others may say unions of crafts more strongly spread influence.
6. Collages should depict people from all walks of life.

Enrich

Have students research several of the strikes that occurred in the 1890s. Have them determine why workers struck, management's position regarding workers' demands, whether violence took place, and the public's attitude toward strikers.

📁 Assign Primary and Secondary Source Readings, pp. 19–20: "The Pullman Strike."

📁 Assign American Portraits 37, 38.

CLOSE

Have students describe the differences and similarities between labor problems in the 1890s and today. Discuss the role of arbitrators.

Visualizing History Instead of broad political reform, Gompers concentrated on "bread and butter issues." These were issues that had a direct effect on workers. **Answer to Caption:** The AFL was interested in practical goals: higher wages, shorter hours, and benefits for its disabled workers.

FOCUS

Bellringer

 Before taking roll, project Section Focus Transparency 9-3 or hand out Section Focus Transparency Activity 9-3. Have students answer the questions.

Motivating Activity

Use the following videos to introduce immigration in the late 1800s. Point out the photograph on page 303 and ask students to discuss what it would be like to move to a country where you cannot speak the language. **L1**

NATIONAL GEOGRAPHIC SOCIETY

 **VIDEODISC**

GTV: A Geographic Perspective on American History

Side 3, Chapter 5
Title: *Making a Mark*
Subject: The impact of immigration, 1870–1910

GTV: The American People: Fabric of a Nation

Side 3, Chapter 1
Title: *The Golden Door*
Subject: The flood of immigration between 1880 and 1920

Patterns of Immigration

Setting the Scene

Section Focus

Between 1860 and 1900 almost 14 million people came to America. Another 14.5 million came between 1900 and 1915. Even more significant than the increase in numbers was the changing character of immigration during these years. The vast majority no longer came from northern and western Europe but from southern and eastern Europe.

Objectives

After studying this section, you should be able to
★ identify the reasons that immigrants came to the United States.
★ distinguish between the "old" and the "new" immigration.

Key Terms

pogrom, anarchism

◄ ADVERTISEMENT URGING IMMIGRATION TO AMERICA

The thirteen colonies had been settled mainly by English settlers. Other settlers from Holland, Sweden, France, Scotland, Ireland, and Germany came later. After 1815, however, increasing numbers of immigrants started to arrive from Ireland. During these early years, a total of only about 400,000 immigrants had come to America. Beginning in the 1850s and continuing after the Civil War, immigration rose sharply.

■ The "Old Immigration"

During the period of "Old Immigration," which started in the 1830s and reached a high point in the 1840s, there was a great wave of immigration to America's shores. Between 1840 and 1850, an additional 1.5 million newcomers journeyed to the United States. Nearly one-half were from Ireland, which was suffering from a potato famine. Between 1846 and 1860, about 1.5 million Irish immigrated to America, settling in New York and Boston, which functioned as ports of entry into the United States.

In the 1840s large numbers of Germans also began to come to America. Some left their homeland because of crop failures. Others came to escape political persecution after the failure of the Revolution of 1848. Still others were German Jews seeking religious freedom. Large numbers of German immigrants settled on farms and in cities in the Midwest—areas that were rapidly growing and had job opportunities. The Germans gave a distinctive flavor to such cities as Cincinnati, Milwaukee, and St. Louis. Then, in the 1850s, after the Gold Rush, Chinese immigrants began to come to the Pacific Coast. Many were hired to help build the railroads. About 100,000 Chinese had settled in the West by the mid-1870s.

Classroom Resources for SECTION 3

Blackline Masters:
 Reproducible Lesson Plan 9-3
Guided Reading Activity 9-3
Linking Past and Present Activity 9
Geography in History Activity 9
Workbook Activity 9-3
Reteaching Activity 9-3
Section Quiz 9-3

Transparencies:
Section Focus Transparency 9-3
Multimedia:
Testmaker
GTV: A Geographic Perspective of American History
GTV: The American People: Fabric of a Nation

During the colonial period, most immigrants were readily accepted. Workers were badly needed in all the colonies.

European agents of railroad companies and steamship lines described America as a land where riches could be had almost for the asking. Perhaps the most persuasive arguments for others to come to this country were the "America letters" written by recent immigrants to their family and friends. "If you wish to be happy and independent, then come here," wrote a German farmer from his new home in Missouri. In the 1840s and 1850s, however, some native-born Americans began to resent the newcomers, especially the Irish immigrants. Some Americans resented them because they dressed and sounded "different" and because they were Catholics.

■ The "New Immigration"

Until the 1880s most newcomers had come from the nations of northern and western Europe. After 1885, however, large numbers came from nations of southern and eastern Europe. The new immigrants were from Italy, Russia, and Poland as well as from the nations of the Austro-Hungarian Empire.

Italians were one of the largest groups of new immigrants. Many came from Sicily and the southern part of Italy. People in this region faced economic misfortune. Unemployment and overpopulation made existence perilous. As a result, millions of Italian Catholics chose to go to America.

Eastern European Jews were another sizable group of new immigrants. Although scattered throughout many countries, the

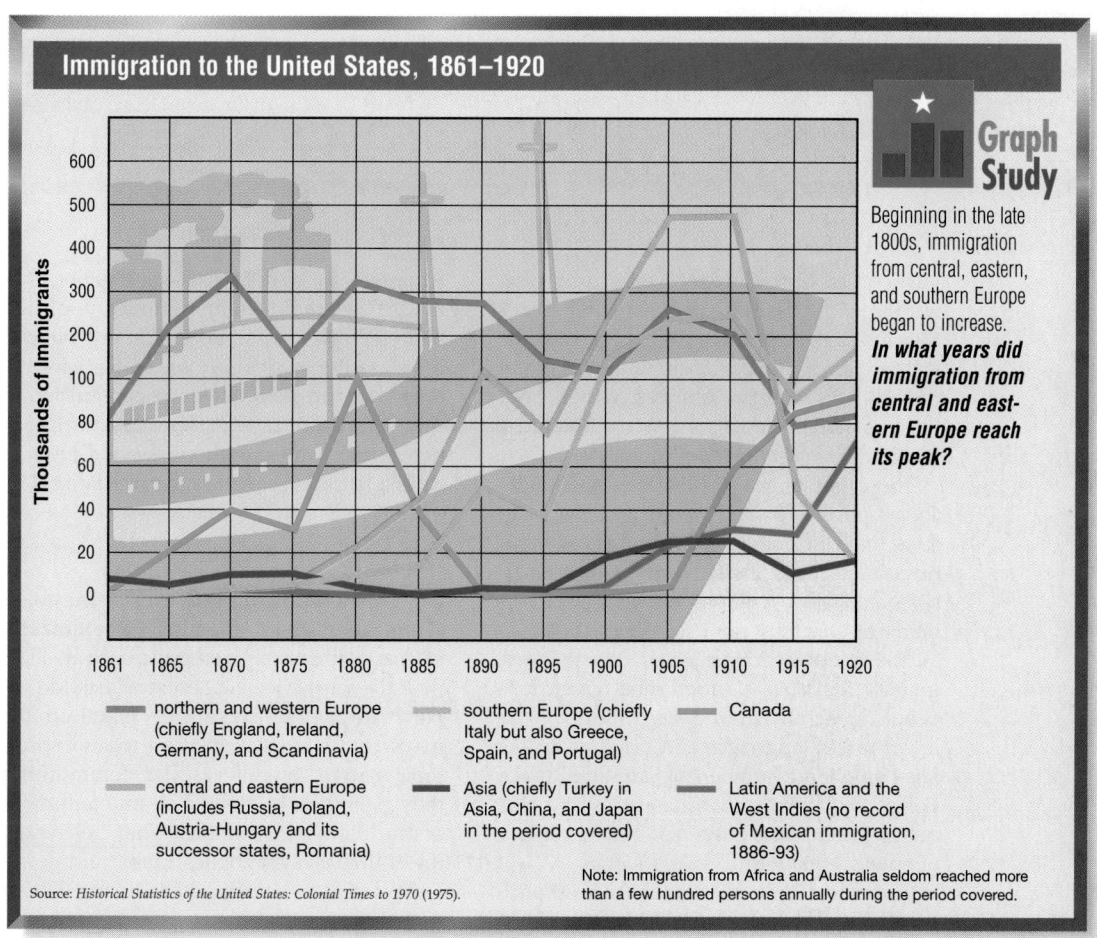

Immigration to the United States, 1861–1920

Graph Study

Beginning in the late 1800s, immigration from central, eastern, and southern Europe began to increase.

In what years did immigration from central and eastern Europe reach its peak?

northern and western Europe (chiefly England, Ireland, Germany, and Scandinavia)

central and eastern Europe (includes Russia, Poland, Austria-Hungary and its successor states, Romania)

southern Europe (chiefly Italy but also Greece, Spain, and Portugal)

Asia (chiefly Turkey in Asia, China, and Japan in the period covered)

Canada

Latin America and the West Indies (no record of Mexican immigration, 1886–93)

Note: Immigration from Africa and Australia seldom reached more than a few hundred persons annually during the period covered.

Source: *Historical Statistics of the United States: Colonial Times to 1970* (1975).

CHAPTER 9 An Urban Society: 1860–1900   **301**

Vocabulary Precheck

Ask students to speculate on the meaning of each key term. Then have them check their guesses by finding the definition in the student text. **LEP**

TEACH
Guided Practice

Demonstrating Reasoned Judgment Discuss which group of immigrants, "old" or "new," was more likely to become rapidly assimilated into American life and why. **L2**

Using Graphs

Answer: between 1905–1910

Graph Skills Practice

What groups immigrated to the United States during the mid- to late 1800s? (*Asians; central and eastern Europeans; southern, northern, and western Europeans; Canadians; Latin Americans.*) In what decade did the greatest number of immigrants enter the United States? (*1905–1915*)

Critical Thinking Activity

Making Deductions Present the following quotation, and ask students to study it and make deductions about why the speaker probably emigrated. (*for economic reasons, was poor in her home country*)

"So when I came to Ellis Island, my Gosh, there was something I'll never forget . . . the first meal we got—fish and milk, big pitchers of milk and white bread, the first time I saw white bread and butter. There was so much milk and I drank it because we didn't have enough milk in my country. And I said, '. . . We're going to have plenty to eat.' " **L1**

Independent Practice

Conducting an Interview

Have students interview a relative, friend, or acquaintance who immigrated to the United States. Have them find out where the person came from, why the person emigrated, what adjustment problems the person experienced, and what humorous misunderstandings may have occurred because of difficulties with English.
L1

📁 Assign Guided Reading Activity 9-3.

Linking Past and Present

According to popular belief, pasta was introduced into Italy by Marco Polo, who brought it back from China. Fifty years before Marco Polo even left for China, however, both the Indians and the Arabs were already eating noodles. Since the Arabs were important traders in Venice during the Middle Ages, it is possible that pasta came to Italy via the Arab lands rather than China.

Discuss food as an important aspect of a national culture.

📁 For additional practice, assign Linking Past and Present Activity 9.

Linking Past and Present

Italian Cuisine

Between 1890 and 1910 about 2.7 million southern Italians immigrated to the United States. Among their contributions to America was a rich and varied cuisine.

Then

Pizza and Pasta

Italian bakery ovens produced the first pizzas, which had been a strictly Neapolitan item in Italy. Opening in 1905, "G Lombardi" on Spring Street in New York's Little Italy became the first known pizzeria in the United States.

Other Italian dishes became lasting contributions to American cuisine. Many people came to love Italian pasta. Macaroni, manicotti, spaghetti, and lasagna were first introduced to Americans by the little shops nestled among the blocks of big-city tenements.

Now

A Continuing Heritage

Americans continue their love affair with Italian food today both at home and when eating out. Entire cookbooks are devoted to Italian cooking. When polled by a culinary news magazine, Americans selected Italian food as the second favorite restaurant fare. Among fast-food chains, Pizza Hut ranks fourth and Domino's Pizza ranks seventh in total sales.

Jews of eastern Europe were confronted with many common problems wherever they lived. For one thing they were often the victims of religious discrimination. In many regions Jews were not allowed to own land, work in certain trades, or move out of areas that had been set aside for them.

These limitations on Jews created widespread poverty. In addition eastern European Jews lived in danger of **pogroms,** or organized massacres. Jewish immigrants seeking personal safety, religious freedom, and economic opportunity came to America.

Slavs made up a third group of new immigrants. "Slavs" is a broad label given to a people, generally from eastern Europe, who have similar languages and customs. In the late 1800s, large numbers of Slavs left Russia, Poland, and other countries to escape economic woes. Many Slavs also came in search of political freedom.

These newcomers were, for the most part, poor. They hoped to find a better life in America. In part it was their labor that made the rapid industrialization of the United States possible. For many people, immigrating to the United States was the only way for them to escape persecution in their homeland. One Jewish immigrant noted that "the only hope for the Jews in Russia is to become Jews out of Russia."

Ethnic Neighborhoods

The new immigrants flocked to the cities. There they lived together in ethnically homogeneous neighborhoods such as "Little Italy" or the Jewish "Lower East Side" in New York City. There they practiced the ways of life they were used to and spoke their native languages. The communities they established revolved around a number of traditional institutions. They re-created the churches, synagogues, clubs, and newspapers of their homeland and adapted them to their new environment.

302   UNIT 3 New Horizons: 1860–1900

Cooperative Learning Activity

Immigrant Contributions to Your Community

Organize students into groups of four to research immigrants in their area. Have each group choose a member who will represent them at meetings. The group representatives should plan together what nationality groups they want to study, what information they want to gather, and how information is to be presented. Students could tape and write first-person accounts of the immigrants' experiences, research what important immigrants are associated with their area, and provide cultural data on the immigrants.
L2 📁

Public Resentment

This huge influx of immigrants created special social problems. Because immigrants lived in their own neighborhoods, practiced their own customs, and spoke their own languages, many Americans wondered if they could ever be assimilated into American life. Some people, especially workers, blamed them for low wages. Others resented that many immigrants were Catholics or Jews.

The railroad strike of 1877 and the Haymarket Square riot of 1886 resulted in many people's fear of immigrants who, it was thought, believed in socialism or even **anarchism,** a belief in no direct government authority over society. A few politicians, notably Senator Henry Cabot Lodge of Massachusetts, were strongly reactionary in their response to the issue of immigration. They wanted immigration from southern and eastern Europe to be stopped completely. In 1896, Senator Lodge argued for a bill that would exclude all prospective immigrants who could not read or write at least 25 words of the United States Constitution in some language. Lodge concluded that such a test would

> *". . . bear most heavily upon the Italians, Russians, Poles, Hungarians, Greeks, and Asiatics . . . races most affected by the test are those who[m] emigration has . . . swelled rapidly . . . and who are most alien to the great body of the United States."*

In the late 1800s, hostility grew toward many of the new racial and ethnic groups coming into the new country. The differences in customs, dress, and language of the new arrivals created a basic distrust of the foreign born by many native-born Americans. Some historians believe that this reaction was a response to the rapid changes occurring in America because of industrialization. For those native-born Americans who were uncertain and disturbed by social change, immigrants became easy targets of hostility.

Organized Opposition

Some Americans formed groups to counter what they considered the immigrant threat. One of these groups, the American Protective Association, was founded in 1887

Visualizing History ▲ THE NEW IMMIGRANTS During the late 1800s, new immigrants poured into the United States, braving the long and difficult journey to start a new life. ***Why did many people view these newcomers as a threat?***

VIDEODISC

GTV: The American People: Fabric of a Nation

Side 3, Chapter 4
Frames 18389-22748
Title: *Generation Gap*
Subject: The immigration experience—for kids

Linking Across TIME

Today, the flow of immigrants to America is higher than in any decade since 1900–1910. Six hundred thousand immigrants arrive yearly. Like those of the late 1800s and early 1900s, today's immigrants also come to escape oppression or to make a better life for themselves and their children.

Visualizing History Discuss the kinds of jobs open to newly arrived immigrants unable to speak English. **Answer to Caption:** They feared the new immigrants would take away their jobs. They also were suspicious of the immigrants' culture and customs.

Cultural Perspectives

Coming and Going In the late 1800s, people from other countries in the Americas could enter and leave the United States without passports whenever they wished. All they had to do was report their name, place of birth, and destination to an immigration officer. In fact, entry was even easier. Mexicans and Canadians could simply walk across the border, and many did so every day.

to protest the large number of Catholic immigrants. In some parts of the country, local laws were passed that prohibited immigrants from holding certain kinds of jobs and denied them other rights. Jewish immigrants, for example, were denied admission to some universities. In addition the immigrants faced actual physical attacks.

The anti-immigration movement was not limited to groups such as the American Protective Association. Some well-known scholars of the time were susceptible to these feelings as well. Historian and future President Woodrow Wilson and frontier historian Frederick Jackson Turner lamented the lessening flow of immigration from northern Europe and the rise in numbers of "inferior stocks" coming to America. One writer considered the new immigration a plot by European governments to "unload the sweepings of their jails and asylums."

Anti-Chinese Sentiment

Public resentment was not limited to newcomers from Europe, however. The Chinese, too, suffered discrimination on the Pacific Coast. The discovery of gold in 1849 and the subsequent demand for cheap labor first brought the Chinese to California. Many found work in the gold fields or on the construction of the Central Pacific Railroad. By 1852 there were some 25,000 Chinese men, women, and children living on the Pacific Coast and thereafter they came at

▲ CHINESE FAMILY IN CALIFORNIA, EARLY 1900S

the rate of 4,000 a year. By the end of the 1870s, there were almost 75,000 Chinese in California alone. Their willingness to work for low wages prompted a violent anti-Chinese movement among the white workers of California. Such feelings intensified during hard economic times. During the depression that followed the Panic of 1873, unemployed workers in California attacked the Chinese. Some Americans began to demand that Chinese immigrants be excluded from the United States.

In 1879 Congress forbade the importing of foreign workers under contract—a law aimed primarily at the Chinese. Then, in 1882, Congress, responding to pressure from the western states, suspended nearly all immigration from China for 10 years.

Section 3 ★ Review

Checking for Understanding

1. **Identify** Henry Cabot Lodge.

2. **Define** pogrom, anarchism.

3. **Explain** why people migrated from Europe to the United States.

4. **Differentiate** the "Old Immigration" from the "New Immigration."

5. **Identify** two attempts that were made to decrease levels of immigration to the United States.

Critical Thinking

6. **Understanding Cause and Effect** How did religious prejudice create problems for some immigrants?

ACTIVITY

7. Find out what groups of immigrants settled in your local area. Present a graphic display using photographs or your own sketches on the cultural influences these people have had on your town or city.

★★

City Life and Problems

Setting the Scene

Section Focus

With the rise of industrialism, the landscape of the nation changed. Railroads crisscrossed the continent. Where farms once stood, factories spewed forth black smoke. Thousands of Americans left the nation's farms hoping to make their fortunes in the city. Millions of immigrants came to better their lives and share in the benefits of the new industrial age.

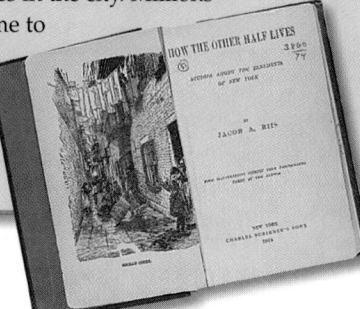

Objectives

After studying this section, you should be able to

★ identify the factors that led to the growth of cities during the late 1800s.

★ list the problems resulting from an increase in the urban population.

Key Term

merchandising

◄ BOOK ON URBAN LIFE BY JACOB RIIS

*A*ll over the nation—but especially in the Northeast—cities were growing rapidly. This urban growth was a result of industrialization. In 1840, 1 out of every 12 Americans lived in a city with a population of more than 8,000. By 1900, however, 1 out of every 3 Americans lived in a large city.

Why were so many people attracted to the cities? One reason was that rising new industries held out the promise of jobs and opportunity. Where else could immigrants—or other Americans, for that matter—fulfill the "rags to riches" dream of making a fortune overnight? The cities of the 1890s held the promise of excitement and activity, in contrast to the isolation of rural farm life. There was running water, modern plumbing, museums, libraries, theaters, shops, convenient transportation, and countless things to see and do.

■ Urbanization

Between 1860 and 1900 American urban areas grew twice as fast as the total population. Chicago, which in the 1830s had been a frontier town with a few hundred residents, became a vast metropolis of almost 2 million people. New York became the second-largest city in the world. During the same span of years, Philadelphia grew from less than 600,000 people to about 1.3 million. Both Boston's and Baltimore's populations increased from about 200,000 to more than one-half million.

Industrial cities were essentially the product of mines, factories, steamships, and railroads. New cities appeared, or old ones mushroomed, near coal and iron deposits (Birmingham, Alabama, and Pittsburgh), sources of water power (Lowell and Lawrence, Massachusetts), shipping centers

LESSON PLAN
SECTION 4, 305–310

FOCUS
Bellringer

Before taking roll, project Section Focus Transparency 9-4 or hand out Section Focus Transparency Activity 9-4. Have students answer the questions.

Motivating Activity

Tell students that between 1850 and 1901 New York City's growth was 460 percent and Chicago's 5,500 percent. Ask them to speculate what problems such rapid growth might have created. *(example answer: overcrowding and unhealthy living conditions, overcrowded schools, an inadequate sewer system, inadequate fire protection)* **L2**

Vocabulary Precheck

Have students think of as many alternative terms for *merchandising* as they can. **LEP**

NATIONAL GEOGRAPHIC SOCIETY

VIDEODISC

GTV: The American People: Fabric of a Nation

Side 3, Chapter 3
Frames 12567-18387
Title: *Home Sweet Home?*
Subject: The urban immigration experience
See GTV Guide for complete lesson plan.

Classroom Resources for SECTION 4

Blackline Masters:
- Reproducible Lesson Plan 9-4
- Guided Reading Activity 9-4
- Critical Thinking Skills Activity 9
- Workbook Activity 9-4
- Reteaching Activity 9-4
- Section Quiz 9-4

Transparencies:
- Section Focus Transparency 9-4

Multimedia:
- Testmaker
- GTV: The American People: Fabric of a Nation
- GTV: A Geographic Perspective on American History

TEACH
Guided Practice
Constructing an Outline
Provide the following outline:

City Life and Problems
I. Factors that led to the growth of cities
II. Problems caused by rapid urbanization
III. Needs of urban dwellers

Divide the class into groups of three. Have each group list subtopics and details for the main topics listed. **L2**

Teaching American Portraits

Jane Addams's (1860–1935) goal in establishing the Hull House was to "share the lives of the poor" and to humanize the city. She believed strongly in the importance of education and had the Hull House staff teach classes in everything from beginning English to cooking to the history of art.

 VIDEODISC

GTV: A Geographic Perspective on American History

Side 3, Chapter 10
Title: *A New Life*
Subject: Migration from rural to urban areas 1890–1920

See GTV Guide for complete lesson plan.

AMERICAN PORTRAITS

Jane Addams
1860–1935

By the time the guns of World War I began blazing in 1914, Jane Addams was already famous as the founder of Hull House—the settlement house that served Chicago's immigrants and urban poor. By then peace had become her passion.

In 1915 Addams urged European leaders to find a way to end the mounting carnage. When the United States entered the war, she was labeled unpatriotic for holding true to her pacifist ideals. After the war ended in 1918, Addams worked to ensure no repetition of the "war to end all wars."

Addams was elected president of the Women's International League for Peace and Freedom in 1915 and held that office until 1929. Her devotion to world peace was recognized in 1931 when she was named corecipient, with educator Nicholas Murray Butler, of the Nobel Peace Prize.

(Baltimore and New York City), and at railroad centers (Omaha and Chicago). Industrial cities, especially in the Northeast, had the greatest growth, but cities in all regions experienced rapid growth. Between 1860 and 1900, Nashville grew from 16,000 to more than 80,000, Minneapolis from 2,500 to more than 200,000, and Los Angeles from 4,000 to more than 100,000.

Once established, cities seemed to generate their own growth. To serve industry such facilities as banks, insurance companies, docks, and warehouses developed. These, in turn, attracted more industry and workers. Immigrants could often find employment only in urban industrialized areas. Yet an even greater number of new workers came from rural areas of the United States.

■ Problems of City Life

The modern industrial city confronted many people with an unfamiliar and often unattractive environment. The new cities were built with less concern for the comforts of the inhabitants than for the profits of builders and real-estate speculators. People poured into the cities faster than housing could be built to accommodate them. Many had no choice but to live in tenements, poorly constructed and cramped five- or six-story buildings, which housed many families. Many of the rooms and tenements had no windows and were often dark, narrow, and airless.

As more and more people were crowded together and the buildings began to deteriorate, city slums developed. Lacking proper sanitation, tenements became foul-smelling and vermin-infested. Typhoid and other diseases often spread rapidly.

Lack of Social Services

Besides inadequate housing, there was a shortage of police and firefighters. City water was impure and sewers were often clogged. Garbage collection was sporadic. In addition there were no attempts at city planning. Little was done to provide for open spaces, parks, and playgrounds or to take advantage of rivers and other natural features. The few open spaces were often used as garbage dumps or left vacant with a scanty growth of grass and weeds competing with cinders and tin cans.

306   UNIT 3 New Horizons: 1860–1900

Special Needs Activity

Writing Disability Some students with writing disabilities feel most comfortable when they are permitted to tape lectures and discussions. This helps bypass the writing problem but creates another problem—time needed to review the lecture and sift through information. This process can be made more efficient if students are cued by the teacher as to when to turn on the recorder for new information. As you discuss the problems resulting from urban population increases, use a prearranged cuing system to help students record appropriate parts of the discussion. **L1, LEP**

Rivers and harbors were polluted by sewage and factory wastes, and the air was fouled by smoke from thousands of chimneys. The new environment cut off people from sun, air, and natural beauty.

New Concerns Arise

The growth of cities created a demand for new sources of water because wells and brooks provided too scanty a supply and were often polluted. New York City, the first of the major cities to meet this problem head-on, built the Croton Aqueduct 25 miles outside the city limits.

Cities also had to come up with more efficient means of intercity transportation. This was accomplished by the horse car and later by the elevated railway, the trolley car, and the subway. The demand for space in preferred localities such as Wall Street in New York or the Loop in Chicago resulted in the creation of huge skyscrapers, which, in turn, added a vertical dimension to transportation—in the form of the elevator.

Rise in Crime

An unexpected problem of urban life, however, was the increase in crime. There had always been occasional violence and theft, but never on a scale demanding an organized police force. There had been nothing resembling modern police until the formation of the Metropolitan Police of London, known as "bobbies," around 1830.

Because the problems experienced by growing urban centers were new, old solutions could not be relied upon. It seemed as if the answers were as varied as the problems. Some people looked back to an earlier morality and sought to enforce the Puritan Sabbath as a means of regenerating the city. As a result restaurants and amusement places were closed. There were even efforts to forbid the running of trains and streetcars.

Public Awareness Spurs Legislation

One who faced the realities of life in factories, shops, and slums was Jacob A. Riis (REES), a Danish American police reporter

Visualizing History

▲ URBAN PROBLEMS Poverty and overcrowding brought on many social problems in large cities throughout the United States. *What problems did residents of tenements in the nation's larger cities face?*

Independent Practice

📁 Assign Guided Reading Activity 9-4.

CURRICULUM CONNECTION

Architecture Have students find and compare illustrations of buildings designed by Henry Richardson and Louis Sullivan. Resource for students: *The Evolution of American Taste: The History of American Style from 1607 to the Present* by William Pierce Randel. **L2**

Visualizing History A young Jewish woman who emigrated from Poland in 1901 was struck by the crowded houses and narrow streets. She asked, "Where are the green fields and open spaces in America?" How does the illustration reflect her sense of wonder?
Answer to Caption: Problems included overcrowding; unsanitary and unhealthful living conditions, including pollution and disease; and shortage of city services, including water and protection.

Sidelight: Tenements

According to Jacob Riis, 1,500,000 people were living in 43,000 tenements in New York City in the 1890s. Tenements were large residences in once-respectable neighborhoods that had been abandoned by their owners and were subdivided for use by several families rather than one. Dividing often led to the shutting off of some levels from other levels, making the use of water and plumbing unavailable to some tenants and dividing rooms into windowless areas. When landlords ran out of residences to subdivide, they built flimsy housing with an eye to heavy use and low maintenance.

▲ A Nation of Cities As the United States became
a nation of cities, public services expanded to
serve the needs of the people. Paved roads, electric street lights, and streetcars improved transportation. *What did critics say about the
appearance of cities?*

for New York newspapers. In the course of
his work, Riis had seen again and again the
connection between slums and human
degradation. In 1890 he focused public
attention on the problem in a best-selling
book, *How the Other Half Lives.* By appealing
to public conscience, Riis secured legislation
that reduced the worst slum conditions,
along with other measures that improved
the lives of city dwellers, such as playgrounds for schools. Among his close
friends was a rising young Republican
politician, Theodore Roosevelt, whom he
"educated" by taking him into tenements,
sweatshops, and jails.

Footnotes to History

Wages and Prices   In 1900 the average
American worker earned 22 cents an hour, or
$12.98 a week based on the typical 59-hour
workweek. A tailor-made suit cost $10; a skirt
$4. Prices for meat at the local market were 7
cents a pound for chicken, 10 cents for beef,
and 12.5 cents for sausage. The average price
for an automobile—$1,550 and out of reach
for most—meant Americans continued to
rely on the horse and buggy and streetcars. In
any case, the nation had just 150 miles of
paved roads.

Settlement Houses Assist Communities

The year before *How the Other Half Lives*
was published, Jane Addams founded, in a
Chicago slum, the most famous settlement
house in the United States, Hull House.
About this neighborhood, Addams wrote:

> ❝ *[T]he streets were inexpressibly
> dirty . . . the street lighting bad.
> . . . Many houses have no water
> save the faucet in the back yard;
> there are no fire escapes. . . .* ❞

Addams, a deeply religious woman,
was inspired by a passionate desire to put
her faith to work. Modeling her endeavor
on Toynbee Hall, a settlement house in
England, Jane Addams was determined to
improve the life of the "other half." Hull
House soon had activities as varied as an
art gallery and a gymnasium as well as hot
lunches for factory workers and classes in
English. Above all, Addams was interested in helping children, believing that "a
fence at the top of a precipice is better than
an ambulance at the bottom." Addams
surrounded herself with young people
who were glad to enlist in a war against
human suffering.

Similar convictions were the motivating
forces behind the founding of other settlement houses, including the Henry Street
Settlement in New York City, the Santa
Maria Institute in Cincinnati, and the South
End House in Boston. In addition to providing immediate services to neighborhood
people, settlement houses were schools
where hundreds of men and women
learned social responsibility.

Many of these people later helped to promote reform legislation, either as political
lobbyists or officeholders. "Graduates" of
Hull House, for example, were instrumental in securing the first playgrounds in
Chicago, better garbage collection, and the
first Illinois factory inspection law. Frances
Perkins, trained in a New York settlement
house, embarked on a political career that
led to her appointment as secretary of labor,
the first woman to serve on a presidential
cabinet.

Critical Thinking Activity

Interpreting Primary Sources Have students
obtain a copy of Jacob A. Riis's book *How the
Other Half Lives* and investigate the legislation
that Riis secured in order to improve slum conditions. Have them research how he went about
securing this legislation. Ask students to present their findings as if they were asking

Congress to pass a law to protect urban
dwellers. **L3**

🖝 For additional practice in using critical
thinking skills, assign Critical Thinking Skills
Activity 9.

Beautifying the City

Among the indictments against sprawling industrial cities were their ugliness and their lack of provision for rest and recreation. Architects and landscape designers were among those who sought remedies.

Public Buildings and Open Spaces

In 1876 New York City opened Central Park, designed by Frederick L. Olmsted and Calvert Vaux, as "a great breathing space for the toiling masses." Olmsted was the first person to use the term *landscape architect* as the name of this kind of work. Olmsted also designed Prospect Park in Brooklyn. Many other cities followed New York's example. In 1892 and 1893 Chicago hosted a World's Fair on fairgrounds designed by Olmsted, with buildings in the classical style surrounded by lagoons and landscaped grassy areas.

The Chicago World's Fair revealed that American architecture was dynamic and original. The best architects now thoroughly understood European styles and adapted them for modern use. The firm of McKim, Mead, and White used the Italian Renaissance style in their design for the Boston Public Library. Henry Richardson adapted Romanesque style in his design for churches, libraries, warehouses, and even department stores.

New Functional Architecture

The Transportation Building at the Chicago Fair, designed by Louis Sullivan, however, was based on a new concept: form follows function. Sullivan believed an architect should create designs that reveal a building's purpose and method of construction. He was one of the first architects to design skyscrapers. His influence, both directly and later through the work of his pupil Frank Lloyd Wright, reached worldwide.

The finest example of a structure in which form expressed function was the Brooklyn Bridge. Completed in 1883, 16 years after it was begun, it was the largest suspension bridge in the world at that time. Hung from great steel cables with a span half again as long as that of any previous bridge, it was designed and constructed by two German Americans, John Roebling and his son Washington Roebling. During the project, John was killed on the job. His son continued directing the work until he himself was injured. The work was then taken over by John's wife who, with her son's direction, completed the project.

Public Libraries

For those who wished to continue their education, American cities provided opportunities that had never existed before. In 1876 the American Library Association was founded to encourage "the best reading for the largest number at the least expense." By 1900 the public libraries, which receive support from taxes, revenues, and private donations, came to be recognized as "no less important than the schoolhouse in the system of popular education."

Downtown Shopping Districts

New means of **merchandising,** or the buying and selling of goods, were created to meet the growing needs of urban populations. One striking example was the department store. Stores such as A. T. Stewart and John Wanamaker were retail centers where nearly all kinds of goods were sold in one location. These stores had an enormous appeal to people of all classes. As a result the downtown areas of cities became centers where

▶ FLATIRON BUILDING, NEW YORK CITY

Linking Across TIME

William Le Baron Jenney designed the first metal-framed skyscraper—a 10-story building erected in Chicago in 1884–1885. By 1931, the Empire State Building dwarfed all other buildings in the world at 102 stories. Today the world's tallest building is the Sears Tower in Chicago. It is 1454 feet high and has 110 stories.

Did You Know?

During construction of the Brooklyn Bridge, John Roebling was killed on the job. His son continued directing the work until he was injured. The work was then taken over by John's wife, who completed the project with her son's direction.

NATIONAL GEOGRAPHIC SOCIETY

 VIDEODISC

GTV: A Geographic Perspective on American History

Side 3, Chapter 15
Title: *A Progress Report*
Subject: Early environmental reforms (1870–1920)

Sidelight: City Planning

When Chicago burned to the ground in 1871, it was both a curse and a blessing. The curse was that most of the city was destroyed; the blessing was that it could be rebuilt with wide straight streets and modern buildings that would serve people better in the next century. Daniel Burnham, one of the architects who gave Chicago the skyscraper, emphasized modern parks, residential areas, and an efficient transportation system in his "Plan of Chicago," which he presented in 1904. Much of his plan was implemented, making Chicago one of the greenest cities today.

Check Understanding

Assign Section 4 Review as homework or an in-class activity.

Evaluate

☑ 🗀 Assign Section Quiz 9-4 or use the Testmaker to create a customized quiz.

Reteach

Have students work in groups to describe the problems of living in a large city from the viewpoint of one of the following: a recent immigrant, a police officer, Louis Sullivan, Jane Addams, or Jacob Riis.

🗀 Have students complete Reteaching Activity 9-4.

🗀 Assign Workbook Activity 9-4.

Enrich

Have students research the "dumbbell tenements" in the library. Have them find out how and why they were built and why they were so terrible to live in. Have volunteers share their findings with the class.

CLOSE

Have students give reasons why the sentiments expressed in the quotation by Jacqueline Shaw Lowell that ends this chapter are still valid today.

people came to shop. Merchants who wanted this new business were active in making sure that the areas were kept clean and attractive. New streets, sidewalks, and buildings were constructed.

Despite some setbacks, citizens made progress solving some of the problems facing the major cities. The availability of electricity enabled shops and factories to remain open after dark and thus stimulated urban nightlife as well.

Efforts by Municipal Governments

Throughout the late 1800s, city governments turned their efforts toward providing the services needed for their citizens. Steps were taken by city leaders to reduce crime, to improve recreational opportunities and living conditions, and to solve some of the public health problems that accompanied the rapid growth of the cities. Methods of identifying criminals, such as the use of photographs, were improved. Electric streetlights added a large measure of safety on city streets.

Many parks were built, usually toward the edges of already congested cities. Public utilities provided electricity, clean water, and sewage services for many urban areas. By 1898 approximately 350 communities had built publicly owned electric light companies, and by 1900 more than 3,500 public waterworks had been constructed nationwide.

The need for better communication spurred the use of a new innovation, the telephone. Within a few years after the telephone was invented in 1876, telephone exchanges were established in more than 80 cities. Within 20 years nearly 800,000 telephones were in use throughout the United States, twice as many as were in use in Europe. The impact of the telephone upon American life was enormous, linking many of the urban and rural areas of the nation almost instantly.

Despite these changes for the better, many social reformers felt that this was only a start. They contended that it was essential to find solutions for problems before the problems ever occurred. More and more reformers urged government to deal with the causes of social and economic problems. Jacqueline Shaw Lowell, the founder of the New York Charity Organization Society, expressed this attitude about the city's problems when she noted:

> 66 *[There are] five hundred thousand wage earners in this city, 200,000 of them women, and 75,000 of those working under dreadful conditions. . . . If the working people had all they ought to have, we should not have the paupers and the criminals. . . . It is better to save them before they go under than to spend your life . . . taking care of them afterwards.* 99

Section 4 ★ Review

Checking for Understanding

1. **Identify** Jacob A. Riis, Jane Addams, Louis Sullivan.

2. **Define** merchandising.

3. **List** the factors that led to the growth of cities during the late 1800s and summarize the problems that developed as the population grew.

4. **Describe** the efforts made to improve life and conditions in the cities.

Critical Thinking

5. **Understanding Analogies** How does Jane Addams's theory that "a fence at the top of a precipice is better than an ambulance at the bottom" explain her focus on children?

ACTIVITY

6. Create a public service announcement to inform new residents about community services provided by local agencies.

Answers to SECTION 4 REVIEW

1. Jacob A. Riis, 307; Jane Addams, 306; Louis Sullivan, 309
2. All vocabulary words are defined in the Glossary.
3. new industries, jobs and opportunities, amenities of city life, excitement and activities, immigration, migration from rural areas
4. aqueducts, better transportation, police departments, legislation, playgrounds, settlement houses, parks, architectural buildings, libraries, department stores
5. Answers will vary. She wants to help children develop so they stay out of trouble rather than help them out of trouble as adults.
6. Public service announcements should show evidence of research.

Urban Pollution and Public Health

Citizens who complain about air pollution, poor water quality, and inadequate garbage disposal in modern cities might feel at home if transported to the New York City of 1866. A report on the sanitary conditions of the city in that year identified the following problems:

(1) filthy streets; (2) neglected garbage and domestic refuse; (3) obstructed and faulty sewers and drains; (4) neglected privies and stables; (5) cattle pens and large stables in the more populous districts; (6) neglected and filthy markets; (7) slaughterhouses and hide and fat depots in close proximity to populous streets; (8) droves of cattle and swine in crowded streets; (9) swill-milk stables; . . . (10) bone boiling, fat melting . . . within the city limits; (11) . . . offensive exhalations . . . in gas manufacture; . . . (12) . . . dumping grounds and manure yards in vicinity of populous streets; (13) . . . management of refuse and junk materials; . . . (14) overcrowding of . . . public conveyances; . . . (15) neglect of dead animals in the streets and gutters of the city.

Such urban problems were not new. Examples can be found even in ancient times. Many cities, having become centers for trade, government, and religion, were large and crowded. Some historians place Rome's population at more than 1 million by the start of the first century A.D. Within 100 years overcrowding resulted in many of Rome's citizens living in apartment houses. Some apartments were 5 or 6 stories high and sheltered about 200 people each. Many of the city's residential structures were flimsy and poorly constructed, and living conditions paralleled those in the impoverished sections of nineteenth-century New York.

The living conditions of the urban poor left a great deal to be desired. Life in the crowded tenements was hazardous at best. Fires were an ever-present threat. In the late 1800s, the amount of damage from urban fires was on the

▲ CITY STOREFRONT, C. 1910

rise. Much of Chicago's downtown area burned in 1871, and two years later Boston experienced a devastating fire.

Another threat was illness. One reason for this was poor diet. Another was unsanitary conditions. Most tenement houses had neither indoor plumbing nor good ventilation.

Making the Geography Connection

1. Categorize the pollution problems under air, soil, and water.

2. Why do you think the speed of urban growth contributes to environmental problems?

ACTIVITY

3. Identify an environmental problem in your state. Write a letter to your state legislator expressing your concerns. Ask whether solving this problem should take precedence over business considerations that might be involved.

311

Answers to Making the Connection

1. Air pollution would include such things as odors from bone boiling and fat melting and offensive exhalations in gas manufacture. Soil pollution might include filthy streets, garbage, stables and cattle pens, animals in the streets, dumping of manure and other refuse, and dead animals. Water pollution could derive from runoff or discharges from any of the items listed.

2. Overcrowding of the cities overtaxes the inadequate disposal systems for removing waste. City services can't expand rapidly enough to keep pace.

3. Student selection and letter will vary.

CHAPTER 9 ★ REVIEW

GLENCOE
TECHNOLOGY

VIDEODISC

Use the MindJogger Videoquiz to review students' knowledge.

MindJogger Videoquiz

Chapter 9
Disc 1, Side B

Available in VHS.

Using Vocabulary
Work should show evidence of familiarity with the terms.

Reviewing Facts
1. monotony, low wages, long hours, conditions, unemployment
2. mobility and diversity of workers, differing goals, public opinion, opposition, lockouts
3. wage increases, shorter hours, health and safety standards
4. opportunity, crop failures, political persecution, religious freedom
5. new industries, jobs and opportunities, amenities of city life, excitement and activities, immigration
6. tenements, crowding, slums, crime, disease, poor sanitation, pollution
7. improved transportation, police, playgrounds, settlement houses, parks, buildings, libraries

Understanding Concepts
1. By enlisting members from each and every facet of society, big

---

Using Vocabulary

Use the following terms in sentences or short paragraphs. Relate them by using two or more of the terms in each sentence or paragraph.

real wages	company town
business cycle	blacklist
lockout	collective bargaining
arbitration	industrial union
injunction	tenement

Reviewing Facts

1. **Discuss** the hardships and problems that plagued industrial workers in the late 1800s and early 1900s.
2. **Report** on the problems facing labor unions in the late 1800s.
3. **Summarize** the achievements of labor unions during the late 1800s.
4. **List** the reasons why people immigrated to the United States.
5. **Cite** reasons for the growth of cities during the late 1800s.
6. **Identify** the problems created by growth in urban populations.
7. **Describe** efforts to improve nineteenth-century city life.

Understanding Concepts

Unity

1. How did Terence Powderly envision the Knights of Labor as being capable of confronting big business? How did his methods and goals differ from other union leaders'?

Conflict

2. With what groups did labor unions have conflict once they were organized? What were some of the reasons for the conflict? Explain how the conflict was resolved.

Critical Thinking

1. **Understanding Stereotypes** What stereotypes of labor unions were created because of the actions of a few union members or nonunion strikers? How did they work against the efforts of organized labor?

2. **Analyzing Photographs** Study the photograph on this page of children on a New York City street in the early 1900s and answer the questions that follow.
   a. What are the individuals in the photograph doing?
   b. What evidence do you see that conveys economic conditions?
   c. What title would you give this photograph?

▲ CHILDREN ON MULBERRY STREET, NEW YORK CITY

3. **Determining Cause and Effect** Explain how technology and industrialization created wealth among business owners. How did the same technology and industrialization create poverty among workers?

4. **Making Comparisons** How did economic hard times in other countries work to the advantage of United States industry? What problems did hard times cause in the United States?

5. **Demonstrating Reasoned Judgment** Thomas Jefferson had dreaded the day when most citizens would shift from farms to the cities. In what way did city life during the later 1800s suggest that his dread was justified?

---

business would be confronted by a union representing all the people.
2. with employers, law enforcement, the public; blamed for unrest and disorder

Critical Thinking
1. stereotyped as anarchists and radicals; became associated with instances of violence

2. a. Children are surrounding a drinking fountain.
   b. children's clothing, lack of shoes
   c. Student titles should tie to city life.
3. These factors concentrated manufacturing in the hands of those who could afford expensive technology.

Workers became vulnerable to business cycles.
4. provided a labor pool to industrialize rapidly; competition for jobs, poverty, labor conflicts
5. Crowding, pollution, unhealthful conditions, and crime in cities weakened traditional values.

History and Geography

Urbanization

A new America emerged during the late 1800s. This new America was shaped by an urban environment that replaced an older agrarian setting.

1. **Human/Environment Interaction** Why did many rural residents move to the cities?

2. **Human/Environment Interaction** How did immigrants try to adjust to life in the United States?

Cooperative Learning Interdisciplinary Activity: Labor History

Work with a partner to research a major strike that occurred in the United States within the last five years. Find information on the workers' grievances. In addition find information on the company's position in the strike. Use this information to take turns as a union representative and a company representative questioning one another during an arbitration meeting.

Practicing Skills

Summarizing

The following excerpt details the Homestead Steel Strike of 1892. Read the material carefully. Then answer the questions that follow.

Strikes did not cease following the tragedy at Haymarket Square. Andrew Carnegie's Homestead Steel Plant in Pennsylvania was the scene of more violence.

The 25,000-member Amalgamated Association of Iron & Steel Workers had negotiated a contract for Homestead workers in 1889. When the union sought to renew the contract in 1892, the company refused. Most of the plant's steelworkers were unskilled and not members of Amalgamated. Homestead officials contended that the union had no right to negotiate for all workers. The company refused a pay raise and countered with an 18 to 26 percent cut for all workers.

As a result, Homestead's 3,000 unskilled workers joined the plant's 800 union members in a strike. The

company manager, Henry Frick, ordered a lockout and called in strikebreakers. The strikers formed picket lines around the plant, which they disparagingly referred to as "Fort Frick."

The company hired the Pinkerton Private Detective Agency to ensure the safety of the strikebreakers. When 300 Pinkerton guards arrived on the morning of July 6, they were met by armed strikers ready for battle. The Pinkertons were forced to surrender and were returned to Pittsburgh. Three guards and seven strikers were killed.

"The strikers are in control," wrote the sheriff of Homestead to Robert Pattison, the governor of Pennsylvania, "Only a large military force . . . will restore order." Pattison responded by sending the Pennsylvania National Guard to Homestead. By July 26 the New York Times could report that "the Homestead Strike has had its back broken." The company took legal action against some of the strike leaders for murder and conspiracy. Amalgamated, once the most powerful trade union in the AFL, was crushed.

Practicing the Skill

1. List in order of occurrence the major events and main ideas expressed in the material.

2. Summarize the text by rewriting the major events and main ideas in your own words.

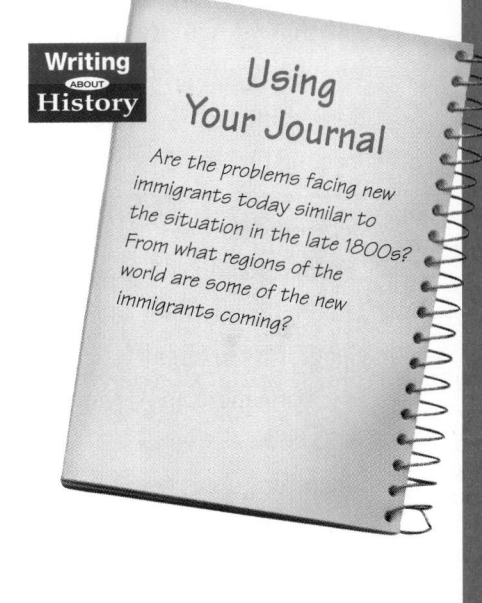

Writing ABOUT History

Using Your Journal

Are the problems facing new immigrants today similar to the situation in the late 1800s? From what regions of the world are some of the new immigrants coming?

Writing ABOUT History Using Your Journal

The ideas students present will vary, but they may mention that many of the problems are the same, including adjustment to new customs and language, and job and housing discrimination.

? Chapter Bonus Test Question

Ask students: In each of the following pairs, the two terms are related in some way. Write a sentence for each pair that explains how the terms are related. (Sample answers: Employers used a *lockout* to retaliate against a *labor union*. A bill was proposed that would require all *immigrants* to pass a *literacy test*.
1. labor union, lockout
2. literacy test, immigrants

History and Geography

1. because of crop failures and an inability to make a living on farms

2. lived together in ethnically homogeneous neighborhoods; recreated the churches, synagogues, clubs, and newspapers of their homeland

Cooperative Learning

Encourage students to list workers' grievances and to find out the company's position on the strike.

Practicing Skills

1. Major events should include: negotiation of workers' contract; refusal to

renew contract; company contends union has no right to negotiate; company offers pay cuts; workers go on strike; company calls strikebreakers; violence; National Guard helps break the strike; union is crushed.

2. Summaries should include a chronological ordering of the significant events.

Daily Lesson Objectives	Teacher Classroom Resources	Multimedia
SECTION 1 **A Tarnished Image** **1 Day** pp. 316–321 1. Identify the major causes of increased political corruption. 2. Give examples of corruption at local, state, and national levels.	📁 Reproducible Lesson Plan 10-1 📁 Performance Assessment Activity 10 📁 Chapter Concepts Mapping Activities 10-A, 10-B 📁 *Vocabulary Activity 10 📁 Cooperative Learning Activity 10 📁 *Guided Reading Activity 10-1 📁 American Portrait 40 📁 Critical Thinking Skills Activity 10 📁 Chapter Map Activity 10 📁 Chapter Skills Activity 10 📁 Primary and Secondary Source Readings, p. 20 📁 Political Cartoons Activities 7, 8 📁 Workbook Activity 10-1 📁 Reteaching Activity 10-1 📁 *Section Quiz 10-1	🔦 Section Focus Transparency 10-1 🔦 Chapter Concepts Transparencies 10-A, 10-B 🔦 Skills Transparency 10 🔦 Map Transparency 10 💿 Vocabulary PuzzleMaker 💿 Testmaker 💿 MindJogger Videoquiz 💿 Focus on Government
SECTION 2 **Calls for Good Government** **1 Day** pp. 323–328 1. Identify the reforms made during the 1870s and 1880s. 2. Describe the tariff controversy.	📁 Reproducible Lesson Plan 10-2 📁 *Guided Reading Activity 10-2 📁 American Portrait 39 📁 Enrichment Activity 10 📁 Workbook Activity 10-2 📁 Reteaching Activity 10-2 📁 *Section Quiz 10-2	🔦 Section Focus Transparency 10-2 💿 Testmaker 💿 Focus on Government 💿 The Presidents: A Picture History of Our Nation
SECTION 3 **Cultural Life** **1 Day** pp. 329–334 1. Discuss developments in literature, art, and higher education. 2. Describe how various leisure activities expanded.	📁 Reproducible Lesson Plan 10-3 📁 *Guided Reading Activity 10-3 📁 Linking Past and Present Activity 10 📁 Geography in History Activity 10 📁 Spirit of American Art and Music, pp. 17, 23 📁 Workbook Activity 10-3 📁 Reteaching Activity 10-3 📁 *Section Quiz 10-3	🔦 Section Focus Transparency 10-3 🔦 U.S. History & Art Transparency 16 🖼 Focus on American Fine Art Prints: *The Boating Party* by Mary Cassatt
CHAPTER REVIEW AND EVALUATION **1 Day**	📁 Chapter 10 Test, Forms A and B 📁 Spanish Chapter 10 Summary 📁 Performance Assessment Activity 10	💿 MindJogger Videoquiz 💿 Student Self-Test & Review Software 🎧 *Chapter 10 Audiocassette Activity and Test

*Also available in Spanish

 OUT OF TIME? If time does not permit teaching the entire chapter, use the Chapter 10 Summary on pages 362–363 and the Chapter 10 audiocassette (English and Spanish) to point out the main ideas of the chapter.

A complete, 1-page lesson plan is provided for each section in the *Reproducible Lesson Plan* booklet.

Key to Ability Levels

Teaching strategies have been coded for varying learning styles and abilities.

L1   Basic activities for all students

L2   Average activities for average to above-average students

L3   Challenging activities for above-average students

LEP Limited English Proficiency activities

Block Schedule

Block scheduling differs from traditional class scheduling in the amount of time allotted to each period. The extended timeframe provided by block scheduling affords you the opportunity to implement a greater number of research-oriented and activity-intense projects to motivate and involve your students. Activities that are particularly suited to use within the block scheduling framework are identified throughout this unit by the following designation:

✔ Performance Assessment Activity

Everyday Life   Have the class work together to create a newspaper or TV newscast that describes an imaginary day in the late 1800s. Divide the class into groups and assign a student from each group to form an editorial board. The board should decide what news, special features, and advertisements to include. Point out that a good way to start is to make lists of the stories, features, and advertisements. Discuss the lists and how to proceed. Ask the board to assign tasks to each group and then review the work submitted by the various groups. The board might duplicate the newspaper for distribution or videotape the newscast for broadcast. After completing the activity, have the students discuss the assignment.

POSSIBLE RUBRIC FEATURES
- Content
- Organization
- Written and Visual Communication Skills
- Creativity
- Collaborative Skills

📁 For additional activities, see Performance Assessment Strategies and Activities.

TEACHER'S CORNER

NATIONAL GEOGRAPHIC SOCIETY

INDEX TO NATIONAL GEOGRAPHIC MAGAZINE

The following articles may be used for research relating to this chapter:

- "A Season in the Minors," by David Lamb, April 1991.

NATIONAL GEOGRAPHIC SOCIETY PRODUCTS AVAILABLE FROM GLENCOE

To order the following products for use with this chapter, contact your local Glencoe sales representative or call Glencoe at 1-800-334-7344:

- *The Presidents: A Picture History of Our Nation* (CD-ROM)
- *GTV: A Geographic Perspective on American History* (Videodisc)
- *GTV: The American People: Fabric of a Nation* (Videodisc)

ADDITIONAL NATIONAL GEOGRAPHIC SOCIETY PRODUCTS

To order the following products for use with this chapter, call National Geographic Society at 1-800-368-2728:

- *The United States as a World Power: From the 1890s to the 1970s* (Filmstrip)
- *The American Presidency* (Filmstrip)
- *Mark Twain: When I Was a Boy* (Video)

Recording Journal Notes
After students have noted abuses, ask them to categorize their findings.

Linking Across TIME

Perhaps the last great political machine was the Cook County Democratic party, run by Chicago Mayor Richard J. Daley. Coming to power in 1955, Daley adopted many of the tactics of the nineteenth-century political bosses. In return, the party workers brought in huge voting majorities for Daley's candidates on Election Day. Daley remained in control of the machine until his death in 1976.

CHAPTER 10
★★★★★★★★★★★★★★★★★★★★★★★★★★★★★★★★★

The Gilded Age
1865–1900

► TIFFANY LAMP

Setting the Scene

Focus

American political life reached a low point between 1865 and 1900. Corruption in the form of graft and bribery became almost routine in local, state, and national governments. Both the Democratic and Republican parties came under the influence of lobbyists and other special interests. Neither party was ready for change, although the assassination of President Garfield prompted civil service reform.

Concepts to Understand

★ How the spoils system and lobbyists fostered **corruption** in government

★ How **public protest** by a free press worked to end political corruption

Read to Discover . . .

★ the major forms of political corruption.

★ new forms of leisure pastimes and amusements that attracted the interest of Americans before 1900.

Journal Notes

As you read the chapter, note the types of corruption and questionable ethics in government during the Gilded Age.

CULTURAL	
• **1873** *One of the first schools of nursing opens at Bellevue Hospital in New York*	• **1876** *National Baseball League formed* • **1883** *Joseph Pulitzer buys the* New York World

1865	1875

POLITICAL	
• **1872** *Crédit Mobilier scheme uncovered*	• **1883** *Pendleton Act passes* • **1884** *Cleveland elected President*

➕ EXTRA CREDIT PROJECT

Literature of the Era Ask interested students to read one of the works of literature mentioned in this chapter—*The Adventures of Tom Sawyer* and *The Adventures of Huckleberry Finn*, by Mark Twain; *The Rise of Silas Lapham*, by William Dean Howells, or *The Red Badge of Courage*, by Stephen Crane—or some other novel of the period. Have students write a brief essay in which they explain how the book they read enhances their understanding of the period.

Concept Mapping Activity

On the chalkboard, reproduce the following generalization and concepts map, and have students copy it in their notebooks.

Political corruption and scandal lead to needed reforms.

Public Protest | Corruption

To reinforce the two chapter concepts, use Chapter 10 Concept Mapping Activities 10-A and 10-B.

Assign Chapter Concepts Transparency Activities 10-A, 10-B.

History AND ART

Visitors to the World's Fair could ride several types of railroads, ascend 1,500 feet in a tethered hot air balloon, or pay fifty cents for two revolutions on the Ferris wheel.

GLENCOE TECHNOLOGY

VIDEODISC

Focus on Government

Side 1, Chapter 20
Title: *The Media and Politics*
Subject: Media's changing roles

History AND ART

Sunset Hour on the West Lagoon
by Williard L. Metcalf

This painting depicts a scene at Chicago's first world's fair, the Columbian Exposition of 1893. The striking beauty of the buildings and grounds spurred beautification programs in many cities.

◀ CROQUET DRESS, LATE 1800s

- **1890** *Reporter Nelly Bly circles globe by train and steamship in 72 days*

- **1895** *William Randolph Hearst purchases the New York Morning Journal*

1885	1895

- **1890** *McKinley Tariff passes*
- **1896** *McKinley elected President*

✔ Performance Assessment

Immigrants and City Machines Examine reasons many urban immigrants found political machines appealing. Point out that during the frigid winter of 1870, Boss Tweed dumped $50,000 worth of coal on street corners in the poorest sections of New York. Members of political machines paid condolence calls when someone died in the family, sent gifts for newborns, and celebrated First Holy Communions and bar mitzvahs. Have students research the following questions and present their findings in the form of an oral report. What were the needs of the immigrants? Despite their awareness of political corruption, why did many immigrants support machine candidates? **L2**

FOCUS

Bellringer

Before taking roll, project Section Focus Transparency 10-1 or hand out Section Focus Transparency Activity 10-1. Have students answer the questions.

Motivating Activity

Ask students to name some present-day political wrongdoings of corrupt officials in their city or state. Write students' responses on the chalkboard. Then have students discuss the following question: Can government reform completely eradicate political corruption? Why or why not? L2

Vocabulary Precheck

Call on students to read aloud the definitions of each "Key Term" from the Glossary. Then have them restate each definition in their own words. L1, LEP

Use the Vocabulary PuzzleMaker Software to create a crossword puzzle. L1

Assign Vocabulary Activity 10.

★★★★★★★★★★★★★★★★★★★★★★★★★★★★★★★★★★★★

A Tarnished Image

Setting the Scene

Section Focus

In the late 1800s, there were scandals at all levels of government. In the eyes of many critics, politics reached a low point. Although that low point was not maintained, it dealt a lasting blow to the image of politicians.

▲ BOSS WILLIAM TWEED

Objectives

After studying this section, you should be able to

★ identify the major causes of increased political corruption.

★ give examples of corruption at local, state, and national levels.

Key Terms

graft, political machine, kickback, ward, lobbyist, township

The Gilded Age was a phrase coined by two authors of the period—Mark Twain and Charles Dudley Warner—in a novel about the corruption of the Grant administration. In the years following the Civil War, the quality of American government left much to be desired. Politicians were irresponsible, loyalties were shallow, and money was tainted.

In this post-Civil War period, the most ambitious and talented people were no longer attracted to politics but to business. Indeed, politics itself became something of a business. The goal of political entrepreneurs was to achieve power and position through political office. Often politicians were able to line their pockets with money. Corruption seemed to flourish at every level of government. At first the corruption was not apparent. Material progress had produced a society that appeared to be bright and attractive. Society and government were not what they appeared to be on the surface, however.

■ Political Machines

Some of the most outrageous examples of **graft,** or thievery in office, were those at the grassroots level of city government. A factor that contributed to corrupt city government was the rapid growth of cities.

Growth of Cities

In 1840 there were only 131 cities in the United States; by 1880 there were 939. In addition cities often doubled, tripled, or even quadrupled in size within a decade. Services for these large populations had to be expanded at a rate never experienced before. Providing increased police and fire

---

Classroom Resources for SECTION 1

Blackline Masters:
- Reproducible Lesson Plan 10-1
- Guided Reading Activity 10-1
- Vocabulary Activity 10
- Cooperative Learning Activity 10
- American Portrait 40
- Critical Thinking Skills Activity 10
- Chapter Map Activity 10

- Chapter Skills Activity 10
- Primary and Secondary Source Readings, p. 20
- Political Cartoons Activities 7, 8
- Workbook Activity 10-1
- Reteaching Activity 10-1
- Section Quiz 10-1

Transparencies:
- Section Focus Transparency 10-1
- Skills Transparency 10
- Map Transparency 10

Multimedia:
- Vocabulary PuzzleMaker
- Testmaker
- Focus on Government

protection, water supplies, and sewage disposal was a daunting task for what often were untrained and ill-paid city officials. At the same time, businesses were eager to get lucrative contracts for paving streets and building new schools. An alliance between business and politics that fostered corruption resulted.

Maintaining Control

The usual democratic restraints on abuses of power did not work well in the cities of this era. Large portions of the population of cities were immigrants who had little or no experience with urban living or with democratic government. Many were accustomed to corruption in government. Both poor immigrants and native-born residents had little time to worry about abstract notions of government. They worked from dawn to dusk just to keep food on the table. Those more well-off, who might have gone into politics, were busy making money in business and real estate. As a result, almost every major city was dominated by a **political machine**—a party-linked political organization that maintained power by controlling votes, controlling the courts, and controlling the police as well.

The strength of a political machine came from the bottom up, not from the top down. Local politicians took care of the needs of their voters. They often provided groceries to families who were needy, organized free celebrations on important national holidays, attended ethnic religious and social events, and even helped get people out of jail. In this way politicians earned the loyalty of their neighborhood citizens. When election time came around, the votes were always there, keeping the helpful politicians in power.

The "Tweed Ring"

The most notorious city machine was the "Tweed Ring" in New York City. In 1868 "Boss" William M. Tweed gained control of New York's Democratic machine, known locally by the name of its central meeting place—Tammany Hall. For the next 3 years, he and his underlings managed to steal millions of dollars of city funds. The usual way this was done involved a process known as the "kickback." A **kickback** was an arrangement whereby contractors would pad, or increase, the amount of their bills for city work and pay or "kick back" a percentage of that amount to politicians in the ring. In one example a county courthouse that should

TEACH
Guided Practice

Demonstrating Reasoned Judgment Have students write a paragraph explaining why corruption in government undermines the democratic process. Have several volunteers read their paragraphs to the class. **L1, LEP**

Visualizing *History* Ask students to look at the "people's door" in the upper left part of the cartoon. What does the closed door symbolize? (*The people's door is shut, suggesting that the Senate does not serve the interests of the people.*) **Answer to Caption:** Lobbyists representing trusts offered senators kickbacks, bribes, and other special favors.

▲ THE TRUSTS Powerful trusts dominate the United States Senate in this 1889 cartoon by Joseph Keppler. The people's entrance to the Senate chambers (upper left) is shown bolted shut. *How did the trusts influence senators?*

Cooperative Learning Activity

Holding a Mock Trial Have students hold a mock trial of William M. Tweed. Before they begin, tell students that although Tweed fleeced the city treasury of millions of dollars, he used some of the money to provide services for his poor constituents. In addition, he argued for publicly funded welfare programs and for the establishment of more schools and hospitals. After the arguments for and against Tweed have been made, ask the class to act as jury and render a verdict. **L2, L3**

↪ Assign Cooperative Learning Activity 10.

Visualizing History ▲ NAST AND TWEED Thomas Nast (left) entertained Americans with biting political cartoons in the late 1800s. The most well-known political machine was run by "Boss" William M. Tweed (right). **Why did corruption in the federal government spread during the Grant administration?**

have cost taxpayers $250,000 actually cost $11 million. One plastering contractor was paid almost $3 million for 9 months' work.

In 1871 the *New York Times* published evidence of Tweed's rampant greed. At the same time, Thomas Nast, a brilliant political cartoonist, ridiculed Tweed in his cartoons for *Harper's Weekly*. Nast's cartoons found their mark and were devastating. Tweed was driven to complain: "I don't care a straw for your newspaper articles: my people don't know how to read, but they can't help seeing them . . . pictures." Tweed and his cronies were convicted of criminal conduct and driven from office.

•••••••••••••••••••••••••••••

Footnotes to History

The National Equal Rights Party New parties entered the political scene during this era. In 1884 suffragist leaders formed the National Equal Rights party. The party convention chose as its presidential candidate Belva A. Lockwood, a noted attorney and the first woman admitted to practice before the Supreme Court. Renominated in 1888, Lockwood was the first woman candidate for the presidency.

In spite of Tweed's removal, Tammany Hall continued to be an active influence in New York politics. This was true because local machine leaders drew their power from the local neighborhoods that they served 24 hours a day. A good deal of the graft, however, was used to help needy residents of the neighborhood **wards,** small administrative divisions of a city.

Occasionally city graft became so flagrant that voters were driven to "throw the rascals out" and put in a reform administration. Such movements often failed. Reform candidates focused on economy and honest administration but failed to understand the reasons why the political machines commandeered so much loyalty and met with such success.

■ Widespread Corruption

Corruption was not limited to local governments. It also occurred at the state and federal levels. In addition to the corruption, government in the late 1800s was affected by a marked lack of leadership. Neither Congress nor the President provided the direction the nation needed.

In State Government

Politics at the state level was nearly as corrupt as in the cities. In many states big business stood to gain or lose large amounts of money as a result of legislative votes on various matters, such as tax rates and internal improvements. Thus, companies spent large sums to influence votes.

In pre-Civil War times, businesspeople influenced politicians by writing letters and inviting them to expensive dinners. After the war the demands on government increased to the point that the amount of money spent by state governments was huge, and the stakes for those seeking state contracts were high. Businesses now began to employ **lobbyists**—people paid to represent a company or a special interest group. Sometimes they tried to influence votes by offering money in the form of campaign contributions. If it was unclear who would win a race, contributions were given to both parties. Such payments were regarded by legislators and lobbyists alike as "insurance" against unfavorable legislation.

At other times money was offered in the form of outright bribes. When Jay Gould controlled the Erie Railroad, he was reported to have spent $500,000 in bribes during a single session of the New York state legislature. Of the relations between the Standard Oil Company and the government of Pennsylvania, one observer wrote, "The Standard has done everything with the Pennsylvania legislature except to refine it."

In Federal Government

In general there was more corruption in state and local politics than in national politics. By far the worst misconduct in the federal government occurred when Grant was President.

Grant had been a great general, but he was a poor President. Although he was personally honest, he seemed unable to distinguish decent people from the dishonest. Dazzled by wealth, he fell under the sway of financial speculators James J. Fisk and Jay Gould, who reaped millions of dollars from their relationship with the President. Members of Grant's family, personal staff, and cabinet peddled influence and jobs in return for cash. At one time Grant's brother managed to hold four jobs by farming out the duties to other men.

Crédit Mobilier

In 1872 the scandals spread to Congress as well. A New York newspaper revealed that officers of the Union Pacific Railroad had formed their own construction company called the Crédit Mobilier. The contracts this company received enabled the railroad officers to reap enormous personal profits. To forestall investigation, the company distributed shares of stock "where it would do the most good." Grant's Vice President and several prominent members of Congress turned out to have accepted these thinly disguised bribes.

When the graft in his administration was uncovered, Grant declared that he would "let no guilty man escape." However, he

Visualizing History

▲ MR. DOOLEY Humorist Finley Peter Dunne's creation, Mr. Dooley, was a shrewd observer of political events. *Which political party were new immigrants likely to join?*

Visualizing History Mr. Dooley, the talkative Irish barkeeper, first appeared in a Chicago newspaper in the 1890s. Dooley spoke for the common man and woman. He provided a humorous perspective on events of the day.
Answer to Caption: the Democratic party, because Democrats actively sought the immigrant vote

 Assign American Portrait 40: Thomas Nast

Linking Across TIME

By the time of the Gilded Age, the pool of citizens eligible to vote had expanded considerably. In the early days of the Republic, only white male property owners over age 21 could vote. By the 1850s, property—and in some states religious—restrictions had disappeared, and most white adult males could vote. In 1870 the Fifteenth Amendment gave African American males the franchise. With the addition of women voters in 1920 and 18-year-old voters in 1971, the voter pool reached its contemporary constituency: all American citizens 18 years and older.

Critical Thinking Activity

Analyzing a Quotation Have students write in their own words the meaning of the following verse written by James Russell Lowell:
Show your State Legislatures; show your Rings;
And challenge Europe to produce such things
As high officials sitting half in sight
To share the plunder and to fix things right;

If that don't fetch her, why you only need
To show your latest style in martyrs,—Tweed!
L2

For additional practice in using critical thinking skills, assign Critical Thinking Skills Activity 10.

Using Graphs

Answer: The elections of 1864, 1868, 1872, 1896, and 1900.

Graph Skills Practice
In which presidential elections did the Democrats win the popular vote? (*1876, 1884, 1888, 1892*)

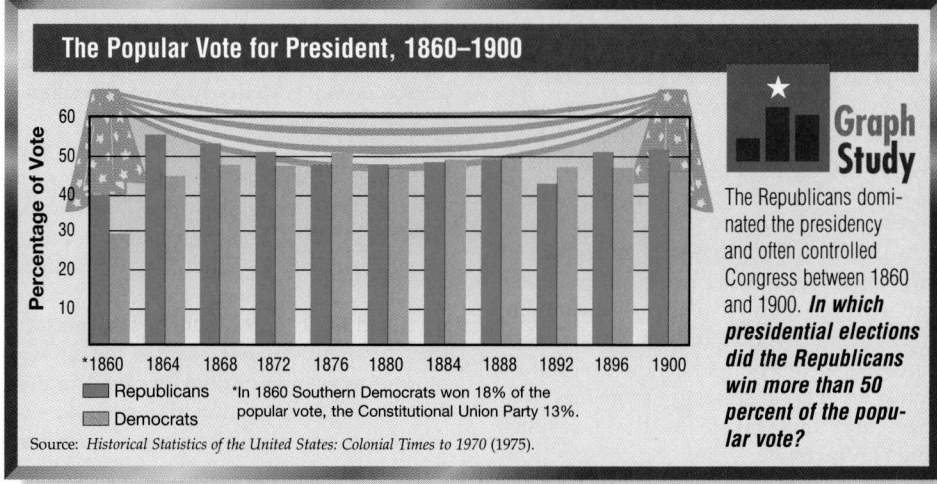

The Popular Vote for President, 1860–1900

Percentage of Vote

*1860 1864 1868 1872 1876 1880 1884 1888 1892 1896 1900

■ Republicans   *In 1860 Southern Democrats won 18% of the
■ Democrats   popular vote, the Constitutional Union Party 13%.

Source: *Historical Statistics of the United States: Colonial Times to 1970* (1975).

Graph Study

The Republicans dominated the presidency and often controlled Congress between 1860 and 1900. *In which presidential elections did the Republicans win more than 50 percent of the popular vote?*

protected many accused of wrongdoing from both investigation and punishment.

■ Postwar Political Parties

Even political analysts often found it difficult to explain the positions Democrats and Republicans took on major issues such as the tariff and railroad regulation. English writer James Bryce wrote:

> *Neither party has, as a party, anything to say on these issues, neither party has any clean-cut principles. . . . All has been lost except office or the hope of it.*

Issues Split Parties

One reason that parties seemed so similar was that they both reflected sectional differences so accurately. At every level, from wards to **townships,** or smaller divisions of a county broken up into local government districts, political parties were popular, and democratic participation was high. They did not avoid any of the issues; rather they were split internally on most of them. In the Northeast, for example, with its strong banking system, both parties favored the gold standard. In the Midwest both parties favored increasing the amount of money in circulation. Republicans in the developing Midwest were protariff, while Southern

Democrats were antitariff. Both parties in the Northeast were divided on the tariff issue.

The humorist "Mr. Dooley," created by Finley Peter Dunne, described a hypothetical candidate for President as someone who was pulled in different directions by varied interests and needed to be all things to all people.

> *Wanted: a good, active Dimmy-crat, sthrong iv lung an' limb; must be . . . a sympathizer with th' crushed an' down throdden people but not be anny means hostile to vested inthrests; must advocate sthrikes, gover'mint be injunction, free silver, sound money, greenbacks, a single tax, a tariff f'r rivinoo . . . at home in Wall sthreet an' th' stock yards, in th' parlors iv th' r-rich an' th' kitchens iv th' poor.*

Although fairly evenly matched in strength, the two parties were hardly identical. Though both parties received support from people in every walk of life, each had a distinctive base of support.

Republicans

The Republicans were supported by Western farmers and merchants, who benefited from Republicans' internal improvements and liberal land policies, and Eastern businesspeople, who benefited from high

Sidelight: Literature

The corruption of the post–Civil War years inspired a number of novels. In *Democracy* (1880), Henry Adams—whose grandfather and great-grandfather were Presidents—ridiculed the "practical" politics of the day. Through the words of a leading character, Adams vividly

showed his contempt: "I declare to you, that . . . I have found no society which has had elements of corruption like the United States. The children in the street are corrupt. . . . The cities are all corrupt, and also the towns and the counties and the States' legislatures and the judges."

tariffs and national banks. The Republicans tended to be old-immigrant Protestants—Presbyterians, Methodists, Congregationalists, or Baptists. The Republicans' problem was to keep together its Eastern and Western wings, which differed on such issues as greenbacks, free silver, tariffs, and banking.

The Republicans' "patron saint" was Abraham Lincoln. As the party that had led during the Civil War, they had great prestige in the North and the West. "The party that saved the nation must rule it," they proclaimed.

While critics attacked the Republicans for keeping alive war hatreds by "waving the bloody shirt," appeals to the memory of the Civil War were much more than that. Republican strength came from genuine devotion to the idea of the United States as a nation rather than as a federation of states. Many Republicans continued to be inspired by the party's early idealism. They felt that government existed to advance the public good.

Democrats

Democrats, too, looked back to the Civil War. From the end of Radical Reconstruction until well into the twentieth century, Southern states formed the "Solid South," never wavering in its allegiance to the Democrats.

The Democrats could not have remained a national party with only Southern support, however. The party depended on an alliance between white Southerners and Northern city machines. Democrats tended to get the support of recent immigrants, many of whom were Catholics or liturgical Protestants, such as Lutherans or Episcopalians. Their religious and cultural background was quite different from that of evangelical Protestants, such as Methodists and Baptists, who formed the core of the Republican party. The Democrats had allies among Western farmers, especially when crop prices were low, and among certain groups of businesspeople and owners of import companies who favored a lower tariff.

The Democratic party had two "patron saints"—Thomas Jefferson and Andrew Jackson. Like these leaders the Democrats claimed to represent the interests of ordinary Americans. In contrast to the Republicans' view that the federal government should take an active role in helping the needy and shaping national growth, the Democrats wanted to keep the federal government on a skimpy allowance and a short leash. "That government governs best which governs least" remained their motto.

During the entire period from 1865 to 1900, Democrats held the presidency for only two terms. Although they usually lost the White House, the Democrats were seldom far out of the running. Democratic candidates often got almost as many popular votes as their victorious opponents, and it was rare that the Republicans did not have to deal with Democrats in control of at least one house of Congress.

Section 1 ★ Review

Checking for Understanding

1. **Identify** William M. Tweed, Thomas Nast, Finley Peter Dunne.

2. **Define** graft, political machine, kickback, ward, lobbyist, township.

3. **Cite** examples of corruption that occurred in government.

4. **State** how the Republican and Democratic parties differed concerning the role of the federal government.

Critical Thinking

5. **Interpreting Satire** In his description of the ideal campaign candidate on page 320, what was Mr. Dooley expressing about politicians?

ACTIVITY

6. Assume the role of an American living in one of the nation's largest cities during the late 1800s. Write a letter to the mayor of your city expressing your concerns over overcrowdedness.

CHAPTER 10 The Gilded Age: 1865–1900 **321**

Answers to SECTION 1 REVIEW

1. William M. Tweed, 317; Thomas Nast, 318; Finley Peter Dunne, 319
2. All vocabulary words are defined in the Glossary.
3. party machine control, kickbacks, graft, bribes, influence peddling
4. Republicans viewed federal government as a union of states having an active role in na-
tion's affairs. Democrats viewed U.S. as a federation of independent states, and federal government as having a limited role.
5. In wanting to please and fearing to offend voters, politicians promised everything but took no real positions.
6. Student letters should express factual concerns.

ASSESS

Check Understanding
Assign Section 1 Review as homework or an in-class activity.

Evaluate
⊙ 🗁 Assign Section Quiz 10-1 or use the Testmaker to create a customized quiz.

Reteach
🗁 Have students complete Reteaching Activity 10-1.

Enrich
Ask students to research what services cities provided in the late 1800s and compare them with the services provided by cities today. Ask students to present their findings in a short report. Choose several volunteers to read their reports to the class.

🗁 Use Chapter 10 Map Transparency Activities and Chapter Map Activity 10.

🗁 Project Skills Transparency 10 and have students complete Skills Transparencies Activity 10.

CLOSE

Have students give reasons why political bosses should not be allowed to control government agencies that provide services for people.

TEACH

Discuss the cartoon described, having students point out the meanings of symbols and words in the cartoon. Ask: Why is a political cartoon a good primary source? (*It reflects issues and feelings of a certain time and point of view.*) How can you determine whether a cartoon portrays a valid point of view? (*Details, such as clothing and political issues, should reflect the period. You should be able to find facts to back up the point of view shown.*)

Students might work together to create political cartoons based on current issues. Have them compare their cartoons for validity and accuracy. **L2**

🖅 Use Chapter Skills Activity 10 to reinforce students' understanding of the skill.

Did You Know?

Before it was exposed in 1871, the Tweed Ring is believed to have stolen as much as $200 million from the city treasury.

🖅 Assign Primary and Secondary Source Readings, p. 20: "A Politician Describes Honest Graft and Dishonest Graft."

🖅 Assign Political Cartoons Activities 7, 8.

Interpreting Political Cartoons

Political cartoons are drawings that express a favorable or unfavorable opinion or point of view. They usually focus on public figures, political events, or economic or social conditions. Benjamin Franklin reportedly drew the first American editorial cartoon in 1754. Since that time, the editorial cartoon has been a regular part of most newspapers.

▲ *Who Stole the People's Money? 'Twas Him.*

Learning the Skill

Historians use editorial cartoons as a way of looking into the past. Cartoons show how a character or an event was viewed at the time it was drawn.

Each cartoon contains useful clues to its meaning. These clues may come from labels or captions, the appearance and action of figures, or the use of symbols—pictures that represent ideas or concepts.

The creator of this cartoon, Thomas Nast, pioneered the use of illustrations and cartoons to comment on significant political issues of the day. None of William "Boss" Tweed's critics leveled more scathing attacks at his notorious Tammany Hall machine than did Nast. In this cartoon, "Who Stole the People's Money?" the answer is "'Twas Him." Tweed appears as the heavyset man in the left foreground of the cartoon.

To interpret a political cartoon, follow these steps:
* **Read** the caption and any other words printed in the cartoon.
* **Analyze** each element in the cartoon.

* **Identify** the clues. What is happening in the cartoon? Who or what is represented by each part of the drawing? What or who do the figures represent? To what do the symbols refer? Studying the clues helps you to identify the subject and to understand the cartoonist's point.

* **Synthesize** these elements to decide the point the cartoonist is making.

Practicing the Skill

1. What is going on in this picture?
2. What words give clues to the cartoon's meaning?
3. What symbols are depicted? What do these symbols represent?
4. What point is the cartoonist making?

APPLYING THE SKILL

5. Cut out and mount on construction paper a series of current political cartoons. Write down the message of each cartoon.

Answers to Practicing the Skill

1. The people pictured seemed to be pinning the blame on someone else.
2. 'Twas Him
3. The dress clothes of the men facing forward reveal their superior economic status to the men at the top; the men pointing their fingers at someone else symbolize the idea of passing the buck.
4. Answers will vary but might include that Nast believed that the corruption in New York City was pervasive. The circle indicates that the organization protects the members by allowing them to "pass the buck."
5. Cartoons should show evidence of student creativity and understanding of the issues.

★★

Calls for Good Government

Setting the Scene

Section Focus

During the 1870s and the 1880s, social reformers like Henry George tried to raise the alarm that official corruption threatened democracy in the United States. If reformers wanted rebellion, they were disappointed, but through their efforts, a slow and steady movement away from the abuses of the Grant administration began. The first hopeful sign was the election of Rutherford B. Hayes in 1876.

Objectives

After studying this section, you should be able to

★ identify the reforms made during the 1870s and the 1880s.

★ describe the tariff controversy.

Key Terms

patronage, rider, free-trader, protectionist

◀ STATE POLITICAL PARTY BANNER, 1890S

[Banner image: MERCER COUNTY DEMOCRACY / ORGANIZED SEPT. 1, 1891 / TRENTON, N.J.]

Before the administration of Rutherford B. Hayes, one of the common practices had been **patronage**—the assumed right of elected officials to control political appointments to unelected positions. Patronage employees made the federal government the epitome of apathy and astonishingly idle.

■ Civil Service Reforms

With the election of Hayes, the tone of national politics began to change. Hayes made some steps toward rescuing the presidency from congressional domination.

Hayes Begins Reforms

After his inauguration in 1877, Hayes named Carl Schurz, owner of a German-language newspaper in St. Louis, Missouri, and United States senator from Missouri, to take charge of the Department of the Interior, which had previously been the scene of some of the worst examples of patronage. This practice was soon curbed. Hayes also forbade the practice of "shaking down" federal workers—forcing them to make political campaign contributions.

Hayes also defied congressional leaders by blocking important appointments favored by individual members of Congress. In addition he refused to sign otherwise acceptable legislation if Congress had attached **riders**—irrelevant amendments—of which he disapproved. He vetoed several appropriations bills with riders attached and finally won a clear-cut victory. Through his actions Hayes not only cut down on corruption but began to restore the balance of power between Congress and the President.

CHAPTER 10 The Gilded Age: 1865–1900 **323**

LESSON PLAN
SECTION 2, 323–328

FOCUS
Bellringer

Before taking roll, project Section Focus Transparency 10-2 or hand out Section Focus Transparency Activity 10-2. Have students answer the questions.

Motivating Activity

Ask students to recall some political, economic, and social aspects of life in the late 1800s in which reforms were needed. (*corrupt urban politics, corrupt business practices, urban poverty, dangerous working conditions, child labor, lack of rights for African Americans and women*) Write students' responses on the chalkboard. Then ask students to suggest some specific changes they think were necessary. (*possible answer: pass a law forbidding child labor*) Mention that details are given in this section about specific government reforms. **L1**

Vocabulary Precheck

Ask students to define each of the "Key Terms." Have a volunteer consult the dictionary for any unfamiliar words. **L1, LEP**

Classroom Resources for SECTION 2

Blackline Masters:
- Reproducible Lesson Plan 10-2
- Guided Reading Activity 10-2
- American Portrait 39
- Enrichment Activity 10
- Workbook Activity 10-2
- Reteaching Activity 10-2
- Section Quiz 10-2

Transparencies:
- Section Focus Transparency 10-2

Multimedia:
- Testmaker
- Focus on Government
- The Presidents: A Picture History of Our Nation

Election of 1880

Hayes's reforms brought him enemies among the Stalwarts, a group of Republican machine politicians who strongly opposed civil service reform. After Hayes declined to run for a second term, the party became divided between the Stalwarts, who wanted to nominate Grant for a third term, and the "Halfbreeds," who opposed Grant. After a prolonged deadlock at the national convention, the Republicans nominated dark horse James A. Garfield, a former Union general.

To blunt the old charge of disloyalty in wartime, the Democrats nominated General Winfield S. Hancock, a Union hero of the Battle of Gettysburg. The intellectual level of the ensuing campaign may be judged by the following excerpt from the speech of a Republican orator:

> *I belong to a party that believes in good crops; that is glad when a fellow finds a gold mine; that rejoices when there are forty bushels of wheat to the acre. . . . [T]he Democratic party is a party of famine; it is a good friend of an early frost; it believes in the Colorado beetle and in the weevil.*

Despite such inflammatory rhetoric, Garfield narrowly won the election by a margin of less than 10,000 votes.

The Pendleton Act

Under Hayes and Garfield, government was cleaner than it had been during the Grant administration, but the spoils system remained a constant source of inefficiency and graft. Disputes over patronage poisoned the relationship between the President and Congress. There was little momentum for reform.

In July 1881, however, as President Garfield entered the Washington, D.C., railroad station, he was shot by a disappointed office seeker. The unbalanced man cried, "I am a Stalwart and Arthur is President now." Garfield clung to life for two months, but in September Vice President Chester A. Arthur, a New York Stalwart, succeeded to the presidency.

Garfield's assassination excited opinion against the spoils system. In 1883 Congress passed the Pendleton Act, which has been called (with some exaggeration) "the Magna Carta of civil service reform." This law allowed the President to decree which federal jobs would be filled according to rules set by a bipartisan Civil Service Commission.

Visualizing History
▲ **ASSASSINATION OF THE PRESIDENT** President Garfield was shot only four months after his inauguration by a frustrated patronage seeker, Charles J. Guiteau. The assassination raised a cry against the spoils system. *After Garfield's death, who became President?*

Cooperative Learning Activity

Campaign Tactics Divide the class into groups of five. Have the groups compose letters to either Grover Cleveland's campaign managers or James G. Blaine's campaign managers. Letters should describe how campaign tactics have changed since 1884. Suggest that letters also include a comparison of tactics then with tactics today. Have groups select representatives to read their letters to the class. **L1, L2**

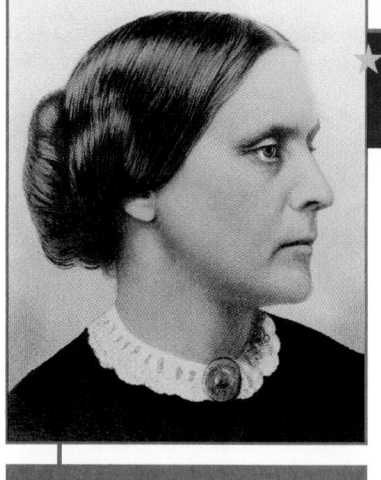

AMERICAN PORTRAITS

Susan B. Anthony
1820–1906

From her Quaker upbringing, Susan B. Anthony learned that men and women were equal before God. She spent most of her 86 years trying to convince others of that equality.

After teaching school for several years, Anthony returned home to help run the family farm. While living in her father's house, she began to focus on the great reform movements of the day. Anthony first joined a temperance group and experienced gender discrimination firsthand when she was refused permission to speak at a temperance rally. Realizing that as long as women were propertyless and voteless they would also remain powerless, Anthony began devoting her considerable energies to securing equal rights for women. Throughout the four decades from the end of the Civil War to her death, she was the nation's foremost crusader for a woman's right to vote.

Candidates competed for these jobs through examinations. Appointments could be made only from the list of those who took the exams. A civil service official could not be removed for political reasons.

Although President Arthur was a veteran of machine politics, he supported the Pendleton Act, placing 14,000 jobs (about one-tenth of the total) under the control of the civil service. The federal government had finally begun a shift away from the spoils system.

■ Cleveland in Office

The reform movement begun by Hayes and continued by Garfield and Arthur did not stop. Thus, the major theme of the presidential election of 1884 was honesty in politics.

Election of 1884

The Republican nominee, Representative James G. Blaine, was a man of great ability and personal charm. However, his reputation was clouded by charges that he had taken money for helping a railroad. As a result some independent reformers in the Republican party, called "Mugwumps," did not support him. The Democrats won Mugwump support by nominating Grover Cleveland, who earned a reputation for integrity as mayor of Buffalo and governor of New York.

The campaign of 1884 was a negative one, focusing less on issues and more on character assassination. Blaine was portrayed as a "tattooed man" with railroad stocks and bonds indelibly engraved on his skin. Cleveland was attacked on the grounds that he had hired a substitute to fight for him in the Civil War and that he had fathered an illegitimate child. Republicans chanted:

Ma! Ma! Where's my pa?
Gone to the White House,
Ha! Ha! Ha!

To which the Democrats countered:

Blaine, Blaine, James G. Blaine,
The continental liar from the
State of Maine.

Cleveland won the election by a narrow margin, becoming the first Democratic President elected since 1856. Balloting in New York was close. Had 600 voters switched to Blaine, he would have won the state—and the presidency. The Republicans retained control of the Senate, but the Democrats gained a majority in the House of Representatives.

Independent Practice

📁 Assign Guided Reading Activity 10-2.

📁 Assign Workbook Activity 10-2.

 **CURRICULUM CONNECTION**

Mathematics Present the following information to students:

In the 1876 election, the popular vote was 4,036,572 for Rutherford B. Hayes, 4,284,020 for Samuel J. Tilden, and 81,737 for Peter Cooper. What was the percentage of popular vote for each candidate? Use a calculator to figure out the answer. *(Hayes 48%, Tilden 49%, and Cooper 1%)* **L1, LEP**

Teaching American Portraits

With her friend Elizabeth Cady Stanton, Anthony formed the National Woman Suffrage Association in 1869. One tactic that Anthony and other association members used was to vote illegally in elections. For this she was fined, but she refused to pay. In 1904, at the age of 84, Anthony took a leadership role in the international women's movement, helping to form the International Woman Suffrage Association.

📁 Assign American Portrait 39: Susan B. Anthony.

Critical Thinking Activity

Detecting Points of View Read the following excerpt from Grover Cleveland's second inaugural address:

"The lessons of paternalism ought to be unlearned and the better lesson taught that while the people should patriotically and cheerfully support the government, its functions do not include support of the people."

Ask: Do you think Cleveland would be a supporter of "big government"? Why or why not? *(No, he did not believe that the government should provide support for the people.)* **L2**

▲ **GROVER CLEVELAND**

Reforms Continue

Unskillful in political maneuvering, Cleveland often met defeat in his dealings with Congress. Nevertheless, his devotion to the public good did much to restore the prestige of the presidency. Cleveland's first problem was to deal with the Democratic office seekers who swarmed to Washington seeking the fruits of his victory. If he were to make appointments on merit alone, he would split his party wide open. If he were to give in to the spoils system, he would lose the support of the Mugwumps and other reformers who had played a decisive part in electing him. As a compromise Cleveland appointed many "deserving Democrats" to office. He also made every effort to see that the new appointees were qualified.

Cleveland entered office with a weak understanding of most national issues but worked intensely at the job. Few Presidents have put in more study to determine what course of action to follow. His Republican predecessors, for example, had signed hundreds of private bills giving pensions to veterans unable to qualify under regular laws. Examining such bills with care, Cleveland found many of them fraudulent. One veteran, for example, asked for a pension for an injury suffered while *intending* to enlist. Cleveland disapproved of so many pension bills that his vetoes totaled more than those of all previous Presidents.

Cleveland worked to improve government efficiency and integrity. He supported the Presidential Succession Act, which established a line of succession to the presidency in the event of the death of the Vice President. He also won repeal of the Tenure of Office Act, which strengthened presidential independence. Interested in preserving public lands, Cleveland reclaimed land from private companies that had not lived up to the terms of their land grants.

■ Tariffs and the Election of 1888

The public question that Cleveland studied most seriously was the tariff. During the Civil War, duties had been raised from an average of 19 percent in 1861 to more than 40 percent in 1865.

▼ **POLITICAL CARTOON ON 1888 CAMPAIGN**

Critical Thinking Activity

Identifying Points of View Point out that many companies in the United States today are moving their manufacturing to foreign countries where labor is cheaper. The manufactured goods are then imported to the United States.

Discuss the economic impact of a tariff on such imported goods. Then have students write a paragraph, from the perspective of a manufacturer, worker, or consumer, on whether tariffs should be levied on imported goods. **L2**

Different Views on Tariffs

High tariff rates, which benefited manufacturers, were constantly attacked by farmers, consumers, shippers, and importers. These **free-traders** argued that a protective tariff was unfair government interference with the normal laws of supply and demand. Tariffs, they said, were subsidies paid to manufacturers out of the pockets of consumers.

Protectionists, on the other hand, defended the tariff as a means of nurturing fledgling industries in the United States. They argued that tariffs kept wages high by shielding them from competition with cheap foreign labor. Previous bills to lower the tariff had been defeated.

Shortly after Cleveland took office, Carl Schurz asked him about his views on the tariff issue. "You know I really don't know anything about it," replied the President. "In my political career as sheriff of Buffalo County, mayor of Buffalo, and governor of New York, it has, of course, not been an issue." Cleveland investigated the problem thoroughly. His studies convinced him that the existing tariff was responsible for the treasury's large surplus. Cleveland argued that the surplus was a sign of overtaxation. He proposed a reduction of the tariff—not because he was a free-trader, but because he was in favor of limited government. Excess money in the treasury, he said, was not good for the economy; it was a temptation to Congress, which was apt to spend it wastefully. The President's dramatic effort to lower the tariff was blocked by House Republicans.

Harrison Elected President

The tariff became the major issue in the presidential election of 1888. Openly avowing protection for the first time, the Republicans collected a record-breaking campaign fund. "Put all the manufacturers of Pennsylvania under the fire," said a Republican campaign manager, "and fry that fat out of them." The Republicans revived Henry Clay's name for the protective tariff, calling their economic program the "American system." Renominating Cleveland, the Democrats campaigned against unnecessary taxation. As in 1880 and 1884, the result was

extremely close. Although he got fewer popular votes than Cleveland, the Republican candidate, Benjamin Harrison, won a majority in the electoral college.

The new President was a quiet, reserved man, whom one observer called a "human iceberg." Harrison was too reserved to make a good Gilded Age politician. Still, he had an able legal mind and a distinguished career as an attorney in Indiana. He had been elected to the Senate in 1881.

Harrison had fought under Sherman at Atlanta and was not shy about "waving the bloody shirt" for votes. An ardent protectionist, he was conservative in fiscal policy and liberal when it came to veterans' pensions.

Treasury Surplus and the Tariffs

Once in office the Republicans promptly disposed of the treasury surplus by spending it, and it was the last time in history that the government held a surplus. Within two years the "Billion-Dollar Congress" had

 ▲ **PRESIDENT HARRISON** Unlike Cleveland before him, President Benjamin Harrison favored attempts to freely spend the mounting treasury surplus. *How long did it take the "Billion-Dollar Congress" to convert the surplus into a deficit?*

 **Visualizing** **H**istory Benjamin Harrison's grandfather was William Henry Harrison, elected President in 1840.
Answer to Caption: less than two years

Did You Know?

Cleveland was originally named Steven Grover Cleveland. By the age of 19, he began signing his name S. Grover Cleveland. A few years later, he dropped the initial.

NATIONAL GEOGRAPHIC SOCIETY

 CD-ROM

The Presidents: A Picture History of Our Naiton

Have students select President Benjamin Harrison from the main menu and the category GAME. Suggest students learn more about Harrison by playing the presidential game with a partner.

GLENCOE TECHNOLOGY

 **VIDEODISC**

Focus on Government

Side 2, Chapter 30
Title: *Presidential Leadership*
Subject: Characteristics and Accomplishments

Sidelight: Etiquette

Rules on how people should behave in public were laid down in books on etiquette. Among the most popular of these books was *Manners and Social Etiquette* (1884), by Mrs. John Sherwood. A sample of the advice she provided: To the question of whether young ladies should allow gentlemen to pay for their theater tickets, Mrs. Sherwood replied, "No." For "in permitting a gentleman to expend money for her pleasures, a lady assumes an obligation to him which time and chance may render oppressive."

ASSESS

Check Understanding

Assign Section 2 Review as homework or an in-class activity.

Evaluate

Assign Section Quiz 10-2 or use the Test-maker to create a customized quiz.

Reteach

Ask students to write five questions on the main ideas in this section. Have students exchange their questions with a partner and answer the questions. Ask the partners to check each other's answers.

Have students complete Reteaching Activity 10-2.

Enrich

Have students draw political cartoons of their own expressing their views of the corruption in the federal government during the late 1800s.

Assign Enrichment Activity 10.

CLOSE

Ask students to name some local issues that played a role in the most recent congressional election and helped one of the candidates to gain or lose votes.

created a deficit, mostly through handouts to special-interest groups. The number of Civil War pensioners increased by more than half—many of them the same ones whom Cleveland had turned down.

Moving on to the election-winning tariff issue, the Republicans passed the McKinley Tariff of 1890, which was the highest in the country's history. It dried up revenue by levying rates so high that some foreign products were kept entirely out of the country.

Nearly every foreign product that competed with American-made products was heavily taxed, including such items as food, clothing, furniture, and tools. Western silver states supported the tariff in exchange for the passage of the Sherman Silver Purchase Act, which authorized the federal government to buy up 4.5 million ounces of silver a month.

Millions of dollars were spent on the improvement of harbors and waterways, coastal defenses, federal buildings, and naval expansion. Congress also passed the Sherman Antitrust Act and provided for admission to the Union of North and South Dakota, Montana, Washington, Idaho, and Wyoming.

Several Issues Hurt Republicans

The Republicans' position on protective tariffs, which had helped them win the presidency in 1888, hurt them two years later. Because there was little competition in the market, prices generally were falling; thus, debts were harder to repay.

Republicans also were hurt nationally by local Republicans in such states as Wisconsin and Massachusetts, who supported compulsory school attendance where instruction was in English. Many Catholic and Lutheran immigrant families in these states wanted public funding for their parochial schools, in which students were taught in their first language. Republicans also pushed Prohibition at the grassroots level.

Democrats used these issues, together with that of a backfiring tariff, to attack the Republicans. The congressional elections of 1890 resulted in a Democratic landslide.

By 1892 the Republicans' position was even worse. Dispiritedly, they renominated Harrison, and the Democrats nominated Grover Cleveland again. Popular discontent with the Republicans was so high that for the first time since before the Civil War Democrats won not only the White House but both houses of Congress.

This time, however, Cleveland won by more than 350,000 popular votes and an electoral majority of 277 to 145. Cleveland became the only President in American history to serve two nonconsecutive terms.

Of larger importance than Cleveland's margin of victory was the support given to a third-party candidate, James B. Weaver. Weaver, who had been the candidate for the Greenback party in 1880, ran in 1892 under the banner of the new People's party, better known as the Populist party. By this time, many Americans were already responding to the Populist philosophy.

Section 2 ★ Review

Checking for Understanding

1. **Identify** Rutherford B. Hayes, James Garfield, Chester Arthur, Grover Cleveland.

2. **Define** patronage, rider, free-trader, protectionist.

3. **Describe** political reforms made during the 1870s and the 1880s.

4. **Explain** the controversy over raising or lowering the tariff.

Critical Thinking

5. **Evaluating Reforms** How could the civil service system limit the patronage system and cut down on corruption?

ACTIVITY

6. Prepare a time line showing the Presidents of the United States from 1876 to 1900.

Answers to SECTION 2 REVIEW

1. Rutherford B. Hayes, 323; James Garfield, 324; Chester Arthur, 324; Grover Cleveland, 325
2. All vocabulary words are defined in the Glossary.
3. curbed patronage and "shaking down" of federal workers, restored political balance, reformed civil service
4. Pro: protectionists said tariffs nurtured new industry and kept wages high. Con: free-traders said tariffs interfered with laws of supply and demand.
5. It prevented the removal of government staff for political reasons; the exam allowed jobs to be awarded on merit.
6. Time lines should include all Presidents.

★★★★★★★★★★★★★★★★★★★★★

Cultural Life

Setting the Scene

Section Focus

The Civil War was also a turning point in cultural life. The period after the war was a time of rapid change. Some satirized the values of post-Civil War society, as in Twain and Warner's description of a poorly maintained Washington Monument. Others celebrated the country's emergence as an industrial giant.

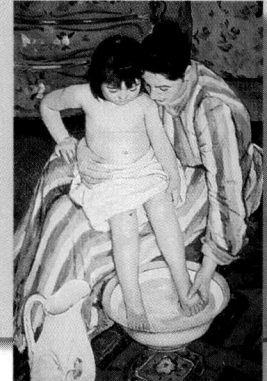

◀ THE BATH BY MARY CASSATT

Objectives

After studying this section, you should be able to

★ discuss developments in literature, art, and higher education.

★ describe how various leisure activities expanded.

Key Terms

antebellum, realism, expatriate, yellow journalism

The United States was quickly becoming an urban, industrialized society. It needed citizens who could understand complex political and economic questions, and it needed literate workers and managers who could staff its offices, shops, and factories.

■ Education

In the late nineteenth century, the nation reformed its educational system. Public education and higher education benefited from the reforms.

Public Education

By 1900 many states had or were working toward compulsory school attendance. In cities, graded schools replaced one-room schoolhouses. The school year, which had

traditionally been squeezed in between fall harvest and spring planting, was lengthened. Many cities also introduced free secondary education, and the number of public high schools increased from a few hundred in 1860 to more than 2,500 in 1890. Yet there remained much room for improvement. In 1900 the average child received only 5 years of schooling.

Private Colleges and Universities

The most far-reaching development in education during the late 1800s was the expansion of higher education. At mid-century most colleges and universities in the United States had poor equipment, scanty libraries, and ill-trained, overworked faculties. Fixed curricula that emphasized ancient Greek and Roman thought included little training in modern languages, history, or science. There were no first-rate graduate

CHAPTER 10 The Gilded Age: 1865–1900   **329**

Classroom Resources for SECTION 3

Blackline Masters:
- ☞ Reproducible Lesson Plan 10-3
- ☞ Guided Reading Activity 10-3
- ☞ Linking Past and Present Activity 10
- ☞ Workbook Activity 10-3
- ☞ Geography in History Activity 10
- ☞ Spirit of American Art and Music, pp. 17, 23
- ☞ Workbook Activity 10-3

- ☞ Reteaching Activity 10-3
- ☞ Section Quiz 10-3

Transparencies:
- 📖 Section Focus Transparency 10-3
- 📖 U.S. History & Art Transparency 16

Multimedia:
- 🖥 Focus on American Fine Art Prints: *The Boating Party* by Mary Cassatt

---

LESSON PLAN
SECTION 3, 329–334

FOCUS
Bellringer

🖐 ☞ Before taking roll, project Section Focus Transparency 10-3 or hand out Section Focus Transparency Activity 10-3. Have students answer the questions.

Motivating Activity

Write the headings Education, Literature, Art, and Architecture on the chalkboard. Ask students to hypothesize how each of these aspects of culture might have changed during the last century. Write students' responses on the chalkboard. Tell them to check their hypotheses as they read this section. **L2**

Vocabulary Precheck

Ask students to define each of the "Key Terms." Have a volunteer consult the dictionary for any unfamiliar words. **L1, LEP**

Linking Across TIME

In 1876 Congress voted funds to complete the Washington Monument. Designed by Robert Mills, a neoclassical architect, the monument was begun in 1848 and completed in 1884. The length of time it took to construct led Mark Twain to suggest that it should carry the title "The Great-Great-Grandfather of His Country."

TEACH

TEACH
Guided Practice

Linking Past and Present
Have students work in small groups to discuss why changes were necessary in education in the late nineteenth century. Have them identify the educational problems that had to be overcome. *(poorly trained, overworked staff, outdated curriculum, poor equipment)* Ask students to compare these problems with the problems inherent in today's educational system. Have students propose some possible solutions to today's educational problems. **L2**

History AND ART

Ungraded schools were common in rural areas. Children from 3 to 18 were often taught in the same classroom.
Answer to Caption: ordinary people in everyday activities

Did You Know?

In the years after the Civil War, educational opportunities expanded for women. By 1890, 13 percent of all college graduates were women. By 1900, that figure increased to nearly 20 percent.

---

schools in law, medicine, or the liberal arts. No American scientific school compared well with the best in Europe.

By 1900 these weaknesses had been vigorously attacked. Responding to the need for more practical education, colleges in the United States reformed their fields of study. Courses in the social and natural sciences were made available, and the elective system, first introduced at Harvard, made it possible for students to choose an individual course of study.

Young scholars from the United States who were trained in the world's best universities—in Germany—brought back higher standards of scholarship and scientific research. Existing private universities were greatly expanded, and new ones were founded—most with the aid of wealthy businesspeople who supported the trend toward making education more useful. More than two dozen new schools were devoted specifically to technical training. The Massachusetts Institute of Technology and others like it supplied industry with highly trained engineers, metallurgists, and chemists. Also during this period the first graduate schools of business, such as the Wharton School of Finance, were established.

State Universities

Along with the growth of privately endowed universities and technical schools came an expansion of state universities. Such institutions owed a great deal to the Morrill Act of 1862, which gave public lands to each state as a grant to finance the endowment of colleges. While the main goal of these schools was to extend knowledge of "agriculture and mechanic arts," they were funded to teach science and classical studies as well. The University of California, Texas A&M, and most of the large state universities of the Midwest began as land-grant colleges.

Universities in the Midwest also played an important role in opening higher education to women for the first time. In the pre-Civil War era, women had been admitted to Oberlin and Antioch colleges in Ohio. After the war, coeducation became common west of the Appalachians. In the more conservative East, women founded private colleges of their own, such as Mount Holyoke, Vassar, Smith, Radcliffe, and Bryn Mawr. These colleges shared the same educational goals as all-male institutions.

The adult public also cried out for more learning. Beginning in 1874 as a summer program to train Sunday school teachers, the

▲ *SNAP THE WHIP* by Winslow Homer, 1872 Winslow Homer's painting captures the joy of a school recess. Homer is known for his vivid use of color and attention to detail. *What subjects did realist artists seek to portray?*

Special Needs Activity

Language Disability It is important for students with language processing weaknesses to hear a variety of language styles accompanied by interpretations so that meanings are clear. This section introduces a number of authors—William Dean Howells, Stephen Crane, and Mark Twain—who wrote in very different styles. Read aloud selections from these authors. (See selection from *Roughing It* by Mark Twain on page 482.) Then ask students to suggest what might make these authors' language difficult to understand. Rewrite selections in contemporary language to assist students' comprehension. **LEP**

The Summer Olympic Games

The first Olympics were held in 776 B.C. to celebrate amateur sports. Resumed in 1896, the first modern games were held in Athens, Greece.

Then

The First Modern Games

The first Olympic Games of the present cycle were held in the rebuilt stadium of Athens. Nearly 290 athletes representing 13 nations participated. The American team dominated the track and field events, winning 9 of the 11 events. Thomas Burke captured the 100-meter dash with a time of 12 seconds. Ellery Clark set the high jump standard at 5'11" and James Connolly's 45' was the best mark for the triple jump. The Games proved a success, and organizers made plans to hold the Games in Paris in 1900.

Now

Bigger, Stronger, and Faster

After a century, the Olympic Games bear little resemblance to the games of 1896. Men and women athletes representing 64 nations competed in 257 events at the Barcelona Games in 1992. Modern performances leave little doubt that today's athletes are stronger and faster. Carl Lewis

▲ FLORENCE GRIFFITH-JOYNER AT THE BARCELONA OLYMPICS

holds the Olympic record for 100 meters with a time of 9.86. Florence Griffith-Joyner's standard for women, 10.49 seconds, eclipses Burke's mark by more than 1½ seconds. High jump competitors regularly clear 7' and more. The record for the triple jump is over 60'.

▲ ATHLETE AT THE FIRST MODERN GAMES

Chautauqua (shuh•TAW•kwuh) Institute in western New York sparked a movement that provided the masses with instruction in such subjects as literature, economics, science, and government through summer school instruction and correspondence school.

■ Literature

United States writers responded to the post-Civil War era in different ways. One popular school of postwar writers looked backward, striving to capture the romance of vanishing rural traditions. A center of such "local-color" writing was the South. Civil War and Reconstruction had swept away an entire way of life, leaving poverty and destruction in its wake. In the 1870s and the 1880s, Southern local colorists wrote nostalgically about **antebellum**—or pre-Civil War—manners, customs, and institutions.

Local colorists also wrote of vanishing ways of life in the small towns and fishing villages of New England, on the farms of the Midwest, on the ranches of the plains, and in the mining camps and boomtowns of the Wild West.

One of America's greatest writers was a local colorist named Samuel Clemens who wrote under the name Mark Twain. Twain wrote vivid and hilarious stories about his travels in the West. His most enduring works—*The Adventures of Tom Sawyer* and *The Adventures of Huckleberry Finn*—are tales of his boyhood home on the Mississippi River. Twain's books were not only acclaimed by critics but loved by the public. He combined shrewd observation and irreverent wit.

Twain's writing bridged the gap between popular and highbrow literature, between ordinary local-color writing and **realism,** a European-influenced movement that strove for accurate representation.

CHAPTER 10 The Gilded Age: 1865–1900   **331**

Independent Practice

📁 Assign Guided Reading Activity 10-3.

CURRICULUM CONNECTION

Language Arts Write the terms *local-color writing* and *realism* on the chalkboard. Have students identify the characteristics of each school of writing.

Linking Past and Present

Over the years, the modern games of the Olympics took on a new look. Women first competed in the Olympics in 1900, and the Winter Games were started in 1924.

📁 For additional practice, assign Linking Past and Present Activity 10.

Assign U.S. History & Art Transparency 16: *In the Garden* by Mary Cassatt.

Assign Focus on American Fine Art Prints: *The Boating Party* by Mary Cassatt.

Critical Thinking Activity

Making Comparisons Present the following information to students:

In the late 1800s grade school was synonymous with learning by rote. Virtually everything was drilled into students' minds through endless repetition. All subjects—arithmetic, reading, spelling, and handwriting—were taught in this manner.

Ask them to compare how students were taught in the late 1800s with how they themselves learned reading, spelling, handwriting, and arithmetic. **L2**

Realist writers wanted to get away from the emotional preoccupations of the romantic movement and the pretty, sentimental themes of popular literature. Realist writers took a close look at real people's lives and problems. William Dean Howells declared that novels should "speak the dialect, the language, that most Americans know." In *The Rise of Silas Lapham,* Howells depicted a crude but likable bumpkin—the new American millionaire. In *The Red Badge of Courage,* Stephen Crane depicted a Union soldier's fear and cowardice under fire. Other realists exposed the seamy underside of urban life. Critics of realism argued that realistic fiction was not uplifting, that its subject matter was often ordinary or even ugly, and that its characters' misdeeds were not always suitably punished.

▲ *THE LITTLE WHITE GIRL* by James Abbott McNeill Whistler, 1864 James Whistler adapted the concepts of Japanese color prints to his own style. **What subjects did realist artists seek to portray?**

■ Art and Architecture

Realism was also an important force in American painting during the Gilded Age. Rejecting the classicism and romanticism of the first half of the century, realist painters portrayed ordinary people in everyday activities. Winslow Homer moved from painting Civil War scenes to subjects such as a schoolyard full of boys playing a rowdy game, a hunter and his dogs, or sailors at sea. Of another great realist painter, Walt Whitman said:

> " *I never knew of but one artist, and that's Tom Eakins, who could resist the temptation to see what they thought ought to be rather than what is.* "

Some of America's greatest painters, however, became **expatriates**—people who choose to live outside their native country. John Singer Sargent, a portraitist of Europe's upper classes, lived in England. James Abbott McNeill Whistler and Mary Cassatt also lived in Europe. Cassatt was influenced by a style of painting called impressionism. Impressionists tried to capture the play of light, color, and pattern as they made immediate impressions on the senses.

The architecture of the Gilded Age was heavy and ornate. It is often called "Victorian," after Queen Victoria of Great Britain who reigned from 1837 to 1901. On the outside, Victorian houses had turrets, towers, porches, and gables. The development of better woodworking machines made it possible to add elaborate "gingerbread" decorations to roofs and porches of houses. The interior decor was similarly ornamented. Rooms were crowded with dark, thickly carved furniture, plush carpeting, heavy curtains, and countless knickknacks on ornate shelves.

Some dismissed the Victorian style as vulgar—a symbol of greed that characterized the Gilded Age. Others have celebrated the gaudiness as a symbol of the period's vitality and exuberance.

Cultural Perspectives

Pulitzer and Publishing Joseph Pulitzer emigrated from Hungary to the United States after being rejected for military service. He served in the Union army and after the war became a reporter for Carl Schurz's German-language daily. In 1878 Pulitzer bought the *St. Louis Dispatch.* Later he acquired the *St. Louis Post,* the *New York World,* the *Evening World,* and other newspapers. Pulitzer is credited with fashioning the modern American newspaper. He founded mass circulation journalism and revolutionized the newspaper to fit the needs of urban society.

The Yellow Press and the Dime Novel

The Industrial Revolution brought some Americans unaccustomed leisure time. As machines took over the work of more and more hands, the time required to produce a shirt, a bucket, a pin, or a table was reduced to a fraction of what it had been. Hours of work, although still long by the standards of the twentieth century, were gradually reduced. As leisure time increased, new forms of entertainment developed.

Penny Newspapers

Journalism took new forms. In the late 1800s, improvements in papermaking and printing made it possible to produce newspapers more cheaply than before. At the same time, newspapers could make their profits entirely from advertisers. Copies were sold below cost to attract the greatest number of readers. These penny newspapers strove to amuse readers as much as to inform them. Their intended audience was not the educated middle and upper classes but clerks, laborers, and homemakers.

The pioneer among the penny newspapers was the *New York World*, purchased by Joseph Pulitzer in 1883. In 15 years its circulation rose from 15,000 to more than 1 million. Pulitzer, dedicating his paper "to the cause of the people rather than the purse-proud potentates," attacked unfair employers and grafting politicians with vigor. The real source of Pulitzer's success, however, was not politics but sensationalism. He was one of the first to use "scare headlines" like "Baptized in Blood" and "Death Rides the Rails." He also introduced the colorized Sunday supplement and the serialized comic strip. From the yellow ink he used in his comics came the term **"yellow journalism,"** which critics applied to the subject matter and style of the *World* and all its imitators. If he could not find news, Pulitzer made it. Once he sent a young reporter, Nelly Bly, to travel around the globe in less time than it took the hero of Jules Verne's popular novel, *Around the World in Eighty Days*.

◀ JOURNALIST NELLY BLY

Dime Novels

Another form of reading matter produced for a mass market was the dime novel, which was designed especially to interest boys. These were adventure stories where heroes such as Mustang Sam and Deadwood Dick fought cattle rustlers and outlaws. Dime novels also portrayed the worlds of business and crime. Moralists suspected that these early paperbacks would corrupt the young. Defenders pointed out, however, that because dime novels were not the work of realists, no bad deed ever went unpunished; no good boy went without his just reward.

• •

Footnotes to History

The Appeal of the Gridiron   Football became a popular spectator sport during the Gilded Age, with college competition proving to be the biggest draw. Rutgers and Princeton played in the first collegiate contest in 1869. Throughout the late 1800s, three big eastern universities—Harvard, Yale, and Princeton—dominated the sport.

Did You Know?

Although organized baseball was played as early as the 1850s, the game really took off after the Civil War. Returning veterans helped to form teams, and by 1866 there were 202 teams in 17 states.

Linking Across TIME

Football became an important spectator sport during the Gilded Age, with college competitions being the biggest draw. The first collegiate game took place in 1869, between Rutgers and Princeton. Seven years later, representatives from eastern colleges gathered to develop a set of rules. The standard design of today's game was established at this meeting. Throughout the 1800s the three big eastern colleges—Harvard, Yale, and Princeton—dominated the sport. Thanksgiving Day games involving these teams drew huge, festive crowds.

Food of the Times

In 1893, at the Chicago World's Fair, Americans were introduced to such processed foods as Cream of Wheat cereal, Aunt Jemima pancake mix, Juicy Fruit gum, and Nabisco's Shredded Wheat.

Sidelight: Circuses

In the late 1800s, circuses were among the most popular forms of entertainment. People seemed to be especially attracted to the oddities—the 120-year-old woman, the bearded lady, the two-headed monster, and so on—that were presented as sideshows. Most of these oddities were frauds, but occasionally they were real. For example, circus owner P. T. Barnum reportedly paid $250,000 for a real white elephant from Siam. Not to be outdone, competitor Adam Forepaugh created his own by painting an Indian elephant with whitewash.

ASSESS

Check Understanding

Assign Section 3 Review as homework or an in-class activity.

Evaluate

Assign Section Quiz 10-3 or use the Testmaker to create a customized quiz.

Reteach

Have students complete Reteaching Activity 10-3.

Assign Workbook Activity 10-3.

Enrich

Have students complete Enrichment Activity 10.

Assign Geography in History Activity 10.

CLOSE

Tell students that between 1870 and 1900 the workday for most people had decreased from 12 to 10 hours and that yearly per capita income rose from $779 to $1,164. Ask students to discuss the impact of these changes on people's lives.

FACT or FICTION?

Vassar College had women's baseball teams in the 1860s.

FACT: Many people were shocked that a college would allow such rough behavior by its students. By 1876 the sport was abandoned, a victim of public outcry.

334

■ Sports and Entertainment

As work became less strenuous, many looked for leisure activities that involved physical exercise. Golf, croquet, and lawn tennis from Great Britain were popular sports with the middle and upper classes. College students brought in other British sports, including rowing, track, and rugby (from which American football was derived).

Baseball, however, was a truly American invention—its earliest form was played before the Civil War. College and club teams sprang up all over the country in the late 1800s. The first professional team was the Cincinnati Red Stockings in 1869; in 1876 the National League was organized. Professional baseball found a ready audience and loyal fans in crowded urban areas where working-class people had little money for entertainment.

The enthusiasm for baseball had started during the Civil War, and it appeared that everyone was playing ball. A writer for a Nevada Territory newspaper noted:

> *The rage for ball playing is very apparent. Old fellows whose hair and teeth are going and gone and young ones who have just got their first breeches and boots on are knocking and tossing and catching ball on the plaza and the streets from daybreak to dark.*

After the modern safety bicycle was substituted for the dangerous "high wheeler," bicycling became a craze. There were hundreds of bicycle clubs; special trains carried cyclists into the country on Sundays, and special bicycle paths were built in parks and suburbs. A transcontinental bicycle route was wanted.

Cities became centers of cultural life. In a day when the motion picture had not yet been invented, theater and vaudeville shows enjoyed great popularity. Large cities boasted opera companies and symphony orchestras, theaters, and museums of fine art.

In 1891 Peter Tchaikovsky, the Russian composer, came to America and conducted one of his own works at the new Carnegie Music Hall in New York City. He wrote home that everything went wonderfully, and that he was received with even greater enthusiasm than he had been in his native land.

▶ HONUS WAGNER OF THE PITTSBURGH PIRATES

Section 3 ★ Review

Checking for Understanding

1. **Identify** Mark Twain, Stephen Crane, James Abbott McNeill Whistler, Joseph Pulitzer, Thomas Eakins.

2. **Define** antebellum, realism, expatriate, yellow journalism.

3. **Discuss** the different kinds of recreations and pastimes that the American people pursued during this era.

Critical Thinking

4. **Supporting Opinions** Argue for or against compulsory education in a democratic society. Support your opinion with facts or arguments that show how your position supports democratic goals.

ACTIVITY

5. Create a collage comparing modern American art and art of the late 1800s.

Answers to SECTION 3 REVIEW

1. Mark Twain, 331; Stephen Crane, 332; James Abbott McNeill Whistler, 332; Joseph Pulitzer, 333; Thomas Eakins, 332
2. All vocabulary words are defined in the Glossary.
3. Penny newspapers, dime novels, magazines, sporting activities, museums, music, theaters

4. Answers will vary. Supporters may say that it provides all children with an education. Opponents may say democracy means choice.
5. Collages should present appropriate comparisons.

Improvements in Printing

During the late 1800s, improvements in printing led to the inexpensive mass production of newspapers, magazines, and books. In 1863 American inventor William A. Bullock produced the first web-fed press. This press printed on huge rolls of paper rather than single sheets. Printer Richard March Hoe perfected the continuous-roll press in 1871. This device made it possible to produce up to 12,000 full newspapers an hour.

In 1886 linotype typesetting machines cut the time required to set type to a fraction of that required to set it by hand. The linotype operator sat at a keyboard. When the operator touched a letter on the keyboard, a lead mold was placed in line with other letters. Each complete line of type was molded onto a single slug, and the slugs were made into printing plates. The linotype allowed text to be assembled much faster into columns and pages.

Improved printing technology led to rapid growth of the publishing industry. It also led to increased competition among newspaper publishers to get out the "latest edition."

Improvements in printing also aided the magazine industry. For nearly 20 years after the Civil War, the magazine industry was limited by technology. For the most part, magazines were monthlies or weeklies that reached a small readership. The leaders in the field included the *Atlantic Monthly* and *Harper's Magazine*.

Improvements in the printing process, however, led to a new form of magazine in the 1880s. Such popular magazines as the *Ladies' Home Journal* and the *Saturday Evening Post* reached larger audiences.

Another development leading directly from improvements in printing concerned the Sunday edition. Throughout the country major city newspapers created Sunday papers of 50 or more pages. Comic strips, which began as Sunday features, were moved into separate colored supplements. By 1900 the formula of the American newspaper—daily and Sunday—was in place. In addition the new techniques helped magazines such as *McClure's* and the *Saturday Evening Post* achieve mass circulation.

▲ NEWSBOY IN THE EARLY 1900S

Making the Science Connection

1. What is a linotype machine?

2. How did improved methods of printing and typesetting affect the publishing industry?

3. How is most publishing done today?

ACTIVITY

4. Create a collage from newspapers and newsmagazines that depicts creative use of artwork, color, and design.

335

CONNECTIONS
History AND SCIENCE

TEACH

Improvements in printing led to an explosion in published materials. For example, the number of daily newspapers in the United States grew from 1,000 in 1880 to about 2,200 by 1900. And the number of bookstores and libraries grew rapidly. Ask students what impact such developments would have on the spread of knowledge. *(They would aid the spread of knowledge.)* **L1**

Did You Know?

To boost readership, newspapers added a comics section. They quickly attracted a loyal following.

Answers to Making the Connection

1. machine that sets type from a keyboard using hot lead slugs

2. They led to growth in the publishing industry and an increase in competition among publishers, especially newspaper publishers.

3. Today, almost all commercial publishing is done by computer.

4. Student collages should provide an eclectic look at design.

Using Vocabulary

Classifications should show cogent connections between terms and connotations.

Reviewing Facts

1. growth of cities, alliance between business and politics, few restraints on abuses of power
2. kickbacks, party machine control, bribes, conflict of interest, influence peddling
3. Hayes, Garfield, Arthur, and Cleveland
4. reform of civil service, balancing of power between the presidency and Congress, improving government efficiency and integrity
5. Some favored tariffs as a means of protecting growing industries and keeping wages high. Others were opposed because government was seen as interfering in the laws of supply and demand and because tariffs amounted to subsidies paid to manufacturers.
6. made compulsory, state-supported colleges, expanded college

Using Vocabulary

Each term below has one of the following connotations: *political, economic,* or *cultural.* Classify each term under its respective connotation. Write a sentence that explains the connection between the term and its connotation.

antebellum	political machine
expatriate	protectionist
free-trader	realism
graft	rider
kickback	yellow journalism

Reviewing Facts

1. **Explain** the increase in political corruption following the Civil War.
2. **Describe** types of corruption that took place in government.
3. **Name** the Presidents who introduced reform or resisted corruption in government.
4. **List** some political reforms made during the 1870s and the 1880s.
5. **Point out** why some were in favor of higher tariffs and others were opposed.
6. **List** changes in higher education.

Understanding Concepts

Corruption

1. How might patronage and the spoils system have allowed for growth in the level of corruption in government?
2. What legitimate purpose do lobbyists serve? What restrictions should be placed on them to avoid wrongdoing?

Public Protest

3. What events described in this chapter suggest that a free press can inspire public protest of corruption in government?
4. Why did the American Presidents after the Grant administration become more sensitive to public demands for reform?

Critical Thinking

1. **Linking Past and Present** What businesses today depend on people having leisure time? Would all these businesses exist if work hours had not been shortened? Explain.
2. **Analyzing Illustrations** Study the advertisement on this page and answer the questions that follow.
   a. What is the product that is featured in the advertisement?
   b. This advertisement appeared in 1885. In what ways would a modern advertisement differ from this example? In what ways would the ads be similar?

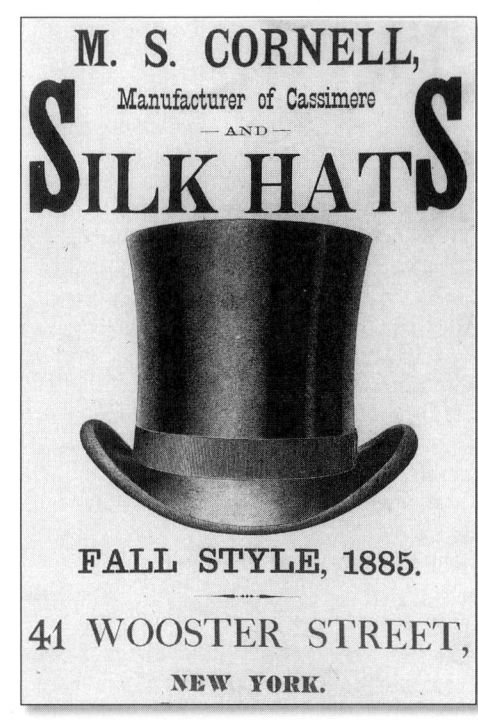

M. S. CORNELL,
Manufacturer of Cassimere
— AND —
SILK HATS
FALL STYLE, 1885.
41 WOOSTER STREET,
NEW YORK.

3. **Determining Cause and Effect** Throughout most of the nation's history, government workers and officeholders have earned substantially less than people in business with comparable ability and responsibility. How might this imbalance lead to corruption in government?

---

curricula, higher education opened to women

Understanding Concepts

1. Jobs were offered or sold as rewards for political support. Elected officials could surround themselves with corrupt jobholders.

2. They educate legislators on specialized issues, provide a way for the public to make views known. They should not be allowed to offer material inducements.
3. published evidence of Tweed's greed, Nast's cartoons about Tweed, revelation of Crédit Mobilier

4. reaction to corruption under Grant, effect of newspaper coverage

Critical Thinking

1. amusement parks, cinemas, organized sports, television, restaurants, night clubs; answers will vary

4. **Extending Concepts** In what types of periodicals do you find forms of yellow journalism today? What kinds of stories do they emphasize? Who might be offended by their contents?

History and Geography

Changing Regions

With rapid growth and industrialization came change in the way people lived as well as growing differences in regional issue interests.

1. **Human/Environment Interaction** How did the growth of cities and urban overcrowdedness affect community services?

2. **Region** Why did Western farmers tend to support the Republican party?

Interdisciplinary Activity: Journalism

Work with a partner to act out an interview between a newspaper reporter and a local political boss or a machine politician. Decide which role each of you will assume. The reporter should review information on corrupt government practices as were presented in the chapter. The politician should review information on party machines. The reporter should prepare a list of questions to ask the politician. The politician should prepare a list of answers to questions that he or she feels may be asked. After the interview, both of you should list what were the most pertinent points brought out in the interview. Compare your findings with those of other groups.

Practicing Skill

Interpreting Political Cartoons

Study the cartoon on this page. Then answer the questions that follow.

1. What is happening in the picture?
2. What words give clues to the cartoon's meaning?
3. Who are the figures in the cartoon?
4. What point is the cartoonist making?

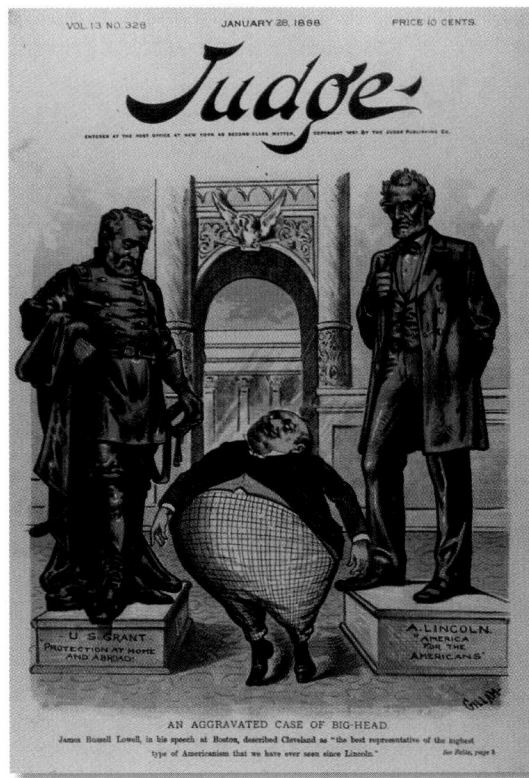

VOL 13 NO.326   JANUARY 28, 1888   PRICE 10 CENTS.

Judge

AN AGGRAVATED CASE OF BIG-HEAD.

James Russell Lowell, in his speech at Boston, described Cleveland as "the best representative of the highest type of Americanism that we have ever seen since Lincoln."   *See Folio, page 2.*

Writing ABOUT History

Using Your Journal

From your journal notes and knowledge of recent problems with some government officials, write a paragraph comparing the corruption and questionable ethics during the Gilded Age with today's problems.

Practicing Skills

1. President Cleveland is between two statues.
2. The title refers to the idea that Cleveland cannot be put in the same class as Grant and Lincoln; the caption to a quote by James Russell Lowell comparing Cleveland to Lincoln.
3. Cleveland is in the center between statues of Grant and Lincoln.
4. that Cleveland should not be put in the same class as either Lincoln or Grant

Writing ABOUT History

Using Your Journal

Students' paragraphs may include questions about campaign contributions, gifts to officeholders, lobbyists' activities, speaking fees for legislators, and other perceived conflicts of interest.

Chapter Bonus Test Question

Ask students if you had represented your state in Congress during the late 1800s, what would have been your position on farm reform? Explain. *(Students should provide reasons to support their position.)*

2. **a.** Silk Hats.
   b. Ads would include price and information about quality, appealing graphics.
3. Government is less attractive to competent people who want to make money.
4. tabloids; emphasize stories on paranormal, and lives of celebrities. Public figures who are slandered or lose privacy.

History and Geography

1. Services for the large populations were difficult to provide.
2. because Western farmers benefited from Republicans' internal improvements and liberal land policies

Cooperative Learning

Encourage students to focus on the corrupt government practices discussed in the chapter.

Daily Lesson Objectives	Teacher Classroom Resources	Multimedia
SECTION 1 **Agrarian Unrest** **1 Day** pp. 340–344 1. Identify the problems farmers faced during the late 1800s. 2. Discuss the rise and fall of the Grange. 3. Analyze the impact of the Interstate Commerce Act.	Reproducible Lesson Plan 11-1 Concept Mapping Activities 11-A, 11-B *Vocabulary Activity 11 *Guided Reading Activity 11-1 American Literary Heritage, p. 29 Critical Thinking Skills Activity 11 Chapter Map Activity 11 Workbook Activity 11-1 Reteaching Activity 11-1 *Section Quiz 11-1	Section Focus Transparency 11-1 Map Transparency 11 Vocabulary PuzzleMaker Testmaker MindJogger Videoquiz
SECTION 2 **Rise and Fall of Populism** **1 Day** pp. 345–350 1. Explain the motivations of the groups that supported greenbacks and free silver. 2. Describe the campaign and results of the election of 1896. 3. Discuss the Populist movement.	Reproducible Lesson Plan 11-2 *Guided Reading Activity 11-2 Geography in History Activity 11 Cooperative Learning Activity 11 American Portraits 42, 44 Reteaching Activity 11-2 Primary and Secondary Source Readings, p. 25 Political Cartoons Activity 11 Workbook Activity 11-2 Reteaching Activity 11-2 *Section Quiz 11-2	Section Focus Transparency 11-2 Skills Transparency 11 Testmaker GTV: A Geographic Perspective on American History The Presidents: A Picture History of Our Nation American Music: Cultural Traditions
SECTION 3 **Other Forces for Reform** **1 Day** pp. 352–356 1. Trace women's involvement in the temperance and suffrage movements. 2. Discuss the political ideas of Karl Marx and Henry George.	Reproducible Lesson Plan 11-3 *Guided Reading Activity 11-3 Linking Past and Present Activity 11 Enrichment Activity 11 Chapter Skills Activity 11 Workbook Activity 11-3 Reteaching Activity 11-3 *Section Quiz 11-3	Section Focus Transparency 11-3 Testmaker Powers of the Supreme Court
CHAPTER REVIEW AND EVALUATION **1 Day**	Chapter 11 Test, Forms A and B Spanish Chapter 11 Summary Performance Assessment Activity 11	MindJogger Videoquiz Student Self-Test & Review Software *Chapter 11 Audiocassette Activity and Test

*Also available in Spanish

 OUT OF TIME? If time does not permit teaching the entire chapter, use the Chapter 11 Summary on pages 362–363 and the Chapter 11 audiocassette (English and Spanish) to point out the main ideas of the chapter.

A complete, 1-page lesson plan is provided for each section in the *Reproducible Lesson Plan* booklet.

Key to Ability Levels

Teaching strategies have been coded for varying learning styles and abilities.

L1 Basic activities for all students

L2 Average activities for average to above-average students

L3 Challenging activities for above-average students

LEP Limited English Proficiency activities

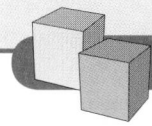

Block Schedule

Block scheduling differs from traditional class scheduling in the amount of time allotted to each period. The extended time frame provided by block scheduling affords you the opportunity to implement a greater number of research-oriented and activity-intense projects to motivate and involve your students. Activities that are particularly suited to use within the block scheduling framework are identified throughout this unit by the following designation:

✓ Performance Assessment Activity

Taking a Stand Have pairs of students create posters advocating or opposing one of the following: Granger laws, the Omaha platform, unlimited coinage of silver, temperance, or the woman suffrage movement. Suggest that partners begin by reviewing the issue they chose and then decide on their point of view. They might afterward list topics that relate to that issue and determine how best to illustrate them. Have the class evaluate the posters in terms of how well each succeeds in presenting the point of view.

POSSIBLE RUBRIC FEATURES

- Content
- Organization
- Research
- Visual Communication Skills
- Creativity
- Collaborative Skills

☞ For additional activities, see Performance Assessment Strategies and Activities.

T E A C H E R ' S   C O R N E R

NATIONAL GEOGRAPHIC SOCIETY

NATIONAL GEOGRAPHIC SOCIETY PRODUCTS AVAILABLE FROM GLENCOE

To order the following products for use with this chapter, contact your local Glencoe sales representative or call Glencoe at 1-800-334-7344:

- *The Presidents: A Picture History of Our Nation* (CD-ROM)
- *GTV: A Geographic Perspective on American History* (Videodisc)
- *GTV: The American People: Fabric of a Nation* (Videodisc)

ADDITIONAL NATIONAL GEOGRAPHIC SOCIETY PRODUCTS

To order the following products for use with this chapter, call National Geographic Society at 1-800-368-2728:

- *The United States as a World Power: From the 1890s to the 1970s* (Filmstrip)
- *The American Presidency* (Filmstrip)

CHAPTER 11
★★★

BEGINNING THE CHAPTER

GLENCOE TECHNOLOGY

VIDEODISC

Use the MindJogger Videoquiz to preview content.

MindJogger Videoquiz

Chapter 11
Disc 2, Side A

 Available in VHS.

Recording Journal Notes

Students are likely to mention in their journals that many Democrats agreed with the principles of the Populist party, thereby raising fears that the third party would divide the Democratic vote.

Linking Across TIME

A coalition of farmers and working people, the Populists called for the direct election of United States senators and an eight-hour working day, as well as other reforms. Although the Populists never won a presidential election, the two major parties eventually adopted many of their reforms.

Politics and Protest
1865–1900

▶ **POLITICAL CAMPAIGN BUTTONS**

Setting the Scene

Focus

In the late nineteenth century, most Americans continued to live on the farm. By the 1880s, however, agriculture was in crisis. Farmers blamed their difficulties on abuses by the railroads, greedy bankers, and Eastern industrialists. Farmers began to band together to fight these problems, which in turn led to the creation of a new political party, the Populists. Populism shared some goals with a larger movement aimed at redistributing the wealth and political power in the United States.

Concepts to Understand

★ Why **economic inequity** developed between farmers and urban workers

★ Why many reformers believed that **social change** would result in a more just and equitable society

Read to Discover . . .

★ some of the problems that American farmers faced in the 1880s.

★ what were the major goals of the Populist party.

Journal Notes

As you read the chapter, note in your journal the answers to these questions: Why was the Democratic party divided in 1896? What effect did this division have on the presidential election?

CULTURAL	•**1874** *National Woman's Christian Temperance Union formed in Cleveland*		•**1881** *Clara Barton founds the American Red Cross*
	1865		**1875**
POLITICAL	•**1871** *Civil Service Reform Act passes*		•**1877** Munn *v.* Illinois •**1878** *Bland-Allison Act passes*

➕ **EXTRA CREDIT PROJECT**

Analyzing the Granger Laws Divide interested students into two groups: defenders of Granger laws and defenders of private businesses. Have the two groups hold a mock court session. The defenders of the Granger laws can represent the viewpoint of the farmers, and the defenders of private businesses can represent the railroads. **L2**

▲ RAILROAD CONDUCTOR'S BADGE

History AND ART

By Industry We Thrive
A Lithograph by Kimmel and Voigt

During the mid- and late 1800s, the lithograph, made by printing from designs on stones or other surfaces, was a popular art form.

• **1891** *Hamlin Garland publishes* Main-Travelled Roads

• **1896** *Henry Ford builds his first automobile*

1885	1895

• **1892** *Populist national convention held in Omaha*

• **1896** *William J. Bryan delivers "Cross of Gold" speech*

CHAPTER 11 CONCEPTS

Concept Mapping Activity

On the chalkboard, reproduce the following generalization and concepts map, and have students copy it in their notebooks.

> People united to have their economic and political needs met.

> Economic Integrity

> Social Change

 To reinforce the two chapter concepts, use Chapter Concept Mapping Activities 11-A and 11-B.

Assign Chapter Concepts Transparency Activities 11-A, 11-B.

History AND ART

By 1870 most people in the United States were employed in industry. For the first time in American history the 1870 census counted farmers as a minority in the workforce.

GLENCOE TECHNOLOGY

VIDEODISC
Economics in Action

Videodisc 1, Side 2, Chapter 14
Title: *Competition and Monopolies*

✓ Performance Assessment

Refer to the Performance Assessment Activity in the Planning Guide on page 338b. When the students have finished their posters, have each group present them to the class. Allow time for class discussion and feedback.

 Use Performance Assessment Activity 11 as an additional assessment technique.

339

FOCUS

Bellringer

Before taking roll, project Section Focus Transparency 11-1 or hand out Section Focus Transparency Activity 11-1. Have students answer the questions.

Motivating Activity

Present the following job description to students:

Wanted: Person to own and manage small business. Applicant must be willing to do physical labor for long hours (12–14), especially during spring and summer. Wages based on current market price of product minus cost of shipment to customers. Payment for services made at point of sale of product.

Tell students that the job describes the work of a farmer in the late 1800s. Discuss why some people might choose such a life. Tell students that they will learn about the problems of farmers in the late 1800s in this section. **L1**

Vocabulary Precheck

Ask students to define each of the "Key Terms." Have a volunteer consult the dictionary for any unfamiliar words. **L1, LEP**

Use the Vocabulary PuzzleMaker Software to create a crossword puzzle. **L1**

Assign Vocabulary Activity 11.

SECTION 1

★★★★★★★★★★★★★★★★★★★★★★★★★★★★★★

Agrarian Unrest

Setting the Scene

Section Focus

In the late 1800s, most people in the United States still lived in rural areas, but the balance was rapidly shifting. The country's attention was on the future—on booming industry and bustling cities. While much of America prospered, farmers were struggling. As conditions grew worse, they organized to protest their exclusion from the table of plenty.

◄ HARVESTING MACHINE AD, LATE 1800S

Objectives

After studying this section, you should be able to

★ identify the problems farmers faced during the late 1800s.

★ discuss the rise and fall of the Grange.

★ analyze the impact of the Interstate Commerce Act.

Key Terms

pooling, cooperative

There appeared, as if from nowhere, a plague of grasshoppers that destroyed not only the wheat but the morale of farmers on the Great Plains. The Norwegian American writer, Ole Rölvaag, described the coming of the grasshoppers in his novel *Giants in the Earth*:

❝ They actually hurt me as they flew against my face and hands. The wagon . . . was literally filled with them. The road was seething. . . . I saw Father standing almost in despair. So thick were the grasshoppers in the cornfield of which both of us had been so proud, that not a spot of green was left to be seen. And within two hours . . . not a leaf was left. . . . ❞

The grasshoppers ate anything green, choked wells to the brim, broke the branches off fruit trees by their weight, and even devoured harnesses and tool handles. They came in clouds that darkened the sky and covered the ground.

■ The Plight of the Farmers

Even clouds of grasshoppers were only one of the hazards of life on the plains. There was always the threat of prairie fires, dust storms, and, worst of all, drought, which combined with hot winds and temperatures over 100°F to bake crops in the ground and to cake farmers' faces with the salt of their sweat.

Farm prices began to decline in the 1880s; the price of wheat fell from 91 cents a bushel in 1883 to 69 cents in 1886. This decline was

---

Classroom Resources for SECTION 1

Blackline Masters:
- Reproducible Lesson Plan 11-1
- Vocabulary Activity 11
- Guided Reading Activity 11-1
- American Literary Heritage, p. 29
- Critical Thinking Skills Activity 11
- Chapter Map Activity 11
- Workbook Activity 11-1

- Reteaching Activity 11-1
- Section Quiz 11-1

Transparencies:
- Section Focus Transparency 11-1
- Chapter Map Transparency 11

Multimedia:
- Vocabulary PuzzleMaker
- Testmaker

largely the result of overproduction of crops. New inventions, such as steam-powered harvesting and threshing machines, had improved crop yields, and more efficient techniques greatly increased farm production. As prices declined farmers had to borrow more and more money. Costs of the new farm machinery that assisted with large harvests were high. Often farmers could afford such equipment only on a mortgage. High, too, were the costs of shipping crops to market. The more farm prices fell, the harder it became for farmers to pay back their loans.

Even farmers who were not investing in mechanized equipment frequently had to borrow money. They had to live for a full year on the payments they received for their crops in the fall. If the money did not last, they were forced to borrow. This meant they were at the mercy of interest rates. It also meant that farmers were pretty much forced to sell their crops as soon as they came in. At that time, of course, because of the large supply, prices were always low. This is why farmer organizations, most notably the Southern Alliance, began to look for other ways to finance and market crops. Many farmers also began to call for railroad regulations for a variety of reasons.

■ Railroad Abuses

Railroads opened vast stretches of the West to settlement, making it possible for farmers to get their crops to markets and to get manufactured goods from the East. Huge sums of money were required to finance the building of a railway system. The promise of quick profits made the railroad an attractive investment for shrewd business leaders. Millions of dollars were raised through the sale of stock to private investors, both American and European.

Because a railroad promised growth and prosperity for those along its path, state and local governments offered loans and land grants in order to obtain railroad connections. Not all the dealings were legal, however.

Unethical Business Practices

Some railroad companies spent millions of dollars in bribes to state legislators and other public officials in exchange for special favors, such as land grants, cash subsidies, pro-railroad laws, and tax exemptions. But they often evaded laws designed to make them provide services in return for the benefits they were granted.

CURRICULUM CONNECTION

Economics Ask: What happens to a crop's price if supply exceeds demand? *(Prices fall.)* **L1, LEP**

Using Graphs

Answer: about 70 cents per bushel

Graph Skills Practice: Why did farm prices peak during the Civil War? *(Supplies were low; demand was great.)*

Linking Across TIME

Today's high-tech farm equipment has increased farm efficiency over 1960 levels almost as dramatically as the steam-powered equipment of the 1900s advanced farm productivity over its 1860 level.

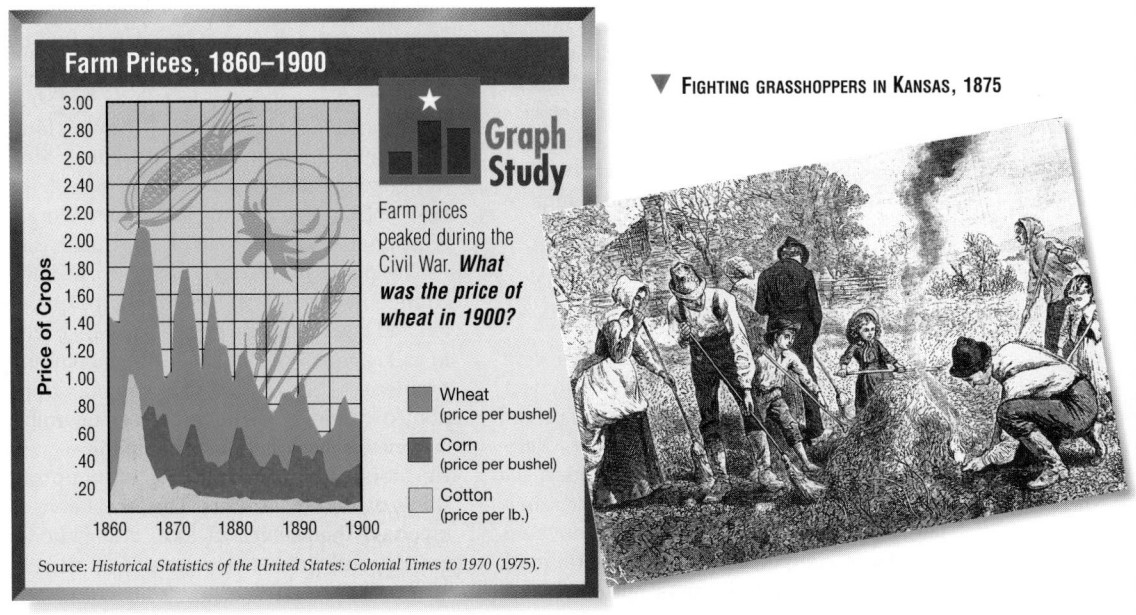

Farm Prices, 1860–1900

Graph Study

Farm prices peaked during the Civil War. **What was the price of wheat in 1900?**

Wheat (price per bushel)
Corn (price per bushel)
Cotton (price per lb.)

Source: *Historical Statistics of the United States: Colonial Times to 1970* (1975).

▼ FIGHTING GRASSHOPPERS IN KANSAS, 1875

CHAPTER 11 Politics and Protest: 1865–1900 **341**

Sidelight: The General Store

The general store was probably the most frequented place in a rural town. It was usually located on Main Street and was stocked with everything from hand tools to quinine to calico for a dress. Farmers came to the store from long distances to load up on supplies and to sell their farm products. Often farm women brought eggs and vegetables that they grew in their gardens. However, a trip to the general store met more than economic needs. It provided a chance to get away from ever-present chores, to see one's friends, to catch up on the local gossip, and to receive mail.

Did You Know?

In 1872 Aaron Montgomery Ward started a mail-order business, sending out a 1-page list of items for sale. By 1874 people were ordering goods from his 72-page catalog. Before long Sears, Roebuck and Company also recognized the vast rural market and began a mail-order business that promised "satisfaction or your money back."

Food of the Times

Americans in the late 1800s consumed huge quantities of baked goods made from wheat or corn. Northerners ate more wheat bread than Westerners or Southerners. Biscuits were a more popular way of preparing wheat in the West and South.

▲ Sears and Roebuck catalog, early 1900s

Another abuse was called "stock watering," the practice of increasing the number of shares of a company without adding to the company's assets. For example, when Jay Gould and James J. Fisk gained control of the Erie Railroad in 1868, they issued $71 million of stock on property worth $20 million. They made money by selling this "watered stock" to the public who did not know of the stock's actual lower value. Such action cheated all the stockholders. It also hurt the public because the railroads had to keep their rates high to pay dividends.

Unfair Pricing

In a day when trucks and highways were not yet dreamed of, railroads often enjoyed a natural monopoly; that is, in certain places there was no competition for services. Railroads took advantage of this situation by charging more for short hauls where they had a monopoly than for long hauls where they faced competition from other railroad lines. Thus, it cost shippers more to send goods from Poughkeepsie, New York, to New York City than to send goods from Chicago to New York City.

Sometimes competing railroad lines divided up traffic serving the same route, a practice known as **pooling.** Railroads pooled to make sure each line had enough traffic to pay costs and debts.

■ The Grange

Feelings against railroad abuses ran high all over the country but were especially strong in the West where there was almost no competition from other forms of transportation. This was because railroads had been favored by huge government subsidies in the form of land. Business owners and workers in the cities as well as farmers resented the railroads.

It was a nationwide farm organization, however, that began a movement against the unfair practices of the railroads. This organization tried to end railroad abuses with laws passed by state legislatures.

From Social Support to Political Action

The Patrons of Husbandry, commonly called the Grange, was an early national farm organization. It was founded in 1867 by Oliver Hudson Kelley. At first the main purpose of the Grange was to relieve the isolation and loneliness in the lives of farm families by providing social activities. Also, recognizing the importance of women on the farm, the Grange was the first fraternal organization to admit women on an equal basis.

The panic of 1873, however, turned the Grange into a reform lobby. As crop prices fell and credit became scarce, farmers began to talk about how to solve their common problems. Local Grange organizations pooled farmers' resources to set up mills, factories, banks, insurance companies, grain elevators, and **cooperatives,** or nonprofit stores owned by farmers. The local Granges involved themselves in local and national politics and pressed for state laws to help farmers.

By 1874 the Grange had 1.5 million members in states throughout the Midwest, the South, and the West. Its solidarity met with such success that several states passed "Granger laws" that fixed maximum freight and passenger rates, forbade railroads to discriminate between places or shippers, and attempted to regulate monopolies of such farmer necessities as grain elevators and warehouses.

Granger Laws Versus Business Interests

Private businesses protested loudly against the Granger laws. Their main argument was that government should not interfere with private enterprise. Railroad lawyers argued that Granger laws were unconstitutional because the Fourteenth Amendment forbade a state to "deprive any person of life, liberty, or property, without due process of law." They viewed a railroad corporation as a legal "person" that should not be deprived of its property by being forced to lower its rates.

Defenders of the Granger laws said railroads that had accepted generous aid from government should not claim to be devotees of laissez-faire capitalism. Further, they argued that laissez-faire rules did not apply to natural monopolies because there was no competition to keep prices down. The Grangers maintained that government must regulate railroads and other such monopolies in order to protect the public.

Supreme Court Decisions

In 1877 the Supreme Court decided in favor of the Granger laws in the case of *Munn* v. *Illinois.* The Court stated that common carriers, such as railroads, and public utilities, such as grain elevators, "stand in the very gateway of commerce" and "take toll of all who pass." Therefore these carriers must "submit to being controlled by the public for the common good."

In spite of such Court decisions, the Granger laws were unsuccessful. The railroads fought the laws by cutting services or threatening to lay no more track until the acts were repealed. Moreover, in the late 1870s, membership in the Grange declined and so did its political activity. The main cause of the Grange's collapse was its venture into business activities. The Grange set up plow and reaper factories, grain elevators, packing plants, and banks. Bitterly opposed by private companies and often not well run, these

★★★★A★★★★★★★ AMERICAN PORTRAITS

Willa Cather
1873–1947

Life on the prairie was a memorable experience for a young girl in the 1880s and the 1890s. The beauty of the land and the hardy determination of the pioneers lasted long in the memory of Willa Cather.

Born in Virginia in 1873, Willa moved with her family to a farm near Red Cloud, Nebraska, at the age of nine. The next eight years would provide the reflections for several novels, written years later.

Cather tried her hand at writing while teaching school in Pittsburgh in 1901 and then became an editor for *McClure's Magazine.* However, her real success did not begin until she started writing about life on the plains. Many of her famous novels, such as *O Pioneers!* (1913), tell of the tough, yet sensitive, nature of the immigrants who matched their determination against the demanding and lonely life on a plains farm.

Teaching American Portraits

When Willa Cather moved with her family to Nebraska, she lived among immigrants and came to admire and respect them. In her novels she draws on her experiences of living among newcomers to the United States. Ask: In Willa Cather's lifetime, what inventions changed life on the farm most, in your opinion? **L1**

Assign American Literary Heritage, p. 29, *O Pioneers!* by Willa Cather.

Did You Know?

Between 1889 and 1893, banks and mortgage companies foreclosed on more than 11,000 farms in Kansas alone. In the late 1970s and early 1980s, thousands of U.S. farmers also lost their land. They, too, had overborrowed. When the price of land dropped and interest rates increased, they defaulted on their loans, and the banks foreclosed.

Critical Thinking Activity

Detecting Bias Write on the chalkboard the following quotation, left incomplete, taken from a Nebraska newspaper.

"There are three great crops raised in Nebraska. One is a crop of corn, one a crop of freight rates, and one a crop of interest. One is produced by farmers, who sweat and toil on the land. The other two are produced by . . . ."

Ask students to study the incomplete quotation and suggest how it might be concluded. *(possible answer: railroads and bankers)* Ask if the author of the quotation displays a bias. *(Yes. The author favors the farmer.)* **L3**

For additional practice, assign Critical Thinking Skills Activity 11.

ASSESS

Check Understanding

Assign Section 1 Review as homework or an in-class activity.

Evaluate

Assign Section Quiz 11-1 or use the Testmaker to create a customized quiz.

Reteach

Have students complete Reteaching Activity 11-1.

Enrich

Have students research the impact of the Interstate Commerce Act on American business today and write a short report on it. Ask volunteers to present their papers to the class.

Assign Map Transparency Activity 11 and Chapter Map Activity 11.

CLOSE

Ask students to explain how the farmers in the late nineteenth century were benefactors as well as victims of the Industrial Revolution.

Granger businesses usually failed. Their collapse discredited the Grange, and by 1880 its membership was less than one-fourth of what it had been in 1874.

The remaining Granger laws were dealt a mortal blow in 1886. In the *Wabash Railway* decision, the Supreme Court held that the states could control railroad traffic only within each state's own borders. They did not have the power to regulate railroad traffic that crossed state borders. Because most railroad traffic crossed state boundaries, the Court's decision effectively wiped out states' regulation of railroad rates.

The fall of the Grangers did not stop other organizations from forming. One especially important local group was started in Texas in the mid-1870s. This group, guided by Dr. C.W. Macune, soon joined with similar groups in Arkansas and Louisiana to form a national alliance. It was called the National Farmers' Alliance and Industrial Union and was referred to as the Southern Alliance.

■ Interstate Commerce Act

The Supreme Court's ruling in the *Wabash* decision made it clear that regulation would have to come at the national level. In 1887 Congress passed the first federal law to regulate interstate commerce. The Interstate Commerce Act declared that the rates that railroads charged must be "reasonable and just"; it forbade pooling, rebates, and higher rates for short rather than long hauls.

The railroad companies were required to publish rates, give advance notice of all rate changes, and make annual financial reports available to the federal government. Enforcement of the law was placed under the Interstate Commerce Commission (ICC), a five-member panel appointed by the President.

As far as its immediate purpose was concerned, the Interstate Commerce Act was a failure. The ICC, lacking power to set rates, could only make recommendations or bring suits in the federal courts. Of 16 such cases that reached the Supreme Court, the Court held for the railroads in 15.

In 1892 Richard Olney, a corporate lawyer who later served as attorney general and secretary of state, wrote to a railroad official urging him not to advocate repeal of the Interstate Commerce Act. "It satisfies popular clamor for government supervision of the railroads," observed Olney, "at the same time that such supervision is almost entirely nominal."

In retrospect, though, the Interstate Commerce Act was a very important law. It established the precedent that the federal government might control large-scale private enterprise if the public good seemed to require it. It also provided a model for the regulatory commissions of today.

Section 1 ★ Review

Checking for Understanding

1. **Identify** the Grange, Interstate Commerce Act.
2. **Define** pooling, cooperative.
3. **Explain** why farmers failed to share in the economy's prosperity.
4. **Describe** the purposes and the goals of the Grange movement.
5. **Analyze** the short-term and long-term effects of the Interstate Commerce Act.

Critical Thinking

6. **Applying Principles** State in your own words the law of supply and demand. Then explain how the law worked against farmers.

ACTIVITY

7. Imagine you are a farmer in the late 1800s. Write a letter to the editor of your local newspaper detailing your proposals for dealing with railroad abuses.

Answers to SECTION 1 REVIEW

1. The Grange, 342; Interstate Commerce Act, 344
2. All vocabulary words are defined in the Glossary.
3. overproduction, low prices, indebtedness due to loans, high costs, natural disasters
4. communal social outlet, setting up cooperatives, lobby for political pressure
5. Short-term: ICC had little power. Long-term: provided model for government control of private enterprise.

6. Farmers produced more crops to meet increased demand, but received lower prices when their supply of crops exceeded the demand.
7. Student letters should focus on relevant issues of the era and be expressed logically and concisely.

★★

Rise and Fall of Populism

Setting the Scene

Section Focus

After the collapse of the Grange movement, farmers in the South and West began to form new organizations. In the 1890s these farmers' alliances grew into a new national political party. American farmers prepared to do battle to maintain their political power against the growing influence of industry.

Objectives

After studying this section, you should be able to

★ explain the motivations of the groups that supported greenbacks and free silver.

★ describe the campaign and results of the election of 1896.

★ discuss the Populist movement.

Key Terms

inflation, deflation, gold standard, third party

◀ **GRANGE FARMER**

"*I*n God we trusted, in Kansas we busted," and "Going home to Mother"—so read signs on the wagons of "busted" farm families returning east during the hard times of the 1880s. Discontent grew to new heights in rural areas. Farm prices continued to fall, money was in short supply, and more and more people were losing their land to creditors.

Many blamed their problems not only on the drought but on human forces as well: greedy bankers, industrialists, and railroad companies that were accused of controlling government policies and bleeding rural areas dry. Like the Grangers, these men and women turned to politics to solve the problems caused by rapid economic change. The farmers' alliances, which spawned the Populist party, succeeded beyond the dreams of the Grangers.

■ Greenbacks and Free Silver

If there was anything that farmers in the late 1800s demanded more strongly than the regulation of natural monopolies or the reduction of the marketers' profits, it was "cheap money." The value of money, like that of any other commodity, changes according to the supply. If the number of dollars in circulation increases while there is no increase in the amount of goods and services for sale, the dollar buys *less*, and prices go up. This situation is called **inflation.** On the other hand, if the number of dollars in circulation decreases while there is no decrease in the amount of goods and services for sale, the dollar buys *more*, and prices go down. This situation is called **deflation.** In the three decades after the

CHAPTER 11 Politics and Protest: 1865–1900 **345**

LESSON PLAN
SECTION 2, 345–350

FOCUS
Bellringer

📁 Before taking roll, project Section Focus Transparency 11-2 or hand out Section Focus Transparency Activity 11-2. Have students answer the questions.

Motivating Activity

Write the following quotation by Mary Ellen Lease, a Kansas lawyer, on the chalkboard, and ask students to name the individuals for whom Lease spoke. (*farmers*)

"We want money, land, and transportation. We want the abolition of National Banks, and we want the power to make loans direct from the government. We want the accursed foreclosure system wiped out."

Ask students: What groups are being attacked in the quotations (*railroads, banks, businesses*)

Tell students that this section tells about farmers' attempts to solve their economic problems through political means. **L2**

Vocabulary Precheck

Ask students to define each of the "Key Terms." Have a volunteer consult the dictionary for any unfamiliar words. **L1, LEP**

Classroom Resources for SECTION 2

Blackline Masters:
📁 Reproducible Lesson Plan 11-2
📁 Guided Reading Activity 11-2
📁 Geography in History Activity 11
📁 Cooperative Learning Activity 11

📁 American Portraits 42, 44
📁 Primary and Secondary Source Readings, p. 25
📁 Political Cartoons Activity 11
📁 Workbook Activity 11-2
📁 Reteaching Activity 11-2
📁 Section Quiz 11-2

Transparencies:
📁 Section Focus Transparency 11-2
📁 Skills Transparency 11

Multimedia:
💿 Testmaker
💿 GTV: A Geographic Perspective on American History
💿 The Presidents: A Picture History of Our Nation
🎵 American Music: Cultural Traditions

TEACH
Guided Practice
Summarizing Content
Have students write a short summary explaining why McKinley won the election, and why Bryan lost it. Then hold a discussion on the following topic: If the election were held today, which candidate would win? Have students support their responses with examples. **L3**

History AND ART

Between 1870 and 1900, more acres of land—431 million—came under new cultivation than in all the nation's history. By 1900 American farmers were producing up to 150 percent more staple crops—cotton, wheat, and corn—than they had in 1870.
Answer to Caption: to help farmers

☞ Assign Geography in History Activity 11.

Did You Know?

For many years American coins were made of gold and silver. Since 1965 the silver was removed from the dime and quarter and reduced to 40 percent in the half dollar. Today only commemorative coins are made of gold.

Civil War, the production of agricultural staples, such as wheat and cotton, nearly quadrupled while the supply of money increased very little. Thus, the prices received by farmers dropped by nearly two-thirds.

The Gold Standard

In 1865, with the value of currency inflated by the wartime issuance of United States notes, or greenbacks, there was $10.60 in circulation for every person in the country. By 1895 per capita circulation had sunk to $4.50. This was partly the result of a movement toward adoption of the **gold standard**. A country that adopted the gold standard made all its currency convertible into gold. Formerly, most countries had been on a bimetallic standard of both gold and silver.

History AND ART

▲ *A PRAYER FOR RAIN* by A.B. Frost, 1894 On the Great Plains, farming had its agonies. Bumper crops brought low prices, and drought brought no crops. *What was the goal of the Populist party?*

The difficulty with the gold standard in the late nineteenth century was that world production of gold did not increase as fast as world production of goods. This restricted the currency supply and drove prices down. Deflation was hard on farmers, who borrowed money more heavily than ever before. This resulted in thousands of farm owners losing their land.

As soon as greenbacks began to be called in during the late 1860s and prices began to drop, farmers started to demand inflation. They protested that bankers and bondholders had lent "50-cent dollars" during the war; they now wanted to be repaid in 100-cent dollars. In the midterm election of 1878, a Greenback party polled more than 1 million votes, electing 15 members to Congress.

The Demand for Free Silver

The Greenback movement declined after the mid-1870s as inflationists turned to free silver. Ever since the gold rush of 1849 had lowered the price of gold, silver miners had sold their silver commercially rather than selling it to the Treasury. In 1873 Congress, unaware of the potential of new silver mines, decided to stop coining silver money and adopted the gold standard. Six years later, after building up a gold reserve, the federal government resumed specie, or coin, payments. These events caused a howl of protest from Western silver miners because new mines, especially the famous Comstock Lode, produced a flood of silver that would no longer be coined. Denouncing what they called "the Crime of '73," silver miners demanded a policy of free silver, meaning that the government should coin all silver brought to the mint. They were joined by farmers of the West and the South who expected that free silver would mean a cheaper dollar and higher prices.

The strength of the silver movement was shown by the Bland-Allison Act of 1878, which was passed over President Hayes's veto. This law required that the Treasury buy from $2 million to $4 million worth of silver a month and issue currency against it. Although adding to the money supply, the Bland-Allison Act did not halt deflation.

Special Needs Activity

Oral Expression Disability Students with oral expression problems often do not ask questions in class. Tell all the students in the class you want them to write down two or three questions based on the information presented in each portion of Section 2. Their questions should relate to something they *do not* understand, such as a word's meaning or the way to answer a question from the Objectives section. Any question related to the material is acceptable. Collect the questions, read them aloud, and discuss ways of finding the answers. **LEP, L1**

■ The Populist Movement

The election of 1892 was notable because for the first time since 1860, a **third party**, a minor political party, won electoral votes. The new organization, the People's, or Populist party, was principally an expression of farmers' grievances.

Government Policies

Ever since the Civil War, federal policies had favored industry over agriculture and the city over the country. In spite of the clamor for a cheaper dollar, the United States remained on the gold standard—to the advantage of creditors—and farm prices went steadily down—to the advantage of urban consumers. The protective tariff raised the price of the goods farmers bought, to the advantage of manufacturers, but American agricultural staples were sold overseas in an unprotected market. Legislation that favored agrarian, or farming, interests proved ineffective. State and federal regulation of railroads had been frustrated by adverse judicial decisions. When drought hit the Great Plains region in the late 1880s, the farmers were in a rebellious mood. In the West in general, economic distress was widespread; after the depression of 1893, feelings became so bitter that many citizens feared a revolution.

Forming a Party

The Populist party originated from two great farmers' organizations, which were formed after the decline of the Grange—the Southern Alliance, which covered the cotton and tobacco belt, and the Northern Alliance, especially strong in the plains region. Although the two alliances failed to merge,

· ·
Footnotes to History

Populist Leaders   Tom Watson from Georgia captured the essence of the new party when he declared that the Populists' chief target was "monopoly—not monopoly in the narrow sense of the word—but monopoly of power, of place, of privilege, of wealth, of progress."

they made similar demands—free silver, more paper money, cheaper credit, government ownership of railroads, and the restoration of railroad bounty lands to the federal government. After several congressional election successes and conferences in Cincinnati in 1891 and St. Louis in February 1892, a new political party was formed. The People's party held a national convention in Omaha in July 1892. Although mostly from farm organizations, delegates also represented the Knights of Labor and the followers of social reformers Henry George and Edward Bellamy.

Following the custom of the time, the convention nominated for President a Civil War veteran, James B. Weaver. There was nothing customary, however, about the Populist party's platform.

▲ **Populist leader Mary Elizabeth Lease**

The Omaha Platform

The preamble of the Omaha platform expressed indignation at the existing political and economic conditions. It condemned the political corruption, the newspapers dominated by business interests, the mortgage burden, and the condition of labor. The influence of social reformers was seen in the statements that "the land is concentrating in the hands of the capitalists" and that governmental injustice breeds "two great classes—tramps and millionaires." Turning to money and banking, the Populists characterized worldwide adoption of the gold standard as "a vast conspiracy against mankind . . . organized on two continents."

The following was perhaps the most zealously radical statement in the preamble of the Omaha platform:

> ❝ *We believe that the powers of government—in other words, of the people—should be expanded . . . as rapidly and as far as the good sense of an intelligent people and the teachings of experience shall justify.* ❞

Independent Practice

Creating Posters Assign students to work in groups to make election posters for Cleveland, Harrison, and Weaver or for Bryan and McKinley. Tell students that the posters must reflect the beliefs of the candidates and their parties. Have each group choose a member to represent the group and present the poster to the class. **L1, LEP**

📂 Assign American Portrait 42: Mary Lease.

Did You Know?

Mary Lease encouraged farmers to "raise less corn and more hell." She warned easterners that "the people are at bay, let the bloodhounds of money beware."

NATIONAL GEOGRAPHIC SOCIETY

 Videodisc

GTV: A Geographic Perspective on American History

Any side, Frame 53448
Subject: In the 1880s and 1890s, western farmers such as these elected independent candidates to legislatures and Congress.

Cooperative Learning Activity

Comparing Catalogs Ask students to work in pairs to obtain a Sears or Montgomery Ward catalog of the late 1800s and choose two sections for further study. Have them list the types of goods sold in the sections they chose. Ask students to compare the early listings with present-day catalogs to find out how descriptions, prices, quantities, and illustrations differ. Have them make generalizations, based on the catalog, about the needs of farm families of the late nineteenth century compared with the needs of families today. **L2** 📦

📂 Assign Cooperative Learning Activity 11.

Visualizing
History

Read to students part of Bryan's spellbinding speech at the 1896 Democratic convention: "You come to tell us that the great cities are in favor of the gold standard. We reply that the great cities rest upon our broad and fertile plains. Burn down your cities and leave our farms, and your cities will spring up again as if by magic; but destroy our farms and grass will grow in the streets of every city in the country." Discuss why these words stirred emotions in support of free silver. **Answer to Caption:** farmers, some laborers, and most debtors

 Assign American Portrait 44: William Jennings Bryan.

Did You Know?

In 1892 Populist governors were elected in Kansas and North Dakota, and the Populist party swept the state of Colorado.

NATIONAL GEOGRAPHIC SOCIETY

 CD-ROM

The Presidents: A Picture History of Our Nation

Suggest students research the issues President Cleveland faced in his two terms in office.

The Omaha platform revealed that it was the agriculturalists—not organized labor—who dominated the Populist party.

The demands of organized labor were given a subordinate position. Excluded from the platform proper, labor's demands were placed among a miscellaneous list of resolutions that were given the title "Expression of Sentiments."

The Omaha platform seems less radical now than it did at that time. The Populists proposed not to overthrow the capitalist system but simply to change the rules. They aimed to achieve their ends not through revolution but through the orderly process of free elections. The Populist platform reveals an important function of third parties in the United States—to bring to public attention measures that the major parties later adopt as their own.

Election of 1892

The Populists' enthusiasm as they entered the campaign of 1892 had a religious tone. They adapted revival meeting hymns as party songs. Huge rallies were addressed not only by men but also by "women with skins tanned to parchment by the hot winds, with bony hands of toil, and clad in faded calico." The balloting revealed the distinct character of various regions in the People's party. All of its 22 electoral votes came from states lying west of the Mississippi River. In the South sympathy with Populist aims was widespread, but there was fear that the new party might divide the Democratic vote and let the Republican party back into power. Southern Democrats with Populist principles—"Popocrats"—nonetheless helped elect their own party's candidate, Grover Cleveland.

 **Visualizing History** ▲ BRYAN AND SILVER The British humor magazine *Puck* shows candidate William Jennings Bryan as a puppet being controlled by the silver-mine owners. ***Besides the mine owners, who supported free silver?***

Sidelight: The Panic of 1893

President Cleveland had barely begun his second term when a series of bank failures and industrial collapses signaled the Panic of 1893. The gold reserve in the U.S. Treasury was depleted due to an excess import of goods, liquidation of U.S. securities in London, and the useless purchase of silver, required by the Sherman Silver Purchase Act. Cleveland called on Congress to repeal the act in order to uphold the gold standard. Farmers felt betrayed by this action, and when Cleveland later borrowed money from J. P. Morgan, they believed that he had sold out to Wall Street.

Cleveland's Second Term

Cleveland's second term proved difficult. Inheriting a treasury deficit from the Harrison administration, he had scarcely taken office when the panic of 1893 burst upon the country. Although Cleveland could not have prevented this disaster, he was blamed for it. Furthermore, he managed to antagonize almost every element in his party. For example, he angered "machine" politicians by putting 120,000 civil service jobs on the merit system. Cleveland also infuriated workers by using troops in the 1894 Pullman strike.

Cleveland Loses Democratic Support

Above all, Cleveland antagonized farmers by defending the gold standard. Fearful that the Sherman Silver Purchase Act would flood the United States Treasury with so much silver that it could not be redeemed in gold, he called a special session of Congress in 1893 and forced repeal of the law. Because most Western and Southern Democrats opposed him, he was able to do this only with Republican support. Even after federal buying of silver ceased, the gold standard was endangered because it was difficult for the government to keep an adequate gold reserve in the treasury. To obtain the precious metal, the Treasury Department sold United States bonds.

In one transaction J. Pierpont Morgan, the most powerful banker on Wall Street, obtained federal bonds so far below their market value that he and the bankers associated with him made $1.5 million. Western fury at the Morgan bond transaction was unbounded. The gold standard was bad enough, but to pay bankers to preserve it seemed to them almost treasonable.

The President's hope of lowering the prohibitive duties of the McKinley Tariff faded when a few Democratic senators joined the Republicans in tacking 633 amendments on a new tariff bill, thereby keeping rates almost at former levels. Cleveland let the resulting Wilson-Gorman Tariff of 1894 become a law without his signature, but he denounced the action of the rebellious senators as "a piece of party perfidy and dishonor."

▲ PRESIDENT GROVER CLEVELAND

Republicans Nominate McKinley

Meanwhile the Republicans had become, more than ever, identified with business interests. A dominant figure in the party was Mark Hanna, an Ohio businessman-politician. Big, bluff, and low-browed, Hanna became, perhaps unjustly, a symbol of the alliance between corporate wealth and politics. Anti-Republican cartoons habitually portrayed him in a suit covered with dollar signs. In 1896 Hanna used his great organizing talents to secure the Republican nomination for his friend William McKinley on a platform pledging high tariffs and maintenance of the gold standard.

Democrats Nominate Bryan

The Democratic national convention opened with such a bitter fight between Gold Democrats and Silver Democrats that it was almost impossible to keep a semblance of order. Then, with dramatic suddenness, the party found a leader in a rather obscure presidential candidate, William Jennings Bryan of Nebraska. Bryan combined a romantic devotion to free silver with a personality, voice, and presence that made him literally a spellbinder:

Linking Across TIME

The Populist party had an impact on politics and government far beyond its showing in national elections. Minor parties have served as vehicles for reform by taking clear-cut stands on controversial issues and proposing bold and original solutions. Among the Populist proposals that were adopted and are still in place today are the federal income tax (Sixteenth Amendment, 1913), direct election of U.S. senators (Seventeenth Amendment, 1913), the secret ballot (late 1890s), and primary elections (Wisconsin, 1903).

Did You Know?

After William Jennings Bryan delivered his speech at the Democratic convention in 1896, people were crying and rejoicing for an hour.

Project Skills Transparency 11 and have students complete Skills Transparencies Activity 11.

Sidelight: Thieves and the Campaign

During William Jennings Bryan's presidential campaign, he was faithfully followed by a band of pickpockets. To make the point that silver was as widely accepted as gold, he would first ask people who carried gold to lift their hands and then those who carried silver to do the same. The thieves worked the packed crowd, relieving both groups of their money.

> ❝ *Burn down your cities and leave our farms, and your cities will spring up again as if by magic; but destroy our farms, and the grass will grow in the streets of every city in the country.* ❞

Speaking at the convention, Bryan used images that seemed to identify the gold standard with evil itself:

> ❝ *You shall not press down upon the brow of labor this crown of thorns—you shall not crucify mankind upon a cross of gold!* ❞

This speech contained hardly a single fact-based argument for a bimetallic standard. It was so charged with emotion that it made free silver a crusade—with Bryan as its standard bearer. Although only 36 years old, he received the Democratic nomination. Most Populists also agreed to support Bryan.

The Campaign for the Presidency

Breaking with tradition, which held that political campaigning was beneath the dignity of one who aspired to the presidency, Bryan traveled the country in search of support. In spite of all his efforts, though, Bryan's cause was doomed. Most large Democratic newspapers abandoned him; the Gold Democrats deserted the Democratic party and ran a separate candidate. Collecting an immense campaign fund, Hanna hired speakers and issued pamphlets aimed at countering the free silver arguments. McKinley was helped by the fact that prices of grain and cotton rose.

The most serious weakness in Bryan's campaign was that free silver was a poor issue on which to base an entire campaign. No one knew what the result of free coinage of silver would be; it would not have ended fluctuation in the value of money, and it might have caused a business panic.

McKinley Wins

The Republicans won the election of 1896 by a decisive margin, carrying all the thickly populated states of the Northeast and Midwest. It was a victory for industry over agriculture, city over country, North and East over West and South.

After their defeat in the election of 1896, the Populists ceased to be a force in politics. Though many at the time felt that all their efforts had failed, those who lived long enough saw most of the planks of their party's platform signed into law.

Section 2 ★ Review

Checking for Understanding

1. **Identify** Populist party, Mark Hanna, William McKinley, William Jennings Bryan.

2. **Define** inflation, deflation, gold standard, third party.

3. **Analyze** the causes of more rapid price declines on farm crops than on many other goods and services.

4. **List** two of the important objectives for the Populist party.

5. **Outline** the issues in the presidential election campaign of 1896.

Critical Thinking

6. **Recognizing Common Goals** The alliance between laborers and farmers was hampered by each group's different interests. What did the two groups have in common that encouraged such an alliance?

ACTIVITY

7. Make a poster of newspaper and magazine ads that advertise political issues or candidates. Write a caption for each illustration that discusses the message that the ad presents.

Answers to SECTION 2 REVIEW

1. Populist party, 347; Hanna, 349; McKinley, 349; Bryan, 350
2. All vocabulary words are defined in the Glossary.
3. While farmers increased the amount of crops they grew, money supply increased very little, creating deflation, which lowered prices.
4. opposed the gold standard; favored government ownership of railroads
5. tariffs, gold or free silver
6. both poor, felt victimized by big business and government support of it
7. Student posters will vary. Students should correctly surmise the messages presented in the advertisements and issues.

Folk Songs of Protest

Songs of protest are threaded throughout American history. In 1777 Americans marched to battle at Saratoga singing "Yankee Doodle." During the 1960s protesters marched for civil rights singing "We Shall Overcome." In the 1890s, too, Populists sang a protest song against bankers called "The Kansas Fool."

THE KANSAS FOOL

We have the land to raise the wheat
And everything that's good to eat;
And when we had no bonds or debt,
We were a jolly, happy set.
With abundant crops raised everywhere,
'Tis a mystery, I do declare,
Why farmers all should fume and fret,
And why we are so deep in debt.

The bankers followed us out west,
And did in mortgages invest;
They looked ahead and shrewdly planned,
and soon they'll have our Kansas land.

CHORUS

Oh Kansas fools! Poor Kansas fools!
The banker makes of you a tool;
I look across the fertile plain,
Big crops—made so by gentle rain;
But twelve-cent corn gives me alarm,
And makes me want to sell my farm.

Other works expressed a tone that was partly serious and partly humorous.

STARVING TO DEATH ON MY GOVERNMENT CLAIM

My name is Tom Hight,
An old bach'lor I am;
You'll find me out west
in the county of fame,
You'll find me out west
on an elegant plain,
Starving to death
on my government claim.

Hurrah for Green County!
the land of the free;
The land of the bedbug,
grasshopper, and flea;
I'll sing of its praises,
I'll tell of its fame,
While starving to death
on my government claim.

Making the Art Connection

1. What complaints do farmers make in the first song?

2. How do these protest songs reflect the fears and concerns of farmers that organized interests were acting against them?

ACTIVITY

3. Write the verses of a current protest song on poster board. Use newspaper and magazine clippings to illustrate the song's message.

351

TEACH

Songs of protest are also associated with the union movement. The Industrial Workers of the World used music to get its message across to attract mine, farm, and textile workers to its ranks. Joe Hill, one of the union's members honored through song, was unjustly executed as a murderer.

Did You Know?

The word *populist* comes from a Latin word meaning "people." Thus a populist is a member of a party claiming to represent the common people.

History and the Humanities

American Music: Cultural Traditions: Have students listen to and analyze the following songs: "No Irish Need Apply" by Mick Moloney, Robbie O'Connell, and Jimmy Keane (2:06) "The Farmer is the Man that Feeds Them All" by Fiddlin' John Carson (3:00)

Answers to Making the Connection

1. Most of the protest is aimed at banking practices, including high interest rates that leave farmers with no money.

2. The second stanza of the first song makes it clear that farmers believed the banks were systematically trying to destroy them. Bankers "followed" them west, "looked ahead and shrewdly planned" to take their land.

3. Answers will vary. Folk music of the 1960s and 1970s, such as Bob Dylan's "Blowing in the Wind," was filled with protest against war and the materialism of society. "We Shall Overcome" is considered an anthem for the civil rights movement. Popular music of the 1980s and 1990s often reflects concerns for the environment and hunger.

★★

Other Forces for Reform

FOCUS

Bellringer

 Before taking roll, project Section Focus Transparency 11-3 or hand out Section Focus Transparency Activity 11-3. Have students answer the questions.

Motivating Activity

Provide the following verse by George Francis Train:

"Kansas will win the
 World's applause
As the sole champion of
 the woman's cause
So light the bonfires, have
 the flags unfurled
To the banner state of all
 the world."

Ask students what feelings and beliefs the writer expresses about women's rights. *(hope and belief that woman suffrage will pass)* **L1**

ABCNEWS INTERACTIVE™

VIDEODISC

Powers of the Supreme Court

Side 1, Chapter 25

Title: *Amendment 18, Prohibition of Liquor*

Subject: Problems during prohibition

Side 1, Chapter 26

Title: *Amendment 19, Woman Suffrage*

Subject: Brief history of woman suffrage

Setting the Scene

Section Focus

Though the Gilded Age is often thought of as a period of greed, corruption, and self-centered individualism, it was also a period of reform. Like the Populists, whose strength lay mainly in the West, reformers in other areas were trying to call attention to problems.

Objectives

After studying this section, you should be able to

★ trace women's involvement in the temperance and suffrage movements.

★ discuss the political ideas of Karl Marx and Henry George.

Key Term

conspicuous consumption

◀ **CARRIE NATION**, FIGHTER FOR PROHIBITION

Reforms of the Civil War and Reconstruction periods encouraged people in the United States to look to government as the agent of social change. In the years of its unquestioned dominance, the Republican party had freed slaves, imposed a new way of life on the South, and opened the West to settlement. After the war, reformers who were dissatisfied with various aspects of life in the Gilded Age also looked to the government for action.

■ Temperance and Women's Rights

The period after the Civil War was not just a time of industrial progress, urban growth, and agrarian and labor discontent. Like the Jacksonian period, it also produced reforms designed to cure the ills of the new industrial society of the United States.

The Temperance Movement

Several reform movements that had begun earlier continued to reach toward their goals. Supporters of Prohibition, for example, formed a national political party in 1869; in 1872 they ran a presidential candidate. The temperance movement had never been more active.

Most effective were two national organizations that waged a ceaseless campaign against the evils of liquor and the saloon: the Anti-Saloon League and the Woman's Christian Temperance Union (WCTU). The WCTU revealed that women were learning the techniques of large-scale organization. Frances Willard, the head of the WCTU, made her group an effective force for causes other than temperance, such as prison reform and protective labor laws. Because women were far more likely than men to favor temperance, temperance advocates usually favored woman suffrage.

Classroom Resources for SECTION 3

Blackline Masters:
- Reproducible Lesson Plan 11-3
- Guided Reading Activity 11-3
- Linking Past and Present Activity 11
- Enrichment Activity 11
- Chapter Skills Activity 11
- Workbook Activity 11-3
- Section Quiz 11-3

Transparencies:
- Section Focus Transparency 11-3

Multimedia:
- Testmaker
- Powers of the Supreme Court

Woman Suffrage

Woman suffrage had its beginnings in the antebellum period; its first leaders were female abolitionists like Elizabeth Cady Stanton, who decided to put the antislavery cause ahead of their own. After the war woman suffrage was championed with renewed vigor.

In 1878 Susan B. Anthony of the National Woman Suffrage Association (NWSA) persuaded a sympathetic senator to propose the first woman suffrage amendment to the Constitution. It was voted down many times in the next 40 years. These defeats reflected the opinion of the majority of the people at the time, both male and female.

At the state level, suffragists had better success. By 1900 about half the states allowed women to vote on school issues, where their special knowledge of children was presumed to be a benefit. On the frontier, where women shared the hardships and dangers equally with men, support for woman suffrage was more widespread. By 1900, four states—Colorado, Wyoming, Utah, and Idaho—had granted women the right to vote.

▼ ELIZABETH CADY STANTON

Women and Unions

Women workers especially suffered exploitation during the new industrial age. By 1900 almost 5 million women were employed in the United States. It was not uncommon for women to work in "sweat shops" for 10 to 14 hours a day, often for less than $4 a week. Most unions, however, refused to accept women as members. One exception, the International Ladies' Garment Workers Union, had women leaders as well as women members. In 1903 a group of women formed the National Women's Trade Union League to campaign for better working conditions.

■ Socialism

Wherever industrialism appeared, there were people driven toward extreme solutions for the problems it created. Something seemed wrong with a system that produced

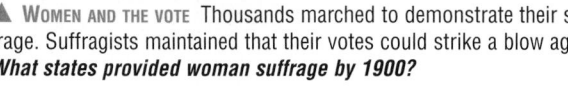

▲ WOMEN AND THE VOTE Thousands marched to demonstrate their support for woman suffrage. Suffragists maintained that their votes could strike a blow against political machines. *What states provided woman suffrage by 1900?*

Vocabulary Precheck

Ask students to guess the meaning of "conspicuous consumption." **L1, LEP**

TEACH
Guided Practice

Chronology Have students list key events in the woman suffrage movement in chronological order. Then discuss students' lists. **L1, LEP**

Visualizing (H)istory In 1890 woman suffrage leaders, including Stanton and Anthony, formed the National American Woman Suffrage Association. The association worked to advance women's rights on both the federal and state levels. In 1910 the association obtained 500,000 signatures on a petition urging the passage of a federal woman-suffrage law. Have students look at the illustration and identify the place and time of the demonstration pictured. (*New York, 1911*)

Answer to Caption: Colorado, Wyoming, Utah, and Idaho

Cultural Perspectives

Discrimination in the Workplace In the late 1800s, discrimination in the workplace was the rule rather than the exception. Women were always paid less than men, even when they did the same work. The best jobs went to native-born white males. African American men were virtually unable to get any factory jobs. Many African American women could find jobs only as domestic workers.

both the idle rich, who lived in mansions, and the unemployed poor, who lived in slums. Some were impelled toward socialism.

Experiments in Socialism

Socialists in the early 1800s did not attempt to change the economic system by gaining control of the government. Instead they tried to effect change by experimenting with cooperative communities. Robert Owen brought his idea of cooperative control of industry from England to New Harmony, Indiana, in 1825. Such socialist communities reached their peak in America in the 1840s.

Karl Marx and Socialism

Socialists of the late nineteenth century were dedicated to changing the entire social and political system, partly because of the influence of Karl Marx. Marx had been a student at the University of Berlin during the emergence of a new philosophical and literary movement that questioned established values. Searching for meaning in history, Marx finally wrote his economic philosophy in *The Communist Manifesto* in 1847 and in *Das Kapital*, the first volume of which was published in 1867. Marx predicted that capitalism was doomed. Fewer and fewer capitalists, he said, would control all wealth,

while the mass of the people would be pushed into the ranks of the proletariat (people without property). Eventually the proletarians would rise and overthrow their masters. History, said Marx, had seen continual class struggles, but the conflict between industrial workers and capitalists would be the last. When the workers eventually took control of society, Marx believed they would establish a classless society.

Marxist socialism appealed to many workers in the industrial countries of Europe. In the United States, however, it gained only a small following.

The American Socialist Party

Eugene V. Debs became a lifelong convert to socialism because of unjust treatment after his imprisonment in an Illinois jail during the Pullman strike. Declaring that in a democracy workers could gain control of the government and use it to change the free enterprise system, he organized the American Socialist party.

■ Dissenting Voices

Socialism was not the only remedy proposed at the time. Other solutions to fix society's ills included a single tax on land and a classless society.

Visualizing History ▲ **AT THE OFFICE** In the early 1900s, professional careers were largely reserved for men, while secretarial jobs were thought to be women's work. *How many women were employed by 1900?*

Linking Past and Present

A Home Away from Home

The bed and breakfast way of travel has long been a part of the American landscape—going back to the 1600s when taverns and inns provided shelter for weary tourists.

Then

The Boardinghouse

The boardinghouse, a lodging house at which meals are provided, became common in many large cities. Many boardinghouses in the late 1800s were established for economic reasons. One immigrant woman wanted to own

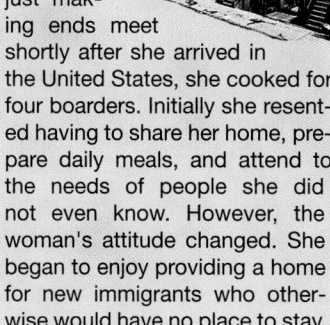

► RIDGE STREET, NEW YORK CITY

her own home in America. Having difficulty just making ends meet shortly after she arrived in the United States, she cooked for four boarders. Initially she resented having to share her home, prepare daily meals, and attend to the needs of people she did not even know. However, the woman's attitude changed. She began to enjoy providing a home for new immigrants who otherwise would have no place to stay.

Now

Bed and Breakfast

A modern form of the boardinghouse is the bed and breakfast home (B&B). A bed and breakfast home is a private residence that is used to accommodate paying guests overnight. Breakfast is provided. B&B is the perfect offering for travelers who prefer a relaxed atmosphere of hospitality and comfort to the more impersonal offerings of hotels or motels.

► BED AND BREAKFAST INN, SUGAR HILL, NEW HAMPSHIRE

Henry George and the Single Tax

Another writer with a proposal for remaking society was Henry George, whose major work *Progress and Poverty* was published in 1879. George attacked the central problem posed by the socialists: Why should the advance of the industrial revolution, with more and more machinery for producing wealth, apparently result in more poverty? George said the problem was that ownership of land—the source of all wealth—was being concentrated in the hands of speculators. These speculators did not put the land to use. They merely waited for it to increase in value, meanwhile charging high rents that drove down wages and business profits. George criticized the growing gap between rich and poor:

 We need not look far from the palace to find the hovel. When people can charter special

steamboats to take them to watering places . . . build marble stables for their horses and give dinner parties which cost . . . a thousand dollars a head, we may know that there are poor girls on the street . . . [facing] starvation. 🙶🙶

George did not propose socialism as a remedy. Instead he urged what he called the "single tax" on land values. The rate of the single tax would be based not on existing value but on *potential* value if the land were used efficiently. Thus there would be no profit in keeping land out of use and waiting for it to increase in worth; owners would either have to develop it themselves or sell it to someone else who would do so. George argued that this would cause prosperity by promoting maximum productivity and by plowing the profits of the land monopoly

CHAPTER 11 Politics and Protest: 1865–1900   **355**

Linking Past and Present

The Kohler family in Kohler, Wisconsin, was one of the factory owners who provided boardinghouses for unmarried immigrant men. For immigrant families the Kohlers built small houses in an area that became a company town. The houses were built so well that the Kohler family turned them into an upscale resort in the 1970s. Ask students to find examples of bed and breakfast inns in or near their community.

🗁 For additional practice, assign Linking Past and Present Activity 11.

Did You Know?

Boardinghouses were known by different names in various cities—"furnished-room houses" in Philadelphia, "rooming houses" in Chicago, and "lodging houses" in San Francisco.

Sidelight: Architecture

The "conspicuous consumption" of the upper class described by Veblen (page 356) was most evident in housing. The dream houses of the upper class were transformed into reality by architect Richard M. Hunt, who had studied at L'Ecole des Beaux-Arts in Paris. He designed both the chateau at Vanderbilt's Biltmore Estates in North Carolina and The Breakers in Newport, Rhode Island. It is said Hunt never had to worry about the cost of his labor or voluminous and expensive construction materials—in other words, he was given a "blank check."

back into society. Although George's ideas had great appeal, the single-tax idea was too radical a change to be accepted completely. However, it did influence methods of taxation both in this country and abroad.

Thorstein Veblen and "Conspicuous Consumption"

Another widely read book, *The Theory of the Leisure Class,* was published in 1899 by Thorstein Veblen. The son of Norwegian immigrants, Veblen had been influenced by Populism in his early days in Wisconsin. Attending Yale and Johns Hopkins University, he became interested in the social sciences, especially economics. His appreciation for science led him to write with the cool detachment of an observer.

Influenced by Darwin's theory of evolution, Veblen believed in the process of natural selection. He contended that the "leisure class," which was made up of those people who had great wealth, was *not* an example of the most fit. In fact Veblen argued that the leisure class hindered progress and evolution. Veblen believed that, like the dinosaur, the leisure class would eventually disappear.

Veblen used the phrase **conspicuous consumption** to describe the life of the upper class. Veblen described conspicuous consumption as the use of vast resources just for show. The phrase had deep meaning because the contrast between wealth and poverty was not hidden. The mansions that lined the streets of cities like New York and Chicago were within a few blocks of immigrant ghettos. However, Veblen's vision of a community of equals governed by an elite group of social planners was judged impractical by most Americans of his time.

Limited Support for Radical Changes

Probably the reason why radical formulas for altering society did not gain wide support was that many Americans did not want change. Even those at the bottom rung of the economic ladder often felt they had bettered their position from an earlier time.

A New England farm boy might find drawing wages of a dollar a day for a 60-hour week in a factory preferable to working from dawn to dark trying to make a living from a rocky farm. An immigrant might be living with her family in a single room and working in a windowless sweatshop, but for the first time in her life she was wearing shoes.

Even the poorest workers believed that in time they would also be able to "get ahead" and become property owners. They fervently believed in the "rags-to-riches" story and felt, like the heroes of the Horatio Alger series, that they could by work, perseverance, and luck rise to a higher station in life. If property rights were destroyed, what would happen to the American dream?

Section 3 ★ Review

Checking for Understanding

1. **Identify** Susan B. Anthony, Eugene V. Debs.

2. **Define** conspicuous consumption.

3. **Discuss** the goals and methods of the temperance movement.

4. **Describe** the movements to gain voting rights for women.

5. **Compare** the solutions proposed by Karl Marx, Henry George, and Thorstein Veblen.

Critical Thinking

6. **Arguing an Opinion**   Why did many states refuse women the right to vote? What arguments would you propose to justify women's right to vote in the late 1800s?

ACTIVITY

7. Create a table comparing major reform issues of the late 1800s with those of today.

Answers to SECTION 3 REVIEW

1. Susan B. Anthony, 353; Eugene V. Debs, 354
2. All vocabulary words are defined in the Glossary.
3. formed organizations and political party
4. formation of National Woman's Suffrage Association, proposal of first woman suffrage amendment
5. Marx predicted overthrow of capitalism by industrial workers and establishment of a classless society. Veblen believed in a society of equals governed by an elite group of experts. George proposed taxing privately owned land's potential value to encourage productivity and discourage speculators.
6. Answers will vary: Women had already involved themselves in important social issues; vote had been extended to African American males, who had formerly been disenfranchised.
7. Student selections for the tables should focus on major issues.

BUILDING SKILLS
Critical Thinking Skills

Recognizing Ideologies

When studying past and current events, recognizing ideologies is a valuable skill to use. An ideology is a set of beliefs and values that guides the actions of a person or a group of people. Often, large organizations and political parties are formed to express a particular ideology.

Learning the Skill

Ask these questions to help you recognize ideologies:

- Which people benefit if the issue passes? If the issue fails? How do they benefit?
- Which people pay or suffer if the issue passes? If the issue fails? How do they pay or suffer?

Throughout United States history, numerous minor political parties have initiated social or political reform. The goals of the minor party often centered on a single issue, and as popular support grew for that issue and public opinion changed, the "cause" was adopted by either the Democratic or Republican party. The minor party thus faded out as its goals were achieved.

The Populist party had an impact far beyond its showing in national elections. Several Populist proposals are in use today. The federal income tax, adopted as part of the Sixteenth Amendment in 1913, accounts for one-half of the monies collected at all levels of government.

The Seventeenth Amendment placed into law the direct election of United States senators. The secret ballot, first used in the late 1890s, became standard practice in all elections. Primary elections are used to settle virtually all contests for majority-party nominations for state and congressional offices and for many local offices. Hundreds of cities and many states permit citizens to use the initiative and referendum, used in South Dakota in the late 1890s, to introduce legislation and vote on proposed laws.

▲ 1891 POLITICAL CARTOON, PARTY OF PATCHES

Practicing the Skill

1. What benefits are associated with the use of a secret ballot? Who might oppose its use? Why?

2. In what way is the proposal for a secret ballot consistent with Populist goals?

3. Who benefits from the initiative and referendum proposal? Explain how these systems work.

APPLYING THE SKILL

4. Choose one of the amendments to the United States Constitution. Write a short essay that explains the amendment and speculates about the political issues or ideologies that may have motivated it.

357

GLENCOE
TECHNOLOGY

 VIDEODISC

Use the MindJogger Videoquiz to review students' knowledge.

MindJogger Videoquiz

Chapter 11
Disc 2, Side A

 Available in VHS.

Using Vocabulary

Responses should tie term and speaker.

Reviewing Facts

1. overproduction, low prices, debt, high costs, and natural disasters
2. fix maximum railway rates, forbid railroad discrimination between places or shippers, regulate other farm-related monopolies (grain elevators, etc.)
3. forbade pooling, rebates, and higher rates for short hauls; required published rates with advance notice of change, financial reports to government
4. lowered prices for crops, made it harder to repay loans
5. Money must be backed by gold. Money supply could not increase faster than the gold supply.
6. elimination of national banks and the gold standard, more government powers, regulation of railroads
7. Marx advocated overthrowing capitalism and establishing a classless society.

Using Vocabulary

Use each of the following terms in a statement that might have been made by each of the following people:

> Railroad owner: pooling
> Farmer: cooperatives
> Banker: inflation

Reviewing Facts

1. **Summarize** the factors that created financial hardships for farmers in the late 1800s.
2. **List** three purposes of the Granger laws.
3. **Specify** what the Interstate Commerce Act required of the railroads.
4. **Explain** why deflation hurt the farmers.
5. **Describe** the gold standard and its effect on the money supply.
6. **State** the reforms the Populists demanded in their platform.
7. **Compare** Karl Marx's solution to poverty with Henry George's.

Understanding Concepts

Economic Inequity

1. In the farmers' view, what groups enriched themselves at the farmers' expense?

Social Change

2. Which groups of people might be expected to support extreme solutions for social problems? What groups would likely oppose such solutions? Why did most Americans vote for more moderate candidates in the late 1900s?

3. What did the Populist party, the Grange, and the followers of Marx, George, and Veblen have in common?

Critical Thinking

1. **Understanding Cause and Effect** Explain how new agricultural technology helped the farmers. How did it financially hurt some farmers?
2. **Comparing Fine Art** Study the two paintings on this page by artist John Singer Sargent. Then answer the questions.
   a. What is the mood in each of these works?
   b. What adjectives would you use to describe these paintings?
   c. Compare the use of color and light in these paintings.
   d. Which painting do you prefer? Explain.

History and Geography

Regionalism and the Election of 1896

The Republican party nominated William McKinley for President in 1896. The Democrats nominated William Jennings Bryan. The Republican platform endorsed the protective tariff, opposed the free coinage of silver, and did not deal with the issues of railroad and trust abuses and labor injunctions. The Democratic platform demanded tariff reduction,

George advocated taxing land's potential value, which would reduce speculation by the rich.

Understanding Concepts

1. railroad owners, manufacturers, banks

2. the unemployed and poorly paid workers; the well-to-do; answers will vary
3. All championed the poor.

Critical Thinking

1. The new technology enabled farmers to increase production while decreasing the amount of work

time. The technology hurt farmers because it was expensive and caused debt and led to overproduction and decreasing prices.
2. a. serene mood
   b. calm, relaxed, friendly
   c. Students should point out that the use of the elements of color and light emphasize the central focus.

called for free silver, and pledged stricter control of trusts and railroads. The map below shows how the nation divided geographically in the election.

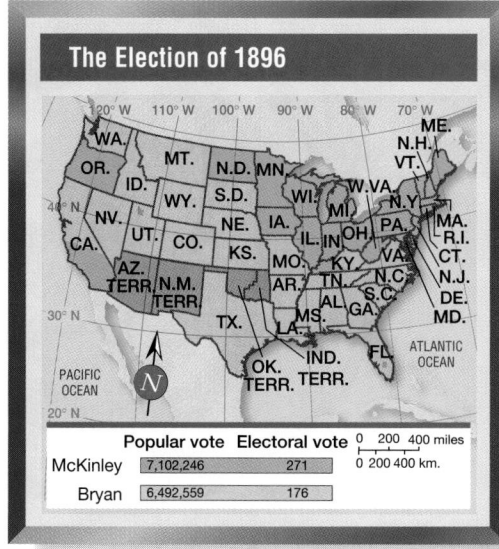

The Election of 1896

	Popular vote	Electoral vote
McKinley	7,102,246	271
Bryan	6,492,559	176

0 200 400 miles
0 200 400 km.

1. **Region** Why was Bryan's main support in the South and West?

2. **Place** In which of the states was the electoral vote divided?

3. **Region** Which candidate received stronger support in the Northeast?

4. **Region** Can you conclude from the map what regions of the nation were likely to support restrictions on industry? Explain.

Cooperative Learning **Interdisciplinary Activity: Economics**

You will be part of a discussion between four people meeting in a Great Plains town in the year 1886. Divide the following roles among yourselves: a farmer, a banker, a railroad owner, and a politician. The purpose of this meeting is to discuss the problems of the farmer. The farmer will begin the meeting by stating his or her main concerns. The other members should discuss ways to answer the

farmer's problems, although each individual should be prepared to argue why he or she cannot agree to a recommended change. End the meeting by having all members agree on two recommendations for helping the farmer.

Practicing Skills

Recognizing Ideologies

Read the statements and express in your own words what ideology each statement is expressing.
1. The American doctrine is that it is the duty of government merely to protect the people while they are taking care of themselves—nothing more than that.

2. There is something radically wrong in our industry. The railroads have never been so prosperous and yet agriculture languishes. The banks have never done a better or more profitable business, and yet agriculture languishes.

3. One of two things is true: either a woman is like a man—and if she is, then a ballot based on brains belongs to her as well as to him; if she is different, then man does not know how to vote for her as well as she herself does.

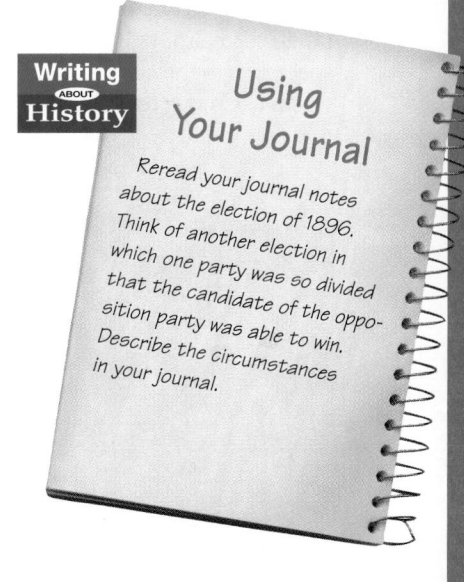

Writing ABOUT History **Using Your Journal**

Reread your journal notes about the election of 1896. Think of another election in which one party was so divided that the candidate of the opposition party was able to win. Describe the circumstances in your journal.

Writing ABOUT History **Using Your Journal**

Students may cite several examples, including 1824, 1836, 1860, and 1868.

? **Chapter Bonus Test Question**

Ask students: Based on what you have read in the chapter, decide whether each of the following is true or false. If it is true, explain why. If it is false, correct it to make it true.
1. Third parties have never been a force in U.S. politics. (*False; many third-party proposals bring to the public's attention measures that the major parties later adopt as their own.*)
2. Populism never gained much support outside farming areas. (*True; Populism was primarily a farmers' movement.*)

---

d. Students should provide reasons for their responses.

History and Geography

1. because his platform would benefit these regions
2. California
3. McKinley
4. the West and Southeast; these regions voted for

Bryan, who ran on a platform pledging stricter control of trusts and railroads

Cooperative Learning

Encourage all members of the group to contribute to the meeting from the perspective of their assigned roles.

Practicing Skills

1. The American government should take action to assure that people are able to take care of themselves.
2. The government should pass laws that favor farming interests.
3. Women should have the right to vote.

Cultural Kaleidoscope

Life in the West

ON THE RANGE

The West and life on the range have always had a special mystique. Television, books, and the movies have kept alive the legend of the Western hero, but the reality of life on the range is overlooked. The work was hard, sometimes boring, and often dangerous. Determination, bravery, and endurance were required to tend great herds of restless and stubborn cattle or to prod a herd great distances on the long drive. Life on the range seems romantic in retrospect, but to the cowhands it was hard and often hazardous.

▶ The rope, or lariat, was an important tool in the hands of a skilled roper. Cowhands used the lariat to rope cattle, pull cattle out of mud, and haul wood to the campfire.

▼ The cowhand's clothing served a useful purpose. Chaps protected the legs during the long hours in the saddle.

◀ The cowhand took special care of the tack, equipment, and grooming tools for the horse. One important piece, the bridle, is used to control the movements of the horse by straps and metal pieces placed on the head and in the mouth of the animal.

360

Cooperative Learning Activity

Famous People of the West Divide the class into small groups. Ask each to research a famous Western figure, such as Andy Adams, Buffalo Bill, Deadwood Dick, Wyatt Earp, Annie Oakley, or Will Rogers (or others of your choosing). Have each group report its findings to the class. **L1**

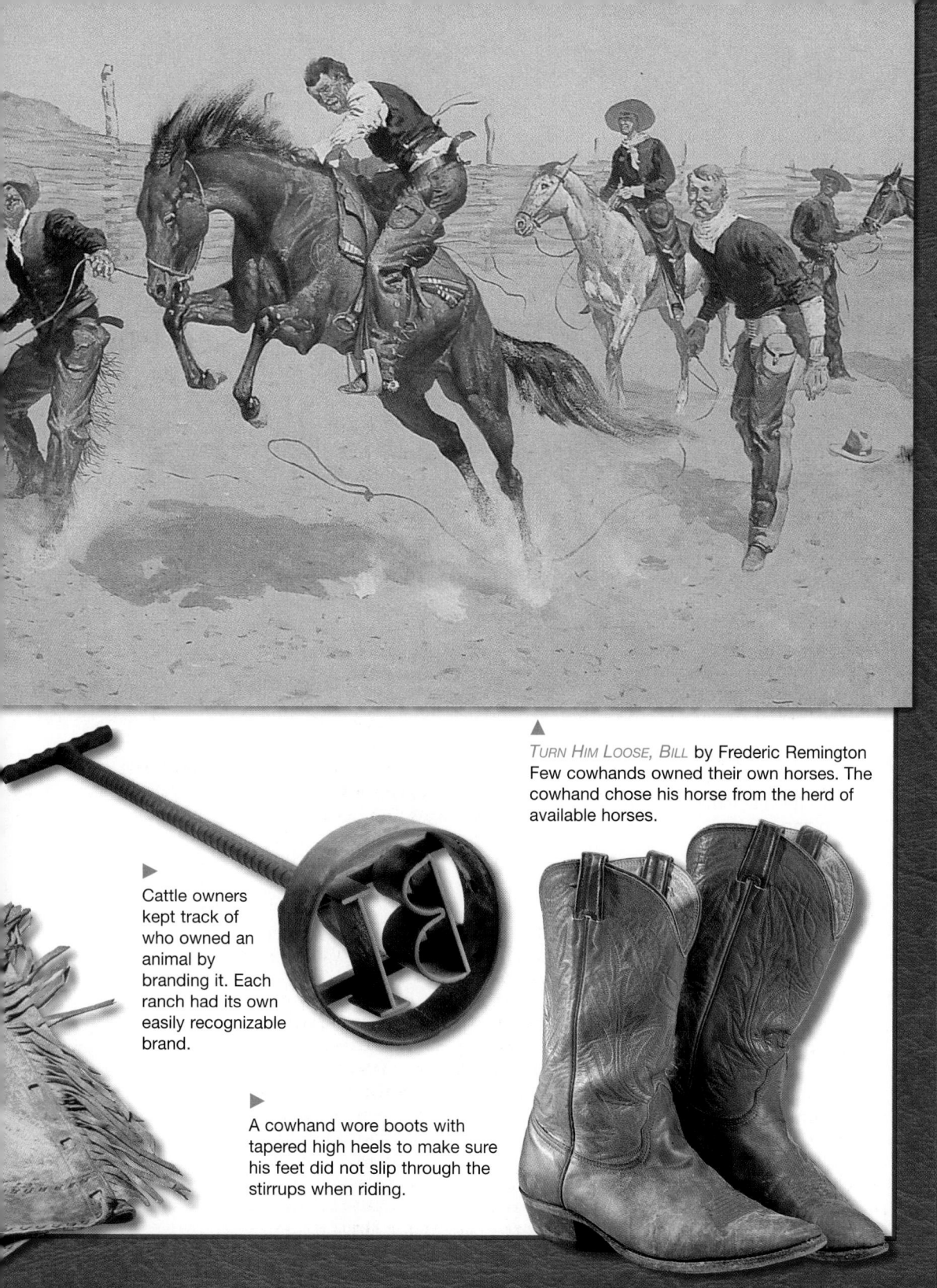

Portfolio Project

Ask students to note representations of cowboys in current advertising and popular culture. With each example, they should try to judge how true to life the image seems.

History and the Humanities

U. S. History & Art Transparency 18, *The Stampede* by Frederic Remington

American Portraits 33-34: Chief Joseph, Helen Hunt Jackson

The Spirit of American Music, p. 25, William Henry Jackson

▲

TURN HIM LOOSE, BILL by Frederic Remington
Few cowhands owned their own horses. The cowhand chose his horse from the herd of available horses.

▶ Cattle owners kept track of who owned an animal by branding it. Each ranch had its own easily recognizable brand.

▶ A cowhand wore boots with tapered high heels to make sure his feet did not slip through the stirrups when riding.

361

The Historian's Craft

For decades, cowboys were portrayed almost exclusively as white Westerners. Historians have explored this stereotype and learned that at least a third of the ranch hands during the height of the cattle kingdom were African Americans or Mexicans. Many were Southerners, who moved west after the defeat of the Confederacy during the Civil War. A useful study of this subject is Joseph B. Frantz and Julian E. Choate, *The American Cowboy: The Myth and the Reality* (1968).

UNIT THREE
DIGEST

0:00 **OUT OF TIME?**

If time does not permit teaching the entire unit or its individual chapters, use the information on these pages along with Chapter Digests Audiocassettes to present the material in a condensed format.

Exploring Unit Themes

The Unit Digest may be used to teach unit coverage when time is limited, to review unit content, or to relate the content of one unit to that of another.

▇ Chapter 7

Have students create a time line showing the major events in the struggle of the Plains peoples.

▇ Chapter 8

Ask students to define "Robber Barons."

▇ Chapter 9

Ask students to research the role of women in the labor movement of the late 1800s.

▇ Chapter 10

Discuss with students the statement:

"The period was poor in purpose and barren in results."

Causes and Effects

Asks students to write a newspaper editorial describing the problems facing farmers in the second half of the nineteenth century, using the information in the chart.

Chapter 7

Into the West

In the early 1860s, many Native American nations lived on the Great Plains with the vast buffalo herds. Then, beginning in 1869, transcontinental railway lines opened the West. The Homestead Act made land easy to obtain, and the railroads actively promoted settlement. Pioneer farmers poured onto the plains by the thousands. The discovery of gold and other minerals and the promise of wealth from cattle also lured many people.

Native Americans fought this intrusion, but their cause was doomed. White hunters slaughtered the buffalo almost to extinction, and farmers, miners, and ranchers took much of their land. In 1890 at Wounded Knee, their resistance came to an end.

Chapter 8

The Rise of Industry

The United States had all the necessary ingredients for industry to grow—abundant natural and human resources, investment money, a free enterprise economic system, and new inventions and technology.

By 1900 huge companies dominated the economy. Their efficiency resulted in cheaper production, higher quality, and lower prices that drove smaller competitors out of business. Corporations, monopolies, and trusts became the norm. Industrial leaders used social Darwinism to justify their actions. The Sherman Antitrust Act, passed in 1890, did little to control business practices.

"BOSTON," by Josiah Flynt

The Plight of the Farmer

CAUSES

- New inventions, more efficient techniques
- Lack of competition among railroads
- Need for machinery; higher shipping costs
- Short money supply

• Farm Woes

EFFECTS

- Decline in prices of farm products
- Farmers' earnings decrease
- Farmers are unable to pay back loans
- Banks lend money to fewer farmers

Cooperative Learning Activity

Creating a Museum Exhibit Divide the class into three groups and assign each group one of the following: a major personality, an important event, or an important technological development of the time period covered in Unit 3. Ask groups to design a museum exhibit illustrating their selected personality, event, or technological development. Suggest that groups use models, sketches, maps, quotations, eyewitness accounts, and so on in their exhibits. Have the groups display their finished exhibits in class. **L2**

Chapter 9

An Urban Society

With industrialization the workforce grew and the workers' lives changed. Machines took over many traditional tasks of the worker. Hours were long, wages were low, and workplaces were hazardous. Unable to improve their lot individually, workers turned to labor unions.

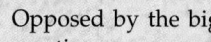

Opposed by the big corporations, management and, to a certain extent, the government, labor unions resorted to strikes. However, even major strikes like the 1894 Pullman strike failed to win significant gains.

An important influence on labor were the large numbers of immigrants who provided unskilled labor for urban industries. They were primarily southern and eastern European and Chinese immigrants who flocked to the cities, where they created their own ethnic communities. Their unfamiliar languages and customs aroused anti-immigration sentiment.

Along with the influx of immigrants, rural Americans came to the rapidly growing cities. In this urban environment that was faced with daunting human and technical problems, a new way of life evolved.

Chapter 10

The Gilded Age

With industrialization and urbanization came political corruption. Scandals arose at every level of government. Political machines dominated almost all major cities.

Government in general lacked leadership, and reform efforts met with limited success. Civil service reform finally came in 1883 with passage of the Pendleton Act.

The society and culture changed as well. Education expanded and improved. Local-color writers like Mark Twain described their locales with realism and detail. Sporting events became a favorite leisure-time activity, as did vaudeville, penny newspapers, and dime novels.

Chapter 11

Politics and Protest

The prosperity of the Gilded Age did not extend to farmers, who were burdened with high costs, low incomes, and heavy debts. They organized into groups such as Granges and farmers' alliances. Ultimately these groups turned to politics.

The farmers joined with labor and other reform groups to form a new national political party—the Populist party. The Omaha platform of the Populist party in 1892 clearly reflected the interests of the farmer. The Populist party had some successes, but the movement died soon after William Jennings Bryan lost the 1896 presidential election.

Farmers were not the only ones seeking reform. The temperance movement had never been more active, and woman suffrage became a popularly debated issue across the country. At the same time, writers such as Karl Marx proposed

socialism as an economic remedy while Henry George favored a "single tax" on land values. However, Americans on the whole were not interested in instituting radical change.

Understanding Unit Themes

1. **Geography and Environment**   Compare the American landscape and the environment in 1860 and 1900.

2. **Conflict and Cooperation**   How did the settlement of the West affect Native Americans? The nation as a whole? How might cooperation have resolved many conflicts?

3. **Influence of Technology**   In what ways did technology influence American life and society between 1860 and 1900?

4. **Cultural Diversity**   What ethnic groups played a role in the settlement of the West and in industrialization?

Chapter 11

Discuss the importance of agriculture in the United States in the late 1800s.

Student Self-Test Software allows students to test their understanding of historical concepts in this unit.

Have students listen to the Chapter Digests on the audiocassettes.

Use the **Testmaker** to create a customized test for Unit 3.

GLENCOE TECHNOLOGY

VIDEODISC

Use the MindJogger Videoquiz to review students' knowledge.

MindJogger Videoquiz

Chapter 7
Disc 1, Side B

Chapter 8
Disc 1, Side B

Chapter 9
Disc 1, Side B

Chapter 10
Disc 1, Side B

Chapter 11
Disc 2, Side A

   Available in VHS.

Flashcards

Use American History Flashcards to reinforce students' knowledge of places and events in American history.

Answers to Understanding Unit Themes

1. In 1860 the United States was primarily rural. In 1900, the United States was an urban nation.
2. destroyed their way of life; opened up opportunity and led to economic expansion. Could have preserved buffalo and Native American hunting lands.
3. Technology enabled railroads to open the West and farmers to cultivate the Great

Plains, cities to grow, production to increase, and transportation to improve.

4. Western settlement: Native Americans, settlers from Eastern states, and U.S. soldiers. Industrialization: Chinese and Irish immigrant railroad workers, immigrants from northern and western Europe followed by those from southern and eastern Europe.

BEGINNING THE UNIT

Present this cause-and-effect chart to students with the effects omitted. Assign students to complete the chart as they read the chapters in the unit.

Events
- Spanish-American War

Causes
- Economic growth of United States
- Expansion of overseas markets
- Shift away from isolationist policy

Effects
- American dominance in the Caribbean
- Expansionist policies in the Pacific and Far East
- Building of Panama Canal
- Emergence as a world power
- Growth of anti-imperialism

History AND ART

George Wesley Bellows was born in Columbus, Ohio, and attended Ohio State University, where he developed his skills in music and athletics as well as in art. He left college in 1904 to study art in New York, where he quickly won national recognition.

0:00 OUT OF TIME?

If time does not permit teaching the entire unit, use the Unit Digest on pages 448–449.

UNIT 4
ENTERING A NEW CENTURY
1867–1920

★★

CHAPTER 12	CHAPTER 13	CHAPTER 14
Imperialism 1867–1908	The Progressive Era 1893–1920	White House Reformers 1900–1914

▲ BANJO, LATE 1800S

364

History AND ART

Cliff Dwellers
by George Wesley Bellows, 1913

Bellows's works often show elements of humor and adventure. His favorite themes, which include landscapes and athletic events, mark him as a uniquely American painter.

Exploring Unit Themes

American Democracy Progressive reforms such as the direct election of senators, the direct primary, municipal government reform, and the initiative, referendum, and recall all gave voters a greater say in the political process. A number of states granted women full suffrage. Jim Crow laws in the South, however, all but denied African Americans the right to vote.

Economic Development The early years of the twentieth century saw greater government involvement in the economy. The power of the trusts was restricted. Laws were passed to improve working conditions and to protect consumers from fraud and poor-quality goods.

The Individual and Family Life Progressive reforms prohibited child labor, mandated work-

Setting the Scene

In an age of optimism, United States foreign policy shifted away from isolationism, and the nation became a major power in international affairs. Americans also took a look at their political institutions and concluded that change was necessary. Progressive-minded reformers sought a more democratic government while working to end a host of social ills.

Themes

- American Democracy
- Economic Development
- The Individual and Family Life
- U.S. Role in World Affairs

Key Events

- Purchase of Alaska and annexation of Hawaii
- Spanish-American War
- Building of the Panama Canal
- States institute direct primary, initiative, and referendum
- Formation of the National Association for the Advancement of Colored People
- Income taxes enacted
- "Bull Moose" party formed
- Federal Reserve System created
- Federal Trade Commission established

Major Issues

- Commercial interests and war with Spain lead to the acquisition of a colonial empire.
- Muckraking literature inspires a new generation of reformers who seek to correct social inequities.
- Reform-minded Presidents extend democracy and protect Americans from big business.

▲ TRAVEL TRUNK

▲ EARLY AIRPLANE

◄ CHILD'S TOY, EARLY 1900S

Portfolio Project

Read the amendments that passed during the time between 1867 and 1920. Choose one and rewrite it in your own words, making clear what the amendment is expected to accomplish.

For more in-depth study of Unit 4, you or your students may use the Internet to research individual topics. An excellent source for information on the American colonial empire is:

World Wide Web:
http://www.maxwell.syr.edu/unofficial/fjzwick/centennial/uscolony.html

Portfolio Project

After students rewrite the amendment they chose, ask them to consider whether it accomplished its objective. Explain that when they have completed the unit, they will be better able to answer that question.

History and the Humanities

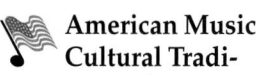
American Music: Cultural Traditions: Spanish-American War: "Battleship of Maine" by the New Lost City Ramblers (3:04) Ragtime: "Maple Leaf Rag" by Scott Joplin (3:12)

U.S. History & Art Transparency 19, *Cliff Dwellers* by George Bellows

Spirit of American Art and Music, p. 31, John Philip Sousa

---

er's compensation insurance, and ensured the quality of consumer goods. These reforms, and the provision of health clinics and recreation parks, improved the quality of life for some. Progressive reforms, however, were of little benefit to African Americans and Native Americans.
U.S. Role in World Affairs After the Spanish-American War, the United States began to take on the responsibilities of a world power. Many Americans nonetheless expressed reservations about the country's new role .
Examining the Themes Tell students that this unit traces the emergence of the United States as an industrial giant and a major world power.

Global Perspectives

FOCUS

Motivating Activity

Tell students that one historian has said of the United States in the late nineteenth and early twentieth centuries that "an exhilarating new spirit of Manifest Destiny swept the nation."

Discuss with students the idea of Manifest Destiny. Ask them to suggest reasons the United States might be caught up in such a spirit during this period. (*becoming a great industrial power; new markets needed for products; Western frontier closing, new areas for expansion sought*) **L1**

TEACH

Guided Practice

Exploring the Time Line
Refer students to the world section of the time line. Ask them to identify worldwide conflicts. (*Sino-Japanese War, Russo-Japanese War, Spanish-American War*) Ask students to consider how these events might affect the United States. (*U.S. could become involved in affairs in the Pacific and in Latin America.*) Tell students that as they read this unit, they will learn how these and other worldwide events interacted with events in the United States. **L1**

The World

	1875		1890	
Asia and Oceania				**1894** *Sino-Japanese War begins*
Europe	**1870** *Franco-Prussian War begins*			**1893** *New Zealand becomes first nation to grant woman suffrage*
Africa	**1869** *Suez Canal opens*			
South America			**1889** *Brazil becomes a republic*	
North and Central America				

The United States

	1875		1890	
Pacific and Northwest				**1894** *Hawaii becomes a republic*
Southeast	**1881** *Booker T. Washington founds Tuskegee Institute*			
Midwest				
Southwest				
Atlantic Northeast		**1886** *Statue of Liberty dedicated*		

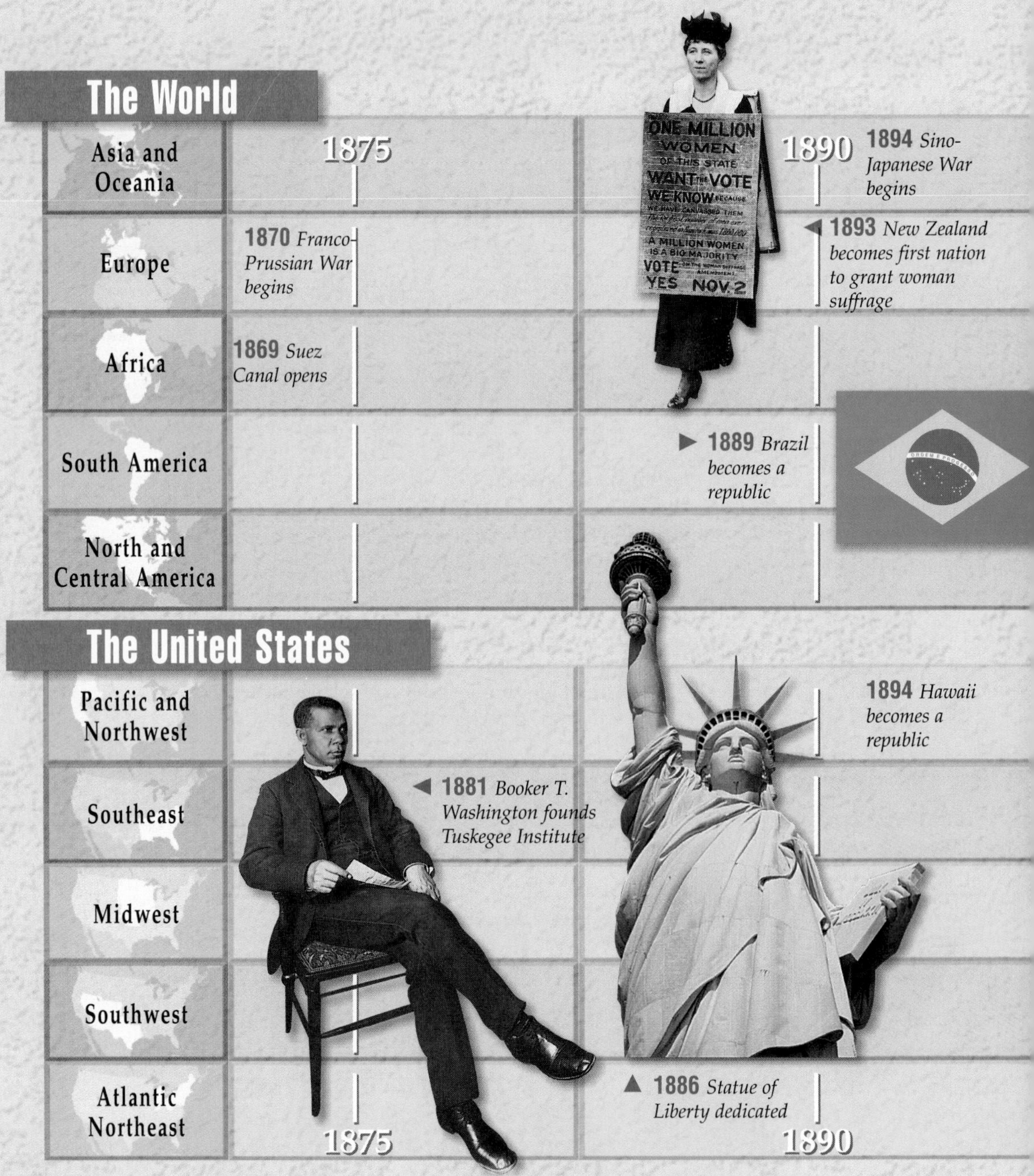

Cultural Perspectives

Adapting to Other Cultures Tell students that the overseas expansion of the United States, which they will read about in this unit, brought the nation into contact with many different groups of people, from the Caribbean and Latin America to East Asia. Many of these people would accept and adapt to ways of life brought by Americans. Americans would also change. They, too, would accept and adapt to the ways of life of the people they encountered.

Linking Across TIME

A trip to the grocery store gives an indication of the Italian influence on American life. Foods like pizza, spaghetti, macaroni, minestrone, parmesan cheese, broccoli, and zucchini are all part of the American diet. However, they were all introduced by the Italian immigrants who came to the United States around the turn of the century.

1905

1920

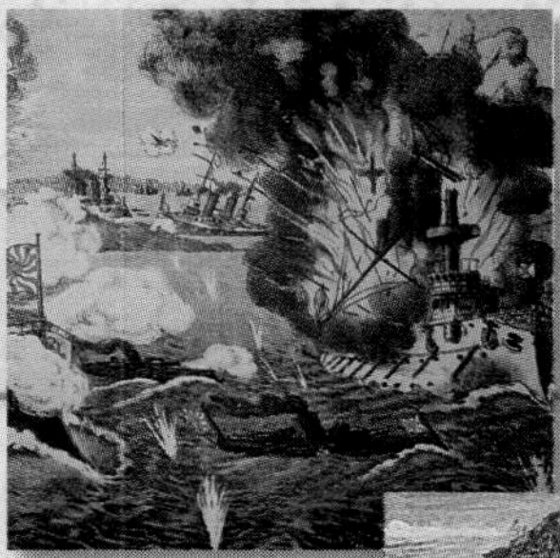

▶ **1904** *Russo-Japanese War begins*

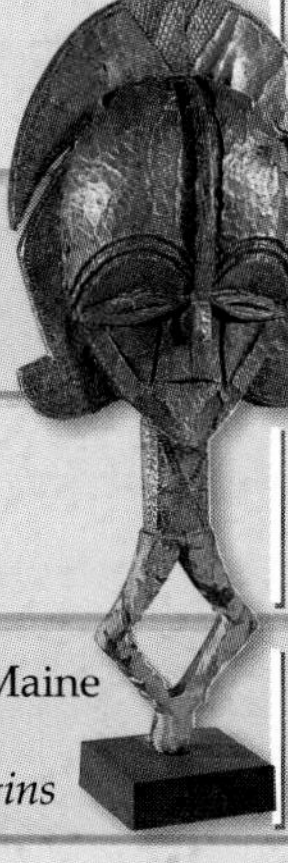

◀ **1908** *Belgium establishes control over the Congo*

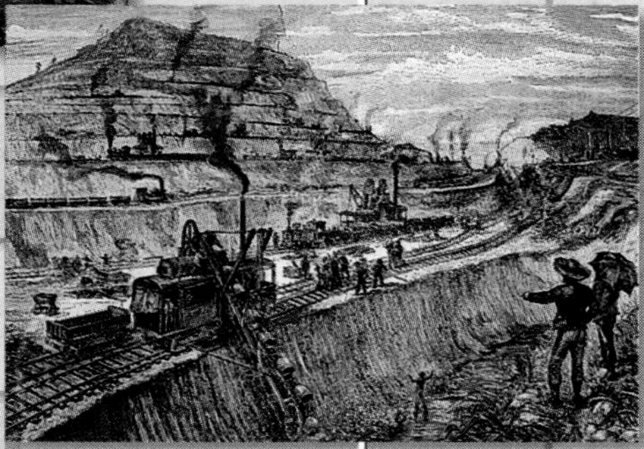

1898 *Battleship* Maine *explodes; Spanish-American War begins*

▲ **1914** *Panama Canal opens*

1898 *Gold discovered at Nome*

▼ **1903** *Wright brothers' first flight*

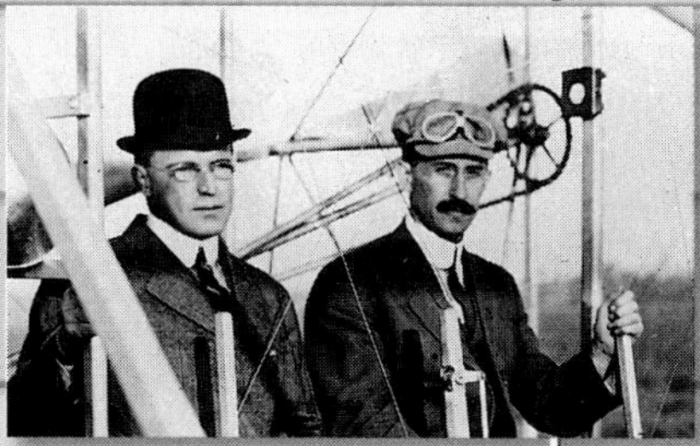

▶ **1908** *Model T Ford produced*

1912 *New Mexico and Arizona become states*

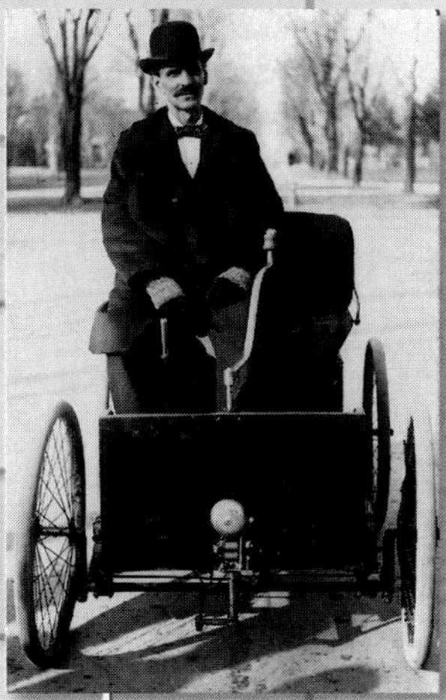

1905

1920

367

Daily Lesson Objectives	Teacher Classroom Resources	Multimedia
SECTION 1 **America Looks Abroad** **1 Day** pp. 370–373 1. Discuss the emergence of the United States from isolationism. 2. Cite two examples of arbitration averting war.	Reproducible Lesson Plan 12-1 Chapter Concept Mapping Activities 12-A, 12-B *Vocabulary Activity 12 *Guided Reading Activity 12-1 Performance Assessment Activity 12 Geography in History Activity 12 Reteaching Activity 12-1 *Section Quiz 12-1	Section Focus Transparency 12-1 Chapter Concepts Transparencies 12-A, 12-B Vocabulary PuzzleMaker Testmaker GTV: A Geographic Perspective on American History MindJogger Videoquiz
SECTION 2 **The Spanish-American War** **1 Day** pp. 375–379 1. List the events that led to the United States's involvement in the Spanish-American War. 2. Explain the reason for the involvement of the Philippines in the war.	Reproducible Lesson Plan 12-2 *Guided Reading Activity 12-2 Critical Thinking Skills Activity 12 Enrichment Activity 12 Workbook Activity 12-2 Reteaching Activity 12-2 *Section Quiz 12-2	Section Focus Transparency 12-2 Testmaker GTV: A Geographic Perspective on American History Focus on Government
SECTION 3 **Becoming a World Power** **1 Day** pp. 380–385 1. Explain why the Philippine Islands were difficult to govern. 2. Discuss the constitutional difficulties involved in colonization.	Reproducible Lesson Plan 12-3 *Guided Reading Activity 12-3 Political Cartoons Activity 12 Linking Past and Present Activity 12 Primary and Secondary Source Readings, pp. 28-30 Chapter Skills Activity 12 Reteaching Activity 12-3 *Section Quiz 12-3	Section Focus Transparency 12-3 Skills Transparency 12 Testmaker Focus on Government
SECTION 4 **A New Arena** **1 Day** pp. 387–391 1. Give examples of Roosevelt's "Big Stick" diplomacy. 2. Discuss the goals and results of the "Open Door" policy in China. 3. Discuss America's concerns over the Russo-Japanese War.	Reproducible Lesson Plan 12-4 *Guided Reading Activity 12-4 Chapter Map Activity 12 Workbook Activity 12-4 Reteaching Activity 12-4 *Section Quiz 12-4	Section Focus Transparency 12-4 Map Transparency 12 Testmaker The Presidents: A Picture History of Our Nation
CHAPTER REVIEW AND EVALUATION **1 Day**	Chapter 12 Test, Forms A and B Spanish Chapter 12 Summary Performance Assessment Activity 12	MindJogger Videoquiz Student Self-Test & Review Software *Chapter 12 Audiocassette Activity & Test

*Also available in Spanish

0:00   **OUT OF TIME?** If time does not permit teaching the entire chapter, use the Chapter 12 Summary on pages 448–449 and the Chapter 12 audiocassette (English and Spanish) to point out the main ideas of the chapter.

A complete, 1-page lesson plan is provided for each section in the *Reproducible Lesson Plan* booklet.

Key to Ability Levels

Teaching strategies have been coded for varying learning styles and abilities.

L1 Basic activities for all students

L2 Average activities for average to above-average students

L3 Challenging activities for above-average students

LEP Limited English Proficiency activities

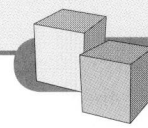

Block Schedule

Block scheduling differs from traditional class scheduling in the amount of time allotted to each period. The extended time frame provided by block scheduling affords you the opportunity to implement a greater number of research-oriented and activity-intense projects to motivate and involve your students. Activities that are particularly suited to use within the block scheduling framework are identified throughout this unit by the following designation:

Performance Assessment Activity

Connecting Past and Present Ask students to draw up a list of territories acquired by the United States in the years between 1865 and 1901. Ask them to locate each on an outline map of the world and then answer the following questions: What is the territory's status today? How does its status today differ from its status in the years between 1854 and 1901? Ask students to choose one territory and research its history since 1900 for a more detailed report on how its status has changed over the years.

POSSIBLE RUBRIC FEATURES

- Content Information
- Main Idea
- Organization Skills
- Map Skills
- Written Communication Skills

For additional activities, see Performance Assessment Strategies and Activities.

TEACHER'S CORNER

NATIONAL GEOGRAPHIC SOCIETY

INDEX TO NATIONAL GEOGRAPHIC MAGAZINE

The following articles may be used for research relating to this chapter:

- "Hawaii's Vanishing Species," by Elizabeth Royte, September 1995.
- "Wrangell-St. Elias: Alaska's Sky-High Wilderness," by Noel Grove, May 1994.
- "Alone Across the Arctic Crown," by Keith Nyitray, April 1993.
- "Kodiak, Alaska's Island Refuge, by John L. Eliot," November 1993.
- "Last Refuge of the Monk Seal, by Diane Ackerman," January 1992.

- "Hard Harvest on the Bering Sea," by Bryan Hodgson, October 1992.
- "Denali, Alaska's Wild Heart," by Douglas H. Chadwick, August 1992.
- "Alaska Highway: Wilderness Escape Route," by Richard Olsenius, November 1991.
- "Hawaii's Volcanic Cradle of Life," by William H. Amos, July 1990.

NATIONAL GEOGRAPHIC SOCIETY PRODUCTS AVAILABLE FROM GLENCOE

To order the following products for use with this chapter, contact your local Glencoe sales representative or call Glencoe at 1-800-334-7344:

- *The Presidents: A Picture History of Our Nation* (CD-ROM)
- *GTV: A Geographic Perspective on American History* (Videodisc)
- *GTV: The American People: Fabric of a Nation* (Videodisc)
- *STV: World Geography* (Videodisc)

- *STV: North America* (Videodisc)
- *Native Americans, Part 2* (CD-ROM)
- *Native Americans: Southwest, Northwest Coast, Arctic* (Transparencies)

ADDITIONAL NATIONAL GEOGRAPHIC SOCIETY PRODUCTS

To order the following products for use with this chapter, call National Geographic Society at 1-800-368-2728:

- *The American Presidency* (Filmstrip)
- *Decades of History: The 20th Century—The Early Years* (Filmstrip)
- *The United States as a World Power: From the 1890s to the 1970s* (Filmstrip)
- *Hawaii: Strangers in Paradise* (Video)

- *Braving Alaska* (Video)
- *Yukon Passage* (Video)
- *Island of the Giant Bears* (Video)

GLENCOE TECHNOLOGY

VIDEODISC

Use the Chapter 12 MindJogger Videoquiz to preview the content of this chapter.

MindJogger Videoquiz

Chapter 12
Disc 2, Side A

 Available in VHS.

Recording Journal Notes

Suggest students divide the countries into two categories: Western Hemisphere and Eastern Hemisphere.

Linking Across
T I M E

Imperialism has been responsible for many conflicts among the nations of the world. Competition among European powers led to World War I. The imperialistic designs of Germany and Japan led to World War II. Throughout history, subjugated people all over the world have rebelled against the rule of outside powers

CHAPTER 12

★★

Imperialism
1867–1908

▼ RED LEATHER BOOTS AND BUTTON HOOK

Setting the Scene

Focus

Foreign policy before the late nineteenth century had been dominated by two ideas. The first was President Washington's isolationist warning against entering into "entangling alliances." The second was President Monroe's warning to Europe against interference in the Americas. War with Spain, however, resulted in a more aggressive foreign policy and the acquisition of overseas colonies. Suddenly, the United States had become a major world power.

Concepts to Understand

★ How increased United States **economic and political power** led to the acquisition of an overseas empire

★ How **confrontation** with Spain resulted in war over Cuba

Read to Discover . . .

★ why Americans moved away from a policy of isolationism.

★ the problems and responsibilities that victory in the Spanish-American War brought the United States.

Journal Notes

Why did the United States become involved in the affairs of other countries? Record each country and the reasons for each as you read this chapter.

CULTURAL	
•**1880** *"General" William Booth organizes the Salvation Army*	•**1891** *University of Chicago founded* •**1893** *World's Columbian Exposition is held in Chicago*

1875	**1885**

POLITICAL	
•**1882** *Chinese Exclusion Act is passed*	•**1893** *Queen Liliuokalani of Hawaii is overthrown*

➕ EXTRA CREDIT PROJECT

Intervention Although United States foreign policy is no longer imperialist, the United States still intervenes in conflicts around the world. Suggest interested students research an example of recent American intervention. Ask them to report their findings, including reasons for the intervention and its outcome. You might conduct a class debate on whether students think the intervention was justified. **L2**

History AND ART
The Return of the Conquerors
by Edward Moran, 1898

Edward Moran painted this work to commemorate the American victory over Spain in the Spanish-American War. In the foreground is Admiral Dewey's flagship *Olympia*.

◀ ADVERTISEMENT FOR CARIBBEAN CRUISE, EARLY 1900S

- **1903** The Great Train Robbery *motion picture produced; first to have a fully developed plot*

- **1910** *Women make up 21 percent of the workforce*

1895	1905

- **1898** *Spanish-American War begins*
- **1899** *Hay initiates Open Door policy*
- **1900** *Boxer Rebellion in China*
- **1904** *Roosevelt Corollary announced*

- **1905** *Roosevelt arbitrates Russo-Japanese War*

CHAPTER 12 Imperialism: 1867–1908   **369**

✔ Performance Assessment

Research A father and a son, Luis Munoz Rivera and Luis Munoz Marin, are key figures in the modern history of Puerto Rico. Have students research the lives of these two men and write a proposal for a public statue, mural, or celebration, showing their contributions to Puerto Rican history. Proposals can describe

events from their lives that might be highlighted in a memorial or celebration. *Famous Puerto Ricans* by Clarke Newlon is a useful reference. **L2** 📁

📁 Use Performance Assessment Activity 12 as an additional assessment technique.

FOCUS

Bellringer

Before taking roll, project Section Focus Transparency 12-1 or hand out Section Focus Transparency Activity 12-1. Have students answer the questions.

Motivating Activity

Ask students to name the President who stated that the independent nations of the Americas were "henceforth not to be considered as subjects for further colonization by any European powers." (Monroe, in what became known as the Monroe Doctrine) **L1**

Vocabulary Precheck

Write the "Key Terms" for this section on the chalkboard. Ask students to use those that they know in sentences. **L1, LEP**

Use the Vocabulary PuzzleMaker Software to create a crossword puzzle. **L1**

Assign Vocabulary Activity 12.

SECTION 1

★★

America Looks Abroad

Setting the Scene

Section Focus

Beginning in the 1500s, European nations built vast colonial empires. By the mid-1800s, many of these colonies had become independent. The Industrial Revolution caused new empire building. Germany, France, Belgium, Portugal, and Japan joined the race for colonies. The United States had grown entirely by expansion. Would the race for empire tempt a once-colonial people to seek colonies?

Objectives

After studying this section, you should be able to

★ discuss the emergence of the United States from isolationism.

★ cite two examples of arbitration averting war.

Key Terms

imperialism, isolationism, reciprocity, arbitration

◀ QUEEN LILIUOKALANI OF HAWAII

*E*uropean colonialism was motivated by trade and adventure, power and profit, idealism and national patriotism. These nations also believed they had a "civilizing mission" toward nonwhite populations. The Industrial Revolution generated a need for markets for manufactured goods and new sources of raw materials. **Imperialism**—the policy of establishing colonies and building empires—answered these needs.

Isolationism, or separation from the political affairs of other countries, was a policy established by George Washington. In his Farewell Address, he warned against entangling alliances. Later the Monroe Doctrine emphasized the United States's desire to keep the Americas separate from Europe. Another factor affecting American foreign policy was the Declaration of Independence—the idea that people had the right to govern themselves.

■ Securing an American Continent

European control of parts of North America by France and Russia ended in the 1860s. The United States challenged a French expansion effort in 1861 and bought Russian territory in 1867.

End of French Expansion

Mexico's reform government under Benito Juárez (HWAHR•uhs) stopped payment of its foreign debts. French, Spanish, and British troops entered the country to force payment. The debts were collected and Spain and Britain left, but the French remained and quickly occupied Mexico City. Ignoring the Monroe Doctrine and taking advantage of the American Civil War, the French emperor Napoleon III overthrew

---

 **Visualizing History**

▲ MINING GOLD IN THE YUKON Many settlers and prospectors came to Alaska after gold was discovered in the region in the late 1800s. *Why did Russia decide to sell Alaska to the United States?*

the Republic of Mexico. In 1864 Napoleon III installed Austrian prince Maximilian as Mexico's emperor.

The United States protested and, after the Civil War, sent nearly 50,000 troops to the border at the Rio Grande. Napoleon's forces withdrew. The Mexicans promptly defeated Maximilian's army and executed Maximilian. The United States proved its willingness to back the Monroe Doctrine with force.

Acquisition of Alaska

Secretary of State William H. Seward believed in Manifest Destiny. He envisioned a great empire and wanted to annex Canada, Hawaii, and several Caribbean islands.

. . . .

Footnotes to History

North to Alaska In August 1896 news spread across the nation that gold had been discovered in the Canadian Yukon Territory, sparking one of the great gold rushes in United States history. Despite the distance and dangers, an estimated 100,000 Americans set out for the Klondike over the next two years. Exploration prompted new discoveries, capped by the gold strike along the beach at Nome. Excavation along the dozen miles along the shore of the Bering Sea yielded the richest tidewater diggings in history.

Seward's only major achievement along this line was the purchase of Alaska in 1867. The undeveloped territory of Alaska, twice the size of Texas, was held by Russia, but the czar saw little value in the territory.

In 1867, when the Russian minister to the United States informed Seward that the czar wanted to sell Alaska, the secretary of state jumped at the chance. In a few hours, Seward arranged a treaty in which the United States would buy Alaska for $7.2 million—less than two cents an acre. After four months of selling the idea to Congress, the transaction was completed.

■ Empire Building

At one time the United States had little need to look beyond its own borders for growth. Raw materials were abundant, and the home market was immense. By the 1890s, the country had developed into a great industrial nation, able to compete with European producers.

Reciprocity

James G. Blaine, secretary of state under Presidents Garfield and Harrison, wanted to open up new markets not by taking on colonies, but by increasing American trade

Linking Across TIME

Hawaii's strategic position made the islands highly attractive to the United States. The U.S. government eventually turned its coaling stop at Pearl Harbor into a naval base that proved invaluable in World War II. Attacked by the Japanese on December 7, 1941, the base sustained crippling casualties. The base not only was rebuilt but also became the center of the victorious Pacific campaign.

Visualizing History **Alaska** Miners found vast reserves of copper in the Copper River area. Other newcomers developed Alaska's fishing industry by building canneries.
Answer to Caption: to protect trade and growing number of Americans living in Hawaii

▲ ANCHORAGE, ALASKA

Visualizing History ▲ ALASKA The wealth of resources found in this scenic state proved Alaska's worth, even though its purchase was originally called Seward's Folly. **Why did some Americans call for the annexation of Hawaii?**

through **reciprocity**—the mutual lowering of tariff barriers. He tried, without much success, to include reciprocity provisions in the McKinley Tariff of 1890. He was able to chair a Pan-American Congress in Washington, D.C., in 1889. The goal of the group, which later became the Pan-American Union, was to promote economic cooperation and trade among the Americas. Success was limited, however, because the United States intervened, often forcibly, in Latin American affairs.

Should Hawaii Be Annexed?

American missionaries and traders first ventured to Hawaii in the early 1800s. American sugar growers followed. By the 1890s Hawaii was closely connected to the United States through commerce and the many Americans living there.

While many nationalities lived in Hawaii, native Hawaiian rulers were controlled by the American business community until the Hawaiian Queen Liliuokalani (lih•LEE• uh•woh•kuh•LAH•nee) came into power in 1891. She was determined to return control to her own people. In response, some American business leaders, with the help of marines from the cruiser *Boston*, took over the government.

The American minister to Hawaii wrote the Department of State that Hawaii was ready to annex. President Cleveland dis-

agreed. He decided that the use of American troops to overthrow the Hawaiian government was a violation of "national honesty." Despite criticism, Cleveland withdrew American soldiers from Hawaii. He also tried, but failed, to oust the revolutionary provisional government and put Liliuokalani back on her throne.

■ Challenging Great Britain

After the Civil War, the United States appeared ready to take a position among the powers of the world. Twice the United States forced Britain to submit to **arbitration,** or the settlement of a dispute by an impartial group.

Civil War Damages

In 1868 Charles Sumner, head of the Senate Foreign Relations Committee, claimed that Great Britain owed the United States more than $2 billion in damages for allowing Confederate ships to use British ports during the Civil War. If the British would not pay, Senator Sumner declared, the United States should take British-controlled Canada.

In 1871 Secretary of State Hamilton Fish arranged for arbitration. Britain did not want to risk war in Canada and feared that a hostile United States might supply Britain's enemies with warships. The United States backed down on its demand for "indirect"

Sidelight: United States Economic Expansion

The late 1800s witnessed a tremendous surge in American agricultural and industrial production. Between 1870 and 1892, for example, the United States increased its gross national product (GNP) from approximately $7.4 billion per year to $14.3 billion per year. The rapid growth in production led, in turn, to increased foreign trade since American markets could not absorb the large quantities of agricultural and manufactured goods that were produced. Between 1870 and 1892, the value of American exports rose from $451 million to $1.1 billion.

damages. In the Treaty of Washington, the United States was awarded $15.5 million, which Britain paid.

Venezuela Border Dispute

President Cleveland requested that the British put a long-standing Venezuela–British Guiana boundary dispute to arbitration. In July 1895 Secretary of State Richard Olney wrote the British government that their refusal to arbitrate violated the Monroe Doctrine. He warned:

> **The United States is practically sovereign on this continent and its fiat is law upon the subjects to which it confines its interposition.**

Britain answered that the Monroe Doctrine had no standing in international law and did not apply to the situation.

Aware of the possibility of war, President Cleveland asked Congress for authorization to appoint a commission to determine the boundary without consulting Britain. Americans responded with excitement, but Britain thought it "monstrous and insulting." For a few days, war seemed a strong possibility.

Fortunately, the British government backed down. Early in January 1896, Britain's attention was diverted from Venezuela by a dispute with Germany involving South Africa. Seeking to improve relations with the United States, Britain agreed to arbitration.

The boundary settlement turned out in Britain's favor and a new era of Anglo-American understanding emerged.

■ Strengthening the Navy

The Venezuelan crisis called attention to the fact that the United States had only three modern battleships. The crisis also popularized the writings of American naval officer Alfred T. Mahan. Mahan believed that as America developed its industry, the nation should look outward. Great nations of the past had built up foreign markets, expanded their merchant fleets, constructed navies to protect their commerce, and planted colonies. Mahan argued that a modern nation needed sea power in order to become great.

At first Mahan had more influence abroad. Kaiser (Emperor) Wilhelm II of Germany studied his books and instructed German naval officers to read them. In Great Britain Mahan was showered with honors. Mahan influenced rising American leaders such as Senator Henry Cabot Lodge and Theodore Roosevelt and helped to shape United States naval policy.

Congress established a Naval Advisory Board in 1881 that pressed for larger naval appropriations. In 1883 Congress authorized construction of 1 more cruiser and 3 battleships. By adding 3 heavier and more powerful ships in 1890 and by voting for 13 new ships in 1895, Congress made it clear that it intended to have a navy capable of matching any enemy on the high seas.

Section 1 ★ Review

Checking for Understanding

1. **Identify** Maximilian, William Seward, Queen Liliuokalani, Charles Sumner.
2. **Define** imperialism, isolationism, reciprocity, arbitration.
3. **Show** how the French challenged the Monroe Doctrine in 1861.
4. **Describe** two instances of confrontation with Great Britain that were settled by arbitration.

Critical Thinking

5. **Understanding Cause and Effect** How did the writings of Captain Alfred T. Mahan lead to expanding the American navy?

ACTIVITY

6. Construct a time line that shows American involvement in Mexico, Alaska, Hawaii, and Venezuela during this era.

ASSESS
Check Understanding
Assign Section 1 Review as homework or an in-class activity.

Evaluate
🔘 🗂 Assign Section Quiz 12-1 or use the Test-maker to create a customized quiz.

Reteach
🗂 Have students complete Reteaching Activity 12-1.

Enrich
🗂 Assign Geography in History Activity 12.

🗂 Assign Cooperative Learning Activity 12.

CLOSE
Have students identify the foreign affairs discussed in Section 1 that were settled based on a policy of isolationism and the foreign affairs that were settled based on a policy of imperialism.

Answers to SECTION 1 REVIEW

1. Maximilian, 371; William Seward, 371; Queen Liliuokalani, 372; Charles Sumner, 372
2. All vocabulary words are defined in the Glossary.
3. French troops invaded Mexico with Spain and Britain to collect debts. Spain and Britain left. France occupied Mexico City and installed Maximilian emperor.
4. a. In 1868 U.S. government claimed $2 million damages for British aid to Confederacy. If Britain refused to pay, U.S. threatened to take control of Canada. Britain negotiated and paid $1.5 million. b. President Cleveland asked Britain to put boundary dispute between Venezuela and British Guiana to arbitration. Britain backed down.
5. showed that a nation needed a strong navy to be great
6. Time lines should include major events.

TEACH

Point out to students that the United States today maintains naval and air bases throughout the world. Discuss with students the advantages and disadvantages of operating bases in distant lands. Ask them if they think it is necessary for the United States to maintain bases in far-flung places. Why or why not? **L1**

Did You Know?

Until the last decade of the nineteenth century, the United States had no battleships. In 1890 Congress authorized the construction of the first three: the *Oregon,* the *Indiana,* and the *Massachusetts.* Each was more than 10,000 tons and bristled with guns.

FACT or FICTION?

Proposals to admit Hawaii as a state began as early as the 1850s.

FACT: In 1854 the U.S. government negotiated a treaty of annexation with the kingdom of Hawaii. It was rejected by the Senate, however, because it contained a provision for immediate statehood. Hawaii did not enter the Union until more than 150 years later when in 1959 it became the fiftieth state.

History AND SCIENCE

GEOGRAPHY   ECONOMICS   **SCIENCE**   MATH   THE ARTS

Coaling Stations and Colonies

By the end of the 1800s, Americans began to think in terms of a different and broader Manifest Destiny. The original concept was changed to include overseas as well as westward expansion. The idea that it was the fate of the United States to extend its boundaries beyond the seas has been called the new Manifest Destiny.

The change in attitude toward foreign affairs was due to certain ideas and developments that occurred in the late 1800s. One such development was imperialism. Nations began to establish empires around the globe to build important new sources of raw materials and provide new avenues for investment.

More justification for imperialism was provided by Captain Alfred Thayer Mahan. Mahan believed that for a country to become a major sea power, its ships needed remote sources of supplies that could not be carried for an entire voyage. While commercial shipping required these supply stations, an armed navy needed them even more. The supplies, according to Mahan, were "first, fuel; second, ammunition; last of all, food."

Fuel became essential to shipping as nations switched from sail to steam power at the turn of the century. No ship could steam away from its home port for any great distance without refueling. A fleet that wanted to trade or fight very far beyond its home waters needed coaling stations in distant lands.

Mahan did not favor unchecked expansionism. Too many supply and fueling bases in foreign lands, he warned, could drain the resources

▲ U.S.S. *IOWA,* C. 1900

of the parent country and could become "a source of weakness, multiplying exposed points, and entailing division of force."

The United States had made some strides earlier in the century. One of these was the development of ironclad ships during the Civil War. However, after the war, the United States allowed its navy to deteriorate.

Mahan's ideas provided a real impetus for change. Influenced by Mahan's concepts, Congress passed the Naval Act of 1890, which appropriated additional money for battleships. By 1900 the United States had the naval power it needed to back up an expanded role in foreign affairs.

Making the Science Connection

1. What supplies did coaling stations provide?

2. How did new technology influence American foreign policy?

3. What was the danger of having too many supply and fueling bases?

ACTIVITY

4. Create a poster that displays examples of twentieth-century technology that have benefited trade and transportation.

Answers to Making the Connections

1. Coaling stations provided fuel, ammunition, and food.

2. The switch to steam-powered ships made it important for the U.S. to have bases for refueling in different lands.

3. They could drain the resources of the parent country.

4. Student posters should display creativity and initiative.

★★★

The Spanish-American War

Setting the Scene

Section Focus

Struggling for freedom under Spanish rule for years, Cubans had gained only greater repression. When a new revolution took place in 1895, Americans were moved by two impulses to intervene. Many urged American support for the repressed Cuban people, while others saw the revolt as an opportunity to expand the American empire.

Objectives

After studying this section, you should be able to

★ list the events that led to the United States's involvement in the Spanish-American War.

★ explain the reason for the involvement of the Philippines in the war.

Key Term

neutrality

◀ TIN TRAY WITH LIKENESS OF THEODORE ROOSEVELT

Americans were outraged when they found that the Spanish Governor-General Valeriano Weyler had ordered Cuban men, women, and children into "reconcentration camps." Weyler, unable to tell civilians from rebels, had set up the camps where 200,000 Cubans, an estimated one-eighth of the population, died of illness and starvation. Some leaders of the Cuban independence movement were naturalized American citizens who had returned to work in Cuba. When captured by Spanish authorities, they demanded protection by the United States.

Not all sentiment supported the Cubans, however. American business interests had invested more than $30 million in Cuba—mostly in sugar plantations—and wanted the revolt to end. Some plantation owners, doubting the capacity of the Cubans for self-government, favored the restoration of Spanish rule. The force of public opinion, however, caused many in the business community to change their minds.

■ Drawn Into War

Although President Cleveland preserved strict **neutrality**, or the refusal to take sides, in the Cuban struggle, he warned that if "the useless sacrifice of human life" went on, the United States might have to abandon the policy of "patient waiting." President McKinley, who came into office in the middle of the conflict, was also committed to neutrality. He even offered to buy Cuba, but was rejected. A peaceful solution seemed possible when Spain recalled General Weyler and offered Cuba a measure of local self-government. Assistant Secretary of the Navy Theodore Roosevelt was impatient

CHAPTER 12 Imperialism: 1867–1908   **375**

LESSON PLAN
SECTION 2, 375–379

FOCUS
Bellringer

Before taking roll, project Section Focus Transparency 12-2 or hand out Section Focus Transparency Activity 12-2. Have students answer the questions.

Motivating Activity

Ask students to name some slogans that are used today to promote various causes. ("Just say no." "Only you can prevent forest fires.") Discuss the pros and cons of using a rallying cry to get one's ideas across. Tell students that in Section 2 they will learn how a famous slogan helped propel the United States into war. **L2**

Vocabulary Precheck

Ask students to define each of the "Key Terms." Have a volunteer consult the dictionary for any unfamiliar words. **L1, LEP**

 VIDEODISC

GTV: A Geographic Perspective on American History

Any side, Frame 53459
Subject: Picture of *Maine* exploding at Havana, Cuba

Classroom Resources for SECTION 2

Blackline Masters:
- Reproducible Lesson Plan 12-2
- Guided Reading Activity 12-2
- Critical Thinking Skills Activity 12
- Enrichment Activity 12
- Workbook Activity 12-2
- Reteaching Activity 12-2
- Section Quiz 12-2

Transparencies:
- Section Focus Transparency 12-2

Multimedia:
- Testmaker
- GTV: A Geographic Perspective on American History
- Focus on Government

TEACH

Guided Practice

Evaluating Have students list developments leading up to the Spanish-American War. Then ask them to evaluate these developments and tell which they think were the most important to the United States's declaration of war. **L2**

Visualizing History Coverage of the *Maine* explosion raised American anger against Spain. President McKinley was trying to resolve American differences with Spain through diplomacy when the explosion occurred. It ended all hope of a negotiated settlement. **Answer to Caption:** No one knows. Each side blamed the other.

Did You Know?

William Randolph Hearst sent artist Frederic Remington to Cuba to cover events after the explosion on the *Maine*. When the expected conflict between the United States and Spain did not immediately materialize, the artist asked if he should return home. Hearst cabled back, "You furnish the pictures, I'll furnish the war."

Visualizing History ▲ THE *MAINE* Coverage of sinking of the *Maine* raised American anger against Spain. *Who was responsible for sinking the ship?*

with McKinley's negotiation with Spain and described the President as having "no more backbone than a chocolate eclair." William Randolph Hearst's *New York Journal* and Joseph Pulitzer's *New York World* fanned public anger with exaggerated and sometimes fabricated stories of Spanish atrocities in Cuba. This "yellow journalism" helped sell papers and encouraged war:

> **❝** How long are the Spaniards to drench Cuba with the blood and tears of her people? . . . How long shall old men and women and children be murdered by the score, the innocent victims of Spanish rage against the patriot armies they cannot conquer?
> . . . How long shall the United States sit idle and indifferent? **❞**

"Remember the *Maine!*"

Public sentiment in favor of war was growing when, on February 9, 1898, the *Journal* printed a private letter written by Enrique Dupuy de Lôme, the Spanish ambassador to the United States, in which he called McKinley "weak and a bidder for the admiration of the crowd. . . . " This comment was a national insult. The ambassador resigned, but the damage to United States–Spanish relations was done.

Six days later the United States battleship *Maine*, anchored off the Cuban capital, Havana, exploded, killing 260 crew members. United States naval experts declared that the explosion came from outside the ship. Spanish experts replied that there were no mines.

The "yellow press" in 1898 expressed no indecision. Papers promptly blamed Spain and even printed diagrams showing just how the deed was done. "Remember the *Maine!*" became the battle cry throughout the United States.

Preparing for War

Congress responded to a torrent of public indignation against Spain by allocating $50 million for war preparations. McKinley, meanwhile, demanded that Spain give Cuba independence. Although at the last moment Spain claimed it was trying to comply, McKinley nevertheless delivered a warlike message to Congress. Congress demanded that Spain evacuate the island. When no reply to this ultimatum was received, Congress declared war on April 25.

While expansionists were excited about the prospects of gaining Cuba, humanitarian forces in Congress attached the Teller Amendment to the declaration of war. In it Congress pledged "to leave the government and control of the Island to the people" as soon as peace was established there.

Special Needs Activity

Summarizing Problems Summarizing requires students to choose key ideas or events and state them in a concise way. Important events and reactions to these events are related in the subsection "Remember the *Maine*." Ask students to pick one of these key events and draw it. *(Most students will choose the explosion on the battleship* Maine*.)* Then have them write a sentence that explains one event that preceded the event they drew and one event that came after it. Label the sequence 1, 2, and 3. Explain that they have summarized a section of text. **L1, LEP**

◼ "A Splendid Little War"

While the army prepared to invade Cuba, the conflict, called by Secretary of State John Hay a "splendid little war," began in the Pacific. Although the McKinley administration had no thought of expanding the territories of the United States, some officials believed that this was a prime opportunity to do so. One such person was Theodore Roosevelt.

The Philippine Connection

When John D. Long, secretary of the navy, was out of his Washington office, Roosevelt took charge. On February 25, 1898, he ordered on his own authority a Pacific squadron stationed in Hong Kong to sail for the Philippine Islands, a Spanish colony for 300 years, if war broke out. Commodore George Dewey, commander of the United States fleet, would try to prevent a Spanish fleet in Manila Bay from going to sea. As soon as war was declared, Dewey's fleet set sail; it penetrated Manila Bay on May 1 and rapidly destroyed the weaker Spanish fleet. The quick victory surprised the President, and an army of occupation was hastily organized to sail from San Francisco to the Philippines.

A native Filipino, Emilio Aguinaldo (AH•gee•NAHL•doh), had led an uprising against Spanish rule of the Philippines in 1896. Aguinaldo was exiled in Hong Kong, where Dewey met him and provided supplies so he could lead a revolt against the Spanish forces that remained in the islands. By the time the American army arrived in the

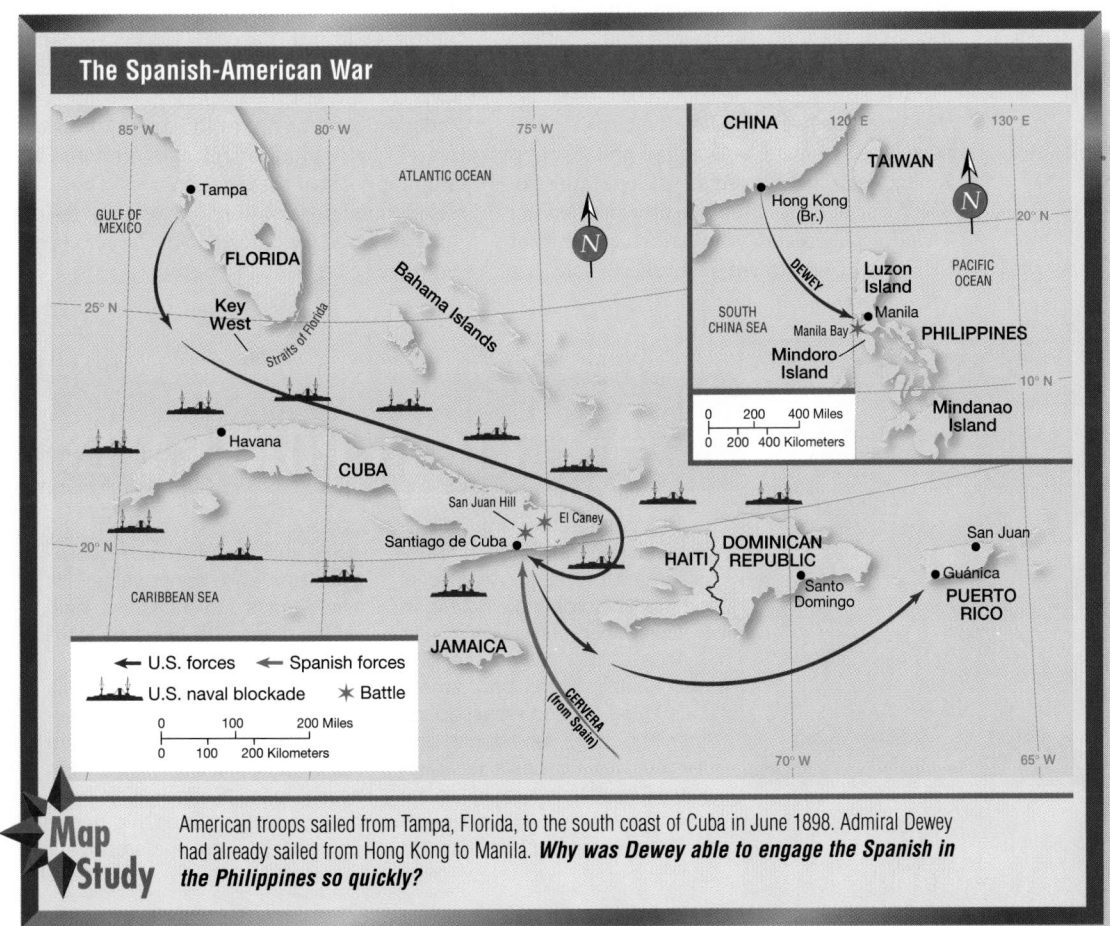

The Spanish-American War

American troops sailed from Tampa, Florida, to the south coast of Cuba in June 1898. Admiral Dewey had already sailed from Hong Kong to Manila. **Why was Dewey able to engage the Spanish in the Philippines so quickly?**

Map Study

Independent Practice

Writing Have students write a feature article for a newspaper about the causes of the Spanish-American War from the point of view of a wife of a crew member of the *Maine*. **L3**

Map Study *Using Maps*

Answer Roosevelt had given orders for him to sail there as soon as war was declared.

Map Skills Practice

Have students study the map and compare the strategy in Cuba with that in the Philippines. *(Students should point out the blockade around Cuba and fighting on land. Dewey sailed into Manila Bay in the Philippines and captured it.)*

GLENCOE TECHNOLOGY

VIDEODISC

Focus on Government

Side 3, Chapter 41
Title: *Foreign Policy and National Defense*
Subject: World affair

Critical Thinking Activity

Making Judgments Ask students to list reasons why a nation might be justified in declaring war on another nation. Have students incorporate their reasons into a paragraph that applies them to the United States declaration of war on Spain in 1898. Invite volunteers to share their papers with the class and discuss why these reasons are justifiable. **L2**

📁 For additional practice in using critical thinking skills, assign Critical Thinking Skills Activity 12.

Teaching
American Portraits

Joseph Pulitzer established the Graduate School of Journalism at Columbia University with a million dollar gift and left another million dollars to the school at his death. He endowed a special fund for the Pulitzer Prizes—16 awards given each year for outstanding accomplishments in journalism, literature, music, and art. Ask students why a newspaper publisher would be interested in giving these awards. *(to encourage writers and artists)* **L1**

Linking Across TIME

The Tenth Cavalry was one of four African American units to serve in Cuba. Although African Americans have fought in every war, and although their courage in Cuba was highly praised, African American soldiers were not considered equals. It was not until 1954 that the army finally abolished segregated units. Until 1941 fewer than 1 percent of African Americans were promoted to officer rank. In 1940 Benjamin O. Davis broke a military race barrier to become the first African American brigadier general.

Philippines, Aguinaldo's forces controlled all the territory except the city of Manila. When the Spanish surrendered and turned the Philippines over to the United States Army, it left unanswered the question of who would rule the islands after the war.

Fighting in Cuba

When war was first declared, McKinley had called for 200,000 volunteers to supplement the regular army, which numbered only 28,000. The War Department was inefficient. Nevertheless, 17,000 troops were declared ready to sail from Tampa, Florida, to Cuba by the middle of June. To fight a war in the tropics, they were issued heavy woolen uniforms left over from the western wars against the Plains peoples. Their ammunition was out-of-date; there were almost no medical supplies; and rations included inedible meat that the soldiers nicknamed "embalmed beef."

After landing on the south coast of Cuba, the Americans advanced on the city of Santiago. One regiment was called the "Rough Riders"—an assortment of college athletes, cowboys, miners, and law officers—led by Theodore Roosevelt, who had resigned from the Navy Department in order to join the

fight. On foot because their horses were still in Florida, they charged up San Juan Hill. By securing the heights overlooking Santiago, they helped capture the city.

The Rough Riders were not alone in this attack. Among the other regiments was the all-black 10th Cavalry Regiment. Many African Americans had responded to the call for soldiers both because they identified with the Cubans' struggle for freedom and because they hoped it would improve their own lot. At least four of these African American soldiers were awarded the Congressional Medal of Honor.

Naval Encounters

At the outbreak of hostilities, an American squadron of new battleships under Admiral William T. Sampson was given the task of intercepting a Spanish squadron under Admiral Pascual Cervera (pahs•KWAHL suhr•VEHR•uh). Knowing that Cervera had left the Cape Verde Islands off the west coast of Africa in April, Americans feared he would attack the undefended Atlantic coast of the United States. They canceled hotel reservations at seaside resorts and prepared for defense, but Cervera headed directly for Santiago harbor.

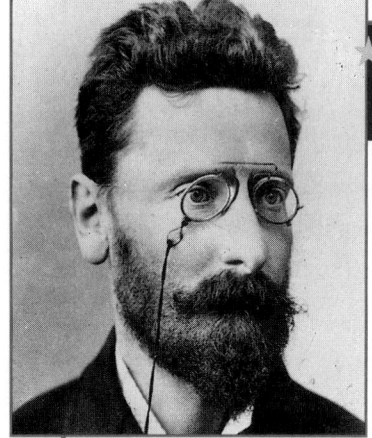

AMERICAN PORTRAITS

After emigrating from Hungary, Joseph Pulitzer made publishing history—and a personal fortune—by creating a new form of newspaper journalism.

As a soldier during the Civil War, Pulitzer noted how Americans loved to read newspapers. After the war, he bought and merged two St. Louis newspapers. Circulation soared as he filled his paper with scandals and attacks on big business. He later bought two New York papers, bringing to them the same successful recipe—sensationalism and controversy. He won a mass audience by running comic strips and covering fashions and sports.

After retiring, he saw his papers engage in "yellow journalism" to compete with William Randolph Hearst's flag-waving newspapers. Pulitzer took back control and returned his newspapers to their flamboyant investigative style.

Joseph Pulitzer
1847–1911

Sidelight: Economics and War With Cuba

By the mid-1890s, tension between Spain and Cuba increased in part because of the Wilson-Gorman Tariff, which the U.S. Congress passed in 1894. This tariff imposed heavy duties on Cuba's major export and economic base—sugar. Before the new tariff, the United States had been the chief market for Cuban sugar.

Because these new duties raised the price of Cuban sugar to prohibitive levels, the sale of Cuban sugar in the United States fell sharply. Decreased sugar sales brought a severe depression to Cuba, which led to discontent and revolts.

Visualizing History ▲ MANILA BAY United States naval ships in the Pacific, under Commodore George Dewey, sailed into Manila Bay on May 1, 1898. *When did Spain and the United States agree to an armistice?*

Sampson's superior force found the Spanish fleet at Santiago and blockaded the harbor. Once the American army took the heights overlooking Santiago, Cervera could surrender or try to break the blockade. On July 3, with little hope of victory, Cervera ordered his ships out of Santiago harbor. In the ensuing battle, all Spanish vessels were sunk. Only one American was killed and one was wounded. Effective Spanish resistance in Cuba ceased with the surrender of Santiago two weeks later. American troops went on to occupy another Spanish possession, the island of Puerto Rico. On August 12 Spain and the United States agreed to an armistice.

The "splendid little war" cost 5,000 American lives, mostly due to disease and food poisoning. The flag of the United States, an emerging world power, flew over distant islands. Had American isolationism ended?

Section 2 ★ Review

Checking for Understanding

1. **Identify** William Randolph Hearst, Joseph Pulitzer, Enrique Dupuy de Lôme, the *Maine,* Theodore Roosevelt, Rough Riders.

2. **Define** neutrality.

3. **List** the key events leading to war with Spain over Cuba.

4. **State** the importance of the naval battle between Sampson and Cervera.

Critical Thinking

5. **Making Judgments** How did the United States justify going to war with Spain given a previous policy of noninvolvement?

ACTIVITY

6. Create a table that compares the Spanish-American War and the Civil War. Include comparisons of length of war, methods of fighting, and battle sites.

379

FOCUS

Bellringer

Before taking roll, project Section Focus Transparency 12-3 or hand out Section Focus Transparency Activity 12-3. Have students answer the questions.

Motivating Activity

Direct students to the two statements on pages 381 and 382, one by President William McKinley and the other by Andrew Carnegie. Ask them to interpret each statement. *(McKinley believed Filipino people were basically inferior to whites; Carnegie was deploring how such an attitude led to violence and the death of Filipinos.)* Tell students that Section 3 traces the conflict between the United States's colonial policies and its commitment to democratic government. **L2**

Vocabulary Precheck

Write "protectorate" on the chalkboard. Ask students to use the term in a sentence. **L1, LEP**

★★

Becoming a World Power

Setting the Scene

Section Focus

After the Spanish-American War the United States was confronted by a host of questions and responsibilities. Congress debated what to do about the Philippine Islands. Commercial and industrial interests argued for annexation, but how could colonialism be reconciled with the principles of the Declaration of Independence?

Objectives

After studying this section, you should be able to

★ explain why the Philippine Islands were difficult to govern.

★ discuss the constitutional difficulties involved in colonization.

Key Term

protectorate

◀ MILITARY RECRUITMENT POSTER

The Spanish-American War and the prospect of expanding in the Pacific brought a change of policy toward the Hawaiian Islands. Cleveland had resisted a move to annex them in 1893, and in 1897 the Senate had turned down an annexation treaty presented by McKinley. Hawaii, the halfway point between California and the Philippines, would be valuable as a naval base, however. In July 1898, before the war ended, the Hawaiian Islands were annexed by a joint resolution of Congress.

■ The Philippines

The armistice left Americans in control of the Spanish-owned Philippine Islands. The debate over whether to acquire and annex the Philippines was a stormy one.

Arguments For and Against Annexing the Philippines

Before entering the Spanish-American War, most Americans had no idea of annexing territory, particularly a territory 6,000 miles from the Pacific coast. McKinley confessed that before Dewey's victory he could not have come within 2,000 miles of placing the Philippine Islands on a map. Once he said, "If old Dewey had just sailed away when he smashed that Spanish fleet, what a lot of strong feelings he would have saved us."

Strong feelings developed against acquiring the islands. Several leading Democrats, including former President Grover Cleveland, were opposed. Many influential private citizens agreed with them. Prominent Republicans such as Speaker of the House Thomas B. Reed and several senators fought annexation as a violation of American tradition.

380   UNIT 4 Entering a New Century: 1867-1920

Classroom Resources for SECTION 3

Blackline Masters:
- Reproducible Lesson Plan 12-3
- Guided Reading Activity 12-3
- Political Cartoons Activity 12
- Linking Past and Present Activity 12
- Primary and Secondary Source Readings, pp. 28-30
- Chapter Skills Activity 12
- Reteaching Activity 12-3

- Section Quiz 12-3

Transparencies:
- Section Focus Transparency 12-3
- Skills Transparency 12

Multimedia:
- Testmaker
- Focus on Government

Senator Henry Cabot Lodge spoke for those who wanted a larger American role in world affairs. Business interests thought of new markets and fields of investment. Public opinion was excited by the prospect of acquiring an empire. Patriotism merged with belief in social Darwinism, or the belief in the "survival of the fittest." If the United States was the most fit to govern the Philippines, why should it haul down the Stars and Stripes and allow Japan or Germany or some other power to step in and take them?

For others, like Reverend Josiah Strong, there was a sense of mission based on racial and religious bias. Strong, in his book *Our Country,* blended social Darwinism with his interest in spreading Christianity. He felt the nationality groups were in a competition from which Anglo-Saxons were destined to emerge victorious.

Settlement With Spain

McKinley, a deeply religious man, wrestled with the problem, then reported that through prayer he had decided to:

> " . . . [E]ducate the Filipinos, and uplift and civilize and Christianize them, and by God's grace, do the very best we could by them, as our fellow men for whom Christ died. "

Actually, Catholic missions had been started in the Philippines in the 1500s. McKinley instructed his peace commissioners to ask for all of the Philippine Islands. When Spain resisted, the United States offered to pay $20 million for them. In the treaty, signed December 10, 1898, Spain gave up control over Cuba and surrendered Puerto Rico, the Pacific island of Guam, and the Philippine Islands. Anti-imperialist feeling in the Senate was so strong that the treaty was ratified by only a two-vote margin. A Senate resolution promising eventual independence to the Filipino people was defeated only by the tie-breaking vote of the Vice President.

The United States encountered problems in trying to govern the Philippines. The

▲ THE BIG STICK To many people around the world, the United States in the late 1800s and early 1900s used its power to spread its influence. *Why did the United States encounter difficult problems in trying to govern the Philippines?*

Critical Thinking Activity

Analyzing a Point of View Pose the following question to students: What problems arise when we view our own culture as so superior to others that we refuse to accept new ideas from another culture? Ask students to write their analysis in the form of a letter to the editor. Have students share their letters with the class. **L2**

TEACH
Guided Practice
Distinguishing Fact from Opinion Provide students with the following exercise:

Read each statement. Write *F* if the statement is a fact or *O* if it is an opinion.

_(O)_ 1. Americans were greatly excited by the idea of acquiring an empire.

_(F)_ 2. Cleveland had fought a move to annex the Hawaiian Islands in 1893.

_(F)_ 3. In 1917 Puerto Rico was granted territorial status.

_(O)_ 4. The U.S. government had no right to spill the blood of Americans to suppress Filipino patriots.

Have students discuss their choices and tell which clue words they used to determine opinion statements. **L1**

Visualizing History Ask students why Roosevelt is shown as a police officer. *(to reflect the United States's new role in the Western Hemisphere)*
Answer to Caption: Filipinos were demanding independence.

📁 Assign Political Cartoons in American History Activity 12: "Big Stick Diplomacy in the Western Hemisphere."

Independent Practice

Creating a Chart Have students use reference books to determine the current status of Puerto Rico, the Philippine Islands, and Cuba. They should organize information into charts that contain the following: Government, Major Industries, Chief Crops, Major Trade Partners.

When charts are completed, have students discuss the current relationship each nation or area has with the United States. Ask how the relationships differ from those at the turn of the century. **L2, L3**

Map Study *Using Maps*

Answer: the Philippines

Map Skills Practice
Have students study the map and create a then-and-now chart showing the political status of United States possessions in 1900 and the current political status of these areas.

Did You Know?

According to the Treaty of Paris, signed in December 1898, the United States gave $20,000,000 for the Philippines. The treaty was only ratified by a two-vote margin because of anti-imperialist feelings in the Senate.

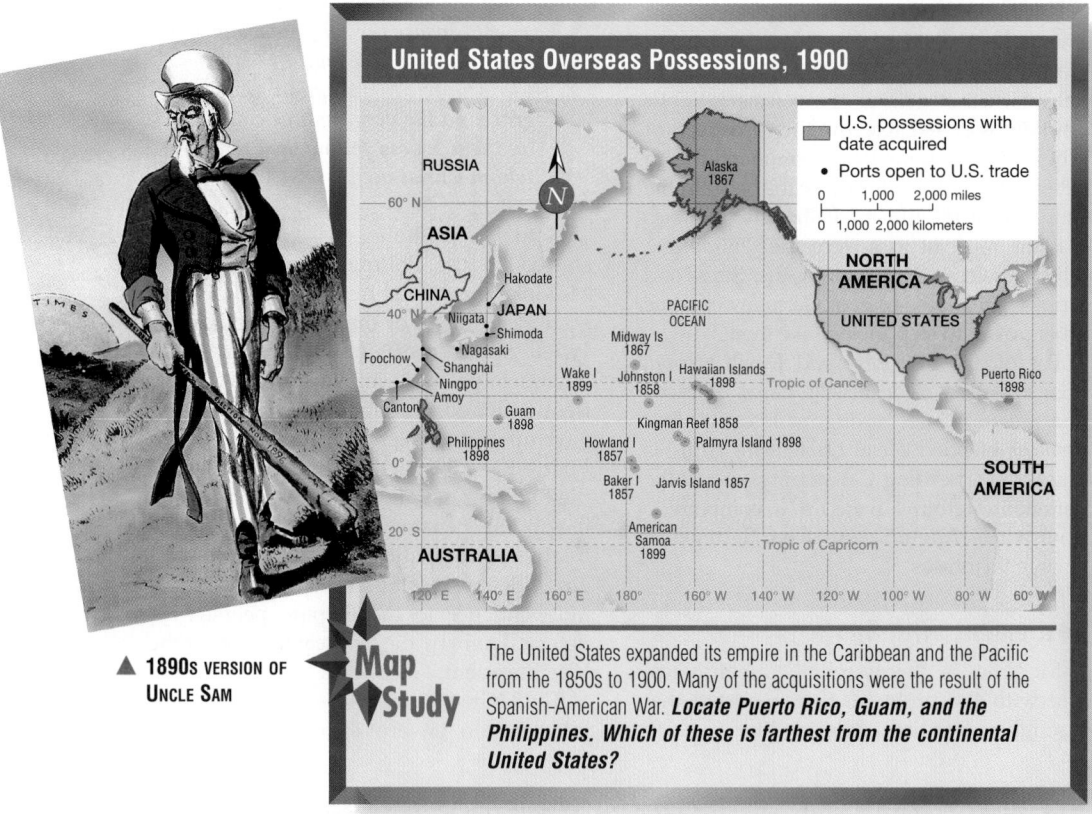

United States Overseas Possessions, 1900

▲ 1890s VERSION OF UNCLE SAM

Map Study The United States expanded its empire in the Caribbean and the Pacific from the 1850s to 1900. Many of the acquisitions were the result of the Spanish-American War. *Locate Puerto Rico, Guam, and the Philippines. Which of these is farthest from the continental United States?*

7,100 islands had 7.5 million people, who were divided into 43 ethnic groups speaking 87 different languages and dialects. The Filipinos ranged from people living in the forests to highly literate city dwellers.

Filipino Resistance

Filipino patriots had helped the American forces capture the islands. Once it became clear that the United States intended to annex the Philippines, however, a new uprising broke out—this time against the Americans. Feeling that they had been cheated out of their independence, Filipino soldiers took to the hills. A revolutionary government was set up under Emilio Aguinaldo. Its leaders adopted a republican constitution. Aguinaldo and the other Filipino leaders knew that if the republic were to succeed, they must gain the loyalty of the people and set up diplomatic relations with other countries.

Fighting between Filipino and United States forces broke out in February 1899. Within two months, the Filipinos had been driven from their capital city, and the government fled. Aguinaldo continued to carry on guerrilla operations that produced some success. Aguinaldo's capture in March 1901, however, for all practical purposes ended the Filipinos' military efforts. More than 60,000 troops—four times the number sent to Cuba—and three years of fighting were required to suppress the Filipino patriots and put down the revolt.

At the conclusion of the fighting, Andrew Carnegie commented to a friend in the government:

     You seem to have finished your work of civilizing the Filipinos; it is thought about 8,000 of them have been completely civilized and sent to heaven. I hope you like it. "

Cultural Perspectives

Contributions The overseas expansion of the United States brought with it great cultural diversity. Today many people from former American colonies live and work in the United States. Suggest that students investigate the cultural diversity of their community, the various peoples who live there and their customs and traditions, their food, music, and so on. Ask students to report their research by describing the contributions of the various groups to the community. **L3**

Many Americans were distressed to find their country at war with an independence movement. Mark Twain suggested that Old Glory should have its white stripes painted black and its stars replaced with skull and crossbones.

Even before the Filipino uprising was put down, President McKinley declared that American policy toward the islands would be for the good of the Filipinos. The President stated,

> *The Philippines are ours, not to exploit but to develop, to civilize, to educate, to train in the science of self-government.*

President McKinley sent two commissions to investigate the conditions in the Philippines and set up a civil government.

There were several changes during the first years of United States rule in the Philippines. The English language replaced Spanish as the language of general usage. The number of American business enterprises grew quickly, largely because Americans were permitted to sell their goods tariff-free in the Philippines. Street names were Americanized.

Resentment against American rule in the Philippines was moderately relieved in 1901 when President Theodore Roosevelt appointed William Howard Taft as the first civilian governor. Genuinely devoted to the interests of the island people, Taft started a program to prepare the Filipinos for self-government, and public schools were established. The United States bought out large foreign landowners and passed laws to keep property in the hands of the Filipinos.

Taft did not believe that the Philippines would be ready for independence for many years, though. In 1907 an elective legislature was set up, and in 1916 the United States promised that the Philippines would have independence eventually. That independence was finally granted in 1946.

Linking Past and Present

Point out to students that CDs have two major advantages over tape cassettes and phonograph records: they last longer, and they let users select any part of the recording quickly. Survey students to find out how many use tape cassettes and how many use compact discs.

For additional practice, assign Linking Past and Present Activity 12.

Did You Know?

Secretary of State Elihu Root answered the question "Does the Constitution follow the flag?" by saying "Je-es, as near as I can make out the Constitution follows the flag—but doesn't quite catch up with it."

FACT or FICTION?

Only reformers opposed imperialism.

FICTION: Opponents of imperialism included not only Jane Addams and Samuel Gompers but also ex-Presidents Benjamin Harrison and Grover Cleveland, industrialist Andrew Carnegie, writers Mark Twain and William James, and many others.

Linking Past and Present

The Sound of Music

The late 1800s produced the first craze of popular music in the United States. Among the reasons for this phenomenon was Edison's phonograph. In 1900 over 150,000 phonographs and 3 million records were bought by the public.

Then

Talking Machines

The phonograph, fondly called the talking machine, was one of the leading sources of entertainment. The phonograph and its accessories were decorated in the popular art of the day. Phonograph records—only 78 rpm were in use—used expendable needles, which were sold in multicolored tin boxes. Many phonograph companies also made a startling number of amplifying horns—the speakers of the day—as well as record turntables and picture records.

Now

Cassettes and Discs

By the 1980s new technology was transforming the industry. The major agents of change were the cassette and the compact disc, often called the CD. The cassette is a plastic cartridge containing magnetic tape on which the music is recorded. The CD is a round, flat platter on which the music is stored by digital code. By the mid-1990's compact discs accounted for more than 60 percent of total sales, cassettes for 36 percent, and records for less than 1 percent.

▲ COMPACT DISCS AND PLAYER

◀ EARLY PHONOGRAPH

CHAPTER 12 Imperialism: 1867–1908 **383**

Cooperative Learning Activity

Conducting a Panel Discussion Invite volunteers to form three groups, one assuming the role of traders or businesspeople, another the role of missionaries, and a third the role of people whose country has just been colonized by the United States. Ask a volunteer to act as the panel arbitrator. Have each group prepare arguments for its viewpoint on colonization and select a spokesperson to present that view. When all views have been presented, ask the class to decide who gave the most convincing argument for or against colonization.
L2, L3

Using Graphs

Answer: 31 years, 1867–1898

Graph Skills Practice
Using the graph, have students work in groups to create a large wall map of the United States and the areas covered in the graph.

Linking Across
TIME

Despite the violence and bloodshed that accompanied the United States acquisition of the Philippines, both the United States and the Philippines gradually began to work toward Philippine independence. In 1916 Filipinos began electing both houses of their legislature and were promised eventual independence. In 1946 independence day finally arrived.

GLENCOE
TECHNOLOGY

VIDEODISC

Focus on Government

Side 3, Chapter 41
Title: *Foreign Policy and National Defense*
Subject: World affairs

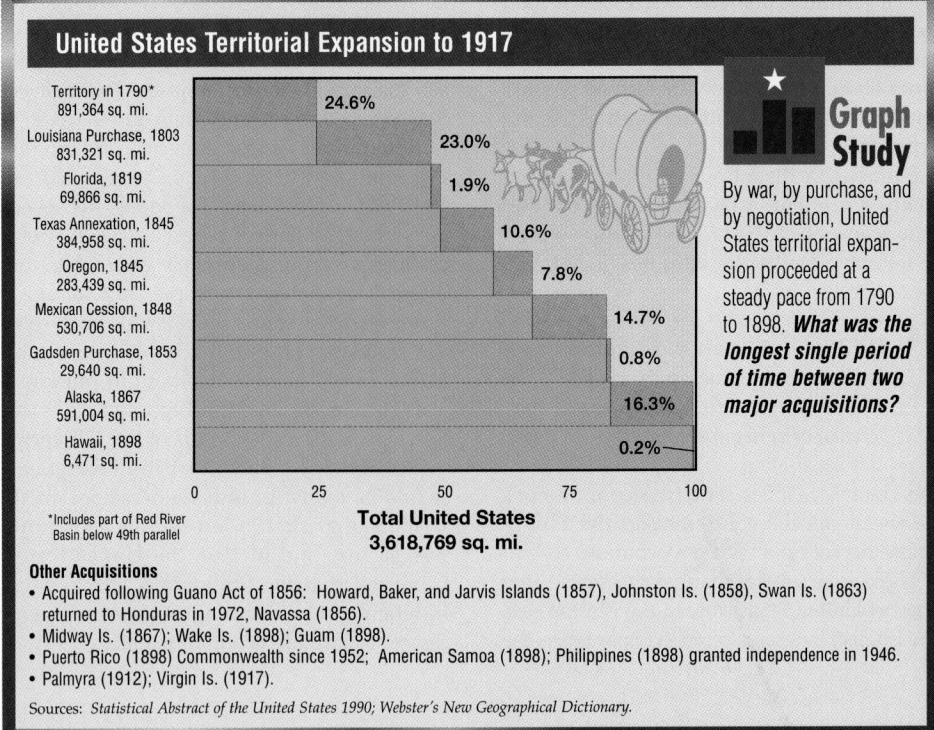

United States Territorial Expansion to 1917

Territory	%
Territory in 1790* 891,364 sq. mi.	24.6%
Louisiana Purchase, 1803 831,321 sq. mi.	23.0%
Florida, 1819 69,866 sq. mi.	1.9%
Texas Annexation, 1845 384,958 sq. mi.	10.6%
Oregon, 1845 283,439 sq. mi.	7.8%
Mexican Cession, 1848 530,706 sq. mi.	14.7%
Gadsden Purchase, 1853 29,640 sq. mi.	0.8%
Alaska, 1867 591,004 sq. mi.	16.3%
Hawaii, 1898 6,471 sq. mi.	0.2%

*Includes part of Red River Basin below 49th parallel

Total United States 3,618,769 sq. mi.

Graph Study

By war, by purchase, and by negotiation, United States territorial expansion proceeded at a steady pace from 1790 to 1898. *What was the longest single period of time between two major acquisitions?*

Other Acquisitions
- Acquired following Guano Act of 1856: Howard, Baker, and Jarvis Islands (1857), Johnston Is. (1858), Swan Is. (1863) returned to Honduras in 1972, Navassa (1856).
- Midway Is. (1867); Wake Is. (1898); Guam (1898).
- Puerto Rico (1898) Commonwealth since 1952; American Samoa (1898); Philippines (1898) granted independence in 1946.
- Palmyra (1912); Virgin Is. (1917).

Sources: *Statistical Abstract of the United States 1990; Webster's New Geographical Dictionary.*

■ Problems of an Overseas Empire

The new possessions posed constitutional problems summarized in the question, "Does the Constitution follow the flag?" Congress, according to the Constitution, may not set tariff duties on goods carried from one part of the United States to another. Did this mean that no duties would be laid on goods from American colonies? The Constitution guarantees to all American citizens certain civil rights. Did constitutional guarantees of civil rights extend to the people of the new colonies who knew nothing of American justice?

The Supreme Court decided that the Constitution did not cover overseas possessions. Puerto Rico, the Court ruled, was a dependency; therefore Congress could set tariffs on its products. Other decisions determined that inhabitants of dependencies enjoyed full civil rights only if granted them by congressional legislation.

Cuba

According to the Teller Amendment, the United States pledged to withdraw from Cuba when order was restored. After three years of civil war, however, the island was in terrible condition. The United States Army remained in Cuba to set up a republican government, oversee Cuban finances, and establish public health programs.

In 1901, to protect its interests in Cuba, the United States Congress added the Platt Amendment to an army bill. This amendment, which governed the relations between Cuba and the United States for 33 years, provided that: (1) Cuba should not make any treaty with another nation that weakened its independence; (2) Cuba should allow the United States the right to buy or lease naval stations; (3) Cuba's public debt should not exceed its capacity to pay; and (4) the United States should have the right to intervene to protect Cuban independence and keep order. These conditions, written into Cuba's constitution and into a treaty with the United

Sidelight: Government for Puerto Rico

The Foraker Act, which settled the status of Puerto Rico, gave that island a governor appointed by the United States, an upper house also appointed by the United States, and a lower house elected by the people. Those who opposed the colonization of Puerto Rico pointed out that this arrangement was very similar to that of British rule over the American colonies.

States, made Cuba an American **protectorate**—a nation or region controlled by a stronger state. The attitude that Cuba was part of "the white man's burden" was reflected in an editorial by William Allen White in Kansas's *Emporia Gazette*:

" *Only Anglo-Saxons can govern themselves. The Cubans will need despotic government . . . to restrain anarchy until Cuba is filled with Yankees.* "

For almost four years, Cuba was under military rule directed by General Leonard Wood. The greatest achievement of Wood's administration was the suppression of yellow fever. An American medical team under Dr. Walter Reed proved the theory of a Cuban physician, Carlos J. Finlay: that yellow fever is transmitted by the stegomyia mosquito. American doctors and volunteers allowed themselves to be bitten by mosquitoes, and some of them died as martyrs to medical progress. Major William C. Gorgas, an Army doctor, carried on a campaign to eliminate mosquitoes from Havana. By 1901, for the first time in centuries, there was no yellow fever in the Cuban capital.

Puerto Rico

The United States had made no prior commitment to withdraw from Puerto Rico as it had done in Cuba. That island's cultural ties with Spain and Latin America through the

Visualizing History

▲ AN OVERSEAS EMPIRE As in most wars, the civilians suffered many hardships. Thousands of Filipinos perished from sickness, starvation, and other indirect effects of war. The Philippines gained independence in 1946. *When was Puerto Rico granted territorial status?*

Roman Catholic Church, the Spanish language, and other traditions had existed for nearly 300 years. Yet, the United States chose to keep the island as its territory.

After a brief period of military rule, Congress gradually allowed Puerto Rico a degree of self-government. The Puerto Rican people demanded either independence or complete self-rule under the American flag. In 1917 they were granted territorial status and made citizens of the United States.

Section 3 ★ Review

Checking for Understanding

1. **Identify** Platt Amendment, "white man's burden," Walter Reed, William Gorgas.

2. **Define** protectorate.

3. **Explain** ways in which the President and Congress resolved the annexation difficulties in the Philippines.

4. **Describe** how problems with Cuba and Puerto Rico were resolved.

Critical Thinking

5. **Making Decisions** Analyze the reasoning of the Supreme Court on constitutional guarantees for overseas possessions. Do you agree?

ACTIVITY

6. Research the origins of these names: *Puerto Rico*, *Venezuela*, and *the Philippines*. Compare your findings with the findings of other students.

CHAPTER 12
SECTION 3

ASSESS

Check Understanding

Assign Section 3 Review as homework or an in-class activity.

Evaluate

◉ 🗁 Assign Section Quiz 12-3 or use the Testmaker to create a customized quiz.

Reteach

🗁 Have students complete Reteaching Activity 12-3.

Visualizing History It took 84,000 U.S. soldiers over 4 years to end rebellion in the Philippines. **Answer to Caption:** 1917

Enrich

Assign Primary and Secondary Source Readings pp. 28-30: "Enthusiasm for War and Expansion" by William Allen White and "Arguments Against Imperialism" by William Jennings Bryan.

CLOSE

Ask students to predict whether the U.S. in the 1900s would follow imperialism or isolationism.

Answers to SECTION 3 REVIEW

1. Platt Amendment, 384; "white man's burden," 385; Walter Reed, 385; William Gorgas, 385
2. All vocabulary terms are defined in the Glossary.
3. set up a committee to prepare Philippines for self-government, established public schools, bought out foreign landowners, and passed laws to protect Filipino property
4. Cuba—through the Platt Amendment, which governed relations between Cuba and U.S. for 33 years. Cuba could

not make treaties that weakened its independence; U.S. had right to buy or lease naval stations; Puerto Rico—given territorial status and inhabitants made U.S. citizens.

5. When Supreme Court decided that Constitution did not cover overseas possessions, Congress felt it could set tariffs on its products. Answers will vary.
6. Ask students to provide the sources they used.

TEACH

Review the basic ideas behind imperialism and anti-imperialism. Point out that as on many political issues, Americans were divided on this one. Ask students to present arguments for and against imperialism. Write their responses on the chalkboard.

After students have read Bryan's speech, discuss how he presented his point of view. Have students who opposed the imperialism argument list ways they could change the minds of those who supported imperialism. **L2**

Project Skills Transparency 12 and have students complete Skills Transparency Activity 12.

Use Chapter Skills Activity 12 to reinforce students' understanding of the skill.

Did You Know?

William Jennings Bryan was nominated three times for President: in 1896, 1900, and 1908. In part his anti-imperialist stand helped defeat him. He did go on, however, to become secretary of state under President Woodrow Wilson. In that post he continued to oppose U.S. expansionist policies.

Analyzing Political Speeches

Free speech lies at the heart of American democracy. It allows us to express opinions and to disagree. One form of free speech is the political speech.

Learning the Skill

To analyze a political speech, use the following steps:

- **Determine** what topic is being discussed.
- **Read** the speech carefully to find out what beliefs or opinions the speaker is expressing.
- **Note** the arguments and evidence presented in support.
- **Decide** whether or not you think the speech is persuasive.

Read this excerpt from William Jennings Bryan's speech before the 1900 Democratic National Convention.

The principal arguments . . . advanced by those who enter upon a defense of imperialism are:

First—That we must improve the present opportunity to become a world power and enter into international politics.

Second—That our commercial interests in the Philippine Islands and in the Orient make it necessary for us to hold the islands permanently.

Third—That the spread of the Christian religion will be facilitated by a colonial policy.

Fourth—That there is no honorable retreat from the position which the nation has taken. . . .

It is sufficient answer to the first argument to say that for more than a century this nation has been a world power. . . .

It is not necessary to own people in order to trade with them. . . .
We do not own Japan or China, but we trade with their people. . . .

The religious argument varies . . . from a passive belief that Providence delivered the Filipinos into our hands, for their good and our glory, to the exultation of the minister who said that we ought to

▲ McKinley tailors an expanding Uncle Sam

"thrash the natives (Filipinos) until they understand who we are," and that *"every bullet sent, every cannon shot and every flag waved means righteousness."*

. . . If true Christianity consists in carrying out in our daily lives the teachings of Christ, who will say that we are commanded to civilize with dynamite and proselyte with the sword?

Practicing the Skill

1. What is the topic of Bryan's speech?
2. What beliefs does he express?
3. What evidence does Bryan give to refute the argument that commercial interests necessitate control of the Philippines?
4. Is the speech persuasive? Why or why not?

APPLYING THE SKILL

5. Select a political issue that is important to you. Draft an outline for a speech on that topic. Be sure to state the issue clearly, give your position or your solution, and present evidence to support your position.

386

Answers to Practicing the Skill

1. whether imperialism is justified
2. that imperialism is not necessary
3. He says that we do not need to own a country in order to trade with it. We traded with Japan and China but we did not own either.
4. Answers will vary, but students should present evidence to support their view.
5. Issues will vary, but students should give their position and present evidence to support their position.

A New Arena

Setting the Scene

Section Focus

Americans expected President Roosevelt to adopt an aggressive foreign policy. Roosevelt was resolved that the United States should be a great power. In the Western Hemisphere, he enlarged the scope of the Monroe Doctrine and secured United States domination of the Caribbean. In the Pacific and East Asia, he attempted to keep a balance of power and restrain first Russian, then Japanese, ambitions.

◀ THEODORE ROOSEVELT, BRONZE RELIEF

Objectives

After studying this section, you should be able to

★ give examples of Roosevelt's "Big Stick" diplomacy.

★ discuss the goals and results of the "Open Door" policy in China.

★ discuss America's concerns over the Russo-Japanese War.

Key Terms

anarchist, corollary, partitioned, sphere of influence, indemnity

---

*I*n the Western Hemisphere, the acquisition of Puerto Rico and the establishment of a protectorate over Cuba gave the United States a new interest in this region. American expansion into the Pacific brought closer contact with East Asian nations, particularly China. Several European countries, along with Japan, were fiercely competing for trading rights in China. The United States entered a new and complex arena of international politics.

■ The Election of 1900

In 1900 William Jennings Bryan, again the Democratic candidate, attempted to make imperialism the paramount issue of the presidential campaign. The Republicans

again nominated McKinley for President. Theodore Roosevelt, who had become governor of New York, received the nomination for Vice President. As much as possible, the Republicans avoided discussion of imperialism because they were divided. The result was an even greater Republican victory than that in 1896.

Six months after his second inauguration, McKinley spoke of the United States's new position in the world. Previously a strong supporter of isolationism, he announced a change of heart, saying:

❝ *Isolation is no longer possible or desirable. God and man have linked the nations together. No nation can longer be indifferent to any other....* ❞

Classroom Resources for SECTION 4

Blackline Masters:

📁 Reproducible Lesson Plan 12-4
📁 Guided Reading Activity 12-4
📁 Chapter Map Activity 12
📁 Workbook Activity 12-4
📁 Reteaching Activity 12-4
📁 Section Quiz 12-4

Transparencies:

🖼 Section Focus Transparency 12-4
🖼 Chapter Map Transparency 12

Multimedia:

💿 The Presidents: A Picture History of Our Nation
📀 Testmaker

FOCUS

Bellringer

📦📁 Before taking roll, project Section Focus Transparency 12-4 or hand out Section Focus Transparency Activity 12-4. Have students answer the questions.

Motivating Activity

Read the following statement by Theodore Roosevelt: "I wish to preach, not the doctrine of ignoble ease, but the doctrine of the strenuous life, the life of toil and effort, of labor and strife...." Ask students what kind of President they think Roosevelt would be. How might he conduct foreign affairs? *(probably be aggressive, likely to dominate the presidency)* **L1**

Vocabulary Precheck

Ask students to define each of the "Key Terms." Have a volunteer consult the dictionary for any unfamiliar words. **L1, LEP**

 CD-ROM

The Presidents: A Picture History of Our Nation

Have students select President Theodore Roosevelt from the main menu and the category GAME. Suggest they learn more about Roosevelt by playing the presidential game with a partner.

TEACH
Guided Practice

Tracing Routes On a world map, have students trace the water route from San Francisco to New York around Cape Horn and use the map's scale to calculate the approximate distance. *(13,000 miles)* Next, have students trace the route by ship from San Francisco to New York City via the Panama Canal and calculate that distance. *(5,200 miles)* Ask students to write a paragraph explaining how the Panama Canal improved United States trade and business. **L1, LEP**

Did You Know?

Theodore Roosevelt was the youngest President in the White House, succeeding McKinley at the age of 42. He was not, however, the youngest *elected* President. John F. Kennedy was 46 years old when he was inaugurated.

Food of the Times

In the early 1800s, the United States was not noted for its cuisine or its fine restaurants. In the latter part of the century, however, a Swiss family named Delmonico brought French cooking to the nation. The family opened a chain of restaurants in New York City. Their success inspired restaurant owners in other cities.

President McKinley explained that America's diversity of products and its efficiency in producing them had so increased that there was an urgent need for more markets. He proposed reciprocity treaties with foreign nations, providing for mutual lowering of tariffs.

McKinley did not live to put his new policy into effect. The day after delivering his speech he was shot by an **anarchist,** one who opposes all forms of government. Just short of 43 years old, Roosevelt became the youngest President.

■ The Big Stick

Theodore Roosevelt had a genius for the dramatic gesture. He told young men, "Don't flinch, don't foul, hit the line hard." Roosevelt's actions were sometimes impulsive, sometimes unwise, but he firmly believed that power imposed responsibility. One of Roosevelt's mottoes in foreign policy was a West African saying, "Speak softly and carry a big stick."

The Panama Canal

The "Big Stick" was most in evidence in the Caribbean. Roosevelt and others believed that in addition to saving time for commercial shipping, a canal would answer the strategic need to shuttle warships between the Atlantic and the Pacific oceans.

This was clearly demonstrated during the Spanish-American War. The battleship *Oregon,* ordered from Puget Sound to Cuba,

· ·

Footnotes to History

Digging the Canal The route of the Panama Canal ran through hills of soft volcanic material. As a shovelful of dirt was removed, more soil slid into place. Massive landslides occurred as the heavier hilltops lost the support of their subsoil. To keep digging was the only solution: First the hilltops were dug away, then the lower layers of soil. Crews dug more than 211 million cubic yards (161 million cu. m) of dirt before the canal was completed.

---

was forced to steam 14,000 miles around Cape Horn—3 times as far as if there had been a canal.

In the 1800s a French company had made a vain and costly effort to cut through Panama. Early in the 1890s, an American company started to dig a canal through Nicaragua but soon abandoned the attempt. In 1901 Britain, which also had an interest in the canal, agreed that the United States could build, control, and fortify a canal, provided that ships of all nations were charged an equal toll.

Immediately, Secretary of State John Hay offered Colombia, which controlled Panama, $10 million and a yearly rent of $250,000 for the right to construct a canal through Panama and control a narrow strip of land on either side. However, feeling that the price was too low and fearful of losing control of Panama, the Colombian senate unanimously refused to ratify the agreement.

Roosevelt was furious. He let it be known that he would not mind if Panama revolted. On November 3, 1903, a revolution broke out, and an independent Republic of Panama was proclaimed. On November 6 the United States recognized Panama's independence. Less than two weeks later the United States and Panama signed a treaty for the canal.

Roosevelt defended his Big Stick diplomacy in Panama on the ground that he advanced "the needs of collective civilization" by speeding up the building of an interocean canal. His action was widely condemned in the United States as unjustifiable aggression. In Latin America it aroused dislike and distrust of the United States.

The engineering difficulties involved in cutting through the Isthmus of Panama were enormous and were compounded by the tremendous health problems encountered in the tropics. In 1885 an English writer wrote of Panama:

> ❝ *In all the world there is not perhaps now concentrated in any so much foul disease. . . . The Isthmus is a damp, tropical jungle, intensely hot, swarming with mosquitoes . . . the home, even as Nature made it, of yellow fever, typhus, and dysentery.* ❞

Cooperative Learning Activity

Creating Cartoons Tell students that Theodore Roosevelt's personality and style made him a favorite with cartoonists. Divide students into groups, and have each portray Roosevelt in a cartoon in which he is involved in an event or an issue. (Students might want to do some research on political cartoons.) Have groups exchange cartoons and explain their meanings. Display the cartoons on a bulletin board. **L2, L3** 🗄

George W. Goethals, a colonel in the Corps of Engineers, directed the engineering feat that completed the canal in 1914. Dr. William C. Gorgas, who had cleaned up Havana, reduced the health threats in Panama.

Venezuela

Roosevelt, like Cleveland, defended Venezuela from possible European aggression, strengthening the Monroe Doctrine. By 1902 Venezuela owed money to citizens of several European countries. Cipriano Castro, the Venezuelan dictator-president, refused either to pay the debts or submit them to arbitration. Roosevelt said the Monroe Doctrine did not protect Latin American nations against punishment for misbehavior.

After consultation with the American State Department, Great Britain and Germany, Venezuela's two principal creditors, blockaded Venezuelan ports to force payment. The blockade was very unpopular in the United States because it was perceived as a violation of the Monroe Doctrine. Feeling was intensified when Venezuelan gunboats were sunk and Venezuelan ports bombarded. Public anger moved Roosevelt to press for an end of the blockade and the submission of the dispute to arbitration. Although both parties agreed to arbitration, Great Britain was quicker to respond than Germany was. This added to Roosevelt's distrust of the rising German empire.

Roosevelt Corollary

In 1903 Argentine foreign minister Luis Drago urged that forcibly collecting debts from bankrupt countries be made a violation of international law. If the United States opposed Drago and allowed foreign nations to block the coasts and bombard the cities of defaulting Latin American nations, the door was left open to further aggression. If, however, the United States outlawed forcible collection of debts, it might be pushed into defending financial dishonesty. The President's reply to the Drago Doctrine became known as the Roosevelt **Corollary,** or addition, to the Monroe Doctrine. Whenever an American republic was guilty of "chronic

Visualizing History ▲ THE PANAMA CANAL Work on the Panama Canal began in 1904 and lasted 10 years. *What difficulties were encountered?*

wrongdoing," said Roosevelt, the United States might have to intervene itself.

Dominican Republic

The Roosevelt Corollary was first applied in the Dominican Republic. In 1905 the United States assumed the responsibility of collecting Dominican customs. The United States Marine Corps collected the duties and divided them to support the Dominican government and to pay that nation's debts to European countries.

Roosevelt's successor, President William Howard Taft, continued Roosevelt's policies but with a shift of emphasis. Taft's secretary of state, Philander C. Knox, promoted American business interests abroad with the slogan, "Every diplomat a salesman." In Latin America this "dollar diplomacy" resulted in increased sales of United States goods—including warships—and in efforts to increase American investments there.

Although Taft described his brand of diplomacy as "substituting dollars for bullets," sometimes he used both. In 1912 he sent marines to Nicaragua to install a more friendly government and to force acceptance of a loan from New York bankers. Such policies increased the unpopularity of the United States in Latin America.

CHAPTER 12
SECTION 4

Independent Practice

Completing a Map Provide students with an outline map of East Asia, including China, Japan, and Korea. Have them complete the map by showing the possessions and spheres of influence of various European nations and the United States in the early twentieth century. Ask students why it was in the interests of the United States for Roosevelt to try to settle the Russo-Japanese War. *(His arbitration helped to maintain the United States's Open Door policy in China.)* **L2**

For additional map practice, assign Map Transparency Activity 12 and Chapter Map Activity 12.

FACT or FICTION?

Theodore Roosevelt was the first American to win the Nobel Peace Prize.

FACT: Roosevelt was awarded the honor in 1904 for his arbitration ending the Russo-Japanese War.

Visualizing History The Panama Canal was regarded as one of the greatest engineering feats of the time. **Answer to Caption:** engineering difficulties, health problems

Sidelight: Technology

The job of constructing the Panama Canal involved three major engineering projects. First the workers had to excavate the Gaillard Cut, which was 300 feet (91 meters) wide across the isthmus. Next they had to build a dam across the Charges River to create an artificial lake. Finally they had to construct the canal's locks.

The hardest job was digging the Gaillard Cut because the hills through which the cut runs consist of soft volcanic material. When workers dug a hole, more rock and earth would slide into the space or push up from below.

Linking Across TIME

Soon after the Panama Canal was completed, many Panamanians began to insist that the United States did not have the right to control the Canal Zone. The United States disagreed, claiming that the treaty of 1903 gave it that right. Over the years the United States set up bases not only in the zone but throughout Panama. Progress toward settling the issue was finally made in 1977, when the United States and Panama signed a treaty. The treaty states that all nations have the right to use the canal but that United States warships have the right to sail through the canal first.

Visualizing History Hay's "Open Door" policy opened the way for a larger American role in Asia. **Answer to Caption:** Both nations wanted control of resource-rich Manchuria.

Did You Know?

John Hay studied law in an office next to Abraham Lincoln. He was Lincoln's assistant private secretary when Lincoln was President.

Visualizing History ▲ SPHERES OF INFLUENCE Cities in China grew into centers of trade. Major international powers divided China into spheres of influence. *What clash of interest led to the Russo-Japanese War?*

■ The Balance of Power in East Asia

Roosevelt realized that the position of the United States in East Asia was weak. He called the Philippines the "Achilles' heel" of American defense; they were easily vulnerable to attack by Japan. China and Russia also posed problems.

China and the Open Door

At the close of the nineteenth century, it looked as though China, like Africa, would be **partitioned,** or divided, among stronger powers. In 1898 and 1899, Russia, Germany, France, and Great Britain forced China to lease its ports, some of them for 99 years. Each "leasehold" was expected to become the center of a **sphere of influence**—an area where a European nation controlled economic development.

The United States and Great Britain, in order to ensure open avenues of trade with China, decided to oppose the parceling out of Chinese territory. Early in 1898 the British government proposed a joint declaration with the United States in favor of the "Open Door"—with the goal of preserving equal

trading opportunities in China for all foreign nations. At that time the United States was cool to the idea, but its annexation of the Philippines changed the American attitude.

John Hay, secretary of state, thought that the days of American isolationism must end. Having defended the acquisition of an overseas empire, he agreed with Great Britain on the policy of an Open Door in China. In September 1899, Hay sent notes to countries with leaseholds in China asking that they keep the ports open to vessels of all nations on equal terms.

Boxer Rebellion

While foreign countries debated control of China, Chinese secret societies were organizing to oust foreign control. One of these was called "the Boxers" by Westerners because of the physical exercises they practiced.

When a falsified story was printed in America suggesting that Westerners were negotiating the dismantling of a Chinese monument, the Boxer Rebellion broke out. With secret aid from the Chinese government, the Boxers intended to wipe out "foreign devils" and their Christian converts. They killed more than 200 foreigners,

---

Critical Thinking Activity

Comparing Remind students that from the time the Monroe Doctrine was adopted to the present time, the United States has always had an interest in the Caribbean and Latin America.

Have students research policies of recent Presidents and compare them with those of Theodore Roosevelt. **L3**

mostly missionaries and their families. For 7 weeks the Boxers laid siege to foreign embassies in Beijing.

During this crisis Hay worked to prevent full-scale retaliation and war against China and to persuade the leaseholding powers not to use the Boxer Rebellion as an excuse to partition the country. In July 1900, he sent a second set of Open Door notes. This time he declared that the policy of the United States was to seek ways to "preserve Chinese territorial and administrative entity."

The United States lacked sufficient military power to enforce Hay's Open Door notes of 1899 and 1900. Equal trading opportunities in China and the preservation of China's territorial integrity lay in maintaining a "balance of power" among the nations with ambitions in East Asia.

Russo-Japanese War

China's two closest neighbors, Japan and Russia, were especially threatening. In 1893 Japan established a protectorate over the independent kingdom of Korea and obtained Formosa and other islands off China's northeast coast. Japan had designs on the resource-rich Chinese province of Manchuria, in which Russia was already established. The Russians hoped to move into Korea. This clash of interests led to the Russo-Japanese War in 1904.

Japan won victories over Russia on both land and sea. By the summer of 1905, both countries were ready to make peace. The Japanese secretly asked Roosevelt if he would serve as go-between. After consulting the czar, Roosevelt formally offered to help make peace. Both nations accepted the President's proposals and sent diplomats to a peace conference in Portsmouth, New Hampshire, in August 1905.

Treaty of Portsmouth

The President induced Japan to give up claims for a money **indemnity,** or payment for damages, and Russia to give up the southern half of the island of Sakhalin (SA•kuh•LEEN). Japan also took over Russian interests in southern Manchuria.

The war altered the balance of power in East Asia. Now it was no longer Russian expansion that was most to be feared, but Japanese. Roosevelt himself believed that there was potential danger of war.

Roosevelt arranged a compromise in 1907 and 1908, known as the Gentlemen's Agreement. In a complicated series of maneuvers, he soothed Japanese anger and showed the Japanese that he was not afraid of them. To check Japanese expansion toward the Philippines, Roosevelt recognized Japan as dominant in Korea and Manchuria.

The resolution of the Russo-Japanese War was an example of Roosevelt's efforts to use arbitration rather than war to settle controversies. Although he upgraded America's military power, he believed that the United States had an obligation as a leader of an interdependent world to act responsibly.

Section 4 ★ Review

Checking for Understanding

1. **Identify** Big Stick diplomacy, John Hay, Drago Doctrine, Roosevelt Corollary, Open Door, Boxer Rebellion, Russo-Japanese War.

2. **Define** anarchist, corollary, partitioned, sphere of influence, indemnity.

3. **Indicate** how President Theodore Roosevelt acted as peacemaker in the Russo-Japanese War.

Critical Thinking

4. **Understanding Cause and Effect** Explain how Roosevelt's Big Stick diplomacy led to ill feeling against the United States throughout Latin America.

ACTIVITY

5. Create a cartoon that illustrates your opinions regarding America's "Big Stick" policy.

Answers to SECTION 4 REVIEW

1. Big Stick diplomacy, 388; John Hay, 388; Drago Doctrine, 389; Roosevelt Corollary, 389; Open Door, 390; Boxer Rebellion, 390; Russo-Japanese War, 391

2. All vocabulary words are defined in the Glossary.

3. Organized the peace conference in Portsmouth, N.H. Japan ceded money claims; Russia ceded Sakhalin and allowed Japan to take over its Manchurian interests in Japan.

4. Such diplomacy created resentment and anger by the U.S. attempting to dominate the economic and political policies of Latin America.

5. Cartoons should display student understanding of the term.

ASSESS
Check Understanding
Assign Section 4 Review as homework or an in-class activity.

Evaluate
Assign the Section 4 Quiz or use the Testmaker to create a customized quiz.

Reteach
Have students write several examples of Roosevelt's Big Stick diplomacy. Then discuss how this diplomacy style affected the United States both economically and politically. (*Economically: made U.S. wealthy because acquired additional markets and sources of raw material. Politically: showed U.S. had power to back up its claims*)

Have students complete Reteaching Activity 12-4.

Assign Workbook Activity 12-4.

Enrich
Theodore Roosevelt said that he considered the presidency a "bully pulpit." Ask students what they think this expression means and if and how Roosevelt's actions reflected this phrase.

CLOSE
Have students read the last paragraph in this section. Ask: Do you agree with its assessment of Roosevelt? Why or why not?

CHAPTER 12 ★ REVIEW

GLENCOE
TECHNOLOGY

 **VIDEODISC**

Use the MindJogger Videoquiz to review students' knowledge.

MindJogger Videoquiz

Chapter 12
Disc 2, Side A

Available in VHS.

Using Vocabulary

Articles will vary but should include all the vocabulary terms.

Reviewing Facts

1. Industrialization increased the need for new markets. Other countries were practicing imperialist policies. Opportunity existed to acquire territory to increase sources of raw materials.
2. British had a powerful navy. The threat of war over the Venezuelan situation of 1895 revealed a weakness of the United States Navy.
3. McKinley wanted to preserve neutrality. The press wanted to go to war to show the strength of the country. McKinley believed that Spain would not grant Cuban independence, and he wanted to intervene to protect Cuban people.
4. the atrocities, the many accusations of yellow press, and protection of American business investments
5. Hawaii was dominated by American interests;

Using Vocabulary

Assume that you are a reporter for an antiadministration newspaper covering the Latin American situation in 1903. Write a feature article describing Theodore Roosevelt's policies using the following vocabulary terms.

imperialism   protectorate
isolationism   sphere of influence
reciprocity   corollary

Reviewing Facts

1. State three reasons why the United States abandoned isolationist policies after the Civil War.
2. Explain how confrontation with Great Britain in 1895–1896 led to strengthening the American navy.
3. Describe the position of the President and press regarding war with Spain over Cuba. Why did McKinley change his mind?
4. List three reasons America went to war over Cuba. Which was most important?
5. Discuss why Hawaii had fewer difficulties accepting its position as a United States possession than did Puerto Rico or the Philippines.
6. Show why Americans favored an Open Door policy in China.
7. Indicate why the United States needed to build the Panama Canal.

Understanding Concepts

Economic and Political Power

1. How did the use of the Big Stick in Latin America increase American wealth and political power?

Confrontation

2. How did a show of force with Great Britain and Germany enhance the American position in Latin America?
3. Why was the United States unable to avoid military confrontation in Cuba?

Critical Thinking

1. **Recognizing Stereotypes** How did adherence to social Darwinism cause the United States to stereotype people who lived in countries under their possession? In what ways did stereotyped thinking influence political and economic policies toward these territories?
2. **Analyzing Fine Art** The painting on this page, *Charge of San Juan Hill,* by Frederic Remington depicts the bravado of the Rough Riders. Analyze the painting and answer the questions that follow.
   a. What is happening in the painting?
   b. What details do you see in this scene?
   c. Do you think Remington has captured the reality of battle? Why or why not? Give reasons to support your answer.

▲ *CHARGE OF SAN JUAN HILL* BY FREDERIC REMINGTON

History and Geography

The Panama Canal

The building of the Panama Canal was regarded as one of the great engineering feats of the time. Many nations attempted to build a canal across Panama. The project, which cost more than $365 million, took seven years to complete. Study the map of the canal, then answer the questions that follow.

Puerto Rico had closer ties to Spain. Philippines were too diverse, too far away, and the least-developed country.
6. its trading interests would be advanced if each nation had equal rights to trade
7. saving time, strategic need

Understanding Concepts

1. acquisition of additional markets and sources of raw materials; showed that the United States had clout to back up its claims
2. showed its willingness to fight to maintain its superior position there

3. honor, pride, patriotism, business interests, and the press and public opinion

Critical Thinking

1. The idea of superior people ruling led to a belief that people in these countries were backward, less advanced, and less competent than Americans.

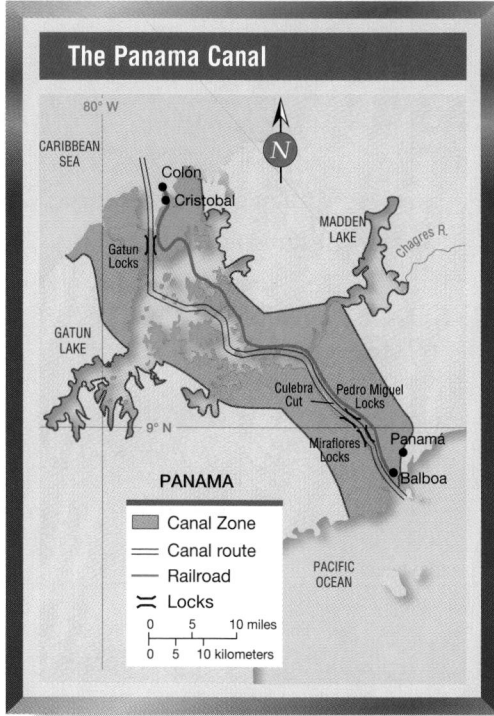

The Panama Canal

CARIBBEAN SEA

Colón
Cristobal

MADDEN LAKE

Gatun Locks

Chagres R.

GATUN LAKE

Culebra Cut

Pedro Miguel Locks

Miraflores Locks

Panamá

Balboa

PANAMA

PACIFIC OCEAN

- Canal Zone
- Canal route
- Railroad
- Locks

0   5   10 miles
0   5   10 kilometers

1. **Location** What cities are located near the path of the canal?

2. **Movement** In what direction would a ship on route to Cristobal from Balboa travel?

3. **Human/Environment Interaction** What military and economic benefits would a canal through Panama provide?

 **Cooperative Learning** **Interdisciplinary Activity: Geography**

Work in a group of three or more to plan a trip from where you live to one of the following cities: Mexico City, Mexico; San Juan, Puerto Rico; Toronto, Canada; Fairbanks, Alaska.

Each member of your group will do one of the following: (a) find historic places to visit; (b) draw the route to follow on a map; or (c) make a list of provisions and clothes to bring. Combine your findings in a travel information packet. Share your trip with the rest of the class.

Practicing Skills

Analyzing Political Speeches

Study the skill activity on page 386. Then read the following excerpt from a speech by Senator Albert Beveridge of Indiana and answer the questions that follow.

The Philippines are ours forever: "territory belonging to the United States," as the Constitution calls them. And just beyond the Philippines are China's illimitable markets. We will not retreat from either. We will not repudiate our duty in the archipelago. We will not abandon our opportunity in the Orient. We will not renounce our part in the mission of our race, trustees under God of the civilization of the world.

1. What is the speaker's topic?

2. What beliefs or opinions does Senator Beveridge express?

3. How does the speaker characterize the role of the United States?

4. How does the speaker describe China's trade and market?

5. Do you consider this speech a persuasive one? Why or why not?

Writing ABOUT History

Using Your Journal

Write a paragraph grouping and summarizing the reasons for becoming involved in the affairs of other countries. What was the major reason?

2. that it is the duty of the United States to be involved in the region
3. God's trustees
4. as without limits
5. Answers will vary but students should give reasons for their opinions.

Writing ABOUT History *Using Your Journal*

Student paragraphs should refer to specific reasons. Answers may vary but will probably say for economic or strategic reasons.

? Chapter Bonus Test Question

Ask students: Describe the relationship between U.S. expansionism and the economic expansion of the nation. (*Expanding industry and business needed more trade and more markets.*)

McKinley believed in civilizing, educating, and training them to be self-governing.

2. **a.** Rough Riders seize the hill under fire.
b. troops are in open area; few trees or places for cover; soldiers are in relatively close proximity; most soldiers are on foot

c. Students should provide reasons to support their answer.

History and Geography

1. Colón, Cristobal, Panamá, Balboa
2. northwest
3. save time for commercial shipping and warships

Cooperative Learning

Encourage students to illustrate their travel information packets and share them with the rest of the class.

Practicing Skills

1. the reason for U.S. involvement in the Pacific

Daily Lesson Objectives	Teacher Classroom Resources	Multimedia
SECTION 1 **Sources of Progressivism** **1 Day** **pp. 396–401** 1. Discuss the role of the muck-rakers in identifying social ills and promoting social change. 2. Explain how methods and strategies used in business and education influenced social reform.	Reproducible Lesson Plan 13-1 Chapter Concept Mapping Activities 13-A, 13-B Performance Assessment Activity 13 *Vocabulary Activity 13 *Guided Reading Activity 13-1 Enrichment Activity 13 American Literary Heritage, pp. 34–35 Primary and Secondary Source Readings, pp. 32-33 Cooperative Learning Activity 13 Workbook Activity 13-1 Reteaching Activity 13-1 *Section Quiz 13-1	Section Focus Transparency 13-1 Chapter Concepts Transparencies 13-A, 13-B Vocabulary PuzzleMaker Testmaker The American History Videodisc MindJogger Videoquiz
SECTION 2 **Progressive Reforms** **1 Day** **pp. 404–410** 1. Explain how reforms strengthened democracy. 2. Describe the advances made by social reformers and government in protecting adult and child workers.	Reproducible Lesson Plan 13-2 *Guided Reading Activity 13-2 American Literary Heritage, pp. 26–28 American Portraits 48 Linking Past and Present Activity 13 Chapter Map Activity 13 Workbook Activity 13-2 *Reteaching Activity 13-2 *Section Quiz 13-2	Section Transparency 13-2 Chapter Map Transparency 13 Testmaker GTV: The American People: Fabric of a Nation
SECTION 3 **Limits of Progressivism** **1 Day** **pp. 412–416** 1. Describe progressive attitudes about immigrants and racial minorities. 2. Explain why African American leadership changed.	Reproducible Lesson Plan 13-3 *Guided Reading Activity 13-3 Critical Thinking Skills Activity 13 Geography in History Activity 13 Chapter Skills Activity 13 American Portrait 46 Primary and Secondary Source Readings p. 31 Workbook Activity 13-3 *Reteaching Activity 13-3 *Section Quiz 13-3	Section Focus Transparency 13-3 Skills Transparency 13 Testmaker GTV: The American People: Fabric of a Nation
CHAPTER REVIEW AND EVALUATION **1 Day**	Chapter 13 Test, Forms A and B Spanish Chapter 13 Summary Performance Assessment Activity 13	MindJogger Videoquiz Student Self-Test & Review Software *Chapter 13 Audiocassette Activity and Test

*Also available in Spanish

0:00   **OUT OF TIME?** If time does not permit teaching the entire chapter, use the Chapter 13 Summary on pages 448–449 and the Chapter 13 audiocassette (English and Spanish) to point out the main ideas of the chapter.

A complete, 1-page lesson plan is provided for each section in the *Reproducible Lesson Plan* booklet.

Key to Ability Levels

Teaching strategies have been coded for varying learning styles and abilities.

L1   Basic activities for all students.

L2   Average activities for average to above-average students

L3   Challenging activities for above-average students

LEP   Limited English Proficiency activities

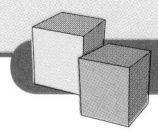

Block Schedule

Block scheduling differs from traditional class scheduling in the amount of time allotted to each period. The extended time frame provided by block scheduling affords you the opportunity to implement a greater number of research-oriented and activity-intense projects to motivate and involve your students. Activities that are particularly suited to use within the block scheduling framework are identified throughout this unit by the following designation:

✔ Performance Assessment Activity

A Picture Essay The Progressive Era was a time of tremendous innovation in painting, as exemplified by the Ashcan School. Divide the class into small groups and assign each one of these artists: Robert Henri, John Sloan, George Luks, William Glackens, Everett Shinn, Ernest Lawson, Arthur Davies, and Maurice Prendergast—the "Eight" of the Ashcan School. Ask each group to create a picture essay of its artist's works with descriptions of his paintings and an analysis of what the artist reveals about American life through his work. Students might also explain how the Ashcan School influenced other American artists.

POSSIBLE RUBRIC FEATURES

- Research Skills
- Content Information
- Organization
- Written and Visual Communication Skills
- Creativity
- Collaborative Skills

🗁 For additional activities, see Performance Assessment Strategies and Activities.

TEACHER'S CORNER

NATIONAL GEOGRAPHIC SOCIETY

NATIONAL GEOGRAPHIC SOCIETY PRODUCTS AVAILABLE FROM GLENCOE

To order the following products for use with this chapter, contact your local Glencoe sales representative or call Glencoe at 1-800-334-7344:

- *The Presidents: A Picture History of Our Nation* (CD-ROM)
- *GTV: A Geographic Perspective on American History* (Videodisc)
- *GTV: The American People: Fabric of a Nation* (Videodisc)

ADDITIONAL NATIONAL GEOGRAPHIC SOCIETY PRODUCTS

To order the following products for use with this chapter, call National Geographic Society at 1-800-368-2728:

- *The American Presidency* (Filmstrip)
- *Decades of History: The 20th Century—The Early Years* (Filmstrip)
- *The United States as a World Power: From the 1890s to the 1970s* (Filmstrip)

BEGINNING THE CHAPTER

Recording Journal Notes
Suggest that students organize their notes under the names of leaders active in the woman suffrage movement.

Linking Across
T I M E

Since the early 1900s, the Supreme Court has expanded the rights of working women. In 1971 the Court ruled that unequal treatment of women based on their gender violates the Fourteenth Amendment and is therefore unconstitutional. A 1986 ruling declared that sexual harassment in the workplace violates the 1964 Civil Rights Act.

The Progressive Era
1893–1920

▲ WOOD AND LEATHER ROCKING HORSE

Setting the Scene

Focus

In the late 1800s, the Grangers and Populists had sought to resist corrupt government and unfair business practices. By 1900 their stalled efforts were given fresh life by a new group of reformers—the progressives. These optimistic, largely urban, middle-class reformers were confident in their ability to improve government and the quality of life. Their reforms were based not only on traditional democratic values but also on the new philosophy of pragmatism and study of the social sciences.

Concepts to Understand

★ Why **reform** efforts were successful in correcting the worst abuses of big business and government

★ How **values and beliefs** shaped the program of the Progressive Era

Read to Discover . . .

★ the types of reform that progressive leaders advocated.

★ the limitations of progressivism.

Journal Notes

Note in your journal, as you read the chapter, how women continued to push for the right to vote.

CULTURAL	• **1890** *Census shows population of the United States at 63 million*	• **1897** *The first subway system is completed in Boston*
	1890	**1900**
POLITICAL	• **1890** *Sherman Silver Purchase Act passes*	• **1902** *Oregon adopts the initiative and referendum*

✚ EXTRA CREDIT PROJECT

Current Reform Movements Reform movements have emerged throughout American history in response to economic, political, and social problems. Interested students might research and report on current reform efforts. Ask them to identify an issue or problem and analyze the movement—its leaders, objectives, and outcomes. Students might conclude their reports by deciding if reform is needed and why. Have them share their work with the class. **L2**

On the chalkboard, reproduce the following generalization and concepts map, and have students copy it in their notebooks.

> A new group of reformers emerges to battle the injustices that had come about as a result of industrialization and urbanization

> Values and Beliefs

> Reform

To reinforce the two chapter concepts, use Chapter Concept Mapping Activities 13-A and 13-B.

Use Chapter Concepts Transparency Activities 13-A, 13-B.

History AND ART

The Lone Tenement, by George Bellows, depicts life in the city in the early 1900s. Bellows was influenced by the so-called Ashcan school, an art movement in the early 1900s that advocated realistic portrayals of urban life.

◀ FRANKLIN SAVINGS BANK

History AND ART

The Lone Tenement
by George Wesley Bellows, 1909

This urban scene displays the artist's vigorous and spontaneous style. Bellows is also remembered for his sports paintings, particularly prizefights.

- **1909** *National Association for the Advancement of Colored People (NAACP) is formed*

- **1920** *Sinclair Lewis's* Main Street *is bestseller*

1910	1920

- **1917** *United States declares war on Germany*

- **1920** *Ratification of woman suffrage*

✔ Performance Assessment

Analyzing Ideas Write the following assessment of the progressives on the chalkboard: "Although they excluded large groups from their efforts, the progressives expanded democracy, reformed education, and improved the quality of life for millions of men, women, and children."

Have students research and write a paper on the views of African American progressives like W.E.B. Du Bois and Ida Baker Wells Barnett. Ask students to answer the following questions in their paper: Would Du Bois and Barnett have agreed with this assessment of progressivism? Why or why not? Do you agree? Give reasons in support of your point of view. After the papers are completed, allow time for class discussion and feedback. **L2**

FOCUS

Bellringer

🔲 📁 Before taking roll, project Section Focus Transparency 13-1 or hand out Section Focus Transparency Activity 13-1. Have students answer the questions.

Motivating Activity

Read this statement by Jacob Riis, an American journalist: "The poor we shall have always with us, but the slum we need not have." Point out that Jacob Riis was one of the strongest advocates of social reform. Ask what idea Riis was expressing. **L2**

Vocabulary Precheck

Ask students to define each of the "Key Terms." Have a volunteer consult the dictionary for any unfamiliar words. **L1, LEP**

🔘 Use the Vocabulary PuzzleMaker Software to create a crossword puzzle. **L1**

📁 Assign Vocabulary Activity 13.

★★

Sources of Progressivism

Setting the Scene

Section Focus

The 1900s saw many challenges and opportunities for change. As city populations exploded with immigrants and rural Americans attracted by jobs, squalid slums and worker discontent also grew. In the face of threats of radical change, a variety of moderate reformers worked to protect, preserve, and improve American society.

Objectives

After studying this section, you should be able to

★ discuss the role of the muckrakers in identifying social ills and promoting social change.

★ explain how methods and strategies used in business and education influenced social reform.

Key Terms

social gospel, pragmatism

◀ LABOR UNION POSTER

*D*espite widespread social, political, and economic change in the late 1800s, the Gilded Age produced no broad effort to improve society. Populism was a large movement, but it was farm based and did not attract urban workers to its goals. The labor movement was also large, but it involved itself primarily with issues related to workers' jobs, wages, and working conditions.

Alternating periods of prosperity and depression accompanied industrialization in the late nineteenth century. Economic contractions shook the United States in the mid-1870s and well into the mid-1880s. The depression that followed the Panic of 1893, however, was the worst the nation had yet seen. As the split between rich and poor became too wide to ignore, Americans of all

classes began to ask hard questions about the nation's political and economic systems, and they saw much that alarmed them.

■ Inequality in America

Not until the 1890s did Americans begin to show widespread concern about the direction in which their society was moving. Increasing poverty was one area of concern.

The Gap Between the Rich and Poor

Millions of American laborers worked long hours for low wages in the late 1800s. Wages of industrial workers averaged $10 to $12 for a 60- to 80-hour week. One of every 5 women worked, frequently for as little as

---

Classroom Resources for SECTION 1

Blackline Masters:
- 📁 Reproducible Lesson Plan 13-1
- 📁 Guided Reading Activity 13-1
- 📁 Vocabulary Activity 13
- 📁 Enrichment Activity 13

- 📁 Primary and Secondary Source Readings, pp. 32-33
- 📁 American Literary Heritage, pp. 34–35
- 📁 Cooperative Learning Activity 13
- 📁 Workbook Activity 13-1
- 📁 Reteaching Activity 13-1
- 📁 Section Quiz 13-1

Transparencies:
- 📖 Section Focus Transparency 13-1
- 📖 Chapter Concepts Transparencies 13-A, 13-B

Multimedia:
- 💿 Vocabulary PuzzleMaker
- 💿 Testmaker
- 💿 The American History Videodisc

$6 to $8 a week, and children received even less. If workers were injured in industrial accidents, were laid off when business slowed, or became unemployed for any reason at all, their income completely stopped. At the other end of the scale were the immensely rich, the people who owned huge yachts, palatial estates, private railroad cars, and summer retreats covering thousands of acres. In 1900, when Andrew Carnegie earned $25 million from his steel company, the average worker made $500.

While 20 percent of the nation's families lived in comfort, 80 percent barely subsisted. A 1904 study estimated that 10 million Americans—12 percent of the nation's population—were "underfed, underclothed, and poorly housed." Relief for the poor was of little help because it was local, unsystematic, and largely dependent on private charity for funds.

It was not just the disparity of wealth that was alarming but also the distribution of political power. Not only did wealthy industrialists seem beyond the reach of government, they even appeared to dominate it. With such vast wealth and power at the top of society and such grinding poverty at the bottom, many Americans feared revolution.

Socialist Solutions

Some Americans turned to socialism as the answer. Edward Bellamy's 1887 novel *Looking Backward 2000–1887* made socialism seem an attractive alternative to the existing industrial society. His book tells the story of a nineteenth-century person in the United States who awakens from a prolonged hypnotic trance to find himself alive in a socialist paradise in the year 2000. All business has been merged into one big trust run by the people themselves; there is work and leisure for all without a trace of poverty or crime. Bellamy's vision of a socialist utopia made such an impact that his book sold 1 million copies, and numerous Nationalist Clubs were founded to advance his ideas.

Bellamy had no real program for action, however, and his followers eventually drifted toward other reform movements. Bellamy's influence, though, was reinforced by other socialist writers. Socialist ideas were widely circulated by popular authors such as Jack London and Upton Sinclair.

Popular labor leader Eugene V. Debs also lost faith in capitalism after being jailed during the Pullman strike of 1894. Declaring that in a democracy workers could gain control of the government and use it to change the free enterprise system, he organized the American Socialist party.

Opposed to Debs and other moderates were radical socialists such as Daniel De Leon, who preached that democratic reform was useless. "We Socialists are not reformers; we are Revolutionists," he

Weekly Wages in the Woolen Industry

Occupation and Location	Men 1890	Men 1900	Women 1890	Women 1900
New England Bobbin hands, doffers, and filling and roving	*Median weekly rates in dollars*			
carriers............................	4.50	5.00	3.00	4.00
Dresser tenders and beamers....................	12.00	8.00	6.00	6.50
General hands, helpers, and laborers....................	6.50	7.00	5.00	5.50
Loom fixers........................	12.50	13.50	—	—
Overseers and foreman..	19.50	19.50	—	—
Spinners............................	7.50	9.50	5.50	6.00
Weavers............................	7.50	9.00	6.50	7.50
All Occupations...............	7.50	8.00	6.50	6.50
Middle States All Occupations...............	7.50	9.00	5.00	5.00
Southern States All Occupations...............	6.50	6.50	3.50	3.50
Central States All Occupations...............	8.50	8.00	4.00	4.00
Pacific States All Occupations...............	9.50	9.50	5.00	5.00
All Sections All Occupations for workers under 16......	3.00	3.50	3.00	3.50

Source: Twelfth Census of the United States, 1900 *Special Reports: Employees and Wages (1903).*

Chart Study Note the differences in pay rates for skilled and unskilled labor for men and women, the regional variations in pay, and the lower wages for children. **Why are no rates shown for female supervisors?**

TEACH
Guided Practice

CURRICULUM CONNECTION

Mathematics Present the following: Urban and Rural Population in the United States, 1900–1930 (in millions of people)

Year	Urban	Rural
1900	30	46
1910	42	50
1920	54	52
1930	69	54

Ask students to predict which population will be greater in 1940, the urban or the rural. *(urban)* **L2**

Using Charts

Answer: Women did not hold such positions in the early 1900s.

Chart Skills Practice What does this chart tell you about the progress of industrial reform in various regions ? *(The West appears to be more advanced in terms of wage reform, the Southern states the least advanced.)*

Cultural Perspectives

An English Social Thinker Edward Bellamy's English counterpart H. G. Wells envisioned the effects of socialism differently. In his 1895 book *The Time Machine,* Wells's hero, a scientist, propels himself into a future world of languid, indifferent people for whom work has been abolished altogether. In the subterranean depths, however, lurk the subhumans who operate the society's machinery. They emerge from the darkness to feed upon the unresisting elite. Wells's pessimistic vision of the "beasts" created by the extremes of socialism was in sharp contrast to Bellamy's paradise.

▲ **WILLIAM BOOTH**

Visualizing History ▲ THE SOCIAL GOSPEL The Salvation Army, after being established in England by General William Booth, was organized in the United States in 1880. It helped provide food, lodging, and hope for the urban needy. *What else did the Salvation Army provide?*

declared. "We care nothing for forms. We want a change of the inside of the mechanism of society. . . ." De Leon argued that even labor unions were traitors to the working class because they compromised with the industrialists. He proposed to organize all workers into new industrial unions that would eventually take over American business.

The Wobblies

Debs and De Leon briefly cooperated in 1905 in founding such a labor union, the Industrial Workers of the World, or "Wobblies." Debs soon withdrew, however, and the IWW rejected De Leon in favor of more radical leaders who preached murder and sabotage. The preamble of the IWW's constitution declared, "The working class and the employing class have nothing in common. There can be no peace so long as hunger and want are found among millions of working people. . . ."

Wherever the IWW existed, there were confrontations, strikes, sabotage, and often violence. The IWW remained strong, however, until after World War I, when Americans rejected radical politics.

More Moderate Voices

Most socialists were more moderate than the Wobblies, however, and the socialist movement gained strength throughout the early 1900s. At its height in 1912, Debs polled nearly 1 million votes as the Socialist party candidate for President. Although this was less than 10 percent of the total votes cast, the socialist movement had an importance greater than its numbers indicated. Other more moderate reformers called "progressives" owed much of their success to a growing public feeling that the only way to save the capitalist system was to improve it.

■ Progressive Leadership

The Progressive Era occupied the first 15 years of the twentieth century. Although the reforms of this period are sometimes called the Progressive movement, that label can be misleading. Unlike the Populists, the progressives were not a political party.

Who the Progressives Were

Although a Progressive party was formed in 1912, progressives also were found in both major parties. Nor were progressives united by a geographic section or by an occupation. Instead, they were a broad and largely unorganized group of reformers who often worked independently, each seeking solutions to a specific problem. Some were local reformers, while others worked for change at state or national levels. The reforms progressives advocated sometimes even conflicted.

Also unlike the Populists, the progressives were generally not the victims of existing conditions. They were mostly urban middle-class professionals who worked as journalists, social workers, educators, and clergy. Although they themselves were not suffering, they sympathized with those who were.

The Social Gospel

Progressives among Catholic priests, Jewish rabbis, and Protestant ministers began to preach a new **social gospel:** that religious organizations should work to improve society as well as to meet the spiritual needs of their congregations. Leaders such as Washington Gladden, Josiah Strong, and Walter Rauschenbush were concerned about social problems. Rauschenbush explained his view:

> 66 *Our business is to make over an antiquated and immoral economic system. . . . Our inherited Christian faith dealt with individuals; our present task deals with society.* 99

In 1908 the National Council of the Churches of Christ was founded to support social reform. In every large city the Salvation Army—a religious group devoted to helping the needy—provided food, lodging, and hope for the despairing and poor. Like the settlement houses of the late 1800s, urban churches began to consider the whole person by providing recreational facilities, adult-education classes, nurseries, and counseling.

Women Reformers

Women also became a driving force for progressive reform. That women figured so largely in the Progressive movement was an indication that their status was improving.

★★★★★A★★★★★★★★ AMERICAN PORTRAITS

Ida Tarbell
1857–1944

After teaching school briefly, Ida Tarbell made her career as a writer and editor. She wrote hundreds of articles and many books, but her reputation as a "muckraker" rests on one book, *The History of the Standard Oil Company*, initially published as articles in *McClure's Magazine*.

Her interest in Standard Oil was deeply personal. Her father claimed that the company had forced him out of the oil tank business and had caused his partner to commit suicide. *McClure's* asked her to write about Standard Oil because of her knowledge of the oil business and because of her flair for writing.

For two years she researched Standard Oil's practices. Her revelations created such a popular furor that Standard Oil was investigated and eventually broken up by the Supreme Court for violating federal antitrust laws.

CHAPTER 13
SECTION 1

Teaching American Portraits

As an editor at *McClure's*, Ida Tarbell exercised great influence over its writers. Lincoln Steffens described her as a tactful, affectionate mediator of their squabbles. Allan Nevins, a biographer of Rockefeller, called her book on Standard Oil "the most spectacular success of the muckraking period...." Ask students what current writers they can think of whose work has revealed information that led to investigative proceedings.

◻ Assign Enrichment Activity 13.

◻ Assign Primary and Secondary Source Readings, pp. 32-33: "The Growth of the Standard Oil Company" by Ida Tarbell.

Sidelight: Jane Addams's Objectives

As a result of Jane Addams's Hull House, the first juvenile court in the United States, the first public playground in Chicago, pensions for mothers, the beginning of industrial medicine, and the union label came about. In 1935 Addams summed up her goals, "To marshal the moral forces capable of breaking what must be broken and building what must be rebuilt; to reconstruct our social relationships through regeneration of the heart; to repair a world shattered by war and sodden self-seeking; to establish moral control over a mass of mechanical achievements."

GLENCOE
TECHNOLOGY

VIDEODISC

The American History Videodisc

Side Two
Frames 11961-13550

Title: *The Progressive Era*

Subject: Sequences concerning the Progressive Era

By 1900 women's colleges in the North and East had been turning out well-trained graduates for two generations. These women were aware of and interested in the various issues of the day. National women's clubs devoted to the study of such issues were common. By 1910 these clubs had nearly 1 million members.

Furthermore, the rights of women were expanding. By 1900 every state recognized the right of women to make a will. Most states recognized the right of women to dispose of their own wages, and some states had given them the right to equal guardianship of children. More importantly, five Western states had adopted woman suffrage.

The settlement-house movement, which women continued to lead, expanded into broader areas of reform such as slum clearance and legislation to limit working hours and outlaw child labor. Florence Kelley left Jane Addams and Hull House in Chicago and founded the National Consumers League, where she organized boycotts of goods produced by children or by workers in unsafe or unhealthful conditions. Another former Hull House social worker, Julia Lathrop, became the first head of the federal Children's Bureau, created in the Department of Labor in 1912 and now part of Health and Human Services. Other female progressives included Carrie Chapman Catt, widely known for her work in the woman suffrage movement. Elizabeth Platt Decker headed the General Federation of Women's Clubs, which attracted nearly 1 million women in the early 1900s to promote the arts, education, and community health.

Striving for Big-Business Efficiency

Ironically, progressive reformers owed a great debt to the big businesses that so many of them detested. Unlike Populists, who believed that common people could solve society's problems, progressives put their faith in experts. Although critical of the methods and power of business leaders, progressives admired their ability to run large companies smoothly and efficiently. Progressives were confident that just like the trained managers, scientists, and efficiency experts who solved business problems, expert reformers could analyze and solve problems that kept society from running smoothly.

■ Educators and Investigators

In the mid-1800s, most American colleges were small, church-supported institutions less concerned with knowledge than with shaping the character of their students. Graduates who wanted to pursue further studies often went to Germany, where universities awarded an advanced degree, the Ph.D. These students brought back to America a learning style that emphasized questioning and research instead of memorizing facts. They pioneered changes in American colleges.

The Influence of Pragmatism

Coupled with educational reform was a new way of thinking known as **pragmatism,** an approach to problem solving that was popularized by Harvard philosopher William James. Pragmatists questioned the absolute truth of science. They believed that scientific laws stated only what was *probably* true and that ideas must be tested to see if they worked.

By the late 1800s many American colleges offered courses in social work, economics, political science, and sociology and granted advanced degrees. Professors such as social scientist Richard Ely at the University of Wisconsin taught students to solve problems pragmatically. At Johns Hopkins University, historian Henry Adams taught students how to do research and told them, "By the instrumentality of scholars great improvement of society is to be made." American colleges thus provided a core of reformers to study society and change it.

Pragmatist John Dewey, who taught at the University of Chicago, argued that the value of government actions should be measured by the good they do. Harvard Law School professor Oliver Wendell Holmes, Jr., was a pragmatist. In his book *The Common*

Critical Thinking Activity

Evaluating Tell students that muckrakers were criticized by many for what was often seen as exaggerated writings. Theodore Roosevelt, although a progressive himself, once called them "liars for hire." Ask students to research primary sources to find some articles by muckraking writers and select a passage or passages to read. Ask students how, if they had lived at the time, they would have reacted to such revelations about social conditions. Do they agree or disagree with Roosevelt's assessment of muckrakers? **L2, L3**

Law, he wrote that law should not be an absolute set of principles but a tool to meet the needs of society. When Holmes was appointed to the Supreme Court in 1902, his ideas began to influence its decisions.

The Muckrakers

Other, more popular, writers played a major role in investigating and exposing a variety of social problems. President Theodore Roosevelt compared these writers to a character in John Bunyan's book, *Pilgrim's Progress,* who constantly looked downward and raked filth, and he labeled them "muckrakers."

Most muckrakers were journalists who wrote for popular magazines like *McClure's Magazine, Cosmopolitan,* and *Collier's.* Although similar to the "yellow journalism" of the period, these articles were not written to boost sales but to expose conditions the writers had found deeply disturbing. For example, in 1902 Lincoln Steffens wrote a series of articles for *McClure's Magazine* that described shocking graft and corruption in city governments across the nation. He was followed in the same magazine by Ida Tarbell's exposé of the corrupt business practices of the Standard Oil Company. In 1906 David Phillips shocked the nation with a series in *Cosmopolitan* about links between big business and 75 United States senators.

Other muckrakers revealed the results of their investigations in books. In 1906 John Spargo's *The Bitter Cry of the Children* wrote about abuses of child labor, and two years

▲ THE MUCKRAKERS The investigative reporting of journalists such as Ida Tarbell, Ray Stannard Baker, and Lincoln Steffens (above) made them frequent contributors to national magazines. ***Why did President Roosevelt call such reporters "muckrakers"?***

later, Ray Stannard Baker's *Following the Color Line* revealed the long pattern of discrimination against African Americans in both the North and the South. Still other muckrakers were novelists who used fiction to criticize existing social conditions. In *The Octopus,* Frank Norris told how railroads dominated wheat farmers in a rich Western valley. Despite their revelations of society's ills, most muckrakers were not activists. They merely identified problems and argued for reform but counted on others to accomplish it.

Section 1 ★ Review

Checking for Understanding

1. **Identify** *Looking Backward,* Wobblies, Ida Tarbell, John Dewey, Oliver Wendell Holmes, muckrakers.

2. **Define** social gospel, pragmatism.

3. **List** five problems in American society that muckraking journalists called attention to in their writing.

Critical Thinking

4. **Understanding Cause and Effect** What relationship do the ideas of philosophy professor William James have to progressive reform?

ACTIVITY

5. Write a letter to a 1910 newspaper that tells why you believe government should or should not get involved in wage reform.

CHAPTER 13 The Progressive Era: 1893–1920 **401**

Visualizing **H**istory Point out that the muckrakers were not the first to write about society's ills, but the first to reach a vast audience.
Answer to Caption: compared them to a literary character who alway looked downward and raked up filth

ASSESS

Check Understanding
Assign Section 1 Review as homework or an in-class activity.

Evaluate
Assign Section Quiz 13-1 or use the Testmaker to create a customized quiz.

Reteach
Have students complete Reteaching Activity 13-1.

Enrich
Have students select one of the muckrakers mentioned in Section 1. Ask them to research and write a biographical sketch of that person.

Assign Cooperative Learning Activity 13.

CLOSE

Have students discuss how living and working conditions during the first decade of the 1900s were different from those during the last decade of the 1900s.

Team Teaching This selection from *Sister Carrie* can be presented in a team teaching context, in conjunction with English or Language Arts.

Historical Setting

At the end of the Civil War, the population of the United States was nearly 40 million. By 1910 it had doubled. This growth, coupled with increased industrialization, led to massive urbanization. By 1900 close to 40 percent of all Americans lived in cities. With the surge in population came the criticism that cities had grown too rapidly and become bleak and soulless.

Background

New literary movements are usually a reaction to their predecessors. Naturalism, however, did not abandon realism but rather took it a step further. Naturalist writers explored basic human drives but saw people as tossed about by fate and their environment, powerless to control their lives.

About the Author

Born in 1871 Theodore Dreiser worked as a journalist in his native Midwest and eventually settled in New York City. His first novel, *Sister Carrie,* published in 1900, drew on the city life he observed around him. The novel was considered objectionable because of its subject matter, and to Dreiser's dissatisfaction, received limited exposure.

American Literary Heritage

▲ THEODORE DREISER

A major literary development in the late nineteenth century was naturalism, which developed out of realist fiction. Naturalist writers carried the vivid detail of realism a step further by depicting environmental factors. In his first novel, *Sister Carrie,* published in 1900, Theodore Dreiser describes the compelling attraction as well as the cold indifference of life in growing cities.

Read to Discover

Why did naturalism, harsh and uncompromising, gain momentum during the years when the United States experienced a population boom? Read how Dreiser describes urban living. The city, with its immense presence and its disregard for the individual, proved the perfect backdrop for naturalistic literature.

Reader's Dictionary

novel	new; original
tacitly	expressed without words
shanty	crudely built dwelling or shelter

Sister Carrie (excerpts)

To Carrie, the sound of the little bells upon the horse-cars, as they tinkled in and out of hearing, was as pleasing as it was novel. She gazed into the lighted street when Minnie brought her into the front room, and wondered at the sounds, the movement, the murmur of the vast city which stretched for miles and miles in every direction.

Mrs. Hanson, after the first greetings were over, gave Carrie the baby and proceeded to get supper. Her husband asked a few questions and sat down to read the evening paper. He was a silent man, American born, of a Swede father, and now employed as a cleaner of refrigerator cars at the stock-yards. . . . His one observation to the point was concerning the chances of work in Chicago.

"It's a big place," he said. "You can get in somewhere in a few days. Everybody does."

It had been tacitly understood beforehand that she was to get work and pay her board. He was of a clean, saving disposition, and had already paid a number of monthly installments on two lots far out on the West Side. His ambition was some day to build a house on them. . . .

"You'll want to see the city first, won't you?" said Minnie, when they were eating. "Well, we'll go out Sunday and see Lincoln Park."

Carrie noticed that Hanson had said nothing to this. He seemed to be thinking of something else.

Cultural Perspectives

Edward Arlington Robinson The naturalist school was represented not only in novels but also in poetry. The preeminent poet of the period was Edward Arlington Robinson. Although his style was traditional, his work reflects a spirit of courage in the face of tragedy. Robinson was concerned with human relationships and how and why people acted the way they did. He was awarded the Pulitzer Prize in 1922, 1925, and 1928.

"Well," she said, "I think I'll look around tomorrow. . . . Which way is the business part?"

Minnie began to explain, but her husband took this part of the conversation to himself.

"It's that way," he said, pointing east. "That's east." Then he went off into the longest speech he had yet indulged in, concerning the lay of Chicago. "You'd better look in those big manufacturing houses along Franklin Street and just the other side of the river," he concluded. "Lots of girls work there. You could get home easy, too. It isn't very far." . . .

In 1889 Chicago had the peculiar qualifications of growth which made such adventuresome pilgrimages even on the part of young girls plausible. . . . It was a city of over 500,000, with the ambition, the daring, the activity of a metropolis of a million. Its streets and houses were already scattered over an area of seventy-five square miles. Its population was not so much thriving upon established commerce as upon the industries which prepared for the arrival of others. The sound of the hammer engaged upon the erection of new structures was everywhere heard. . . .

The entire metropolitan center possessed a high and mighty air calculated to overawe and abash the common applicant, and to make the gulf between poverty and success seem both wide and deep.

Into this important commercial region the timid Carrie went. She walked east along Van Buren Street through a region of lessening importance, until it deteriorated into a mass of shanties and coal-yards, and finally verged upon the river. She walked bravely forward, led by an honest desire to find employment and delayed at every step by the interest of the unfolding scene, and a sense of helplessness amid so much evidence of power and force which she did not understand. . . .

Through the open windows she could see the figures of men and women in working aprons, moving busily about. The great streets were wall-lined mysteries to her. . . .

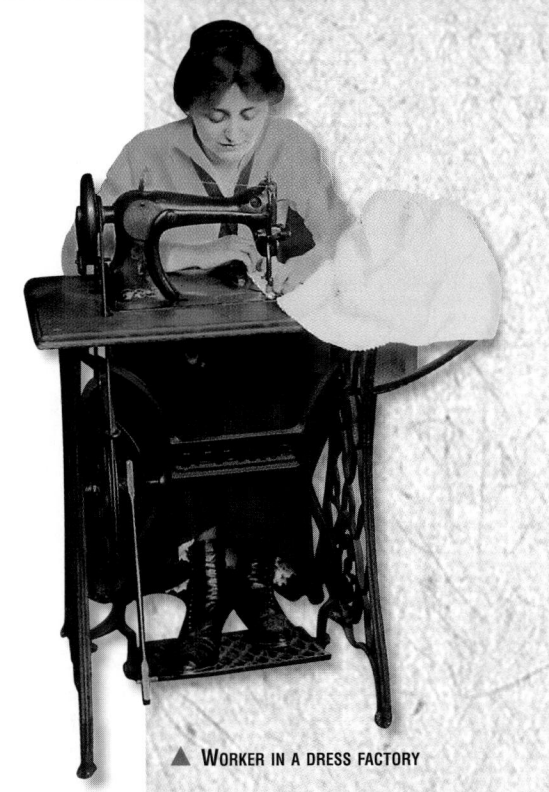

▲ WORKER IN A DRESS FACTORY

Responding to Literature

1. Why do you think Carrie came to live with her sister?

2. What kind of attitude about life in the city does Mr. Hanson demonstrate?

3. Do large cities today hold the attraction that they held for Carrie and other ambitious men and women at the turn of the century? Why or why not?

ACTIVITY

4. Create a table that shows the advantages and the disadvantages of living in a large city as opposed to a small town or rural living.

INTEGRATING
Language Arts

Developing Student Understanding

Ask students to name some positive and negative characteristics of city life, as compared with rural life. (*Positive: more employment and cultural opportunities, greater exposure to multicultural living, more diverse educational opportunities; Negative: overcrowding, greater ethnic and racial tensions, a more hectic pace of life*)

Explain that many naturalist writers of the early 1900s explored the lives of people in the cities, examining not only what made cities exciting but also the forces that overwhelmed people and often led to tragedy. **L2**

Other Works of Naturalist Writers

Naturalist writers included Upton Sinclair, whose 1906 novel, *The Jungle,* presented a stomach-churning and unforgettable portrait of the meatpacking industry. Frank Norris's 1901 novel, *The Octopus,* exposed a corrupt railroad industry that cheated small businesses while favoring large businesses.

History and the Humanities

Assign American Literary Heritage, pp. 34–35, *The Call of the Wild* by Jack London.

Answers to Responding to Literature

1. She believes that she will find new opportunities and a new life in the city.
2. His life revolves around work and money.
3. Answers will vary. Students might argue that cities have employment, educational, and social opportunities not available in small towns or rural areas. Others might defend the values of small town life, such as a healthy environment, a relaxed pace, more concerned people.
4. Student tables should display information concisely and objectively.

★★

Progressive Reforms

FOCUS
Bellringer

🖐️ 📁 Before taking roll, project Section Focus Transparency 13-2 or hand out Section Focus Transparency Activity 13-2. Have students answer the questions.

Motivating Activity

Discuss the requirements students must meet in order to apply for a job. Is there a minimum age? Must students have work permits? Social security numbers? Why are these rules necessary? How do these job requirements compare with job requirements at the beginning of the twentieth century? Point out to students that changes in child labor laws are only one of the reforms that occurred as a result of the Progressive Movement. Suggest that as students read Section 2 they look for other reforms that expanded and strengthened democracy. **L1**

Vocabulary Precheck

Ask students to define each of the "Key Terms." Have a volunteer consult the dictionary for any unfamiliar words. **L1, LEP**

Setting the Scene

Section Focus

Progressive reforms affected government, consumer's rights, and education. People began to speak out against children working in mines, mills, and factories and to back temperance and woman suffrage. Although early accomplishments were mainly local changes, later reforms occurred at state and national levels.

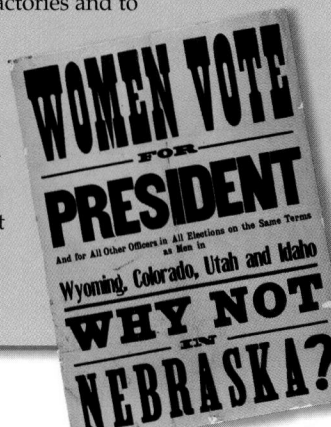

◀ WOMAN SUFFRAGE POSTER

Objectives

After studying this section, you should be able to

★ explain how reforms strengthened democracy.

★ describe the advances made by social reformers and government in protecting adult and child workers.

Key Terms

direct primary, initiative, referendum, recall

---

*J*t is fitting that the earliest evidence of progressive activism dealt with cities. Being primarily city residents, progressives were viewed as representative of the increasing importance of the nation's urban centers. What is perceived as the initial progressive reform came even before the muckrakers began to write. This reform was inspired not by a book or a magazine article but by a natural disaster.

■ Reforms in Government

In 1900 a hurricane roared in from the Gulf of Mexico and devastated the coastal city of Galveston, Texas. When the political machine that controlled city government proved incapable of responding to the disaster, local reformers and business leaders

convinced the state legislature to allow them to take control. In April 1901, the mayor and city council were replaced by five commissioners chosen in a nonpartisan election. Four of the commissioners were local business leaders who applied their management experience to running the city, and it quickly recovered. Reformers in other cities were impressed. Galveston's experience demonstrated the benefits of running a city like a business.

Changes in City Government

From the commission plan developed another progressive reform—the city-manager plan. In this reform an elected city council hired a professional manager to run city government, much as the directors of a business would hire a superintendent to run a factory.

Classroom Resources for SECTION 2

Blackline Masters:
📁 Reproducible Lesson Plan 13-2
📁 Guided Reading Activity 13-2
📁 American Literary Heritage, pp. 26–28
📁 American Portraits, p. 48
📁 Linking Past and Present Activity 13
📁 Chapter 13 Map Activity
📁 Reteaching Activity 13-2

📁 Section Quiz 13-2
Transparencies:
📊 Section Transparency 13-2
📊 Chapter Map Transparency 13
Multimedia:
💿 Testmaker
💿 GTV: The American People: Fabric of a Nation

Early city managers often were engineers, because much of the business of running a modern city—such as sewage disposal, water supply, and paving streets—was technical. By 1915 more than 400 cities had adopted commission or city-manager plans.

Even in cities where progressives could not reshape government, reform mayors fought powerful combinations of political bosses, unethical business leaders, and corrupt city officials. Reform mayors such as Tom Johnson in Cleveland, Samuel "Golden Rule" Jones in Toledo, and Hazen Pingree in Detroit gained national attention. All three left successful businesses to battle corruption in city government and to force streetcar lines, electric companies, and other utilities to behave in the public interest.

Voting Reforms

At the state level, political reform was first achieved in Wisconsin. Robert La Follette, after twice failing to become Republican

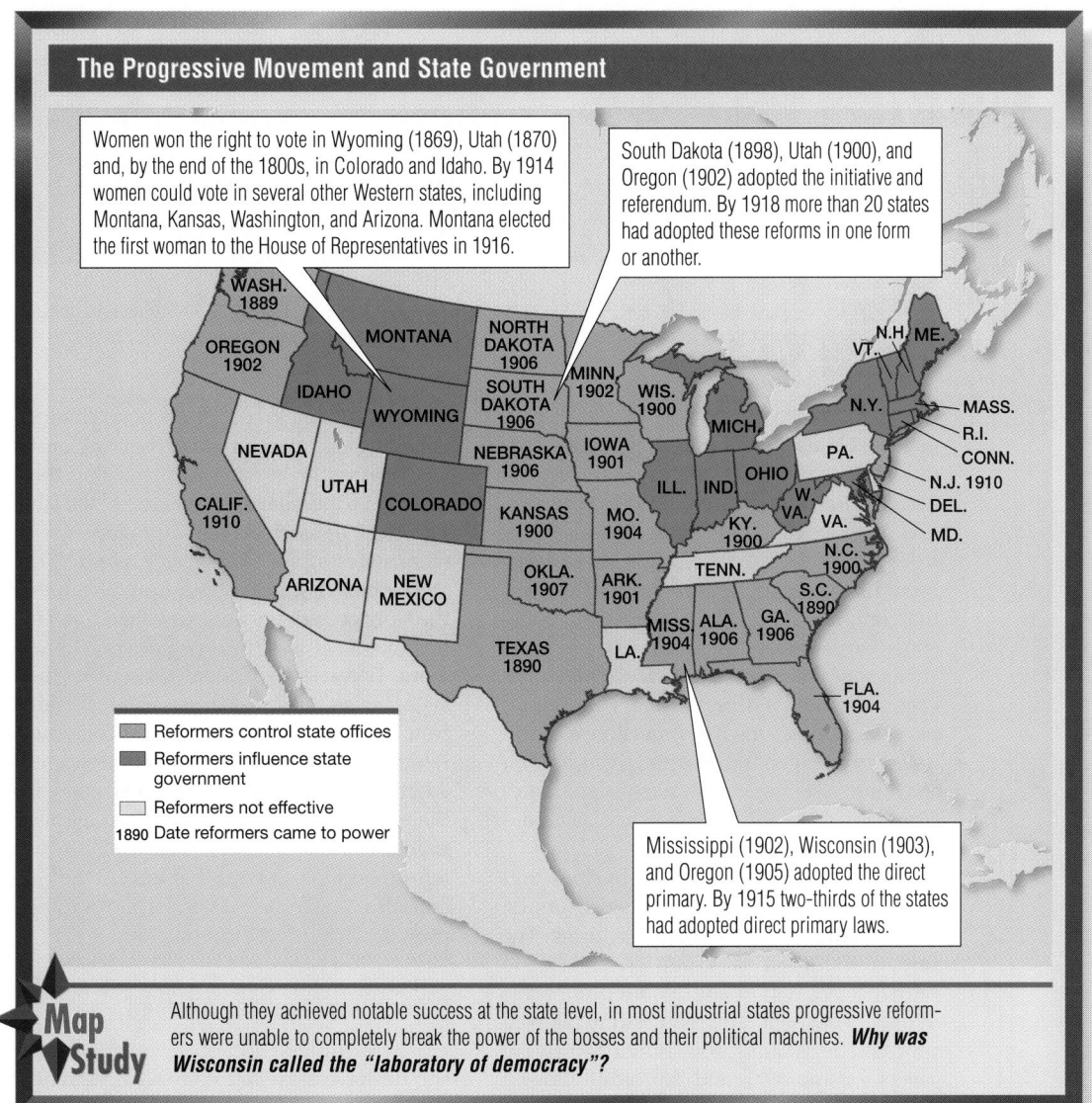

The Progressive Movement and State Government

Women won the right to vote in Wyoming (1869), Utah (1870) and, by the end of the 1800s, in Colorado and Idaho. By 1914 women could vote in several other Western states, including Montana, Kansas, Washington, and Arizona. Montana elected the first woman to the House of Representatives in 1916.

South Dakota (1898), Utah (1900), and Oregon (1902) adopted the initiative and referendum. By 1918 more than 20 states had adopted these reforms in one form or another.

WASH. 1889
OREGON 1902
IDAHO
MONTANA
WYOMING
NORTH DAKOTA 1906
SOUTH DAKOTA 1906
MINN. 1902
WIS. 1900
MICH.
N.H. ME.
VT.
N.Y.
MASS.
R.I.
CONN.
NEVADA
UTAH
COLORADO
NEBRASKA 1906
IOWA 1901
ILL. IND.
OHIO
PA.
N.J. 1910
DEL.
CALIF. 1910
KANSAS 1900
MO. 1904
KY. 1900
W. VA.
VA.
MD.
ARIZONA
NEW MEXICO
OKLA. 1907
ARK. 1901
TENN.
N.C. 1900
S.C. 1890
TEXAS 1890
LA.
MISS. 1904
ALA. 1906
GA. 1906
FLA. 1904

▮ Reformers control state offices
▮ Reformers influence state government
▯ Reformers not effective
1890 Date reformers came to power

Mississippi (1902), Wisconsin (1903), and Oregon (1905) adopted the direct primary. By 1915 two-thirds of the states had adopted direct primary laws.

Map Study Although they achieved notable success at the state level, in most industrial states progressive reformers were unable to completely break the power of the bosses and their political machines. *Why was Wisconsin called the "laboratory of democracy"?*

Guided Practice

Categorizing Organize students into four groups. Give each group one of the following topics: Tax Reform, Regulation of Public Utilities, Protection of Workers, Advances in Education. Ask students in each group to make a list of subtopics and details that indicate specific reforms in each area. Create a class outline on the chalkboard entitled "Some Progressive Reforms." Summarize the activity by discussing which reforms probably had the greatest impact on the lives of average citizens. **L2**

Map Study *Using Maps*

Answer: A great many of the progressive reforms were adopted there.

Map Skills Practice Based on this map, ask students to make a statement about the overall success of reformers at the state level. (*Reformers had more success in influencing state government than in actually controlling those governments.*)

🖐️ 🗂️ For additional map practice, use Map Transparency Activity 13 and Chapter Map Activity 13.

Special Needs Activity

Study Strategy Many words in this section have specific definitions that are not always apparent from the content of the text. Have students write these words that appear in bold type in the Reforms in Government subsection: **direct primary, initiative, referendum, recall.** Direct them to look up the words in an unabridged dictionary and write all the definitions given. Then ask students to compare the definitions in the dictionary with the use in the text and put an asterisk by the definition that is the same as the meaning in the text. **L1, LEP**

 **Visualizing History**

▲ **THE RIGHT TO VOTE** Women parade for the right to vote in New York. Suffragists (left) are forced to eat during a hunger strike. *Which region of the nation was first to grant woman suffrage?*

candidate for governor, finally was elected in 1900. He used his office to attack the tradition of party nominating conventions. Because party bosses controlled the selection of convention delegates, they also controlled the selection of election candidates. From his own experience, La Follette knew that reformers had little chance of being chosen to run for office. In 1903 he pressured the state legislature to require that each party hold a **direct primary,** a preliminary election in which voters choose candidates for the general election. This reform took the nomination of party candidates from the bosses and their political machines and gave it to the people.

To reduce the control that big business and the party bosses had over state legislators, La Follette introduced three other reforms. The **initiative** allowed a group of citizens to introduce legislation and required the legislature to vote on it. The **referendum** allowed proposed legislation to be submitted to the voters for approval, and the **recall** allowed voters to remove an elected official from

office by holding a special election. Although none of these ideas originated in Wisconsin, La Follette's great success in enacting them there gave the state a reputation as "the laboratory of democracy," and progressives in other states copied Wisconsin's reforms.

The most significant political reform that the progressives accomplished at the national level was the direct election of senators. Because they were chosen by their state legislatures, senators were shielded from direct public pressure. Progressive reformers felt that if its members were elected, the Senate would be more responsive to the public will and less influenced by powerful business interests. The call for this reform became so great that in 1913 the Seventeenth Amendment to the Constitution provided for direct election of senators.

Slow Progress for Women

It was difficult to argue that the people should have a greater voice in government affairs without including women, especially

Sidelight: Reformers in the Cities

Three notable progressives were responsible for urban reform. When he became mayor of Detroit in 1898, Hazen Pingree improved the quality of life with new parks and schools and work for the unemployed. Samuel Jones, mayor of Toledo, established municipal ownership of public utilities and cleaned up corruption in the police at the turn of the century. In 1901 in Cleveland, Tom Johnson placed higher taxes on railroad and utility properties, lowered streetcar fares, and built recreational facilities.

because they were increasingly holding jobs in factories, business offices, and schools, as well as taking prominent roles in reform movements. In addition, some progressives believed that if women gained the right to vote, their influence would help push through other reforms. By 1914, 11 Western states had granted women full suffrage. In the East, women promoted their cause by holding parades and circulating petitions. Many women believed, however, that a constitutional amendment would be needed to gain the vote nationwide.

■ Consumer Protection

A basic principle that American business inherited from Great Britain was *caveat emptor,* Latin for "let the buyer beware." This meant that people who purchased worthless life insurance, bread made with sawdust, or colored water labeled as medicine had only themselves to blame for not being more careful. Progressives argued that consumers had no way of knowing when meat was prepared under unsanitary conditions, children's cough syrup was dosed with opium, or other products were similarly misrepresented.

Regulating the Insurance Industry

In 1905 Charles Evans Hughes, a lawyer who worked for the New York legislature, investigated the insurance industry. He uncovered bribery of elected officials and huge salaries insurance executives paid to themselves and to family members they hired. Consequently, New York—and later other states—passed laws to regulate insurance companies and to protect the interests of policyholders.

Making Buildings Safer

At the local level, protection for consumers often came in the form of city zoning laws. The laws regulated how land and buildings could be used. Building codes prohibited some of the worst features of tenements by setting minimum requirements for light and air, fire escapes, room size, and sanitation.

Ensuring the Safety of Food and Medicine

Passage of pure food and drug laws demonstrated the effectiveness of the muckrakers in influencing consumer protection. Articles in *Collier's* about harmful medicines in 1906 convinced the chief chemist of the Department of Agriculture to perform experiments on himself and then to call for regulation. Even more sensational was the publication in 1906 of Upton Sinclair's best-selling book, *The Jungle,* a fact-based novel that portrayed horribly unsanitary conditions in slaughterhouses:

> 66 *There would be meat that had tumbled out on the floor, in the dirt and sawdust, where workers had tramped and spit uncounted billions of [tuberculosis] germs. There would be meat stored in great piles in rooms; and the water from leaky roofs would drip over it, and thousands of rats would race about on it.* 99

An outraged President Theodore Roosevelt demanded reform, and Congress responded with legislation. The Pure Food and Drug Act established a government agency, the Food and Drug Administration, to protect consumers from unsafe medicines and foods. The Meat Inspection Act was passed on the same day in 1906. These laws regulated the content and inspection of food, prohibited the use of addictive drugs in nonprescription medicines, and required accurate labels on food and drug products. State governments followed with similar legislation to regulate food and drugs that did not cross state lines.

■ Protecting Workers

"I aimed at the public's heart," Upton Sinclair complained, "and by accident I hit it in the stomach." Sinclair did not intend *The Jungle* to focus public attention on impure food. Instead he wanted to expose

Linking Across TIME

A legacy of the progressives' concern with protecting people from harmful substances can be seen in the work of the Food and Drug Administration (FDA) and the Environmental Protection Agency (EPA). The EPA, which regulates toxic substances, registers some 22,000 pesticides and requires some 75 toxicity tests for each pesticide. Companies are often required to wait several years for a substance to be approved and licensed for sale and use.

 Assign American Literary Heritage, pp. 26–28: from *The Jungle* by Upton Sinclair.

NATIONAL GEOGRAPHIC SOCIETY

GTV: The American People: Fabric of a Nation

Side 3, Chapter 5
Frames 22750-28981
Title: *Sending a Message*
Subject: Citizenship and voting rights

Sidelight: Mother Jones and Child Labor

Mary Harris Jones ("Mother Jones") was a well-known labor leader in the late 1800s and early 1900s. She devoted much of her life to speaking and organizing efforts to help improve the conditions of workers, especially children. At the age of 73, Jones organized and led the March of the Mill Children from Pennsylvania to New York. Three children dressed as Revolutionary soldiers led the group and carried signs that read, "We Want to Go to School" and "Prosperity, Where Is Our Share?" The marchers were seeking the President's support for a law prohibiting child labor.

Visualizing
History

▲ CHILD LABOR One concern for reformers was protecting children, such as these workers in a Pennsylvania coal mine. Because canaries are very sensitive to poisonous gases, they were used to detect such gases in coal mines. *How was child labor reform achieved?*

the terrible working conditions in slaughterhouses. One of the grim realities of industrialization was the frequency of industrial accidents.

Workers' Compensation

Workers who suffered industrial accidents had little protection. Employers argued that industrial accidents were not caused by unsafe conditions but by carelessness, and they often fired employees who were seriously disabled. Progressives joined labor union leaders to pressure state legislatures for workers' compensation laws. These laws established insurance funds into which employers made payments. Workers who were injured by industrial accidents were paid from the fund. In 1902 Maryland was first to pass such legislation, and by 1911 10 of the states had workers' compensation laws on the books. Workers' compensation laws not only

helped injured workers, they improved working conditions for all workers because employers with low accident rates paid lower insurance premiums. Related progressive legislation established state agencies to inspect factories, limited workers' hours, and attempted to end crowded, unsanitary work environments.

Protecting Women: *Muller* v. *Oregon*

Many progressives were especially interested in improving working conditions for women. By 1900 about 20 percent of all workers were women, and progressive reformers believed women workers needed special protection. In 1903 Oregon passed a law limiting female factory workers to a 10-hour day. Employers challenged the law as violating a woman's civil right to work as long as she chose, and in 1908 the case was appealed to the Supreme Court.

Critical Thinking Activity

Evaluating Effectiveness Have students research some social-service organizations that are active in their community. Suggest they focus on such questions as how these organizations help the people of the community. Which organization is the most important, and why do you think so? What kind of organization do you think your

community needs that it does not have? Have students write a report answering these questions. When students present their reports, conduct a class discussion on how students think social-service organizations in their community might be improved. **L3**

To defend the law in *Muller* v. *Oregon*, progressive attorney Louis D. Brandeis presented research that convinced the Court that long working hours damaged women's health, and the Oregon law was upheld. After the *Muller* decision, several other states quickly passed similar laws.

Muller v. *Oregon* was a revolutionary legal decision. For the first time, the Court looked beyond legal principles and precedents and applied pragmatism to the law. The Court began to weigh what was best for society when it decided cases. In so doing, it took the first step toward becoming an instrument of social reform.

Protecting Children

Probably the most emotional progressive labor reform was the campaign against child labor. Although children had always worked on family farms, urban children found factory work dangerously monotonous and conditions often unhealthy or unsafe. Reformers established a National Child Labor Committee in 1904 to campaign for the abolition of child labor.

Muckraker John Spargo's 1906 book, *The Bitter Cry of the Children*, presented detailed evidence of the conditions of child labor in America. He told of anthracite coal mines, where thousands of "breaker boys" were hired at age 9 or 10 to pick slag out of coal and were paid 60 cents for a 10-hour day. He described how the work permanently bent their backs and often crippled their hands. He revealed that in textile mills more than one-eighth of the employees were less than 16 years old and that some children entered cotton factories at age 7 or 8. Public opinion was so stirred by such information that by 1914 all but one state set a minimum age for employment and many established other limits on child labor as well. At the federal level, the newly established Children's Bureau had few powers, but it investigated and published information that helped the campaign to improve the well-being of child workers.

Linking Past and Present

★★★★★★★★★★★

Scouting

While many progressive reformers often focused on social issues, others concentrated on providing organized activities for boys and girls.

Then_____

Beginnings

Organizations such as the Boy Scouts of America (founded in 1910) and the Girl Scouts of America (1912) arose to provide supervised activities that stressed traditional values.

"BE PREPARED"

"DO A GOOD TURN DAILY"

Scouts hiked during the school year, camped in the summer, and attended weekly meetings packed with instructions, drills, and games. Scouting channeled adolescent energy into the wholesome pursuit of specialized merit badges acquired by passing tests on woodcraft, reconnaissance, and citizenship skills.

Now_____

The Growth of Scouting

The scouting program of work, play, and companionship continues today. The program is part of an international organization, encompassing members in more than 100 nations. Currently, in the United States, about 10 million individuals hold membership in the Boy Scouts and Girl Scouts. Scouting has touched the lives of a wide and very diverse group of individuals. More than 90 pilots and scientists selected as astronauts and mission specialists, including Neil Armstrong and Dr. Anna Fisher, were active in scouting. Others with backgrounds in scouting include baseball great Henry Aaron and John F. Kennedy, the first scout to become President.

★★★★★★★★★★★★★★★★★★★★★★★★★★★★★★

ASSESS

Check Understanding

Assign Section 2 Review as homework or an in-class activity.

Evaluate

◉ 🗁 Assign Section Quiz 13-2 or use the Test-maker to create a customized quiz.

Reteach

Ask students to identify and explain the ways in which progressives attempted to make government more democratic and efficient.

🗁 Have students complete Reteaching Activity 13-2.

Enrich

Tell students that in the latter part of the twentieth century the direct primary has been severely criticized for a variety of reasons. One is that because primaries are stretched out over a period of time, only wealthy candidates can afford to go the distance. Also, voters lose interest after a while. Ask students to write letters to their representatives in Congress suggesting ways that direct primaries might be reformed to address the charges of the critics.

CLOSE

Ask the students to discuss the elements of direct democracy that have survived from the Progressive Era.

■ Varieties of Reform

In addition to reforming labor practices, many progressives insisted that business be regulated. Because of their great influence and power, large corporations commonly gained tax breaks from state legislatures.

Robert La Follette, the governor of Wisconsin, determined that railroads paid less than half the property taxes of other businesses. He obtained reform laws to tax railroads on a more equal basis. La Follette also established a commission to regulate the railroads in the state.

On the federal level, Congress began to tax corporate profits in 1909. Although the Supreme Court in 1895 had declared an income tax unconstitutional, in 1913 the Sixteenth Amendment empowered the federal government to levy such a tax.

Public Utilities

The Progressive Era also was a time when reformers called for regulation of public utilities such as streetcar lines, waterworks, and electric-light companies. Many states set up public service commissions with the power to control the rates charged by public utilities. Some city reformers called for city governments to buy them out and run the utilities directly. By 1915, for example, all but 1 of the 36 largest cities owned or operated their own waterworks.

Health, Recreation, and Education

Progressive reform was also felt in other areas. It resulted in playgrounds and dental clinics for children. Private charities multiplied and broadened their social usefulness. Progressives also began to show concern about America's natural resources. State and federal governments passed conservation laws and set aside public recreation areas.

The reform impulse also resulted in great progress in education. Many states passed laws requiring children to attend school, and the number of high schools more than doubled between 1900 and 1920. The school year was lengthened and the curriculum enriched by courses in music, art, home economics, and industrial arts.

The Fight Against Alcohol Use

Long at the forefront of the temperance movement was the Woman's Christian Temperance Union (WCTU), founded in 1874. By 1890, it already had 150,000 members.

Like so many progressive reforms, temperance was first accomplished at the local level. By 1914 nearly half the people of the United States lived in areas where the sale of alcohol was illegal, and 12 states had passed statewide Prohibition laws. In 1919 Prohibition became nationwide when the Eighteenth Amendment was added to the Constitution.

Section 2 ★ Review

Checking for Understanding

1. **Identify** Galveston, Seventeenth Amendment, Charles Evans Hughes, Upton Sinclair, *Muller* v. *Oregon,* John Spargo, WCTU.

2. **Define** direct primary, initiative, referendum, recall.

3. **Describe** the commission plan as a form of city government.

4. **Discuss** three reforms that came out of the Progressive movement that promoted more direct involvement by citizens in government.

Critical Thinking

5. **Understanding Cause and Effect** Explain why progressive reforms strengthened the cause of woman's suffrage.

ACTIVITY

6. Identify reforms that are being demanded today. On a chart, compare these with reforms sought by progressives in terms of who will benefit from the reforms, who opposes them and why, and overall goals.

Answers to SECTION 2 REVIEW

1. Galveston, 404; Seventeenth Amendment, 406; Charles Evans Hughes, 407; Upton Sinclair, 407–408; *Muller* v. *Oregon*, 408; John Spargo, 409; WCTU, 410
2. All vocabulary words are defined in the Glossary.
3. City government is divided into departments; mayor and city council are replaced by elected commissioners.
4. direct primary, initiative, referendum, recall, and the direct elections of senators
5. Many reformers were women, and it was difficult to reform society and extend democracy without confronting the irony that women were denied the vote on the basis of gender.
6. Charts should address each of the comparisons appropriately.

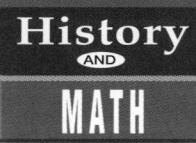
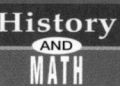
Urbanization

Demography is the study of population. Demographers measure population density (how many people live in a given area), distribution (where people live), and migration patterns (movement from one place to another). They collect and examine other information about people—births and deaths, marriages, ages, and national backgrounds. Their findings

The greatest growth occurred in the industrial cities of the Northeast, but cities in all regions experienced rapid growth. Nashville went from just less than 17,000 people to more than 80,000, Minneapolis from 2,500 to more than 200,000, and Los Angeles from 4,400 to more than 100,000. Cities such as Detroit, Cleveland, Buffalo, Milwaukee, Indianapolis, Columbus, Toledo, Omaha, and Atlanta doubled, or even tripled, in size.

Urban Population, 1860–1920				
Year	Percent Rural	Percent Urban	Cities 2,500 to 50,000	Cities over 50,000
1860	80.2	19.8	376	16
1870	74.3	25.7	638	25
1880	71.8	28.2	904	35
1890	64.9	35.1	1290	58
1900	60.3	39.7	1659	80
1910	54.3	45.7	2153	109
1920	48.8	51.2	2578	144

often explain how changes in a society have affected people.

The table on this page shows demographic information for the period from 1860 through 1920. During this period, great cities became an important part of the national scene. Cities were vital centers of physical, social, and cultural change during this period. One of the most obvious changes was their sheer growth.

Urban growth was not new. Most American cities had been growing steadily since colonial times, and New York City already had more than 1 million residents by 1860. The rate of growth, however, rose significantly. By 1900 New York's population had more than tripled.

During the same span of years, Chicago's population rose from 440,000 to about 1.7 million, Philadelphia grew from 565,000 people to approximately 1.3 million, while population in both Boston and Baltimore increased from about 200,000 to more than 500,000.

Not only was there a growth in city population, but the entire nation was undergoing urbanization—a rise in the proportion of the total population living in urban settings. In 1860, less than 20 percent of the population of the United States lived in towns and cities with populations of 2,500 or more. By 1900 that figure had reached about 40 percent. By 1920, a majority of Americans would be city dwellers.

Making the Math Connection

1. According to the table, when did urban dwellers first outnumber rural dwellers?

2. What percentage of Americans in 1880 lived in rural settings?

ACTIVITY

3. Create a bar graph that shows urban growth from 1860 through 1920.

411

Answers to Making the Connection

1. 1920
2. 71.8

3. Bar graphs should use the percentage figures under Percent Urban for the years listed.

FOCUS

Bellringer

🔖 📁 Before taking roll, project Section Focus Transparency 13-3 or hand out Section Focus Transparency Activity 13-3. Have students answer the questions.

Motivating Activity

Read to students the following statement by Booker T. Washington:

"In all things that are purely social we [the two races] can be as separate as the fingers, yet one as the hand in all things essential to mutual progress."

Point out to students that Washington was the most influential black leader at the turn of the century. He thought African Americans could not gain equality with whites all at once. Ask students to interpret Washington's statement. Tell students that in this section they will learn how progressives viewed African Americans as well as new immigrants and how these views affected minority groups. **L1**

Vocabulary Precheck

Write "literacy test" on the chalkboard. Have a volunteer skim the section to find the term and read it in context. **L1, LEP**

★★★
Limits of Progressivism

Setting the Scene

Section Focus

While progressivism resulted in many lasting changes, reform had its limits. Much progressive reform was based on traditional American attitudes about race, sex, and nationalism. As a result, not all Americans shared equally in the benefits of reform.

◀ WOODEN ICE SKATES, EARLY 1900S

Objectives

After studying this section, you should be able to

★ describe progressive attitudes about immigrants and racial minorities.

★ explain why African American leadership changed.

Key Term

literacy test

$\mathcal{T}$he achievements of progressive reform at the national level were less far-reaching than its successes at local and state levels. It was more difficult to create nationwide demands for reform than to organize effective campaigns on a smaller scale. The federal government also was more difficult to prod into action. The Senate, chosen by boss-dominated state legislatures until 1913, was a highly conservative body. In the House of Representatives, powerful figures such as committee heads and the speaker usually resisted change.

The Supreme Court became somewhat less conservative than it had been in the 1890s, as progressives Oliver Wendell Holmes (1902), Charles Evans Hughes (1910), and Louis D. Brandeis (1916) were appointed to the Court. Yet the majority of justices seldom were willing to extend federal power into new areas.

Partly because of the attitude of the courts, many of the evils described by the muckrakers were considered outside the constitutional sphere of the federal government's powers, making national reform nearly impossible.

The benefits of progressivism were spread unevenly in other ways, too. Many middle-class progressives feared labor unions almost as much as they did trusts. So although progressives worked with labor leaders to improve working conditions, few objected when businesses organized effectively to prevent unions in their plants—often with cooperation from local courts and police. Therefore, wage gains during the Progressive Era went only to skilled workers. The earning power of unskilled workers actually dropped because prices increased more rapidly than their rates of pay.

Classroom Resources for SECTION 3

Blackline Masters:
📁 Reproducible Lesson Plan 13-3
📁 Guided Reading Activity 13-3
📁 Critical Thinking Skills Activity 13
📁 Geography in History Activity 13
📁 Workbook Activity 13
📁 Chapter Skills Activity 13

📁 American Portraits, p. 46
📁 Primary and Secondary Source Readings, p.31
📁 Reteaching Activity 13-3
📁 Section Quiz 13-3

Transparencies:
🔖 Section Focus Transparency 13-3
🔖 Skills Transparency 13

Multimedia:
 Testmaker
⊙ GTV: The American People: Fabric of a Nation

Reformers and Immigrants

Among the many factors that held down the wages of unskilled workers was the continuing flood of immigrants to the United States, averaging one million a year during the Progressive Era—largely from southern and eastern Europe. This "New Immigration" caused widespread alarm, as immigrant men and women competed for unskilled jobs in American mines, mills, and factories.

In addition, the newcomers seemed to have more difficulty fitting in to established American culture than the "old immigrants" from northern and western Europe. Pressure from labor-union leaders and such organizations as the Immigration Restriction League persuaded Congress in 1897, 1913, and 1915 to enact laws requiring all immigrants to pass **literacy tests,** tests to show they could read English. All three laws were vetoed, but such a law passed over President Woodrow Wilson's veto in 1917.

Reform and Immigrant Cultures

Many progressives feared the socialist ideas that immigrants brought from Europe. As middle-class reformers, progressives wanted to change capitalism, not abolish it. Many also worried about preserving existing values and culture. Therefore, many progressive reforms were aimed at weakening the political strength of immigrant numbers and instilled in newcomers what reformers thought were proper American values.

In calling for reform of city government, one writer complained about:

> 66 [t]he mass of ignorant voters, who now help the vicious bosses to govern our cities. . . . A colony of Italians, Scandinavians, Germans, or Irish, preserving their national language and their national ideas, and living as foreigners among us is very difficult to reach, but their votes count just as much as the votes of the most highly educated men among us. 99

▲ ADULT CLASSES Many businesses organized English classes for their employees. The classes were held in the plant so that workers could attend at the end of their shift. *Why would employers consider learning English important?*

Cooperative Learning Activity

Comparing Viewpoints Divide the class into groups, and assign each group one of the following roles: a newly arrived immigrant, a progressive reformer, a political boss, a labor union leader. Direct students to formulate the views of each of these people concerning immigration and reform. Ask each group to present its viewpoint to the class and answer questions. You might suggest that students write a summary of each of the viewpoints presented and discuss the merits of each. **L2, L3**

Independent Practice

Debate Ask students to summarize the arguments of Booker T. Washington and those of W.E.B. Du Bois. After they have completed their summaries, ask them to write a few paragraphs explaining with whose views they most agree and why. You might suggest they conclude by comparing the arguments of Washington and Du Bois with those of African American leaders today. **L2**

📁 Assign Guided Reading Activity 13-3.

📁 Assign American Portrait 46: Ida B. Wells-Barnett.

📁 Assign Primary and Secondary Source Readings p.31: "Advice to African Americans" by Booker T. Washington.

Visualizing
History Although progressives largely ignored the problems of African Americans, some were actively involved in the founding of the National Association for the Advancement of Colored People (NAACP). In fact, with the exception of Du Bois, all of the founders were white. However, the group's leaders and members were mainly African Americans.
Answer to Caption: the NAACP

Visualizing History ▲ **STRIVING FOR JUSTICE** Booker T. Washington (right) and W.E.B. Du Bois were among the most important African American leaders of the period. Both men had the same goals, but they took different approaches to those goals. *What organization did Du Bois help form?*

When progressives reformed government by defeating political bosses and machines, they also destroyed the system that provided immigrant groups with a political voice, political jobs, and political power.

Education and Resistance

As reformers obtained child labor laws and school attendance laws, they forced immigrant children out of factories and into classrooms. Many states made the study of American history a required course in public schools during the Progressive Era. Educator John Dewey advised that it was essential to teach students to be good citizens.

With the great increase in immigration in the late 1800s, other functions were thrust upon the schools. Besides teaching intellectual skills and citizenship, the schools taught patriotism and gave Americans a sense of unity. In this way, schools assisted in the work of assimilating newcomers into American culture by teaching the English language and stressing American values.

In the late 1800s American education was rapidly becoming free, public, and almost universal. In fact, by 1900 most states had compulsory education laws. These laws required that children attend school for a certain part of each year.

As a result, enrollment increased. In 1870 less than 60 percent of all children ages 5 to 17 were enrolled in elementary and secondary schools. By 1900 the figure was over 72 percent. The number of public high schools increased from about 150 in 1870 to nearly 6,000 by 1900. The greatest growth occurred in the Northeast and the Midwest.

The benefits of public school education, however, were not shared by everyone. Most pupils were middle- and upper-class children who chose to go to a public school rather than to be privately educated. Many immigrant children did not complete their schooling. Many poor immigrants needed their children to work to add to the family income. Forced to work at an early age, they sometimes did not even finish elementary school.

■ Progressives and Race

The most conspicuous limit to progressivism was its attitude about race. Like most white Americans at that time, most progressives believed that nonwhite races were inferior. Therefore, reformers did not object

Cultural Perspectives

Adjusting to a New Country Immigrants to the United States formed groups to help them adjust to their new country and to overcome the prejudices of native-born Americans. These groups usually were connected to churches, synagogues, and schools and were often social and athletic clubs. The immigrants formed their own ethnic societies, such as German American clubs, Slovak American clubs, the Polish National Alliance, the Italian-American Society, and the National Council of Jewish Women. Newspapers in the immigrants' native languages served as a link among the newcomers. Many of these newspapers still exist in large American cities.

to the segregation of Japanese Americans in San Francisco schools in 1906, nor did they oppose sharp cuts in Japanese immigration that began in 1907.

Ignoring the Problems of African Americans

In addition, progressives accepted widespread discrimination against African Americans. Although many progressives sympathized with their plight, most reformers agreed with Theodore Roosevelt, who stated that Africans "as a race and in the mass are altogether inferior to whites."

Few progressives objected to the Jim Crow laws that Southern states had passed after Reconstruction to restore segregation. In 1896, when the Supreme Court ruled in *Plessy* v. *Ferguson* that segregation was constitutional as long as separate facilities were equal, no progressive campaign was launched for reform. While Southern whites were lynching African Americans and barring them from voting or holding public office, progressives were crusading for primary elections, direct election of senators, and other reforms to spread democracy. Like most whites, progressives generally accepted the South's Jim Crow system, partly because of indifference and partly because African Americans in the North also were restricted to low-paying jobs, segregation, and inferior social status.

The Struggle for Equality Continues

These circumstances help explain a shift in African American leadership during the Progressive Era. At the turn of the century the most influential African American leader

• •

Footnotes to History

Separate but Equal For nearly 50 years after the *Plessy* decision, the separate but equal doctrine was used to justify segregation in the United States. In the late 1930s and the 1940s, the Supreme Court began to challenge the doctrine in a series of decisions that have had far-reaching implications. The most important decision came in 1954 involving African American students in Topeka, Kansas.

was Booker T. Washington. Formerly enslaved, Washington founded Alabama's Tuskegee Institute in 1881 to train African Americans in 30 trades. Washington argued that equality would be achieved not through campaigns for reform but when African Americans gained the education and skills to become valuable members of their communities. In 1895 he spelled out this view:

> **❝** . . . [T]he agitation of questions of social equality is the extremist folly. . . . [P]rogress in the enjoyment of all privileges that will come to us must be the result of severe and constant struggle rather than of artificial forcing. No race that has anything to contribute to the market of the world is long in any degree ostracized. **❞**

Yet as the great changes in society that accompanied progressive reform bypassed African Americans, a new leadership arose that rejected Washington's approach to achieving equality. The most prominent new African American leader was W.E.B. Du Bois,

Visualizing History

▲ EDUCATION Progressives believed in compulsory public education to keep children out of factories and to provide them with proper values. ***Why did many states require high school students to study American history?***

Linking Across TIME

The NAACP was not the first African American national civil rights organization. In 1890 newspaper editor Thomas Fortune formed the Afro-American League of the United States. Located in Chicago it worked to promote civil rights. More radical in its approach was the Niagara Movement, whose members demanded an immediate end to racial discrimination, equal justice and housing, and full voting rights. Its views were attacked by moderates like Booker T. Washington, and it failed to attract much support, but it helped to lay the foundation for the emergence of the NAACP.

Visualizing History Remind students that the majority of progressives were from the middle class. Discuss how their status might affect their ideas about the education of children from working-class and immigrant families.

Answer to Caption: They believed it was essential in order to create good citizens.

Critical Thinking Activity

Comparing Attitudes Remind students that in the later decades of the twentieth century, many immigrants came to the United States from Asia and various nations in the Western Hemisphere. Have students research examples of current attitudes toward newcomers and compare them with the attitudes toward immigrants at the beginning of the century. **L3**

📁 For additional practice in using critical thinking skills, assign Critical Thinking Skills Activity 13.

Visualizing History

▲ **IN THE CITIES** The rapid growth of cities led to a push for building codes and zoning laws. Other areas of progressive reform included child labor and foods. *In what other areas did progressives help change American society?*

a Harvard-educated history professor at Atlanta University. Du Bois argued that suffrage was the way to end white supremacy, stop the lynching of African Americans, and gain better schools. In 1905 Du Bois and 28 other leaders convened at Niagara Falls to demand full political rights and responsibilities for African Americans as well as an end to racial discrimination.

This call resulted in the founding of the National Association for the Advancement of Colored People (NAACP) in 1909. "The power of the ballot we need in sheer self-defense," Du Bois said, "else what shall save us from a second slavery?" Du Bois edited the NAACP's magazine, *The Crisis*. In fiery editorials he called for African Americans to fight openly against injustice and discrimination.

The End of the Progressive Era

Despite the failure of most progressives to be concerned about such questions, progressive reform helped change American society in a number of ways. Although they excluded large groups from their efforts, the progressives expanded democracy, reformed the education system, and improved the quality of life for millions of men, women, and children.

Except for the two amendments to the Constitution in 1919 and 1920, progressivism in America ended as the United States entered World War I. Americans turned from reforming their own society to a crusade to "make the world safe for democracy."

Section 3 ★ Review

Checking for Understanding
1. **Identify** *Plessy* v. *Ferguson,* Booker T. Washington, W.E.B. Du Bois.

2. **Define** literacy test.

3. **Describe** how some progressive reforms worked to limit the political power of immigrants.

4. **Discuss** the status of African Americans during the Progressive Era.

Critical Thinking
5. **Making Comparisons** Compare the methods of Booker T. Washington and W.E.B. Du Bois for increasing African Americans' participation in society.

ACTIVITY
6. Create a poster that illustrates three Progressive Era accomplishments.

BUILDING SKILLS
Critical Thinking Skills

Making Inferences

▲ **A** GROUP OF IMMIGRANT WOMEN AT WORK

When you use the facts an author presents to draw a conclusion that is not explicitly stated, you are making an inference. Knowing how to make valid inferences will help you to understand and learn from everything you read.

Learning the Skill

To make an inference, follow these steps:
- **Read** carefully for stated facts and ideas.
- **Summarize** the information and list the important facts.
- **Decide** what conclusions might be drawn beyond what the author has said directly.
- **Examine** each inference critically to make sure that it is based on careful analysis of the information you have. Ask: On what evidence do I base this inference?

Read this excerpt, then answer the questions that follow.

In unaired rooms, mothers and fathers sew by day and by night. Those in the home sweatshop must work cheaper than those in the factory sweatshops. . . . And the children are called in from play to drive and drudge beside their elders. . . .

All the year in New York and in other cities you may watch children radiating to and from such pitiful homes. Nearly any hour on the East Side of New York City you can see them—pallid boy or spindling girl—their faces dulled, their backs bent under a heavy load of garments piled on head and shoulders, the muscles of the whole form in a long strain . . . [w]hile in the same city, a pet cur is jeweled and pampered on a fine lady's velvet lap on the beautiful boulevards.

Practicing the Skill

Based on this passage, which of the following inferences might be made about the author's views?
1. Workers would be better off if they moved out of the city.
2. Efforts are needed to remedy working and living conditions for the poor.
3. The work has a harmful effect on the children's health.
4. Wealthy people should take action to alleviate working conditions for the poor.

APPLYING THE SKILL

5. Paste a political cartoon from a newspaper or magazine on a piece of paper or posterboard. List three valid inferences based on the work.

417

TEACH

Have students read the excerpt and apply the steps. Ask: What possible inferences might be made about children's situation during this time? (*Possible answer: Children were overworked and not protected from abusive treatment.*) On what part of the passage did you base the inference? (*Students should cite the parts that provided the basis for the inferences.*)

Project Skills Transparency 13 and have students complete Skills Transparency Activity 13.

Use Chapter Skills Activity 13 to reinforce students' understanding of the skill.

Did You Know?

The term *sweatshop* comes from what was called the *sweating system,* a system of subcontracting. A garment manufacturer, for instance, gave materials to a middleman, who then subcontracted the work to tailors and seamstresses who worked at home or in small shops.

VIDEODISC

Use the MindJogger Videoquiz to review students' knowledge.

MindJogger Videoquiz

Chapter 13
Disc 2, Side A

Available in VHS.

Using Vocabulary
Articles should be concise and include all the terms.

Reviewing Facts

1. exposed unsafe working conditions, corruption in politics, and other social problems

2. Most Americans just survived. Exploitation of the powerless—workers, women, children, and immigrants—was widespread.

3. commission plan and city manager form of government and public ownership or regulation of public utilities

4. It was more difficult to convince people nationwide.

5. Reformers admired big business's methods and expert management and applied them.

6. minimum employment age and other laws to reform child labor, workers' compensation, regulation of working conditions

7. Although most socialist goals were not realized, socialists made progressive reforms seem mild—and acceptable —in comparison.

CHAPTER 13 ★ REVIEW

Using Vocabulary

Imagine that you are a muckraker who is investigating the need for urban reform. Use the following words to write an article summarizing the corruption and stating your recommendations.

social gospel	referendum
recall	pragmatism
direct primary	initiative

Reviewing Facts

1. **Discuss** the role of the muckrakers in promoting social change.

2. **Describe** the inequalities that existed between the upper and lower classes of society.

3. **List** the improvements in city government achieved through progressive reform efforts.

4. **Explain** why reform was more successful at state and local levels than at the national level.

5. **State** the connection between progressive reform and big business management methods.

6. **Identify** reforms that improved the lives of industrial workers.

7. **Indicate** the importance of the socialist movement in early twentieth-century reform.

8. **Discuss** why progressives were not considered to be radical reformers.

Understanding Concepts

Reform

1. To what extent did reform in government extend democracy in the Progressive Era?

2. What changes did labor reforms bring to other areas of society in the early 1900s?

Values and Beliefs

3. Describe the values of the people who preached the social gospel and pioneered social programs.

4. How did progressives' beliefs about immigrant cultures influence their reform activities?

Critical Thinking

1. **Understanding Cause and Effect** To what extent were progressive reformers inspired by the Populists? Consider the membership, goals, and approach to problem solving of each reform group.

2. **Analyzing Artifacts** Study the picture on this page from *Harper's Weekly* and answer the questions that follow.

   a. What is the purpose of this picture?

   b. What is the central focus of the picture?

   c. Do you think this picture is effective? Explain your answer.

3. **Making Comparisons** Compare the commission plan of government to the city-manager plan and explain how each expressed the progressive approach to government.

4. **Interpreting Points of View** Assume you were a recent immigrant during the Progressive Era. What reforms would you feel strongest about? Why?

---

8. Most progressives believed in reforming capitalism rather than abolishing it.

Understanding Concepts

1. It reduced the power of political bosses and gave voters more power.

workers' compensation, child labor reform increased school enrollment as interest in children's welfare was manifested by a juvenile justice system and in the formation of organizations for young people

3. Many reformers sympathized with the sufferings

of others. Some reformers wanted to change the values and behavior of the less fortunate.

4. Their reforms were designed to make immigrants' values and behavior more "American."

History and Geography

The Progressive Movement in America

Use the map on page 405 and information from Chapter 13 to help you answer each of the following questions.

1. **Location** In what year did reformers gain control of state offices in Oklahoma?

2. **Region** In what states in the western and southwestern United States did Progressives have little impact?

3. **Human/Environment Interaction** Which progressive reforms were specifically designed to help

   a. rural residents

   b. urban residents

   c. both rural and urban residents

4. **Location** Which progressive reforms are associated with the following cities and states:

   a. Oregon

   b. Maryland

   c. New York

   d. Wisconsin

   e. Galveston, Texas

Cooperative Learning ## Interdisciplinary Activity: Health

Worker safety was an important part of the progressive program. Reformers realized that safety and accidents can touch every aspect of daily living. Although many accidents occurred at home, the workplace also posed a threat to safety. Organize into groups of four to complete the following activity on worker safety.

Research and compile information on three of your state's workers' safety laws. Include information on when the laws were passed and their intended goals. Include, if possible, information or statistics on worker safety. Conclude from your research whether the laws have been beneficial in promoting worker safety.

Have members of your group who are employed list and illustrate specific safety measures that are taken at their workplaces. Discuss why employers place so much emphasis on safety.

Share your findings with the other students. Display the information on the class bulletin board.

Practicing Skills

Making Inferences

When making inferences apply your own knowledge, experience, and opinions to form conclusions. Reread the material on consumer protection on page 407, then answer the questions that follow.

1. Many men and women worked to protect consumers. What inference can you make about their motivations?

2. What inference can you make about the effects of the book *The Jungle* on consumer protection efforts?

3. Is the following statement a valid inference: "Progressive reform made great inroads in many areas, but perhaps its strongest influence occurred in the regulation of building codes." Why or why not?

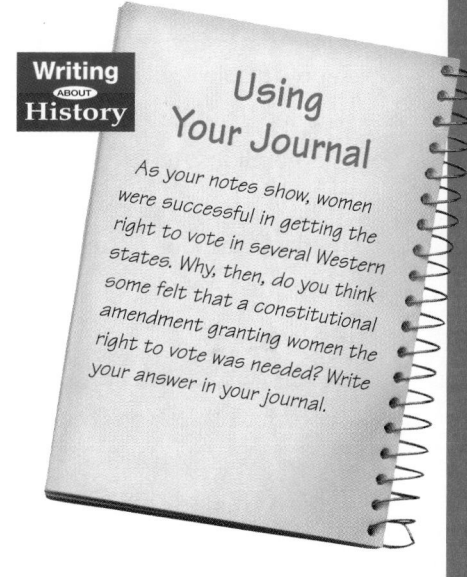

Writing ABOUT History

Using Your Journal

As your notes show, women were successful in getting the right to vote in several Western states. Why, then, do you think some felt that a constitutional amendment granting women the right to vote was needed? Write your answer in your journal.

   c. voting reforms, consumer protection laws, child labor reform

4. a. working conditions for women

   b. workers' compensation

   c. regulation of the insurance industry

   d. voting reforms

   e. city government

Cooperative Learning

Students might report their findings about workers' safety laws in the form of a chart.

Practicing Skills

1. They believed that consumers had the right to know what they were purchasing.

2. It resulted in laws being passed to protect consumers from unsafe medicines and foods.

3. No. The inference is not based on the information from the chapter.

Writing ABOUT History **Using Your Journal**

Students should recognize that a constitutional amendment has the power of the federal government behind it to enforce it.

Chapter Bonus Test Question

Ask students: What was the significance of the Progressive Movement? *(The innovations and reforms progressives championed paved the way for later reforms.)*

Critical Thinking

1. Although progressives supported some Populist reforms, progressivism was city-based and national in appeal, and Populism was regional and rural.

2. a. to show changes brought about by the automobile

   b. the man

   c. Answers may vary, but students should support their opinions.

3. Both based on business management techniques.

4. Students should provide valid reasons for their choices.

History and Geography

1. 1907

2. Nevada, Utah, Arizona, New Mexico

3. a. Few reforms were aimed solely at rural.

   b. reforms in city government

419

Daily Lesson Objectives	Teacher Classroom Resources	Multimedia
SECTION 1 **The Square Deal** **1 Day** pp. 422–426 1. Explain why Roosevelt was known as a "trustbuster." 2. Identify the series of events that led to settlement of the 1902 coal strike. 3. Examine Roosevelt's conservation efforts. 4. Discuss Roosevelt's legacy to the United States.	Reproducible Lesson Plan 14-1 *Guided Reading Activity 14-1 *Vocabulary Activity 14 Chapter Concept Mapping Activities 14-A, 14-B Primary and Secondary Source Readings, pp. 34–35 Enrichment Activity 14 Geography in History Activity 14 Reteaching Activity 14-1 *Section Quiz 14-1	Section Focus Transparency 14-1 Chapter Concepts Transparencies 14-A, 14-B MindJogger Videoquiz Vocabulary PuzzleMaker Testmaker GTV: A Geographic Perspective on American History
SECTION 2 **The Taft Presidency** **1 Day** pp. 428–431 1. Explain the impact of the Payne-Aldrich Tariff. 2. Examine reaction to the Ballinger-Pinchot controversy. 3. Describe reactions to Taft's leadership.	Reproducible Lesson Plan 14-2 *Guided Reading Activity 14-2 Linking Past and Present Activity 14 American Portrait 45 Primary and Secondary Source Readings, p. 36 Reteaching Activity 14-2 *Section Quiz 14-2	Section Focus Transparency 14-2 Testmaker The Presidents: A Picture History of Our Nation
SECTION 3 **The Election of 1912** **1 Day** pp. 432–435 1. Discuss the formation of the Progressive party. 2. Explain how a split in the Republican party helped lead to Woodrow Wilson's election in 1912.	Reproducible Lesson Plan 14-3 *Guided Reading Activity 14-3 Chapter Skills Activity 14 Chapter Map Activity 14 Political Cartoons Activity 13 Reteaching Activity 14-3 *Section Quiz 14-3	Section Focus Transparency 14-3 Map Transparency 14 Testmaker Powers of the President The Presidents: A Picture History of Our Nation
SECTION 4 **Wilson's Progressivism** **1 Day** pp. 437–443 1. Explain why Wilson had congressional support for his programs. 2. List the accomplishments of Wilson's domestic program.	Reproducible Lesson Plan 14-4 *Guided Reading Activity 14-4 Critical Thinking Skills Activity 14 Cooperative Learning Activity 14 Reteaching Activity 14-4 *Section Quiz 14-4	Section Focus Transparency 14-4 Testmaker Economics in Action American Music: Cultural Traditions
CHAPTER REVIEW AND EVALUATION **1 Day**	Chapter 14 Tests, Forms A and B Spanish Chapter 14 Summary Performance Assessment Activity 14	MindJogger Videoquiz Student Self-Test & Review Software *Chapter 14 Audiocassette Activity and Test

*Also available in Spanish

0:00 **OUT OF TIME?** If time does not permit teaching the entire chapter, use the Chapter 14 Summary on pages 448–449 and the Chapter 14 audiocassette (English and Spanish) to point out the main ideas of the chapter.

> A complete, 1-page lesson plan is provided for each section in the *Reproducible Lesson Plan* booklet.

Key to Ability Levels

Teaching strategies have been coded for varying learning styles and abilities.

L1 Basic activities for all students

L2 Average activities for average to above-average students

L3 Challenging activities for above-average students

LEP Limited English Proficiency activities

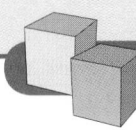

Block Schedule

Block scheduling differs from traditional class scheduling in the amount of time allotted to each period. The extended time frame provided by block scheduling affords you the opportunity to implement a greater number of research-oriented and activity-intense projects to motivate and involve your students. Activities that are particularly suited to use within the block scheduling framework are identified throughout this unit by the following designation:

✓ Performance Assessment Activity

Linking Past and Present Ask students to choose one of the following reforms addressed by progressive presidents: regulation of business, protection of workers, social issues, the environment. Then have them create a report that shows how that issue was addressed in the early 1900s and the way it is viewed today. Each report should account for similarities and differences in the way the problem is defined and in proposed solutions to it. This activity may be done individually or in small groups.

POSSIBLE RUBRIC FEATURES
- Content Information
- Research Skills
- Organization
- Collaborative Skills
- Written and Visual Communication Skills
- Presentation

☞ For additional activities, see Performance Assessment Strategies and Activities.

TEACHER'S CORNER

NATIONAL GEOGRAPHIC SOCIETY

NATIONAL GEOGRAPHIC SOCIETY PRODUCTS AVAILABLE FROM GLENCOE

To order the following products for use with this chapter, contact your local Glencoe sales representative or call Glencoe at 1-800-334-7344:

- *The Presidents: A Picture History of Our Nation* (CD-ROM)
- *GTV: A Geographic Perspective on American History* (Videodisc)
- *GTV: The American People: Fabric of a Nation* (Videodisc)

ADDITIONAL NATIONAL GEOGRAPHIC SOCIETY PRODUCTS

To order the following products for use with this chapter, call National Geographic Society at 1-800-368-2728:

- *The American Presidency* (Filmstrip)
- *Decades of History: The 20th Century—The Early Years* (Filmstrip)
- *The United States as a World Power: From the 1890s to the 1970s* (Filmstrip)

GLENCOE TECHNOLOGY

 VIDEODISC

Use the Chapter 14 MindJogger Videoquiz to preview the content of this chapter.

MindJogger Videoquiz

Chapter 14
Disc 2, Side A

 Available in VHS.

Recording Journal Notes

To help students get started, ask them to list the three progressive Presidents—Roosevelt, Taft, and Wilson—leaving space for specific information on each one.

Linking Across TIME

Although the reforms carried out by the progressive Presidents addressed specific issues of their time, these areas remain concerns today. Among contemporary problems are issues relating to discrimination in the workplace (worker protection) and the disposal of hazardous waste (correcting a social ill).

420

CHAPTER 14
★★★

White House Reformers
1900–1914

▶ **EARLY TELETYPEWRITER**

Setting the Scene

Focus

After the turn of the century, progressive reforms at the national level were aided by three strong-minded Presidents: Theodore Roosevelt, William Howard Taft, and Woodrow Wilson. These Presidents had different political philosophies, styles, and temperaments. Yet each worked to control big business, gain protection for workers, and protect the American people from social ills.

Concepts to Understand

★ How **interests and positions** of the progressives were translated into federal legislation

★ How business practices worked to limit **economic competition**

Read to Discover . . .

★ in what ways Roosevelt was successful or disappointing as a progressive leader.

★ what progressive reforms were achieved by Wilson as President.

Journal Notes

Note instances in your reading where Presidents appealed directly to the nation in order to gain support for new or controversial programs.

CULTURAL	
• **1902** *First Rose Bowl game played* • **1903** *Orville Wright flies first heavier-than-air airplane*	• **1906** *San Francisco earthquake causes extensive damage* • **1907** *Electric washing machine invented*
1900	**1904**
• **1901** *Theodore Roosevelt becomes President*	• **1906** *Pure Food and Drug Act passed*
POLITICAL	

➕ EXTRA CREDIT PROJECT

Roosevelt and Progressivism Theodore Roosevelt had a varied career before he became President. Among other things, he served as a New York State representative, a rancher, a New York City police commissioner, an officer in the Spanish-American War, and governor of New York. Ask interested students to research what Roosevelt accomplished in each of these careers, with particular emphasis on the way each related to his progressivism. Have students present their findings to the class in the form of brief oral reports. **L2**

Concept Mapping Activity

On the chalkboard, reproduce the following generalization and concepts map, and have students copy it in their notebooks.

Reformers make some progress in solving economic and social problems

Interests/ Positions

Economic Competition

 To reinforce the two chapter concepts, use Chapter Concept Mapping Activities 14-A and 14-B.

 Use Chapter Concepts Transparency Activities 14-A, 14-B.

History AND ART

Thomas Moran said of this painting, "I cast all my claims to being an artist into this one picture of the Great Canyon and am willing to abide by the judgment of it."

NATIONAL GEOGRAPHIC SOCIETY

VIDEODISC

GTV: A Geographic Perspective on American History

Side 3, Chapter 15
Title: *A Progress Report*
Subject: Early environmental reforms, 1870–1920

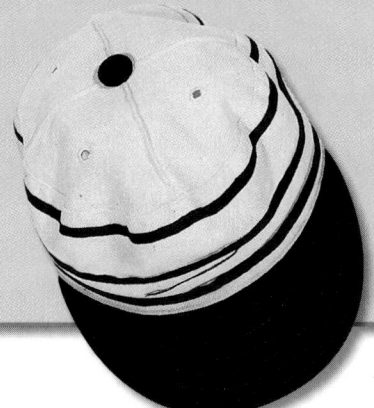

History AND ART

The Grand Canyon of the Yellowstone
by Thomas Moran, 1872

On a government expedition to the West, Moran made sketches for a series of paintings. His work prompted Congress to designate Yellowstone a national park.

◀ BASEBALL CAP, EARLY 1900s

- **1908** *First Model T Ford automobile produced*

- **1913** *Congress designates Mother's Day as the second Sunday in May*

| 1908 | 1912 |

- **1908** *William Howard Taft elected President*

- **1912** *Woodrow Wilson elected President*
- **1912** *Progressive party is formed*
- **1913** *Federal Reserve System created*

✔ Performance Assessment

Analyzing Immigration Laws Point out that, between 1880 and 1924, more than 27 million immigrants entered the United States. The numbers alarmed nativists and awakened anti-immigrant feeling. Ask students to research the nation's immigration laws from 1790 to 1917. Ask them to consider the causes and effects of each law. Then ask students to consider what restrictions, if any, they would place on immigration today. Have students put their findings in a paper, a chart, or an original artistic display. After students complete their projects, ask them to justify restrictions and brainstorm possible consequences. **L3**

★★★★★★★★★★★★★★★★★★★★★★★★★★★★★★★

The Square Deal

FOCUS

Bellringer

Before taking roll, project Section Focus Transparency 14-1 or hand out Section Focus Transparency Activity 14-1. Have students answer the questions.

Motivating Activity

Remind students that they have studied 25 Presidents so far in this text. Ask them to identify those they feel were effective. Have them suggest what special qualities made these Presidents good leaders. **L1**

Vocabulary Precheck

Write "conservation" on the chalkboard. Have a volunteer skim the section to find the term and read it in context. **L1, LEP**

Use the Vocabulary PuzzleMaker Software to create a crossword puzzle. **L1**

Assign Vocabulary Activity 14.

Setting the Scene

Section Focus

When Theodore Roosevelt succeeded William McKinley as President, leaders of industry feared that he would use the power of his office to break up existing trusts. With Roosevelt's first speeches, their worst fears were realized. The President made it clear that he intended to carry out his "Square Deal," based on the idea that every individual is "entitled to no more and to receive no less."

◄ INDUSTRIAL FLATIRON

Objectives

After studying this section, you should be able to

★ explain why Theodore Roosevelt became known as a "trustbuster."

★ identify the series of events that led to settlement of the 1902 coal strike.

★ examine Roosevelt's efforts for conservation of wilderness areas.

★ discuss Roosevelt's legacy to the United States.

Key Term

conservation

When Theodore Roosevelt received the Republican vice-presidential nomination in 1900, the powerful Republican leader Mark Hanna warned that there would be only one life between "that cowboy" and the White House. When the election resulted in a Republican victory, Hanna turned to McKinley and said, "Now it is up to you to live." However, after McKinley's assassination in 1901, Theodore Roosevelt—the "cowboy," the reformer, the progressive—did indeed become President of the United States.

■ The Trustbuster

Roosevelt described his approach to social problems as the "Square Deal," a belief that all people should have an equal opportunity to succeed through strong personal ethics, a sense of fairness, and adherence to the spirit of the law. Roosevelt also promised America that he would continue McKinley's policies unbroken. Not having become President by election, Roosevelt felt he did not have the authority to push a general program of reform through Congress. During this time, however, industries were merging at an all-time high rate. This rash of mergers prompted Roosevelt to urge Congress to pass legislation regulating big business.

Popular Support for Regulation

When Congress did not respond, Roosevelt turned to the American people to garner support for his program. The response was overwhelming. Government leaders responded with a series of moves designed

422   UNIT 4 Entering a New Century: 1867–1920

Classroom Resources for SECTION 1

Blackline Masters:
- Reproducible Lesson Plan 14-1
- Guided Reading Activity 14-1
- Vocabulary Activity 14
- Primary and Secondary Source Readings, pp. 34–35
- Enrichment Activity 14

- Geography in History Activity 14
- Workbook Activity 14-1
- Reteaching Activity 14-1
- Section Quiz 14-1

Transparencies:
- Section Focus Transparency 14-1

Multimedia:
- MindJogger Videoquiz
- Vocabulary PuzzleMaker
- Testmaker
- GTV: A Geographic Perspective on American History

to limit the trusts. First, the attorney general took the Northern Securities Company to court. In 1904 the Supreme Court overturned previous court decisions and ruled that Northern Securities, which had tried to attain a monopoly of northwestern railroads, had violated the Sherman Act.

Legislation to Assist Antitrust Suits

Roosevelt was not opposed to all trusts. He believed the government should leave honest corporations alone. Only the trusts that damaged the public or worked outside the law should be regulated or broken up. In his own words, "We draw the line against misconduct, not against wealth."

Roosevelt also understood that trust-busting suits could not prevent monopolies. Well-considered cases brought to court at the appropriate time, however, could force even the most powerful trust to obey the law. Roosevelt's reputation as a trustbuster grew.

Eventually, Congress followed Roosevelt's lead and, in 1903, passed the Expedition Act, which gave federal antitrust suits precedence on the dockets of circuit courts. An act of Congress also established the Department of Commerce and Labor, empowered to investigate interstate commerce. In addition, the Department of Justice started more trust-busting suits against corporations than they had at any time during the three previous administrations.

■ The Coal Strike of 1902

One of the most prolonged strikes in United States history started in May 1902, when nearly 150,000 workers walked out of the anthracite mines of eastern Pennsylvania. Terrible conditions precipitated this strike: low wages, frequent layoffs, and the requirement to live in cheaply built company towns. The strikers drew widespread public support.

▲ ON STRIKE The major weapon for men and women workers against management was the strike. Coal miners at Shenandoah, Pennsylvania, demonstrate to win better pay and working conditions during the 1902 coal strike. *How was the strike settled?*

CHAPTER 14
SECTION 1

TEACH
Guided Practice

Recognizing Cause and Effect Provide students with copies of the following cause-and-effect chart, omitting the causes and effects. Have them complete the chart. **L1**

Events
- Roosevelt asked Congress to pass legislation regulating big business.
- Roosevelt made speeches to the American people asking for support of his reform program.

Causes
- Industrial mergers reached an all-time high.
- U.S. Steel Corporation tried to attain a monopoly of northwestern railroads.

Effects
- Congress passed the Expedition Act.
- Congress established the Department of Commerce and Labor.

Visualizing History In 1869 about half of the nation's industrial power came from water; by 1900 steam engines supplied 80 percent of the nation's industrial power. Coal kept those steam engines running.
Answer to Caption: Roosevelt's representative, Root, met with Morgan, who forced the mine operators to back down.

Special Needs Activity

Reading Disability One problem many students with reading comprehension or attention problems have is working through a section of material in a timely fashion. They tend to lose their sense of purpose in the reading or become distracted by movement or noise. One way to help them stay focused on their objectives is to set both a goal and a time limit. Start students in Section 1 with a search for the names of the representative of the United Mine Workers and the spokesperson for the mine employers. Give one minute as the time goal. **L1, LEP**

📁 Assign Guided Reading Activity 14-1.

Did You Know?

Theodore Roosevelt had a high opinion of himself. When he published his memoirs of the Spanish-American War, the publisher ordered an extra supply of the letter "I."

Food of the Times

As early as 1883, the federal government was investigating the use of additives to prevent spoilage of canned and processed foods. Government agents tested the preservatives used in milk, meat, butter, and cocoa as well as in canned vegetables and fruits. Their findings and Upton Sinclair's novel *The Jungle* led to the Pure Food and Drug Act of 1906.

📁 Assign Primary and Secondary Source Readings, pp. 34–35: "The Triangle Shirtwaist Company Fire" by Leon Stein.

▲ FACTORY WORKERS ON STRIKE

Management and Labor in a Deadlock

John Mitchell, who represented the United Mine Workers, asked mine operators to consider allowing an independent party to determine whether miners' wages were adequate. But George F. Baer, principal spokesperson for the mine employers, refused Mitchell's suggestion, saying that "anthracite mining is a business and not a religious, sentimental, or academic proposition." Baer further alienated a public already sympathetic to the workers when he refused to listen to the miners' complaints, to submit to arbitration, or to recognize the United Mine Workers as the true representative of the mine workers. This attitude and the strong conviction behind the miners' position caused the strike to drag on, with no prospect of settlement. Appeals for action poured in to the President.

Presidential Action Helps Resolve the Strike

Roosevelt had no power to force an agreement, yet he resolved to use whatever influence he had to end the strike. Early in October, Roosevelt invited representatives of the operators to meet union representative Mitchell at the White House. Nothing was accomplished in a stormy session, but public opinion soured even more toward the employers.

Faced with this deadlock, Roosevelt considered a legally questionable seizure of the mines by federal troops, but after a conference between Elihu Root, the President's representative, and J. Pierpont Morgan, whose banking firm indirectly controlled most of the anthracite mines, Morgan was able to put enough pressure on the operators to force them to back down. Morgan's action was apparently prompted by concern that United States businesses would suffer if the strike continued. Roosevelt's action in using the prestige of his office and his personal influence to settle the strike was recognized in this country and abroad as an important precedent. The London *Times* commented:

> ❝ *The President has done a very big and entirely new thing. We are witnessing not merely the end of the coal strike, but the definite entry of a powerful government on a novel sphere of operation.* ❞

■ Efforts at Conservation

Even before Theodore Roosevelt became President, the nation was adopting a policy of **conservation,** the planned management of natural resources to prevent destruction or neglect. In 1872 an act of Congress created Yellowstone National Park, and the 1890s saw the establishment of four more national parks. In 1891 Congress enacted the Forest Reserve Act, empowering Presidents to set aside land for national forests and withdraw forest lands from the public domain. In this way, land could be set aside for preservation rather than left available for private claim or purchase.

Action Based on Personal Commitment

Roosevelt's efforts to preserve the nation's natural resources stemmed from a deep love for America's wilderness. His beliefs made conservation popular. He stimulated public

Cooperative Learning Activity

Discussing Conservation Organize students into groups of four. Have each group focus on the topic "Conservation became a household word during Roosevelt's presidency." Give each student a set of colored chips. When a student wishes to speak, he or she must place a chip in the center of the table. Give the groups 10 or 15 minutes to discuss what measures are being taken toward conservation in their communities and across the country today. All students must spend their chips in the time given for discussion. Ask one student in each group to summarize his or her group's discussion. **L2** 📁

interest in the subject by writing, by taking publicized holiday trips to the West, and by constantly pushing for better conservation laws. Roosevelt also used the power and prestige of the presidential office to promote the cause.

Laws to Preserve Our Natural Legacy

The Newlands Act of 1902, supported by Roosevelt, provided federal aid to irrigation projects in arid states. He also enforced laws against the illegal occupation of public lands. Using the Forest Reserve Act, Roosevelt more than tripled the amount of land previously set aside for national forests.

Roosevelt also enlisted states' aid in the conservation effort. In May 1908 he called a national conference on conservation that resulted in the creation of more than 40 state conservation commissions and a National Conservation Commission, which began an inventory of the nation's natural resources.

Wisconsin senator Robert La Follette, though often critical of Roosevelt, predicted that future historians would conclude that Roosevelt's greatest achievement was not the Square Deal, but the preservation of the nation's natural resources for the benefit of all.

■ Further Regulation

As the presidential election of 1904 approached, the "Old Guard" of the Republican party was unhappy at the prospect of four more years of the Rough Rider in the White House. The New York *Sun* accused Roosevelt of "bringing wealth to its knees" and "putting labor unions above the law." It seemed possible that Mark Hanna might try to block Roosevelt's nomination, but Hanna died in February 1904. Roosevelt had popular opinion behind him and was, as even his enemies admitted, the ablest politician of the day. He received the unanimous nomination from the Republican national convention.

After being elected to a full term in 1904, Roosevelt felt confident enough to respond to the growing public clamor for stricter regulation of the railroads. The Interstate Commerce Commission had only limited success in controlling the unfair practices and political influence of these powerful businesses. Newspaper editor William Allen White spoke for many when he wrote:

> *The railroads cannot name senators, pack state conventions, run legislatures, and boss politics generally . . . and then successfully maintain that they are private carriers doing a private business.*

Did You Know?

On one occasion when President Theodore Roosevelt was hunting, he supposedly refused to shoot a bear cub that crossed his line of fire. Following the incident, *Washington Post* cartoonist Clifford K. Berryman drew a cartoon of Roosevelt turning away from the helpless cub. Seeing the cartoon, candy-store owner Morris Michtom began to make toy bear cubs in 1903, naming them "Teddy Bears."

Visualizing
History Naturalists like John Muir led the campaign to create Yosemite National Park in California.
Answer to Caption: It provided federal aid for irrigation projects.

NATIONAL GEOGRAPHIC SOCIETY

 VIDEODISC

GTV: A Geographic Perspective on American History

Side 3, Chapter 12
Title: *The Price of Progress*
Subject: Pros and cons of progress

Visualizing
History

▲ CONSERVATION Theodore Roosevelt was an avid supporter of the conservation movement. Roosevelt worked to protect wildlife and scenic areas. *What was the purpose of the Newlands Act?*

Sidelight: *The Jungle*

Perhaps no book can match Upton Sinclair's *The Jungle* in terms of public popularity *and* impact on government policy. Sinclair continued his muckraking ways, publishing a number of controversial novels. He also ran for Congress and the governorship of California on the Socialist ticket.

ASSESS
Check Understanding

Assign Section 1 Review as homework or an in-class activity.

Evaluate

🔲 📁 Assign Section Quiz 14-1 or use the Testmaker to create a customized quiz.

Reteach

Have students write a paragraph summarizing Roosevelt's "Square Deal" achievements.

📁 Have students complete Reteaching Activity 14-1.

Enrich

📁 Assign Enrichment Activity 14.

📁 Assign Geography in History Activity 14.

CLOSE

Ask students if they think Roosevelt would have been reelected based on his accomplishments. Have them give reasons for their answers.

Some leaders proposed that the railroads be owned and operated by the government. Thinking such a step would lead to far-reaching disaster, Roosevelt urged tighter regulation as an alternative. As a result of popular support, clever politics, and willingness to compromise, Roosevelt was able to push the Hepburn Bill through the Senate 18 months after he urged Congress to act.

The Hepburn Act of 1906 strengthened the Interstate Commerce Act of 1887 in several ways. It abolished the "free pass" that railroads granted to politicians and other influential people. It widened the jurisdiction of the Interstate Commerce Commission to include express companies, pipelines, and sleeping-car companies. Railroad corporations were restrained from operating other businesses.

Most important of all, the Interstate Commerce Commission was granted power to fix rates, although its decisions could be appealed to the courts. Complaints to the commission soon multiplied 40 times, and a great many rates were lowered.

Roosevelt also urged legislation to address abuses in the food and meatpacking industries. The Meat Inspection Act of 1906 gave government the right to inspect meats sold in interstate commerce and the right to enforce cleaner conditions in meatpacking plants.

■ Assessing Roosevelt's Progressive Policies

In spite of Roosevelt's many accomplishments, Congress offered much resistance to his ideas. His legislative achievement was so unimpressive that some critics accused Roosevelt of producing "more noise than accomplishment."

Roosevelt and Politics

Roosevelt failed to effect a revision of the tariff, regarding the issue as "political dynamite." He did use the issue to his advantage, however, occasionally threatening to bring it up unless congressional leaders supported other legislative measures. Roosevelt also never seriously supported long-overdue efforts to make the banking system more stable and the currency system more flexible.

One reason for the failure to produce much reform legislation was Roosevelt's feeling that politics was "the art of the possible." His philosophy of reform was one of gradualism: he was willing to accept half a loaf if he could not get the whole. Furthermore, the Republican leaders in Congress, carryovers from the McKinley-Hanna period, were unsympathetic to progressive legislation.

Roosevelt and History

Although Roosevelt accomplished less than he seemed to promise, he restored the people's faith in the power of the federal government to serve their interests. Through his Square Deal philosophy, he promoted the idea that the cure for the evils of unrestrained individualism was not socialism but moderate reform. Above all he created a demand for reform. According to one historian, "Roosevelt was the best publicity man progressivism ever had."

Section 1 ★ Review

Checking for Understanding

1. **Identify** J. Pierpont Morgan, Expedition Act, Forest Reserve Act, Hepburn Act, Square Deal.

2. **Define** conservation.

3. **Explain** why Roosevelt preferred regulation to trust-busting.

4. **State** Roosevelt's part in the 1902 coal strike.

Critical Thinking

5. **Understanding Cause and Effect** Analyze how Roosevelt's conservation policies grew out of his love for the American wilderness.

ACTIVITY

6. Draw a political cartoon that illustrates Roosevelt's "Square Deal."

Answers to SECTION 1 REVIEW

1. J. Pierpont Morgan, 424; Expedition Act, 423; Forest Reserve Act, 425; Hepburn Act, 426; Square Deal, 422, 426
2. All vocabulary words are defined in the Glossary.
3. Roosevelt believed that trust busting did not stop the rise of monopolies. Regulation forced business leaders to obey laws.

4. used prestige of the office and personal influence to settle the strike
5. He wrote about conservation, took holiday trips to the West, and constantly pushed for better conservation laws.
6. Cartoons should display understanding of Roosevelt's policies.

The Conservation Movement

By the beginning of the twentieth century it was becoming clear that the natural resources Americans had long taken for granted were—in fact—in danger of being used up. Theodore Roosevelt, a champion of conservation, made an effective case for the wise and scientific use of natural resources by people of all ages.

To the Society of American Foresters in 1903, Roosevelt said, "First and foremost, you can never afford to forget for one moment what is the object of forest policy. . . . Your attention should be directed not to the preservation of the forests as an end in itself, but as the means for preserving and increasing the prosperity of the nation."

Roosevelt's 1907 Arbor Day message to schoolchildren said in part, "Within your lifetime the nation's need for trees will become serious. . . . You will want what nature once so bountifully supplied and man so thoughtlessly destroyed; and because of that want you will reproach us, not for what we have used, but for what we have wasted. . . ."

Roosevelt abhorred the way the country's national resources were being exploited. For example, irreplaceable resources such as natural gas were wasted, and fires and floods, caused by poor management of land and water services, were common. Roosevelt wanted not only to protect wildlife and scenic areas, but also to ensure efficient use of soil, minerals, and forests.

The National Reclamation Act, also known as the Newlands Act of 1902, was the first major conservation law passed under Roosevelt. It provided for replacing natural services and set aside funds from public land sales for irrigation projects in the West.

During Roosevelt's terms, the size of the national forests were increased from about 40 million acres to more than 190 million acres. Roosevelt also worked to preserve other valuable lands as well. At his direction, the Department of the Interior set aside 80 million acres of coal lands.

▼ ARAPAHO NATIONAL FOREST, COLORADO

Making the Geography Connection

1. What did Roosevelt suggest was the object of forest policy?

2. How did Roosevelt's conservation program relate to the Square Deal?

ACTIVITY

3. Imagine you are a reporter researching environmental issues in the United States. Use your text and other resources to decide which issues you will address. Write a newspaper story in which you discuss how you think these issues will continue to affect the nation.

427

CONNECTIONS

History AND GEOGRAPHY

TEACH

Point out that Roosevelt was both a conservationist and an avid hunter. On one East African safari, he and his son shot 17 lions, 12 elephants, 11 buffalo, and 20 rhinoceroses—including 9 rare white rhinoceroses. Ask students if they think one can be both a conservationist and a hunter. **L1**

Did You Know?

In 1908 Roosevelt called a National Conservation Congress. It was attended by 44 governors and hundreds of experts. It led to annual governors' meeting and the creation of state conservation commissions.

NATIONAL GEOGRAPHIC SOCIETY

 VIDEODISC

GTV: A Geographic Perspective on American History

Side 3, Chapter 15
Title: *A Progress Report*
Subject: Early environmental reforms, 1870–1920

See GTV Guide for complete lesson plan.

Answers to Making the Connection

1. To preserve and increase the prosperity of the nation.

2. Government regulation and protection of forests and other natural resources were necessary to conserve them for the benefit of all people and prevent their exploitation by a select few.

3. Student newspaper stories should focus on an important issue and present arguments cogently and effectively.

★★

The Taft Presidency

FOCUS
Bellringer

 Before taking roll, project Section Focus Transparency 14-2 or hand out Section Focus Transparency Activity 14-2. Have students answer the questions.

Motivating Activity

Review with students the meaning of the words *lobbyists* (well-organized pressure groups) and *insurgents* (people who act contrary to the policies and decisions of their political party). Ask students to name lobby groups today and what these groups do. **L1**

Vocabulary Precheck

Ask several volunteers to use the term "income tax" in a sentence. **L1, LEP**

NATIONAL GEOGRAPHIC SOCIETY

CD-ROM

The Presidents: A Picture History of Our Nation

Have students select President Taft from the main menu and the category GAME. Suggest they learn more about Taft by playing the presidential game with a partner.

Setting the Scene

Section Focus

In 1908 Theodore Roosevelt declined to run for reelection, accepting the custom that limited Presidents to two terms. Although his successor, William Howard Taft, was a supporter of Roosevelt's progressive policies, Taft's presidency led not only to a split between Taft and Roosevelt but also to a division of the Republican party itself.

Objectives

After studying this section, you should be able to

★ explain the impact of the Payne-Aldrich Tariff.

★ examine the public reaction to the Ballinger-Pinchot controversy.

★ describe the reactions of Roosevelt and the public to Taft's leadership.

Key Term

income tax

◀ ROOSEVELT AND TAFT IN CONFLICT

Although a distinguished public servant, having served as a judge, as governor of the Philippines, and as Roosevelt's secretary of war, Taft was a reluctant President. His true ambition lay in the judicial, not the executive, branch of government. Remarking on the snow, sleet, and rain that pelted the people coming to his Inaugural Address, Taft said, "Even the elements do protest."

■ Taft in Difficulty

Taft began his term as President by addressing the tariff issue, largely ignored during Roosevelt's eight-year term. Since passage of the Dingley Tariff of 1897, prices had advanced more rapidly than wages, and many blamed the resulting high cost of living on unduly high tariff rates. Some, including Taft, also believed that high rates encouraged monopoly.

Subversion of Tariff Reform

Congress met in March 1909, and within less than a month the House of Representatives passed a measure, introduced by Sereno Payne of New York, that provided for substantial reductions in the tariff without abandoning the principle of protection. Under the leadership of conservative Senator Nelson W. Aldrich of Rhode Island, however, more than 800 amendments were tacked onto the House bill. Many of these amendments were designed to conceal higher rates, such as changing a duty on certain small articles from so much "per hundredweight" to so much "per hundred."

428 UNIT 4 Entering a New Century: 1867–1920

Classroom Resources for SECTION 2

Blackline Masters:
- Reproducible Lesson Plan 14-2
- Guided Reading Activity 14-2
- Linking Past and Present Activity 14
- American Portraits, p. 45
- Primary and Secondary Source Readings, p. 36
- Reteaching Activity 14-2
- Section Quiz 14-2

Transparencies:
- Section Focus Transparency 14-2

Multimedia:
- Testmaker
- The Presidents: A Picture History of Our Nation

When Aldrich attempted to railroad the amended bill through the Senate, he was met with resistance in his own party. Several Republican senators, nicknamed "the Insurgents," used their privilege of unlimited debate to reveal the way Aldrich and his allies were carrying out the demands of high-tariff lobbyists instead of the people. Too late, Taft attempted to persuade the Old Guard leaders to reduce the rates, but they made only slight concessions before the bill received Senate approval.

By the time the bill reached Taft's desk, the Payne-Aldrich Tariff contained high duties on iron ore, coal, and hides and increases on other materials. The bill, however, allowed for a corporation tax, established a tariff commission to make a scientific study of rates, and provided for some flexibility in rates at the discretion of the President. For these reasons, and because he feared a split between the Old Guard and the Insurgents in his own party, Taft signed the bill despite its weaknesses.

Continuing Controversy

Another blow was dealt to Taft's popularity when a conflict developed between Taft's secretary of the interior, Richard A. Ballinger, and the chief forester, Gifford Pinchot. Ballinger reopened for private purchase certain lands in Montana, Wyoming, and Alaska that had been withdrawn while Roosevelt was President. Pinchot, a well-known conservationist, protested these actions and publicly accused Ballinger of fraud. Taft, convinced of Ballinger's innocence—later confirmed by a congressional investigating committee—dismissed Pinchot for insubordination. But the public viewed Taft's action as a move against the conservation effort begun by Roosevelt, and Taft's popularity plummeted. Even though Ballinger was exonerated of the charges, he eventually resigned his post.

Immediately following the Ballinger-Pinchot controversy came an outbreak of Insurgent Republicanism in the House of Representatives, which took the form of an attack on the Old Guard speaker of the House, Joseph G. "Uncle Joe" Cannon. The speaker had come to enjoy a power over legislation greater in some ways than that of the President. He appointed all committees, he decided what bills should be referred to which committees, and by almost absolute control over debate he could push some measures through without discussion and see that others never reached the floor.

The conservative Cannon used the powers of this office to hold up progressive legislation. He also cooperated with Aldrich during the tariff debacle in 1909. Furthermore, Cannon had long been an opponent of conservation. With the motto "Not one cent for scenery," he had stalled the creation of national parks and forests.

Finally, in March 1910, a coalition of Democrats and Republican Insurgents forced a change in the rules of the House that stripped the speaker of much of his power. This attack on Cannon hurt Taft, who in order to keep party harmony aligned himself with

▲ ROOSEVELT AND TAFT In this cartoon, a smiling Roosevelt celebrates with Taft, his chosen successor. Soon, however, Roosevelt and Taft found themselves at odds. *Why did Taft dismiss Gifford Pinchot?*

CHAPTER 14 White House Reformers: 1900–1914 **429**

TEACH
Guided Practice
Making Value Judgments
Ask students to list the successes of the Taft administration. (*sample responses—established Tariff Board, began a federal budget, supported the Sixteenth and Seventeenth Amendments*) Discuss students' lists, and then ask them what they think was Taft's greatest achievement. **L2**

📁 Assign Guided Reading Activity 14-2.

📁 Assign American Portrait 45: Gifford Pinchot.

FACT or FICTION?
William Howard Taft was the first President to make regular use of the presidential automobile.

FACT: Taft rode in the car but did not drive it himself. It would probably have been too difficult for him to squeeze behind the steering wheel, since he weighed over 300 pounds.

Visualizing History Because Roosevelt backed Pinchot, Taft's action further widened the rift between Taft and the former President.
Answer to Caption: for insubordination

Critical Thinking Activity

Analyzing Effectiveness Have students compare the accomplishments of Roosevelt's administration with those of Taft's administration. (*Roosevelt: Northern Securities dissolution, Expedition Act, established the Department of Commerce and Labor, settled coal strike, Newlands Act of 1902,* *Hepburn Act; Taft: prosecuted twice as many antitrust cases as Roosevelt, established Tariff Board, started federal budget, supported Sixteenth and Seventeenth Amendments*) Next, ask students who they think was the greater reformer—Roosevelt or Taft. Have them give reasons for their answers. **L2**

Independent Practice

Journalism Have students imagine they work as newspaper reporters. Their assignment is to cover the speech that Theodore Roosevelt is giving at Osawatomie, Kansas, during the congressional election of 1910. In their articles students should include the subject, content, delivery of the speech, and audience response. **L3**

Linking Past and Present

Point out to students that today more than 85 percent of the ready-to-eat cereals made in the United States are fortified with nutrients. The amounts of nutrients in these fortified cereals are beyond the amounts of nutrients that the whole grain from which the cereal is made would contain. The extra synthetic nutrients are sprayed on the fortified cereals. These nutrients include vitamins A and C, niacin, and thiamin. Ask students why they think fortified cereals are popular.

☞ For additional practice, assign Linking Past and Present Activity 14.

Linking Past and Present

Breakfast Cereals

Early attempts to make a ready-to-eat dry breakfast cereal resulted in tasteless fare. These failures did not discourage two brothers, Will and John Kellogg, who ran a sanitarium in Battle Creek, Michigan. While there, the brothers experimented with a variety of grains and textures.

Then

Growth and the Cereal Industry

Success came with flavoring and roasting very thin flakes of grain. Almost immediately, the brothers recognized its sales potential. In 1906 Will Kellogg organized the Kellogg Company to manufacture cereal products as breakfast foods. The company became a huge success, partly because of its innovative advertisements and promotions. It was the first cereal company to aim its advertising directly at children, sparking a host of imitators. A patient at the sanitarium, C.W. Post, decided to start his own cereal company. Its products included a cereal first called Elijah's Manna, which was later renamed Grape-Nuts. To differentiate it from the more than 40 other cereal companies based in Battle Creek alone, Kellogg had his own signature printed on each package.

Now

20 Billion Bowls

Today, ready-to-eat cereals are available in dozens of flavors, forms, and textures. They are combinations of such cereal grains as wheat, corn, oats, and rice. Supplementary contents include sugars, colorings, and flavorings.

These ingredients are cooked together under pressure; dried; ground, flaked, or shredded; then toasted and packaged. To make puffed cereals, grains are heated in a pressure chamber. When the pressure is released, water vapor expands each grain to many times its original size.

People in the United States eat more than 20 billion bowls of cereal yearly.

---

the speaker. Thus, by signing the Payne-Aldrich Tariff, by supporting Ballinger against Pinchot, and by backing Cannon, Taft gave the impression that he had "sold the Square Deal down the river." An Insurgent senator described Taft as "a large good-natured body entirely surrounded by people who know exactly what they want." Popular indignation was so great that the congressional elections of 1910 resulted in a sweeping Democratic victory, with Democrats taking the majority in the House and Democrats and Republican Insurgents wresting control of the Senate from the Old Guard.

■ "New Nationalism"

During his retirement Roosevelt tried hard to maintain faith in the man he had chosen as his successor, but he found public opinion toward Taft had worsened. In spite of Roosevelt's intention to remain out of politics, Taft's disappointing performance as President soon drew Roosevelt back into the political arena.

Roosevelt aligned himself with the Insurgents in the Republican party, who had started to call themselves "Progressive Republicans," or simply "Progressives." In a speech at Osawatomie, Kansas, during the congressional election of 1910, Roosevelt spoke of a new set of policies that he called the "New Nationalism." In words that recalled the Populist platform of the 1890s and foreshadowed the New Deal of the 1930s, Roosevelt said:

❝ *We are face to face with new conceptions of the relations of property to human welfare. . . .*

Cooperative Learning Activity

Taft's Achievements Organize students into groups of four or five. Ask each group to consider the accomplishments of Taft's administration. Using one piece of paper per group, have each group member take a turn writing a statement about Taft's achievements. Have each group share its statements with the class. Then discuss any missing information. **L2**

The man who wrongly holds that every human right is secondary to his profit must now give way to the advocate of human welfare, who rightly maintains that every man holds his property subject to the general right of the community to regulate its use to whatever degree the public welfare may require it. "

In his New Nationalism speech, Roosevelt outlined a much more radical program of action than he had ever proposed while in the presidency. He favored both state and federal legislation to actively promote human welfare, including laws to protect women and children in the labor force and workers' compensation for those injured on the job.

Attacking the courts for declaring certain progressive legislation unconstitutional, Roosevelt suggested that state judges be subject to recall and that Supreme Court decisions be reversible by popular vote. By taking such stands, Roosevelt established his position as the natural leader of the Progressive Republicans.

■ Taft's Successes

Despite Taft's political problems, his administration experienced several successes. Although it was Roosevelt who was nicknamed the "trustbuster," Taft actually prosecuted twice as many antitrust cases in four years as his predecessor had in seven. Taft established the Tariff Board to investigate tariff rates, and under his leadership a federal budget began to take shape. Taft also supported the Sixteenth Amendment, giving Congress power to collect **income taxes,** or taxes on the income of individuals and companies, and the Seventeenth Amendment, calling for direct election of United States senators. In addition, during his administration two new states—New Mexico and Arizona—were admitted to the United States.

Taft genuinely supported Roosevelt's Square Deal policies, but unlike Roosevelt, who claimed an executive right to do anything not forbidden, Taft's judicial background allowed him to use "only those powers expressly authorized by law." Taft also lacked his predecessor's gift for dramatizing issues and enlisting public support. To some degree, Taft brought his political troubles on himself. He had a very different temperament from other politicians, and he had a hard time keeping up with the incessant work of the office. He did not really want to be President; his greatest ambition—later fulfilled—was to sit on the Supreme Court. In the end, Taft's administration would be remembered for its failures rather than its achievements.

Section 2 ★ Review

Checking for Understanding

1. **Identify** Payne-Aldrich Tariff, Richard Ballinger, Joseph Cannon, New Nationalism, "the Insurgents."

2. **Define** income tax.

3. **List** the reasons the public thought Taft was destroying the Square Deal.

4. **Explain** Theodore Roosevelt's return to national politics with the New Nationalism program.

Critical Thinking

5. **Making Judgments** Analyze how Taft's leadership led to increasing the power and authority of the federal government.

ACTIVITY

6. Ask various people in your community how they feel about the current President's performance. Limit your questions to one issue, such as the budget. Report your findings to the class.

ASSESS

Check Understanding

Assign Section 2 Review as homework or as in-class activity.

Evaluate

Assign Section Quiz 14-2 or use the Testmaker to create a customized quiz.

Reteach

Have students complete Reteaching Activity 14-2.

Enrich

Assign Primary and Secondary Source Readings p. 36: "What the Progressive Party Was Like" by William Allen White.

CLOSE

Ask students: Based on what you have learned in this section, do you think Theodore Roosevelt will run in the 1912 presidential election against Taft?

FACT or FICTION?

Taft and Roosevelt, his predecessor, had been at odds from the beginning of Taft's term as President.

FICTION: Roosevelt had selected Taft as his successor, using his powerful influence to have Taft nominated at the Republican National Convention of 1908. Roosevelt did not break with Taft until 1911, in the wake of the Ballinger-Pinchot controversy.

Answers to SECTION 2 REVIEW

1. Payne-Aldrich Tariff, 429; Richard Ballinger, 429; Joseph Cannon, 429; New Nationalism, 430–431; "the Insurgents," 429

2. All vocabulary words are defined in the Glossary.

3. Taft's support of Payne-Aldrich Tariff, of Ballinger's proposal to reclaim land set aside for national forests, and of Joseph Cannon.

4. announced return to politics in "New Nationalism" speech, which focused on human-welfare needs

5. Taft prosecuted many cases; Roosevelt; established Tariff Board to investigate rates; supported new amendments.

6. Student questions should be expressed clearly and fairly.

431

FOCUS

Bellringer

 Before taking roll, project Section Focus Transparency 14-3 or hand out Section Focus Transparency Activity 14-3. Have students answer the questions.

Motivating Activity

Ask if any students have ever served as volunteers in an election campaign. Ask those who have to describe the various techniques that are used to get a candidate elected. Then discuss with the class the major elements needed to run a successful political campaign. (money, enthusiasm, campaign staff, publicity, volunteers, and so on) Tell students that this section describes the election of 1912. **L1**

Vocabulary Precheck

Write "inheritance tax" on the chalkboard. Have a volunteer skim the section to find the term and read it in context. **L1, LEP**

NATIONAL
GEOGRAPHIC
SOCIETY

CD-ROM

The Presidents: A Picture History of Our Nation

Have students select Presidents Roosevelt, Taft, and Wilson from the main menu. Suggest they compare the lives of these leaders.

★★★

The Election of 1912

Setting the Scene

Section Focus

With his New Nationalism speech, Theodore Roosevelt returned to the political arena. As the election of 1912 approached, he remained convinced that Taft was unfit for another term as President, and it was not in Roosevelt's nature to sit on the sidelines. Thus the great question in American politics as the campaign began was whether Roosevelt would run again for the presidency.

Objectives

After studying this section, you should be able to

★ relate the events that led to the formation of the Progressive party.

★ explain how a split in the Republican party helped lead to Woodrow Wilson's election in 1912.

Key Term

inheritance tax

◀ POLITICAL CARTOON, 1912 PRESIDENTIAL ELECTION

Senator Robert La Follette, a man of great ability and a leader of the recently formed National Progressive Republican League, had the support of many Progressive Republicans for the 1912 presidential nomination. When La Follette suffered a temporary nervous collapse, however, the Progressives turned to Roosevelt. Explaining that his no-third-term pledge referred to a third consecutive term, Roosevelt declared himself a candidate against Taft for the Republican nomination.

■ Roosevelt Challenges Taft

The heated, emotional struggle for control of the Republican party reached its climax at the national convention in June.

Conservatives rallied behind Taft, as did many former supporters of the Square Deal who thought Roosevelt too radical or who disliked his running for a third term. Except for some devoted followers of La Follette, the Progressive Republicans lined up for Roosevelt. In states where convention delegates were chosen in primary elections, Roosevelt was generally the choice of the voters.

The Taft forces, however, had the immense advantage of controlling the party machinery. The convention chairperson Elihu Root kept such a tight hold on proceedings that he was accused of driving a steam roller over the Roosevelt forces. The convention's Credentials Committee gave 235 of 254 convention seats to Taft. When Taft received the nomination on the first ballot, Roosevelt charged the Republican party leaders with stealing the nomination. He stood ready, he said, to carry on the battle for progressive principles outside the party.

Classroom Resources for SECTION 3

Blackline Masters:
- Reproducible Lesson Plan 14-3
- Guided Reading Activity 14-3
- Chapter Skills Activity 14
- Chapter Map Activity 14
- Political Cartoons in American History Activity 13
- Reteaching Activity 14-3
- Section Quiz 14-3

Transparencies:
- Section Focus Transparency 14-3
- Map Transparency 14

Multimedia:
- Testmaker
- The Presidents: A Picture History of Our Nation
- Powers of the President

Formation of Progressive Party

In August a convention met in Chicago to found a new political party—the Progressive party. The delegates were a curious mixture—college professors, social workers, newspaper editors, former Rough Riders, wealthy people motivated by social conscience, and some professional politicians.

Senator Albert J. Beveridge, who had followed Roosevelt out of the Republican party, called on the new party to work for a nobler America. The Progressives, said Beveridge, stood for "social brotherhood" as opposed to "savage individualism," for a "representative government that represents the people," as opposed to invisible government controlled by corrupt bosses and the "robber interest."

The Progressive platform demanded reforms such as a more direct democracy through such means as the initiative and referendum, for conservation of natural resources for the general welfare, for woman suffrage, and for labor reforms such as the prohibition of child labor.

In addition, Progressives called for revision of the currency system and the introduction of an **inheritance tax,** which would be a percentage of the value of an inheritance, levied on the privilege of an heir to receive this property.

The party nominated Theodore Roosevelt for the presidency and immediately acquired a party symbol when the former President announced that he felt "as strong as a bull moose." The Progressive party had a strong enthusiasm and one of the most popular individuals in public life. It also had abundant campaign funds, supplied by wealthy businesspeople who believed that capitalism could survive only if it was reformed.

The Bull Moose crusade was a forlorn hope, however. Most of the Progressives were amateurs with little or no knowledge of practical politics. Party machinery could not be set up in thousands of election districts overnight. All that Roosevelt accomplished by bolting from the Republican party was to give control of the Republican party to the Old Guard, and to ensure the election of a Democratic President.

The New Freedom

When the Democratic convention met at Baltimore in June 1912, there was discord between the progressive wing, to which William Jennings Bryan belonged, and the conservative wing, whose delegates represented city political machines. Although disclaiming any desire for another nomination,

Visualizing History
▲ ROOSEVELT THE CAMPAIGNER
Theodore Roosevelt was a vigorous and effective campaigner. The Progressive party platform included a minimum-wage law for women, workers' compensation laws, and strong regulation of child labor. *Who were the Republican and Democratic candidates in the 1912 election?*

▼ THE BULL MOOSE, SYMBOL OF THE PROGRESSIVE PARTY

"Look up, not down—
Look out, not in—
Look forward, not backward—
And lend a hand."

Founders' Day
October 27, 1912
THE
Progressive Party

TEACH
Guided Practice

Making Comparisons Ask students to create a chart comparing the philosophies of the New Nationalism and the New Freedom. Students should use New Nationalism and New Freedom as vertical headings and Progressivism and Big Business as horizontal headings. *(New Nationalism: Progressivism—supported; Big Business—accepted as fact of life, but proposed regulations to keep it under control. New Freedom: Progressivism—supported; Big Business— viewed monopolies as evils, antithesis of free competition)* Ask students to discuss the similarities and differences between the philosophies. **L2**

Visualizing History Many observers note that Roosevelt's enthusiasm and earnest approach was very effective on the campaign trail.
Answer to Caption: Taft and Wilson

📁 Assign Political Cartoons in American History Activity 13: "A Third Party."

Critical Thinking Activity

Analyzing Ideas Point out that during Taft's presidency, Congress passed much progressive legislation, a great deal of it with Taft's backing. For example the Mann-Elkins Act extended the jurisdiction of the ICC to include telegraph and telephone lines, and the Railroad Valuation Act empowered the ICC to establish a basis for fixing fair rates. Furthermore, Congress established postal savings banks to protect the small depositor, and the parcel post to help the small shipper. Ask: Does this legislation conflict with or confirm the image Progressives painted of Taft and the Republicans? **L3**

Independent Practice

Analyzing Quotations

Present these statements by Roosevelt:

"The most successful politician is he who says what everybody is thinking most often and in the loudest voice."

"No man is justified in doing evil on the ground of expediency."

Ask students, based on his record, whether Roosevelt practiced what he preached. Have them write examples to support their opinions. **L1**

📁 Assign Guided Reading Activity 14-3.

ABCNEWS INTERACTIVE™

🔘 **VIDEODISC**

Powers of the President

Side 1, Chapter 7
Title: *Political Party System*
Subject: Role of political parties in election of a President

▲ **TAFT AND SONS** Theodore Roosevelt once said, "Taft has the most lovable personality I have ever come in contact with." Their friendship was wrecked, however, on the realities of politics and ambition. ***On what ballot was Taft nominated in 1912?***

Bryan was influential in seeing that the Democratic platform was as progressive as that of the Bull Moose party itself. After a protracted struggle, Woodrow Wilson, who had won national fame as a reform governor of New Jersey, received the nomination on the 46th ballot, partly through the help of Bryan.

Two Progressive Platforms

In the campaign Taft was not active, privately expressing the opinion that Wilson was sure to win. The real battle took place between Roosevelt and Wilson. Both men supported progressivism, although under different labels. Wilson countered Roosevelt with what he called the "New Freedom."

Although there appeared to be little distinction between the philosophies of the two candidates, they did in fact differ. Roosevelt's New Nationalism accepted big business as a fact of life and proposed a more powerful federal government and a strong executive to keep it under control. Wilson's New Freedom viewed monopolies as enemies of free competition. He also advocated the use of federal power to ensure more equality of opportunity.

The differences between Wilson and Roosevelt were striking. Roosevelt had long been the best-known political figure in the United States. Wilson, a former university president and college professor, had been active on the American political scene for only three years. Roosevelt, the former Rough Rider, was thought of by the public as a strong fighter in a war on privilege. While Roosevelt enjoyed mixing with all sorts of people, Wilson was aloof.

One writer likened Roosevelt to a great national spectacle, like Niagara Falls. People jammed the halls when he spoke, but it is not certain that they came so much to listen as to gape.

On the campaign platform Wilson's tall, angular figure displayed an ease of manner and his homely face exhibited a warmth he often lacked in personal relations. From his early teens, he had often dreamed of persuading people through eloquence. Even his strongest enemies admitted that he

★★★ **AMERICA'S FLAGS** ★★★

The Twenty-fifth Flag Statehood for both Arizona and New Mexico increased the number of stars to 48 in 1912. This flag served as the American flag from 1912 to 1959, more years than had any other flag.

★★★★★★★★★★★★★★★★★★★★★

Cooperative Learning Activity

Third Parties Have students work in groups of four or five to discuss the following topic: why it has been so difficult for third parties to develop in the American political system. Suggest that students consider the history of the Bull Moose party as they develop their answers. Call on students randomly to report their groups' progress. **L1** 📦

could be very persuasive. Although Wilson lacked the magnetism of his rival Roosevelt, he knew how to touch people's conscience and appeal to their sense of reason.

An attempt to assassinate Roosevelt gave him an opportunity to demonstrate his courage and self-possession. On his way to deliver a speech in Milwaukee he was shot in the chest. Pausing only long enough to make sure that his assailant received protection of the police, Roosevelt insisted on delivering his speech before receiving medical attention. Not seriously wounded, he was later able to resume his campaign at full speed.

Results of the Election

The results of the election fulfilled Taft's prediction of victory for Wilson. Although he won the presidency, Wilson actually had fewer popular votes than Roosevelt and Taft combined. Because of the split in the Republican vote, however—and also a surprisingly strong Socialist party vote—Wilson carried 40 of the 48 states, with a total of 435 electoral votes; his opponents together received only 96 electoral votes. So, for the first time since Grover Cleveland's election in 1892, a Democrat became President of the United States.

Wilson's Previous Career

Woodrow Wilson had gained national prominence as a foe of privilege and as an individual with strong powers of leader-ship. During eight years as president of Princeton University, he not only raised standards and improved teaching, but also fought social privilege as represented by social clubs. As governor of New Jersey he fought political bosses who represented special interests, not the interests of the people as a whole. Under his leadership, the New Jersey legislature enacted an elaborate program of progressive measures.

The extraordinary successes gained by the "scholar in politics" can be explained partly by the fact that from childhood he had been ambitious to hold high office. Not only had he trained himself in public speaking, but he had also devoted much of his life to studying the techniques of effective political leadership. A long-time admirer of the British government, he developed the theory that the President, like the British prime minister, should take the initiative in guiding and promoting legislation. The President alone, in his opinion, stood for the interests of the entire nation.

In addition to books on government, Wilson had written a history of the United States and many articles, mostly on political topics. He was well informed on domestic issues, especially the tariff. A Southerner who had lived his adult life in the North, a Democrat who admired Alexander Hamilton as well as Thomas Jefferson, a scholar who knew the past as well as the present, Wilson was able to see public questions in perspective.

CHAPTER 14
SECTION 3

ASSESS
Check Understanding
Assign Section 3 Review as homework or an in-class activity.

Evaluate
Assign Section Quiz 14-3 or use the Test-maker to create a customized quiz.

Reteach
Have students complete Reteaching Activity 14-3.

Enrich
Ask students to construct a flow chart illustrating the history of the Bull Moose party. Then have them describe the impact of the party on the 1912 election.

CLOSE
Ask students to predict the kinds of legislation that Wilson might try to pass during his administration and why. Have them write their predictions in their notebooks.

Section 3 ★ Review

Checking for Understanding
1. **Identify** Bull Moose party, New Freedom.
2. **Define** inheritance tax.
3. **Explain** why Roosevelt left the Republicans and helped form the Progressive party.
4. **Describe** the significant details of the Progressive party platform.
5. **Summarize** the electoral voting for each of the major candidates in the 1912 presidential election.

Critical Thinking
6. **Recognizing Stereotypes**   Analyze whether supporters of the Progressive party were radical reformers or dreamers.

ACTIVITY
7. Imagine you are a volunteer working for one of the presidential candidates in the 1912 election. Prepare a poster that explains your candidate's position on one major issue.

Answers to SECTION 3 REVIEW

1. Bull Moose party, 433; New Freedom, 433
2. All vocabulary words are defined in the Glossary.
3. Old Guard Republicans nominated Taft. Roosevelt felt cheated and took his supporters, forming the Progressive party.
4. more direct democracy through initiative and referendum, conservation of natural resources, woman suffrage, labor reforms, revision of currency systems, inheritance tax

5. Wilson carried 40 states, winning huge majority in electoral vote over Roosevelt and Taft.
6. They fitted these stereotypes to a degree, since they were idealists who talked about, wrote about, and crusaded for reform. However, they were not radical activists, and reforms they wanted were realistic.
7. Issues and posters will vary. Students' work should indicate that they understand the candidate's position on the issue.

TEACH

Remind students that any generalizations made from election maps must be supported. Review the map key. Ask: What information is provided? *(popular and electoral votes for Wilson, Roosevelt, and Taft)* How are the electoral victories identified on the map? *(by color)* What generalizations can be drawn from the map? *(Wilson won most of the electoral votes in the South and West.)*

Discuss the guidelines for making supporting statements. Ask: Why are election maps useful to historians and politicians? *(They show areas of support.)* What sources could be used to back up information on election maps? *(actual election counts)* **L2**

📁 Use Chapter Skills Activity 14 to reinforce students' understanding of the skill.

Did You Know?

Although Wilson led his rivals in the Electoral College by a wide margin (435 to 88 for Roosevelt and 8 for Taft), he got only 41.9 percent of the popular vote. William Jennings Bryan received more votes in 1908.

🕹️ 📁 For additional map practice, use Map Transparency Activity 14 and Chapter Map Activity 14.

436

BUILDING SKILLS
Critical Thinking Skills

Supporting Generalizations

A generalization is a statement that offers a general characteristic rather than a specific one. Sometimes when making a point or offering an interpretation, an author may make a generalization and then give supporting statements. At other times, however, you may be given only a generalization without supporting statements, or supporting statements without a generalization. In such cases you will need to use your understanding of the content and thought processes to supply what's missing—either the generalization or the supporting statement.

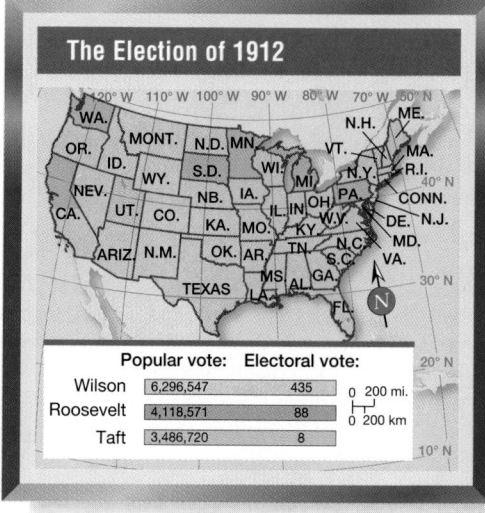

The Election of 1912

	Popular vote:	Electoral vote:
Wilson	6,296,547	435
Roosevelt	4,118,571	88
Taft	3,486,720	8

0 200 mi.
0 200 km

Learning the Skill

As a historian, it is important to back up generalizations with supporting statements or evidence. Here are guidelines for making supporting statements.

- Supporting statements must relate directly to the generalization.
- They must be logical.
- They must be based on fact.

Study the map of the election of 1912, noting how the guidelines have been applied to the following generalizations.

Generalization:
- The Southern states had a great influence on the election of the Democratic candidate, Woodrow Wilson.

Supporting statement:
The election map shows that all electoral votes from the Southern states went to Woodrow Wilson. (This statement relates directly to the generalization, is logical, and is based on fact.)

Generalization:
- The citizens who voted preferred Woodrow Wilson.

Supporting statement:
Woodrow Wilson won the election of 1912. (This statement relates directly to the general-

ization and is logical, but it is not based on fact. The majority of citizens who voted did not vote for Wilson.)

Practicing the Skill

1. Write a supporting statement for the following generalizations.

   a. Despite his popularity with the public, Theodore Roosevelt often had great difficulty getting "Square Deal" measures through Congress.

   b. Taft continued Roosevelt's reform program, but the public lost confidence in his leadership.

APPLYING THE SKILL

2. Review information in Section 3 about Theodore Roosevelt's reentry into the national political arena. Write a generalization about the goals and objectives of the Progressive party. Then support your generalization with facts.

Answers to Practicing the Skill

1. **a.** Possible supporting statements: Roosevelt tried to win public support when Congress failed to pass legislation to regulate big business. Although Roosevelt favored a revision of the tariff, he did not get Congress to act. **b.** Although it was Roosevelt who was nicknamed the "trust buster," Taft actually prosecuted twice as many antitrust cases in four years as had his predecessor.

Unlike Roosevelt, Taft's judicial background allowed him to use "only those powers expressly authorized by law."

2. Answers will vary. Student generalizations should indicate that they understand the aims of the Progressive party.

★★★

Wilson's Progressivism

Setting the Scene

Section Focus

Before becoming President, Woodrow Wilson had held only one political office, governor of New Jersey from 1910 to 1912. In those two years, he had successfully worked for an elaborate program of progressive laws. Wilson began his first presidential term determined to obtain major social reform at the federal level.

Objectives

After studying this section, you should be able to

★ explain why Wilson had congressional support for his programs.

★ list the accomplishments of Wilson's domestic program, including legislation on tariffs and on trusts.

Key Terms

rediscount, price-cutting, interlocking directorate

◀ NUTCRACKER IN LIKENESS OF WOODROW WILSON

The new President entered office with several handicaps. He was a minority President, chosen by only 42 percent of the voters. With no experience in national politics, he knew few Democratic party leaders. In addition, the Democratic party at the time comprised a loose alliance of local interests not expected to work well together. Long out of office, the Democrats lacked people with experience in government at the federal level.

■ Wilson and Congress

Although inexperienced in national politics, Wilson enjoyed certain advantages upon entering office. The 1912 election results sent Congress a clear message that most Americans demanded progressive legislation. If the Democrats did not support the President in the creation of this legislation, warned a

member of Congress, they would be "turned into the wilderness for 40 years more." No prominent Democratic leaders opposed Wilson, as Republicans Cannon and Aldrich had thwarted Taft. On the contrary, Wilson enjoyed the loyal support of most Democrats—including Bryan, the most influential man in the party, whom Wilson appointed secretary of state.

Wilson's first Inaugural Address was one of the shortest and most eloquent ever delivered. He began by asking the meaning of the Democratic triumph at the polls. His answer was that it meant little "except when the Nation is using that party for a large and definite purpose." To Wilson, the purpose was to do away with the evils that, along with many blessings, industrialism had brought. The President described these evils as the "inexcusable waste" of natural resources, the "human cost" of unrestrained individualism, and the use of government "for private and selfish purposes." Wilson

CHAPTER 14 White House Reformers: 1900–1914   **437**

Classroom Resources for SECTION 4

Blackline Masters:
☞ Reproducible Lesson Plan 14-4
☞ Guided Reading Activity 14-4
☞ Critical Thinking Skills Activity 14
☞ Cooperative Learning Activity 14
☞ Workbook Activity 14
☞ Reteaching Activity 14-4
☞ Section Quiz 14-4

Transparencies:
🔦 Section Focus Transparency 14-4
🔦 Skills Transparency 14

Multimedia:
💿 Testmaker
💿 Economics in Action
🎏 American Music: Cultural Traditions

LESSON PLAN
SECTION 4, 437–443

FOCUS
Bellringer

📁 Before taking roll, project Section Focus Transparency 14-4 or hand out Section Focus Transparency Activity 14-4. Have students answer the questions.

Motivating Activity

Have students imagine that Woodrow Wilson has asked them to help him prepare his inaugural address. Based on what they know, ask students to suggest a goal for Wilson to outline in his speech. Tell students to note Wilson's three major goals as they study Section 4. **L2**

Vocabulary Precheck

Ask students to define each of the "Key Terms." Have a volunteer consult the dictionary for any unfamiliar words. **L1, LEP**

Did You Know?

Born in Staunton, Virginia, Woodrow Wilson was the first southerner—and just the second Democrat—elected President since the Civil War. He recognized his aloofness as a weakness. "I have a sense of power in dealing with men collectively which I do not feel always in dealing with them singly," he confessed.

TEACH
Guided Practice
Analyzing Alternatives

Have students write responses to the following:

If you had been a farmer, business owner, or consumer around 1914, how would the Federal Reserve Act have improved your economic situation? *(provided banks with enough money to extend loans to businesspeople and farmers, assured a steady supply of goods to consumers, protected depositors from bank "runs")*

Use students' answers as a starting point for a discussion of the success of Wilson's business reform program. **L3**

Visualizing
History
Woodrow Wilson had been an attorney and gained eminence as one of the leading experts in political economics and jurisprudence.
Answer to Caption: called for reform of tariff and banking system, equality of business opportunity, improvements in agriculture, and conservation of natural resources

Visualizing
History

▲ **INAUGURATION OF A NEW PRESIDENT** The shortcomings of industrial America were widely recognized when Woodrow Wilson became President in March 1913, so it was no surprise that his brief Inaugural Address was devoted to domestic reform. *What goals did Wilson set forth in his Inaugural Address?*

also stated his goals—not, he said, Democratic or Republican goals but goals for all the nation. After calling for reform of tariffs and banking, equality of business opportunity, improvements in agriculture, and conservation of natural resources, he concluded:

> *This is not a day of triumph. It is a day of dedication. Here muster not the forces of party, but the forces of humanity. . . . I summon all honest men, all patriotic, all forward-looking men to my side. God helping me, I will not fail them, if they will but counsel and sustain me!*

■ The Underwood Tariff

The President lost no time in embarking on his program of reform. Like Taft, Wilson at once called Congress into special session. Appearing in person before Congress—the first President to do so in 100 years—he delivered a special message on the tariff. This short speech made headlines nationwide and illustrated Wilson's long-standing belief that the President's greatest power lay in focusing public attention on important issues.

Wilson's message charged that high tariffs had:

> *. . . built up a set of privileges and exemptions from competition behind which it was easy . . . to organize monopoly; until . . . nothing is obliged to stand the tests of efficiency and economy.*

Lower rates, he claimed, would help businesses by putting them under "constant necessity to be efficient, economical, and enterprising. . . ." Opening the American market to foreign products would at the same time open foreign markets to American goods. Wilson warned, however, against undue haste, making it clear that he did not favor removing protective duties entirely.

Cooperative Learning Activity

National Finances Divide students into groups of five, assigning each group member a number between one and five. Then point out that the Aldrich Commission reported that the financial organization of the United States was flawed in four ways. Give groups a certain amount of time for discussion. Select a number, and call on a student with that number to explain one of the ways the financial organization of the United States was flawed. If the answer is incomplete, continue to call on students with the same number. Call another number for another explanation, and so on. **L2, L3**

The House of Representatives soon passed a bill, sponsored by Alabama representative Oscar W. Underwood, embodying the President's recommendations. The real fight occurred in the Senate, where previous attempts to lower the tariff had foundered, and where the Democrats had only a six-vote majority. Lobbyists swarmed to Washington, pressuring senators to alter the bill. But before senatorial opposition could crystallize, Wilson again appealed to the people. He denounced the "insidious" lobbyists and asked an aroused public to insist that Congress put an end to "this unbearable situation." The President then held personal conferences with Democratic senators and wrote letters to those threatening to oppose him. Under such varied and unrelenting pressure from the executive office, the Senate voted to accept the House bill with little change.

The Underwood Tariff Act represented the first substantial drop in import duties since 1857. It attempted to fix duties at a level where costs of production in the United States and abroad would be equalized, thus lowering the duty paid on almost 1,000 articles. It removed protection entirely from industries that already competed successfully with foreign producers.

A most important section of the Underwood Tariff Act was the provision for levying an income tax, now legalized by the Sixteenth Amendment. Originally introduced merely to make up for losses in revenue created by lower tariffs, the income tax became the federal government's chief source of revenue in a very short time.

■ The Federal Reserve Act

As the tariff debate reached a crescendo, Wilson appeared before Congress to introduce the second major item in his reform program: a revision of the banking and currency system. The purpose of the revision was to provide businesses with cheaper and more available credit. Like the tariff message, Wilson's speech was so brief that many influential newspapers published the entire text.

Flaws in the Banking System

In 1907 a sharp panic had revealed serious weaknesses in the American banking and currency system. There were runs on banks, many of which closed or stopped lending as a result. In 1908 Congress set up the National Monetary Commission, headed

◀ **FEDERAL RESERVE SYMBOL**

 **Visualizing History**

▲ **STRUCTURE OF THE FEDERAL RESERVE** By 1994 the United States had more than 11,000 commercial banks. Nearly 40 percent of these were member banks that belonged to the Federal Reserve System. *What flaws in the banking system was the Federal Reserve System set up to correct?*

Independent Practice

Analyzing Vocabulary To make certain that students understand the meaning of the business and economic terminology in this section, have them write a paragraph in which they correctly use the following terms: *antitrust, price-cutting, contract tying, intercorporate investment, interlocking directorates.* **L1**

Visualizing History When the Federal Reserve takes actions that increase the amount of money in circulation, it is following a *loose money policy.* Conversely the actions it takes to reduce the money supply are called a *tight money policy.*

Answer to Caption: Answers include instability of banks in time of crisis, inflexible currency, no central control, and too much concentration in certain areas to exclusion of rural and isolated districts.

GLENCOE TECHNOLOGY

 VIDEODISC
Economics in Action

Disc 2, Side 1, Chapter 21
Title: *The Federal Reserve and Monetary Policy*
Subject: Explains how the Federal Reserve System controls the money supply

---

Sidelight: Baseball Traditions

The tradition of having the President open the baseball season by throwing out the first ball originated with President William Howard Taft. So did the seventh-inning stretch. During a game he was attending, Taft stood up in the middle of the seventh inning because he was uncomfortable—his large, 300-pound frame did not fit too well in the narrow seat. Many people in the crowd thought Taft was about to leave, so, out of respect, they also rose. When he sat back down, so did the crowd. People generally felt that Taft had shown good sense by standing up and stretching, and this action soon became an integral part of the game.

📂 Assign Guided Reading Activity 14-4.

Did You Know?

The law creating the Federal Reserve System was the first reorganization of the banking system since the Civil War.

Linking Across TIME

When the Federal Reserve System, or Fed, was established in 1913, its powers were more limited than today. In its early days, the Fed served as the nation's central bank. It cleared the checks of member banks and regulated banking activities. Since the United States went off the gold standard in 1933, the Fed has served as watchdog over the nation's money supply. By controlling the supply of money, the Fed seeks to keep the economy from expanding too fast, or slipping into a recession.

📂 Project Skills Transparency 14 and have students complete Skills Transparency Activity 14.

---

by conservative Senator Aldrich, to investigate the situation and propose change. After four years of study, the Aldrich Commission reported that the financial organization of the United States was flawed in four respects.

First, American banking lacked stability in times of crisis. Banks did not keep enough money on reserve to cover sudden withdrawals, and there was not enough cooperation between banks.

Second, America's currency was inflexible. The amount of money in circulation was based on the amount of gold and silver in the treasury, plus the bonds held by the national banks. The present system provided no way to increase or decrease the supply of money according to the investment needs of the country.

Third, there was no central control of banking practices. In other modern industrialized countries, central banks, such as the Bank of England and the Bank of France, directed banking policy. Nothing similar had existed in this nation since Andrew Jackson had destroyed the second Bank.

Finally, the commission found that too much bank capital was concentrated in New York City and on Wall Street. Meanwhile, other parts of the country, especially isolated rural districts, often suffered from a lack of adequate banking facilities and credit.

Although few questioned the list of ills in the banking and currency system, government leaders disputed the cure. Bankers favored a great central bank, privately controlled, like the first and second Banks of the United States. Many progressives, especially Bryan, called for strict federal control of banking and credit. It was Wilson's difficult task to select a plan that would work and at the same time win support from both bankers and Bryan's followers.

Central Banking Authority

The plan Wilson finally chose was called the Federal Reserve Act. Again, under constant pressure from the President, Congress finally passed the law in December 1913. The Federal Reserve Act promptly became one of the most important and useful pieces of legislation in United States history.

The new system provided for 12 Federal Reserve Banks situated throughout the country. All national banks were required to join them, and other banks could join if they wished. The Federal Reserve did not deal directly with individuals but instead serviced member banks. These "banks for bankers" concentrated reserves, so they could provide support to individual banks in times of temporary difficulty such as a "run." They also provided for local investment needs and made it easier to move funds from one part of the country to another.

The Federal Reserve Act provided a compromise between private and public control. The Federal Reserve Banks themselves were privately owned, a majority of their directors being elected by the member banks. Overall control of the Federal Reserve Banks, however, remained in the hands of a Federal Reserve Board, whose 7 members were appointed by the President, subject to approval by the Senate, for 14-year terms. Thus the center of the nation's financial power moved from Wall Street in New York City to Washington, D.C.

Flexible Money Supply

Before passage of the Federal Reserve Act, local banks frequently lacked funds to make sound loans to businesspeople and farmers. For want of adequate funds, stores and factories closed, and crops rotted. The Federal Reserve Act greatly improved this situation by providing for a new form of "flexible" currency known as Federal Reserve notes. The new money went into circulation when local banks needing cash brought businesspeople's promissory notes to Federal Reserve Banks. In return, the Federal Reserve Bank issued Federal Reserve notes, assessing the member bank a small fee called a **rediscount.**

When a Federal Reserve Bank bought promissory notes, it could print and issue more paper money, using those notes as part of the security, or collateral, thereby protecting the value of the currency. Then, when the notes were paid and the money came back to the Bank, the currency was retired.

Critical Thinking Activity

Analyzing Effectiveness The Federal Reserve Act is said to be one of the most important pieces of legislation in the history of the United States. Ask students to explain how this act successfully provided the United States with a banking system responsive to the needs of a great industrial nation. (*It set up a new banking system under which the country was divided into 12 banking* *districts, each with a Federal Reserve Bank that supervised the activities of member banks and controlled credit.*) **L3**

📂 For additional practice in using critical thinking skills, assign Critical Thinking Skills Activity 14.

The Federal Reserve Banks also controlled the amount of money in circulation by raising or lowering the rediscount rate, or the rate at which they charged for rediscounting. Raising the rate discouraged banks from lending and so "contracted" the currency; lowering the rate encouraged lending and "expanded" the currency. Thus currency and credit in any Federal Reserve District expanded or contracted according to the economic needs of that region.

On the whole, the Federal Reserve Act made the banking system responsive to the needs of a great industrial nation. It succeeded in its first great test, during World War I, when it assisted industrial expansion and helped finance the war effort.

■ Wilson Regulates Trusts

Shortly after signing the Federal Reserve Act, Wilson asked Congress to pass an antitrust law more effective than the Sherman Antitrust Act. Denying any desire to interfere with legitimate business activities, his message to Congress proposed various methods of preventing the "indefensible and intolerable" abuses of private monopoly.

Federal Trade Commission

Late in 1914, Congress responded to Wilson's requests by passing two laws. The first, the Federal Trade Commission Act, established a Federal Trade Commission to

Map Study *Using Maps*

Answer: Twelve districts and Federal Reserve banks within those districts reflect regional centers of finance, industry, and agriculture.

Map Skills Practice
Describe the regions the following Federal Reserve banks served: San Francisco (*West*), Dallas (*Southwest*), Chicago (*Great Lakes*), Boston (*Northeast*).

Did You Know?

The President was named Thomas Woodrow Wilson after his maternal grandfather, a Presbyterian minister. After graduating from Princeton, he began calling himself T. Woodrow Wilson. Soon after he dropped the first initial.

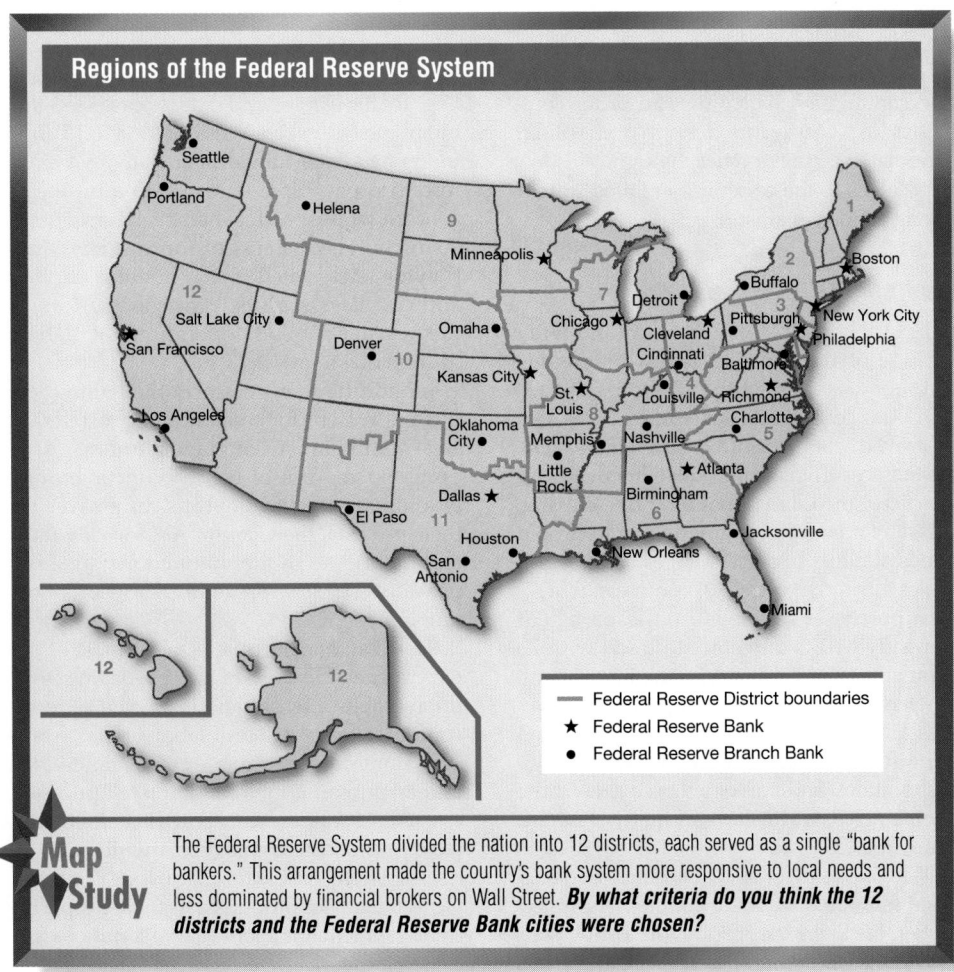

Regions of the Federal Reserve System

Federal Reserve District boundaries
★ Federal Reserve Bank
● Federal Reserve Branch Bank

Map Study
The Federal Reserve System divided the nation into 12 districts, each served as a single "bank for bankers." This arrangement made the country's bank system more responsive to local needs and less dominated by financial brokers on Wall Street. **By what criteria do you think the 12 districts and the Federal Reserve Bank cities were chosen?**

Sidelight: Eugene Debs

The fourth candidate running for President in 1912 was Eugene V. Debs of the Socialist party. Debs campaigned tirelessly, undertaking a whistle-stop tour of the country on which he made as many as 20 appearances a day. He was a powerful and spellbinding speaker, and his speeches were a mixture of socialist idealism and allusions to the greatness of America's past. In the election Debs received almost 900,000 votes—6 percent of all votes cast. It appeared that the Socialist party would become a major force in American politics, but the Red Scare after World War I ended most of its support.

Teaching American Portraits

In 1909 W.E.B. Du Bois and other members of the Niagara Movement joined with a number of white liberals to form the National Association for the Advancement of Colored People (NAACP). He was named the first editor of the association's journal, *Crisis*.

Although the NAACP's initial aim was to halt the rash of lynchings of African Americans, its long-term goal was to win racial equality and end segregation. Over time the NAACP grew in membership and in influence. Have students research the activities of the NAACP today.

Did You Know?

Before becoming President, Woodrow Wilson had gained national prominence as a foe of privilege. During eight years as president of Princeton University, he not only raised standards and improved teaching, but also fought social privilege as represented by snobbish undergraduate clubs. As governor of New Jersey, he successfully fought the bosses who represented special interests, not the interest of the people as a whole. Under his leadership the New Jersey legislature enacted an elaborate program of progressive measures.

★★★★**A**★★★★★★★
AMERICAN PORTRAITS

W.E.B. Du Bois
1868–1963

The first African American to receive a Harvard Ph.D., W.E.B. Du Bois was a distinguished educator who refused to accept racial inequality. Du Bois initiated the Niagara Movement in 1905 to fight racial discrimination against African Americans in the United States.

For 24 years, Du Bois served as editor of the NAACP's journal, *The Crisis*, using it as a tool to assert demands for racial justice and equality. Between 1910 and 1930, his influence shaped not only the NAACP but a generation of African American intellectuals and activists.

In 1919 he organized the first Pan-African Congress, which promoted the idea that all people of African descent throughout the world should work together to combat the effects of discrimination. *Pan-Africanism* is still strong today among nations in Africa, where Du Bois moved in 1961.

investigate and regulate business practices. The commission had power to order companies to "cease and desist" from unfair conduct. In actual practice, though, Wilson's appointees to the commission failed to take strong actions against trusts.

Clayton Antitrust Act

In October 1914, less than a month after passage of the Federal Trade Commission Act, Congress passed the Clayton Antitrust Act. This act forbade several practices that destroyed competition or prevented new businesses from being developed. These practices included ruinous **price-cutting**, whereby a large company deliberately sold goods at a loss to drive weaker competitors out of business; "tying" of contracts, whereby a purchaser of goods from a particular company had to agree not to trade with its competitors; and intercorporate investment, whereby a company bought part ownership in a rival concern. The act also outlawed **"interlocking" directorates** between large corporations and banks, whereby the same people acted as directors in many different companies.

The Clayton Act also contained two sections favorable to trade unions. As noted earlier, the Sherman Act, by forbidding conspiracies, had proven more effective against labor unions than against business monopolies. In the Danbury Hatters' case, fought out in the federal courts from 1903 to 1915, a union had been ruined financially by being forced to pay triple damages to a business concern whose product had been boycotted. To discourage such use of antitrust laws, the Clayton Act stated that "nothing in the antitrust laws shall be construed to forbid the existence and operation of labor . . . organizations."

In addition, ever since the jailing of Eugene V. Debs for contempt of court in the 1894 Pullman strike, labor unions had protested the use of court injunctions forbidding strikes and boycotts. In answer to their protests, the Clayton Act forbade federal courts to issue injunctions against peaceful strikes, picketing, boycotts, or union meetings.

The Clayton Antitrust Act lost most of its effectiveness because of loose wording and unfavorable interpretations by the federal courts. The protection of labor unions from suits under the Sherman Act was limited to unions pursuing their "legitimate" purposes—and it was the courts that defined the word *legitimate*. Injunctions might still be issued when "necessary to prevent irreparable damage to property or to a property right," which again left a large loophole for conservative judges.

Cultural Perspectives

Dealing With Segregation In a policy that became known as the Atlanta Compromise, Booker T. Washington, the founder of the Tuskegee Institute, encouraged Southern African Americans to accept segregation and to concentrate on quietly uplifting themselves. Some Northern African Americans, however, railed against the compromise in general and

Washington in particular. W.E.B. Du Bois, for example, said Washington "apologizes for injustice. He belittles the emasculating effects of caste distinctions . . . . The way for people to gain their reasonable rights is not by voluntarily throwing them away." Encourage students to find out more about both men and their impact on American life.

Wilson's Other Accomplishments

The Clayton Act completed the legislative program that Wilson had originally promoted. Wilson, however, did not stop there, turning his attention to other domestic issues.

Domestic Legislation

Additional legislation passed during his first term included the establishment of 12 regional Federal Farm Loan Banks, endowed with public funds in order to provide loans for agriculture. A Federal Highways Act, designed to help farmers get their produce to market, allotted federal funds to states for road construction and development. Wilson also supported the Keating-Owen Child Labor Act, which prohibited the employment of children under age 14 in factories producing goods for interstate commerce. The Adamson Act, passed under threat of a nationwide tie-up in transportation, established an 8-hour day for railroad workers.

Under Wilson's directed eye, much constructive legislation had been passed quickly. Wilson supplied a skillful and dynamic leadership, sometimes keeping Congress in session throughout the hot summer months. Chauncey Depew, a noted conservative Republican, said that for a man regarded as a mere theorist, Wilson had accomplished "the most astonishing practical results."

Segregation in the Capital

The reforms Wilson achieved did not have "practical results" for African Americans, however, as the President brought Jim Crow to Washington. The nation's capital had been desegregated since Reconstruction, but Wilson strongly believed in separating the races. His administration segregated drinking fountains, rest rooms, and lunch counters in government office buildings and assigned jobs according to race.

A number of prominent African American leaders like W.E.B. Du Bois, who had supported Wilson in 1912, turned against him. African American newspaper editor William Monroe Trotter blamed Wilson's New Freedom for a "new slavery for your Afro-American fellow citizens." Yet the President exemplified the racial prejudice of many other progressive reformers.

Wilson also opposed woman suffrage at first. Later, however, he modified his position. During this second term, the Nineteenth Amendment gave women the right to vote.

Wilson's efforts during the beginning of his first term focused almost exclusively on domestic matters. In fact, foreign affairs did not even receive mention in his first Inaugural Address. But by the end of his term, world events overshadowed these domestic achievements. Wilson's role as architect and promoter of progressive legislation was all but forgotten. It was obscured by growing tensions in foreign affairs that resulted in tragedy for him and for the world.

Section 4 ★ Review

Checking for Understanding

1. **Identify** Underwood Tariff, Federal Reserve Board, Federal Trade Commission, Clayton Antitrust Act.

2. **Define** rediscount, price-cutting, interlocking directorate.

3. **Explain** how the Federal Reserve System works.

4. **Describe** the provisions of the Clayton Antitrust Act that limited the power of monopolies.

Critical Thinking

5. **Making Judgments**   Evaluate the effect of Wilson's antitrust legislation and the creation of the Federal Reserve System on the economy of the nation.

ACTIVITY

6. Create a table using the headings: Work, School, and Housing. Under each, state the ways your life would be different if you lived in a segregated society.

ASSESS
Check Understanding
Assign Section 4 Review as homework or an in-class activity.

Evaluate
◉ 🗀 Assign Section Quiz 14-4 or use the Test-maker to create a customized quiz.

Reteach
🗀 Have students complete Reteaching Activity 14-4.

🗀 Assign Workbook Activity 14-4.

Enrich
🗀 Assign Cooperative Learning Activity 14.

CLOSE
Refer students to the statement by Woodrow Wilson that opens this section. Discuss with students if Wilson's actions as President were based on his concern for the American people.

Answers to SECTION 4 REVIEW

1. Underwood Tariff, 438; Federal Reserve Board, 440; Federal Trade Commission, 441; Clayton Antitrust Act, 442
2. All vocabulary words are defined in the Glossary.
3. Federal Reserve banks situated nationwide with reserve funds for member banks; flexible currency system to provide loans as needed; printed money using notes as collateral; money withdrawn when notes paid.
4. forbade the following: price-cutting by large companies,

tying contracts, intercorporate investment, and interlocking directorates
5. inspired public confidence by reforming banking system, encouraging growth of business through promise of fair trade practices, and generating overall domestic prosperity
6. Student statements should be valid and tied to realistic expectations.

Using Vocabulary

Paragraphs will vary but should include all the vocabulary terms.

Reviewing Facts

1. included government regulation of big business and railroads, trust busting, and conservation of natural resources
2. educators, editors, literary figures, philanthropists, and former Rough Riders who supported reform
3. established the Tariff Board, supported the Sixteenth and Seventeenth Amendments, prosecuted many antitrust cases.
4. Both wanted to regulate big business through government control and protect the public interest, but Roosevelt saw big business— even monopolies—as necessary; Wilson did not. Wilson wanted to eliminate monopolies and trusts.

Understanding Concepts

1. Taft yielded on the tariff question. The amended Payne-

Using Vocabulary

Write a paragraph describing Wilson's New Freedom program. Use the following terms:

progressivism	labor
antitrust	monopoly
free competition	income tax

Reviewing Facts

1. **Describe** the progressive beliefs of Theodore Roosevelt.
2. **Identify** the sources of support for Roosevelt's Square Deal and New Nationalism.
3. **Cite** two important achievements of William Howard Taft's administration.
4. **Compare** the progressivism of Woodrow Wilson and Theodore Roosevelt based on their respective programs.

Understanding Concepts

Interests and Positions

1. Show how Taft's policies seemed to go against Roosevelt's Square Deal.

Economic Competition

2. In what way did big-business practices and tactics in the early 1900s slow or inhibit economic competition?

Critical Thinking

1. **Linking Past and Present** Compare Theodore Roosevelt's approach to conservation of natural resources with those of Presidents during the 1980s and 1990s.
2. **Analyzing Political Cartoons** Study the cartoon on this page showing President Woodrow Wilson, then answer the questions that follow.

   a. Do you think the cartoonist has a favorable or unfavorable view of Wilson? Explain.

b. What point is the cartoonist making?
c. What symbols did the cartoonist use to get his message across to the viewer?
d. What would be an appropriate title for the cartoon?

History and Geography

Conservation and the Environment

Conservation is the care and protection of natural resources including the land, lakes, rivers, and forests; oil, natural gas, and other energy sources; and wildlife. Review the information on conservation in the chapter, then answer the questions that follow.

1. **Human/Environment Interaction** When was the National Reclamation Act passed? What was its purpose?
2. **Human/Environment Interaction** What efforts did state government make to promote conservation?

Aldrich Tariff favored manufacturing interests by raising duties on most goods. He also supported Joseph Cannon and allowed the sale of reserved public lands.
2. Price-cutting allowed big companies to sell goods at a loss and wipe out compe-

tition; intercorporate investment whereby one company bought part ownership in rival concern; interlocking directorships between large corporations and banks allowed the same people to be directors in different companies.

Critical Thinking

1. Students should use valid reasoning in drawing their comparisons.
2. a. The cartoonist presents Wilson in a favorable light: fast-moving and energetic.
   b. Answers will vary, but students should note that Wilson is a leader.

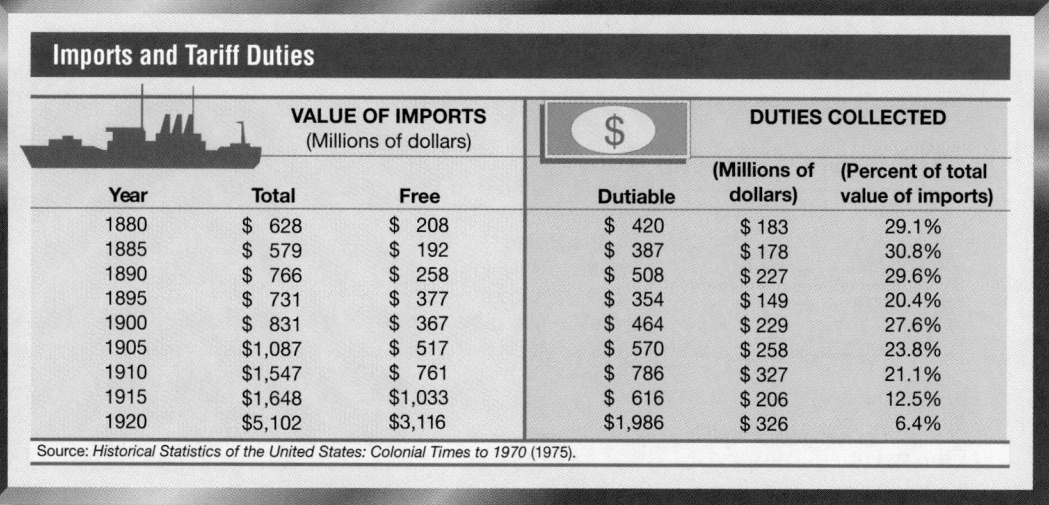

Imports and Tariff Duties

	VALUE OF IMPORTS (Millions of dollars)			DUTIES COLLECTED		
Year	Total	Free		Dutiable	(Millions of dollars)	(Percent of total value of imports)
1880	$ 628	$ 208		$ 420	$ 183	29.1%
1885	$ 579	$ 192		$ 387	$ 178	30.8%
1890	$ 766	$ 258		$ 508	$ 227	29.6%
1895	$ 731	$ 377		$ 354	$ 149	20.4%
1900	$ 831	$ 367		$ 464	$ 229	27.6%
1905	$1,087	$ 517		$ 570	$ 258	23.8%
1910	$1,547	$ 761		$ 786	$ 327	21.1%
1915	$1,648	$1,033		$ 616	$ 206	12.5%
1920	$5,102	$3,116		$1,986	$ 326	6.4%

Source: *Historical Statistics of the United States: Colonial Times to 1970* (1975).

Interdisciplinary Activity: Mathematics

Cooperative Learning

With a partner, use almanacs, magazines, and other reference books to obtain information about the salaries of professional athletes, business leaders, college presidents, governors, and the President of the United States. Present your findings in the form of a bar graph. Then write a paragraph indicating whether you believe the President should earn more or less money than others on the graph and give reasons why.

Practicing Skills

Supporting Generalizations

Use what you have learned about supporting generalizations to examine the data in the table above and to answer the questions below.

1. What is the subject of this data?

2. What years are covered in the table? How many years separate each row of data?

3. Explain the trend in the total value of imports represented on this table.

4. Explain the trend in total duties collected in the time period covered by the table.

5. Write a generalization with supporting statements on the value of American imports from 1880 to 1920.

6. Write a generalization with supporting statements on the amount of duties collected from 1880 to 1920.

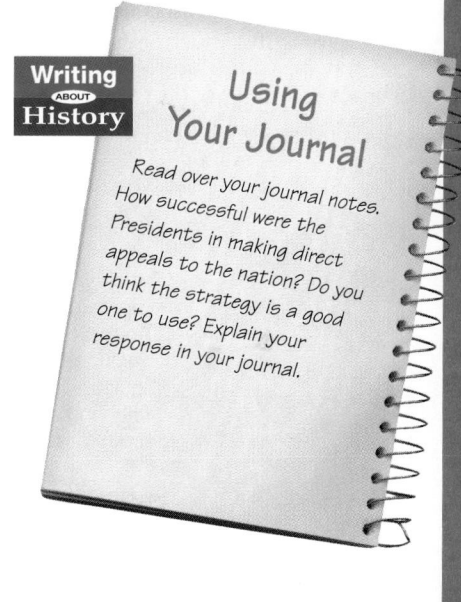

Writing ABOUT History

Using Your Journal

Read over your journal notes. How successful were the Presidents in making direct appeals to the nation? Do you think the strategy is a good one to use? Explain your response in your journal.

crease was gradual, until 1915. Between 1915 and 1920 the value of imports more than tripled.

4. increased for every time period, except three

5. Possible generalization: The value of imports to the United States increased between 1895 and 1920. Supporting statements:

6. Possible generalization: After the passage of the Underwood Tariff Act, duties on imports made up a smaller part of the total value of imports. Supporting statement: After the passage of the Underwood Tariff Act in 1913, duties as a percentage of the total value of imports decreased from 21.1% in 1910 to 12.5% in 1915 and 6.4% in 1920.

Writing ABOUT History
Using Your Journal

Students should offer reasons for their opinions.

❓ Chapter Bonus Test Question

Ask: Which of the Progressive era Presidents was the true "trust buster"? Give reasons in support of your answer. *(Answers will vary. Theodore Roosevelt was the first to regulate trusts, but Taft prosecuted more cases. Wilson initiated legislation that strengthened the Sherman Antitrust Act and established a Federal Trade Commission.)*

---

c. Answers will vary, but students might note that the cartoonist wants Americans to support Wilson.
d. Titles will vary.

History and Geography

1. The 1902 act provided for replacing natural services and set aside funds from public land sales for irrigation projects in the West.
2. More than 40 state conservation commissions were established.

Cooperative Learning

Stress to students to label the axes on the bar graph and to use increments of dollars that will be appropriate to the totals presented.

Practicing Skills

1. value of imports and duties collected
2. 1880–1920; five years
3. The total value of imports rose in every five-year period except two. The in-

445

Cultural Kaleidoscope

Transportation

Moving Into The Fast Lanes

As America evolved into a world power at the turn of the twentieth century, it also began to look differently at itself. The frontier was nearly gone and in its place, from 1880 to 1914, booming industrial expansion became a hallmark of American culture. No symbol better expresses this period than the automobile. Although the auto was invented in the nineteenth century, it is truly a twentieth-century phenomenon that touched and changed the way Americans lived.

Beginning in 1908, the Ford Model T reached unparalleled sales, justifying its nickname of the car that put the world on wheels.

In the early 1900s, car bodies tended to look similar to each other. By 1912, designers began to create distinctive hood ornaments.

Some automakers outfitted their vehicles with horns operated by hand or by foot. Some luxury cars included two horns—a quiet one for use in the city and a louder one for country driving.

There had been only a handful of automobiles on American highways by 1895. By 1920 there were nearly 5 million, and the automobile was beginning to remake American life.

446

No better proof of the impact of the automobile exists than in the popular songs of the day.

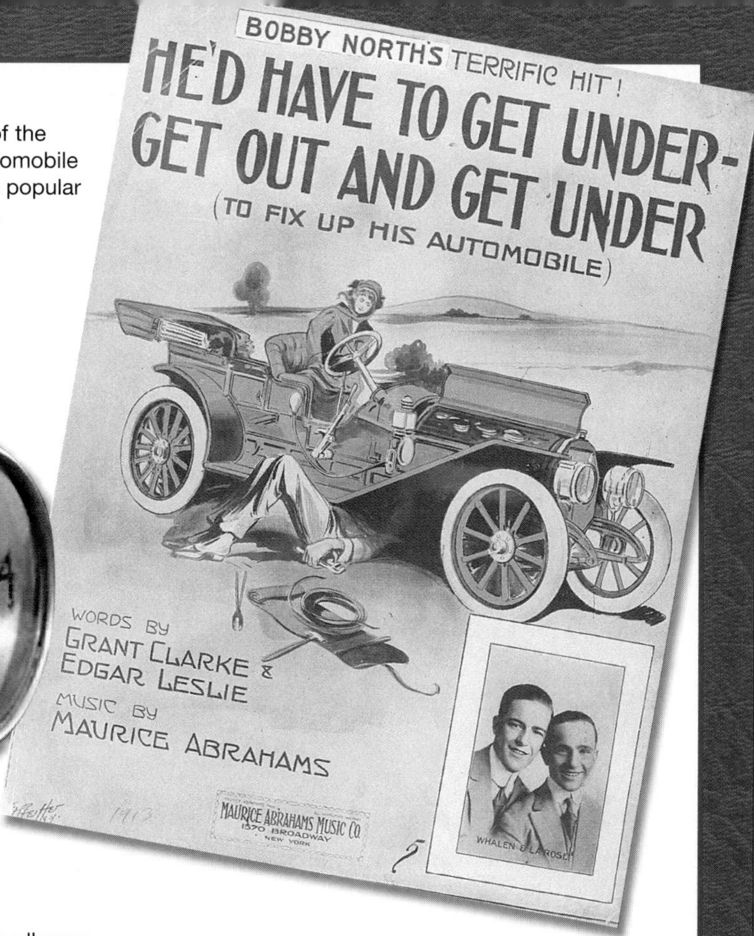

BOBBY NORTH'S TERRIFIC HIT!
HE'D HAVE TO GET UNDER-
GET OUT AND GET UNDER
(TO FIX UP HIS AUTOMOBILE)

WORDS BY
GRANT CLARKE &
EDGAR LESLIE
MUSIC BY
MAURICE ABRAHAMS

MAURICE ABRAHAMS MUSIC CO.
1570 BROADWAY
NEW YORK

WHALEN & LAROSCH

Headlights were once called headlamps and were typically constructed of brass.

Modern cars still have four wheels and run on gasoline. Yet they look very different from cars of 80 years ago. Shown is the front compartment of the 1914 Mercer Raceabout.

447

Portfolio Project

Ask students to keep a file of the vanity license plates they spot over a two- or three-week period. What vanity plate would they choose for themselves?

History and the Humanities

American Music: Cultural Traditions: McKinley's Assassination: "Whitehouse Blues" by Charlie Poole and the North Carolina Ramblers (3:25)

The Spirit of American Art and Music, pp. 29, 31: Georgia O'Keeffe and John Philip Sousa

American Portraits, p. 43, Miguel Antonio Otero, Jr.

The Historian's Craft

Historians are interested in the economic and social effects of important events, including the development of new technology. (One example from earlier times: the invention of the cotton gin.) Over the years, historians have documented a host of sweeping changes that the automobile has produced, including the spread of suburbs, the deterioration of inner cities, the development of a huge network of roads, the decline of railroads, and such phenomena as fast-food restaurants, drive-ins, shopping malls, and motels.

0:00 OUT OF TIME?

If time does not permit teaching the entire unit or its individual chapters, use the information on these pages along with Chapter Digests Audiocassettes to present the material in a condensed format.

Exploring Unit Themes

The Unit Digest may be used to teach unit coverage when time is limited, to review unit content, or to relate the content of one unit to that of another.

■ Chapter 12

Have students work as a group to construct a large world map showing the territories acquired by the United States in the late 1800s. Display the map and use it as the starting point for a debate on the following: The burdens of imperial rule kept the United States from establishing a fair and equitable society at home.

■ Chapter 13

Ask students to research one of the progressive reforms and write a report. Reports should include the situation before the reform, what the reform changed, and who benefitted from the reform. Invite students to read their reports to the class.

Causes and Effects

Ask students to write a newspaper article about reforms regarding child labor. Students use the information on the chart.

Chapter 12

Imperialism

In the last decades of the nineteenth century, Americans reassessed and abandoned their traditional isolationist policy. Because of growing industrial power, trade and contacts with Latin America increased. In the Pacific, American interest in Hawaii led to its annexation in 1898.

In 1898 the United States went to war with Spain. Americans sympathized with an independence movement in Cuba seeking to overthrow

Child Labor

CAUSES

- Young children worked 10-hour days in poor conditions
- Children had to work because their families could not survive without extra income

• **Reform**

EFFECTS

- A national child labor committee was formed to promote abolition of child labor
- John Spargo wrote *The Bitter Cry of the Children*
- By 1914 nearly every state had set minimum age of employment
- The Children's Bureau was established as a branch of the Department of Labor

Spanish control. The Spanish-American War was over in six months.

As a result of the war, the United States gained a colonial empire and with it the challenge of governing overseas territories—Puerto Rico, Guam, and the Philippines. Questions soon arose over whether native people living in colonial possessions were entitled to the same civil rights as American citizens. Eventually the Supreme Court of the United States ruled that the Constitution did not cover overseas possessions.

As the United States expanded into the Pacific, Americans were anxious to renew trade opportunities with the Chinese. To protect any potential trade between the two countries, Secretary of State John Hay asked the Chinese in 1899 to grant an "Open Door" trade policy.

President Theodore Roosevelt strengthened American involvement in world affairs. He defended Venezuela from possible European aggression and he issued the Roosevelt Corollary, a statement that attempted to justify United States intervention in Latin America. In addition, Roosevelt negotiated an end to the Russo-Japanese War. Perhaps most important, Roosevelt prevented Colombia from putting down an insurrection in Panama City. This action allowed Panamanians to establish the Republic of Panama. Roosevelt quickly negotiated a treaty for the rights to build a canal across Panama.

Chapter 13

The Progressive Era

Beginning about 1900 a large, loosely organized group of urban, middle-class professionals—including journalists, social workers, educators, ministers, and socially conscious politicians—became concerned about the need for social change in the United States. These reformers—called "progressives"—were the first to thoroughly investigate social problems that they felt were unjust and undemocratic. Progressives were concerned that if society's problems were not solved, democracy and capitalism might be threatened.

The goal of progressives was an efficient, smoothly functioning nation where each social problem could be managed by experts trained in

Cooperative Learning Activity

The Workings of Local Government Organize students into three groups to find out more about how their local government works. Suggest that one group do library research to gather information. Ask another group to interview local officials, and the third to attend a board or council meeting. Have groups com-

pare their findings and prepare a report on the impact of progressive reform on the structure and function of their local government. **L2**

that area. The many areas in which the progressives focused their efforts included the following: reform of the political system, business regulation, consumer protection, limits on immigration, tax reform, protection of working women and children, labor and education reform, and temperance. Journalists called "muckrakers" brought many of these problem areas to public attention, and most Americans supported calls for change. Reform occurred first at local and state levels.

Although progressives had the nation's best interests at heart, some reforms came at the expense of immigrants and racial minorities. Reformers tried to extinguish immigrant cultures, and they neglected African Americans almost completely.

Chapter 14

White House Reformers

Theodore Roosevelt, William H. Taft, and Woodrow Wilson were reform Presidents. They sought to improve the welfare of the average American citizen, regulate big-business practices, and conserve the nation's natural resources.

Roosevelt supported the progressive movement with his domestic goal to give everyone a "Square Deal." He soon became known as a "trustbuster."

Roosevelt also helped settle the coal strike of 1902. Roosevelt's greatest achievement lay in the area of conservation.

During Taft's administration the Constitution was strengthened with the Sixteenth Amendment's passage (providing for an income tax) and the Seventeenth Amendment (allowing direct election of senators). Taft also created the Tariff Board to investigate duties.

One of Wilson's first acts as President was to help pass the Underwood Tariff Act, which lowered import duties and introduced a federal income tax. Wilson achieved a progressive legislative program. He implemented a reform of banking and currency practices, secured passage of a labor reform bill, and engineered legislation regulating trusts.

Understanding Unit Themes

1. **American Democracy**   In what ways did reforms in government help the middle class and hinder African Americans?

2. **Economic Development**   How did the opening of new markets in East Asia and the acquisition of territories create economic growth in the United States?

3. **The Individual and Family Life**   In what ways did social and political reforms improve the quality of life for many?

4. **U.S. Role in World Affairs**   How did American foreign policy change around 1900? Give examples of this change.

5. **U.S. Role in World Affairs**   How did Roosevelt's role in resolving the Russo-Japanese War show that the United States had become a world leader?

■ **Chapter 14**

Ask students to compare President Roosevelt's Square Deal with President Wilson's New Freedom. Suggest they focus on such questions as: What were the aims of the two programs? How successful were the programs in accomplishing their aims? Who benefitted from these programs?

◉ **Student Self-Test** Software allows students to test their understanding of historical concepts in this unit.

∩ Have students list to the Chapter Digests on the audiocassettes.

◉ Use the Testmaker to create a customized test for Unit 4.

GLENCOE TECHNOLOGY

 VIDEODISC

Use the MindJogger Videoquiz to review students' knowledge.

MindJogger Videoquiz

Chapter 12
Disc 2, Side A

Chapter 13
Disc 2, Side A

Chapter 14
Disc 2, Side A

 Available in VHS.

Flashcards

Use American History Flashcards to reinforce students' knowledge of places and events in American history.

Answers to Understanding Unit Theme

1. The middle class gained political rights. African Americans were still subject to poll taxes, literary tests, and segregation.
2. more goods, stronger investments, new industries developed to process raw materials.
3. stronger voice in government, working conditions improved
4. abandoned isolationism, began to expand overseas
5. In asking to mediate the dispute, Roosevelt believed the U.S. had an obligation to be a world leader, acting responsibly and with restraint.

BEGINNING THE UNIT

Present the cause-and-effect chart to students with the effects omitted. Assign students to complete the chart as they read the chapters in the unit.

Event
- Stock market crashes.

Causes
- U.S. enters World War I.
- U.S. rejects League of Nations.
- Nationalist spirit grows.
- U.S. economy expands.

Effects
- Great Depression
- Crisis in industry and agriculture
- Capitalist system in jeopardy
- "New Deal"

History AND ART

During the Great Depression the federal government established a program to help unemployed artists. The Federal Arts Project employed thousands of artists in many different capacities. It was the beginning of government support of the arts.

0:00 OUT OF TIME?

If time does not permit teaching the entire unit, use the Unit Digest on pages 538–539.

UNIT FIVE
CRUSADE AND DISILLUSION
1914–1932

★★

CHAPTER 15	CHAPTER 16	CHAPTER 17
World War I Era 1914–1920	The Decade of Normalcy 1920–1928	The Depression Begins 1928–1932

▼ WALL TELEPHONE

▲ DUSTER COAT

History AND ART

Third Avenue
by Charles Goeller, 1933–1934

Scenes of city life during the Great Depression were important themes for many artists.

450

Exploring Unit Themes

Conflict and Cooperation During World War I, the American people readily cooperated with the government in support of the war effort. During the Great Depression, however, many Americans turned against the government. Some became disillusioned when the government failed to stop the country's economic plunge. Others blamed the Great Depression on government policies.

Influence of Technology Technology greatly influenced the lives of Americans in war and in peace. New weapons made war a deadlier game. At home, radio and movies and the advent of the automobile completely revolutionized American life.

Setting the Scene

The spirit of progressive reform dwindled as the United States drifted toward the conflict of World War I. Once the war ended, the national mood was no longer progress and optimism but "normalcy" and isolation. During the 1920s, Americans elected conservative Republican leaders.

Themes

- Conflict and Cooperation
- Influence of Technology
- The Individual and Family Life
- United States Role in World Affairs

Key Events

- World War I begins in Europe
- Germany resumes unrestricted submarine warfare
- Congress declares war on Germany
- The Senate rejects the Treaty of Versailles and the League of Nations
- Teapot Dome oil scandal
- Stock market crash
- Bonus Army marches on Washington

Major Issues

- Violation of neutral rights leads the United States to declare war on Germany.
- Despite Wilson's leadership, an isolationist mood defeats the Treaty of Versailles and the League of Nations.
- Prosperity of the 1920s fails to reach African Americans and farmers.
- Widespread depression and human misery after the crash prompts the federal government to provide direct relief.

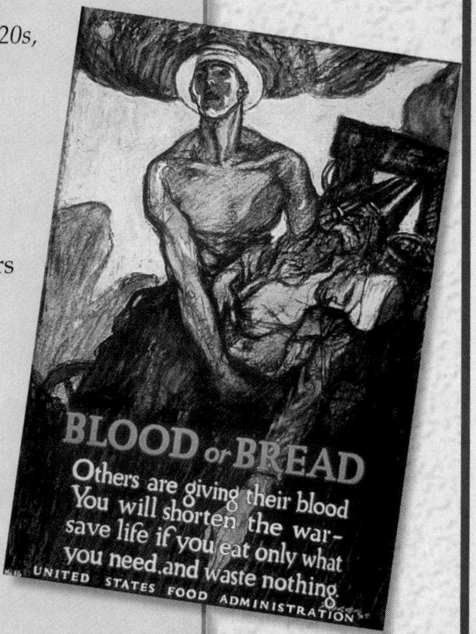

BLOOD or BREAD
Others are giving their blood
You will shorten the war—
save life if you eat only what
you need, and waste nothing.
UNITED STATES FOOD ADMINISTRATION

▲ GOVERNMENT POSTER, WORLD WAR I

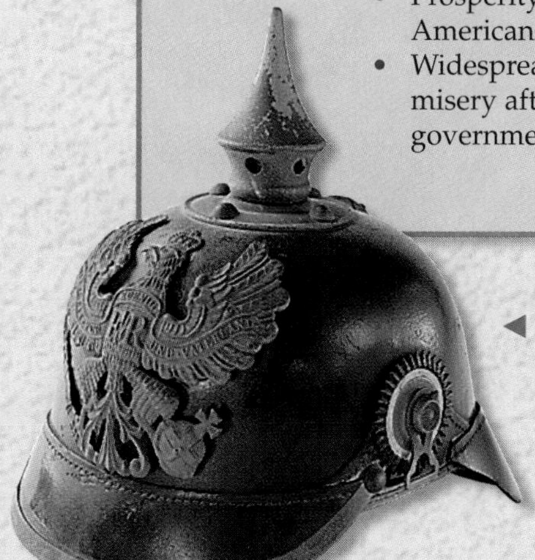

◀ GERMAN HELMET, EARLY 1900S

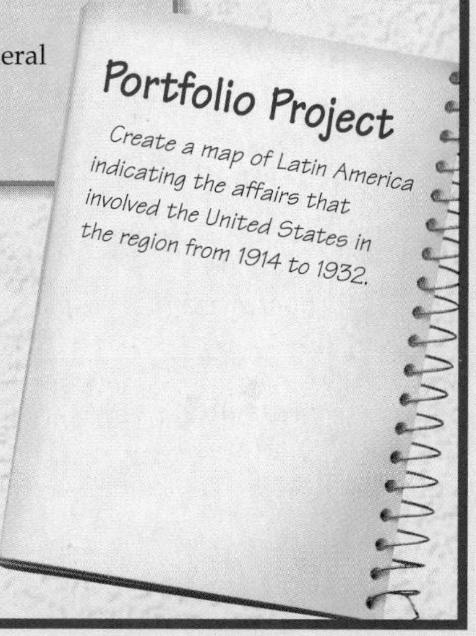

Portfolio Project

Create a map of Latin America indicating the affairs that involved the United States in the region from 1914 to 1932.

Portfolio Project

Suggest students review the United States's relations with Latin America in the late 1800s and early 1900s. Have them compare those policies with United States involvement in the region as indicated on their maps.

History and the Humanities

American Music: Cultural Traditions: War Song Hits: "For Your Country and My Country," "Good Bye Broadway, Hello France," "Over There" by Columbia Quartette (2:53)

U.S. History and Art Transparencies 20–22: *I Want You for the U.S. Army* by James Montgomery Flagg, *Allies Day, May 1917* by Childe Hassam *Yellow Cactus Flower* by Georgia O'Keeffe

FOCUS

Motivating Activity

Remind students that World War I resulted in a new world order—old empires were dismantled, and new nations were created. Provide students with maps showing the world before and after World War I. Discuss with students the territorial and political changes that occurred. Then ask them to speculate on what issues might remain unresolved in the future. *(new nations created in eastern and central Europe; Middle East changed by breakup of Ottoman Empire; some European nations received territories of others)* **L2**

TEACH

Guided Practice

Exploring the Time Line
Explain that during the early 1900s, rival European nations divided into two major military alliances: Great Britain, France, and Russia; Germany and Austria-Hungary. Ask students how such alliances might lead to conflict in Europe. *(A dispute could involve several nations.)* In case of a conflict, why might it be difficult for the United States to remain neutral? *(U.S. trade and business would be affected; U.S. likely would favor Great Britain and France.)* **L2**

Global Perspectives

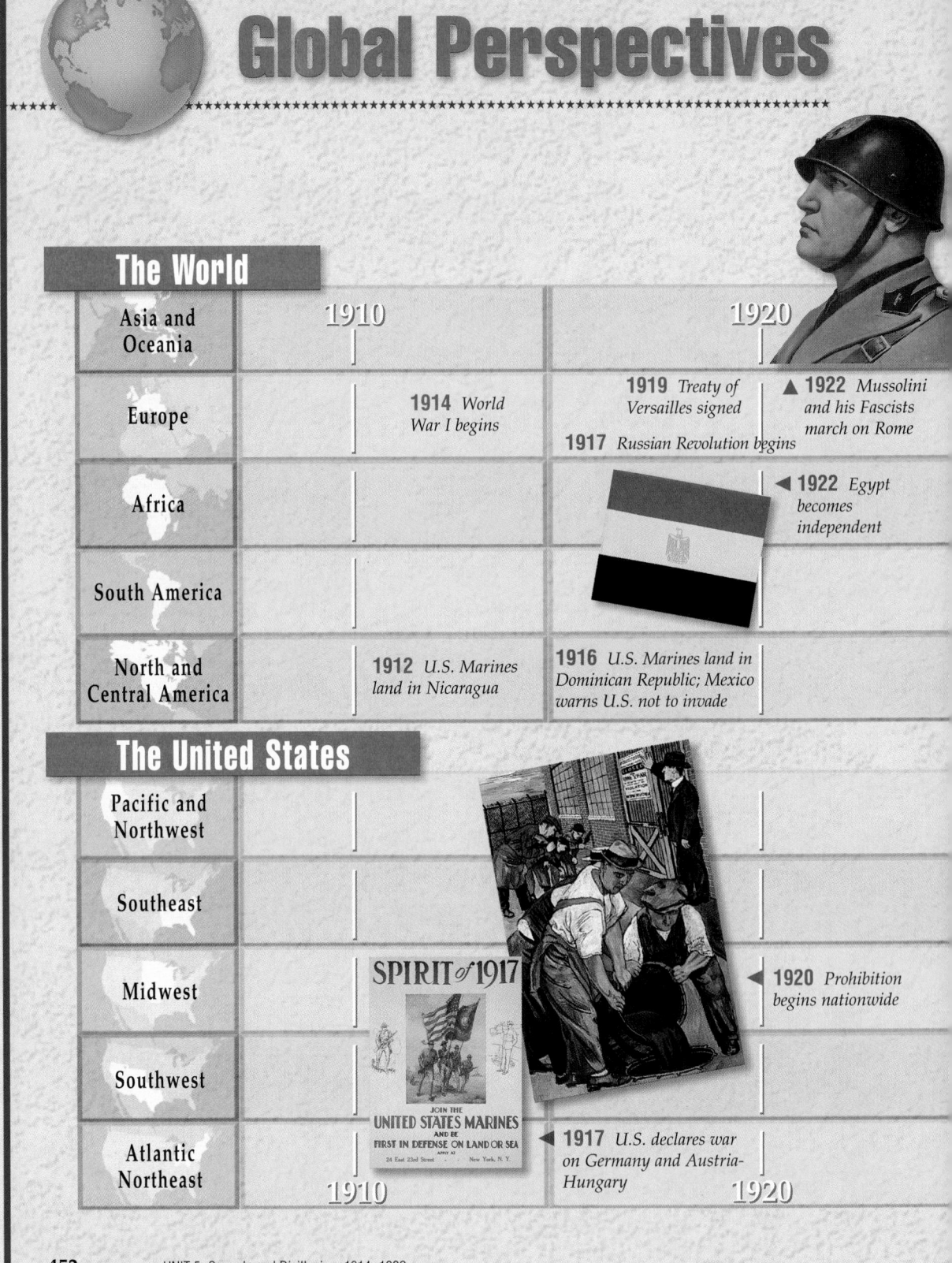

The World

	1910		1920	
Asia and Oceania				
Europe		**1914** *World War I begins*	**1919** *Treaty of Versailles signed* **1917** *Russian Revolution begins*	▲ **1922** *Mussolini and his Fascists march on Rome*
Africa				◄ **1922** *Egypt becomes independent*
South America				
North and Central America		**1912** *U.S. Marines land in Nicaragua*	**1916** *U.S. Marines land in Dominican Republic; Mexico warns U.S. not to invade*	

The United States

	1910		1920	
Pacific and Northwest				
Southeast				
Midwest				◄ **1920** *Prohibition begins nationwide*
Southwest				
Atlantic Northeast			**1917** *U.S. declares war on Germany and Austria-Hungary*	

SPIRIT of 1917

JOIN THE
UNITED STATES MARINES
AND BE
FIRST IN DEFENSE ON LAND OR SEA
APPLY AT
24 East 23rd Street   New York, N. Y.

Cultural Perspectives

The Influence of Jazz During the 1920s, in what is called the Great Migration, thousands of African Americans left the South for Northern cities in hopes of finding a better life. They brought with them a musical form new to the North—jazz. In such cities as New Orleans, African American musicians had for years been adapting old spirituals and work songs to create new rhythms. Jazz musicians such as Louis Armstrong, "King" Oliver, and "Jelly Roll" Morton helped popularize jazz among white Americans. Many music historians think that jazz was the only serious American music to emerge in the early twentieth century, and it continues to leave its mark on popular American music.

While the great migration of Eastern Europeans to the United States came at the end of the 1800s, the first Eastern European immigrants arrived nearly 200 years before. John Smith, the leader of Jamestown, wanted to exploit the colony's pine trees for pitch and turpentine. So he sent to Poland, where the manufacturing of naval stores was well established, for skilled workers. The first Polish artisans arrived in 1608, probably as indentured servants. Colony records listed them as free members of the community some 11 years later.

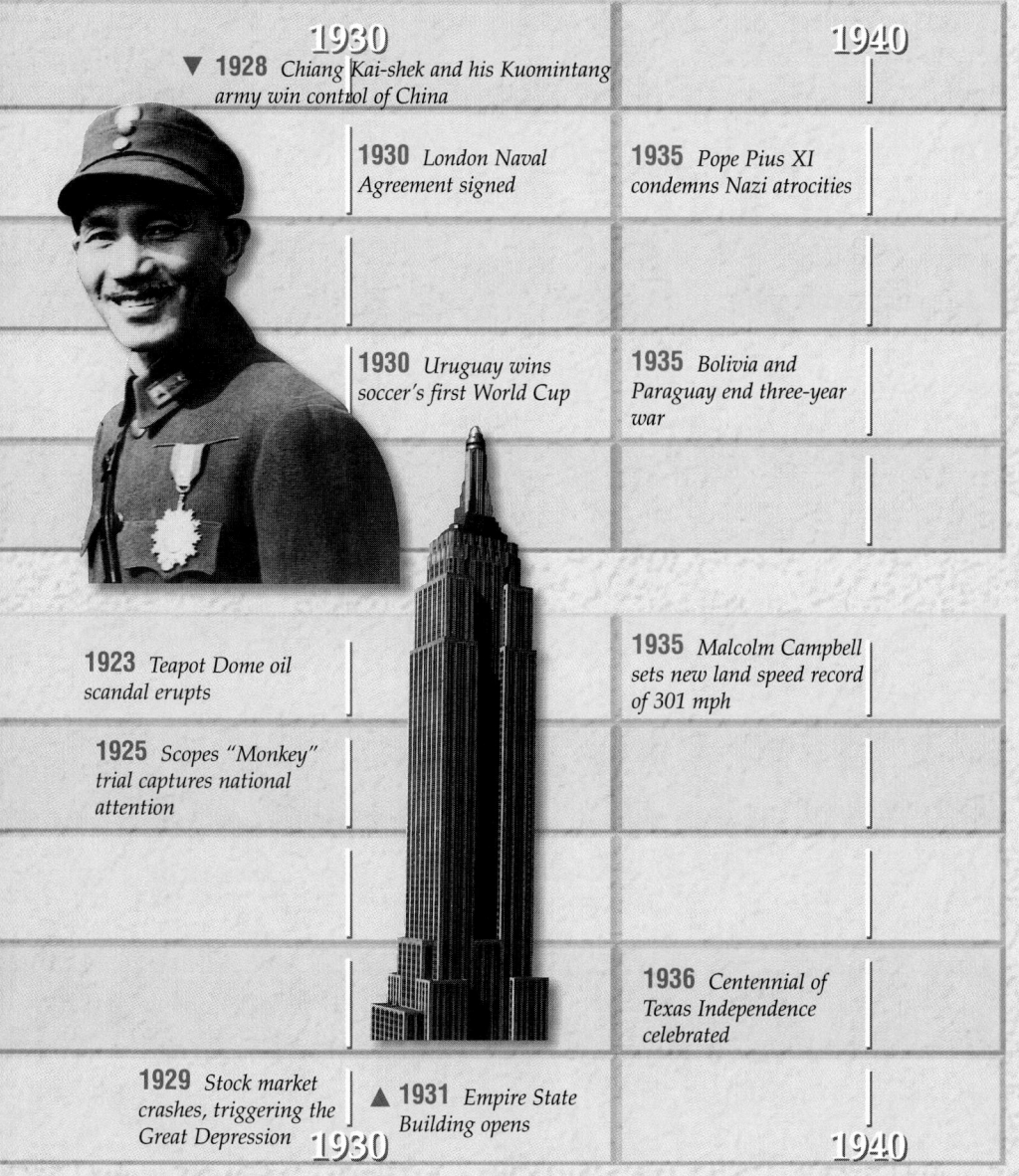

1930   1940

▼ **1928** *Chiang Kai-shek and his Kuomintang army win control of China*

1930 *London Naval Agreement signed*

1935 *Pope Pius XI condemns Nazi atrocities*

1930 *Uruguay wins soccer's first World Cup*

1935 *Bolivia and Paraguay end three-year war*

1923 *Teapot Dome oil scandal erupts*

1935 *Malcolm Campbell sets new land speed record of 301 mph*

1925 *Scopes "Monkey" trial captures national attention*

1936 *Centennial of Texas Independence celebrated*

1929 *Stock market crashes, triggering the Great Depression*

▲ **1931** *Empire State Building opens*

1930   1940

UNIT 5 Crusade and Disillusion: 1914–1932   **453**

LESSON PLAN
Global Perspectives

Independent Practice

Linking World Events
Have students note the dates of the Russian Revolution. Tell them that when the Bolsheviks seized power in Russia, they called on the workers of the world to revolt. Point out that labor unrest in the United States in 1919 convinced some Americans that a Bolshevik plot existed to overthrow the government. Have students research this "Red Scare" and write an editorial expressing their view of the government's action. **L3**

ASSESS
Studying the Time Line

1. Apart from Europe, on what world region did American foreign policy focus in this period? (*Latin America*)
2. When did World War I begin? When did the United States enter the war? (*1914; 1917*)
3. What events depicted on the time line occurred in 1922? (*Mussolini marches on Rome and Egypt becomes independent.*)

Cooperative Learning Activity

Forming Questions Divide students into three groups, and assign each group one chapter in the unit. Ask each group to skim its chapter and write the headings of the sections in the chapter. Then direct the groups to turn those headings into questions. (*Example: What were the results of Wilson's moral diplomacy?*) Have groups share their questions and speculate about the answers. When the unit is completed, encourage students to compare their speculations with the text. **L3**

Daily Lesson Objectives	Teacher Classroom Resources	Multimedia
SECTION 1 **Prelude to War** **1 Day** pp. 456–460 1. Describe Wilson's foreign policy toward Latin American nations. 2. Identify the causes of World War I. 3. Explain why the United States had difficulty remaining neutral during the war.	Reproducible Lesson Plan 15-1 Concept Mapping Activities 15-A, 15-B *Guided Reading Activity 15-1 *Vocabulary Activity 15 Critical Thinking Skills Activity 15 Chapter Skills Activity 15 Enrichment Activity 15 Reteaching Activity 15-1 *Section Quiz 15-1	Section Focus Transparency 15-1 Chapter Concepts Transparencies 15-A, 15-B Skills Transparency 15 Vocabulary PuzzleMaker Testmaker Lessons of War MindJogger Videoquiz
SECTION 2 **America Enters the War** **1 Day** pp. 462–467 1. Identify the events that led the United States to enter World War I. 2. Describe the role of the United States in helping the Allies to achieve victory over the Central Powers.	Reproducible Lesson Plan 15-2 *Guided Reading Activity 15-2 Primary and Secondary Source Readings, pp. 37–40 Chapter Map Activity 15 Linking Past and Present Activity 15 Geography in History Activity 15 Reteaching Activity 15-2 *Section Quiz 15-2	Section Focus Transparency 15-2 Map Transparency 15 Testmaker GTV: A Geographic Perspective on American History
SECTION 3 **War on the Home Front** **1 Day** pp. 468–472 1. Explain how the war was financed. 2. Describe how public opinion was shaped by the government. 3. Discuss the goals of Wilson's Fourteen Points.	Reproducible Lesson Plan 15-3 *Guided Reading Activity 15-3 Cooperative Learning Activity 15 Workbook Activity 15-3 Reteaching Activity 15-3 *Section Quiz 15-3	Section Focus Transparency 15-3 Testmaker Powers of the Congress
SECTION 4 **After the War** **1 Day** pp. 473–478 1. Describe the outcome of the Versailles peace conference. 2. Explain why the Senate rejected the Treaty of Versailles. 3. Identify domestic problems that arose after the war.	Reproducible Lesson Plan 15-4 *Guided Reading Activity 15-4 Political Cartoons Activity 14 Enrichment Activity 15 Workbook Activity 15-4 Reteaching Activity 15-4 *Section Quiz 15-4	Section Focus Transparency 15-4 Testmaker GTV: A Geographic Perspective on American History
CHAPTER REVIEW AND EVALUATION **1 Day**	Chapter 15 Test, Forms A and B Spanish Chapter 15 Summary Performance Assessment Activity 15	MindJogger Videoquiz Student Self-Test & Review Software *Chapter 15 Audiocassette Activity and Test

*Also available in Spanish

 0:00
OUT OF TIME? If time does not permit teaching the entire chapter, use the Chapter 15 Summary on pages 538–539 and the Chapter 15 audiocassette (English and Spanish) to point out the main ideas of the chapter.

A complete, 1-page lesson plan is provided for each section in the *Reproducible Lesson Plan* booklet.

Key to Ability Levels

Teaching strategies have been coded for varying learning styles and abilities.

L1   Basic activities for all students

L2   Average activities for average to above-average students

L3   Challenging activities for above-average students

LEP   Limited English Proficiency activities

Block Schedule

Block scheduling differs from traditional class scheduling in the amount of time allotted to each period. The extended time frame provided by block scheduling affords you the opportunity to implement a greater number of research-oriented and activity-intense projects to motivate and involve your students. Activities that are particularly suited to use within the block scheduling framework are identified throughout this unit by the following designation:

✓ Performance Assessment Activity

Foreign Policy   Recall with students that the United States's foreign policy from 1900 through World War I was based on three different theories: Roosevelt's "Big Stick" diplomacy, Taft's dollar diplomacy, and Wilson's moral diplomacy. Have students individually or in small groups choose a key region of the world and research the current U.S. foreign policy in regard to that region. How is today's policy similar to those of the early 1900s? What differences seem most striking? Suggest students draw conclusions about the effectiveness of today's policies compared with those that characterize the early 1900s. Encourage students to share their findings with the class.

POSSIBLE RUBRIC FEATURES
- Content Information
- Research Skills
- Organization
- Writing and Communication Skills
- Critical Thinking Skills

🗁 For additional activities, see Performance Assessment Strategies and Activities.

TEACHER'S CORNER

NATIONAL GEOGRAPHIC SOCIETY

INDEX TO NATIONAL GEOGRAPHIC MAGAZINE

The following articles may be used for research relating to this chapter:

- "Riddle of the Lusitania," by Robert D. Ballard, April 1994.
- "The Bolshevik Revolution," by Dusko Doder, October 1992.

NATIONAL GEOGRAPHIC SOCIETY PRODUCTS AVAILABLE FROM GLENCOE

To order the following products for use with this chapter, contact your local Glencoe sales representative or call Glencoe at 1-800-334-7344:

- *The Presidents: A Picture History of Our Nation* (CD-ROM)
- *GTV: A Geographic Perspective on American History* (Videodisc)
- *GTV: The American People: Fabric of a Nation* (Videodisc)

ADDITIONAL NATIONAL GEOGRAPHIC SOCIETY PRODUCTS

To order the following products for use with this chapter, call National Geographic Society at 1-800-368-2728:

- *Last Voyage of the Lusitania* (Video)
- *1914–1918: World War I* (Video)
- *1917: Revolution in Russia* (Video)
- *The American Presidency* (Filmstrip)
- *Decades of History: The 20th Century—The Early Years* (Filmstrip)
- *The United States as a World Power: From the 1890s to the 1970s* (Filmstrip)

CHAPTER 15
★★

World War I Era
1914–1920

► CONGRESSIONAL
MEDAL OF HONOR

BEGINNING THE CHAPTER

GLENCOE TECHNOLOGY

 VIDEODISC

Use the Chapter 15 MindJogger Videoquiz to preview the content of this chapter.

MindJogger Videoquiz

Chapter 15
Disc 2, Side B

 Available in VHS.

Recording Journal Notes
Encourage students to record their observations under such topics as Outbreak of War in Europe, American Neutrality, United States Declaration of War, and The War Effort.

Explain that World War I spurred technological development, not only in weaponry but also in other areas. Medical advances were made in the treatment of the wounded. The use of the wireless for battlefield communication laid the groundwork for radio broadcasting, which began in 1920.

Setting the Scene

Focus

When Europe went to war in 1914, the United States sought to stay out of the conflict. Both sides disregarded American neutrality. Germany's use of unrestricted submarine warfare and economic ties to Great Britain eventually led the United States into the bloody struggle. Mobilization called for many sacrifices by the American people. The Senate, however, rejected Wilson's proposed peace settlement, and wartime fervor led to intolerance.

Concepts to Understand

★ How **conflict** became evident in American society during and after World War I

★ How Wilson's idealism and American **economic interests** led to controversy over foreign policy

Read to Discover . . .

★ why the United States declared war on the German Empire in 1917.

★ why the United States did not join the League of Nations.

Journal Notes

What was the general attitude of the American people during World War I? Record your observations as you read the chapter.

CULTURAL	
•**1915** *First transcontinental telephone is hooked up*	•**1917** *Temperance movement leads to prohibition laws in 29 states*

1914	**1916**

POLITICAL	
•**1914** *World War I begins when Austria-Hungary declares war on Serbia*	•**1916** *Germany agrees to restrict submarine warfare* •**1917** *United States declares war on Germany*

✚ EXTRA CREDIT PROJECT

Submarine Warfare Explain to students that in 1915 a German submarine sank the British liner *Lusitania*, among whose passengers were more than 100 Americans. The United States responded strongly and even hinted at using force to stop submarine attacks. Events surrounding the sinking were controversial at the time and still are. Interested students might investigate the circumstances and form their own conclusions. **L3** 🖥

World War I posters

History AND ART

Allies Day
by Childe Hassam, 1916

Hassam depicts a vision of the Avenue of the Allies in red, white, and blue brush strokes.

▲ WORLD WAR I POSTERS

- **1918** *Daylight saving time is first adopted*

- **1918** *Wilson proclaims his Fourteen Points*

- **1919** *Sherwood Anderson publishes Winesburg, Ohio*

- **1919** *Versailles peace conference is held*
- **1920** *Nineteenth Amendment is ratified*

| 1918 | 1920 |

On the chalkboard, reproduce the following generalization and concepts map, and have students copy it in their notebooks.

> The conflicting interests of the world powers lead to world war.
>
> Conflict   Economic Interests

 To reinforce the two chapter concepts, use Concept Mapping Activities 15-A and 15-B.

Use Chapter Concepts Transparency Activities 15-A, 15-B.

History AND ART

In this painting, Hassam has captured the feelings of patriotism the nation was experiencing after having joined the Allied cause of World War I.

ABCNEWS INTERACTIVE™

 VIDEODISC

Lessons of War

Side One, Chapter 7
Title: *Can War Be Justified?*
Subject: The circumstances under which nations may claim that waging a war is justified

✔ Performance Assessment

African American Migration Have students research and report on the movement of African Americans from the South to the North known as the Great Migration. This massive exodus began during World War I when Northern industries needed workers to fill jobs left vacant by workers drafted into the armed forces. It was accelerated by the naval war, which all but stopped immigration from abroad.

Have students identify both "push" and "pull" factors for the Great Migration. Students may provide their findings in a written report accompanied by photographs, artwork, and graphs and tables. **L2** 📦

FOCUS

Bellringer

Before taking roll, project Section Focus Transparency 15-1 or hand out Section Focus Transparency Activity 15-1. Have students answer the questions.

Motivating Activity

Read to students this statement from President Wilson's response to the sinking of the British passenger ship *Lusitania:* "There is such a thing as a nation being so right that it does not need to convince others by force that it is right." What is Wilson's main point? (*It is not necessary to go to war to resolve every dispute.*) **L1**

Vocabulary Precheck

Write "contraband" on the chalkboard. Have a volunteer skim the section to find the term and read it in context. **L1, LEP**

Use the Vocabulary PuzzleMaker Software to create a crossword puzzle. **L1**

Assign Vocabulary Activity 15.

★★★★★★★★★★★★★★★★★★★★★★★★★★★

Prelude to War

Setting the Scene

Section Focus

On the day he took office, President Woodrow Wilson remarked to a friend that it would be an irony of fate if his administration had to deal mainly with foreign affairs. But Wilson's administration soon was confronted with difficult and complex foreign problems that involved the fate of the world.

◄ *REVOLUTION* BY JOSÉ CLEMENTE OROZCO, 1920

Objectives

After studying this section, you should be able to

★ describe Wilson's foreign policy toward Latin American nations.

★ identify the causes of World War I.

★ explain why the United States had difficulty remaining neutral during the war.

Key Term

contraband

President Wilson's focus on domestic issues was demonstrated in his first Inaugural Address in 1913. He was comfortable with and well-informed on matters such as the tariff and banking. But in foreign affairs neither Wilson nor those he counted on for advice were experienced.

■ Wilson's Moral Diplomacy

As President, Wilson resolved to "strike a new note in international affairs" and to see that "sheer honesty and even unselfishness . . . should prevail over nationalistic self-seeking in American foreign policy." However, other forces at work at home and abroad frustrated his hope to lead the world by moral example.

Political Unrest in Mexico

For nearly 30 years, Mexico had been ruled by a dictator, Porfirio Díaz (pawr•FEE•rih•oh DEE•AHS). He brought stability and encouraged foreign investment in Mexico's economic development. When Díaz was overthrown in 1911, Mexico entered a period of political chaos.

Francisco Madero (frahn•SEES•koh muh•DEHR•oh) came to power. Investors in Mexico feared that the new president would confiscate all property owned by foreigners. Businesspeople and foreign diplomats plotted with units of the Mexican army to overthrow Madero. Before Wilson took office, General Victoriano Huerta (veek•toh•ree•AH•noh WEHR•tuh) seized power, and Madero was murdered—presumably on Huerta's orders.

American capitalists supported Huerta in the belief that he would support business

---

Classroom Resources for SECTION 1

Blackline Masters:
- Reproducible Lesson Plan 15-1
- Guided Reading Activity 15-1
- Vocabulary Activity 15
- Critical Thinking Skills Activity 15

- Chapter Skills Activity 15
- Enrichment Activity 15
- Workbook Activity 15-1
- Reteaching Activity 15-1
- Section Quiz 15-1

Transparencies:
- Section Focus Transparency 15-1
- Skills Transparency 15

Multimedia:
- Vocabulary PuzzleMaker
- Testmaker
- Lessons of War
- MindJogger

interests. Other countries with large Mexican investments recognized the new ruler. Repulsed by Huerta's brutality, Wilson refused to recognize the new government. He was convinced that without United States support "the unspeakable Huerta" would be overthrown.

Wilson Intervenes

Because Huerta remained in power, Wilson looked for a reason to intervene. In April 1914, American sailors on shore in the city of Tampico (tam•PEE•koh) clashed with Mexican authorities. Seeing a chance to overthrow Huerta, Wilson sent marines to seize the Mexican port of Veracruz (VEHR•uh•KROOZ). Although Wilson expected the Mexican people to welcome his action, anti-American riots broke out in Mexico and throughout Latin America. The President's intervention also was condemned in the European press.

Shocked by world reaction, Wilson accepted an offer from the ABC powers (Argentina, Brazil, and Chile) to mediate the dispute. The ABC powers supported Wilson by recommending that Huerta go into exile.

Venustiano Carranza (vay•noos•TYAH•noh kuh•RAN•zuh) was installed as Mexico's president.

Yet trouble continued between the United States and Mexico. Mexican forces opposed to Carranza conducted raids into the United States. Led by Pancho Villa (PAHN•choh VEE•yuh), guerrillas burned the town of Columbus, New Mexico, and killed 18 Americans. Wilson sent 6,000 troops under General John J. Pershing across the border to find and capture Villa. A year-long expedition failed to capture the guerrillas and resulted in a clash with the Mexican army. Tensions eased in January 1917 when Wilson's growing concern over the war in Europe caused him to recall the troops.

In the Caribbean

Wilson followed Roosevelt's example by ordering marines in Nicaragua, Haiti, and the Dominican Republic to preserve order and set up governments viewed by Americans as more stable than those in control. In 1917 the United States expanded its naval power in the Caribbean by purchasing Denmark's strategically valuable Virgin Islands.

▲ MARINES IN VERACRUZ In April 1914 President Woodrow Wilson ordered American forces into Mexico to seize the port of Veracruz. *How did Latin American nations respond to American intervention?*

TEACH
Guided Practice
Determining Motives
Direct students to list ways in which the Wilson administration attempted to repudiate "Dollar Diplomacy" in Mexico. L2

📁 Assign Guided Reading Activity 15-1.

Visualizing History Ask students why Wilson's intervention in Mexico failed, and how that failure might affect Mexican–American relations. **Answer to Caption:** Anti-American riots broke out in Mexico and other Latin American nations.

ABCNEWS INTERACTIVE™

💿 **VIDEODISC**
Lessons of War

Side One, Chapter 5
Title: *How Wars Begin— World War I*
Subject: The circumstances and events which led to World War I.

Sidelight: Views of Wilson's Diplomacy

Concerning the Mexican Revolution, President Wilson cautioned "watchful waiting." Interventionists termed his policy "deadly drifting." One critic joked about Wilson's diplomacy when he made up a dance step called the Wilson Tango. It consisted of one step forward, two steps back, one to the side, and then a hesitation.

Visualizing
History Pancho Villa fought for the poor. He gathered around him tenant farmers or those who had lost their land. The fight for land was one of the key elements in Mexico's civil wars. **Answer to Caption:** Wilson sent troops to find and capture Villa.

Did You Know?

For a time Pancho Villa's forces held Mexico City. He finally was defeated by Mexican general Alvaro Obregón, who in 1920 rebelled against Carranza and became Mexico's president.

■ War in Europe

While Wilson was dealing with problems in Mexico and the Caribbean, Europe began one of the bloodiest wars in its history. After almost 50 years of general peace, tensions built up.

Setting the Stage for War

In the late 1800s, as Europe became industrialized and nations sought to establish empires, tensions arose among colonizing nations. Within Europe itself, nationalism also heightened rivalries and tension. Much of central and eastern Europe was ruled by empires that included several nationality groups, each with its own language. Many of these groups wanted to form independent nations by joining with similar groups in other nations. In Austria-Hungary, for example, Slavic groups resented being ruled by the Germans and Magyars (Hungarians). They wanted to join other Slavic peoples to form a South Slav, or Yugoslav, nation in the Balkans.

The Balkans were an area of Slavic peoples in southeastern Europe that for decades had been fought over by three major powers—Russia, Austria-Hungary, and the Ottoman Empire (Turkey and its provinces). In 1908 Austria-Hungary annexed two Balkan territories once ruled by the Turks, Bosnia and Herzegovina (HEHRT•suh•goh•VEE•nuh). Serbia, a Balkan nation on Austria-Hungary's border, called on Russia, its historic protector, for help. The Russians, weakened from their defeat by Japan in 1905 and wanting the Balkans for themselves, did nothing.

This instability and the complex rivalries led to an arms race as each country sought to defend itself. The arms race generated more mistrust and helped military leaders achieve more power and influence in European governments.

Formation of Alliances

The European nations made alliances with one another for mutual self-defense. The Triple Alliance drew together Germany, Austria-Hungary, and Italy. Fearing isolation

Visualizing
History ▲ **PANCHO VILLA** Many Americans viewed Pancho Villa as nothing more than a bandit. To Mexico's poor, however, he was a democratic savior. *What action did Wilson take against Villa?*

in Europe, France and Russia agreed to help each other if either became involved in war with Germany or Austria-Hungary. France arranged a separate partnership with Great Britain known as the Entente Cordiale (AHN•TAHNT KAWR•DYAHL), meaning "cordial understanding." After Russia's defeat in 1905 reduced Britain's fear of Russian power, all three nations came together to form the Triple Entente.

War Begins

Tensions were high in June 1914, when Archduke Franz Ferdinand, heir to the throne of Austria-Hungary, visited Bosnia. His assassination by Slavic nationalist Gavrilo Princip provided the incident that ignited Europe into war. Austria-Hungary declared war on Serbia on July 28, 1914.

One month after the assassination, war exploded in Europe. To protect its status as a European power, Russia felt it had to defend Serbia. Believing that Germany would aid Austria-Hungary, Russian armies mobilized along the borders of both nations. Germany demanded that Russia halt its threatening acts and that France pledge neutrality in the event of a war between Russia and Germany. Both Russia and France rejected Germany's demands. On August 1 Germany declared war on Russia;

Critical Thinking Activity

Explaining Causes Write the following terms on the chalkboard: *imperialism, nationalism, militarism, balance of power.* Have students define each term. Using the text and additional research, ask them to explain how each contributed to war in Europe. Ask if students think any one nation or group of nations was primar-

ily responsible for World War I. Have each give evidence to support his or her opinion. **L3**

🗀 For additional practice in using critical thinking skills, assign Critical Thinking Skills Activity 15.

on August 3 it declared war on France. The German army crossed neutral Belgium on its way to invade France.

Responding to the invasion of Belgium, Great Britain declared war on Germany. Europe was divided into two camps. Those fighting for the Triple Entente were called the Allies. Italy (which switched sides in 1915), France, Russia, and Great Britain formed the backbone of the Allies. What remained of the Triple Alliance—Germany and Austria-Hungary—joined with the Ottoman Empire and Bulgaria to form the Central Powers.

■ United States Neutrality

As war consumed Europe, Americans hoped the vast Atlantic Ocean would keep them out of the conflict. President Wilson stated that this was "a war with which we had nothing to do."

Taking of Sides

Despite a neutral stance, America could not help but take sides. Immigrants of European nationality groups gave many Americans roots that influenced their opinions. Many of the 8 million German Americans were sympathetic to their homeland. Many Irish Americans, seething from British domination of Ireland, also hoped for a German victory. In general, however, the common heritage shared by the United States and Britain, and America's historic links with France, put American public opinion on the side of the Allies.

Both Sides Strain Neutrality

America's neutrality did not protect it from either the Allies or the Central Powers. The British imposed a blockade on the Central Powers. They planted mines in the North Sea, forced neutral ships into port for inspection, opened American mail, and redefined **contraband,** or prohibited materials, so that not even food could be shipped to Germany. Trade between the United States and the Central Powers shrank.

At the same time, exports from the United States to the Allies nearly quadrupled, as war materials and food from America helped the Allies. Ties between the United States and the Allies became closer when the United States government lent the Allies $2 billion. The American public purchased another $2 billion in British and French war bonds.

To retaliate against the British blockade, cut off Britain's war supplies, and starve Britain into submission, the Germans relied on a new weapon—the submarine. The "U-boat" broke long-established rules of warfare by sinking unarmed ships. International law required that unarmed ships not be sunk without providing for the safety of passengers and crews.

In 1915 the British passenger liner *Lusitania* was sunk. Nearly 1,200 passengers drowned—including 128 Americans. Some Americans felt that this act was grounds for war. But others thought that people who traveled on ships of warring nations did so

▲ ASSASSINATION AT SARAJEVO The assassination of Archduke Ferdinand and his wife proved to be a fateful event. Within a month, the continent of Europe was ablaze with war. *How did the United States react to the start of war?*

CHAPTER 15 World War I Era: 1914–1920 **459**

Linking Across TIME

German submarines, or U-boats, wreaked havoc during the first years of World War II, just as they did during World War I. From 1940 to 1942, U-boats sank thousands of tons of Allied shipping in the Atlantic. After the United States joined the Allies, however, American shipyards built many more warships. Accompanying Allied convoys across the Atlantic, those warships located the marauding Germans with sonar and radar. By mid-1943 the Allies were sinking U-boats faster than Germany could replace them.

Cooperative Learning Activity

Debating Form the class into groups to debate the question of whether the United States should enter the war in Europe. Groups may use arguments from the section as well as any of their own. Encourage them to formulate arguments as though the decision has not been made and the strength of their arguments will make the difference. Call on a member of each group to summarize the main arguments for both sides. **L2**

 **Visualizing Ⓗistory**

▲ WAR ON THE SEAS United States neutrality was put to a test when German submarines attacked American vessels in the Atlantic. *Why were submarine attacks considered a barbaric act of war?*

at their own risk, especially when Germany had taken out newspaper ads warning Americans not to travel on the *Lusitania*.

The Sussex Pledge

Wilson steered a middle course on the issue of the U-boats. He refused to take extreme measures against Germany. How-ever, he sent several messages to Germany insisting that its government safeguard the lives of noncombatants in the war zones.

Late in March 1916, Wilson's policy was tested when a U-boat torpedoed the French passenger ship *Sussex,* injuring several

Americans on board. Although Wilson's advisers favored breaking off relations with Germany, the President chose to issue a final warning. He demanded that the German government abandon submarine warfare or risk war with the United States. Germany did not want to strengthen the Allies by drawing the United States into the war. So it offered to compensate Americans injured on the *Sussex* and promised with certain condi-tions to sink no more merchant ships with-out warning. The Sussex Pledge, as it was called, met the foreign-policy goals of both Germany and the President by keeping the United States out of war a little longer.

Section 1 ★ Review

Checking for Understanding

1. **Identify** Victoriano Huerta, Pancho Villa, Aus-tria-Hungary, Serbia, Triple Alliance, Triple Entente, *Lusitania,* U-boat.

2. **Define** contraband.

3. **Cite** two causes of World War I.

4. **Describe** two trends that made American neutrality difficult.

Critical Thinking

5. **Evaluating Tactics** Can German U-boat attacks on the *Lusitania* and *Sussex* be justified? Explain.

ACTIVITY

6. Check sources such as local newspa-pers and municipal reports to see how people in your community reacted to the beginning of World War I.

Answers to SECTION 1 REVIEW

1. Huerta, 456; Villa, 457; Austria-Hungary, 458; Serbia, 458; Triple Alliance, 458; Triple Entente, 458; *Lusitania,* 459; U-boat, 459
2. All vocabulary words are defined in the Glossary.
3. nationalism, imperialism
4. Trade with Britain increased profits for

American business, and Germany's subma-rine warfare threatened maritime commerce.
5. Yes: There are no rules in war. No: Killing civilians is not justified by military goals.
6. Students should provide list of sources and include details.

BUILDING SKILLS
Social Studies Skills

Interpreting a Political Map

The ability to read and understand a map is a skill that may be applied in many areas; it is particularly useful in the study of history. There are many kinds of maps in use today. In this text, you have studied several different types: historical, physical, thematic, and political.

Learning the Skill

Historical maps show places and events from the past. Physical maps show natural features such as mountains, valleys, plains, and bodies of water. Thematic maps deal with specialized information, often on a single topic such as population density, land use, languages, and natural resources.

A political map shows the political boundaries or borders of a state, country, and/or region. Political maps change whenever political borders change. A political map of the world today looks very different from one only 10 years old.

Follow these procedures when you evaluate a political map:

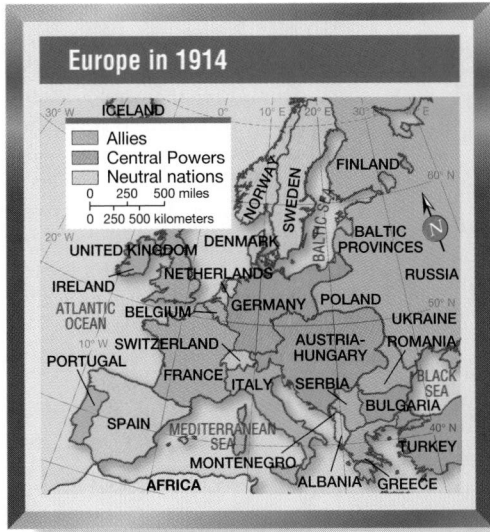

- **Determine** the time period covered by the map. This may be given in the title, although some political maps supply the date in the copyright.
- **Read** the map title and scale.
- **Examine** the legend. What information, other than political boundaries, is provided by the map?
- **Analyze** the lines of latitude and longitude. These lines are constant—they do not change. Use them when you compare change in boundaries over time. Boundaries are usually represented by a solid dark line.

Practicing the Skill

Apply the information from the chapter and the guidelines shown as you analyze the map of Europe in 1914.

1. What countries shown on this map maintained neutrality during World War I?

2. How might location have influenced neutrality?

3. Explain this statement: In 1914 the borders of the United Kingdom were determined by geography, not just politics.

4. Compare the map on this page with the map of Europe on page 474. What became of Austria-Hungary? What happened to Serbia? To the Baltic Provinces?

APPLYING THE SKILL

5. Make a map of the county in which you live. Include your community and other cities as well as important physical features. Make a legend that shows the symbols or colors used on the map and what they mean.

461

FOCUS

Bellringer

Before taking roll, project Section Focus Transparency 15-2 or hand out Section Focus Transparency Activity 15-2. Have students answer the questions.

Motivating Activity

Ask students to list reasons for going to war. Compile a class list on the chalkboard. Then ask students to speculate which reasons might bring the United States into World War I. Explain that as they read Section 2, they will be able to compare their speculations with the reasons described in the text.

Vocabulary Precheck

Write "armistice" on the chalkboard. Have a volunteer skim the section to find the term and read it in context. L1, LEP

★★★

America Enters the War

Setting the Scene

Section Focus

In the presidential election of 1916, the Democrats again chose Woodrow Wilson as their candidate. This time the campaign focused on Wilson's diplomatic skills, using the slogan "He kept us out of the war." Americans, however, gave his policies a less-than-ringing endorsement. When the election votes were counted, Wilson won, but it was a very close race.

Objectives

After studying this section, you should be able to

★ identify the events that led the United States to enter World War I.

★ describe the role of the United States in helping the Allies to achieve victory over the Central Powers.

Key Term

armistice

◀ DISTINGUISHED SERVICE CROSS

*I*n 1916 Wilson ran for reelection on a peace ticket under the slogan "He kept us out of the war." Although Wilson never used the slogan himself, he emphasized that he had kept "peace with honor."

Wilson defeated the Republican candidate Charles Evans Hughes in a close election. Following his reelection, Wilson devoted his energies to finding a peaceful solution to the war. The President realized the only sure way to keep Americans out of the European conflict was to end this terrible war altogether.

A quick victory eluded both sides, as defensive weapons proved superior to offensive tactics. The war was especially gruesome. The use of poison gas and such other new weapons as the tank and the machine gun, along with enormous casualty lists, ended the optimism that had pervaded western Europe before the war.

■ "Peace Without Victory"

On December 18, 1916, Wilson asked the warring nations to state their peace terms. As a neutral party, he hoped to negotiate a settlement, but both sides responded with terms that their opponents would not accept. In spite of these replies, Wilson addressed the Senate on January 22, 1917, calling for "peace without victory." "A victor's peace," he argued, "would leave a sting, a resentment, a bitter memory upon which terms of peace would rest only as upon quicksand. Only a peace between equals can last."

Submarine Warfare Resumes

The Germans soon dashed Wilson's hope of mediating an end to the war. German losses on the battlefield and the shortages

---

Classroom Resources for SECTION 2

Blackline Masters:
- Reproducible Lesson Plan 15-2
- Guided Reading Activity 15-2
- Primary and Secondary Source Readings, pp. 37–40
- Chapter Map Activity 15
- Linking Past and Present Activity 15

- Geography in History Activity 15
- Workbook Activity 15-2
- Reteaching Activity 15-2
- Section Quiz 15-2

Transparencies:
- Section Focus Transparency 15-2
- Map Transparency 15

Multimedia:
- Testmaker
- GTV: A Geographic Perspective on American History

caused by the British blockade forced Germany to resume unrestricted submarine warfare. German naval commanders claimed they could starve Britain into submission in five months if the German government gave U-boats permission to sink ships on sight. The Germans felt that even if this violation of their Sussex Pledge drew the United States into the war, the Americans could not raise an army and transport it to Europe in time to prevent the Allies from collapsing. Therefore, Germany decided to risk American involvement and, on January 31, 1917, announced that all vessels in waters near Great Britain, France, and Italy would be sunk without warning.

On February 3, 1917, Wilson responded to this threat by breaking off diplomatic relations with Germany. When goods piled up in American ports because ships feared to sail, he asked Congress for the power to arm merchant ships. This measure passed the House of Representatives easily, but an 11-person filibuster blocked the bill on the Senate floor. The President refused to be stopped by the effort of this "little group of willful men." Finding the authority in a 1797 law, Wilson armed the merchant ships.

Drawn Into War

Meanwhile, other events caused the nation's antagonism toward Germany to mount. The British government revealed that it had intercepted a cable from the German foreign minister, Arthur Zimmermann, to the German ambassador in Mexico. Zimmermann instructed the ambassador to arrange an alliance between Mexico and Germany in the event that the United States entered the war. To encourage Mexico's cooperation, Germany promised that Mexico would regain Texas, Arizona, and New Mexico upon a German victory. American newspapers published the Zimmermann Note, outraging the public. Then, between March 12 and March 19, four American merchant ships were sunk without warning. Two days later Wilson called a special session of Congress to consider "grave questions of national policy."

On April 2, 1917, Wilson appeared before Congress with a heavy heart. In one of the most eloquent speeches ever delivered in the Capitol, the President asked the members of Congress to declare war on Germany:

 **Visualizing History** ▲ PREPARING FOR WAR Americans register for the draft. The World War I era produced this classic recruitment poster, which has been used ever since. *What events drew the United States into the war?*

TEACH
Guided Practice
Making Comparisons
Have students create a chart comparing the strengths and weaknesses of the Allied Powers and the Central Powers early in 1917. Suggest that they divide the chart into two vertical columns headed Allied Powers and Central Powers, with Strengths and Weaknesses along the left-hand side. When they have completed the chart, have them assess ways in which the United States's involvement affected the strengths and weaknesses of both sides. **L3**

☞ Assign Guided Reading Activity 15-2.

Visualizing History By 1918 a flood of American soldiers was arriving in France. The Committee on Public Information mobilized support for the war through posters like this one.
Answer to Caption: Germany's unrestricted submarine warfare, the Zimmermann Note, the sinking without warning of four American merchant ships

☞ Assign Primary and Secondary Source Readings, pp. 37–40: "Peace Without Victory" by Woodrow Wilson and "The Zimmermann Note" by Barbara W. Tuchman.

Critical Thinking Activity

Analyzing Assumptions Write the word *assumption* on the chalkboard. Point out to students that in late 1916 Germany assumed that the United States would not be able to mobilize in time to make any difference to the war in Europe. Ask students to list the actions Germany took that were based on this assumption. Then have them make a list of actions Germany might have taken had it not made this assumption, including any actions that might have ended the war. **L2**

▲ JOHN J. PERSHING

Visualizing
History

▲ TRENCH WARFARE Much of World War I was fought from trenches where soldiers spent days, or even weeks, in mud and unsanitary conditions. *What was the status of the conflict when the United States entered the war?*

> " *It is a fearful thing to lead this great, peaceful people into war, into the most terrible and disastrous of all wars, civilization itself seeming to be in the balance. But the right is more precious than peace, and we shall fight for the things which we have always carried nearest our hearts—for democracy, for the right of . . . free peoples as shall bring peace and safety to all nations and make the world itself at last free. To such a task we dedicate our lives and our fortunes, everything we have. . . . [T]he day has come when America is privileged to spend her blood and her might for the principles that gave her birth and happiness and the peace which she has treasured. God helping her, she can do no other.* "

In his war message, the President insisted that the United States's quarrel was only with the "military masters" of Germany, and he expressed friendship for the German people. Maintaining that the United States had "no selfish ends to serve," Wilson stated that the people of the United States would be fighting to make the world "safe for democracy" and to promote "peace and safety to all nations." Four days after Wilson's message, Congress, after a spirited debate, declared war on Germany by the overwhelming margins of 82 votes to 6 in the Senate and 273 to 50 in the House.

■ Status of the Allies

When the United States entered the war, the Allies seemed in danger of defeat. U-boats were sinking ships at a rate that threatened to wipe out the entire merchant tonnage of the world; the British Isles had only a two-month supply of food with no relief in sight. Late in 1917 the Italians suffered a severe defeat at the village of Caporetto. Russia's military effort slackened and then ceased after the overthrow of the czar and the Bolshevik, or communist, revolution. In March 1918, Russia signed the Treaty of Brest-Litovsk, surrendering to Germany immense areas of land including Ukraine.

With one of the richest grain-growing areas in the world now in its possession, Germany hoped to relieve severe food shortages. Russia's withdrawal from the conflict also freed German armies to fight on the Western Front—the area along the French-German border where the war had been stalemated for nearly four years.

The World at War: World War I

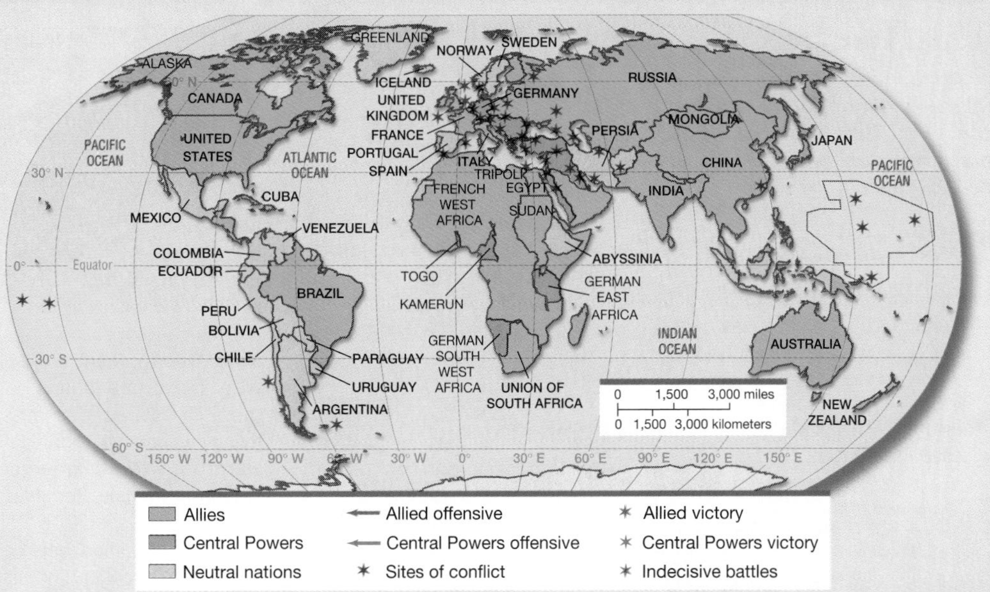

Allies ─ Allied offensive ✴ Allied victory
Central Powers ─ Central Powers offensive ✴ Central Powers victory
Neutral nations ✴ Sites of conflict ✴ Indecisive battles

The Western Front

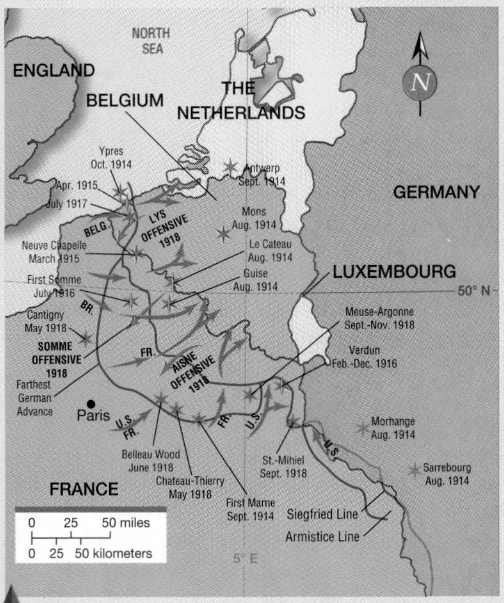

The Eastern Front

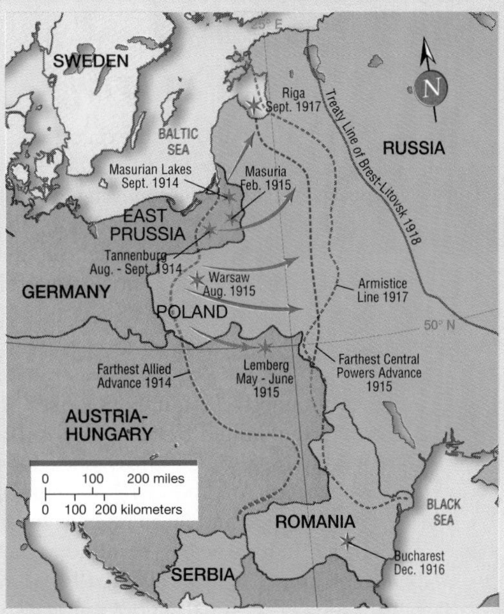

Although most action in World War I occurred in Europe, it was truly a world conflict. Note the battles outside Europe, the intercontinental alliances, and Europe's division of Africa. **When did the Battle of Belleau Wood take place?**

Map Study *Using Maps*

Answer: June 1918

Map Skills Practice

After students have studied the maps on this page, have them write a paragraph explaining why World War I was not confined to Europe alone. *(Students should recognize that worldwide alliances and the colonial empires held by various European countries expanded the conflict.)*

For additional map practice, use Chapter 15 Map Transparency Activities and Chapter Map Activity 15.

Linking Across TIME

Stars and Stripes, the GI newspaper staffed entirely by soldiers, was first published in 1918. In addition to being a source of information and morale for soldiers, it provided many young journalists and cartoonists with their first jobs. Two well-known cartoonists whose work appeared in *Stars and Stripes* were Milt Caniff ("Terry and the Pirates") and Bill Mauldin, who would win the Pulitzer Prize in 1945 for his Willie and GI Joe cartoons.

Sidelight: American Pilots in France

Colonel Stanton's "Lafayette, we are here" declaration was not the first reference to the French general by the Americans. A squadron of American pilots led by French commanders had been flying hundreds of missions against Germany since 1916. Called the Lafayette Escadrille, it consisted mostly of French pilots and well-off Americans who loved flying. Because the United States was officially neutral, American pilots had to reach France in secret, usually through the French Foreign Legion, whose recruitment procedures were notoriously lax.

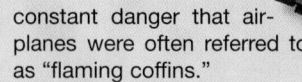

Linking Past and Present

Aerial Warfare

Aviation technology opened up a new dimension to war. For the first time combat took place not only on land and at sea, but also in the air.

Then

Flaming Coffins

Controlled air flight was less than 20 years old when World War I broke out. Fire was such a constant danger that airplanes were often referred to as "flaming coffins."

At first, the planes were used for reconnaissance, surveying and scouting, and for photographing enemy positions. Later, they were used for bombing. Both the Allies and the Central Powers developed a machine gun that was synchronized to fire through the whirling propeller of a flying plane.

Now

The Stealth and Missiles

An important part of modern warfare strategy is the use of stealth aircraft and missiles to strike at the enemy's air defense. Stealth is a name for military aircraft, both fighters and bombers, that are difficult for radar to detect. Stealth aircraft were used for the first time in warfare during the Gulf War. Cruise missiles, flying too low for radar detection, were used to strike targets considered too risky for piloted aircraft. In the assault on Baghdad, some of the initial strikes came from Tomahawk cruise missiles.

▼ STEALTH FIGHTER-BOMBER

▼ AMERICAN FLYING ACE EDDIE RICKENBACKER

■ Raising an Army

The Allies did not expect the United States to participate in combat because in the spring of 1917 American forces numbered only 200,000. In addition, the army possessed only 1,500 machine guns, 55 obsolete airplanes, and no heavy artillery.

The Draft

Although these numbers looked discouraging, the United States mobilized rapidly. On May 18, 1917, Congress passed the Selective Service Act, requiring all men between the ages of 21 and 30 to register for military service. In June nearly 10 million young men signed up. The draft eventually extended to all men between 18 and 45 and resulted in the induction of 2.8 million men into the armed forces. Another 2 million men and women volunteered for military service.

Twelve weeks after war had been declared, the first United States soldiers landed in France. On July 4, symbolically recalling the American-French partnership during the American Revolution, Colonel Charles E. Stanton stood at the tomb of France's great war hero, Marquis de Lafayette, and said, "Lafayette, we are here." More than 2 million American soldiers comprising 42 infantry divisions reached France before the war ended. This vast new reservoir of military strength was an important factor in the Allied victory.

African Americans

Among those drafted to serve in the war were some 370,000 African Americans; of these, 200,000 served overseas. African American soldiers encountered rampant discrimination and prejudice in the army, where their units were completely segregated from white units. In addition, African Americans were not allowed to serve in the Marine Corps, and the 10,000 in the navy were restricted to the lower ranks.

Critical Thinking Activity

Supporting Opinions Many historians believe that the most significant factors in the defeat of the Central Powers were the entrance of the United States into the war and the collapse of the Russian Empire. Do you agree with this assessment? What evidence can you find to support the conclusion? Is there evidence to refute it? Ask students to write a paragraph explaining their opinion. Have them cite evidence in support. **L1**

Still, in the bitter battles along the Western Front, African American soldiers fought valiantly, winning praise from both the French commander, Marshal Henri Pétain (ahn•REE pay•TAN), and the United States commander, General John Pershing. African American soldiers in one infantry regiment won 21 American Distinguished Service Crosses and 68 French military decorations. The entire 369th Infantry won the highly prized French decoration, the Croix de Guerre (KRWAH dih GEHR), for gallantry.

■ Victory on Land and Sea

In the spring and early summer of 1918, Germany made a last desperate effort to win the war and nearly succeeded. Starting in March, the Germans almost penetrated the British lines; a second drive in June threatened Paris. United States troops helped to stop the advance, distinguishing themselves in a counterattack at Château-Thierry (SHA•TOH TYEH•REE), a town less than 50 miles from Paris.

The tide turned in mid-July as Marshal Ferdinand Foch (FAWSH), supreme commander of the Allied armies, ordered a great counteroffensive along the Western Front close to the German border. Pershing requested that American troops be assigned a section of

the front for themselves—an area near Verdun. In mid-September 550,000 "doughboys"—the nickname given American soldiers—won an overwhelming victory at St.-Mihiel (san mee•yehl). Then an even larger force drove toward the key city of Sedan, breaking through well-defended portions of the German lines.

By early November, the Allies were poised to advance onto German soil. Realizing the war was lost, the Germans signed an **armistice,** or temporary stop to the fighting, on November 11, 1918.

American naval forces joined the British in waging war against Germany's deadly U-boats. The invention of the depth charge, an underwater explosive, provided the Allies with a new weapon, but its effective use demanded hundreds of patrol vessels to watch for U-boats and protect Allied ships by escorting them out of dangerous areas. So, in addition to 79 destroyers, the United States supplied more than 100 small "sub-chasers" plus a variety of former yachts, tugs, and fishing boats—"almost any craft which could carry a wireless, a gun, and depth charges was boldly sent to sea." By the end of 1917, the number of U-boat casualties was slashed in half. In 1918 the United States Navy took the principal role in laying mines across the North Sea, which prevented U-boats from reaching the Atlantic Ocean and isolated those already at sea from ports and supplies.

◀ WORLD WAR I SHELL

Section 2 ★ Review

Checking for Understanding

1. **Identify** Zimmermann Note, Selective Service Act, John Pershing, doughboys.

2. **Define** armistice.

3. **Explain** the meaning of the phrases "peace without victory" and "Lafayette, we are here."

4. **Summarize** the events that brought the United States into the war.

Critical Thinking

5. **Assessing Outcomes** Would Germany have won if the United States had not entered the war? Explain your position.

ACTIVITY

6. Prepare the text for a radio news broadcast on one of the major battles of World War I.

CHAPTER 15
SECTION 2

ASSESS
Check Understanding
Assign Section 2 Review as homework or an in-class activity.

Evaluate
🔘 📁 Assign Section Quiz 15-2 or use the Testmaker to create a customized test.

Reteach
Have students identify each of the following and explain his role in World War I: Newton D. Baker (*U.S. secretary of war*), Henri Pétain (*French commander*), John J. Pershing (*commander of American Expeditionary Forces*), Ferdinand Foch (*supreme commander of Allied forces*), Arthur Zimmermann (*German foreign minister*).

📁 Have students complete Reteaching Activity 15-2.

Enrich
📁 Assign Geography in History Activity 15.

CLOSE
Remind students that Woodrow Wilson ran in 1916 under the slogan "He Kept Us Out of War." Ask students if they would have voted for him and why.

Answers to SECTION 2 REVIEW

1. Zimmerman Note, 463; Selective Service Act, 466; doughboys, 466; John Pershing, 467.
2. All vocabulary words are defined in the Glossary.
3. no total winners or losers, recognized France's support of American Revolution
4. resumption of submarine warfare, growing antagonism against Germany, Zimmermann Note

5. Answers will vary. Until the United States's entrance, German U-boats were threatening Great Britain. American supplies kept Britain from starving, and American troops, besides supplying manpower, boosted morale, especially after Russia made a separate peace.
6. Student broadcast texts should show creativity and indicate understanding of battle's significance.

467

FOCUS

Bellringer

 Before taking roll, project Section Focus Transparency 15-3 or hand out Section Focus Transparency Activity 15-3. Have students answer the questions.

Motivating Activity

Ask students to imagine that they are young people at the time of World War I. Have them list some of the things they could do to contribute to the war effort on the home front. Tell them that in this section they will learn how Americans at home contributed to victory abroad. **L1**

Vocabulary Precheck

Ask students to guess what the phrase "victory garden" means and how it originated. **L1, LEP**

ABCNEWS INTERACTIVE™

VIDEODISC

Powers of the Congress

Side One, Chapter 16
Title: *Provide for the Common Defense*
Subject: Role of Congress

★★

War on the Home Front

Setting the Scene

Section Focus

In order to raise and equip vast armies, increase the size of the navy elevenfold, and keep munitions and food flowing to the Allies, massive reorganization of American business, industry, and agriculture was needed. Victory in World War I was due, in large part, to the great efforts and sacrifices made on the home front.

Objectives

After studying this section, you should be able to

★ explain how the war was financed.

★ describe how public opinion was shaped by the government.

★ discuss the goals of Wilson's Fourteen Points.

Key Term

victory garden

◀ WORLD WAR I POSTER

The United States found itself ill-equipped for battle when it entered World War I. The most immediate domestic concern that Congress faced was to keep the United States and Allied armies supplied by gearing United States industry to the war machine. In addition, the federal government needed to raise money to pay for the war and to mobilize the American people to support the war effort.

■ Mobilizing the Economy

To accomplish these goals, Wilson and Congress applied the Progressive Era's ideals of efficiency, control, and conformity in society to the war effort at home. "It is not an army that we must shape and train for war," said the President, "it is a nation."

Organizing Industries

The government's solution to the problem of supplying the troops was to place most industries under the control of federal agencies. The most important of these—the War Industries Board—handled purchasing for both the Allies and the United States. Under the leadership of Bernard Baruch, a Wall Street stockbroker, the War Industries Board attempted "to operate the whole United States as a single factory dominated by one management." Enlisting the most able businesspeople in America to direct the war effort, the government received the cooperation of business to convert factories to war production. Federal officials determined how raw materials would be allocated and what prices should be fixed.

The Fuel Administration was in charge of boosting coal and oil production, while encouraging people to conserve. The agency

468   UNIT 5 Crusade and Disillusion: 1914–1932

Classroom Resources for SECTION 3

Blackline Masters:

- Reproducible Lesson Plan 15-3
- Guided Reading Activity 15-3
- Cooperative Learning Activity 15
- Workbook Activity 15-3
- Reteaching Activity 15-3
- Section Quiz 15-3

Transparencies:
- Section Focus Transparency 15-3

Multimedia:
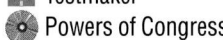
- Testmaker
- Powers of Congress

introduced such conservation methods as daylight savings time and shortened work-weeks for nonwar-related factories. The Railroad Administration took charge of the railroads and ran them as a single system. The War Labor Board worked to prevent labor disputes.

Labor unions generally supported the war effort, hoping that cooperation would result in goodwill from the government and big business. Union leaders saw in the war opportunities for higher pay, better working conditions, and the right to organize and bargain collectively. Membership in unions doubled, and unions won concessions, such as the eight-hour day that industries had long opposed.

Involvement of Women

Wartime also meant increased opportunities for American women. Millions of jobs given up by men who volunteered or were drafted were filled by women. For the first time, women were welcomed in many occupations. Female workers became an essential part of the nation's war effort in war industries and defense plants.

Despite the progress toward social and economic equality the war offered them, many women wondered how the United States could be fighting to save democracy and still deny them the vote at home. Activists for woman suffrage continued to work during the war.

Involvement of African Americans

African Americans might well have asked similar questions because Southern states continued to deny them the right to vote. Also, African American soldiers fighting in Europe encountered far less discrimination from Europeans than they had experienced in their own country.

Nevertheless, the war offered new opportunities for African Americans at home. Job opportunities and high wages during the

 **Visualizing History** ▲ **AT HOME** During the war more and more women became a vital part of the labor force. In addition, women volunteered for noncombat duty on the war front or for a military Home Guard in the United States. *What happened to the suffrage movement during the war?*

Critical Thinking Activity

Evaluating Government Actions Ask students to identify actions the government took to organize the war effort (*regulating industry, encouraging greater production, propaganda, keeping an eye on dissenters, and so forth*). After students identify the actions, have them list the effects of those actions. Then discuss why government tends to expand its control in wartime. Ask students if they think all of the government's actions on the home front in World War I were necessary. **L3**

TEACH
Guided Practice
Analyzing Cause and Effect
Have students write a series of diary or journal entries concerning the economic changes brought about by the mobilization for war from the point of view of one or more of the following: a union member, a wife and homemaker, a factory worker not involved in war production, and a worker involved in munitions production. Ask each writer to record how his or her life has changed under the new economic system now in place. **L2**

Did You Know?

Throughout the conflict, Americans observed daylight saving time, established in Europe during the war, to save electricity. Factories cut back production of women's corsets to save steel. Toymakers curtailed the manufacture of many toys to save tin.

Visualizing History Point out that on the home front, women did work previously considered suitable only for men. They worked in factories and offices and took on such jobs as delivering milk and ice.
Answer to Caption: objected to the idea that the nation was fighting for democracy yet denied women the vote

▲ POSTER SUPPORTING BONDS

war pulled 500,000 African Americans from Southern farms to munitions-producing Northern factories. Most were offered only unskilled or semiskilled jobs, but by war's end, more than 100,000 African Americans held jobs as skilled workers or factory supervisors.

Although discrimination against African American workers led to race riots in 26 Northern cities in 1919, African Americans in the North made significant economic gains during the war. As a result, migration northward continued after the war ended. One African American wrote a letter to a Chicago newspaper explaining this "great migration." African Americans, he said, were

> 66 . . . compelled to go where there is better wages and sociable conditions, believe me . . . many places here in [Alabama] the only thing that a black man gets is a peck of meal and from 3 to 4 lbs. of bacon per week, and he is treated as a slave. 99

Impact of War on Civilians

The war had a great impact on the lives of all American civilians. Using the slogan "Food Will Win the War—Don't Waste It," the Food Administration, directed by Herbert Hoover, supervised efforts to reduce food consumption. Families were encouraged to "Hooverize" by "serving just enough" and by having Wheatless Mondays and Meatless Tuesdays.

Citizens were also encouraged to plant **victory gardens,** gardens for raising their own vegetables. To increase wheat production, the federally financed Grain Corporation guaranteed farmers first $2.00, then $2.26 per bushel. In 1918 it bought the entire American wheat crop. The combined efforts of the Food Administration and the American public were tremendously successful.

The Cost of War

World War I was costly. By its end the United States was spending about $44 million a day, or a total of about $33 billion. Of that amount, $10 billion went to the Allies as loans. The government raised about one-third of the money to finance the war through taxation. Income taxes were increased, although only wealthier families paid income taxes at that time. Corporations also paid higher taxes, including an "excess profits" tax, designed to return war profits to the government. The government also levied excise duties on items as varied as theater tickets, chewing gum, and phonograph records.

The government borrowed the rest of the money—more than $20 billion—from the American people by selling four issues of Liberty Bonds and a postwar issue of Victory Bonds. Posters, rallies, and "Liberty Loan sermons" encouraged people to buy the bonds.

Purchasing bonds became an act of patriotism. Even children were urged to use their pennies to buy War Savings Stamps. Boy Scouts sold the stamps under the slogan "Every Scout to Save a Soldier." Twenty-one million people—more than one-fifth of the nation's population—subscribed to the Fourth Liberty Loan.

Controlling Public Opinion

Success of the war effort depended heavily on voluntary civilian cooperation. Therefore, the government wanted to make sure that Americans understood and supported the nation's war aims.

Selling the War to Americans

The Committee on Public Information under the leadership of journalist and author George Creel was established to "sell" the war to America. Creel described his job as "the world's greatest adventure in advertising." He recruited advertising people, commercial artists, authors, songwriters, entertainers, public speakers, and motion-picture companies to help him.

Millions of pamphlets were distributed explaining the causes and aims of the war. Thousands of "four-minute men" spoke at movie theaters and public halls and gatherings in support of the war effort. Although this flood of propaganda reinforced the President's image of the war as a moral crusade, it also helped promote widespread intolerance.

Control of War Protesters

To prevent spying and resistance to the war effort, Congress passed the Espionage and Sedition acts. Severe penalties imposed by these laws silenced most war opposition. Loyalty Leagues, organized by Creel, encouraged Americans to spy on their neighbors and to report those who might be "disloyal." In addition, the postmaster general was given authority to ban certain newspapers, magazines, and pamphlets from the mail. Thousands of people were imprisoned, sometimes for opinions expressed in private conversations. People were arrested for criticizing the President, for questioning the American form of government, for criticizing the army or even military uniforms. Socialist leader Eugene Debs was arrested and sentenced to 10 years in prison for merely telling an audience to "resist militarism, wherever found." People were even jailed for criticizing the Red Cross and the YMCA.

War fever was responsible for the vigorous enforcement of these laws, and the courts generally upheld the principle behind them. About 3,000 cases involving convictions under the Espionage and Sedition acts were heard on appeal in federal courts. After the war some of these cases

★★★★★★★★★★★★★★★★
AMERICAN PORTRAITS

George M. Cohan
1878–1942

By the time he wrote "Over There"—the most popular song of World War I—George M. Cohan was already one of America's biggest stars. At the age of 14, he was creating songs and skits for his family's vaudeville act. By his early 20s, he was writing, producing, and starring in hit Broadway shows.

Claiming that he had been born on the 4th of July (actually July 3), Cohan discovered early in his career that he could excite crowds with such patriotic appeals as his "I'm a Yankee Doodle Dandy."

When American troops left for France in 1917, he quickly penned "Over There," touching the chord of nationalistic fervor sweeping the country. His song became America's war anthem. In 1940 Congress awarded Cohan a Medal of Honor for "Over There" and "You're a Grand Old Flag," another patriotic song.

Teaching American Portraits

George M. Cohan wrote his most famous song, "Over There," on the day war was declared. He sat down at the piano and wrote what he said was just a bugle call. All wars have inspired songs. You might suggest that students research other songs of World War I and study the lyrics. How do they reflect the attitudes of the time? Are they idealistic, humorous, optimistic, patriotic, sentimental?

Linking Across
TIME

The mass media of the World War I period consisted only of newsprint. Film had not yet developed as a medium for spreading ideas, nor had the radio. Considering these limitations, World War I propaganda was extremely effective. Decades later, following World War II, an overwhelming media system of radio, television, film, and print was in place, creating a network that helped foster the "cold war" by projecting an image of the Soviet Union and communism as a threat to the security of the United States.

📁 Assign Cooperative Learning Activity 15.

Sidelight: Expanding Role of Women

When men went off to fight, American women began to work at jobs they could not have dreamed of before the war. Necessity drove them into such areas as typesetting and operating linotype machines, and it also opened up jobs as mechanics, bricklayers, and streetcar operators. Some women became blacksmiths or telegraph operators. Thousands worked to keep their family farms going while the men were away. Although these gains were short-lived (many returned to their traditional roles as homemakers after the war), the experience left women with a new sense of their own worth and ability.

Assess

Check Understanding

Assign Section 3 Review as homework or an in-class activity.

Evaluate

🔘 📂 Assign Section Quiz 15-3 or use the Test-maker to create a customized test.

Reteach

Under the section headings Mobilizing the Economy and Controlling Public Opinion, ask students to summarize the government's actions and their effectiveness in helping the war effort.

📂 Have students complete Reteaching Activity 15-3.

Enrich

Have students write newspaper editorials questioning the moral implications of using advertising to "sell" a war to a nation. What are the effects of such a campaign? Invite volunteers to read their editorials to the class. Then ask students what might have happened in 1917 to anyone who wrote such an editorial.

Close

Based on the description of government actions in the subsection Controlling Public Opinion, ask students to draw an inference about the differing attitudes of the American people toward the war.

reached the Supreme Court. In the landmark case *Schenck v. United States* (1919), Justice Oliver Wendell Holmes, writing for a unanimous Court, stated:

> ❝ *When a nation is at war, many things that might be said in time of peace are such a hindrance to its efforts that their utterance will not be endured so long as [soldiers] fight and that no Court could regard them as protected by any constitutional right. . . .* ❞

The Court refused, however, to support punishment when no "clear and present danger" of hurting the United States existed or when the accused was jailed for unpopular political beliefs.

Persecution of Germans

War fever was also to blame for the mistreatment and persecution of German Americans. Despite Wilson's insistence that Americans were "the sincere friends of the German people," anti-German sentiment ran high. Many school systems banned the teaching of the German language, and orchestras stopped performing the music of Beethoven, Schubert, and Wagner.

■ Wilson's Fourteen Points

While the war was foremost in the President's mind, Wilson never ceased to think

◀ LIBERTY LOAN POSTER

ahead to peace. In January 1918, Wilson went before Congress to present his goals for a lasting peace. With his Fourteen Points (see Appendix), the President hoped to establish a new world order.

The Fourteen Points were based on "the principle of justice to all peoples." The President proposed to eliminate the general causes of war through disarmament, freedom of the seas, and open diplomacy instead of secret agreements. Wilson also addressed the right of peoples to live under a government of their own choosing. Finally, he proposed an international peacekeeping organization.

Although Wilson's words appealed to a world weary of war, other Allied leaders did not support him. They wanted German territory and to punish Germany. A formidable challenge lay ahead for the President if he were to see his dream of peace realized.

Section 3 ★ Review

Checking for Understanding

1. **Identify** Bernard Baruch, War Industries Board, George Creel, Liberty Bonds, Espionage and Sedition acts, Fourteen Points.

2. **Define** victory garden.

3. **Describe** three ways that Americans at home supported the war effort.

4. **List** the two ways the government raised money for the war.

Critical Thinking

5. **Defending an Opinion** Was government action to suppress opposition to the war justified? Explain your reasoning.

ACTIVITY

6. Suppose that the United States were at war today. Write a law that specifies who is eligible to be drafted and what to do about people who refuse to serve.

Answers to SECTION 3 REVIEW

1. Bernard Baruch, 468; War Industries Board, 468; Liberty Bonds, 470; George Creel, 471; Espionage and Sedition acts, 471; Fourteen Points, 472
2. All vocabulary words are defined in the Glossary.
3. purchase of Liberty Bonds and War Savings Stamps, conservation of fuel and food, increased production
4. through taxes and borrowed money
5. Answers will vary. *Pro*—During wartime, measures to prevent disloyalty and weakening of resolve are necessary. *Con*—Free speech rights never can be revoked. The government overstepped its powers in stifling opposition to the war.
6. Student laws should be logical and binding.

After the War

Setting the Scene

Section Focus

As Kaiser Wilhelm abdicated the German throne and fled, Germany signed an armistice. Now the Allies faced the task of constructing a framework for peace. Wilson still had support at home and enjoyed great popularity abroad. The opportunity to carry out his peace plan seemed at hand. However, his political blunders and the demands of Allied leaders doomed his chances.

Objectives

After studying this section, you should be able to

★ describe the outcome of the Versailles peace conference.

★ explain why the Senate rejected the Treaty of Versailles.

★ identify domestic problems that arose after the war.

Key Terms

covenant, deport

◀ WORLD WAR I HELMET

---

idterm elections in the United States in November 1918 showed a changing attitude toward Wilson and his policies. Realizing that Democrats faced heavy losses in the elections, the President appealed to voters to show support for his peace program by returning Democrats to Congress. Instead, voters elected Republican majorities in both houses.

■ The Peace Plan Opposed

Shortly after the election, Wilson announced his intention to head the American delegation to the peace conference. His decision was not received well by those who thought that as President his place was at home. Wilson faltered again when he failed to include any prominent Republicans in the American delegation to the conference.

Peace Conference

The peace conference opened at the palace of Versailles in January 1919, but most of the sessions took place in Paris. Delegates from 27 nations attended. The proceedings, however, were dominated by the leaders of the three most powerful nations—the United States's President Wilson, Britain's Prime Minister David Lloyd George, and France's Premier Georges Clemenceau (KLEH•muhn•SOH). With Vittorio Orlando, the Italian premier, these men became known as "the Big Four." Because their meetings were held in secret, Wilson was robbed of an effective weapon—direct appeal to public opinion. Secrecy also seemed to violate the Fourteen Points, which pledged "open covenants openly arrived at." Nevertheless, the President scored an immediate triumph by forcing plans for a League of Nations into the

CHAPTER 15 World War I Era: 1914–1920   **473**

Classroom Resources for SECTION 4

Blackline Masters:
- Reproducible Lesson Plan 15-4
- Guided Reading Activity 15-4
- Political Cartoons in American History Activity 14
- Enrichment Activity 15
- Workbook Activity 15-4
- Reteaching Activity 15-4
- Section Quiz 15-4

Transparencies:
- Section Focus Transparency 15-4

Multimedia:
- Testmaker
- GTV: A Geographic Perspective on American History

LESSON PLAN
SECTION 4, 473–478

FOCUS

Bellringer

Before taking roll, project Section Focus Transparency 15-4 or hand out Section Focus Transparency Activity 15-4. Have students answer the questions.

Motivating Activity

Read aloud the following words of President Wilson: "It must be a peace without victory. . . . Victory would mean peace forced upon the loser, a victor's terms imposed upon the vanquished. . . ."

Ask students what the quotation suggests about the way Wilson would treat a defeated Germany. **L2**

Vocabulary Precheck

Ask students to define each of the key terms. Have a volunteer consult the dictionary for any unfamiliar words. **L1, LEP**

 VIDEODISC

GTV: A Geographic Perspective on American History

Side 4, Chapter 1
Title: *Modern Times*
Subject: World War I: before and after
See GTV Guide for complete lesson plan.

473

TEACH
Guided Practice
Making Generalizations

Write the following on index cards: Economic Controls, Demand for Consumer Goods, Peacetime Production, Wartime Government Spending, Inflation, Government Price Guarantees, Demand for Food, Wartime Crop Prices.

Direct students to take turns drawing a card, and use the phrase written on the card in a sentence that describes the United States economy either during or following the war. Write students' contributions on the board. When all the cards have been used, ask them to form generalizations about whether war is good or bad for the economy and why. **L2**

Map
Study *Using Maps*

Answer: Palestine

Map Skills Practice

Have students use the map to name the Arab territories that went to Great Britain and France. (*Great Britain gained Iraq, Trans-Jordan, Egypt, and Palestine; France gained Syria, Tunisia, Algeria, and French Morocco.*) Ask students what generalizations they can form concerning British and French colonization. (*Both Great Britain and France expanded their empires as a result of World War I.*)

▲ WORLD WAR I
INFANTRY BOOTS

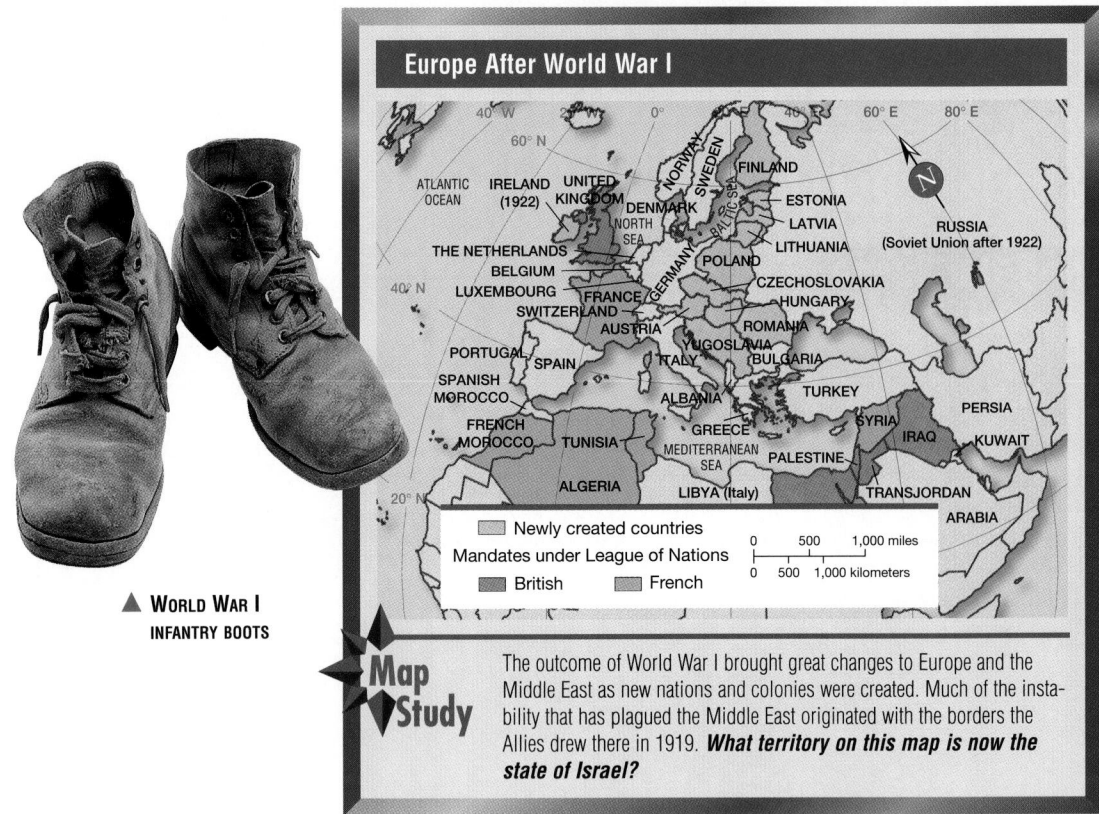

Europe After World War I

Newly created countries
Mandates under League of Nations
British   French

Map Study

The outcome of World War I brought great changes to Europe and the Middle East as new nations and colonies were created. Much of the instability that has plagued the Middle East originated with the borders the Allies drew there in 1919. **What territory on this map is now the state of Israel?**

peace treaty. In mid-February the **covenant,** or charter, of the League, written by Wilson himself, was accepted by the conference.

Opposition Grows

During Wilson's absence his political influence in the United States weakened alarmingly. The likelihood that Wilson's peace program would fail became evident when 39 Republican senators and senators-elect—far more than enough to prevent ratification of a treaty—signed a statement opposing the League of Nations. Instead of trying to repair the rift, however, Wilson publicly denounced the "narrow, selfish, provincial purposes" of his opponents and insisted that the League be part of the peace treaty. At the peace table, he tried to appease his critics at home by calling for changes designed to protect American interests. To accept such changes, the Allies required Wilson to make further concessions in their favor.

Treaty of Versailles

Despite Wilson's hopes, it was a victor's peace. In the Middle East, the Ottoman Empire lost territory. In Europe, Austria-Hungary was split up. The greatest humiliation was reserved for the Germans, however. Germany lost territory and was stripped of its colonies. In addition, Germany was required to pay for damage it had done in Europe and to repay the Allies for the cost of the war. Although many of the Fourteen Points were ignored, Wilson trusted the League of Nations to right injustices after the desire for revenge subsided.

Difficulty at Home

The peace settlement complete, in July 1919 President Wilson came home to face his foes. Although he hoped Americans would support the treaty, they criticized it from all sides. In Congress a small group of

Special Needs Activity

Reading Disability Significant problems often arise because of a lack of decoding skills, and reading comprehension is weakened. By the time the student finishes a paragraph, he or she might have forgotten the beginning. For students who have very poor reading skills, have a good reader tape-record Section 4 so that the student can listen while following along in the text. Remind students to look at all the pictures and maps in the section.

senators branded the League a "treacherous and treasonable scheme," while a much larger group wanted the Senate to ratify the treaty but with amendments that would preserve the nation's freedom to act independently.

Instead of compromising, Wilson insisted that the Senate ratify the treaty without changes. Convinced that he could defeat his opposition by appealing to public opinion, Wilson went directly to the people. Starting in Ohio in September, he traveled 8,000 miles and made 37 major speeches in less than a month on behalf of the treaty. Almost everywhere his reception was warm; he seemed to be regaining popular support. Had his strength held out, he might have won the battle, but the physical strain proved too great for the President. He collapsed in Colorado on September 25 and was forced to abandon his speaking tour. Shortly after returning to the White House, Wilson suffered a stroke that paralyzed one side of his body and impaired his speech. He was bedridden for months, isolated from even his closest advisers.

With the President silenced, in November 1919, and again in March 1920, the Senate refused to ratify the Versailles treaty. Instead, the United States negotiated a separate peace treaty with each of the Central Powers in 1921.

America's Postwar Problems

The fate of the treaty was only one of the problems the United States faced after World War I. Demobilizing the armed forces, returning to a peacetime economy, and coping with fears of espionage presented the country with serious challenges.

Demobilization

The United States began to demobilize as soon as the hostilities ended. Within a short time, the army was reduced to less than 500,000, and economic controls were lifted. The businesspeople left Washington, D.C.,

and industry converted to peacetime production. With Wilson preoccupied with the peace treaty and later incapacitated, the nation received little overall direction. Industry enjoyed a brief postwar boom, resulting from the increased demand for consumer goods that had been scarce during the war. Unfortunately, government spending during the war brought inflation that nearly doubled the cost of living by 1919, and prices rose to a point where many consumers could not afford to pay for new items. Consequently, after 1920 business activity slowed. Farmers were especially hard-hit. Slackening demands for food and the end of government price guarantees caused agricultural prices to plummet. Many farmers who took advantage of high wartime crop prices and went into debt to expand their farms now faced bankruptcy.

▲ *SIGNING OF THE TREATY OF VERSAILLES* by John Johansen, 1919 The greatest obstacle at the peace conference was that many countries were interested chiefly in gaining territory and inflicting punishment on Germany. ***Who played major roles in treaty negotiations?***

Independent Practice

Expressing an Opinion Have students research the conflict over the ratification of the Treaty of Versailles and the acceptance of the League of Nations. Ask them to write a letter to the editor explaining why they believed the League is to the advantage or disadvantage of the United States. **L2**

📁 Assign Guided Reading Activity 15-4.

Did You Know?

Robert LaFollette, progressive reformer and former governor of Wisconsin, became a senator in 1906. He opposed United States membership in the League of Nations. LaFollette believed that the Treaty of Versailles was unjust and that the United States, if it joined the League, would have to uphold the treaty.

History AND ART The demands of European leaders to punish Germany and protect the interests of their own nations did not fit with President Wilson's goals concerning a postwar world. He only agreed to the treaty because it called for a League of Nations.
Answer to Caption: the United States, Great Britain, France, and Italy

---

Cooperative Learning Activity

Writing Interview Questions Organize students into four groups, and have each group draw up a list of interview questions for one of the principals at the Versailles peace conference: David Lloyd George of Great Britain; Vittorio Orlando of Italy; Georges Clemenceau of France; and Woodrow Wilson of the United States. When students have completed their lists, have them compare questions. Which questions would remain the same or similar from man to man? Which would change depending upon the person being interviewed? Have a reporter from each group summarize the main ideas of the interview questions. **L2** 📦

Linking Across
TIME

The labor unrest that followed World War I was repeated after World War II. During the war workers received large increases in wages. After the war, unions wanted to maintain those wages and even increase them. Therefore, miners, auto workers, and railroaders conducted a series of strikes. In response Congress passed the Taft-Hartley Act in 1946. The act made it more difficult for unions to strike and strengthened the ability of the National Labor Relations Board to enforce collective bargaining between labor and management. The Taft-Hartley Act is still in effect.

Visualizing History During the war, the government fueled antiforeign feelings by warning Americans about spies and foreign agents. These feelings led some to view all immigrants with suspicion.

Answer to Caption: They viewed them as radical and suspected them of plotting revolution.

Visualizing History

▲ ANTI-IMMIGRANT SENTIMENT A 1920 cartoon shows immigrants taking jobs from Americans. *How did many Americans view labor leaders?*

Labor Unrest

High prices also contributed to labor unrest after the war, and when the War Labor Board disbanded, the truce between employers and organized labor ended. A record number—3,600—strikes occurred in 1919, most meeting with little success. Four of them—the Seattle general strike, the Boston police strike, the steel strike, and the coal strike—were highly disruptive and had effects that lasted well into the 1920s.

In January 1919, only 2 months after the armistice, 35,000 shipyard workers from Seattle, Washington, went on strike to gain an increase in their wages. The next month union workers in all Seattle industries walked off their jobs in support of the shipyard strikers. Many city residents viewed the strike as revolutionary. They responded by hoarding food and fuel and by purchasing guns. Seattle's mayor blamed the situation on dangerous radicals and after 5 days used the state militia to break the strike.

In September 1919, another major city was hit by labor unrest as Boston's police force went on strike for better wages and working conditions. Looters soon were in the streets, smashing windows and stealing goods. When the mayor was unable to restore order, Massachusetts governor Calvin Coolidge

called out the state guard. A new police force was hired, and Coolidge received national acclaim for his view that "There is no right to strike against the public safety by anybody, anywhere, anytime."

Later that month more than 350,000 steelworkers went on strike across the nation, demanding better wages, an 8-hour rather than a 12-hour day, and the right to join a union. Two-thirds of the strikers were immigrants. Most of the office workers and supervisors who refused to join the strike were American-born. The companies blamed the strike on radicals who told "these foreigners . . . that if they would join the union they would get Americans' jobs." When the companies hired replacement workers, violence broke out, and federal troops were called in to protect them. After 4 months, the strikers gave up with no gains.

While the steel strike was under way, 450,000 coal miners walked off their jobs nationwide. Overworked and underpaid, the strikers demanded a 60 percent pay increase and a 30-hour week. Since at the time coal was the nation's major energy source, the government responded quickly. Obtaining a court order, it forced the strikers back to work. Eventually, however, coal miners won a large pay increase to an average of $7.50 a day.

Red Scare

Many Americans had long suspected a link between labor unrest and political radicalism. The strikes of 1919 helped fuel a larger "Red Scare" than the United States experienced after the war. When the Bolsheviks seized power in Russia in 1917, they called on workers everywhere to revolt. In 1919 communism seemed to have great appeal among the poverty-stricken peoples of war-torn Europe. Although the overwhelming majority of American labor leaders were not allied with the Communists, nevertheless, many Americans suspected them of planning revolution.

The same laws used to quiet opposition and suppress civil liberties during the war were now turned against radicals. Immigrants—especially those with Russian

Critical Thinking Activity

Analyzing Policy Have students debate the following issue: All foreign-born Americans who hold ideas foreign to the United States government, whether or not they advocate the overthrow of the government, should be deported. Ask a class member to keep track of the argu-

ments, both pro and con, by writing them on the board. Suggest that students examine each pro argument in the context of the First Amendment. Ask under what circumstances the First Amendment might not apply. **L3**

names—came under suspicion. Attorney General A. Mitchell Palmer rounded up 6,000 immigrants that the government suspected of being Communists and **deported**—expelled from the country—nearly 600 of them. Some of the immigrants deported had become American citizens, and some were deported without trials.

Racial Tension

Accompanying the Red Scare was a wave of racism. Racial tensions rose as white soldiers returning from Europe found themselves competing for jobs and housing with African Americans who had come north during the war. During the summer of 1919, race riots broke out in many Northern cities. The worst was in Chicago, where nearly 40

people were killed and more than 500 injured. One journalist described the scene:

66 *During this wild week mobs of whites pursued and beat and killed [African Americans]. Other mobs of [African Americans] pursued and beat and killed whites. . . . Armed bands in motor trucks dashed wildly up and down the streets, firing into houses. . . .* 99

Few cities in the United States escaped racial violence in the early 1920s. Even after the Red Scare died down, racial intolerance lived on in organizations such as the Ku Klux Klan, which spread from the South to become a powerful national force.

Map Study *Using Maps*

Answer: encouraged the movement

Map Skills Practice
Ask students which region of the United States was most progressive in granting woman suffrage before 1920. *(West)* What clues does the map give about attitudes toward equality for women in the various regions of the United States? *(Southeast traditional, East and Midwest less so but not ready for full suffrage, West progressive, open to equality for women, at least politically)*

CURRICULUM CONNECTION

Health A deadly killer claimed twice as many lives as artillery, machine guns, and poison gas immediately after World War I. An epidemic of influenza probably broke out in an army barracks in Kansas and spread across the United States and to all parts of the world. From 1918 through mid-1919, more than 20 million people died throughout the world.

Assign Political Cartoons in American History Activity 14: "The Gates to Immigration Close."

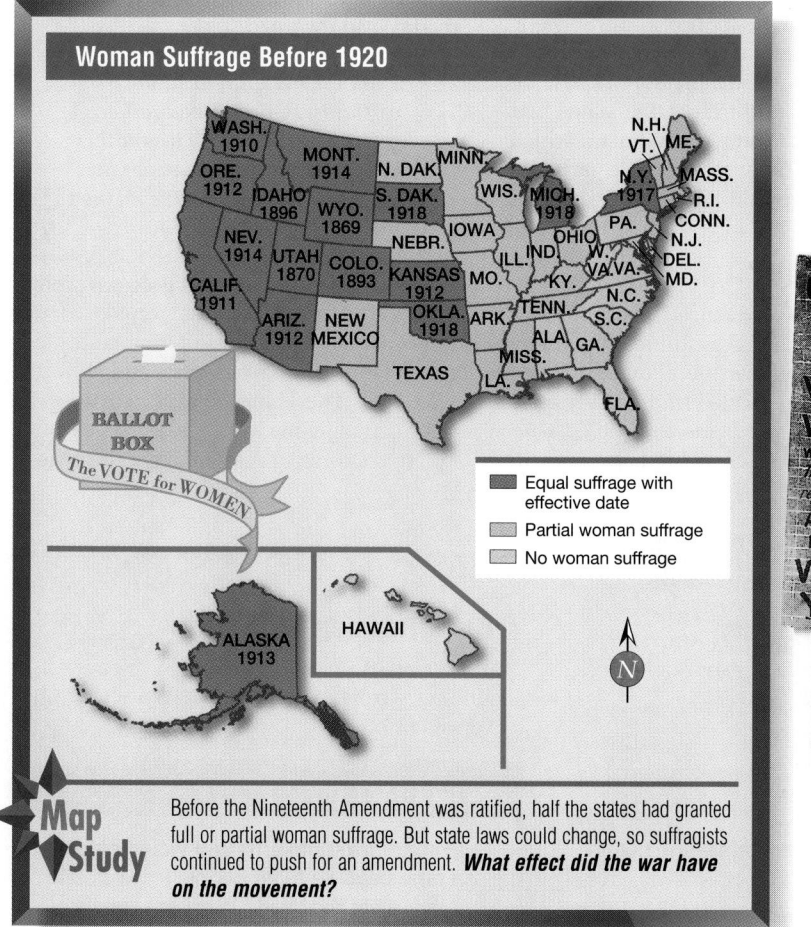

Woman Suffrage Before 1920

WASH. 1910
ORE. 1912
IDAHO 1896
MONT. 1914
N. DAK.
MINN.
WIS.
MICH. 1918
N.H.
VT.
ME.
N.Y. 1917
MASS.
R.I.
CONN.
WYO. 1869
S. DAK. 1918
IOWA
OHIO
PA.
N.J.
NEV. 1914
UTAH 1870
COLO. 1893
NEBR.
ILL.
IND.
W. VA.
VA.
DEL.
MD.
CALIF. 1911
KANSAS 1912
MO.
KY.
N.C.
ARIZ. 1912
NEW MEXICO
OKLA. 1918
ARK.
TENN.
S.C.
TEXAS
MISS.
ALA.
GA.
LA.
FLA.

BALLOT BOX
The VOTE for WOMEN

ALASKA 1913
HAWAII

- Equal suffrage with effective date
- Partial woman suffrage
- No woman suffrage

N

Map Study

Before the Nineteenth Amendment was ratified, half the states had granted full or partial woman suffrage. But state laws could change, so suffragists continued to push for an amendment. **What effect did the war have on the movement?**

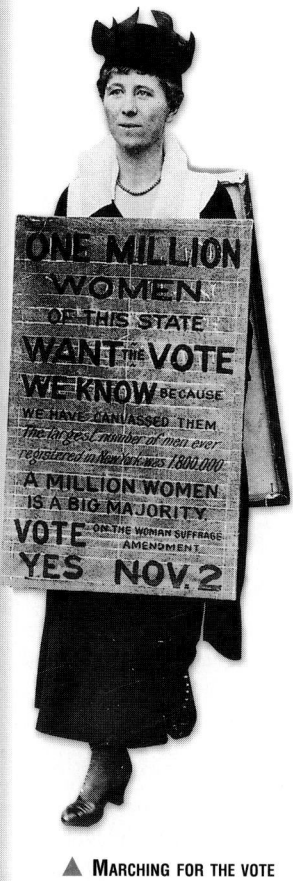

ONE MILLION WOMEN OF THIS STATE WANT THE VOTE WE KNOW BECAUSE WE HAVE CANVASSED THEM *The largest number of men ever registered in New York was 1,800,000.* A MILLION WOMEN IS A BIG MAJORITY VOTE YES NOV. 2 ON THE WOMAN SUFFRAGE AMENDMENT

▲ MARCHING FOR THE VOTE

CHAPTER 15 World War I Era: 1914–1920 **477**

Sidelight: Carry Nation

Carry Nation, a fiery temperance crusader, is best remembered for smashing up saloons with an axe. Beginning in Kansas, she traveled through the Midwest, lecturing on the evils of liquor and storming barrooms. Nation also

tried, unsuccessfully, to alert people to the dangers of smoking tobacco. "I can see," she once said, "where I have made mistakes—many of them—but they were mistakes of the head and not the heart."

478

■ Wilson's Legacy

Despite a lack of presidential leadership as Wilson's second term drew to a close, Congress and the states implemented important laws. However, Congress would not approve joining the League of Nations.

In 1920 Congress passed the Esch-Cummins Act, which turned the operation of railroads back to their owners. This statute gave the Interstate Commerce Commission almost complete power to fix rates as well as to regulate railroad financing.

Prohibition

World War I helped to add two amendments to the Constitution. Prohibition, which had made gains before the war began, made even greater advances during the war. "Hooverizing" put American citizens in the mood to sacrifice, and war needs compelled the federal government to forbid the use of grain to manufacture liquor. By January 1919, two-thirds of the states had ratified the Eighteenth Amendment, which prohibited "the manufacture, sale, or transportation" of intoxicating beverages.

The Nineteenth Amendment

The war also advanced the cause of women's rights. It was difficult to deny demands that women be allowed to vote after they had performed traditionally male jobs in factories and fields and served with courage and devotion behind the lines in Europe. On the eve of the 1920 presidential election, after decades of struggle, women gained suffrage when the Nineteenth Amendment was ratified.

A Warning

Wilson's final year and a half in office left the country virtually leaderless. The President had recovered sufficiently to transact routine business, but his energies still were focused on getting the United States into the League of Nations. Retaining a belief that the American people would not retreat from world leadership, he urged that the election of 1920 be a "great and solemn referendum" on the League issue.

The 1920 election saw Wilson's party and the League repudiated at the polls. The country wanted to turn its back to world responsibilities. In 1923, shortly before he died, Wilson warned:

> ❝ *I can predict with absolute certainty that within another generation there will be another world war if the nations of the world do not concert the method by which to prevent it.* ❞

Few people listened to Wilson's warning, however. Most Americans wanted to put their memories of war, suffering, and sacrifice behind them. "The war to end all wars" was over. The United States had done its part in making the world "safe for democracy." It was time to start enjoying the peace.

Section 4 ★ Review

Checking for Understanding

1. **Identify** Treaty of Versailles, League of Nations, Eighteenth Amendment, Nineteenth Amendment.
2. **Define** covenant, deport.
3. **List** the provisions of the Versailles treaty.
4. **Describe** the economic problems of the United States after the war.

Critical Thinking

5. **Analyzing Motives** Explain why "peace without victory" was so difficult to achieve at Versailles.

ACTIVITY

6. Prepare a list of items you would place in a time capsule to let people know in 300 years what the World War I era was like.

Answers to SECTION 4 REVIEW

1. Treaty of Versailles, 474; League of Nations, 473–474; Eighteenth Amendment, 478; Nineteenth Amendment, 478.
2. All vocabulary words are defined in the Glossary.
3. a League of Nations, Germany stripped of colonies, reparations from Germany to Allies
4. rising prices, slow business activity, low farm prices, labor unrest
5. Some of the Allies had suffered greatly during the war. They were intent on rewards, revenge, and reparations.
6. Student lists should show creativity.

Changing the Map of Europe

Part of President Wilson's peace program following World War I called for self-determination of nations. Before the war Europe was a complex mosaic, or pattern, of distinct ethnic groups. Many of these groups lived within the borders of nations dominated by other ethnic groups. Wilson believed that national boundaries should be drawn to give each ethnic population its own nation.

Other powers at the Versailles peace conference, however, had their own plans. Allied leaders wanted to weaken the Central Powers by dividing their land. Some Allies also wanted their enemies' territory for themselves.

Germany's land area was greatly reduced. Germany's colonies were given over to the Allies as mandates, territories ruled by the Allies with the approval of the League of Nations. Alsace and Lorraine were returned to France. The French also received control of the coal-rich Saar Basin for 15 years.

The Allies signed individual peace treaties with other nations, most of them centering on territorial topics that focused on partitioning the Austro-Hungarian Empire. With the end of the Hapsburg dynasty, Hungary became independent, and Austria was left a small, economically weak country.

From the ashes of the old Russian and Austro-Hungarian empires, new nations emerged in eastern Europe. Among these countries were Finland, Estonia, Lithuania, Latvia, Poland, Czechoslovakia, and Yugoslavia.

▲ THE BIG FOUR MEET AFTER WORLD WAR I

Wilson's secretary of state, Robert Lansing, noted that the boundaries created after the war were artificial and did not follow ethnic population patterns. Lansing stated that they would last only as long as dissatisfied nations were too weak to change them. He believed that when one nation became confident of its strength and began to seek to remedy these boundaries, a new war would take place. Twenty years later that became the case.

Making the Geography Connection

1. How did Wilson think national boundaries should be determined in Europe after World War I?

2. What new nations were created in eastern Europe after the war?

ACTIVITY

3. Select a European nation and create a time line showing important events in its history from 1900 to 1920.

479

Answers to Making the Connection

1. Wilson believed that nation states should be created based on ethnic population.
2. Finland, Estonia, Lithuania, Latvia, Poland, Czechoslovakia, and Yugoslavia
3. Time lines should show evidence of student research. Students might include significant cultural events as well as political events.

CHAPTER 15 ★ REVIEW

GLENCOE
TECHNOLOGY

VIDEODISC

Use the MindJogger Videoquiz to review students' knowledge.

MindJogger Videoquiz

Chapter 15
Disc 2, Side B

Available in VHS.

Using Vocabulary

Headlines should use the vocabulary correctly.

Reviewing Facts

1. based on morality and idealism; sent troops to protect democratic governments
2. Nationalism created allegiances but also fostered unrest among ethnic minorities. Countries pledged to defend their allies if attacked.
3. submarine warfare, the Zimmermann Note
4. The economy was largely under government control. Liberties were restricted.
5. drove back Germans at St. Mihiel and Sedan (also accept Château-Thierry and Verdun); navy used convoys and depth charges to thwart U-boat attacks
6. punitive to Germany and included reparations payments, loss of territory, and a League
7. Congress refused to ratify the treaty
8. Strikes were unsuccessful; the Red Scare made Americans fearful of unions; unemployment

Using Vocabulary

Imagine that you have kept a diary of events of World War I. Write headlines of three diary entries using each of the following terms in a headline.

covenant   deport
contraband   victory garden
armistice

Reviewing Facts

1. **Discuss** Wilson's foreign-policy views and how they related to his actions in Latin America.
2. **State** how nationalism and alliances created the conditions that led to World War I.
3. **Identify** two reasons the United States declared war on Germany.
4. **Cite** changes in economic and political policies that were imposed in the United States during World War I.
5. **List** two actions taken by the American military that helped win the war.
6. **Describe** the terms of the Versailles treaty.
7. **Explain** why Wilson was frustrated with Congress after the war.
8. **Summarize** the social difficulties confronting the United States after the war.

Understanding Concepts

Conflict

1. Identify the two types of nationalism that existed in Europe and explain why each was a factor in causing World War I.
2. Explain how Wilson's ideals influenced his actions and made compromise difficult.

Economic Interests

3. Explain how economic and political interests in the United States were factors in its inability to remain neutral in World War I.
4. Analyze how competing interests made the adoption of Wilson's Fourteen Points difficult.

Critical Thinking

1. **Evaluating Foreign Policy** Consider the United States's neutrality policy before entering the war. Evaluate the feasibility of this policy. Consider the events that forced the United States to abandon neutrality and enter the war.
2. **Expressing Viewpoints** During World War I the government worked to control public attitudes about the war. In your opinion, was it necessary for the government to take such actions? Explain your viewpoint.
3. **Analyzing Fine Art** Study the mural by José Clemente Orozco entitled *Revolutionists* on this page, then answer the questions that follow.
   a. What themes are illustrated?
   b. What was happening in Mexico in the early 1900s that may have inspired this work?
   c. Why would a wall mural be a good way to spread a message?

4. **Analyzing Graphs** Study the graph on page 481, then answer the questions that follow.
   a. When the United States declared war, fewer than 25,000 soldiers were prepared to fight. What was the first month that the United States had 1 million troops in the army? By

was high; prices rose; racial tension.

Understanding Concepts

1. Nationalism encouraged aggressive growth and expansion, leading to jealousy, distrust, and competition for empires. Internally,

the demands of ethnic nationality groups destabilized some nations and caused international rivalry.
2. insisted on his idealistic goals; refusal to compromise meant fewer goals reached
3. The United States was connected to Europe through trade. Blockades

affected commerce. British heritage, the fact that the Allies were democracies, and anti-German feelings hindered neutrality.
4. Allies wanted revenge, territorial rewards, and to punish Germans for the war. Americans were divided over nation's role.

what month were there 1 million American soldiers in Europe?

b. About what percentage of the United States Army was in Europe by the end of 1917? By the armistice a year later?

c. What information does this graph provide about the efficiency of America's mobilization?

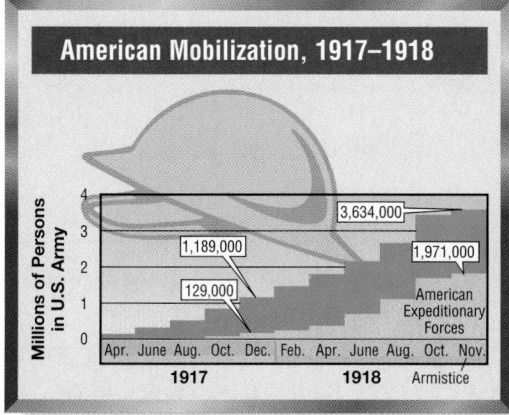

American Mobilization, 1917–1918

Millions of Persons in U.S. Army

3,634,000

1,189,000

1,971,000

129,000

American Expeditionary Forces

Apr. June Aug. Oct. Dec. | Feb. Apr. June Aug. Oct. Nov.

1917 | **1918** — Armistice

History and Geography

World War

War in Europe engulfed many nations. Review the chapter and the maps on page 465 to help you answer these questions.

1. **Movement** In which direction did forces of the Central Powers advance into Russia?

2. **Region** Which nations in South America were allied with the Central Powers? The Allies?

3. **Location** What major battles were fought in France in 1915?

Cooperative Learning Interdisciplinary Activity: Journalism

Work with a partner to write two newspaper editorials on the United States government's methods of controlling public opinion during World War I—

one supporting the government's policies and the other opposing them. Before writing, collaborate on a list of pros and cons about the government's activities, including the Espionage and Sedition acts and the Committee on Public Information. Then each of you should take opposite positions and write an editorial. When you have finished, exchange your editorials. After reading your partner's work, write a "letter to the editor" as a rebuttal to his or her position.

Practicing Skills

Interpreting a Political Map

Study the map of Europe after the war that appears on page 474, then answer the questions that follow.

1. Of these nations, which one was newly created after the war: Spain, Poland, or Syria?

2. What territories and nations were under French control?

3. Do you agree with the following assessment: Newly created nations were generally located in western Europe. Explain.

Writing ABOUT History

Using Your Journal

From your notes on attitudes during World War I and your knowledge of events in the Persian Gulf in 1990–1991, compare the general feelings during each conflict.

History and Geography

1. eastern
2. with Central Powers: none; with Allies: Brazil
3. Neuve Chapelle

Cooperative Learning

Encourage students to write a list of pros and cons about the government's activities as a basis for their editorials.

Practicing Skills

1. Poland
2. French Morocco, Tunisia, Algeria, Syria
3. Disagree; they were formed in Eastern Europe from Germany and Austria-Hungary

Writing ABOUT History

Using Your Journal

Responses will vary, but in World War I, Americans tried to remain neutral; in the Gulf War, there was little hesitation about stopping Iraqi aggression.

Chapter Bonus Test Question

Ask students: How did World War I affect the foreign policy of the United States in the years after the war? *(United States grew disillusioned with overseas involvement and wanted to stay out of world affairs.)*

Critical Thinking

1. not feasible considering U-boat activity, blockades
2. Some will argue that the suppression of civil rights never is warranted. Others will focus on issues of national security and the unity needed in a national emergency.

3. a. Students should note that the artist is focusing on the plight of the poor.
b. struggle for power that brought hardships and political chaos
c. Students might note that the dimensions of a mural provide dramatic means to illustrate ideas.

4. a. December 1917; August 1918
b. about 11 percent; about 54 percent
c. It took more than a year after the United States declared war for significant American forces to reach Europe. This belies claims of rapid mobilization.

Daily Lesson Objectives	Teacher Classroom Resources	Multimedia
SECTION 1 **The Harding Years** **1 Day** pp. 484–490 1. Describe the accomplishments of the Washington Conference. 2. Explain the provisions of the National Origins Act. 3. Describe the scandals in the Harding administration.	Reproducible Lesson Plan 16-1 Chapter Concept Mapping Activities 16-A, 16-B *Guided Reading Activity 16-1 *Vocabulary Activity 16 Supreme Court Case Study 9 Primary and Secondary Source Readings, p. 41 Political Cartoons in American History Activity 15 Workbook Activity 16-1 Reteaching Activity 16-1 *Section Quiz 16-1	Section Focus Transparency 16-1 MindJogger Videoquiz Vocabulary PuzzleMaker Testmaker The Presidents: A Picture History of Our Nation
SECTION 2 **The Coolidge Era** **1 Day** pp. 492–497 1. Discuss the changes to industry Henry Ford introduced. 2. Outline the problems of farmers and the government's response. 3. Describe the background and details of the Kellogg-Briand Pact.	Reproducible Lesson Plan 16-2 *Guided Reading Activity 16-2 Critical Thinking Skills Activity 16 Enrichment Activity 16 Chapter Map Activity 16 American Portrait 56 American Literary Heritage, p. 33 Workbook Activity 16-2 Reteaching Activity 16-2 *Section Quiz 16-2	Section Focus Transparency 16-2 Chapter 16 Map Transparency Skills Transparency 16 Testmaker The Presidents: A Picture History of Our Nation
SECTION 3 **The "Roaring Twenties"** **1 Day** pp. 500–506 1. Describe changes in women's lives during the 1920s. 2. Outline developments in the arts and education during this period.	Reproducible Lesson Plan 16-3 *Guided Reading Activity 16-3 Geography in History Activity 16 Supreme Court Case Study 18 Linking Past and Present Activity 16 Primary and Secondary Source Readings, pp. 42–43 Cooperative Learning Activity 16 Chapter 16 Skills Activity Spirit of American Art and Music, pp. 32–34 Workbook Activity 16-3 Reteaching Activity 16-3 *Section Quiz 16-3	Section Focus Transparency 16-3 Testmaker American Music: Cultural Traditions
CHAPTER REVIEW AND EVALUATION **1 Day**	Chapter 16 Test, Forms A and B Spanish Chapter 16 Summary Performance Assessment Activity 16	MindJogger Videoquiz Student Self-Test & Review Software * Chapter 16 Audiocassette Activity and Test

*Also available in Spanish

 OUT OF TIME? If time does not permit teaching the entire chapter, use the Chapter 16 Summary on pages 538–539 and the Chapter 16 audiocassette (English and Spanish) to point out the main ideas of the chapter.

A complete, 1-page lesson plan is provided for each section in the *Reproducible Lesson Plan* Booklet.

Key to Ability Levels

Teaching strategies have been coded for varying learning styles and abilities.

L1 Basic activities for all students

L2 Average activities for average to above-average students

L3 Challenging activities for above-average students

LEP Limited English Proficiency activities

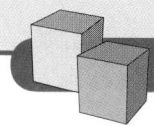

Block Schedule

Block scheduling differs from traditional class scheduling in the amount of time allotted to each period. The extended time frame provided by block scheduling affords you the opportunity to implement a greater number of research-oriented and activity-intense projects to motivate and involve your students. Activities that are particularly suited to use within the block scheduling framework are identified throughout this unit by the following designation:

✓ Performance Assessment Activity

History Through Ads The prosperity of the 1920s brought a host of new products to a public eager to buy. To encourage and attract consumers, a new industry developed: the advertising industry. Ask students to work in pairs or small groups to research ads of the period and prepare written or oral reports on their findings. For example, some might focus on foods. What do those ads tell about the American diet? The nation's favorite foods? Eating habits? Another group might explore ads for such household items as refrigerators and vacuum cleaners. Still another might focus on ads for various forms of transportation. Groups might be encouraged to compare their findings with comparable ads today. Their reports should analyze both similarities and differences.

POSSIBLE RUBRIC FEATURES
* Research Skills
* Content Information
* Organization
* Written and Visual Communication Skills
* Creativity
* Collaborative Skills

📁 For additional activities, see Performance Assessment Strategies and Activities.

TEACHER'S CORNER

NATIONAL GEOGRAPHIC SOCIETY

NATIONAL GEOGRAPHIC SOCIETY PRODUCTS AVAILABLE FROM GLENCOE

To order the following products for use with this chapter, contact your local Glencoe sales representative or call Glencoe at 1-800-334-7344:

* *The Presidents: A Picture History of Our Nation* (CD-ROM)
* *GTV: A Geographic Perspective on American History* (Videodisc)
* *GTV: The American People: Fabric of a Nation* (Videodisc)

ADDITIONAL NATIONAL GEOGRAPHIC SOCIETY PRODUCTS

To order the following products for use with this chapter, call National Geographic Society at 1-800-368-2728:

* *The American Presidency* (Filmstrip)
* *Decades of History: The 20th Century—The Early Years* (Filmstrip)
* *The United States as a World Power: From the 1890s to the 1970s* (Filmstrip)
* *Building a Nation: The Story of Immigration* (Filmstrip)
* *Immigration: The Triumph of Hope* (Video)
* *The Superliners: Twilight of an Era* (Video)

GLENCOE TECHNOLOGY

VIDEODISC

Use the Chapter 16 MindJogger Videoquiz to preview the content of this chapter.

MindJogger Videoquiz

Chapter 16
Disc 2, Side B

 Available in VHS.

Recording Journal Notes
Suggest students categorize their notes under such headings as music, dance, art, poetry, fiction, nonfiction.

Linking Across
TIME

Reflecting the sophisticated spirit of the 1920s that many Americans aspired to, magazines such as *Vanity Fair* and *Smart Set*, known as "highbrow" publications, were founded. Both ultimately faded (although *Vanity Fair* was revived in the 1980s). What did not disappear was *Reader's Digest*, with its "digested" articles and positive outlook, founded in 1921.

CHAPTER 16
★★★
The Decade of Normalcy
1920–1928

▶ THE CLOCHE, POPULAR WOMAN'S HAT OF THE 1920S

Setting the Scene

Focus

The decade that followed World War I differed considerably from the Progressive years that came before it. Voters turned to conservative leaders who promised to turn the country away from European affairs and inward to "normalcy." For many Americans this shift meant preserving the values of rural America and enjoying prosperity. For others it meant a fascination with a dazzling new assortment of consumer goods, entertainment, and changing fashions.

Concepts to Understand

★ Why shifts in government policies and increased production resulted in **economic change**

★ How **social change** affected the arts, the role of women, and minorities

Read to Discover . . .

★ ways United States involvement in international relations changed following World War I.

★ what signs of social tension were evident in the 1920s.

Journal Notes

What was the Harlem Renaissance? Jot down details about it as you read the chapter.

CULTURAL
- **1920** *First commercial radio broadcast is aired*
- **1922** *Lincoln Memorial is dedicated*
- **1925** *John Scopes trial over teaching evolution in Dayton, Tennessee, occurs*

| 1920 | 1923 |

POLITICAL
- **1920** *Warren Harding is elected*
- **1921** *Washington Conference is held*
- **1923** *Calvin Coolidge becomes President after Harding's death*

482 UNIT 5 Crusade and Disillusion: 1914–1932

➕ **EXTRA CREDIT PROJECT**

The Sacco-Vanzetti Case Explain to students that a negative side of the 1920s was the Red Scare, which reflected fears and prejudices often directed at immigrants. One episode was the trial and execution of Nicola Sacco and Bartolomeo Vanzetti, Italian immigrants and confessed anarchists accused of robbery and murder. The Sacco-Vanzetti case attracted worldwide attention. Interested students might research the case. Have them share their findings with the class and offer evidence to support their points of view about the case. **L2**

History AND ART

Dance Hall
by Thomas Hart Benton, 1930

Thomas Hart Benton excelled at mural painting, concentrating on Midwestern legend, history, and daily life.

▲ TROMBONE USED IN JAZZ GROUP, 1920S

- **1927** *First "talking" motion picture,* The Jazz Singer, *is released*

- **1929** *Chicago mobsters murder seven rival gang members in the St. Valentine's Day Massacre*

1926	1929

- **1926** *United States intervenes in Nicaragua*
- **1928** *Kellogg-Briand Pact is negotiated*

- **1929** *Herbert Hoover becomes President*

 Performance Assessment

Refer to the Performance Assessment Activity in the Planning Guide on page 482b. When the students have finished their reports about ads in the 1920s, have them present their findings to the class. Allow time for class discussion and feedback.

☞ Use Performance Assessment Activity 16 as an additional assessment technique.

Concept Mapping Activity

On the chalkboard, reproduce the following generalization and concepts map, and have students copy it in their notebooks.

Rapid social change and political conservatism mark the 1920s.

Social Change	Economic Change

☞ To reinforce the two chapter concepts, use Concept Mapping Strategies and Activities 16-A and 16-B.

☞ Assign Chapter Concepts Transparency Activities 16-A, 16-B.

History AND ART

Thomas Hart Benton was one of the leaders of regionalism, or art based on depictions of regional themes. Benton celebrated the vital and energetic men and women who tamed the frontier and built new towns and cities. In many of his murals, he divided one scene from another with arbitrary borders. The change in scale and his use of overlapping images give the effect of a photo montage, a picture made by combining several different images. Educated at the Art Institute of Chicago, Benton began his career as a cartoonist for the *Joplin* (Missouri) *American* in 1906.

483

FOCUS

Bellringer

📙 🗂 Before taking roll, project Section Focus Transparency 16-1 or hand out Section Focus Transparency Activity 16-1. Have students answer the questions. Discuss student responses.

Motivating Activity

Warren G. Harding noted that "America's present need is not heroics but healing, not nostrum but normalcy, not revolution but restoration...." Ask students to put the main idea of Harding's statement into their own words. (*Americans are tired of action; they want to rest, to remain unbothered.*) Ask students to consider Harding's assessment as they read Section 1 and decide if they agree with his conclusion.

Vocabulary Precheck

Ask students to define each of the "Key Terms." Have a volunteer consult the dictionary for any unfamiliar words. **L1, LEP**

🎧 Use the Vocabulary PuzzleMaker Software to create a crossword puzzle. **L1**

🗂 Assign Vocabulary Activity 16.

★★★★★★★★★★★★★★★★★★★★★★★★★★★★★★★★★★★★★★

The Harding Years

Setting the Scene

Section Focus

The internationalism of Woodrow Wilson was reversed under the administrations of the next three Presidents— all Republicans. The party's slogan "America First" hailed the country's unparalleled prosperity, characterized by remarkable achievements in the field of business.

◀ **1920 REPUBLICAN CAMPAIGN PIN**

Objectives

After studying this section, you should be able to

★ describe the accomplishments of the Washington Conference.

★ explain the provisions of the National Origins Act.

★ describe the scandals in the Harding administration.

Key Terms

reparation, technological unemployment, open shop, welfare capitalism

---

The end of the war created new problems for the United States. After the dismantling of the War Industries Board, business lost the profitable military contracts of the war years. Four million recently demobilized service men and women needed work. In 1920 and 1921, unemployment soared, as did prices. Labor unrest was reflected in the United States Steel strike and the Boston police strike of 1919.

■ The Election of 1920

Several prominent men sought the Republican nomination in 1920, the prize going to a dark horse, Ohio senator Warren G. Harding. Harding's running mate was Massachusetts governor Calvin Coolidge. To oppose Harding, the Democrats chose Ohio governor James M. Cox, a loyal Wilson

supporter. Cox's running mate was Franklin D. Roosevelt, who, like his distant cousin, Theodore, had served as assistant secretary of the navy. The strategy chosen by Cox was as Wilson desired—to campaign for the League of Nations.

The Republicans were divided on the issue. Harding said he favored "a society of free nations" to keep peace. Most prominent Republicans took this to mean that Harding supported their decision to join the League, but anti-League Republicans seemed certain that Harding opposed it. Thus, as journalist Walter Lippmann pointed out, Harding received support from "men and women who thought a Republican victory would kill the League, plus those who thought it was the most practical way to procure the League."

The election was an overwhelming Republican victory. Harding carried every northern and western state and even broke

UNIT 5 Crusade and Disillusion: 1914–1932

Classroom Resources for SECTION 1

Blackline Masters:
🗂 Reproducible Lesson Plan 16-1
🗂 Guided Reading Activity 16-1
🗂 Vocabulary Activity 16
🗂 Supreme Court Case Study 9
🗂 Primary and Secondary Source
 Readings, p. 41

🗂 Political Cartoons in American
 History Activity 15
🗂 Workbook Activity 16-1
🗂 Reteaching Activity 16-1
🗂 Section Quiz 16-1

Transparencies:
📙 Section Focus Transparency
 16-1

Multimedia:
💿 MindJogger Videoquiz
💿 Vocabulary PuzzleMaker
💿 Testmaker
💿 The Presidents: A Picture
 History of Our Nation

the Democratic Solid South by carrying Tennessee. A key to the election results may be found in the President's reassuring slogan—"a return to normalcy"—coined by Harding during his campaign. It suggested a return to "the good old days," to the conditions that prevailed before the shocks of World War I.

Postwar Foreign Policy

After his election, Harding announced that his administration would not lead the United States into the League of Nations "by the side door, back door, or cellar door." The United States was too powerful, too economically interconnected, and too widely involved in world affairs to retreat into isolationism, however, and participated actively in many League conferences.

War Debt

One international problem that demanded a solution was $10.3 billion in Allied war debts owed to the United States for food and war materials. The debtor nations had difficulty meeting their payments. They argued that high American tariffs had closed the United States market to their imports and slowed their economic recovery. Furthermore, debtor nations argued, because the United States had lost fewer people in the war than the other Allies, it should be willing to pay more of the financial cost. The United States government, however, took the position that the Allies had gained territory and **reparations,** or payments for damages, as a result of the victory while the United States had claimed no reward, and that to cancel these debts would destroy faith in international agreements.

Eventually the United States made agreements with 17 of the 20 debtor nations, reducing the debts by 30 to 80 percent. Most of the money the Allies paid actually came from Germany. To pay its reparations, Germany obtained private bank loans from other countries—especially the United States.

The Washington Conference

At the time of the Harding administration, the United States, Great Britain, and Japan were experiencing costly and competitive naval buildups that originated during the war. There was also friction in East Asia, caused mainly by conflicts over commercial rights in China and by Western suspicion of Japan's recent territorial gains. After World War I, Japan had acquired all of Germany's Pacific islands north of the equator as well as the Chinese port of Kiaochow (jee•OW•JOH). Japan also treated the rest of the Chinese province of Shantung as its own.

In the hope of resolving these problems, the administration hosted an eight-nation conference in Washington, D.C. The negotiations, which lasted from November 1921 to February 1922, led to three important treaties.

The Four-Power Treaty

The Four-Power Treaty, signed by the United States, Great Britain, France, and Japan, was an agreement among the four

 **NOT ROOM FOR BOTH** By showing the League of Nations agreement trying to replace the Constitution in ruling the nation, this artist expressed concern that joining the League would deprive the United States of the freedom to set its own policies. *What role did the 1920 election play in resolving this issue?*

TEACH
Guided Practice
Supporting Generalizations Have students write examples to support the following generalization:

The widespread desire for peace and quiet following World War I influenced leaders of the United States to enter into unrealistic treaties that were doomed to fail. **L2**

📁 Assign Guided Reading Activity 16-1.

Visualizing (H)istory Discuss with students the United States's refusal to join the League of Nations. Remind them that the United States joined the United Nations after World War II. Has this interfered with U.S. foreign policy? **Answer to Caption:** Republicans won the election and rejected membership in the League.

NATIONAL GEOGRAPHIC SOCIETY

 CD-ROM

The Presidents: A Picture History of Our Nation

Have students select President Harding from the main menu and the category GAME. Suggest they learn more about Harding by playing the presidential game with a partner.

Special Needs Activity

Study Strategy Remind students that some questions require factual information (who, what, when, where). This information is directly accessible by finding facts within the text. Have students turn to the subsection Scandals Among Harding's Advisers. Ask them to create one question of each type, such as: Who was involved in the worst scandal under Harding? What was the name of the scandal? When did it happen? Where is Teapot Dome located? **LEP, L1**

Independent Practice

Analyzing Statistics

Have students construct a double bar graph to show the effects of the immigration quota acts of the 1920s. Give students these figures: immigrants from northern/western Europe, average per year from 1907 to 1914—183,301; Act of 1921—138,551; Act of 1924—203,346; Act of 1929—114,469; immigrants from southern/eastern Europe, average per year from 1907 to 1914—474,662; Act of 1921—341,655; Act of 1924—99,487; Act of 1929—27,046.

When students have completed their graphs, ask them to form a generalization about the statistics. *(From 1907 to 1914, there were almost three times as many immigrants from southern/eastern Europe as from northern/western Europe. By 1929 there were about five times fewer immigrants from southern/eastern Europe as from northern/western Europe. Accept comparable generalizations.)* **L2**

Using Graphs

Answer: Membership declined as unions seemed less necessary to workers.

Graph Skills Practice

Suggest students research statistics for various groups and create a similar graph for each group. How do the earnings of each group compare with the overall earnings of all workers?

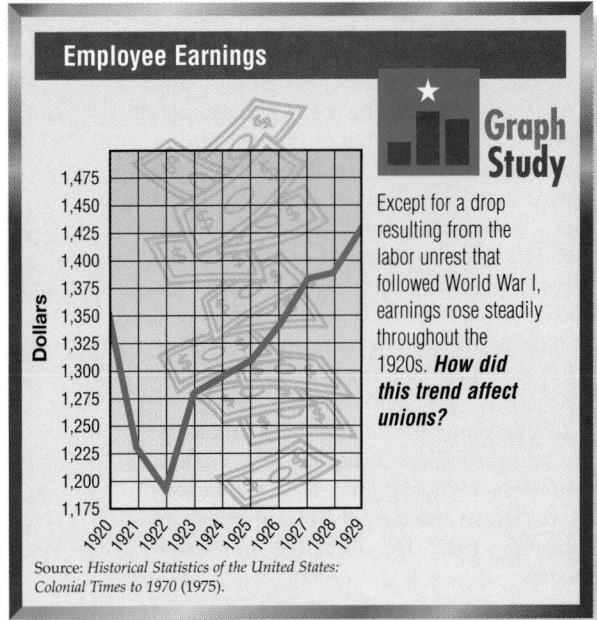

Employee Earnings

Graph Study

Except for a drop resulting from the labor unrest that followed World War I, earnings rose steadily throughout the 1920s. **How did this trend affect unions?**

Source: *Historical Statistics of the United States: Colonial Times to 1970* (1975).

great powers to respect one another's Pacific holdings. In case of disagreements or a threat from another nation, the signers also agreed to confer "fully and frankly."

The Five-Power Treaty

Under the Five-Power Treaty, the 5 naval powers of the United States, Great Britain, Japan, France, and Italy agreed to freeze their navies at 1921 levels and thus avoid the financial strain of further naval buildups. The signers further agreed to halt the building of large warships for 10 years; some ships under construction would even be scrapped. The treaty also included an agreement by the United States and Great Britain not to build new fortifications or naval bases in the western Pacific. This provision gave Japan control of nearby waters in exchange for agreeing to remain at inferior naval strength.

The Nine-Power Treaty

The Nine-Power Treaty—signed by the United States, France, Great Britain, Japan, Italy, Belgium, China, the Netherlands, and Portugal—put the "Open Door" China

policies of John Hay into a treaty. The signers agreed to preserve equal commercial rights in China and to refrain from "taking advantage of conditions in China to seek special rights or privileges." Following this policy, Japan soon withdrew from the province of Shantung.

Although the immediate results of the Washington Conference were encouraging, the conference failed to reach an agreement limiting military forces on land. Moreover, the treaties had notable shortcomings. Under the Five-Power Treaty, naval powers could still build unlimited numbers of smaller combat vessels, such as submarines and destroyers. In addition, the Four-Power Treaty did not commit the signers to active military defense of their allies; indeed, such a commitment might have been unacceptable to the United States. The Nine-Power Treaty made no provision for enforcement of the Open Door policy.

■ Business Normalcy

From the start, Harding's handling of domestic problems made it apparent that normalcy meant a general retreat from government regulation of business. Although the federal government actively aided businesses by levying protective tariffs, promoting foreign trade, and breaking strikes, its policy in other matters was laissez-faire. There was little effort to enforce the antitrust laws that regulated business mergers. Reflecting the dominant feeling of the time, regulatory agencies such as the Interstate Commerce Commission and the Federal Trade Commission were largely unsympathetic to policies restricting private enterprise.

The Fordney-McCumber Act

The new trend was immediately seen in the tariff laws. In 1922 Congress passed the Fordney-McCumber Act, raising import duties to high levels. This protected agriculture as well as certain young industries, such as rayon, china, and the optical-glass and chemical products for which the United States seized patents from Germany during

Sidelight: Presidential Gaffes

President Harding's linguistics were a source of both laughter and embarrassment to Americans. The word *normalcy* was his own mispronunciation of the word *normality* and did not exist until he coined it. Democrat William McAdoo, Woodrow Wilson's son-in-law, said

the President's speech was like "an army of pompous phrases moving over the landscape in search of an idea." Harding himself said he liked to *bloviate,* a word meaning "to speak bombastically and at length."

the war. Because the Fordney-McCumber Act authorized the President to raise or lower duties by as much as 50 percent, rates often went still higher.

Creating the Bureau of the Budget

Because World War I had raised the national debt from less than $10 per person to over $200, the Harding and Coolidge administrations attempted to lower this burden by making the government more fiscally responsible. In 1921 Congress created the Bureau of the Budget in the Treasury Department.

The efforts of the Bureau of the Budget to introduce savings were especially supported by Coolidge, who felt so strongly about curbing the nation's expenditures that he devoted serious attention to routine federal purchases such as lead pencils and typewriter ribbons. After the Washington Conference, there was no threat of war on the horizon, and even military expenditures were greatly lowered.

Changes in Taxation

Andrew Mellon, secretary of the treasury from 1921 to 1932 and a wealthy man, believed that heavy taxes on excess profits "penalized success" and discouraged investment in productive enterprise. At Mellon's insistence, Congress abolished the wartime excise and excess profits taxes and reduced tax rates on incomes by nearly two-thirds. Even with these cuts, the nation's prosperity produced enough tax revenue to reduce the national debt by $8 billion between 1921 and 1929.

■ Labor and Labor Unions

Between 1921 and 1928, the average annual wage for workers rose from $1,227 to $1,384. However, new manufacturing caused **technological unemployment**—jobs lost when occupations become obsolete. Although people replaced by machines usually found jobs elsewhere, the transition was sometimes difficult. Not only were they often forced to leave home to find employment, but they also frequently lost the benefit of long years spent learning a particular skill.

The introduction of jukeboxes and sound films, to cite an extreme example, caused widespread unemployment among musicians. Although the assembly line lowered the costs of production, many laborers could not stand the monotony and nervous tension caused by working at a speed set by the machine.

Union Decline

The "prosperity decade" saw labor unions decline in strength. Even the American Federation of Labor, one of the largest organizations, had difficulty holding its members in the face of antiunion activities. Employers joined to promote the **open shop**—a shop where workers do not have to

Visualizing History

▲ **KKK** Members of the Ku Klux Klan parade down Pennsylvania Avenue in Washington, D.C., in September 1926. The KKK spread from the South to gain national power in the 1920s. *How did the Klan as well as many other Americans react to increased immigration after World War I?*

CURRICULUM CONNECTION

Economics The individual American's portion of the national debt increased to $200 after World War I. In 1990 the estimated liability for each taxpayer because of the savings and loan scandal (separate from the amount owed on the national debt) was $3,000.

Visualizing History At its height in 1923, the Klan claimed a membership of 4 million. The Klan was politically powerful in Texas, Oregon, Georgia, Oklahoma, Alabama, and Indiana. After 1924 membership began to decline when corruption among its leaders was exposed. **Answer to Caption:** They discriminated against immigrants; the government passed restrictive immigration laws.

Did You Know?

In contrast to Harding's material excess, Vice President Calvin Coolidge's frugality was legendary. His concern for waste continued when he reached the White House. He expected small change from servants sent out to buy newspapers. He also inspected the White House iceboxes and criticized menus that appeared extravagant.

Critical Thinking Activity

Analyzing Viewpoints Have students analyze the financial philosophy of Andrew Mellon, secretary of the treasury. Mellon believed that the wealthy should not be penalized in the form of taxes on excess profits, inheritances, and large incomes. Such taxes would discourage investment, the effects of which would "trickle down" to improve the lot of all. Students may either write individual arguments supporting or challenging this philosophy or divide into groups and debate the question. **L2**

Linking Across
TIME

As in the 1920s, some Americans today resent recent immigrants. In California, where Hispanics make up more than one-fourth of the state's population, resentment is caused by the misguided belief that Hispanics refuse to learn to speak English. A recent study showed, however, that 90 percent of Hispanic children do speak English and that 25 percent of the children speak no Spanish at all.

Graph Study

Answer: 1925

Graph Skills Practice
Suggest students work in pairs or groups to research immigration in the 1980s and create a bar graph similar to this one showing the areas from which immigrants came.

Assign Supreme Court Case Studies 9: *Gitlow* v. *New York* (1925)

join a union. Labeled the "American Plan," in practice the open shop meant a shop closed to union members. To further reduce the power of unions, companies promoted **welfare capitalism,** a system to make employees feel more a part of the business by enabling them to buy shares of stock, by instituting profit sharing, and by providing such fringe benefits as medical care, retirement pensions, and recreational facilities. Moreover, wages and conditions improved somewhat during the 1920s. With some improvement in their standards of living and the relative weakness of unions, striking seemed pointless to many workers.

Strikebreaking

Although Herbert Hoover, secretary of commerce, persuaded President Harding to make a successful personal appeal to the leaders of the steel industry to abandon the 12-hour day, the federal government was usually on the side of the employers. Thus Attorney General Harry M. Daugherty helped to break railroad and coal strikes in 1922 by obtaining injunctions that prohibited every conceivable union activity, including

picketing, making public statements to the press, and jeering at strikebreakers. In 1919 the Indiana State Guard—and eventually federal troops—protected strikebreakers at United States Steel. In addition, the Supreme Court continually whittled away at the protections that unions thought they had secured by the Clayton Act of 1914. Once again, injunctions were freely used to stop strikes and boycotts.

■ Restricting Immigration

In the decade before World War I, approximately 1 million persons a year came to live in the United States, over two-thirds of these from countries in southern and eastern Europe. To slow down this tide of immigration, Congress passed in 1917 an act requiring a literacy test, designed to exclude large numbers of immigrants.

The act, however, had little effect. New immigrants congregated in such cities as New York and Chicago, where opportunities for employment were greatest. Established immigrants resented the new immigrants' increasing political power. Even more, they

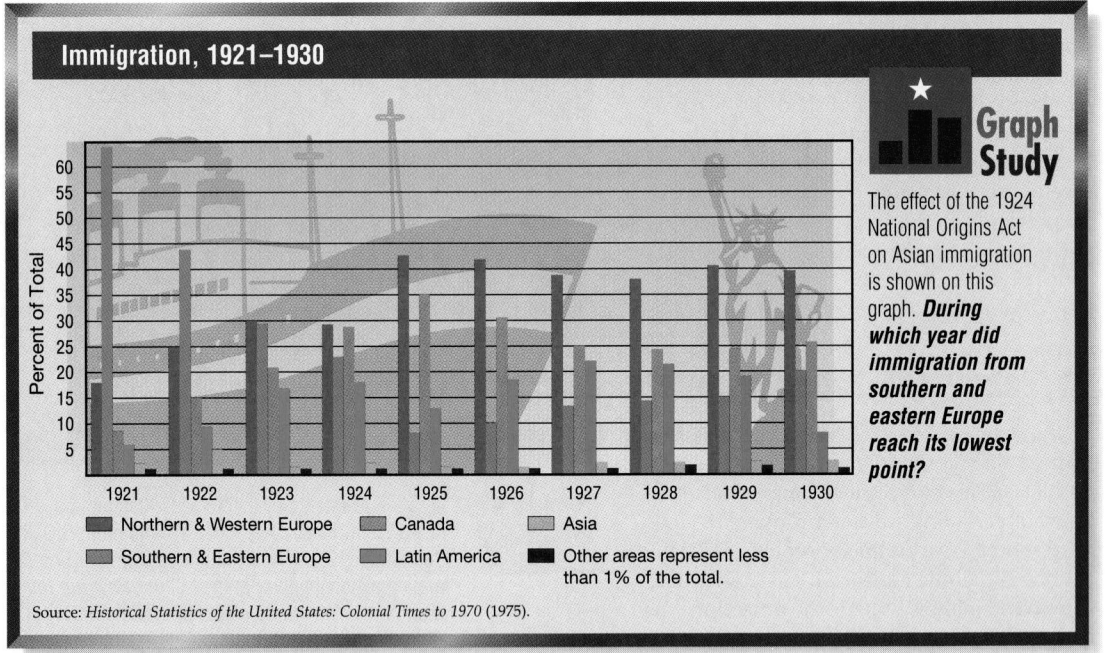

Immigration, 1921–1930

Graph Study

The effect of the 1924 National Origins Act on Asian immigration is shown on this graph. *During which year did immigration from southern and eastern Europe reach its lowest point?*

Legend:
- Northern & Western Europe
- Southern & Eastern Europe
- Canada
- Latin America
- Asia
- Other areas represent less than 1% of the total.

Source: *Historical Statistics of the United States: Colonial Times to 1970* (1975).

Cooperative Learning Activity

The Immigration Acts Divide the class into five groups. Have each group represent one of the following: a member of a conservative labor union, a resident of a new immigrant community, an older immigrant from northern or western Europe, an employer of immigrants, and a Japanese businessman. Give each group time to prepare a speech about the immigration acts of the 1920s. Then have each group choose a representative to deliver the speech giving that group's viewpoint about immigration. Conduct a class discussion on the pros and cons of each argument. **L3**

feared that the newcomers, most of whom were Catholic, would overthrow traditional Protestant values. Conservative labor unions were angered by the willingness of poor immigrants to work for very low wages. Employers, who had previously favored unrestricted immigration as a means of hiring cheap labor, now came to fear that the new immigrants were radicals who would fight for a communist revolution.

The National Origins Act

During and after World War I, feeling against "hyphenated-Americans" was stimulated by anti-German hysteria, by the Red Scare, and by the Ku Klux Klan. When immigrants came to the United States, fleeing their war-torn countries in the hopes of finding wealth and opportunity, Congress took quick action. In 1921 Harding signed the Emergency Quota Act, which cut the number of people admitted to the United States. According to this act, only 3 percent of the total number of people in any national group already living in the United States in 1910 would be admitted during a single year.

Three years later the National Origins Act made restriction a permanent policy. This 1924 law temporarily reduced the quota still further. It also provided that after 1927 a total of only 150,000 immigrants would be admitted to the United States per year, their nationalities apportioned on the basis of the 1920 census. This meant that more than 85 percent of the new immigrants would be from Europe—mainly from Great Britain, Ireland, Germany, and Scandinavia.

The intention of the National Origins Act was clearly to discriminate against certain nationalities and races. This became even more apparent when immigrants from Asia and Africa were either assigned very small quotas or barred entirely. Japanese immigration was completely excluded. The Japanese regarded the law as a national insult, and the day it went into effect was declared a day of public mourning and national humiliation in Japan. The incident discredited moderate Japanese politicians who sought to cooperate with the United States and advanced the cause of reactionary militarists in Japan.

 **History AND ART** ▲ *THE PASSION OF SACCO AND VANZETTI* by Ben Shahn, 1932 Many Americans rallied to the defense of Nicola Sacco and Bartolomeo Vanzetti. *Why did this case arouse controversy?*

Sacco and Vanzetti

An event that for many came to symbolize mistrust of immigrants in the United States was the trial of Nicola Sacco and Bartolomeo Vanzetti. These two Italian immigrants and anarchists were accused in 1921 of killing two men during a robbery in Massachusetts. They were convicted, but

History AND ART

The artist Ben Shahn took many of his subjects from the darker side of life. He was particularly interested in people who were victims of injustices. **Answer to Caption:** Many thought the men had not received a fair trial and were convicted because they were immigrants and radicals.

Linking Across TIME

Scandals in presidential administrations might seem commonplace in contemporary times, but in the 1920s they were rare enough to cause a great deal of concern, and for those involved, a sense of shame and responsibility. Albert Fall was the first cabinet member to serve time in jail. Jesse Smith, a friend of Attorney General Harry Daugherty, committed suicide after it was discovered that he had arranged settlements between the Department of Justice and law violators. Charles Cramer, legal adviser of the Veterans' Bureau, also committed suicide after he was involved in misuse of the bureau's funds.

📁 Assign Primary and Secondary Source Readings p. 41: "What Harding Was Like" by Alice Roosevelt Longworth.

Sidelight: Religion and Business

The Puritan link between being accepted by God and success in business surfaced again in the 1920s. Bruce Barton, who founded the phenomenally successful advertising agency Batten, Barton, Durstine, and Osborn, claimed that Christians were obligated to build businesses. His book *The Man Nobody Knows* presented Jesus as a businessman. Barton's favorite quote from the Bible was Jesus' response to his parents when they found him in the temple, "Wist [Know] ye not that I must be about my Father's business?" The fact that Jesus was referring to spiritual affairs did not seem to bother Barton. In 1936 Barton was elected to Congress.

ASSESS
Check Understanding
Assign Section 1 Review as homework or an in-class activity.

Evaluate
Assign Section Quiz 16-1 or use the Testmaker to create a customized quiz.

Reteach
Have students write a paragraph or two describing how the issues in the 1920 presidential campaign, as well as the election outcome, reflected the attitudes of Americans following World War I.

Have students complete Reteaching Activity 16-1.

Assign Workbook Activity 16-1.

Enrich
Assign Political Cartoons in American History Activity 15.

CLOSE
Ask students to think about the "normality" or *normalcy* Americans wanted after World War I. Have them write their definition of *normalcy* and give examples of personal and political behavior that they believe fits their definition.

many thought they never received a fair trial. It was believed that the trial judge was prejudiced against the defendants because of their ethnic backgrounds and political beliefs. For years attempts were made to obtain a retrial, but in 1927 Sacco and Vanzetti were executed. In his final statement in court, Vanzetti continued to maintain his innocence of the crime, saying:

> ❝ . . . [M]y conviction is that I have suffered for things that I am guilty of. I am suffering because I am a radical and indeed I am a radical; I have suffered because I was an Italian and indeed I am an Italian. . . . ❞

The question of the guilt or innocence of Sacco and Vanzetti has never been answered with certainty. Their trial made many people think critically about the American justice system, however.

■ Scandals Among Harding's Advisers

Although President Harding was personally honest, there was more corruption in his administration than in any previous one. Harding's poker-playing friends, known as "the Ohio Gang," used their ties to the President and the attorney general to sell government appointments, pardons, and immunity from prosecution.

Less than 18 months after Harding took office, his administration was racked by scandal. It was discovered that Charles R. Forbes, the director of the Veterans Bureau and a close friend of Harding, had made illegal deals that had netted him hundreds of thousands of dollars in commissions. When this fact became public, the attorney for the Bureau, who was also involved, shot himself. His suicide was closely followed by that of Jesse Smith, a close friend of Attorney General Harry M. Daugherty, who himself was later accused of corruption while in office.

The worst scandal involved Harding's secretary of the interior, Albert B. Fall, who secretly leased to private interests some oil lands, which had been set aside for the navy at Teapot Dome, Wyoming, and Elk Hills, California. In return Fall received bribes totaling more than $300,000. Eventually the Senate investigated the Teapot Dome scandal, and Secretary Fall went to prison.

When Harding learned what was going on, he complained privately that he had been betrayed. He said that he had no troubles with his enemies, but his friends—they were a different story. In the summer of 1923, Harding traveled to Alaska, deeply concerned and depressed over the scandals in his administration. On his return he became severely ill. He died on August 2, shortly before news of the scandals broke to the public.

Section 1 ★ Review

Checking for Understanding
1. **Identify** Fordney-McCumber Tariff, Washington Conference, National Origins Act.

2. **Define** reparation, technological unemployment, open shop, welfare capitalism.

3. **Cite** two foreign-policy problems the United States faced after the war and explain their significance.

Critical Thinking
4. **Analyzing Changes** Explain why the election of Harding fit America's mood and why this mood had changed since 1917.

ACTIVITY
5. Select one of the years shown on the graph on page 488. Display the information for that year in a circle graph.

Answers to SECTION 1 REVIEW

1. Fordney-McCumber Tariff, 486; Washington Conference, 485; National Origins Act, 489
2. All vocabulary words are defined in the Glossary.
3. collecting war debts, maintaining world peace
4. During the war Americans saw the need to intervene in Europe. After the war Americans wanted peace and a return to the "good old days." Harding's noncontroversial style and his "normalcy" pledge reflected these feelings.
5. Circle graphs will vary. Ask students to explain the steps necessary to complete the activity.

Household Technology

". . . [T]he wise woman," proclaimed a 1920s electric company ad, "delegates to electricity all that electricity can do." Inventions such as electric irons, vacuum cleaners, and washing machines changed the lives of urban middle-class housewives in the decade of the 1920s. But these devices changed only the way women spent their time, not how much time they spent.

One study revealed that upper middle-class homemakers employed only half as many full-time servants as their mothers had. These women did work their mothers had hired others to do. Although some women found that laborsaving devices gave them more leisure time, others said that the dirt and soot caused by automobile traffic and nearby factories made their homes dirtier than those of the previous generation. Most of the women surveyed said they spent less time on housework than their mothers, but parenting and other demands had increased. "So many things our mothers didn't know about, we feel that we ought to do for our children," said one woman.

The technological innovations were developed by such creative individuals as Charles Steinmetz. Steinmetz gained recognition in electrical science, and General Electric offered him a job with an excellent salary and superb research facilities.

Known as the "Electrical Genius of GE," Steinmetz made contributions to science and science engineering that sped the nation into an age of electricity. More than 200 patents flowed from his work, which included the study, explanation, and harnessing of alternating current. Before Steinmetz, it had been impossible to transmit electricity more than 3 miles without using multiple generators.

▲ VACUUM CLEANER ADVERTISEMENT, 1920S

Making the Science Connection

1. What laborsaving devices aided American housewives during the 1920s?

2. What benefits were derived from the work of Charles Steinmetz?

ACTIVITY

3. Find a photo or drawing of a household innovation that in your opinion has provided the greatest benefits. Write a paragraph explaining your reasons for choosing that particular item.

491

Answers to Making the Connection

1. electric iron, vacuum cleaners, washing machines

2. About 200 patents flowed from his work on the alternating current. Now it was possible to transmit electricity more than 3 miles without using multiple generators.

3. Paragraphs will vary but should include valid reasons for choosing the item.

TEACH

Electric irons, vacuum cleaners, and washing machines had been invented earlier, but they came into widespread use in the 1920s because of the assembly-line technique developed during this decade. By 1926 nearly 16 million homes had been wired for electric lighting. Almost 80 percent of these homes had electric irons, 37 percent had vacuum cleaners, and more than 25 percent had washing machines, toasters, or fans. The following items made their first appearance during this decade: electric food disposal (1920), self-winding wristwatch (1922), spin dryer (1924), automatic potato peeler (1925), embossed and inlaid linoleum (1925), and pop-up toaster (1926).

Ask students to consider the appliances in their homes and decide which are the most time-saving. Ask them if they think modern Americans need all the appliances they can get. L1

CURRICULUM CONNECTION

Science The technological innovations enjoyed by American households in the 1920s were made possible in part by an increase in the availability of electricity. Before 1914, 20 percent of American homes had electricity. By the end of the 1920s, 70 percent of households enjoyed electric power.

FOCUS

Bellringer

 Before taking roll, project Section Focus Transparency 16-2 or hand out Section Focus Transparency Activity 16-2. Have students answer the questions. Discuss student responses.

Motivating Activity

Tell students that Coolidge was firmly convinced that government should be run by businessmen for businessmen. As students read Section 2, ask them to note how Coolidge's philosophy was put into action. **L1**

Vocabulary Precheck

Ask students to speculate on the meaning of "domestic market." Then have them check their guesses by finding the definition in the student text. **LEP**

CD-ROM

The Presidents: A Picture History of Our Nation
Have students select TIME LINE from the main menu. Suggest they write headlines noting major events during President Coolidge's term in office.

SECTION 2

★★★★★★★★★★★★★★★★★★★★★★★★★★★★★★★★

The Coolidge Era

Setting the Scene

Section Focus

When awakened to hear that Harding had died, Vice President Coolidge was at his boyhood home in Vermont. His father, a justice of the peace, administered the oath of office in the flickering light of a kerosene lamp. This homey scene typified the small-town values that the new President held—values which many Americans still shared and cherished.

Objectives

After studying this section, you should be able to

★ discuss the changes to industry Henry Ford introduced.

★ outline the problems of farmers and the government's response.

★ describe the background and details of the Kellogg-Briand Pact.

Key Term

domestic market

◀ **AUTOMOBILE ADVERTISEMENT, 1920S**

𝒞oolidge had traits often associated with small-town America. He was conservative, cautious, and given to few words. In public speeches and magazine articles, he preached the old-fashioned virtues of honesty, thrift, and hard work. His philosophy of government was simple: economy and laissez-faire. To take as little action as possible was with Coolidge almost a principle of life; he once said, "Four-fifths of all our troubles in this life would disappear if we would only sit down and keep still."

■ The Election of 1924

By 1924 the scandals of the Harding administration had surfaced, hurting the Republican party. This presented the Democratic party with a ready-made issue for the presidential campaign.

The Democrats Are Divided

The Democrats threw away their chances for victory at their national convention, however. The party was deeply divided over two issues: Prohibition—which the rural regions favored and the cities opposed—and more importantly, the Ku Klux Klan.

This secret society, which took its name and ritual from the Southern organization of Reconstruction times, was designed to intimidate African Americans, Catholics, Jews, immigrants, and "foreign ideas," such as the League of Nations. By the mid-1920s the Klan had become a force in American politics, despite its willingness to use terror and violence.

At the 1924 Democratic convention, the rivals for the nomination were William G. McAdoo of California and Governor Alfred E. Smith of New York. McAdoo

Classroom Resources for SECTION 2

Blackline Masters:
- Reproducible Lesson Plan 16-2
- Guided Reading Activity 16-2
- Critical Thinking Skills Activity 16
- Enrichment Activity 16
- Chapter Map Activity 16
- Workbook Activity 16-2
- Reteaching Activity 16-2

- Section Quiz 16-2

Transparencies:
- Section Focus Transparency 16-2
- Chapter 16 Map Transparency
- Skills Transparency 16

Multimedia:
- Testmaker
- The Presidents: A Picture History of Our Nation

favored Prohibition and received most of his support from the western and southern regions of the United States. Governor Smith was a Roman Catholic and opponent of Prohibition. His strongest backing came mostly from urban areas of the Northeast. Smith's supporters wanted an outright condemnation of the Ku Klux Klan, a move that Southern and Western delegates blocked.

The two candidates were deadlocked for so long that the cowboy-humorist Will Rogers suggested that the eventual nominee might be born at the convention. By the time a compromise candidate—John W. Davis of West Virginia—was nominated on the one-hundred-and-third ballot, the Democrats had lost all chance of winning the election.

The Republicans Win

The Republicans campaigned on the slogan "Keep Cool with Coolidge"; the way to keep business thriving, they said, was not to "rock the boat" but to keep in power the party that favored business. This strategy was successful. In an election that attracted only half the eligible voters to the polls, Coolidge won easily.

■ Business

During the 1920s many Americans went almost dizzy with prosperity. As business boomed and wages rose, former luxuries became necessities. A combination of increased leisure time for both men and women, new gadgets, new amusements, and more money to spend resulted in something approaching glorification of wealth and of the material comforts that went with it.

The Impact of the Automobile

The outstanding symbol of the new age was the automobile. In the early twentieth century, when the manufacture of automobiles in the United States was just beginning, driving cars was a sport for the wealthy. It was Henry Ford who almost single-handedly changed the automobile from a toy of the wealthy to a necessity for all. Ford's famous "Model T"—affectionately known as the "Tin Lizzie"—was so cheap that most families could afford it. Ford applied many of the familiar techniques of successful industrialists, such as the use of standardized parts and the formation of a vertical organization to combine different

Will Rogers
1879–1935

★★★★★ **AMERICAN PORTRAITS**

Part Native American, Will Rogers grew up in the West and became a cowboy while in his teens. He landed jobs with Wild West shows, where he would mix in a few jokes while doing his rope-twirling act. Aiming good-natured barbs at famous people, he became known as the "cowboy philosopher."

By 1920 Will Rogers was a star of both stage and screen. Starting in 1926, his daily newspaper column spread his humorous views of life and politics throughout the nation. Claiming "I don't make jokes—I just watch the government and report the facts," he always poked fun in a lighthearted way and was never hostile; one of his favorite sayings was "I never met a man I didn't like."

By the late 1920s audiences were listening to his commentary on radio. To Americans, Rogers had become a national treasure.

Sidelight: Prosperity for Whom?

Although the 1920s was a decade of general prosperity, the percentage of wealth enjoyed by ordinary people declined sharply. The percentage of disposable income received by the top 5 percent of the population rose from 23.96 in 1920 to 34.06 by 1928. (Compare these figures to 16.9 for 1987.) The other 95 percent of the population (approximately 118 million of the nation's 122 million people) actually received more than 10 percent less of the total disposable income in a nine-year span.

TEACH
Guided Practice
Identifying Problems
Write the following on the chalkboard: farm products, farm costs, foreign market, Prohibition, automobile, eating habits, credit and marketing industries, Calvin Coolidge. Invite students to choose an issue and make one statement telling how the issue is related to the poor economic conditions of farming and farmers in the 1920s. (*Examples: Prohibition—reduced need for grain crops; foreign market—decreased because many countries owed money to the United States and thus did not buy U.S. products.*) **L3**

Teaching American Portraits
Will Rogers's style allowed him to get away with criticizing the government. An angrier delivery probably would have earned him enemies if not censorship. However, when he drawled with tongue in cheek that "we'll hold the distinction of being the only nation in the history of the world that ever went to the poorhouse in an automobile," everyone from the unemployed worker to Henry Ford could chuckle, though some more cynically than others, at the truth of his perception.

Ask students to name modern-day comedians who structure their acts around politics. Ask them which comedians they think will last and why. **L1**

Independent Practice

Technology Have students enlist their families in this activity to see whether a task can be completed more quickly using an assembly-line technique or by having one person do it. Tasks such as washing and drying dishes, setting the table, preparing a meal, and other common household activities might be used. Ask students to time both the family assembly-line completion of an activity and the student's completion. Invite volunteers to report their findings to the class. **L1, LEP**

Using Graphs

Answer: lower auto prices, installment buying, consumer attitudes about prosperity and spending

Graph Skills Practice
Between which years was there a tremendous surge in auto sales? *(1921–1923)* What might account for that surge? *(reduced cost of autos because of efficiency of assembly line)*

Did You Know?

Henry Ford was a pacifist and objected to U.S. entrance into World War II. However, after the sneak attack on Pearl Harbor, Ford changed his tune and produced B-24 bombers, armored tanks, and other war vehicles.

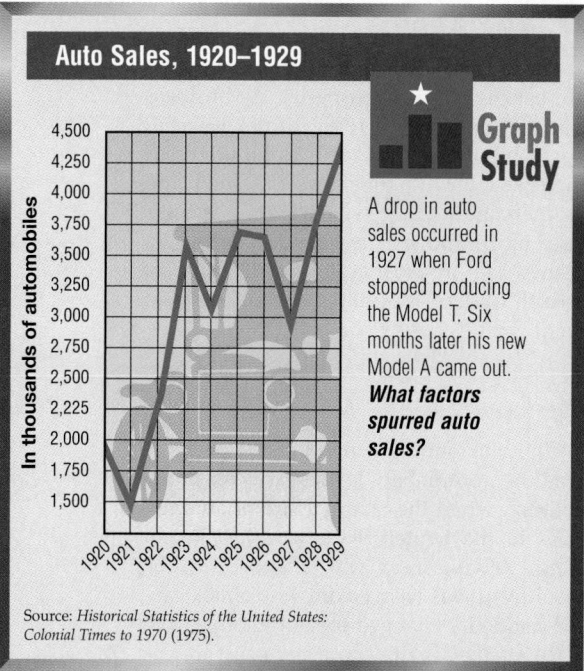

Auto Sales, 1920–1929

In thousands of automobiles

4,500
4,250
4,000
3,750
3,500
3,250
3,000
2,750
2,500
2,225
2,000
1,750
1,500

1920 1921 1922 1923 1924 1925 1926 1927 1928 1929

Source: *Historical Statistics of the United States: Colonial Times to 1970* (1975).

Graph Study

A drop in auto sales occurred in 1927 when Ford stopped producing the Model T. Six months later his new Model A came out. **What factors spurred auto sales?**

operations. But Ford's greatest achievement was the assembly line, which divided operations into such simple tasks that most of the work could be done by unskilled labor. Furthermore, by bringing the parts to the workers, assembly lines sped up production so fast that Ford could boast that:

> ... [R]aw iron ore at the docks at 8:00 Monday morning could be marketed as a complete Ford car on Wednesday noon, allowing 15 hours for shipment.

Ford's economies so reduced costs that an American automobile, which sold for an average price of $2,123 in 1907, could be bought for as little as $290 in 1924. While reducing costs, he staved off unionization by nearly doubling wages in 1914 to $5 a day. Other employers resented Ford because his pay scale was so high that it caused discontent among their own workers. It was Ford's belief that mass-production methods and low prices would produce an immense market for goods. This turned out to be correct,

and the simplicity of the formula spawned imitators. By the mid-1920s other great trusts, notably General Motors and Chrysler, were competing successfully with Ford.

The impact of the automobile on life in the United States was revolutionary. Although small businesses generally continued to decline, new fields for small enterprises—garages, gas stations, diners, and tourist homes—appeared. Draft animals disappeared from farms as tractors took their places. The isolation of rural areas lessened, as cars put towns within easy reach of many farmers, and put the country within reach of city dwellers.

The Growth of Big Business

It seemed that Americans had discovered a magic formula for producing wealth and fulfilling human wants on a scale never before thought possible. Its ingredients were mass production, standardized products, and a nationwide market. This formula tended to favor big businesses over small because only big businesses could set up assembly lines, do the research necessary for constant development of new products, and afford nationwide advertising. It was natural then that the 1920s should see much concentration of industry. Mergers and holding companies helped to concentrate industry by reducing competition. The chain store soon became a familiar sight on Main Street, capturing one-fourth of the grocery business by 1929.

Whereas many Americans had formerly regarded big business as an enemy, they now relied on it both to supply cheap products and to create new opportunities for wealth. The stock market provided striking evidence of this when, for the first time in history, some members of the general public began to buy securities. The prices of shares of stock, especially those connected with new industries, mounted to dizzying heights. More and more purchasers "invested in the future."

With wealthier Americans speculating in the stock market, money to run business came from more and more diverse sources. Business, on the other hand, was becoming

Cooperative Learning Activity

Effects of the Automobile Divide the class into groups of five students each. In each group one student is a minister, another an advertising executive, a third an assembly-line worker, a fourth a farm wife, and a fifth a union leader. Pose this question: How did the automobile industry affect the social, economic, and industrial life in the United States? Have each student answer from the point of view of his or her "character." Ask each group to select a reporter to summarize the group's ideas. **L2**

more and more concentrated. One device used by businesspeople to concentrate financial power was the "pyramiding" of holding companies, whereby it was possible—with a relatively small outlay of capital—for businesspeople to gain control of immense industrial properties.

The Plight of Agriculture

Farmers were the one great economic group that did not share in the Coolidge prosperity. The average income for farmers in 1929 was less than one-third of the average income for the rest of the country.

Falling Prices and Shrinking Markets

Technological advances led to greater production, which caused a slump in farm prices even while farmers' costs mounted. As one account puts it:

> "*Freight rates, wages, taxes, farm implements, and the like, all of which went into the farmers' cost of production, remained high or came down via the stairway, while farm prices took the elevator.*"

Farm prices took disastrous slides in 1920 and 1921 and did not recover. Wheat went from almost $2.50 a bushel to less than $1.50. The foreign market dwindled because the United States had changed from a debtor to a creditor nation. Before World War I, foreign investments in the United States exceeded American investment abroad; the principal means of making up this unfavorable credit balance was for the United States to export agricultural staples, such as wheat and cotton. During the war the balance shifted the other way, principally because of United States loans to the Allies. With the return of peace, countries owing the United States money preferred not to buy its products. Great Britain, for example, often bought wheat from Argentina or Canada, especially after the Fordney-McCumber Tariff reduced the American market for British goods.

The **domestic market,** the market composed of buyers and sellers within the country, also diminished. New fabrics such as rayon lessened the demand for cotton; the

Visualizing History ▲ ON THE ASSEMBLY LINE Finishing touches are put on a Model A at a Ford plant in Dearborn, Michigan. ***What effect did assembly-line production have on the price of automobiles?***

Critical Thinking Activity

Supporting Generalizations Write the following sentence on the chalkboard: The business technology of the 1920s created an era of prosperity. Have students find three facts in the section to support this generalization. Write supporting facts on the board as students state them. *(Luxuries became necessities; wages rose; most families could afford automobiles; for the first time in history, some members of general public bought securities.)* **L1**

For additional practice in using critical thinking skills, assign Critical Thinking Skills Activity 16.

CHAPTER 16
SECTION 2

Assign Guided Reading Activity 16-2.

Research In the 1920s the government gave little if any attention to the plight of American farmers. Point out that in later decades farmers received, and continue to receive, aid from the government. Have students research the kinds of aid the government extends to farmers today. Ask them to draw conclusions about the aid in terms of its effect on farm production and consumer prices. **L2**

Did You Know?

Calvin Coolidge, often referred to as Silent Cal, was an austere, taciturn man. Theodore Roosevelt's daughter, Alice Roosevelt Longworth, once described him as a man who looked as if he "had been weaned on a dill pickle."

Visualizing History Assembly-line production is still the method by which automobiles, as well as many other products, are produced. On some modern assembly lines, robots have replaced workers.
Answer to Caption: reduced the cost of automobiles

▼ FARMERS ON THEIR WAY TO WORK, 1920s

▲ *WHEAT* by Thomas Hart Benton, 1967 During his later career, Thomas Hart Benton chronicled America's past. *Why did the domestic market for agricultural products diminish during the 1920s?*

substitution of tractors and trucks for draft animals reduced the need for fodder. Faced with decreasing demands for the traditional staples, farmers might have been expected to shift to other products—but that was easier said than done. A Southern tenant farmer usually had no skill at anything but raising cotton. A Dakota wheat farmer usually lacked the capital and the knowledge to change, say, to dairy farming, which in any case was not well suited to that region. Moreover, many farmers had borrowed heavily during the war to buy new land at inflated prices. The only obvious way to pay off the debt was to raise more crops. But more crops meant unsalable surpluses; unsalable surpluses meant low prices. Low prices made the debt burden even heavier.

The Influence of the Farm Bloc

Early in Harding's administration, members of Congress from the Midwest and Plains states formed the Farm Bloc. It included about 25 senators and 100 representatives from both parties. Strong enough to hold a balance of power in Congress, the Farm Bloc forced through several laws favoring farmers. The Capper-Volstead Act of 1922 made farm cooperatives free of antitrust laws; the Intermediate Credits Act of 1923 set up federal banks to make loans to aid farm cooperatives.

None of the laws, however, dealt with the farmers' major problem: surpluses they could not sell. If wheat farmers were to benefit from the 42-cent-a-bushel protective tariff, which eliminated foreign competition, they somehow had to limit the amount of wheat put on that market.

The Farm Bloc supported the McNary-Haugen Bill. This bill proposed that the federal government buy crop surpluses and sell them abroad, while protecting the United States market with a high tariff. This would immediately raise the domestic price. Whatever losses the government suffered would be covered by an equalization fee—a tax

Sidelight: A New Form of Communication

As the automotive industry expanded, another technology also was spreading its wings. Airmail was common by the early 1920s, although the beginnings of this service were not so auspicious. Started in 1918, the service connected New York City, Philadelphia, and Washington, D.C. When President Wilson one day dropped in to observe, he saw the plane bound for Philadelphia repeatedly fail to take off. Then someone remembered to fill it with gas. Next the pilot flew in the wrong direction and crash-landed in a field. Finally the mail was sent by rail.

▲ FARM LANTERN, 1920s

charged against producers. Supporters of the bill claimed that it would help farmers as the tariff helped manufacturers.

Twice the bill passed Congress, but both times President Coolidge vetoed it. The idea would not work, he insisted, and furthermore, a "healthy economic condition is best maintained through a free play of competition." Thus, farmers failed to obtain protections similar to those many businesses received at the time.

■ Foreign Affairs

During the 1920s both Republican Presidents worked to promote world peace through individual agreements. During Coolidge's administration, France and the United States took the lead in promoting a treaty that attempted to "outlaw war." Called the Kellogg-Briand Pact after the American secretary of state and the French foreign minister who proposed it, the treaty was eventually ratified by 64 nations, each agreeing to abandon war "as an instrument of national policy" and to settle disputes by peaceful means.

A serious weakness of the pact was that it had no means of enforcement. No provisions were set down in the event there were acts of aggression among signer nations.

Although the United States generally participated in talks and treaties with European and Asian nations during this period, its manner toward Latin America remained protective. The Harding and Coolidge administrations—following the Roosevelt Corollary to the Monroe Doctrine—occasionally sent troops to "preserve order" in Caribbean countries. They became increasingly aware, however, that the Latin American people acutely resented such intervention. Although not willing to give up the right to intervene, Secretary of State Charles Evans Hughes believed troops should be sent to Latin America only to promote political stability, not to assist American investors. Accordingly, in the mid-1920s, United States Marines withdrew from the Dominican Republic and Nicaragua, where they had been sent in the previous decade to maintain order.

Section 2 ★ Review

Checking for Understanding

1. **Identify** Henry Ford, assembly line, Farm Bloc, McNary-Haugen Bill.

2. **Define** domestic market.

3. **List** three ways that the automobile changed American life.

4. **Summarize** the farmers' situation during the 1920s and how government reacted to their plight.

Critical Thinking

5. **Supporting an Opinion**   Did Coolidge regard farming in the same way he viewed big business? Explain.

ACTIVITY

6. Select a nation and research the laws, customs, and information you would need to know to export a product.

Answers to SECTION 2 REVIEW

1. Henry Ford, 493; assembly line, 494; Farm Bloc, 496; McNary-Haugen Bill, 496

2. All vocabulary words are defined in the Glossary.

3. mobility, new enterprises to support automobiles, and lessened isolation of rural areas

4. Farmers, hurt by low prices and Coolidge's veto of the McNary-Haugen bill, did not prosper.

5. Answers will vary. Coolidge did not extend to farmers the same protection and supports he gave to big business. The Fordney-McCumber Tariff hurt farmers while it helped manufacturing. Coolidge refused to support the McNary-Haugen bill.

6. Findings will vary. Students should demonstrate an understanding of the relationships.

ASSESS
Check Understanding
Assign Section 2 Review as homework or an in-class activity.

Evaluate
🔘 🗂 Assign Section Quiz 16-2 or use the Testmaker to create a customized quiz.

Reteach
Have students write in their own words the main idea of each of the following quotes:
"We want less government in business and more business in government." (Harding)
"The business of America is business." (Coolidge)

🗂 Have students complete Reteaching Activity 16-2.

🗂 Assign Workbook Activity 16-2.

Enrich
🗂 Assign Enrichment Activity 16.

🗂 For map practice, use Map Transparency Activity 16 and Chapter Map Activity 16.

🗂 Project Skills Transparency 16 and have students complete Skills Transparencies Activity 16.

CLOSE
Ask students to summarize the fundamentals of the philosophy of government during the 1920s and identify its strengths and weaknesses.

American Literary Heritage

Historical Setting

In the 1920s Americans seemed determined to compensate for lost time. The "Roaring Twenties" boasted flourishing jazz musicians and a renewed interest in dance. Radio proved to be a marvel of the era. The movie industry blossomed, and in 1927 the first "talkie" was released.

Background

Poetry depends on the creation of a particular mood, which reflects the outlooks and sentiments with which the poet approaches his or her topic. The emotional stance of the poet is essential to mood. The poems here capture the spirit of restlessness, the emphasis upon youthful vigor, and the deepening cultural expansion that characterized the United States during the 1920s.

About the Authors

Edna St. Vincent Millay (1892–1950) was a significant poet in New York City's Greenwich Village, where she embraced a bohemian existence. Langston Hughes (1902–1967) was a central figure in the Harlem Renaissance, which addressed issues of cultural pride while presenting protest pieces.

▲ EDNA ST. VINCENT MILLAY

After World War I, divergent movements in American literature grew up in New York's Harlem and Greenwich Village and in the nation's heartland. Two poets who typify these movements are Edna St. Vincent Millay and Langston Hughes.

▲ LANGSTON HUGHES

Read to Discover

Edna St. Vincent Millay captures the tireless energy of youth and the fun of being young and in love in New York City. Langston Hughes absorbed the poetry of everyday language and uses rhythms of the jazz age to reflect the pride of African Americans.

Reader's Dictionary

wan	weak; dim or faint
shawl	a fabric garment used to cover the head or shoulders
boogie-woogie	percussive style of playing blues music featuring inventive melodic variations

Recuerdo

by Edna St. Vincent Millay

We were very tired, we were very merry—
We had gone back and forth all night on the ferry.
It was bare and bright, and smelled like a stable-
But we looked into a fire, we leaned across a table,
We lay on a hill-top underneath the moon;
And the whistles kept blowing, and the dawn
   came soon.
We were very tired, we were very merry—
We had gone back and forth all night on the ferry;
And you ate an apple, and I ate a pear,
From a dozen of each we had bought somewhere;
And the sky went wan, and the wind came cold,
And the sun rose dripping, a bucketful of gold.
We were very tired, we were very merry,
We had gone back and forth all night on the ferry.
We hailed, "Good morrow, mother!" to a
   shawl-covered head,
And bought a morning paper, which neither
   of us read;
And she wept, "God bless you!" for the
   apples and pears,
And we gave her all our money but our
   subway fares.

Cultural Perspectives

Writers and Influences Point out that in the 1920s both white and African American writers responded to the forces around them. Although African American writers often used literature to protest or to address themes of concern to them, they, like white writers, were influenced by the spirit of restlessness and change that surrounded them.

Dream Boogie

by Langston Hughes

Ain't you heard
The boogie-woogie rumble
Of a dream deferred?
Listen closely:
You'll hear their feet
Beating out and beating out a—
You think
It's a happy beat?
Listen to it closely:
Ain't you heard
something underneath
like a—
What did I say?
Sure,
I'm happy!
Take it away!
Hey, pop!
Re-bop!
Mop!
Y-e-a-h!

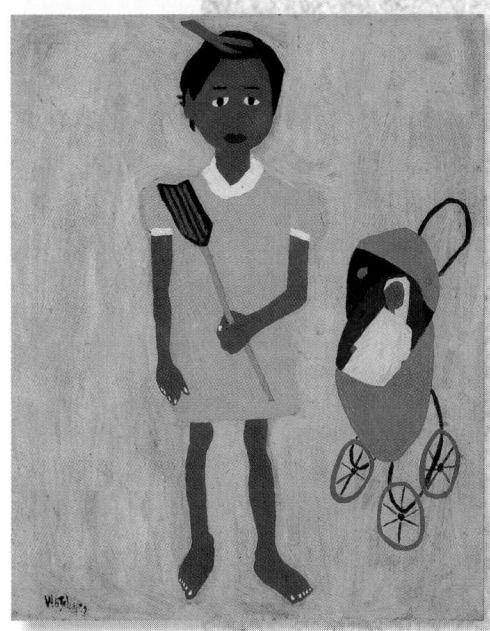

▲ *Li'l Sis* by William H. Johnson, 1944

▲ *Ferry Boat Trip* by William H. Johnson, 1934

Responding to Literature

1. What period of time is covered in "Recuerdo"?

2. How many speakers are there in "Dream Boogie"? What device is used to set them apart?

3. What differences and similarities in voice can you find between the authors of these selections?

4. What views of American life in the 1920s do Millay and Hughes embody?

ACTIVITY

5. Write a poem of at least 8 lines to describe a walk in the park.

Answers to Responding to Literature

1. It covers the space of a single night through dawn of the following morning.
2. There are two. The second voice is represented by the lines in italics.
3. "Recuerdo"—the voice is one of youthful optimism and high spirits; "Dream Boogie"—the dual voice echoes the hope tempered by cynicism that prevails in the African American community to this day.
4. "Recuerdo" contains a view of a nation that is something of a playground. The Hughes piece contains a mixed view of life in a land where black skin remains a barrier to fair and equal treatment.
5. Poems should show vivid imagery.

The "Roaring Twenties"

FOCUS

Bellringer

Before taking roll, project Section Focus Transparency 16-3 or hand out Section Focus Transparency Activity 16-3. Have students answer the questions. Discuss student responses.

Motivating Activity

Write the following on the chalkboard and ask students which experiences make them feel more part of a crowd and which make them aware of their individuality:

reading a book
watching television
viewing a film in a theater

Discuss students' responses, and explain that developments during the 1920s changed the lives of individuals and groups of Americans in many ways.
L1

Vocabulary Precheck

Ask students to break down the compound term "postwar disillusionment" to determine the meaning.
L1, LEP

Setting the Scene

Section Focus

The 1920s saw striking changes in American society. Radio and film became immensely popular. The arts flowered. "Coolidge prosperity" provided more leisure time and more spending money for new gadgets. The availability of credit helped many to buy more than they could afford. Women adopted new standards of behavior. To many, however, these changes suggested a loss of important traditional values.

Objectives

After studying this section, you should be able to

★ describe changes in women's lives during the 1920s.

★ outline developments in the arts and education during this period.

Key Term

postwar disillusionment

◄ COOLIDGE CAMPAIGN POSTER, 1924

From a Long Island airfield on May 20, 1927, a small plane called the *Spirit of St. Louis* took off for France. Twenty-five-year-old Charles Lindbergh set off to make the first nonstop solo flight across the Atlantic. Thirty-three and one-half hours later, Lindbergh landed near Paris. Huge crowds greeted him. An American naval vessel brought him home, and even greater crowds welcomed him back to the United States. "Lucky Lindy," as he was called, became a hero of the age.

President Coolidge called him "a boy representing the best traditions of his country." In an era when the ideals and heroes of history were questioned, when politics was riddled with graft, and when machines seemed to be replacing people, Lindbergh helped people restore some confidence in themselves. He proved that Americans were still capable of pioneering, even in the machine age. Quiet, courageous, and self-reliant, Lindbergh showed that not all the old values of life had disappeared, despite the changing priorities of modern society.

■ New Directions in Society

The rapid changes caused by the progress of technology in the 1920s brought with them some serious problems. Automobiles, though they offered an exciting new freedom of movement, also killed as many Americans in 1928 and 1929 as had lost their lives in battle during World War I. Cities lost some of their attractiveness as automobiles enabled people and businesses to move to the suburbs. The easily available "canned entertainment" provided by radio and motion

Classroom Resources for SECTION 3

Blackline Masters:
- Reproducible Lesson Plan 16-3
- Guided Reading Activity 16-3
- Geography in History Activity 16
- Supreme Court Case Study 18
- Linking Past and Present Activity 16

- Primary and Secondary Source Readings, pp. 42–43
- Cooperative Learning Activity 16
- Chapter Skills Activity 16
- Spirit of American Art and Music, pp. 32–34
- Workbook Activity 16-3

- Reteaching Activity 16-3
- Section Quiz 16-3

Transparencies:
- Section Focus Transparency 16-3

Multimedia:
- Testmaker
- American Music: Cultural Traditions

Visualizing History

▲ LINDBERGH'S HISTORIC FLIGHT Because a huge fuel tank blocked his plane's windshield on his transatlantic flight, Lindbergh used a periscope to see. Lindbergh's heroics inspired other pilots like Amelia Earhart (right). *In what way was Lindbergh a symbol of the 1920s?*

pictures seemed to discourage Americans from creating their own amusements.

Prohibition

Unfortunately, during the 1920s crime became big business. Gangsters such as Al Capone and Dutch Schultz consolidated the illegal liquor trade on many of the same principles used to consolidate the automobile and steel industries. The Prohibition Bureau, set up to enforce the law against the distilling and sale of liquor, was understaffed, underpaid, graft-ridden, and ineffective. Although liquor consumption dropped substantially during Prohibition, illegal drinking by millions created an illegitimate billion-dollar industry. The entrepreneurs in this illegal business became wealthy enough

to buy beautiful homes in Florida, steel-plated limousines, and fabulous jewels, such as Capone's 11.5-carat diamond ring. Some gangsters became powerful enough to corrupt local governments.

Rural America, with its traditional values and churchgoing ways, tended to support Prohibition, but the cities generally opposed it. The customary diets of several urban ethnic groups included liquor, and many city dwellers resisted Prohibition as the work of religious crusaders. Regardless, Prohibition was never fully enforced. Many people supported Prohibition publicly while privately continuing to drink.

Despite the success of the illegal liquor trade, Prohibition actually gained in popularity during the 1920s. In 1928 voters elected more supporters of Prohibition to

CHAPTER 16 The Decade of Normalcy: 1920–1928 **501**

TEACH
Guided Practice
Making Comparisons
Suggest students imagine they are twentieth-century de Tocquevilles traveling through the United States. They are particularly struck by the changing status of women and want to write an article about these changes.

Ask volunteers to read their papers aloud. Then hold a discussion comparing the status of women in the 1920s with the status of women today. **L2**

📁 Assign Guided Reading Activity 16-3.

📁 Assign Geography in History Activity 16.

📁 Assign Supreme Court Case Study 18: *Olmstead* v. *United States* (1928).

Visualizing History Discuss with students the characteristics that made Charles Lindbergh and Amelia Earhart heroic figures to Americans of the 1920s.

Answer to Caption: helped Americans regain confidence in themselves and showed that even in a machine age people still could pioneer

Critical Thinking Activity

Using Primary Sources Studying a work of art or literature can help students understand the attitudes and behavior of people in a particular historical period. Suggest students choose an artist or writer from the 1920s and examine his or her work. Ask them to report what they learned about the period from the work. **L3**

Independent Practice

Identifying Consequences
Have students write a paragraph to describe the "dark side" of each of these 1920s' phenomena, which in general were perceived as social goods: the automobile, Prohibition, new freedom for women, new educational theories. When students have completed their paragraphs, ask them why they think society is willing to tolerate the dangers that accompany technology. **L3**

CURRICULUM CONNECTION

Law The sensationalized case of the kidnapping of Charles Lindbergh's son led Congress to pass the Lindbergh Law, which makes kidnapping a federal offense if the kidnapper takes the victim across state lines.

Food of the Times

In the 1920s a native of Brooklyn came home from a trip with an idea that changed the way Americans eat. After Clarence Birdseye watched Native Americans preserve fish and game by freezing it, he hit on a way to turn the idea into a business. He patented his process in 1925. Within three years frozen vegetables could be purchased in hundreds of food stores.

▲ MOVIE POSTER, 1920S

Congress than ever before, as well as a "dry" President, Herbert Hoover. The popularity of Prohibition was a sign of continuing faith in the possibility of achieving a better life, of a longing for the ideals that had eroded in the horrors of World War I. Traditional standards of behavior were changing as Americans left the villages for the cities and the farms for the factories. Prohibition seemed a way to halt this change in values.

Women in the 1920s

The 1920s saw women express greater personal freedom. A dramatic new woman of the 1920s—the "flapper"—demanded the same freedom enjoyed by men. She sometimes smoked cigarettes and drank liquor and dressed in a way her mother and grandmother would not have believed possible. While most women in the 1920s

• •

Footnotes to History

Pastimes Recreation became the order of the day in the 1920s. Crossword puzzles, word games, and the Chinese game of Mah Johng became national obsessions. Thanks in great part to the efforts of sports journalists, athletes became larger-than-life heroes.

were not flappers, these new women demonstrated how modern behavior was changing.

American family life was also changing. Couples had fewer children because of increased knowledge about family planning, divorce rates increased, and more women than ever before sought employment outside the home.

Women in the Workplace

Having achieved the right to vote, women sought financial independence as well. Many young single women became salesclerks in department stores, secretaries, or telephone operators, for example. In 1920, 25 percent of female workers were in clerical and sales work. Eventually the employees in those particular jobs became almost exclusively female. Graduates of women's colleges began to seek jobs in business rather than in more traditional jobs such as teaching. But many women, especially married women who had to work to support families, were confined to jobs with long hours, poor conditions, and low wages. Women who worked outside the home suffered severe discrimination, often receiving only 50 to 60 percent of a man's wages for the same work. Further, women continued to meet with difficulty when trying to enter prestigious professions such as science and law.

Individual women made great contributions in many fields—often under difficult circumstances. Amelia Earhart learned to fly planes and became the first woman to complete a solo flight across the Atlantic. Singers Bessie Smith and Billie Holliday were innovative interpreters in jazz and blues. Dorothy Thompson became a famous journalist. Mary McLeod Bethune—an African American woman born into poverty—founded her own college, founded the National Council of Negro Women, and served as a government consultant.

Women in the Home

Most Americans—both men and women—continued to believe that a married woman's place was in the home. Thus, in

Cooperative Learning Activity

Debating Prohibition Invite volunteers to form two groups to debate the pros and cons of Prohibition. Give students time to prepare their arguments. As each group presents its argument, summarize it on the chalkboard. Make sure groups cite evidence to support their viewpoints. When the debate is concluded, discuss the arguments with the class. Ask the class to decide which are most valid. **L1**

Commercial Radio

The 1920s ushered in a host of technologies still used today. Among the most significant breakthroughs was commercial radio.

Then_____

The 1920s

In one of the first commercial broadcasts, radio station KDKA in Pittsburgh broadcast news of President Harding's landslide victory in November 1920. Within the next two years, nearly 600 radio stations began operation. One million Americans tuned in daily to hear their favorite radio

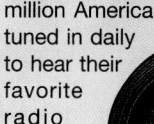

▶ **RADIO, 1920s**

programs. Dramas, adventures, and comedies, each with a cast of actors and a sound effects technician, were performed live in the radio studio as the broadcast aired. Radio, like so many technologies that emerged in the post-World War I period, served to shrink the world, bringing immediate contact and communication, and a common experience to people in all parts of the world.

Now_____

The Scope of Broadcasting

By the mid-1990s, nearly 11,000 radio stations operated in the United States, and Americans owned more than 500 million radios—on average, each household has about six. One survey indicates that four of every five American teenagers and adults listen to radio every day.

▲ **RADIO AND CASSETTE PLAYER**

Many of the radiocasts in the United States are designed for entertainment, chiefly recorded music. Most stations focus on one kind of music, such as rock, classical, or country and western. Other stations specialize in providing information such as newscasts, talk shows, and sporting events. Long a staple of radio, the talk show gained many listeners during the 1980s and 1990s. Talk shows provide a forum for discussion on a variety of topics and interviews with people from many professions.

---

spite of a spirit of independence, most women continued to be bound by the belief that their role was different from that of men, that they were to be mothers and homemakers. With new electric technology, the nature of being a homemaker changed. New household appliances, such as refrigerators and vacuum cleaners, commercial laundries, and canned food made hard, time-consuming domestic duties much easier. Many who stayed at home and became mothers, particularly in middle-class families, managed motherhood by listening to child-rearing experts who promoted regularly scheduled feedings for children and regimented routines for such children's extracurricular activities as music lessons and clubs.

■ Cultural Achievements

American culture thrived in the 1920s. Literature, architecture, music, painting, movies, radio—all flourished during this time.

American Literature

Some writers of the period, such as novelist Willa Cather and poet Robert Frost, tried to recapture the spirit and traditions of rural America; others, such as poet Carl Sandburg, examined what was happening in America's cities. In Eugene O'Neill, the United States produced its finest playwright. O'Neill found material in many aspects of American life—from the rage of a worker in

CHAPTER 16 The Decade of Normalcy: 1920–1928 **503**

The first commercial broadcasting station was WJW in Detroit, Michigan, which went on the air in August 1920. From then on, radio was a major form of communication. By the mid-1920s, Americans could listen to presidential candidates debating the issues of the day. Radio had an enormous influence on family life as families gathered around the radio to listen to their favorite programs. Although radio has been eclipsed by television, it is still alive and well. Suggest students research radio in their area. How many stations are there? What kinds of broadcasting do they deliver? How does radio influence community life today?

🗀 For additional practice, assign Linking Past and Present Activity 16.

Did You Know?

In November 1920 station KDKA in Pittsburgh broadcast the news of Harding's victory in one of the first commercial broadcasts in history. By 1927 the nation had close to 700 stations, and the Federal Radio Commission was established to regulate broadcasting.

Sidelight: A Disillusioning Episode

If the scandals in his cabinet broke Warren Harding's heart, another scandal shattered the idealism of American baseball fans. In 1919 eight members of the Chicago White Sox were accused of taking mob money to throw the World Series to the Cincinnati Reds. The accused, called the Black Sox, were not greedy businessmen but exploited and poorly paid players, some of whom had been promised and then denied raises. The owners, gamblers, and gangsters cleaned up; the players, though formally acquitted in court, were banned from professional baseball for life. The scandal set the tone of disillusionment that would permeate the decade.

Linking Across
T I M E

The Ku Klux Klan was one of the reactionary forces that manifested itself during the 1920s. The Klan, whose name comes from the Greek word *kyklos,* meaning "circle," has had four periods of influence in the United States. The first was in the post–Civil War period, when it rose as a reaction to Reconstruction. It enjoyed a resurgence in the 1920s, when membership reached more than 3 million, much of it in the Midwest. Membership rose again from the late 1940s to the 1970s. There was yet another rise in the 1980s. Today membership is only about 6,000.

Visualizing
History A well-known educator, Mary McLeod Bethune founded a college for African Americans in Daytona Beach, Florida. Later, in the 1930s, she headed the Division of Negro Affairs of the National Youth Administration, a New Deal agency whose goal was to improve conditions for African Americans. **Answer to Caption:** Increased intolerance of racial or ethnic diversity was general in the 1920s.

Visualizing
History ▲ WORKING FOR JUSTICE Activists like Mary McLeod Bethune fought to pass a federal law against lynching. *What attitudes might explain why lynching and other such incidents increased in the 1920s?*

the hold of a steamship in *The Hairy Ape,* to family tension in a decaying New England town in *Desire Under the Elms.* Ernest Hemingway, who had driven an ambulance on the Italian front during World War I, wrote about the meaningless violence of war in *A Farewell to Arms.* His fiction created a new literary style characterized by direct, simple, spare prose. The poet T. S. Eliot saw a world filled with "hollow men" and, in *The Wasteland,* one that would end "not with a bang but a whimper."

Postwar disillusionment, disappointment or dissatisfaction with the way things were after the war, was often manifested as criticism of American life. Henry Ford said that "history is bunk," and a school of "debunking" historians reexamined the past and reevaluated more accurately the facts behind

the myths of many American heroes. Many American writers did the same. In his novels *Main Street* and *Babbitt,* Sinclair Lewis depicted the absurdities of life in small-town America. H. L. Mencken mocked the "vast . . . herd of good-natured animals" who made up most of the machine-age society. Mencken saw no hope for improvement. "If I am convinced of anything," he wrote, "it is that Doing Good is in bad taste."

The Arts

Achievements in American literature were matched in the arts. New city skyscrapers and suburban homes expanded the opportunities of architects like Frank Lloyd Wright, who achieved worldwide fame for his bold use of new materials and for architectural designs free of traditional influence. In jazz, which started with African American Dixieland bands in New Orleans, America produced a new form of music. At first seen as corrupting the morals of young people, jazz was soon accepted as an important art form. In the fine arts, the American scene was brilliantly portrayed by such painters as Reginald Marsh, Thomas Hart Benton, George

◄ SINGER AND ACTRESS
ETHEL WATERS

Critical Thinking Activity

Classifying On a line across the chalkboard, write the following: Theme, Author/Artist, Work. Invite volunteers to come to the board and fill in entries under Theme. Then have other volunteers classify authors/artists and

their works according to the themes. Discuss with the class whether any of the themes expressed in the literature and art of the 1920s are important in society today. **L2**

Bellows, and Edward Hopper. In photography, Alfred Stieglitz achieved an international reputation.

Also during this period, the young motion-picture industry mushroomed. The first feature-length film appeared in 1915. By 1929 there were about 100 million paid admissions to movie theaters every week—proof that moviegoing had gained respectability. During the 1920s the motion-picture industry moved from New York to southern California. Mary Pickford, Charlie Chaplin, Douglas Fairbanks, Gloria Swanson, and Clara Bow were among the first stars of the silent screen. In 1927 Warner Brothers introduced "talking" pictures, which made the movies more popular than ever.

▲ THE SCOPES TRIAL Opposing attorneys Clarence Darrow (left) and William Jennings Bryan pose during the Scopes trial. Scopes was later freed on appeal, but the trial proved too much for Bryan, who died a week after it ended. *What basic clash of values in 1920s society did the trial illustrate?*

■ Changes and Challenges in Education

A significant amount of the new wealth of the 1920s went into education, both through taxes for new public schools and through private donations to colleges and universities. The introduction of the school bus made possible the gradual replacement of bare, one-room country schoolhouses with large, well-equipped central schools. High school was no longer the privilege of the well-off but was also attended by the children of farmers and workers—although graduation from high school remained the exception rather than the rule. Both high school and college enrollment increased steadily.

A philosophy of education, long championed by John Dewey, emphasized learning through direct experience and experiment rather than through memorization. Greater emphasis was placed on science, which Dewey viewed as a way of using both thought and activity to investigate nature.

Some religious groups found these new educational theories threatening and were able to gain laws in some states to prevent the teaching of evolution in public schools. This set the stage for a battle between science and religion. It came in 1925, at the trial of John T. Scopes, a teacher in Dayton, Tennessee, who was willing to be arrested for teaching evolution to his high school class. The American Civil Liberties Union (ACLU) had raised money to test the new antievolution law in Tennessee and had asked Scopes if he would volunteer for the cause. The famous attorney Clarence Darrow defended Scopes, while William Jennings Bryan aided the prosecution for the antievolution forces. After a sensational trial, Scopes was convicted, but Bryan, who took the witness stand as an expert on the Bible, was made to look foolish through Darrow's penetrating questioning. The Scopes case symbolized the tensions of the 1920s, as some Americans tried to resist the tide of social change and to preserve older values and beliefs.

■ The Harlem Renaissance

World War I had been a liberating experience for many African Americans. This was especially true of those who went abroad.

Did You Know?

The annual average salary in 1925 for public school teachers was $1,263, at a time when the average salary for clerical workers was $2,239. Because teachers' salaries were so low, especially at the elementary-school level, most teaching positions were filled by women. In 1925 only about one in five teachers was a man, most of whom were high-school teachers. Rural education, typically inferior to urban education, employed many teachers who had not even graduated from high school. Only about a third as many children in rural areas went to high school as did children in urban areas.

Visualizing History Tennessee's law against the teaching of evolution remained on the books until 1967. One historian noted that the trial was a conflict between rural and urban values.
Answer to Caption: It was a clash between modern emphasis on experiment and experience in education and traditional ideas of education.

Sidelight: Agents of Prohibition

Isador Einstein, known as Izzy, and his partner, Moe Smith, worked as a team to trap lawbreakers during Prohibition. Masters of disguise, they were a flamboyant pair who used any number of methods to enforce the law. Izzy was particularly adept at going through any neighborhood, for he spoke five languages. He once nabbed an unsuspecting speakeasy owner by disguising himself as a pickle salesman. Together Izzy and Moe made some 4,000 arrests and hauled in around 15 million dollars worth of alcohol.

For the first time they were freed from the second-class citizenship they suffered in the United States. But the prejudice and discrimination that awaited them at home helped to create a spirit of pride and protest, forging a new unity and a new African American:

> *... who had pride in heritage and self and who, through poetry, music, dance, and the theater, was able to create works of beauty out of travail and sufferings, as well as out of the more humorous facts of life.*

A striking outcome of this new spirit among African Americans was the "Harlem Renaissance." In New York City, the intellectual capital of the United States, a number of highly talented African Americans rose to fame. Some were in the performing arts, including actors Charles Gilpin and Richard B. Harrison, singers Roland Hayes and Ethel Waters, dancer Bill Robinson, and singer-actor Paul Robeson. Others were scholars, including sociologist E. Franklin Frazier and economist Abram L. Harris. Still others were writers, such as poets Countee Cullen and Langston Hughes and novelists Jessie H. Fauset, Zora Neale Hurston, and Walter White. The use of the American experience as a theme for novels, poems, paintings, and sculpture was new in a society that until now had recognized few African American artists.

▲ WRITER COUNTEE CULLEN

More influential than the intellectuals and artists among African Americans themselves was a dynamic leader from Jamaica, Marcus Garvey. A spokesman for "Negro Nationalism," which exalted African American culture and traditions, Garvey formed the Universal Negro Improvement Association, which soon boasted a million members. Garvey told his followers they would never find justice in America and proposed to lead them to Africa. People were not interested, but Garvey stimulated the pride of African Americans in their history and heritage.

Section 3 ★ Review

Checking for Understanding

1. **Identify** Amelia Earhart, Mary McLeod Bethune, John T. Scopes.
2. **Define** postwar disillusionment.
3. **Cite** the factors that resulted in increased crime in the 1920s.
4. **Summarize** changes in women's personal and economic status during the 1920s.
5. **Discuss** significant contributions that the Harlem Renaissance made to the arts.

Critical Thinking

6. **Evaluating Achievements** How are the advances made by women in the 1920s significant to the lives of American women today?

ACTIVITY

7. Read a short story or poem by one of the writers associated with the Harlem Renaissance. Select photographs that express the work's main ideas and paste them on a piece of posterboard.

Answers to SECTION 3 REVIEW

1. Amelia Earhart, 501; Mary McLeod Bethune, 504; John T. Scopes, 505
2. All vocabulary words are defined in the Glossary.
3. Prohibition created an illegal liquor industry.
4. gained more personal freedom, took jobs outside the home
5. a blooming of the arts including jazz, painting, and literature
6. Answers will vary. Some careers did become available to them, although they were not equal to men's in status or salary. These changes largely carried over and progressed through time to the present day.
7. Student work should demonstrate understanding of main idea.

BUILDING SKILLS
Critical Thinking Skills

Distinguishing Fact from Opinion

A fact is a statement or piece of information that can be verified by evidence. An opinion, on the other hand, presents a personal viewpoint that cannot be proved true or false.

Learning the Skill

Use these steps to help distinguish between fact and opinion.

- **Read** the statement carefully.
- **Ask:** What evidence supports this statement? What makes me confident that this statement is valid?
- **Look** for words and phrases that indicate opinion. Examples are *I think, I believe, probably, seems to me, may, might, could, ought, in my judgment,* or *in my view.*
- **Examine** the material for expressions of approval and disapproval such as *good, bad, poor,* and *unsatisfactory.* Be aware of such superlatives as *greatest, worst, finest,* and *best.*
- **Locate** and analyze such superlatives as *greatest, worst, finest,* and *best.*
- **Look** for words that have negative meanings such as *squander, contemptible,* and *disgrace.*
- **Note** the use of generalizations that include words like *none, every,* and *always.*
- **Look** for specific data that supports a statement of fact. If the statement can be proven, it is factual. For example, it is a fact that *George Washington served as the first President.*
- **Determine** whether information is fact or opinion.

    If the statement refers to situations that are desirable or undesirable, important or unimportant, or likely or unlikely, then the statement is an opinion. For example, it is an opinion that *George Washington was the greatest President.* This assertion is based on someone's preferences or ideas.

▲ *THE CREATION* BY AARON DOUGLAS

Practicing the Skill

Decide whether each statement below is fact or opinion and explain what evidence would be needed to support it.

1. The post-World War I period brought an upsurge of African American literature and art that culminated in the Harlem Renaissance.
2. Aaron Douglas was the best-known visual artist, but equally accomplished work was produced by Laura Wheeler Waring.
3. The painting *The Creation* is the best work of American art of the 1900s.

APPLYING THE SKILL

4. Paste a photo or drawing of one of your favorite musical or visual artists on a poster. List at least three facts and three opinions about the artist.

507

Answers to Practicing the Skill

1. Fact: can be supported by reading a text or encyclopedia
2. Opinion: uses superlatives such as *best-known*
3. Opinion: uses *best,* a word of approval
4. Facts and opinions will vary. Student work should demonstrate understanding of difference between fact and opinion.

TEACH

Tell students that the ability to distinguish between fact and opinion is an important skill that can be used in a variety of experiences and situations. Ask students to give examples of instances in which it is important to be able to recognize the difference between fact and opinion. Then ask students to explain why the source of certain facts and opinions is important. **L1**

📁 Use Chapter Skills Activity 16 to reinforce students' understanding of the skill.

Did You Know?

During the Harlem Renaissance, Aaron Douglas illustrated books written by such writers as Countee Cullen and Langston Hughes.

History and the Humanities

🎵🇺🇸 **American Music: Cultural Traditions:**
Early Jazz/Blues: "Muskrat Ramble" by Louis Armstrong and his Hot Five (2:35); "Downhearted Blues" by Bessie Smith (3:24)

📁 Assign **The Spirit of American Art and Music,** pp. 33–34: Elizabeth Catlett.

Using Vocabulary
Letters will vary but should use the terms accurately.

Reviewing Facts
1. his personality, his promise of "normalcy"
2. the Washington Conference, solution to war debts, Kellogg-Briand Pact, involvement in Latin America
3. protective tariffs, *laissez-faire* government, lower taxes
4. fear, Red Scare, labor pressure, prejudice
5. Mass production, standardized products, and a nationwide market helped lower prices and make products available to all.
6. Tariffs created a backlash overseas and reduced markets for the oversupply of crops. These factors lowered prices.
7. radio, motion pictures, jazz, new literary styles, modern architecture, Harlem Renaissance, improved home products, women feeling more independent, African Americans slowly entering some professions

508

CHAPTER 16 ★ REVIEW

Using Vocabulary

Imagine that you are the chairperson of a large industrial company in the 1920s. Write a letter to the President using the terms below.

welfare capitalism
open shop
technological unemployment

Reviewing Facts

1. **State** two reasons Harding was elected President in 1920.
2. **Summarize** foreign-policy actions of Harding and Coolidge.
3. **List** three ways that Harding and Coolidge helped stimulate business in America.
4. **Explain** why Congress enacted the Emergency Quota Act and the National Origins Act.
5. **Discuss** how Henry Ford's innovations contributed to the growth of the economy.
6. **Describe** ways farmers were affected by tariffs and improved technology.
7. **Cite** evidence that the 1920s changed the arts and the lives of women and African Americans.

Understanding Concepts

Economic Change
1. Explain why urban dwellers of all economic levels would support the economic changes of the 1920s.
2. Why did union membership decline during the 1920s? Speculate on the effect of an economic downturn on union membership.

Social Change
3. Art, literature, and music thrived in the 1920s. What changes in society do you think inspired artists, writers, and musicians?
4. Explain why the 1920s was a period of both advances and setbacks for women and African Americans.

Critical Thinking

1. **Drawing Conclusions** Explain how changes in business and manufacturing during the 1920s sparked a revolution in social customs, arts, and entertainment.
2. **Analyzing Fine Art** Study the painting of singer and actor Paul Robeson on this page by artist Betsy Graves Reyneau, then answer the questions that follow.
   a. What does the painting tell you about the artist's view of Robeson?
   b. What title would you give this painting?

▲ PAUL ROBESON IN THE ROLE OF OTHELLO

3. **Evaluating Alternatives** What was the overriding goal of the treaties negotiated during the Harding and Coolidge administrations? Would the United States have been better served by joining the League of Nations? Explain your position.
4. **Making Inferences** Although this was a prosperous era for many Americans, scandals in politics and organized crime increased. Explain how the new prosperity and Prohibition may have worked to make corruption more tempting.

Understanding Concepts
1. Middle- and lower-income Americans benefited in the form of higher wages, cheaper products, and plentiful jobs.
2. wages rose and workers remained happy; probable increase

3. Some commented on social changes by painting or writing about a slower, simple past. Others drew upon the social changes to create new artistic forms, such as jazz.
4. While both groups made advances, they were still victims of prejudice.

Critical Thinking
1. Business changes allowed for more leisure time and pursuit of the arts. They also freed women from some of their burdens.
2. a. possibilities: austere, strong, intense.
   b. Student titles should reflect the mood.

History and Geography

Immigration

1. **Location** Why did many immigrants to America settle in large cities such as New York and Chicago?

2. **Movement** Why did levels of immigration fall after 1921?

3. **Human/Environment Interaction** Why do you think homogeneous ethnic communities develop in many major cities?

Interdisciplinary Activity: Language Arts

Cooperative Learning

Work in groups of four to evaluate the changes that took place in the 1920s. One member of each group should assume one of the following roles: business owner, farmer, African American, flapper. The goal of your group is to write four paragraphs that discuss the changes from these four perspectives. Have each group member read the paragraph describing the changes that affected him or her.

Practicing Skills

Distinguishing Fact from Opinion

Read the following passages. Review the information on distinguishing fact from opinion on page 507. Then tell whether each sentence expresses factual information or an opinion.

Passage A

In 1917 Congress adopted and submitted to the States the Eighteenth Amendment, known as the Prohibition Amendment. It prohibited the "manufacture, sale, or transportation of intoxicating liquors."

Prohibition was more than a protest against "Demon Rum." It also was a defense of the old rural America against the threat of urbanization and social change. As such, it was a legal triumph for the conservatives in American society.

Passage B

The Republican party isn't a "poor man's party." Republican prosperity has erased that degrading phrase from our political vocabulary. Republican efficiency has filled the working-man's dinner pail—and his gas tank besides—made the telephone, radio, and sanitary plumbing standard household equipment. And placed a whole nation in the silk stocking class. Republican prosperity has reduced hours and increased earning capacity, silenced discontent, put the proverbial "chicken in every pot" and a car in every backyard to boot.

Passage C

Advertising aimed at the emotions rather than at the mind, selling a way of life centered on the happy home and the healthy family. Photographs were skillfully contrived to make people believe they were denying themselves unnecessarily if they did not share the joy others derived from owning, eating, or using a certain product. Advertising copywriters played on the desire for prestige. In the words of one author of the time: "When all is said and done, this much can be said in behalf of advertising, that it gives a certain illusion, a certain sense of escape in the machine age. It creates a dream world."

Still another factor was the motion picture, which did more than just entertain. It gave Americans who lived in small towns a glimpse of a glamorous lifestyle far different from the one they and their neighbors knew.

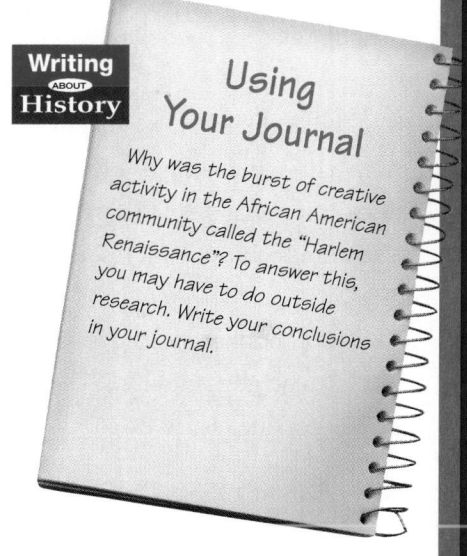

Writing ABOUT History

Using Your Journal

Why was the burst of creative activity in the African American community called the "Harlem Renaissance"? To answer this, you may have to do outside research. Write your conclusions in your journal.

class discussion evaluating the changes described by each group.

Practicing Skills

Passage A
Sentence 1—fact
Sentence 2—fact
Sentence 3—opinion
Sentence 4—opinion
Sentence 5—opinion

Passage B
All sentences are opinions.

Passage C
All sentences are opinions.

Writing ABOUT History

Using Your Journal

Students should understand the term *renaissance* as a re-birth or reawakening.

? Chapter Bonus Test Question

Ask students: In which era do you think new technology played a greater role in people's lives, the 1920s or the 1990s? (*Responses will vary but students should cite evidence to support their answers.*)

---

3. The treaties were attempts to preclude future wars by disarmament and conflict resolution. Joining the League may have made it effective, thus simplifying international role-making.

4. Prosperity can breed a hunger for more material goods, thus tempting people to take bribes, engage in crime and so on.

History and Geography

1. Opportunities were greatest there.

2. In that year President Harding signed the Emergency Quota Act, which cut the number of people admitted.

3. Provide familiar surroundings and a feeling of belonging in an otherwise unfamiliar environment

Cooperative Learning

Encourage students to include specific changes for their particular perspective. Hold a

Daily Lesson Objectives	Teacher Classroom Resources	Multimedia
SECTION 1 **The Stock Market Crashes** **1 Day** pp. 512–517 1. Explain how Hoover's philosophy affected his economic policy. 2. Explain the major causes of the Great Depression.	Reproducible Lesson Plan 17-1 Performance Assessment Activity 17 Concepts Mapping Activities 17-A, 17-B *Vocabulary Activity 17 *Guided Reading Activity 17-1 Geography in History Activity 17 Enrichment Activity 17 Workbook Activity 17-1 Reteaching Activity 17-1 *Section Quiz 17-1	Section Focus Transparency 17-1 Chapter Concepts Transparencies 17-A, 17-B Skills Transparency Activity 17 Vocabulary PuzzleMaker Testmaker MindJogger Videoquiz GTV: A Geographic Perspective on American History
SECTION 2 **Hoover's Policies** **1 Day** pp. 519–524 1. List the ways in which Hoover tried to end the Depression. 2. Describe the change in policy toward Latin America under Hoover. 3. Describe the Hoover-Stimson Doctrine and evaluate its effectiveness.	Reproducible Lesson Plan 17-2 *Guided Reading Activity 17-2 Cooperative Learning Activity 17 Critical Thinking Skills Activity 17 Chapter Skills Activity 17 Workbook Activity 17-2 Reteaching Activity 17-2 *Section Quiz 17-2	Section Focus Transparency 17-2 Testmaker STV: North America Powers of the President The Presidents: A Picture History of Our Nation
SECTION 3 **The Depression Worsens** **1 Day** pp. 526–533 1. Compare the condition of workers and farmers in the early 1930s. 2. Discuss the mood of the country as the election of 1932 approached.	Reproducible Lesson Plan 17-3 *Guided Reading Activity 17-3 Primary and Secondary Source Readings, pp. 44–46 Linking Past and Present Activity 17 Chapter Map Activity 17 Workbook Activity 17-3 Reteaching Activity 17-3 *Section Quiz 17-3	Section Focus Transparency 17-3 Map Transparency 17 Testmaker GTV: A Geographic Perspective on American History Powers of the President The Presidents: A Picture History of Our Nation
CHAPTER REVIEW AND EVALUATION **1 Day**	Chapter 17 Test, Forms A and B Spanish Chapter 17 Summary Performance Assessment Activity 17	MindJogger Videoquiz Student Self-Test & Review Software *Chapter 17 Audiocassette Activity and Test

*Also available in Spanish

 OUT OF TIME? If time does not permit teaching the entire chapter, use the Chapter 17 Summary on pages 538–539 and the Chapter 17 audiocassette (English and Spanish) to point out the main ideas of the chapter.

A complete, 1-page lesson plan is provided for each section in the *Reproducible Lesson Plan* booklet.

Key to Ability Levels

Teaching strategies have been coded for varying learning styles and abilities.

L1 Basic activities for all students

L2 Average activities for average to above-average students

L3 Challenging activities for above-average students

LEP Limited English Proficiency activities

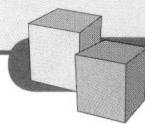

Block Schedule

Block scheduling differs from traditional class scheduling in the amount of time allotted to each period. The extended time frame provided by block scheduling affords you the opportunity to implement a greater number of research-oriented and activity-intense projects to motivate and involve your students. Activities that are particularly suited to use within the block scheduling framework are identified throughout this unit by the following designation:

✔ Performance Assessment Activity

Charting the Economy Point out that business cycles or fluctuations have been occuring almost since the founding of the United States. Even before the Great Depression, severe recessions in the 1820s and in 1873 bankrupted thousands of companies and forced hundreds of banks to close. Have pairs or small groups create a chart by listing signs of prosperity and of economic problems. For each indicator, have students identify its effects. For example, increased production of consumer goods was a sign of prosperity. Effects include both easy credit and overbuying by people who could not afford it. Have students share their charts with the class. Discuss which factors, if any, are at work in the current economy.

POSSIBLE RUBRIC FEATURES
- Content Information
- Classifying
- Organization
- Collaborative Skills
- Recognizing Cause and Effect

☞ For additional practice, use Performance Assessment Strategies and Activities.

TEACHER'S CORNER

NATIONAL GEOGRAPHIC SOCIETY

NATIONAL GEOGRAPHIC SOCIETY PRODUCTS AVAILABLE FROM GLENCOE

To order the following products for use with this chapter, contact your local Glencoe sales representative or call Glencoe at 1-800-334-7344:

- *The Presidents: A Picture History of Our Nation* (CD-ROM)
- *GTV: A Geographic Perspective on American History* (Videodisc)
- *GTV: The American People: Fabric of a Nation* (Videodisc)

ADDITIONAL NATIONAL GEOGRAPHIC SOCIETY PRODUCTS

To order the following products for use with this chapter, call National Geographic Society at 1-800-368-2728:

- *1929–1941: The Great Depression* (Video)
- *The American Presidency* (Filmstrip)
- *Decades of History: The 20th Century—The Early Years* (Filmstrip)

BEGINNING THE CHAPTER

Recording Journal Notes

To help organize their information, you might suggest that students record their observations under various headings.

Linking Across

T I M E

An economic depression was not a new phenomenon in the United States. Just before World War I, there were signs of economic weakness. The Great Depression of the 1930s, however, was more than a panic and a temporary crisis. Later recessions and economic downturns, such as those of the 1970s and early 1990s, were never as severe as the Great Depression of the 1930s.

The Depression Begins
1928–1932

▶ **APPLE VENDOR DURING THE DEPRESSION**

Setting the Scene

Focus

Most Americans believed that the election of Herbert Hoover as President in 1928 would continue a decade of prosperity. This optimism quickly disappeared. A prolonged slump in agriculture, industrial overproduction, high tariffs, and the stock market crash all contributed to the worst economic depression in the nation's history. By 1932 millions of Americans were out of work. When Hoover's best efforts to revive the economy proved unsuccessful, the nation turned to a new President.

Concepts to Understand

★ Why **economic change** from prosperity to depression was triggered by the stock market crash

★ How **political policy** changed as a result of the Depression

Read to Discover . . .

★ how President Hoover tried to lift the country out of the Depression.

★ why Hoover's political leadership was not more successful.

Journal Notes

As you read the chapter, record in your journal how the American people conflicted with the government during the Depression.

CULTURAL			
	• *First color motion pictures are demonstrated by George Eastman*	• *Ernest Hemingway publishes* A Farewell to Arms	• *Sinclair Lewis is the first American to win Nobel Prize for Literature*
	1928	**1929**	**1930**
	• *Hoover is elected*	• *Stock market crashes*	• *Hawley-Smoot Tariff is passed*
POLITICAL			

✚ EXTRA CREDIT PROJECT

The SEC and the Economy The stock market of the 1920s was largely unregulated. Following the crash of 1929 and the onset of the Great Depression, the federal government stepped in and created the Securities and Exchange Commission (SEC) in 1934 to oversee the stock market. Suggest interested students research the operation and powers of the SEC and evaluate its effectiveness in preventing problems. Discuss student reports with the class, and ask how important the role of the SEC is in keeping the economy on an even keel. **L2**

History
AND
ART

Tenement Flats
by Millard Sheets, 1934

Millard Sheets's painting evokes feelings of life during the Great Depression.

◀ PROHIBITION AGENT'S BADGE

- *"The Star-Spangled Banner" becomes official U.S. national anthem*

- *Amelia Earhart is first woman to fly solo across the Atlantic*

- *San Francisco Ballet founded*

| **1931** | **1932** | **1933** |

- *Hoover vetoes Veteran Bonus*

- *RFC is established*
- *Bonus Army marches on Washington, D.C.*

- *Franklin D. Roosevelt becomes President*

✓ **Performance Assessment**

Refer to the Performance Assessment Activity in the Planning Guide on page 510b. When the students have finished their charts of effects of economic indicators, have each group present its findings to the class. Allow time for class discussion and feedback.

▱ Use Performance Assessment Activity 17 as an additional assessment technique.

Concept Mapping Activity

On the chalkboard, reproduce the following generalization and concepts map, and have students copy it in their notebooks.

> A chain of economic problems ends prosperity and ushers in a deepening depression that affects all Americans.

| Economic Change | Political Party |

▱ To reinforce the two chapter concepts, use Concept Mapping Activities 17-A and 17-B.

🗂 ▱ Use Chapter Concepts Transparency Activities 17-A, 17-B.

History
AND
ART

Many people lost their homes during the Great Depression because they were unable to meet mortgage payments or pay rent. Millard Sheets's painting depicts life in tenements during this era.

NATIONAL GEOGRAPHIC SOCIETY

 VIDEODISC

GTV: A Geographic Perspective on American History

Side 4, Chapter 3
Title: *Thinking Big*
Subject: Depression, Dust Bowl, New Deal

511

FOCUS

Bellringer

✍ Before taking roll, project Section Focus Transparency 17-1 or hand out Section Focus Transparency Activity 17-1. Have students answer the questions. Discuss student responses.

Motivating Activity

Ask students to think of an event that was so important to them that they have always remembered the day. Discuss how the event affected them. Tell them that the stock market crash of 1929 was such an event. **L1**

Vocabulary Precheck

Ask students to define each of the key terms. Have a volunteer consult the dictionary for any unfamiliar words. **L1, LEP**

⊙ Use the Vocabulary PuzzleMaker Software to create a crossword puzzle. **L1**

✍ Assign Vocabulary Activity 17.

★★

The Stock Market Crashes

Setting the Scene

Section Focus

When Calvin Coolidge declared, "I do not choose to run in 1928," he cleared the way for Herbert Hoover to head the Republican ticket. Many people believed that electing Hoover President would help continue the prosperity. With the great stock market crash of 1929, however, and the chain of economic problems that followed, this optimism disappeared.

◀ HOOVER CAMPAIGN BUTTON, 1928

Objectives

After studying this section, you should be able to
★ explain how Hoover's philosophy affected his economic policy.
★ explain the major causes of the Great Depression.

Key Terms

armory, securities, speculation, on margin, installment buying

---

*H*erbert Hoover easily won the Republican nomination in 1928. A successful geologist, he had spent eight years as secretary of commerce in the Harding and Coolidge administrations. The Democrats chose Alfred E. Smith, four-time governor of New York. Their race for the presidency was marked by the influence of a new invention—the radio.

■ The Election of 1928

The most visible issue in the election campaign was Prohibition. Both candidates vowed to continue enforcing Prohibition. The Prohibition issue, however, masked other important differences between the candidates. Hoover represented rural, agrarian

interests; Smith represented urban, industrial interests.

Religion was at the core of a smear campaign against Smith's Catholicism. Wild tales circulated alleging that Catholics had turned certain Washington church sites into **armories,** or storehouses for guns. Some believed that the White House under Smith would become a branch of the Vatican. Hoover was embarrassed by these accusations and tried to quash them.

Late in the campaign, Hoover made a speech to offer his ideas on the proper relationship of government to business. Government, Hoover claimed, should be "an umpire instead of a player in the economic game." Government had a part to play— conservation of natural resources, scientific research, and flood control were places where Hoover believed government could

---

Classroom Resources for SECTION 1

Blackline Masters:
✍ Reproducible Lesson Plan 17-1
✍ Vocabulary Activity 17
✍ Guided Reading Activity 17-1
✍ Geography in History Activity 17

✍ Enrichment Activity 17
✍ Workbook Activity 17-1
✍ Reteaching Activity 17-1
✍ Section Quiz 17-1

Transparencies:
🖉 Section Focus Transparency 17-1
🖉 Skills Transparency 17

Multimedia:
⊙ Vocabulary PuzzleMaker
⊙ Testmaker
◎ MindJogger Videoquiz
◎ GTV: A Geographic Perspective on American History

make useful contributions. To him, personal liberty depended on economic freedom. He reminded his listeners that:

> *Our experiment in human welfare has yielded a degree of well-being unparalleled in the world. . . . We are nearer to the ideal of abolition of poverty and fear from the lives of men and women than ever before in any land.*

Prosperity was the campaign issue that proved most damaging to the Democrats. The almost uninterrupted prosperity the country had enjoyed during the 1920s was associated in the minds of many voters with the Republican party. Republican campaign slogans such as "two cars in every garage" gave the Democrats no chance of winning the election.

Hoover won an impressive victory in the electoral college with a vote of 444 to 87, taking 58 percent of the popular vote and carrying all but 8 states. His appeal to rural Protestant voters even broke the Democrats' traditional hold on the Solid South, resulting in a Republican win in 5 Southern states. Although Smith lost the election, he won nearly twice as many votes as had the Democratic candidate in 1924. Of greater significance, Hoover became the first presidential winner to lose in the nation's 12 largest cities. A shift in the rural-urban balance of political power in America was in the wind.

■ Hoover in the White House

When he took office in March 1929, Herbert Hoover still radiated optimism. In his Inaugural Address, he predicted that the United States would soon be "in sight of the day when poverty will be banished from this nation."

 ▲ *PROHIBITION RAID* by Thomas Hart Benton, 1929 An unwanted result of Prohibition was the stimulus it gave to illegal activity. Thomas Hart Benton's *Prohibition Raid* is symbolic of the time. **What did the Wickersham Commission recommend?**

▲ CRIME FIGHTER ELIOT NESS

TEACH
Guided Practice
Making Comparisons
Have students write on their papers the four Ps that guided the outcome of the 1928 presidential election: personal prestige, prosperity, Prohibition, Protestantism. Ask them to give one example for each, showing how it worked for Hoover and against Al Smith. **L1**

History AND ART

The rise of organized crime was due partly to Prohibition. Bootleggers, who dealt in the illegal traffic of alcohol, made millions of dollars selling liquor to the public. Eventually the critics of Prohibition won out. In 1933 the Twenty-first Amendment repealed national Prohibition. **Answer to Caption:** recommended that Prohibition should continue

NATIONAL GEOGRAPHIC SOCIETY

 CD-ROM

The Presidents: A Picture History of Our Nation

Have students select the category Presidents' Birthplaces. Suggest they find whether President Hoover carried his home state in the 1928 and 1932 elections.

Critical Thinking Activity

Making Comparisons Economists today are undecided about the possibility of another Great Depression. Some similarities exist between today's economy and that of the 1920s. Suggest students research elements of the current economy (health of the stock market; problems of industry, business, and wage earners; state of agriculture; and so on) and compare them to those of the 1920s. Ask students to form an opinion about whether or not another such severe depression could occur. **L3**

Prohibition

Hoover did not believe that government should let economic events run their course but rather that it should help people to help themselves. He appointed commissions to investigate problems such as housing, retirement pensions, unemployment insurance, child welfare, and conservation. One commission, headed by former Attorney General George W. Wickersham, devoted 2 years to investigating Prohibition. The 11 members of the commission disagreed among themselves on whether Prohibition should continue. Most felt that the "noble experiment" was ineffective and promoted crime, yet the commission as a whole recommended that Prohibition be continued.

Farmers' Problems

The plight of farmers was an issue that demanded more immediate action. In April 1929, Hoover called Congress into special session to pass farming legislation. Members of Congress from farm states demanded that the federal government buy surplus farm products and sell them abroad. Hoover opposed this on the grounds that "no government agency should engage in buying and selling and price-fixing of products." Instead, the President proposed that the federal government help farmers use their own organizations to market produce more efficiently and adjust supply to demand.

Following this recommendation, Congress passed the Agricultural Marketing Act of 1929, which created a Federal Farm Board with $500 million at its disposal to help existing farm organizations and to form new ones. The Farm Board established national cooperatives—such as the National Livestock Marketing Association and the American Cotton Cooperative Association—and then loaned these organizations money to help keep prices stable. It was too little, too late. Farmers were soon worse off than ever.

■ The Crash of 1929

The market value of **securities,** or stocks and bonds, on the New York Stock Exchange more than tripled between 1925 and 1929—from $27 billion to $87 billion. In the summer of 1929, for example, a share of General Motors rose from $268 to $391 and by September 2 rose even higher—to $452 per share.

Speculation

As prices rose, more and more people began speculating. **Speculation** is engaging in a risky business venture on the chance that a quick or sizable profit can be made. People bought

 **Visualizing History**

▲ EFFECTS OF THE CRASH One day after the stock market crash, Walter Thornton advertised his car for sale. Panic hit the stock market as people frantically tried to sell. *What effect did speculation have on the stock market in 1929?*

Sidelight: A Get-Rich-Quick Scheme

A popular scheme to make a quick profit in the 1920s was speculation in land. The biggest boom in real estate was in Florida, where the climate and the possibility of vacation resorts attracted scores of speculators. The value of land in Florida soared, and those who were there first realized big profits. Many, however, bought land sight unseen and ended up with swampland. The land rush in Florida ended in 1926 when a devastating hurricane swept the state.

shares they thought would rise in price quickly, and after prices went up they would sell the stocks for a profit.

To maximize the potential profits on their investments, speculators commonly bought stock **on margin.** To buy stock in this way one made a small cash down payment and borrowed the rest from a stockbroker. For example, for $2,000 a person could buy 100 shares on margin rather than pay cash for 10 shares of stock at $200 per share. The purchaser simply put down 10 percent of the price (or $20 per share) and borrowed the other $18,000 from a broker, who would then hold the shares of stock as collateral for the loan. So long as prices continued to rise, investors could sell the stock later, repay the loan, and reap the profit.

Stock Market Begins to Decline

Some bankers, brokers, and economists were concerned, however, because they knew the stocks for many companies were greatly overpriced in comparison to the earnings and profits the companies were making. Yet most investors were swept along on the tide of the day's optimism. Meanwhile, the market continued its dizzying climb. By the end of 1929, brokers' loans to those who had bought on margin exceeded $7 billion. The Federal Reserve Board tried to restore stability to the market by advising banks not to loan money for buying stocks on margin, but few banks listened.

In September 1929, the market started to waver as some professional speculators sensed danger and began to pull out, and prices slipped. Late in October real disaster struck. On Thursday, October 24, almost 13 million shares of stocks were frantically traded. As stocks' values dropped below the amounts borrowed to purchase them, brokers demanded that investors repay their loans. If they could not, the brokers offered the stock for sale.

Black Tuesday

Recognizing what was going on, investment bankers tried to shore up market prices by purchasing as many shares as they could.

The effort was not enough to stabilize an overvalued market. On October 29—Black Tuesday—the bottom fell out. Some 16 million shares were sold, causing such a collapse that by mid-November the average price of securities had been cut nearly in half. This cost investors about $30 billion, a sum that represented almost one-third of the value of all goods and services produced in the United States in 1929. The loss was equal to the total wages of all Americans that year.

About 1.5 million Americans had been involved in purchasing stock. Many investors lost their entire life savings.

It was the failure of banks that hit people the hardest. Banks loaned money to brokerage houses, which in turn bought stock themselves or loaned money to investors for speculative stock purchases. When loan payments were not forthcoming, many banks went bankrupt. In the aftermath, millions of people who had never bought stock but had trustingly kept their money in savings accounts lost everything as the banks closed.

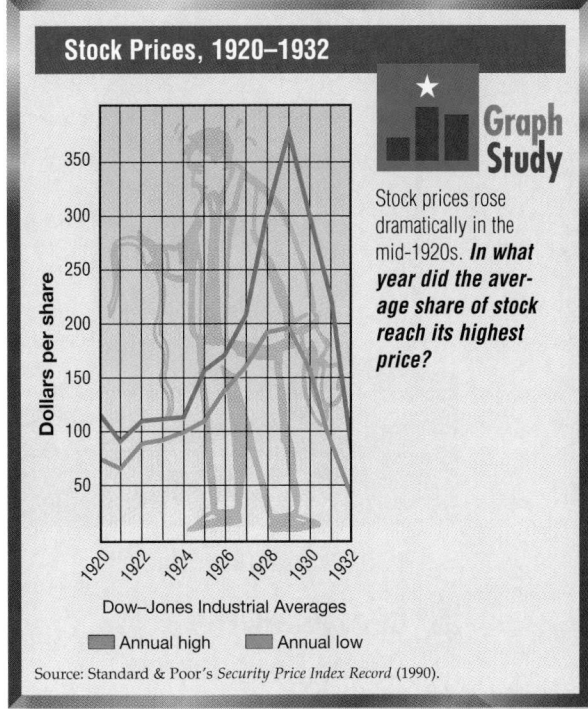

Stock Prices, 1920–1932

Graph Study

Stock prices rose dramatically in the mid-1920s. *In what year did the average share of stock reach its highest price?*

Dollars per share

Dow–Jones Industrial Averages

Annual high   Annual low

Source: Standard & Poor's *Security Price Index Record* (1990).

Using Graphs

Answer: 1929

Graph Skills Practice
Ask students to use the information on the graph and in the text to summarize the course of the American economy in the 1920s.

CURRICULUM CONNECTION

Economics The ability of the consumer to obtain easy credit expanded in the 1920s. Between 80 and 90 percent of purchases for large household items were made through time payments.

Did You Know?

In the 1920s the average price for such items as washing machines, refrigerators, and vacuum cleaners was $97.50, $87.50, and $28.95 respectively.

Cooperative Learning Activity

Examining Issues Divide the class into several groups. Assign each group an event or issue covered in Section 1 (for example, the 1928 election, work of the Wickersham Commission, policies of Hoover, speculation on the stock market, problems of farmers, high tariffs, the crash on "Black Tuesday"). Ask each group to compose a headline and write an article examining the issue or event. Have the groups share their articles with the class. **L1, L2**

ASSESS
Check Understanding
Assign Section 1 Review as homework or an in-class activity.

Evaluate
⊙ 📁 Assign Section Quiz 17-1 or use the Testmaker to create a customized quiz.

Reteach
Ask students to list the major causes of the Depression and their effects on business, labor, and agriculture.

📁 Have students complete Reteaching Activity 17-1.

📁 Assign Workbook Activity 17-1.

Enrich
Suggest students do a "Kelley Chart" to illustrate what would happen to a family caught in a major depression today. Have them imagine that the Kelleys are steelworkers with two children, one in college and one in high school. What items are they likely to be paying for on credit? What assets are they likely to have? What are their major monthly bills? Have students create a chart showing how a depression would affect the Kelleys.

📁 Assign Geography in History Activity 17.

📁 Assign Enrichment Activity 17.

📦 Project Skills Transparency 17 and have students complete Skills Transparency Activity 17.

▲ TELEGRAPHIC TICKER

■ Causes of the Great Depression

The collapse of the stock market was only a prelude to a catastrophic economic decline from which the United States did not recover for 12 years. The causes of the Great Depression were so complex that economists have debated the issue ever since.

Overproduction and Underconsumption

One cause of the Depression was overproduction. Laborsaving machinery had increased the production capacity of the nation's industries so much that far more goods were produced than the American population could consume. For a time, consumer purchasing power was bolstered by **installment buying**—an agreement whereby a purchaser made a down payment and paid the rest of the cost in periodic regular installments to which an interest charge was added. By the late 1920s, most consumers who could afford high-cost items such as refrigerators, cars, or stoves had bought them on an installment plan. Consumer spending began to decrease. From January to September 1929, for example, the number of automobile purchases dropped by one-third.

Another cause of the Depression was underconsumption. In the 1920s the rich got richer much faster than the rest of the people. Some 30,000 families at the top of the economic pyramid had as much income as did the 11 million families at the bottom. Though production increased, employment stood still and workers' wages went up very slowly. In 1929 more than two-thirds of the nation's families were earning less than $2,500 per year, a sum said to be the minimum income for a decent quality of life. About one-fifth of the nation lived in dire poverty. Thus there was insufficient purchasing power to support the nation's mass-production industries.

Agricultural Slump and Surpluses

A prolonged slump in agriculture, which affected the economic life of the entire country, was another factor. Farmers were heavily indebted to banks, which held mortgages on farmlands throughout the nation. The declining value of farms made it harder for farmers to get credit. Banks that had invested heavily in farm mortgages were in danger of failing.

In addition, huge farm surpluses produced a drop in farm prices so great that farmers often spent more money growing and marketing their products than they received in selling them. The resulting loss in farmers' purchasing power further reduced the consumption of manufactured goods—a condition that only added to the problem of underconsumption.

Tariffs and Taxes

The Great Depression was not solely a result of economic practices. Many of the economic policies of the Harding and Coolidge administrations during the 1920s set the stage for problems by the end of the decade. Policies such as the high Fordney-McCumber Tariff, combined with an insistence on collecting war debts, interfered with world trade and destroyed foreign markets for American products, especially in agriculture. The Mellon tax policies, which aided the upper class, contributed to the uneven distribution of wealth. Failure to curb or discourage the stock market's early boom made the ultimate crash more severe.

Critical Thinking Activity

Debating an Issue Have students debate the following proposition: The people who manipulated the stock market and used other means to make money before the crash were just as guilty as those who broke the Prohibition laws and should have been charged and tried as lawbreakers. After students have debated the issue, have them discuss why they think white-collar crime is dealt with so much less severely in this society than other kinds of crime. **L3**

Once started, the Great Depression took on a momentum of its own. Individuals with mortgages on their homes, who had bought cars and other goods on credit and who had purchased stocks on margin, "lost their shirts." They stopped buying, for example, luxuries like radios, causing radio manufacturers to close down plants or run them only part-time. Thousands of workers were laid off as orders were canceled for copper, wood cabinets, and glass radio tubes. Montana copper miners, Minnesota lumberjacks, and Ohio glassworkers in turn lost their jobs.

Because these jobless workers could not meet mortgage payments or repay loans, they lost their property. Banks that had lent them money failed, wiping out the savings of their depositors. Such chain reactions closed down more and more factories, drove more and more firms into bankruptcy, and put more and more Americans out of work.

Russell Hunter, a brass worker in the Naugatuck Valley region of Connecticut, known as the "Brass Valley," describes what the early years of the Depression were like:

❝ *During Hoover's time, we went on short time. After a while, when things really were bad, in 1932, we were working sometimes five hours a week, one day a week. That was tough, trying to raise a family. Nobody lost their jobs completely. They shared [the work] to give every-body something to do. Still, you had to go on welfare. People got by going on the welfare. At that time, people were losing their homes, automobiles. . . .* ❞

The mood of the country was changing. Feelings of optimism were giving way to feelings of fear.

GNP, Stock Values, and Unemployment

Year	Gross National Product (in billions)	Stock Values, New York Stock Exchange (in billions)	Unemployment (Percent)
1920	$140.0	$5.5	5.2
1921	127.8	4.7	11.7
1922	148.0	5.7	6.7
1923	165.9	5.9	2.4
1924	165.5	5.9	5.0
1925	179.4	7.6	3.2
1926	190.0	8.6	1.8
1927	189.8	10.5	3.3
1928	190.9	13.7	4.2
1929	203.6	17.9	3.2
1930	183.5	14.4	8.7
1931	169.3	7.5	15.9
1932	144.2	3.8	23.6

Chart Study Study each column heading, noting the years that show the greatest change. **What was the worst year of the Great Depression for both business and labor?**

Using Charts

Answer: 1932

Chart Skills Practice
Have students look at the column showing GNP. What happened to the GNP between 1927 and 1932? (*rose steadily and then fell sharply*) How did this affect the value of stocks? (*also rose steadily and then fell sharply*) What was the effect on wage earners? (*Unemployment declined and then rose sharply.*) Using this chart, summarize the state of the nation's economy in the 1920s. (*A period of prosperity and high employment was followed by a sudden and steep decline in the economy and a huge rise in unemployment.*)

CLOSE

Have students read the excerpt from Hoover's speech on page 513. Ask students how the events that later occurred in 1929 relate to the validity of President Hoover's assessment.

Section 1 ★ Review

Checking for Understanding

1. **Identify** Wickersham Commission, Agricultural Marketing Act.
2. **Define** armory, securities, speculation, on margin, installment buying.
3. **State** two reasons Hoover won the presidential election in 1928.
4. **Explain** how speculation caused the stock market to rise.
5. **List** four causes of the Great Depression.

Critical Thinking

6. **Synthesizing Ideas** Who was to blame for stock market speculation? Explain.

ACTIVITY

7. For one week, keep track of references in the media to unemployment, consumer spending, manufacturing trends, recession, and prices. After each entry, indicate whether the information was, in your view, positive or negative.

CHAPTER 17 The Depression Begins: 1928–1932   **517**

Answers to SECTION 1 REVIEW

1. Wickersham Commission, 514; Agricultural Marketing Act, 514
2. All vocabulary words are defined in the Glossary.
3. Any two: Hoover's dignified radio style, his stand on Prohibition, campaign, economic prosperity
4. People could buy stocks without putting up much of their own money, rapidly inflating stock prices.
5. World War I war debts, surpluses in agricultural production, overproduction, and underconsumption
6. The government encouraged speculation by not restricting credit availability. Many Americans overextended themselves.
7. Findings will vary but students should note the economic effects with their entries.

TEACH

The ability to buy on credit has fed the boom-bust cycles of the nation's economy. The Federal Reserve Board's lack of action during the 1920s to keep stock prices from becoming credit-inflated and its subsequent reluctance to inject badly needed cash into the post-crash economy intensified the seeming prosperity of the 1920s and the depths of the Great Depression. Even though these mistakes serve as major influences on current Federal Reserve Board policies, the stock market crash of 1987, the junk-bond collapse, and severe banking problems were not prevented.

CURRICULUM CONNECTION

Economics *The New York Times* index of 25 industrial stocks reached 100 in 1924, 181 in 1925, dropped a little in 1926, and rose to 245 by 1927. In 1928 the index rose to 331 and peaked at 452 in early September 1929. The index lost 31 points on October 31. By mid-November its value was 224.

History
AND
ECONOMICS

THE ARTS GEOGRAPHY SCIENCE MATH

The Stock Market

"Sooner or later," said economist Roger Babson on September 5, 1929, "a crash is coming . . . factories will be shut down . . . men will be thrown out of work . . . the result will be a serious business depression." However, most analysts assured Americans that the stock market was healthy and thriving.

A stock exchange is an organized system for buying and selling shares, or blocks of investments, in corporations. In the late 1920s, the value of stocks on the New York Stock Exchange climbed to dizzying heights. To take advantage of the boom, investors borrowed money to buy stocks, a practice known as buying on margin.

In other words, speculators were using their own money to make a relatively small down payment on the stock and borrowing the remainder of the purchase price from a stockbroker. The broker in turn borrowed the money lent to the speculator from a bank. The brokers' loans were call loans—loans that could be called in at any time by the borrower or lender.

The 1920s seemed to be a period of never-ending prosperity. The values of common stock had been increasing steadily year after year. In 1926 more than 450 million shares of stock were traded on the New York Stock Exchange. In 1927 the total rose to more than 570 million. Speculators believed they could make a quick profit in the market. Bankers knew they could make money by lending to brokers. Brokers knew they could come out ahead by lending to customers. Everyone, it seemed, was trying to get rich quickly.

The boom could last only as long as investors added money to the pool. By 1929 everyone with money to invest had bought into the market, and it ran out of new customers. Prices stopped rising. People sold shares to pay the interest on their loans. As shares were sold, prices fell. Panicked investors tried to minimize their losses.

On October 29, less than two months after Babson's prediction, the market crashed. The crash was a symptom, not a cause, of the Great Depression.

▼ WALL STREET

Making the Economics Connection

1. What series of events occur when the stock market crashes?

2. Why did people begin selling shares of stock in the fall of 1929?

ACTIVITY

3. Research information on stock market figures during the months of September and October 1929. Compare these figures with those from a two-week period today. Are any of the companies the same? How much do their shares cost today?

Answers to Making the Connection

1. People stop buying stocks, prices stop rising, people sell to pay off loans, prices fall, people panic.

2. People were afraid that they would not get back the money they invested.

3. Findings will vary. Student work should demonstrate a basic understanding of the workings of the stock market.

Hoover's Policies

Setting the Scene

Section Focus

Before 1929 the federal government had responded to economic depressions by considering different monetary or tariff policies. During the Great Depression, however, the government was forced to seek more vigorous remedies for the nation's vast economic problems. Failing to succeed in domestic policies, President Herbert Hoover made peace the cornerstone of his administration.

Objectives

After studying this section, you should be able to

★ list the ways in which Hoover tried to end the Depression.

★ describe the change in policy toward Latin America under Hoover.

★ describe the Hoover-Stimson Doctrine and evaluate its effectiveness.

Key Term

moratorium

▲ UNION LABEL SYMBOL

*N*o sooner had the stock market collapsed than President Hoover asked leaders of industry, finance, and labor to come to the White House. The President asked labor leaders to abandon or postpone wage demands, industry leaders to keep employment high, and bankers to continue lending.

Hoover and other leaders tried to restore public confidence by issuing optimistic statements. Their rosy predictions were contradicted by worsening conditions, however, and the phrase "prosperity is just around the corner" became a joke. The Republican campaign slogan "Two cars in every garage" had become "Two families in every garage." The President's position was made all the more difficult because he was blamed for the Depression.

■ Domestic Economic Concerns Loom

In dealing with Congress and the public, Hoover was limited by his inflexible views. A man of great ability and possessing a sincere desire to serve the nation, he lacked the practical political experience that comes from being a legislator or state executive. Even with such skills, his position would have been difficult. Republican party leaders never gave him their wholehearted support, and members of the Farm Bloc were in open revolt. As a result of the midterm elections of 1930, the Democrats made gains in the Senate and won control of the House of Representatives. This shift in power led to a Congress that was hostile to Hoover's policies during the last two years of his administration.

CHAPTER 17 The Depression Begins: 1928–1932 **519**

Classroom Resources for SECTION 2

Blackline Masters:
- 🗃 Reproducible Lesson Plan 17-2
- 🗃 Guided Reading Activity 17-2
- 🗃 Cooperative Learning Activity 17
- 🗃 Critical Thinking Skills Activity 17
- 🗃 Chapter Skills Activity 17
- 🗃 Reteaching Activity 17-2
- 🗃 Section Quiz 17-2

Transparencies:
- 🗃 Section Focus Transparency 17-2

Multimedia:
- 🔲 Testmaker
- 🔘 STV: North America
- 🔘 Powers of the President
- 🔘 The Presidents: A Picture History of Our Nation

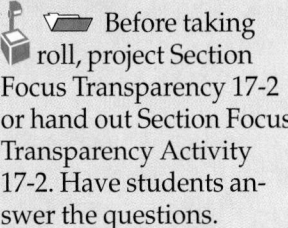

TEACH

Guided Practice

Expressing an Opinion
Have students write letters to the editor about the plight of American farming during the 1920s and early 1930s. They may write from the point of view of a farmer, a food buyer, a member of the Farm Board, a businessperson. Letters should reflect the writers' beliefs in the importance of farming and suggest solutions to the crisis, while criticizing or approving solutions already being offered. **L2**

NATIONAL GEOGRAPHIC SOCIETY

VIDEODISC

STV: North America

Side 2
Frames 03405-09639
Title: *The Central Lowlands*
Subject: The Great Plains

Did You Know?

Despite prejudice and discrimination, an African American leader, Oscar De Priest from Chicago, was elected to Congress in 1928. De Priest was the first African American to attain that position since 1901 and the first Northern African American to serve in Congress.

Tariffs

Like President Taft in 1909, Hoover was unable to control Congress on the tariff issue. The Hawley-Smoot Tariff started in the House as a protection for farmers, but by the time it passed the Senate, it had turned into the highest protective tariff in peacetime history. It raised the average duty on raw agricultural materials and other items above the Fordney-McCumber Act levels.

By the time the Hawley-Smoot bill reached the President's desk in 1930, more than 1,000 leading economists had signed a letter urging him to veto it. They argued that it would help inefficient producers, raise consumer prices, reduce foreign markets, and cause ill will toward the United States in other countries. This opinion was voiced by many newspapers, bankers, and even by a number of manufacturers. Now Hoover faced a dilemma. If he used his veto power, he would isolate himself politically by breaking with the Republican values he held so strongly. Furthermore, he would abandon the one feature of the bill he had fought so hard for—a revised Tariff Commission with the authority to raise and lower rates. He therefore signed the bill in spite of the warnings.

Within a year, 25 nations retaliated with laws to restrict purchases of American goods, causing foreign trade with the United States to drop rapidly. Some American corporations managed to avoid international barriers by establishing factories overseas. Ironically, an act designed to promote American economic recovery instead created employment overseas.

Farmers

American farmers, beleaguered throughout the 1920s, were hit even harder. Farmers' income was cut by more than half between 1929 and 1932; their burden of debt became unbearable. During this crisis the Farm Board tried to maintain the price of wheat and cotton by buying up the surplus of these crops. The Farm Board also attempted—without success—to persuade farmers to plant less, in order to reduce the amount of farm produce grown and thus to prevent further surplus crops. The immense quantities of wheat and cotton held by the government actually drove prices down, however, because buyers feared that the government would sell these surpluses as soon as prices rose. Finally, in 1931 the Farm Board acknowledged defeat and stopped its purchases. Immediately prices dropped even lower. By 1932 farmers were receiving only 38 cents a bushel for wheat that in 1929 had sold at $1.04. Even Hoover's relatives in Iowa suffered from the depressed farm economy. Harry Terrell, a farmer who lived in the same neighborhood as President Hoover in Iowa, described conditions in the following way:

> ❝ *I was born across the road from the farm of Herbert Hoover's uncle. I knew the Hoover family, distant cousins of the President. Even people like them, they had times just like the rest of us. . . . Corn was going for eight cents a bushel. One county insisted on burning corn to heat the courthouse, 'cause it was cheaper than coal."* ❞

■ Hoover's Strong Resolve

Hoover was deeply affected by all the misery and poverty around him, but as a staunch believer in private enterprise, he feared direct government handouts would destroy personal initiative. Hoover therefore offered government help to banks and businesses in the hope that restored financial health at the top of the economic pyramid would eventually trickle down to relieve unemployment at the bottom. Keeping his attitude positive and his resolve strong, Hoover sought to inspire confidence in a people ravaged by hopelessness and despair: "Ninety percent of our difficulty in depression is caused by fear."

Special Needs Activity

Memory Disability New information is learned more quickly and completely when it can be associated with already known information. Memory is aided by activating the "schema" or knowledge frames as underpinnings for the information that presently needs to be remembered. Part of Section 2 deals with American reaction to Japanese aggression in China. Before students read this section, discuss more recent American reactions to aggression by foreign powers. Cite examples such as Iraq's invasion of Kuwait and the struggle for dominance in Bosnia.

▲ *Drought-Stricken Area* by Alexander Hogue, 1934 The collapse of farm prices was compounded by a terrible drought in 1930. ***How did President Hoover feel about providing direct relief to the unemployed?***

In 1932, after Hoover's initial resistance, Congress established the Reconstruction Finance Corporation (RFC). With $2 billion in resources, the RFC made loans to hard-pressed railroads, insurance companies, banks, and even state and local governments—but not to individuals. The RFC favored projects that were "self-liquidating"; that is, projects designed to pay their way so the government would eventually get back its money. Thus projects such as toll bridges and dams that would produce electric power were favored over those that could have been socially useful but brought in no revenue, such as playgrounds, schools, and city halls.

There was a point beyond which Hoover refused to use the power of the federal government. He feared that too much reliance on federal action would result in the "paternalism" and "state socialism" he had warned against in 1928. He opposed direct federal relief for the unemployed because he believed it would weaken the self-respect of those who received it, undercut the efforts of private charity, and that it would destroy the tradition of local responsibility for the unfortunate. Hoover, therefore, vetoed the Garner-Wagner bill in 1932, which would have given direct aid to the unemployed. He also

vetoed the Norris bill, which would have put the government in the business of producing and selling electricity in the Tennessee Valley—thus setting up direct competition with private companies.

■ Efforts for Peace

The desire for world peace was strong during these hard times, partly because preparation for war was costly, and partly because few had forgotten the horrors of World War I.

As a Quaker and a pacifist, Herbert Hoover believed that war was morally wrong; as administrator of Belgian relief between 1914 and 1917, he saw firsthand the devastation of World War I. Hoover was committed to world peace. As he stated in 1928:

❝ *I think I may say that I have witnessed as much of the horror and suffering of war as any other American. From it I have derived a deep passion for peace. Our foreign policy has one primary objective, and that is peace.* ❞

CHAPTER 17 The Depression Begins: 1928–1932   **521**

CURRICULUM CONNECTION

Government Despite cynics' response to what they called "the millionaires' dole," the Reconstruction Finance Corporation turned out to be successful. It also set the stage for the New Deal of Franklin Delano Roosevelt. The Norris bill would also be reborn in the Roosevelt era as the Tennessee Valley Authority.

ABCNEWS INTERACTIVE™

VIDEODISC

Powers of the President

Side Two, Chapter 9
Frames 12225-14316

Title: *World Leader*

Subject: Directing foreign policy

Hoover's peace efforts were aided by his many years spent overseas. The most widely traveled man ever to occupy the White House, he had visited every continent and knew many foreign leaders personally.

Latin America

As secretary of commerce, Hoover had come to understand Latin America's distrust of the United States. Before his inauguration in March 1929, he made goodwill tours of 10 Latin American countries. Hoover stressed that the United States wished to be a friend to its neighbors in Latin America. Many expressed doubts about how effective Hoover's efforts would be. Hoover's Latin American policies reflected a sincere desire to improve relations. In addition to successfully arbitrating a long-standing boundary dispute between Chile and Peru, Hoover abandoned military intervention in Latin American countries.

The Clark Memorandum, written by Undersecretary of State J. Reuben Clark, argued the position that the Roosevelt Corollary to the Monroe Doctrine had no historical basis. Clark wrote, "The Monroe Doctrine states a case of the United States v. Europe, not of the United States v. Latin America." In other words, the Monroe Doctrine could no longer be used to justify American intervention in Latin America.

In accordance with this principle, Hoover withdrew troops from Nicaragua and refused to intervene in the affairs of Latin American states that, because of political chaos, had repudiated their debts to the United States. While this nonintervention policy helped to convince many Latin Americans that the United States had no aggressive intentions, it won Hoover little goodwill. The Hawley-Smoot Tariff had hurt Latin America's economy, and the region's resentment of the power of the United States did not disappear.

Visualizing History ▲ **SOUP KITCHEN** People line up at a 1930s Chicago soup kitchen, operated by gangster Al Capone. Government made few efforts to help citizens fight the effects of the Depression. *What was the Garner-Wagner bill intended to provide?*

Cooperative Learning Activity

Analyzing Ideas Remind students that Herbert Hoover was a Quaker, a member of a religious group that believes in pacifism. Suggest students research the Quakers and write a paragraph analyzing the difficulty of following pacifist beliefs in modern times. Encourage students to explore how Hoover's Quaker heritage may have affected his policies. **L3**

📁 For additional practice in using critical thinking skills, assign Critical Thinking Skills Activity 17.

Disarmament

Hoover strongly favored disarmament, not only because of his personal beliefs but also because military spending and increased taxes depleted valuable resources. Shortly after taking office, Hoover made arrangements for a new conference in London on naval disarmament. Its goal would be to extend the limits on battleships that had been set in the Five-Power Treaty signed in 1921–1922.

After four months of talks, the London Naval Conference of 1930 produced a treaty fixing ratios for the submarines, cruisers, and destroyers of the United States, British, and Japanese navies. Italy refused to sign. France, fearing aggression by Germany and Italy, said that it favored disarmament only if other powers would agree to give France assurance of protection. In the end, France chose not to sign.

Ever since 1927 a disarmament conference hosted by the League of Nations had been meeting at Geneva. Its work was hampered by the activities of lobbyists for arms manufacturers and by mutual mistrust among the delegates. For five years it had gotten nowhere, focusing on such trivial issues as the influence of fog on war. In 1932 President Hoover proposed to the Geneva Conference that the nations of the world either entirely abandon aggressive weapons or cut existing arms by one-third. No action resulted. With Adolf Hitler's rise to power in Germany, however, and Japanese invasions into China, disarmament now seemed like an invitation to aggression. Hoover's proposal could have succeeded only if the United States had been willing to join an alliance of nations committed to "collective security," whereby members would all agree to come to the aid of any member nation who was threatened with aggression.

War Reparations

By 1931 Germany was in the throes of a serious depression. Germans could not continue paying war reparations to the Allies without defaulting on their debts to American private investors. Hoover, like Harding and Coolidge before him, believed that

 ▲ **War Debts** This cartoon suggests that Germany, despite its ability to pay, was making little effort to make payments owed to the United States and its allies. *What political movements did Germany's economic woes help bring about?*

reparations were "a European problem." But heavy war debts and rising unemployment caused great discontent among the German people and led directly to the rapid growth of two antidemocratic parties—the Communist party and the Nazi party.

Moratorium

The Allies were unlikely to cancel German reparation payments, which they used to pay off their own war debts to the United States. To address the problem, in 1931 Hoover proposed an international **moratorium,** or suspension, for one year of all war-debt payments to the United States. Hoover's aim was to protect United States investments in Germany and to save the German Republic from collapse, as well as to stimulate international trade. Secretary of State Henry L. Stimson urged that war debts and reparations be canceled completely, but Hoover refused. To do so would have been a highly unpopular measure and would have worsened Hoover's already poor relations with Congress.

Linking Across
T I M E

In the 1980s, as in the 1930s, American corporations shared similar desires for opening up foreign markets as well as promoting American trade and goodwill abroad. Big-hitter McDonald's opened franchises in Europe and the Soviet Union. Coca Cola opened a plant in Japan. IBM, Xerox, and ITT established factories in Mexican border towns. A bonus for the latter three is cheap labor. Mexican workers earn an average of 55 cents an hour. In addition, the Mexican government does not have strict environmental laws against pollution and does not encourage unions.

Visualizing History Discuss with students why Hoover's disarmament proposals failed. Ask if they might have succeeded had the United States been willing to join in an international alliance with other nations.
Answer to Caption: the Communist party and the Nazi party

Sidelight: Aid to the Soviet Union

Although the United States was hostile to the Communist regime in the Soviet Union, farmers and businesspeople saw the Soviet Union as a new market. Farmers especially wanted to sell their produce to the Soviets. In 1921 Hoover, then secretary of commerce, complied, and some $78 million in food relief was given to the Soviet Union. Hoover believed that some economic relations with the Communists would help make their economy more capitalistic. The aid did not have that effect. It did, however, shore up the Soviet regime and saved millions of Russians from starvation.

ASSESS

Check Understanding

Assign Section 2 Review as homework or an in-class activity.

Evaluate

◉ 🗁 Assign Section Quiz 17-2 or use the Test-maker to create a customized quiz.

Reteach

Have students write several paragraphs to show how the Depression, both in the United States and abroad, affected the foreign policy decisions of the Hoover administration.

🗁 Have students complete Reteaching Activity 17-2.

🗁 Assign Workbook Activity 17-2.

Enrich

Suggest students write dialogues between Hoover and the leaders of labor, industry, and finance whom he asked to meet with him at the White House after the 1929 crash. What did Hoover ask of these men? What might their responses have been? Have students dramatize their dialogues.

CLOSE

Have students reread Hoover's statement on page 521, which states the objective of his foreign policy. Ask them to discuss whether Hoover's foreign policy met this objective and tell why or why not.

■ The Hoover-Stimson Doctrine

The Hoover administration encountered problems in the Far East. In September 1931, Japan seized China's rich province of Manchuria. Taking advantage of the civil war in China and the weak condition of the Western nations, Japanese armies speedily overran Manchuria. This action was in direct violation of the Nine-Power Treaty of 1922, which guaranteed China's sovereignty, and the Kellogg-Briand Pact, which outlawed wars of aggression. It also breached the Charter of the League of Nations, to which both China and Japan belonged.

The Intent of the Doctrine

China appealed to the League of Nations, which turned to the United States for help. President Hoover, however, refused to consider either economic or military action. Instead, he sent an army officer to serve on a League commission to investigate Japanese actions in Manchuria. Secretary Stimson proclaimed in 1932 that the United States would refuse to recognize the legality of any territorial arrangement that violated the Kellogg-Briand Pact. The Hoover-Stimson Doctrine, designed to enlist world opinion against aggressor nations, did nothing to aid China and served only to irritate the Japanese.

Although the nonrecognition policy had been worked out by Hoover and Stimson together, it meant different things to each of them. Stimson wanted the policy to act as a warning, which later might be backed up by economic or military aid. According to Hoover, the statement itself was enough. The United States, he said, did not exist to police the world. Economic sanctions might lead to war, he said, and Japanese aggression in Asia did not "imperil the freedom of the American people." Hoover then said that should the United States be obliged to

> ❝ . . . *arm and train Chinese, [we would] find ourselves involved in China in a fashion that would excite the suspicions of the whole world.* ❞

Nor were the British and French governments willing to apply sanctions. The failure of Western nations to take action only encouraged Japanese expansion into China and Southeast Asia.

Public Opinion

The American public was not prepared to support any interventionist effort that could potentially involve the United States in war once again. This feeling was evident in 1931 when Congress overwhelmingly overrode Hoover's veto and voted to give independence to the Philippines within 10 years. This measure pleased Filipino leaders; it also pleased the United States business community, who wanted to keep Filipino products out of America. However, a major reason for passage of the bill was that the American people no longer wanted to defend the islands, upholding the American anti-imperialist past.

Section 2 ★ Review

Checking for Understanding

1. **Identify** Hawley-Smoot Tariff, Reconstruction Finance Corporation, Clark Memorandum, Hoover-Stimson Doctrine.

2. **Define** moratorium.

3. **Summarize** why Hoover disapproved of relief programs and direct involvement in business.

Critical Thinking

4. **Predicting Consequences** What message did the United States and its allies send by not taking action against Japan?

ACTIVITY

5. Create newspaper headlines to announce the major events covered in this section.

Answers to SECTION 2 REVIEW

1. Hawley-Smoot Tariff, 520; Reconstruction Finance Corporation, 521; Clark Memorandum, 522; Hoover-Stimson Doctrine, 524
2. All vocabulary words are defined in the Glossary.
3. suppressed self-initiative, hurt self-respect, destroyed tradition of local responsibility, put government in competition with private business
4. encouraged Japanese and German expansion through nonintervention
5. Headlines will vary but should be concise and explanatory.

Writing a Persuasive Argument

A persuasive argument is one in which the reader or listener is urged to do something or believe in the same thing as does the writer or speaker.

Learning the Skill

The following guidelines will help you organize and write a persuasive argument:

a. **Research** the topic. What are the facts, and how do people feel about it?

b. **Tailor** your argument to your audience. Exactly who are you trying to persuade? Keep in mind that many people will share your point of view if they see some benefits for themselves.

c. **Support** your argument with solid facts and examples.

d. **Save** the most persuasive arguments for last, then end your paper by summarizing.

Imagine that the following is a paper that you wrote as Herbert Hoover defending his war-debt moratorium. Note how the guidelines were applied:

I am writing to you, the people of France, as you continue to heal the wounds inflicted by the Great War. My heart and thoughts are with you. Look around you. In what condition is Europe? There is depression, unemployment, and debt. Germany, for all its past offenses, is teetering on the brink of collapse. Europe, like America, is fighting the effects of this demoralizing depression. International trade is at dangerously low levels, and the spectre of debt hangs over all of us like a shadow. The time has come to close the gap between how we feel about that Great War, and what we know to be the just and proper way to revive our ailing economies. Let us consider our children's future, and not so much our temporary feelings of outrage for a war that is over. Abide with me in my decision to place a one-year, international moratorium on all war debts. It is time to let go of the past and resurrect the quality of life that has been obscured by this spectre of debt.

▲ PRESIDENT HERBERT HOOVER

Practicing the Skill

1. To whom did President Hoover address his views?

2. What do you think is his most persuasive argument? Explain.

3. How did Hoover summarize his argument?

APPLYING THE SKILL

4. Use the guidelines above to write a persuasive argument for or against the Hawley-Smoot Tariff.

TEACH

Use the guidelines to discuss Herbert Hoover's defense of the war debt moratorium. Ask: At the time of the writing, what was the economic condition of France and the United States? (*Both countries were in a depression.*) Why does Hoover compare suffering in America with suffering in France? (*He wanted to create a feeling of commonality between the nations.*) What arguments does Hoover use to persuade the French to go along with his plans? Point out the way Hoover summarizes his argument. Is it persuasive? Why or why not? (*Answers will vary, but appeals to future generations and to letting go of the past are powerful.*) **L2**

☞ Use Chapter Skills Activity 17 to reinforce students' understanding of the skill.

Did You Know?

When the moratorium ended, Hoover demanded that European nations resume payments. All but Finland, whose obligation was tiny, had no choice but to default.

525

Answers to Practicing the Skill

1. to the French people
2. The future of the world's children is perhaps the most persuasive argument. It makes the reader realize that feelings of revenge could affect the world for years to come.
3. with an appeal to let go of the past and to restore the quality of life that had been lost
4. Persuasive arguments will vary but should use the guidelines presented in the feature.

FOCUS

Bellringer

 Before taking roll, project Section Focus Transparency 17-3 or hand out Section Focus Transparency Activity 17-3. Have students answer the questions.

Motivating Activity

Ask students to consider negative emotions and activities a major depression might cause in a nation. Then have them consider what positive emotions and behavior a widespread crisis might precipitate. **L2**

Vocabulary Precheck

Write "lame duck" on the chalkboard. Have a volunteer skim the section to find the term and read it in context. **L1, LEP**

NATIONAL GEOGRAPHIC SOCIETY

 **VIDEODISC**

GTV: A Geographic Perspective on American History

Side 4, Chapter 3
Title: *Thinking Big*
Subject: Depression, Dust Bowl, New Deal

★★

The Depression Worsens

Setting the Scene

Section Focus

Between Election Day in November 1932 and Inauguration Day in March 1933, the nation's economy hit rock bottom. National income had dropped from $81 billion to $41 billion. Over 25 percent of the nation's workers were unemployed, and many others worked only part-time. Thousands of businesses were bankrupt, thousands of banks had closed, and farmers were in revolt.

Objectives

After studying this section, you should be able to

★ compare the condition of workers and farmers in the early 1930s.

★ discuss the mood of the country as the election of 1932 approached.

Key Term

lame duck

▶ **DEPRESSION SCRIP, EMERGENCY MONEY**

The Depression was uneven in its impact. While many people lost their jobs, the majority of Americans did not. Instead, many found their hours reduced. The few who kept their jobs and did not have their hours or wages cut actually were better off because prices declined. Even so, for most Americans the mood was gloomy—and for good reason. In 1932 over 30,000 companies closed. In just 2 months in 1931 over 800 banks failed, wiping out the life savings of thousands of depositors.

All over the United States, families not able to pay their rent or mortgages were evicted from their homes. Some ended up in communities of makeshift shacks on the outskirts of cities.

■ Want in the Land of Plenty

As the Depression deepened, fear and despair replaced the buoyant optimism of the 1920s. "I'm afraid, every man is afraid," steel industrialist Charles M. Schwab admitted. "I don't know, we don't know, whether the values we have are going to be real next month or not."

Fear

Loss of confidence affected all sorts of people. Some who lost their jobs suffered such emotional effects that they became unemployable. "My father spent two years

---

Classroom Resources for SECTION 3

Blackline Masters:
- Reproducible Lesson Plan 17-3
- Guided Reading Activity 17-3
- Primary and Secondary Source Readings, pp. 44–46
- Linking Past and Present Activity 17

- Chapter Map Activity 17
- Workbook Activity 17-3
- Reteaching Activity 17-3
- Section Quiz 17-3

Transparencies:
- Section Focus Transparency 17-3
- Map Transparency 17

Multimedia:
- Testmaker
- GTV: A Geographic Perspective on American History
- Powers of the President
- The Presidents: A Picture History of Our Nation

painting his father's house," one man later remembered. "He painted it twice. It gave him something to do."

Business leaders hesitated to build new factories or to bring out new products. Frightened bankers became unwilling to lend money, even to borrowers with good character and ample collateral. On the stock market, security prices dropped dramatically. Stock in Radio Corporation of America (RCA) dropped from $101 per share in 1929 to $2.50 in 1932.

Starvation

One of the great ironies of the Depression was that starvation existed in the midst of plenty. The productive capacity of farmers did not slacken. On the contrary, farmers' problems resulted, in part, from their ability to grow more food than they were able to sell. Already in a depression throughout most of the 1920s, the collapse of the farm economy after 1929 wreaked havoc on rural America. Despite Hoover's programs, grain prices dropped so low that farmers heated their homes by shoveling their crops into their furnaces. They protested low agricultural prices by declaring "farmers' holidays" and tried to prevent food shipments to cities. In Iowa farmers blockaded highways and dumped milk trucks in an attempt to make milk scarce and raise its price. In Oregon they slaughtered sheep because mutton prices were lower than what it cost to ship the animals to market. Meanwhile, in America's cities people picked through garbage looking for scraps of meat.

Virginia Durr, an Alabama activist for tenant farmers' rights, described the suffering when she said, "Have you ever seen a child with rickets shaking, as with palsy? No proteins, no milk. And the companies pouring milk into the gutters. . . . People with nothing to eat and they killed the pigs."

▶ APPLE SELLER, NEW YORK CITY, 1932

Visualizing History

▲ "HOOVERVILLES" Many families lost their homes during the Great Depression because they were unable to meet mortgage payments or pay rent. Some of the homeless found living quarters in shacks constructed of tin and old crates. Villages of these makeshift shacks, such as this one in Seattle, Washington, sprouted up throughout the nation. *How did the rate of unemployment change between 1930 and 1933?*

TEACH
Guided Practice
Making a Chart Ask students to make a class chart showing the people or organizations that appeared during the Depression to offer economic solutions. **L1, LEP**

Visualizing History Scenes such as these were commonplace in cities across the nation during the Great Depression. Not only were people homeless but in spite of soup lines, thousands searched through garbage dumps for food.
Answer to Caption: number of jobless more than tripled

📁 Assign Primary and Secondary Source Readings, pp. 44-45: "The Problems of Unemployment."

ABCNEWS INTERACTIVE™

◎ **VIDEODISC**

Powers of the President

Side Two, Chapter 11 Frames 15800-17889
Title: *Protector of the Peace*
Subject: Maintaining domestic tranquillity

Cooperative Learning Activity

Creating Visual Displays Have students work in groups to create visual displays of the effects of the Depression. They may make posters, photo essays, or newspaper headlines, or draw illustrations. Each group should choose a focus: the effects on children, on the land, on families, or on employment. Ask a reporter for each group to explain the group's display to the class. Displays can be mounted in the classroom for the duration of the unit. **L1, L2** 📦

Independent Practice

Research Have students research photographs and political cartoons from the Depression era and display them on a bulletin board. Ask them to write captions describing the illustrations. Then conduct a class discussion, asking such questions as: What images were used repeatedly as symbols of these times? How were politicians portrayed in cartoons?

Discuss with students the kinds of images used to symbolize problems in today's society. **L3**

📂 Assign Guided Reading Activity 17-3.

Linking Past and Present

Point out to students that there are other games that have long histories and are popular around the world, such as spinning tops, playing with marbles, and cat's cradle. Ask students to describe games that they play or have played that were also played by their parents or grandparents.

📂 For additional practice, assign Linking Past and Present Activity 17.

Linking Past and Present

★★★★★★★★★★★★★★★

The Game of Monopoly

Board games are a favorite American pastime, and one of the more popular is Monopoly. The game, in which each player's goal is to make money while forcing the opponents into bankruptcy, originated and flourished, oddly enough, during the height of the Great Depression.

Then_____

Atlantic City Vacations

Charles Darrow was a tinkerer, continually designing puzzles,

games, and toys. The unemployed Philadelphia engineer hoped that if one of his creations proved popular, his family could once more afford their cherished excursions to Atlantic City. One thought prompted another, and one night in 1931 Darrow sat down at his kitchen table to design a game. He sketched in the name of Atlantic City streets on a board. He carved little wooden houses, hotels, and tokens. He printed direction cards and title deeds, and added dice and play money. Soon Darrow was taking orders from Philadelphia department stores. The popularity of the game spread when the Parker Brothers Game Company began distributing Monopoly nationwide. Within a short time, the company was producing nearly

20,000 sets a week—and Darrow could afford as many Atlantic City vacations as he wanted.

Now_____

Worldwide Popularity

Monopoly has become popular in many other parts of the world. Published in more than 25 nations in 19 languages, Monopoly is challenged only by Scrabble as the best-selling trademarked game in the world. Sets merchandised in other nations are adapted to represent native locales. The British version of the game, for example, uses the names of London streets.

★★

■ The Human Cost of the Depression

Although business leaders promised Hoover that they would not cut wages of remaining workers, as the Depression deepened, their situation changed.

Wage Cuts and Unemployment

In October 1931, United States Steel Corporation cut salaries and wages by 10 percent, and employers in other industries soon followed. By 1933 salaries had decreased 40 percent and hourly wages by 60 percent. The average family's income fell from $2,300 in 1929 to $1,600 in 1932. More layoffs followed the wage cuts. In 1930, 4 million workers were unemployed; by 1933 the number of jobless Americans more than tripled.

In cities throughout the country breadlines and soup kitchens appeared on sidewalks as local governments and private charities struggled to feed the poor. In some cases the lines stretched for blocks as people waited for their only good meal each day.

As unemployment grew, Hoover's Reconstruction Finance Corporation began to loan money to state governments for relief, but these and other relief funds proved woefully inadequate. Toledo, Ohio, for example, could only spend 2 cents for each relief meal it served. New York City provided only $2.39 per week to each family on relief. In many other cities, after private charity was exhausted, there was nothing.

Hoovervilles

Throughout the nation, families who could not pay their rent or make their mortgage payments were evicted from their homes. Some moved in with relatives if they could. The less fortunate ended up in makeshift communities dubbed "Hoovervilles" on the outskirts of cities. One woman later remembered Oklahoma City's Hooverville:

Sidelight: Talking Pictures

Although the first talking pictures were released in 1927, it was not until after the crash that most motion picture theaters were equipped for sound. By then weekly movie attendance reached 110 million out of a population of 121 million. As the Depression grew, the new medium found inventive ways to provide viewers with escape from their troubles. By far the most successful creations were the extravagant musicals. The plots were simple or nonexistent, and the musicals projected upbeat and unreal worlds. Movie musicals could not have existed before the 1930s and have never been more popular since.

> *Here were all these people living in rusted-out car bodies. I mean that was their home. There were people living in shacks made of orange crates. One family with a whole lot of kids was living in a piano box. This wasn't just a little section, this was maybe ten miles wide and ten miles long. People living in whatever they could junk together.* 〞

People who were even less fortunate slept in doorways or on park benches. Desperate men grubbed in garbage cans to feed their families. Nearly every street corner had its apple seller. So many apples were available because of a surplus of the fruit in the Pacific Northwest. To reduce the surplus, the International Apple Shippers Association set up a system for unemployed people to sell the apples. A person could get a credit for $1.75 for a crate of 100 to 120 apples, then turn around and sell the apples for 5 cents each, making a small profit. However, as more and more people tried to make money this way, apple vendors reacted by raising the price to $2.25 a crate. Unless a person sold more than half a crate, he or she made no profit.

Other jobless Americans banded together in hunger riots, smashing into grocery stores and grabbing whatever food they could carry. Begging increased dramatically, and the song "Brother, Can You Spare a Dime?" became a bitter testimony to veterans who remembered fighting a war to protect American values and to make the world safe for democracy.

■ The Bonus Army

In May 1932, some 1,500 unemployed army veterans and their families marched on Washington, D.C., to demand early payment of the bonus Congress had promised to pay them in 1945. Within sight of the White House, some set up a Hooverville in an area across the Potomac River known as Anacostia Flats. Others occupied abandoned buildings in the area. As they demonstrated daily in front of the White House and the Capitol, their numbers increased to more than 20,000.

The government tried to keep the protesters peaceful. President Hoover supported their right to express their views and even provided them with army tents, cots, and field kitchens. When Congress

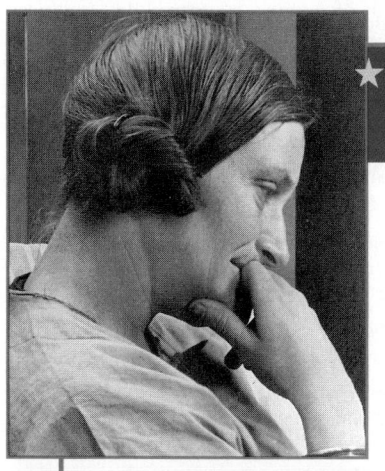

★★★★★**A**★★★★★★★★
AMERICAN PORTRAITS

Dorothea Lange
1895–1965

By the time she finished high school, Dorothea Lange had chosen her career. She wanted to be a photographer—even though she had never used a camera.

After taking a photography course, Lange journeyed from New York to San Francisco, where she ran a portrait business for 10 years. Then the Depression struck. Lange became a documentary photographer, her compassion showing clear-ly in her photos. By the mid-1930s she was documenting the life of California's migrant laborers, work that earned her a position with the Farm Security Administration (FSA). Her FSA photos revealed poverty's brutal effects on rural Americans. Lange later traveled through the dust bowl states, capturing people's suffering in a book called *An American Exodus, A Record of Human Erosion.*

Cultural Perspectives

Minority Groups and the Depression Remind students that although all classes of society, except for the very rich, suffered during the Depression, minority groups were particularly hard hit. Divide the class into three groups, and assign a minority group to each: African Americans, Hispanics, Native Americans. Have students research their group and report on their particular problems and what attempts if any were made to resolve them. When groups report their findings, conduct a class discussion on such questions as: How were their problems the same? How were they different? Were there similarities in ways they tried to solve their problems? What problems were not resolved?

Teaching American Portraits

Dorthea Lange did with photography what John Steinbeck did with literature in *The Grapes of Wrath.* Lange's most famous portrait photo, *Migrant Mother,* is exhibited in the Library of Congress. In 1960 a panel at the University of Missouri included it as one of the 50 best photographs of the first half of this century. In 1966, a year after her death, Lange was honored by a retrospective show of her works at the Museum of Modern Art in New York City. Have students consider the idea of photographers picturing people suffering and in distress. How do you think such pictures affect the viewer? **L1**

Did You Know?

Many Americans found ways to get along as best they could with what they had. Some held "rent parties," inviting guests to give a donation to help pay the rent. Others thought that going "back to the land" might help solve the problem. Others simply sought escape in the popular film comedies and musicals of the time.

▱ Assign Primary and Secondary Source Readings, p. 46: "The Bonus March."

Visualizing **History** Although Hoover was blamed for the excessive force used against the bonus army, it was General MacArthur who gave the orders and disobeyed Hoover's directive not to use force. **Answer to Caption:** with fear and excessive force

VIDEODISC

Powers of the President

Side Two, Chapter 10
Frames 14322-15791
Title: *Manager of the Economy*
Subject: The President and the economy

---

rejected their demands, most of the veterans left Washington. About 2,000 refused to leave, however. After a clash between the veterans and the local police, Hoover called in the army. General Douglas MacArthur, commander of the troops, carried out the President's orders to clear the veterans from federal buildings. Using tanks, machine guns, and tear gas, his troops drove the veterans out of Washington and burned their camp. Historian Frederick Lewis Allen described the sudden chaos that resulted:

> **Cavalrymen were riding into the crowd, infantrymen were throwing tear-gas bombs, women and children were being trampled and choking from the gas; . . . [People] were running wildly, pell-mell across uneven ground, screaming as they stumbled and fell. The troops moved slowly on, scattering before them veterans and homegoing government clerks alike. . . . That evening, the Washington sky glowed with fire. Even after midnight the troops were still on their way with bayonets and tear-gas bombs.**

Many Americans blamed Hoover for the use of brutal and excessive force against the veterans. He seemed more than ever an inflexible leader.

■ Fear of Revolution

During this time of bewilderment and despair, fear of revolution started to spread. Lloyds of London, a British insurance company, began to write policies for riot insurance in the United States. Looking for scapegoats, Americans blamed the Depression on the very people they had admired and willingly followed a few years earlier— industrialists and bankers. Public outrage

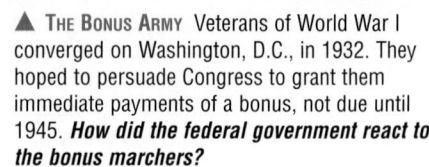

Visualizing **History**

▲ **THE BONUS ARMY** Veterans of World War I converged on Washington, D.C., in 1932. They hoped to persuade Congress to grant them immediate payments of a bonus, not due until 1945. *How did the federal government react to the bonus marchers?*

increased when a Senate investigation charged that some of the nation's wealthiest were trying to get away without paying taxes on their huge incomes. Others were accused of using unscrupulous business practices to increase their own wealth in the midst of such widespread poverty and suffering.

Radical Alternatives

The unrest in society offered hope to both Socialists and Communists, who preached that the Depression marked the end of capitalism, which would soon be replaced by a system that distributed goods more fairly. Both groups proposed that government control the means of production and distribution. Both promised that a planned economy would result in greater abundance for all. "Folks are restless," observed Mississippi Governor Theodore Bilbo, "communism is gaining a foothold. . . . In fact, I'm getting a little pink myself."

Sidelight: A Tradition Begun in the Depression

The lighting of the Christmas tree at Rockefeller Center in New York City is a tradition televised for the nation each year. The first Christmas tree in what was to become Rockefeller Center (at the time it was a block of rubble from demolished townhouses) was decorated with tin cans and paper in 1931. The decorators were New York City workers who still had jobs. The official Rockefeller Center tree tradition was inaugurated two years later.

Such radical alternatives were weakened because Socialists and Communists bitterly opposed each other and destroyed each other's credibility. The Socialists proposed to gain their power by persuasion and the ballot box. The Communist party, however, held that capitalism could not be overthrown without violent revolution—what Earl Browder, the general secretary of the party, called the "omelet theory." Just as it was impossible to make an omelet without breaking eggs, Browder explained, it was impossible to make a revolution without breaking heads.

Using the Forces of Democracy

Fears of a revolution in the United States proved to be unfounded, however. Although many Americans were suffering, were angry, and wanted a change, protest movements tended to be splintered. No single leader emerged to galvanize them or act as a unify-

ing force. Most Americans clung to their democratic traditions and expressed their anger at the ballot box.

■ The Election of 1932

As the presidential election of 1932 approached, the Democrats sensed victory for the first time since 1916.

The Candidates

The Democratic national convention rejected Al Smith's bid for renomination and instead chose New York Governor Franklin D. Roosevelt as their candidate. The former assistant secretary of the navy had run as the candidate for Vice President in 1920. In 1928, while Smith was losing the presidential election to Hoover, Roosevelt had won New York's race for governor and

▲ *HOME RELIEF STATION* by Louis Ribak, 1935–1936 The painting expresses the frustration felt by the American people during the Depression years. *What did the election of 1932 reveal about American public opinion concerning the Hoover administration and its response during the most difficult years of the Depression?*

NATIONAL GEOGRAPHIC SOCIETY

CD-ROM

The Presidents: A Picture History of Our Nation

Have students select Time Line from the main menu. Suggest they write headlines noting major events during President Hoover's term in office.

History AND ART

Home-relief stations were generally set up by church-sponsored groups or private charities.
Answer to Caption: that the Hoover administration was incapable of dealing with the deepening depression

Food of the Times

The main sources of food for thousands during the Great Depression were soup from the "soup kitchens" and bread from the "bread lines." Those who had a little money might treat themselves to the "blue-plate special" offered by diners.

Critical Thinking Activity

Analyzing Historical Issues Have students consider the following issue: Americans were so discouraged by the Depression and the failure of the Republicans to alleviate its effects that they would have voted for anyone the Democrats offered in 1932, as long as the candidate offered a change. Ask students if they think Roosevelt's platform would have been accepted by a less demoralized populace, or whether he really did speak to something valuable and long lasting in the American people at that time. Have students present their analysis orally for class discussion. **L2**

531

Linking Across TIME

After 60 years of government involvement in the economy, millions of Americans are still homeless and jobless. Pictures of homeless men, women, and children huddled in makeshift quarters or of centers to feed the hungry in the 1980s and early 1990s are difficult to distinguish from those of the earlier period.

Ask students if they think government today is doing enough to resolve the problem of homelessness. Ask what suggestions they can offer.

Visualizing History The American people responded enthusiastically at the polls to Roosevelt's call for action to rescue the nation from the Great Depression.
Answer to Caption: The entire country was seized by a banking panic.

ASSESS
Check Understanding
Assign Section 3 Review as homework or an in-class activity.

Visualizing History ▲ INAUGURATION DAY During the ride to Roosevelt's inauguration, Hoover seemed glum while Roosevelt appeared confident. *What happened to the American economy between Election Day 1932 and Inauguration Day 1933?*

in the process proved himself to be a remarkable vote-getter. In 1930 he had been reelected by a huge majority.

The Campaign

The Democratic platform of 1932—the briefest in United States political history—urged the repeal of Prohibition and made general proposals for reform and recovery. The Democrats' most effective asset, however, was Roosevelt himself. Setting the tone for

• •
Footnotes to History

The Roosevelt Campaign Franklin D. Roosevelt had been stricken with polio in 1921 and could not walk without braces and canes. Very few photographs were taken of Roosevelt in a wheelchair. Determined to prove that his disability would not affect his performance as President, Roosevelt set out on a grueling cross-country campaign trip.

what became a whirlwind campaign, he flew by plane to the Democratic convention to become the first candidate to accept a presidential nomination in person.

In his acceptance address, he pledged "a new deal for the American people." In later speeches, however, he was vague and described the "New Deal" in broad terms only. It remained clear that Roosevelt intended to take action that would help "the forgotten man at the bottom of the economic pyramid." He summed up the history of the Hoover administration in four sentences:

> **First, it encouraged speculation and overproduction through its false economic policies. Second, it attempted to minimize the crash and misled the people as to its gravity. Third, it erroneously charged the cause to other nations of the world. And finally, it refused to recognize and correct the evils at home which it had brought forth; it delayed reform, it forgot reform.**

The Republicans, meanwhile, gloomily renominated Hoover, who suffered the problem of having to defend his policies in the midst of a terrible depression. He maintained that hard times were the result of economic collapse abroad—for which his administration could not be held responsible. Hoover flatly rejected Roosevelt's position that government had "a positive duty to see that no citizen shall starve." "You cannot," warned Hoover, "extend the mastery of government over the daily life of a people without somewhere making it master of people's souls and thoughts."

On Election Day, the Republican victories of the 1920s were completely reversed as Roosevelt carried 42 of the 48 states. This landslide revealed not only a widespread willingness to blame the Republicans for the Depression but also a desire to use government as an agency for human welfare.

Yet even at the bottom of the worst depression in history, few Americans favored the overthrow of capitalism, either by violent or peaceful means. The election

Sidelight: Hoover Dam

One project undertaken by the Hoover administration that rivaled New Deal programs was the construction of a huge dam on the Colorado River at the Arizona-Nevada border. One of the highest concrete dams in the world, the structure was finished in 1936 at a cost of about $385 million. The dam controls the flooding of the

Colorado River and provides hydroelectric power for much of the Southwest. Today environmentalists are concerned that the uneven flow of the Colorado River, controlled by the dam, is causing deterioration of the canyon's walls and beaches.

results revealed that the Socialists polled 900,000 votes and the Communists only 100,000. This meant that their combined share was a little more than 2 percent of all of the votes cast.

Banking Panic

In the time between Roosevelt's election in November and his inauguration in March, the Twentieth Amendment was added to the Constitution, changing the date of the presidential inauguration from March 4 to January 20. Had this amendment gone into effect sooner, it would have been better for the country. For four months Hoover as President was a **lame duck,** an officeholder with little influence, because his term was about to end. During this time the nation was virtually leaderless. The new President—Franklin D. Roosevelt—was without power to act.

During this short time, the entire banking system disintegrated, and the economy ground almost to a standstill. Although thousands of smaller banks had already failed, most of the larger banks seemed to be able to hold firm during this time. Despite Roosevelt's promise that upon becoming President he would take action to rescue the nation from the Depression, in early 1933 the entire country was seized by a banking panic. Having lost faith in the nation's economy, thousands of depositors withdrew their money from banks and hoarded cash and gold. Given such a situation, even the most stable banks were bound to stop payments

 ▲ DEPRESSION LIFE These three children, ages 5, 12, and 7, were discovered living in an abandoned house. Many Americans demanded action to escape such economic woes. *What candidate won the 1932 election?*

eventually because there was not enough gold in circulation to cover all deposits.

As the situation deteriorated, state governors issued proclamations closing the banks of their states until confidence could be restored. By March 4—the day Roosevelt would take the oath of office—almost every private bank in the country was closed or placed under restriction by state regulation. From 1930 to the eve of the inauguration, more than 5,400 banks had shut down. The people of the nation waited anxiously to see what the new President would do.

Section 3 ★ Review

Checking for Understanding

1. **Identify** bonus army, General Douglas MacArthur.

2. **Define** lame duck.

3. **Describe** the mood of the country as the Depression worsened.

4. **Explain** why farmers destroyed crops and livestock even though people were hungry.

Critical Thinking

5. **Identifying Problems** What part did the public's lack of confidence in government play in the banking crisis?

ACTIVITY

6. Write a day's entry in the diary of a 17-year-old looking for work during the Great Depression.

Evaluate

☞ Assign Section Quiz 17-3 or use the Testmaker to create a customized quiz.

Reteach

☞ Have students complete Reteaching Activity 17-3.

☞ Assign Workbook Activity 17-3.

Enrich

Invite students to discuss how Franklin Delano Roosevelt's paralysis from polio and subsequent actions served as a metaphor for people's lives throughout the Depression. What other metaphors of this kind can students find throughout history or today?

☞ Assign Chapter Map Activity 17.

☞ Assign Map Transparency Activity 17.

CLOSE

Suggest students write a short analysis of what happened to make people's attitudes change toward government intervention in the economy between 1920 and 1930.

Visualizing
History Point out that estimates indicate that about 1 million people, including about 200,000 children, became drifters.
Answer to Caption: Democratic candidate Franklin D. Roosevelt

Answers to SECTION 3 REVIEW

1. bonus army, 529; General Douglas MacArthur, 530
2. All vocabulary words are defined in the Glossary.
3. Americans became fearful, confused, and angry. Some blamed the wealthy.
4. It cost too much to send it to market, and to

sell the crops and livestock would lower prices even further.
5. People withdrew money from the banks and hoarded cash and gold.
6. Diary entries will vary. Students should show awareness of effects of the Depression on workforce.

Using Vocabulary

Imagine that you must write a handbook on tips for investing in the stock market. Write an entry about speculation that explains the pros and cons. Use these terms:

speculation   on margin
securities   installment buying

Reviewing Facts

1. **Explain** how overproduction or underconsumption was one cause of the Great Depression.

2. **Describe** the effects of the Hawley-Smoot Tariff.

3. **Summarize** Hoover's actions to combat the Depression and the philosophy behind the actions.

4. **List** two defeats Hoover had in foreign policy.

5. **Cite** reasons for the rise of communism and socialism during the Depression.

6. **State** three reasons Franklin D. Roosevelt won the election of 1932.

7. **Discuss** the banking crisis of 1933 and relate it to the overall mood of Americans.

Understanding Concepts

Economic Change

1. Was America's appetite for money and consumer goods a cause of the Great Depression? Explain how activities such as stock market speculation and installment buying contributed to the crisis.

2. How did economic changes affect American faith and beliefs about the United States? Why do you think some Americans feared a revolution? Explain the increased activity among the Socialists and Communists in America.

Political Policy

3. Explain why Hoover's political beliefs were popular while the economy was doing well but increasingly unpopular during the Depression.

4. Do you think Roosevelt, using the platform he proposed in 1932, would have won the 1928 presidential election? Explain your answer.

Critical Thinking

1. **Contrasting Ideas** Explain the difference between laissez-faire economics and Hoover's beliefs about government in the economy.

2. **Analyzing Trends** Study the graph on farm prices, then answer the questions that follow.

   a. What is the time period in the graph?

   b. When were wheat and corn prices the highest? The lowest?

   c. What is the overall trend in the prices of wheat, corn, and cotton?

   d. How did this trend affect farmers during the Great Depression?

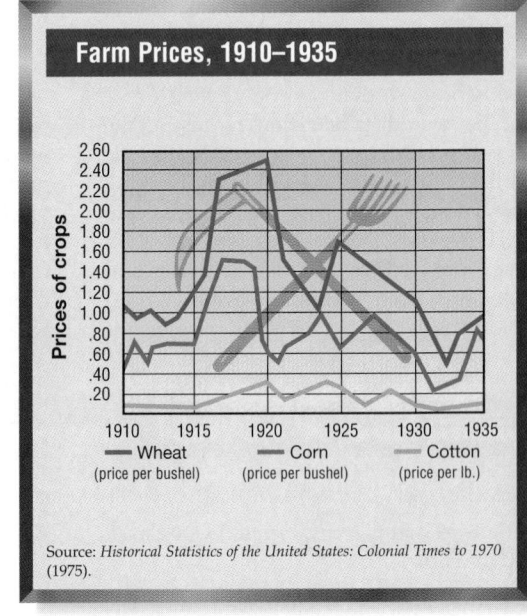

Farm Prices, 1910–1935

Prices of crops

2.60 / 2.40 / 2.20 / 2.00 / 1.80 / 1.60 / 1.40 / 1.20 / 1.00 / .80 / .60 / .40 / .20

1910   1915   1920   1925   1930   1935

— Wheat (price per bushel)   — Corn (price per bushel)   — Cotton (price per lb.)

Source: *Historical Statistics of the United States: Colonial Times to 1970* (1975).

3. **Analyzing Choices** Explain why the Hoover-Stimson Doctrine was ineffective. Make a list of reasons why Americans might have been unwilling to go to war in the early 1930s.

Using Vocabulary

Handbook entries will vary but should demonstrate an understanding of the economic terms.

Reviewing Facts

1. insufficient purchasing power to buy goods that were being mass-produced cheaply

2. The tariff raised import duties. Other nations raised their duties, shrinking U.S. exports.

3. Hawley-Smoot tariff, established RFC, vetoed direct relief; The philosophy was based on helping the economy heal itself without much government help.

4. League refused to back disarmament; could not deter Japanese aggression; Latin America

5. People looked for change, thought capitalism was dying, reacted against materialism.

6. energetic personality, his promise to help needy and use government power

7. demand for cash intensified, people lost confidence, removed deposits, hoarded gold

Understanding Concepts

1. Americans were swept up in the mood of the 1920s. However, prosperity built on credit lasts only as long as the real confidence that supports it. The crash served as the great altering force.

2. Many could find no work, and some feared starvation. Political ideologies that promised to redistribute wealth were attractive.

3. They greatly contributed to both the boom and the bust.

4. Probably not. In 1928 the economy was booming, and Americans believed in Hoover's philosophy of individual initiative.

Critical Thinking

1. Hoover did not completely believe in *laissez-faire* policies since it was the role of government to guarantee

4. **Identifying Assumptions** Compare the Democratic and Republican platforms in the election of 1932. What assumptions did the Republicans make about what American voters were thinking?

5. **Making Predictions** Research recent newsmagazines such as *Newsweek, U.S. News and World Report, TIME,* or *Business Week* for a summary report on the state of the economy. Compare the information in the report with the description of the economy prior to the Depression in your text. List any similarities and differences between the two time periods. Predict whether another depression could occur.

History and Geography

Agriculture and the Depression

1. **Human/Environment Interaction** Why did the Farm Board want farmers to plant fewer crops?

2. **Human/Environment Interaction** What conservation measures did President Hoover support?

Cooperative Learning Interdisciplinary Activity: Economics

Work in groups of three to analyze the causes of the Great Depression. Assign each group member two of the causes listed on pages 515–517 of your text. Have each group member make a list of economic and social effects that might have resulted from his or her cause. For example, if your subject is underconsumption, explain how this factor affected store owners, manufacturers, and consumers. When you have finished your individual lists, create a master list entitled "How the Great Depression Changed America."

Practicing Skills

Writing a Persuasive Argument

Refer to the skills lesson on Writing a Persuasive Argument on page 525 to help you practice this skill.

Imagine that you are an American citizen at the time of the Great Depression. Use information from Chapter 17 to write a persuasive argument on one of the following topics.

1. Why President Hoover was/was not justified in his refusal to give direct aid to victims of the Great Depression.

2. Installment buying was/was not a major cause of economic woes.

3. The United States should/should not follow a policy of isolation.

4. Documentary photography captured/did not capture the sufferings during the Great Depression.

▲ **DEPRESSION FAMILY PHOTOGRAPHED BY DOROTHEA LANGE**

Writing ABOUT History Using Your Journal

Compare and contrast the conflict of Americans with government during the Depression with the ways they cooperated with government during World War I.

History and Geography

1. in order to reduce the amount of farm produce grown and thus to prevent further surplus
2. scientific research and flood control

Cooperative Learning

Encourage students to include as many effects as they can for each of the causes.

Practicing Skills

For questions 1–4, persuasive arguments will vary. Students should apply the four guidelines presented on page 525.

Writing ABOUT History Using Your Journal

Responses will vary, but students should recognize that people pulled together for a common cause, and the economy was boosted by the war. People were pulled apart by the Depression, and the government did little to alleviate conditions, creating disillusionment and tensions.

? Chapter Bonus Test Question

Ask: How did a platform of intervention in the economy affect the election of 1932? *(Americans wanted government to help alleviate economic conditions, which were growing worse under a Republican administration.)*

justice, but to do so with limited intervention.
2. **a.** 1910–1935
   b. wheat: 1920—highest, 1932—lowest; corn: 1916—highest, 1931—lowest
   c. a decrease
   d. hit hard because prices were not maintained but fluctuated

3. The doctrine did not offer any real incentive for Japan to leave Manchuria. The human and economic costs of World War I and the Depression left little money to finance armament and even less spirit to use armaments in war.

4. Americans did not want direct federal aid. 2. Americans would not blame him for the Depression.
5. Predictions will vary but students should note the similarities and differences between the two time periods.

Cultural Kaleidoscope

The 1920s

Fashions in the 1920s

During the 1920s, postwar America rebelled against many of the social values that were in place at the turn of the century. Nowhere was this revolution more evident than in the fashions of the period. The flapper, embodying independence and social rebellion, became the model for the new woman.

Poised and chic couples set a sophisticated style of dress in the 1920s.

During the 1920s straight, unfitted dresses were in vogue. Skirts seemed to rise and fall with the stock market. When Wall Street boomed during the 1920s, skirt lengths rose above the knee.

The straw hat, or boater, was the common headwear for men.

Many women adopted a new kind of hat style, a drooping, bell-shaped hat called a cloche.

536

◄ Bow tie

▼ Artist John Held, Jr., helped create the image of youth in the 1920s. His art often appeared on the cover of popular magazines.

► Woman's earring

► The changes in society gave women a greater measure of intellectual and economic independence.

537

Cultural Kaleidoscope

Portfolio Project

Ask students to collect advertisements and other illustrations from newspapers and periodicals showing current versions of the items pictured in this kaleidoscope. Ask students to write a brief caption that summarizes the difference between the two styles. They might also write a brief report explaining how contemporary fashions reflect the roles of women in society today. (For example, running shoes might symbolize women's desire for comfort and their interest in keeping fit; they are also a unisex fashion.) **L2**

History and the Humanities

U.S. History & Art Transparency 22, "Yellow Cactus Flower" by Georgia O'Keeffe

American Literary Heritage, pp. 39–41, from *Main Street*, by Sinclair Lewis

Primary and Secondary Source Readings pp. 42–43, *What Is a Flapper?* by Samuel Crowther

The Spirit of American Art and Music, pp. 43–44, Duke Ellington

The Historian's Craft

Although popular culture glorified the "new women" of the 1920s, scholars gather evidence to see how much change actually occurred. For instance, statistics show that although men's earning increased in the 1920s, women's earnings fell. Also many firms fired women as soon as they got married. A study of laws passed or enforced during the period reveal that though women could now vote, in many states they could not serve on juries, hold office, or own a business. As one contemporary historian writes: "It is now clear that flappers were the exception rather than the rule in the 1920s."

UNIT FIVE
DIGEST

Exploring Unit Themes

The Unit Digest may be used to teach unit coverage when time is limited, to review unit content, or to relate the content of one unit to that of another.

■ Chapter 15

Remind students that the United States tried to stay out of World War I. Then ask them to consider what is sufficient provocation for going to war.

■ Chapter 16

Read to the class the following excerpt from Frederick Lewis Allen's *Only Yesterday:* "... [L]ike the suddenly liberated vacationist, the country felt that it ought to be enjoying itself more than it was, and that life was futile and nothing mattered much. ..." Discuss with students whether this is an accurate picture of the United States in the 1920s.

Causes and Effects

Ask students to write a magazine article in which they describe the causes and effects of the stock market crash of 1929, using the information in the chart.

Chapter 15

World War I Era

Wilson, an idealist who believed in fair play, wanted the United States to stop using military force and economic pressure as a tool of foreign policy. However, he ended up imitating his Republican predecessors by sending American troops into the Caribbean. Latin Americans came to resent his "moral imperialism" as much as Theodore Roosevelt's "Big Stick."

When war erupted in Europe in 1914, the United States declared neutrality. But British and French propaganda, American business interests, and German submarine warfare persuaded Americans to side with the Allies.

An apparent conspiracy between Mexico and Germany against the United States and the sinking of four American merchant ships ended American neutrality. Congress declared war on Germany in April 1917.

Unprepared for war, Americans mobilized with incredible speed. The production of armaments became a top priority, and government agencies such as the War Industries Board reorganized the economy to supply them. The draft was reinstated and propaganda was produced to influence public opinion. The government raised money for the war effort through taxes and selling bonds.

When the balance of the war tipped in favor of the Allies, an armistice was signed in November 1918. The Allies rejected most of Wilson's peace plan. After the war the United States experienced economic and social unrest, punctuated by strikes and race riots.

The Stock Market Crash of 1929

CAUSES

- Unrestricted availability of credit
- Greatly inflated sense of prosperity
- The government's "hands-off" policy toward business

● The Market Crashes

EFFECTS

- Massive unemployment
- Economic downturn
- Loss of confidence in financial institutions
- Questioning of government policy
- Trend toward social consciousness

Chapter 16

The Decade of Normalcy

By the 1920s Americans wanted to get on with their lives, forget about public affairs, and stay out of wars. Warren G. Harding understood this when he promised "normalcy," a return to the values and practices of the past. The United States was now too enmeshed in world affairs to return to isolationism and continued to be involved in foreign diplomacy.

President Harding and his Republican successor Calvin Coolidge eased restrictions on business and looked after business interests. These policies seemed to work as the growth of new, urban industries fueled an economic boom during the 1920s. The growing prosperity was a key factor in the decline of labor unions' strength.

Major social changes and cultural achievements took place during the 1920s. Prohibition brought on a crime wave. The success of radio advertising increased the demand for consumer goods. The automobile affected more than the economy; it seemed to change the American way of life. Along with their newly won suffrage, American women demanded economic opportunity. In the "Harlem Renaissance," African Americans reflected a new spirit of pride and protest.

After World War I, however, feelings against immigrants led Congress to seriously restrict all immigration into the United States.

Cooperative Learning Activity

Paraphrasing Divide the class into small groups, and have students turn to President Wilson's Fourteen Points in the Documents section. Ask the groups to read the document and work to rewrite or paraphrase the Fourteen Points, making them readily understandable to junior high school students. Have groups compare their paraphrased documents. Some groups might like to test the effectiveness of their work by teaching the document to a junior high school class. **L2**

▲ Bonus Army skirmish, 1932

Have students construct an economic time line showing the major developments of the era.

 Student Self-Test Software allows students to test their understanding of historical concepts at the unit, chapter, or section levels.

⌒ Have students listen to the Chapter Digests on the audiocassettes.

 Use the Testmaker to create a customized test for Unit 5.

GLENCOE TECHNOLOGY

 **VIDEODISC**

Use the MindJogger Videoquiz to review students' knowledge.

MindJogger Videoquiz

	**Chapter 15** Disc 2, Side B
	**Chapter 16** Disc 2, Side B
	Chapter 17 Disc 2, Side B
	Available in VHS.

Flashcards

Use American History Flashcards to reinforce students' knowledge of places and events in American history.

Chapter 17

The Depression Begins

Herbert Hoover slid into the presidency in 1928 full of optimism. In foreign policy Hoover practiced a "Good Neighbor" policy with Latin American republics. In domestic policy he assured Americans that as long as business thrived, the country would prosper.

Farmers, however, were already experiencing a depression, and government relief proved ineffective. On Black Tuesday, October 29, 1929, the stock market crashed, losing much of its value. This touched off a business and economic decline from which the country did not recover for more than a decade. The Great Depression was caused not only by stock market speculation but also by the effects of World War I, the depressed condition of agriculture, and unwise government policies.

By the end of the 1920s, thousands of Americans were jobless, and many farmers lost their land. Hoover offered to help banks and businesses but opposed direct federal relief to the unemployed because he feared that government handouts would destroy Americans' drive to work.

The American economy had hit rock bottom by the 1932 presidential election. Signs of instability and rebellion appeared everywhere. In the election, Democrat Franklin D. Roosevelt won the presidency by a wide margin.

Understanding Unit Themes

1. **Conflict and Cooperation** Explain why Americans felt so willing to cooperate with their government during World War I but felt in conflict with it during the Depression.

2. **Influence of Technology** How did technological innovation alter the lives of Americans in both war and peace?

3. **The Individual and Family Life** Trace the social changes covered in the unit from war to peace, from prosperity to depression.

4. **U. S. Role in World Affairs** In what specific ways did the United States's role in world affairs change during this time?

Answers to Understanding Unit Themes

1. Concerted efforts produced results during World War I. During the Great Depression, however, many Americans became disillusioned because of the government's inability to make their lives better.
2. Military technologies prolonged war. Automobile led to migration.
3. made economic sacrifices; more women worked; the Great Depression was a time of hardship.
4. Wilson was an idealist and wanted to stop using military force and economic pressure in foreign relations. Harding and Hoover pursued peace by trying to improve foreign relations and by pushing for disarmament.

BEGINNING THE UNIT

Provide this cause-and-effect chart to students with the effects omitted. Assign students to complete the chart as they read the chapters in the unit.

Events
- The New Deal

Causes
- The Stock Market Crash of 1929
- The Great Depression
- The Dust Bowl
- The election of Franklin Roosevelt

Effects
- The expansion of the federal government
- American involvement in World War II
- Postwar prosperity

History AND ART

This wartime painting of Flying Grumman Wildcat Fighters filling the skies above an old-fashioned hay wagon illustrates the changes that were taking place in the 1930s and 1940. Encourage students to speculate about the causes and effects of those changes.

0:00 OUT OF TIME?

If time does not permit teaching the entire unit, use the Unit Digest on pages 662–663.

UNIT SIX
TIMES OF CRISIS
1932–1960

CHAPTER 18
The New Deal
1932–1939

CHAPTER 19
World War II
1933–1945

CHAPTER 20
The Cold War
1945–1952

CHAPTER 21
Search for Stability
1952–1960

▲ M-1 RIFLE, FIRST USED DURING WORLD WAR II

▲ WPA PLAY POSTER, 1936

History AND ART

B-17 Base in England
by Peter Hurd, 1943

Less than 25 years after World War I, the United States found itself at war again. This war, however, was far different. It was a fight for survival, and before it was over, it involved almost every nation in the world.

540

Exploring Unit Themes

American Democracy During the New Deal years, the federal government's role in the economy grew. The government also assumed responsibility for the neediest members of society by providing work, relief, and assistance.

Civil Rights and Liberties While African Americans made some gains during the New Deal and war years, they still did not enjoy equality with whites, and attempts to pass civil rights legislation were defeated. Women's rights followed a similar pattern—gains made during the New Deal and war years were largely rolled back in the 1950s.

Conflict and Cooperation After World War II, the United States entered into a number of mutual defense alliances. It also played a leading role in

Setting the Scene

Several major crises deeply affected the United States between 1930 and 1960. A great depression endangered the nation's economic system, and foreign military power threatened its national security. Americans committed themselves to economic recovery and to fighting—first, the Axis Powers in World War II, and later, the spread of communism.

Themes

- American Democracy
- Civil Rights and Liberties
- Conflict and Cooperation
- U.S. Role in World Affairs

Key Events

- New Deal legislation
- Dust Bowl
- Japanese attack Pearl Harbor
- Surrender of Germany and Japan
- United Nations Charter
- Cold War
- Truman Doctrine
- North Atlantic Treaty Organization
- Korean War
- Polio vaccine
- Suez Crisis
- Castro controls Cuba

Major Issues

- New Deal programs attempt to relieve economic hardships and pull the United States out of the Great Depression.
- Aid to the Allies and the Japanese attack on Pearl Harbor pulls the United States into World War II.
- The desire to contain communism leads the United States to assume a more active role in world affairs.

▼ WORLD WAR II POSTER

Together We WIN

▲ FLYING GRUMMAN WILDCAT FIGHTER, 1942

Portfolio Project

Identify something you consider a symbol of the era and describe the ideas and emotions connected with it. Try to include visual materials.

the founding of the United Nations, an international organization dedicated to solving conflict through peaceful negotiations.

U.S. Role in World Affairs The Japanese attack on Pearl Harbor drew the United States into a fighting role in World War II. The United States emerged as the major power in the postwar world, assuming leadership in the reconstruc-

tion of war-torn Europe and the fight against the spread of communism.

Examining the Themes Point out that this unit describes a series of crises that shook and ultimately transformed the United States. Have students identify the changes each of these crises brought about.

interNET CONNECTIONS

For more in-depth study of Unit 6, you or your students may use the Internet to research individual topics.

World Wide Web:
Franklin D. Roosevelt Library and Museum:
http://www.academic.marist.edu/fdr/fdrintro.htm
World War II:
http://www.lib.muohio.edu/~skimmel/wwii/index.html

Portfolio Project

After students have chosen their symbols and completed the first draft of their work, ask them to edit one another's writing.

History and the Humanities

American Music: Cultural Traditions: New Deal "Franklin D. Roosevelt's Back Again" by Bill Cox and Cliff Hobbs (2:50) World War II "Boogie Woogie Bugle Boy" by the Andrews Sisters (2:47)

U.S. History & Art Transparency 24: *Migrant Mother, 1936* by Dorothea Lange

Global Perspectives

LESSON PLAN
Global Perspectives

FOCUS
Motivating Activity
Have students review the information on the world section of the time line. Then ask them to suggest titles for each of the three decades that sum up the developments of those decades. For example, the 1930s might be titled "The Rise of Totalitarianism." Ask students to do the same thing for the United States section of the time line. Have students compare their titles. **L1**

TEACH
Guided Practice
Exploring the Time Line
The Suez Crisis of 1956 had a chilling effect on the United States's relations with its allies. American leaders were angered that Britain, France, and Israel took action without consulting them. The British and French governments countered by accusing John Foster Dulles, Eisenhower's secretary of state, of collusion with the Soviet Union. While this bitterness dissipated over time, during 1956 there was serious talk of dismantling NATO. Have students compare the Suez Crisis with the Persian Gulf Crisis in terms of allied relations. **L2**

The World

	1930	1940
Asia and Oceania		
Europe		
Africa		
South America		
North and Central America		

◄ **1934** *Hitler becomes Der Führer of Germany*

1939 *World War II begins in Europe*

1938 *Venezuela becomes the third-largest oil-producing nation in the world*

The United States

	1930	1940
Pacific and Northwest		
Southeast		
Midwest		
Southwest		
Atlantic Northeast		

► **1941** *Japanese attack on Pearl Harbor brings United States into World War II*

1937 *Parts of the Southwest and the Great Plains become a dust bowl*

◄ **1933** *Newly inaugurated President Franklin D. Roosevelt launches New Deal*

542   UNIT 6 Times of Crisis: 1932–1960

Cultural Perspectives

Revival of Religion The United States experienced a revival of religion during the 1950s. In a 1954 survey, 56 percent of the men and 69 percent of the women claimed to be active participants in worship services. Protestantism, Roman Catholicism, and Judaism were recognized as the three "American faiths," and there was now a growing tolerance among their members toward differences in religious beliefs. Popular religious leaders included Jewish rabbi Joshua Loth Liebman, the Catholic priest Monsignor Fulton J. Sheen, and the Protestant evangelist Billy Graham. All three had large followings, wrote books, and made extensive use of radio or television.

Linking Across TIME

The Chinese and Japanese have played a major role in American life, especially in California and Hawaii, since the mid-1800s. They may have set foot on the North American continent hundreds of years before. Some scholars believe that Hui Shen, a Chinese missionary, explored the Pacific coast of North America as early as the 400s! There is solid evidence to suggest that Chinese sailors regularly visited California in the mid-1500s. Before the closing of Japan in the 1600s, Japanese sailors, too, probably ventured as far as California.

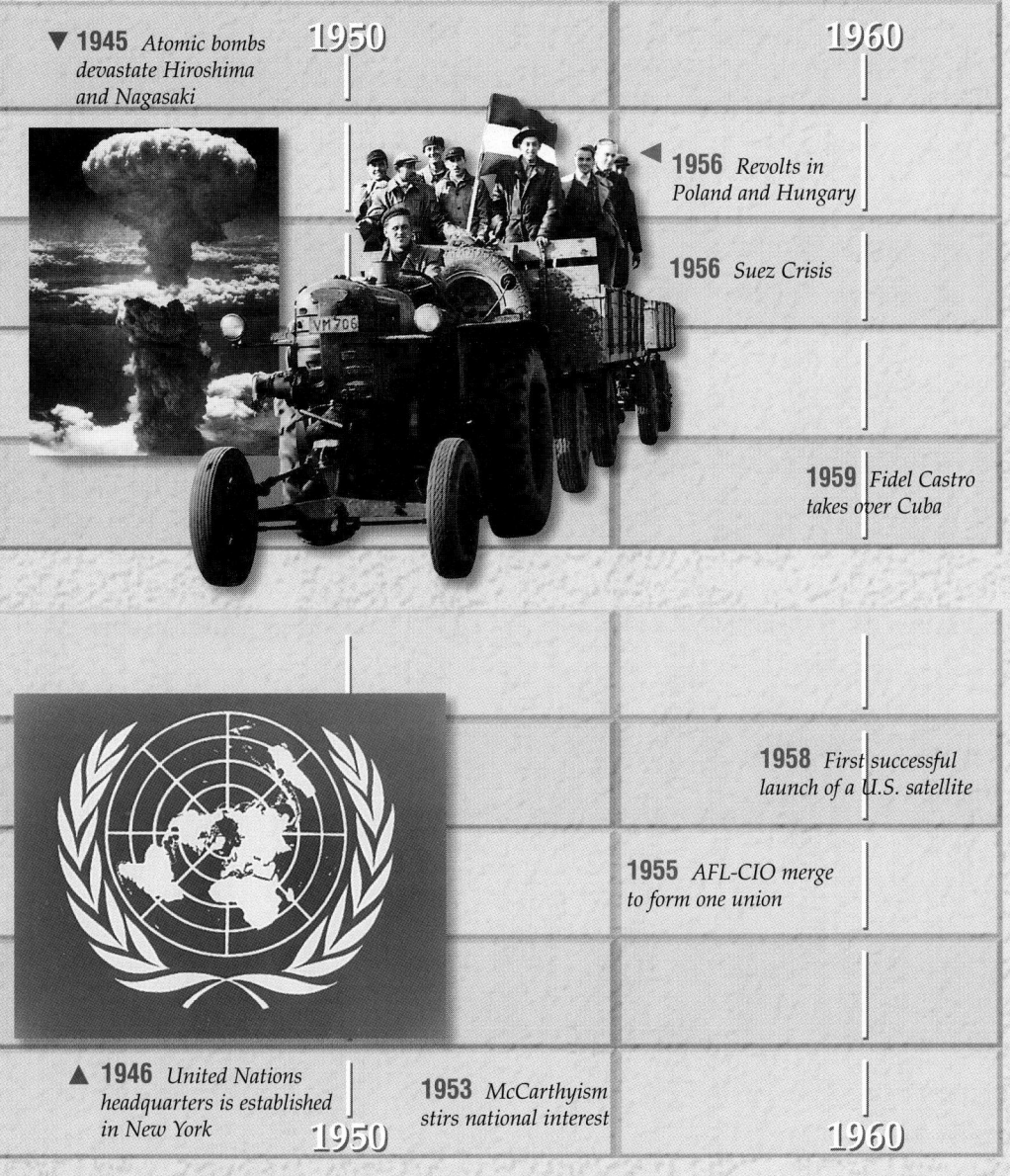

1950

1960

▼ **1945** *Atomic bombs devastate Hiroshima and Nagasaki*

◄ **1956** *Revolts in Poland and Hungary*

1956 *Suez Crisis*

1959 *Fidel Castro takes over Cuba*

1958 *First successful launch of a U.S. satellite*

1955 *AFL-CIO merge to form one union*

▲ **1946** *United Nations headquarters is established in New York*

1950

1953 *McCarthyism stirs national interest*

1960

543

Daily Lesson Objectives	Teacher Classroom Resources	Multimedia
SECTION 1 **Roosevelt Takes Charge** **1 Day** pp. 544–550 1. Identify the traits that made Franklin Roosevelt an effective leader. 2. Describe how Roosevelt gained ideas and support for his New Deal.	Reproducible Lesson Plan 18-1 Concepts Mapping Activities 18-A, 18-B *Vocabulary Activity 18 *Guided Reading Activity 18-1 Workbook Activity 18-1 Reteaching Activity 18-1 *Section Quiz 18-1	Section Focus Transparency 18-1 Chapter Concepts Transparencies 18-A, 18-B MindJogger Videoquiz GTV: A Geographic Perspective on American History GTV: The American People: Fabric of a Nation
SECTION 2 **Reform, Relief, and Recovery** **1 Day** pp. 551–557 1. Give examples of how Roosevelt's policies helped and hurt the rural poor. 2. Compare the effectiveness of measures aimed at farmers and city workers.	Reproducible Lesson Plan 18-2 *Guided Reading Activity 18-2 Political Cartoons in American History Activity 16 Cooperative Learning Activity 18 Chapter Map Activity 18 Geography in History Activity 18 Workbook Activity 18-2 Reteaching Activity 18-2 *Section Quiz 18-2	Section Focus Transparency 18-2 Map Transparency 18 Testmaker Powers of the President The American History Videodisc American Music: Cultural Traditions
SECTION 3 **The Second New Deal** **1 Day** pp. 559–566 1. List the groups that challenged Roosevelt. 2. Outline the steps taken to achieve reform. 3. Identify the events that led to the end of the New Deal.	Reproducible Lesson Plan 18-3 *Guided Reading Activity 18-3 Linking Past and Present Activity 18 Chapter Skills Activity 18 Workbook Activity 18-3 Reteaching Activity 18-3 *Section Quiz 18-3	Section Focus Transparency 18-3 Skills Transparency 18 Testmaker Economics in Action Focus on Government The Presidents: A Picture History of Our Nation
SECTION 4 **The Impact of the New Deal** **1 Day** pp. 567–573 1. Identify changes that the New Deal caused in American society. 2. Evaluate the effects of the New Deal on life today.	Reproducible Lesson Plan 18-4 *Guided Reading Activity 18-4 Critical Thinking Skills Activity 18 Enrichment Activity 18 Workbook Activity 18-4 Reteaching Activity 18-4 *Section Quiz 18-4	Section Focus Transparency 18-4 U.S. History & Art Transparencies 23, 24 Testmaker Focus of Government
CHAPTER REVIEW AND EVALUATION **1 Day**	Chapter 18 Test, Forms A and B Spanish Chapter 18 Summary Performance Assessment Activity 18	MindJogger Videoquiz Student Self-Test & Review Software *Chapter 18 Audiocassette Activity and Test

*Also available in Spanish

 OUT OF TIME? If time does not permit teaching the entire chapter, use the Chapter 18 Summary on pages 662–663 and the Chapter 18 audiocassette (English and Spanish) to point out the main ideas of the chapter.

A complete, 1-page lesson plan is provided for each section in the *Reproducible Lesson Plan* booklet.

Key to Ability Levels

Teaching strategies have been coded for varying learning styles and abilities.

L1   Basic activities for all students

L2   Average activities for average to above-average students

L3   Challenging activities for above-average students

LEP   Limited English Proficiency activities

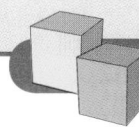

Block Schedule

Block scheduling differs from traditional class scheduling in the amount of time allotted to each period. The extended time frame provided by block scheduling affords you the opportunity to implement a greater number of research-oriented and activity-intense projects to motivate and involve your students. Activities that are particularly suited to use within the block scheduling framework are identified throughout this unit by the following designation:

✔ Performance Assessment Activity

Researching Popular Culture   Organize students in groups of four or five to research the popular culture of the Depression years. Each group might focus on a different aspect of culture. For example, one might research films of the time, while another investigates music, literature, radio programs, or the popular magazines of the day. Invite each group to report its findings to the class in the form of an oral report. The reports should explain what students learned about life during the Depression from their research. In addition, you may wish to have the groups prepare a collage that portrays an individual actor, filmmaker, writer, or artist of the era. Encourage groups to compare and contrast their findings.

POSSIBLE RUBRIC FEATURES

- Content Information
- Research Skills
- Organization
- Writing and Communication Skills
- Critical Thinking Skills

📁 For additional activities, see Performance Assessment Strategies and Activities.

TEACHER'S CORNER

NATIONAL GEOGRAPHIC SOCIETY

NATIONAL GEOGRAPHIC SOCIETY PRODUCTS AVAILABLE FROM GLENCOE

To order the following products for use with this chapter, contact your local Glencoe sales representative or call Glencoe at 1-800-334-7344:

- *The Presidents: A Picture History of Our Nation* (CD-ROM)
- *GTV: A Geographic Perspective on American History* (Videodisc)
- *GTV: The American People: Fabric of a Nation* (Videodisc)

ADDITIONAL NATIONAL GEOGRAPHIC SOCIETY PRODUCTS

To order the following products for use with this chapter, call National Geographic Society at 1-800-368-2728:

- *1929–1941: The Great Depression* (Video)
- *The American Presidency* (Filmstrip)
- *Decades of History: The 20th Century—The Early Years* (Filmstrip)

GLENCOE TECHNOLOGY

VIDEODISC

Use the Chapter 18 MindJogger Videoquiz to preview the content of this chapter.

MindJogger Videoquiz

Chapter 18
Disc 2, Side B

 Available in VHS.

Recording Journal Notes

To help students get started, ask them to watch for accomplishments of Eleanor Roosevelt and Frances Perkins. Encourage them to investigate what each woman contributed to the Roosevelt administration.

Linking Across TIME

Point out that the New Deal had its roots in Progressive legislation of the early 1900s. Franklin Roosevelt's activist style resembled that of his cousin, Theodore. Many of the officials who developed New Deal programs had served as officials in the administration of Woodrow Wilson.

CHAPTER 18
★★

The New Deal
1932–1939

▶ SHOVEL, CIVILIAN CONSERVATION CORPS

Setting the Scene

Focus

When Franklin D. Roosevelt took the oath of office, Congress and the American people were eager to follow the President's leadership. Within months, laws were passed to provide relief, recovery, and reform of the economic system. Two years later, however, millions of Americans were still unemployed, and the New Deal came under increasing criticism. Throughout Roosevelt's second term, many programs were reshaped to permanently change the way government relates to its citizens.

Concepts to Understand

★ How New Deal **economic reform** differed from previous policies

★ Why the **political leadership** of Roosevelt was effective at bringing about New Deal reforms

Read to Discover . . .

★ how New Deal legislation attempted to end the Depression.

★ what long-term effects the New Deal programs had on American society.

Journal Notes

What role did women play in the Roosevelt administration? Note the details in your journal.

CULTURAL
- **1932** American speed skaters and bobsledders earn medals in the Winter Olympics

1932

POLITICAL
- **1933** Repeal of Prohibition
- **1933** "Hundred Days" begins after Roosevelt's inauguration

- **1934** Severe drought in the Great Plains creates a dust bowl
- **1935** Middletown is published

1934

- **1934** Securities and Exchange Commission is established
- **1935** Social Security Act is passed

✚ EXTRA CREDIT PROJECT

The National Mood Before Franklin Roosevelt took office, many Americans feared that the country would soon erupt in revolution. They believed that the nation's social fabric was weakened by the Great Depression. Ask interested students to interview someone who lived through the early 1930s. Interviewers should encourage their subjects to recall what people were talking about at the time. What were their concerns? Expectations? Hopes for the future? Ask these students to share their findings with the class. **L2**

▲ NEW DEAL POSTERS

CHAPTER 18 CONCEPTS

Concept Mapping Activity

On the chalkboard, reproduce the following generalization and concepts map, and have students copy it in their notebooks.

The government attempts to stimulate the national economy and to shelter individuals from the effects of the Depression.

Economic Reform	Political Leadership

📁 To reinforce the two chapter concepts, use Concept Mapping Activities 18-A and 18-B.

📁 Use Chapter Concepts Transparencies 18-A, 18-B.

History AND ART

We Demand
by Joe Jones, 1934

Depression painter Joe Jones emphasized working people in his art. In *We Demand*, he concentrated on the efforts of workers to organize the protest to improve their wages and conditions of employment.

History AND ART

Depression-era paintings like *We Demand* by Joe Jones celebrated workers. These paintings suggested the heroic qualities in ordinary people.

- **1936** *Tornadoes kill more than 400 Southerners in 5 states*
- **1938** *Thornton Wilder's play* Our Town *wins Pulitzer Prize*

1936	1938

- **1936** *Roosevelt is reelected*
- **1937** *Roosevelt attempts to pack the Supreme Court*
- **1938** *Fair Labor Standards Act passes*

NATIONAL GEOGRAPHIC SOCIETY

 VIDEODISC

GTV: The American People: Fabric of a Nation

Side 3, Chapter 8
Title: *Shoulder to Shoulder*
Subject: Building on America's diversity during the Depression

✓ **Performance Assessment**

Analyzing Ideas Point out that Congress passed the Indian Reorganization Act in 1934. Part of the original proposal that was rejected included a plan to set up special courts that took into account Native American traditions and customs in decisions involving a conflict between self-governing Native American communities and state and local governments. Ask students to work in groups on a report to answer the following questions. Why do you think lawmakers turned down that part of the proposal? What are some arguments in its favor? Against it? Have students research recent court battles between Native Americans and state governments over land claims. Have each group present its findings to the class. **L2**

FOCUS

Bellringer

Before taking roll, project Section Focus Transparency 18-1 or hand out Section Focus Transparency Activity 18-1. Have students answer the questions. Discuss student responses.

Motivating Activity

Ask students what they think President Roosevelt meant when he said, "The only thing we have to fear is fear itself." *(Fearing what might happen is often far worse than what actually does happen.)* **L1**

Vocabulary Precheck

Write *fireside chat* on the chalkboard. Ask students to use the term in a sentence. **L1, LEP**

Use the Vocabulary Puzzlemaker Software to create a crossword puzzle. **L1**

Assign Vocabulary Activity 18.

★★★

Roosevelt Takes Charge

Setting the Scene

Section Focus

President Roosevelt's Inaugural Address attempted to lift the gloom and fear that had blanketed the country. At last, a new President promised action against the Depression. Congress and the American public—some in eager anticipation and others out of desperation—were ready to follow the President's lead.

Objectives

After studying this section, you should be able to

★ identify the traits that made Franklin Roosevelt an effective leader.

★ describe how Roosevelt garnered ideas and support for his New Deal.

Key Term

fireside chat

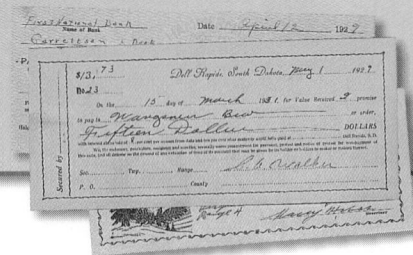

▲ PERSONAL BANK CHECKS

Within his Inaugural Address Franklin D. Roosevelt made the same promises about the nation's recovery that Herbert Hoover and his advisers had been making since 1929. Roosevelt promised that the nation "will endure as it has endured, will revive and will prosper." Unlike Hoover, however, the new President reflected the popular mood of the nation by blaming bankers, "the unscrupulous moneychangers," for allowing starvation in the midst of plenty. The nation was in a kind of war, he said, and strong presidential leadership was needed. Sketching the need for various relief and reform measures, the new President called for immediate legislation. If Congress failed to act quickly, Roosevelt promised to ask for executive authority "as great as the power that would be given to me if we were in fact invaded by a foreign foe."

■ A Strong Leader

Before taking office, Roosevelt displayed little evidence of the leadership he would offer in his 12 years in the White House. One writer described him as "an amiable man . . . who without any important qualifications for the office, would very much like to be President." His outstanding attribute was his name, which his cousin Theodore Roosevelt had made well known in American politics.

Early Life

The only son of wealthy parents, FDR, as his friends called him, attended the best schools. At the time of his election, Roosevelt had been in politics for more than 20 years, yet his views on many issues were unknown. Nor did many Americans realize that he had overcome a serious physical handicap.

546   UNIT 6 Times of Crisis: 1932–1960

Classroom Resources for SECTION 1

Blackline Masters:
- Reproducible Lesson Plan 18-1
- Guided Reading Activity 18-1
- Vocabulary Activity 18
- American Portrait 55

- Primary and Secondary Source Readings, pp. 47-48
- Workbook Activity 18-1
- Reteaching Activity 18-1
- Section Quiz 18-1

Transparencies:
- Section Focus Transparency 18-1

Multimedia:
- Vocabulary PuzzleMaker
- Testmaker
- MindJogger Videoquiz
- GTV: A Geographic Perspective on American History
- GTV: The American People: Fabric of a Nation

In 1921, at age 39, Roosevelt was stricken with polio. Fighting back against the crippling disease, he regained the use of his hands and arms, but he remained paralyzed from the waist down. His painful recovery toughened him and, at the same time, gave him genuine sympathy for the less fortunate. Playwright Robert Sherwood, a close associate, described his toughness and compassion:

> **"** *I tried continually to study him, to try to look beyond his charming and amusing and warmly affectionate surface into his heavily forested interior. But I never understood what was going on in there. . . . He could be a ruthless politician, but he was the champion of friends and associates who for him were political liabilities . . . and of causes which apparently competent observers assured him would be political suicide.* **"**

A Master Politician

Both friends and foes agreed that, despite his complexity, Roosevelt was master of the art of politics. Few Presidents had such varied political training—at local, state, and federal levels—in elected and appointed offices. Elected to the New York legislature in 1910, at the height of the Progressive Era, Roosevelt learned about local government. As assistant secretary of the navy during World War I, he had an insider's view as the Wilson administration organized the federal government to wage war. As governor of New York when the stock market crashed, FDR dealt with many of the same problems he would face as President.

Perhaps Roosevelt's greatest strength as a politician was his warm and understanding approach to people. Where Hoover had withdrawn to the isolation of the White House as the Depression settled in, Roosevelt reached out by radio to the American people in a series of **fireside chats.** These were informal talks in which the President calmly but confidently explained in simple

Visualizing History ▲ A MANDATE FOR CHANGE Farmers in debt, workers without jobs, and bankrupt business owners wanted the government to take bolder action. Americans responded enthusiastically to Franklin D. Roosevelt's call for action to fight the Great Depression. ***What personal qualities did Roosevelt bring to the presidency?***

CHAPTER 18 The New Deal: 1932–1939 **547**

TEACH
Guided Practice
Analyzing Data Provide students with the following data about the volume of shares traded on the New York Stock Exchange for the years 1920 through 1935:

1920—(227,636,000)
1925—(459,717,623)
1929—(1,124,800,410)
1930—(810,632,546)
1935—(381,635,752)

Have students incorporate the data into a line graph and explain what the graph suggests about the nation's attitude toward the buying of stocks after the Stock Market Crash of 1929. (*Possible response: buying of stocks, which reached wild proportions before 1929, was not as popular a form of investment after 1930. Also, most Americans would not have had much confidence in the stock market.*) **L2**

Visualizing History Franklin Roosevelt's personal warmth and an aristocratic appearance served him well. **Answer to Caption:** toughness, a warm and understanding approach to people, pragmatism, a willingness to experiment, skill in dealing with the press

Special Needs Activity

Memory Difficulties Students with memory difficulties find that they remember lists and facts if they use a cuing system to stimulate recall. Explain how memory prompts can be used effectively by directing students' attention to page 547. Point out that the information in the first three paragraphs on Roosevelt's qualities as a leader might be presented as the three "Ps"—**P**olitical skill, **P**ersonality, and Use of the **P**ress. Thinking of the three "Ps" will help them recall the information. **LEP, L1**

Independent Practice

Journalism Have students write a newspaper report on President Roosevelt's fireside chat announcing the "bank holiday." Suggest that students focus their reports on Roosevelt's attempt to reassure the American public that the country's financial institutions were sound. Also suggest that they include a concise and interesting headline. **L2**

CURRICULUM CONNECTION

Language Arts The term *New Deal* was coined by Raymond Moley and Samuel Rosenman, two members of Franklin Roosevelt's "brain trust." It was intended to conjure up images of Woodrow Wilson's New Freedom and Teddy Roosevelt's Square Deal.

Visualizing
History At the time Frances Perkins joined Roosevelt's cabinet, she had been active in labor relations for over 20 years in New York State. **Answer to Caption:** the first woman appointed to a cabinet post

 Assign American Portrait 55: Frances Perkins.

 Assign Primary and Secondary Source Readings pp. 47-48: "First Cabinet Meeting" by Frances Perkins.

548

---

terms the nation's problems and how the New Deal planned to defeat the Depression. Millions of radio listeners felt that the President was talking directly to them. After a fireside chat, Roosevelt sometimes received as many as 50,000 letters a day.

Roosevelt also knew how to use the press better than his predecessor. Hoover had avoided reporters and refused to answer questions unless they were written out in advance. In contrast, FDR allowed reporters to barrage him with questions during frequent press conferences. This approach made him popular with the press—important shapers of public opinion—and focused public attention on Washington, D.C., and his New Deal programs. "Gone is the fortress that was the White House," wrote one reporter after Roosevelt took office.

Getting Things Done

A product of the Progressive Era, FDR retained the progressives' approach to solving society's problems. As President he was a pragmatist and an experimenter. He sometimes asked three or four people with conflicting opinions to do the same job and compared the results. FDR compared himself to a quarterback on a football team who called a play, and if it did not work, tried another. Action, he felt, was better than inaction. Most Americans, desperate for relief from the effects of the Depression, agreed with him.

The "Brain Trust"

Roosevelt also had trust in the ability of experts to plan for society. Even before receiving the Democratic nomination for President, he gathered a group of professors from Columbia University to advise him. This group of economists, political scientists, and attorneys was nicknamed the "brain trust" by the press. After Roosevelt became President, the brain trust stayed on to help him plan New Deal recovery programs. In selecting his cabinet, FDR named people who presented a variety of viewpoints and ideas—Northerners and Southerners, liberals and conservatives. He

named Republican Harold Ickes as secretary of the interior, and for secretary of agriculture he chose Henry A. Wallace, whose father had the job under Harding. For secretary of labor Roosevelt named the first woman cabinet officer, former child labor reformer Frances Perkins. Other women held important positions in almost every New Deal agency. Like Secretary Perkins, many of these women had been social workers. Now the President was calling upon them to administer the federal government's social and relief programs.

Eleanor Roosevelt as Adviser

Outside the brain trust, the adviser that Roosevelt relied on most was his wife, Eleanor. Because of his paralysis, FDR moved with difficulty in a wheelchair or with heavy braces on his legs. As a result, he asked Eleanor to assume a significant role in his administration. The President called her his "eyes and ears" outside the White House. During the first year of the New Deal, she traveled extensively to attend political rallies, tour factories, visit coal mines, and contact many people that FDR might not otherwise have met. At cabinet meetings, the President

Visualizing
History ▲ SECRETARY OF LABOR Frances Perkins was appointed secretary of labor by Roosevelt. A long-time advocate of minimum wage and maximum hour laws, child-labor restrictions, and other progressive reforms, she was one of only two cabinet members to serve throughout Roosevelt's four terms. ***What was unique about her appointment?***

Cooperative Learning Activity

Making Comparisons Divide the class into groups of four or five students. Have each group discuss the following statement: The New Deal was a continuation of the Progressive Era. Have group members take turns offering information from Section 1 that supports or opposes the statement. Then have the groups use this information to decide whether or not they agree with the statement. Have a representative from each group report on the group's decision. **L2**

AMERICAN PORTRAITS

Eleanor Roosevelt
1884–1962

Eleanor Roosevelt did not herself hold public office until she was a 61-year-old widow. But as First Lady she fought tenaciously for social justice and added a sense of compassion to the New Deal.

Although painfully shy as a young girl, Eleanor Roosevelt emerged as a vibrant public personality during the 1920s when her husband, FDR, was recovering from polio. She did all she could to keep his name in the public mind. After Roosevelt's election, she spoke for people who otherwise would have been ignored—women, the poor and the underprivileged, and African Americans.

Sensitive to racial injustice, she spoke up so strongly for civil rights that she won African American support for the New Deal. A lecturer and columnist, Eleanor Roosevelt later worked for global human rights in the United Nations.

---

would report, "My missus says that people are working for wages well below the minimum . . . in the town she visited last week." Eleanor Roosevelt shared Franklin's concern for the victims of the Depression—close friends thought that her concern was even deeper than his—and the belief that decisive government action was needed to conquer society's ills.

■ The First New Deal

President Roosevelt fulfilled his promise to provide "action now." Americans waited to see what he would do.

Restoring Faith in Banks

On Sunday, March 5, 1933, the day after his inauguration, Roosevelt called a special session of Congress. On Monday he used an old law still on the books to suspend the nation's banking activity. Many Americans had lost faith in banks after the crash, withdrew their money, and kept it at home. Banks needed depositors' funds to make loans that would help recovery, but, in many areas, the loss of deposits was so great that banks had to close their doors. After a week in office, the President went on the radio

with his first fireside chat. He explained that only healthy banks would be allowed to reopen. He assured Americans that it would be "safer to keep money in a reopened bank than under the mattress." The next day most banks began to do business again, and in a few days deposits exceeded withdrawals. As the President's calm assurances restored public confidence in the nation's financial system, the bank crisis ended.

The Hundred Days

That first week was just the beginning of feverish activity. In the "Hundred Days" between March 9 and June 16, 1933, Congress passed 15 major bills, more than had ever been enacted in such a short time. Most were bills that the President submitted and that Congress passed with little debate. Seldom had a President enjoyed such overwhelming support.

Meeting "Each Day's Troubles"

Roosevelt took office with no clear idea of how to solve the nation's economic crisis. "There's nothing to do," he said, "but meet each day's troubles as they come." The New Deal, therefore, was not a carefully worked

CHAPTER 18 The New Deal: 1932–1939 **549**

Critical Thinking Activity

Analyzing Media Have students listen to a number of the fireside chats given by Franklin Roosevelt. (These are available on cassette tapes at some libraries.) Then ask students if they listen to or watch broadcasts of presidential speeches or press conferences. Have students discuss how these press conferences and speeches compare with Roosevelt's fireside chats. Then point out that Roosevelt's broadcasts restored public confidence in the government and gave the American people hope for the future. **L3**

Teaching American Portraits

Point out that Eleanor Roosevelt used the position of First Lady to champion various causes. Ask students which causes they would like to see championed by someone close to the President. **L1**

ASSESS
Check Understanding

Assign Section 1 Review as homework or an in-class activity.

Evaluate

 Assign Section Quiz 18-1 or use the Testmaker to create a customized quiz.

Reteach

Have students complete Reteaching Activity 18-1.

Assign Workbook Activity 18-1.

NATIONAL GEOGRAPHIC SOCIETY

 **VIDEODISC**

GTV: A Geographic Perspective on American History

Side 4, Chapter 3
Title: *Thinking Big*
Subject: Depression, Dust Bowl, New Deal

Enrich

Have students research the contributions to the New Deal of one of the following members of Roosevelt's "brain trust": Raymond Moley, Rexford Tugwell, Adolph Berle, Eleanor Roosevelt, Harry Hopkins, Harold Ickes, Frances Perkins, or Henry Wallace. Have students present their information in an oral report.

CLOSE

Write the following statement on the chalkboard:
Franklin Delano Roosevelt was the right person to occupy the presidency at this time.

Ask students to discuss this statement based on what they learned in Section 1.

Visualizing History In many movies of the period, bank executives were portrayed as cold-hearted figures who foreclosed on mortgages and called in loans. In fact, they had few other choices.
Answer to Caption: suspended the nation's banking activity, thus preventing further runs on banks; reassured Americans that they would not lose their bank deposits

 ▲ **BANK CLOSINGS** Afraid for the safety of their savings, panicked depositors line up outside a bank. Such "runs"—when all depositors tried to withdraw their money at the same time—usually caused those banks to fail, making their depositors' fears come true. *How did Roosevelt handle the bank crisis?*

out reform plan. Instead, it was a series of measures quickly drawn up to attack the Depression in many ways at once. Some laws were in response to special demands. Some were even passed against the President's wishes, but he signed them to avoid holding up other legislation. However, New Deal programs had three general purposes: recovery from the Depression, relief for its victims, and reform of the economic system.

From 1933 to early 1935, the dominating goals of the Roosevelt administration were recovery and relief. During the "First New Deal," as this phase was called, the President and his advisers thought that a series of temporary measures could get the economy moving again. From this beginning, recovery would come on its own momentum. Therefore, little additional legislation followed the Hundred Days of the First New Deal. The administration merely implemented the laws that the Senate and the House had created and waited for recovery to occur.

Section 1 ★ Review

Checking for Understanding

1. **Identify** FDR, brain trust, Frances Perkins, the Hundred Days.

2. **Define** fireside chat.

3. **Cite** the political experience that prepared Roosevelt to lead the nation out of the Depression.

4. **Explain** Roosevelt's approach to solving problems.

Critical Thinking

5. **Making Comparisons** Compare Roosevelt's style in managing the crisis to Hoover's. Why did the public support Roosevelt?

ACTIVITY

6. Analyze the painting that opens this chapter. Draw a political cartoon that expresses the painting's main idea.

Answers to SECTION 1 REVIEW

1. FDR, 546; brain trust, 548; Frances Perkins, 548; the Hundred Days, 549
2. All vocabulary words are defined in the Glossary.
3. a progressive background, served in New York legislature, assistant secretary of Navy in Wilson administration, governor of New York
4. emphasized openness to new ideas, experimentation, and action

5. Roosevelt was informal and warm, more in tune with the nation's mood, and willing to seek public support, such as by blaming the Depression on bankers. He used the media to keep the public informed. Hoover was aloof and isolated, which made him unpopular with the press and public.
6. Student work should focus on average worker or worker unity.

★★

Reform, Relief, and Recovery

Setting the Scene

Section Focus

Many of the laws passed during the Hundred Days were popularly known by their initials—AAA, NRA, TVA, and CCC. People jokingly called them the New Deal's "alphabet soup," yet the programs gave the American people a sense of hope. Many were intended as stopgap measures, but their effects are still felt today.

◀ **WPA** POSTER, **LATE 1930S**

Objectives

After studying this section, you should be able to
★ give examples of how Roosevelt's policies helped and hurt the rural poor.
★ compare the effectiveness of measures aimed at farmers and city workers.

Key Terms

deficit spending, pump priming, dole, foreclosure

---

*B*oth Hoover and Roosevelt believed that prosperity would return with a little help to spark the economy. So, like Hoover, FDR sought the help of the business community and spoke of an alliance of "business and banking, agriculture and industry, and labor and capital." But he differed from Hoover in the amount and variety of legislation he proposed and in his willingness to call on the full powers of the federal government to solve national problems.

■ Financial Reform

In June 1933 Congress passed the Glass-Steagall Act. This law prohibited banks from investing in the stock market and created a Federal Deposit Insurance Corporation (FDIC) to insure depositors' savings. Although the program was opposed by the

American Bankers' Association as "unscientific, unjust, and dangerous," federal insurance made people feel that their money would be safe in banks.

Congress also responded to the demand that the government prevent stock market fraud. The Federal Securities Act of 1933 required companies that issued or marketed stocks and bonds to provide complete and truthful information to purchasers. Congress followed this act in 1934 with the Securities and Exchange Commission (SEC) to regulate the stock market.

When Roosevelt took office, he faced strong pressure to inflate the currency. A number of senators and representatives wanted to stimulate recovery by putting into circulation billions of dollars in new paper money. Roosevelt, however, rejected inflation and took a conservative approach in his early efforts to achieve recovery. Still, he realized that to keep relief agencies from

CHAPTER 18 The New Deal: 1932–1939   **551**

LESSON PLAN
SECTION 2, 551–557

FOCUS
Bellringer

🔖 📂 Before taking roll, project Section Focus Transparency 18-2 or hand out Section Focus Transparency Activity 18-2. Have students answer the questions. Discuss student responses.

Motivating Activity

Ask students to read the following quotation from a campaign speech by FDR: "The country needs and, unless I mistake its temper, the country demands bold, persistent experimentation." Then ask students to suggest slogans that sum up what Roosevelt felt the American people were asking him to do. (*Sample slogans: "WE WANT ACTION NOW!"; "DON'T JUST SIT THERE, DO SOMETHING!")* Have students share their ideas with the class. Then point out that in Section 2 they will see that Roosevelt kept up a frenzied rate of activity throughout the first New Deal. **L1**

Vocabulary Precheck

Ask students to define each of the "Key Terms." Have a volunteer consult the dictionary for any unfamiliar words. **L1, LEP**

Classroom Resources for SECTION 2

Blackline Masters:
📂 Reproducible Lesson Plan 18-2
📂 Guided Reading Activity 18-2
📂 Political Cartoons in American History Activity 16

📂 Cooperative Learning Activity 18
📂 Chapter Map Activity 18
📂 Geography in History Activity 18
📂 Workbook Activity 18-2
📂 Reteaching Activity 18-2
📂 Section Quiz 18-2

Transparencies:
🔖 Section Focus Transparency 18-2
🔖 Map Transparency 18

Multimedia:
📷 Testmaker
💿 Powers of the President
💿 The American History Videodisc
🎵 American Music: Cultural Traditions

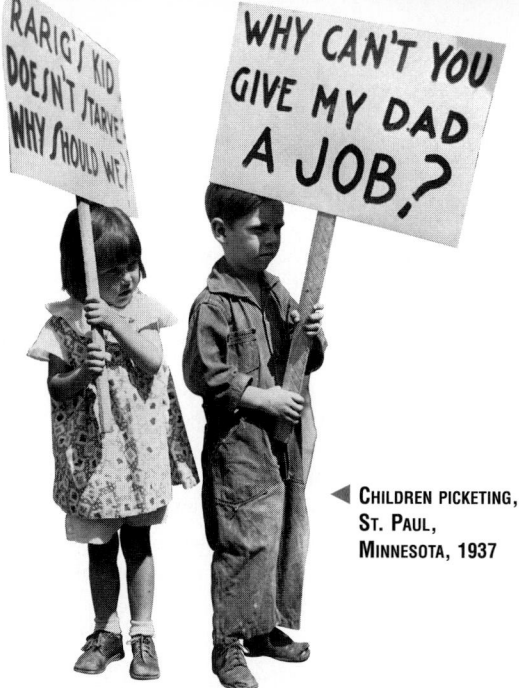

◄ CHILDREN PICKETING, ST. PAUL, MINNESOTA, 1937

closing and millions of Americans from starving, **deficit spending** was necessary. In other words, the federal government's annual spending would have to exceed its income.

■ Help for the Jobless

From deficit spending, the New Deal moved to **pump priming**—pouring government money into the economy through loans and federal spending in the hope of stimulating recovery. Roosevelt called for government to give money directly to people who would spend it. Increased spending would increase demand for consumer goods, New Dealers claimed, which would stimulate production and create jobs.

By 1933, 12 million to 15 million Americans—1 of every 4 workers—was unemployed, and many were on the verge of starvation. At first Roosevelt, like Hoover, thought that local agencies should handle relief until industry and agriculture recovered enough to provide jobs. It soon became clear, however, that states, cities, and local charities had exhausted their resources.

The Federal Government Steps In

In May 1933 Congress established a Federal Emergency Relief Administration (FERA). FERA made outright grants to states and municipalities to distribute as they chose. They generally provided a **dole**—direct gifts of money, food, and clothing. Although the dole was the cheapest and quickest form of relief, its critics were concerned that people who received handouts would lose their self-respect and job skills, making them even more unemployable. So once the federal government had met the need for emergency relief, New Dealers searched for alternatives to the dole.

The Public Works Administration (PWA), created in June 1933, offered jobs instead of handouts. Under the direction of Secretary of the Interior Harold Ickes, the program provided jobs on construction projects—improving highways and building dams, sewer systems, waterworks, schools, and other government buildings. The PWA generally worked through private contractors, and Ickes broke down long-standing racial barriers in the construction trades by insisting that contractors hire African Americans.

In the autumn of 1933, Harry Hopkins, head of the FERA, won approval for a Civil Works Administration (CWA) to hire jobless persons. During the winter of 1933–1934, the CWA employed 4 million people—300,000 of them women. The CWA built or improved 1,000 airports, 500,000 miles of roads, 40,000 school buildings, and 3,500 parks, playgrounds, and playing fields. But the cost of all this was tremendous—$1 billion in just five months. In the spring of 1934, Roosevelt gave in to fierce criticism from conservatives and cancelled the program.

The TVA

One early New Deal program combined emergency relief and pump priming with long-term economic and social planning. In May 1933, after Roosevelt's prodding, Congress established the Tennessee Valley Authority (TVA), designed to promote the development of a seven-state region.

Before the TVA, the natural resources of the Tennessee Valley had long been exploited.

Critical Thinking Activity

Relating Past to Present Briefly review the recent savings and loan crisis. Then ask students to compare this crisis with the banking crisis of the 1930s by answering the following questions: How were the two crises the same? How were they different? What approaches used to solve the 1930s crisis might have been used to settle the 1990s crisis? What do we know today that might have helped Roosevelt settle the 1930s crisis? Discuss students' answers. **L2**

Forests were leveled, and heavy rainfalls caused erosion and disastrous floods. Poor farmers attempted to work worn-out land, and many people were on relief.

Employing as many as 40,000 workers at a time, the TVA built 20 dams for flood control and improved 5 others. The TVA also moved farmers from marginal lands, reforested millions of acres, built power plants and fertilizer factories, and even started new towns. But the most notable change was the immense amount of cheap electricity that the TVA produced. Its increased availability allowed farmers to install refrigerators, milking machines, and other equipment. Cheap power also attracted industry.

Despite its obvious benefits, the TVA had its critics. Some charged that funds for the TVA should be used to support programs nationwide. Above all, the TVA was attacked by the power companies. One goal of the TVA was to provide a basis to determine fair electricity rates all over the country. But private power companies argued that to use the TVA for this purpose was unfair because the government charged large parts of the cost of electricity production to the cost of flood control and navigation. For the federal government to take over the production of private power, they argued, was unfair and communistic. Although the power companies were powerful enough to prevent any more regional authorities like the TVA, the New Deal did build other power plants, the most famous of which was the Grand Coulee Dam in Washington state.

The CCC

The most generally admired New Deal relief agency was the Civilian Conservation Corps (CCC), established in March 1933. It offered outdoor work to unemployed single men, 18 to 25 years old, at $30 per month, $22 of which went back to their families. By midsummer the CCC had established 1,500 camps. During its existence, the CCC helped conserve the nation's natural resources by putting 3 million young men to work planting trees, fighting forest fires, building reservoirs, and stopping soil erosion.

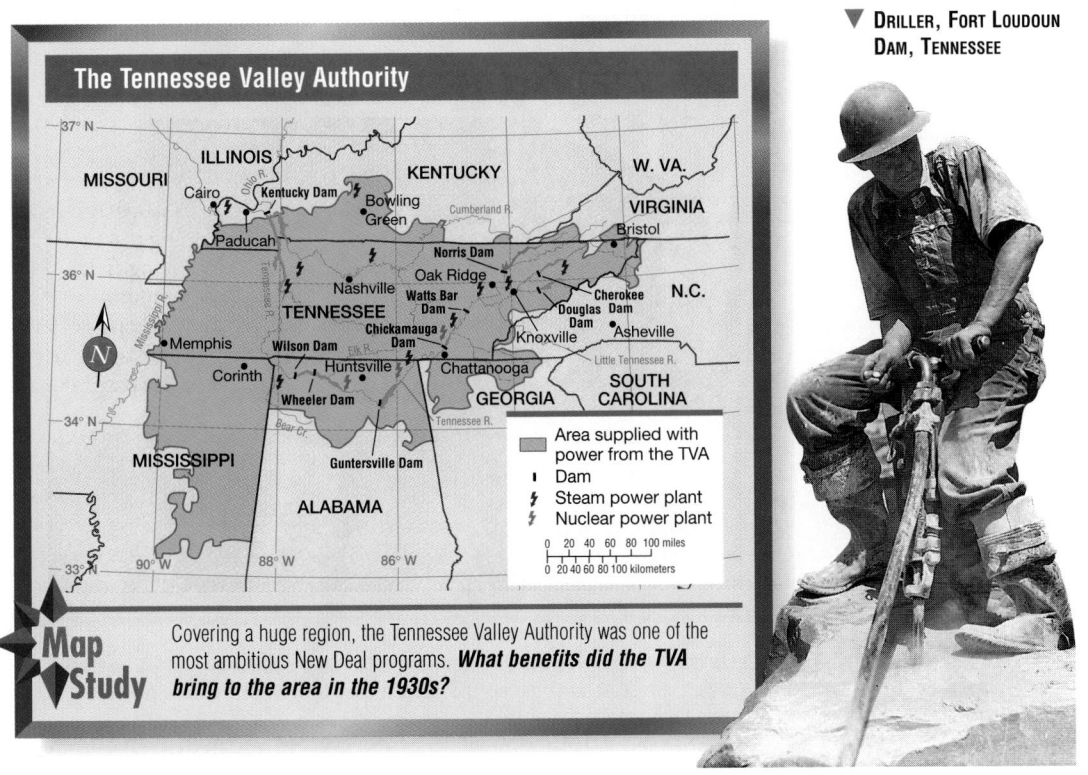

The Tennessee Valley Authority

Covering a huge region, the Tennessee Valley Authority was one of the most ambitious New Deal programs. **What benefits did the TVA bring to the area in the 1930s?**

▼ DRILLER, FORT LOUDOUN DAM, TENNESSEE

CHAPTER 18 The New Deal: 1932–1939   **553**

■Map
▼Study   *Using Maps*

Answer: flood control, cheap power, economic growth and development, jobs

Map Skills Practice
Which states were provided with electricity by the Tennessee Valley Authority? (*Alabama, Georgia, Kentucky, Mississippi, North Carolina, Tennessee, Virginia*)

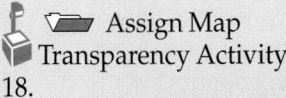 For additional map practice, assign Chapter Map Activity 18.

 Assign Map Transparency Activity 18.

CURRICULUM CONNECTION

Government Introduce students to the concept of regional planning. Since TVA covered several states, no single state could run the program. The project also was too large for one state to finance.

Cooperative Learning Activity

Organize students into groups of four or five and have group members work together to write an answer to the following question: Were the measures President Roosevelt took to help the unemployed simply "make work" government programs, or did they have a truly positive impact on the economy? Explain your answer.

Answers should be developed in three stages—brainstorming, first draft, and final draft. Call on groups randomly to report their progress. **L1, L2** 📦

For additional practice, assign Critical Thinking Skills Activity 18.

Visualizing History The young men employed by the CCC, many of whom lacked prior job experience, were most likely to be out of work in an economic downturn. Have students consider why. *(lacked seniority, work experience)*
Answer to Caption: Spending fuels the economy by encouraging production of goods and services.

FACT or FICTION?

Young unemployed women could not take part in the CCC.

FICTION: While women complained that they were excluded, a few special camps were set up for them. But only 8,000 participated in a program that put over 3 million young men to work.

■ Relief for Agriculture

The impoverished condition of farmers in the Tennessee Valley was by no means unique in 1933. Since 1929 banks had foreclosed on the property of 10 percent of the nation's farmers. In **foreclosure** actions, when a borrower cannot make loan payments, the bank seizes the property that was put up as security for the loan. Farmers threatened to stop producing food unless their debt burden and agricultural prices improved. The New Deal provided relief for heavily indebted farmers by placing a five-year moratorium, or freeze, on mortgage foreclosures. But New Dealers recognized that the root of the farmers' plight was low agricultural prices, and that this situation was related to a problem that had plagued farmers since the end of World War I —overproduction.

The Agricultural Adjustment Act

Roosevelt proposed an unusual approach: stop agricultural surpluses by paying farmers to *not* produce crops. In May 1933, Congress passed the Agricultural Adjustment Act (AAA), under which the government paid farmers who reduced production of basic crops like cotton, wheat, tobacco, hogs, and corn. Funds for these payments came from a tax levied on flour mills, slaughterhouses, and other businesses that processed food.

In 1933 cotton farmers plowed under a quarter of their acreage, and hog producers killed 6 million piglets instead of fattening them for market. In 1934 and 1935, farmers withdrew 10 million acres from production and received more than $1 billion in benefit payments. Surpluses were greatly reduced by 1936, and total farm income rose by more than 50 percent.

Large commercial farmers, who concentrated on one crop, benefited more than smaller farmers who raised several. The crop reduction program actually hurt some people. In the West and Southwest, Mexican migrant workers suffered when growers raised less produce and so hired fewer pickers. Tenant farmers and sharecroppers were forced off the land they worked as owners took it out of production. About 150,000 white tenants and almost 195,000 African American tenants left farming during the 1930s. To stop this trend, the New Deal created the Farm Security Administration to give loans to help tenants purchase land.

Visualizing History ▲ **JOBS** Unemployment was a major problem during the Depression. Many New Deal programs were aimed at putting men and women back to work. **Why were jobs important to economic recovery?**

Critical Thinking Activity

Evaluating Tactics Point out that union leaders criticized the NRA because they felt it allowed employers to ignore the right of the unions to collective bargaining. In 1934 workers all over the country struck, demanding the right to organize. Ask students the following question: Did the workers have the right to strike to get their demands met? Why or why not? *(Answers will vary. Supporting argument: strikes most effective means of getting employers to meet demands. Opposing argument: strikes hurt economy; ongoing negotiations better tactic.)* **L2**

▲ THE CCC Many work programs for the unemployed were started during the Roosevelt administration. The CCC offered outdoor work to unemployed single men. *What work did the CCC do?*

ABCNEWS INTERACTIVE™

VIDEODISC

Powers of the President

Side Two, Chapter 10
Title: *Manager of the Economy*
Subject: The President and the Economy

American Music: Cultural Traditions Have students listen to and discuss "Talking Dust Bowl" by Woody Guthrie (2:40)

But only 3,400 African American farmers received any of this money. Landless farmers joined other urban and rural migrants who wandered the country in search of jobs.

The Dust Bowl

In 1934 and 1935 a terrible disaster struck the Great Plains and added to the number of farmers on the move. The origins of the disaster arose during World War I, when high crop prices tempted farmers to grow wheat and cotton on what traditionally had been grazing lands. Plows broke up the deep, tough sod that had prevented erosion and conserved moisture in this semiarid region. When the years from 1933 to 1935 were unusually dry, the area began to turn to desert. Dust storms carried away so much topsoil that a haze obscured the sun, sometimes as far away as the Atlantic coast. Between 1934 and 1939, nearly 350,000 farm families left the dust bowl.

To take care of immediate distress, Congress provided the farmers in the dust bowl with funds for new seed and livestock. For long-term solutions, the Department of Agriculture helped farmers plant millions of trees in shelter belts to cut wind velocity and help retain moisture. The government also encouraged farmers to return the land to grazing. Yet there was much criticism of New Deal farm policies. Many farmers did not like being told what to raise or how much to plant. To others, decreasing food supplies when people were hungry seemed immoral. However, the New Deal provided more direct assistance to farmers than to any other group, and saved thousands of farm families from poverty and despair.

Native Americans and the New Deal

The New Deal worked to change long-standing government policies affecting Native Americans, including a reversal of

Sidelight: Woody Guthrie

One of those who abandoned the Dust Bowl and headed west for the promised land of California was Woody Guthrie. He soon gave up farmwork and devoted his whole time to songwriting and performing. Guthrie wrote songs about the everyday lives of working people—the hardships of the migrant workers, the struggle to organize unions, and the fight for racial equality and freedom. Once considered radical and subversive, Guthrie's songs—most notably "This Land Is Your Land"—are now national treasures.

Using Graphs

Graph Skills Practice:
Point out the drop in union membership in the 1930s. Ask what may have caused it. *(the Great Depression)* Then ask what caused the rise in membership in the 1940s. *(New Deal legislation)*

Answer: Section 7a of the NIRA required that every NRA code recognize workers' right to join unions and to bargain.

Did You Know?

During the New Deal years, people had more time on their hands and less money than they had in the 1920s. This had a great impact on how people used their leisure time. Sports that were rather expensive to play—golf, for instance—declined in popularity. For example, there were as many as 1,155 private golf clubs in the United States in 1930. This number fell to 763 by 1936.

the gradual loss of land and tribal authority. Earlier, the federal government had opted for a number of different policies with widely divergent goals.

With the end of the frontier wars in the late 1800s, the federal government had at long last abandoned a policy that could fairly be summarized as expulsion and extermination. The General Allotment Act in 1887 provided for the division of reservation land into plots to be granted to individual Native Americans. This arrangement was based on the idea that the best thing for Native Americans was to make them as much like other Americans as possible.

The education system reinforced this idea: children were taken from home at an early age, crowded into boarding schools, and given some "book learning" before being sent back to the reservation. They acquired little knowledge of the culture of their ancestors. Meanwhile, older people received just enough food to sustain them.

However well-meaning, this policy was scarcely better than the old policy. By 1934 Native Americans held only 48 million of the 133 million acres they had possessed in 1887. Although Native Americans were citizens of the United States, state laws often discriminated against them, and the federal government generally ran their affairs for them.

Some improvement began during the Coolidge administration with a reorganization of health services for Native Americans. Later, President Hoover appointed two dedicated individuals as commissioner and deputy commissioner of Indian Affairs. They began a reform of the workings of the department.

The Indian Reorganization Act

More action on Native American affairs was taken during the New Deal years. The Roosevelt administration promoted a new approach that was made law in the Indian Reorganization Act in 1934. This act repealed the allotment policy and returned to tribal ownership Native American lands previously open to sale.

According to John Collier, commissioner of Indian Affairs, the act had a worthwhile

purpose. It would enable Native Americans "to earn a decent livelihood and lead self-respecting, organized lives in harmony with their own aims and ideals."

Instead of promoting individual ownership, the federal government now encouraged Native Americans to revert to their own traditions. Instead of being weakened, tribal organization was strengthened. Native Americans were encouraged to become members of the federal Indian Service. Children were now taught the traditions of their own people in school. Ceremonies, art forms, and handicrafts were revived.

New Benefits

The new arrangements brought benefits that could be seen in the reversal of two disturbing trends: Native American landholdings increased after 1934, and the Native American population once again began to increase. Since then Native Americans, now a rapidly growing minority group, have continued to fight in the courts and legislatures for religious freedom, water rights, and land claims.

■ Industrial Relief

Roosevelt's advisers believed that industry, like agriculture, suffered from overproduction. In June 1933 the New Deal tried to help industry with the National Industrial Recovery Act (NIRA).

The NIRA

To control production, the NIRA provided that representatives of labor and of management from competing companies draw up "codes of fair competition" in each industry. These codes set the prices of products to eliminate discount selling. They shortened workers' hours in order to create more jobs, and they established minimum-wage levels. To spread production among as many firms as possible, factories were limited to two shifts a day. To direct this complex program, the act created the National Recovery Administration (NRA).

Sidelight: Relations With the Soviet Union

Relations between the United States and the Soviet Union began to improve in November 1933 when, at President Roosevelt's request, Soviet Commissar for Foreign Affairs Maxim Litvinov visited Washington, D.C. At a formal ceremony, the United States recognized the Soviet government for the first time. In addition, the Soviets pledged to stop broadcasting anti-American propaganda and interfering in American internal affairs.

Power to enforce the codes was very limited, so the NRA used the power of public opinion to enlist the cooperation of business. Those that signed code agreements were given signs with blue eagles and the words "We Do Our Part." Consumers were encouraged to purchase goods only from businesses that displayed the signs. The NIRA, however, never worked out as planned. Prices rose faster than wages. Businesses complained that large companies wrote the codes to favor themselves and to put small competitors out of business.

Workers Turn to Unions

Probably no group suffered more than people who worked for hourly wages. By 1933 one-third of these workers were unemployed. The earnings of the rest had shrunk as their rates or hours were cut. The idea spread that the best way to restore workers' wages and purchasing power was to strengthen labor unions. Under Section 7a of the NIRA, every NRA code guaranteed workers the right to organize unions and to bargain collectively with their employers. As a result, between May and October 1933, American Federation of Labor (AFL) membership jumped by about a million workers.

In 1934 a wave of strikes swept the nation as workers demanded the right to organize for improved wages and job security. Many of these strikes became violent, and most resulted in defeat for the workers, as police generally sided with employers. Although sympathetic to organized labor, the only

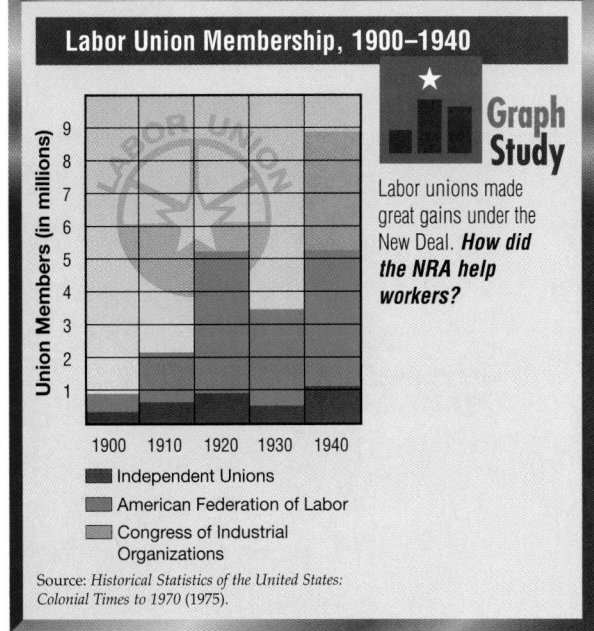

Labor Union Membership, 1900–1940

Union Members (in millions)

Graph Study

Labor unions made great gains under the New Deal. *How did the NRA help workers?*

- ■ Independent Unions
- ■ American Federation of Labor
- ■ Congress of Industrial Organizations

Source: *Historical Statistics of the United States: Colonial Times to 1970* (1975).

way the NRA could punish a company was to take away its Blue Eagle symbol. Workers began to demand stronger labor laws.

New Solutions Needed

As the nation entered 1935, American spirits sagged. Despite the New Deal, farm prices and industrial wages were well below 1929 levels, and workers remained unemployed and poor. To many Americans, the New Deal was taking too long and accomplishing too little. FDR clearly saw that he must find other means to restore prosperity.

Section 2 ★ Review

Checking for Understanding

1. **Identify** FDIC, FERA, PWA, CCC, AAA, NRA, Section 7a.
2. **Define** deficit spending, pump priming, dole, foreclosure.
3. **List** three programs designed to create jobs by employing workers on projects to benefit the nation.
4. **State** effects of the farm program.

Critical Thinking

5. **Making Judgments** During widespread unemployment, is government money better used as a dole or for more expensive work-relief programs? Why?

ACTIVITY

6. Create a table that lists the positive and negative aspects of the New Deal farm program.

ASSESS
Check Understanding
Assign Section 2 Review as homework or an in-class activity.

Evaluate
☑ 📁 Assign Section Quiz 18-2 or use the Testmaker to create a customized test.

Reteach
Ask students to summarize in writing the purpose, provisions, and degree of success of the Agricultural Adjustment Act and the National Industrial Recovery Act.

📁 Have students complete Reteaching Activity 18-2.

📁 Assign Workbook Activity 18-2.

Enrich
Have students obtain copies of John Steinbeck's *Grapes of Wrath* and read excerpts that describe migrant life during the Depression. One excerpt from the book can be found on pages 572–573 at the end of this chapter. Then lead the class in a discussion of the hardships migrant workers of the 1930s faced.

CLOSE
Remind students that Roosevelt's goals when he took office were relief, recovery, and reform. Ask them to evaluate his success in achieving these goals.

Answers to SECTION 2 REVIEW

1. FDIC, 551; FERA, 552; PWA, 552; CCC, 553; AAA, 554; NRA, 556; Section 7a, 557
2. All vocabulary words are defined in the Glossary.
3. Civil Works Administration, Public Works Administration, Tennessee Valley Authority, Civilian Conservation Corps
4. People with jobs would spend money.

Consumer spending would stimulate production and create the jobs necessary for recovery.
5. Answers will vary. Dole is expedient financially, but work programs preserve dignity and projects benefit society.
6. Tables should present a valid appraisal of the policies.

▲ FARM IN THE DUST BOWL

TEACH

The term "dust bowl" was first used by Associated Press reporter Robert Geiger in a story published in April 1935. Mention that the dust storms continued on and off for 10 years. The westerly winds carried the dust as much as 300 miles into the Atlantic, depositing it on ships that plied the ocean. Ask students to identify a similar situation to the Dust Bowl going on today. (*Most students will suggest the desertification of the Sahel region of Africa.*) **L2**

 Assign Geography in History Activity 18.

CURRICULUM CONNECTION

Geography The first of the great dust storms began on November 11, 1933. In South Dakota the sky was pitch dark by noon. Historian William Manchester writes that by the time the sun reappeared "fields had been replaced by sand while roads, trees, sheds, fences, and machinery had disappeared beneath great hanging dunes of soil. By then the wind was headed for Texas. A towering pall darkened Chicago and was visible as far east as Albany."

The Dust Bowl

As the entire nation struggled to cope with the Depression, farmers in Kansas, Oklahoma, and Texas suffered from the scourges of drought and dust. From the 1890s to the 1920s, grasslands in this part of the Great Plains were put to the plow, and when rain fell, they were bountiful. But in the 1930s, the rains failed. As crops withered, leaving bare dirt exposed, the region's high winds lifted the fine topsoil to create dust storms called "dusters."

Large-scale mechanized farming on the plains after 1900 exposed huge areas of soil. Farmers eager to maximize yields overtilled the soil and burned wheat stubble to kill weeds. These poor soil-conservation practices and the long drought created a dust bowl on the plains throughout most of the 1930s, as millions of tons of airborne powdery topsoil buried crops and killed livestock.

The dust bowl took its toll on people too. People sat helpless while their farms blew away. They sometimes lost their way and died in the thick storms while only yards from their houses. Thousands of families abandoned their land to seek work in the fields and orchards of California, Oregon, and Washington. Many migrants, however, could not find work even after they reached their destination. Those who stayed on their land were encouraged to plant crops that conserved the soil.

Making the Geography Connection

1. How did humans change the natural environment of the Great Plains in the early twentieth century?

2. How was a dust bowl created in this region?

ACTIVITY

3. On a piece of posterboard, paste photographs that show modern methods of irrigation and agricultural practices. Write a paragraph in which you argue whether another dust bowl in the United States is possible.

558

Answers to Making the Connection

1. By plowing and planting crops, they broke up the grasslands that covered the topsoil and held it together.
2. The development of large-scale mechanized farming exposed huge areas of soil which dried out in the drought and was carried away by the wind.
3. Student paragraphs should show valid reasoning to support the position taken.

SECTION 3

★★

The Second New Deal

Setting the Scene

Section Focus

Some of Roosevelt's critics planted seeds of dissatisfaction with the New Deal by appealing to the jobless, the displaced, the underpaid, and the elderly. These victims of the Depression were fertile ground for the radical ideas floating about in 1935. FDR recognized that the New Deal must be reassessed and redirected. Yet even after strong voter support in the 1936 presidential election, Roosevelt faced continued opposition.

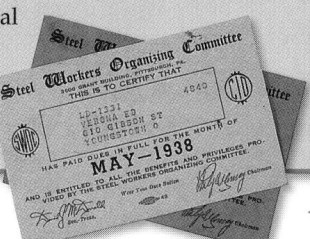

◀ UNION CARDS

Objectives

After studying this section, you should be able to

★ list the special-interest groups that challenged Roosevelt.

★ outline the steps the Second New Deal took to achieve reform.

★ identify the events that led to the end of the New Deal.

Key Terms

coalition, craft union, industrial union, recession

For the 10 million unemployed Americans in 1935, Senator Huey Long's slogan, "Every Man a King," was an appealing fantasy but a far cry from their reality. They received just enough relief to keep themselves and their families alive. Their miserable dole seemed hardly worth the humiliation it caused. Millions of elderly Americans faced a similar stark reality, without savings, without adequate medical care, and without hope.

■ Attacks on the New Deal

The radical critics of the New Deal posed a strong threat to the Roosevelt administration. As time passed, the ranks of New Deal critics grew. Some wanted a more active government. Others felt that the government was interfering too much in American life.

Three Prominent Attackers

Every week Father Charles E. Coughlin, the "Radio Priest" whose broadcasts reached 40 million listeners, bitterly attacked Roosevelt. Originally a New Deal supporter, Coughlin accused the President of turning the New Deal into a "raw deal." His political organization, the National Union for Social Justice, called for such socialistic measures as heavy taxes on the wealthy and a guaranteed income for everyone. Gradually, Coughlin began expressing anti-Semitic, or anti-Jewish, views. In 1942 Catholic leaders ordered him to stop broadcasting.

An even more dangerous rival to Roosevelt was Huey Long, senator from Louisiana. With the backing of the rural poor, he became extremely powerful in his home state and used it as a base on which to build national popularity. With his folksy, humorous manner, Long knew how to win

LESSON PLAN
SECTION 3, 559–566

FOCUS
Bellringer

📁 Before taking roll, project Section Focus Transparency 18-3 or hand out Section Focus Transparency Activity 18-3. Have students answer the questions. Discuss student responses.

Motivating Activity

Ask students to discuss their feelings about a new school policy, such as unannounced searches of lockers. Direct the discussion so that two opposing views develop: "They went too far" and "They didn't go far enough." Then tell students that this was exactly where Roosevelt found himself in 1934. Conservatives accused him of going too far. Radicals and liberals, however, said that he could do much more. Point out that in Section 3 students will see how Roosevelt responded to his critics. **L1**

Vocabulary Precheck

List this section's key terms on the chalkboard. Have students develop questions for which each term is an answer. **L1, LEP**

Classroom Resources for SECTION 3

Blackline Masters:
📁 Reproducible Lesson Plan 18-3
📁 Guided Reading Activity 18-3
📁 American Literary Heritage, pp. 42–44
📁 American Portrait 53

📁 Primary and Secondary Source Readings, p. 49
📁 Linking Past and Present Activity 18
📁 Chapter Skills Activity 18
📁 Workbook Activity 18-3
📁 Reteaching Activity 18-3
📁 Section Quiz 18-3

Transparencies:
📁 Section Focus Transparency 18-3
📁 Skills Transparency 18

Multimedia:
📁 Testmaker
📁 Economics in Action
📁 Focus on Government
📁 The Presidents: A Picture History of Our Nation

TEACH
Guided Practice
Analyzing Ideas Huey Long's ideas were so appealing to some people that they were willing to excuse his tactics, which included fixing elections and harassing opponents. When accused of violating the Louisiana constitution, Long replied, "I'm the Constitution around here now!" Ask students to discuss what dangers these beliefs present. **L2**

Visualizing

History Encourage interested students to compare Father Coughlin to contemporary figures who use radio as a forum for their political views.
Answer to Caption: less money and property for the wealthy, guaranteed income for everyone

GLENCOE
TECHNOLOGY

VIDEODISC

Economics in Action

Disc 1, Side 1, Chapter 3
Title: *Economic Systems and the American Economy*
Subject: How a free enterprise system works

Visualizing History

▲ **NEW DEAL CRITICS** Father Charles Coughlin (left) reached millions of listeners before the Catholic Church made him stop his radio broadcasts. Until his assassination, Senator Huey Long (right) was equally popular. *What idea did these leaders share?*

audiences. He proposed confiscating the property of the rich and giving every family a home, $2,000 a year, and a free college education for their children. His followers organized hundreds of "Share-Our-Wealth" clubs.

Less colorful than Father Coughlin or Senator Long, but just as threatening, was Dr. Francis Townsend. A former public health official, Townsend was shocked by the plight of older Americans who were no longer able to compete for jobs. He proposed a plan that he claimed would provide relief for the elderly and at the same time stimulate economic recovery, calling for the federal government to pay all Americans over age 60 a pension of $200 per month. Recipients would be required to spend their entire pension check within 30 days. Townsend claimed that not only would this help older Americans, but the money they pumped into the economy would create jobs. The pensions could be financed by a national sales tax on consumer goods, Townsend argued. His innovative plan attracted millions of devoted advocates.

Fighting Back

Roosevelt's annual address to Congress in January 1935 answered his attackers. He admitted that "we have not weeded out the

overprivileged and we have not effectively lifted up the underprivileged." The President announced a "Second New Deal" to put recovery on a new course. This new phase showed greater concern for the less fortunate and abandoned efforts to enlist the support of business.

The political groups supporting the New Deal also changed. Roosevelt had played down partisanship to gain the support of moderate and progressive Republicans. Now he devoted his energies to achieving his goals through the Democratic party alone. To strengthen it, he attempted to form a **coalition,** or combination, of separate groups whose members could be counted on to vote for Democrats. To the traditional source of Democratic political power—the South and Northern urban political machines—Roosevelt attempted to add labor unions, farmers, and African Americans. Many of the Second New Deal's programs were intended to appeal to these groups.

■ Work Relief and Social Security

The most immediate result of the New Deal's shift in attitude was the President's demand for large-scale work relief.

Sidelight: Roosevelt's Press Conferences

Throughout his presidency Franklin Roosevelt averaged about two press conferences a week. These were informal affairs, with as many as 200 reporters cramming into the Oval Office to hear Roosevelt's pronouncements. He would answer questions off the cuff, and he seemed to know each reporter by name. With a mixture of charm, openness, and familiarity, Roosevelt built a working relationship with the press unmatched by any other United States President.

Responding to Roosevelt's request, Congress appropriated funds in April 1935 for "work relief and to increase employment by providing useful projects." An immense new agency, the Works Progress Administration (WPA) was set up under the direction of Harry Hopkins to provide a chance for all people to use their skills to earn an income.

The WPA employed writers, teachers, librarians, actors, musicians, and artists. A "junior WPA," the National Youth Administration (NYA) helped high school and college students stay in school by giving them part-time work, such as typing and library cataloguing. Existing work-relief programs were expanded. The government, through the Reconstruction Finance Corporation, lent large sums to businesses and to local governments. The Civilian Conservation Corps increased the number it employed. The Public Works Administration finally rolled into high gear and provided hundreds of thousands of jobs.

Unemployable men and women needed help during the Depression as much as the unemployed. Persons with no source of support and no ability to earn an income had no place to go. To remedy this problem, Congress in 1935 passed the Social Security Act. Under this program, the federal government financed state unemployment insurance plans through payroll taxes paid by employers. Federal grants to states provided care for dependent mothers and children. The core of the program was retirement benefits, paid for by taxes on workers and employers, that people could collect when they stopped working at age 65.

The Social Security Act had flaws. For example, the act did not protect some groups who needed it most, such as farm workers and domestic help. Since 65 percent of all African American employees in the 1930s fell into these two categories, the act neglected this group the most. Yet the Social Security Act was a landmark in reforming society. It set the policy that an industrial society was responsible for those who, through no fault of their own, are unable to work.

■ Business and Labor

Several pieces of legislation demonstrated Roosevelt's efforts to appeal to the political coalition he was forming. Early in the New Deal, taxes remained at levels set in the 1920s. Now Congress passed tax increases on the incomes of wealthy Americans, inheritance taxes on the property of deceased persons, and higher taxes on corporations. Although the law was attacked as communistic, Roosevelt was more interested, some felt, in heading off the various "share-the-wealth" schemes than he was in actually redistributing the nation's wealth.

The Wagner Act

Next to the Social Security Act, the most important and lasting legislation of the Second New Deal was the National Labor Relations Act, also called the Wagner Act,

Visualizing **H**istory

▲ ATTACK ON THE NEW DEAL Some Americans thought the New Deal was too restrictive to free enterprise. This cartoonist shows Uncle Sam tied down by New Deal agencies and laws, much as Gulliver was bound by the Lilliputians in the book *Gulliver's Travels*. **Why might critics have thought this way?**

Did You Know?

Huey Long founded a political dynasty that wielded power in Louisiana for more than 50 years. During that time, some seven members of his family held political office at the state or national level.

Visualizing **H**istory Discuss the way the cartoonist views the government and the American people. Ask: Who today might share the views expressed in this cartoon? *(those who would like to reduce the size of the federal government)*
Answer to Caption: The New Deal represented an unprecedented expansion of the government into areas of the private sector. Many Americans were unaccustomed to so high a degree of government regulation of business.

📁 Assign American Literary Heritage, pp. 42–44, *A Curtain of Green* by Eudora Welty.

📁 Project Skills Transparency 18 and have students complete Skills Transparency Activity 18.

Cooperative Learning Activity

Creating Posters Divide the class into three groups. Assign each group one of the following organizations: Father Coughlin's National Union for Social Justice, Huey Long's Share-Our-Wealth Clubs, Dr. Francis Townsend's Old-Age Revolving Pensions, Inc. Have group members work together to design and construct a poster encouraging people to join their organization. Remind groups that their posters should include strong visual images and catchy slogans. Display finished posters on the bulletin board. **L2**

▲ *An Incident in Contemporary American Life, 1942,* by Mitchell Jamieson WPA artists painted murals in many government offices. Mitchell Jamieson's mural of African American opera singer Marian Anderson's famous concert before an integrated audience of 73,000 at the Lincoln Memorial is in the offices of the United States Department of the Interior in Washington, D.C. *What political favor did Roosevelt want from African Americans?*

passed in July 1935 after the Supreme Court declared the National Industrial Recovery Act unconstitutional. The Wagner Act set up a National Labor Relations Board (NLRB), which could hold secret elections in factories to find out whether workers wanted to unionize. The board could arbitrate grievances, reinstate workers fired for supporting unions, and order employers to stop antiunion activities.

The Wagner Act stimulated a burst of labor union activity. But the AFL was ill-equipped in both philosophy and structure to organize workers in mass-production industries such as radio, steel, automobiles, and textiles. The AFL was a federation of **craft unions**—unions where all members had the same skill. In mass-production industries, however, workers from many crafts or skills often worked in a single plant. To have several unions undermined unity. So some labor leaders proposed that factory workers be organized in an **industrial union**—a union to which all workers in a single industry belong, regardless of the job they perform. When the AFL rejected this approach, these leaders abandoned it to form the Congress of Industrial Organizations (CIO).

The CIO

"If I went to work in a factory, the first thing I'd do would be to JOIN A UNION," read the slogan signed by President Roosevelt on union recruiting posters, as the CIO moved into industries that the AFL had long neglected. By 1936 the CIO had signed up enough steelworkers to threaten a nationwide strike. Instead, in March 1937 the nation's largest steel producer, the United States Steel Corporation, recognized the union as bargaining agent for its workers, established a 40-hour workweek, and increased wages. Just beginning to recover from the Depression, the company was not willing to risk a major strike. The smaller producers did not follow this lead, however, and bloody strikes broke out around the country. But by 1941, the steelworkers' union had contracts with the entire industry.

Meanwhile, the CIO moved into the automobile industry, where management discouraged worker unity by exploiting racial and religious tensions among African Americans, Southern whites, and Catholic ethnic groups. Although hourly wages in the industry were high, seasonal layoffs reduced the average worker's annual earnings to less than $1,000. Workers also resented the

---

Critical Thinking Activity

Supporting a Position Point out that conservative critics charged that the New Deal amounted to unnecessary interference in the American economy. Then ask students to write a few paragraphs supporting one of the following position statements: (1) The economy was in a shambles and only the federal government had the power to rescue it. (2) Given time, the economy would have righted itself without government action.

Have volunteers read their answers to generate a class discussion on the role of government in the economy. **L3**

"speed-ups" that occurred when management increased the rate at which cars moved along the assembly line.

The Autoworkers Strike

The CIO did not want to challenge the auto industry until the struggle with the steel companies had ended. The nation's autoworkers, however, were impatient for change and took matters into their own hands. They instituted a strike strategy called the sit-down strike. Rather than walking off their jobs, the striking autoworkers remained in the factory. The company could not hire new workers to continue production, nor could it remove the strikers by force without risking violence to the factory. One striker later remembered:

> " We were nervous. We didn't know we could do it. Those machines had been kept going as long as we could remember. When we finally pulled the switch and there was some quiet, I finally remembered something . . . that I was a human being, that I could stop those machines. . . . "

The sit-down strike was not originated by the autoworkers, nor was it unique to them. The radical International Workers of the World first used the technique against General Electric in 1906. But in the late 1930s factory workers, taxi drivers, maids, secretaries, and salesclerks sat down at their jobs to protest their pay and working conditions.

Union success in the auto, steel, and other industries swelled the ranks of organized labor during the Second New Deal. The CIO grew especially rapidly because it was willing to organize women workers, whom the AFL had ignored. From less than 3 million in 1933, union membership more than tripled by 1939. Organized labor showed its appreciation for the Wagner Act and other New Deal programs by giving political support to the Democrats.

■ The 1936 Election

The Democrats renominated Roosevelt for President in 1936, and they enthusiastically endorsed the New Deal. The business community, however, contributed to his 1936 campaign only about one-fifth as much as it contributed in 1932, and many newspapers turned against FDR. The Republican nominee, Kansas governor Alfred M. Landon, denounced Roosevelt for endangering the "American system of free enterprise." He labeled Social Security as "unjust, unworkable, stupidly drafted, and wastefully financed," and attacked many other New Deal programs.

Four years of New Deal programs, however, had forged a new political coalition for the Democrats. Farmers, labor unions, retirees, and many ethnic groups supported Roosevelt and his programs. African American voters abandoned an allegiance to the Republican party that dated back to Reconstruction to support the party of Roosevelt. FDR's New Deal had not offered special programs for African Americans, but it had not tried to exclude them either. African American workers, who often were the first fired when hard times hit, owed much to New Deal relief programs, and they showed their gratitude at the polls. On Election Day, Roosevelt won in a landslide, and Democrats elected huge majorities to the House and Senate.

■ The New Deal and the Supreme Court

Before he could continue the New Deal in his second term, Roosevelt believed he had to eliminate opposition on the Supreme Court. During 1935 and 1936 the Court struck down New Deal programs, including the NIRA and AAA. Never before had the Court declared so much legislation unconstitutional. Roosevelt and his supporters believed that "9 old men" on the Court, 7 of whom had been appointed by Republican Presidents, were interfering with the New Deal's attempts at recovery. Laws that helped millions of people,

CHAPTER 18
SECTION 3

CURRICULUM CONNECTION

Government The social security system set up by the Social Security Act of 1935 is operated by one of the biggest agencies of the federal government. The Social Security Reform Act of 1983 fine-tuned the system's short-range and long-range financing and benefits. These changes were necessary because of the growing number of elderly in the United States.

FACT or FICTION?

As Maine goes, so goes the country.

FACT: Until 1936, results in Maine were such a solid indicator of who would win the presidential election that the saying became a political rule-of-thumb.

NATIONAL GEOGRAPHIC SOCIETY

 CD-ROM

The Presidents: A Picture History of Our Nation

Have students view "Franklin D. Roosevelt" and use the information to write a brief biography to include in their portfolios.

Sidelight: The Federal Theater

Among the most exciting and innovative projects of the WPA was the Federal Theater. In 1936 a gifted young director named Orson Welles staged Shakespeare's *Macbeth*, setting it in the West Indies and using an all African American cast. Another all African American production, *Swing Mikado*, was copied extensively by commercial theater companies. Many Federal Theater productions used the "living newspaper" technique—often taking on the style and methods of radio and documentary cinema to build morality plays about current events.

Linking Past and Present

Point out to students that the number of farms has decreased in the last 50 years, while the number of acres per farm has increased. In 1940 there were about 6 million farms in the United States. By 1993 that number had dwindled to a little more than 2 million. The number of acres per farm in 1940 was about 174, while in 1993 that number increased to 473. Ask students what these figures indicate about farming in the United States today. **L1**

📁 For additional practice, assign Linking Past and Present Activity 18.

📁 Assign Primary and Secondary Source Readings, p. 49: "FDR Takes on the Supreme Court."

ASSESS

Check Understanding

Assign Section 3 Review as homework or an in-class activity.

Evaluate

📁 Assign Section Quiz 18-3 or use the Testmaker to create a customized quiz.

Reteach

📁 Have students complete Reteaching Activity 18-3.

📁 Assign Workbook Activity 18-3.

Linking Past and Present

★★★★★★★★★★★★★

Government and the Farmer

When their problems became widespread, farmers joined cooperatives and turned to the government for help. In farm crises before the 1930s, the federal government always left competition and the free enterprise system intact among farm businesses.

Then

New Deal Policies

The Great Depression of the 1930s, however, triggered actions

◀ FARMING IN VIRGINIA, 1930S

that altered the face of agriculture. Farmers, long thought of as free and independent, became largely dependent on government assistance. The Agricultural Adjustment Act of 1933, for example, offered farmers payments to reduce production.

Now

Supports and Controls

The period since World War II has seen almost continuous battles over how much government control should be exercised over farm production. The farmers' own efficiency sometimes works against the government's solution. When production is slowed by one method, such as limiting acreage planted, farmers turn to technology to pull ahead again. They improve their farming meth-

▲ WHEAT HARVESTING TODAY

ods to make those fewer acres yield more than before.

Nor have price supports, another New Deal remnant, been the answer. Under this program, if market prices for certain crops fall below a guaranteed price, the government buys them. An immensely expensive program, it reaches few small farmers. Government efforts to preserve the independent farmers continue. But with each farm crisis, large agribusinesses gradually replace smaller farms.

★★★★★★★★★★★★★★★★★★★★★★★★★★★★★★★★★★★★

passed by large majorities in Congress, were being rejected by the Court, often by margins of 5 to 4.

Roosevelt considered his landslide reelection to be a mandate to curb the Supreme Court. In February 1937 the President presented legislation allowing him to appoint an additional justice to the Supreme Court for each justice over 70 years of age. Although the Court's size would increase from 9 to 15, Roosevelt argued that it needed "an infusion of younger blood." The "court-packing" bill caused a furor even in the President's own party. Many Americans were alarmed by the threat it posed to the system of checks and balances. Enough Democrats joined the Republicans in Congress to defeat Roosevelt's proposal. Although he suffered a major setback and lost many supporters, the President claimed that he had "lost the battle but won the war." While debate on the "court-packing" bill raged in Congress, in

two 5-to-4 decisions, the Court upheld the constitutionality of the two major laws of the Second New Deal—the Social Security Act and the Wagner Act.

■ Later New Deal Measures

By 1937 the economy had recovered nearly to 1929 levels, although widespread unemployment still remained. Roosevelt's financial advisers urged a cutback in spending and a balanced federal budget. Federal Reserve banks tightened credit, and the WPA cut the number of its employees in half.

The economy quickly slumped into a **recession,** a mild downturn in the business cycle, that critics called a "Roosevelt Depression." Huge crop surpluses collapsed agricultural prices, and industrial production dropped by one-third, almost to 1932 levels.

Sidelight: Dissension in Roosevelt's Cabinet

The recession caused dissension within Roosevelt's cabinet. Secretary of the Treasury Henry Morgenthau argued that the New Deal was not able to bring about economic recovery because businesses feared that continued government spending would cause inflation. Morgenthau felt that the government should

balance its budget and let businesses lead the way in economic recovery. However, Harry Hopkins and Harold Ickes argued that Roosevelt's quick spending cuts caused the recession. They felt that an increase in government spending was the only way to bring about economic recovery.

The President blamed the slump on businesses that, he claimed, failed to reinvest profits in production and on monopolies that kept prices artificially high. To meet the economic crisis, the President again expanded the work-relief programs of the WPA and stepped up military spending. People went back to work and prices rose. But the recession proved that hard times were not yet over.

In 1938 Congress passed a number of New Deal measures that carried out earlier policies. A Fair Labor Standards Act abolished child labor and placed a ceiling on hours and a floor under wages, at least for workers in businesses classified as "interstate commerce." A new Farm Security Administration promoted the well-being of impoverished farmers. A new AAA attempted to cope with surpluses by paying farmers not only to produce less but also to improve the soil and to control erosion. In addition, a food-stamp plan helped to distribute farm surpluses among those on relief.

These were some of the last New Deal programs. In the fall of 1937, when Roosevelt called a special session of Congress, not one of his proposals was enacted. Both in 1937 and in 1938 Congress rejected the President's request to reorganize the executive branch. These defeats were largely the result of a coalition of Republicans and conservative Southern Democrats who increasingly opposed the President in Congress. Roosevelt tried to weaken this coalition by supporting liberal Democrats against incumbents in the 1938 primary.

 ▲ PACKING THE COURT Although Roosevelt was overwhelmingly reelected in 1936, most people reacted negatively in 1937 to his attempt to pack the Supreme Court. *In this cartoon, what does the donkey's reaction symbolize?*

Roosevelt's attempted "purge" of his own party ended in defeat. In most cases, the conservative Democrats won. In the November election the Republicans staged a modest comeback, picking up seats in both houses of Congress. The coalition of Republicans and Southern Democrats was growing powerful and could block further extension of the New Deal.

Roosevelt accepted the judgment of the voters in the 1938 election. In January 1939 he announced that he would propose no further New Deal programs. Instead, he turned his attention to the growing threat of war in Europe.

Section 3 ★ Review

Checking for Understanding

1. **Identify** Father Coughlin, Huey Long, WPA, NLRB, CIO, court-packing.

2. **Define** coalition, craft union, industrial union, recession.

3. **Explain** the steps in Dr. Townsend's recovery plan.

4. **Describe** steps the New Deal took toward reform after 1935.

Critical Thinking

5. **Contrasting Ideas** How did the second New Deal differ from the first in its objectives, support base, program focus, and success?

ACTIVITY

6. Draw a political cartoon on one of these topics: opponents Huey Long and Franklin Roosevelt or labor unions and the New Deal.

CHAPTER 18
SECTION 3

GLENCOE TECHNOLOGY

◉ **VIDEODISC**

Focus on Government

‖‖‖‖‖‖‖‖‖‖‖‖

Side 2, Chapter 37
Title: *Making Connections, The Rules of the Supreme Court*
Subject: Procedures and rules

Enrich

Arrange for a union member or official to talk to students about the changes in unions since the 1930s and the importance of the 1930s to the growth of organized labor in the United States. Students should prepare questions ahead of time.

CLOSE

Have students use an economics text to find out the ways in which the American economic system was changed by the laws enacted during the second New Deal. Ask for volunteers to present their findings to the class.

Visualizing History No President since has tried to change the actual number of the justices on the Supreme Court.
Answer to Caption: the refusal of many members of Roosevelt's own party to go along with his plan

---

Answers to SECTION 3 REVIEW

1. Father Coughlin, 559; Huey Long, 559; WPA, 561; NLRB, 562; CIO, 562; court-packing, 564

2. All vocabulary words are defined in the Glossary.

3. Pensions to the elderly would relieve their suffering; requiring the pensions to be spent would stimulate production and create jobs.

4. focus on long-term reforms such as improving power of workers, graduated income tax, permanent social welfare programs

5. First—emphasized widespread but temporary emergency relief and recovery programs; Second—lasting reform of system focused on less fortunate in society at the expense of business support

6. Student cartoons should focus on a significant issue.

BUILDING SKILLS
Critical Thinking Skills

TEACH

Encourage students to recall times when they accurately predicted outcomes and to remember the information on which they based their predictions. Why might a predicted outcome, although reasonable, not occur? *(An unexpected action changes the course of events.)* Then ask volunteers to read the list of actions listed on page 566 and identify the organizing principle of the list. *(a chronology of events that impacted the labor movement)* **L2**

📁 Use Chapter Skills Activity 18 to reinforce students' understanding of the skill.

Did You Know?

The New Deal's pro-labor position had a dramatic effect on union membership. In 1933 less than 3 million workers belonged to labor unions. Two years later membership rose to 4.5 million.

Predicting Consequences

Consequences are the effects and repercussions that result from a decision or action. Sometimes the consequences of an action take you by surprise. More often, with a little forethought you can anticipate possible consequences.

Learning the Skill

To help predict consequences you can:

- **Restate** the action or decision under consideration.
- **Link** the action with relevant prior circumstances.
- **Map** out all possible outcomes or consequences.
- **Analyze** the possibilities. Are some consequences more likely to occur than others?

Much of the government activity of the 1930s revolved around improving economic conditions and employment opportunities. The American labor movement worked toward these goals long before Roosevelt's New Deal. But the progress of the labor movement was impacted, either negatively or positively, by the actions and decisions of employers, Congress, and the courts.

Read each of the items described below. Predict what might have happened to the American labor movement if these events had *not* occurred.

- Court interpretation of the Sherman Antitrust Act of 1890 finds that union strikes are "in restraint of trade or commerce."
- Clayton Act of 1914 holds that the courts cannot stop peaceful strikes, pickets, or boycotts.

- Fair Labor Standards Act of 1938 outlaws child labor and limits maximum workday hours.
- Taft-Hartley Act of 1947 halts strikes that might endanger national health and safety.

Practicing the Skill

1. Predict the effect of the Clayton Act on a local factory owner whose workers are on strike.
2. Predict the effect of the Fair Labor Standards Act on a family's financial situation.
3. Predict the effect of the Taft-Hartley Act on police and firefighters.

APPLYING THE SKILL

4. On a sheet of paper, paste a copy of a current newspaper article that discusses a public policy. Predict one or more consequences that may occur from the policy. On what basis did you make your predictions? How confident are you of your predictions?

566

Answers to Practicing the Skill

1. could lose money without workers to produce the product
2. A family's finances could decrease with the limit of maximum workday hours and a limit on the amount of money to be made in a day.
3. limited their ability to strike
4. Newspaper articles and predictions will vary. Students should present valid reasons to support their predictions.

★★

The Impact of the New Deal

Setting the Scene

Section Focus

Just as Roosevelt's fireside chats over the radio reached the American people, his New Deal programs touched their lives. From relief for the poor, to wages and working conditions, to regulation of the nation's economy and financial markets, programs affected society at every level. The New Deal involved the federal government in American life to an extent unprecedented in the nation's history.

▶ **WPA POSTER, 1940**

Objectives

After studying this section, you should be able to

★ identify changes that the New Deal caused in American society.

★ evaluate the effects of the New Deal on life today.

Key Term

ethnic group

*Sociologists Robert and Helen Lynd in 1929 published a study of values, behaviors, and everyday life in the 1920s in a typical American city that they called "Middletown." (It was actually Muncie, Indiana.) In 1935 they returned to "Middletown" for a follow-up study and found that the Depression and the New Deal had profoundly affected the families living in that community.

■ The New Deal and Society

The Depression affected every part of society. Its impact was felt at home and at work. The New Deal brought relief for some, but problems remained. In 1937 President Roosevelt said, "I see one-third of a nation ill-housed, ill-clad, ill-nourished."

Adapting to the Depression at Home

During the Depression, both births and divorces decreased as people could not afford either event. Older people moved in with working relatives. Many families rented rooms to boarders or moved to smaller and less expensive homes. Housewives took in laundry and sewing to help support their families. Sales of prepared food declined, and many people canned foods at home.

Changes at Work

Competition among adults for jobs resulted in stronger child labor laws, and the number of working children declined during the 1930s. Consequently, the number of high school and college students rose.

In Middletown, the Lynds noted that when a man lost his job and could not find

CHAPTER 18 The New Deal: 1932–1939 **567**

LESSON PLAN
SECTION 4, 567–571

FOCUS
Bellringer

Before taking roll, project Section Focus Transparency 18-4 or hand out Section Focus Transparency Activity 18-4. Have students answer the questions. Discuss student responses.

Motivating Activity

Display U.S. History and Art Transparency 23, *Fallingwater* by Frank Lloyd Wright, and Transparency 24, *Migrant Mother* by Dorothea Lange. Have students discuss how the works reflect the times—the 1930s. As they read this section, have students focus on how the culture of the 1930s reflected the changes that the New Deal caused in American society. **L2**

Vocabulary Precheck

Write *ethnic group* on the chalkboard. Have a volunteer skim the section to find the phrase and read it in context. **L1, LEP**

Classroom Resources for SECTION 4

Blackline Masters:
- Reproducible Lesson Plan 18-4
- Guided Reading Activity 18-4
- Critical Thinking Skills Activity 18

- Spirit of American Art and Music, pp. 33–34
- Enrichment Activity 18
- Workbook Activity 18-4
- Reteaching Activity 18-4
- Section Quiz 18-4

Transparencies:
- Section Focus Transparency 18-4
- U.S. History & Art Transparencies 23, 24

Multimedia:
- Testmaker
- Focus on Government

Art Refer students to the illustration on page 567 and point out that many artists employed by the WPA painted murals that detailed events of the time. Have students pretend they have been commissioned to create a mural for a public building today. Their mural should depict scenes of the 1990s. Have students brainstorm to decide what political and social topics best express the conditions of today. **L2**

Visualizing History Southern legislators blocked New Deal programs for African Americans.
Answer to Caption: none

GLENCOE
TECHNOLOGY

 VIDEODISC

Focus on Government

Side 1, Chapter 11
Title: *Lecture Launcher, Assuring Equal Justice For All*
Subject: Ongoing civil rights struggle

▲ A. PHILIP RANDOLPH As a young man, A. Philip Randolph quickly became aware of the discrimination African Americans faced in employment. He became a leader in the labor movement. *What civil rights measures were enacted during the New Deal?*

another, traditional family roles often were reversed, "with the woman taking a job for whatever money she could earn and the man caring for the household." Still, women were accused of taking men's jobs, and businesses often refused to hire married women.

Most women who worked outside the home, with the exception of farm and domestic workers, benefited from the New Deal. Women's wages rose and working conditions improved. The greatest direct assistance to women came from the Women's Division of the WPA. It employed between 300,000 and 400,000 women, some in traditionally female white-collar jobs such as teacher, nurse, and librarian. But most worked on canning and sewing projects. Their pay was low, but it often made the difference between food and famine.

■ Minorities

African Americans did not fare well under the New Deal. In addition, the government failed to enact any major civil rights measures during this period.

African Americans Get Mainly the Same Old Deal

As the poorest of the poor, African Americans often fell through the cracks of broad legislation such as the AAA and the Social Security Act. For example, although the AAA gave money to rural landowners, in the South 80 percent of all African American farmers owned no land. In addition, Roosevelt offered no civil rights program and did little to challenge the segregation that continued to exist throughout the nation, and he tolerated job discrimination. Even some government agencies refused to hire African Americans. Those that did, such as the CCC and armed forces, segregated African Americans and whites. In addition, African Americans received lower wages than white workers and were not assigned to certain jobs.

Nevertheless, Roosevelt appointed more African Americans to government posts than any President before him. Although most African American officials filled secondary posts, they influenced the President as an unofficial "black cabinet." Heading the cabinet was Mary McLeod Bethune, director of the Negro Affairs Division of the National Youth Administration. A personal friend of Eleanor Roosevelt, she often expressed the cabinet's concerns to the First Lady, who then carried them to FDR.

One concern of African Americans during the Depression was an increase in lynching and other acts of mob violence against them. Roosevelt supported a 1934 federal antilynching bill that held local sheriffs accountable for the frequent lynchings of African Americans in the South. But he never made the bill a legislative priority, and it finally died in the Senate in 1938.

One reason New Deal programs for African Americans were so limited was the opposition of powerful congressional committee heads who were from the South. As a result Roosevelt accepted NRA codes, for example, that permitted a lower minimum wage in the South than in the rest of the nation. FDR felt that if he pushed these Southern legislators too strongly, he would lose their support.

Cooperative Learning Activity

Women's Wages Mention that in 1937 the U.S. Supreme Court, in the decision of *West Coast Hotel* v. *Parrish* upheld a minimum wage law for women. This judgment reversed two previous rulings. Organize students into two groups. Have the members of one group work together to research the cases dealing with women's wages that the Supreme Court reviewed during the New Deal years. Ask the other group to research how women's wages changed during the New Deal. Have the two groups share their findings. **L3**

White Ethnic Groups Do Well

In general, the federal government responded more favorably to white **ethnic groups,** groups of people who shared the same culture, religion, and customs. During the 1930s the federal Office of Education sponsored a radio series called "Americans All . . . Immigrants All." The show celebrated the cultural vitality of a democracy made up of people from many lands. It also indicated the Democrats' awareness of the political power that ethnic groups could exercise if they were organized. Immigrants and their children made up 40 percent of the white population at that time. They tended to vote in groups and could swing elections, especially in large urban areas. Americans of Irish, Italian, and Polish descent became major partners in the New Deal coalition.

■ Popular Culture

The 1930s were somber years compared to the fads and frivolity of the 1920s. Literature and the arts generally turned to more realistic themes about poverty and human suffering.

Literature

Grim times provided powerful themes for American authors such as John Dos Passos, whose trilogy of novels called *U.S.A.* focused on fictional characters who lost their ideals and became hardened by society. Perhaps the most powerful novel of the era was John Steinbeck's *Grapes of Wrath,* the story of a family who left their Oklahoma farm in the dust bowl and headed to the migrant labor camps of California.

There was also much escapism in popular culture, as people turned to entertainment when things became grim. The best-selling book of the decade was Margaret Mitchell's *Gone With the Wind.* Although set in the South during the Civil War and Reconstruction, it offered a hopeful account of Scarlett

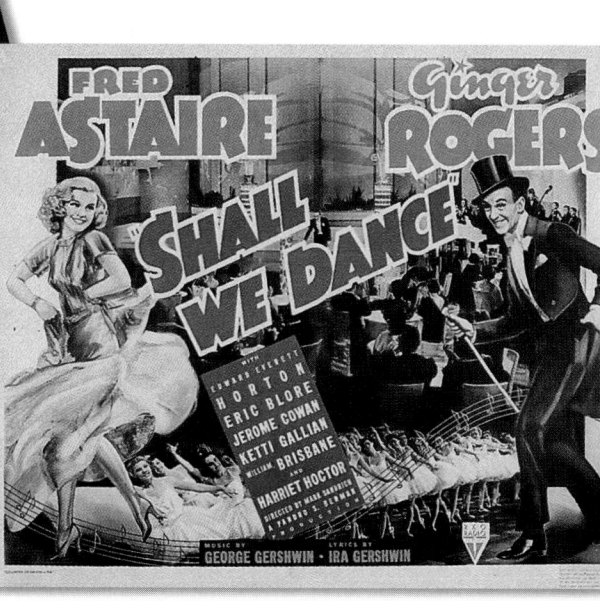

Visualizing History ▲ AT THE MOVIES The decade of the 1930s was a golden era for motion pictures. Popular fare included the Fred Astaire and Ginger Rogers musicals and Disney favorites such as *Snow White and the Seven Dwarfs. How many Americans attended the movies every week?*

Did You Know?

During the early months of 1933, the rate of foreclosures on private homes was about 1,000 per week. Congress quickly took action, establishing the Home Owners Loan Corporation (HOLC) on June 13, 1933. The HOLC helped owners refinance their debts into a single mortgage. By 1936 the HOLC had made loans covering 1 million mortgages.

Visualizing History The movies of Fred Astaire and Ginger Rogers offered Depression audiences "escapist" entertainment, frequently presenting the stars in luxurious settings and beautiful costumes. The movies featured witty dialogue, a mixture of romantic and comic dance routines, popular songs, and gifted entertainers. **Answer to Caption:** 85 million

📁 Assign The Spirit of American Art and Music, pp. 33–34: Elizabeth Catlett.

Critical Thinking Activity

Linking Past and Present Tell students that in 1936 about 38 percent of families in the United States—11.7 million families—had annual incomes of less than $1,000. The poverty line at that time was $1,330. Ask students to use sources such as the *Statistical Abstract of the United States* to find the most recent poverty figures. Have students compare the poverty situation today and in the mid-1930s. Then ask them to discuss the following question: What changes made in the 1930s may have helped us in dealing with poverty today? **L2**

📁 For additional practice, assign Critical Thinking Skills Activity 18.

Independent Practice

Analyzing Policies Write the following on the chalkboard:

African Americans—New Deal or Raw Deal?

Have students compare their tables. Interested students might like to use resources in the library to develop New Deal/Raw Deal tables for other minority groups, such as Native Americans and Mexican Americans. **L2**

📁 Assign Guided Reading Activity 18-4.

Visualizing
History *Gone With the Wind* was also one of the first color films made. It was released in 1939—the year that saw the release of another film classic, *The Wizard of Oz*. Victor Fleming directed both films.
Answer to Caption: radio

▲ MASS ENTERTAINMENT Clark Gable and Vivien Leigh starred in the movie of the 1930s best-selling novel, *Gone With the Wind*. The film was a big hit because people got nearly 4 hours of entertainment for just 10 to 25 cents. *What other mass entertainment medium was popular in the 1930s?*

O'Hara's efforts to rebuild her life and had much meaning for readers who had gone through the 1929 crash and the Depression.

Entertainment

As "talkies"—films with sound—became common during the 1930s, about 85 million people escaped the realities of the Depression for a few hours each week at the movie theater. There they watched movies that were often about the lives of happy and successful people. Continued improvements in sound technology ushered in the era of musicals, and audiences delighted at the dance routines of Fred Astaire and Ginger Rogers. Cartoon characters, such as Mickey Mouse, made audiences laugh, and as color-film technology spread, full-length animated features like Walt Disney's *Snow White and the Seven Dwarfs* provided more fantasy and escape.

• •

Footnotes to History

The 40-Hour Workweek During the 1930s, more leisure time was available, partly because working hours were reduced. The 40-hour week became standard. With the growth of unions, NRA codes and, finally, the Fair Labor Standards Act, the shorter workweek remained.

At home families could listen to network radio programs broadcast coast-to-coast. Daytime radio offered "soap operas," where characters suffered through daily crises. At night comedy, adventure, and musical variety programs dominated the airwaves. And the performances of Arturo Toscanini conducting the NBC Symphony of the Air brought classical music for the first time to millions of radio listeners.

The Automobile

Just as books, movies, and the radio provided Americans with an emotional outlet from the realities of the Depression, the automobile made them feel that they could physically escape their problems. Americans' love affair with cars, which began during the prosperity of the 1920s, continued throughout the poverty-stricken 1930s. The number of automobiles increased from 26 million in 1933 to 32 million by 1940. During the depths of the Depression, almost half the families in the United States owned a car, even though many could not afford to buy gasoline.

Yet despite the expense, many Americans continued to drive their cars during the 1930s. By late in the decade, thanks to government work projects, a maze of paved highways crisscrossed the nation. Large numbers of people took off down these two-lane roads,

Cultural Perspectives

The Plight of Mexican Americans Mexican Americans suffered greatly during the Depression, and the New Deal relief agencies provided them with considerable assistance. The Farm Security Administration built permanent migrant camps in areas of large-scale agricultural employment, such as the San Joaquin Valley in California. The FERA provided immediate relief during the worst part of the Depression. And while the WPA provided employment, it also created a renewed interest in Mexican arts and crafts.

some searching for employment and others pioneering what became an American institution—the family vacation by car.

The Influence of the New Deal

In the arts, as in so many other areas of society, the New Deal played a role. The WPA helped unemployed actors, artists, writers, and musicians. The Federal Theatre Project sponsored performances of Shakespeare as well as children's plays. Some 6,500 writers put together state and regional guidebooks and recorded life stories of formerly enslaved people, immigrants, and Native Americans.

The Federal Arts Project had artists paint murals and sculptors create statues, many of which still can be viewed today. The artistic works of William Gropper, Peter Blume, and Jack Levine reflected social concerns. Photographers like Dorothea Lange and artists like Ben Shahn documented people's lives during the Depression. Arts projects were among the most controversial New Deal programs, however. Critics called them socialistic. In 1939 Congress cut off funds for the theater project, and the other arts programs were discontinued as employment rose during World War II.

To many people who lived through it, the New Deal seemed to have changed American society. Yet it was not the revolutionary assault on capitalism that some of its critics charged. The New Deal changed the lives of farmers through crop subsidies and rural electrification. It changed the lives of indus-

▲ Comic Strip Hero Little Orphan Annie

trial workers by strengthening labor unions and expanding collective bargaining. It provided Social Security and welfare programs for the aged, the unemployed, and dependent children. In so doing, it turned a government that previously had responded more to business groups into a government open to labor, farmers, and other interests.

Yet the New Deal did not adopt national planning of the economy, as some of Roosevelt's advisers had expected. Rather than government owning industry, the New Deal emphasized federal regulation of private enterprise. Rather than overturning capitalism, New Dealers believed that they had helped to save it.

Section 4 ★ Review

Checking for Understanding

1. **Identify** black cabinet, John Steinbeck, Margaret Mitchell, soap operas, Federal Arts Project.

2. **Define** ethnic group.

3. **Summarize** the impact of the New Deal on African Americans.

4. **Discuss** popular forms of entertainment in the 1930s.

Critical Thinking

5. **Seeing Relationships** Analyze how the Depression influenced themes in American art and literature during the 1930s.

ACTIVITY

6. Research the effect of the New Deal in your community. Find out if the federal government supported any local projects in conservation, construction, or the arts.

CHAPTER 18 The New Deal: 1932–1939 **571**

Answers to SECTION 4 REVIEW

1. black cabinet, 568; John Steinbeck, 569; Margaret Mitchell, 569; soap operas, 570; Federal Arts Project, 571
2. All vocabulary words are defined in the Glossary.
3. no specific programs to address African American problems; many general programs bypassed or slighted African Americans
4. Popular novels focused on grim themes of people struggling to overcome adversity; movies and radio provided escapist entertainment; autos became increasingly popular.
5. Both arts focused on the hard lives of working people.
6. Students should discuss any New Deal impact on the community.

CHAPTER 18
SECTION 4

ASSESS
Check Understanding
Assign Section 4 Review as homework or an in-class activity.

Evaluate
Assign Section Quiz 18-4 or use the Testmaker to create a customized quiz.

Reteach
Have students complete Reteaching Activity 18-4.

Assign Workbook Activity 18-4.

Enrich
Discuss with students the problems faced by African Americans during the Depression and the response of the New Deal to those problems. Then have students research and write a report on the contributions to society during the New Deal of one of the following: Mary McLeod Bethune, Marian Anderson, or Robert C. Weaver. Ask for volunteers to read their reports to the class.

Have students complete Enrichment Activity 18.

CLOSE
Have students summarize in their own words the impact of the New Deal. Suggest that they include in their summaries what impact, if any, the New Deal has on our lives today.

Block Schedule

Team Teaching

This selection from *The Grapes of Wrath* can be presented in a team teaching context, in conjunction with English or Language Arts.

Historical Setting

The crash of 1929 resulted in bank closings, severe business losses, and 14 million unemployed Americans. Tragically it was during the Depression that the Dust Bowl dried up and blew away. Its tenant farmers, too, were tossed to the wind.

Background

During the Great Depression, radio and film offered escapist fare for Americans who momentarily sought to forget their troubles. Yet, there were artists who chose to reveal the Depression in ugly, gritty terms. With *The Grapes of Wrath*, Steinbeck illustrates the harshness of the Depression.

About the Author

Born in Salinas, California, in 1902, John Steinbeck was to set much of his literature in the Salinas Valley. He had intended to earn a degree in marine biology but interrupted his studies at Stanford University to pursue a writing career. It was not until 1935 that he gained any recognition. He received the Pulitzer Prize for *The Grapes of Wrath*.

▲ JOHN STEINBECK

In *The Grapes of Wrath*, John Steinbeck chronicles the hardships of the Joads, an Oklahoma farm family whose plight resembles that of the downtrodden everywhere. As you read the excerpt from Steinbeck's novel, look for statements that reveal the beliefs, concerns, and attitudes of tenant farmers during the 1930s.

Read to Discover

When the economy collapsed in 1929, millions of American lives collapsed with it. People everywhere lost their jobs. In the nation's Dust Bowl, farmers had to leave the land that their families had worked for generations.

Reader's Dictionary

auger — large tool for boring into the earth
tenant — one who holds or possesses land

The Grapes of Wrath (excerpts)

The owners of the land came onto the land, or more often a spokesman for the owners came. They came in closed cars, and they felt the dry earth with their fingers, and sometimes they drove big earth augers into the ground for soil tests. The tenants, from their sun-beaten dooryards, watched uneasily when the closed cars drove along the fields. And at last the owner men drove into the dooryards and sat in their cars to talk out of the windows. . . .

If a bank or a finance company owned the land, the owner man said, The Bank—or the Company—needs-wants-insists-must have-as though the Bank or the Company were a monster, with thought and feeling, which had ensnared them. . . . The owner men sat in the cars and explained. You know the land is poor. You've scrabbled at it long enough, God knows. . . .

The owner men went on leading to their point: You know the land's getting poorer. You know what cotton does to the land; robs it, sucks all the blood out of it.

The squatters nodded—they knew, God knew. If they could only rotate the crops they might pump blood back into the land. Well, it's too late. And the owner men explained the workings and the thinkings of the monster that was stronger than they were. . . .

The squatting men raised their eyes to understand. Can't we just hang on? Maybe the next year will be a good year. God knows how much cotton next year. And

Cultural Perspectives

Steinbeck and the World John Steinbeck became popular all over the world because of his ability to tell unforgettable stories and his empathy for disadvantaged people. His socially relevant books made him a favorite author in the former Soviet Union and in developing countries. Later Steinbeck also wrote about life in Russia, England, and France. As an indication of his international popularity, Steinbeck received the Nobel Prize for Literature in 1962. After he received the award President Lyndon Johnson asked him to serve as goodwill ambassador to the United Nations.

with all the wars—God knows what price cotton will bring. Don't they make explosives out of cotton? And uniforms? Get enough wars and cotton'll hit the ceiling. Next year, maybe. They looked up questioningly.

We can't depend on it. The bank—the monster has to have profits all the time. It can't wait. It'll die. . . .

The squatting men looked down again. What do you want us to do? We can't take less share of the crop—we're half starved now. The kids are hungry all the time. We got no clothes, torn an' ragged. If all the neighbors weren't the same, we'd be ashamed to go to meeting.

And at last the owner men came to the point. The tenant system won't work any more. One man on a tractor can take the place of twelve or fourteen families. Pay him a wage and take all the crop. We have to do it. We don't like to do it. But the monster's sick. Something's happened to the monster.

But you'll kill the land with cotton. We know. We've got to take cotton quick before the land dies. Then we'll sell the land. Lots of families in the East would like to own a piece of land.

The tenant men looked up alarmed. But what'll happen to us? How'll we eat?

You'll have to get off the land. The plows'll go through the dooryard. . . .

It's not us, it's the bank. A bank isn't like a man. Or an owner with fifty thousand acres, he isn't like a man either. That's the monster.

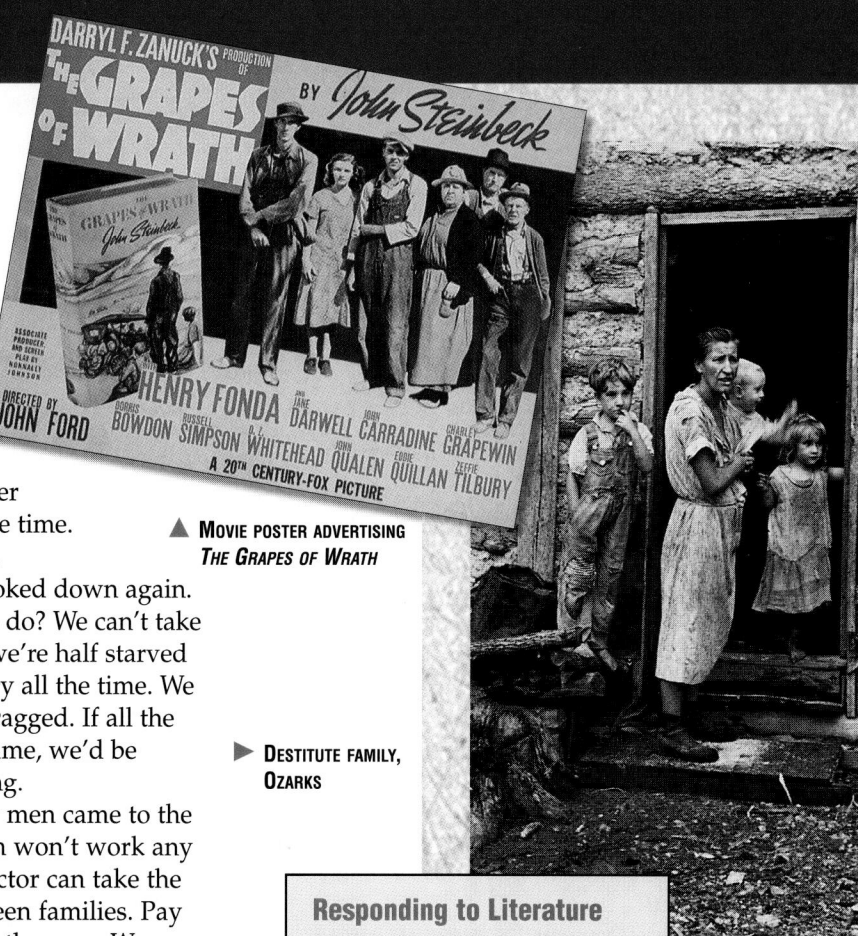

▲ MOVIE POSTER ADVERTISING *THE GRAPES OF WRATH*

► DESTITUTE FAMILY, OZARKS

Responding to Literature

1. Locate passages where the tenant men are beseeching or protesting.

2. What is the "monster"? Do you think this is an apt metaphor? Why or why not?

3. Steinbeck clearly sides with the tenant farmers. What arguments could be made for the banks and the owners? Which viewpoint do you favor?

ACTIVITY

4. Write a dialogue in which a parent explains to a son or daughter why they must move from their home in the Dust Bowl.

CHAPTER 18 The New Deal: 1932–1939 **573**

GLENCOE TECHNOLOGY

 VIDEODISC

Use the MindJogger Videoquiz to review students' knowledge.

MindJogger Videoquiz

Chapter 18
Disc 2, Side B

 Available in VHS.

Using Vocabulary

Sentences should include all the vocabulary terms.

Reviewing Facts

1. to identify which banks were secure so that confidence could be restored
2. Before: financial reform and emergency relief and recovery; After: work relief programs, lasting business, labor, taxation, and social welfare reform.
3. fireside chats, press conferences, public appearances
4. farmers—Resettlement Administration, AAA, TVA, FSA; workers— NIRA, NLRB; unemployed—CWA, PWA, CCC, TVA, WPA, Social Security; unemployable—social security
5. paid farmers to reduce production, which raised prices; moratorium on mortgage foreclosures; loans to tenants to buy their own land; helped poor farmers get a new start on good land.
6. Government supported labor unions through NIRA and NLRB. CIO

Using Vocabulary

Write sentences about Roosevelt's New Deal using these vocabulary words.

deficit spending	foreclosure
dole	recession
pump priming	

Reviewing Facts

1. **Explain** the purpose of the bank holiday in the first Hundred Days.
2. **Compare** the purposes of New Deal legislation before and after 1935.
3. **Cite** the means Roosevelt used to advocate, promote, and gain public support for his New Deal programs.
4. **Identify** specific New Deal programs that provided help to various types of needy people in society.
5. **Describe** Roosevelt's attempts to help farmers.
6. **Discuss** developments and achievements within organized labor movements during the 1930s and the role that the New Deal played in these developments.
7. **Specify** groups that did not fully share in the benefits of the New Deal.
8. **List** ways the New Deal supported the arts during the Depression.
9. **Explain** the lasting effects that came from the New Deal policy.

Understanding Concepts

Economic Reform

1. Which New Deal programs would you classify as achieving lasting economic reform? Explain your reasons for your choices.
2. Describe the ways in which "pump priming" is intended to work. How is its use supposed to aid the nation's recovery in times of recession or depression?

Political Leadership

3. Much of the success of the New Deal relied on the charismatic personality and leadership of Franklin Roosevelt. Explain how he used these assets to gain support for his controversial and complicated New Deal policies.
4. One mark of a good leader is the ability to choose and utilize able administrators. Explain to what extent this was true of Franklin Roosevelt.

Critical Thinking

1. **Finding Explanations** Though farmers received substantial assistance during the New Deal and have since, many farmers have continued to suffer economically. What problems inherent in farming could possibly account for this recurring difficulty?

The Federal Budget and Deficit

	Federal Receipts (in billions of dollars)	Federal Deficit (in billions of dollars)	Gross Federal Debt (in billions of dollars)	Per Capita Federal Debt (total dollar amt.)
1940	6.9	-2.7	43.0	325
1939	6.6	-2.9	40.4	309
1938	7.0	-.1	37.2	286
1937	5.6	-2.8	36.4	283
1936	4.2	-3.5	33.8	264
1935	3.8	-2.4	28.7	226
1934	3.1	-3.3	27.1	214
1933	2.1	-2.6	22.5	179
1932	2.0	-2.7	19.5	156

Source: *Historical Statistics of the United States: Colonial Times to 1970* (1975).

2. **Analyzing Statistics** Use the table on this page and information from the chapter to help you answer these questions.
   a. What is the subject of the table? How many years does the information presented in the table cover?

---

achieved contracts in major industries.
7. African Americans, tenant farmers, some private industries
8. work of Federal Arts Project, Federal Theater Project, FSA, WPA
9. government's role in economic planning and regulation, expanded social welfare programs

Understanding Concepts

1. Social Security benefits, labor laws, banking and securities reform, commitment to public assistance
2. Government puts money

into the economy; increased consumption, spurring production and jobs.
3. displayed activist approach, openness to ideas
4. dependence on experts; Eleanor Roosevelt and Frances Perkins provided role model for women

b. What year was the federal deficit at its highest level? What was happening in the United States at that time?

c. During the time period shown, did the federal government ever spend less money than it received?

d. If the federal deficit decreased in 1940, why didn't the federal debt also decrease?

3. **Understanding Cause and Effect** Why do you suppose Roosevelt abandoned his efforts to enlist the support of the business community for the New Deal reforms that he launched during his second term as President?

4. **Demonstrating Reasoned Judgment** Assume the nation has entered a depression today. As a member of Congress devoted to economic reform, write an argument proposing and supporting deficit spending to stimulate the economy and to finance expanded government assistance programs. Include reasons an economist might express in favor of such programs. Also think carefully about the reasons why some of your constituents would favor such policies and why others would oppose them.

History and Geography

The Effects of the Great Depression

1. **Place** How did the problems of urban people compare with those in agricultural areas?

2. **Region** What problems faced residents of the Dust Bowl?

3. **Human/Environment Interaction** Could the problems of the Dust Bowl have been prevented? If so, how? If not, why?

Cooperative Learning | Interdisciplinary Activity: Debate

Working in a group of three, assume roles of government officials during Roosevelt's term. One member should assume the role of a Roosevelt supporter in Congress and present an argument to Congress for enlarging the Supreme Court. The second member should assume the role of an anti-Roosevelt senator and address Congress, refuting the need to enlarge the Court. The third member will listen to both arguments and decide which is the more effective. All group members should then be prepared to argue either position before the class if called upon by the teacher.

Practicing Skills

Predicting Consequences

Review the skill on predicting consequences on page 566. Then read the following statements and predict consequences for each.

1. Engineers develop an effective, efficient electric-powered automobile.

2. The laws are changed to provide for the direct election of the Supreme Court.

3. You decide to work in a field that does not appeal to you but that will provide financial security.

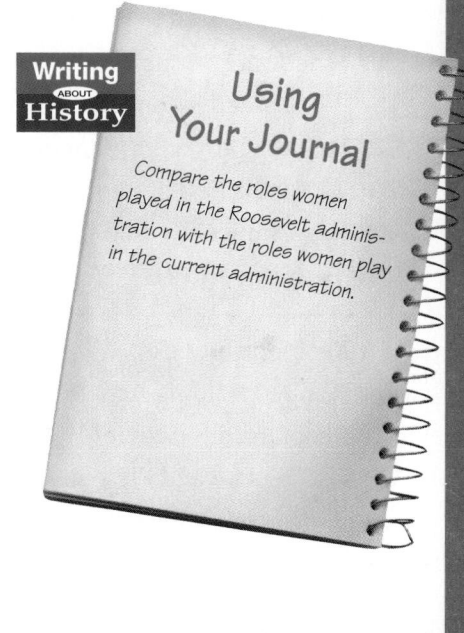

Writing ABOUT **History**

Using Your Journal

Compare the roles women played in the Roosevelt administration with the roles women play in the current administration.

vented erosion and conserved moisture. Other students might indicate that the unusual drought over the long time period would have resulted in a Dust Bowl in any case.

Cooperative Learning

You might ask groups to role-play the government officials presenting their arguments to Congress.

Practicing Skills

1. Possible prediction: Degree of air pollution would lessen.
2. Possible prediction: Judges would be too concerned about public opinion in rendering their decisions.
3. Possible prediction: You might feel unfulfilled in your work.

Writing ABOUT **History** | Using Your Journal

Ask students to provide examples.

? Chapter Bonus Test Question

Ask students: Choose a President among FDR's predecessors to compare with Roosevelt, in terms of both substance and style. (*Answers will vary but should reflect an understanding of Roosevelt's ideology and style of governing.*)

Critical Thinking

1. Answers include: overproduction has kept prices down.
2. **a.** federal budgets and deficits; 9 years
   b. 1936; Depression
   c. no
   d. The debt is cumulative.
3. knew he would have to adopt more radical and permanent reforms that business would find even less acceptable
4. Arguments and reasons will vary but should include reasons that would be expressed by an economist.

History and Geography

1. The situations of both were desperate.
2. finding a way to renew the topsoil for planting; needed funds for seed and livestock
3. Students might indicate that by limiting growing farmers might have pre-

Daily Lesson Objectives	Teacher Classroom Resources	Multimedia
SECTION 1 **World Affairs, 1933–1939** **1 Day** pp. 578–582 1. Discuss how the Depression influenced American foreign policy. 2. Explain the reasons for Japan's aggression in Asia.	Reproducible Lesson Plan 19-1 Concept Mapping Activities 19-A, 19-B *Guided Reading Activity 19-1 *Vocabulary Activity 19 Critical Thinking Skills Activity 19 Workbook Activity 19-1 Reteaching Activity 19-1 *Section Quiz 19-1	Section Focus Transparency 19-1 Chapter Concepts Transparencies 19-A, 19-B MindJogger Videoquiz GTV: A Geographic Perspective on American History Lessons of War
SECTION 2 **Moving Closer to War** **1 Day** pp. 583–588 1. Discuss Germany's conquest of Europe. 2. List the steps by which Roosevelt increased support to the Allies.	Reproducible Lesson Plan 19-2 *Guided Reading Activity 19-2 Workbook Activity 19-2 Reteaching Activity 19-2 *Section Quiz 19-2	Section Focus Transparency 19-2 Testmaker Lessons of War Historic America Electronic Field Trips
SECTION 3 **The United States at War** **1 Day** pp. 589–597 1. Discuss the course of the war in Europe and in Asia. 2. Describe the Atlantic Charter and the agreements the Allies reached at the Yalta Conference.	Reproducible Lesson Plan 19-3 *Guided Reading Activity 19-3 Chapter Map Activity 19 American Portrait 57 Primary and Secondary Source Readings, pp. 50–52 Political Cartoons in American History Activity 18 Workbook Activity 19-3 Reteaching Activity 19-3 *Section Quiz 19-3	Section Focus Transparency 19-3 Map Transparency 19 GTV: A Geographic Perspective on American History Historic America Electronic Field Trips Lessons of War Powers of the President Focus on Government
SECTION 4 **War on the Home Front** **1 Day** pp. 599–604 1. Discuss efforts to mobilize the economy for war production. 2. Explain the war's impact on women, African Americans, and Japanese Americans.	Reproducible Lesson Plan 19-4 *Guided Reading Activity 19-4 Chapter Skills Activity 19 Linking Past and Present Activity 19 Enrichment Activity 19 Geography in History Activity 19 Reteaching Activity 19-4 *Section Quiz 19-4	Section Focus Transparency 19-4 Skills Transparency 19 Testmaker Lessons of War GTV: The American People: Fabric of a Nation
CHAPTER REVIEW AND EVALUATION **1 Day**	Chapter 19 Test, Forms A and B Spanish Chapter 19 Summary Performance Assessment Activity 19	MindJogger Videoquiz Student Self-Test & Review Software *Chapter 19 Audiocassette Activity and Test

*Also available in Spanish

 OUT OF TIME? If time does not permit teaching the entire chapter, use the Chapter 19 Summary on pages 662–663 and the Chapter 19 audiocassette (English and Spanish) to point out the main ideas of the chapter.

A complete, 1-page lesson plan is provided for each section in the *Reproducible Lesson Plan* booklet.

Key to Ability Levels

Teaching strategies have been coded for varying learning styles and abilities.

L1   Basic activities for all students

L2   Average activities for average to above-average students

L3   Challenging activities for above-average students

LEP   Limited English Proficiency activities

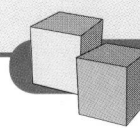

Block Schedule

Block scheduling differs from traditional class scheduling in the amount of time allotted to each period. The extended time frame provided by block scheduling affords you the opportunity to implement a greater number of research-oriented and activity-intense projects to motivate and involve your students. Activities that are particularly suited to use within the block scheduling framework are identified throughout this unit by the following designation:

✓ Performance Assessment Activity

Shifting Opinions In the 1930s many Americans wanted to keep the nation out of another world war. Gradually attitudes began to change. Have students, working alone or in small groups, choose an individual or a group to research. What was the attitude of that individual or group toward the Germans or the Japanese at the time the Olympics were held in Berlin? In 1939, when the war began in Europe? In December 1941, when Pearl Harbor was bombed? During the course of the war? Have students present their findings to the class in the form of a written or oral report. The reports should describe how and why attitudes changed from 1936 through 1945.

POSSIBLE RUBRIC FEATURES

- Research Skills
- Content Information
- Organization
- Written and Oral Communication Skills
- Creativity
- Critical Thinking Skills

📁 For additional practice, use Performance Assessment Strategies and Activities.

T E A C H E R ' S   C O R N E R

NATIONAL GEOGRAPHIC SOCIETY

INDEX TO NATIONAL GEOGRAPHIC MAGAZINE

The following articles may be used for research relating to this chapter:

- "Blueprints for Victory," by John F. Shupe, May 1995.
- "The Wings of War," by Thomas B. Allen, March 1994.
- "Douglas MacArthur: An American Soldier," by Geoffrey C. Ward, March 1992.
- "Pearl Harbor: A Return to the Day of Infamy," by Thomas B. Allen, December 1991.
- "Remembering the Blitz," by Cameron Thomas, July 1991.
- "The Bismarck Found," by Robert D. Ballard, November 1989.
- "Living With Radiation," by Charles E. Cobb, Jr., April 1989.

NATIONAL GEOGRAPHIC SOCIETY PRODUCTS AVAILABLE FROM GLENCOE

To order the following products for use with this chapter, contact your local Glencoe sales representative or call Glencoe at 1-800-334-7344:

- *The Presidents: A Picture History of Our Nation* (CD-ROM)
- *GTV: A Geographic Perspective on American History* (Videodisc)
- *GTV: The American People: Fabric of a Nation* (Videodisc)
- *STV: World Geography* (Videodisc)
- *STV: North America* (Videodisc)

ADDITIONAL NATIONAL GEOGRAPHIC SOCIETY PRODUCTS

To order the following products for use with this chapter, call National Geographic Society at 1-800-368-2728:

- *Lost Fleet of Guadalcanal* (Video)
- *Decades of History: The 20th Century—The Early Years* (Filmstrip)
- *The United States as a World Power: From the 1890s to the 1970s* (Filmstrip)

BEGINNING THE CHAPTER

GLENCOE TECHNOLOGY

 **VIDEODISC**

Use the Chapter 19 MindJogger Videoquiz to preview the content of this chapter.

MindJogger Videoquiz

Chapter 19
Disc 3, Side A

Available in VHS.

Recording Journal Notes

To help students get started, ask them to make a list of the major combatants in World War II—Germany, Japan, and Italy on the Axis side, and Britain, France, the United States, and the Soviet Union on the Allied side.

Linking Across TIME

By the mid-1930s, it was obvious that war in Europe was again on the way. The U.S. had twice been drawn into European wars, once in 1812 and again in 1917. Fearing that history would repeat itself, Congress passed the Neutrality Acts.

CHAPTER 19
★★★★★★★★★★★★★★★★★★★★★★★★★★★★★★★★★★★

World War II
1933–1945

▶ **SILVER STAR, AWARDED FOR GALLANTRY IN ACTION**

Setting the Scene

Focus

The Depression of the 1930s was worldwide. When a new war engulfed Europe, Roosevelt sought to aid the British. After Japan attacked Pearl Harbor in 1941, America entered the war directly. Initially, Allied prospects were bleak, but by 1944 the tide had turned. Victory in the Pacific, however, came only after the use of nuclear weapons.

Concepts to Understand

★ Why **international alliances** were formed between Germany, Italy, and Japan

★ How the Allies prevented Germany and Italy from winning the **military conflict** in Europe

Read to Discover . . .

★ what events led the American people to abandon isolationism and neutrality.

★ why Roosevelt was more successful than Wilson in helping to form a world peacekeeping body.

Journal Notes

Consider the interests, fears, and concerns of the nations involved in World War II. Record examples in your journal as you read the chapter.

CULTURAL	• **1931** *Pearl Buck publishes* The Good Earth	• **1936** *Babe Ruth and Ty Cobb named to baseball's Hall of Fame*
	1930	**1935**
POLITICAL	• **1933** *United States recognizes the government of the Soviet Union*	• **1939** *Germany attacks Poland; war in Europe begins*

576 UNIT 6 Times of Crisis: 1932–1960

✚ **EXTRA CREDIT PROJECT**

Working With Geography Just as many Americans could not locate Middle Eastern countries on a map until the Persian Gulf War began in January 1991, many Americans in the 1940s had not heard of European and Japanese combat locales until the nation took part in World War II. On an outline map of the world, ask interested students to identify the Allied and Axis powers. Also encourage them to provide a thumbnail sketch of each nation including key geographical features, major products, main ethnic groups, and involvement in World War I. **L2**

◄ TANK BOOTS, 1943

- **1940** *Color television is demonstrated by the Columbia Broadcasting System*
- **1942** *Sugar and gasoline are rationed*

1940

- **1940** *Selective Service Act passed*
- **1941** *Japanese attack Pearl Harbor*

- **1945** *Tennessee Williams's play* The Glass Menagerie *opens in New York*

1945

- **1944** *Allies invade Normandy*
- **1945** *Nuclear weapons first used*

Performance Assessment

Expressing Opinions Provide the following information: In March 1942, United States General John DeWitt ordered the evacuation of all Japanese from the western half of Washington, Oregon, and California and from southern Arizona. Most of the evacuees were American citizens. DeWitt explained, "It makes no difference whether a Japanese is theoretically a citizen. He is still a Japanese. . . . " Note that thousands of Japanese Americans served in the armed forces during the war. The bravery of the all-Japanese American 442nd Regimental Combat Team made it the most highly decorated unit in U.S. military history. Organize the students into groups. Have each group write a response to DeWitt's statement. **L1**

FOCUS

Bellringer

Before taking roll, project Section Focus Transparency 19-1 or hand out Section Focus Transparency Activity 19-1. Have students answer the questions.

Motivating Activity

Ask students if they have ever been at home doing a job that needed to be done when a friend called and asked them for help. Then point out that President Roosevelt was in a similar situation. Direct students to read the Section Focus, and tell them they will learn how Roosevelt attempted to deal with problems both at home and abroad in the late 1930s. **L1**

Vocabulary Precheck

Ask students to define each of the "Key Terms." Have a volunteer consult the dictionary for any unfamiliar words. **L1, LEP**

Use the Vocabulary PuzzleMaker Software to create a crossword puzzle. **L1**

Assign Vocabulary Activity 19.

★★★

World Affairs, 1933–1939

Setting the Scene

Section Focus

Like President Woodrow Wilson, for whom he had worked during World War I, Franklin D. Roosevelt was greatly interested in world affairs. But when he entered the White House in 1933, recovery from the Depression kept most of his energy and attention focused on the United States. As Europe again moved toward war, however, the President experienced growing concern with events overseas.

◄ **MILITARY ALUMINUM CANTEEN**

Objectives

After studying this section, you should be able to

★ discuss how the Depression influenced American foreign policy.

★ explain the reasons for Japan's aggression in Asia.

Key Terms

fascism, totalitarian, appeasement

---

*L*ike his distant cousin Theodore, Franklin D. Roosevelt was acquainted with the world beyond the shores of the United States. He had made more than a dozen trips to Europe, and he had firsthand knowledge of the Caribbean area. Through family connections with the China trade, he had acquired an interest in Asia. He resembled Theodore Roosevelt, too, in realizing that as a world power the United States had a commitment to help preserve the peace of the world. As a former associate of Woodrow Wilson, he believed in world organization to promote international cooperation and to solve disputes.

For most of his first two terms, however, Franklin D. Roosevelt focused on domestic affairs. Events in Europe and Asia seemed distant when compared to the crisis of the Depression. In addition, the President rec-

ognized that Americans, pressed by hard times at home, cared little about the world at large. So although Roosevelt believed that German expansion posed a threat to the United States, he was cautious in his efforts to alert the nation to this danger. Only when dealing with affairs in the Western Hemisphere did Roosevelt act with his typical bold political style.

■ New Deal Foreign Policy

At his first inaugural in 1933, President Roosevelt pledged that the United States would be a "good neighbor" in the family of nations. He pledged to respect the sovereign rights of all nations in the Western Hemisphere. A few weeks later, he applied the phrase "Good Neighbor" specifically to the administration's Latin American policy.

Classroom Resources for SECTION 1

Blackline Masters:
- Reproducible Lesson Plan 19-1
- Guided Reading Activity 19-1
- Vocabulary Activity 19
- Cooperative Learning Activity 19
- Critical Thinking Skills Activity 19

- Political Cartoons in American History Activity 17
- Workbook Activity 19-1
- Reteaching Activity 19-1
- Section Quiz 19-1

Transparencies:
- Section Focus Transparency 19-1

Multimedia:
- Testmaker
- MindJogger Videoquiz
- GTV: A Geographic Perspective on American History
- Lessons of War

Peaceful Intentions in Latin America

President Roosevelt and Secretary of State Cordell Hull worked to improve relations with the United States's southern neighbors. Later that year, at the Pan-American Conference at Montevideo, Uruguay, the United States agreed to a resolution that "no state has the right to intervene in the internal affairs of another." Roosevelt demonstrated his commitment to the Good Neighbor policy by recalling American troops from Haiti and Nicaragua, where they had been protecting American property since the 1920s. When Cuba erupted in revolution in 1933, Roosevelt used diplomacy, not troops, to help restore order. When Mexico seized American-owned oil companies in 1938, Roosevelt resisted demands for military action and sought a peaceful settlement.

Domestic Recovery Determines Foreign Decisions

During Roosevelt's first years in office, the United States seemed less inclined to cooperate with Europe. The New Deal adopted a policy of economic isolation, and its recovery programs included attempts to solve agricultural and industrial production problems without considering the rest of the world. In 1933 delegates from more than 60 nations met in London to bring about cooperation in confronting world depression. Roosevelt wrecked the conference by rejecting proposals to peg the value of the dollar to any other currency. He feared that such a move would hurt his efforts to raise American farm prices.

Only when the United States had achieved some recovery from the Depression was the President willing to consider economic cooperation with other nations. Secretary of State Hull believed world prosperity and goodwill could be gained by reducing tariffs. At Hull's urging, Congress passed the Reciprocal Trade Agreements Act of 1934, allowing the State Department to make treaties with other countries to mutually lower import duties. Within six years, the United States had reached such agreements with more than a dozen nations.

Recognition of the Soviet Union

Another change in foreign policy took place when the United States recognized the government of the Soviet Union. Since the Bolshevik Revolution of 1917, the United States had refused to recognize the communist government. After their revolution, the Soviets tried to encourage communism throughout the world. By 1933, however, the USSR was beset by serious economic problems at home and seemed less of a threat. Much more threatening was the rising power of Japan, the Soviets' rival in Asia. The President hoped that a strong Soviet Union could slow Japanese expansion. In addition, Roosevelt saw the Soviets' need for food and industrial equipment as a market for American farmers and manufacturers. "The United States would probably

Visualizing ▲ JAPANESE EXPANSION Japanese
History forces first moved into Manchuria in 1931. Japan established the puppet state of Manchukuo a year later. *How did Roosevelt hope to slow Japan's aggression in Asia?*

TEACH
Guided Practice

History Divide students into groups of three. Ask each student to play one of the following: Japan's leader, Hitler, or Mussolini. Have each discuss and list reasons for his aggressive policies in the early to mid-1930s and list the countries his armies invaded. During class discussion, have each person share the lists. **L2**

CURRICULUM CONNECTION

Language Arts The word *fascist* comes from the Latin word *fasces*, or the rods and axes that Roman officials carried in ancient times to show that Rome was strong and unified.

Visualizing
History Japan had been building its military forces for decades. In the early part of the century, Japanese soldiers won an impressive victory in the Russo-Japanese War (1904–1905). As a result of this war, Japan gained international status as a great military power.
Answer to Caption: Roosevelt hoped that by recognizing the Soviet Union, he could slow Japanese aggression in Asia.

Special Needs Activity

Language Disability It is not unusual for students with language-based learning disabilities to know a variety of strategies for studying text, but to forget to employ these strategies appropriately. Ask students to preview Section 1 to determine the topics presented. List the topics on the board: the Good Neighbor policy, American isolationism, the rise of Hitler and Mussolini. Ask students to think of strategies and skills they have employed throughout this text that might be of help in learning the information in the section. **LEP, L1**

Visualizing (H)istory
▲ **MUSSOLINI** Italy's dictator Benito Mussolini gives the Fascist salute during an address. After Italy surrendered to Allied forces, Mussolini was captured and executed by the Italian people. *What plans did Mussolini have in common with Adolf Hitler?*

recognize the Devil," Will Rogers joked, "if it could sell him pitchforks." Recognition of the Soviet Union helped improve relations but did little to increase trade or to check Japanese militarism.

Aggression and Appeasement

American hopes to concentrate on domestic affairs, relatively isolated from foreign concerns, were quickly dashed. Events in the world began to send off alarms of trouble ahead.

Japanese Expansion in the Pacific

Between 1872 and 1925, Japan's population nearly doubled, causing severe problems for that small island nation. To sustain industrial growth, Japan needed larger markets for its products and more raw materials for its factories. To meet these needs and to ease overcrowding in the home islands, Japan pursued a policy of expansion in the Pacific.

During World War I, Japan supported the Allies but used the war to increase its influence in China. After the war Japan was bitter toward the West. The Washington Conference of 1921 cost Japan most of its gains in China and limited Japan's naval power. When the United States joined other Western nations in 1924 in banning immigrants from Japan, its leaders looked to military solutions for their nation's problems.

In September 1931, Japanese troops invaded and occupied mineral-rich Manchuria in northeastern China. When the League of Nations demanded that Manchuria be returned to China, Japan ignored the order.

Threats From Germany and Italy

On March 5, 1933, the day after Roosevelt took office, the German parliament voted Adolf Hitler, the National Socialist (Nazi)

Cooperative Learning Activity

Analyzing Reasons Divide the class into small groups. Have students in each group "huddle up" and discuss the following question: What were the reasons for the American public's desire to maintain neutrality in the late 1930s? Call upon a student randomly in each group to report the group's progress. (*A basic answer* *should include the following: People for neutrality felt that the United States had shed enough blood in World War I and had not made the world safe nor helped the spread of democracy.*) **L2**

📁 For additional practice, assign Cooperative Learning Activity 19.

leader, the power he needed to begin a program of conquest in central and eastern Europe. In Italy, dictator Benito Mussolini made similar plans to control the Mediterranean and to expand Italy's empire in Africa.

Mussolini and Hitler followed a new political doctrine known as **fascism** (FASH•ihz•uhm), a form of government in which a dictator and supporters cooperate to seek more power for their nation, usually at the expense of rights for individuals. Each ruler established a **totalitarian** state—a nation that totally controls the life of its people. The Fascists in Italy and the Nazis in Germany set up all-powerful official parties. Both whipped up support with huge patriotic rallies, parades, music, and appeals to national pride and racial hatred, and both used force to silence all opposition.

Each dictator blamed his country's problems after World War I on undesirables in society. Mussolini accused Italy's Communists of causing strikes and social unrest.

The Nazis blamed Germany's economic chaos on its Jewish population. They restricted Jews, boycotted Jewish-owned stores, and destroyed synagogues. Both Hitler and Mussolini hinted that another war might be necessary to right the wrongs they felt had been done to their countries by the Treaty of Versailles.

The glorification of war by Italy, Germany, and Japan was not idle talk. In 1935 Mussolini attacked and took control of Ethiopia in Africa. In 1937 Japanese armies invaded the rest of China. In March 1938 Hitler marched into Austria. In 1936 General Francisco Franco rebelled against the republican government of Spain, and German and Italian tanks, bombers, and troops helped Franco win a bitter civil war that lasted until 1939.

Bargaining for Peace

The response of Great Britain and France was **appeasement,** a policy of giving aggressor nations what they wanted in order to avoid war. Like the Americans, the British and French were disillusioned by World War I and wanted peace. Much as they disliked Italian, German, or Japanese expansion, they disliked the thought of war

Visualizing History GERMANY UNDER HITLER In 1935 Adolf Hitler announced that he intended to ignore the Versailles treaty and began to rearm Germany. In 1936 his army reoccupied the Rhineland on Germany's border with France. *How did Great Britain and France respond when Hitler began to act aggressively in Europe?*

Did You Know?

The American public, unwilling to support Roosevelt's push to abandon isolationism in the late 1930s, turned to celebrating the "blessings of democracy and the wonders of technology" at the New York World's Fair, which opened on April 30, 1939, and cost $150 million. The fairgrounds in Flushing Meadows covered 1,216 acres, was planted with 1 million tulips imported from Holland and 10,000 trees, and sported 300 futuristic exhibit buildings for the Fair's 1,500 exhibitors.

Visualizing History Both Hitler and Mussolini used such gestures as salutes to create a bond of authority between themselves and their public, a sense of solidarity based on discipline and power. **Answer to Caption:** They gave in to Hitler's demand for part of Czechoslovakia in return for a promise to ask for nothing more.

ABCNEWS INTERACTIVE™

 VIDEODISC

Lessons of War

Side Two, Chapter 3
Title: *Appeasement: Munich Pact*

Critical Thinking Activity

Expressing an Opinion Ask students to reread pages 580–581 and write their answers to the following questions: What reasons did the leaders of Great Britain and France have for appeasing Hitler? Do you feel these reasons were justified? How would you have felt if you were a French or British citizen? A citizen of Czechoslovakia? **L2**

For additional practice, assign Critical Thinking Skills Activity 19.

ASSESS

Check Understanding

Assign Section 1 Review as homework or an in-class activity.

Evaluate

🔲 📁 Assign Section Quiz 19-1 or use the Testmaker to create a customized quiz.

Reteach

Have students summarize the reasons for the Neutrality Acts passed in the mid-1930s.

📁 Have students complete Reteaching Activity 19-1.

📁 Assign Workbook Activity 19-1.

Enrich

Direct students to select a historical figure mentioned in Section 1. Have them use library resources to find out more about this individual. Then ask them to prepare a short biographical sketch about the person to present to the class.

📁 Assign Political Cartoons in American History Activity 17.

CLOSE

Ask students to recap the events that led to Roosevelt's calling for the abandonment of U.S. isolationism. Then remind them that public opinion did not support Roosevelt's proposal. Ask students to predict what might change people's minds.

even more. Pacifism reached new heights: a majority of the students in the debating union at Britain's Oxford University voted that on no account would they go to war for king or country. Appeasement reached its peak at the Munich Conference of September 1938 when British and French leaders allowed Hitler to annex part of Czechoslovakia in return for his promise to make no further territorial demands. British Prime Minister Neville Chamberlain returned from Germany to tell a jittery world that the Munich Pact meant "peace for our time." Winston Churchill, however, who soon would replace Chamberlain as prime minister, observed that "Britain and France had to choose between war and dishonor. They chose dishonor. They will have war."

Neutrality

The American people were also determined to avoid war. World War I had left the United States with a huge domestic debt and billions of dollars in foreign debts that could not be collected. Americans also wanted to avoid war for a number of other reasons. A congressional investigation of the munitions industry revealed that American manufacturers had made large profits by supplying arms and credit to the Allies during the years 1914–1917. This led to the notion that American participation in World War I had been arranged by "merchants of death," assisted by British propagandists. There was increasing feeling that William Jennings Bryan had been correct in 1914 in urging that the United States supply no arms to the belligerents,

make them no loans, and abandon defense of neutral rights on the high seas. To prevent being drawn into war again, Congress passed Neutrality Acts in 1935, 1936, and 1937. These laws barred the transportation or sale of arms to warring nations and banned loans to nations at war outside the Western Hemisphere.

The restrictions of the Neutrality Acts did not please Roosevelt who believed they would "drag us into the war instead of keeping us out." He had wanted legislation that would allow him more discretion—for example, to embargo supplies on one side but not to the other. On October 5, 1937, he warned the American people that war was contagious:

❝ *Innocent people are being cruelly sacrificed to a greed for power and supremacy. . . . Let no one imagine that America will escape. . . . War is contagion, whether it be declared or not.* ❞

Roosevelt signed the Neutrality Acts without protest. However, he would have preferred some freedom to distinguish between aggressors and victims. The President believed that Germany, Italy, and Japan were "bad neighbors" who were bent on war. In a speech in October 1937, Roosevelt called for the abandonment of isolation, but American public opinion forced him to drop any idea of collective action against aggressor nations. "It's a terrible thing," Roosevelt remarked, "to look over your shoulder when you're trying to lead—and find no one there."

Section 1 ★ Review

Checking for Understanding

1. **Identify** "Good Neighbor" policy, Adolf Hitler, Benito Mussolini, Francisco Franco, Munich Conference, Neutrality Acts.

2. **Define** fascism, totalitarian, appeasement.

3. **Examine** Japan's objectives in its aggressive expansion in Asia.

Critical Thinking

4. **Evaluating Policy** Should one country intervene militarily in the affairs of another to protect property owned by its citizens? Explain.

ACTIVITY

5. Create a time line depicting the main events that led to war.

Answers to SECTION 1 REVIEW

1. "Good Neighbor" policy, 578; Adolf Hitler, 580; Benito Mussolini, 581; Francisco Franco, 581; Munich Conference, 582; Neutrality Acts, 582
2. All vocabulary words are defined in the Glossary.
3. ease overcrowding at home, provide raw materials and markets for growing industry
4. Answers will vary. Some may say United

States owes protection to American businesses abroad; others may argue that when American companies go to other countries, out of reach of American power, they take their chances; still others may note that the United States would oppose such intervention in its affairs by another country.
5. Timelines should include significant events such as invasions and Munich.

★★★

Moving Closer to War

Setting the Scene

Section Focus

As war in Europe became a certainty, a great debate took place among Americans over what role the United States should play. Isolationists opposed any American involvement in European affairs and wanted the United States to act independently in the world. On the other side of the debate, internationalists believed that America's own security was linked to the success of Europe's struggle against Hitler.

Objectives

After studying this section, you should be able to

★ discuss Germany's military conquest of Europe during the late 1930s and early 1940s.

★ list the steps by which the Roosevelt administration increased American support to the Allies and the effects these steps had.

Key Terms

blitzkrieg, lend-lease

◄ BRONZE STAR, AWARDED FOR HEROISM

The most outspoken isolationists in Congress were progressive Republicans mainly from the Midwest and the West. Their primary support came from a number of newspapers, most notably those in the William Randolph Hearst chain. On the radio Roosevelt's New Deal critic, Father Charles Coughlin, also lined up with the isolationists. An America First Committee sponsored rallies around the country against the war. A frequent speaker was the popular pilot Charles Lindbergh who warned that "the only way our American life and ideals can be preserved is by staying out of this war." The internationalists were strongest in the Democratic party and generally represented states in the South and the Northeast. They looked to President Roosevelt for leadership.

■ Europe at War Again

As Churchill had predicted, the Munich agreement failed to appease Hitler, who in March 1939 swallowed up the rest of Czechoslovakia and demanded territory in Poland. Britain and France pledged to defend Poland from Hitler, and they asked the Soviet Union to join in an alliance to contain Germany. In August 1939, however, Soviet dictator Joseph Stalin signed a nonaggression pact with Germany. By removing the threat of war on two fronts, the pact cleared the way for Hitler to invade Poland. Hitler still doubted that Britain and France would resist him, however.

▲ PURPLE HEART

Classroom Resources for SECTION 2

Blackline Masters:
- Reproducible Lesson Plan 19-2
- Guided Reading Activity 19-2
- Workbook Activity 19-2
- Reteaching Activity 19-2
- Section Quiz 19-2

Transparencies:
- Section Focus Transparency 19-2

Multimedia:
- Testmaker
- Lessons of War
- Historic America Electronic Field Trips

LESSON PLAN
SECTION 2, 583–588

FOCUS

Bellringer

Before taking roll, project Section Focus Transparency 19-2 or hand out Section Focus Transparency Activity 19-2. Have students answer the questions. Discuss student responses.

Motivating Activity

Have students turn to page 585 and direct their attention to Winston Churchill's words from a speech in which he offers his people only "blood, tears, sweat, and toil" and pledges to fight the Germans to the end. Ask: As an American, how would you have responded to these words in 1940? Tell them that they will find out more about the events surrounding this speech in Section 2. **L1**

ABCNEWS INTERACTIVE™

VIDEODISC

Lessons of War

Side One, Chapter 7
Title: *Can War Be Justified?*
Subject: Circumstances under which nations may claim that waging war is justified

Vocabulary Precheck

List this section's key terms on the chalkboard. Have students develop questions for which each term is an answer. **L1, LEP**

TEACH
Guided Practice

Analyzing Policies Have students write answers to the following questions: Why was the giving of destroyers to Britain in exchange for bases a dangerous precedent-setting decision? *(It expanded the power of the President in international crises.)* What was a major reason Roosevelt won reelection in 1940? *(Americans did not want to gamble on a leadership change in time of crisis.)* What caused Congress to revise the Neutrality Acts? *(increased German attacks on American ships supplying Britain)* Discuss students' answers. **L2**

Visualizing History The photograph and cartoon illustrate the power and goal of the Nazis.
Answer to Caption: Hitler wanted to control the world.

THE FALL OF POLAND By the late 1930s, Hitler had rebuilt the German military force, and he was ready to embark upon a course of intimidation and conquest. German forces invaded Poland in September 1939. The conquest of Poland took little more than a month. *What point does the cartoon express?*

Outbreak of War

Before dawn on September 1, 1939, German forces crossed into Poland in an attack so fast and brutal that a new word was coined—**blitzkrieg,** meaning "lightning war." This time Britain and France decided to fight, and on September 3 they declared war on Germany.

President Roosevelt declared that the United States would remain neutral, but he added, "Even a neutral cannot be asked to close his mind or his conscience." Within weeks he asked Congress to lift the Neutrality Acts' arms embargo that prevented Britain and France from buying American weapons. Although Congress was flooded with telegrams urging it to "keep America out of the blood business," after weeks of debate, it agreed to sell arms to the Allies if they paid cash and carried the goods in their own ships.

Near Disaster at Dunkirk

After a lull in the fighting over the winter of 1939–1940, Hitler launched an invasion of Norway and Denmark. Next, the German armies swept into the Netherlands and Belgium, where for the first time they met resistance from British and French troops. In May 1940, German forces defeated the Allied army and drove it to the sea at the French town of Dunkirk on the Belgian border. Cut off from retreat by land, the army was saved when 300,000 British and French troops were evacuated across the English Channel in a heroic nine-day rescue effort aided by 600 private boats.

Battle of Britain

In June 1940, Italy invaded France and declared war on Great Britain. In response, President Roosevelt announced that, although

Sidelight: Rationing in Wartime

During the early years of World War II, Germany was one of the best-fed of the European combatant nations. Germany's rationing plan provided its citizens with 2,000 calories per day—95 percent of the calories received in peacetime. Soviet citizens received about 1,800 calories per day, while people in occupied Belgium, the Netherlands, Finland, and Norway received less than 1,800. Citizens of the Baltic states, Poland, France, Italy, and Greece were lucky to get 1,500 calories per day.

the United States would not enter the war, it would extend as much aid as possible to the democracies. On June 22 France surrendered, and Britain faced the threat alone.

As the German air force bombed British airfields, factories, and cities to prepare the way for German armies to cross the English Channel, Britain found leadership in its new prime minister, Winston Churchill. Offering only "blood, toil, tears, and sweat," he pledged:

> ❝ . . . we shall defend our island, whatever the cost may be. We shall fight on the beaches. We shall fight on the landing grounds. We shall fight on the fields and in the streets. We shall fight in the hills. We shall never surrender . . . until, in God's good time, the New World, with all its power and might, steps forth to the rescue and liberation of the Old. ❞

■ America Abandons Neutrality

Prime Minister Churchill asked the United States for a loan of 50 destroyers to protect British shipping from German submarines. Recognizing that the isolationists in Congress would block approval of the loan, Roosevelt decided to act on his own. In September 1940, by executive order, he transferred 50 old World War I destroyers to Britain in return for the use of bases in Newfoundland and the Caribbean.

Meanwhile, for months London suffered bombing day and night by hundreds of German planes. The fighter pilots of the Royal

▶ WATCHING THE GERMAN ARMY ENTER PARIS

Visualizing History

▲ DUNKIRK As the trapped British and French armies awaited evacuation at Dunkirk, they were bombarded by German planes and artillery. The largest retreat in military history was accomplished by the British navy and private boats ranging from yachts to tugboats, all protected by the Royal Air Force. Huge amounts of equipment were left behind, but Britain's army was saved from total destruction. *What effect did the fall of France have on American foreign policy?*

Independent Practice

Debate Divide the class into two groups. One group will represent isolationists; the other, internationalists. After doing further research on these movements of the 1930s, have the students debate the following topic: The United States should have entered the war in 1940. The students should present sound arguments for their positions. **L2**

📁 Assign Guided Reading Activity 19-2.

CURRICULUM CONNECTION

Language Arts Besides *blitzkrieg*, Germany used other war tactics such as *sitzkrieg*, in which there existed a lull in hostilities, only to be followed by a series of German attacks against countries without a declaration of war.

Visualizing History This painting highlights the drama of the Dunkirk rescue by focusing on the many small boats that evacuated thousands of British and French soldiers.

Answer to Caption: The fall of France worried many Americans. Although it did not result in a declaration of war, the U.S. did reinstitute the draft and increase its defense spending.

Cooperative Learning Activity

Isolationism Pose the following question to students: What were some reasons for the shift in American public opinion away from isolation? Give students time to think of a response. Have them pair up and discuss their responses. Ask students to share their responses with the class. *(Students might cite that the fall of France and the threat to Britain shook many Americans out of the belief that events outside the Western Hemisphere were none of their business. Students might also include Roosevelt's appropriation for defense and the passage of the Selective Service Act in 1940.)* **L2, L3**

FACT or FICTION?

Isolationist sentiment in the United States arose in part from the fact that the nation was an ocean away from the conflict in Europe and Asia.

FACT: In the days before intercontinental missiles and supersonic jet flights, the Atlantic and Pacific oceans made many Americans feel protected within their own borders.

Visualizing **History** Point out that the Nazis established major death camps at Auschwitz, Treblinka, and Majdanek in Poland. Two-thirds of the Jewish population in Europe perished at these and other camps. **Answer to Caption:** They began to heed Roosevelt's warnings.

ABCNEWS INTERACTIVE™

Historic America Electronic Field Trips

Side 2, Chapter 9
Title: *Holocaust Memorial Museum*

Subject: Tour of Washington, D.C., site honoring victims of Holocaust

Ask: Why is it important to remember the Holocaust? (*to make sure it can never happen again*)

Visualizing History ▲ **ARRESTING OPPONENTS** Hitler's secret police, the Gestapo, arrested Jews and other opponents of the government by the thousands. Many were sent to large prisons called concentration camps. Resistance by the imprisoned against Nazi atrocities took many forms, including trying to escape and rebelling against their captors. *How did Americans react to the fall of France and the threat to Britain?*

Air Force, however, kept the Germans from gaining control of the skies over Britain and forced Hitler to abandon his invasion plans. "Never in the field of human conflict," said Churchill, "was so much owed by so many to so few."

America Realizes Its Peril

The fall of France and the threat to Britain shook many Americans out of their belief that events outside the Western Hemisphere were none of their business. The possibility that Hitler and Mussolini might add the British and French fleets to their own made the Atlantic Ocean suddenly seem narrower, and Congress began to heed Roosevelt's warnings. It appropriated billions of dollars for defense and passed a Selective Service Act in September 1940, the first peacetime draft in American history, adding 800,000 men to the armed forces.

Roosevelt's Leadership Endorsed

In the presidential election of 1940, the debate between internationalists and isolationists was carried on in both major parties. The Republicans nominated a newcomer to politics—Wendell Willkie, a Wall Street lawyer and utility company executive, best known for his criticism of the New Deal. For Democrats the question was whether Roosevelt would seek a third term, breaking the precedent set by George Washington. With the United States facing war in Europe and Asia, Roosevelt felt his experience was needed. He kept silent until the Democratic convention, then announced that he would accept the nomination.

At first, both candidates agreed on foreign-policy issues. But when Willkie slipped in the polls, he began to warn that Roosevelt's reelection would mean war. Roosevelt's promise to keep American troops out of war, Willkie said, was no better than his

586 UNIT 6 Times of Crisis: 1932–1960

Critical Thinking Activity

Supporting an Opinion Remind students of the embargo cutting off exports of scrap metal to Japan, ordered by Roosevelt in 1940. The embargo was later extended to include other products with military uses. Discuss the embargo imposed against Iraq in 1990 and Haiti in 1994. Ask students to write their opinions on whether embargoes are successful in preventing war and to explain the reason for their answers. **L1, L2**

promise to balance the budget. In November 1940, Roosevelt won reelection. With the world in crisis, most American voters did not want to gamble on a change in leadership.

Aid to a Desperate Britain

The British government was running out of money to pay for weapons, so the President proposed that the United States abandon its "cash and carry" policy. But not wanting to revive the old war-debts controversy, Roosevelt suggested a **lend-lease** policy, wherein the United States would merely lend goods to Britain, which the British could return or replace after the war. Lend-lease again stirred debate, but public opinion was shifting in Roosevelt's favor. A poll in January 1941 showed that 60 percent of Americans believed that it was more important to help Britain than to keep out of war. In March 1941, large majorities in both houses of Congress passed lend-lease, authorizing the President to send American supplies and weapons to other nations on any terms he thought would protect the security of the United States.

Battle for the Atlantic

It was one thing to enact lend-lease, however, and another to get supplies across the Atlantic in time to help. When Hitler attacked Yugoslavia and Greece in the spring of 1941, the Nazis overran those countries before lend-lease aid could reach them. When Hitler's bombers failed to knock out Britain, he ordered his submarine fleet to starve that nation into submission.

In trying to make sure that lend-lease supplies reached their destination, the United States was drawn step-by-step into the critical battle of the Atlantic. As German U-boats sank British and American supply ships almost daily, Roosevelt ordered the United States Navy to protect merchant shipping. By the fall of 1941, American and German warships were exchanging fire, and in October a German U-boat sank an American destroyer, killing more than 90 members of its crew. Congress responded by revising the Neutrality Acts to allow merchant ships to be armed.

Germany Turns on a Former Ally

While German-American tensions were escalating in the Atlantic, in June 1941 Hitler, wanting Russia's vast wheat and oil supplies, suddenly attacked the Soviet Union. As German armies quickly advanced into the USSR, Stalin signed an alliance with Great Britain, and the United States offered lend-lease aid. American isolationists were outraged that Roosevelt would aid the Soviets. But Churchill knew that American aid to the Soviet Union would reduce German pressure on Britain. In supporting Roosevelt's decision, he remarked:

> " *I have only one purpose, the destruction of Hitler. . . . If Hitler invaded Hell I would at least make a favorable reference to the Devil in the House of Commons.* "

By the end of November 1941, very few Americans were preaching isolation. Most agreed with Roosevelt that the United States must be an "arsenal of democracy" to sup-

Visualizing History

▲ STRATEGY SESSION Before the United States entered the war, Roosevelt and Churchill met to coordinate Allied strategy and to make peacetime plans. Out of this meeting off the North American coast in August 1941, plans emerged for the United Nations. **How did Churchill feel about helping Stalin?**

Visualizing History Churchill and Roosevelt formed a strong working partnership in the early years of the war. Some Americans saw that partnership as a threat to U.S. neutrality.
Answer to Caption: Churchill felt that it would reduce German pressure on Britain.

CURRICULUM CONNECTION

Geography During the bombing of Great Britain from September 1940 to May 1941, large areas of London and the entire city of Coventry were reduced to rubble.

ABCNEWS INTERACTIVE™

 VIDEODISC

Lessons of War

Side One, Chapter 12
Title: *Laws of War*
Subject: A review of the rules that place limits on types of weapons

---

Sidelight: The U.S.S. *Reuben James*

Several incidents in 1941 increased tensions between the United States and Germany. In September a German submarine attacked an American destroyer, the *Greer*, which was on its way to Iceland. Roosevelt used this incident to order the navy to protect the merchant vessels of all nations. On October 20, 96 American sailors died when the destroyer U.S.S. *Reuben James* sank after being hit by a German torpedo. As a result Roosevelt pushed through Congress a measure that authorized the arming of U.S. merchant ships and permitted these ships to carry war supplies to Britain.

ASSESS
Check Understanding
Assign Section 2 Review as homework or an in-class activity.

Evaluate
◉ ▭ Assign Section Quiz 19-2 or use the Test-maker to create a customized quiz.

Reteach
Provide students with the following event: Congress passes the Lend-Lease Act. Ask students to identify a cause and an effect. *(Cause: Roosevelt desires new ways to aid Britain's war efforts; Effect: America sends supplies and weapons to Britain.)*

▭ Have students complete Reteaching Activity 19-2.

Enrich
Have students use library resources to find more information about the evacuation of Dunkirk. Ask them to share their information in the form of oral reports. They might use statistical information to accompany their reports.

▭ Assign Workbook Activity 19-2.

CLOSE
Remind the class that Roosevelt hoped that the United States would become "the great arsenal of democracy." Ask students to discuss the ways in which the United States was fulfilling Roosevelt's hope based on what they learned in Section 2.

ply Great Britain and the Soviet Union against Hitler. In fact, about 15,000 Americans were already at war, most in British or Canadian uniforms.

■ Aggression in the Pacific

While the American public's attention was fixed on the Atlantic and Europe, events were taking place in the Pacific and Asia that would eventually plunge the United States into war. Already in China, Japan moved against European colonies in Southeast Asia. This vast region contained the rice, rubber, tin, zinc, and oil needed for Japan's expanding industries. With France defeated, Britain on its knees, and the Soviets retreating in front of German armies, the United States was the only remaining obstacle to Japanese ambitions in the Pacific.

Embargo

In September 1940, Japan allied with the Axis Powers, the countries of Germany and Italy. The United States quickly responded by cutting off exports of scrap metal to Japan. As Japan continued its aggression in Asia, President Roosevelt extended the embargo to include other products that had possible military uses. In July 1941, he told the Japanese that the United States would help them find raw materials if they abandoned their policy of conquest. When Japan rejected his proposal, the President

halted all trade with Japan and ordered American forces in the Pacific to prepare for war.

Appeal for Peace

On October 18, 1941, the Japanese prime minister, Prince Fumimaro Konoye, resigned. Konoye had been willing to negotiate with the United States because he did not believe Japan could defeat America in a war. The new prime minister, General Hideki Tojo, did not share Konoye's views. He favored war to eliminate American and British influence in Asia.

By late November, as the United States continued to insist that Japan honor the Open Door policy, Japanese leaders decided that if the dispute did not quickly come to a favorable conclusion, they would attack. Nonetheless, on November 20, negotiations were opened in Washington, D.C. Representing the United States was Secretary of State Cordell Hull. Ambassador Admiral Kichisaburo Nomura and special envoy Saburo Kurusu represented Japan.

The Talks Stall

As negotiations deadlocked, Roosevelt realized that war was inevitable. On December 6, the President appealed for peace directly to Japan's Emperor Hirohito. American officials did not know that, on November 26, a Japanese fleet had put to sea, headed for the United States's main naval base in the Pacific—Pearl Harbor in Hawaii.

Section 2 ★ Review

Checking for Understanding

1. **Identify** Winston Churchill, Selective Service Act, Pearl Harbor.

2. **Define** blitzkrieg, lend-lease.

3. **Describe** why hostilities developed between the United States and Japan.

4. **Explain** the importance of the presidential election of 1940.

Critical Thinking

5. **Citing Evidence** What actions and policies demonstrated that Congress and Roosevelt recognized the possibility that the United States would be drawn into war?

ACTIVITY

6. Write a radio news story on a bombing raid on London.

Answers to SECTION 2 REVIEW

1. Winston Churchill, 585; Selective Service Act, 586; Pearl Harbor, 588
2. All vocabulary words are defined in the Glossary.
3. Japan's ambitions and America's policies long had clashed. With Europe at war, Japan viewed the United States as its only barrier to expansion. When negotiations failed, Japan attacked.
4. Foreign policy was an issue settled in favor of interventionists by reelection of Roosevelt; opened way to supplying arms to Allies.
5. Roosevelt appropriated $13 billion for defense. Selective Service Act drafted 800,000 men immediately.
6. News stories should be factual and provide vivid detail.

★★★

The United States at War

Setting the Scene

Section Focus

Three days after Congress declared war on Japan, Germany and Italy declared war on the United States. Americans now faced war in both Europe and Asia. Japan's unprovoked attack had ended the public debate over foreign policy. The American people were now united in their determination to win the war.

◀ UNITED STATES POSTER AFTER BOMBING OF PEARL HARBOR

Objectives

After studying this section, you should be able to

★ discuss the course of the war in Europe and in Asia.

★ describe the Atlantic Charter and the agreements the Allies reached at the Yalta Conference.

Key Term

Holocaust

---

*W*ith little warning, Japanese bombers attacked the American fleet based at Pearl Harbor. Shortly after noon on Sunday, December 7, 1941, President Roosevelt had just finished lunch when he received an urgent telephone call from Frank Knox, the secretary of the navy. The secretary had just received a wire from Hawaii: "Air Raid on Pearl Harbor. This is no Drill."

In 2 hours, Japanese planes sank many vessels, including 5 battleships and 3 destroyers, and heavily damaged many others. The attack also destroyed about 250 airplanes, and about 4,500 people were killed or wounded. Only the fleet's aircraft carriers, out of the harbor on maneuvers, escaped the devastation.

■ The World at War

However determined the American people were to defeat the Axis Powers—Germany, Italy, and Japan—the immediate outlook was bleak.

Japanese Victories in the Pacific

The destruction of the American fleet removed Japan's only obstacle in the Pacific. For six months the Japanese won victory after victory, capturing American bases at Guam and Wake Island, conquering Britain's colonies at Hong Kong and Singapore, and occupying the independent kingdom of Thailand. In April 1942, American forces on the peninsula of Bataan in the

---

LESSON PLAN
SECTION 3, 589–597

FOCUS
Bellringer

Before taking roll, project Section Focus Transparency 19-3 or hand out Section Focus Transparency Activity 19-3. Have students answer the questions.

Motivating Activity

Ask students what military strategy they think would be most effective in fighting a two-front war. L2

Vocabulary Precheck

Ask students to consult the dictionary to find the origin of the word *holocaust* and its meanings. L1, LEP

NATIONAL GEOGRAPHIC SOCIETY

 VIDEODISC

GTV: A Geographic Perspective on American History

Side 4, Chapter 6
Title: *Echoes of War*
Subject: Effects of World War II on America

Classroom Resources for SECTION 3

Blackline Masters:
- Reproducible Lesson Plan 19-3
- Guided Reading Activity 19-3
- Chapter Map Activity 19
- American Portrait 57

- Primary and Secondary Source Readings, pp. 50–52
- Political Cartoons in American History Activity 18
- Workbook Activity 19-3
- Reteaching Activity 19-3
- Section Quiz 19-3

Transparencies:
- Section Focus Transparency 19-3
- Map Transparency 19

Multimedia:
- Testmaker
- GTV: A Geographic Perspective on American History

- Historic America Electronic Field Trips
- Lessons of War
- Powers of the President
- Focus on Government

TEACH
Guided Practice

Analyzing Movement Ask students to draw on a map how Japan, Italy, and Germany moved into other countries to take them over. *(Italy: Ethiopia; Germany: Rhineland, Austria, Czechoslovakia, Poland; Japan: Manchuria, main part of China)* **L2**

📁 Provide maps from Outline Map Resource Book, pp. 28 and 39 to complete the activity.

Visualizing History The anti-Japanese sentiment implied by the racial epithet in the newspaper headline was widespread during the war.
Answer to Caption: silenced many who had previously opposed involvement in the war and ended support for American isolationism

ABCNEWS INTERACTIVE™

💿 **Historic America Electronic Field Trips**

Side Two, Chapter 8
Title: *USS Arizona Memorial*

Subject: Tour of the memorial

Ask: What does the memorial commemorate? *(honors those who died in attack on Pearl Harbor)*

Philippines finally surrendered. Meanwhile, the Japanese forces conquered Burma and the East Indies.

German Success in Europe

Axis forces occupied nearly all of Europe, and Britain was besieged. In North Africa, German General Erwin Rommel, "the Desert Fox," led an Italian-German force toward the Suez Canal, pushing the British back to the borders of Egypt. By summer 1942 the Germans had pushed deep into the Soviet Union, capturing the rich farmland of Ukraine and threatening the cities of Stalingrad, Leningrad, and Moscow. Success or failure of the war in Europe depended on whether the Soviet Union could hold out until the United States and Britain could launch an offensive on the western front.

Even before Japan attacked Pearl Harbor, American strategists had decided that in the event of war, United States forces would concentrate on defeating Hitler before dealing with Japan. Not only did the United States have closer ties with the countries occupied by Germany, but Germany seemed a greater threat to the Western Hemisphere, where Nazi sympathies were strong in several Latin American nations. Churchill agreed with this plan, observing that

> 66 *. . . [T]he defeat of Germany . . . will leave Japan exposed to an overwhelming force, whereas the defeat of Japan would by no means bring the World War to an end.* 99

Turning Point of the War

Meanwhile, German troops launched a second attack on the Soviets in 1942. In the spring they moved toward the oil fields near the Caspian Sea, and by midsummer

Visualizing History ▲ **PEARL HARBOR** Japan's surprise attack on Pearl Harbor severely damaged the United States Pacific Fleet. In addition, about 250 warplanes were destroyed and more than 2,400 Americans were killed. *How did the attack affect American public opinion about isolationism?*

Cooperative Learning Activity

Analyzing Propaganda Divide the class into groups of three. Have each group analyze the propaganda used by both the Axis Powers and the Allied Powers during World War II. Assign each member of the group one of the following tasks: researching the information, writing descriptions and summaries of the information, and analyzing the propaganda. Have the members of each group combine their tasks to make a presentation to the class. Groups should include visual examples of the propaganda in their presentations. **L2** 📁

World War II in Europe and Africa

Legend:
- ■ Major Axis Powers
- ■ Greatest extent of Axis control
- □ Allied or Ally-controlled
- ← Allied forces
- ← Supply lines

0   500   1,000 miles
0   500   1,000 kilometers

SUPPLY LINES FROM U.S.

D-DAY June 6, 1944

Nov. 8, 1942

Aug. 15, 1944

July 10, 1943

Oct. 23, 1942

FINAL SOVIET DRIVE July-August, 1944

SUPPLY LINE TO SOVIET UNION

Map Study Churchill and Roosevelt delayed an attack in Europe to first fight in the Mediterranean. Some historians believe this was a plan to weaken Soviet power in postwar Europe. **What reasoning might support such a theory?**

Map Study *Using Maps*

Answers: Originally Stalin had cooperated with Hitler. Churchill's distrust of Stalin's intentions was well known. Delaying the invasion forced the Soviets to face the Germans alone, increased Soviet losses, and weakened them as a postwar power.

Map Skills Practice

Ask students to identify the major Axis Powers shown on the map. (*Germany, Italy*)

For additional map practice, assign Chapter Map Activity 19.

Assign Map Transparency Activity 19.

VIDEODISC

Lessons of War

Side Two, Chapter 8
Title: *At the Front*
Subject: Contributions of minorities in World War II

---

they were more than halfway to their goal. Stalin pleaded with the Allied leaders Roosevelt and Churchill for an invasion of western Europe that would take some pressure off the Soviet Union. Churchill told him that such a second front in Europe was a year away. Soviet troops were left to face the Germans alone.

In September 1942, the Red Army made a desperate and heroic stand at Stalingrad. For four months, Soviet and German troops battled house-to-house for control of the city. Although the German invasion was halted, Stalingrad was reduced to rubble and the Soviets suffered more casualties defending it than the United States did in the entire war. Stalin never forgave Roosevelt and Churchill for allowing this to happen.

In November the Soviet army counterattacked. Taking advantage of the Russian winter, the Red Army surrounded Hitler's freezing forces. In February 1943, the tattered remains of the invading German army, only one-third of its 330,000 men still alive, surrendered.

CHAPTER 19 World War II: 1933–1945   **591**

Critical Thinking Activity

Analyzing Events World War II resulted in the devastation of lives and property. Ask students the following question: Could World War II have been avoided? Why or why not? (*Answers will vary. Some students might say that it could have been avoided if the Allies had not used the policy of appeasement with Hitler in the late 1930s;* *they might also indicate that it could have been avoided if the League of Nations had been given greater powers after World War I. Other students might say that a war could not have been avoided because force was the only way to stop the military aggression of Germany and Japan.*) **L2**

Independent Practice

Mathematics Have students use library resources to compare World War II with World War I. The comparison should include the number of nations participating, the number of soldiers mobilized, the number of lives lost, and the amount of money spent. The report should be accompanied by charts and graphs that illustrate the statistics. **L2**

📁 Assign American Portrait 57: Benjamin Oliver Davis, Jr.

CURRICULUM CONNECTION

Meteorology Poor weather postponed the D-Day operation, named Operation Overlord, for 24 hours, and weather looked unfavorable for the next day as well. Eisenhower knew that if he did not go ahead, the tidal and moon conditions would delay the invasion several months.

Visualizing History The code name for the planned invasion was "Operation Overlord." Most of the Allied troops landed from the water, but large numbers also came from the air on gliders and as paratroopers.

Answer to Caption: forced Hitler to move troops from the eastern front to fight Allied forces in France

German Weak Point Exposed

In North Africa, American and British forces, working first separately and then together, pushed Rommel and his Afrika Korps into Tunisia. Under the command first of Major General Lloyd R. Fredendall and then of Major General George S. Patton, American forces checked Rommel's drive at Kasserine Pass and took El Guettar and Bizerte. Under General Bernard L. Montgomery, the British took Tripoli and Tunis. By May, Rommel had fled, nearly 250,000 Axis troops had surrendered, and the campaign in North Africa was over.

Allied victories in North Africa cleared the way for an attack on what Churchill called "the soft underbelly" of Europe. In August 1943, British and American forces took Sicily, and in September they invaded the Italian mainland. After his defeat in Sicily, Mussolini was overthrown, and the new Italian government quickly surrendered. German troops still occupied Italy, however, and put up fierce resistance in the mountainous terrain. Not until June 1944 did the Allies enter Rome. Axis forces remained in control of northern Italy.

■ Victory in Europe

American and British air forces had already begun round-the-clock bombing of German industrial and transportation centers. But Hitler's armies had to be defeated on the ground.

Normandy Invasion

On June 6, 1944, the greatest amphibious force in history—176,000 troops carried in 5,000 vessels—crossed the English Channel to land along a 60-mile stretch of coastline in France. Planning for the "D-Day" invasion at Normandy had been under way for more than two years.

▼ **AMERICAN SOLDIER IN FRANCE, 1944**

Visualizing History ▲ **D-DAY** American troops, under heavy fire from German defenders, stormed the coast of France from Coast Guard landing barges. British, Canadian, and free French forces also participated in the invasion. *How did the Normandy invasion take pressure off Soviet forces?*

Sidelight: Ernie Pyle

Journalist Ernie Pyle was a famous World War II correspondent. He traveled with the U.S. armed forces and covered campaigns in Europe, North Africa, and the Pacific. In 1944 Pyle won the Pulitzer Prize for journalism. The popular motion picture *G.I. Joe* was based on his European campaign in Italy. Ernie Pyle was killed by the Japanese while reporting on the war.

Under the command of American General Dwight D. Eisenhower, a million Allied forces were in France within a month after D-Day. On July 25 the Americans broke through the German line. By early August, General George Patton and his forces were racing across northern France through open countryside. In August American and British troops broke out of Normandy and struck rapidly eastward, entering Paris on August 25, 1944. In September they crossed the western border of Germany.

Rapid Soviet Advance From the East

At the same time, the Soviets closed in from the east. In January 1944, the Red Army freed Leningrad from an 890-day German siege, during which 800,000 residents died. By spring Soviet troops had freed Ukraine, and in July they entered Poland. In August Romania and Bulgaria surrendered, opening the Balkans to the Soviets. In December they entered Hungary. By the end of 1944, most of eastern Europe was in Soviet hands.

Germany Surrenders

In December 1944, Hitler ordered a counterattack in Belgium. Although Allied lines "bulged," the Germans could not break through. The Battle of the Bulge was the last German offensive. In March 1945, the Allies crossed the Rhine River and moved into the heart of Germany. Meanwhile, the Soviets pushed from the east, taking Berlin in April 1945. In April, Hitler committed suicide in his underground shelter in Berlin, and on May 7, 1945, German leaders agreed to an unconditional surrender. Franklin D. Roosevelt, who led the nation through the Depression and the war, however, did not witness this event. Only days before Hitler's suicide, the President died of a massive cerebral hemorrhage.

Crimes Against Humanity

As they entered Germany, Allied armies discovered evidence of one of the most terrible acts of the war—the Nazi **Holocaust,**

Visualizing History ▲ CONCENTRATION CAMPS The condition of survivors in Nazi death camps such as Belsen, Auschwitz, and Buchenwald horrified the world. *Why were the death camps created?*

or deliberate extermination of millions of European Jews and other civilians. As early as 1942, the United States government had received reports that Hitler had ordered the murder of all Jews in German-occupied territories. Only in 1944 did Roosevelt respond to criticism within his own administration that the United States was passively accepting the murder of Jews. He created a War Refugee Board, but for 6 out of 10 Jews in Europe, action came too late. Not until Allied troops reached the Nazi death camps—at Auschwitz, Dachau, Buchenwald, and elsewhere—and found the survivors and the gas chambers in which so many had died was the horrible truth fully realized. The Nazis had killed 12 million people, of whom 6 million were Jews.

Linking Across TIME

One key scientific gain during the war was the improvement and wide use of radar. Allied radar could detect incoming enemy aircraft long before these planes reached their target. As a result Allied fighter planes and antiaircraft were prepared when attacking planes arrived. Radar also provided accurate weather information for Allied aircraft crews.

Visualizing History Many Americans refused to believe the rumors circulating during the war about the systematic exterminations practiced in the concentration camps. Photographs like this awakened many Americans to facts they had tried to ignore.
Answer to Caption: systematically murder Jews and other minorities the Nazis regarded as racially inferior

Did You Know?

On the day following the attack on Pearl Harbor, Congress declared war against Japan. The only member of Congress to vote against war was Jeannette Rankin of Montana, who had also voted against America's entry into World War I.

Sidelight: Human Cost of War

Over 54 million military personnel and civilians died in World War II. The Soviet Union lost over 20 million people, China lost about 13 million, Poland lost 6½ million people (more than 22 percent of its population), Germany lost about 5 million, Japan over 1,800,000, France just under 500,000, Great Britain over 450,000, and the United States just under 300,000.

Map Study *Using Maps*

Answer: They were the two strategic islands closest to Japan and could be used to launch attacks against Japan itself.

Map Skills Practice

Have students use the arrows on the map to follow the drives of the American forces to reconquer the Pacific by tracing the campaign from year to year. The dates show when each campaign started and ended. When was the Battle of Leyte Gulf fought? *(October 23–26, 1944)*

FACT or FICTION?

If it had not been for the Navajos, the marines might never have taken Iwo Jima.

FACT: A group of Navajos in the Marine Signal Corps confused the Japanese with a code based on the Navajo language.

 VIDEODISC

Lessons of War

Side One, Chapter 6
Title: *Can a Battle Change History?*
Subject: The Battle of Midway

■ War in the Pacific

In May 1942, American warships defeated a Japanese fleet in the Battle of the Coral Sea. In June Japanese forces tried to take the Midway Islands, an atoll in the central Pacific about 1,200 miles (1,920 kilometers) northwest of Hawaii. The naval and air Battle of Midway that ensued was a great victory for the Allies, resulting in the first major defeat of the Japanese navy. It slowed the Japanese advance across the central Pacific, brought an end to the threat to Hawaii, and ended Japanese naval superiority in the Pacific. Japan still held many heavily fortified Pacific islands. So the Allies

World War II in the Pacific

Legend
Japanese Empire, 1936
Extent of Japanese control, 1942
Allies
Neutral nations
← Allied troop movements
✳ Major battles
Atomic bomb explosions

Map labels: SOVIET UNION, BERING SEA, ALEUTIAN ISLANDS, SAKHALIN, ATTU, KISKA, KURILE IS., MONGOLIA, MANCHUKUO (MANCHURIA), CHINA, Chungking, KOREA, JAPAN, Tokyo, NEPAL, INDIA, Hiroshima, Nagasaki, KYUSHU, Midway June 3-6, 1942, Pearl Harbor Dec. 7, 1941, MIDWAY ISLAND, 1942, HAWAIIAN ISLANDS, BURMA, OKINAWA, 1945, PACIFIC OCEAN, Hong Kong (Br.), FORMOSA, IWO JIMA, WAKE ISLAND, THAILAND, LUZON, MARIANA IS., FRENCH INDOCHINA, Manila, PHILIPPINE IS., SAIPAN, MARSHALL IS., 1944, MALAYA, Singapore, GUAM, ENIWETOK, KWAJALEIN, GILBERT IS., 1942-43, Leyte Gulf Oct. 23-26, 1944, CAROLINE ISLANDS, SUMATRA, BORNEO, 1944-45, JAPANESE MANDATE, TARAWA, NETHERLANDS EAST INDIES, BISMARCK ARCH., Coral Sea May 7-8, 1942, ELLICE ISLANDS, INDIAN OCEAN, NEW GUINEA, SOLOMON IS., GUADALCANAL, AUSTRALIA, CORAL SEA

Map Study

While a joint British-American force freed Southeast Asia from Japanese occupation, American forces recaptured strategic islands as the forces moved northward toward the Philippines and Japan itself.
What strategic importance does the map show for Iwo Jima and Okinawa?

Cultural Perspectives

Contributing to the War Effort The over 16 million men and women who fought for the United States in World War II represented every cultural background, religious affiliation, and ethnic group in the nation. Although many faced discrimination in the armed forces, the overwhelming majority served their country with distinction. Encourage students to choose a particular group and research its contributions to the war effort. Of special interest is the role played by the 10,000 Japanese Americans who volunteered for service in World War II despite the fact that their families were held in "relocation centers."

adopted a military strategy called "island hopping"—to cut Japanese supply lines by capturing key islands and to use them as bases to attack other Japanese strongholds, especially the Philippines and eventually Japan itself.

Guadalcanal

In August 1942, Americans took the first step in the long and bloody road to Tokyo when marines landed on Guadalcanal in the Solomon Islands. The struggle for Guadalcanal was fought on the ground, at sea, and in the air, lasting six months. Not until 1943 did Japan's resistance there come to an end.

In attacking the United States, Japan had failed to realize the industrial power of America and its ability to mobilize that power rapidly. Of the 19 ships sunk at Pearl Harbor, 17 were returned to duty by December 1942, and new ships were constantly added. The navy worked out new ways of fueling and repairing ships at sea, allowing fleets to stay at sea for long periods of time.

During 1943 and 1944, American forces "island-hopped" toward the Philippines and Japan. In October 1944, Allied forces under the leadership of American General Douglas MacArthur landed in the Philippines. MacArthur's advance was matched by amphibious operations directed by Admiral Chester Nimitz against Japanese-held islands in the central Pacific.

Iwo Jima and Okinawa

In 1945 the last of Japan's island outposts fell with the taking of Iwo Jima (EE•woh JEE•muh) in March and Okinawa (oh•kuh•NAH•wuh) in June. Though Iwo Jima measures only a few square miles, American marines suffered more than 20,000 casualties in capturing it. Japan now began to use kamikazes (KAH•mih•KAH•zeez), suicide pilots who flew bomb-laden planes into American ships. During the invasion of Okinawa, kamikazes scored 279 hits on United States vessels.

By the summer of 1945, after Germany was defeated, all Allied power was turned against Japan. The Soviet Union agreed to declare war on Japan and confront Japan's forces in Manchuria. But the conquest of the Japanese islands was left to the United States. America's long-range B-29 bombers had been bombing Japan from bases on recaptured Pacific islands since June 1944. In one raid alone in March 1945, more than 83,000 Tokyo civilians were incinerated by American incendiary bombs. But despite such heavy casualties, Japan's military leaders rejected calls for unconditional surrender. American commanders worried that an invasion of Japan would meet heavy resistance and might cost a million lives.

Hiroshima and Nagasaki

Since early in the war, American scientists had secretly been developing an atomic bomb. First tested in New Mexico in July 1945, it gave Harry Truman, who became President after Roosevelt's death, another choice, and Soviet leader Stalin told Truman to "make good use of it."

After the Japanese government rejected Truman's final warning to surrender or risk "utter destruction," on August 6 an atomic bomb destroyed 60 percent of Hiroshima, a major Japanese industrial city. When Japan still refused to surrender, a second bomb was dropped on the city of Nagasaki on August 9, causing almost as much destruction as the first. The two attacks took about 150,000 Japanese lives. When reports of the death and devastation reached Tokyo, the stunned emperor, telling his people that "the unendurable must be endured," asked for peace. The final surrender took place on September 2, 1945, on the battleship *Missouri* anchored in Tokyo Bay.

◀ AMERICAN MILITARY HELMET NICKNAMED THE "STEEL POT"

ABC**NEWS**
INTERACTIVE™

○ **VIDEODISC**

Powers of the President

Side One, Chapter 33
Title: *Waging War*
Subject: Powers of the Commander in Chief

Did You Know?

The U.S.S. *Arizona* was one of the battleships sunk by the Japanese at Pearl Harbor. A memorial structure was placed over the partly sunken ship in tribute to those who died in the attack. The ship remains where it came to rest on December 7, 1941.

GLENCOE
TECHNOLOGY

○ **VIDEODISC**

Focus on Government

Videodisc 3, Chapter 55
Title: *The United Nations*
Subject: Field trip to United Nations

🖙 Assign Primary and Secondary Source Readings, pp. 50–51: "Americans at War" by Ernie Pyle.

Sidelight: *Adagio for Strings*

After announcing the death of President Franklin D. Roosevelt from a cerebral hemorrhage, the NBC Radio Network played Samuel Barber's *Adagio for Strings*. Since that time, this sad, serene piece of music has been linked to occasions of public mourning. It has been used as a lament in hundreds of funerals and memorials all over the world.

CURRICULUM CONNECTION

Military History World War II was the first war in which women were given regular military status. About 350,000 women signed up. Most joined the Women's Army Corps (WACS) and the women's branch of the navy (WAVES).

Visualizing History Some Americans believed that the physically weakened Roosevelt, who died two months after the Yalta Conference, gave Stalin too much ground at Yalta.
Answer to Caption: agreed to occupy Germany after the war, encourage representative governments in eastern Europe, establish an organization for world peace, and secretly give the Soviets territories in Japan and China

ASSESS

Check Understanding
Assign Section 3 Review as homework or an in-class activity.

Evaluate
Assign Section Quiz 19-3 or use the Testmaker to create a customized quiz.

Visualizing History ▲ MEETING AT YALTA Looking tired and drawn, Roosevelt (center) poses with Stalin (right) and Churchill during a break in their meetings at Yalta. Two months later, Roosevelt was dead. *What agreements were reached at Yalta?*

■ Wartime Diplomacy

The first planning for peace took place in August 1941 when Roosevelt and Churchill met on a ship off the coast of Newfoundland. At that meeting they issued the Atlantic Charter, a statement of principles on which depended "hopes for a better future for the world." Much like Wilson's Fourteen Points, the Atlantic Charter looked forward to a world where people would have the right to choose their form of government.

After Pearl Harbor, Roosevelt turned his attention to forming an alliance among the nations fighting against Hitler. On January 1, 1942, representatives of the 26 countries at war with the Axis Powers agreed to support the principles of the Atlantic Charter. They promised full economic and military support in the war, and they agreed not to make a separate peace.

In holding the great alliance together, Roosevelt and Churchill kept constantly in touch. Although they often did not agree on strategy, neither wavered in admiration for the other. Working closely with the other major Allies was more difficult. Japanese troops had pushed China's government deep into the interior, and Chinese leaders were unhappy that the war in Europe was the top priority. General Charles de Gaulle (dih•GOHL), leader of the French government in exile, disapproved of the United States's recognizing a government in south France that was friendly to the Nazis.

Cooperation with the Soviet Union proved the most difficult problem. Stalin had almost never been outside of his country and was suspicious of capitalist nations. Even so, the alliance between the United States and Great Britain and the Soviet Union lasted until the end of the war. Germany could not be defeated without Soviet aid, and the Soviets depended on supplies from Britain and the United States.

Planning for War and Peace

Cooperation in plans for war and peace was worked out in a series of international conferences. At Casablanca, Morocco, in January 1943, Roosevelt and Churchill agreed to demand "unconditional surrender" from the Axis Powers, assuring the Soviet Union that its allies would not sign a separate peace treaty with Germany.

At Cairo, Egypt, in November 1943, Roosevelt and Churchill met Chinese leader

Sidelight: Eleanor Roosevelt and the UN

President Truman appointed Eleanor Roosevelt one of the first American delegates to the new United Nations. In 1947 she was named chairperson of the UN Commission on Human Rights. After a year and a half of her determined leadership, the commission produced the Universal Declaration of Human Rights.

This document states the basic principles of freedom and liberty for the people of the member states and territories under United Nations jurisdiction. The document still serves as a model for democratic governments all over the world.

Chiang Kai-shek (jee•AHNG ky•SHEHK) and agreed that Japan should be stripped of its Pacific empire and Korea given independence. From Cairo, Roosevelt and Churchill flew to Tehran, capital of Iran, to meet with Stalin. There they promised that the D-Day invasion of France would be launched the next year. In return Stalin agreed to begin a new offensive against Germany at the same time from the east.

The Yalta Conference

In February 1945, Roosevelt, Churchill, and Stalin met for the last time at Yalta, in the Soviet Union. They agreed publicly that the United States, Britain, and the Soviet Union, along with France, should occupy Germany after the war, but they promised to encourage some form of representative government for the other peoples of Europe. They also agreed on a conference to be held at San Francisco in April 1945 to establish a world peace organization.

Secret agreements at Yalta covered the terms on which the Soviet Union could enter the war against Japan after Germany was defeated. The Soviets were promised Japanese territories, and that they could keep Outer Mongolia, in China, and obtain an ice-free naval port. In return, Stalin agreed to support the Nationalist government of Chiang Kai-shek instead of the Chinese Communists who were challenging Chiang for power.

Although the Yalta agreements later were attacked as a "sellout," at the time it seemed vital to keep the Soviet Union from making a separate peace with Germany when American and British forces were still fighting in the west. Even more important, the United States wanted Soviet support in the war against Japan.

Roosevelt's Death

When he reported to Congress on his Yalta trip, Roosevelt looked tired and pale. Two months later, on April 12, 1945, the President died suddenly at Warm Springs, Georgia. The nation he led for more than 12 years was shocked, and newspapers that printed daily lists of soldiers and sailors who had died in action added the name: "Roosevelt, Franklin D., Commander in Chief."

The United Nations

Two weeks after Roosevelt's death, representatives of 50 nations met at San Francisco to make plans for a new world organization. But the talks at San Francisco were made more difficult by rising suspicions among the Allies. The Soviet Union was keeping a firm hand on Poland and seemed to be breaking its Yalta promises. Still, the meeting at San Francisco produced a charter for the United Nations (UN). The preamble of the UN Charter pledged all the countries signing it to "faith in fundamental human rights," to "justice and respect" for the terms of peace treaties, and to the goal of living together. In July 1945, when the Senate ratified the Charter by a vote of 89 to 2, the United States became the first nation to join the UN.

Section 3 ★ Review

Checking for Understanding

1. **Identify** D-Day, Dwight Eisenhower, Harry Truman, Atlantic Charter, Yalta Conference.

2. **Define** Holocaust.

3. **Summarize** the progression of the war in Asia, Europe, Africa, and the Pacific.

4. **List** the meetings held among Allied leaders between 1941 and 1945.

Critical Thinking

5. **Anticipating Consequences** In a wartime alliance, what risk is carried by each nation that agrees not to make a separate peace?

ACTIVITY

6. Research information on the United Nations. Make a chart illustrating the organization's various roles.

CHAPTER 19
SECTION 3

Reteach

Have students analyze the different strategies employed in fighting the war on the European front and on the Pacific front.

📁 Have students complete Reteaching Activity 19-3.

📁 Assign Workbook Activity 19-3.

Enrich

Have students choose one of the following neutral countries and research the reasons for its neutrality during World War II: Ireland, Spain, Sweden, and Turkey. Have students write a report and share their information in a class discussion.

📁 Assign Political Cartoons in American History Activity 18.

CLOSE

Read students the following quotation by President Truman announcing the use of the atomic bomb: "[The Japanese] may expect a rain of ruin from the air, the like of which has never been seen on this earth." Then have them discuss the ways in which the atomic bomb changed the nature of international politics.

Answers to SECTION 3 REVIEW

1. D-Day, 592–593; Dwight Eisenhower, 593; Harry Truman, 595; Atlantic Charter, 596; Yalta Conference, 597
2. All vocabulary words are defined in the Glossary.
3. Allied offensives began in Africa, then Italy; D-Day invasion as Soviets pushed west, converging on Berlin; Americans defeated Japanese fleets at Coral Sea and Midway
4. Atlantic, January 1941; Casablanca, January 1943; Quebec,

August 1943; Cairo, November 1943; Teheran, November 1943; Yalta, April 1945
5. Risk: In a joint peace settlement, a nation might not get what it wants because of the aims of its allies; Gain: stronger and more unified military effort against enemy.
6. Charts should include peacekeeping, fact-finding, and aid functions.

TEACH

Early in 1939 U.S. physicists saw the application of nuclear energy to military weapons. It was German-born physicist Albert Einstein who informed President Roosevelt of the potential military use of nuclear fission. The Manhattan Project was set up in 1942 to build a nuclear bomb, and on July 16, 1945, the first nuclear device was tested in a desert in New Mexico.

📁 Assign Primary and Secondary Source Readings, p. 52: "A Marine at Nagasaki After the Atomic Blast" by Studs Terkel.

ABCNEWS INTERACTIVE™

 VIDEODISC

Lessons of War

Side One, Chapter 11
Title: *Weapons of War*
Subject: The quest for technological advantage in warfare

| GEOGRAPHY | ECONOMICS | **History AND SCIENCE** | MATH | THE ARTS |

The Atomic Bomb

"We must not be the most hated and feared people in the world," a physicist wrote, urging President Truman not to use the atomic bombs that would kill some 150,000 mostly civilian Japanese.

Rumors that the Nazis might develop an atomic bomb spurred American and British efforts to build one. Scientist Albert Einstein wrote President Roosevelt urging that a major research program begin at once so that the nation would be the first with the bomb.

The secret project, later called the Manhattan Project, was carried out primarily at facilities in Oak Ridge, Tennessee and, later, at Los Alamos, New Mexico. American physicist J. Robert Oppenheimer was the director, and he persuaded many top physicists to join the project. On July 16, 1945, the bomb was tested atop a steel tower in a lonely desert track at Alamogordo, New Mexico, called *Jornada del Muerto*, Journey of Death.

President Truman did not know the bomb existed until a few weeks before his decision to use it. Truman, who had taken office after President Roosevelt's death on April 12, received word of the test results in Potsdam, Germany, where he was in conference with Churchill, Stalin, and their top advisers. Roosevelt had told Churchill about the bomb. Although some historians disagree about why atomic bombs were dropped on Japan and about the ethical issues involved, President Truman believed the bombing was justified: "The dropping of the bombs stopped the war, saved millions of lives."

▲ THE DEVASTATION AT HIROSHIMA

Making the Science Connection

1. Why did the United States start the Manhattan Project?

2. Given the present concerns about the dangers of nuclear war, do you think the United States was right to develop nuclear weapons? Why or why not?

ACTIVITY

3. Research information on nuclear testing. Present findings in a written report about how current testing regulations differ from the 1940s and 1950s.

Answers to Making the Connection

1. American leaders were concerned that Nazi Germany was close to creating an atomic bomb.
2. Answers will vary. Some students might argue that under no circumstances should the United States use nuclear weapons.

Others may argue that nuclear weapons should be used for defensive purposes only or to save the lives of American military personnel.
3. Reports will vary but should include a comparison of nuclear testing regulations.

War on the Home Front

Setting the Scene

Section Focus

To fight the Axis Powers, the United States had to mobilize people and resources more quickly than ever before. By 1944 more than 11 million men and women were in uniform. As the number of industrial workers also rose to new heights, the war accomplished what the New Deal had never been able to—it ended the Depression's unemployment.

We Can Do It!

◄ ROSIE THE RIVETER, SYMBOL OF WOMEN WORKERS DURING WORLD WAR II

Objectives

After studying this section, you should be able to
★ discuss efforts to mobilize the economy for war production.
★ explain the war's impact on women, African Americans, and Japanese Americans.

Key Term

wildcat strike

Americans were amazed at the speed with which industry turned to making war materials. When in May 1940 President Roosevelt talked of producing 50,000 airplanes a year, some thought he was asking the impossible. Yet, by 1944 the number of planes produced annually had risen to about 100,000. Mass production was so effective in the ship industry that the average time for building a freighter dropped from a year to less than 2 months. In 4 years American shipyards put to sea tonnage equal to the entire merchant fleet of all the other countries of the world.

■ The Production Battle

As in World War I, federal agencies took on the direction of private companies doing war work. After a Senate investigation revealed corruption and mismanagement among companies involved in war production, in January 1942 Roosevelt gave a War Production Board strong regulatory power. Its head, Donald Nelson, could seize vital materials, order industrial plants to convert to war production, and prohibit manufacture of products he considered unessential to the war effort.

Rapid Conversion to War Production

Within weeks of Pearl Harbor, production of bicycles, beer cans, refrigerators, toothpaste tubes, and more than 300 other items was cut back or banned. Automobile manufacturers were ordered to convert production to tanks and other war supplies. Entire new industries were created. Synthetic rubber, for example, became important when Japan's conquest of Southeast Asia cut off America's supply of natural rubber. By the end of 1942,

CHAPTER 19 World War II: 1933–1945   **599**

LESSON PLAN
SECTION 4, 599-604

FOCUS
Bellringer

Before taking roll, project Section Focus Transparency 19-4 or hand out Section Focus Transparency Activity 19-4. Have students answer the questions.

Motivating Activity

Ask students what they know about the treatment given to Japanese Americans who were living in the United States during World War II. Tell students they can check the accuracy of their ideas as they read Section 4. **L1**

Vocabulary Precheck

Write *wildcat strike* on the chalkboard. Have a volunteer skim the section to find the phrase and read it in context. **L1, LEP**

ABCNEWS
INTERACTIVE™

VIDEODISC

Lessons of War

Side Two, Chapter 9
Title: *In the Crossfire*
Subject: Home fronts, here and abroad

Classroom Resources for SECTION 4

Blackline Masters:
▱ Reproducible Lesson Plan 19-4
▱ Guided Reading Activity 19-4
▱ Chapter Skills Activity 19
▱ Linking Past and Present Activity 19

▱ Enrichment Activity 19
▱ Geography in History Activity 19
▱ Supreme Court Case Study 17
▱ Workbook Activity 19-4
▱ Reteaching Activity 19-4
▱ Section Quiz 19-4

Transparencies:
Section Focus Transparency 19-4
Skills Transparency 19

Multimedia:
Testmaker
Lessons of War
GTV: The American People: Fabric of a Nation

TEACH
Guided Practice

Determining Cause and Effect Present the cause-and-effect concept map below, omitting the effects. Have students complete the map. **L1**

Event
- inflation due to World War II production

Causes
- increased employment
- increase in workers' earnings
- rise in prices of consumer goods

Effects
- government sets price ceiling on consumer products
- government rations goods
- 1943 act outlaws strikes against war industries

Linking Past and Present

Tell students that the jeep was first mass-produced for the armed forces in 1940. Standard jeeps can maneuver well over mud or rugged terrain. Modern jeeps can travel at speeds of more than 144 miles per hour. Ask students why they think the jeep is a popular vehicle in the United States today.

Assign Linking Past and Present Activity 19.

---

nearly 33 percent of American production went to war materials, and by 1944 nearly 50 percent. Production of all goods nearly doubled, and America's production of war materials matched the total output of Germany, Italy, and Japan combined.

In May 1941, Roosevelt set up the Office of Scientific Research and Development to mobilize science and technology for the war effort. Among the many inventions that came from this agency were DDT, which controlled insects and made jungle fighting more tolerable; the bazooka, a weapon that enabled an infantry soldier to destroy a tank; and radar, which determined the position and speed of airplanes and ships.

Financing the War

To raise funds for the war effort, the federal government increased taxes and sold war bonds in amounts ranging from $25 to $10,000. In 1942 the government extended the income tax for the first time to include middle- and lower-income people. To make collection easier, the government in 1943 began to require that employers deduct taxes from workers' paychecks before they received them.

The war increased employment, and workers' earnings rose as war production brought longer workweeks and overtime. As people had more money to spend, and as the shift to war materials made consumer goods scarce, prices rose. To combat inflation, in 1942 Congress created the Office of Price Administration, which set price ceilings on consumer products and began to ration goods that were in short supply. By war's end 20 items—including sugar, meat, butter, coffee, gasoline, fuel oil, and shoes—required government-issued rationing coupons to be presented at the time of purchase. Despite attempts to hold down prices, however, the cost of living rose 29 percent during the war, leading to demands for higher wages.

To help prevent strikes, a National War Labor Board was established to settle labor disputes by mediation. Although this task was made easier by the no-strike pledges

---

Linking Past and Present

The Jeep

General George C. Marshall, U.S. Army chief of staff during World War II, once described the jeep as "America's greatest contribution to modern warfare." From Normandy to North Africa, from World War II to the Gulf War, the Jeep played a vital military role.

Then

General Purpose

The small, durable military motor vehicle called the jeep derived its name from the initials G.P., an abbreviation for "General Purpose Vehicle," its official title. Supremely functional, the jeep had an 80-inch wheel base, 1/4

ton capacity, and three seats, with room for a .30-caliber machine gun mount. Equipped with four-wheel drive, the jeep was able to overcome such battlefield stumbling blocks as ice or mud and was sturdy enough to be dropped by parachute onto rugged terrain. Nearly 650,000 jeeps were manufactured during World War II.

Now

Clones and Copies

Imitations, clones, and copies of the jeep design mushroomed after the war. Research and development yielded, among other military land vehicles, an all-steel vehicle, an all-aluminum version, and the High Mobility Multi-Purpose Wheeled Vehicle (the Humvee).

▼ CIVILIAN HUMVEE

Cooperative Learning Activity

Creating a Teaching Tool Group students into home teams of four or five, and then have them number off to form "expert groups." Expert groups consist of one member from each home team. Tell students in the expert groups to read Section 4 and find out how the government geared the nation's economy for war production. *(Federal government agencies took on the direction of private companies doing war work and obtained promises from unions not to strike during the war.)* Students in the expert group should discuss their findings and create a teaching tool that will help in sharing the material with their home teams. **L1, L2**

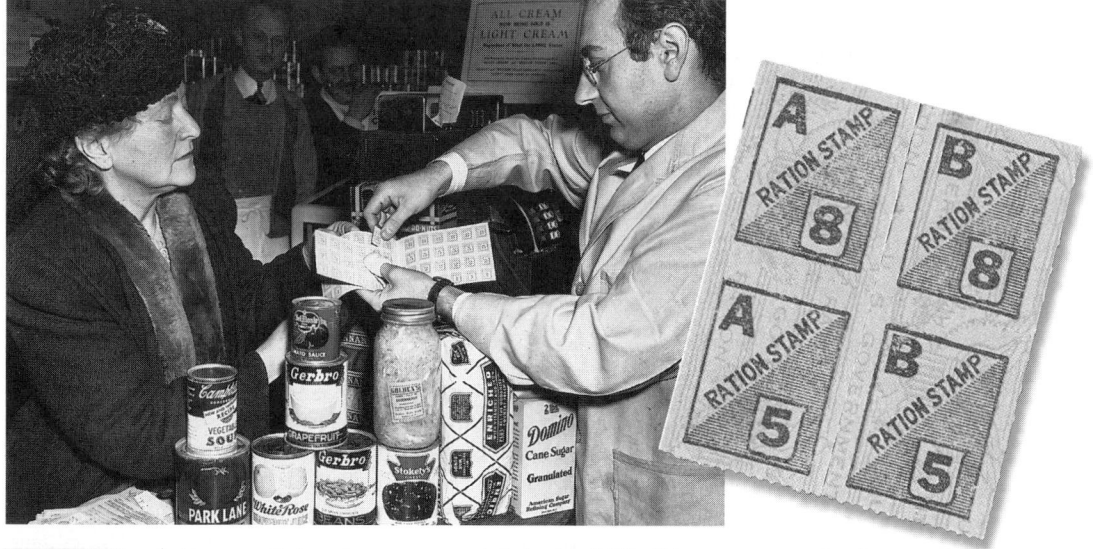

Visualizing History

▲ **RATIONING** Ration stamps were used during World War II in an attempt to distribute essential goods fairly. Meat, butter, sugar, and gasoline were among the items that were rationed. ***How did the cost of living change during the war years?***

that both the AFL and the CIO made after Pearl Harbor, there were many small **wildcat strikes**—work stoppages without union approval—and a short national strike by 500,000 coal miners. Even though most labor unions kept their no-strike pledge, an act passed in 1947 outlawed strikes against war industries.

■ The War and Social Change

The need for defense workers altered traditional patterns of American society. As millions of men joined the armed services, more women than ever before entered the labor force. "If you can drive a car, you can run a machine" became an advertising slogan for industries.

Women Assume Nontraditional Roles

The government, newspapers, radio, and newsreels encouraged women to take factory jobs as a patriotic duty, and 5 million American women entered the workforce during the war. "Rosie the Riveter," who first appeared in overalls in a Lockheed Aircraft poster, became a national symbol of the vital contribution women were making to the war effort.

More than ever before, women filled jobs that were not traditional for females. They worked on production lines, in steel mills, on the docks, and in other jobs that required heavy manual labor. Outside war industries, women also took over such traditionally male jobs as driving buses and trucks and working as train conductors, lumberjacks, and barbers. Most of these new workers were married and had children. Yet women still encountered resistance from male workers. As one female aircraft worker described it:

Footnotes to History

Women Pilots Of the more than 25,000 women who applied to become members of the Women's Airforce Service Pilots (WASPs), about 2,000 were accepted, and 1,074 won their wings. Their duties included ferrying planes from the factories to the airfields, testing rebuilt aircraft, and hauling gunnery targets. After the war, women were not permitted to fly for the military again until 1977.

CHAPTER 19 World War II: 1933–1945 **601**

Food of the Times

During the war sugar, coffee, processed and canned foods, meat, fish, and dairy products were all rationed. To compensate for the scarcity of meat, some homemakers cooked meatless dishes. Others used horse meat, which was unrationed. To make up for shortages of fresh vegetables, many families planted victory gardens. By 1943 they produced 40 percent of the nation's vegetables.

CURRICULUM CONNECTION

Social History During World War II rationing affected the clothing industry. Cuffs disappeared from men's trousers, and the vest passed out of style in an effort to conserve cloth.

Visualizing History Some of the products shown in the photograph are still available today. Interested students could visit a grocery store to look for these brands and check their current prices.
Answer to Caption: The cost of living rose 29% as consumer goods grew scarcer and wages went up.

Critical Thinking Activity

Evaluating Decisions In 1942 the government removed over 100,000 persons of Japanese birth and ancestry from their homes on the Pacific Coast to poorly constructed relocation centers. Ask students the following question: Do you think the government ever has the right to relocate or keep a group in detention? Why or why not? *(Answers will vary. Students who oppose the relocation policy might suggest that it was a violation of the Bill of Rights; those who agree with the policy might indicate that sometimes the country's security takes precedence over the issue of a group's rights.)* **L2**

Independent Practice

Art During World War II, many posters were used to encourage Americans to cooperate in the all-out war effort needed to bring victory. Using the information in Section 4, have students make their own posters in which they encourage the American public to contribute to the war effort. Display students' completed posters. **L2**

📁 Assign Guided Reading Activity 19-4.

📁 Assign Workbook Activity 19-4.

CURRICULUM CONNECTION

Economics By 1943 the United States was producing twice the amount of war goods as all the enemy countries combined. By the end of the war, American industry had produced 296,000 aircraft, 102,000 tanks, 93,000 naval and cargo vessels, and 373,000 artillery pieces.

Visualizing History

The photographs shown here were probably posed. Women in factories wore overalls so that their clothing would not get caught in equipment. They also tied back their hair or wore nets so that it would not get caught in the machinery. **Answer to Caption:** offered job training, funds for child care

---

> *The men really resented the women very much. . . . [A]fter a while they realized that it was essential that the women worked there, 'cause there wasn't enough men, and the women were doing a good job.*

To encourage women to work, the government offered job-training courses, and Congress appropriated funds for child-care centers, but even this was not enough to meet the need. Federal and state governments suspended laws that limited the hours women could work, and women's wages rose as the concept of equal pay for equal work spread. Although at first most women considered their new employment to be temporary, by war's end 80 percent said they wanted to keep their jobs.

Opportunities for African Americans

The need for workers also speeded the shift of African Americans from farming to manufacturing. Many African Americans left the South and moved to cities in the Northeast, the Midwest, and California to work in war industries. Some companies hired few African Americans before the war, but by 1945 thousands of African Americans had jobs in defense plants.

Resentment Toward Social Change

Between 1941 and 1945, one of every five Americans relocated to another part of the country. The movement of so many Americans to fill jobs in war industries created housing shortages, crowded schools, and heightened social tensions. Old-timers resented the newcomers, regardless of their race. In California there were prejudices against "Okies," white migrants from Oklahoma and Texas who arrived in the 1930s to look for work after losing their farms in the Dust Bowl. In many cities prejudices arose against newly arrived African Americans. The police were needed to help African American families move into public housing in Detroit, when angry mobs tried to block them. It took federal troops to break a strike of streetcar operators in Philadelphia, who protested against the promotion of African American workers.

The federal government's response to racial discrimination during the war was uneven. In 1941 African American labor leader A. Philip Randolph threatened to lead 100,000 protesters on Washington, D.C., to

▲ **NEW OPPORTUNITIES** World War II offered increased job opportunities for women and for African Americans. Although women's wages rose, they still averaged 60 percent less than men's wages. *How did the government encourage women to work?*

Sidelight: Japanese Internment Camps

The Japanese internment camps were bleak and dismal. One in Santa Anita was formerly a racetrack, and detainees lived in horse stalls along with the stench of manure and the biting of horseflies. In the camp in Puyallup, Washington, the detainees were supplied with only one washroom for every 100 families. In many camps there was no electric lighting, which forced the detainees to use highly flammable kerosene lamps or candles.

AMERICAN PORTRAITS

Charles Drew
1904–1950

Born and raised in the segregated city of Washington, D.C., Charles Drew refused to let racial prejudice bar him from professional success. After graduating from Amherst College in Massachusetts, he earned his M.D. degree at Canada's McGill University.

In the 1930s Drew conducted pioneering research on blood plasma, and he established a model blood plasma bank. When the United States entered World War II, Drew was asked to head the military's blood plasma program. By collecting, storing, transporting, and transfusing donated blood plasma, this program saved the lives of countless wounded soldiers. But in 1942 Drew resigned when the military refused to accept blood donations from African Americans unless their blood was segregated from the blood of white donors and was given only to black soldiers.

Teaching American Portraits

There is a sad ending to the life of Charles Drew. In 1950, at age 46, he was in a car accident in North Carolina. Drew was taken to a white hospital where he was refused treatment. Before he could be moved to another hospital, he bled to death. Ask students to explain the irony of this event.

demand an end to discrimination in defense jobs and the armed forces. In order to stop the march, Roosevelt established the Fair Employment Practices Commission to promote minority hiring in government offices and in companies that had war contracts. But while it opposed discrimination, the commission did not reject segregation. Even the military remained segregated, and although hundreds of thousands of African Americans served in uniform in every capacity from cooks to fighter pilots, most served in all-black units.

Detention of Japanese Americans

The most significant racial discrimination of the war involved the removal of Japanese Americans from the West Coast. About 90 percent of all Japanese Americans, outside Hawaii, lived in California and the Pacific Northwest. Because of immigration restrictions after 1924, two-thirds had been born in the United States and were citizens by birth. Yet government officials were suspicious of their loyalty. When war broke out, residents of California, Oregon, and Washington feared that with the Pacific fleet at Pearl Harbor severely damaged, they were vulnerable to invasion at any time. Californi-

ans, in particular, were concerned that their neighbors of Japanese descent might engage in sabotage. Army General John DeWitt investigated and reported that:

> **The Japanese race is an enemy race and while many second and third generation Japanese born on United States soil have become 'Americanized,' the racial strains are undiluted. . . . It, therefore, follows that along the vital Pacific Coast over 112,000 potential enemies of Japanese extraction are at large today.**

Based on such reports, beginning in February 1942, the government moved 110,000 Japanese Americans to detention centers surrounded by barbed wire and patrolled by soldiers and confined them there for the duration of the war.

The order to evacuate Japanese Americans from the West Coast came quickly. Detainees had as little as 48 hours to make arrangements for their homes, businesses, and farms. Many had to sell their property at a loss or abandon it. Bargain hunters descended on them, taking advantage of their plight.

American industry in World War II would not have been so productive had the American people not fully supported the war effort. Such support was in marked contrast to the detachment with which Americans traditionally had viewed Europe's great conflicts.

NATIONAL GEOGRAPHIC SOCIETY

 VIDEODISC

GTV: The American People: Fabric of a Nation

Side 4, Chapter 2
Title: *United We Stand?*
Subject: Japanese internment during World War II

Critical Thinking Activity

Interpreting Primary Sources Obtain a copy of *Farewell to Manzanar* by Jeanne Wakatsuki-Houston and James D. Houston, which describes Jeanne Wakatsuki's experiences in a Japanese relocation camp. Read excerpts to the students, and discuss with them the conditions in which the Japanese Americans were forced to live. Have them speculate how they might have felt toward the American government if they had been sent to a relocation center like the one to which Wakatsuki was sent. **L2**

ASSESS

Check Understanding

Assign Section 4 Review as homework or an in-class activity.

Evaluate

⊙ ☞ Assign Section Quiz 19-4 or use the Testmaker to create a customized quiz.

Reteach

☞ Have students complete Reteaching Activity 19-4.

Enrich

☞ Have students complete Enrichment Activity 19.

☞ Assign Geography in History Activity 19.

🎒 ☞ Project Skills Transparency 19 and have students complete Skills Transparency Activity 19.

CLOSE

Have students compare Americans' World War II patriotism with that during the Persian Gulf War.

▲ INTERNMENT OF JAPANESE AMERICANS During World War II, persons of Japanese descent were sent to internment camps. More than 70,000 were Nisei, or American-born. *How did the Supreme Court rule on the detainees' appeal to protect their rights?*

Arriving at one of 10 detention camps in isolated areas of Utah, Wyoming, Arizona, and other sparsely settled Western states, they were put to work at menial, low-paying jobs. Their military guards searched their quarters for "weapons," sometimes confiscating kitchen knives, scissors, and even knitting needles. Entire families lived out the war in a single room in army-style barracks furnished with cots and bare light bulbs. Since the authorities had no plans for running the camps, the detainees established their own camp governments, schools, and newspapers.

Almost immediately detainees appealed to the courts to protect their rights. When the issue came before the Supreme Court in December 1944, in *Korematsu* v. *United States*, the justices upheld the government's policy as necessary for national security.

Despite their unhappy experience, most Japanese Americans remained loyal to the United States. Thousands served in segregated military units. A Japanese American army unit recruited from detention camps fought in the Italian campaign and was the army's most decorated unit in American military history. However, the government's policy toward Japanese Americans at home became a blot on the nation's war record.

Section 4 ★ Review

Checking for Understanding

1. **Identify** War Production Board.
2. **Define** wildcat strike.
3. **Explain** how the productive capacity of the industries of the United States aided the Allies' war effort.
4. **Contrast** the war's effects on African Americans and on Japanese Americans.

Critical Thinking

5. **Formulating Hypotheses** Why were Japanese Americans detained during the war while Americans of German or Italian descent were not?

ACTIVITY

6. Imagine you are a World War II defense worker. Write a diary entry describing your first day on the job.

Answers to SECTION 4 REVIEW

1. War Production Board, 599
2. All vocabulary words are defined in the Glossary.
3. converted many industries to war production, produced materials to supply troops, amount of manufactured goods doubled
4. African Americans in defense jobs and armed services, though segregated; shift from farming to manufacturing, migration to North; white resentment and race riots
5. Japan attacked Pearl Harbor, and Americans feared an attack on the West Coast, where there were many Japanese Americans.
6. Diary entries should include realistic detail.

BUILDING SKILLS
Critical Thinking Skills

Interpreting Points of View

A person's point of view is the way in which he or she interprets topics or events. There are a number of factors that affect a person's point of view, including age, gender, ethnic background, and religion. The ability to interpret points of view will help you to determine the objectivity of an argument or the accuracy of a description.

Learning the Skill

Use the following steps to help you interpret points of view in written material:

- **Read** the material and identify the main idea.
- **Gather** background information on the topic and the author.
- **Identify** any aspects of the topic that the author has emphasized or excluded.
- **Identify** any words or phrases that suggest a personal opinion.
- **Identify** the author's point of view on the topic.

Read the following excerpt from "The Good War, An Oral History of World War Two." The speaker, Peter Ota, was 15 when he was interned, or sent to a detention camp for Japanese Americans in 1942. Later, he served in an armored division of the United States Army.

We came back to Los Angeles at the end of the war, believing that there was no other way but to be American. We were discouraged with our Japanese culture. My feeling at the time was, I had to prove myself. I don't know why I had to prove myself. Here I am, an ex-GI, born and raised here. Why do I have to prove myself? We all had this feeling. We had to prove that we were Americans, okay?
. . . My children were denied a lot of the history of what happened. . . . I think this stems from

▲ JAPANESE AMERICAN CHILDREN AT INTERNMENT CAMP

another Japanese characteristic: when shame is put on you, you try to hide it. We were put into camp, we became victims, it was our fault. We hide it.

Practicing the Skill

1. What is Ota's background?
2. How does Ota explain the silence of Japanese Americans on the internment camps? Do you agree or disagree with Ota's explanation?

APPLYING THE SKILL

3. Think about a topic on which you and a friend disagree. Analyze each point of view. Then, in a brief paragraph, describe the compromises each side might make to resolve your differences.

605

GLENCOE
TECHNOLOGY

 VIDEODISC

Use the MindJogger Videoquiz to review students' knowledge.

MindJogger Videoquiz

Chapter 19
Disc 3, Side A

Available in VHS.

Using Vocabulary

Statements will vary but should include each of the vocabulary terms.

Reviewing Facts

1. economic problems; European nations did not want war; Americans believed it was a European problem.
2. wanted raw materials, land, and markets
3. sold arms, provided destroyers, lend-lease, exchanged fire with German ships, extended lend-lease, armed merchant ships
4. first focus on Germany and Italy; North Africa, 1942: U.S. and British forces defeat Germans; Mediterranean, 1943: invasion of Sicily, Italy surrenders; Europe, 1944: Allied army invades and liberates France, moves into Germany while Soviets press Germany from the east; Asia, 1942: defeat Japan's fleet in naval battles; Asia, 1942–1945: capture key islands in Pacific, retake Philippines, bomb Japan; Japan,1945: drop atomic bombs on Japan

606

Using Vocabulary

Use each of the following words in a statement about the aggressor nations in World War II, the kind of warfare they conducted, and world response.

appeasement   Holocaust
fascism   totalitarian

Reviewing Facts

1. **List** reasons for isolationist policies in the United States and appeasement in Europe.
2. **State** the reasons for Japan's territorial ambitions in Asia.
3. **Chronicle** the steps by which the United States progressed from neutrality to war.
4. **Discuss** the priorities and sequence of the Allies' military campaigns in World War II.
5. **Explain** the difficulties Roosevelt and Churchill faced in dealing with Chiang Kai-shek, de Gaulle, and Stalin.
6. **Describe** how World War II affected women and minorities in the United States.

Understanding Concepts

International Alliances

1. How did World War II underscore the importance of an international organization such as the United Nations?
2. Explain the importance of Germany's 1939 nonaggression treaty with the Soviet Union to Hitler. Why do you suppose the Soviet Union signed it?

Military Conflict

3. Analyze Hitler's strategy for war. After his early victories, where did he go wrong?
4. Why did kamikaze missions pose such a deadly threat to American forces? What does this strategy suggest about the values and patriotism of the Japanese?

Critical Thinking

1. **Evaluating Policy** Economic problems at home was one reason that the United States initially avoided involvement in World War II. What subsequent developments suggest that this policy may have been self-defeating?
2. **Analyzing Fine Art** Study the painting of V-J Day on this page, then answer the questions.
   a. Does the painting have a central focus?
   b. Could you understand the meaning of this painting if it did not have a caption?

▲ *V-J Day—Crowds cheering at Times Square* by Edward Dancig, 1947

3. **Linking Past and Present** In 1990 the United Nations Security Council demanded that Iraq withdraw its forces from Kuwait. Had the United Nations existed in 1935, could it have prevented World War II? Explain your answer.
4. **Analyzing Trends** How did the nation's role in the United Nations illustrate the dramatic change World War II had made in long-range United States foreign policy?

5. They distrusted Stalin and Soviet intentions; not convinced that the other two leaders really represented their people.
6. More women worked outside homes; minorities and women gained jobs and higher wages. Many Japanese Americans were interned.

Understanding Concepts

1. showed lack of unity and resolve against aggression
2. It freed Hitler to attack in Europe without threat of a two-front war. After World War I, the Soviets were eager to avoid war.

3. After removing any Soviet threat with a pact, he blitzed through Europe; he went wrong in that he could not eliminate Britain, attacked Soviet Union, and did not anticipate United States aid.
4. Such attacks were difficult to prevent because the pilot was determined to

5. Analyzing Graphs Study the graph on this page and answer the questions that follow.

a. Which decade depicted on the graph shows the smallest increase in the number of women joining the labor force? The largest increase?

b. Summarize the apparent relationship between the world wars and the employment of women.

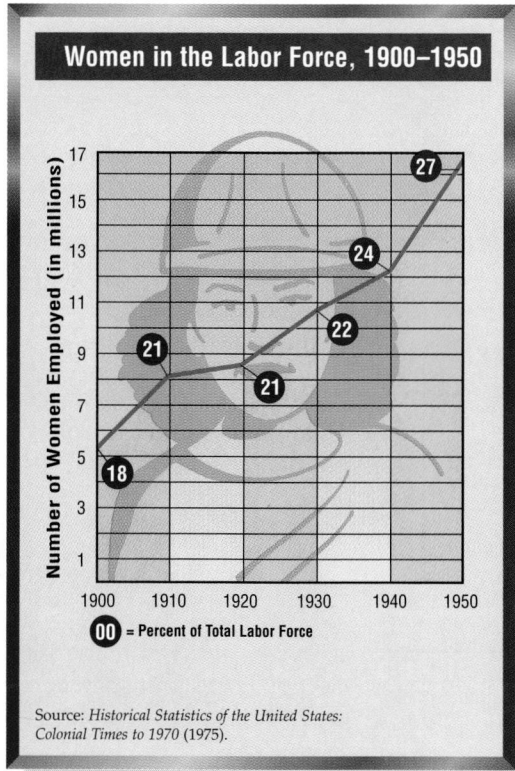

Women in the Labor Force, 1900–1950

Number of Women Employed (in millions)

27
24
22
21
21
21
18

1900 1910 1920 1930 1940 1950

00 = Percent of Total Labor Force

Source: *Historical Statistics of the United States: Colonial Times to 1970* (1975).

History and Geography

War in the Pacific

Study the map on page 594, then answer the questions that follow.

1. Region Compare the area under Japanese control in 1942 with that of 1936.

2. Place What battle shown on the map was fought in May 1942?

3. Location Between which lines of latitude is Iwo Jima located?

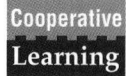

Cooperative Learning Interdisciplinary Activity: Law

As a class, create a courtroom with students role-playing a panel of judges, a three-member prosecution team, three defense attorneys, a jury, three defendants, and an audience. Put the following people on trial for crimes against humanity: Adolf Hitler—for beginning World War II and establishing the Nazi death camps; a German military officer—for carrying out orders to execute Jews in a death camp; General Hideki Tojo—for ordering kamikaze attacks against Allied forces.

Practicing Skills

Interpreting Points of View

Read the editorial page of a newspaper and choose an editorial, column, or letter to the editor with a point of view that conflicts with your own. Analyze the author's view, and write a brief paragraph comparing his or her view with your own.

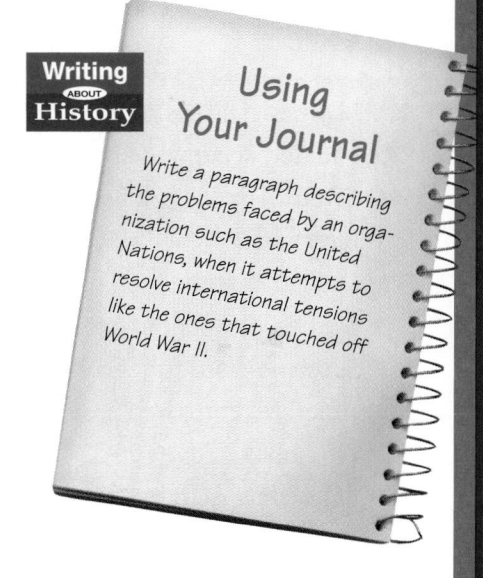

Writing ABOUT History

Using Your Journal

Write a paragraph describing the problems faced by an organization such as the United Nations, when it attempts to resolve international tensions like the ones that touched off World War II.

3. between 140°E and 150°E

Cooperative Learning

You might videotape students' role-playing situations and hold a class discussion.

Practicing Skills

Students should explain how the cartoon's point of view contrasts with their own.

Writing ABOUT History **Using Your Journal**

Paragraphs should include references to conflicts arising from competing interests. Students may refer also to specific countries and crises.

? Chapter Bonus Test Question

Ask: Give an example of the way the war heightened prejudices against minorities. How do you account for that response? (*Possible answers include internment of Japanese Americans and discrimination against African Americans.*)

---

sacrifice his life; demonstrated that the pilots valued honor before life.

Critical Thinking

1. Although the New Deal did not keep the United States out of the war, the war's demand for goods and workers ended the Great Depression.

2. a. no
b. Even without a caption, the painting suggests joy and celebration.
3. Some may note that the UN did not prevent war in 1991.
4. U.S. leadership in creating the UN after World War II signaled a departure from

isolationism and a commitment to international cooperation.
5. a. 1910–1920; 1940–1950
b. During wartime more women enter the workforce.

History and Geography

1. grew dramatically
2. Battle of the Coral Sea

Daily Lesson Objectives	Teacher Classroom Resources	Multimedia
SECTION 1 **The Start of the Cold War** **1 Day** pp. 610–615 1. Describe the changes in Eastern Europe and the factors that made communism strong after World War II. 2. Outline the foreign policy goals of the Truman administration. 3. Explain how the United States became a world power after World War II.	Reproducible Lesson Plan 20-1 *Guided Reading Activity 20-1 Concept Mapping Activities 20-A, 20-B *Vocabulary Activity 20 Chapter Map Activity 20 Chapter Skills Activity 20 Outline Map Resource Book, p. 29 Workbook Activity 20-1 Reteaching Activity 20-1 *Section Quiz 20-1	Section Focus Transparency 20-1 Chapter Concepts Transparencies 20-A, 20-B Testmaker Vocabulary PuzzleMaker MindJogger Videoquiz Communism and the Cold War
SECTION 2 **The Cold War in Asia** **1 Day** pp. 617–621 1. Cite the outcome of the United States' occupation of Japan. 2. Explain the political situation in China after the war. 3. Explain why the United Nations waged a limited war in Korea.	Reproducible Lesson Plan 20-2 *Guided Reading Activity 20-2 Cooperative Learning Activity 20 Political Cartoons in American History Activity 22 Geography in History Activity 20 Workbook Activity 20-3 Reteaching Activity 20-2 *Section Quiz 20-2	Section Focus Transparency 20-2 Skills Transparency 20 Testmaker Communism and the Cold War
SECTION 3 **Cold War America** **1 Day** pp. 622–628 1. Explain changes in the American labor force after the war. 2. Describe the condition of African Americans during the 1940s. 3. Evaluate the Truman presidency.	Reproducible Lesson Plan 20-3 *Guided Reading Activity 20-3 Critical Thinking Skills Activity 20 Enrichment Activity 20 Linking Past and Present Activity 20 Political Cartoons in American History Activity 20 Supreme Court Case Study 20 American Portrait 54 Workbook Activity 20-3 Reteaching Activity 20-3 *Section Quiz 20-3	Section Focus Transparency 20-3 Testmaker GTV: A Geographic Perspective on American History GTV: The American People: Fabric of a Nation Communism and the Cold War The Presidents: A Picture History of Our Nation
CHAPTER REVIEW AND EVALUATION **1 Day**	Chapter 20 Test, Forms A and B Spanish Chapter 20 Summary Performance Assessment Activity 20	MindJogger Videoquiz Student Self-Test & Review Software *Chapter 20 Audiocassette Activity and Test

*Also available in Spanish

 OUT OF TIME? If time does not permit teaching the entire chapter, use the Chapter 20 Summary on pages 662–663 and the Chapter 20 audiocassette (English and Spanish) to point out the main ideas of the chapter.

A complete, 1-page lesson plan is provided for each section in the *Reproducible Lesson Plan* booklet.

Key to Ability Levels

Teaching strategies have been coded for varying learning styles and abilities.

L1   Basic activities for all students

L2   Average activities for average to above-average students

L3   Challenging activities for above-average students

LEP Limited English Proficiency activities

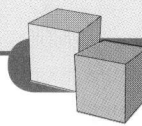

Block Schedule

Block scheduling differs from traditional class scheduling in the amount of time allotted to each period. The extended time frame provided by block scheduling affords you the opportunity to implement a greater number of research-oriented and activity-intense projects to motivate and involve your students. Activities that are particularly suited to use within the block scheduling framework are identified throughout this unit by the following designation:

Performance Assessment Activity

Documenting a Life Divide students into small groups and ask each to imagine that its members have been asked to prepare a documentary about a major historical figure of the Cold War. Tell them that before a director shoots a film, he or she creates a storyboard that serves as a guide to the director and the camera crew. Ask them to develop a storyboard for the figure their group chose. Possibilities include Harry Truman, Joseph Stalin, Joseph McCarthy, George Marshall. After groups have completed their research, ask them to assemble their information—including maps, photographs, and other artwork—onto a storyboard. It should describe the individual's life in chronological order, highlight his or her involvement in the Cold War. Encourage groups to present their storyboards to the class.

POSSIBLE RUBRIC FEATURES
- Content Information
- Organization
- Written and Visual Communication Skills
- Collaborative Skills
- Creativity
- Research Skills

For additional practice, use Performance Assessment Strategies and Activities.

T E A C H E R ' S   C O R N E R

NATIONAL
GEOGRAPHIC
SOCIETY

NATIONAL GEOGRAPHIC SOCIETY PRODUCTS AVAILABLE FROM GLENCOE

To order the following products for use with this chapter, contact your local Glencoe sales representative or call Glencoe at 1-800-334-7344:

- *The Presidents: A Picture History of Our Nation* (CD-ROM)
- *GTV: A Geographic Perspective on American History* (Videodisc)
- *GTV: The American People: Fabric of a Nation* (Videodisc)

ADDITIONAL NATIONAL GEOGRAPHIC SOCIETY PRODUCTS

To order the following products for use with this chapter, call National Geographic Society at 1-800-368-2728:

- *Decades of History: The 20th Century—The Middle Years* (Filmstrip)
- *The United States as a World Power: From the 1890s to the 1970s* (Filmstrip)
- *1945–1989: The Cold War* (Video)
- *The Rise and Fall of the Soviet Union* (Video)

GLENCOE
TECHNOLOGY

 VIDEODISC

Use the Chapter 20 MindJogger Videoquiz to preview the content of this chapter.
MindJogger Videoquiz

Chapter 20
Disc 3, Side A

 Available in VHS.

Recording Journal Notes

To get students started, discuss the hearings held by the Un-American Activities Committee of the House of Representatives and the Army-McCarthy hearings in the Senate.

Linking Across
T I M E

Point out that the iron curtain effectively isolated Eastern Europe from 1946 until 1989. In that year the Soviet program of *glasnost* flowered, and many Soviet satellites declared their independence from Moscow. The most dramatic of these declarations came when East Germans broke through the Berlin Wall in 1990.

CHAPTER 20
★★★

The Cold War
1945–1952

▼ REBUILDING BERLIN, THE MARSHALL PLAN AT WORK

Setting the Scene

Focus

Within months after the end of World War II, the United States and the Soviet Union entered into a period of intense confrontation and rivalry. American leaders sought to maintain workable links with the Soviets while trying to check communism in Europe. Later this containment policy was applied to China, but it could not prevent the outbreak of war in Korea. At home, Americans sought to adjust to a peacetime economy.

Concepts to Understand

★ Why the **political and economic power** of the United States and the Soviet Union were set against each other

★ How effective presidential **leadership** resulted in aggressive foreign and domestic policies

Read to Discover . . .

★ ways the United States sought to contain the Soviet Union.

★ the effect the cold war had on Americans at home.

> ### Journal Notes
>
> How did the fear of communism become a serious threat to American democracy during the Truman administration? Record relevant points as you read the chapter.

CULTURAL	• **1945** Harvey *by Mary Chase wins Pulitzer Prize for plays*	• **1947** *Jackie Robinson first plays for Brooklyn Dodgers*
	1944	**1946**
POLITICAL	• **1945** *Harry S Truman becomes President on death of Franklin D. Roosevelt*	• **1946** *Winston Churchill makes "iron curtain" speech* • **1947** *Truman Doctrine announced*

➕ **EXTRA CREDIT PROJECT**

Research Several nations in Eastern Europe have a long history of being overrun by more powerful nations. Ask interested students to research the history of one country in the region. Tell them to keep the following questions in mind: At what times in history has the nation been conquered? By whom? How did living under foreign rule affect the nation and its people? What is its status today? Ask students to share their findings with the rest of the class.
L2

Concept Mapping Activity

On the chalkboard, reproduce the following generalization and concepts map, and have students copy it in their notebooks.

The United States takes on the challenge of world leadership and the protection of Western Democracy.

Political and Economic Power

Leadership

 To reinforce the two chapter concepts, use Concept Mapping Activities 20-A and 20-B.

 Use Chapter Concepts Transparencies 20-A, 20-B.

History AND ART

Norman Rockwell's paintings appeared regularly in the *Saturday Evening Post*.

History AND ART

The Homecoming
by Norman Rockwell, 1945

New opportunities for housing and education eased the transition from military to civilian life for returning veterans. At the same time, Americans faced new challenges at home and abroad.

▲ PRESIDENT HARRY S TRUMAN AND GENERAL DOUGLAS MACARTHUR

ABCNEWS INTERACTIVE™

VIDEODISC

Communism and the Cold War

Side One, Chapter 3
Title: *End of Alliance*
Subject: Summary of events near end of World War II which led to the Cold War

- **1948** *Largest telescope in the world is dedicated at Mount Palomar Observatory*

- **1950** *National Council of Churches of Christ is formed, representing 30 denominations*

1948	1950

- **1948** *Berlin airlift*
- **1949** *Communist forces take China*
- **1949** *NATO created*

- **1950** *North Korea invades South Korea*

CHAPTER 20 The Cold War: 1945–1952   **609**

✓ Performance Assessment

Refer to the Performance Assessment Activity in the Planning Guide on page 608b. When the students have finished their storyboards about a major historical figure of the Cold War, have them present the storyboards to the class. Allow time for class discussion and feedback.

 Use Performance Assessment Activity 20 as an additional assessment technique.

SECTION 1

FOCUS

Bellringer

Before taking roll, project Section Focus Transparency 20-1 or hand out Section Focus Transparency Activity 20-1. Have students answer the questions. Discuss student responses.

Motivating Activity

Read Harry Truman's statement: "[H]istory will remember my term of office as the years when the cold war began to overshadow our lives." Then ask why they think President Truman's words were effective in describing the effects of World War II. **L2**

Vocabulary Precheck

Ask students to define each of the "Key Terms." Have a volunteer consult the dictionary for any unfamiliar words. **L1, LEP**

Use the Vocabulary PuzzleMaker Software to create a crossword puzzle. **L1**

Assign Vocabulary Activity 20.

The Start of the Cold War

Setting the Scene

Section Focus

The Allies' goal of establishing democratic governments throughout Europe after World War II proved to be elusive. To Churchill and Truman, democracy meant political and economic systems like those in Great Britain and the United States. Western democracy was unacceptable to Stalin, who began to establish Soviet-style communism in Eastern Europe. To implement a policy of containment, the Truman administration provided massive economic aid to war-torn Western Europe, joining with these countries in the first peacetime alliance in United States history.

Objectives

After studying this section, you should be able to

★ describe the changes in Eastern Europe and the factors that made communism strong after World War II.

★ outline the foreign policy goals of the Truman administration.

★ explain how the United States became a world power after World War II.

Key Terms

communism, satellite nation, purge, buffer, guerrilla, containment, collective security

◀ UN FLAG

*P*resident Truman's policies from the beginning of his administration showed his determination and the high degree to which he was personally involved in handling both domestic and international affairs. On his desk he kept a sign: "The buck stops here." In times of great crisis, Truman showed an extraordinary capacity for quick, effective, yet restrained action.

■ East-West Suspicions

In 1945, during the first months of his administration, President Truman concentrated his attention on winning the war against Germany and Japan. Like Roosevelt, he supported the creation of the United

Nations as a world peacekeeping organization. But Truman was much more suspicious than Roosevelt had been of the Soviet Union and its dictator, Joseph Stalin.

Soviet Control of Eastern Europe

When the war ended, the alliance between the United States, Great Britain, and the Soviet Union unraveled. While there was a common enemy, Western democracies and Soviet leaders had overlooked their political, economic, and social differences. After the war, suspicions returned. Soviet expansion into Eastern Europe heightened American fears of **communism,** a system in which society as a whole, represented by the Communist party, owns and controls property and the means of production.

Classroom Resources for SECTION 1

Blackline Masters:
- Reproducible Lesson Plan 20-1
- Guided Reading Activity 20-1
- Vocabulary Activity 20
- Chapter Map Activity 20

- Chapter Skills Activity 20
- Outline Map Resource Book, p. 29
- Workbook Activity 20-1
- Reteaching Activity 20-1
- Section Quiz 20-1

Transparencies:
- Section Focus Transparency 20-1

Multimedia:
- Testmaker
- Vocabulary PuzzleMaker
- MindJogger Videoquiz
- Communism and the Cold War

As fighting ended, Soviet troops occupied much of Eastern Europe. The Soviet leaders, who had promised free elections in these nations, did not follow through. In Hungary, where free elections were held in November 1945, communist candidates received only 17 percent of the vote. Unwilling to lose control, Stalin later suppressed elections in Hungary and in the other nations of Eastern Europe. Then, under elections supervised by Soviet troops, voters gave 90 percent of the vote to communist candidates in Poland. This pattern was repeated in all Soviet-occupied areas, helping to establish communist governments throughout Eastern Europe. Nations that were held under Soviet domination came to be called **satellite nations.**

To restore the devastated Soviet economy, the Soviets removed whole factories, transportation equipment, and machinery from the satellite nations. Stalin also ordered **purges,** or forced removals, of leaders of satellite nations who were deemed disloyal.

The Iron Curtain

The leaders of Western Europe and the United States watched with grave concern as the Soviet Union crushed all opposition in the nations of Eastern Europe after 1945. Former Prime Minister Winston Churchill identified the new threat in a speech in March 1946 at Fulton, Missouri. With President Truman on the platform, Churchill warned:

> 66 . . . [F]rom Stettin on the Baltic to Trieste on the Adriatic, an iron curtain has descended across the continent. Behind that line lie all the capitals of the ancient states of central and eastern Europe. 99

The phrase "iron curtain" would be used to describe Soviet policy in Europe from 1945 to 1989. The West, said Churchill, must meet this challenge with force, if needed, because the Communists had no respect for weakness. Truman and his advisers agreed that a "get tough" policy was their only choice.

Visualizing History ▲ **An Iron Curtain** Former Prime Minister Winston Churchill and President Truman appear together during Churchill's speech at Fulton, Missouri. *What message did Churchill give to the American people?*

CHAPTER 20 The Cold War: 1945–1952 **611**

TEACH
Guided Practice

Geography Have students use their texts to compare the geographical divisions of prewar and postwar Europe, using two outline maps of Eastern Europe and European Russia. Ask students to label countries as they existed before World War II on one map and the new geographical divisions of postwar Eastern Europe and the "iron curtain" on the other map. **L2**

Provide each student two copies of the map from Outline Map Resource Book on page 29 to complete the activity.

Visualizing History Point out that Churchill urged a "vigilant association of English-speaking peoples" to counter the Soviet threat.
Answer to Caption: that Soviets were closing off Eastern Europe

 Videodisc

Communism and the Cold War

Side One, Chapter 6
Title: *The Arms Race*
Subject: The race to build weapons

Special Needs Activity

Reading Disability It is often difficult for students with vocabulary deficits to understand the emotional impact of words and how these words shape our feelings about events. In the section "The Strength of Communism," students study the message communism brought to people. Ask them to note the promises communism made (*abolish poverty, privilege, and private property; provide productive work and classless society*). Talk about the difference between "forces of progress" and "forces of oppression." Discuss the meaning and the emotional impact of each phrase. **L1, LEP**

■ The Strength of Communism

Following World War II, the United States began to withdraw troops from Europe, leaving the Soviet army as the most powerful military force in Europe. As a result of the German invasion, the Soviet Union had lost 20 million people and suffered devastation of land, property, and industry. Feeling threatened by Western powers, the Soviet Union wanted to create a **buffer,** or safety zone, on its western border. Soviet troops stationed there ensured that the nations of Eastern Europe would remain its allies.

Communism's Promises

The Communists promised to abolish poverty, privilege, and private property. They guaranteed productive work, shelter, education, health care, and a classless society in the new "people's democracies" of war-torn Eastern Europe.

The Communists saw the world as divided between forces of progress and forces of oppression. Soviet rhetoric incited revolts in other impoverished nations, as people living in poverty listened eagerly to the Communists' plans. Communists began to organize resistance to governments they considered to be reactionary and imperialist. Sometimes they organized groups of **guerrilla** forces—armed bands that were not a part of a regular military unit—to foment civil war.

Containment

President Truman responded with a policy of **containment**—preventing the further spread of communism. This policy was based on the belief that foreign policy goals of Soviet leaders included conquering other nations—not simply the securing of their own borders. Containment, however, did not win universal support.

Some who opposed the policy believed that it was too soft. Angry with the advance of communism, they called for a quick and decisive victory over the Soviet Union. Another view was expressed by Walter Lippmann, a newspaper columnist. Lippmann argued that Soviet troops remained in Eastern Europe to protect the Soviets' western border. He warned that the United States could not contain the Soviet Union everywhere. Such a policy, he said, would require the United States to defend all anticommunist governments—no matter how repressive or unpopular they might be.

Lippmann published his newspaper columns on containment in a book called *The Cold War.* The title, a term coined by Lippmann to refer to a state of war that did not involve actual bloodshed, came to be used by everyone, including the President, to describe the icy rivalry that existed between the United States and the Soviet Union.

■ Aid to Europe

The cold war was like no other struggle that had ever engaged the United States. It required a constant state of military preparedness; it called for military support for countries believed to be in danger of a communist takeover. It had other economic costs, as both the United States and the Soviet Union tried to "buy" allies with gifts ranging from food to steel mills.

The Truman Doctrine

The policy of containment began in Europe. Great Britain, in financial trouble, was forced to notify United States officials early in 1947 that it would withdraw its soldiers from Greece and end aid to Turkey. United States diplomats in Greece warned that this could lead to a communist takeover. Already, they said, Soviet-supported guerrillas were controlling much of the country. It was feared that if Greece fell to the Communists, Turkey would be next.

President Truman decided that the United States must act. In March 1947 he told Congress that if the United States was not willing to give aid to Greece and Turkey to contain communism, democratic governments everywhere would be threatened. Truman's warning that the nation faced a crisis was clear:

Cooperative Learning Activity

Researching Topics Divide the class into two groups. Assign each group member one of the following two topics. Have them answer the question that corresponds to their topic: "East-West Suspicions" (What was the main reason the alliance between the United States and the Soviet Union began to shatter after the war ended?) "The Strength of Communism" (Why did the message of communism sound compelling to the people of Europe?) Randomly call on various group members to share their responses with the remainder of the class. **L2**

> *I believe that it must be the policy of the United States to support free peoples who are resisting attempted subjugation by armed minorities or outside pressures. . . . If we falter in our leadership, we may endanger the peace of the world—and we shall surely endanger the welfare of our own nation.*

Truman's policy, known as the Truman Doctrine, proposed that the United States provide military and economic aid to Greece and Turkey. Immediately approved by Congress, the Truman Doctrine superseded the Monroe Doctrine, shifting the United States away from peacetime isolationism.

The Marshall Plan

Soon after the Truman Doctrine went into effect, the administration proposed a plan for economic aid to Europe. The situation in Europe was desperate in 1947. There were shortages of food, fuel, and raw materials, and European nations needed money to rebuild industries and transportation systems.

The Truman administration realized that economic woes in France, Italy, and other Western European countries might lead to the election of communist governments. The nation's leaders were also concerned that Europe's faltering economy would affect United States markets.

In June 1947, Secretary of State George C. Marshall went beyond the Truman

Europe After World War II

Legend:
- British
- French
- American
- Russian
- Air corridors
- Iron Curtain
- ◎ Jointly occupied cities

Map Study

After being invaded twice in less than 30 years, the Soviets especially feared future German power. Thus, after World War II, the Allies agreed to divide and occupy Germany. ***What other nation was divided after the war?***

Critical Thinking Activity

Evaluating Policies Point out to students that cold war tensions between the United States and the Soviet Union increased with the escalation of the arms race. Ask the following question: "Do you think the United States could have countered Soviet aggression in some other way? Why or why not?" (*Answers will vary.*

Those who answered yes might suggest that the United States could have dealt with it through international conferences or the UN. Those who answered no might suggest that the only way the United States could have dealt with it was through military superiority) **L2**

Independent Practice

📁 Assign Workbook Activity 20-1.

 **CURRICULUM CONNECTION**

Language Arts Ask students to read and analyze Winston Churchill's entire speech delivered in Fulton, Missouri, in which he mentions the "iron curtain." Ask the students what they think he meant by the term. **L1**

Did You Know?

Senator Robert A. Taft opposed the Marshall Plan and called it a "global . . . give-away program." He was concerned that the plan would bankrupt the United States.

Map Study   *Using Maps*

Answer: Austria

Map Skills Practice

What was the purpose of the Berlin airlift? (*to break the Soviet blockade of West Berlin without confronting the troops in East Germany*)

📁 For additional map practice, assign Chapter Map Activity 20.

Berlin remained a focal point throughout the Cold War. In 1961, the government of East Germany built the Berlin Wall to prevent its people from moving to West Germany. The dismantling of the Berlin Wall in 1989 foreshadowed the end of Communist domination of Eastern Europe.

 **Visualizing History**

▲ THE BERLIN AIRLIFT When the Soviets closed off the routes from the West to Berlin, American and British cargo planes carried on an around-the-clock airlift. Berlin children, standing in the rubble of their shattered city, watch an American bomber fly in with supplies. *What effect did the airlift have on the Soviet blockade?*

Doctrine to propose a massive recovery plan for European nations. Under the Marshall Plan, American aid in the form of money, supplies, and machinery would help to end Europe's "hunger, poverty, desperation, and chaos." The United States offered the Marshall Plan to all nations in Europe—including the Soviet Union. Believing that the plan would promote the interests of United States capitalism, the Soviet Union and Eastern European communist nations turned it down.

The nations of Western Europe, on the other hand, welcomed the Truman administration's offer. Drawing up detailed plans for restoring production and controlling inflation, they also agreed to change trade laws—tariffs and quotas that blocked the flow of commerce.

The Marshall Plan was an enormous success. During the Truman years, the United States gave more than $13 billion in loans and grants to the nations of Western Europe. To administer aid effectively, the 16 Western European nations formed the Organization for European Economic Cooperation, the first step toward European economic unity.

■ The Berlin Airlift

At the end of the war, the Allies had decided on a joint occupation of Germany. The United States, Great Britain, France, and the Soviet Union each controlled a zone, or section, of Germany. They also each controlled a section of the capital, Berlin, in the Soviet-controlled zone.

Failing to reach agreement with the Soviet Union, the Western powers in May 1948 announced plans to join their three sections of Germany to form an independent nation. The Soviet Union responded by closing off all traffic from West Germany to Berlin. They thought that this move would force the West to back down from its control of West Berlin. President Truman saw this action as a test of Western determination. Instead of sending troops through the land corridor to Berlin and risking war, Truman ordered a massive airlift to supply Berlin's 2 million people. Night and day for more than 10 months, British and United States cargo planes carried food, medicine, clothing, raw materials, and even coal to Berlin. In May 1949, the Soviet Union finally lifted its blockade. Truman said:

Cooperative Learning Activity

Creating a Map On an outline map of Europe, have students work in groups of three to show the division between East and West by indicating the European countries that made up the NATO alliance in 1949 and those that made up the Warsaw Pact in 1955. *(NATO: Belgium,* *Denmark, France, Iceland, Italy, Luxembourg, the Netherlands, Norway, Portugal, the United Kingdom. Warsaw Pact: Albania, Bulgaria, Czechoslovakia, East Germany, Hungary, Poland, Romania, the Soviet Union.)* **L2**

> " *When we refused to be forced out of Berlin, we demonstrated to the people of Europe that with their cooperation we would act, and act resolutely, when their freedom was threatened.* "

■ North Atlantic Treaty Organization

Believing that rebuilding their economies without rebuilding their military strength might invite Soviet aggression, five Western European states formed an alliance in March 1948. They invited the United States, the world's only atomic power, to join their alliance. With Senate approval, Truman began talks to create a North Atlantic Treaty Organization (NATO), which formed in April 1949.

NATO linked into a military alliance the United States, Great Britain, Canada, Belgium, Italy, France, the Netherlands, Luxembourg, Iceland, Denmark, Norway, and Portugal. Greece, Turkey, and West Germany joined later. NATO was based on **collective security,** an agreement by which "an armed attack against one or more of them in Europe or North America shall be considered an attack against all of them." General Dwight D. Eisenhower, commander of NATO's forces, exercised sole authority over the atomic weapons that the United States committed to the defense of NATO.

Then, in September 1949, the Soviet Union exploded its first atomic bomb. Much sooner than military experts had expected, the United States had lost its nuclear monopoly. Faced with this new threat, Congress quickly passed the NATO appropriations bill. In 1955 the Soviet Union and its satellites countered NATO by establishing their own military alliance—the Warsaw Pact. The arms race was well under way.

Within a few years, both the United States and the Soviet Union developed a new and more powerful weapon—the hydrogen bomb. Later, other nations, including Great Britain, France, and China, also built nuclear weapons.

▲ GENERAL DWIGHT D. EISENHOWER

Section 1 ★ Review

Checking for Understanding

1. **Identify** cold war, Truman Doctrine, Marshall Plan, NATO, Berlin airlift.

2. **Define** communism, satellite nation, purge, buffer, guerrilla, containment, collective security.

3. **Explain** how the Soviet Union controlled its satellite nations.

4. **Summarize** the Truman administration's major foreign policy goals.

Critical Thinking

5. **Analyzing Policies** How did exercising the Truman Doctrine in Greece nullify the Monroe Doctrine of 1823?

ACTIVITY

6. Select a nation mentioned in Section 1 and create a time line of important events in the nation's history between World War II and the present.

ASSESS

Check Understanding
Assign Section 1 Review as homework or an in-class activity.

Evaluate
▣ 🗁 Assign Section Quiz 20-1 or use the Testmaker to create a customized quiz.

Reteach
Have students list the foreign policy goals of the Truman administration after World War II.

🗁 Have students complete Reteaching Activity 20-1.

Enrich
Ask students to assume the role of political leaders during the late 1940s who oppose the policy of containment because they believe that it will lead to unlimited intervention in the affairs of other countries. Have students prepare a speech to Congress that outlines the reasons for their beliefs.

CLOSE

Ask students the following questions: What did the Truman Doctrine, the Marshall Plan, NATO, and the Berlin Airlift have in common? *(They were all a part of the policy of containment.)*

Answers to SECTION 1 REVIEW

1. cold war, 612; Truman Doctrine, 612; Marshall Plan, 613; NATO, 615; Berlin airlift, 614
2. All vocabulary words are defined in the Glossary.
3. by crushing all opposition to itself in the Eastern European nations
4. containment of Soviet expansion; aid economic and political recovery abroad; moral and political leadership
5. U.S. gave economic and military aid to non-communists. Monroe Doctrine promised U.S. would not intervene in European affairs.
6. Time lines should focus on significant events in the nation's history.

TEACH

Point out that maps can chronicle events in a war, the political and economic development of an area, the change in population—almost any collection of facts about a place can be shown on a map.

Review the guidelines for using maps to form hypotheses. Have students write hypotheses for each of the maps on page 620. *(The Korean conflict began when North Korea invaded the southern part of the nation. The conflict was a stalemate.)* Discuss how the statements could be proved or disproved. **L2**

📁 Use Chapter Skills Activity 20 to reinforce students' understanding of the skill.

Did You Know?

During the Berlin airlift, a plane flew into the city every three minutes. Without the supplies those planes carried, West Berliners would have had to back down.

BUILDING SKILLS
Critical Thinking Skills

Hypothesizing

Hypothesizing is the process of forming a tentative explanation based on available evidence. A hypothesis offers a possible answer to a problem, or an explanation for why a situation or condition exists.

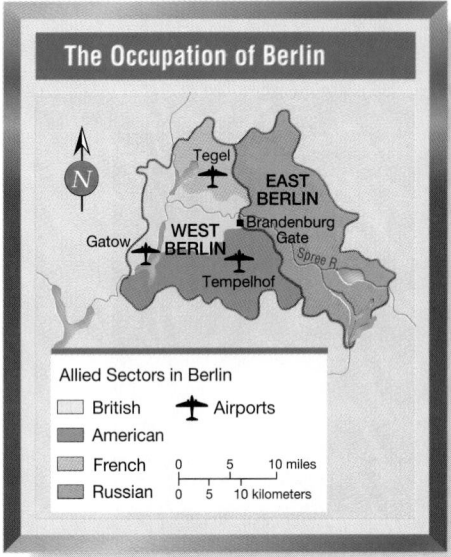

The Occupation of Berlin

Allied Sectors in Berlin
- ☐ British ✈ Airports
- ■ American
- ▨ French   0   5   10 miles
- ▨ Russian   0   5   10 kilometers

Learning the Skill

A hypothesis cannot be judged right or wrong until it is confirmed or disproved by additional evidence. The following guidelines will help you form hypotheses.

- **Analyze** the information that is being presented and write it as a statement.
- **Form** possible hypotheses that may explain the statement you have written.
- **Gather** additional evidence about the situation and test each hypothesis.
- **Accept** or reject each hypothesis.

Study the map on this page showing the Allied occupation of Berlin. Note how the guidelines on hypothesizing have been applied.

a. Berlin was divided and occupied by the Allies. The Soviets occupied East Berlin. West Berlin was divided into French, British, and American sectors.

b. *Hypothesis:* Berlin was divided because the Allies wanted to keep the city for themselves.
   Hypothesis: Berlin was divided among the Allies because the Western nations did not want the Soviets to have control of it.
   Hypothesis: Berlin was divided so that its citizens would have self-government.
   Hypothesis: Berlin was divided because the Western Allies feared Soviet intentions.

c. Gather additional evidence to test these hypotheses. Historians use many sources of information to understand an event. Written primary sources are often the most reliable record of what happened.

d. The information provided from reading Chapter 20 and from doing additional research might indicate that the second hypothesis best explains the statement.

Practicing the Skill

1. In Section 1 you read about the Marshall Plan. Form a hypothesis to explain why the United States instituted this plan.

2. Accept or reject the following hypothesis and explain your reasoning: The policy of containment was intended to hold back the spread of communism.

APPLYING THE SKILL

3. On Saturday morning you find a note in your pocket in your own handwriting that says "study Tues./Wed. civics/multiple choice." You do not remember writing the note or what it means. Explain how you can use hypothesizing and your knowledge of your own habits to figure out the note.

616

Answers to Practicing the Skill

1. Hypotheses will vary. Possible hypothesis: President Truman wanted to prevent Communists from gaining control of Western Europe.
2. Answers will vary. Students might indicate that in 1947 President Truman provided military and economic aid to Greece and Turkey to prevent a Communist takeover there.

3. After analyzing the note, the student might surmise that a civics test in multiple-choice format is scheduled for Wednesday and to set aside time the day before for study. The student could call another student in the class to verify.

★★★

The Cold War in Asia

Setting the Scene

Section Focus

In Asia the end of World War II brought peace only to the people of Japan. Under the United States's occupation, the Japanese renounced militarism, disbanded their army, democratized their society, and embarked on a program of economic development that brought them unprecedented prosperity. In contrast, the rest of Asia was caught up in the cold war. As tensions grew, the cold war escalated into a hot war.

Objectives

After studying this section, you should be able to

★ cite the outcome of the United States's occupation of Japan.

★ explain the political situation in China after the war.

★ explain why the United Nations waged a limited war in Korea.

Key Term

defense perimeter

◄ CHINESE COMMUNIST LEADER MAO ZEDONG

At the close of World War II, the aims of the United States in Asia were to restore peace, help Asian peoples to resist foreign rule, and restore Asian trade with the world. The United States felt it had a special commitment to the Philippines, Japan, and China.

On July 4, 1946, the United States carried out its promise of independence for the Philippines. In return for special business rights and the lease of military bases, the United States gave the Philippine nation tariff concessions in American markets and $600 million to repair war damage. Later, when communist-led guerrilla groups revolted against the government, the United States sent money and weapons to put down the rebellion. Despite difficult economic and political problems, the Philippines became an independent, democratic nation.

■ The Occupation of Japan

In July 1945, shortly before the United States dropped atomic bombs on Hiroshima and Nagasaki, the leaders of Great Britain, the United States, and the Soviet Union met in Potsdam, near Berlin. They discussed how they would deal with Germany and Japan after the war.

The agreement regarding Japan provided that Japanese militarists be punished and Japan disarmed, Japanese rule be restricted to

CHAPTER 20 The Cold War: 1945–1952 **617**

LESSON PLAN
SECTION 2, 617–621

FOCUS

Bellringer

Before taking roll, project Section Focus Transparency 20-2 or hand out Section Focus Transparency Activity 20-2. Have students answer the questions. Discuss student responses.

Motivating Activity

Recall with students the events that led to the end of World War II in Japan. *(the dropping of atomic bombs on Hiroshima and Nagasaki)* Then ask them to state how they would deal with postwar Japan. **L1**

Vocabulary Precheck

Write *defense perimeter* on the chalkboard. Have a volunteer skim the section to find the phrase and read it in context. **L1, LEP**

 VIDEODISC

Communism and the Cold War

Side Two, Chapter 4

Title: *Revolution in China*

Subject: Transformation of China into a communist country

Classroom Resources for SECTION 2

Blackline Masters:
- Reproducible Lesson Plan 20-2
- Guided Reading Activity 20-2
- Cooperative Learning Activity 20
- Political Cartoons in American History Activity 22
- Geography in History Activity 20
- Reteaching Activity 20-2
- Section Quiz 20-2

Transparencies:
- Section Focus Transparency 20-2
- Skills Transparency 20

Multimedia:
- Testmaker
- Communism and the Cold War

TEACH

Guided Practice

Chronology Provide the following activity for students:

Place the following events in chronological order.

(6) **a.** MacArthur was removed from command of the UN forces.

(3) **b.** North Korea invaded South Korea.

(2) **c.** Philippines become independent.

(4) **d.** American forces staged landing at Inchon.

(1) **e.** The civil war between the Nationalists and Communists in China began again.

(5) **f.** Chinese troops crossed the border to aid the North Koreans. **L1, L2**

Did You Know?

Matsushita Konoskuke, a Japanese entrepreneur, introduced an electric rice saucepan that revolutionized Japanese cooking. This was the beginning of Panasonic electronics.

Teaching American Portraits

Douglas MacArthur and his father are the only father and son to have both received the Congressional Medal of Honor. This medal is given only to people who perform extraordinary acts of heroism. The army, navy, and air force each has its own medal.

---

their home islands, and the Japanese be reeducated so that a democratic Japanese nation could be formed. American troops would occupy Japan until these aims were accomplished. To carry out this Potsdam Declaration, General Douglas MacArthur was named Supreme Commander of the Allied Powers.

Under MacArthur's leadership, Japan's military was dismantled. A few militarists were tried and convicted of war crimes and hanged. Under American direction, a new constitution provided for elected representative government and woman suffrage. Most other aspects of Japanese culture remained intact. The emperor remained as a symbol of Japan's unity, but he was no longer to be looked upon as a god.

MacArthur encouraged economic opportunity and trade unionism, and he attempted to redistribute large rural tracts to landless Japanese. A reorganized school system taught democratic values. The Allies had planned to make Japan pay reparations for war damages, but MacArthur realized that the Japanese lacked the resources to pay such compensation. Instead, Japan received nearly $2 billion in aid. The Japanese people accepted the reforms. In a treaty signed in San Francisco in 1951, the country gained back its independence. Japan achieved a remarkable recovery, eventually establishing itself as the leading economy of Asia.

■ Communist Triumph in China

Japan's surrender left China a divided nation. The Communists under Mao Zedong [MAU dzuh•DUNG] controlled the north, the Nationalists led by Chiang Kai-shek held the southwest, and Japanese armies occupied the center. The United States helped the Nationalist armies take the land the Japanese had held. In planning for peace, President Roosevelt had insisted to Churchill and Stalin that China be treated as a power. As a result, China gained a permanent seat on the UN Security Council.

Civil War

Since the early 1930s, a civil war between the Nationalist government and the Communists had ravaged China. During World War II, both sides stopped fighting one another and fought the Japanese. In the war against Japan, Mao's Communists grew to

★★★★AMERICAN PORTRAITS

Douglas MacArthur
1880–1964

Douglas MacArthur was born into a military family. His father won the Congressional Medal of Honor during the Civil War and later became the army's top-ranking general. Following in his father's footsteps, MacArthur saw action during World War I and was twice wounded. By 1918 he had risen to the rank of general. When Japan attacked Pearl Harbor, MacArthur was stationed in the Philippines, where he led its defense.

Ordered to retreat in 1942, he pledged: "I shall return." He kept his promise in 1944 by leading the liberation of the islands. After the war, as commander of U.S. occupation forces in Japan, he wrote its constitution. From July 1950 until President Truman fired him in April 1951, MacArthur commanded UN forces in Korea. Some Republican leaders urged MacArthur to run for President, but he declined and retired.

618 UNIT 6 Times of Crisis: 1932–1960

Cooperative Learning Activity

Citing Examples After the class has read the material in Section 2, divide it into three or four groups. Ask students to provide examples of how the policy of containment was at work in the United States's relations with Asia. Have them take turns contributing answers by writing their ideas on a sheet of paper and passing the paper to the other members of their group. When all the members of the group have contributed their ideas, ask one member to share the answers with the rest of the class. **L2**

☞ For additional practice, assign Cooperative Learning Activity 20.

Visualizing History ▲ AMERICANS IN KOREA President Truman ordered American forces to the Korean peninsula in June 1950 after North Korean troops invaded South Korea. In the conflict with North Korea, the United States was directly fighting a communist nation for the first time. *What was the outcome of the conflict?*

be a strong guerrilla force. Through his promise of land reform, as well as military and political pressure, Mao's forces were able to extend their control over much of mainland China. The civil war of the 1930s had greatly weakened the Nationalists.

After Japan surrendered, the conflict between the Communists and the Nationalists again flared. To prevent the extension of communist power, Truman sent General George C. Marshall to China. Marshall was unsuccessful. As the Communists gained strength, Chiang asked Truman to send military aid. Marshall, now secretary of state, advised that it was more important to spend the limited foreign-aid resources of the United States on saving Western Europe from Stalin rather than on saving China from Mao. In addition, a fact finder Truman sent to China reported no attempt to save it from the Communists could succeed because:

> " *The only basis on which national Chinese resistance to Soviet aims can be revitalized is through the presently corrupt, reactionary and inefficient Chinese National government.* "

Having already given Chiang's forces $2 billion in aid, the State Department judged that further help would not save the Nationalists from their own internal weaknesses. By the end of 1949 Mao Zedong's forces had forced Chiang's army off the mainland to Taiwan and a few other small islands.

Aftermath of Communist Victory

Truman's China policy came under bitter political attack. Nationalist supporters accused Truman of "writing off" Chiang and losing China to the Communists. Truman believed, however, that most Americans would not support the massive military intervention needed to save Chiang's government.

The United States recognized the Nationalist government in Taiwan as the government of all of China and blocked attempts by Mao's government to gain a seat in the United Nations. To protest the exclusion of the Chinese communist government, the Soviet Union walked out of the United Nations Security Council and boycotted its proceedings.

CHAPTER 20 The Cold War: 1945–1952 **619**

Visualizing History Because Congress never declared war, the U.S. involvement in the struggle in Korea has never been officially called a "war," but rather a "conflict." **Answer to Caption:** a stalemate in Korea left a divided country

🗂 Assign Political Cartoons in American History Activity 22.

Critical Thinking Activity

Making Judgments The Truman administration's policy toward China was met with criticism. Have the students answer the following questions: Could the United States have saved China from Communist domination? If so, how? If not, why not? (*Students' answers will vary. Some might suggest that the United States should have given the Nationalists more military and economic aid to fight communism. Other students might suggest that the conflict in China was a civil war, and as such was beyond the control of the U.S. government.*) **L2**

Independent Practice

Debating Have students write arguments in favor of or against the following statement: President Truman had no choice but to fire General Douglas MacArthur. **L2**

📁 Assign Guided Reading Activity 20-2.

📁 Assign Workbook Activity 20-2.

◆**Map**
◆**Study** *Using Maps*

Answer: September 15

Map Skills Practice

Where was the prewar boundary between North Korea and South Korea? *(the 38th parallel)*

ABCNEWS INTERACTIVE™

💿 **VIDEODISC**

Communism and the Cold War

‖‖‖‖‖‖‖‖‖‖‖‖‖‖‖

Side Two, Chapter 7
Title: *Korean War*
Subject: Images of the Korean War, including newsreel footage

📁 Project Skills Transparency 20 and have students complete Skills Transparency Activity 20.

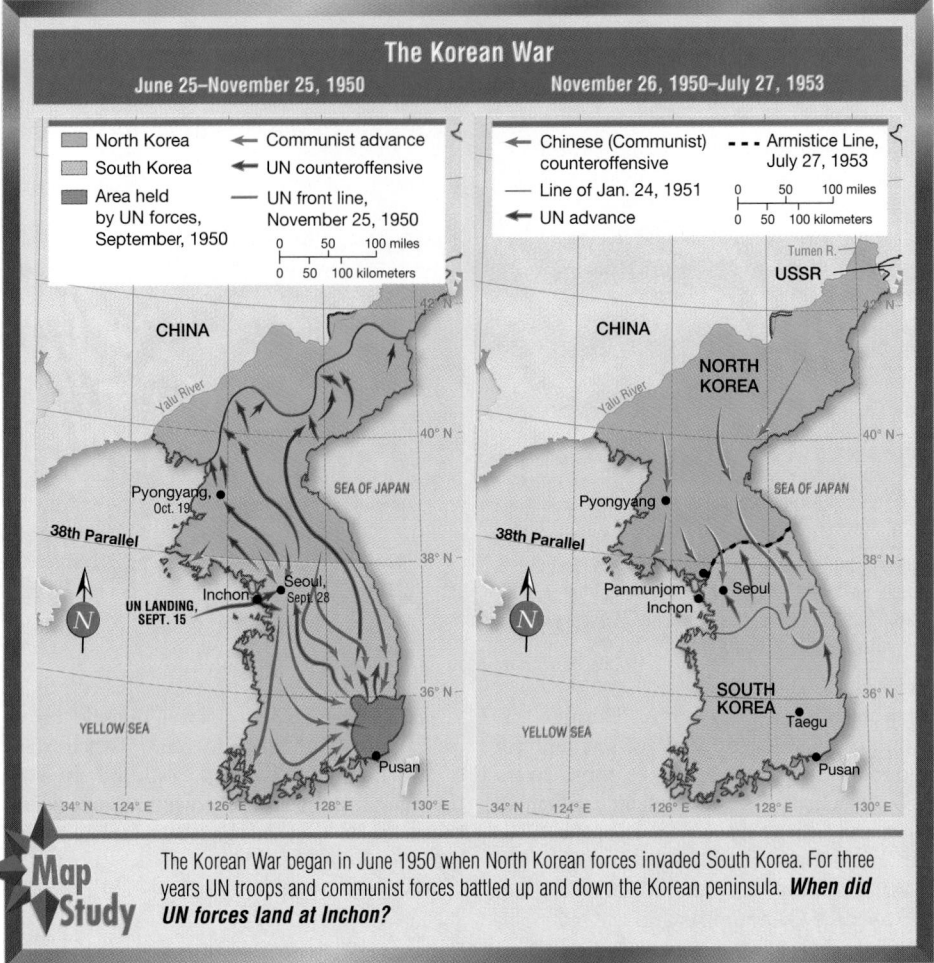

The Korean War
June 25–November 25, 1950   November 26, 1950–July 27, 1953

◆**Map**
◆**Study**

The Korean War began in June 1950 when North Korean forces invaded South Korea. For three years UN troops and communist forces battled up and down the Korean peninsula. *When did UN forces land at Inchon?*

War in Korea

When the Japanese surrendered, Soviet Union troops occupied Korea north of the 38th parallel and set up a communist government. As with other Soviet satellite states, North Korea sealed itself off from other countries of the world. A 1948 UN fact-finding commission was not allowed to travel north of the 38th parallel.

In the south the United States supported the government of Syngman Rhee, who was chosen in UN-supervised elections. In 1948 the UN recognized the South Korean Republic as the government of all Korea.

United States military and diplomatic experts advised that Korea should be viewed as outside the **defense perimeter,** or area that could be protected, of the United States because of the great cost of defending it. The next year the United States withdrew most of its troops from Korea.

On June 25, 1950, North Korean troops invaded South Korea. The Truman administration was not sure whether North Korea was acting by itself or as the agent of the Soviet Union or China. The invasion, however, became a vital test for the UN. Calling an emergency meeting of the Security Council, the United States won a vote to order North Korea to withdraw its troops. On June 27, 1950, as the invasion continued, the Security Council called on all UN members to aid South Korea.

President Truman appointed General MacArthur to command all UN troops in

Sidelight: TV from Coast to Coast

In the six years following World War II, television grew from a limited East Coast industry into a nationwide series of broadcasting stations linked by networks. By 1951 about 100 stations across the country participated in the first transcontinental television broadcast—Truman's opening address to the delegates of the Japanese Peace Treaty Conference in San Francisco. That year more than 6 million television sets could be tuned to news or special events programs, such as the Kefauver hearings on organized crime, or to lighter programming, such as *I Love Lucy* or a variety of quiz shows.

Korea and instructed him to limit the fighting to South Korean territory below the 38th parallel. Truman also ordered United States military forces to Korea without asking Congress to declare war.

During the summer of 1950, North Korean troops pressed UN forces down the Korean peninsula until they had their backs to the water at Pusan (POO•SAHN), a major port in South Korea. In the fall, however, General MacArthur planned a surprise landing midway up the peninsula at the South Korean port of Inchon.

This landing gave the UN troops the offensive, and MacArthur was given authority by the UN Security Council to liberate North Korea and unite it with the South. By November, UN troops were as far north as the Yalu River valley, bordering communist China, when 200,000 Chinese troops crossed the border to aid the North Koreans. MacArthur's troops were once again pushed back.

Truman Fires MacArthur

A major disagreement soon developed between MacArthur and Truman over the

Footnotes to History

A New Korea The division of Korea left South Korea with a weakened economy. Today, however, industrial development has made South Korea's economy one of the world's fastest-growing. Among its most important industries are electronics, textiles, and automobiles.

conduct of the war. MacArthur wanted the United States to bomb China and to help Chiang Kai-shek invade China from Taiwan. Truman, however, did not want to risk war with China. In April 1951, Joseph Martin, Republican leader of the House of Representatives, released a letter he had received in which MacArthur criticized the President. MacArthur's letter was a deliberate challenge to the principle that the civilian power of the President must be superior to that of the military. Truman felt he had no choice but to remove MacArthur from command. He explained, "I could do nothing else and still be President of the United States."

The Senate Foreign Relations and Armed Services Committee opened hearings to determine the circumstances of MacArthur's dismissal. Two months of hearings dispelled much of the controversy. Truman's decision emerged as acceptable to the country.

The Conflict Ends

Years of fighting had produced a stalemate in Korea. Presidential candidate Dwight Eisenhower in 1952 pledged to "go to Korea," to settle hostilities. The war continued until 1953, when a cease-fire was declared. Korea was left a divided country, much as it had been before the war began. The Korean struggle was costly for the United States, which lost more than 54,000 troops. But as a result, many neutral nations drew closer to the United States, and noncommunist ones began to arm for their own defense.

Section 2 ★ Review

Checking for Understanding

1. **Identify** Chiang Kai-shek, Mao Zedong, Douglas MacArthur.

2. **Define** defense perimeter.

3. **Explain** why the United States's China policy failed.

4. **Summarize** the important events that led to the Korean War.

Critical Thinking

5. **Choosing a Position** Explain the two positions represented by Truman and MacArthur on Korea. Which position would you have chosen?

ACTIVITY

6. Create a chart that lists the advantages and disadvantages of civilian control of the military.

ASSESS

Check Understanding
Assign Section 2 Review as homework or an in-class activity.

Evaluate
◉ 🗁 Assign Section Quiz 20-2 or use the Testmaker to create a customized quiz.

Reteach
Ask students to write a paragraph identifying the role of the United States in the 1940s in the Philippines, Japan, China, and Korea.

🗁 Have students complete Reteaching Activity 20-2.

Enrich
Ask students to answer the following question in writing, giving reasons for their response: Was the United States right in giving Japan $2 billion in aid after World War II?

🗁 Assign Geography in History Activity 20.

CLOSE
Ask students: After studying Section 2, do you think that President Truman's foreign policy toward Asia was a sound one? Why or why not?

Answers to SECTION 2 REVIEW

1. Chiang Kai-shek, 618; Mao Zedong, 618; Douglas MacArthur, 618
2. All vocabulary words are defined in the Glossary.
3. backed corrupt Nationalists, ignored Mao's appeal, concentrated resources in Europe
4. Soviet troops set up Communist government in North Korea, UN recognizes South Korea as lawful government of all Korea, United States withdraws troops, North Korea invades South Korea.
5. MacArthur—invade China, cut supply lines, help Chiang; Truman—restrict war to Korea; students' opinions will vary.
6. Comparisons should be objectively stated.

FOCUS

Bellringer

Before taking roll, project Section Focus Transparency 20-3 or hand out Section Focus Transparency Activity 20-3. Have students answer the questions. Discuss student responses.

Motivating Activity

Read the following quotation, which expresses President Truman's views about a free society.

"I think small business, the small farmer, the small corporation are the backbone of any free society, and when there are too many people on relief and too many people at the top who control the wealth of the country, then we must look out." Ask students to paraphrase this statement. **L1**

Vocabulary Precheck

Ask students to define each of the "Key Terms." Have a volunteer consult the dictionary for any unfamiliar words. **L1, LEP**

SECTION 3

★★★★★★★★★★★★★★★★★★★★★★★★★★★★★★★★★★

Cold War America

Setting the Scene

Section Focus

Life in cold war America was marked by a search for security. African Americans and women sought to keep the gains they had made during the war, and many Americans struggled to maintain their standard of living in the face of postwar inflation. For some, security meant exposing the subversives they suspected were operating in society and at high levels of their government. In the face of mounting opposition, Truman attempted to pursue policies that addressed these concerns.

Objectives

After studying this section, you should be able to

★ explain changes in the American labor force after the war.

★ describe the condition of African Americans during the 1940s.

★ evaluate the Truman presidency.

Key Terms

jurisdictional strike, featherbedding, subversive

◀ SENATOR ROBERT TAFT

World War II brought great changes to the nation's economy. War industries solved the unemployment problem of the Depression. In fact, with 16 million people in the United States armed services, there was actually a shortage of workers in industry. The number of African American workers in defense industries more than tripled. Six million women joined the labor force, a rise of nearly 60 percent.

■ Prosperity Continues

When the war ended in 1945, people were fearful of depression. In the past, when government spending for war materials stopped and soldiers returned home to look for jobs, unemployment spread. Even if the

factories kept running, some newly hired African American and women workers now feared that they would be replaced by returning soldiers.

Fears of a depression proved groundless. After a slight drop in business activity, the number of Americans with jobs actually increased. Several factors contributed to the continuing prosperity. As the United States kept feeding not only its own people but millions of people overseas, farm income remained high. During the war Americans, due to rationing and scarcity of consumer goods, had saved $30 billion. Now they spent their savings for postponed purchases. In addition, Congress stimulated postwar business by cutting wartime taxes nearly $6 billion. Instead of depression, consumer demand stimulated a sharp rise in prices, or inflation. Defense spending,

622   UNIT 6 Times of Crisis: 1932–1960

Classroom Resources for SECTION 3

Blackline Masters:
- Reproducible Lesson Plan 20-3
- Guided Reading Activity 20-3
- Critical Thinking Skills Activity 20
- Enrichment Activity 20
- Linking Past and Present Activity 20

- Political Cartoons in American History Activity 20
- Supreme Court Case Study 20
- American Portraits 54
- Workbook Activity 20-3
- Reteaching Activity 20-3
- Section Quiz 20-3

Transparencies:
- Section Focus Transparency 20-3

Multimedia:
- Testmaker
- GTV: A Geographic Perspective on American History

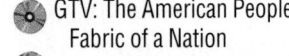

- GTV: The American People: Fabric of a Nation
- Communism and the Cold War
- The Presidents: A Picture History of Our Nation

which had dropped to $15 billion by 1949, escalated to $50 billion by 1953, pouring even more money into the economy. In addition, the Marshall Plan restored markets in Europe for American goods.

In some ways the cold war economy of the 1950s resembled the wartime economy of the 1940s. The government's military spending continued to stimulate industrial production, while a portion of the labor force continued in military service.

Women

Immediately following World War II, soldiers returning from service took the places of many women who were employed in factories. In the automobile plants the proportion of women on assembly lines dropped from 25 percent in 1944 to 7.5 percent in 1946. The head of the Women's Bureau, a federal agency set up to protect women's interests, stated that "women ought to be delighted to give up any job and return to their proper sphere in the kitchen." Federal and state aid to child-care centers in factories was stopped.

Yet continued prosperity created new job opportunities. By 1952 more than 2 million more women were employed than in 1946. The kinds of work available to women were changing. This change was dramatically reflected in the experience of African American women. Between 1940 and 1950 the percentage of African American women employed as domestic servants dropped from 72 to 48 percent. The number of those working as farm laborers fell from 20 percent to 7 percent. At the same time, the percentage hired by factories rose from 7 percent to 18 percent. The rise in female employment did not mean that women had gained economic equality, however. Women in industries earned less than two-thirds as much as men.

■ Gains for African Americans

As a group, African Americans benefited from the postwar economic boom. Many made the transition from farming to manufacturing, from rural areas to cities, from the South to other regions of the country. The number of African American workers in white-collar, skilled, and supervisory jobs nearly tripled, increasing from about 300,000 to nearly 900,000. As opportunities for African Americans opened up fields such as law, nursing, and professional sports, average income—even adjusted for inflation—almost doubled.

▼ 1953 Packard convertible

Visualizing History

▲ Purchasing Power The United States enjoyed an economic boom in the early postwar years. Increasing consumer demand for necessities as well as luxury items fueled inflation, however. *How did job opportunities for women change during the early 1950s?*

CHAPTER 20 The Cold War: 1945–1952 **623**

CHAPTER 20
SECTION 3

TEACH
Guided Practice

Economics Remind students that shortly after government spending for war materials stopped and troops returned home at the end of World War I, there was a depression. Explain that many people feared this would happen again. Have students write an essay explaining the economic factors that contributed to the prosperity of the 1950s.

After the essays are completed, ask students to discuss the reasons for the continued prosperity in the 1950s. **L2**

NATIONAL GEOGRAPHIC SOCIETY

 Videodisc

GTV: A Geographic Perspective on American History

Side 4, Chapter 8
Title: *Shifting Winds*
Subject: Population movements since the 1940s

Visualizing History Point out that farmers in the fall of 1946 stopped sending beef to market to protest the rigidity of government controls.
Answer to Caption: Prosperity brought new opportunities for women.

Cooperative Learning Activity

Identifying Causes and Solutions Divide the class into five groups. Assign each group one of the following topics discussed in Section 3: inflation in the postwar years, the desire of American women for full equality, civil rights for African Americans, resentment of the Taft-Hartley Act by labor unions, the fear of communism at home. The students in each group should discuss the assigned topic, the factors that caused the problem to arise, and the methods used in attempting to solve it. At the end of the discussion, have a representative of each group report the highlights of the group's findings to the rest of the class. **L2**

Independent Practice

Math Ask students to choose a consumer product, such as food, medical care, fuel, housing, or clothing. Have them research the prices of this product from 1946 to the present and plot their findings on a line graph. Students should also plot the national family income for the same years. Have them draw conclusions about the effects of inflation on consumers. A useful source of information is *The Statistical Abstract of the United States*. **L2**

 Assign Guided Reading Activity 20-3.

Did You Know?

Reliable day care facilities were first called for by working women during World War II.

NATIONAL GEOGRAPHIC SOCIETY

 **VIDEODISC**

GTV: The American People: Fabric of a Nation

Side 4, Chapter 3
Title: *Up and Out*
Subject: Movement of African Americans to the North

Changing social attitudes helped these advances. The war against Germany and the cold war both played a part. The horrifying racism of the Nazis helped to make some Americans more sensitive to racism in their own country. They began to realize that not only African Americans, but also Asian Americans, Hispanic Americans, and other minorities had been treated unfairly and denied social and economic opportunities.

During this period, African Americans worked hard to gain civil rights. During the war, the membership of the National Association for the Advancement of Colored People (NAACP) rose from 100,000 to 351,000. The NAACP hired teams of able lawyers to bring a series of lawsuits to the federal courts to end violations of the constitutional rights of African American citizens. Like women, however, African Americans fell short of gaining full equality in the 1940s.

In the North, African Americans often lived in crowded inner-city areas. Wages averaged about 60 percent of those paid to white workers. African American workers were still likely to be "last hired, first fired." In the South old patterns of segregation and racism remained. African American Southerners resented that their children had to attend separate schools that were often ill-equipped and understaffed. They objected to Jim Crow laws that forced them to use segregated facilities. Even worse, most African American Southerners were denied the vote, either by custom or by law. Almost none held political office.

■ Inflation in the Postwar Years

Government spending on wartime military programs and for postwar domestic programs brought prosperity and inflation. During periods of inflation the amount of money in circulation increases and prices rise sharply as the demand for goods exceeds the supply.

Because increased taxes were not sufficient to pay the costs of war, the federal government ran a large deficit during World War II. The national debt rose from $50 million to nearly $270 billion. The government borrowed much of this money from Federal Reserve Banks. Using the federal bonds that the government gave as security, the banks issued new money. As a result, there was four times as much money in circulation in 1945 as there was in 1938.

As inflation drove prices up, the purchasing power of paychecks decreased. When consumers could not buy as much, factories slowed production, returning to a 40-hour week, and employers stopped paying overtime. Workers, losing purchasing power, demanded pay raises and often went on strike. In 1946 there were nearly 5,000 strikes, in which nearly 4.6 million workers took part—a record that is unlikely to be surpassed. Some strikes hit industries basic to the national economy such as steel, transportation, and coal. When railroad workers went on strike, President Truman asked Congress for power to draft them into the army. Fortunately, however, the strike ended before this measure was necessary.

■ The Taft-Hartley Act

Union activities were a major issue in the congressional elections of 1946. The anxiety caused by the strikes in basic industries helped conservative, antilabor candidates. The Republicans showed new vigor as they ran on the slogan, "Had enough?" For the first time in 18 years, they gained control of both the Senate and the House.

An immediate result of this swing toward conservatism was the Taft-Hartley Act, passed over President Truman's veto in 1947. Intended to keep unions from abusing their power, the act outlawed practices such as the closed shop, which forced business owners to hire only union members; **jurisdictional strikes,** which forced businesses to recognize one union instead of another; **featherbedding,** which limited workers' output in order to create more jobs; and high fees charged to workers for joining a union. In addition, unions were forbidden to use their money to support political campaigns.

Critical Thinking Activity

Supporting a Position The Taft-Hartley Act created controversy for the Truman administration. Have the students determine their position on the following statement: The President should have the right to halt economically damaging strikes for a "cooling off" period. Students should provide reasons for their position. *(Students' answers will vary, but their positions need to be substantiated with specific reasons.)* **L2**

 For additional practice, assign Critical Thinking Skills Activity 20.

Linking Past and Present

★★★★★★★★★★★★★★★★★★★★★★★★★★★★★★★★★★★★

Women and Sports

Over the past 50 years, a revolution has taken place in women's sports. Still, resistance to women's sports did not disappear overnight.

Then

Play Days

Even in the 1950s American physical educators disparaged women's sports. Arguing that organized, competitive sports were "unfeminine" and a "male domain," they tried to channel female athletes' energy into "Play Days" and other forms of mild exercise. Opportunities for females in interscholastic and intercollegiate sports, in which schools compete against one another, were limited. Males outnumbered females in interscholastic competition by as much as 20 to 1. At the intercollegiate level, the ratio approached 10 to 1.

► BABE DIDRICKSON ZAHARIAS

Now

Changing Attitudes

The rise in the level of women's sports participation is undeniable evidence of strong and dramatic change. Part of the change is due to new attitudes. Campaigns on behalf of female athletics by Billie Jean King, Wilma Rudolph, and many others helped shatter the myth that women and competitive sports did not mix. By 1990, nearly 2 million females were taking part in interscholastic sports participation—an increase of 600 percent in a 20-year span—and nearly 100,000 on the intercollegiate level.

★★★★★★★★★★★★★★★★★★★★★★★★★★★★★★★★★★★★

CHAPTER 20
SECTION 3

Linking Past and Present

Ask students to interview adults in their families, such as parents and grandparents, to find out what opportunities in athletics high school girls had when the adults were in high school. Have students compare those opportunities with the ones high-school girls have today.

📁 For additional practice, assign Linking Past and Present Activity 20.

📁 Assign American Portrait 54: Mildred Ella Didrikson Zaharias.

Did You Know?

Despite the Taft-Hartley Act, union membership rose from 14.3 million persons (which was 35.5 percent of the labor force) in 1945 to more than 18 million persons by 1955 (which was 33.2 percent of the labor force).

NATIONAL GEOGRAPHIC SOCIETY

💿 CD-ROM

The Presidents: A Picture History of Our Nation

Have students view "Harry S Truman" and use the information to write a brief biography to include in their portfolios.

The Taft-Hartley Act was a very controversial measure. Its supporters claimed the law held irresponsible unions in check the way the Wagner Act of 1935 restrained antiunion activities of employers. Labor leaders called the act a "slave labor" law. They claimed it erased many of the gains that unions had made since 1933. In addition, they deeply resented that union leaders had to swear they were not members of the Communist party.

■ Election of 1948

As the presidential election of 1948 drew near, the Democratic party was divided. Southern Democrats objected to Truman's civil rights program, which included proposals to end racial, religious, and ethnic discrimination, to abolish immigration quotas, and to integrate the armed forces.

The Candidates

Many white Southerners left the Democratic party to form the "Dixiecrat" party, which nominated South Carolina Governor Strom Thurmond for President. Other Democrats thought Truman was taking too hard a line against the Soviet Union. They supported the Progressive party ticket led by former Vice President Henry Wallace. Truman appeared certain to lose the election; he had lost the support of both the right wing and the left wing of his party. The Democrats renominated Truman only after party leaders failed to persuade General Eisenhower to accept the nomination.

The Republicans united behind their candidate for President, Governor Thomas E. Dewey of New York. Dewey was so confident that he would win that he avoided discussing issues and simply called on Americans to join him in building unity.

CHAPTER 20 The Cold War: 1945–1952   **625**

Cultural Perspectives

James Baldwin A vivid description of African American life in the postwar years was created by James Baldwin in his novel *Go Tell It on the Mountain*. The novel describes a day in the lives of members of a church in Harlem, and, through flashbacks, their ancestors. Baldwin was recognized as a leading African American novelist noted for his powerful treatment of bigotry and oppression in American society.

Did You Know?

In 1947 Jackie Robinson signed with the Brooklyn Dodgers to become the first African American baseball player in the major leagues. He was named to the Baseball Hall of Fame for his hitting, fielding, and leadership. He continued playing through the 1956 season. Off the field Robinson fought for civil rights. He died in 1972.

Map Study *Using Maps*

Answer: the South

Map Skills Practice

Why did Truman win? *(He attacked the "do-nothing" Congress. He made a whistle-stop campaign and made more than 350 speeches.)*

📁 Assign Political Cartoons in American History Activity 20.

The Campaign

Far behind in the public-opinion polls, President Truman pursued an aggressive campaign from the beginning. First, he called the Republican Congress back into special session and asked them to carry out the promises of the Republican party platform by passing civil rights and other progressive legislation. When they failed to act, Truman had his campaign theme: The "do-nothing, good for nothing" Republican 80th Congress. Setting out on a "whistle stop" tour of the country by train, Truman covered 30,000 miles, giving some 350 speeches along the way.

Right up to Election Day, the pollsters predicted a Republican victory. But Truman won 2 million more votes than Dewey and piled up a 303-to-189 margin in the electoral college. Truman had held together the New Deal coalition. He won labor support for his veto of the Taft-Hartley Act. He won support from African American voters for his civil rights proposals. He won the farmers' vote for his support of high farm price supports. Not only did Truman defeat Dewey, but the Democrats regained their majority in Congress.

The Fair Deal

In his Inaugural Address in January 1949, Truman called for a Fair Deal, a return to and expansion of Roosevelt's New Deal policies. President Truman asked for slum clearance, federal subsidies for public schools, government-backed medical insurance, aid to farmers, and higher minimum wages. Although the Democrats held a majority, the new Congress was still influenced by an alliance of Republicans and conservative Southern Democrats. Together they blocked most of Truman's proposals to Congress.

In 1949 postwar prosperity slipped into a recession. Unemployment reached 7 percent of the labor force. The recession lasted only a few months, however. A tax cut passed in 1948 took effect, making more money available. The New Deal's built-in stabilizers such as price supports for agriculture and Social Security benefits helped to lessen the effect of the economic downturn. Beginning in 1950, the Korean War changed the economic picture sharply. Rearmament now competed with the demand for consumer goods. The war also fueled anticommunist sentiment at home.

▲ TRUMAN DISPLAYS HEADLINE THAT WRONGLY PROJECTED DEWEY AS THE WINNER

The Election of 1948

Popular vote:	Electoral vote:
Truman	24,105,812	303
Dewey	21,970,065	189
Thurmond	1,169,063	39

0 200 400 miles
0 200 400 kilometers

Map Study

The Democratic party split in 1948. *From which region did Thurmond receive his strongest support?*

Sidelight: Fighting Inflation

To combat inflation President Truman wanted to continue wartime controls on wages, prices, and rents. Business leaders objected, stating that such controls prevented them from putting more factories into full production. They argued that once consumer demand was met prices would stabilize. Under these circumstances there was little the Truman administration could do. During 1946 wholesale prices on 28 basic commodities rose by 25 percent. Prices continued to rise for the next 2 years.

■ Fear of Communists

The cold war and the Korean War heightened fear of communism in the United States. A communist spy ring, which had been sending atomic secrets to the Soviet Union, was uncovered in Canada. To Americans, this explained the Soviets' success in developing an atomic bomb so early. Americans began to suspect that there might be other communist sympathizers and spies in the government, universities, press, and the arts—all working to undermine American democracy. In a period of international tensions, national insecurity led to a search for scapegoats.

Constitutional Rights

The question arose: Should the rights of Communists be protected by the Constitution? In 1949, 11 members of the Communist party in the United States were convicted of conspiracy. The courts held that since the Communist party was organized to overthrow the United States government by force, its members were not entitled to protection by the free speech rights of the First Amendment. Although there were relatively very few Communist party members in the United States, the suspected communist conspiracy led to extensive precautions. Many people were forced to take loyalty oaths before being hired for jobs. Government officials were subjected to security checks.

Loyalty Oaths

During the postwar period, a tendency grew among many Americans to mistake criticism of American institutions for disloyalty. As Judge Harold Medina told the jury that convicted the 11 Communists of conspiracy, taking away the right to criticize does not make a country stronger. Instead, allowing abuses of rights to go unchecked makes it weaker. In several rulings during this period, however, the Supreme Court found state loyalty oaths to be constitutional. The Court noted that the states had a constitutional right to assurance that an employee was not engaged in subversive activity.

 **Visualizing History**

▲ **CHARGES OF SUBVERSION** In the early 1950s, Senator Joseph R. McCarthy (left) claimed that Communists had infiltrated educational institutions and high levels of government. *What cold war events stirred McCarthy and others?*

Subversives

The "loss" of China to the Communists and the stalemated Korean War helped to create this mood in the United States that was much like the Red Scare in the years following World War I. Critics of Truman accused the President of having lost China, alleging that his close advisers were Communists or communist tools. Senator Robert A. Taft, Republican leader in the Senate, claimed that the State Department was "riddled" with **subversives,** or individuals attempting to overthrow the government. Taft said that State Department officials had:

> ❝ . . . surrendered to every demand of the Soviet Union and promoted, at every opportunity, the communist cause in China. ❞

In 1948 the House Committee on Un-American Activities heard testimony from Whittaker Chambers, a magazine editor. Chambers admitted that he had been a communist spy in the 1930s and said that he had received secret documents from Alger Hiss, then a high-ranking State Department official. At first, few people believed Chambers's story. However, Richard M. Nixon, a

CHAPTER 20 The Cold War: 1945–1952 **627**

ASSESS

Check Understanding

Assign Section 3 Review as homework or an in-class activity.

Evaluate

🔘 🗁 Assign Section Quiz 20-3 or use the Testmaker to create a customized quiz.

Reteach

Have students write an essay describing the changes that occurred in the United States labor force during the 1940s.

🗁 Have students complete Reteaching Activity 20-3.

🗁 Assign Workbook Activity 20-3.

Enrich

🗁 Have students complete Enrichment Activity 20.

CLOSE

Discuss with students what they think were three of the greatest accomplishments and three of the most serious problems of the Truman administration.

---

young representative from California, pressed the case forward. Finally, Chambers produced several rolls of microfilm of secret documents he claimed to have received from Hiss. Hiss denied these charges. Though not convicted of spying, Hiss was found guilty of lying under oath.

McCarthyism

Increased fears of communist subversion were fertile ground for more reckless voices. At a Lincoln's Day speech in February 1950, Senator Joseph R. McCarthy of Wisconsin accused the Democratic party of "twenty years of treason." McCarthy charged that Roosevelt had deliberately sacrificed the navy at Pearl Harbor and had "sold out" to the Soviet Union at Yalta. In addition, McCarthy claimed to have a list of "card-carrying Communists" in the State Department.

While McCarthy never produced the list, nor a shred of evidence to support his charges, he ruined the careers of many government officials. A growing atmosphere of hysteria inspired other "witch-hunts." Private groups used the communist label to drive liberal professors out of colleges. They made sure books they believed to be subversive were removed from schools. They had many broadcasters, writers, and entertainers barred from television and kept many actors from working on the stage and in films.

Years later a Senate committee determined that McCarthy's accusations and investigations had been groundless. The use of indiscriminate, unfounded political accusations to destroy or assassinate the character of one's opponent came, in time, to be known as McCarthyism.

■ Truman's Legacy

In 1952 President Truman announced that he would not run for reelection. By the time Truman left office, he had become unpopular. The successful Soviet atomic bomb explosion, the defeat of the Nationalists in China, and the problems with carrying out the war in Korea, all contributed to charges that Truman was "soft on communism." Other Americans thought his loyalty program had hurt innocent people.

Instances of corruption in high places were also discovered—some of the President's closest aides had received valuable gifts in return for political favors. Although Truman was not personally involved, the "Truman scandals" gave the Republicans a ready-made issue for the 1952 elections.

The problems Truman faced were new and complex. Congress was often suspicious or hostile, yet Truman got many of his programs enacted. Americans were tired of foreign involvements, yet he managed to keep the nation from retreating into isolationism. Truman's reputation as leader rose after he left the White House. Most of the Fair Deal measures he called for eventually became law. His policy of "containment" was continued by other Presidents. He set the United States on a course that included an unwavering defense of democracy everywhere.

Section 3 ★ Review

Checking for Understanding

1. **Identify** Taft-Hartley Act, Joseph McCarthy.
2. **Define** jurisdictional strike, featherbedding, subversive.
3. **List** reasons why economic growth continued after World War II.
4. **Discuss** gains made by African Americans in their struggle for equality.

Critical Thinking

5. **Making Comparisons** Compare gains made by African Americans in their struggle for equality with the limitations on their achievements.

ACTIVITY

6. Draw a political cartoon that focuses on the effect Senator Joseph McCarthy had on the American people.

628

Answers to SECTION 3 REVIEW

1. Taft-Hartley Act, 625; Alger Hiss, 628; Joseph McCarthy, 628
2. All vocabulary words are defined in the Glossary.
3. Farm income increased; wartime savings provided buying power; military spending increased; European markets restored through Marshall Plan, employment.
4. more and varied jobs, changing attitudes toward enhanced self-awareness, African American organizations
5. African Americans often lived in crowded inner-city areas; wages averaged about 60 percent of those of white workers; African Americans in the South were forced to use segregated facilities and often denied the right to vote.
6. Cartoons should clearly depict point of view.

▲ FLORIDA FAMILY MOVING NORTH

African American Migration

African American migration from the rural South to Northern and Western cities between 1910 and 1950 was one of the largest migrations in American history. African Americans migrated in search of greater economic opportunity and a better life than the drought, boll weevils, racism, and poverty they were accustomed to in the South. Much of the African American migration took place during the two world wars.

During World War I, industrial agents traveled the South promising jobs with high wages and free transportation to the North. Soon the African American population of cities such as Chicago, Cleveland, and Detroit swelled. Detroit alone saw an increase of over 600 percent.

In the 1940s rural Southern African Americans streamed into Northern and Western cities for two main reasons. First, around 1940 cotton farming became mechanized. Far fewer workers were needed, and many African Americans

became jobless. Second, many saw great opportunity in wartime industries.

Although social and economic gains in the cities were limited by racial prejudice, African Americans acquired a political voice. Their migration forever changed the face of American politics and society.

Making the Geography Connection

1. Where did African Americans migrate to during the period from 1910 to 1950?

2. Why did they migrate from the rural South?

ACTIVITY

3. Prepare a chart of population in 1970, 1980, and 1990 for several cities in your state. Write a paragraph that accounts for the population trends.

629

Answers to Making the Connections

1. to northern and western cities
2. in search of greater economic opportunity and a better life

3. Explanations should be based on valid inferences.

GLENCOE
TECHNOLOGY

VIDEODISC

Use the MindJogger Videoquiz to review students' knowledge.

MindJogger Videoquiz

Chapter 20
Disc 3, Side A

 Available in VHS.

Using Vocabulary
Paragraphs will vary but should include all the vocabulary terms.

Reviewing Facts
1. fear for western border, appeal to poor, anti-government; control or suppress elections
2. promised to abolish poverty, privilege, private property; guaranteed productive work
3. Negative: would bankrupt U.S. and weaken UN; would provoke Soviet Union. Positive: cost of not acting; inability of UN to deal with problems; Russian expansionist ambitions
4. massive economic aid, tariff concessions, establishment of democratic governments, education, agrarian reform
5. Did not stop Mao, insufficient aid to Nationalists; limited Korean war
6. Soviet occupation of North Korea; U.S. recognized South Korea; withdrew troops in 1949; Soviets trained, equipped North Korean army to attack South Korea

Using Vocabulary

Use the following vocabulary terms to write a paragraph describing the Soviet establishment of an iron curtain and the development of the cold war.

communism	satellite nation
containment	subversive
purge	buffer

Reviewing Facts

1. **Discuss** how and why the Soviets created a buffer of satellite states.

2. **Explain** why communism appealed to people in certain parts of the world.

3. **Summarize** arguments for and against containment and the Truman Doctrine.

4. **Cite** actions taken in the Philippines and Japan after World War II that led to successful economic recovery.

5. **Examine** the reasons for the charge that Truman was soft on communism.

6. **Detail** events leading to war in Korea.

7. **List** the advances made by African Americans.

8. **Explain** how the Truman agenda for prosperity at home and abroad enabled him to win in 1948.

Understanding Concepts

Political and Economic Power

1. Explain how communism concentrates economic power in the hands of those who hold political power.

2. How did the United States use its position as the strongest and wealthiest nation in the world to shape economic recovery in Europe?

Leadership

3. Analyze the qualities that made President Truman an effective leader.

4. Compare the goals and leadership styles of Stalin and Mao Zedong.

Critical Thinking

1. **Applying Ideas** What does the term "cold war" mean and how does it apply to this era?

2. **Applying Principles** How was the Truman Doctrine applied in assisting Greece, by the Marshall Plan, and in creating NATO?

3. **Testing Conclusions** According to some experts, the United States failed to save China because of its loyalty to the Nationalists and its ignorance of China's true situation. Test this theory using information from the text.

4. **Making Comparisons** Write a report comparing the purposes and provisions of the Monroe Doctrine and the Truman Doctrine. Address such questions as: What were the foreign policy objectives that the United States tried to accomplish in each case? What commitment of resources was required to support each doctrine? Explain what the differences indicate about fundamental change in foreign policy between the 1820s and the 1940s.

5. **Analyzing Political Cartoons** Study the political cartoon on this page and answer the questions that follow.

   a. Whom do the individuals in the cartoon represent?

   b. What is the cartoonist saying about Truman's power?

---

7. more upper-level jobs, increased membership of NAACP, equal treatment in armed services
8. civil rights proposals—the African American vote; farmers' subsidies—farm vote; veto Taft-Hartley—labor vote

Understanding Concepts

1. Society, as represented by state, controls means of production. State controlled by those with political power.
2. Leadership role UN; aid Greece, Turkey, prevent Communist takeover; Marshall Plan; started NATO to protect against Soviet expansion
3. hard-working, willing to act, take responsibility
4. Both determined to establish communist governments; use force; persuasive and powerful

History and Geography

Postwar Europe

Study the map on page 613 and answer the questions that follow.

1. **Location** What countries occupied Germany?
2. **Location** What cities were under joint occupation?
3. **Movement** Into what city did air corridors flow? What was the purpose of the corridors?
4. **Region** Which countries were most susceptible to Soviet expansion? Explain.

 **Interdisciplinary Activity: Debate**

Working in groups of three, conduct a debate about the possible alternatives of United States foreign policy in Europe after World War II. One member should propose and support pulling troops out of Europe to lessen the Soviets' perceived need for a buffer of satellites. Another should support the contention that the Soviets wanted to conquer other nations as well as secure their own borders, and only a heavy military presence in Europe would contain them. The third member should decide which position was best supported and write an opinion that examines the best points of each argument. All members should be prepared to argue either position in front of the class if called on by the teacher.

Practicing Skills

Hypothesizing

Study the graphs on the Marshall Plan and European recovery on this page, then read each of the following hypotheses. Indicate whether each hypothesis is correct, incorrect, or not answerable from the information provided on the graph.

1. A large majority of the Plan's funds went to Eastern European nations.
2. Agricultural production grew at a faster rate than industrial production.

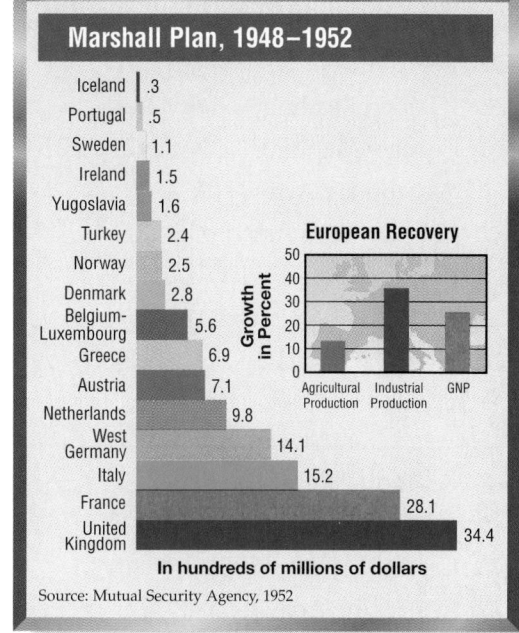

Marshall Plan, 1948–1952

	In hundreds of millions of dollars
Iceland	.3
Portugal	.5
Sweden	1.1
Ireland	1.5
Yugoslavia	1.6
Turkey	2.4
Norway	2.5
Denmark	2.8
Belgium-Luxembourg	5.6
Greece	6.9
Austria	7.1
Netherlands	9.8
West Germany	14.1
Italy	15.2
France	28.1
United Kingdom	34.4

European Recovery

Growth in Percent — Agricultural Production, Industrial Production, GNP

Source: Mutual Security Agency, 1952

3. Construction became the strongest European industry after the war.
4. Industrial production grew at its fastest rate in Western Europe.

Writing ABOUT History

Using Your Journal

Compare the threat of communism after World War II with the threat of communism after World War I.

REVIEW ★ CHAPTER 20

History and Geography

1. Britain, France, the United States, Soviet Union
2. Berlin, Vienna
3. Berlin; to airlift supplies to Berlin
4. the Eastern European countries because they bordered the Soviet Union

Cooperative Learning

Call on groups to debate their positions in front of the class. Compare the opinions of the class with the ones of individual group members.

Practicing Skills

1. incorrect
2. incorrect
3. not answerable
4. not answerable

Writing ABOUT History

Using Your Journal

Responses will vary but should reflect the very different positions of the Soviet Union after each war.

? Chapter Bonus Test Question

Ask: In which location were African Americans most likely to establish a political power base during this era? *(industrial cities in the North)*

Critical Thinking

1. cold war—war of nerves, not shooting war; atmosphere of hostility
2. help free people resist aggressors, Greek civil war; economic aid to strengthen free societies; cooperation in agreeing to coordinate recovery efforts; eliminate hunger, poverty, chaos; collective security against threat of Communist expansion
3. underestimated Mao's strength and appeal to peasants; Chiang government corrupt, out of tune with needs of majority; no real commitment to China
4. Answers should indicate the changes in foreign policy between the 1820s and 1940s.
5. a. President Truman and Congress
   b. that he is overextending powers

Daily Lesson Objectives	Teacher Classroom Resources	Multimedia
SECTION 1 **The Eisenhower Years** **1 Day** pp. 634–637 1. Describe President Eisenhower's style of leadership. 2. Explain how Senator Joseph McCarthy's influence came to an end.	Reproducible Lesson Plan 21-1 *Guided Reading Activity 21-1 Concept Mapping Activities 21-A, 21-B *Vocabulary Activity 21 Chapter Skills Activity 16 Writer's Guidebook Lessons 2-6 Reteaching Activity 21-1 *Section Quiz 21-1	Section Focus Transparency 21-1 Chapter Concepts Transparencies 21-A, 21-B Vocabulary PuzzleMaker MindJogger Videoquiz GTV: The American People: Fabric of a Nation Communism and the Cold War The Presidents: A Picture History of Our Nation
SECTION 2 **The Straight Road** **1 Day** pp. 639–642 1. Explain Eisenhower's economic policies. 2. Discuss the plight of the small farmer in the 1950s.	Reproducible Lesson Plan 21-2 *Guided Reading Activity 21-2 Critical Thinking Skills Activity 21 Reteaching Activity 21-2 *Section Quiz 21-2	Section Focus Transparency 21-2 Testmaker Powers of the President Economics in Action
SECTION 3 **An Affluent Society** **1 Day** pp. 643–648 1. Describe the effect of affluence on American life. 2. Give examples of advances in medical technology.	Reproducible Lesson Plan 21-3 *Guided Reading Activity 21-3 Linking Past and Present Activity 21 American Portrait 62 Primary and Secondary Source Readings, p. 56 Reteaching Activity 21-3 *Section Quiz 21-3	Section Focus Transparency 21-3 Skills Transparency 21 GTV: A Geographic Perspective on American History Communism and the Cold War American Music: Cultural Traditions
SECTION 4 **Foreign Policy** **1 Day** pp. 650–657 1. Discuss Eisenhower's approach to foreign policy and the Eisenhower Doctrine. 2. Describe how the fear of nuclear war affected the cold war.	Reproducible Lesson Plan 21-4 *Guided Reading Activity 21-4 Cooperative Learning Activity 21 Chapter Map Activity 21 Geography in History Activity 21 Workbook Activity 21-4 Reteaching Activity 21-4 *Section Quiz 21-4	Section Focus Transparency 21-4 Map Transparency 21 Testmaker Communism and the Cold War Powers of the Congress
CHAPTER REVIEW AND EVALUATION **1 Day**	Chapter 21 Test, Forms A and B Spanish Chapter 21 Summary Performance Assessment Activity 21	MindJogger Videoquiz Student Self-Test & Review Software *Chapter 21 Audiocassette Activity and Test

*Also available in Spanish

0:00   **OUT OF TIME?** If time does not permit teaching the entire chapter, use the Chapter 21 Summary on pages 662–663 and the Chapter 21 audiocassette (English and Spanish) to point out the main ideas of the chapter.

A complete, 1-page lesson plan is provided for each section in the *Reproducible Lesson Plan* booklet.

Key to Ability Levels

Teaching strategies have been coded for varying learning styles and abilities.

L1 Basic activities for all students

L2 Average activities for average to above-average students

L3 Challenging activities for above-average students

LEP Limited English Proficiency activities

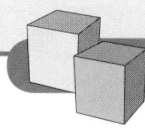

Block Schedule

Block scheduling differs from traditional class scheduling in the amount of time allotted to each period. The extended time frame provided by block scheduling affords you the opportunity to implement a greater number of research-oriented and activity-intense projects to motivate and involve your students. Activities that are particularly suited to use within the block scheduling framework are identified throughout this unit by the following designation:

✓ Performance Assessment Activity

Scientific Breakthroughs Divide students into small groups and ask each to research scientific developments during the 1950s in one of the following fields: medicine, communications, computers, or aviation and space science. Students who research medicine might focus on the work of Dr. Jonas Salk. Point out that in 1952 a record number of 58,000 cases of polio was reported in the United States. Dr. Salk finally developed an effective vaccine against polio and in doing so became the medical hero of the 1950s. Have each group create a poster to highlight achievements in the field it researched. Invite groups to share their posters with the class.

POSSIBLE RUBRIC FEATURES
- Content Information
- Organization
- Visual Communication Skills
- Collaborative Skills
- Creativity
- Research

☞ For additional practice, use Performance Assessment Strategies and Activities.

TEACHER'S CORNER

NATIONAL GEOGRAPHIC SOCIETY

NATIONAL GEOGRAPHIC SOCIETY PRODUCTS AVAILABLE FROM GLENCOE

To order the following products for use with this chapter, contact your local Glencoe sales representative or call Glencoe at 1-800-334-7344:

- *The Presidents: A Picture History of Our Nation* (CD-ROM)
- *GTV: A Geographic Perspective on American History* (Videodisc)
- *GTV: The American People: Fabric of a Nation* (Videodisc)

ADDITIONAL NATIONAL GEOGRAPHIC SOCIETY PRODUCTS

To order the following products for use with this chapter, call National Geographic Society at 1-800-368-2728:

- *Decades of History: The 20th Century—The Middle Years* (Filmstrip)
- *The United States as a World Power: From the 1890s to the 1970s* (Filmstrip)
- *1945–1989: The Cold War* (Video)
- *The American Presidency* (Filmstrip)

BEGINNING THE CHAPTER

Recording Journal Notes

To help students get started, remind them of the various postwar crises of the Truman administration—the Berlin blockade and airlift, the Korean War, and the domestic anti-communist fervor.

Linking Across TIME

Point out that the 1950s was a period of relative tranquility after decades of crisis. As they faced the second half of the twentieth century, Americans saw their country as the most properous and powerful nation in the world. Yet they remained uneasy, not sure that the peace and prosperity would last.

Search for Stability
1952–1960

▼ **1957 CHEVROLET**

Setting the Scene

Focus

A war hero, Dwight D. Eisenhower became one of the most popular Presidents of modern times. His domestic and foreign policies were stable and consistent. At home, the nation was generally prosperous. In foreign policy he continued Truman's efforts at containment. The cold war expanded into the Middle East, Africa, and Latin America. Covert operations increased, and American troops were sent into Lebanon.

Concepts to Understand

★ Why the United States's **international leadership** led to the use of covert operations in other countries

★ How **economic growth** stimulated the economy during the 1950s

Read to Discover . . .

★ how President Eisenhower viewed his role as President.

★ how the lives of most Americans improved following World War II.

Journal Notes

As you read the chapter, record in your journal the efforts of the United States to contain the spread of communism.

CULTURAL		
• **1952** *Ralph Ellison publishes Invisible Man*	• **1955** *Jonas Salk develops vaccine to prevent polio*	
1950	**1953**	
• **1950** *McCarthy charges communist influence in government*	• **1953** *Truce in the Korean War reached*	
POLITICAL • **1952** *Eisenhower elected President*	• **1954** *Geneva Conference divides Vietnam*	

✚ EXTRA CREDIT PROJECT

Demographics In the 1950s many women married young and were expected to stay at home and care for their children or work at jobs reserved for women. Ask interested students to gather statistical information about women's roles in the years from 1950 to 1960: What was the average age for marriage? How many children did the average woman have? What percentage of women worked outside the home? What jobs did these women hold? Encourage students to share their findings with the class. **L2**

Snack Bar
by Isabel Bishop, 1954

The 1950s was an era of social change for many Americans. Artist Isabel Bishop captures the lonely aspects of urban life and the nature of the fast-food culture.

History **ART**

◀ BASEBALL PLAYER JACKIE ROBINSON

● **1957** *The musical* West Side Story *premieres in New York*

● **1960** *There are more than 45 million television sets in American homes*

1956	1959

● **1955** *Formation of the AFL-CIO*
● **1956** *Suez crisis erupts*

● **1959** *Castro comes to power in Cuba*
● **1960** *Soviets shoot down a United States U-2 surveillance plane*

✔ Performance Assessment

Refer to the Performance Assessment Activity in the Planning Guide on page 632b. When the students have finished their posters about scientific developments in the 1950s, have them present the posters to the class. Allow time for class discussion and feedback.

▭ Use Performance Assessment Activity 21 as an additional assessment technique.

CHAPTER 21 CONCEPTS

Concept Mapping Activity

On the chalkboard, reproduce the following generalization and concepts map, and have students copy it in their notebooks.

The nation searches for economic and political stability in a world of crisis.

International Leadership	Economic Growth

▭ To reinforce the two chapter concepts, use Concept Mapping Activities 21-A and 21-B.

 ▭ Use Chapter Concepts Transparencies 21-A, 21-B.

History **ART**

In *Snack Bar* Isabel Bishop captures the lonely aspects of urban life and the nature of our fast-food culture. Bishop was one of many artists employed by federal art projects during the Great Depression.

 NATIONAL GEOGRAPHIC SOCIETY

VIDEODISC

GTV: The American People: Fabric of a Nation

Side 4, Chapter 4
Title: *Greener Pastures*
Subject: Development and impact of suburbs

633

FOCUS

Bellringer

Before taking roll, project Section Focus Transparency 21-1 or hand out Section Focus Transparency Activity 21-1. Discuss student responses.

Motivating Activity

Ask students what kind of President they think the American people wanted in the early 1950s. *(Students might indicate that people wanted someone who would make the country stable and make them feel secure.)* As the students read this section, tell them to focus on the type of leadership the American people received from President Eisenhower. **L1**

Vocabulary Precheck

Write *presidential succession* on the chalkboard. Have a volunteer skim the section to find the term and read it in context. **L1, LEP**

Use the Vocabulary PuzzleMaker Software to create a crossword puzzle. **L1**

Assign Vocabulary Activity 21.

SECTION 1

★★★

The Eisenhower Years

Setting the Scene

Section Focus

As the Truman presidency ended, the fear of communism preoccupied the nation. In Asia the United States was engaged in a long and frustrating war with the Communists. In other parts of the world, a dangerous cold war between communism and American interests intensified. The nation was ready for new leadership to guide it through these troubling times.

◄ EISENHOWER CAMPAIGN BUTTON

Objectives

After studying this section, you should be able to

★ describe President Eisenhower's style of leadership.

★ explain how Senator Joseph McCarthy's influence came to an end.

Key Term

presidential succession

After 7 years of the Truman administration and 20 years of Democratic leadership, the Republicans hoped that 1952 would be their year. They knew Americans were worried about the continuing war in Korea and the tense cold war. Americans were also concerned with the charges of communist infiltration in the government. President Truman's reputation was damaged by news reports that some of his officials had accepted bribes. These issues gave the Republicans their rallying cry for the election. They ran against "Korea, communism, and corruption."

■ The Election of 1952

As their candidate, the Republicans picked one of the most popular war heroes, Dwight D. Eisenhower.

When asked to run for President in 1948, Eisenhower refused. By 1952, however, he became concerned that isolationists might regain the White House and agreed to run. He won the Republican nomination after a hotly contested race with Senator Robert A. Taft of Ohio. As his running mate, Eisenhower chose Richard M. Nixon, a 39-year-old senator from California who had made his reputation pursuing alleged Communists in government.

"I Like Ike"

The Republicans adopted the slogan "It's time for a change!" Eisenhower, known as "Ike," promised to end the war in Korea and took a hard line against corruption. "I like Ike" became the Republican rallying cry.

Eisenhower's promise to keep his administration clean was soon regarded with skepticism. Charges were disclosed that Richard

---

Classroom Resources for SECTION 1

Blackline Masters:
- Reproducible Lesson Plan 21-1
- Guided Reading Activity 21-1
- Vocabulary Activity 21

- Chapter Skills Activity 16
- Writer's Guidebook Lessons 2-6
- Workbook Activity 21-1
- Reteaching Activity 21-1
- Section Quiz 21-1

Transparencies:
- Section Focus Transparency 21-1

Multimedia:
- Testmaker
- Vocabulary PuzzleMaker

- MindJogger Videoquiz
- GTV: The American People: Fabric of a Nation
- Communism and the Cold War
- The Presidents: A Picture History of Our Nation

Nixon had received gifts from California businesspeople totaling $18,000 while he was a senator. For a while, it looked as though Nixon might be dropped from the ticket. But in a nationwide speech broadcast on radio and television, he insisted the funds had been used for legitimate political purposes. He did admit that his family had kept one gift, a cocker spaniel puppy named "Checkers." The "Checkers speech" saved Nixon, who remained on the Republican ticket.

Eisenhower Defeats Stevenson

The Democrats nominated Adlai Stevenson, governor of Illinois. Stevenson was a thoughtful and eloquent liberal, but his campaign was burdened by the need to defend the actions of the Truman administration.

It is doubtful that Stevenson ever had a chance to win against the popular Eisenhower. If he did, he lost it two weeks before Election Day, when Eisenhower promised to make a trip to Korea if elected. The election was a landslide for Eisenhower. He received in excess of 6 million popular votes more than Stevenson and carried the electoral college by 442 to 89 votes. The Republicans also gained an eight-seat majority in the House. The Senate was evenly divided between Democrats and Republicans.

■ A New Style of Leadership

Although Eisenhower was a career soldier, he did not run the White House like an officer commanding an army. Instead, he acted as the chief administrator or leader of the White House team.

Hidden-Hand Presidency

Under Eisenhower the cabinet assumed new importance and acted as a genuine advisory board. For the first time in history, the cabinet had a full-time secretary, an agenda, and regularly kept minutes. Eisenhower made Sherman Adams, former governor of

Visualizing
History

▲ **EISENHOWER BECOMES PRESIDENT** Dwight D. Eisenhower proved to be a popular campaigner and was the first Republican to be elected President since 1928. *How great was his margin of victory over Stevenson in 1952?*

TEACH
Guided Practice
Interpreting Primary Sources Play a recording of portions of the McCarthy hearings, especially the Army-McCarthy hearings. (The recordings are available in many libraries.) Have students share their reactions to the hearings with the class. **L2**

🗁 Assign Guided Reading Activity 21-1.

Visualizing
History   Dwight Eisenhower had never been a candidate for political office before he ran for President. Few people even knew his party affiliation before 1952. **Answer to Caption:** Eisenhower received a landslide margin of 6 million popular votes.

NATIONAL GEOGRAPHIC SOCIETY

💿 **CD-ROM**
The Presidents: A Picture History of Our Nation
Have students select President Eisenhower from the main menu and the category GAME. Suggest students learn more about Eisenhower by playing the presidential game with a partner.

Cooperative Learning Activity

Arriving at a Consensus Divide the class into groups of four or five. Have the students in each group use the information in Section 1 to discuss the following question: How did President Eisenhower establish a new style of leadership? Each student in the group should take a turn. *(Students should indicate that Eisenhower acted as the leader of the White House team; his cabinet acted as a real advisory board; Eisenhower's chief of staff had great power by controlling access to the President.)* Have a group leader take notes and present the group's consensus to the class. **L2**

Independent Practice

Writing Have students write a report explaining the provisions of the Twenty-fifth Amendment. It outlines the procedures for times when the President is disabled as well as how these procedures are to be put into effect. **L2**

📁 Assign Writer's Guidebook Lessons 2-6.

📁 Assign Workbook Activity 21-1.

Did You Know?

The problem of presidential incapacity was not new. William H. Harrison suffered from pneumonia for a month before his death in 1841. In 1881 James Garfield lingered for two months before he died from an assassin's bullet. In 1919 Woodrow Wilson suffered a paralyzing stroke that rendered him unable to participate in upcoming treaty negotiations.

VIDEODISC

Communism and the Cold War

Side One, Chapter 11
Title: *Communists in our Midst: McCarthyism*
Subject: McCarthyism

New Hampshire, his chief of staff. Adams wielded great power by controlling access to the President.

The advantages of Eisenhower's kind of administration were clear. If, for some reason, the President was unable to lead, the government would not come to a standstill. Cabinet members could easily take over day-to-day operations. Indeed, Eisenhower suffered serious illnesses three times during his presidency, and each time the White House staff carried on with little difficulty. Critics claimed that the President was abdicating his responsibilities. At crucial times he seemed unaware of decisions made by his aides. Historians later described Eisenhower's management style as a "hidden-hand presidency."

The Bricker Amendment

Eisenhower hoped to establish good working relations with Congress, but members of his own party sometimes made this difficult. Still angry over the secret agreements that President Roosevelt had made with Stalin and Churchill at Yalta, Republican senator John Bricker of Ohio introduced a bill to limit presidential power. The Bricker Amendment required Senate ratification of all agreements made by the President with other nations. It also prohibited the President from making a treaty that conflicted with the laws of any state.

A Narrow Victory

Eisenhower believed that the Bricker Amendment would limit the President's

• •

Footnotes to History

A New Cabinet Post During his first term, President Eisenhower worked to reorganize the government. The Department of Health, Education, and Welfare was created in 1953. Oveta Culp Hobby, commander of the Women's Air Corps during World War II, became the head of the department. She was the second woman in American history to hold a cabinet post. Frances Perkins, secretary of labor during Franklin Roosevelt's presidency, was the first.

power to deal effectively with other nations. It would also allow any state to disrupt United States foreign policy. Although most Republicans in Congress supported the Bricker Amendment, the Eisenhower administration fought hard against it. In February 1954, the bill was defeated by a single vote. Wearily, the President commented:

> ❝ *If it is true that when you die the things that bothered you most are engraved on your skull, I am sure I'll have there the mud and dirt of France during the invasion and the name of Senator Bricker.* ❞

■ McCarthy's Influence Ends

Some Americans believed that a Republican President would put an end to Senator Joseph McCarthy's charges that the government was filled with Communists. But McCarthy continued his crusade and subjected many government officials to humiliating investigations.

For a time McCarthy succeeded in giving the impression that he was saving the country from communism. A public opinion poll taken in 1954 reported that 50 percent of the people favored him and 29 percent opposed him. Senators wary of McCarthy's influence with the voters were reluctant to oppose him.

Although the President privately disapproved of McCarthy and his methods, Eisenhower refused to attack him publicly. The President believed that if he fought McCarthy, he would only give him more publicity. This tactic, however, deprived McCarthy's opponents in Congress of Eisenhower's leadership.

McCarthy's underhanded tactics were finally exposed to the public in 1954. In televised hearings regarding possible communist subversion in the army, Americans observed McCarthy's callous disregard of law and fairness. After the hearings ended, the Senate passed a resolution condemning McCarthy for his conduct.

Critical Thinking Activity

Assessing Motivation During the 1950s the fear of Communist subversion hung over the country and was fanned by Senator Joseph McCarthy. Ask students if they think that McCarthyism was a "necessary evil" in order to protect America's vital interests during the cold war. *(Some students might indicate that* *McCarthyism was an overreaction and that it resulted in infringement of the civil rights of many falsely accused people. Other students might indicate that the United States was very vulnerable during that time and couldn't afford to take any chances of Communist subversion.)* **L2**

The Election of 1956

In September 1955, President Eisenhower suffered a heart attack. Although the President recovered rapidly, the nation's confidence was shaken. The stock market dropped more sharply than it had since 1929. Then, within the next two years, Eisenhower suffered two major illnesses.

Presidential Disability

The President's health focused attention on the question of **presidential succession,** the order in which others fill the office of President. Although Eisenhower had kept the government running smoothly during his illnesses, Americans wondered what would happen if the President remained ill. The Constitution provides that the Vice President becomes President if the President is unable to handle the duties of office. However, it does not say who is to decide whether the President is, or is not, able to serve.

The matter was addressed in 1967 after ratification of the Twenty-fifth Amendment, which outlines procedures when the President is disabled. Moreover, it deals with the situation when a President feels capable of continuing in office but is thought by others to be incapable.

In 1956 the Republicans renominated Eisenhower. The Republicans claimed that the Eisenhower administration had brought peace and prosperity to the nation. Eisenhower had ended the war in Korea and avoided other world conflicts. The Democrats, nominating Adlai Stevenson for a second time, capitalized on fear about the President's health. They played upon the public's concern that Vice President Nixon might become President.

Eisenhower Is Reelected

Eisenhower won by a greater margin than in 1952. Eisenhower's personal popularity led him to a decisive victory. He won 35.6 million popular votes to Stevenson's 26 million. Eisenhower had 457 electoral votes while Stevenson had 74. The President's popularity did not rub off on his party, however. Democrats won control of both the House of Representatives and the Senate. The Democrats had a slight majority in the Senate, 49 to 47 seats, and a sizable majority in the House. Consequently, Eisenhower became the first President in more than 100 years to take office without his party controlling either house of Congress.

In his second term, Eisenhower was more independent of his party than any other President in the twentieth century. Many conservative Republicans regarded Eisenhower as too liberal in domestic affairs and too interventionist in foreign affairs. However, "modern Republicans" and some Democrats supported the President. His policies won support from the two Democratic leaders in Congress, House Speaker Sam Rayburn and Senate Majority Leader Lyndon Johnson. On domestic issues, an alliance developed between "modern Republicans" and moderate-to-liberal Democrats.

Section 1 ★ Review

Checking for Understanding

1. **Identify** Richard Nixon, "Checkers speech," Adlai Stevenson, Bricker Amendment.

2. **Define** presidential succession.

3. **Explain** the need for an amendment concerning presidential succession.

4. **State** reasons for Eisenhower's appeal to moderate Democrats.

Critical Thinking

5. **Evaluating Performance** Describe Eisenhower's leadership style and discuss its advantages and disadvantages.

ACTIVITY

6. Write a one-page editorial in which you argue whether a military official should or should not be President.

ASSESS
Check Understanding
Assign Section 1 Review as homework or an in-class activity.

Evaluate
Assign Section Quiz 21-1 or use the Testmaker to create a customized quiz.

Reteach
Have students write a paragraph describing Eisenhower's style of leadership and how it differed from that of his predecessors.

Have students complete Reteaching Activity 21-1.

Enrich
Have students look for quotes that show opposing viewpoints by two of the people mentioned in this section.

CLOSE
Have students cite recent events involving Congress and the President. What is the current President's relationship with Congress?

Answers to SECTION 1 REVIEW

1. Richard Nixon, 634; "Checkers speech," 635; Adlai Stevenson, 635; Bricker Amendment, 636
2. All vocabulary words are defined in the Glossary.
3. Eisenhower's heart attack and illnesses; need for amendment saying who would succeed if President suffered extended illness or there was disagreement over capacity to serve

4. middle course economics; retained some New Deal assistance; independent of party
5. Decentralized "staff" approach, cabinet, advisers; shared decision making; Advantages: could carry on in President's absence; Disadvantages: President isolated; could be unaware of staff decisions
6. Students should provide cogent reasoning to support their position.

BUILDING SKILLS
Critical Thinking Skills

Analyzing Symbols

BUILDING SKILLS

TEACH

Remind students that events can be symbolic. Neil Armstrong's walk on the moon can symbolize modern technology. Have students review the guidelines presented for understanding symbolism. Discuss historical events that have become symbols. For example the Vietnam War has come to symbolize the failure of American diplomacy; Jackie Robinson's integrating baseball has become a symbol of the American struggle to integrate society.

✍ Use Chapter Skills Activity 21 to reinforce students' understanding of the skill.

Did You Know?

When asked why he pushed the United States to send an astronaut to the moon, President John F. Kennedy replied, "Because it is there. . . . The moon and planets are there, and new hopes for knowledge and peace are there."

▲ COLD WAR CARTOON

Neil Armstrong was the first person to walk on the moon. This accomplishment had a powerful impact on people all over the world. One reason this event had such an impact was that people saw his walking on the moon as a symbol, and they attached extra meaning to it.

Learning the Skill

A *symbol* is something used to represent or stand for something else—often an abstract idea, concept, or feeling. Symbols are all around us, even though we often do not recognize them as such. All words, for example, are symbols for objects or ideas.

A familiar symbol is the American flag, which stands for the United States and patriotic pride. Other familiar symbols include the color purple, which stands for royalty; lions, which stand for courage; and the skull and crossbones, which symbolizes death.

Armstrong's moon walk symbolizes human progress, the power of modern technology, and our never-ending curiosity about the universe. The following guidelines will help you discover symbolism in history:

- Think about the event or condition being studied. What is the main activity in it?
- What overall condition led to this main activity?
- Who or what situation could be affected by this activity?
- What consequences could there be for those who are affected?
- What statement could be made that would demonstrate the symbolism, or meaning, of this event?

For example, possible statements of the symbolism in McCarthyism include:

a. McCarthyism symbolized a callous disregard for law and fairness.

b. McCarthyism symbolized cold war mistrust between two superpowers.

Practicing the Skill

1. Analyze the political cartoon on this page. What do the two figures symbolize?

2. Why do you think the cartoonist used those two figures? What other figures might he have chosen?

APPLYING THE SKILL

3. Create a table with two columns. In the first column, write down the symbols used to represent your school. In the second column, answer these questions: What does each symbol stand for? How does the symbol represent that idea?

Answers to Practicing the Skill

1. The eagle represents the United States. The bear represents the Soviet Union.
2. Answers will vary but might include that the eagle is a symbol of the United States; the bear might have been used to represent the Soviet Union because it is an animal that can be unpredictable and aggressive. Alternative symbols will vary but should appropriately symbolize the United States and the Soviet Union.
3. Tables will vary. Sample answers for column 1: mascots, school song, flag. Sample answers for column 2: A team mascot might look fierce; a service organization might show hands at work.

★★★

"The Straight Road"

Setting the Scene

Section Focus

Democratic administrations had leaned toward the interests of labor. When Eisenhower accepted the presidential nomination, he promised that in economic matters he would "travel the straight road down the middle." As a result, the nation enjoyed an unprecedented period of prosperity and witnessed the rapid development of big business and agribusiness.

Objectives

After studying this section, you should be able to

★ explain the Eisenhower administration's economic policies.

★ discuss the plight of the small farmer in the 1950s.

Key Term

agribusiness

◀ LABOR UNION SYMBOL

Throughout both of his administrations, Eisenhower steered a course between conservatism and liberalism. Ike's middle course pleased most Americans. At the beginning of his administration it looked as though he might try to undo the New Deal. Like Hoover, Eisenhower believed that the role of government should be limited. Eisenhower advocated cutting the budget, reducing taxes, and ending government regulation of business. He condemned the Tennessee Valley Authority as "creeping socialism" and tried unsuccessfully to arrange for private industry to build new power plants in Tennessee, Alabama, and Kentucky.

Eisenhower and the New Deal

Despite this conservative agenda, Eisenhower recognized that New Deal programs were strongly supported by most Americans. He wrote in a private letter:

> ❝ *Should any political party attempt to abolish Social Security, unemployment insurance, and eliminate labor laws and farm programs, you would not hear of that party again in our political history.* ❞

The debate during Eisenhower's presidency was not over ending such New Deal programs as Social Security or the minimum wage, but over how much larger to allow them to become. With President Eisenhower's encouragement, Congress extended Social Security to 7 million more people and increased benefits. Congress also extended unemployment compensation to 4 million more people. Eisenhower tried to persuade Congress to enact a health insurance program partly funded by the federal government, but Congress rejected the legislation.

CHAPTER 21 Search for Stability: 1952–1960 **639**

Classroom Resources for SECTION 2

Blackline Masters:
- 🗂 Reproducible Lesson Plan 21-2
- 🗂 Guided Reading Activity 21-2
- 🗂 Critical Thinking Skills Activity 21
- 🗂 Reteaching Activity 21-2
- 🗂 Section Quiz 21-2

Transparencies:
- 🗂 Section Focus Transparency 21-2

Multimedia:
- Testmaker
- Powers of the President
- Economics in Action

LESSON PLAN
SECTION 2, 639–642

FOCUS

Bellringer

🗂 Before taking roll, project Section Focus Transparency 21-2 or hand out Section Focus Transparency Activity 21-2. Have students answer the questions. Discuss student responses.

Motivating Activity

Have students recall the New Deal programs, especially Social Security. Ask them how the American people might have felt if these programs were undone. As students read this section, have them focus on Eisenhower's economic policies and on how these policies differed from those of his predecessors. **L1**

Vocabulary Precheck

Write *agribusiness* on the chalkboard. Have a volunteer skim the section to find the term and read it in context. **L1, LEP**

VIDEODISC

Powers of the President

Side One, Chapter 25
Title: *Call For Legislation*
Subject: The President's role

TEACH
Guided Practice

Finding Main Ideas Have students summarize the main ideas in Section 2 by writing a newspaper headline for each subhead in the section. For example, a headline for the first subhead might read "Government Supportive of Big Business." **L1, LEP**

Visualizing History Until his death in 1970, Walter Reuther was the most respected labor leader in the United States. Presidents sought his advice and his support in political campaigns.
Answer to Caption: The merger increased the strength of organized labor and made it easier to form local unions.

GLENCOE
TECHNOLOGY

VIDEODISC

Economics in Action

Disc 2, Side 1
Chapter 18

Title: *The American Labor Force*

Subject: The history of labor unions and their role today

■ Business and Labor

Big business also had an ally in the White House. During the 1950s, 3,000 companies merged with the 500 largest corporations without any antitrust challenges by the government. The nation's 100 largest companies controlled more than 30 percent of all industrial production. Some corporations, such as General Motors and American Telephone and Telegraph, had annual budgets that were larger than those of many countries.

The American labor movement grew more slowly than big business, but it continued to gain strength. In 1955 the American Federation of Labor (AFL) and the Congress of Industrial Organizations (CIO) merged, forming the AFL-CIO. The merger increased the strength of organized labor and made it easier for workers to form local unions.

Organized labor tried hard to win pay increases. During the 1950s, take-home pay and buying power rose sharply. Workers also enjoyed longer paid vacations. Walter Reuther, United Auto Workers president, observed that the movement was developing a "whole new middle class."

Organized labor was not very successful in its efforts to organize the lowest-paid factory workers and office workers. Often, these workers were women or minorities. The growth in AFL-CIO membership actually slowed by 1957.

Union growth was also adversely affected by congressional investigations into corrupt union practices. The investigations revealed that strong-arm tactics were used by some unions to force employers into accepting the unions. The Teamsters' Union, accused of misappropriating funds, was expelled from the AFL-CIO. These revelations began to turn public opinion against unions.

■ Farm Problems

Despite the prosperity of the 1950s, it was a difficult time for many of the nation's farmers. Between 1948 and 1956, the farmers' share of the national income dropped from 9 to 4 percent. While the average American enjoyed a per capita income of $1,629, the farm population averaged $632 a year.

Visualizing History ▲ LABOR UNIONS MERGE George Meany (left), president of the AFL, and Walter Reuther, president of the CIO, shake hands on the merger of the two unions. *How did the joining of these unions help organized labor?*

Cooperative Learning Activity

Examining Economic Policy Ask students the following question: How were the economic policies of President Eisenhower more conservative than those of his predecessors? Have students use the information in Section 2 to answer the question. After they think of a response, have them pair up to discuss their responses.

Ask volunteers to share their responses with the class. *(Student responses should indicate that Eisenhower believed that the role of government should be limited. He advocated cutting the budget, reducing taxes, and ending government regulation of business.)* **L2**

AMERICAN PORTRAITS

Betty Friedan
1921–

Betty Friedan (free•DAN) was one of the first to analyze the lives of women. When she began her analysis, most women were homemakers or worked in low-paying jobs.

In 1957 she began a year-long study of her Smith College classmates. She discovered that many of these well-educated women were leading unhappy lives. With additional research it became clear to Friedan that American women were failing to find fulfillment in life. Instead, they were succumbing to "the feminine mystique"—a belief that they were supposed to ignore their talents and interests and live only for the achievements of their family.

In 1963 Friedan published *The Feminine Mystique*, a book that sparked the modern women's liberation movement. In 1966 she helped found the National Organization for Women (NOW) to lead the fight for equal rights.

Question of Price Supports

Eisenhower was reluctant to have the government continue to guarantee farmers set prices for their products. The heart of the issue, according to the administration, was

> *... whether our farms are to continue to be operated by freemen. Or ... to offset some very real and obvious problems that farmers now face, will government go in the opposite direction and subsidize agriculture in such a manner that it also takes control?*

But without strong price supports from the government, the small family farmer faced economic ruin. Overproduction from better seeds, fertilizers, and mechanization kept farm prices low. Legislation reduced but did not end price supports or the farm surplus.

Many small farm families gave up and sold out to large farm owners who raised only a single crop and used the latest machinery and agricultural methods. Because of their efficiency, the large farm owners could cut their costs and still make a profit. More small farmers were unable to compete with the **agribusinesses,** or modern large-scale farms that covered 1,000 acres or more. By 1959 half of the nation's farm-land belonged to 4 percent of the farmers.

Seasonal Workers

There were other problems associated with America's changing agricultural patterns. Large farm owners hired seasonal workers to cultivate and harvest their crops. Many of the workers were Mexican Americans from California and the Southwest, but as many as 400,000 workers were Mexicans allowed into the United States on short-term visas. Unprotected by the National Labor Relations Act or federal minimum wage laws, these migrant workers labored long hours for little pay and endured terrible living conditions. Their children grew up with little, if any, education.

■ Prosperity and Recession

Much of the economic growth of the 1950s was due to a tremendous increase in consumer credit. Effective advertising enticed Americans to borrow more money to buy houses, cars, and consumer goods.

Independent Practice

Working With Statistics
Have students find the gross national product (GNP) for the years 1950–1959 in *The Statistical Abstracts of the United States* and report their findings on a line graph. Based on the GNP for each of these years, have them generalize about the state of the economy during the 1950s. **L2**

 Assign Guided Reading Activity 21-2.

CURRICULUM CONNECTION

Economics When the war in Europe cut farm production there, demand increased for American farm products. Prices rose, and U.S. farm income went up. When the war ended in Europe, and their farm production resumed, demand for U.S. farm products declined, as did farm income.

Teaching American Portraits

In 1981 Betty Friedan wrote *The Second Stage,* in which she acknowledged the end of the anger that fueled the women's movement in the 1960s and 1970s. Instead she predicted that women would make advances quietly and would work with men as their allies, not their enemies.

Critical Thinking Activity

Determining Cause and Effect Four solutions to the disposal of the overabundance of production in the 1950s were used in different degrees. They were (1) built-in obsolescence—a new model car every year; (2) the creation of new consumer demand—advertising; (3) shipping excess goods to "needy" nations—food and technology; and (4) government-sponsored public programs—highways, public housing. The space exploration program and the military buildup are other examples of what society could do with an oversupply of production capability. Discuss what changes each solution would undergo if overabundance vanished. **L2**

ASSESS

Check Understanding

Assign Section 2 Review as homework or an in-class activity.

Evaluate

Assign Section Quiz 21-2 or use the Test-maker to create a customized quiz.

Reteach

Have students summarize the Eisenhower administration's economic policies by making a chart with these headings: Big Business, Labor, and Farmers.

Have students complete Reteaching Activity 21-2.

Enrich

Have students research and report on the Soil-Bank Bill that Congress passed in 1956. The report should include how soil banks started, how they were used, and their effect on farm income today.

Assign Critical Thinking Skills Activity 21.

CLOSE

Ask students to create a cause-and-effect chart for the following event: In the mid-1950s, Eisenhower attempted to hold down government spending.

This growing demand, in turn, encouraged industries to produce more goods and hire more people.

President Eisenhower worried that this rapid growth of the economy would lead to inflation, or rapidly rising prices. Because of this he tried to hold down domestic and military spending. But in 1957 and 1958, his attempts to balance the budget set off a recession. Sales dropped and manufacturers laid off workers. Unemployment rose to 7.6 percent of the workforce. Eisenhower resisted congressional pressure for a tax cut to stimulate the economy. Finally, late in 1958, boom times returned again.

Although President Eisenhower remained a popular leader during the late 1950s, he was sharply blamed by some critics for not moving quickly enough. Some detractors charged that the President ignored important national issues such as civil rights and the protection of natural resources.

At the same time, the administration also had to deal with a number of scandals. The most publicized scandal revolved around Sherman Adams, the President's closest adviser. In the spring of 1958, congressional hearings disclosed that Adams had received gifts from a wealthy Boston industrialist who was under investigation by the government. Adams was forced to resign. The recession and the scandals hurt the Republican cause during the 1958 elections, and the Democrats strengthened their control of both houses, winning 15 additional seats in the Senate and 48 seats in the House. Despite these difficulties, Eisenhower

received praise for some of his efforts. In foreign policy, he sought to ease world tensions. During his last year in office, the President visited an unprecedented number of nations on a goodwill tour. He affirmed that

> *Our basic aspiration is to search out methods by which peace in the world can be assured with justice for everybody.*

At home, he backed government grants to help in the building of more schools for the nation's expanding school-age population. Eisenhower also supported the National Defense Education Act of 1958. This law provided a $295 million fund to provide loans to college students for their education.

In 1959 two new states were added to the union. On January 3 Eisenhower issued a proclamation making Alaska the 49th state—the first new state since Arizona and New Mexico joined the Union in 1912. On August 21, Hawaii became the 50th state.

★★★ AMERICA'S FLAGS ★★★

The Stars and Stripes Today The 50-star flag of the United States was raised for the first time on July 4, 1960. New stars were added in 1959 for Alaska and in 1960 for Hawaii. The Stars and Stripes has been through 27 versions in all.

★★★★★★★★★★★★★★★★★★★★★★★★

Section 2 ★ Review

Checking for Understanding

1. **Identify** creeping socialism, AFL-CIO, migrant workers.

2. **Define** agribusiness.

3. **Characterize** the economic philosophy and practice of Eisenhower.

4. **List** two problems connected with farming in the 1950s.

Critical Thinking

5. **Comparing Trends**   Compare developments in business and agriculture during the 1950s, including the impact on workers.

ACTIVITY

6. Imagine you are President Eisenhower's speech writer. Write a short speech incorporating the President's economic goals.

Answers to SECTION 2 REVIEW

1. creeping socialism, 639; AFL-CIO, 640; migrant workers, 641

2. All vocabulary words are defined in the Glossary.

3. minimal regulation, allow mergers; taxes and government spending low, but provide assistance for needy, security for citizens

4. Farm surplus brought low prices; without price supports small farmers couldn't compete with agribusiness, left land; agribusiness used imported labor, overworked, underpaid.

5. Mergers increased big-business share, agribusinesses increased share of farmland. Business profits high, farmers' minimal or none. Business labor gained higher wages, better conditions.

6. Students should display an understanding of Eisenhower's position.

★★★★★★★★★★★★★★★★★★★★★★★★★★★★★★★★★★★★

An Affluent Society

Setting the Scene

Section Focus

The economic growth of the 1950s brought great changes to the nation. For the first time, most Americans enjoyed a life of abundance. This prosperity greatly changed the way people lived. Advances in technology and medicine coupled with economic prosperity gave Americans great confidence in the future.

Objectives

After studying this section, you should be able to

★ describe the effect of affluence on American life.

★ give examples of advances in medical technology.

★ explain the pressures of conformity in the 1950s.

Key Term

automation

◀ THE TELEVISION GENERATION

After World War II, Americans were ready to settle down and enjoy a period of peace and prosperity. Industry responded to the demands of Americans by turning out huge quantities of new goods. New communities and housing developments were built as people moved from the cities to the suburbs. Americans were on the move, and they relied heavily on the automobile for this new mobility. People anxiously awaited each year's new car models with their added gadgets and longer "tail fins." Highways stretched across the country carrying more and more traffic. A new suburban lifestyle evolved among middle-class Americans.

New technology and continuing prosperity allowed many Americans to enjoy more leisure time. At the same time, the number of available leisure activities increased.

■ An Economy of Abundance

In 1958 economist John Kenneth Galbraith published *The Affluent Society*, in which he claimed that America's postwar prosperity was a new phenomenon. In the past, Galbraith said, all societies were based on an "economy of scarcity," in which the productivity of the economy was limited by a lack of resources and overpopulation.

In the 1950s, however, the United States and a few other highly industrialized nations were experiencing what Galbraith called an "economy of abundance." Up-to-date technology enabled these nations to produce an endless variety and amount of goods and services for their people. The citizens of these countries were enjoying a standard of living never before thought possible. Poverty was disappearing, except

CHAPTER 21 Search for Stability: 1952–1960   **643**

Classroom Resources for SECTION 3

Blackline Masters:
- Reproducible Lesson Plan 21-3
- Guided Reading Activity 21-3
- Linking Past and Present Activity 21
- American Portrait 62
- Primary and Secondary Source Readings, p. 56
- Reteaching Activity 21-3
- Section Quiz 21-3

Transparencies:
- Section Focus Transparency 21-3
- Skills Transparency 21

Multimedia:
- Testmaker
- The American People: Fabric of a Nation
- Communism and the Cold War

LESSON PLAN
SECTION 3, 643–648

FOCUS

Bellringer

Before taking roll, project Section Focus Transparency 21-3 or hand out Section Focus Transparency Activity 21-3. Have students answer the questions. Discuss student responses.

Motivating Activity

Ask students to list 10 things that make them happy. Then ask them to count how many things on their lists are material goods. Discuss with the students the importance of material wealth. As they read this section, have them focus on the ways that affluence affected American life. **L1**

Vocabulary Precheck

Write *automation* on the chalkboard. Have a volunteer skim the section to find the term and read it in context. **L1, LEP**

NATIONAL GEOGRAPHIC SOCIETY

 VIDEODISC

GTV: The American People: Fabric of a Nation

Side 4, Chapter 4
Title: *Greener Pastures?*
Subject: Development and impact of suburbs

TEACH
Guided Practice

Debate Have students debate the following point:

Suburbs are better places to live than cities.*(The basic pro argument might include the point that suburbs are often safer than cities and are less crowded. The basic con argument might include the point that cities offer a more diverse way of life, because the people are generally not as homogeneous as people in suburbs. Cities also generally offer a greater variety of cultural activities.)* **L2**

Visualizing
History Early computers were large because information was stored on envelope-sized rectangular cards with holes punched in them. Each card could store only a few pieces of information. Today a tiny silicon chip can store millions of pieces of information.
Answer to Caption: for bookkeeping functions like billing and inventory control

Assign Guided Reading Activity 21-3.

Project Skills Transparency 21 and have students complete Skills Transparency Activity 21.

Visualizing History

▲ COMPUTERS COME OF AGE Early computers, such as the UNIVAC, occupied entire rooms and used vacuum tubes rather than microchips to process information. *How did most businesses first use computers?*

within such groups as the unskilled, uneducated, and new immigrant population.

Some critics accused Galbraith of overstating the situation, but the facts and figures seemed to support it. Americans produced more than they could use, and this new wealth was being distributed throughout the population. During the 1920s the wealthiest 5 percent of the population received 35 percent of the country's income, but by 1960 this group received only 18 percent.

Life for most Americans was easier than ever before. They earned more money than they needed for such necessities as food and housing. With their surplus income, they purchased automobiles, household appliances, and other luxury items. The number of Americans owning their own homes went up from 40 percent to 60 percent between 1940 and 1960. Americans also had more free time as working hours were reduced and they were given holidays with pay. Not only were Americans better off, but they were more secure. Unemployment insurance and Social Security now covered the majority of jobholders.

Technological and Scientific Progress

The United States made spectacular leaps in the field of science. With more money to spend, an increase in the number of university-trained scientists, and a growing commitment to the future, the United States led the world in new technological developments. America's factories and industries began to use **automation,** the technique of operating a production system using mechanical or electronic devices. With automated production methods, goods could be produced more efficiently and quickly than with human workers.

During the 1950s the use of computers began to revolutionize American industry. Businesses used computers for many purposes. Computers took over bookkeeping functions such as billing and inventory control. They were also used for such things as making hotel reservations, sorting bank checks, guiding satellites, predicting election results, forecasting weather conditions, identifying fingerprints, and setting type for printing.

Cooperative Learning Activity

Research Divide the class into groups of five to six. Have each group report on attitudes toward children and child-rearing practices in the United States from colonial times to the present. The reports should include information on Puritan child-rearing practices and child labor during the 1800s. Each group should assign a specific responsibility to each member in the group, such as research, writing, or graphic presentation. Have each group present their report to the rest of the class. **L2, L3**

Automation and computers in the workplace caused many workers to lose their jobs. In the long run, however, computers and automation created more jobs than they eliminated. And the new jobs usually demanded a higher level of education.

Breakthroughs in medicine during the 1950s were also impressive. In April 1955, Americans learned of one of the most important discoveries in the history of medicine. After many years of research, United States scientist Dr. Jonas Salk had developed a vaccine for preventing the dreaded childhood disease known as polio. The Salk vaccine was proven effective after a huge test run on 1,830,000 schoolchildren. Within a few years, cases of polio nearly disappeared.

By 1960 other major illnesses, including pneumonia, tuberculosis, and diphtheria, were nearly wiped out. Life expectancy in the United States increased. While cancer and heart disease continued to be serious threats to the lives of Americans, researchers made important advances in diagnosing and treating these diseases.

From Cities to Suburbs

In the 1950s the automobile changed the face of America. No longer did people have to live near their places of work. Those who lived and worked in the city could move to less-crowded places. This migration of city residents caused rapid growth of suburbs. In the years after World War II, cities became ringed by seemingly endless housing developments carved out of the less densely settled country land. Shopping centers with vast parking lots were built to serve the new suburban population. Businesses and factories also began relocating from the cities to the suburbs, where their workers now lived. The Highway Act of 1956 contributed to the growth of the suburbs by adding 41,000 miles to the interstate highway system.

Meanwhile, cities began to experience serious problems. To handle the flood of automobile traffic, new highways had to be built, often destroying whole urban neighborhoods. Those who were left behind to live in the cities often included poor people and the members of minority groups. With a declining population, cities faced growing financial problems. Taxes could no longer keep up with the demands for such services as public transportation, police protection, housing, and education.

Pressures to Conform

In the affluent 1950s, a new house in the suburbs, a larger television in the living room, and the newest model automobile in the garage represented the fulfillment of the

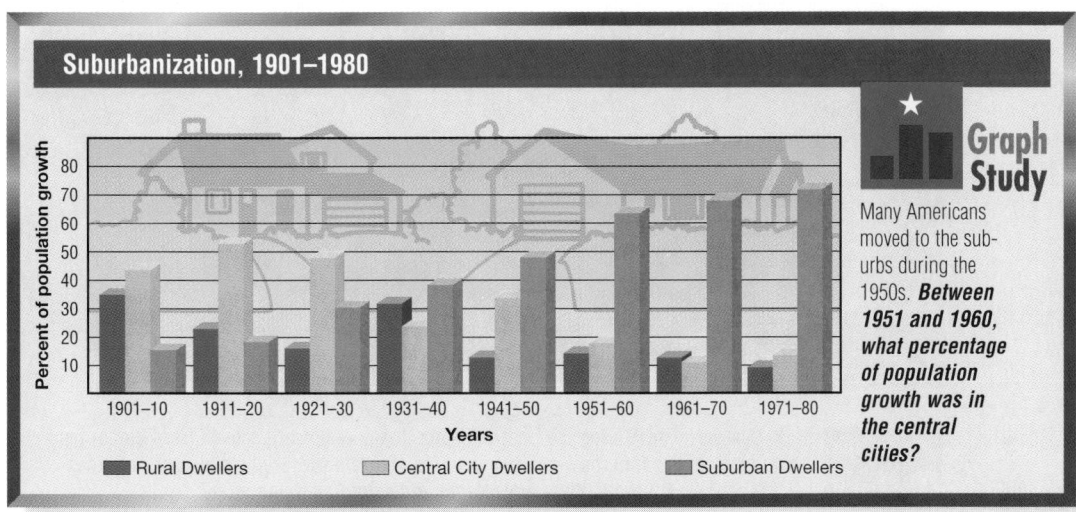

Suburbanization, 1901–1980

Percent of population growth (y-axis): 10, 20, 30, 40, 50, 60, 70, 80

Years (x-axis): 1901–10, 1911–20, 1921–30, 1931–40, 1941–50, 1951–60, 1961–70, 1971–80

Legend: ■ Rural Dwellers ■ Central City Dwellers ■ Suburban Dwellers

Graph Study

Many Americans moved to the suburbs during the 1950s. **Between 1951 and 1960, what percentage of population growth was in the central cities?**

Cultural Perspectives

Alaska and Hawaii In 1959 two new states were added to the Union. Alaska became the forty-ninth state and Hawaii the fiftieth. Both states are home to people from many different ethnic groups. Encourage students to research the ethnic heritage of each state and then share their findings with the class by preparing a poster.

CHAPTER 21
SECTION 3

Independent Practice

History Ask students to use the information in Section 3 to make a chart listing the advances in technology and medicine during the 1950s. (*Technology: the use of automation to produce goods; the use of computers in businesses; the use of television for entertainment and communication. Medicine: Salk vaccine against polio; the treatment and near elimination of pneumonia, tuberculosis, and diphtheria.*) Have them research other advances in technology and medicine not mentioned in the section and add them to the chart. Hold a class discussion on students' additions. **L2**

📁 Assign Workbook Activity 21-3.

Did You Know?

Among the most popular television shows of the 1950s were family situation comedies like *I Love Lucy, Father Knows Best*, and *Leave It to Beaver*; westerns like *Gunsmoke* and *Wagon Train*; and detective shows like *Peter Gunn* and *77 Sunset Strip*.

Using Graphs

Answer: 20 percent

Graph Skills Practice
In what decade did half of all Americans live in suburbs? (*1941–50*)

"American Dream." For many young couples, the suburbs offered comfort, security, and a pleasant place to raise their children. Yet it soon became clear that this new lifestyle had problems of its own.

Critics noted that a strong pressure to conform characterized American suburban life. Suburban neighborhoods were usually filled with people who were very much alike. They were generally typified as being young, with comfortable incomes, and having jobs in the service industries. Often this conformity led to discrimination or ostracism of those who seemed "different." For example, in many suburbs racial and religious minorities were unable to buy homes. To some extent, the high cost of homes in the suburbs was the reason, but prejudice was an even more important factor. Often suburban residents refused to sell homes to minority families. If minority families did move to the suburbs, others in the community made them feel unwelcome.

Many writers criticized the trend toward conformity in American life in the 1950s. Nonfiction works, such as David Reisman's *The Lonely Crowd* (1950) and William H. Whyte's *The Organization Man* (1956), and novels such as Sloan Wilson's *The Man in the Gray Flannel Suit* (1956), tried to explain the pressure to conform. Sometimes, as represented in *The Man in the Gray Flannel Suit*, these pressures were so subtly pervasive as to make people feel they had little control over their own lives:

> **❝** [I]t seemed as though all I could see was a lot of bright young men in gray flannel suits rushing around New York in a frantic parade to go nowhere. They seemed to be pursuing neither ideals nor happiness—they were pursuing a routine. . . . I thought I was on the sidelines watching that parade. . . . It was quite a shock to glance down and see that I too was wearing a gray flannel suit. **❞**

The pressures to conform in business were especially great. Employees who wanted to advance to better positions took care to adhere to the company's rules. This often meant being loyal to the corporation and being "one of the team." Outside work

Visualizing History

▲ **SUBURBAN LIFE** During the postwar years, many Americans moved from the farms and cities to the suburbs—and many young people discovered a new cast of heroes such as Davy Crockett. *What advantages did suburban living offer?*

Sidelight: Mies van der Rohe

The most common new buildings of the 1950s were the split-level homes of the suburbs and the steel skyscrapers of the city. Mies van der Rohe probably had the greatest impact on architecture during this time. His tall and straight structures of glass, brick, and steel set the style for new buildings in cities. His idea of "less is more" became the basis for building designs by those who imitated his style. The John Hancock Center in Chicago was based on van der Rohe's style.

Linking Past and Present

The Drive-in Theater

The drive-in movie theater is a uniquely American institution. By the very early 1950s, the drive-in had fully arrived.

Then

Movies Under the Stars

Part of the drive-in's appeal was that it met a wish on the part

▼ DRIVE-IN, EARLY 1950S

of families to spend more time together—an important aim, particularly after the disruptions of World War II. Drive-ins provided an inexpensive night out and erased the problem of hiring a baby-sitter. Theater operators provided play areas for children; by the mid-1950s, an estimated 90 percent of drive-ins either contained a children's playground or planned to build one.

Operators provided patrons with such items as car heaters in the winter and window nets in the summer to keep out insects. Other enticements included baby bottle warmers, barbecue pits, and laundromats. Some of the measures to attract customers were clever, but decidedly offbeat. One theater in Asbury Park, New Jersey, provided space for 500 cars and 25 airplanes.

Now

Industry in Decline

Spiraling real estate costs and competition from indoor theaters, television, and the video stifled the drive-in's appeal. From a peak of more than 4,000 in 1958, the number of drive-in theaters has plunged to less than 1,000 today. Yet so deep-rooted is the drive-in experience that for many Americans it is still the perfect night out.

it meant having the "right" type of family life and belonging to the "right" clubs and religious groups. Social critics complained that Americans were in danger of losing their individuality.

■ Changes in Family Life

During the 1950s there were renewed social pressures on women to remain at home. Women's magazines ran articles such as "Should I Stop Work When We Marry?" and "The Business of Running a Home." The immensely popular *Pocket Book of Baby and Child Care* by Dr. Benjamin Spock said that raising children was more important and rewarding than the extra money or satisfaction that a woman might get from a job. Many women who had gone to college or had careers traded their aspirations and jobs for marriage and motherhood. The number of women who worked continued to rise,

but women lost ground in the workplace. They were still paid less than men for doing the same work. They were also shut out of better jobs with higher salaries.

After World War II, more women dropped out of school and married at an early age. The nation's birthrate increased so rapidly that people refer to the period between 1945 and 1961 as the "baby boom." During the baby boom, more than 65 million children were born in the United States.

Parents in the prosperous 1950s wanted their children to have all the things that they had not been able to have during the Depression and war years. They gave their children an increasing amount of material goods and emphasized the benefits of living the "good life." Parents also allowed their children greater freedom than they themselves had known as youngsters. Critics pointed to this new "permissiveness" as the major cause of the rise in juvenile delinquency.

Sidelight: Television and the Movies

One of the greatest effects of television in the 1950s was on the movie industry. Between the late 1940s and 1960, nearly half of the 18,000 movie theaters in the United States closed. This was largely the result of more people turning to television for entertainment. The movies lost

more of their audience as improvements in television technology were made. By the end of the 1950s, it was apparent that the great days of the movie industry were over. Ask students what effect the rise of the videotape industry has had on the movie industry today.

▲ WATCHING TELEVISION The most popular of the 1950s television shows were comedies, variety shows, and "Westerns" starring Roy Rogers (above), Hopalong Cassidy, and other stars. *Why were some people worried about the effects of watching television?*

Republican party and the Democratic party spent millions on television advertising and broadcasts. Although television stirred greater interest in voting, it also posed disturbing questions. Would television give an unfair advantage to the candidate who used television most effectively and who could afford to buy the most airtime?

Some critics also worried that television would have a negative effect on American culture. In the early 1950s, pollster George Gallup voiced concern that:

> ❝ [O]ne of the real threats to America's future place in the world is a citizenry which daily elects to be entertained and not informed. ❞

Supported by advertisers trying to reach the widest audience, television programs often appealed to the lowest common denominator of public taste. In order to avoid offending potential customers, advertisers would not buy time on programs that dealt with controversial issues. As a result, television furnished entertainment that was intended "to fix the attention but not engage the mind."

Yet the 1950s has often been called the "Golden Age of Television." Many of the country's most talented writers, comedians, musicians, and actors flocked to the new medium. There they could reach an audience of millions.

■ The Impact of Television

One of the symbols of the prosperity of the 1950s was the television set. In 1945 fewer than 1 in every 20,000 people had a television. But within a few years, televisions were everywhere, and they were almost as common as telephones.

Beginning with the election of 1952, television brought national politics into American living rooms. During the campaign, both the

Section 3 ★ Review

Checking for Understanding

1. **Identify** John Kenneth Galbraith, Jonas Salk, Benjamin Spock, baby boom.
2. **Define** automation.
3. **Discuss** changes that occurred in American life as a result of abundance, affluence, and the growth of technology.
4. **List** ways in which early computers were used in the 1950s.
5. **Report** how minority groups were adversely affected by pressures to conform.

Critical Thinking

6. **Analyzing Results** Examine the ways the television and the automobile changed the American lifestyle during the 1950s. How would your life be different without them?

ACTIVITY

7. Research the distribution of population by age for each decade from 1940 to 1990. Present your findings in the form of a graph. Then, write three generalizations from your findings.

▲ CHUCK BERRY

◄ ELVIS PRESLEY,
ROCK-AND-ROLL
STAR OF THE 1950S

Origins of Rock and Roll

During the Eisenhower years, many teen-agers rebelled against the pressure to conform by rejecting the mellow pop music favored by their parents. Teens of the 1950s preferred the heavily accented beats and repetitious lyrics of rock and roll.

Rock and roll developed in the mid-1950s. It was a derivation of the rhythm and blues that African American musicians had created for black audiences years before. It also often had some elements of country music. In rock and roll, the tempo was quicker, the accented beats were moved, and electrically amplified instruments—mostly guitars—were used.

Because rock and roll was such a departure from the sentimental love songs of the past, it shocked and dismayed many parents. Teenagers, however, were sold. One of the first rock hits, recorded in 1955, was Bill Haley and the Comets' *Rock Around the Clock,* which sold 17 million copies. In 1956 Elvis Presley came on the rock scene. In his performances he moved to the beat of the music. With songs like *Don't Be Cruel* and *Jailhouse Rock,* Presley set the musical style for a decade. The lyrics of most rock-and-roll music remained about love, although some writers and performers, most notably Chuck Berry, treated the subject with wit and humor.

Making the Art Connection

1. How did rock-and-roll music evolve?
2. Why did rock and roll shock and dismay parents?

ACTIVITY

3. Paste photographs or drawings on a posterboard of the musician or musical group that you think represents the best of modern rock and roll. Write a caption that includes your definition of rock and roll.

649

TEACH

The moral indignation and trend toward censorship directed toward rock and roll was self-defeating. Point out that these forces themselves were causes of the rebellious nature of rock and roll's popularity.

Did You Know?

Elvis Presley's black leather jacket and ducktail haircut became standard dress for young men.

History and the Humanities

 **American Music: Cultural Traditions:** Early Rock and Roll: "Rocket 88" by Jackie Brenston and his Delta Kings (2:46); "Rock Around the Clock" by Bill Haley and the Comets (2:12)

Answers to Making the Connection

1. Rock and roll was a derivation of the rhythm and blues of black musicians with some elements of country music. In rock and roll, the tempo was quicker, the accented beats were moved, and electrically amplified instruments (mostly guitars) were used.
2. Rock and roll was such a departure from the sentimental tunes of the past.
3. Artwork and captions will vary.

Bellringer

 Before taking roll, project Section Focus Transparency 21-4 or hand out Section Focus Transparency 21-4. Have students answer the questions. Discuss student responses.

Motivating Activity

Review with the class earlier events in the cold war. (*Students should recall the Truman Doctrine, the Marshall Plan, and the Korean War.*) Review with students the policy of containment adopted by President Truman. As they read this section, tell them to focus on the ways that President Eisenhower continued the policy of containment. **L1**

Vocabulary Precheck

Write *covert* on the chalkboard. Have a volunteer skim the section to find the term and read it in context. **L1, LEP**

VIDEODISC

Communism and the Cold War

Side One, Chapter 6
Title: *The Arms Race*
Subject: Development of the arms race between the United States and the Soviet Union

---

Setting the Scene

Section Focus

In the 1950s affluence at home contrasted sharply with political upheaval abroad. Forces were changing the international landscape. The Eisenhower administration aggressively waged a campaign against communism. Fully aware of the consequences of nuclear war, Eisenhower attempted to manage international conflict through cooperative alliances.

LIFE — John Glenn's Personal Album — MAKING OF A BRAVE MAN

◀ ASTRONAUT JOHN GLENN

Objectives

After studying this section, you should be able to

★ discuss Eisenhower's approach to foreign policy and the Eisenhower Doctrine.

★ describe how the fear of nuclear war affected the cold war.

★ discuss why American relations with Latin America were poor in the 1950s.

Key Term

covert

$\mathcal{D}$uring the 1950s the Eisenhower administration labored to contain communism, particularly in newly independent nations in Asia and Africa. Eisenhower used diplomacy, military power, and secret activities to achieve these goals.

President Eisenhower and Secretary of State John Foster Dulles (DUH•luhs) expanded the nation's network of alliances in order to contain communism. In Western Europe, the United States took a leading role in NATO. In Southeast Asia, the United States helped to create the Southeast Asian Treaty Organization (SEATO). In the Middle East, the United States counted on the cooperation of the Central Treaty Organization (CENTO), and in Latin America, the United States promoted the Organization of American States (OAS). These alliances created a formidable counterbalance to the influence of the Soviet Union.

■ The Influence of Dulles

President Eisenhower's foreign policy was greatly influenced by Dulles. After serving in the United States Senate in the late 1940s, Dulles had years of experience in high-level diplomacy, particularly with Asian nations. Secretary Dulles favored a vigorous foreign policy, denouncing Truman's "containment" policy as inadequate. Instead, he advocated "liberation" of Eastern European nations that were under Soviet domination:

❝ *If our policy is to stay where we are, we will be driven back. It is only by keeping alive the hope of liberation, by taking advantage of that wherever opportunity arises, that we will end this terrible peril which dominates the world. . . .* ❞

Classroom Resources for SECTION 4

Blackline Masters:
- Reproducible Lesson Plan 21-4
- Guided Reading Activity 21-4
- Cooperative Learning Activity 21
- Geography in History Activity 21
- Workbook Activity 21-4
- Reteaching Activity 21-4
- Section Quiz 21-4

Transparencies:
- Section Focus Transparency 21-4
- Map Transparency 21

Multimedia:
- Testmaker
- Communism and the Cold War
- Power of the Congress

Dulles threatened "massive retaliation" against communist aggression. "If you are scared to go to the brink [of nuclear war], you are lost," he said. Accordingly, the Department of Defense reduced the size of the regular army and increased its nuclear arsenal.

Eisenhower tempered Dulles's tough stance and took a more cautious approach. He insisted that "there is no alternative to peace." A nuclear war might well mean the end of civilization. Therefore, the Eisenhower administration continued Truman's policy of containment.

■ War and Peace in Asia

Containing communism became a global challenge for Eisenhower. In Asia the end of one conflict was followed by the start of another one.

End of the Korean War

Carrying out his campaign promise, Eisenhower went to Korea in December 1952. Peace negotiations to end the Korean War, however, seemed to go nowhere. Exasperated, Eisenhower threatened the Communists with possible use of nuclear weapons. Finally in July 1953, after long and bloody fighting, the United Nations Command and the North Koreans reached a settlement. Korea was divided along a line close to the 38th parallel.

Southeast Asia

The United States then was faced with a new problem in Southeast Asia. After Japan surrendered Indochina in 1945, France tried to regain control of its colonies. The people, however, wanted to rule themselves. Ho Chi Minh, a Communist, headed an independence movement called the Vietminh to drive the French from Vietnam, one of the countries of Indochina. The United States stayed out of the fighting but supplied weapons and supplies to the French.

In 1954 the Vietminh surrounded French troops at Dien Bien Phu. The French asked the United States to bomb communist positions. Eisenhower believed that a French defeat might lead to communist domination of all of Southeast Asia.

Secretary Dulles favored giving military support to France. But when Eisenhower could get no support from the leaders of Congress or from other Western nations, he decided to stay out of the war. Dien Bien Phu fell in May 1954, and the French soon withdrew from Indochina.

Visualizing History

▲ EISENHOWER AND DULLES President Eisenhower delegated much of the conduct of foreign affairs to his secretary of state, John Foster Dulles (left). *What policy did Dulles favor to fight communist aggression?*

TEACH
Guided Practice

Geography Have students locate the following places on a map of the world: Israel, Egypt, the Commonwealth of Independent States, Great Britain, France, the Suez Canal. Then ask them to explain how these places were involved in what became the Suez crisis. **L1, LEP**

Visualizing History John Foster Dulles's younger brother was Allen W. Dulles, the head of the Central Intelligence Agency (CIA) from 1953 to 1961. Their personal relationship resulted in close coordination between the two departments. **Answer to Caption:** massive retaliation

ABCNEWS INTERACTIVE™

 VIDEODISC

Communism and the Cold War

Side Two, Chapter 8
Title: *Vietnam War*
Summary: Perspectives on the conflict

Special Needs Activity

Study Strategy Sometimes students have difficulty with the kind of knowledge that informs them how skills and strategies work. This kind of information is called "procedural" knowledge. It works in combination with declarative knowledge to specify the task the learner confronts and the active steps that he or she will take to perform the appropriate strategy. In order to learn procedural knowledge, students must practice and get feedback. Before students read about the Eisenhower Doctrine, ask them what they will need to do in order to "discuss its impact." **L1, LEP**

▲ THE UNITED STATES AND IRAN Shah Mohammad Reza Pahlavi came to power in Iran in 1953 with the help of secret American funds. He was later overthrown during the Iranian revolution of 1979. **Why did Eisenhower involve the CIA in Iran?**

At a conference in Geneva, Switzerland, in 1954, Vietnam was divided along the 17th parallel. North of that line, Ho Chi Minh's communist forces took control. To the south, a United States-supported government under Ngo Dinh Diem was set up. Diem's regime was dictatorial, inefficient, and unpopular. Communist-supported guerrillas began to fight against Diem's government. The United States provided most of the money for South Vietnam's defense. President Eisenhower had avoided war in Vietnam, but he had tied American prestige to the survival of Diem's unpopular and dictatorial government.

■ The Eisenhower Approach

When it came to solving foreign problems, Eisenhower preferred using diplomacy and **covert,** or secret, activities carried out by the Central Intelligence Agency (CIA).

In Iran and Guatemala

In 1953 President Eisenhower became concerned when the Iranian prime minister seized control of the Anglo-American Oil Company. The President feared that Iran was aligning itself with the Soviet Union, which would endanger oil supplies to Western nations. Under Eisenhower's orders, the CIA secretly funded a successful revolt by the young shah of Iran. Later Iran signed an agreement allowing United States, British, and French companies to share in Iranian oil production.

In 1954 the CIA helped to remove another unfriendly government. The Guatemalan government of Colonel Jacobo Arbenz Guzman had seized property of the American-owned United Fruit Company. The United States learned that Guzman was getting weapons from communist nations. Concerned that Guatemala would become a communist foothold in Latin America, the Eisenhower administration funded a coup that overthrew the government.

In both Iran and Guatemala, the revolutions appeared to have been inspired from within the nation. Only later did people learn of the CIA's role.

Secretary Dulles believed the events in Vietnam, Iran, and Guatemala were evidence of the Soviet Union's intention to spread communism. He argued that newly emerging nations should choose sides in the worldwide struggle between communism and democracy.

"Third World" Neutrality

In 1955 representatives from 29 Asian and African states met and signed an agreement calling for racial equality and self-determination. Two thousand delegates, from countries containing more than half the world's population, saw themselves as the "Third World." They declared their intention to remain independent of both the "First World"—the West—and the "Second World"—the Soviet Union.

The policy of neutralism was hotly debated. Some observers compared neutralism to isolationism and defended it as necessary for new and comparatively weak nations. Others attacked neutralism. Secretary Dulles took the position that no nation had the right to remain neutral in a conflict between "tyranny and freedom."

■ Middle East Powder Keg

During the 1950s the United States was drawn into the affairs of the Middle East. Before World War II, American businesses had begun to exploit the area's rich oil supplies. After the war the United States became increasingly dependent on Mideast oil. Americans were anxious to protect this oil supply. Many Americans also were interested in the survival of Israel, established in 1948 as a Jewish homeland.

The Middle East was like a "powder keg ready to explode." Arab nations believed that Israel was on land belonging to the Palestinians. They threatened to destroy Israel. Also, deep divisions existed among the Arab nations. Poverty and discontent were widespread. Finally, Soviet expansion posed a threat to Western oil supplies.

The first explosion came in 1956 in Egypt. Egypt's President Gamal Abdel Nasser was anxious to gain military superiority over the Jewish state. To get weapons, Egypt signed a commercial treaty with the Soviet Union, exchanging cotton—Egypt's major cash crop—for tanks and guns. The United States had tried to forge friendly relations with Egypt by offering to loan the nation money to build a giant dam across the Nile River. But Nasser's overtures toward the People's

Republic of China and the Soviet bloc forced Dulles to cancel the loan. Nasser responded by seizing the Suez Canal in July 1956.

The British, French, and Israelis decided to attack Egypt and reclaim the Suez Canal, which provided a vital trade link between Europe, the Middle East, and Asia. Acting independently of the United States, they invaded Egypt in October.

The world seemed on the verge of another major war. During a heated debate in the United Nations, the United States voted with the Soviet Union to condemn the actions of Israel, Great Britain, and France. This pressure forced the three nations to agree to withdraw from Egypt.

The Suez crisis greatly embarrassed the United States. Three of its strongest allies had acted alone. The affair might have shattered the Western alliance if Soviet action to crush the Hungarian revolution had not persuaded them to close ranks again.

Visualizing **H**istory

▲ NASSER AND THE SUEZ CRISIS
Warfare in the Middle East was close at hand after Egyptian leader Nasser seized the Suez Canal. Then Egypt was invaded by Britain, France, and Israel. *What caused Britain, France, and Israel to withdraw?*

Linking Across TIME

Tensions between Egypt and Israel have been the focus of several Middle East conflicts. In 1978, in a dramatic turnabout, Egypt became the first Arab state to make peace with Israel. The 1978 peace accords were engineered by Egypt's Anwar Sadat, Israel's Menachem Begin, and U.S. President Jimmy Carter.

Visualizing
History
The Suez Canal, which connects the Mediterranean and Red seas, was opened in 1869. It cut 4,000 miles off voyages between Britain and India.

Answer to Caption: In the United Nations, the U.S. joined the Soviet Union in condemning the invasion.

ABCNEWS INTERACTIVE™

 VIDEODISC

Powers of the Congress

Side One, Chapter 16
Title: *Provide for the Common Defense*
Subject: Explores role of Congress

Critical Thinking Activity

Evaluating an Action The overthrow of the leftist Guatemalan government was made possible by the activities of the CIA. Ask students the following question: Is secret aggression, such as that by the CIA, justifiable? Why or why not? *(Answers will vary. Some students might indicate* *that such action is justifiable because it is necessary for our country's and the world's security. Other students might indicate that such action is not justifiable because it undermines the sovereignty of another country.)* **L2**

FACT or FICTION?

In 1958 U.S. scientists began testing Earth's ozone.

FACT: Scientists wanted to discover what effects, if any, had been caused by atmospheric testing of nuclear weapons and by the growing number of high-altitude flights by military and commercial jet aircraft.

Visualizing History As a result of the Hungarian crisis, the United States dropped its call for the liberation of Eastern Europe.
Answer to Caption: Soviet troops overwhelmed Hungarian fighters.

Visualizing History

▲ **CONFLICT IN HUNGARY** The Hungarian revolt began when workers and students demonstrated for reform in 1956. Here, Hungarian citizens capture a Soviet tank in strife-torn Budapest. *How did the revolt end?*

The Eisenhower Doctrine

After the Suez crisis, the Soviets supported Egypt and offered to help build a new dam, the Aswan, across the Nile. President Eisenhower worried that the Soviets would gain new strength in the region. In January 1957, Eisenhower asked Congress to give him authority to use United States military forces to defend any Middle Eastern country that requested help against the forces of "international communism." Congress overwhelmingly approved the so-called Eisenhower Doctrine.

A year later the president of Lebanon asked Eisenhower to send troops to protect his government. He feared that Nasser and the Soviet Union might encourage a revolt in Lebanon.

In July 1958, American soldiers entered Lebanon. American troops remained in Lebanon until new elections established a stronger government. By taking this action, the United States showed that it intended to play a leading role in the Middle East. Yet the basic problems of the Middle East—poverty, rivalry and strife, and the threat of communist aggression—still defied solution.

The NATO Alliance

After President Eisenhower took office in 1953, he attempted to strengthen NATO under a unified command. But France was fearful of German resurgence and strongly opposed the plan. Western defenses were strengthened, however, when West Germany was allowed to rearm and join NATO.

The NATO alliance faced other difficulties. Europeans had mixed feelings about the United States. European Socialists and Communists regarded the United States as a materialistic nation where workers were exploited in order to increase the profits of a few great trusts. Conservatives believed Europe would be Americanized. In Britain and France, many people blamed the United States for their nation's loss of power in the world. But Soviet aggression persuaded Western Europe and the United States to maintain a common front.

Political uprisings in two of its satellites prompted the Soviet Union to reassert its control over Eastern Europe. In October 1956, anti-Soviet riots broke out in some Polish cities. The Soviet Union ultimately agreed to Polish demands for more freedoms. In Hungary, however, what began as

Sidelight: Nationalism and Independence

The years following World War II saw major political change in Africa. A large number of new nations were formed during this time. Once colonies ruled by European powers, many of these new nations found sovereignty difficult. Differences between groups within nations sometimes led to revolution and intertribal war. Many new nations needed help and asked for it but at the same time feared it because of the link between democracy and capitalism and imperialism and colonialism.

peaceful protests ended with open fighting. When communist leaders tried to put down the unrest, the Hungarians turned against them. On October 30, 1956, after less than a week of fighting, Budapest radio told the Hungarians: "You have won!" For five days jubilant Hungarians tasted freedom. Then on November 4, Soviet tanks and troops rolled through Budapest and overwhelmed its defenders. In the United States there was sympathy for the Hungarians, but little could be done without risking war.

■ Trouble in Latin America

While the United States worried about communist gains in Europe, Asia, and Africa, it ignored Latin America. There, the great poverty of the majority of the people and the concentration of land and power in the hands of a few created a breeding ground for political instability.

Latin Americans had good cause to believe they were "forgotten neighbors." They saw the United States pouring billions of dollars into remaking Europe's economy and strengthening weak governments in Asia. Yet Latin America received little United States foreign aid.

In 1958 Vice President Nixon made a good-will visit to Latin America. In some of the countries he visited, Nixon faced hostile demonstrations. In Peru and Venezuela, mobs threw stones and beat sticks against Nixon's car. This shocking attack on the Vice President brought home to people of the United States their neglect of Latin America's problems.

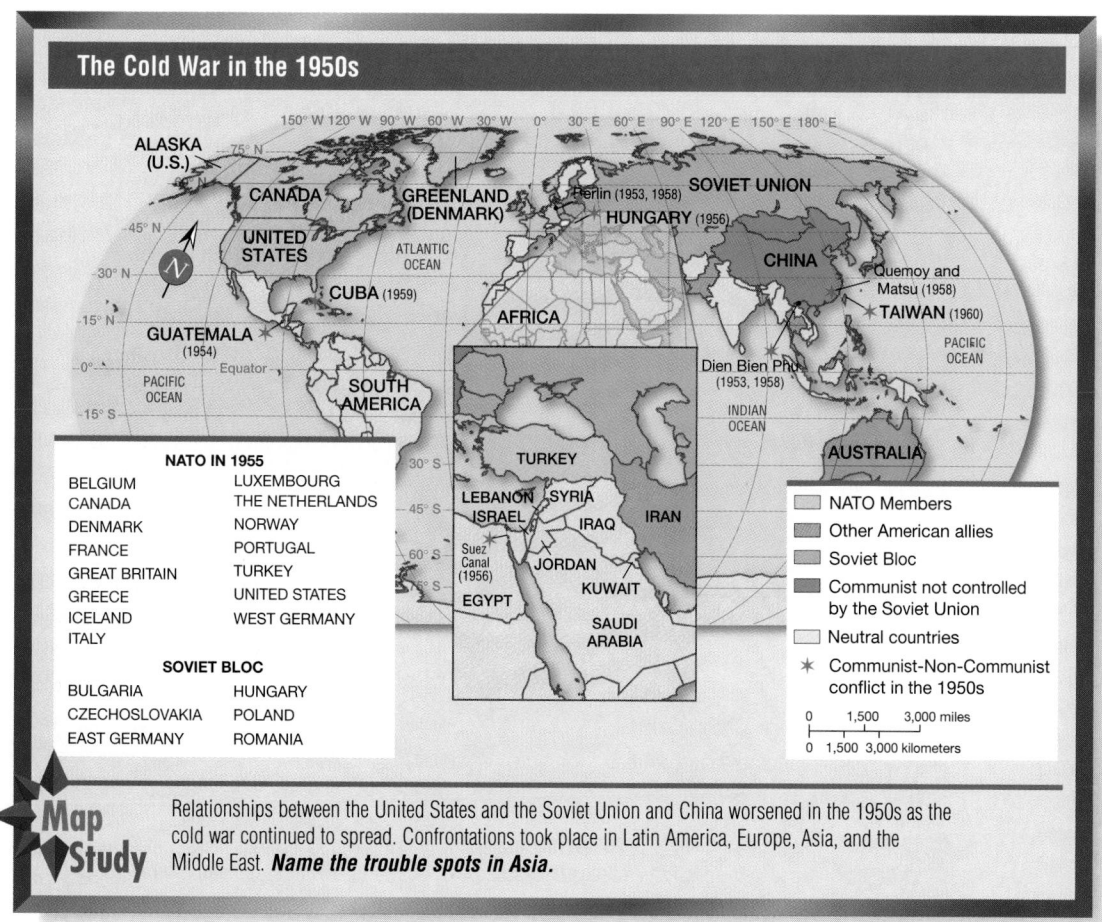

The Cold War in the 1950s

NATO IN 1955

BELGIUM	LUXEMBOURG
CANADA	THE NETHERLANDS
DENMARK	NORWAY
FRANCE	PORTUGAL
GREAT BRITAIN	TURKEY
GREECE	UNITED STATES
ICELAND	WEST GERMANY
ITALY	

SOVIET BLOC

BULGARIA	HUNGARY
CZECHOSLOVAKIA	POLAND
EAST GERMANY	ROMANIA

☐ NATO Members
▨ Other American allies
☐ Soviet Bloc
■ Communist not controlled by the Soviet Union
☐ Neutral countries
✳ Communist-Non-Communist conflict in the 1950s

0   1,500   3,000 miles
0   1,500   3,000 kilometers

Map Study Relationships between the United States and the Soviet Union and China worsened in the 1950s as the cold war continued to spread. Confrontations took place in Latin America, Europe, Asia, and the Middle East. **Name the trouble spots in Asia.**

Did You Know?

After Stalin's death in 1953, the Soviet Union engaged in summit meetings with the United States, France, and Great Britain. Have students compare the relationship between the Soviet Union and the United States in the 1950s and that between Russia and the United States today.

Map Study *Using Maps*

Answers: Dien Bien Phu (Vietnam), Quemoy and Matsu (islands off the China mainland), and Taiwan (Nationalist China on the island of Formosa)

Map Skills Practice
Ask: Which trouble spot shown on the map eventually led to the United States's involvement in the Vietnam conflict? *(Dien Bien Phu)*

📁 Assign Chapter Map Activity 21.

📁 Assign Geography in History Activity 21.

📁 Assign Map Transparency Activity 21.

Cooperative Learning Activity

Analyzing Government Policy Divide the class into small groups. Ask the students the following question: What factors contributed to the poor relations between the United States and Latin America in the 1950s? Have students in each group take turns contributing answers by writing the answer on a piece of paper and passing the paper to the left. When every student in each group has contributed an answer, discuss the groups' responses. *(The United States largely ignored the political situation in Latin America; Latin America received a small percentage of U.S. foreign aid; the Cuban government befriended and received military support from the Soviet Union.)* **L2**

ABCNEWS
INTERACTIVE™

VIDEODISC

Communism and the Cold War

Side One, Chapter 12
Title: *Espionage*
Subject: Cold War espionage

Events in Cuba further soured United States-Latin American relations. In 1959 a resistance movement headed by Fidel Castro forced the resignation of Cuba's corrupt dictator, Fulgencio Batista. Castro became a popular figure in the United States, and there was hope that the two nations would establish friendly relations. But American enthusiasm for Castro waned when he made friendly moves toward the Communists, denounced the United States, and seized private property. Castro also sought the military support of the Soviet Union. In response, President Eisenhower cut the quota of sugar the United States imported from Cuba and broke off relations with the Castro government.

■ Thaws in the Cold War

During the Eisenhower administration, the cold war spread to all continents. Yet there were signs that a "thaw" was possible. After Stalin's death in 1953, the Soviet people were allowed a little more freedom. The new premier, Nikita Khrushchev, denounced Stalin as a brutal tyrant. The Soviets now talked of peaceful coexistence and said that war in the atomic age would be so horrible that "the living will envy the dead."

In July 1955, Eisenhower met with the leaders of the Soviet Union, France, and Great Britain in Geneva, Switzerland. He made a strong plea for nuclear disarmament, saying that it would:

❝ *. . . ease the fears of war in the anxious hearts of people everywhere. . . . It would make [it] possible for every nation, great and small, developed and less developed, to advance the standards of living of its people. . . .* ❞

The summit, however, settled nothing. In 1958 tensions between the superpowers escalated once more, this time over the divided city of Berlin. The Soviets threatened to cut off Western access to Berlin unless the West recognized the East German government. When the crisis cooled down, both sides made new efforts to reduce world tensions. In 1959 Vice President Nixon and Premier Khrushchev exchanged visits. Khrushchev met with President Eisenhower at Camp David, where they made plans for a second summit meeting.

The new thaw was short-lived. Two weeks before the second summit meeting was to be held, in May 1960, an American U-2 surveillance plane was shot down over the Soviet

Visualizing
Ⓗistory

▲ COLD WAR RELATIONS During the era of the cold war, UN forces were sent to keep peace in Africa, the Middle East, and other hot spots. *What signs pointed toward a thaw in the cold war?*

Critical Thinking Activity

Seeing Relationships Fear of nuclear war lay behind the offensive and defensive decisions of both the superpowers and provided a background for the machinations of the politics of economically developing nations. The threat of a complete military "solution" to a disagreement led to hostilities played out in specific "theaters," with influence being the objective. Many leaders of economically developing countries recognized this by playing the United States against the Soviet Union. Discuss the shift from military muscle to economic might in fighting the cold war and how the threat of nuclear war influenced this change. **L2**

▲ U-2 PILOT GARY POWERS

■ Eisenhower's Farewell

The U-2 incident and the failure of East-West negotiations brought Eisenhower's years in office to a frustrating close. After the death of Secretary Dulles in 1959, Eisenhower took over more of the direction of foreign policy himself. He traveled widely in Europe, Asia, the Middle East, and Latin America to promote "peace and goodwill" and a "better understanding of America." But he was unable to lessen the tensions of the cold war and the threat of nuclear confrontation.

Still, Eisenhower remained a popular President, as near to a "father figure" as any President since George Washington. Like Washington, Eisenhower gave a farewell address. In it he warned against the influence of the military-industrial complex:

66 *We must never let the weight of this combination (of the military and industry) endanger our liberties or democratic processes. We should take nothing for granted. Only an alert and knowledgeable citizenry can compel the proper meshing of the huge industrial and military machinery of defense with our peaceful methods and goals, so that security and liberty may prosper together.* 99

The President's message was impressive because it came from a man who had spent most of his life as a soldier.

Union. The CIA had sent it to spy on and photograph Soviet nuclear sites and missile bases. Khrushchev denounced Eisenhower as a prisoner of the "war mongers" and refused to take part in the meeting. Relations between East and West once again turned colder.

ASSESS
Check Understanding
Assign Section 4 Review as homework or an in-class activity.

Evaluate
◉ 🗁 Assign Section Quiz 21-4 or use the Test-maker to create a customized quiz.

Reteach
Have students write a report on Eisenhower's foreign policy approach in the following countries: Vietnam, Iran, Egypt, and Lebanon.

🗁 Have students complete Reteaching Activity 21-4.

Enrich
Have students research the present situation concerning the Suez Canal. They might find out who is running it and how important it is to the world today compared with its importance during the Eisenhower administration.

🗁 Assign Workbook Activity 21-4.

CLOSE
Write the following statement on the chalkboard: President Eisenhower took American foreign policy in a new direction.

Ask students to discuss this statement based on what they learned in Section 4.

Section 4 ★ Review

Checking for Understanding

1. **Identify** John Foster Dulles, SEATO, CENTO, OAS, Ho Chi Minh, Gamal Abdel Nasser, Fulgencio Batista, Fidel Castro, U-2.

2. **Define** covert.

3. **Describe** the Eisenhower administration's foreign policy.

4. **State** reasons why European attitudes toward the United States changed in the 1950s.

Critical Thinking

5. **Making Predictions** How might economically developing nations view the cold war?

ACTIVITY

6. Imagine you were a journalist in 1961 when President Eisenhower left office. Write a profile of Eisenhower for a popular publication, focusing on his personal traits and his leadership style.

CHAPTER 21 Search for Stability: 1952–1960   **657**

Answers to SECTION 4 REVIEW

1. John Foster Dulles, 650; SEATO, 650; CENTO, 650; OAS, 650; Ho Chi Minh, 649; Gamal Abdel Nasser, 653; Fulgencio Batista, 656; Fidel Castro, 656; U-2, 657
2. All vocabulary words are defined in the Glossary.
3. containment, covert CIA action, avoid war, try to thaw cold war, achieve nuclear disarmament

4. saw United States as materialistic exploiter of workers; feared Europe being Americanized; British and French resented lack of support
5. Answers will vary. Unaligned with either, might feel unfairly imperiled by minority. No stake in race, but cannot sit out a nuclear war.
6. Profiles will vary but should depict valid portrayal.

GLENCOE
TECHNOLOGY

VIDEODISC

Use the MindJogger Videoquiz to review students' knowledge.

MindJogger Videoquiz

Chapter 21
Disc 3, Side A

Available in VHS.

Using Vocabulary
Statements will vary but should include both words.

Reviewing Facts
1. war hero, father figure, optimism, trust, strong, no war
2. whether to continue price supports or leave farmer at mercy of elements and prices
3. Liberal: extended Social Security and increased benefits; tried to get health insurance program. Conservative: little regulation of business, low taxes.
4. Automation produced goods faster; electronics revolutionized industry; improved farm machines increased yields, shortened hours. Television opened new medium for advertising.
5. More Americans moved to suburbs; bought homes, autos, luxury goods; more leisure time.
6. Dulles: no reconciliation with Communists, containment inadequate, take offensive. Eisenhower: seek peace, negotiate, avoid

Using Vocabulary

Use these vocabulary words in a statement about the influence of technology on business and agriculture.

agribusiness   automation

Reviewing Facts

1. **State** reasons why Americans elected Ike by overwhelming majorities in 1952 and 1956.
2. **Explain** the Eisenhower administration's dilemma regarding the farm problem.
3. **Show** how Eisenhower's policies toward health and welfare programs and big business reflected his middle-course economic policy.
4. **Identify** technological advances of the 1950s that contributed to the strength of the American economy.
5. **Describe** the effects of economic growth and affluence on American life.

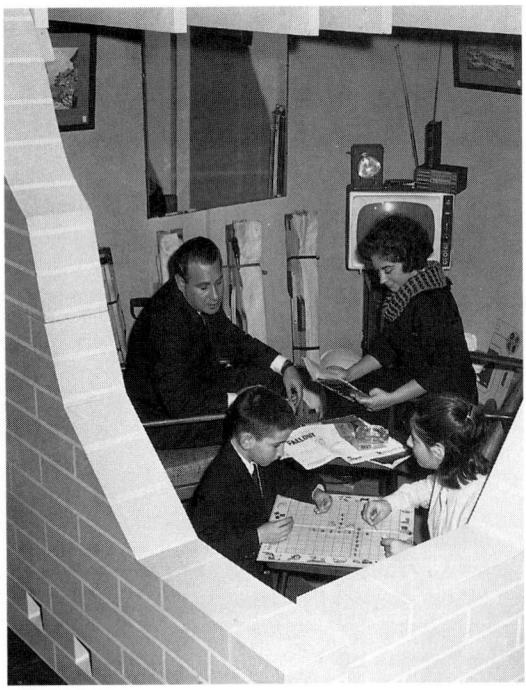

6. **Cite** the differences between Dulles's and Eisenhower's approaches to foreign policy.
7. **Discuss** how the following groups were affected by the pressure to conform: (1) middle-class families, (2) African Americans, (3) women.
8. **Speculate** about the effects of the nuclear threat on the conduct of the cold war.

Understanding Concepts

International Leadership

1. If you were to examine Eisenhower's leadership style as commander of NATO forces, how would you expect it to differ from his international leadership style as President? Why?
2. What is your opinion of Eisenhower's use of covert operations to remove unfriendly foreign governments? Explain.

Economic Growth

3. What factors stimulated economic growth in the 1950s?
4. How did the growth of the television industry both reflect and stimulate economic growth?

Critical Thinking

1. **Demonstrating Reasoned Judgment** Find an example of Eisenhower's actions that supports both national security and global security. Did he take any steps in the interest of national security at the possible expense of global security? Support your answer.
2. **Locating Examples** What lifestyle changes reflected the "economy of abundance" during the 1950s?
3. **Analyzing Photographs** Study the photograph of the bomb shelter on this page, then answer the questions that follow.
   a. What do you think the photographer was trying to show with this picture?
   b. Do you think this photograph was part of an advertisement, a news story, or for another purpose? Explain.

military involvement, seek nuclear disarmament.
7. (1) house in suburbs like others, big cars, right clubs, schools, correct dress, behavior (2) more discrimination, keep out of suburbs (3) back to home, child-rearing
8. probably shifted focus away from military solu-

tions to diplomacy, formation of alliances

Understanding Concepts

1. more authoritative, less sharing of decision; military based on obedience and discipline
2. may say necessary to pro-

tect United States or United States has no right to impose system
3. business mergers; technological advances; higher wages; peace
4. Most American homes had TV. Advertisers pitched to wide audience, increased product sales, demand.

4. Supporting an Opinion Respond to President Eisenhower's domino theory. Do you believe it justifies the containment policy? Explain.

5. Assessing Outcomes Do you agree with President Eisenhower's statement that control of the military-industrial complex is necessary "so that security and liberty may prosper together"? Why or why not?

6. Making Comparisons When NATO was established in 1949, each country promised to come to the aid of the others in case of attack. In 1991 NATO dispatched three squadrons of German, Italian, and Belgian jet fighters to Turkey, a member of NATO, to strengthen its border with Iraq in case of war. How does this 1991 NATO action carry out the intent of the charter?

History and Geography

The Western and Eastern Blocs

Use the map on page 655 and information from Chapter 21 to help you answer the questions that follow.

1. Location In which Western Hemisphere nations did cold war conflicts occur?

2. Location What conflicts took place in Europe during this period?

3. Place What features of the Suez Canal made it the center of conflict in the mid-1950s? What nations were involved in the conflict?

Cooperative Learning Interdisciplinary Activity: Sociology

Working in a group of four, research life in the United States during the Eisenhower administration. Divide the research assignments so that different members are responsible for finding information about news events, movies, television shows, popular music, theater, art achievements, literary publications, advances in science and technology, sports events, and fashion trends for those years. Have members record their findings. Combine the reports to form a history of American life and lifestyles during the Eisenhower years.

Practicing Skills

Analyzing Symbols

Refer to the skills lesson on page 638 to help you practice this skill. For each of the following names, phrases, or terms, select an appropriate symbol, draw the symbol, and write a caption that explains the association.

- *The Affluent Society*
- suburbanization
- automation
- *The Man in the Gray Flannel Suit*
- baby boom
- massive retaliation
- Hungary
- Fidel Castro
- Middle East powder keg
- cold war thaw
- U-2

Study the list below. What does each item symbolize to you?

- The American Flag
- The Constitution
- The White House
- The Statue of Liberty

Writing ABOUT History

Using Your Journal

Write a paragraph discussing the success or failure of the Eisenhower administration to contain communism.

6. It carried out the idea of collective security.

History and Geography

1. Cuba and Guatemala
2. in Berlin and in Hungary
3. It was a trade link between Europe, the Middle East, and Asia. Britain, France, Israel, and Egypt were involved.

Cooperative Learning

Encourage students to form a book that describes American life and lifestyles during the Eisenhower years. Display completed books.

Practicing Skills

Students should include a caption that explains the association of symbol to item. Students' descriptions of what symbols mean to them will vary.

Writing ABOUT History

Using Your Journal

Students will present various positions but should review the major East-West crises of the period.

? Chapter Bonus Test Question

Ask: How did President Eisenhower try to keep the cold war from turning into a shooting war? *(tried to reduce tensions, reduce threat of Soviet nuclear war, contain Soviet expansion)*

Critical Thinking

1. Summits, good will missions, and plea for nuclear disarmament support both. Covert overthrow of unfriendly government may establish dangerous precedent, harm global security.
2. suburbs, home ownership, autos, television, luxury goods, leisure time interests
3. **a.** Answers should include a view of life in a shelter.
   b. Students should include valid reasons to support their answers.
4. Some will cite domino theory and support containment policy, or say not our affair. Others may say spread of communism limited to areas with poverty or political repression.
5. Those who agree might indicate that both the military and industry have a stake in accelerating arms race. Those who disagree might indicate that the complex is not dangerous and can manage itself.

Cultural Kaleidoscope

Making Connections

History and Technology

Since its beginnings, the United States has protected innovators by issuing patents. A patent is a grant given an inventor that prevents anyone else from making, using, or selling his or her invention. It usually runs for 17 years. The Constitution provides for patents in Article I, Section 8, and the first one was issued in 1790.

More About...
Credit Cards

Although credit cards were issued in the 1930s by oil companies in order to increase sales at service stations, the first multipurpose card dates back to 1950. Francis X. McNamara, dining out in New York City with clients, discovered that he'd left his wallet at home. He called his wife, who obligingly drove in from the suburbs with money. McNamara, determined to avoid such embarassment in the future, went home and thought up the Diners Club.

A Changing Society

Innovations

From important discoveries and innovations like computers, penicillin, open heart surgery, and the polio vaccine to more mundane accomplishments like TV dinners, the period from the 1930s to the 1960s was a time of discovery and unbounded imagination. New technology transformed the nature of work and helped Americans enjoy more leisure time. At the same time, the number of available leisure activities increased. By the 1950s Americans were enjoying a standard of living far beyond any they had previously known.

Progress in electronics began to revolutionize home entertainment. Probably no form of entertainment has matched the effects of television. Developed in the 1930s, television went on the market in the late 1940s. Fewer than 1 million households had a set in 1949. Within four years, the number had soared to 20 million.

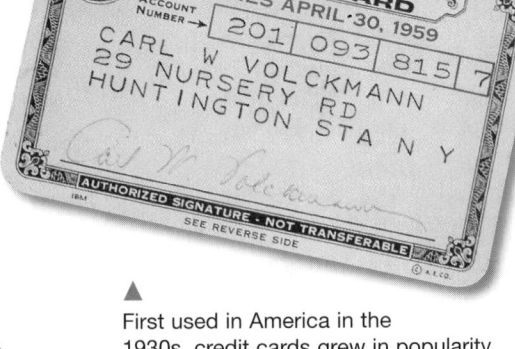

First used in America in the 1930s, credit cards grew in popularity during the 1950s when computers allowed for fast and accurate billing.

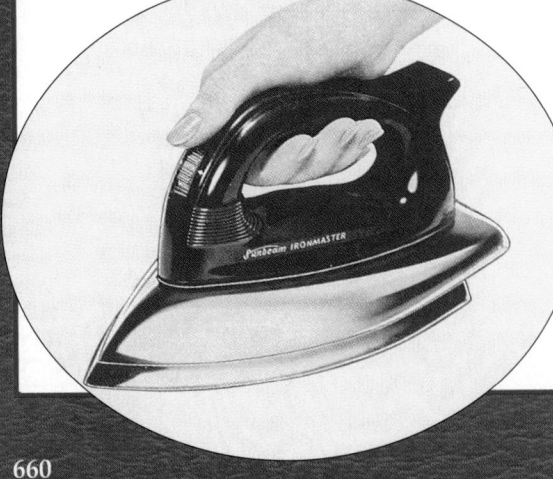

The electric iron, like this model, became a necessary domestic appliance.

660

Cooperative Learning Activity

Reporting on Innovations Divide the class into small groups. Assign each one an innovation featured in this spread, such as antibiotics, refrigeration, or television (or others of your choice). Have each group research its innovation and report to the class. **L1**

▶ With new means of refrigeration widely available after World War II, Americans could store quantities of food for months on end. By 1956, 9 of 10 American families owned a refrigerator. Other symbols of the affluent society: by 1956, 3 of 4 families owned at least one auto, 3 out of 5 owned their own home. In 1945 only 9,000 private swimming pools were in use. In 1957 alone more than 50,000 pools were installed.

▲ Between the 1920s and the advent of the television age, millions of Americans learned about the important events of the day from radio. By the mid-1930s, two-thirds of American homes had at least one radio—less than half that many had telephones.

▶ More and more Americans, it seems, were eating canned foods. Hormel's Spiced Ham, better known as Spam, quickly established a strong position. Part of the impetus came during World War II when Spam's price and shelf life made it a staple of the soldier's diet. In Korea, Spam is considered an imported luxury item.

Portfolio Project

Have students keep a log of their leisure activities for a week. Among the specifics they might note: what the activity is, whether they engage in it alone or with others, and how much time they spend on it. They might also speculate about whether their parents and/or grandparents could have spent their leisure time pursuing the same activities.

History and the Humanities

📁 **The Spirit of American Art and Music,** pp. 39–40, 43–44: Aaron Copeland, Duke Ellington

🎵 **American Music: Cultural Traditions:** Cold War: "Old Man Atom" by Sam Hinton (3:10)

🖼 **Focus on American Fine Art Print 16,** *New York, New Haven and Hartford* by Edward Hopper

661

The Historian's Craft

The innovations shown here were all designed to appeal to, and be purchased by, consumers. Historians study advertisements in order to understand the impact of various innovations.

Among other things, they note the audience being targeted and the motives (competition, anxiety, thrift, and so on) to which they appeal.

Exploring Unit Themes

The Unit Digest may be used to teach unit coverage when time is limited, to review unit content, or to relate the content of one unit to that of another.

■ Chapter 18

Have students construct a chart showing the New Deal legislation mentioned in Chapter 18.

■ Chapter 19

Ask students to list the reasons American leaders gave for entering World War II.

■ Chapter 20

Remind students that the postwar years brought some interesting words and phrases into everyday language—"cold war," "containment," and "iron curtain," for example. Ask students to find and note the meaning and origin of these and other new political terms introduced in Chapter 20.

Causes and Effects

Ask students to write a paragraph summarizing the information on the chart. Paragraphs should reflect the connections between the causes and the effects.

Chapter 18

The New Deal

Franklin D. Roosevelt's New Deal was a two-part program of emergency measures and long-range planning with three specific aims—recovery from the Depression, relief for victims of the Depression, and reform of the nation's economic system.

During Roosevelt's first days in office, Congress enacted an unprecedented number of new programs. The second phase of the New Deal emphasized social reform rather than short-term emergency measures. Out of these efforts came large-scale public works programs and a Social Security system.

Roosevelt won reelection in 1936 by a landslide. However, problems with the Supreme Court and other setbacks in Congress slowed the pace of the New Deal. But by then its programs already had altered the role of government in American life.

Rebuilding Europe

CAUSES

- Communist guerrillas control much of Greece
- European countries suffer economic devastation after World War II

↓

• The Marshall Plan

↓

EFFECTS

- Congress responds by voting military and economic aid to Greece
- Western European economies prosper

Chapter 19

World War II

During FDR's first and second administrations, the Good Neighbor policy committed the United States to a policy of nonintervention in Latin America. In Europe, FDR recognized the Soviet Union and sought to maintain neutral relations with other nations.

When war in Europe broke out in 1939, German victories prompted the United States to aid the Allied nations of Britain and France. In 1941, after Japanese planes bombed Pearl Harbor, the United States declared war on Japan and Germany. For the second time in 25 years, the American economy converted to war production and transformed the nation's way of life.

By the time an ailing Roosevelt was reelected to a fourth term, Germany and Japan had suffered major defeats on all fronts. Germany surrendered in May 1945. Japan surrendered after American planes dropped atomic bombs on Hiroshima and Nagasaki. Before the war ended, the United Nations formed in hopes of maintaining international peace and cooperation.

Cooperative Learning Activity

Writing Letters Divide the class into groups of four or five. Have groups select one of the following topics: Tennessee Valley Authority, social security, United Nations, G.I. Bill, House Committee on Un-American Activities, cold war, affluent society. Have groups write a letter to someone who might have played a part in the early history of their chosen topic. The letters should explain changes concerning their topics that have taken place in the intervening years. Groups should select representatives to read their letters to the class. **L2**

Chapter 20

The Cold War

After World War II, the Soviet Union drew an "iron curtain" between Eastern Europe and the rest of Europe. An intense war of words, rivalry, and confrontation soon developed between the West and the Soviet Union.

Western fear that communism would spread led to a policy of containment. The Marshall Plan also gave massive economic aid to war-torn Western Europe. The United States, Canada, and nations of Western Europe established the North Atlantic Treaty Organization (NATO); Eastern European communist countries responded with the Warsaw Pact.

Meanwhile, the cold war spread to Asia. In 1949 Mao Zedong established a communist government in China, despite American efforts to prevent it. In Korea, Americans fought a "hot war" to stop a communist takeover of the peninsula.

At home the Truman administration pushed for economic and social reform. Inflation was rising, and labor resorted to strikes to increase wages. Fear generated by the cold war led to a search for Communists in the federal government.

In the early 1950s, the country began a long period of economic prosperity. The growing economy created millions of new jobs. Encouraged by their new economic strength, African Americans began to lobby for their civil rights.

Chapter 21

Search for Stability

In 1953, Dwight D. Eisenhower brought a new style of leadership to the White House. Although friendly to corporations, Eisenhower also expanded New Deal programs. Despite inflation and a brief recession, business leaders and working women and men prospered. Farmers, however, did not fare well.

For many Americans, affluence and a new confidence in the future came with economic growth. A new way of life evolved as families moved from the cities to the suburbs and wage earners commuted to work.

Under Eisenhower, America's cold war containment policy continued through diplomacy, aid, and covert operations. His efforts to lessen tensions and reduce the Soviet nuclear threat, however, failed.

Understanding Unit Themes

1. **American Democracy**   How did the role of government in American democracy change during the Depression and the New Deal? What changes persist to the present?

2. **Civil Rights and Liberties**   Throughout the 1930s and 1940s, women gained new employment opportunities and a recognized place in the workforce. How do you account for the ground they lost in the 1950s?

3. **Conflict and Cooperation**   How does the purpose of the United Nations differ from that of NATO, the Warsaw Pact, and the alliances of World War II?

4. **U.S. Role in World Affairs**   Describe United States efforts to contain the spread of communism worldwide from 1948–1960. What were the results of these efforts?

UNIT 6 DIGEST

■ Chapter 21

Remind students that prosperity brought changes in lifestyle for many Americans during the 1950s. Have them research and write a report on everyday life in the "affluent society."

 Student Self-Test Software allows students to test their understanding of historical concepts in this unit.

🎧 Have students listen to the Chapter Digests on the audiocassettes.

Use the Testmaker to create a customized test for Unit 6.

GLENCOE
TECHNOLOGY

💿 VIDEODISC

Use the MindJogger Videoquiz to review students' knowledge.

MindJogger Videoquiz

 Chapter 18
Disc 2, Side B

 Chapter 19
Disc 3, Side A

 Chapter 20
Disc 3, Side A

 Chapter 21
Disc 3, Side A

 Available in VHS.

Flashcards

Use American History Flashcards to reinforce students' knowledge of places and events in American history.

Answers to Understanding Unit Themes

1. more government intervention; supported labor, work relief, and assistance programs; social security benefits; regulated banking and business practices; intervened to stimulate or otherwise adjust economy

2. Labor not needed. Pressure to conform sent women back to homes.

3. United Nations is unaligned international peacekeeping organization.

4. China—supported Chiang Kai-shek against Mao; failed. Korea—sent troops to help Rhee drive out North Koreans; fought to a draw; country divided. Indochina—supplied Diem against Communist forces. Continued involvement led to Vietnam War. Europe—could not end Soviet control of satellites but contained its further expansion.

BEGINNING THE UNIT

Provide this cause-and-effect chart to students with effects omitted. Assign students to complete the chart as they read the chapters in the unit.

Event
- War in Vietnam

Causes
- Struggle for civil rights
- U.S. intervention globally against communism
- Beginning of U.S. involvement in Southeast Asia

Effects
- Americans divided over war in Vietnam
- War undermines economic and social progress
- Protests and conflict challenge the government
- Government resists policy changes
- Watergate scandal erodes confidence in government
- Challenge to government's role in society brings change
- Struggle to redefine government continues

History AND ART

Ask students to discuss what advantages and disadvantages a mural artist faces.

0:00 OUT OF TIME?

If time does not permit teaching the entire unit, use the Unit Digest on pages 800–801.

664

UNIT SEVEN
REDEFINING AMERICA
1954–PRESENT

★★

CHAPTER 22	CHAPTER 23	CHAPTER 24	CHAPTER 25	CHAPTER 26
The Civil Rights Era 1954–1975	The Vietnam Era 1954–1975	Camelot to Watergate 1960–1976	Search for Solutions 1976–1992	Toward a New Century 1992–

▲ VIETNAM VETERAN'S HAT

History AND ART

Mural on Building
Davenport, Iowa

Vivid images abound in this colorful mural commemorating American leaders and important events.

664

Exploring Unit Themes

Civil Rights and Liberties During this period, through demonstrations and civil disobedience, African Americans won repeal of discriminatory laws and more opportunities to share in the American dream. Women, too, made progress in their drive for equal rights.

Conflict and Cooperation In the early 1960s the belief grew—especially among young Americans—that by working together people could overcome problems, but bitter feelings over the Vietnam War left young Americans at odds with their government. During the 1980s, however, American confidence was restored.

Cultural Diversity The United States continued to be a haven for immigrants seeking freedom or opportunities for a better life. Today, the new

Setting the Scene

American society from the mid-1950s to the present has been described as a roller coaster. Americans were taken to new heights of optimism and confidence but lows of doubt and frustration as well. In addition, growing awareness of new technology redefined the way Americans lived and worked.

Themes

- Civil Rights and Liberties
- Conflict and Cooperation
- Cultural Diversity
- U.S. Role in World Affairs

Key Events

- Desegregation in public schools
- Kennedy's assassination
- War in Vietnam
- Watergate scandal
- Camp David Peace Accords
- Persian Gulf War
- Congress approves NAFTA

Major Issues

- The growing civil rights movement opens the political process for thousands of Americans.
- Involvement in Vietnam polarizes Americans at home and tarnishes the nation's image abroad.
- Illegal activities by high-level government officials result in the Watergate scandal.
- Democratic movements lead to the end of the Soviet Union.
- The United States and allies liberate Kuwait after Iraqi invasion.
- America seeks to redefine its role in the new world order and meet rising challenges at home.

▲ TALL SHIPS, PART OF BICENTENNIAL CELEBRATION

▲ POLITICAL CAMPAIGN BUTTONS

Portfolio Project

Make a poster for an imaginary benefit concert similar to the "Live Aid" concert. Select a topic from the leading challenges facing America in the late 1990s. Make sure to note this topic on the poster, along with the location of the concert and what artists will be performing.

INTRODUCING
UNIT 7

interNET CONNECTIONS

For more in-depth study of Unit 7, you or your students may use the Internet to research individual topics.

Information on Vietnam:
http://grunt.space.swri.edu/visit.htm

World Wide Web:
Martin Luther King, Jr.: http://www-leland.stanford.edu/group/King
The Kennedy Assassination Home Page: http://www.rt66.com/~rharris/jfk.html

Portfolio Project

Suggest students narrow the focus of their topic. For instance, if they study the environment, ask them to select an aspect of the environment that is of concern to them.

History and the Humanities

U.S. History and Art Transparencies **29, 32:** *Day of the Fair* by Andrew Wyeth; *Still Life With Red Car 1986* by Frank Romero

Focus on American Fine Art Prints **19,** *Springtime in the Pedernales* by Porfirio Salinas

immigrants are mostly from Latin America and Asia.

U.S. Role in World Affairs During most of this period, the United States assumed a cold war stance. The collapse of communism in the Soviet Union and throughout Eastern Europe beginning in the late 1980s, however, brought much of the cold war to an end.

Examining the Themes Tell students that this unit traces the many events and issues that have confronted the United States since the 1950s.

FOCUS

Motivating Activity

Remind students that on the evening of January 16, 1991, even before the United States government had made any official statements, the American people knew that the Gulf War to repel the invasion of Kuwait by the forces of Iraq had begun. Reporters from the news network CNN provided vivid, live word-pictures of the aerial bombardment of Iraq's capital of Baghdad.

Ask students to draw conclusions about the impact of satellite communications by discussing the following statement: Today, there are no local events, only global events. (*Students may suggest that instant communications makes people more aware of global events.*) **L1**

TEACH

Guided Practice

Exploring the Time Line
Direct students' attention to the World Events section of the time line and have them note events that reflect changes around the world. Conduct a class discussion about how these changes might affect policies of the United States. (*For example, building the Berlin Wall—U.S. might step up cold war policies against USSR; collapse of communism—U.S. redefine policy toward USSR and Eastern Europe.*) **L2**

Global Perspectives

The World

	1950	1954		1965	1966
Asia and Oceania		1954 French are defeated in Vietnam			1966 China's Cultural Revolution begins
Europe				1961 Berlin Wall built	
Africa			◄ 1960 "Year of Africa" —many countries become independent		
South America					
North and Central America			1959 St. Lawrence Seaway opens		

The United States

Pacific and Northwest			◄ 1959 Alaska and Hawaii become states		
Southeast		1955 Rosa Parks inspires Montgomery bus boycott		1965 Freedom March from Selma to Montgomery	
Midwest		1954 Brown v. Board of Education *decision*			
Southwest				◄ 1966 First artificial heart implanted	
Atlantic Northeast	1950			1965	

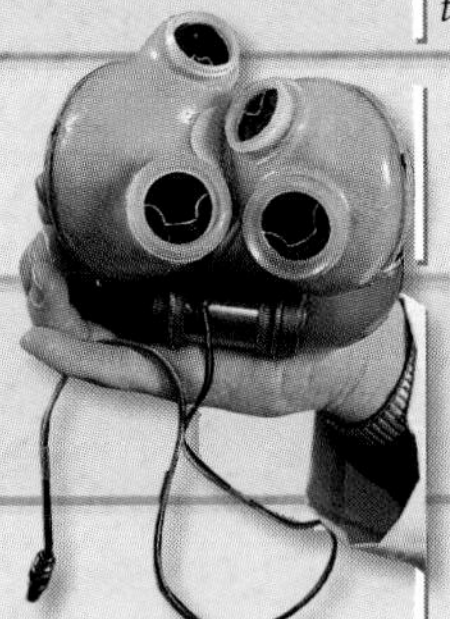

666   UNIT 7 Redefining America: 1954–Present

Cultural Perspectives

Immigration Trends In the late 1980s, Asia, the Caribbean, and Latin America were the major sources of immigration to the United States. The largest numbers of newcomers were from Colombia, the Dominican Republic, Ecuador, Guyana, Haiti, Jamaica, India, China, the Philippines, and South Korea. At the same time, however, people emigrated from another 150 countries. It is not surprising, then, that the United States has been called the world in microcosm.

Linking Across TIME

The United States has long been known as a nation of immigrants. Throughout its history, people from other countries came to its shores seeking a better way of life. In the late 1980s, the major sources of immigration to the United States were Asia, the Caribbean, and Latin America. Among the countries that sent the most immigrants were China, Colombia, the Dominican Republic, Ecuador, Guyana, Haiti, India, Jamaica, the Philippines, and South Korea. At the same time, however, immigrants came from another 150 countries. It is not surprising then that some people have called the United States the world in microcosm, or miniature.

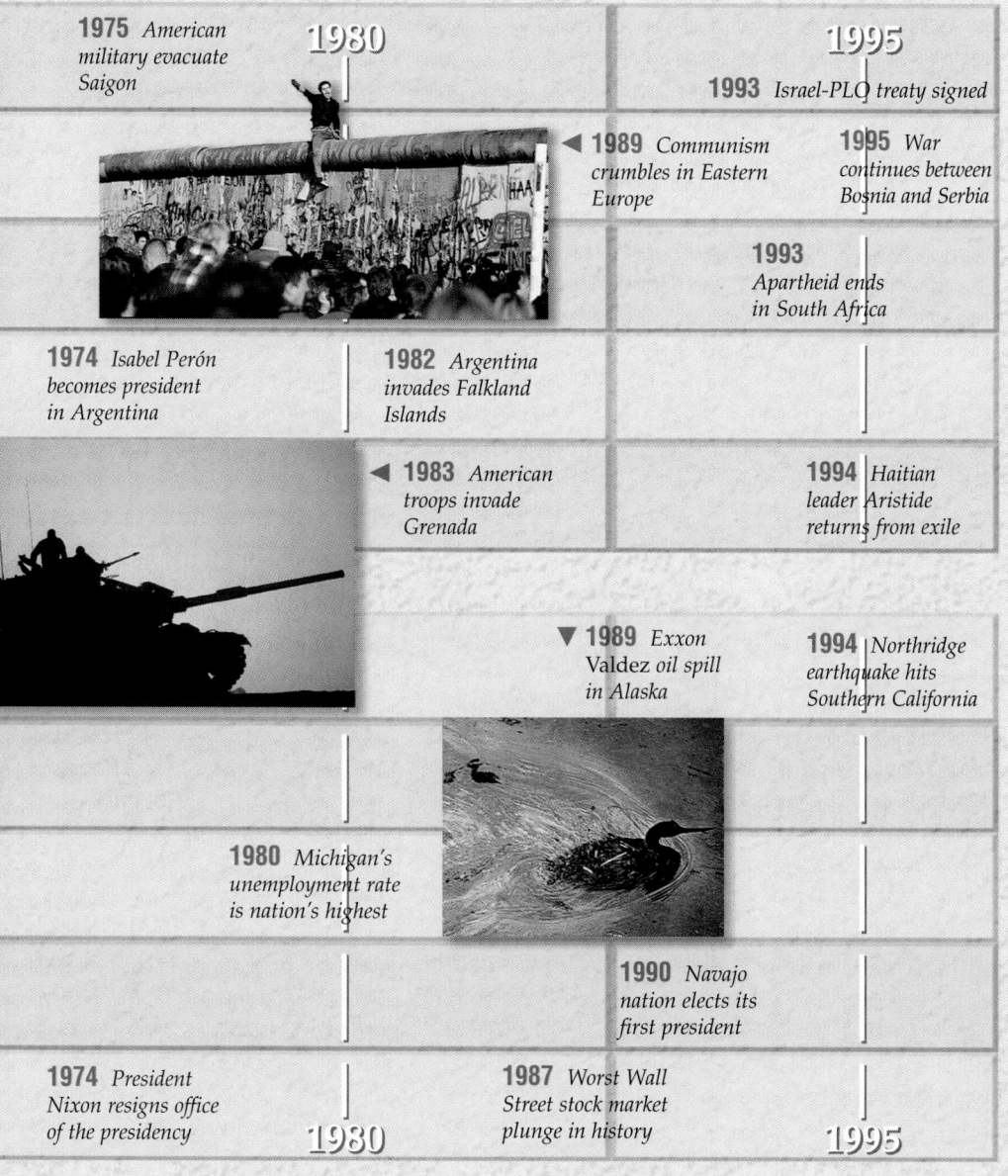

1980

1975 *American military evacuate Saigon*

◀ **1989** *Communism crumbles in Eastern Europe*

1974 *Isabel Perón becomes president in Argentina*

1982 *Argentina invades Falkland Islands*

◀ **1983** *American troops invade Grenada*

▼ **1989** *Exxon Valdez oil spill in Alaska*

1980 *Michigan's unemployment rate is nation's highest*

1974 *President Nixon resigns office of the presidency*

1980

1987 *Worst Wall Street stock market plunge in history*

1995

1993 *Israel-PLO treaty signed*

1995 *War continues between Bosnia and Serbia*

1993 *Apartheid ends in South Africa*

1994 *Haitian leader Aristide returns from exile*

1994 *Northridge earthquake hits Southern California*

1990 *Navajo nation elects its first president*

1995

Cooperative Learning Activity

Constructing Time Lines Divide the class into two groups and assign one group the world, the other, the United States. Have each group research and construct a time line for its area for the last 15 years. Suggest that groups have at least five entries for each region in its area. Display the finished time lines on the bulletin board and use them as a starting point for a class discussion on global interdependence. **L2**

Independent Practice

Linking World Events
Point out that the opening of the St. Lawrence Seaway in 1959 enabled oceangoing vessels to travel as far inland in the United States as the Great Lakes. Ask students to write a report on how the seaway changed the patterns of trade in the United States. Suggest that they illustrate their reports with maps, graphs, and charts. A useful source of information is *The United States and Canada, Present and Future* by Richard S. Thoman. **L3**

ASSESS
Studying the Time Line

1. Which 1950s entry in the world section of the time line is related to a 1970s entry in the United States section? *(1954—French defeated in Vietnam)*
2. In what sense have the events in the Europe column of the world time line come "full circle?" *(Berlin wall symbolic of division between communist and free Europe; crumbling of communism led to fall of Berlin Wall.)*
3. "Americans must not be ignorant of the world, for what happens thousands of miles away may have a resounding impact on their lives." Ask students to support this statement with information from the time lines. *(Answers will vary but may include war between Bosnia and Serbia.)*

Daily Lesson Objectives	Teacher Classroom Resources	Multimedia
SECTION 1 **A New Beginning** **1 Day pp. 670–674** 1. Discuss the effects of the *Brown* v. *Board of Education* decision. 2. Describe major events in the early civil rights movement.	Reproducible Lesson Plan 22-1 *Guided Reading Activity 22-1 Concept Mapping Activities 22-A, 22-B *Vocabulary Activity 22 Supreme Court Case Study 22 Linking Past and Present Activity 22 Reteaching Activity 22-1 *Section Quiz 22-1	Section Focus Transparency 22-1 Chapter Concepts Transparencies 22-A, 22-B MindJogger Videoquiz GTV: The American People: Fabric of a Nation Powers of the Supreme Court Martin Luther King, Jr.
SECTION 2 **Successes and Setbacks** **1 Day pp. 676–680** 1. Describe advances made in civil rights during the Kennedy-Johnson administrations. 2. Describe the setbacks and difficulties the civil rights activists faced during the 1960s.	Reproducible Lesson Plan 22-2 *Guided Reading Activity 22-2 Chapter Map Activity 22 Geography in History Activity 22 Workbook Activity 22-2 Reteaching Activity 22-2 *Section Quiz 22-2	Section Focus Transparency 22-2 Map Transparency 22 Skills Transparency 22 Testmaker GTV: The American People: Fabric of a Nation Martin Luther King, Jr.
SECTION 3 **New Directions** **1 Day pp. 682–686** 1. List some of the factors responsible for discontent among some African Americans. 2. Explain what new philosophies were developed by African Americans to deal with the discontent.	Reproducible Lesson Plan 22-3 *Guided Reading Activity 22-3 Cooperative Learning Activity 22 Critical Thinking Skills Activity 22 Workbook Activity 22-3 Reteaching Activity 22-3 *Section Quiz 22-3	Section Focus Transparency 22-3 Testmaker Set on Freedom™: The American Civil Rights Movement Martin Luther King, Jr.
SECTION 4 **The Impact of Civil Rights** **1 Day pp. 687–691** 1. Describe the gains made by women and minorities. 2. Explain why the Equal Rights Amendment was not ratified.	Reproducible Lesson Plan 22-4 *Guided Reading Activity 22-4 American Literary Heritage, p. 51 Enrichment Activity 22 Workbook Activity 22-4 Reteaching Activity 22-4 *Section Quiz 22-4	Section Focus Transparency 22-4 Testmaker GTV: The American People: Fabric of a Nation The American Indian
CHAPTER REVIEW AND EVALUATION **1 Day**	Chapter 22 Test, Forms A and B Spanish Chapter 22 Summary Performance Assessment Activity 22	MindJogger Videoquiz Student Self-Test & Review Software *Chapter 22 Audiocassette Activity and Test

*Also available in Spanish

 OUT OF TIME? If time does not permit teaching the entire chapter, use the Chapter 22 Summary on pages 800–801 and the Chapter 22 audiocassette (English and Spanish) to point out the main ideas of the chapter.

A complete, 1-page lesson plan is provided for each section in the *Reproducible Lesson Plan* booklet.

Key to Ability Levels

Teaching strategies have been coded for varying learning styles and abilities.

L1 Basic activities for all students

L2 Average activities for average to above-average students

L3 Challenging activities for above-average students

LEP Limited English Proficiency activities

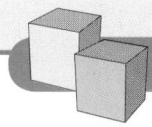

Block Schedule

Block scheduling differs from traditional class scheduling in the amount of time allotted to each period. The extended time frame provided by block scheduling affords you the opportunity to implement a greater number of research-oriented and activity-intense projects to motivate and involve your students. Activities that are particularly suited to use within the block scheduling framework are identified throughout this unit by the following designation:

✔ Performance Assessment Activity

A Chronology of a Movement Organize students in groups of four or five. Have each select six events discussed in this chapter that they consider important to the civil rights movement. For each event, groups should tell when and what happened, how this event contributed to the struggle for equality, and how they think the history of this period might have been different if the event had not occurred. Groups might also suggest a picture or visual image to represent the event. Have groups share their choices with the class. Then as a class, create an illustrated time line of the civil rights movement.

POSSIBLE RUBRIC FEATURES

- Content Information
- Research Skills
- Organization
- Writing and Communication Skills
- Critical Thinking Skills
- Collaborative Skills

☞ For additional practice, use Performance Assessment Strategies and Activities.

TEACHER'S CORNER

NATIONAL GEOGRAPHIC SOCIETY

INDEX TO NATIONAL GEOGRAPHIC MAGAZINE

The following articles may be used for research relating to this chapter:

- "Philadelphia's African Americans", by Roland L. Freeman, August 1990.
- "I Dream a World: America's Black Women," by Brian Lanker, August 1989.

NATIONAL GEOGRAPHIC SOCIETY PRODUCTS AVAILABLE FROM GLENCOE

To order the following products for use with this chapter, contact your local Glencoe sales representative or call Glencoe at 1-800-334-7344:

- *The Presidents: A Picture History of Our Nation* (CD-ROM)
- *GTV: A Geographic Perspective on American History* (Videodisc)
- *GTV: The American People: Fabric of a Nation* (Videodisc)

ADDITIONAL NATIONAL GEOGRAPHIC SOCIETY PRODUCTS

To order the following products for use with this chapter, call National Geographic Society at 1-800-368-2728:

- *Decades of History: The 20th Century—The Middle Years* (Filmstrip)

VIDEODISC

Use the Chapter 22 MindJogger Videoquiz to preview the content of this chapter.

MindJogger Videoquiz

Chapter 22
Disc 3, Side A

 Available in VHS.

Recording Journal Notes

Suggest students organize their notes into categories such as demonstrations, boycotts, marches, freedom rides, sit-ins.

Linking Across
T I M E

Point out that African American leaders had been working toward full equality since the Civil War ended but they made only limited progress until the 1950s. By the 1960s, African Americans had made considerable gains in securing enforcement of their voting rights. During those years a number of African Americans were elected to Congress and served as mayors of large cities.

668

CHAPTER 22
★★★ L2 ★★★★

The Civil Rights Era
1954–1975

▶ **CELEBRATING KWANZAA,** HOLIDAY BASED ON TRADITIONAL AFRICAN FESTIVAL

Setting the Scene

Focus

During the 1950s, African Americans rebelled against their second-class status. The ranks of civil rights advocates swelled, and African Americans, joined by some white liberals, began following the nonviolent ideas of Dr. Martin Luther King, Jr. They fought for equality first in the South and eventually in the North. Met with violence at every turn, many African Americans abandoned King's ideas and developed new philosophies. Whatever their ideas, these civil rights activists inspired hope to other minorities.

Concepts to Understand

★ Why efforts to gain **civil rights** created an effective movement for change

★ How the **civil rights** movement led to social upheaval

Read to Discover . . .

★ legislation that addressed civil rights issues.

★ the kind of impact the civil rights movement had on other minorities.

Journal Notes

What was life like for civil rights activists during the 1950s and 1960s? Note details about it in your journal as you read the chapter.

CULTURAL

- **1959** *Jazz pioneer Ornette Coleman releases* The Shape of Jazz
- **1962** *Richard Wright pens* Another Country
- **1964** *Dr. King wins Nobel Peace Prize*

1954	1960

POLITICAL

- **1955** *Montgomery bus boycott begins*
- **1957** *Congress passes the first civil rights legislation since Reconstruction*
- **1964** *Civil Rights Act is passed*
- **1965** *"March for Freedom" begins*
- **1965** *Voting Rights Act is passed*

✚ **EXTRA CREDIT PROJECT**

Charting Voter Registration Explain that the Voting Rights Act of 1965 was a major step in ensuring voting rights for African Americans. The act led to massive voter registration drives in the South. Invite interested students to research the growth in African American voter registration in the Southern states following passage of the act. Have students create a chart showing, for example, the years 1960 and 1966. (The *Statistical Abstract of the United States* is a source for such information.) Ask them to present their charts to the class and discuss their findings. Which states showed the greatest increase? The least increase? What might account for the differences among the states? **L2** 📖

*Concept Mapping
Activity*

On the chalkboard, repro-
duce the following gener-
alization and concepts
map, and have students
copy it in their notebooks.

African American
leaders offered a new
vision of equality, which
brought about reform
and change in
American society.

Civil
Rights

Social
Change

To reinforce the two
chapter concepts, use
Concept Mapping
Activities 22-A and 22-B.

Use Chapter
Concepts Transparen-
cies 22-A, 22-B.

**Visualizing
History**

The civil rights march
on Washington, D.C.,
in 1963 was the culmi-
nation of hundreds of
protests and demon-
strations that took
place across the nation.

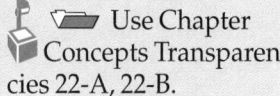

NATIONAL
GEOGRAPHIC
SOCIETY

 VIDEODISC

GTV: The American
People: Fabric of a Nation

Side 4, Chapter 5
Title: *The War at Home*
Subject: The civil rights
movement
**See GTV Guide for
complete lesson plan.**

**Visualizing
History**

The March on Washington, 1963

The August 1963 March on Washington for equal rights was
the largest and most peaceful protest in the nation's history.
Dr. Martin Luther King, Jr., electrified the listeners with his "I
Have a Dream" address.

◀ STATUE OF LIBERTY

- **1966** Soul on Ice *states Black Panther
aims*
- **1972** *Joseph Walker publishes* The River
Niger
- **1973** *Toni Morrison publishes* Sula

1966	1972

- **1967** *Carl Stokes is elected mayor of
Cleveland, Ohio*
- **1968** *Martin Luther King, Jr.,
is assassinated*
- **1972** *Congress approves Equal Rights
Amendment*

CHAPTER 22 The Civil Rights Era: 1954–1975   **669**

✓ Performance Assessment

Influence of the Civil Rights Movement The civil
rights movement inspired other minorities to
demand social justice. Divide students into
small groups and ask each to research the effects of the movement on Hispanics, women,
Native Americans, and the disabled. Have each
group report its findings to the class. Then discuss similarities and differences among the
groups. Which made the greatest gains in the
1960s and 1970s? What work remains to be
done? **L2**

For additional practice, assign
Performance Assessment Activity 22.

SECTION 1

A New Beginning

FOCUS

Bellringer

Before taking roll, project Section Focus Transparency 22-1 or hand out Section Focus Transparency Activity 22-1. Have students answer the questions. Discuss student responses.

Motivating Activity

Read the following song verse to students.
"We shall overcome, we shall overcome,
We shall overcome someday.
Oh, deep in my heart, I do believe,
We shall overcome someday."
Point out that songs were an important aspect of the civil rights movement. **L1**

Vocabulary Precheck

Ask students to define each of the "Key Terms." Have a volunteer consult the dictionary for any unfamiliar words. **L1, LEP**

Use the Vocabulary PuzzleMaker Software to create a crossword puzzle. **L1**

Assign Vocabulary Activity 22.

Setting the Scene

Section Focus

Almost a century after passage of the Fourteenth and Fifteenth Amendments, African Americans were still victims of discrimination and segregation. In the South these attitudes were entrenched not only in custom but also in law. The battle to obtain equal rights for African Americans would have to be fought in the courts, in the news media, and in the consciences of the American people. For the civil rights movement, the 1950s marked a new beginning in the ongoing struggle for equality.

Objectives

After studying this chapter, you should be able to

★ discuss the effects of the *Brown v. Board of Education* decision.

★ describe major events in the early civil rights movement.

Key Terms

nonviolent resistance, federalized

▶ DR. MARTIN LUTHER KING, JR.

he end of Reconstruction left African Americans economically and politically second-class citizens. The sharecropping system and "Jim Crow" segregation laws worked to deny them their rights as citizens. African American leaders began to work toward restoring their full civil rights in the early decades of the twentieth century, but the movement did not come into full flower until almost 50 years later.

During the 1950s and the early 1960s, African Americans boldly rejected their second-class status and the humiliating practice of forced separation. They fought for equal opportunities in jobs, housing, and education. They fought against segregated schools, buses, and trains; they fought against separate facilities in restaurants, hotels, libraries, and hospitals. They won an important ally when the Supreme Court issued several decisions against racial discrimination. But the main force behind the civil rights movement came from citizens—African American and white—who banded together in an effective protest movement.

■ Brown v. Board of Education

One of the Supreme Court's most significant rulings of the 1950s came in May 1954. Three years earlier, Linda Brown's parents had sued the school board of Topeka, Kansas, for not allowing their daughter to attend an all-white school, miles closer to their home than the segregated elementary school she was assigned to attend.

The Supreme Court ruled in *Brown v. Board of Education of Topeka, Kansas* that it was unconstitutional to separate schoolchildren by race. The *Brown* decision reversed the

Classroom Resources for SECTION 1

Blackline Masters:
- Reproducible Lesson Plan 22-1
- Guided Reading Activity 22-1
- Vocabulary Activity 22
- Supreme Court Case Study 22
- Linking Past and Present Activity 22

- Primary and Secondary Source Readings, pp. 57–60
- American Literary Heritage, p. 50
- Workbook Activity 22-1
- Reteaching Activity 22-1
- Section Quiz 22-1

Transparencies:
- Section Focus Transparency 22-1

Multimedia:
- Testmaker
- Vocabulary PuzzleMaker
- MindJogger Videoquiz

- GTV: The American People: Fabric of a Nation
- Powers of the Supreme Court
- Martin Luther King, Jr.
- American Music: Cultural Traditions

Court's decision in *Plessy* v. *Ferguson*, an 1896 ruling that had upheld the constitutionality of "separate but equal" public accommodations. *Plessy* had become the basis for Jim Crow laws and legal segregation in many states.

The Southern Manifesto

The Supreme Court's ruling in *Brown* v. *Board of Education* called for major changes in many states, especially those in the South. Some border states integrated their schools, but the South remained segregated. The governor of Virginia threatened to close the state's public schools and send white children to private schools. A group of 101 southern members of Congress signed a "Southern Manifesto," which called the Court's ruling "a clear abuse of judicial power" and pledged use of "all lawful means to bring about a reversal of this decision."

■ Boycotts and Demonstrations

The decisions of the Warren Court gave legal support to African Americans' struggle for civil rights. But most civil rights battles, particularly in the South, were fought by brave men and women who broke down barriers of segregation one by one.

Rosa Parks Takes a Stand

In December 1955, an African American seamstress from Montgomery, Alabama, became one of the first to take a stand. At the end of the workday, Parks boarded a segregated bus in which all the seats allotted for African Americans were filled; she took a seat in the front, which was reserved for white riders. Because Parks refused to give up her seat, she was arrested.

The arrest of Rosa Parks aroused anger in Montgomery's African American community. Many of its leaders believed that now was the time to challenge Alabama's segregation laws. At a meeting held at the Dexter Avenue Baptist Church, a boycott of the city's buses was called. The 26-year-old minister of the church, Dr. Martin Luther King, Jr., was asked to lead the boycott.

On the day of Rosa Parks's trial, almost all the African American riders who usually took the buses began a nearly year-long boycott. Because a majority of the regular bus riders were African American, the bus company lost much of its business.

Visualizing
Ⓗistory

▲ ROSA PARKS Rosa Parks refused to give up her seat to a white bus rider. She meets with her lawyer after she was charged with breaking the law. *What actions did civil rights leaders take to protest Parks's arrest?*

Cooperative Learning Activity

Creating a Documentary Have students work in small groups to produce a television-style documentary on the civil rights movement during the 1950s. Each group should write a script that covers the main events described in the section. Ask students to create interviews with on-the-scene participants in the movement such as Linda Brown, Rosa Parks, and Dr. Martin Luther King, Jr. The scripts should conclude with speculations about the gains of the civil rights movement and its challenges for the future. One student in each group might act as narrator to present the scripts to the class for discussion. **L2** 📦

TEACH
Guided Practice

Interpreting Primary Sources Provide students with copies of the following excerpt from Chief Justice Earl Warren's court decision:

"Today, education is perhaps the most important function of state and local governments. . . ."

Ask students to explain why education is important to all citizens, regardless of ethnic origin. *(Possible response: serves as foundation of good citizenship, awakens cultural values; prepares for later professional training; helps young people adjust to environment)* **L1**

🗂 Assign Supreme Court Case Study 22: *Brown* v. *Board of Education of Topeka*.

Visualizing
Ⓗistory Many people came to regard Rosa Parks's action as the true beginning of the civil rights movement of the 1950s and 1960s.
Answer to Caption: a boycott of city buses

ABCNEWS
INTERACTIVE™

 VIDEODISC

Powers of the Supreme Court

Side Two, Chapter 22
Title: *Brown* v. *Board of Education of Topeka (KS)*
Subject: Issues behind the landmark case

Linking Past and Present

Tell students that the SCLC played a major role in the 1963 civil rights march in Washington, D.C. It also played a major role in voter-registration drives and anti-discrimination drives, especially in the South. Ask students how effective nonviolent protest is in effecting change.

☞ For additional practice, assign Linking Past and Present Activity 22.

Independent Practice

☞ Assign Guided Reading Activity 22-1.

Constructing a Time Line

Have students research and construct a time line of the major developments in African Americans' struggle for equal rights in the twentieth century. *(protest movements, formation of groups, court cases, and so forth)* Suggest students summarize their findings in a paragraph or two. **L2**

ABCNEWS INTERACTIVE™

💿 **VIDEODISC**

Martin Luther King, Jr.

‖‖‖‖‖‖‖‖‖‖‖‖‖

Side One, Chapter 11

Title: *1956 Montgomery Bus Boycott: Rosa Parks*

Subject: Rosa Parks describes what happened

Linking Past and Present

★★★★★★★★★★★

violence and confrontation without conflict.

Churches and Civil Rights

From the beginning of the civil rights movement, African American churches played a central role in devising strategies and mobilizing volunteers. The message of the gospel became the message of the movement. The churches called for protest without retaliatory

Then_____

Organizing for Freedom

Many leaders of the Southern Christian Leadership Conference (SCLC) and other organizations were ministers. In 1957 Martin Luther King, Bayard Rustin, and others had founded the SCLC in the wake of the Montgomery bus boycott.

The SCLC took a leading role in the Freedom Rides challenging segregation on public transportation and other public accommodations. Dr. King's first SCLC drive in the North was launched in Chicago in July 1966 for open housing.

Now_____

New Directions

Led by Dr. King's family and friends, the SCLC continues the fight against segregation and discrimination through nonviolent civil protest. In expanding its scope, the SCLC today also concentrates on such problems as crime and drug abuse. Membership in the organization is open to all, but most of the leaders are African American Protestant ministers.

★★★

Rosa Parks was convicted and fined $10. Dr. King and other African American leaders were arrested for sponsoring an "illegal boycott." Then, in November 1956, the Supreme Court ruled that segregation in public transportation was illegal. The bus company ended its policy of segregation. The African American citizens of Montgomery, assured of equal treatment, resumed riding the buses. The Montgomery bus boycott galvanized the civil rights movement, and in Martin Luther King, Jr., that movement found an inspiring leader.

King Preaches Nonviolence

African American churches and their ministers took the lead in organizing the civil rights movement. Dr. King, a Baptist minister, drew from his own faith and also from techniques of the Indian leader Mohandas Gandhi. Like Gandhi, King encouraged the use of **nonviolent resistance,** or peaceful means to effect change. He told people to disobey unjust laws but asked them to love their oppressors and never fight with them even if provoked. He explained that public opinion, not violence, would force authorities to change unjust laws:

> ❝ *Injustice must be exposed, with all the tension its exposure creates, to the light of human conscience and the air of national opinion before it can be cured.* ❞

In 1957, to carry on this nonviolent struggle against discrimination in public places all over the South, King and other African American leaders founded the Southern Christian Leadership Conference (SCLC). In addition to the SCLC and its student branch—the Student Nonviolent Coordinating Committee—there were many other groups organized to promote civil rights.

Sidelight: Thurgood Marshall

The lawyer who argued the *Brown* case before the Supreme Court was Thurgood Marshall, who had been fighting for equal rights in court since the 1930s. In 1967, he became the first African American to be appointed to the Supreme Court, where he served until his retirement in 1991.

Among them were such long-established African American organizations as the National Association for the Advancement of Colored People (NAACP), which fought discrimination in many legal cases, including *Brown* v. *Board of Education;* the National Urban League, which established community programs for minorities in cities; and the Congress of Racial Equality (CORE), which worked for economic and political opportunities for African Americans. Dr. King remained at the forefront of the movement as it continued to grow in the 1960s. In 1964 he received the Nobel Peace Prize for his nonviolent leadership.

■ Crisis in Little Rock

Not wanting to create controversy, the Eisenhower administration and Congress refused to pass civil rights legislation. As a result, civil rights groups turned to the courts for settlement of their grievances.

In 1953 Eisenhower appointed Earl Warren as chief justice of the United States Supreme Court. Warren began to move the Court toward a more liberal interpretation of the Constitution in decisions on individual rights. Also in 1953 the NAACP brought a number of civil rights cases before the Court. Thurgood Marshall, the NAACP's leading lawyer, wanted the Court to strike down state laws that required racial segregation in public schools. He argued that African American children were not getting the same quality of education as white children.

On May 17, 1954, the Court handed down a historic decision in *Brown* v. *Board of Education of Topeka.* It overturned the 1896 *Plessy* v. *Ferguson* decision that segregation was constitutional so long as equal facilities were provided for both races. The Court declared

> 66 *We conclude that in the field of public education, the doctrine of "separate but equal" has no place. Separate educational facilities are inherently unequal.* 99

In *Brown* v. *Board of Education of Topeka,* the Supreme Court did not set a deadline for

ending segregation. However, in May 1955, the Court called for the implementation of integration "with all deliberate speed."

Civil Rights Legislation

The ruling needed the active support of President Eisenhower, but the President believed that the federal government should remain neutral concerning controversial issues that affected state and local governments. He remarked, "I don't believe you can change the hearts of men with laws and decisions."

In 1957 Congress passed the first civil rights law since Reconstruction. The act created a civil rights division within the Department of Justice and gave the government the power to seek court injunctions against those who denied any citizen's constitutional rights.

Confrontation

In September 1957, the state of Arkansas tested the federal government's policies on civil rights. A federal court had ordered that nine African American students be admitted

▲ CRISIS IN LITTLE ROCK Central High School in Little Rock, Arkansas, became the focus of court-ordered desegregation in 1957. After Governor Orval Faubus used the Arkansas National Guard to prevent nine African American students from attending, Eisenhower sent federal troops to Little Rock. *How was the crisis resolved?*

Visualizing **H**istory   Little Rock seemed an unlikely place for a showdown on school segregation. Just five days after the *Brown* decision, the Little Rock school board announced its willingness to obey the new law. Then on September 2, Governor Faubus appeared on statewide television to announce he had ordered state National Guard soldiers to surround the school.

Answer to Caption: Federal troops remained in Little Rock for the rest of the year, and African American students were able to attend school. Central High closed for the 1958–59 academic year.

American Music: Cultural Traditions Have students listen to "We Shall Not Be Moved" by the Freedom Singers (2:19).

CURRICULUM CONNECTION

Civics In 1989, Linda Brown, now Linda Brown Smith, was concerned that integration was not proceeding quickly enough. To make sure her grandson received an equal education, she attempted to reopen the *Brown* case. It did not get to the courts because she and her local board of education resolved their differences.

Critical Thinking Activity

Comparing Philosophies Martin Luther King, Jr., took many of his nonviolent ideas from those of Mohandas K. Gandhi, leader of India's liberation movement against the British. Ask students to research Gandhi's philosophy and his work. Have them compare the two philosophies. How are they similar? Different? What impact did each leader have on his nation? How successful was each in reaching his goals? Have students present their findings orally for class discussion. **L3**

ASSESS
Check Understanding
Assign Section 1 Review as homework or an in-class activity.

Evaluate
Assign Section Quiz 22-1 or use the Test-maker to create a customized quiz.

Reteach
Have students complete Reteaching Activity 22-1.

Assign Workbook Activity 22-1.

Enrich
Assign Primary and Secondary Source Readings, pp. 57–60: "Blocked from Central High School" and "Martin Luther King, Jr.'s Letter from Birmingham Jail."

CLOSE
Suggest a volunteer read aloud Martin Luther King's statement on page 672. Ask students to discuss the following questions: Based on what you know of the civil rights movement, how effective was nonviolent direct action? Is breaking the law in a just cause ever acceptable? Why or why not?

▲ PROTESTING FOR RIGHTS

to the all-white Central High School in Little Rock, Arkansas. The state's governor, Orval Faubus, defied federal authority and sent National Guard troops to prevent the students from attending.

President Eisenhower tried to persuade Governor Faubus to obey the court order. The governor withdrew the troops, but without their presence the African American students were exposed to an angry mob that threatened them with physical harm. Forced to act to maintain order, Eisenhower sent in 1,000 paratroopers and **federalized**, or put

under the jurisdiction of the federal government, 10,000 members of the Arkansas National Guard to surround the school so that the students could enter safely.

As Daisy Bates, then the president of the Arkansas NAACP, later remembered:

❝ . . . the nine [African American] pupils marched solemnly through the doors of Central High School, surrounded by twenty-two soldiers. An Army helicopter circled overhead. Around the massive brick schoolhouse 350 paratroopers stood grimly at attention. . . . Within minutes a world that had been holding its breath learned that the nine pupils . . . had finally entered the 'never-never-land.' ❞

Troops remained in Little Rock for the rest of the year, however, and Central High School was closed for the 1958–1959 academic year.

As the Eisenhower administration drew to a close, the nation remained racially divided. Custom and years of intimidation kept many African Americans from voting. Between 1957 and 1960, the Justice Department brought only 10 suits to secure voting rights for African Americans. Only 25 percent of African American adults voted in states of the Deep South, and only 5 percent in Mississippi. The movement for civil rights was just beginning.

Section 1 ★ Review

Checking for Understanding
1. **Identify** *Brown* v. *Board of Education,* Earl Warren, Southern Manifesto, Rosa Parks, Martin Luther King, Jr.
2. **Define** nonviolent resistance, federalized.
3. **Explain** Martin Luther King's philosophy of nonviolence.
4. **Describe** why Eisenhower sent federal troops into Little Rock.

Critical Thinking
5. **Analyzing a Viewpoint** How would you evaluate Eisenhower's stand on civil rights? Explain why many African Americans in the South would not be content with this approach.

ACTIVITY
6. Write newspaper headlines for three major events of the 1950s civil rights movement.

Answers to SECTION 1 REVIEW
1. *Brown* v. *Board of Education,* 670; Southern Manifesto, 671; Rosa Parks, 671; Martin Luther King, Jr., 671–672; Earl Warren, 673
2. All vocabulary words are defined in the Glossary.
3. King advocated disobeying unjust laws without using violence. He suggested followers should love their oppressors.
4. to maintain order and protect students
5. Answers may include that Eisenhower had to take action to enforce federal law. Because desegregation was not a matter of changing "hearts of men"—it was African Americans' legal right to equal opportunity.
6. Headlines should focus on significant events.

African American Women Pioneers in Film

In a 1946 issue, the NAACP magazine, the *Crisis*, noted "There are very few [African American men] working on the technical and production side of film-making. There have been one or two . . . writers, a few musicians, and a handful of dance directors." The situation was even more limiting for African American women. Some had made their mark on the other side of the camera. Performers such as Hattie McDaniel, Dorothy Dandridge, and Louise Beavers showcased their talents in many films—almost always, however, playing servant roles.

In the 1980s and 1990s, African American women began to make their mark in film directing, writing, and in other areas of movie production. One of the most influential remains Kathleen Collins. Her work as a teacher, director, playwright, and screenwriter inspired a generation of African American women filmmakers. In such films as *The Cruz Brothers and Mrs. Malloy* (1980) and *Losing Ground* (1982), Collins worked on the belief that "if I can be very faithful to [my own view] and manage to find a way to say it, it will mean something to other people."

Documentary filmmaker Michelle Parkerson has won acclaim for a number of compelling profiles of artists and performers.

Her first film, *But Then, She's Betty Carter* (1980), offers the story of the noted jazz stylist. *Gotta Make This Journey* (1983) tells the story of a female a cappella singing group. *A Litany of Survival* (1993) chronicles the story of one of Parkerson's heroes, poet and essayist Audre Lord.

Writer, producer, and director Julie Dash garnered acclaim and honors for *Daughters of the Dust* (1992). This poignant film, set in the Georgia Sea Islands, tells the story of the women of a family at the turn of the century. For Dash, the film's essence is "the fear of going away from home and not being able to come back, the fear of abandoning one's culture."

▲ FILMMAKER JULIE DASH

Ruth Carter has made a significant contribution in costume design. Her responsibilities include both designing and making costumes. In works such as *School Daze* and *What's Love Got to Do With It* she has taken on the challenging assignments of re-creating the clothes and styles of the 1950s and 1960s. She was nominated for a 1992 Academy Award for Best Costume Design for her work on *Malcolm X*.

Making the Art Connection

1. What positions in film were open to African American women before the 1940s?

2. Who are the subjects of Michelle Parkerson's documentaries? What do they have in common?

3. In what area of filmwork has Ruth Carter contributed?

ACTIVITY

4. View a film written, directed, or produced by an African American woman. Write a review of the film describing the plot, technique, and main point of the story.

675

CONNECTIONS

History AND THE ARTS

TEACH

Tell students that Julie Dash's first short film was *Diary of an African Nun*, a film adapted from a short story by Alice Walker. The feature-length film *Daughters of the Dust* was the first by an American-born African American female filmmaker to be released commercially in the United States. Discuss with students what perspectives films by African American women can bring to the viewers. **L2**

Did You Know?

Hattie McDaniel was the first African American woman to sing on American radio. In the 1930s and 1940s she appeared in many films, generally in the roles of a maid. She won an Academy Award for her role in the movie *Gone With the Wind*.

☞ Assign American Literary Heritage, p. 50: from *I Know Why the Caged Bird Sings* by Maya Angelou. Have students discuss the excerpt.

Answers to Making the Connection

1. playing servant roles
2. women; they are artists
3. in costume design

4. Reviews should present the main events that take place in the story, unique or special techniques used in the film, and the film's point of view.

FOCUS

Bellringer

 Before taking roll, project Section Focus Transparency 22-2 or hand out Section Focus Transparency Activity 22-2. Have students answer the questions. Discuss student responses.

Motivating Activity

Write the terms *New Frontier* and *Great Society* on the chalkboard. Invite students to tell what kind of images these terms evoke (*a new beginning, new challenges, new opportunities; progress, prosperity, equality*) Explain that as the civil rights movement gained momentum, the government took a more active role in supporting it. **L1**

Vocabulary Precheck

Write *sit-in* on the chalkboard. Have a volunteer skim the section to find the term and read it in context. **L1, LEP**

NATIONAL GEOGRAPHIC SOCIETY

VIDEODISC

GTV: The American People: Fabric of a Nation

|||||||||| (barcode)

Side 4, Chapter 5
Title: *The War at Home*
Subject: The Civil Rights movement
See GTV Guide for complete lesson plan.

676

★★★

Successes and Setbacks

Setting the Scene

Section Focus

During the Kennedy-Johnson years, there were successes and setbacks for the civil rights movement. Kennedy moved slowly at first. However, violent events soon forced his hand, and he used the federal courts as well as troops to enforce desegregation in the South. Lyndon Johnson continued the former President's policies and succeeded in getting them passed into law.

◄ "IN A FREE GOVERNMENT . . . " BY JACOB LAWRENCE

Objectives

After studying this section, you should be able to

★ describe advances made in civil rights during the Kennedy-Johnson administrations.

★ describe the setbacks and difficulties the civil rights activists faced during the 1960s.

Key Term

sit-in

As the 1960s began, leaders for the civil rights movement—both African Americans and liberal whites—stepped up the tactics of nonviolent resistance throughout the South. Although eventually many of these tactics resulted in great gains for the movement, they generally were met with violence. People were attacked and killed, and only the federal government was strong enough to do something about it.

■ Students Stage Sit-ins

During the winter of 1959 and 1960, civil rights groups held marches, demonstrations, and boycotts to end segregation in public places. They especially challenged the practice of not serving African Americans at many southern lunch counters. In February 1960, four African American students sat down at a segregated lunch counter in a local store in Greensboro, North Carolina. They refused to leave until they were served. Their action was known as a **sit-in,** and before long students were staging sit-ins all over the South. By September 1961, 70,000 students were using this tactic to produce social change.

By 1960 the crusade for civil rights had become a national movement. As a result, many Americans were now beginning to recognize the moral evil of racial discrimination. King wrote:

❝ *The law cannot change the heart—but it can restrain the heartless. It will take education and religion to change bad internal attitudes—but legislation and court orders can control their external aspects.* ❞

676 UNIT 7 Redefining America: 1954–Present

Classroom Resources for SECTION 2

Blackline Masters:
🗁 Reproducible Lesson Plan 22-2
🗁 Guided Reading Activity 22-2
🗁 Chapter Map Activity 22
🗁 Geography in History Activity 22
🗁 Workbook Activity 22-2
🗁 Reteaching Activity 22-2
🗁 Section Quiz 22-2

Transparencies:
🖉 Section Focus Transparency 22-2
🖉 Map Transparency 22
🖉 Skills Transparency 22

Multimedia:
💿 Testmaker
💿 GTV: The American People: Fabric of a Nation
💿 Martin Luther King, Jr.

Kennedy and Civil Rights

In contrast to Eisenhower's cautious stand on civil rights, President Kennedy had promised vigorous support of the movement. Kennedy was aware of the support he needed from African American voters to win the 1960 election. Yet his slim victory over Nixon, coupled with the fear of losing southern Democratic support in Congress, made him act less forcefully than the words of his campaign had seemed to promise.

Kennedy's cautious attitude disappointed white liberals and African American leaders. He waited until 1962 to sign an executive order ending segregation in government-owned housing. And although Kennedy appointed African Americans to his administration as well as to federal judicial positions, he also appointed some judges who supported segregation. Events in the South, however, soon forced Kennedy to take a more active role in civil rights.

The Freedom Riders

In the spring of 1961, civil rights activists volunteered as "Freedom Riders" to ride buses into segregated terminals throughout the South. In May busloads of Freedom Riders were attacked by mobs in the Alabama cities of Anniston and Birmingham. A bus was fire-bombed and riders were beaten and clubbed. As more and more Freedom Riders poured into southern cities, local police were unable or unwilling to protect them from angry racists. The President was forced to use federal marshals to restore order. The Justice Department also pressured the Interstate Commerce Commission to bring lawsuits against those terminals that refused to comply with regulations on desegregation.

While Kennedy was in office, from 1961 to 1963, the Department of Justice brought six times as many lawsuits to protect African American voting rights as it did under Eisenhower, from 1958 to 1960. As a result, by 1964, the percentage of African American citizens registered to vote in the Deep South had risen from 25 to 40 percent, largely because of the work of the Freedom Riders.

Violence in Birmingham

Violence that broke out in Birmingham was the last straw for Kennedy. From that point on, Kennedy wholeheartedly sided

▲ CHALLENGING SEGREGATION Civil rights groups challenged the practice of not serving African Americans at many southern diners. Here, two African Americans refuse to leave a segregated Raleigh, North Carolina, lunch counter until they are served. *What was their tactic called?*

CHAPTER 22 The Civil Rights Era: 1954–1975 **677**

TEACH
Guided Practice
Sociology
Lead a discussion on the effectiveness of the protest methods used by the civil rights movement. **L2**

Visualizing **Ⓗistory** The first sit-in was not elaborately planned. Four freshmen from North Carolina Agricultural and Technical College sat at a lunch counter. The next day they came back, accompanied by more than 20 other students.
Answer to Caption: the sit-in

ABCNEWS INTERACTIVE™

 VIDEODISC
Martin Luther King, Jr.

Side One, Chapter 16
Title: *1963 Birmingham: King Arrested*
Subject: Report on the 1963 march

Side One, Chapter 17
Title: *1963 Birmingham: King's Letter From Jail*
Subject: King reads a portion of letter

Side One, Chapter 18
Title: *1963 Birmingham: Street Violence*
Subject: Violence in Birmingham

CURRICULUM CONNECTION

Music Have students locate recordings or lyrics of such civil rights protest songs as "We Shall Overcome," "Keep Your Eyes on the Prize," and "If You Miss Me From the Back of the Bus." Ask students to note the lyrics and consider what made these songs so powerful among civil rights activists. **L2**

Did You Know?

Although the Kennedy administration supported civil rights, it did not always support the tactics used by civil rights activists. Both the President and Robert Kennedy, then attorney general, tried to dissuade Martin Luther King from proceeding with the march on Washington in 1963. King refused, and the march went forward.

Visualizing History After crossing the Edmund Pettus Bridge outside Selma on the way to Montgomery, the marchers were set upon with tear gas and clubs.
Answer to Caption: a civil rights demonstration in Birmingham, Alabama

Visualizing History ▲ THE ROAD TO MONTGOMERY Dr. Martin Luther King, Jr., led a five-day march from Selma to Montgomery, Alabama, in March 1965. Marches were an effective way for African Americans to protest discrimination. *What demonstration did King lead in April 1963?*

with Martin Luther King and the civil rights activists. In April 1963, King led a demonstration in Birmingham, Alabama. On the orders of Police Commissioner Eugene "Bull" Connor, police used fire hoses, clubs, and snarling dogs on demonstrators, including women and children. National television carried the sight of this violence into millions of homes across America. Viewers were shocked and outraged. Kennedy sent 3,000 troops to restore peace in the city. In June he proposed a new civil rights bill that would outlaw segregation throughout the nation.

■ Trouble in Southern Universities

During Kennedy's administration the Department of Justice brought numerous suits for desegregation of schools. In September 1962, James Meredith, a 29-year-old African American air force veteran, sought entrance to the University of Mississippi. Although Meredith was backed by a court order, Governor Ross Barnett declared,

"Never! We will never surrender to the evil and illegal forces of tyranny." Kennedy immediately sent in federal marshals and eventually the Mississippi National Guard to enable Meredith to enter the university safely. Meredith was able to attend classes, but two people were killed in a mob action.

Another confrontation between state and federal powers took place in June 1963—this time in Alabama. Governor George Wallace symbolically stood in a doorway to prevent desegregation of the University of Alabama at Tuscaloosa. Kennedy immediately federalized the Alabama National Guard and ordered the troops to make sure African Americans were allowed to enter. As a result, Wallace backed down.

The violence of such confrontations convinced Kennedy that federal legislation against segregation and discrimination was needed. Kennedy quickly proposed laws that would forbid segregation in stores, restaurants, hotels, and theaters and that would prohibit discrimination in employment. But progress on school desegregation was slow. Most African American school children in the South continued to attend all-black schools.

678 UNIT 7 Redefining America: 1954–Present

Cultural Perspectives

Music of Protest Popular music of the 1960s reflected the mood and temper of the times. Folksingers such as Bob Dylan and Joan Baez, carried political messages in their lyrics. Rock music was revolutionized with the advent of the Beatles, and the Detroit "Motown" sound introduced new African American singers. Music of the 1960s culminated in the rock festival of 1969 at Woodstock, New York, when thousands gathered to display what many Americans thought of as the "counterculture."

The March on Washington

In August 1963, for the 100th anniversary of the Emancipation Proclamation, African American leaders planned to hold the largest civil rights demonstration in the nation's history. This "March on Washington for Jobs and Freedom" would press for the passage of Kennedy's proposed civil rights bill, which was being debated in Congress.

King's Dream of Freedom

More than 200,000 demonstrators, both African American and white, converged on the nation's capital. They sang hymns and spirituals as they gathered near the Lincoln Memorial. As one 15-year-old African American girl described it:

> ❝ *There was this sense of hope for the future—the belief that this march was the big step in the right direction. It could be heard in the voices of the people singing and seen in the way they walked. It poured out into smiles.* ❞

At the Lincoln Memorial the marchers heard eloquent speeches, especially from Dr. Martin Luther King, Jr., who, in a famous address, described his dream of freedom and equality for all people:

> ❝ *I have a dream that one day this nation will rise up and live out the true meaning of its creed: 'We hold these truths to be self-evident; that all men are created equal' . . . And when this happens, and when we allow freedom to ring, when we let it ring from every village and hamlet, from every state and every city, we will be able to speed up that day when all God's children . . . [will] join hands and sing in the words of the old . . . spiritual: 'Free at last, Free at last, Thank God Almighty, we're free at last.'* ❞

The leaders of the march then left for a meeting with President John F. Kennedy at the White House.

A New Civil Rights Act

The March on Washington was a historic event for the civil rights movement. It not only awakened millions to the plight of African Americans living in the South but also confirmed for Congress the widespread support for a civil rights bill.

Progress was slow. In 1963, 9 years after the *Brown* decision, only one-half of one percent of African American public school children in the 11 former Confederate states were attending desegregated schools. Some southern communities desegregated public facilities only after boycotts and sit-ins. Others refused, however, and some even used violence to intimidate nonviolent protestors.

After President Kennedy's assassination on November 22, 1963, President Johnson was determined to continue Kennedy's civil rights policies. So he accepted

Visualizing History

▲ JAMES MEREDITH In 1962, against the wishes of the governor of Mississippi, the Supreme Court ordered that James Meredith (center) be allowed to enroll at the University of Mississippi. *What action did the federal government take to enable Meredith to enter the university safely?*

Linking Across TIME

Reformers and protesters in the United States have always relied on some form of media to get across their messages. Rebelling colonists published cartoons and pamphlets. During the civil rights movement, the medium was television.

Visualizing History James Meredith became the first African American to graduate from the University of Mississippi.
Answer to Caption: The President ordered federal and state troops to enable Meredith to enter the university in safety.

ABCNEWS INTERACTIVE™

⊙ **VIDEODISC**

Martin Luther King, Jr.

Side One, Chapter 21
Title: *1963 March on Washington: Newsreel*
Subject: Newsreel account of the August 28, 1963, march on Washington

Side One, Chapter 22
Title: *1963 March on Washington: "I Have a Dream . . . ."*
Subject: Portions of King's speech

Sidelight: Memorial to a Struggle

In 1989, the Southern Poverty Law Center dedicated the Civil Rights Memorial in honor of those who died during the struggle for civil rights in the South. Located in Montgomery, Alabama—the scene of so many of the events in that cause—the memorial serves to inform and educate young people about the civil rights movement. The monument was designed by Maya Lin, the creator of the Vietnam Veterans Memorial in Washington, D.C.

ASSESS

Check Understanding

Assign Section 2 Review as homework or an in-class activity.

Evaluate

 Assign Section Quiz 22-2 or use the Test-maker to create a customized quiz.

Reteach

Have students complete Reteaching Activity 22-2.

Enrich

Assign Chapter Map Activity 22.

Assign Geography in History Activity 22.

Assign Map Transparency Activity 22.

CLOSE

Ask for examples of how the civil rights movement brought social and political change to American society.

Map Study *Using Maps*

Answer: Texas, Arkansas, Tennessee, and Florida

Map Skills Practice

Ask students to explain the change in registration of African American voters in Alabama from 1960 to 1966. (*Less than 1 in 6 African Americans were registered in 1960. By 1966 nearly 1 in 2 were.*)

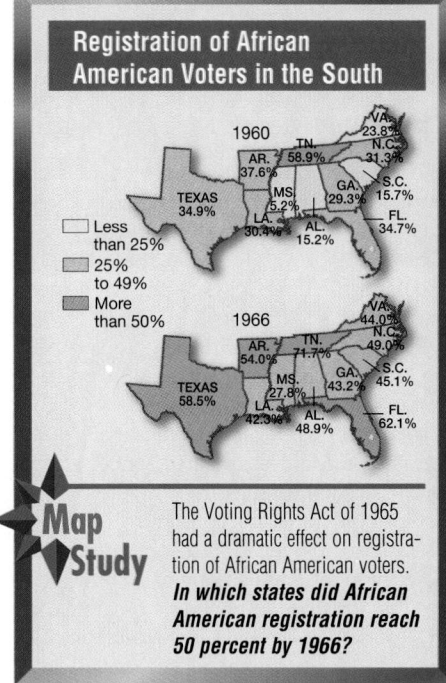

Registration of African American Voters in the South

1960

VA. 23.8%
N.C. 31.3%
TN. 58.9%
AR. 37.6%
TEXAS 34.9%
MS. 5.2%
GA. 29.3%
S.C. 15.7%
LA. 30.4%
AL. 15.2%
FL. 34.7%

☐ Less than 25%
▨ 25% to 49%
▩ More than 50%

1966

VA. 44.0%
N.C. 49.0%
TN. 71.7%
AR. 54.0%
TEXAS 58.5%
MS. 27.8%
GA. 43.2%
S.C. 45.1%
LA. 42.3%
AL. 48.9%
FL. 62.1%

Map Study

The Voting Rights Act of 1965 had a dramatic effect on registration of African American voters. **In which states did African American registration reach 50 percent by 1966?**

the challenge of getting Kennedy's proposed bill passed. It had passed the House of Representatives in February 1964 but was stalled in the Senate where southern segregationists intended to kill it. Even though Johnson himself was from the South, he had broken with the segregationists early in his career. Johnson was aided in his goal by national remorse over Kennedy's assassination. To take advantage of this, the President called for speedy action:

> *No memorial . . . could more eloquently honor President Kennedy's memory than the earliest possible passage of the civil rights bill. . . .*

On July 2, the President signed into law the Civil Rights Act of 1964. The strongest civil rights act since Reconstruction stated that all citizens should have equal access to such public facilities as parks and libraries and to such private businesses serving the public as restaurants and theaters. It forbade discrimination in education and strengthened the right to vote. It also outlawed job discrimination because of race, sex, religion, or national origin. Passage of the Voting Rights Act of 1965 helped pave the way for more African Americans to vote. Activist John Lewis said:

> *These elections signal a new level of maturation in American politics. They demonstrate the willingness of white voters to set aside racial differences, and they reflect the fact that many minorities have gained the broad political experience and skills to make them solid candidates for major office.*

The Voting Rights Act of 1965 also helped other minorities. It set aside a New York state law requiring voters to be able to read English, enabling such groups as Puerto Ricans and Mexican Americans to vote.

Section 2 ★ Review

Checking for Understanding

1. **Identify** Freedom Riders, Eugene "Bull" Connor, James Meredith, March on Washington.

2. **Define** sit-in.

3. **Summarize** the advances and setbacks of the civil rights movement during Kennedy's presidency.

Critical Thinking

4. **Evaluating Events** The March on Washington is seen as one of the major events of the civil rights movement. Why is this so?

ACTIVITY

5. Create a poster encouraging people to vote. Include an attention-getting slogan.

Answers to SECTION 2 REVIEW

1. Freedom Riders, 677; Eugene "Bull" Connor, 678; James Meredith, 678; March on Washington, 679

2. All vocabulary words are defined in the Glossary.

3. Advances: segregation ended in government-owned housing, blacks appointed to government offices, proposed civil rights bill, federal protection and lawsuits; Setbacks: Kennedy's cautious approach, slow pace of school desegregation, attempts to prevent African Americans from registering at universities, violence against African Americans

4. united people of different races, religions, and backgrounds, giving hope that hatred, prejudice, and discrimination might end

5. Posters should display creativity and a short, memorable slogan.

BUILDING SKILLS
Critical Thinking Skills

Identifying Cause and Effect

▲ REGISTERING TO VOTE, BATESVILLE, MISSISSIPPI

Understanding cause and effect involves considering why an event occurred. A cause is the action or situation that produces an event. An effect is the result or consequence of an action or situation.

Learning the Skill

To understand cause and effect, follow these steps:

• Identify two or more events or developments.

• Decide whether one event caused the other. One useful way to determine this is to look for language clues. Such words as *because, as a result of, for this reason,* and *thus* often indicate a cause-and-effect relationship.

Read the following passage, then answer the questions that follow.

Despite federal laws that granted them the right to vote, many African Americans in the South were deprived of their rights by threats and violence or by unfair eligibility tests. Dr. Martin Luther King,

Jr., decided it was time to push for voting rights, and selected Selma, Alabama, as the starting point for the campaign. This was because in Selma most of the African Americans who applied to vote were turned down. Dr. King wanted to dramatize this injustice.

In January 1965, King organized a voter registration drive in Selma. The county sheriff, however, deputized whites and attacked groups of African Americans with dogs and cattle prods as they tried to register. In March, King organized a "march for freedom" from Selma to the state capitol in Montgomery, 50 miles away. Police armed with billy clubs, bullwhips, and tear gas, urged on by angry mobs, met the marchers, who reached Montgomery only after President Johnson sent federal troops to provide protection.

National outrage over the events in Selma helped speed the passage of the Voting Rights Act of 1965. It did away with literacy tests in many southern states and provided for federal assistance in registering African Americans. Steps were also taken to eliminate the poll tax, forbidden by the Twenty-fourth Amendment yet still used to keep the poor from voting. As a result, more than 400,000 people, mostly African Americans who had not previously voted, were registered within a single year.

Practicing the Skill

1. Why did Dr. King select Selma as the starting point of the voting campaign?

2. What effect did the events at Selma have on subsequent legislation?

APPLYING THE SKILL

3. Write three sentences that show a cause-and-effect relationship. For each of the sentences, construct a cause-and-effect diagram by writing the cause on the left and the effect on the right. Connect the two parts of the sentence with an arrow. Show any words that indicate cause and effect.

Answers to Practicing the Skill

1. to dramatize the injustice of voting discrimination in the city
2. National outrage helped speed passage of the Voting Rights Act of 1965.
3. Sentences should show clear and precise cause-and-effect relationships.

BUILDING SKILLS

TEACH

Review *cause* and *effect* by asking students to define these terms. (*A cause is any condition, person, or event that makes something happen. What happens as a result of a cause is known as an effect.*) L1

🗔 Project Skills Transparency 22 and have students complete Skills Transparency Activity 22.

🗔 Use Chapter Skills Activity 22 to reinforce students' understanding of the skill.

Did You Know?

When many African Americans in the South registered to vote, they were threatened with the loss of their jobs. One woman who was fired as a timekeeper on a cotton plantation in Mississippi was Fannie Lou Hamer. When she lost her job, she immediately joined SNCC and became actively involved in the voter registration drives of the summer of 1961.

ABCNEWS
INTERACTIVE™

VIDEODISC

Martin Luther King, Jr.

Side One, Chapter 3

Title: *Ted Koppel: MLK Overview*

Subject: Brief overview of the life of Dr. Martin Luther King, Jr.

New Directions

FOCUS

Bellringer

📁 Before taking roll, project Section Focus Transparency 22-3 or hand out Section Focus Transparency Activity 22-3. Have students answer the questions. Discuss student responses.

Motivating Activity

Explain to students that in 1964, Martin Luther King, Jr., received the Nobel Peace Prize for his use of nonviolent resistance in the civil rights movement. At the same time, more radical African Americans were beginning to question the effectiveness of nonviolence. Ask students to write a paragraph or two speculating on how they think more militant leaders might affect the civil rights movement. Point out that this section describes discontent among African Americans and describes actions they took. **L2**

Vocabulary Precheck

Ask students to define each of the "Key Terms." Have a volunteer consult the dictionary for any unfamiliar words. **L1, LEP**

Setting the Scene

Section Focus

As the civil rights movement progressed, African Americans found their situation unchanged in many ways. Laws had not altered prejudice, and improvement in their economic status had practically ceased. As many African Americans were stopped from exercising their rights, some began to change their ideas about how to go about gaining equality.

Objectives

After studying this section, you should be able to

★ list some of the factors responsible for discontent among some African Americans.

★ explain what new philosophies were developed by African Americans to deal with the discontent.

Key Terms

racism, black nationalism, black power, assimilation, busing

◀ **MALCOLM X** HAT

*D*espite gains made at the national, state, and local levels through peaceful change in cooperation with whites, progress in civil rights was slow. It was especially slow in social and economic areas. Unemployment for African Americans, for example, was much higher than the national average. As a result, by the mid-1960s a growing number of African Americans adopted a new, more radical approach to the problem of **racism,** that is, racial prejudice or discrimination. They believed in taking immediate action not only to gain political and legal rights, but to end discrimination in housing, education, and employment. Instead of following King's philosophy of integration and nonviolence, radical groups began to put forward a new theory and expressed their willingness to use violence to protect themselves and to achieve just treatment.

■ New Leadership

Many whites reacted with alarm to the new direction in the civil rights movement. They were especially worried about groups that openly preached black revolution. These whites felt the new philosophies African Americans were developing threatened their way of life.

The Black Muslims

The Nation of Islam, known as the Black Muslims, was originally founded in the early 1930s, and was led by Elijah Muhammad. This group appealed to African Americans to embrace the Islamic faith and preached **black nationalism.** This philosophy stated that African Americans should completely separate themselves from whites and form their own self-governing communities—their own

682 UNIT 7 Redefining America: 1954–Present

Classroom Resources for SECTION 3

Blackline Masters:
- 📁 Reproducible Lesson Plan 22-3
- 📁 Guided Reading Activity 22-3
- 📁 Cooperative Learning Activity 22
- 📁 Critical Thinking Skills Activity 22
- 📁 Workbook Activity 22-3
- 📁 Reteaching Activity 22-3
- 📁 Section Quiz 22-3

Transparencies:
- 📁 Section Focus Transparency 22-3

Multimedia:
- 📀 Testmaker
- 📀 Set on Freedom™: The American Civil Rights Movement
- 📀 Martin Luther King, Jr.

nation. They also advocated a program of self-defense. Their ideas—popularized by a talented speaker and minister known as Malcolm X—received national attention in the early 1960s. In his autobiography, Malcolm X talked about his views:

> " . . . I'm not for wanton violence, I'm for justice. . . . I feel that when the law fails to protect [African Americans] from whites' attacks, then those [African Americans] should use arms, if necessary, to defend themselves. . . . "

By 1964, however, Malcolm X came to favor an integrated society instead of separatism. Therefore, he broke with the Black Muslims. Apparently as a result of his public disagreements with them, he was shot and killed in February 1965. Although in the end Malcolm X came to favor integration, his earlier ideas continued to influence many young African Americans after his death. By the late 1960s, the Student Nonviolent Coordinating Committee (SNCC) and the Congress of Racial Equality (CORE), which had originally supported King's tactics, had become more radical.

Black Power

In May 1966, the head of SNCC, Stokely Carmichael, developed the idea of **black power** to further racial equality. This philosophy stated that blacks should "take back control of all aspects of their lives—social, political, and economic. As expounded by the black nationalists, it meant separation from white society, by violent means if necessary."

The philosophy of black power moved away from the idea of **assimilation**—the policy of incorporating different racial or cultural groups into the dominant society—and preached racial distinctiveness, pride, and leadership.

Many members and leaders of the civil rights movement had been white liberals. Now groups like SNCC and CORE moved whites out of leadership positions. African Americans began to reexamine their African heritage. Some took African names or wore "Afro" hairstyles and African-style clothing. They demanded that schools adopt programs in African-American studies.

Black power created a deep division among civil rights activists. This new idea was firmly rejected by such groups as the NAACP, which saw it as a threat to law and order. However, it would be black power that, from this point on, would more strongly influence the future development of the civil rights movement.

The Black Panthers

One of the most militant black-power groups was the Black Panthers. Founded in 1966 by Huey Newton, Bobby Seale, and Eldridge Cleaver, the Black Panthers urged African Americans to arm themselves and confront white society in order to force whites to grant them equal rights. Cleaver's *Soul on Ice* (1967) served as a statement of Black Panthers' aims:

Visualizing History

▲ NATION OF ISLAM The Nation of Islam, founded in Detroit, Michigan, by Wali Farad, gained many converts during the 1950s and 1960s. *What were the goals and objectives of black nationalism?*

Cooperative Learning Activity

Debating Form volunteers into two groups to conduct a debate. Ask one group to present arguments supporting African American nationalism, the other to oppose it. Give students time to consider their arguments. Have each side present its views to the class. Make sure each side presents evidence to support its views. As the students discuss the pros and cons, encourage the class to reach a consensus. **L3**

📁 For additional practice, assign Cooperative Learning Activity 22.

TEACH
Guided Practice
Summarizing Discuss with students the discontent among many African Americans. Then have them summarize in a report the tactics used by groups such as SNCC, CORE, and the Black Panthers and conclude by explaining the effect of these tactics on the attitudes of white Americans. **L1**

Did You Know?

The name *Black Panthers* reflected the group's militant stand. Members dressed in black from the berets on their heads to their black leather boots.

Visualizing History The Nation of Islam, a subgroup of the Islamic religion, is commonly known as the Black Muslims.
Answer to Caption: separation from whites; form self-contained communities; self-defense

---

GLENCOE
TECHNOLOGY

💿 **VIDEODISC**

Set on Freedom™: The American Civil Rights Movement

Side A, Chapter 24
Title: *The Assassination of Malcolm X*

Independent Practice

Oral History Have students draw up questions in order to conduct an interview with someone who lived through the civil rights movement. Help students prepare questions that will get the interviewee to tell how his or her life changed as a result of the civil rights movement. **L2**

 Assign Guided Reading Activity 22-3.

Teaching American Portraits

Tell students that Malcolm X encouraged young people to think of themselves as part of an African majority not an African American minority. He believed that there could be no unity between African Americans and white Americans until African Americans themselves were united. Ask students why they think such a message might appeal to young people. *(would give them a sense of pride and belonging, might make some feel superior)*

> *What the white man must be brought to understand is that the black man . . . does not intend to be tricked again into another hundred-year forfeit of freedom. Not for a single moment or for any price will the black men now rising up in America settle for anything less than their full . . . share . . . in the sovereignty of America.*

■ The Battle in the North

Although the major battles for civil rights were fought in the South, the movement's leaders recognized that segregation and prejudice also existed in the North. King shifted his demonstrations from the South to such northern cities as Chicago, where he protested housing discrimination, unemployment, and urban poverty. Northern African American populations tended to be concentrated in the inner cities, where poverty was widespread and discontent was high.

Discontent Leads to Riots

Frustration over urban conditions led to a series of riots in many cities. Often occurring in the heat of summer, these riots were sometimes triggered by an incident between police and African American citizens. When riots erupted, looting and burning also broke out.

The first major riot took place in the Harlem section of New York City in July 1964. Other riots broke out that year in Philadelphia and Chicago. In August 1965, a riot in the African American neighborhood of Watts in Los Angeles left 34 people dead, more than 3,000 arrested, and $20 million in property damage. The summer of 1966 brought new disruptions in New York, Atlanta, Cleveland, Detroit, Chicago, San Francisco, and Los Angeles. Federal troops and National Guardsmen entered Detroit in July 1967, after much of the city was in flames. When the riot was over, 40 people had been killed and hundreds more were injured. Thousands were left homeless, and many businesses were in ashes.

Most of the riots took place outside the South, in parts of the United States where African Americans supposedly enjoyed

★★★ AMERICAN PORTRAITS

Malcolm X
1925–1965

Born Malcolm Little in Omaha, Nebraska, this future religious leader and activist became a member of the Nation of Islam while serving a prison sentence for burglary. As was the custom in this religious sect, Malcolm dropped his "slave" name in favor of the letter X.

Malcolm X became a powerful and eloquent minister in the Nation of Islam. He taught the religious faith while advocating a position of independent African American political action, black power, pride, and self-defense. The Nation of Islam, sometimes referred to as the Black Muslim movement, stressed the need for African American unity, and advocated a position of separation in a time when most civil rights workers dedicated themselves to achieving racial and economic integration.

Malcolm X eventually broke with the Nation of Islam, moderated his separatist stance, and agreed to work with other civil rights activists to fight racism, discrimination, and injustice. However, Malcolm was assassinated shortly thereafter by rival members of the Nation of Islam.

Critical Thinking Activity

Evaluating Have students write an essay comparing the strategies of the Kennedy administration and those of the Nixon administration concerning the civil rights movement. Ask students to evaluate the two in terms of their effects on the progress of the movement. Have them conclude with a statement describing how government can influence the course of reform and change in a society. **L2**

 For additional practice, assign Critical Thinking Skills Activity 22.

Visualizing History

▲ SUMMER OF 1965 Members of the National Guard patrol the streets of the Watts section of Los Angeles in August 1965. Watts was the site of one of many urban racial confrontations to erupt in the United States during the middle and late 1960s. *What event set off a wave of riots in April 1968?*

VIDEODISC
Martin Luther King, Jr.

Side One, Chapter 38
Title: *Memphis, the Final Stop*

Side One, Chapter 39
Title: *His Final Speech April 3*

Side One, Chapter 40
Title: *ABC Special Report, April 4, 1968*

equal rights. Adam Clayton Powell, Jr., an African American member of Congress from New York City, offered an explanation. In the South, he said, what African Americans wanted was relatively easy for whites to give: the right to sit at a drugstore counter or in the front of a bus. In the North, African Americans had long been able to sit where they pleased. Now they wanted "a bigger piece of the pie"—better jobs, more money, better places to live. Some white jobholders and property owners felt threatened.

The Kerner Commission

In response to the violence spreading across America, President Johnson appointed a National Advisory Commission on Civil Disorders, known as the Kerner Commission, to look into the problem. The Kerner Commission laid responsibility for the ghettos at the feet of white society.

Although African Americans suffered greater loss of life and property, the riots tended to harden white prejudices. The urgently requested commission report was quietly received and produced little change.

The Death of Martin Luther King, Jr.

Despite the Kerner Commission report, violence continued to grow. Then in 1968 the violence reached a climax with the assassination of Dr. Martin Luther King, Jr. In April of that year, King was in Memphis, Tennessee, to support a strike of African American sanitation workers. He was planning a national poor people's campaign to promote economic gains for African Americans and all poor people.

There had been many threats against King's life over the years. Dr. King, however, had always dismissed them. Yet prophetically, King told a church meeting the night of April 3:

> ...I've been to the mountain top, and I don't mind.... I've looked over and I've seen the Promised Land. I may not get there with you, but I want you to know tonight that we as a people will get to the Promised Land.

The next day, he was killed by a sniper. Ironically, the murder of the great teacher of

Visualizing History The Watts riot was the first of a series of racial disorders that hit cities throughout the United States in the summers of 1965, 1966, and 1967.
Answer to Caption: assassination of Martin Luther King, Jr.

Special Needs Activity

Study Strategy The development of metacognitive understandings in students is aided by teacher explanation. This means that the teacher describes critical features of the strategy. Summarizing is one strategy that students have practiced before. Have students read the subsection titled *The Kerner Commission*. Explain to them that summarizing is a process of restating the information in the text. Then explain each component of summarizing: reading, thinking about essential elements of the text, framing the information in succinct units, and writing it. **L1, LEP**

ASSESS
Check Understanding
Assign Section 3 Review as homework or an in-class activity.

Evaluate
◎ ☞ Assign Section Quiz 22-3 or use the Testmaker to create a customized quiz.

Reteach
Ask students to reread the subheads in Section 3 and state the main ideas under each subsection.

☞ Have students complete Reteaching Activity 22-3.

☞ Assign Workbook Activity 22-3.

Enrich
Suggest interested students investigate the report of the Kerner Commission. Have them summarize its major points. Ask them to write a paragraph explaining why it was largely ignored.

CLOSE
Ask students to trace the events that signaled the transition from the nonviolent resistance of the civil rights movement to more militance.

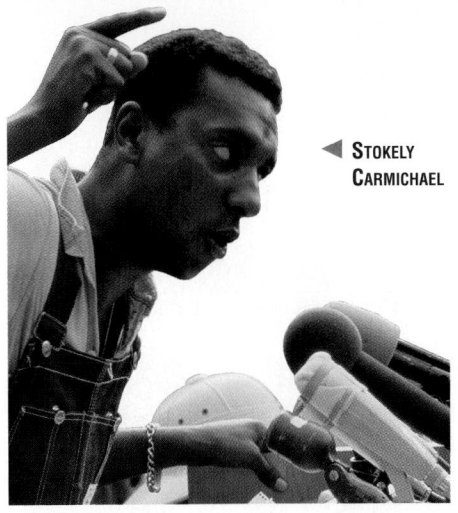
◀ STOKELY CARMICHAEL

nonviolence set off a week of rioting, arson, and looting in 125 American cities. It was as if King's death swept away the last bit of faith in a peaceful solution. "America," announced Stokely Carmichael, "must be burned down in order for us to survive." Rioting took place in Washington, D.C., just blocks from the White House. President Johnson ordered troops to enforce a curfew and protect government buildings.

■ The Civil Rights Movement After 1968

Between the *Brown* decision and King's death, the civil rights movement made great gains. After King died, however, the movement's leaders feared that they would begin to lose some of their hard-won victories.

Richard Nixon, who won the presidency in 1968, had his own agenda. He wanted the Republicans to win control of both the White House and Congress in 1972. To do that, he needed to lure southern Democrats into the Republican ranks.

To this end, Nixon developed a "southern strategy." He appointed a southern justice to the Supreme Court. The President also reversed a Johnson administration policy that cut off federal funds to racially segregated school systems. Although federal policy had been affirmed in 1968 by the Supreme Court in *Green* v. *County School Board,* Nixon ignored the Court's ruling and instructed the Justice Department to support school boards that were seeking to delay desegregation.

Contrary to Nixon's hopes, his appointments to the Supreme Court did not guarantee a reversal of the *Green* decision. Instead, the Court affirmed integration by means of **busing**—transporting children to a school outside their residential area to achieve racial balance in that school. White Americans in the South and most other regions of the nation resisted busing, and Nixon denounced it. The Nixon administration's open opposition to busing for desegregation intensified public controversy over the issue.

Nixon's agenda moved many people and much of government policy to the right, away from the liberal policies of the Kennedy-Johnson years. Many civil rights gains were lost or delayed. However, despite the setback, the movement continued. It would make gains in the future and strongly influence other minorities.

Section 3 ★ Review

Checking for Understanding
1. **Identify** the Nation of Islam, Malcolm X, Stokely Carmichael, Kerner Commission, Watts, "southern strategy."

2. **Define** racism, black nationalism, black power, assimilation, busing.

3. **Summarize** the goals of the black-power movement.

Critical Thinking
4. **Making Comparisons** Explain how the views of Malcolm X on the problem of racism differed from those of Martin Luther King, Jr.

ACTIVITY
5. Use photographs and drawings to illustrate a poster on the life and accomplishments of Dr. Martin Luther King, Jr.

Answers to SECTION 3 REVIEW
1. the Nation of Islam, 682; Malcolm X, 683; Stokely Carmichael, 683; Watts, 684; Kerner Commission, 685; "southern strategy," 686
2. All vocabulary words are defined in the Glossary.
3. to separate all aspects of African American life from white society and maintain racial distinctiveness, pride, and leadership
4. King believed in nonviolent resistance, integration, and equality for all Americans; Malcolm X believed that African Americans should use weapons if necessary to protect themselves and that African Americans should live separately from white Americans. He later modified his views.
5. Posters should show major events in King's life.

★★★

The Impact of Civil Rights

Setting the Scene

Section Focus

All the efforts made by civil rights activists during the 1950s and 1960s had a far greater impact than just to help African Americans gain equality in America. Other disadvantaged groups—women, Hispanics, and Native Americans—found new hope in the African Americans' struggle and formed movements of their own. These movements found support because of the atmosphere in the nation as a whole. Because of the civil rights struggle and the Vietnam War, a great number of people had begun to question the status of American society and the policies of the government.

Objectives

After studying this section, you should be able to

★ describe the gains made by women and minorities.

★ explain why the Equal Rights Amendment was not ratified.

Key Terms

feminist, sexism, bilingualism

▶ SHIRLEY CHISHOLM

LESSON PLAN
SECTION 4, 687–691

FOCUS
Bellringer

 Before taking roll, project Section Focus Transparency 22-4 or hand out Section Focus Transparency Activity 22-4. Have students answer the questions. Discuss student responses.

Motivating Activity

Ask students to consider how women and minority groups are portrayed today in television and films. Have them speculate about the ways the movement for equal rights for women and minorities may have affected these portrayals. Explain that Section 4 traces the impact of the struggle for equal rights on women and minorities. **L2**

Vocabulary Precheck

Ask students to define each of the "Key Terms." Have a volunteer consult the dictionary for any unfamiliar words. **L1, LEP**

uring the 1960s and 1970s, young Americans became leaders in promoting social justice. They were determined to close the gap between the realities of American life—discrimination, poverty, and social inequalities—and the nation's ideal of "liberty and justice for all."

■ The Women's Rights Movement

Women constituted more than 50 percent of the population in the United States in the 1970s. However, their political, economic, legal, and social status resembled that of a disadvantaged minority. Minority women faced a special problem in that they encountered sexual and racial discrimination at the same time.

Status of Women

In 1977 women held less than 5 percent of the elective offices in the United States. There had been few female senators or governors, no Supreme Court justices, and no mayors of major cities in the history of the republic. Of the 435 members of the House of Representatives, only 18 were women. In her autobiography *Unbought and Unbossed*, Shirley Chisholm, the first African American woman to serve in the House of Representatives, wrote:

❝ *When I decided to run for Congress, I knew I would encounter both anti-black and anti-feminist sentiments. What surprised me was the much greater virulence of the sex discrimination.* ❞

NATIONAL GEOGRAPHIC SOCIETY

 **VIDEODISC**
GTV: The American People: Fabric of a Nation

Side 4, Chapter 1
Title: *America's Choir*
Subject: A profile of Americans in the 90s
See GTV Guide for complete lesson plan.

Classroom Resources for SECTION 4

Blackline Masters:
🗂 Reproducible Lesson Plan 22-4
🗂 Guided Reading Activity 22-4
🗂 American Literary Heritage, p. 51
🗂 Enrichment Activity 22
🗂 Workbook Activity 22-4
🗂 Reteaching Activity 22-4
🗂 Section Quiz 22-4

Transparencies:
🖌 Section Focus Transparency 22-4
Multimedia:
📀 Testmaker
📀 GTV: The American People: Fabric of a Nation
📀 The American Indian

TEACH
Guided Practice

Point out to students that the women's movement is often referred to as the "women's liberation movement." Ask students to write a short news feature titled "Women's Liberation," explaining why the movement was so named. **L1**

CURRICULUM CONNECTION

Sociology In the past, many people lumped women together with minority groups, using such references as "women and other minorities." In fact, women in the United States are not a minority but make up a little more than the majority of the population.

Visualizing
History The same year that Congress voted to submit the ERA, it also passed the Equal Employment Opportunity Act, which provided the power to enforce the sex discrimination provisions of the 1964 Civil Rights Act through the courts.
Answer to Caption: It failed to obtain the votes needed for ratification.

▼ GLORIA STEINEM

▶ PHYLLIS SCHLAFLY

Visualizing History ▲ ERA MARCHERS The Equal Rights Amendment, submitted to the states in 1972 for ratification, aroused strong feelings among supporters and opponents. *What happened to the Equal Rights Amendment?*

Representative Chisholm was elected for a second term in 1970. In 1972 she ran against George McGovern for the Democratic nomination for President. She served in Congress for the next decade and continued to support equal rights for minorities and women. After serving in Congress, she then turned her talent to teaching on the college level. About her accomplishments, she noted:

> 66 *I hope that my having made it, the hard way, can be some kind of inspiration, particularly to women.* 99

In 1960 women made up one-third of the nation's workforce. Yet, most of their jobs offered less pay and prestige than those positions that men held. For every dollar on average that a man earned on a job in the 1960s, a woman with the same job earned only 59 cents. During the rest of the 1960s and into the next decade the economic situation of women improved slightly.

In 1976 the United States Department of Labor reported that full-time working men averaged 75 percent more pay than full-time working women. Dissatisfied with the slow progress, many women began calling for stronger action.

The publication in 1963 of *The Feminine Mystique* by Betty Friedan had inspired demands for change. Friedan rejected the notion that the destiny of women was only to be wives and mothers. She described how the media had created an image of women that was designed to imprison them in their households and bar serious consideration of them as competitors in the labor market.

National Organization for Women

In 1966 Betty Friedan joined with other **feminists,** or women activists, to establish the National Organization for Women (NOW). The organization's Statement of Purpose read:

> 66 *... [To] take action to bring women into full participation in the mainstream of American society now, assuming all the privileges and responsibilities thereof in truly equal partnership with men.* 99

Among its early successes, NOW helped end separate classified employment ads for men and women, and airline rules that required female flight attendants to retire at

688   UNIT 7 Redefining America: 1954–Present

Critical Thinking Activity

Comparing Suggest students compare the women's movements in the nineteenth and early twentieth centuries with that of the 1960s and 1970s. How were the leaders similar? What differences seem most striking? How were their objectives alike? How did each movement influence American society? Which was the more militant or radical? Students might present their comparisons orally or as a report to the class. **L2**

age 32. In the 1960s and 1970s, NOW and similar groups helped increasing numbers of women to enter professions. Banks, realtors, and department stores were forced to grant loans, mortgages, leases, and credit that they long had denied to female applicants.

The Equal Rights Amendment

Following intense lobbying by women's groups, in 1972 Congress voted to submit the Equal Rights Amendment (ERA) to the states for ratification. This amendment stated that "equality of rights under the law shall not be denied or abridged by the United States or by any state on account of sex."

Not all women supported ERA, however. Phyllis Schlafly, founder of STOP ERA, dismissed the women's rights movement as "a series of sharp-tongued, high-pitched, whining complaints by unmarried women." STOP ERA supporters contended that the ERA would force women to give up their traditional roles as wives and mothers, and that they would lose certain legal protections in the family and in the workplace. As a result of a vigorous campaign by STOP ERA and other groups, the Equal Rights Amendment failed to obtain the votes needed for ratification.

Women Make Progress

Despite the failure of the ERA, women continued to make progress. **Sexism**—treating people differently because of their gender—was recognized and outlawed in the workplace by 1971. Princeton, Yale, and other traditionally all-male colleges began to open their doors to females.

Women were also becoming increasingly important in the business world. By the mid-1970s, nearly half of all married women worked outside the home; almost all who had graduated from college worked.

Women also were becoming an important force in politics in the 1970s. By the 1980s, there were more women than ever in both the Senate and the House of Representatives, as well as on the Supreme Court, in the cabinet, and in state government offices. In 1984, Representative Geraldine Ferraro became the first female major-party candidate to run for Vice President.

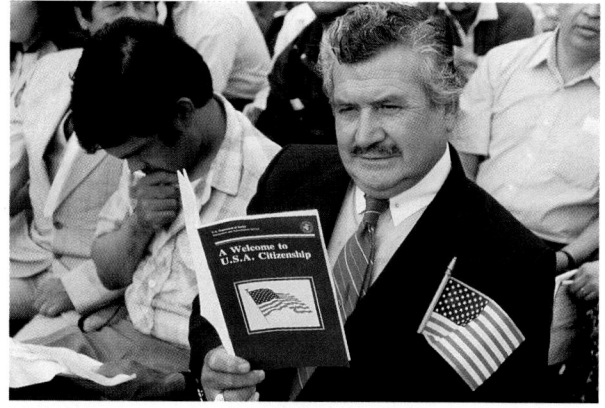

 ▲ HISPANIC AMERICANS By the 1970s Hispanic Americans were the second-largest minority in the United States. *What group made up the largest number of Hispanics?*

■ Hispanic Activism

At this time, Hispanics also became active in campaigning for equal rights. By the 1970s Hispanic Americans had become the second-largest minority in the United States, next to African Americans. Spanish-speaking people made up almost 8 percent of the population and were the largest minority group in several states. New York City alone had about 2 million Spanish-speaking people. Part of Miami, Florida, became known as "Little Havana" because it was home to hundreds of thousands of Cuban immigrants.

Mexican Americans made up the largest group of Hispanic peoples. For years, thousands of Mexican Americans labored as

· ·

Footnotes to History

Muñoz Marín and Puerto Rico Puerto Rican newspaper editor Luis Muñoz Marín formed his own political party after Liberal party leaders expelled him, partly because he called for independence from the United States. Muñoz Marín founded his own party and, in 1942, organized Operation Bootstrap to attract mainland industry to the island. In 1948 Muñoz Marín was overwhelmingly elected Puerto Rico's first governor. He persuaded the United States to approve a commonwealth status for the island in 1952. When he died in 1980, he was mourned as a national hero.

Independent Practice

Supporting an Opinion Tell students that the struggle for full civil rights for all Americans continues in the 1990s. Ask students to write an editorial in which they identify groups that still experience discrimination. Have them explain the issues involved, why the prejudice persists, and possible solutions. **L3**

📁 Assign Guided Reading Activity 22-4.

Linking Across TIME

Betty Friedan was a major leader in the women's movement. Her book *The Feminine Mystique* stirred tremendous controversy and became a bible for many women in the struggle for equal rights. In the early 1990s, Friedan again became the center of controversy when she seemed to back away from her earlier, more radical views.

Visualizing History Among Hispanic Americans who worked to secure equal rights was Rodolfo Gonzalis who organized the Crusade for Justice and was active in the Chicano movement.
Answer to caption: Mexican Americans

Cooperative Learning Activity

Making a Graph Divide students into three groups and assign one of the following to each: women, Hispanics, Native Americans. Ask each group to research recent economic gains in terms of earnings and employment and create a line or bar graph showing trends in the last 10 years. When the graphs are completed, have groups present them to the class and summarize their findings. **L2** 📦

Linking Across
T I M E

The struggle of Native Americans for equality and justice has been a long one. The federal government has gone back and forth in its efforts to either assimilate Native Americans or separate them onto reservations. Today, Native Americans are fighting in the courts to regain land rights and have organized to lobby for their cause.

Facts on File

CD-ROM

The American Indian

Students can learn more about the Native American movement by selecting the category HISTORY and BIOGRAPHY from the main menu.

migrant farm workers, moving from place to place to harvest seasonal crops. They were not protected by federal minimum-wage laws, unemployment insurance, or Social Security.

In 1965 Cesar Chavez organized a nationwide coalition and asked Americans to boycott California grapes picked by nonunion labor. After enduring five years of such persistent protest, most California grape growers relented and agreed to sign a contract with Chavez's union, the United Farm Workers.

During the 1970s, Hispanic Americans began to organize. The League of United Latin American Citizens (LULAC) won suits in federal courts to guarantee Hispanic Americans the right to serve on juries, to send their children to unsegregated schools, and to be taught in Spanish as well as in English. The use of two languages is called **bilingualism.** As their political strength grew, more Hispanic Americans were elected to local and state offices as well as to Congress.

◀ RUSSELL MEANS, AIM LEADER

■ Native Americans Organize

Like the Hispanics, Native Americans organized during the 1960s and 1970s. Their plight captured national attention when a 1966 study revealed that Native Americans suffered from malnutrition and disease to such an extent that their life expectancy was only 46 years. They had less formal education than any other minority group, and their family income was less than one-half the national average.

Termination Policy

After World War II, the federal government tried to incorporate Native Americans into white society. A new policy called "termination" was established in 1953. This meant that the federal government stopped recognizing Native American nations as legal entities that were separate from state government. Now, the nations would be subject to the same local governments as whites. The government in Washington worked to make Native Americans give up their cultures and adapt to white society.

Native Americans were so angry that they began speaking out more forcibly. A group of younger Native Americans had breathed life into the National Congress of American Indians (NCAI), set up in 1944. As a result of their activity, President Eisenhower put a stop to termination without consent. Later Presidents did

▲ AMERICAN INDIAN MOVEMENT FLAG

Critical Thinking Activity

Analyzing Gains Although women and minorities have gained many rights and opportunities as a result of the civil rights movement, much remains to be done. Ask students to identify areas where they think more could be done to ensure that all Americans have equal rights.

Have students write their ideas in the form of a letter to their representative in Congress. Invite volunteers to read their letters and discuss with the class the areas they feel are most important. **L2**

not revive it during the 1960s. They made some efforts to provide tribes with government money.

Declaration of Indian Purpose

In 1961, more than 400 representatives of 67 Native American nations met in Chicago to draw up a bill of rights for Native Americans. They called it the Declaration of Indian Purpose, and in it they committed themselves to Indian nationalism and intertribal unity. The delegates also stated their belief in "red power," and demanded an end to federal control of Native American affairs. "We simply want to run our lives our own way," said one young leader.

As a result, in 1968, the Congress passed the Indian Civil Rights Act, which guaranteed Native American reservation dwellers some of the rights provided to other citizens under the Bill of Rights.

However, some Native Americans wanted to take more direct action. In the state of Washington, men from more than 50 Native American groups led a "fish-in." They deliberately broke game laws and risked imprisonment to protest the loss of their former fishing and hunting grounds.

In 1973 a more militant group, the American Indian Movement (AIM), seized the reservation at Wounded Knee, South Dakota. They demanded that lands taken from Native Americans in violation of federal treaties be returned. They also demanded that development programs on reservations be managed

by their own governments, and not the federal Bureau of Indian Affairs. The takeover ended after a standoff between federal agents and Native Americans, and federal policies toward Native Americans began to change.

The Pueblo of Taos, New Mexico, regained Blue Lake, a place sacred to their religious life. In 1975 a federal court declared that the Passamaquoddy and the Penobscot nations had a valid claim to more than half the state of Maine and to $25 billion in damages and unpaid rents.

▲ NATIVE AMERICANS Native Americans fought in the nation's wars and honored those who gave their lives for freedom. Many pressed for economic and political equality and compensation for the loss of their land. *What action did Native Americans take at Wounded Knee in 1973?*

Section 4 ★ Review

Checking for Understanding

1. **Identify** Shirley Chisholm, Betty Friedan, NOW, ERA, Phyllis Schlafly, Cesar Chavez, LULAC, "red power," AIM.

2. **Define** feminist, sexism, bilingualism.

3. **List** three inequalities between men and women that existed in the 1970s.

4. **State** two demands that were made by Hispanics and Native Americans.

Critical Thinking

5. **Analyzing Point of View** Analyze the women's rights movement in the 1970s. What stereotypes of women persist today?

ACTIVITY

6. Research the history of one of the immigrant groups in your community. Write a one-page report detailing their unique contributions.

CHAPTER 22 The Civil Rights Era: 1954–1975 **691**

ASSESS
Check Understanding
Assign Section 4 Review as homework or an in-class activity.

Evaluate
🔲 🗂 Assign Section Quiz 22-4 or use the Testmaker to create a customized quiz.

Reteach
🗂 Have students complete Reteaching Activity 22-4.

🗂 Assign Workbook Activity 22-4.

Enrich
🗂 Assign Enrichment Activity 22.

🗂 Assign American Literary Heritage, p. 51: "Tomorrow" by Peter Blue Cloud.

CLOSE
Have students summarize the section and explain why the period can be called "a time of change."

Visualizing History The American Indian Movement was founded in Minnesota by Dennis Banks and Clyde Bellecourt. **Answer to Caption:** They seized the reservation and demanded the land be returned.

CHAPTER 22 ★ REVIEW

GLENCOE
TECHNOLOGY

 **VIDEODISC**

Use the MindJogger
Videoquiz to review
students' knowledge.

MindJogger Videoquiz

Chapter 22
Disc 3, Side A

Available in VHS.

Using Vocabulary
Paragraphs should follow
thematically or chrono-
logically and include all
the vocabulary words.

Reviewing Facts
1. public schools desegregated; Southern resis-
tance created
2. King emerged as leader
of civil rights move-
ment; bus company
ended segregation.
3. Supreme Court deseg-
regation ruling, 1954;
Montgomery bus boy-
cott, 1955; formation of
SCLC, 1957; Civil
Rights Act, 1957; Little
Rock desegregation
battle, 1957; sit-in
movement, 1960; free-
dom rides, 1961; James
Meredith entered U. of
Mississippi, 1962;
Birmingham demon-
stration, 1963; March
on Washington, 1963
4. pushed through Voting
Rights Act
5. divided civil rights
movements into mod-
erates and radicals;
pride in heritage
6. economic, social, and
political equality
7. Native Americans have
gained more control
over their own lives

692

Using Vocabulary

Using the following vocabulary terms, write a
paragraph describing the development of the civil
rights movement.

nonviolent resistance	sit-in
federalized	racism
black nationalism	black power
assimilation	busing

Reviewing Facts

1. **List** two results of the Supreme Court's *Brown* v.
Board of Education ruling.
2. **Cite** two results of the Montgomery bus boycott.
3. **Arrange** in chronological order significant events
in the civil rights movement that occurred
between 1953 and 1963.
4. **Describe** how Johnson followed through on
Kennedy's policies regarding civil rights.
5. **List** two results of the black-power movement.
6. **Describe** the aims and objectives of the women's
rights movement.
7. **Summarize** advances made by Native American
peoples.

Understanding Concepts

Civil Rights

1. Explain the factors in American society that
helped the civil rights movement grow.
2. Evaluate the importance of leadership to the
civil rights movement in the 1950s and 1960s.
3. Compare the results of the late 1960s riots with
the goals of the black-power movement. Use this
information to formulate an opinion of the use of
violence in demonstrations.
4. Why did the civil rights movement cause so
much turmoil? Explain how the demands of
African Americans affected other minorities and
what the results were.

Critical Thinking

1. **Evaluating Tactics** Though Martin Luther
King, Jr.'s, methods for change were nonviolent,
they were not passive. What were some challenges faced by nonviolent civil rights demonstrators? Why was their nonviolence an effective
tactic?
2. **Analyzing Fine Art** Study the mural that
appears on this page. Then answer the questions
that follow.
   a. Describe what the mural is showing.
   b. What can you tell about the artist by looking
   at the mural?
   c. What can you tell from the mural about the
   artist's feelings toward African American
   culture?

3. **Interpreting Demographic Data** *Demographics*
is the data used to show the characteristics of a
human population in terms of size, growth, density distribution, and vital statistics. Study the
graph on page 693 and answer the questions that
follow.
   a. What demographic information does the
   graph show?
   b. What do the numbers in parentheses represent? What change does this information
   show?
   c. What does the information indicate about the
   problems a small group might have effecting
   change through the political process?

and have gained back or
been compensated for
some lands.

Understanding Concepts
1. Answers may include unequal opportunity.
2. Possible response: leadership was essential—
boycotts, sit-ins, and

demonstrations required
effective organization.
3. Students are likely to suggest that the riots led many
Americans to oppose the
goals of the movement.
4. The movement attempted
to bring reform and change
and threatened the status
quo. The gains won by
African Americans encour-

aged other groups to
protest and demand equal
rights. Results varied, but
both Native Americans
and Hispanics gained more
opportunities and social
and political rights.

Critical Thinking
1. Demonstrators faced physical and psychological

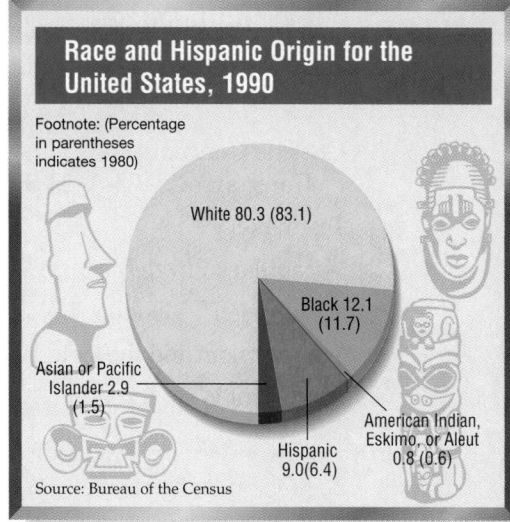

Race and Hispanic Origin for the United States, 1990

Footnote: (Percentage in parentheses indicates 1980)

White 80.3 (83.1)

Black 12.1 (11.7)

Asian or Pacific Islander 2.9 (1.5)

Hispanic 9.0(6.4)

American Indian, Eskimo, or Aleut 0.8 (0.6)

Source: Bureau of the Census

History and Geography

Native Americans and the Land

1. **Human/Environment Interaction** What effect did the Indian Civil Rights Act have on Native American reservations?

2. **Human/Environment Interaction** What action did Native Americans take to protest the loss of their fishing and hunting grounds?

3. **Human/Environment Interaction** How did the federal courts rule in the conflict over land claims in Maine?

Cooperative Learning — Interdisciplinary Activity: Sociology

You will work in a group with two others to analyze three activist movements of the 1970s: the women's rights movement, the Hispanic movement, and the Native American movement. The goal of your group is to find as many similarities between these movements as you can. Each group member should choose one of these movements. First, work individually to make a list of the goals of each movement and the methods used to attain them. Next,

work with your partners to compile a master list of similarities between the three movements. Present your list to the class and discuss the findings.

Practicing Skills

Identifying Cause and Effect

Consider the following statements. Each of these statements includes a cause and an effect. For each statement make a cause-and-effect diagram by writing the cause on the left and the effect on the right. Then connect the two parts of the statement with an arrow.

1. As a result of serving in the military during wartime, African Americans were in a better position to demand their full rights as Americans.

2. President Truman could not get Congress's support for his civil rights program, largely because of a split in the Democratic party.

3. When it became clear that the Eisenhower administration and Congress would not consider legislation, civil rights groups turned to the courts for settlement of their grievances.

4. Loopholes in the Civil Rights Act of 1957 led to a call for stronger legislation.

Writing ABOUT History

Using Your Journal

Discuss how civil rights activists alive today might react to this statement: Though the journey has been rough and hard, the results are worth it.

state of Maine and to $25 billion in damages and unpaid rents

Cooperative Learning

Students might present the comparisons in chart form. Discuss why the movements would be comparable.

Practicing Skills

1. first part of sentence— cause; second part— effect
2. first part—effect; second part—cause
3. first part—cause; second part—effect
4. first part—cause; second part—effect

Writing ABOUT History

Using Your Journal

Most students are likely to agree. Many gains were made and the example of the civil rights movement continues to inspire people.

? Chapter Bonus Test Question

Ask: What kinds of gains do you think African Americans and other minorities might experience in the first decades of the next century. (*Responses will vary but should include political and economic issues.*)

---

abuse. Repercussions could have included backlash and lessened federal protection for violent activists.

2. **a.** Students may note that a celebration is depicted.
b. Answers may include artist preferred bright, vivid scenes.

c. shows pride in African American culture

3. **a.** the background of citizens in 1990
b. the percentage of the population in 1980
c. might lead them to pursue political strategies other than running for elective office

History and Geography

1. It guaranteed reservation dwellers some of the rights provided to other citizens under the Bill of Rights.

2. They led a "fish-in," deliberately breaking game laws and risking imprisonment.

3. that the nations had a valid claim to more than half the

Daily Lesson Objectives	Teacher Classroom Resources	Multimedia
SECTION 1 **Cold War Challenges** **1 Day**　pp. 696–700 1. Discuss Kennedy's responses to Soviet and international communism. 2. Explain the purposes of the Alliance for Progress and the Peace Corps.	Reproducible Lesson Plan 23-1 *Guided Reading Activity 23-1 Concept Mapping Activities 23-A, 23-B *Vocabulary Activity 23 Critical Thinking Skills Activity 23 Enrichment Activity 23 Primary and Secondary Source Readings, pp. 54–55 Reteaching Activity 23-1 *Section Quiz 23-1	Section Focus Transparency 23-1 Chapter Concepts Transparencies 23-A, 23-B Testmaker Vocabulary PuzzleMaker MindJogger Videoquiz Communism and the Cold War Lessons of War
SECTION 2 **War in Vietnam** **1 Day**　pp. 702–706 1. Explain how the Gulf of Tonkin incident led to the escalation of the war in Vietnam. 2. Explain why the Tet offensive was the turning point of the Vietnam War.	Reproducible Lesson Plan 23-2 *Guided Reading Activity 23-2 Chapter Map Activity 23 Political Cartoons in American History Activity 25 Chapter Skills Activity 23 Reteaching Activity 23-2 *Section Quiz 23-2	Section Focus Transparency 23-2 Map Transparency 23 Skills Transparency 23 Testmaker Communism and the Cold War Powers of the President
SECTION 3 **Protest and Reaction** **1 Day**　pp. 708–712 1. List reasons for opposition to the war. 2. Describe the youth counter-culture.	Reproducible Lesson Plan 23-3 *Guided Reading Activity 23-3 Linking Past and Present Activity 23 Cooperative Learning Activity 23 Reteaching Activity 23-3 *Section Quiz 23-3	Section Focus Transparency 23-3 Testmaker Powers of the President
SECTION 4 **Secrecy and Summitry** **1 Day**　pp. 713–717 1. Explain why Nixon pursued détente in foreign policy. 2. List and describe the steps that President Nixon took to end American involvement in Vietnam.	Reproducible Lesson Plan 23-4 *Guided Reading Activity 23-4 Primary and Secondary Source Readings, pp. 64–65 Spirit of American Art and Music, p. 47 Enrichment Activity 23 Geography in History Activity 23 Reteaching Activity 23-4 *Section Quiz 23-4	Section Focus Transparency 23-4 Testmaker Communism and the Cold War Powers of the President Historic America Electronic Field Trips
CHAPTER REVIEW AND EVALUATION **1 Day**	Chapter 23 Test, Forms A and B Spanish Chapter 23 Summaries Performance Assessment Activity 23	MindJogger Videoquiz Student Self-Test & Review Software *Chapter 23 Audiocassette Activity and Test

*Also available in Spanish

 0:00　OUT OF TIME? If time does not permit teaching the entire chapter, use the Chapter 23 Summary on pages 800–801 and the Chapter 23 audiocassette (English and Spanish) to point out the main ideas of the chapter.

A complete, 1-page lesson plan is provided for each section in the *Reproducible Lesson Plan* booklet.

Key to Ability Levels

Teaching strategies have been coded for varying learning styles and abilities.

L1 Basic activities for all students

L2 Average activities for average to above-average students

L3 Challenging activities for above-average students

LEP Limited English Proficiency activities

Block Schedule

Block scheduling differs from traditional class scheduling in the amount of time allotted to each period. The extended time frame provided by block scheduling affords you the opportunity to implement a greater number of research-oriented and activity-intense projects to motivate and involve your students. Activities that are particularly suited to use within the block scheduling framework are identified throughout this unit by the following designation:

✓ Performance Assessment Activity

Analyzing Foreign Policy Have students choose one of the Presidents highlighted in this chapter and write a speech defining that President's approach to foreign problems. The speeches should begin by describing administration objectives. Point out that the United States has several basic foreign policy goals it hopes to achieve. These include national security, international trade, promoting world peace, maintaining democratic ideas, and protecting human rights. Then ask students to outline policies based on one or more of these goals, and conclude with a critical examination of the results of those policies. Students might work alone on the speeches or in small groups. Encourage speechwriters to read their address to the class.

POSSIBLE RUBRIC FEATURES

- Research Skills
- Content Information
- Organization
- Written and Oral Communication Skills
- Critical Thinking Skills

📁 For additional practice, use Performance Assessment Strategies and Activities.

T E A C H E R ' S   C O R N E R

NATIONAL GEOGRAPHIC SOCIETY

INDEX TO NATIONAL GEOGRAPHIC MAGAZINE

The following articles may be used for research relating to this chapter:

- "The New Saigon," by Tracy Dahlby, April 1995.
- "The Mekong," by Thomas O'Neill, February 1993.
- "Hong Kong—Plight of the Boat People," by Larry Kohl, February 1991.
- *Vietnam: The Hard Road to Peace,* (A Special Edition), November 1989.

NATIONAL GEOGRAPHIC SOCIETY PRODUCTS AVAILABLE FROM GLENCOE

To order the following products for use with this chapter, contact your local Glencoe sales representative or call Glencoe at 1-800-334-7344:

- *The Presidents: A Picture History of Our Nation* (CD-ROM)
- *GTV: A Geographic Perspective on American History* (Videodisc)
- *GTV: The American People: Fabric of a Nation* (Videodisc)

ADDITIONAL NATIONAL GEOGRAPHIC SOCIETY PRODUCTS

To order the following products for use with this chapter, call National Geographic Society at 1-800-368-2728:

- *Decades of History: The 20th Century—The Middle Years* (Filmstrip)
- *The United States as a World Power: From the 1890s to the 1970s* (Filmstrip)
- *The American Presidency* (Filmstrip)
- *The Vietnam War* (Filmstrip)
- *The Changing Faces of Communism Series: Vietnam* (Video)
- *1945–1989: The Cold War* (Video)

GLENCOE TECHNOLOGY

 VIDEODISC

Use the Chapter 23 MindJogger Videoquiz to preview the content of this chapter.

MindJogger Videoquiz

Chapter 23
Disc 3, Side B

 Available in VHS.

Recording Journal Notes

To help students get started, suggest that they list the major events of the Vietnam War era as they read the chapter. They can then record details about the role of the President during these events and what his feelings might have been at the time.

Linking Across **TIME**

Twenty-six senators cosponsored a bill authorizing the fund to build a Vietnam memorial on public grounds in Washington, D.C. The bill had widespread support and was passed unanimously in both houses of Congress. On July 1, 1980, President Jimmy Carter signed the bill into law.

CHAPTER 23
★★★
The Vietnam Era
1954–1975

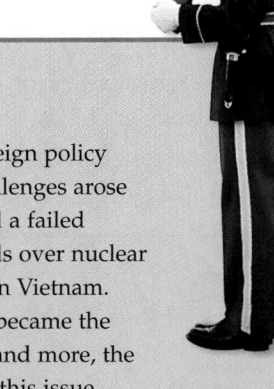
▶ SOLDIER STANDING GUARD

Setting the Scene

Focus

President Kennedy's handling of foreign policy was tested strenuously as cold war challenges arose during the Vietnam Era. Kennedy faced a failed Cuban invasion, a missile crisis, quarrels over nuclear testing, and the beginnings of the war in Vietnam. During the Johnson years, this conflict became the focus of attention for the nation. More and more, the American people became divided over this issue.

Concepts to Understand

★ How social upheaval divided the nation and affected **foreign policy** during the Vietnam Era

★ Why public opinion was divided over the conduct of the **war** in Vietnam

Read to Discover . . .

★ lessons Kennedy learned from his handling of foreign policy.

★ what events set off political turmoil during this period.

Journal Notes

What do you think it would have been like to be President of the United States during the Vietnam War? Note details about it in your journal as you read the chapter.

CULTURAL
- **1955** *Ford offers seatbelts as optional equipment*
- **1964** *The Beatles appear on* The Ed Sullivan Show

| 1955 | 1960 |

- **1959** *Castro takes power in Cuba*
- **1961** *Peace Corps is established*
- **1962** *Cuban missile crisis*

POLITICAL

✚ **EXTRA CREDIT PROJECT**

Designing a Magazine Cover Divide interested students into groups of three. Have each group create a magazine cover, its table of contents, and the editorial message for an issue called "The Year in Review." The magazine cover should highlight the articles inside. Ask students to design the cover, to write the "Table of Contents," and to write a short "Message From the Editor" paragraph. The magazine cover should reflect one of the major events mentioned in the chapter, such as the cold war challenges of the 1960s, the war in Vietnam, student protests. Have students present their project to the class. Post their work on the bulletin board. **L2**

History
AND
ART

Con Thien
by John Gordon, 1967

An American soldier in a Vietnam bunker waits out heavy shelling during an attack near the demilitarized zone.

◀ VIETNAM VETERANS STATUE,
WASHINGTON, D.C.

- **1967** *Green Bay Packers win first Super Bowl, 35–10, over Kansas City Chiefs*
- **1968** *Peace talks to end Vietnam War begin in Paris*
- **1968** *Robert Kennedy is assassinated; Nixon becomes President*

| 1965 | 1970 |

- **1970** *First Earth Day observed as millions protest pollution*
- **1970** *Kent State University students riot*
- **1971** *Pentagon Papers are published*
- **1972** *President Nixon visits China*

CHAPTER 23 The Vietnam Era: 1954–1975   **695**

On the chalkboard, reproduce the following generalization and concepts map, and have students copy it in their notebooks.

President Kennedy's and President Johnson's attempts to continue New Deal policies at home and cold war containment abroad fell short of expectations; the nation continued at war and was thrown into domestic turmoil.

| Foreign Policy | War |

📁 To reinforce the two chapter concepts, use Concept Mapping Activities 23-A and 23-B.

🕹️ 📁 Use Chapter Concepts Transparencies 23-A, 23-B.

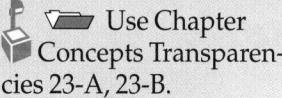

History
AND
ART

The statue of the servicemen was sculpted by Frederick Hart. Cast in bronze, it is 7 feet (2.1 meters) tall.

ABCNEWS
INTERACTIVE™

  VIDEODISC

Communism and the Cold War

Side Two, Chapter 5
Title: *How We Saw Them*
Subject: American view of communism

Performance Assessment

Designing a Brochure Point out that in 1975, after the fall of the South Vietnamese government, the United States agreed to admit those Vietnamese who wanted to settle in the nation. These immigrants were given refugee status and such aid as free English classes, job counseling and training, and day care. These services helped many Vietnamese make a successful transition to American life. Discuss why Americans felt an obligation to help the Vietnamese. Then organize the students into groups and ask each group to design a brochure that would help the newcomers adjust to life in the United States in the 1970s. Encourage the groups to share their brochures. Discuss how they might be updated for new arrivals in the 1990s. **L2**

FOCUS

Bellringer

✋ 📂 Before taking roll, project Section Focus Transparency 23-1 or hand out Section Focus Transparency Activity 23-1. Have students answer the questions. Discuss student responses.

Motivating Activity

Ask students how they think most Americans would respond if the President announced that missiles in Cuba were pointed at the United States. Tell them that this happened in 1962. Ask what they think should be done. Compare with President Kennedy's actions. **L1**

Vocabulary Precheck

Ask students to define each of the "Key Terms." Have a volunteer consult the dictionary for any unfamiliar words. **L1, LEP**

📀 Use the Vocabulary PuzzleMaker Software to create a crossword puzzle. **L1**

📂 Assign Vocabulary Activity 23.

★★

Cold War Challenges

Setting the Scene

Section Focus

President Kennedy entered office with little firsthand experience in international affairs. Yet he had to meet such challenges as the buildup of nuclear arms, anti-United States feeling in Latin America, and instability in economically developing nations in Africa and Asia. He achieved some triumphs, but in other cases his inexperience led him into mistakes.

Objectives

After studying this section, you should be able to

★ discuss Kennedy's responses to Soviet and international communism.

★ explain the purposes of the Alliance for Progress and the Peace Corps.

Key Terms

reactionary government, credibility gap

◀ CUBAN LEADER FIDEL CASTRO

*P*resident Kennedy's basic aims in foreign policy were similar to those of Truman and Eisenhower. His major concern was the threat of communism, and he declared that he would not relax efforts to contain it.

■ Crises in Cuba

In 1959 Fidel Castro had led a movement to overthrow Fulgencio Batista—the corrupt dictator then ruling Cuba—and had set up a new government. Castro soon established ties with the Soviet Union and began to adopt Marxist-influenced policies. As a result, the Eisenhower administration began to view Cuba as a threat to democracy in the Western Hemisphere. Eisenhower authorized the Central Intelligence Agency to train and arm Cuban exiles secretly for the overthrow of Castro.

The Bay of Pigs Invasion

The CIA believed that an invasion of Cuba by these exiles would touch off a popular uprising against Castro. Kennedy's military advisers approved the project. In office less than three months, Kennedy agreed that the invasion should proceed.

On April 17, 1961, a force of 1,400 Cuban exiles came ashore at the Bay of Pigs on the south coast of Cuba. From the start the invasion went poorly. There was no popular uprising by the Cuban people. Within hours Castro's forces had the invaders surrounded.

The failed invasion hurt the prestige of the new Kennedy administration and strengthened Castro's position in the world. It also allowed Soviet leader Nikita Khrushchev to pose as the defender of Latin America against United States imperialism.

Classroom Resources for SECTION 1

Blackline Masters:
- 📂 Reproducible Lesson Plan 23-1
- 📂 Guided Reading Activity 23-1
- 📂 Vocabulary Activity 23
- 📂 Critical Thinking Skills Activity 23

- 📂 Enrichment Activity 23
- 📂 Primary and Secondary Source Readings, pp. 54–55
- 📂 Workbook Activity 23-1
- 📂 Reteaching Activity 23-1
- 📂 Section Quiz 23-1

Transparencies:
- ✋ Section Focus Transparency 23-1

Multimedia:
- 📀 Testmaker
- 📀 Vocabulary PuzzleMaker
- 📀 MindJogger Videoquiz
- 📀 Communism and the Cold War
- 📀 Lessons of War

The Alliance for Progress

The Castro movement, known as "Fidelismo," threatened to spread to other countries in Latin America. Promoted by Cuban agents, it often found support among the poverty-stricken and those seeking more political power. Kennedy announced a new economic program for Latin America—called the Alliance for Progress—that emphasized social reform and political freedom. Its purpose was to develop long-term economic growth among 19 Latin American nations, thus making it less likely that poverty would drive people in these countries to support communist-inspired revolutions. Over a 10-year period, the United States pledged $20 billion to help Latin American countries provide better schools, housing, and health care.

Even though United States aid to Latin America quadrupled, the results were uneven. In some countries—notably Chile, Colombia, Venezuela, and the Central American republics—the Alliance succeeded in promoting reform. In others, however, much of the money was diverted for the benefit of the military and the wealthy.

The Cuban Missile Crisis

On October 22, 1962, President Kennedy appeared on television and made a chilling announcement. U-2 spy planes from the United States had taken photographs proving that the Soviet Union had placed missiles in Cuba. The medium-range missiles were capable of reaching Atlanta and New Orleans; intermediate-range missiles were capable of reaching as far north as Pittsburgh and Detroit and as far west as Denver. Kennedy ordered a naval blockade to keep the Soviets from delivering any more missiles, and he demanded that the Soviets

dismantle all their missile sites in Cuba. War seemed imminent.

Secretly, the Soviet Union offered to remove the missiles if the United States promised never to invade Cuba. As negotiations continued, Khrushchev added another demand: that the United States remove its own missiles from the Soviet border of Turkey. President Kennedy rejected this demand because it would weaken the NATO alliance. The President's brother, Attorney General Robert Kennedy, suggested they ignore the new proposal and accept the Soviet Union's first offer.

After five agonizing days, when the world appeared on the brink of nuclear disaster, the Soviet ships turned back from the blockade. Soviet leaders also decided to withdraw their missiles from Cuba. President Kennedy won strong public support for his firm stand.

■ The Peace Corps

To help developing nations fight poverty and disease, Kennedy set up the Peace Corps in 1961. Like the Alliance for Progress, the Peace Corps was organized to help prevent the spread of communism.

Peace Corps Volunteers

After a period of rigorous training, Peace Corps volunteers went to countries that had asked for their assistance. There they lived among the people and helped them solve local problems. They laid out sewage systems in Bolivia, trained medical technicians in Chad, and built a model town in Pakistan. A high proportion of volunteers taught English and practical skills. In return they received only a living wage and a small vacation allowance. By late 1963 there were 11,000 Peace Corps volunteers serving in 40 countries.

Peace Corps volunteers in economically developing nations of Africa, Asia, and Latin America witnessed firsthand the problems and potential of newly independent nations. Many countries often lacked the necessary institutions to make the transition from colonial status to political and economic independence.

Footnotes to History

The Brink of War The Cuban missile crisis grew volatile because installation of Cuban missile bases would cut the warning time for an attack on the United States from 15 minutes to under 3 minutes. Kennedy's firmness and cool judgment erased the shame of the Bay of Pigs and boosted the United States's prestige.

Sidelight: Kennedy's Foreign Policy

In 1961 President Kennedy had to set a new path in foreign policy that would accommodate the changes occurring in the world. There had been much talk of "the end of the postwar world." Europe, for example, no longer recognized the United States as the leader of the free world. During his 1960 campaign, Kennedy charged that the United States had lost its "position of pre-eminence" under Eisenhower and stated his intent to regain that position through disarmament and détente with the Soviet Union.

TEACH

Guided Practice

Geography Ask students to discuss Kennedy's foreign policy challenges by asking: How did President Kennedy's policy in Latin America change over time? Why did many people consider the Bay of Pigs incident a mistake? How was the Cuban missile crisis resolved? **L2**

🗁 Assign Primary and Secondary Source Readings, pp. 54–55: "The Cuban Missile Crisis."

FACT or FICTION?

During the Kennedy administration, a "hot line" was installed between the White House and the Kremlin.

FACT: The purpose of this direct telephone line between the government centers of the United States and the Soviet Union was to prevent an accidental nuclear attack.

ABCNEWS INTERACTIVE™

 VIDEODISC

Communism and the Cold War

Side One, Chapter 16
Title: *Cuban Missile Crisis*
Subject: Summary of the crisis

Independent Practice

Analyzing Point of View

Write the following on the chalkboard:

The Kennedy presidency is sometimes represented as the point in time when the world began to make the great turn toward peace.

Have students write a brief paragraph supporting or opposing this point of view. Ask them to support their arguments with details from this section. **L2**

📁 Assign Guided Reading Activity 23-1.

Visualizing History During its first 29 years, the Peace Corps sent volunteers to work in Africa, Asia, Latin America, and the Pacific islands. Beginning in 1989, however, the Peace Corps sent volunteers to several Eastern European countries. **Answer to Caption:** 1963 treaty that banned atomic testing in the atmosphere, in outer space, and underwater

ABCNEWS
iNTERACTiVE™

VIDEODISC

Communism and the Cold War

Side One, Chapter 15
Title: *Berlin Wall*
Subject: Newsreel reports of the building of the Berlin Wall

Visualizing History

▲ SUMMIT MEETING When Khrushchev and Kennedy met at Vienna in June 1961, the two leaders treated one another with wary politeness. ***What agreement did they reach on nuclear testing?***

Nationalism in Africa

By 1961, 27 newly independent nations had been formed from European colonies in Africa. When Europeans established boundary lines of the colonies in the 1800s and early 1900s, they failed to take into account the existing ethnic and cultural divisions. Even decades later, it was difficult to obtain loyalty to the new nation-states.

Since the beginning of colonial rule, nationalist groups in Africa had resisted European control, often violently. Following World War II, these relatively small efforts for freedom swelled into powerful mass movements.

In 1961 ethnic rivalries in the Congo, later renamed Zaire, broke out into civil war. When the mineral-rich province of Katanga attempted to secede because of tribal and regional differences, two Congolese leaders called for Soviet military aid. The United States, however, backed the efforts of the United Nations to arrange a cease-fire. In 1963, after intervention by UN troops, the Congo was reunited. Other attempts at superpower intervention were generally rebutted as most African nations developed a policy of nonalignment.

■ Challenges From the Soviet Union

Although holding to the containment policy, Kennedy sought means of relieving the tensions of the cold war. In his Inaugural Address he had said, "Let us never negotiate out of fear, but let us never fear to negotiate." In June 1961, he met with Khrushchev in the Austrian capital, Vienna. The two men treated each other with wary politeness, but they could find no area of agreement. Khrushchev may have thought that he could intimidate Kennedy, who had recently been embarrassed by the Bay of Pigs disaster. The Soviet leader handed Kennedy a near-ultimatum on East Germany and Berlin. He insisted that the Western powers recognize the German puppet state and that the four-power postwar occupation of Berlin, which was completely surrounded by East Germany, come to an end. The President refused.

The Berlin Wall

The communist answer was to build a wall through Berlin, blocking free movement between their section of Berlin and the

---

Critical Thinking Activity

Analyzing Point of View Ask students to discuss the following statement made by President Kennedy as it applies to his foreign policy and to American foreign policy.

"The United States is neither omnipotent nor omniscient—that we are only six percent of the world's population—that we cannot impose our will upon the other ninety-four percent of mankind—that we cannot right every wrong or reverse every adversity—and that therefore there cannot be an American solution to every world problem." **L2**

📁 For additional practice, assign Critical Thinking Skills Activity 23.

rest of the city. This weakened the economy of West Berlin, which had drawn much of its labor from the Soviet sector. The wall also prevented the flight of refugees seeking to escape the oppression of East Germany. Those attempting to escape were shot down by East German police.

In June 1963, Kennedy visited West Berlin. A vast, cheering crowd gathered to hear him at the city hall. The President told them:

66 *Freedom has many difficulties and democracy is not perfect, but we have never had to put up a wall to keep our people in. . . . All free men, wherever they may live, are citizens of Berlin, and therefore, as a free man I take pride in the words, 'Ich bin ein [I am a] Berliner.'* 99

The Berlin Wall stood for nearly 30 years as a menacing symbol of the cold war division between East and West.

Quarrels Over Nuclear Testing

In 1961 the Soviet Union broke a three-year moratorium on testing nuclear weapons in the atmosphere. The Soviets exploded more than 40 bombs, one with 3,000 times the power of the bomb that destroyed Hiroshima. Kennedy attempted to persuade the Soviets to ban above-ground testing because nuclear fallout pollutes the atmosphere of the whole world. The Soviets would not agree to a method of inspection satisfactory to Americans. Not wanting the Soviet Union to gain nuclear superiority, the United States also resumed testing.

In August 1963, the United States, the Soviet Union, and Great Britain signed a test-ban treaty that prohibited atomic tests in the atmosphere, in outer space, and underwater. It did not, however, ban underground testing or reduce the total number of nuclear weapons. In September 1963, the Senate ratified the treaty by a vote of 80 to 19.

Dominican Intervention

Cold war tensions were again heightened when the United States intervened in the Dominican Republic. In April 1965, Lyndon Johnson, who was then in the White House, received word that rebels were trying to overthrow the rightist military government that controlled the island country. Fearing that the rebels

Visualizing
History

▲ BARRIER TO FREEDOM The Berlin Wall dividing the East German and West German parts of the city was hastily constructed in August 1961. West Berliners decorated their side and questioned the wall's existence. *Why was the wall built?*

Visualizing
History Not long after the Berlin Wall was constructed, stories began to emerge about *wall-jumpers*—people who illegally crossed the wall regularly. One told of three East Berliners who were addicted to American movies. Every weekend they would sneak into West Berlin and take in all the latest Hollywood releases, returning in time for work on Monday morning. **Answer to Caption:** to protest the West's refusal to recognize the East German government and to end the four-power occupation of the city; also prevented East Germans from fleeing to West Germany

Did You Know?

The Vienna summit began with a good-natured exchange of jokes. Khrushchev suggested that he should be credited with Kennedy's victory at the polls, for if he had released Gary Powers—the U-2 pilot shot down over the soviet Union in 1960—before the election, Nixon would have trounced Kennedy by some 200,000 votes. "Don't spread the story around," Kennedy replied. "If you tell everybody that you like me better than Nixon, I'll be ruined at home."

CHAPTER 23 The Vietnam Era: 1954–1975 **699**

Cultural Perspectives

Immigration From Cuba Cubans began arriving in the United States after the Cuban missile crisis in 1962. For several months, 3,000 people a week arrived, largely for political reasons. Between 1965 and 1970, more than 360,000 Cubans immigrated to the United States. Many settled in and around Miami, Florida. Others established large communities in New York and New Jersey.

ASSESS

Check Understanding

Assign Section 1 Review as homework or an in-class activity.

Evaluate

Assign Section Quiz 23-1 or use the Test-maker to create a customized quiz.

Reteach

Have students complete Reteaching Activity 23-1.

Assign Workbook Activity 23-1.

Enrich

Have students complete Enrichment Activity 23.

CLOSE

Tell students that in his popular history of the United States, Samuel Eliot Morison closed the chapter on the Kennedy years with these lines from the musical *Camelot:* "Don't let it be forgot That once there was a spot For one brief shining moment That was known as Camelot."

Ask students to discuss why they think Morison associated the Arthurian legend with Kennedy.

were controlled by communists, Johnson ordered 20,000 marines to the Dominican Republic. This was the first time the United States had openly sent troops to the Caribbean since 1926.

Many Latin Americans criticized this military action. They charged that fear of a communist takeover, similar to that of Cuba by Fidel Castro, was leading the United States to support **reactionary governments,** or extremely conservative governments with oppressive policies. Nonetheless, most members of Congress continued to support the President. By a margin of 312 to 52, the House of Representatives voted in support of sending American troops to prevent a communist takeover anywhere in Latin America. But the Dominican incident raised suspicions of a **credibility gap,** a lack of believability growing out of the difference between official statements and practices.

■ Israel and Korea

Two other incidents caused friction with the Soviet Union during the 1960s. One had to do with Israel. The other was the *Pueblo* incident in Korea.

Arab-Israeli War

Hostilities between Israel and the Arab nations in the Middle East were common and continuing. The United States, which had traditionally supported Israel since its found-ing in 1948, continued that support during the Arab-Israeli War of 1967. The Soviet Union, on the other hand, backed and armed Egypt, Syria, and Jordan, the three Arab nations involved. Being on opposite sides in this conflict heightened cold war tensions between the two superpowers. However, the speed of Israel's victory prevented an out-and-out clash between the two countries.

Later in 1967, President Johnson met with Soviet Premier Aleksey Kosygin at Glassboro, New Jersey, to try to smooth relations between the United States and the Soviet Union. Although they discussed their nations' views and goals, they came to no agreement.

The *Pueblo* Incident

In January 1968, the North Koreans seized a United States ship, the *Pueblo,* and its 83 crew members. The *Pueblo* was a spy vessel, which used electronic equipment to obtain information about communist North Korea. As long as the ship stayed in international waters at least 12 miles from shore, its activities were considered legal. North Korea, however, claimed that the *Pueblo* had illegally entered its waters.

American officials were stunned. Some people wanted to retaliate, but President Johnson could not afford a conflict with North Korea while the United States was involved in the Vietnam War. As a result, the crew members remained prisoners for nearly a year.

Section 1 ★ Review

Checking for Understanding

1. **Identify** Bay of Pigs, Nikita Khrushchev, Alliance for Progress, Peace Corps, Berlin Wall, *Pueblo.*

2. **Define** reactionary government, credibility gap.

3. **Explain** why the Bay of Pigs invasion failed.

4. **State** two possible reasons why Khrushchev sent missiles to Cuba.

Critical Thinking

5. **Making Inferences** Besides being an economic policy, the Alliance for Progress was an attempt to stop communism. Explain this aspect of the program.

ACTIVITY

6. Write a speech in which you defend or criticize President Kennedy's actions during the Cuban missile crisis.

Answers to SECTION 1 REVIEW

1. Bay of Pigs, 696; Nikita Khrushchev, 696; Alliance for Progress, 697; Peace Corps, 697; Berlin Wall, 698; *Pueblo,* 700

2. All vocabulary words are defined in the Glossary.

3. No popular uprising against Castro occurred once Cuban exiles invaded.

4. to protect Cuba; wanted missile-launching site close to U.S.; to pressure U.S.

5. Promoting economic growth: improving education, housing, and health care; and redistribution of land would alleviate poverty and discontent on which communism thrived.

6. Speeches should point out position clearly and be supported with valid reasoning.

Changing Nature of Warfare

Technology always affects the conduct of war. In fact, changes in the way wars are fought are often the result of changes in technology.

During the Revolutionary War, armies were outfitted with flintlock muskets—notoriously inaccurate. The soldier fired at the enemy when he saw "the whites of his eyes," a distance of less than 50 yards. With the Civil War and the introduction of a more accurate bullet, rifles were deadly up to 300 yards.

In some ways the Civil War was the first modern war. It was the first war in which railroad lines were vital, and the first in which telegraph lines, ironclad ships, and observation balloons were used as a matter of course. It foreshadowed World War I, since the armies often dug in, and sometimes fought from elaborate trenches. It also represented a step toward the concept of "total war," with less and less distinction between civilians and soldiers.

Over time, battles became increasingly impersonal, as soldiers killed and were killed by unseen enemies. Field telephones, first used in World War I, enabled soldiers to direct their fire thousands of feet behind enemy lines.

Airplanes were introduced, and pilots dropped bombs by hand from open cockpits. Bombing quickly became more sophisticated, and by World War II, bombers flying over enemy territory in Europe dropped hundreds of bombs in a single mission.

Modern-day warfare has become even more detached. Weapons systems are computer-controlled. Pilots use radar to direct heat-seeking missiles at enemies miles away.

During the Vietnam War, United States pilots flew huge B-52s on bombing raids over North Vietnam. Helicopters supplied food and ammunition to United States field forces, transported troops, and promptly evacuated the wounded.

▶ **MARINE DURING GULF WAR**

▲ **WORLD WAR I SOLDIERS**

Making the Science Connection

1. How did technological advances affect battlefield tactics? Which advance do you think has had the greatest effect on modern warfare?

2. How do today's radio and television influence the perception of war on the home front?

ACTIVITY

3. Select an implement of modern warfare and research its development. Place your findings on a time line.

701

Answers to Making the Connection

1. In general the conduct of battles has grown more and more impersonal as weapons have become more powerful. Now, soldiers kill and get killed by unseen enemies.

2. Radio and television bring the reality of war into each person's home. This can dramatically influence feelings about war, particularly when the reason for participation in the war is complicated or controversial.

3. Student work should show research. You may wish to have students include a bibliography.

FOCUS

Bellringer

Before taking roll, project Section Focus Transparency 23-2 or hand out Section Focus Transparency Activity 23-2. Have students answer the questions.

Motivating Activity

Make a line of dominoes standing on end. Knock the first one over so that the rest fall in turn. Ask students what the "domino theory" meant in relation to Southeast Asia. Ask: How did the domino theory influence Americans? *(created fear)* Tell students to keep the domino theory in mind as they read Section 2. **L1**

Vocabulary Precheck

Ask students to define each of the "Key Terms." Have a volunteer consult the dictionary for any unfamiliar words. **L1, LEP**

Did You Know?

President Eisenhower first coined the phrase "domino theory" in 1954.

War in Vietnam

Setting the Scene

Section Focus

Perhaps the biggest cold war challenge was the war in Vietnam. Kennedy increased the number of military advisers in South Vietnam, but his tragic death prevented him from finding a solution. Although Kennedy's intentions for the future were not clear, Johnson continued the established policy of containment and honored the commitments made by Eisenhower and Kennedy.

Objectives

After studying this section, you should be able to

★ explain how the Gulf of Tonkin incident led to the escalation of the war in Vietnam.

★ explain why the Tet offensive was the turning point of the Vietnam War.

Key Terms

war of national liberation, escalation, search-and-destroy strategy

◀ SOLDIER'S BOOTS, VIETNAM WAR

*I*n setting United States policy in Vietnam, both Kennedy and Johnson were torn between a wish to limit American involvement in a country halfway around the world and fear of a communist victory that would swallow up all of Southeast Asia. Ultimately, however, involvement increased and, before long, American troops were engaged in combat.

■ Trouble in Southeast Asia

During the Kennedy years, the Soviet Union lent its support to **wars of national liberation.** These were wars to free a nation from the control of another country, and they took place in many economically developing nations.

War in Laos

When Kennedy took office in 1961, the Southeast Asian nation of Laos was in danger of falling to communist guerrilla forces. The CIA and the Joint Chiefs of Staff pressed for a strong defense of Laos. Kennedy, on the other hand, believed a diplomatic solution could be found. In the end Kennedy avoided war by striking a compromise with Khrushchev—first by agreeing to a cease-fire and then by establishing a neutral government. Fighting between the Laos government and the guerrilla forces soon resumed, however.

Kennedy and Vietnam

Another hot spot was Vietnam, a former French colony in Southeast Asia. It had been divided into North and South Vietnam in 1954. North Vietnam was controlled by the communist government of Ho Chi Minh.

702   UNIT 7 Redefining America: 1954–Present

Blackline Masters:
 Reproducible Lesson Plan 23-2
Guided Reading Activity 23-2
Chapter Map Activity 23
Political Cartoons in American History Activity 25

Chapter Skills Activity 23
Workbook Activity 23-2
Reteaching Activity 23-2
Section Quiz 23-2

Transparencies:
Section Focus Transparency 23-2
Map Transparency 23
Skills Transparency 23

Multimedia:
Testmaker
Communism and the Cold War
Powers of the President

South Vietnam was controlled by a noncommunist government supported first by France and then by the United States. In the late 1950s the Vietcong—South Vietnamese communist guerrillas—began fighting to overthrow the United States-backed government of Ngo Dinh Diem and to reunite South Vietnam with the North. Both Eisenhower and Kennedy responded by sending military aid and advisers to South Vietnam. By late 1963 Kennedy had increased the number of advisers to 16,000.

Kennedy's Vietnam policy was complicated because Diem was a corrupt and unpopular dictator, a French-educated, upper-middle-class Catholic who ruled a largely Buddhist country. Middle- and lower-class Buddhists distrusted both Diem and the West. In his efforts to remain in power, Diem took increasingly harsh and undemocratic measures.

■ Johnson's Choices

During the 1964 campaign Johnson ran as the candidate of peace and restraint. "We seek no wider war," he repeatedly promised. "We don't want our American boys to do the fighting for Asian boys." At the same time,

the President did not want to appear weak or to leave the door open for a communist victory in Vietnam.

As the military situation in Vietnam continued to deteriorate, the war dominated the foreign policy of the administration. When President Johnson entered the White House, South Vietnamese President Ngo Dinh Diem had just been assassinated. Within three months, another revolution took place in South Vietnam. This was followed by a series of governments, as one military faction after another gained power in South Vietnam.

The President faced disagreeable choices. He could admit defeat and pull out. If the "domino theory" was correct, the rest of Southeast Asia would soon fall to the communists. Another option was continuing limited support of South Vietnam's government, but the instability of that government would probably mean eventual defeat. Finally, he could actively enter the war and attack North Vietnam. This would mean the loss of lives and vast expense, and also the possibility of war with the People's Republic of China.

By the summer of 1964 Johnson began to move cautiously toward the third alternative. In secrecy the United States began limited

Visualizing History
▲ ESCALATION By the end of 1965, there were nearly 200,000 American troops in Vietnam. By the end of 1968, the total had increased to more than 500,000. *What was the Gulf of Tonkin Resolution?*

TEACH
Guided Practice
Expressing an Opinion
Present the following statement to students:
    The Gulf of Tonkin incident had a long-term and unexpected significance.
    Ask students if they agree or disagree with this statement. Why or why not? Have them explain their answers in a brief paragraph. *(The incident moved Johnson to order American forces into the conflict. Involvement escalated at a steady pace. Peace overtures failed, and Americans became divided.)* **L2**

Visualizing History The Green Berets were specially trained to infiltrate behind enemy lines and counter guerrilla activity.
Answer to Caption: allowed the President to "take all the necessary steps" to prevent further aggression in Vietnam

ABCNEWS
INTERACTIVE™

 VIDEODISC
Communism and the Cold War

Side Two, Chapter 8
Title: *Vietnam War*
Subject: Summary of Vietnam War

Critical Thinking Activity

Analyzing Effects Review with students the Gulf of Tonkin incident. Have them identify information that was withheld from Congress and the American people. Then ask students to write newspaper editorials focusing on the effects of misinformation on Congress. Have students predict how the Gulf of Tonkin Resolution might affect the future of U.S. involvement in Vietnam. They should conclude their editorials with recommendations that the President or Congress might take to prevent similar incidents.

Independent Practice

Oral History Have students conduct a 15-minute interview with a Vietnam veteran from their community. **L2**

 Assign Workbook Activity 23-2.

 Visualizing **History** GI slang referred to helicopters as TWA—teenie-weenie airlines. They were used on a massive scale during the Vietnam War. With gas turbine replacing piston engines, the helicopters had remarkable range and maneuverability.

Answer to Caption: to counter the Vietcong guerilla tactics

ABCNEWS INTERACTIVE™

 **VIDEODISC**

Powers of the President

Side Two, Chapter 15
Title: *The Vietnam War*
Subject: Case study of checks and balances concerning U.S. involvement in Vietnam

SideTwo, Chapter 16
Title: *Use of Force*
Subject: President Johnson requests Gulf of Tonkin Resolution

 **Visualizing** **History**

▲ THE AIR WAR As American involvement in Vietnam grew, helicopters were used extensively because they were effective at pinpointing enemy positions. *What were the goals of search-and-destroy missions?*

bombing of positions held by the Vietcong and supported limited commando raids on North Vietnam's coast.

■ Escalation

Johnson reported that North Vietnamese torpedo boats fired on two American destroyers in the Gulf of Tonkin on August 2 and 4, 1964. Calling these attacks unprovoked, he asked Congress for authorization to bomb North Vietnam.

Gulf of Tonkin Resolution

On August 7 the Senate and House quickly passed the Gulf of Tonkin Resolution, authorizing the President to "take all necessary steps, including the use of armed force" to prevent further aggression. In effect, Congress, with only two dissenting votes, handed its war powers over to the President.

Johnson, however, had kept important information from Congress. The two American destroyers had been assisting the South Vietnamese military in conducting electronic spying on North Vietnam. It was unclear whether the ships had been attacked. Fur-

thermore, Johnson did not reveal that a draft of the resolution had been prepared three months before the attack, in case such an event occurred.

President Johnson regarded the Gulf of Tonkin Resolution as a blanket approval of the war effort from Congress. At the suggestion of his military advisers, he ordered the bombing of bases in North Vietnam.

Until August 1964, the fighting in South Vietnam had been between South Vietnamese government troops and the Vietcong. After the Gulf of Tonkin incident, however, North Vietnam began sending its own troops to fight in the South. As the United States expanded its role, the civil war grew into a major conflict between American and communist forces.

In February 1965, after the Vietcong attacked an American base in South Vietnam, Johnson ordered an **escalation,** or military expansion, of the war. He ordered American planes to begin bombing targets in North Vietnam, and, in April 1965, made the fateful decision that American ground forces should engage in combat.

In the Vietnam War the United States faced a far more difficult situation than it had in Korea. In Korea the United States

Cooperative Learning Activity

Research and Teaching To review the Vietnam War, divide the class into groups of three. Have each group discuss how the lack of success in a limited war in Vietnam ultimately divided the nation. Assign each member of the group one of three topics: the significance of the Gulf of Tonkin Resolution, the growing divisions within Johnson's cabinet, and the reasons for American opposition to the war. Ask students to research each topic in the text and teach the other group members the information. Call on students randomly to check each group's progress. **L3**

fought as an agent of the United Nations, with widespread support from noncommunist countries. Now the United States stood almost alone in its military support of South Vietnam's government, and much of world opinion was hostile to American policy in Vietnam. The South Vietnamese communists had strong support in rural areas and military aid from North Vietnam. Most noncommunist South Vietnamese were indifferent or opposed to their government, no matter what group happened to be in power.

A Different Kind of War

Military operations turned into a "dirty, ruthless, wandering war" without a battlefront. The Vietcong guerrillas used hit-and-run tactics. Not as well equipped as the Americans, the Vietcong and North Vietnamese used ambushes, boobytraps, and small-scale attacks. They moved swiftly by night and by day hid in the jungles or in friendly villages. Using terrorism against civilians, the Vietcong controlled much of the countryside.

Search and Destroy

To counter such tactics, American troops adopted a **search-and-destroy strategy.** American forces tried to search out enemy troops, bomb their positions, destroy their supply lines, and force them out into the open for combat. By 1966 American planes had dropped nearly the same tonnage of bombs in Vietnam as had been dropped in the Pacific in World War II.

Napalm, a jellied gasoline that explodes, splatters, and clings to whatever it touches, was dropped from airplanes. In order to improve visibility, American planes sprayed chemical defoliants—Agent Orange, for example—that stripped leaves from trees and shrubs, turning farmland and forest into wasteland. American troops burned villages believed to be hiding communist supporters.

■ Resistance to Peace

The United States poured increasing numbers of troops into Vietnam. During the

height of the conflict, more than 500,000 American soldiers were serving in Vietnam. The number of American dead continued to rise: from 5,008 in 1966 to 9,377 in 1967 and 14,489 in 1968.

Once the United States had escalated the fighting, there seemed to be no way of leaving without damaging its international prestige. North Vietnam's leader, Ho Chi Minh, kept his forces in battle despite the massive bombing of his country, believing that North Vietnam could simply outlast the United States in the war.

Between 1965 and 1967, American officials estimated that some 2,000 attempts were made to open direct negotiations, all unsuccessful. Other nations, including Great

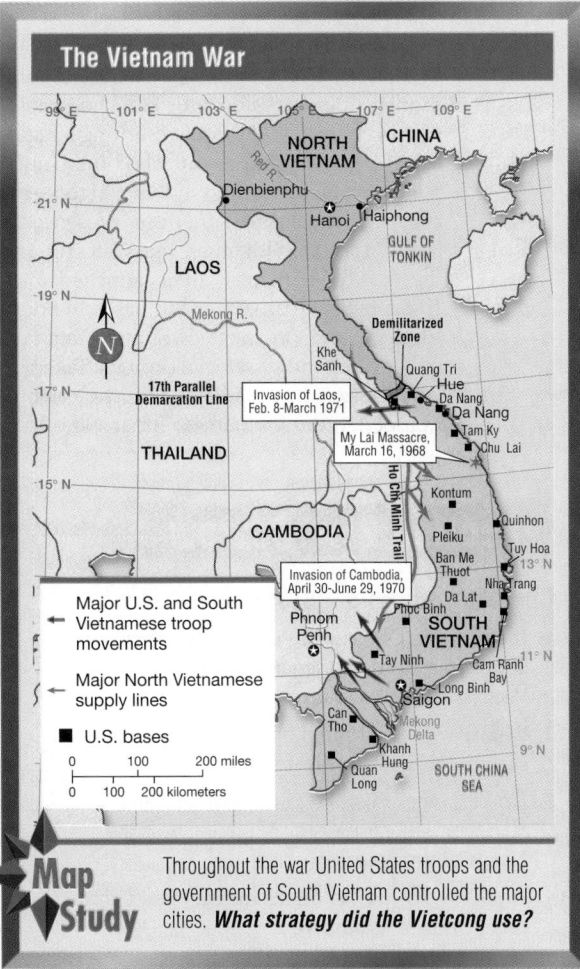

The Vietnam War

Major U.S. and South Vietnamese troop movements

Major North Vietnamese supply lines

■ U.S. bases

Map Study

Throughout the war United States troops and the government of South Vietnam controlled the major cities. **What strategy did the Vietcong use?**

Linking Across TIME

The Vietnam War caused controversy into the 1990s. Still unresolved was whether the American government would compensate war veterans who claimed that exposure to the jungle defoliant Agent Orange was to blame for their high cancer rate. In 1987 the government said that no such connection could be proven because it was impossible to assess a veteran's contact with the herbicide. In 1990 an opposing report said that records of troop movements could establish exposure to Agent Orange.

Map Study *Using Maps*

Answer: guerrilla tactics, striking and then disappearing

Map Skills Practice
Where is the border between North and South Vietnam? *(17th parallel)*

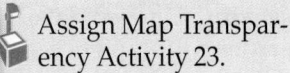 For additional map practice, assign Chapter Map Activity 23.

Assign Map Transparency Activity 23.

Special Needs Activity

Study Strategy Reciprocal teaching is a technique that keeps the learner active. Being an active learner is important for students who have either reading comprehension or attention difficulties. Have students select one portion of

Section 2 to teach to another student. Ask them to read the passage and then to teach it to a partner. Discuss with the class if they learn best when they are the teacher or the student. **L1, LEP**

ASSESS

Check Understanding

Assign the Section 2 Review as homework or an in-class activity.

Evaluate

Assign Section Quiz 23-1 or use the Testmaker to create a customized quiz.

Reteach

Have students complete Reteaching Activity 23-2.

Enrich

Have students research Agent Orange. Ask them to find out the effects of this defoliant on Vietnam and its effect on the health of American soldiers after the war. Have students report their findings to the class.

Assign Political Cartoons in American History Activity 25.

CLOSE

Discuss President Johnson's actions during the war. Remind students that President Lincoln did not consult with Congress before the start of the Civil War. Ask: Should the President be permitted to make executive decisions on matters of national defense without the consent of Congress? Have students write a brief editorial defending their point of view and share it with the class.

Britain, Poland, and the Soviet Union, offered plans to negotiate between the two sides. None succeeded.

■ Tet and Retreat

At the end of 1967, General William Westmoreland, American commander in Vietnam, had assured the country that the end of the war was in sight. Vastly enlarged American forces expanded the "search-and-destroy" missions. American bombers destroyed North Vietnamese factories, roads, bridges, and cities. Secretary of State Dean Rusk said the enemy "was hurting very badly."

Vietcong Attack Turns the Tide

January 30, 1968, marked a turning point in the war. The supposedly exhausted communist guerrillas abruptly launched major offensive strikes. Early that morning a handful of Vietcong soldiers attacked the United States Embassy compound in Saigon—the very center of the American presence in South Vietnam. Together, the Vietcong and the North Vietnamese then launched massive attacks on all American bases in South Vietnam and on most of South Vietnam's major cities and provincial capitals. Taken by surprise by the assault during the celebration of Tet, the Vietnamese lunar New Year,

Americans and South Vietnamese sustained heavy losses. After fierce fighting, they finally drove back the communist offensive.

Militarily, the communists were defeated. Politically, however, they scored a victory. The American people were shocked that the enemy that was supposedly on the verge of defeat could launch such a large-scale attack. Television coverage of the attack and the destruction that followed shook the nation's confidence. When General Westmoreland requested an additional 209,000 troops for Vietnam—in addition to the 500,000 already there—it seemed like another admission that the United States could not win the war.

Peace Talks Begin

Finally, on March 31, 1968, Johnson announced that he would halt nearly all bombing of North Vietnam. He offered to send special negotiators to hold peace talks with the North Vietnamese and the Vietcong. A few days later, on April 3, North Vietnam accepted Johnson's offer to begin peace negotiations. Diplomats from the United States and North Vietnam met in Paris in May 1968, but they could not agree on terms. Prospects for peace in Vietnam grew dim. After a lull, the war continued, and the number of American troops in Vietnam reached a new high. It would be five long years of continued bitter struggle, however, before the United States left the war in Vietnam behind.

Section 2 ★ Review

Checking for Understanding

1. **Identify** Ho Chi Minh, Vietcong, Gulf of Tonkin Resolution, General William Westmoreland, napalm.

2. **Define** war of national liberation, escalation, search-and-destroy strategy.

3. **Explain** what mistake Johnson's military advisers made about the Vietcong and the North Vietnamese.

4. **Explain** why the Tet offensive was the turning point of the Vietnam War.

Critical Thinking

5. **Expressing Problems Clearly** Some political analysts called Vietnam a "quagmire." Write two statements that explain the difficult choices the United States faced in Vietnam.

ACTIVITY

6. Interview friends and relatives who lived during the Vietnam War era to see how people in your community reacted to the conflict. Present a written summary of your findings.

Answers to SECTION 2 REVIEW

1. Ho Chi Minh, 702; Vietcong, 703; Gulf of Tonkin Resolution, 704; General William Westmoreland, 706; napalm, 705
2. All vocabulary words are defined in the Glossary.
3. underestimated the will and ability of the Vietcong and the North Vietnamese to keep fighting despite American military escalation
4. It brought home to Americans that the North Vietnamese were not close to crumbling and the

United States was not close to winning the war.
5. President Johnson was torn between his desire to contain and end the war, and his belief that the fall of South Vietnam would lead to a Communist takeover of the entire region. It became evident that military might alone would not win the war.
6. You might wish to have students write their interview questions as the first part of the assignment.

BUILDING SKILLS
Social Studies Skills

Interpreting Military Maps

The Tet Offensive, 1968

* Places attacked during Tet offensive

0   100   200 miles
0   100 200 kilometers

In your study of American history, you often use maps. Maps are especially helpful for studying the progression of war. A military map shows the area where battles occur, where victories have been won, and who controls various sites.

Military maps vary in the level of detail provided. Some military maps show only the major battles fought over the course of a war. Others may show detailed troop movements and defensive positions during a particular battle or over a specific period of time.

Learning the Skill

On January 30, 1968, Viet Cong and North Vietnamese forces launched a major attack throughout South Vietnam. This was unexpected, as a truce had been declared for Tet, or the lunar New Year. Study the map of the Tet offensive. Nearly 8,400 communist troops infiltrated South Vietnam's major cities and government installations during the offensive. Although the invading troops failed to capture any major cities, more than 30 cities were attacked, with the heaviest fighting in Saigon and Hue. After you read the guidelines that follow, answer the questions.

a. **Read** the map title. This will indicate the location and time period covered on the map.

b. **Read** the items listed in the map key. This tells what the symbols on the map represent. For example, areas under the control of a particular nation or region may be represented by a color. Battle sites may be symbolized by crossed swords, a shell burst, or a star. Military movements and offensives may be illustrated with solid or broken lines and arrows.

c. **Study** the map itself. This will reveal the actual events or sequence of events that took place. Notice the geography of the area and try to determine how it would affect military strategy.

Practicing the Skill

1. What time period is represented on the map?

2. From the map, can you tell the outcome of the attacks?

3. Where are the attack sites with respect to North Vietnam?

APPLYING THE SKILL

4. Locate a map of the Vietnam War in an encyclopedia or historical work. List the information presented in the map. Answer the question: How do such maps help summarize the events in a war?

707

BUILDING SKILLS

TEACH

Discuss the guidelines for interpreting military maps, and apply them to the map shown. Point out that students' prior knowledge of an event or a location helps them interpret parts of the map. Ask: Why are only certain towns and cities identified on the map? (*Only places where battles occurred are shown.*)

Review the symbols shown in the map key, and have students locate each on the map. What generalizations about the war can students make using this map? For example, was the action limited to one part of Vietnam? (*No, battles took place throughout the country.*) **L1**

📽 🗁 Project Skills Transparency 23 and have students complete Skills Transparency Activity 23.

🗁 Use Chapter Skills Activity 23 to reinforce students' understanding of the skill.

Did You Know?

Although the Tet offensive failed, the North Vietnamese won a psychological victory. It convinced many Americans that the war could not be won.

FOCUS

Bellringer

 Before taking roll, project Section Focus Transparency 23-3 or hand out Section Focus Transparency Activity 23-3. Have students answer the questions. Discuss student responses.

Motivating Activity

Obtain music recordings from the mid-1960s that represented mainstream society (for example, Frank Sinatra) and the counterculture (for example, the Beatles). Play each selection. Ask students to characterize each recording with adjectives. List the adjectives on the board, and discuss student answers. Point out that in the 1960s each type of music was popular among different groups of people, reflecting their conflicting philosophies and lifestyles. **L1**

Vocabulary Precheck

Ask students to define each of the "Key Terms." Have a volunteer consult the dictionary for any unfamiliar words. **L1, LEP**

VIDEODISC

Powers of the President

Side Two, Chapter 18
Title: *Vietnam Protests*
Subject: Sights and sounds of antiwar protests

708

★★

Protest and Reaction

Setting the Scene

Section Focus

As casualties mounted, there was strong opposition to the war among a growing number of Americans. They lost confidence in their government. Soon, large numbers of disillusioned youths began demonstrating against United States involvement in Vietnam. In the middle of all the chaos, *Newsweek* reported that the United States was "divided and confused as never since the Great Depression."

◀ ANTIWAR BUTTON

Objectives

After studying this section, you should be able to

★ list reasons for opposition to the war.

★ describe the values and beliefs of the youth counterculture.

Key Terms

student deferment, conscientious objector, teach-in, commune, counterculture

---

*A*fter Tet, criticism of American involvement in Vietnam increased. One of the nation's most trusted news broadcasters, Walter Cronkite, reported:

❝ *We have too often been disappointed by the optimism of the American leaders to have faith any longer in the silver linings. . . . To say that we are closer to victory today is to believe, in the face of evidence, the optimists who have been wrong in the past. To suggest we are on the edge of defeat is to yield to unreasonable pessimism. To say that we are mired in stalemate seems the only realistic, yet unsatisfactory conclusion.* ❞

Hearing Cronkite's broadcast, President Johnson turned to his aides and said, "It's all over." He recognized that he had lost the battle for public opinion.

■ Growing Opposition to War

Gradually, as America moved deeper into the Vietnam War, opposition grew. The United States's reasons for fighting in Southeast Asia began to be questioned.

Senate Hearings on the War

Beginning in January 1966, the Senate Foreign Relations Committee held "educational" hearings on Vietnam. The televised hearings carried the senators' doubts about the war to millions of American homes.

Classroom Resources for SECTION 3

Blackline Masters:
- Reproducible Lesson Plan 23-3
- Guided Reading Activity 23-3
- Primary and Secondary Source Readings, pp. 62–63
- Linking Past and Present Activity 23
- Cooperative Learning Activity 23
- Supreme Court Case Studies 36, 37
- Workbook Activity 23-3

- Reteaching Activity 23-3
- Section Quiz 23-3

Transparencies:
- Section Focus Transparency 23-3

Multimedia:
- Testmaker
- Powers of the President

Hawks and Doves

Before long, Americans became divided into two groups. Those who supported the war were called "hawks" and those who opposed, "doves." For a long time, polls showed that most Americans sided with the "hawks." But doubts began to grow. By May 1967, even Secretary of Defense Robert McNamara had begun to question America's role in the war.

■ Student Protests

Many of those opposed to the war were students who openly protested America's involvement in Vietnam. The antiwar movement was centered on college campuses, which had also been the source for activists in the civil rights movement.

Protests Against the Draft

A number of the antiwar protests focused on the draft. Many of those facing the draft did not understand why the war was being fought or why they should go. Students also protested against the government's unfair practices. A person with a limited education from a low-income family was far more likely to be sent to fight in Vietnam than someone with a good education from an upper-income family, and African American soldiers made up a disproportionately large number of American soldiers fighting overseas.

One policy that contributed to this inequity was the practice of giving **student deferments.** Young men were safe from the draft as long as they were enrolled in college. In 1966 alone, there were 1.8 million deferments. Some men who did not serve were **conscientious objectors.** They received this status by belonging to an organized religious body with pacifist views. About 500,000 young men simply refused to report when they were drafted. Some fled to other countries, such as Canada or Sweden. Around 3,000 young men went to prison rather than fight in a war they opposed. Some antiwar protesters used the tactics of civil disobedience and demonstrations that they had learned from the civil rights movement.

Visualizing History

▲ DEMONSTRATIONS AND CONFRONTATION Reacting against the antiwar demonstrations, many Americans began to counter with demonstrations in support of American troops. Many antiwar demonstrations were accompanied by violence. In May 1970, six students were killed during separate confrontations at Jackson State and Kent State (above right). *Why did many students protest the war?*

CHAPTER 23 The Vietnam Era: 1954–1975   **709**

TEACH
Guided Practice

Debate Tell students that television and newspapers brought the war into homes of Americans and divided the nation. Divide the class into two groups. Appoint one student to be the moderator between the groups. Have the first group advocate the "hawk" viewpoint. Have the second group advocate the "dove" viewpoint. Have the moderator reconcile the differences between groups. **L3**

Visualizing History News of the killings at Kent State traveled quickly to college campuses all over the country. Hundreds of other universities and colleges closed in protest and sympathy.
Answer to Caption: Answers will vary but might include: questions arose over American involvement, disproportionate number of poor fighting overseas.

Did You Know?

Ho Chi Minh City (formerly Saigon) proclaimed 1990 its "Year of Tourism." The tunnels once used by the Vietcong guerrillas—a network of 200 miles—were one of the featured tourist attractions.

📁 Assign Primary and Secondary Source Readings, pp. 62–63: "The Reality of Vietnam."

Critical Thinking Activity

Analyzing Reactions Tell students that in 1964 the Vietnam War was not a national issue. Two factors, however, would soon bring it to national attention. The first incident was the controversy surrounding the Gulf of Tonkin incident. The second was campaign speeches in which Johnson pledged he would not "send American boys halfway around the world to do a job that Asian boys ought to be doing for themselves." Have students analyze in writing how both of these events became crucial issues by 1967 and 1968. **L2**

Independent Practice

Sociology Have students interview a parent or an older friend on his or her opinion of the counterculture or black power movements of the late 1960s. **L2**

📁 Assign Guided Reading Activity 23-3.

Linking Past and Present

Point out to students that because more is known about PTSD today, recovery rates for the disorder have improved. With recognition and treatment more than half of PTSD victims can recover completely. The odds of recovery are better when symptoms appear soon after the trauma, when the person was psychologically healthy before the incident, and when there is a strong support system.

📁 For additional practice, assign Linking Past and Present Activity 23.

ABCNEWS INTERACTIVE™

💿 **VIDEODISC**

Communism and the Cold War

Side One, Chapter 25

Title: *Music of the Cold War*

Subject: Montage of music reflecting the political moods during the cold war

Surviving the War

The military kept accurate records of Americans who died fighting in Vietnam. No one, however, was keeping track of what happened to those who survived.

Then_____

Coming Home

Many Vietnam veterans adjusted smoothly to civilian life. Others, however, were left with deep

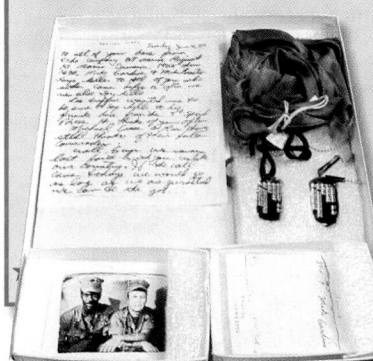

◄ COLLECTION OF VETERAN'S ITEMS

psychological problems. These veterans were often described as suffering from "shell shock" or "combat fatigue." Yet a significant number continued to suffer trauma years later.

Now_____

PTSD

Research indicated that these veterans were experiencing post-traumatic stress disorder (PTSD), a condition in which a person who has experienced a traumatic event feels severe and long-lasting aftereffects. The event that triggers the disorder overwhelms a person's normal sense of reality and ability to cope. Typical symptoms include involuntary "flash-backs" or recurring nightmares during which the victim reexperiences the ordeal.

The National Vietnam Veterans Readjustment Study indicated that one-third of male Vietnam veterans and more than one-fourth of females serving in the Vietnam theater had full post-traumatic stress disorder at some time during their lives.

PTSD is also common among survivors of natural disasters, such as floods or tornadoes, and victims of human aggression, such as assault. PTSD can be extremely long-lasting. Studies show that survivors of Nazi concentration camps and soldiers returning from war may display symptoms decades after the traumatic event.

The Veterans Administration provides counseling to veterans who have postwar readjustment problems in the areas of family relationships, education, and in their personal lives.

Some university students and teachers held **teach-ins** to study the history of the war and to protest against its expansion.

Violence on Campus

While most protests were peaceful, some turned violent. One occurred in April 1968 at Columbia University in New York City. It began when students seized college buildings and ended in a riot marked by both police brutality and student retaliation.

Two of the most tragic episodes of the antiwar movement took place in May 1970. After President Nixon announced the invasion of Cambodia, protests erupted on scores of campuses. At Kent State University in Ohio, rioting reached such an intensity that the National Guard was sent in. On May 4, a contingent of guardsmen, harassed by students,

fired into the crowd, killing 4 students and wounding 10. On May 14, at Jackson State University in Mississippi, student protest was suppressed by the state police, who fired randomly into a dormitory. Two students were killed, 9 were wounded. These events precipitated a nationwide student strike. Hundreds of colleges and universities suspended classes or closed down completely.

The campus violence that erupted was not limited to the United States. During this time and before, there were student riots in Rio de Janeiro, London, Paris, Rome, Madrid, Warsaw, and Prague. In Prague, student protests triggered a rebellion that led to the overthrow of the communist regime that had ruled Czechoslovakia since 1948. However, after a few months 200,000 Soviet troops crushed the revolt and reestablished control.

710   UNIT 7 Redefining America: 1954–Present

Cooperative Learning Activity

Designing a Museum Project Divide the class into small groups. Have the groups design a museum project on the 1960s counterculture. Groups may select the music, fashion trends, literature, individuals, and events they feel are most significant in the study of this cultural movement. Encourage students to use music, scenarios, photographs, and primary sources in

their projects. Have each team present their projects to the class. **L2** 📁

📁 For additional practice, assign Cooperative Learning Activity 23.

📁 Assign Supreme Court Case Studies 36, 37: *Gregory* v. *Chicago* (1969) and *Tinker* v. *Des Moines School District* (1969).

New Beliefs and Values

Some young people rebelled against established values and searched for a new set of beliefs. They studied different religions and philosophies. In an attempt to achieve expanded awareness, some experimented with drugs that cause hallucinations. They proclaimed their freedom of expression and individuality by wearing long hair and unconventional clothing. Some even left family and comfortable homes to live in **communes**—communities in which living quarters, food, and work were shared.

In their rejection of their parents' values, the "hippies," or "flower children" as they were frequently called, were said to have established a **counterculture**—with values and practices that conflicted with those of established society. The counterculture was symbolized in an outdoor rock concert, the Woodstock festival held in New York in August 1969. More than 400,000 people attended what *TIME* called "history's biggest happening."

A Conservative Backlash

The actions and protests of the Woodstock generation caused a reaction among a growing number of conservative Americans who had become angry over the demonstrations, the riots, and a war that seemed to be going nowhere. The sight of long-haired draft protesters outraged many who did not hesitate to support their government in time of war. Many working-class Americans were offended by the actions of students they considered privileged. The deep anger these Americans felt soon developed into a backlash against the antiwar movement.

■ 1968: The Turning Point

By 1968, a kind of turning point had been reached in American society. With the Tet offensive and the protests, polls showed that the majority of Americans had turned against the President's handling of the war.

Johnson had become so unpopular that he seldom appeared in public for fear of hostile crowds. Even the President's own party was divided over the war.

The Race for President

By this time, Eugene McCarthy, a Democratic senator from Minnesota—and a dove—had announced that he was going to challenge Johnson for the Democratic party's presidential nomination. Although Johnson won the first primary election in New Hampshire, his margin of victory was narrow. McCarthy received more than 40 percent of the votes. Then, four days after this primary, Democratic Senator Robert Kennedy, who also opposed the war, announced that he too would run for the nomination.

Johnson had always intended to run for reelection in 1968. When he realized just how little support he had, however, he made a decision that was surprising to many. The President decided to drop out of the race. On March 31, 1968, he stunned the nation by announcing, "I shall not seek, and I will not accept, the nomination of my party for another term as your President." With Johnson withdrawn, Vice President

Visualizing History

▲ ASSASSINATION During the 1968 Democratic primaries, Robert F. Kennedy won a number of victories. On June 5, 1968, the night of his victory in the California primary, Kennedy was assassinated. *What two Democratic candidates remained in the race?*

CHAPTER 23 The Vietnam Era: 1954–1975 **711**

Visualizing History Robert Kennedy campaigned so hard that reporters traveling with him complained of the pace. Kennedy was usually up by 7:00 A.M. and often didn't quit shaking hands and meeting people until 3:00 in the morning.
Answer to Caption: McCarthy and Humphrey

Sidelight: Protest Buttons and Patches

Protest buttons were a nearly universal way for young people to express their views of society during this period. This development could have grown out of the long-time American tradition of campaign buttons. The Vietnam War, poverty, racial and gender discrimination, and pollution were all targets of their protests. The message T-shirt also had its beginnings in this era. Cloth patches carried the symbols of the day, including the peace symbol; a rainbow, a symbol of optimism; and the ecology flag designed in 1970 for the first Earth Day.

ASSESS
Check Understanding
Assign Section 3 Review as homework or an in-class activity.

Evaluate
Assign Section Quiz 23-3 or use the Test-maker to create a customized quiz.

Reteach
Have students complete Reteaching Activity 23-3.

Assign Workbook Activity 23-3.

Enrich
Interested students might want to find out more about American folk-singers such as Joan Baez, Bob Dylan, and Judy Collins, who used their lyrics for social and political causes. Have students report briefly on these people and why they became the voices of the antiwar movement in the late 1960s.

CLOSE
Summarize this section by asking students what achievements were made by student protesters and counterculture members. Ask: What evidence in our culture shows that changes have taken place?

Hubert Humphrey became the administration candidate and the preferred choice for many longtime Democrats.

Soon it appeared that Kennedy was pulling in front of McCarthy and Humphrey. Kennedy's program and popularity seemed broad enough to rebuild the Democratic coalition shattered by Vietnam. Then on June 5, 1968, just after winning the Democratic primary in California, Kennedy was assassinated by an Arab nationalist, angry at Kennedy for his support of Israel.

In August the Democrats held their national convention in Chicago. Now that Kennedy was dead, Humphrey was expected to win the nomination. However, furious at the Vice President's support of the war, about 10,000 protesters gathered in Chicago. Chicago Mayor Richard Daley, himself a Democrat, advised his police to get tough with the protesters. While violence reigned outside, the convention nominated Hubert Humphrey for President and Senator Edmund Muskie of Maine for Vice President.

The Candidates

The splintering of the Democratic party made the Republican candidate, Richard M. Nixon, the front-runner in the election of 1968. Although defeated in his campaign for President in 1960 and for governor of California in 1962, Nixon had remained active in national politics. For his vice-presidential running mate, Nixon chose Spiro T. Agnew, governor of Maryland.

In his campaign, Nixon promised to unify the nation, return dignity to the presidency, stabilize American foreign policy, and lead a war against crime in the streets. He said he had a plan for ending the war in Vietnam, but he did not provide details.

A third candidate, George Wallace, governor of Alabama, ran as an Independent in all 50 states. Wallace was against federally enforced civil rights, including desegregation and busing; black power; "pointy-headed intellectuals"; and social unrest. As a result of his civil rights stand, he attracted support in the South. Wallace also appealed to blue-collar workers in the North as well as the South. Leaders of organized labor, however, campaigned hard for Humphrey and moved much of the blue-collar vote back to the Democrats.

The Election of 1968

On Election Day, Nixon won, though the vote was very close. He received 31.8 million votes, while Humphrey had 31.3 million and Wallace, 9.9 million. In the electoral college, Nixon won 301 votes to 191 for Humphrey and 46 for Wallace. However, although the people had elected a Republican President, the Democrats kept their majorities in both houses of Congress.

Speaking to reporters after his election, Nixon recalled seeing a young girl carrying a sign at one of his rallies that said: "Bring Us Together." This, he promised, would be his chief effort as President.

Section 3 ★ Review

Checking for Understanding

1. **Identify** hawks, doves, Robert McNamara, Eugene McCarthy, Hubert Humphrey.

2. **Define** student deferment, conscientious objector, teach-in, commune, counterculture.

3. **List** two reasons why some Americans began to oppose United States involvement in Vietnam.

4. **Explain** how the conservative backlash developed.

Critical Thinking

5. **Synthesizing Ideas** How did the war in Vietnam and increasing violence at home affect Americans' confidence in President Johnson?

ACTIVITY

6. Create a political cartoon illustrating the growing division between the "hawks" and the "doves." Title your cartoon "... Meanwhile, back on the home front."

Answers to SECTION 3 REVIEW

1. hawks, 709; doves, 709; Robert McNamara, 709; Eugene McCarthy, 711; Hubert Humphrey, 712
2. All vocabulary words are defined in the Glossary.
3. belief that Vietnam was not strategically important, the realization and horror at American deaths and the deaths of noncombatants
4. Protests and fear of radicalism led to defense of conservative values.
5. American perception that the war in Vietnam was not winnable increased opposition. Violence led to the perception that there was no law and order in the country.
6. Cartoons should depict position clearly.

★★★★★★★★★★★★★★★★★★★★★★★★★★★★★★★★★★★★

Secrecy and Summitry

Setting the Scene

Section Focus

The foreign policy of the Nixon administration was one of secrecy and surprise. Also during his administration, Nixon secretly plotted the bombing of Cambodia and the expansion of the war in Indochina. As opposition to the war heated up, government documents came to light that indicated Nixon, along with Kennedy and Johnson, had deceived the public about what was really going on in the Vietnam War. Finally, Nixon gave in and began withdrawing American troops.

Objectives

After studying this section, you should be able to

★ explain why Nixon pursued détente in foreign policy.

★ list and describe the steps that President Nixon took to end American involvement in Vietnam.

Key Terms

détente, summit, shuttle diplomacy

◄ VIEW AT THE VIETNAM MEMORIAL

Surprising both his supporters and his critics, Richard Nixon as President shed his long-held image as a "cold warrior." He opened a dialogue with the communist leaders of China and entered into a series of agreements with the Soviet Union. Nixon recognized the legitimacy of the communist regimes of Eastern Europe.

■ A New Policy

Like Woodrow Wilson, President Nixon took almost sole charge of foreign policy. To help him handle foreign policy matters, Nixon appointed Henry A. Kissinger, a brilliant political scientist, as his national security adviser. Kissinger's job was to present the President with policy options in which the probable consequences of each policy were outlined. Kissinger also undertook secret missions abroad. In 1973 Nixon appointed Kissinger secretary of state.

Nixon, like Wilson, wanted to be remembered as a peacemaker. In his Inaugural Address he proclaimed:

“ *After a period of confrontation, we are entering an era of negotiation. Let all nations know that during this administration our lines of communication will be open. We seek an open world—open to ideas, open to the exchange of goods and people. . . .* ”

CHAPTER 23 The Vietnam Era: 1954–1975   **713**

LESSON PLAN
SECTION 4, 713–717

FOCUS
Bellringer

Before taking roll, project Section Focus Transparency 23-4 or hand out Section Focus Transparency Activity 23-4. Have students answer the questions. Discuss student responses.

Motivating Activity

Write the word *détente* on the board. Ask students if they know its meaning. *(easing of tensions between the superpowers)* Point out that détente was one of the main features of Nixon's foreign policy. **L1**

Vocabulary Precheck

Ask students to define each of the "Key Terms." Have a volunteer consult the dictionary for any unfamiliar words. **L1, LEP**

ABCNEWS INTERACTIVE™

VIDEODISC

Communism and the Cold War

Side One, Chapter 20
Title: *Détente*
Subject: Overview of détente between United States and the Soviet Union

---

Classroom Resources for SECTION 4

Blackline Masters:
- 🗀 Reproducible Lesson Plan 23-4
- 🗀 Guided Reading Activity 23-4
- 🗀 Spirit of American Art and Music, p. 47
- 🗀 Enrichment Activity 23
- 🗀 Geography in History Activity 23
- 🗀 Reteaching Activity 23-4
- 🗀 Section Quiz 23-4

Transparencies:
- Section Focus Transparency 23-4

Multimedia:
- Testmaker
- Communism and the Cold War
- Powers of the President
- Historic America Electronic Field Trips

TEACH
Guided Practice

Research Have students research a significant summit meeting and create posters illustrating its goals and accomplishments. **L2**

Visualizing History Point out that the word *détente* is derived from the French word for "relaxation." **Answer to Caption:** relaxation from tensions between two countries

Food of the Times

Nixon's trip to China led to a renewed interest in China—including Chinese food. Chinese restaurants across the United States tried to duplicate many of the dishes served at the many banquets the President attended.

ABCNEWS INTERACTIVE™

 VIDEODISC

Powers of the President

Side One, Chapter 29
Title: *Making Treaties*
Subject: The President's role in making treaties

Visualizing History

▲ OPENING THE LINES OF COMMUNICATION President Richard Nixon worked to improve relations with the communist superpowers. The thaw in relations was reflected in the President's visits to the Soviet Union (left) and China (right). ***What is détente?***

Nixon Proclaims Détente

Nixon proclaimed a policy of **détente,** or relaxation of tensions between the United States and the communist bloc. He maintained that it would be a "safer world and a better world if we have a strong, healthy United States, Europe, China, Russia, and Japan, each balancing the other."

To achieve this balance Nixon proposed a meeting between the United States and the Soviet Union to discuss strategic arms limitations. The SALT negotiations, as they were called, began in Helsinki, Finland, in 1969. Before the conclusion of SALT I in 1972, the two sides had agreed to ban biological warfare and limit the growth of nuclear weapons.

SALT culminated in the May 1972 Moscow **summit,** or diplomatic meeting, between the superpowers. In addition to signing the SALT agreement, Nixon and the Soviet leader, Leonid Brezhnev, also agreed to increase trade, exchange scientific information, and cooperate in preventing pollution.

Nixon and China

President Nixon also sought improved relations with China. He began by lifting trade and travel restrictions. The President also withdrew the Seventh Fleet from

defending Taiwan, an island which China claimed as its own.

The Chinese responded to Nixon's initiatives in a variety of ways. More important, the Chinese accepted Henry Kissinger's proposal that he visit Beijing secretly to open discussions with Chinese leaders. During Kissinger's meeting with Chinese Premier Zhou En-lai (JOH EHN•lye), he arranged for President Nixon to visit China in February 1972. President Nixon's sensational announcement that he would visit Beijing foreshadowed the 1971 admission of the government of the People's Republic of China to the United Nations.

■ War in Vietnam

During the 1968 presidential campaign, Nixon declared that he had a plan for ending the Vietnam War. After his inauguration he resumed negotiations with the North Vietnamese, but they produced little.

The President faced a dilemma: if he continued United States involvement in the war, public opposition would increase. If he withdrew United States troops without a peace agreement, he would be the first President of the United States ever to lose a war.

714 UNIT 7 Redefining America: 1954–Present

Sidelight: Nixon's Foreign Policy

Although President Nixon escalated the Vietnam War, he gained stature from his achievements in foreign policy, especially as the sponsor of détente. In 1969 he announced a "Nixon Doctrine" based on his willingness to forgo future military intervention like that in Vietnam. In Moscow he negotiated the limiting of strategic missiles and ended the production of biological weapons. Also, in 1971 the United States relaxed its opposition, and the People's Republic of China was admitted to the United Nations, replacing the Chinese Nationalist government of Taiwan.

The Pentagon Papers

To make matters worse, in June 1971, the *New York Times* published a secret Department of Defense study. *The Pentagon Papers,* as they were called, documented that for two decades, four Presidents had escalated the nation's involvement in Indochina.

The Pentagon Papers were evidence of the growing power of the executive branch. They contained details of decisions made by Presidents and their advisers without the consent of Congress. *The Pentagon Papers* also showed how the administrations acted to deceive Congress and the public about Vietnam.

President Nixon was outraged over the "leaking" of the secret documents. He ordered the Justice Department to go to court to stop further publication of the papers. Nixon hoped the Supreme Court would affirm the government's right to restrain publication in matters of national security, but the Court decided that *The Pentagon Papers* were not vital to national security.

The federal government then brought charges against Daniel Ellsberg, one of the authors of *The Pentagon Papers,* for leaking the documents to the press. President Nixon also authorized a group of people who were called "the Plumbers" to break into the office of Ellsberg's psychiatrist to collect information about him. When their activities came to light, the charges against Daniel Ellsberg were dropped.

The United States in Vietnam, 1950–1975

1950	**May 8** President Truman sends U.S. aid and advisers to French forces in Indochina
1954	**May 7** French defeated by Communists at Dien Bien Phu
	July 20–21 Geneva Conference provides cease-fire and divides Vietnam
1957	Vietcong begin attacks in South Vietnam
1960	**Dec. 20** Vietcong form National Front for the Liberation of South Vietnam
1961	**Nov. 16** President Kennedy increases number of U.S. advisers in Vietnam
1963	**Nov. 1** Ngo Dinh Diem assassinated
1964	**July 24** U.S. rejects French President de Gaulle's plan to neutralize all of Indochina
	Aug. 2–4 Gulf of Tonkin—N. Vietnam attacks a U.S. destroyer and U.S. retaliates
	Aug. 7 Gulf of Tonkin Resolution—Congress grants President Johnson authority to use force against aggression
1965	**Feb. 7–8** First U.S. bombing of North Vietnam
	March 2 Rolling Thunder bombing campaign begins against North Vietnam
	March 8–9 President Johnson sends 3,500 Marines (first combat troops) to join 23,500 U.S. advisers
1966	**March 2** U.S. forces number 215,000
	Dec. 31 U.S. forces number 389,000
1967	**May 19** First U.S. air strike against central Hanoi
1968	**Jan. 30–Feb. 24** Tet offensive by Vietcong
	March 31 President Johnson announces cessation of bombing of N. Vietnam north of 20th parallel and that he will not seek reelection
	May 10 Paris Peace Talks begin between U.S. and N. Vietnam
1969	**January 25** First full session of Paris Peace Talks with Vietcong and S. Vietnam also represented
	March 16 My Lai massacre (revealed in November 1969)
	June 8 President Nixon announces the withdrawal of 25,000 U.S. troops from Vietnam
	Sept. 3 Death of Ho Chi Minh
	Oct. 15 Vietnam Moratorium Day—nationwide antiwar demonstrations across the U.S.
1970	**Feb. 20** Presidential adviser Henry A. Kissinger opens secret peace negotiations in Paris
	April 29 U.S. troops invade Cambodia
	May 4 Four antiwar students killed during demonstrations at Kent State University, Ohio
	July 24 Senate votes to repeal Gulf of Tonkin Resolution
1971	**Nov. 12** President Nixon limits U.S. ground forces in Vietnam to a defensive role
1972	**April 15–20** Widespread antiwar demonstrations in U.S.
	June 17–22 Watergate break-in and arrests
	Aug. 12 Last U.S. ground combat troops leave Vietnam
	Dec. 18–30 Bombing of Hanoi and Haiphong resumed to break stalled peace negotiations
1973	**Jan. 27** Cease-fire in Vietnam agreed upon
	Feb. 12 N. Vietnam releases first U.S. prisoners of war
1974	**Aug. 9** President Nixon resigns
1975	**April 29–30** North Vietnamese capture Saigon; American personnel evacuated; Vietnam War ends

Source: *The New York Times,* April 30, 1985; *An Encyclopedia of World History,* 5th ed. (1972); Gorton Carruth, *What Happened When* (1989); James S. Olson, *Dictionary of the Vietnam War* (1988)

Chart Study

American involvement in Vietnam grew rapidly after the first combat troops arrived in 1965. In 1975 troops from North Vietnam moved into South Vietnam, and it came under communist control. **When did the Tet offensive take place?**

Cooperative Learning Activity

Analyzing Foreign Policy To review Nixon's foreign policy, divide students into small groups. Have the students in each group read the section individually to review Nixon's contributions and setbacks in foreign policy. Ask them to take notes as they read. Then have students meet in their groups to create a chart based on the information in their notes and on their reading. Have each group select a spokesperson to report to the class on the group's analysis. For accountability, call on individual students at random. **L2**

Independent Practice

Chronology Have students make a time line of the major events in President Nixon's foreign policy. **L1, LEP**

📁 Assign Guided Reading Activity 23-4.

Linking Across TIME

Twenty years after the People's Republic of China opened its door and let the West in, Chinese students demonstrated for democracy in Tiananmen Square, in Beijing, China. During the demonstrations, students erected a "Goddess of Democracy" statue symbolizing their desire for change and closely resembling the Statue of Liberty. The demonstrations lasted for seven weeks in May and June 1989, until government troops were finally sent in to crush them.

Using Charts

Answer: January 30–February 24, 1968

Chart Skills Practice

Ask students to answer the following: When did U.S. forces surpass 200,000 in number? *(March 2, 1966)*

📁 Assign Primary and Secondary Source Readings pp. 64–65: "Remembering the Vietnam War."

715

ABCNEWS
INTERACTIVE™

VIDEODISC

Communism and the Cold War

Side Two, Chapter 10

Title: *Middle East*

Subject: The 1973 Yom Kippur War

Teaching American Portraits

The Civil Rights Memorial is inscribed with a quote from Martin Luther King, Jr., which comes from the Bible: "Until justice rolls down like waters and righteousness like a mighty stream." Ask students to discuss the meaning of these words. **L2**

ABCNEWS
INTERACTIVE™

VIDEODISC

Historic America Electronic Field Trips

Side Two, Chapter 10

Title: *Vietnam Veterans Memorial*

Subject: Views of monument honoring Americans who served

Ask: In what ways is the memorial unique? *(made of black granite; names of the war's dead are inscribed)*

 Assign Spirit of American Art and Music: p. 47, Maya Lin.

★★★A★★★★★★★ AMERICAN PORTRAITS

Maya Lin
1959–

Maya Lin was a 21-year-old architecture student at Yale University when her design for the Vietnam Veterans Memorial was selected in a national competition. Lin's simple but powerful and unique design joined two gleaming black granite walls inscribed with the names of the war's 58,000 dead and missing. While Maya's work was initially controversial, today the memorial is a symbol of national healing.

Maya was born and raised in Athens, Ohio. Her parents, both of whom had emigrated from China in the 1940s, were college professors. Maya was a good high school student, with a particular aptitude for mathematics.

In 1988, Maya Lin designed the Civil Rights Memorial in Montgomery, Alabama. Recently she completed a memorial at Yale University and designed the interior of the Museum of African Art in New York City.

President Nixon's response to the publication was a further sign that the credibility of his administration was eroding. Nixon himself, it was revealed, had ordered the secret bombing of North Vietnamese sanctuaries in Cambodia in 1969. In April 1970, Nixon, without consulting Congress, ordered an invasion of Cambodia to drive the North Vietnamese out of the country. Protests against the war now intensified.

Nixon Announces Vietnamization

To quiet opposition to the war, Nixon announced a policy of "Vietnamization." Vietnamization consisted of two steps: the phased withdrawal of United States troops, and their replacement by conscripts from Vietnam. Nixon hoped that Vietnamization, combined with saturation bombing of North Vietnam, would allow the United States to withdraw from the war "with honor."

By the end of the war, the total tonnage of bombs dropped by the United States on Vietnam was more than twice that dropped by the United States on all targets in both World War II and the Korean War.

Finally, on January 23, 1973, the United States, South Vietnam, North Vietnam, and the Vietcong signed a cease-fire agreement, ending the military presence of the United States in Vietnam. The war, however, did not end for the people of Vietnam. Although United States troops withdrew from South Vietnam, North Vietnamese troops did not.

The End of the War

In 1974 the weakened forces of South Vietnam abandoned distant outposts they could no longer defend, and North Vietnamese forces captured several provincial capitals. In January 1975, North Vietnam launched a major offensive. By late March they drove South Vietnamese troops from a region known as the Central Highlands, approximately 160 miles north of Saigon. While thousands of civilians retreated with the soldiers, many died in the gunfire or from starvation. The South Vietnamese army soon collapsed, and by early April, the North Vietnamese army had reached the outskirts of Saigon.

Hoping to stall the communist drive, President Gerald Ford, Nixon's successor, requested more than $700 million in military aid for South Vietnam. Congress, however, approved only $300 million, to be used chiefly to evacuate Americans from Saigon. On April 29, as North Vietnamese troops overtook Saigon, the United States carried out an emergency evacuation of all remaining Americans and many South Vietnamese refugees.

Critical Thinking Activity

Expressing an Opinion Ask students to answer the following question: Do you agree or disagree with Nixon's attempt to stop the publication of the *Pentagon Papers* leaked by a Pentagon expert, Daniel Ellsberg, to the press? Why or why not? In their answers, ask students to discuss under what circumstances, if any, the government should misrepresent the atrocities of war and United States participation in order to protect the innocence of the American people. Have students explain their answers in a brief paragraph. **L3**

The war ended when the Saigon government surrendered on April 30, 1975. North and South Vietnam were formally united as the Socialist Republic of Vietnam on July 2, 1976.

■ War in the Middle East

On October 6, 1973, the Jewish holiday of Yom Kippur, Egyptian and Syrian troops launched surprise attacks against Israeli forces. Their objective was to recapture the territory Egypt and Syria had lost to Israel during the Six-Day War of 1967. Caught by surprise, the Israeli troops were pushed back, but they quickly regrouped and launched their own attack, pushing into Syria and across the Suez Canal into Egypt.

Israel appealed to the United States for help, and President Nixon responded with a massive airlift of $2 billion in military supplies. At the same time, the Soviet Union continued to supply Egypt and Syria.

Even as the United States and the Soviet Union gave aid to the opposing sides, they worked through the United Nations Security Council to arrange a cease-fire. In late October, the nations of Israel, Egypt, and Syria agreed to terms. By the end of 1973, a UN peacekeeping force had been sent to the Middle East to police the region.

After the conflict, Secretary of State Henry Kissinger worked with Israel and Egypt to reduce tensions in the Middle East. For the next two years, he engaged in **shuttle diplo-**

▲ THE FALL OF SAIGON On April 28, 1975, President Ford ordered the emergency helicopter evacuation of all Americans remaining in Vietnam. *When did the United States end its military involvement in Vietnam?*

macy, flying back and forth between the capitals of the two nations in an effort to produce a lasting peace. Kissinger's efforts yielded two important results. Early in 1974 Golda Meir, the prime minister of Israel, and Anwar el-Sadat, the president of Egypt, agreed to establish diplomatic relations again between their countries. Then in September 1975, Israel and Egypt agreed to withdraw their forces from the cease-fire line. Although significant problems remained, a measure of peace had been achieved in the Middle East.

Section 4 ★ Review

Checking for Understanding

1. **Identify** Henry Kissinger, Leonid Brezhnev, SALT, Zhou En-lai, *The Pentagon Papers,* Daniel Ellsberg, Vietnamization.

2. **Define** détente, summit, shuttle diplomacy.

3. **List** three steps taken during Nixon's presidency to end United States involvement in Vietnam.

4. **Describe** how Henry Kissinger's shuttle diplomacy helped to end war in the Middle East.

Critical Thinking

5. **Evaluating Foreign Policy** Evaluate the pros and cons of Nixon's use of secrecy in China and Vietnam.

ACTIVITY

6. Refer to the chart on page 715. Study the information and answer the following in a written paragraph: Why has the Vietnam War been called the most tragic war in the history of the United States?

ASSESS

Check Understanding
Assign Section 4 Review as homework or an in-class activity.

Evaluate
◉ 🗁 Assign Section Quiz 23-4 or use the Test-maker to create a customized quiz.

Reteach
🗁 Have students complete Reteaching Activity 23-4.

🗁 Assign Workbook Activity 23-4.

Enrich
🗁 Assign Enrichment Activity 23.

🗁 Assign Geography in History Activity 23.

CLOSE
Tell students that President Nixon might have ended the U.S. involvement in Vietnam in 1969 and concentrated on domestic events. Ask: Why do you believe Nixon chose to continue and even escalate the war? What would you have done?

Visualizing History On April 29, 1975 U.S. helicopters removed approximately 1,000 Americans and 5,500 Vietnamese. **Answer to Caption:** April 30, 1975

Answers to SECTION 4 REVIEW

1. Henry Kissinger, 713; Leonid Brezhnev, 714; SALT, 714; Zhou En-lai, 714; *Pentagon Papers,* 715; Daniel Ellsberg, 715; Vietnamization, 716
2. All vocabulary words are defined in the Glossary.
3. withdrawal of troops, saturation bombing, peace negotiations
4. Kissinger flew between capitals of the fighting nations to maintain negotiations.

5. Supporters will point out that delicate negotiations require secrecy. Opponents will point out that the public has the right to know about the actions of their government.
6. Paragraphs might include that the war resulted in deaths and division in the country.

Using Vocabulary

Articles will vary but should include all the vocabulary words.

Reviewing Facts

1. In Vienna Kennedy and Khrushchev quarreled over Berlin, resulting in building of Berlin Wall. In Cuba they came to brink of war over Soviet missiles, resulting in removal of missiles. Both agreed to Nuclear Test Ban Treaty.

2. Communist guerrillas attempted to take over the governments of Laos and Vietnam. Kennedy had to decide on how much the United States should be involved. Negotiated cease-fire in Laos. Sent U.S. advisers to Vietnam.

3. little popular support for South Vietnamese government; Vietnamese Communists were militarily strong and had widespread support; difficult for American troops to fight against the hit-and-run tactics of the enemy

718

Using Vocabulary

Imagine you are a reporter who is covering the diplomatic meeting between the superpowers at Moscow in May 1972. Use the following vocabulary words to write an article describing the history of the United States's cold war struggle against communism.

reactionary government
credibility gap
war of national liberation
search-and-destroy strategy

summit
escalation
détente

Reviewing Facts

1. **Summarize** Kennedy's relations with Khrushchev.

2. **Explain** the many foreign policy challenges that Kennedy faced in Southeast Asia.

3. **State** two reasons why it was difficult for the United States to win the war in Vietnam.

Understanding Concepts

Foreign Policy

1. Explain how Americans' perceptions of communism influenced United States policy to support South Vietnam.

War

2. Evaluate the effectiveness of violent versus nonviolent demonstrations. What were the results of nonviolent demonstrations in the early 1960s?

Critical Thinking

1. **Making Inferences** What lessons about military intervention could President Kennedy have learned from the Bay of Pigs?

2. **Analyzing Art** Study the photograph on this page of the Vietnam Veterans Memorial, then answer the questions that follow.

   a. Compare the Vietnam Memorial with other national monuments and memorials. In what way is the design of the Memorial unique?

b. The Vietnam Veterans Memorial is one of the most visited of our nation's monuments. Why do you think this is so?

History and Geography

The Vietnam War

Study the map on page 705 and answer the questions that follow.

1. **Region** What nations besides North and South Vietnam were the sites of battles or invasions?

2. **Location** What is the relative location of China to North Vietnam?

Cooperative Learning ## Interdisciplinary Activity: Political Science

Work with two other group members to explore the options facing President Kennedy during the Cuban missile crisis. List two potential consequences of each option.

Practicing Skills

Interpreting Military Maps

Two kinds of terrain maps are shown on page 719—a terrain model and a topographic map. The two maps show roughly the same area of Vietnam. The terrain model is a representation of the shape of the land, with hills and valleys shown. Although the actual model is only two-dimensional, the

Understanding Concepts

1. American policy in Vietnam was founded on containment and the "domino theory" belief that if Vietnam fell, so would the rest of Southeast Asia.

2. Answers will vary. Nonviolent measures had some success in identifying areas of discrimination. Some national legislation was passed to deal with these. The 1960s riots did bring attention to the goals of the black-power movement, but one might question the cost involved, which included deaths and the destruction of property.

Critical Thinking

1. Answers will vary. Kennedy probably learned not to intervene without local support. The Alliance for Progress and Peace Corps attempted to enlist local support to thwart the spread of communism.

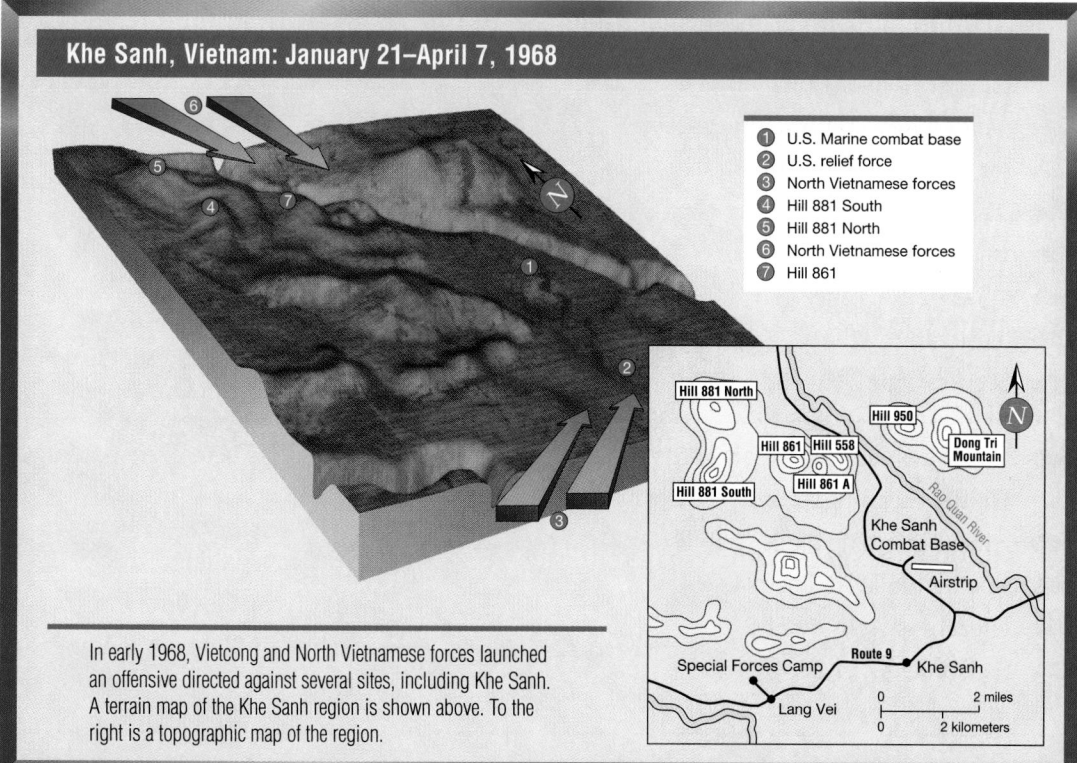

Khe Sanh, Vietnam: January 21–April 7, 1968

1. U.S. Marine combat base
2. U.S. relief force
3. North Vietnamese forces
4. Hill 881 South
5. Hill 881 North
6. North Vietnamese forces
7. Hill 861

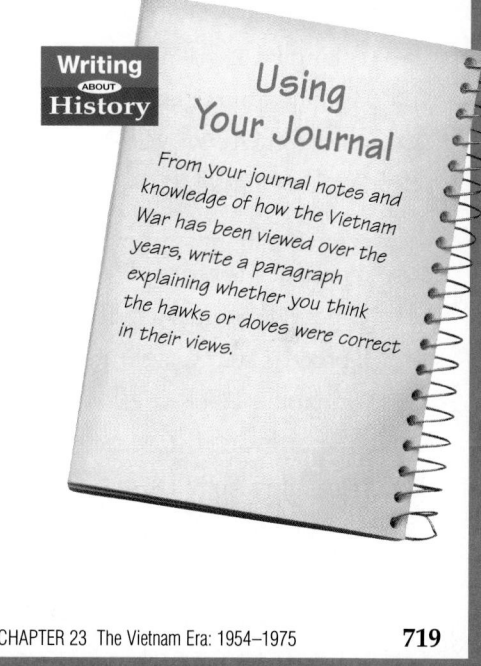

Hill 881 North
Hill 950
Hill 861 Hill 558
Dong Tri Mountain
Hill 881 South Hill 861 A
Rao Quan River
Khe Sanh Combat Base
Airstrip
Special Forces Camp Route 9 Khe Sanh
Lang Vei
0 2 miles
0 2 kilometers

In early 1968, Vietcong and North Vietnamese forces launched an offensive directed against several sites, including Khe Sanh. A terrain map of the Khe Sanh region is shown above. To the right is a topographic map of the region.

shading and shapes of the dark areas make the model appear three-dimensional.

The topographic map is a two-dimensional map showing elevations using contour lines. A contour line represents points that are all at the same elevation. Each contour line represents a successively higher or lower elevation. The vertical distance between contour lines is the same for all lines in a particular topographic map.

Use the two terrain maps to answer the following questions.

1. The three-dimensional terrain model shows the paths of North Vietnamese forces during one part of the Tet offensive. Over what land features did the North Vietnamese forces travel?

2. Why do you suppose there are no distance or elevation scales on the three-dimensional model?

3. Can elevation of the hills in either map be determined? Why or why not?

Writing ABOUT **History**

Using Your Journal

From your journal notes and knowledge of how the Vietnam War has been viewed over the years, write a paragraph explaining whether you think the hawks or doves were correct in their views.

Writing ABOUT **History** Using Your Journal

Students' answers should reflect an understanding of the views of the group they choose to support—hawks supported the war, doves opposed it.

Chapter Bonus Test Question

Ask students: Which of the following events was the most significant to American life? Give reasons in support of your choice.
• Cuban missile crisis
• Tet offensive
• Vietcong signing of the cease-fire agreement
(*Answers will vary but should reflect an understanding that significance is measured by an event's long-term effects.*)

2. a. Answers will vary but may include its dimensions and the names printed on it.
b. Answers will vary but may include that many Americans had relatives or friends who served.

History and Geography
1. Laos and Cambodia
2. north of North Vietnam

Cooperative Learning
Ask students to present their options and consequences in the form of a flow chart. Discuss students' charts.

Practicing Skills
1. valleys and relatively flat land
2. For the purpose of the map—show troop movements—distances are not important.
3. No, neither map has any scale or markings for elevation.

Daily Lesson Objectives	Teacher Classroom Resources	Multimedia
SECTION 1 **Kennedy's New Frontier** **1 Day** pp. 722–726 1. Describe important legislation Kennedy proposed during his term of office. 2. Describe the impact of Kennedy's death on the nation.	Reproducible Lesson Plan 24-1 *Guided Reading Activity 24-1 Concept Mapping Activities 24-A, 24-B Chapter Map Activity 24 American Portrait 64 Workbook Activity 24-1 Reteaching Activity 24-1 *Section Quiz 24-1	Section Focus Transparency 24-1 Chapter Concepts Transparencies 24-A, 24-B MindJogger Videoquiz Communism and the Cold War Powers of the President The Presidents: A Picture History of Our Nation
SECTION 2 **The Great Society** **1 Day** pp. 728–732 1. Explain how Johnson's belief in consensus helped win the 1964 election. 2. Discuss Johnson's efforts to fight poverty.	Reproducible Lesson Plan 24-2 *Guided Reading Activity 24-2 Critical Thinking Skills Activity 24 Chapter Skills Activity 24 Reteaching Activity 24-2 *Section Quiz 24-2	Section Focus Transparency 24-2 U.S. History & Art Transparency 31 Focus on Government The Presidents: A Picture History of Our Nation
SECTION 3 **An Imperial Presidency** **1 Day** pp. 734–738 1. Describe how Nixon tried to deal with the economic problems of the early 1970s. 2. Explain how Nixon handled the war on crime and the energy crisis.	Reproducible Lesson Plan 24-3 *Guided Reading Activity 24-3 *Vocabulary Activity 24 Linking Past and Present Activity 24 Supreme Court Case Studies 29, 32 Reteaching Activity 24-3 *Section Quiz 24-3	Section Focus Transparency 24-3 Skills Transparency 24 Vocabulary PuzzleMaker Powers of the President The Presidents: A Picture History of Our Nation
SECTION 4 **The Watergate Scandal** **1 Day** pp. 739–743 1. Explain how the constitutional process solved the Watergate crisis. 2. List the ways in which Congress sought to reassert its constitutional powers.	Reproducible Lesson Plan 24-4 *Guided Reading Activity 24-4 Supreme Court Case Study 42 Enrichment Activity 24 Geography in History Activity 24 Reteaching Activity 24-4 *Section Quiz 24-4	Section Focus Transparency 24-4 Testmaker Powers of the President Powers of the Congress
CHAPTER REVIEW AND EVALUATION **1 Day**	Chapter 24 Test, Forms A and B Spanish Chapter 24 Summaries Performance Assessment Activity 24	MindJogger Videoquiz Student Self-Test & Review Software *Chapter 24 Audiocassette Activity and Test

*Also available in Spanish

0:00   **OUT OF TIME?** If time does not permit teaching the entire chapter, use the Chapter 24 Summary on pages 800–801 and the Chapter 24 audiocassette (English and Spanish) to point out the main ideas of the chapter.

A complete, 1-page lesson plan is provided for each section in the *Reproducible Lesson Plan* booklet.

Key to Ability Levels

Teaching strategies have been coded for varying learning styles and abilities.

L1 Basic activities for all students

L2 Average activities for average to above-average students

L3 Challenging activities for above-average students

LEP Limited English Proficiency activities

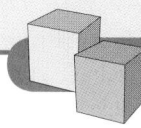

Block Schedule

Block scheduling differs from traditional class scheduling in the amount of time allotted to each period. The extended time frame provided by block scheduling affords you the opportunity to implement a greater number of research-oriented and activity-intense projects to motivate and involve your students. Activities that are particularly suited to use within the block scheduling framework are identified throughout this unit by the following designation:

✔ Performance Assessment Activity

Domestic Policy Have students choose one of the Presidents highlighted in this chapter and write a speech defining his approach to domestic problems. The speeches should begin by describing his objectives, then outline policies based on those objectives, and conclude with a critical examination of the results of those policies. Students might work alone on the speeches or in small groups. Encourage speechwriters to read their address to the class. The class might compare the way different Presidents approached the nation's domestic problems. Students might also focus on a single President and compare his domestic policy with his approach to foreign affairs. What similarities do they detect? What differences seem most striking? How do they account for those differences?

POSSIBLE RUBRIC FEATURES

- Research Skills
- Content Information
- Organization
- Written and Oral Communication Skills
- Critical Thinking Skills

📁 For additional activities, see Performance Assessment Strategies and Activities.

T E A C H E R ' S   C O R N E R

NATIONAL GEOGRAPHIC SOCIETY

INDEX TO NATIONAL GEOGRAPHIC MAGAZINE

The following articles may be used for research relating to this chapter:

- "Diminishing Returns," by Michael Parfit, November 1995.
- "Hawaii's Vanishing Species," by Elizabeth Royte, September 1995.
- "Earth Day: 25 Years Old," by Frank Graham, Jr., April 1995.
- "The Endangered Species Act," by Douglas H. Chadwick, March 1995.
- "The Everglades: Dying for Help," by Alan Mairson, April 1994.
- "New Eyes on the Universe," by Bradford A. Smith, January 1994.
- "Chesapeake Bay—Hanging in the Balance," by Tom Horton, June 1993.
- "Silence of the Songbirds," by Les Line, June 1993.
- "Our Disappearing Wetlands," by John G. Mitchell, October 1992.
- *World; Endangered Earth,* (A Special Edition), December 1988.

NATIONAL GEOGRAPHIC SOCIETY PRODUCTS AVAILABLE FROM GLENCOE

To order the following products for use with this chapter, contact your local Glencoe sales representative or call Glencoe at 1-800-334-7344:

- *The Presidents: A Picture History of Our Nation* (CD-ROM)
- *GTV: A Geographic Perspective on American History* (Videodisc)
- *GTV: The American People: Fabric of a Nation* (Videodisc)

ADDITIONAL NATIONAL GEOGRAPHIC SOCIETY PRODUCTS

To order the following products for use with this chapter, call National Geographic Society at 1-800-368-2728:

- *Decades of History: The 20th Century—The Middle Years* (Filmstrip)
- *The United States as a World Power: From the 1890s to the 1970s* (Filmstrip)
- *The American Presidency* (Filmstrip)
- *1945–1989: The Cold War* (Video)

Recording Journal Notes
Suggest that students also include actions by Congress to curb presidential power and future abuses.

Linking Across TIME

Underscore the continuity of history by pointing out that an issue that troubled George Washington—what kind of relations should the United States have with foreign nations—still worries Presidents today. Have students suggest other issues that can be traced back through our history.

CHAPTER 24

★★

Camelot to Watergate
1960–1976

▶ **HYDRANT DECORATED FOR NATION'S BICENTENNIAL**

Setting the Scene

Focus

During the brief administration of John F. Kennedy, his leadership and the American people were repeatedly tested by staggering challenges at home and abroad. During Johnson's administration federal spending for social programs, along with the cost of the war in Vietnam, strained the government's budget. The Nixon administration was troubled by questions about illegal activities that led to Nixon's resignation and left the nation with deep wounds.

Journal Notes

In what ways has corruption affected politics in America? Note details in your journal as you read the chapter.

Concepts to Understand

★ How presidential leadership shaped **domestic policy**

★ How the limits of **presidential power** are defined by the other branches of government

Read to Discover . . .

★ how Kennedy's and Johnson's approaches to economic problems differed from Nixon's.

★ what developments caused Nixon to resign the presidency.

CULTURAL	• **1964** *The Beatles come to America*	• **1968** *Cost of mailing a letter increases to 6 cents* • **1969** *Neil Armstrong walks on the moon*
	1960	**1965**
POLITICAL	• **1963** *Kennedy assassinated; Lyndon Johnson becomes President*	• **1968** *Nixon appoints Warren Burger head of Supreme Court* • **1969** *Nixon announces new federalism*

✚ EXTRA CREDIT PROJECT

Writing a Political Speech Ask interested students to write a campaign speech for a presidential candidate in 1960, 1964, or 1968. The speeches should address the issues of the day and offer the candidates' views on those issues.

Encourage volunteers to read their speeches to the class. Discuss similarities and differences within a given election and between elections. **L2**

Concept Mapping Activity

On the chalkboard, reproduce the following generalization and concepts map, and have students copy it in their notebooks.

The style of leadership and the domestic policies of President Kennedy and President Johnson differed from those of President Nixon.

Domestic Policy

Presidential Power

To reinforce the two chapter concepts, use Concept Mapping Activities 24-A and 24-B.

Use Chapter Concepts Transparencies 24-A, 24-B.

History AND ART

Norman Rockwell's *The Peace Corps in Ethiopia* depicts a young American volunteer giving instruction on using a plow.

History AND ART

The Peace Corps in Ethiopia, 1966
by Norman Rockwell

Rockwell's painting depicts a young American volunteer giving instructions on the use of a plow. Peace Corps volunteers worked in many developing countries around the world.

◀ PRESIDENT JOHN F. KENNEDY

- **1971** *Amtrak passenger service begins*
- **1976** *Bicentennial celebration of the United States*

1970	1975

- **1973** *Vice President Agnew resigns*
- **1974** *Watergate scandal unfolds; Nixon resigns*
- **1975** *Several of Nixon's aides are convicted*

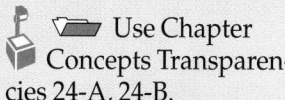

ABCNEWS INTERACTIVE™

 VIDEODISC

Powers of the President

Side Two, Chapter 23
Title: *Watergate Scandal*
Subject: Montage of news reports about the scandal

 Performance Assessment

Refer to the Performance Assessment Activity in the Planning Guide on page 720b. When groups have finished their speeches about presidential domestic policy, have them present them to the class. Allow time for class discussion and feedback.

Use Performance Assessment Activity 24 as an additional assessment technique.

721

FOCUS

Bellringer

Before taking roll, project Section Focus Transparency 24-1 or hand out Section Focus Transparency Activity 24-1. Have students answer the questions. Discuss student responses.

Motivating Activity

Read aloud the following excerpt from President Kennedy's Inaugural Address:

"Let the word go forth from this time and place, to friend and foe alike, that the torch has been passed to a new generation of Americans born in this century, tempered by war, disciplined by a cold and bitter peace."

Ask students: What qualities do you associate with the term "new generation of Americans"? *(youth, optimism, promise, opportunity, idealism, bravery)* **L1**

Vocabulary Precheck

Ask students to define each of the "Key Terms." Have a volunteer consult the dictionary for any unfamiliar words. **L1, LEP**

★★

Kennedy's New Frontier

Setting the Scene

Section Focus

By the late 1950s, many people in the United States felt it was time to attack the nation's problems vigorously. Despite the prosperity of the postwar years, poverty was still prevalent. Eisenhower, the first President to be legally limited to two terms, would soon be leaving office. The people looked to his still-unchosen successor to provide strong, active leadership.

Objectives

After studying this section, you should be able to

★ describe important legislation Kennedy proposed during his term of office.

★ describe the impact of Kennedy's death on the nation.

Key Terms

mandate, pragmatist, urban renewal

◀ DECORATIVE FLAG, COMPUTER ART

*W*ashington, D.C., glittered during the Kennedy years. As never before, millions became familiar with the occupants of the White House. The public's enchantment with Kennedy was not shared by Congress, however. Many of Kennedy's most important legislative efforts would have to wait until after his death to become law.

■ The Election of 1960

In the 1960 presidential campaign, the Republicans chose Vice President Richard M. Nixon and the Democrats chose Senator John F. Kennedy of Massachusetts. As his vice-presidential running mate Nixon chose UN Ambassador Henry Cabot Lodge. To win Southern support, Kennedy chose Texas Senator Lyndon B. Johnson.

The backgrounds of the two presidential candidates presented striking contrasts. Kennedy was a Catholic and the second-oldest son of a wealthy family. Nixon, born in California, was from far more humble origins, and his Quaker mother had struggled to keep the family together.

There were also similarities between the two men. Both were young: Nixon was 47 years old, and Kennedy was 43. Nixon and Kennedy were experienced legislators, both having served in the House of Representatives or in the Senate. Nixon had also served eight years as Eisenhower's Vice President.

The Impact of Television

The political differences between the candidates were small. Both were considered "cold warriors" who believed that communism was the chief threat to the way of life in

---

Classroom Resources for SECTION 1

Blackline Masters:
- Reproducible Lesson Plan 24-1
- Guided Reading Activity 24-1
- Chapter Map Activity 24

- American Portrait 64
- Workbook Activity 24-1
- Reteaching Activity 24-1
- Section Quiz 24-1

Transparencies:
- Section Focus Transparency 24-1

Multimedia:
- Testmaker
- MindJogger Videoquiz
- Communism and the Cold War
- Powers of the President
- The Presidents: A Picture History of Our Nation

the United States. Senator Kennedy hoped to take advantage of Republican weaknesses and challenged Nixon to a series of televised debates. Nixon was the more skilled debater, and most who heard the debates on radio declared Nixon the winner. Yet, the millions more who watched on television thought a well-prepared, poised, and youthful Senator Kennedy won the debates. The debates were one of the earliest examples of the strong impact television would have on politics in the United States.

The Issue of Religion

Political observers wondered whether Kennedy's religion would be an obstacle to his election. No Catholic had ever been elected President, and some believed that a Catholic could not make official decisions independent from the Roman Catholic Church. Kennedy answered by stressing his belief in the separation of church and state. He declared he would resign, rather than violate either his conscience or the interests of the nation.

Kennedy won the election, finally laying to rest the idea that a Roman Catholic could not be elected President. Analyzing his victory, Kennedy concluded, "It was TV more than anything else that turned the tide." However, he carried the election by one of the narrowest margins in American history. He won the popular vote by 120,000 out of 68 million votes cast and the electoral college by 303 to 219. In several states a difference of only a few thousand votes would have swung the electoral votes the other way. As a result, Kennedy did not enter office with a clear **mandate,** or endorsement of his ideas, from the American people. Nevertheless, though he was cautious at first, the new President moved ahead with his domestic program.

▶ **KENNEDY-NIXON DEBATE**

▲ THE 1960 ELECTION At the start of the 1960 election campaign, polls showed Richard Nixon in the lead. Kennedy, who had been less in the public eye than Nixon, began to draw enthusiastic responses on the campaign trail and revealed that he was highly informed and poised under fire. *What impact did the televised debates have on voters?*

CHAPTER 24 Camelot to Watergate: 1960–1976 **723**

TEACH
Guided Practice
Journalism Divide the class into small groups. Have each group produce a newsletter in which it describes the successes and failures of Kennedy's domestic programs. **L2**

Did You Know?

John Kennedy, his wife, and their two small children were the youngest family to live in the White House since Theodore Roosevelt's days.

Visualizing History Nixon and Kennedy were the first presidential candidates to debate on television. **Answer to Caption:** They may have swung the election in Kennedy's favor.

NATIONAL GEOGRAPHIC SOCIETY

CD-ROM

The Presidents: A Picture History of Our Nation

Have students view "John F. Kennedy" and use the information to write a brief biography to include in their portfolios.

Special Needs Activity

Study Strategy Many students will not use a learning strategy unless they are fully aware of its benefits. Explain the benefits of summarizing by saying: "Summarizing is a way of remaining actively involved in reading by committing yourself to making decisions about information in the text so that it is compact enough to be easily remembered." Then ask these questions about the material on the 1960 presidential election: Which point should be included in a summary—that Kennedy and Nixon took part in a televised debate or that Kennedy was the son of wealthy parents? Why? **L1, LEP**

Independent Practice

Research Divide the class into small groups. Assign to each one aspect of Kennedy's domestic policies to research and critique. Sample topics might include the Housing Act of 1961, the Area Redevelopment Act, and increased funding for NASA. Ask groups to describe the program to the class and then assess its successes and failures. **L3**

 Assign Guided Reading Activity 24-1.

Map Study *Using Maps*

Answer: Northeast and the South

Map Skills Practice
Where did Nixon make his strongest showing? *(the West)*

 For additional map practice, assign Chapter Map Activity 24.

 Assign Map Transparency Activity 24.

VIDEODISC

Powers of the President

Side Two, Chapter 73

Title: *Patronage*
Subject: Robert Kennedy becomes attorney general

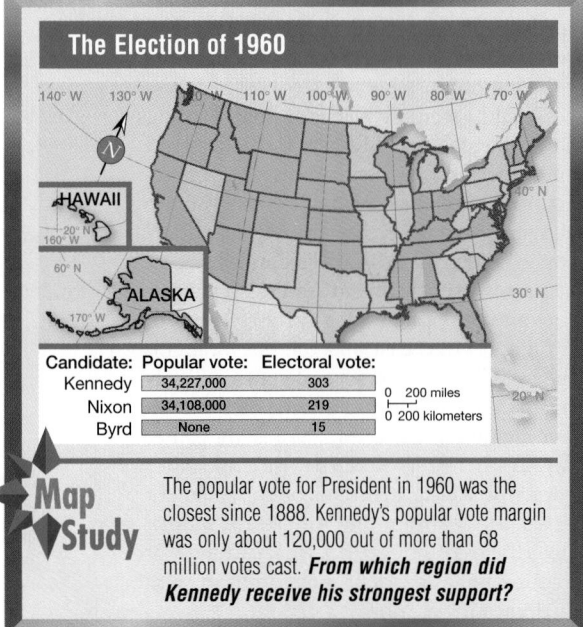

The Election of 1960

Candidate:	Popular vote:	Electoral vote:
Kennedy	34,227,000	303
Nixon	34,108,000	219
Byrd	None	15

Map Study

The popular vote for President in 1960 was the closest since 1888. Kennedy's popular vote margin was only about 120,000 out of more than 68 million votes cast. *From which region did Kennedy receive his strongest support?*

■ The New Frontier

Kennedy devoted his Inaugural Address to defining the role of the United States in a divided world. The torch, he said, had been "passed to a new generation," committed to the rights for which the United States had stood since the Revolution. He warned the communist world that the United States would remain strong, but he also urged both sides to renew the search for peace. He wanted both to join forces against the common enemies of "tyranny, poverty, disease, and war itself." In ringing tones, he declared:

> *My fellow Americans, ask not what your country can do for you. Ask what you can do for your country. My fellow citizens of the world: Ask not what America can do for you, but what together we can do for the freedom of man.*

The Kennedy administration became known as the "New Frontier." For the first time, the future of the United States lay in the hands of those born in the twentieth century. The President and his closest advisers

---

were intelligent and tough-minded. They were sure of their ability to make the country and the world better places to live in.

In public the new President mixed idealism with realism and informality with dignity. Although he showed a great deal of idealism, Kennedy was also a **pragmatist**—one who searches for practical solutions to problems. Above all, Kennedy seemed to have the gift of leadership that inspired trust and devotion. Kennedy's qualities seemed to appeal not only to those in the United States but to people all over the world.

■ Kennedy's Economic Program

Essentially, Kennedy's New Frontier was a continuation of Roosevelt's New Deal and Truman's Fair Deal. Kennedy promised to stimulate the economy with tax cuts and increased federal spending.

Promoting Economic Growth

In 1960, though the country was still prosperous, the economy was slowing down. When Kennedy became President, the nation's rate of economic growth was only 3 percent a year. Kennedy looked for ways to increase growth and create more jobs. In stimulating the economy, he chose not to rely on federal spending, which tends to cause inflation. Instead, he sought to increase business production and efficiency. His administration also asked businesses to hold down prices and labor leaders to hold down requests for pay increases.

Conflicts With Steel Companies

Prodded by Secretary of Labor Arthur Goldberg, labor unions in the steel industry agreed to reduce their demands for higher wages. Despite this agreement, several steel companies raised prices sharply in 1962. Kennedy denounced the steel company executives and threatened to have the Department of Defense buy cheaper steel from foreign companies. He also instructed

---

Sidelight: Kennedy's Wit

President Kennedy's press conferences were marked by witty asides and friendly banter with reporters. For example, when chided by a reporter for appointing his younger brother, Robert, as attorney general, Kennedy replied, "I can't see that it's wrong to give him a little legal experience before he goes out to practice law." On a visit to France, during which the French press seemed more interested in what his wife was wearing, Kennedy announced, "I am the man who accompanied Jacqueline Kennedy to Paris, and I have enjoyed it."

the Justice Department to investigate whether the steel industry was guilty of price-fixing. The steel companies backed down and cut their prices. To achieve this victory, however, Kennedy had strained his relations with the nation's business leaders. As a result of his actions to stimulate the economy, Kennedy achieved his aim of raising the growth rate, which doubled during his administration.

Legislative Victories

Kennedy was able to win some legislative victories in his domestic program. After getting a bill for federal aid to public schools passed, he tried to wipe out areas of poverty, notably in the Appalachian Mountain region, in much of the South, and in the nation's inner cities. Kennedy supported the Area Redevelopment Act, designed to encourage industries to move into economically depressed areas. His Housing Act of 1961 called for $5 billion for **urban renewal,** or programs to improve homes and neighborhoods in the inner cities.

Perhaps his most significant victory was increased funding for the National Aeronautics and Space Administration (NASA). Kennedy challenged the nation and NASA with the goal of putting an astronaut on the moon by 1970. There were those who objected to spending an estimated $20 billion for the space program, but Kennedy saw space exploration as a challenge to the nation's prestige and a symbol of cold war rivalry with the Soviet Union.

Conflict With Congress

Although Kennedy achieved some legislative victories, conflict with Congress prevented him from getting much of his domestic program passed. Despite the fact that the Democratic party enjoyed large majorities in both houses, a coalition of conservative Southern Democrats dominated Congress, rejecting many New Frontier measures.

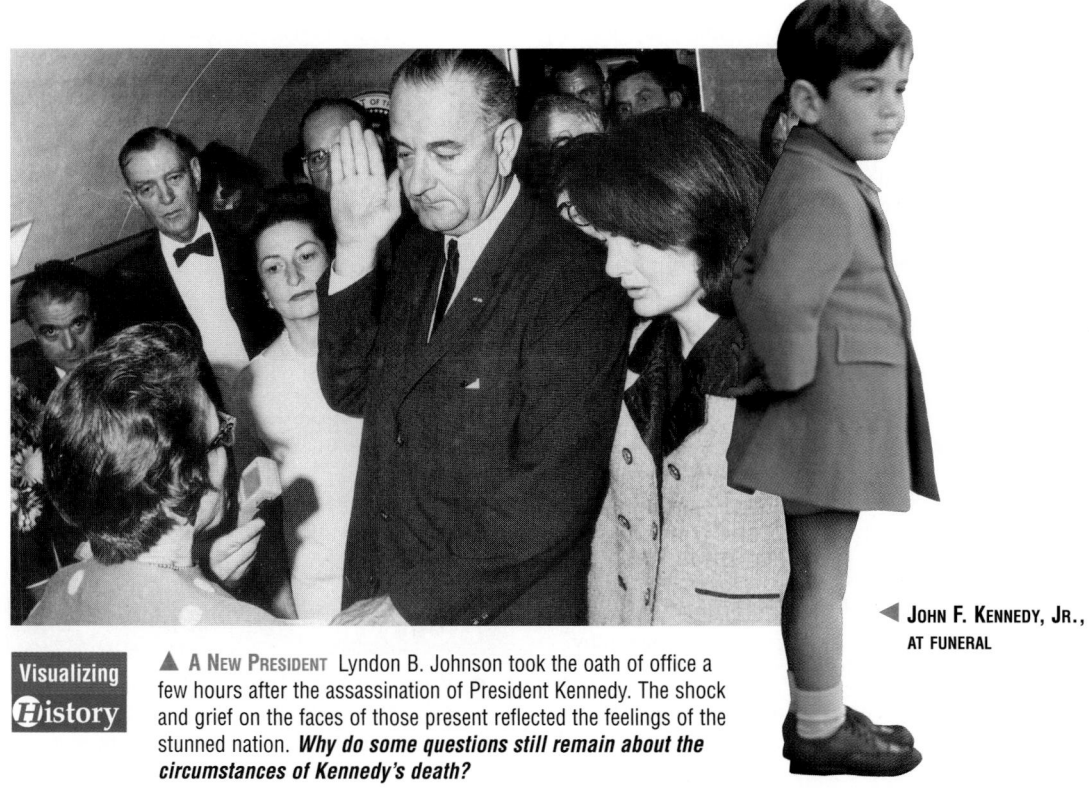

Visualizing History

▲ A New President Lyndon B. Johnson took the oath of office a few hours after the assassination of President Kennedy. The shock and grief on the faces of those present reflected the feelings of the stunned nation. *Why do some questions still remain about the circumstances of Kennedy's death?*

◀ John F. Kennedy, Jr., at funeral

CHAPTER 24 Camelot to Watergate: 1960–1976   **725**

 Assign American Portrait 64: Robert F. Kennedy.

Visualizing History Kennedy had prepared a major speech on U.S. foreign policy. Cut down by an assassin's bullet on the streets of Dallas, he never delivered the speech. By unanimous consent, it was entered into the Congressional Record a few days later. **Answer to Caption:** Theories persist because the Warren Commission's report did not answer all the questions.

Did You Know?

In 1961 Russian cosmonaut Yuri Gagarin became the first man to travel in space. Later that year Alan Shepard became the first American in space.

ABCNEWS INTERACTIVE™

 VIDEODISC

Powers of the President

Side One, Chapter 15
Title: *Presidential Vacancy*
Subject: Kennedy's assassination and Johnson's swearing in—in Dallas

Sidelight: The Death of a President

The shock and sadness of President Kennedy's untimely death reached far beyond the borders of the United States. In Britain the cast of the irreverent television satire program *That Was the Week That Was* threw out their prepared script and did a show memorializing Kennedy. In the former Soviet Union, young people openly wept on the streets of Moscow. In a remote town in Sudan, a storekeeper etched a dark border on his receipts because "the greatest man in the world is dead today."

Food of the Times

The research for space travel in the 1960s led to the development of freeze-dried foods. Within a short time, they found their way to supermarkets across the nation.

ASSESS

Check Understanding

Assign Section 1 Review as homework or an in-class activity.

Evaluate

Assign Section Quiz 24-1 or use the Testmaker to create a customized quiz.

Reteach

Have students complete Reteaching Activity 24-1.

Assign Workbook Activity 24-1.

Enrich

Have students write a letter to President Kennedy thanking him for his actions on a particular issue or urging him to support some other kind of legislation. Select students to read their letters to the class.

CLOSE

Summarize the section by referring students to the chapter generalization. Ask them to give examples of how President Kennedy offered a new vision and sense of idealism to the American people.

When Kennedy proposed that the government recognize the problems of cities by creating a new cabinet department for urban affairs, Congress voted down the proposal. Kennedy also asked for a national health insurance program, Medicare, to help older citizens pay their medical bills. The Senate defeated this bill, which was opposed by many doctors. The President called the Senate's action a "serious defeat for every American family."

■ Tragedy in Dallas

Kennedy hoped to achieve a greater mandate for his domestic program in the election of 1964. To that end, he traveled to Dallas, Texas, to smooth party differences and gather support. In Dallas, on November 22, 1963, the President was assassinated.

The sense of tragedy and grief that many felt was caught by a conversation between the newspaper columnist Mary McGrory and Daniel Moynihan, a member of Kennedy's staff. In response to McGrory's remark that "we'll never laugh again," Moynihan replied, "Heavens, Mary, we'll laugh again. It's just that we'll never be young again." It was this feeling of youth snuffed out, of promise unfulfilled, that made Kennedy's death seem peculiarly tragic to many.

The country and the world were deeply shocked and saddened at this loss. Americans everywhere grieved over the President's death. In Italy, people brought flowers to the gates of the American embassy in Rome. In India, crowds wept in the streets of New Delhi. In Africa, President Sékou Touré of Guinea said, "I have lost my only true friend in the outside world."

The Warren Commission

Kennedy's alleged assassin, Lee Harvey Oswald, was himself shot to death only two days after the assassination. This event led to speculation that Oswald was killed to protect others who may have helped plan the crime. In 1964, a national commission headed by Chief Justice Warren concluded that Oswald was indeed the assassin and that he acted alone. The commission's report did leave important questions unanswered, though, and theories still persist that Oswald acted as part of a conspiracy. None of those theories has gained wide acceptance, however.

Johnson Takes Over

Kennedy was succeeded in office by Vice President Lyndon B. Johnson. Johnson took the oath of office on the plane that carried Kennedy's body from Dallas back to Washington, D.C. From Kennedy, Johnson inherited both unsolved problems and unfulfilled promises.

In domestic policy, Kennedy's New Frontier program was stalled in Congress. Yet, only two years after his death, most of these programs became law. The public reaction to the young President's tragic death, combined with the political skills of Lyndon Johnson, made possible sweeping social reform.

Section 1 ★ Review

Checking for Understanding

1. **Identify** New Frontier, Housing Act of 1961, NASA.

2. **Define** mandate, pragmatist, urban renewal.

3. **List** three economic programs undertaken by President Kennedy.

4. **Explain** why many of Kennedy's domestic programs were not passed.

Critical Thinking

5. **Analyzing Results** How did the lack of a mandate affect Kennedy's ability to govern?

ACTIVITY

6. Write the title "The New Frontier" at the top of a piece of poster board. Paste photographs of important events during the Kennedy administration.

Answers to SECTION 1 REVIEW

1. New Frontier, 724; Housing Act of 1961, 725; NASA, 725
2. All vocabulary words are defined in the Glossary.
3. tax cuts, requests to business and labor to hold down prices and wages, and poverty-fighting programs like Area Redevelopment Act and Housing Act
4. Congress dominated by conservative coalition of Republicans and Southern Democrats
5. Answers will vary but many students will suggest the lack of a mandate made him more cautious.
6. Posters should reflect a wide range of national and international events.

▼ PHOTOGRAPH OF EARTH FROM THE MOON

▲ ASTRONAUT IN SPACE

Space Race

Americans were stunned by the news that the Soviets had put a satellite—*Sputnik I*—into orbit around the earth in October 1957. Physicist Edward Teller called the launch a Soviet victory in "a battle more important and greater than Pearl Harbor." President Eisenhower told the panicked nation that only its pride, not its security, was damaged.

Americans, however, were threatened by what they considered Soviet technical superiority. In response, Congress passed the National Defense Education Act, which financed science and foreign-language programs in schools. In addition, the National Science Foundation's curriculum-development budget was dramatically increased. Congress also created the National Aeronautics and Space Administration (NASA) in 1958. Huge sums of money were allocated to develop space technology and to compete with the Soviets in space.

In the spring of 1961, Alan Shepard, Jr., became the first American to make a space flight. On February 20, 1962, Lieutenant Colonel John Glenn became the first American to orbit the earth. Shortly after Shepard's flight,

Kennedy challenged the nation to a great undertaking. He pledged that America would land an individual on the moon by 1970. In July 1969 Commander Neil A. Armstrong, Colonel Edwin E. Aldrin, Jr., and Lieutenant Colonel Michael Collins took off in Apollo.

When they reached the moon, Collins remained aboard the command spacecraft while Aldrin and Armstrong descended to the surface in a lunar module. Millions watched on television as Armstrong became the first human being to set foot on the surface of the moon.

Making the Science Connection

1. How did Americans feel about the success of *Sputnik*?

2. What actions were taken in response to *Sputnik*?

ACTIVITY

3. Investigate major events in the American space program from 1960 to the present. Use your findings to create a space time line.

727

TEACH

The launching of *Sputnik II* a month later caused even more concern in the United States. Much larger than its predecessor and carrying a passenger—a dog named Laika—*Sputnik II* was propelled into space by an incredibly powerful rocket. Such a rocket, American scientists surmised, could be modified to carry missiles against the United States. Ask students to discuss whether they think American security concerns were justified. **L1**

CURRICULUM CONNECTION

Science In 1958 the United States sent up its first satellite, *Explorer I*. It marked the beginning of a "space race."

ABCNEWS INTERACTIVE™

  VIDEODISC

Communism and the Cold War

Side One, Chapter 14
Title: Sputnik *Launches the Space Race*
Subject: The beginning of the space race

Answers to Making the Connection

1. They were stunned.
2. passed the National Defense Education Act, which financed educational, science, and foreign-language programs; increased the National Science Foundation's budget; cre-

ated NASA; committed to moon landing by 1970

3. Space time lines will vary but should include major events in the space program.

FOCUS

Bellringer

 Before taking roll, project Section Focus Transparency 24-2 or hand out Section Focus Transparency Activity 24-2. Have students answer the questions. Discuss student responses.

Motivating Activity

Tell students that Lyndon Johnson was a veteran of more than 20 years in Congress. Ask students to put themselves in the place of an American legislator and explain why Johnson was more successful in passing legislation than was Kennedy. In what way did consensus help Johnson in Congress? Have students summarize their beliefs in writing. **L2**

Vocabulary Precheck

Ask students to speculate on the meaning of *consensus*. Then have them check their guesses by finding the definition in the section text. **L1, LEP**

NATIONAL GEOGRAPHIC SOCIETY

CD-ROM

The Presidents: A Picture History of Our Nation

Have students select President Lyndon Johnson from the main menu and the category GAME. Suggest they learn more about Johnson by playing the presidential game with a partner.

★★★★★★★★★★★★★★★★★★★★★★★★★★★★★★★★★★★★★

The Great Society

Setting the Scene

Section Focus

Lyndon Johnson was a big man, with great energy and ambition. Sharing the same goals as Kennedy, Johnson carried into legislation the former President's war on poverty. As a former Senate leader, Johnson conceived and skillfully guided through Congress more significant domestic legislation than had been passed since the New Deal.

◀ *SILENT SPRING* BY RACHEL CARSON

Objectives

After studying this section, you should be able to

★ explain how Johnson's belief in consensus helped him win the 1964 election.

★ discuss Johnson's efforts to fight poverty in the United States.

Key Term

consensus

---

*A*ided by the Kennedy cabinet and relying on his long experience in government, Lyndon Johnson quickly made the transition from Vice President to President. On November 27, 1963, five days after John F. Kennedy's assassination, Johnson appeared before a joint session of Congress. His words assured the nation's representatives that he intended to carry out Kennedy's programs:

> *... the ideas and ideals which [Kennedy] so nobly represented must and will be translated into effective action. John Kennedy's death commands what his life conveyed—that America must move forward.*

Elected to the House of Representatives in 1937 and the Senate in 1948, Johnson was at home in Congress. During the 1950s he was the powerful Democratic majority leader of the Senate. Although a Southerner, Johnson had taken a moderate position on most issues and had been a leader in passing the Civil Rights Act of 1957.

■ The Election of 1964

As President, Johnson continued an effective policy of working through **consensus,** or general agreement, that he had developed in Congress. With skilled bargaining, compromising, and even verbal arm-twisting, Johnson reinforced his favorite biblical quotation, "Come let us reason together." He took over the responsibilities of the Chief Executive with firmness and strength, determined to pursue the Democratic party's goals of social justice.

In the election of 1964, Johnson used these goals to campaign for President. His campaign plan offered something for everyone: business and labor, rich and poor, young and

728 UNIT 7 Redefining America: 1954–Present

Classroom Resources for SECTION 2

Blackline Masters:
- Reproducible Lesson Plan 24-2
- Guided Reading Activity 24-2
- Critical Thinking Skills Activity 24
- Chapter Skills Activity 24
- Workbook Activity 24-2
- Reteaching Activity 24-2
- Section Quiz 24-2

Transparencies:
- Section Focus Transparency 24-2
- U.S. History & Art Transparency 31

Multimedia:
- Testmaker
- Focus on Government
- The Presidents: A Picture History of Our Nation

old, African American and white. Known as "the Great Society," Johnson's domestic program was an effort to expand upon Kennedy's ideas as well as to make a contribution of his own. It was designed to fight poverty, discrimination, unemployment, pollution, and other social ills of America. At the same time, he pledged to provide major tax cuts for individuals and corporations.

To offer voters "a choice, not an echo," Republicans selected an outspoken conservative, Barry Goldwater, to run against Johnson and his liberal running mate, Hubert Humphrey. The Arizona senator ran a determined, uncompromising campaign. His opposition to the Civil Rights Act of 1964 turned away African American voters. His coolness to Social Security made older people fearful. His support of the open shop hurt him with organized labor. Above all, Goldwater's suggestion that military commanders should be allowed to decide for themselves whether to use nuclear weapons made many people nervous.

As predicted, Johnson's wide appeal won him more than 60 percent of the popular vote. Goldwater carried only his home state of Arizona and five Southern states, where former "Dixiecrats" switched to the Republican party. In addition, the Democrats increased their majorities in both houses of Congress. The Great Society had won an overwhelming mandate.

■ War on Poverty

In the mid-1960s the United States had the highest standard of living in the world. But behind the Great Society program was a new awareness that many Americans did not share in the general prosperity.

The Other America

Contributing to this awareness was a book by Michael Harrington entitled *The Other America*, published in 1962. In response to economist John Kenneth Galbraith, who wrote in *The Affluent Society* that only "pockets" of poverty remained, Harrington claimed that as many as 40 million Americans—one-fourth of the population—were poor. He charged:

Visualizing
History

▲ HELP FOR NEGLECTED AMERICANS The War on Poverty reached into Appalachia where poor soil and lack of education affected many lives. *Why did some writers and leaders call for the government to help the poor?*

CHAPTER 24 Camelot to Watergate: 1960–1976 **729**

TEACH
Guided Practice

History Tell students that the "Great Society" was the major theme of President Johnson's administration. Read aloud to students the program that he introduced in a commencement speech at the University of Michigan on May 22, 1964:

"... We have the opportunity to move not only toward the rich society and the powerful society, but upward to the Great Society."

Ask students to explain what hopes Johnson had for Americans. *(a better life for all)* Then have them list the programs of the Great Society in four basic categories: Civil Rights, Education, War on Poverty, and Health. **L2**

🗂 Assign Guided Reading Activity 24-2.

Did You Know?

President Johnson nominated the first African American, Thurgood Marshall, to the U.S. Supreme Court in June 1967.

Visualizing
History The government established the poverty level—the income below which a family lacks the means to meet its basic needs.
Answer to Caption: Some contended that it was impossible for many people to escape poverty on their own.

Cooperative Learning Activity

Simulating a Television Broadcast Divide students into groups of five. Have each simulate a television-style broadcast of the 1964 presidential election returns. One member should act as a moderator and the others as reporters at polling places across the United States. The moderator should ask each reporter why Johnson is winning by such a wide margin. Point out that Johnson won 61.1 percent of the electoral vote and captured 44 states, which included African American and Irish constituents. Goldwater carried only Arizona and 5 states in the Deep South. **L2** 📦

Independent Practice

Conducting a Survey

Have students conduct a survey of 12 people who live in their communities. Ask them to find out each person's age, employment, and interests. Have them write a paragraph explaining how each person could benefit from the following Great Society programs: 1964 Equal Opportunity Act, 1965 Immigration Act, 1965 Voting Rights Act, 1965 Elementary and Secondary Education Act, and Medicare. **L1, LEP**

 Assign Workbook Activity 24-2.

Teaching American Portraits

As Cesar Chavez sought support from migrant workers, he reminded them: "No union movement is worth the life of a single grower or his child or a single worker or his child."

Ask students: What turned the tide in Chavez's strike against grape growers? **L1**

GLENCOE
TECHNOLOGY

 **VIDEODISC**

Focus on Government

Side One, Chapter 9
Title: *Citizenship in the United States*
Subject: Concept of Citizenship

Cesar Chavez
1927–1993

★★★★AMERICAN PORTRAITS

Born to Mexican American migrant workers, Cesar Chavez picked crops in the Southwest as a child and young man. At age 25, he began organizing farm workers to win better pay and working conditions.

Early in the 1960s, Chavez founded a union for migrant farm workers and later merged it with another to form the first large-scale organization of farm workers. He then organized a strike against grape growers.

The strike drew national attention as Chavez borrowed tactics from the civil rights movement—marches and a 25-day fast.

Yet the grape growers would not settle. The tide began to turn in 1968 when Chavez asked the American people to boycott grapes. Growers' profits tumbled as consumers began to side with the workers. The strike lasted until 1970, when the growers finally agreed to settle.

> " *The United States contains an underdeveloped nation, a culture of poverty. Its inhabitants do not suffer the extreme poverty of the peasants of Asia . . . yet the mechanism of the misery is similar. They are beyond history, beyond progress, sunk in a paralyzing, maiming routine.* "

Most of the American people knew little of the great mass of human misery, said Harrington. The poor were hidden away in the slums of central cities, in rural areas—especially in Appalachia and the Deep South—and on Native American reservations. Many of the poor were elderly people leading "lives of quiet desperation" in secluded rooms.

It was not possible for these people to "pull themselves up by their bootstraps," Harrington believed. Automation had done away with the jobs of many workers, and small farmers could no longer compete with agribusiness. Then, too, displaced factory workers and farmers did not have the opportunity for the training and work experience needed for new jobs. Further, pensions and Social Security did not adequately cover medical expenses for older citizens.

Johnson Declares War

Johnson announced his strategy in his first State of the Union Address on January 8, 1964: "This administration . . . declares unconditional war on poverty in America." A new Office of Economic Opportunity (OEO) aimed its billion-dollar budget at illiteracy, unemployment, and disease. The OEO-sponsored VISTA (Volunteers in Service to America) sent workers to improve conditions in poor neighborhoods. Job Corps provided training for the unskilled, while Project Head Start helped poor children prepare for school. The Elementary and Secondary Education Act of 1965 gave direct massive federal aid to public and parochial schools. A similar act provided college scholarships for needy students.

The Great Society's War on Poverty extended federal influence into areas that had traditionally been handled by local governments, private enterprise, or religious groups. In some cases OEO was granted power to overrule local governments.

The emphasis was not simply on relief but on helping poor people help themselves. For example, community action programs taught people to organize protests and put pressure on landlords, employers, and even government agencies to effect change.

Cultural Perspectives

Breaking Political Barriers President Johnson named Robert Weaver as head of the Department of Housing and Urban Development. Weaver was the first African American in United States history to serve in a President's cabinet. Lisle Carter, also an African American, was named as assistant secretary in the Department of Health, Education, and Welfare. Encourage students to research the accomplishments of these and other African Americans who broke political barriers in the 1960s.

Medicare

After nearly 20 years of opposition by those who believed that the government should stay out of health care, Congress passed the Medicare Act. Medicare provided people over age 65 with hospital care. Medical centers were to be set up in areas where such facilities were lacking. The act provided funds for medical schools to increase enrollments and reduce the shortage of doctors.

Immigration Reform

To many thousands of immigrants, the United States already represented a "great society"—a land of newfound opportunity and freedom. The doors of this great society had opened wide to immigrants from northwestern Europe and nearly closed to others, because of a quota system that the United States established in 1924.

Out of 157,000 immigrants admitted each year, Great Britain and Ireland were allotted 83,000; India, with a population of 450 million, and Andorra, with a population of 6,400, each were allotted 100. Presidents Truman, Eisenhower, and Kennedy had been unable to persuade Congress to change this system.

Standing beneath the Statue of Liberty, which welcomed immigrants to the country, Johnson signed the Immigration Act of 1965. The law replaced national quotas with global quotas and favored those with special skills. As a result, immigration to the United States from Asia and Latin America increased sharply.

Under Johnson's leadership Congress passed a great number of other important laws in a few months. "We did reach consensus," he concluded. "I think we did convince the vast majority of Americans that the time for procrastinating had passed."

His programs were well-received in part because people saw benefits for themselves. Some businesspeople, for example, benefited from the War on Poverty because of the increased purchasing power of poor people. Johnson's program also included subsidies to farmers.

Rising Costs End Great Society

Great Society programs required large sums of money. Federal spending for social purposes rose from $54 billion in 1964 to $98 billion in 1968. Federal budget problems and national inflation made Great Society spending an issue for debate. The $20-billion-a-year cost of the Vietnam War made things worse.

Guns and Butter

At first, Johnson tried to finance the war with taxes, explaining that the nation could afford both guns and butter. New social programs and rising war costs made the federal deficit climb to $28 billion by 1968. The President realized that without additional taxes, either social or military programs would have to be cut. He asked Congress for a tax increase. Congress refused unless the President would cut the budget. Johnson chopped $6 billion out of proposed domestic spending, marking the end of the Great Society.

End of an Era

Lyndon Johnson left office in January 1969 a discouraged man. Unable to build a Great Society at home and wage a war at the same time, he had to waive his chance for another term. The American people had rejected Johnson's policies in Vietnam. Supporters of Nixon, he knew, were not sympathetic to the Great Society programs. The nation had become deeply divided.

The 1960s had begun as a time of youth, optimism, and confidence in the future and ended in war, riots, and extreme violence. Three national heroes—President John F. Kennedy, Dr. Martin Luther King, Jr., and Senator Robert Kennedy—had been assassinated. Tens of thousands of young Americans had been killed or wounded in the most unpopular war the United States had ever fought. The New Frontier and the Great Society programs, designed to make life better for the poor and the needy, had also become casualties of the war.

Did You Know?

President Johnson signed the Elementary and Secondary Education Act at his one-room schoolhouse in the presence of his first teacher, the Voting Rights Act in the room where Lincoln had signed the Emancipation Proclamation, and the Immigration Act in the shadow of the Statue of Liberty.

FACT or FICTION?

The Highway Beautification Act allocated funds to control and minimize the use of billboards along the nation's highways.

FACT: Lady Bird Johnson played an active role in convincing Congress to enact the law in 1965. It passed by a single vote.

NATIONAL GEOGRAPHIC SOCIETY

CD-ROM

The Presidents: A Picture History of Our Nation

Tell students that some political scientists and critics believe that had it not been for the Vietnam War, President Johnson might have gone down as the greatest President of the century. Ask students to research the biography of LBJ to find evidence to support or refute this hypothesis.

Critical Thinking Activity

Evaluating Policies Tell students that Franklin Roosevelt appointed 27-year-old Lyndon Baines Johnson to serve as the national youth administrator for the state of Texas. Under Johnson's leadership thousands of boys returned to high school, and thousands more found work on government or private projects. Ask students how Johnson's early experiences under Franklin Roosevelt's New Deal influenced his Great Society legislation in the 1960s. Discuss student answers. **L3**

For additional practice, assign Critical Thinking Skills Activity 24.

ASSESS

Check Understanding

Assign Section 2 Review
as homework or an in-
class activity.

Evaluate

Assign Section
Quiz 24-2 or use the Testmaker to create a custom-
ized quiz.

Reteach

Have students com-
plete Reteaching Activity
24-2.

Enrich

Have students think
about how they would
choose a President if they
were eligible to vote in the
next election. Ask them to
write down three domes-
tic and three global issues
that concern them most.

CLOSE

Tell students that Presi-
dent Johnson thought of
the Great Society as an
extension of the Bill of
Rights, because like the
Bill of Rights, it reflected
the concern of people who
fought for freedom in
their time. Ask: What
rights did the Great
Society seek?

732

Visualizing
History

▲ END OF THE GREAT SOCIETY
President Johnson felt increasing
criticism because of the growing
dissent over the war and increas-
ing opposition within his own party. *What decision
did the President make in 1968 regarding his
political future?*

After the unhappy events of 1968, the
year itself ended on an ironic note of hope
and progress. Late in December 1968 the
United States succeeded in sending the first
astronauts into orbit around the moon. During one of the most difficult years in American history, the nation had scored a great
technological achievement. The photographs sent back from space made planet
Earth seem small, peaceful, and beautiful. It
brought a new feeling to Americans that no
matter how difficult, the problems they
faced could be solved.

Growing Concern for the Environment

During the 1960s, greater emphasis was
placed on the environment. Many conservation projects had been started during the
Great Depression, mostly as a means of providing work for the unemployed. During the
same period, the dust bowl demonstrated
the need for soil conservation. As time went
on, scientists discovered more about the
effects of pollutants on the environment, and
people became more concerned with environmental health.

The individual most responsible for
launching the environmental movement
and prompting new regulations was Rachel
Carson. An aquatic biologist by training, Carson wrote about the sea with great insight.
Her most important book, *Silent Spring*
(1962), dealt with the environment. Long
aware of the threat posed by careless use of
toxic chemicals, she researched carefully and
wrote movingly about how modern industry
and agriculture were poisoning the planet.
Silent Spring sparked a federal investigation
that backed her conclusions and led to
tougher laws regarding harmful chemicals.
Rachel Carson died soon after publication of
Silent Spring, unaware of the ecology movement that her work would inspire.

Section 2 ★ Review

Checking for Understanding

1. **Identify** Barry Goldwater, *The Other America,*
Office of Economic Opportunity, Medicare Act.
2. **Define** consensus.
3. **Explain** the Great Society.
4. **List** four programs that were part of the War
on Poverty.
5. **Identifying Central Issues** How did the war
in Vietnam and violence in the United States
affect Americans' confidence in President
Johnson?

Critical Thinking

6. **Classifying Information** Make a list of guidelines that you would use to classify Americans
who live in poverty. Would your classification
meet government standards?

ACTIVITY

7. Make a pictorial history of the 1960s
using photographs from old magazines.
Write an introduction to your history and
a caption under each photograph.

Answers to SECTION 2 REVIEW

1. Barry Goldwater, 729; *The Other America,* 729;
Office of Economic Opportunity, 730; Medicare
Act, 731
2. All vocabulary words are defined in the
Glossary.
3. battling unemployment, discrimination,
pollution
4. VISTA, Job Corps, Head Start, Elementary

and Secondary Education Act of 1965
5. increased opposition to Johnson; perception
that there was no law and order
6. Answers will vary but students should provide sound reasoning to support their
position.
7. Pictorial histories may focus on social or
historical events and issues.

BUILDING SKILLS
Critical Thinking Skills

Drawing Conclusions

Drawing conclusions allows you to understand ideas that are not stated directly. To draw conclusions, use the available facts and your own knowledge and experience to form a judgment or opinion about the material.

Learning the Skill

Here are some steps to follow in learning to draw conclusions.
- Review the facts that are stated directly.
- Use your knowledge and insight to develop some conclusions about these facts.
- Look for information to check the accuracy of your conclusions.

Read the selection about artist Robert Rauschenberg, then answer the questions that follow.

▼ *KITE* BY ROBERT RAUSCHENBERG, 1963

The decade of the 1960s was a fresh period in American art when artists experimented with a variety of media, materials, techniques, and styles. Robert Rauschenberg mastered the technique of *collage,* a two-dimensional art form using a variety of images.

Rauschenberg came into prominence in the mid-1950s when he began to incorporate pieces of discarded cloth, wood, crumpled printed materials, and other manufactured objects, such as tin cans or bottles, onto his canvases. He referred to these works as "combine paintings."

The bold drips and splatters of Rauschenberg's brushwork, as well as his use of geometric shapes and colors, reflect his debt to abstract expressionism, an artistic movement that came into vogue after World War II. Yet his works also point to the emergence of pop art in the 1960s, an artistic style that used commonplace subject matter from popular culture.

Practicing the Skill

1. Interpret the meaning of Rauschenberg's title *Kite.*

2. How does *Kite* capture the dynamic change of a nation?

3. What conclusions can you draw about the artist's intent in using images of the bald eagle and the military flag? The images of the troops and an army helicopter?

APPLYING THE SKILL

4. Study a physical-political map of your state, then draw conclusions about the economic future. Consider such questions as: How might the state's bodies of water be used in the future? Are they strategic for trade? Is the terrain mountainous or flat? Does the land have agricultural potential? Present your findings in a one-page report.

733

★★

An Imperial Presidency

FOCUS

Bellringer

 Before taking roll, project Section Focus Transparency 24-3 or hand out Section Focus Transparency Activity 24-3. Have students answer the questions. Discuss student responses.

Motivating Activity

Ask students to list the domestic problems Nixon faced and the methods he used to deal with them. **L1**

Vocabulary Precheck

Ask students to define each of the "Key Terms." Have a volunteer consult the dictionary for any unfamiliar words. **L1, LEP**

Use the Vocabulary PuzzleMaker Software to create a crossword puzzle. **L1**

Assign Vocabulary Activity 24.

NATIONAL GEOGRAPHIC SOCIETY

CD-ROM

The Presidents: A Picture History of Our Nation

Have students view "Richard M. Nixon" and use the information to write a brief biography to include in their portfolios.

Setting the Scene

Section Focus

Under Nixon the office of the President became more powerful, threatening the balance among the three branches of government. Although Nixon used presidential powers chiefly in foreign affairs, he also expanded them for his own purposes at home. Although he projected a new image during the campaign, the specter of the ruthless Richard Nixon of his early career haunted the White House. His time in office came to be known as the "imperial presidency."

Objectives

After studying this section, you should be able to

★ describe how Nixon tried to deal with the economic problems of the early 1970s.

★ explain how Nixon handled the war on crime and the energy crisis.

Key Terms

stagflation, balance of payments, new federalism, revenue sharing

◀ SEAL OF THE REPUBLICAN NATIONAL COMMITTEE

To Americans and foreigners alike, the United States in the late 1960s had lost its direction. Not only was it losing the war in Vietnam, but its industries were losing their competitive edge. A sense of defeat and decay became apparent. Deep social, political, and racial divisions were threatening to tear society apart. Richard Nixon claimed that he had a "plan to end the war in Vietnam" and "bring Americans together." His promise of peace in Vietnam and tranquility at home appealed to many.

■ Nixon's Political Career

Richard M. Nixon was the first President in modern times to be elected after having lost a previous bid for the presidency. After losing the 1962 California gubernatorial race, his political career seemed over. In the 1968 campaign, however, he changed his public image. The old Nixon had been intensely partisan and ruthless. When he had run for Congress from California in 1946 as a newly discharged naval officer, he charged that his opponent had strong ties to communist organizations. Political opponents called him opportunistic and self-serving.

The new Nixon, however, impressed observers as calm, broad-minded, and statesmanlike. He promised that his administration would be "open to new ideas, open to men and women of both parties, open to the critics as well as those who support us." Bringing the nation together proved difficult, however. With the Democrats in control of Congress, Nixon saw many of his domestic proposals rejected.

Classroom Resources for SECTION 3

Blackline Masters:

- Reproducible Lesson Plan 24-3
- Guided Reading Activity 24-3
- Vocabulary Activity 24
- Linking Past and Present Activity 24
- Supreme Court Case Studies 29, 32
- Reteaching Activity 24-3
- Section Quiz 24-3

Transparencies:

- Section Focus Transparency 24-3
- Skills Transparency 24

Multimedia:

- Vocabulary PuzzleMaker
- Powers of the President
- The Presidents: A Picture History of Our Nation

The War Against Crime

One of Nixon's domestic successes was his war against crime. During the 1968 campaign, Nixon spoke out against permissive attitudes toward the rights of those accused of crimes. Nixon criticized the record of the Supreme Court under Chief Justice Earl Warren. He denounced Supreme Court decisions that curtailed the powers of the police in the interrogation of suspects and that forbade the use of electronic "bugging" equipment for gathering evidence. Such decisions, Nixon maintained, violated "the first civil right of every American to be free of domestic violence." He promised to fill vacancies on the Supreme Court with judges who would not "weaken the peace forces as against the criminal forces."

Nixon eventually succeeded in his campaign to change the liberal thrust of the Court. When Chief Justice Warren resigned shortly after Nixon took office, the President nominated Warren Burger, a respected conservative judge, to take his place. He also placed three other conservative justices on the Court. The Burger Court, known to critics as the Nixon Court, did not abolish the protections of criminal suspects set up by the Warren Court. It did, however, whittle them down. Its harder line against criminals was dramatically revealed when it reversed the opinion of the Warren Court that capital punishment was a violation of the Bill of Rights.

Nixon's Economic Policies

Nixon inherited difficult economic problems. The combined costs of President Johnson's War on Poverty and the Vietnam War had produced a large federal budget deficit and mounting inflation. Between 1964 and 1969, the dollar lost one-fifth of its purchasing power.

Stagflation

The President tackled inflation by curtailing the supply of money. By the end of 1970, however, it was apparent that the plan was not working. Restricting the supply of money drove interest rates up, and higher interest rates discouraged investment. Unemployment increased, and the stock market

Visualizing History

▲ THE BURGER COURT The Supreme Court is generally referred to by the name of its chief justice. Thus, in 1969, when Warren E. Burger became chief justice, the Supreme Court became known as the Burger Court. *Why had President Nixon criticized the Warren Court?*

TEACH

Guided Practice

Interpreting Primary Sources Present the following excerpt from Nixon's acceptance speech:

"When the strongest nation in the world can be tied down for four years in a war in Vietnam with no end in sight, when the richest nation in the world can't manage its own economy, when the nation with the greatest tradition of the rule of law is plagued by unprecedented racial violence, . . . then it's time for new leadership for the United States of America."

Have students clarify Nixon's goals during his presidency. *(unity, "law and order," peace, economic prosperity)* Then ask them to give an example from Section 3 of how Nixon addressed each goal. **L3**

🗀 Assign Guided Reading Activity 24-3.

Visualizing History President Nixon made four appointments to the Supreme Court. He appointed Burger, Harry Blackmun, Lewis Powell, and William Rehnquist.
Answer to Caption: He criticized its permissive attitude toward the rights of those accused of crime and denounced the curtailing of police powers.

🗀 Assign Supreme Court Case Studies 29, 32: *Escobedo v. Illinois* (1964); *Miranda v. Arizona* (1966).

Critical Thinking Activity

Writing a Persuasive Speech Ask students to write a persuasive speech in which they critique Nixon's plans to fight inflation and unemployment. Students may use the text, encyclopedias, and historical works to supplement their arguments. Have volunteers read their speeches to the class. **L2**

🗀 Assign Writer's Guidebook Lessons 1–6.

Linking Past and Present

★★★★★★★★★★★★★★★

Shopping Malls

A 1973 report on New Jersey's Cherry Hill Mall observed that the shopping mall had become to the suburb what Main Street once was to the small town—the focus of community life.

Then

Something for Everyone

Mall construction was at a peak during the early 1970s.

Cities and suburbs across the United States became home to enclosed malls featuring, under one roof, a fairly predictable array of small specialty stores for books, gifts, and shoes.

Large malls typically included major department stores as dependable "anchors" for sales and customers, as well as several popular restaurants. Malls were enormously successful in not only attracting shoppers, but also walkers and joggers.

Now

A City Under One Roof

Compared to its early counterpart, the mall in the 1990s grew in size and in scope—serving as an entertainment complex as well as a retail center. The nation's largest is Bloomington, Minnesota's Mall

▲ MALL OF AMERICA, BLOOMINGTON, MINNESOTA

of America. Opened in the summer of 1992, the mall contains 350 stores, 8 night clubs, a 14-screen movie theater, an 18-hole miniature golf course, and a 7-acre amusement park over its 4.2 million square feet. On average, the mall attracts more than 700,000 shoppers per week—200,000 on Saturday nights alone. A special Christmas season promotion offers bargain airfares to passengers who fly in for a day of shopping.

★★★

declined. The slowdown in business activity reduced federal revenues, and inflation accelerated. This economic slowdown, coupled with inflation, was called **stagflation.**

To meet the problem of stagflation, Nixon turned to other, less conservative measures. In August 1971 he announced his New Economic Policy, which called for a 90-day freeze on wages, prices, and rents. This was followed by a system of wage and price controls in November. In January 1973 the President relaxed controls, and prices rose sharply. In response, a new freeze was imposed in June.

President Nixon also took steps to end the recession by stimulating the economy. He proposed tax cuts for both businesses and individuals, hoping that when the demand went up, production would rise and unemployment would fall. After making some revisions in the President's proposals, Congress enacted tax cuts in December 1971.

The President also used deficit spending to fight recession.

These measures, however, failed to solve the problem of stagflation. Although the tax cuts and deficit spending helped to ease the recession, they added to inflation. On the other hand, while the controls slowed inflation for a time, they did little to help the economy grow or to lower unemployment.

A Balance of Payments Deficit

Inflation caused prices to rise not only on domestic goods, but on exports. So, fewer exports were purchased. This resulted in a balance of payments deficit. The **balance of payments** is the difference between the money paid to and received from other nations. In this case, the nation was spending more than it received. Between 1970 and 1971, the nation's balance of payments deficit jumped from $4 billion to $22 billion.

The deficit was evidence that the United States had lost its dominance in world markets. Between 1950 and 1970, for example, the United States's share of world automobile production dropped from 76 to 31 percent, and the same phenomenon was occurring in the textile, shoe, and electrical equipment industries.

A serious effect of the balance of payments deficit was that it weakened other nations' confidence in the value of the dollar. Because world trade depends on stable money and because the dollar was the major currency in the world, the dollar crisis threatened to disrupt trade.

Trying to improve the economic situation, Nixon acted decisively. To combat inflation, in August 1971 he announced, as noted earlier, a 90-day freeze on prices and wages. To discourage imports, he placed an additional duty of 10 percent on all goods purchased from abroad. He also allowed the dollar to decline in value in relation to foreign currencies, making it more expensive for Americans to buy goods from other countries. Therefore, goods made in the United States became cheaper than foreign-made goods, and that promoted exports.

Although Nixon's policies brought some relief, inflation, chronic unemployment, and the loss of foreign markets remained a problem throughout his presidency. The measures also caused ill will in nations that depended on American markets for their products.

The New Federalism

Nixon also announced his **new federalism,** which was intended to reduce the federal government's role in the economy and turn many of its tasks over to state and local governments. Following the President's lead, Congress passed a series of **revenue-sharing** bills that granted federal funds to local agencies to use as they saw fit.

■ The Energy Crisis

Another problem concerned energy. In the fall of 1973, Arab nations placed an embargo on crude oil shipments from the Middle East.

The purpose of the embargo was to force the United States to stop supporting Israel in its struggle with the Arab states. Support for Israel did not change, but the embargo produced an energy crisis in America—and near panic. In some areas the price of petroleum shot up nearly 400 percent, and there were shortages of gasoline for cars and heating oil for homes, schools, and businesses.

Although the United States had about one-sixteenth of the world's population, Americans consumed about one-third of the world's energy. Most of this energy came from such nonrenewable resources as oil, gas, and coal. Coal reserves were abundant in America but supplied less than 20 percent of the nation's energy needs. By 1973, the United States was importing about 6 million barrels of oil each day, or about 36 percent of the oil needed to heat homes and to keep factories and automobiles running.

President Nixon announced a plan to make the country self-sufficient in energy by 1980. He called for higher taxes on imported oil and encouraged Americans to take conservation measures, such as lowering their thermostats at home and at work. Congress passed a law requiring states to lower the speed limit on highways to 55 miles per hour to save gasoline and approved the construction of a pipeline in Alaska for the shipment of newly discovered oil to refineries. Congress provided some tax incentives to

▼ SIGN OF THE TIMES

Temporarily... 10 GALLONS PER CUSTOMER We appreciate your business & cooperation.

ASSESS
Check Understanding
Assign Section 3 Review as homework or an in-class activity.

Evaluate
 Assign Section Quiz 24-3 or use the Testmaker to create a customized quiz.

Reteach
Have students complete Reteaching Activity 24-3.

ABCNEWS
INTERACTIVE™

VIDEODISC

Powers of the President

Side Two, Chapter 9
Title: *World Leader*
Subject: Role of President as a world leader; includes Nixon in China

 CURRICULUM CONNECTION

Environmental Studies
Industrial nations that make up 25 percent of the world's population consume about 75 percent of the world's energy, 85 percent of its forest products, and 70 percent of its steel.

Sidelight: The Moon Landing

During the Nixon administration, the United States reached the moon. On July 16, 1969, the U.S. spacecraft *Apollo 11* left Cape Kennedy. Four days later Neil Armstrong, Edwin Aldrin, and Michael Collins became the first men to reach the moon. As Americans watched on television, two of the astronauts planted an American flag. Neil Armstrong, stepping onto the moon's surface, commented, "That's one small step for a man, one giant leap for mankind." Nixon called the astronauts and said, "Because of what you have done the heavens have become a part of man's world."

CLOSE

Summarize the section by telling students that Nixon portrayed himself as a promoter of peace. Ask: In what way did he accomplish this at the beginning of his term?

Visualizing
Ⓗistory Congress approved construction of an Alaska pipeline to help reduce the nation's dependence on imported oil. Construction of the 800-mile (1,287.2-km) pipeline was completed in 1977. It can transport up to 2 million barrels of crude oil a day from the Arctic Coastal Plain to the port of Valdez. From there the oil is shipped by tanker to refineries. **Answer to Caption:** higher taxes on imported oil, new conservation measures

Visualizing
Ⓗistory

▲ **ENERGY CRISIS** One of the nation's most important concerns during the Nixon administration was the energy crisis. Long lines of cars at gas stations were a sign of the times. *What actions did the administration take to conserve energy?*

encourage energy research and put the nation on year-round daylight saving time for two years.

After the Arab nations lifted the oil embargo in March 1974, most Americans forgot about the energy crisis mentality. They began once again to use fuel in increasing quantities. However, fuel prices began a steep rise as the oil shortage continued. In the 1960s the major oil-exporting nations had formed the Organization of Petroleum Exporting Countries (OPEC). By 1970 OPEC had begun to raise prices, and over the next decade the cost of oil increased from less than $2 a barrel to more than $30 a barrel. The increases in the price of oil by the OPEC members contributed to the problems that plagued the American economy throughout the 1970s.

Section 3 ★ Review

Checking for Understanding

1. **Identify** Warren Burger.

2. **Define** stagflation, balance of payments, new federalism, revenue sharing.

3. **Point out** how Nixon affected the criminal justice system.

4. **Describe** two features of Nixon's economic policies.

Critical Thinking

5. **Evaluating Policy** Write an evaluation of Nixon's policy for handling inflation.

ACTIVITY

6. Imagine you are one of President Nixon's speechwriters. Write a press release in which you detail the President's plans to fight inflation and unemployment.

Answers to SECTION 3 REVIEW

1. Warren Burger, 735
2. All vocabulary words are defined in the Glossary.
3. He placed conservative justices on Supreme Court, changing the Court's liberal thrust and diminishing the rights of criminal suspects.
4. reduced federal spending and curtailed the supply of money

5. Answers will vary. Though Nixon's policies brought some relief, inflation, unemployment, and the loss of foreign markets remained problems.
6. Press releases will vary but should show understanding of administration policies.

★★★

The Watergate Scandal

Setting the Scene

Section Focus

The public disclosure of Richard Nixon's involvement in the Watergate scandal culminated in his resignation from office. It also led Congress and the Supreme Court to reassert their constitutional powers. Although confidence in the government was shaken by Watergate, the Bicentennial, or the 200th anniversary of the American Revolution, was cause for celebration.

Objectives

After studying this section, you should be able to

★ explain how the constitutional process solved the Watergate crisis.

★ list the ways in which Congress sought to reassert its constitutional powers.

Key Terms

executive privilege, impound, deregulation

◀ STREET SIGN, WASHINGTON, D.C.

*N*ot surprisingly, the Republican party nominated President Nixon as its candidate in the election of 1972. Nixon ran against Senator George McGovern of South Dakota, who won the Democratic nomination with the support of a coalition of activists—young people, African Americans, and women.

■ A Crisis in the Presidency

Almost from the beginning, however, the McGovern campaign derailed itself. McGovern's running mate, Senator Thomas Eagleton, was forced to withdraw when it was disclosed that he had been hospitalized for depression. In addition, Democratic party regulars and labor union leaders were cool, if not hostile, toward the liberal McGovern's candidacy.

In contrast, President Nixon conducted a perfect campaign. The almost-complete withdrawal of United States troops from Vietnam defused the war issue, and the summits in Beijing and Moscow signaled an easing of cold war tensions. Moreover, the President solidified his support among "middle Americans" by calling for law and order, by opposing busing, and by making continuous appeals to patriotism.

On Election Day the President received 61 percent of the popular vote and won every electoral vote except those of Massachusetts and the District of Columbia.

CREEP

It was later learned, however, that this tremendous victory was not won entirely fairly. During the campaign the President and his political advisers organized the Committee to Reelect the President (CREEP) and collected more than $50 million for Nixon's reelection campaign, some

CHAPTER 24 Camelot to Watergate: 1960–1976   **739**

Classroom Resources for SECTION 4

Blackline Masters:
- Reproducible Lesson Plan 24-4
- Guided Reading Activity 24-4
- Primary and Secondary Source Readings, pp. 68–69
- Supreme Court Case Study 42
- Enrichment Activity 24
- Geography in History Activity 24
- Reteaching Activity 24-4

- Section Quiz 24-4
Transparencies:
- Section Focus Transparency 24-4
Multimedia:
- Testmaker
- Powers of the President
- Powers of the Congress

LESSON PLAN
SECTION 4, 739–743

FOCUS
Bellringer

Before taking roll, project Section Focus Transparency 24-4 or hand out Section Focus Transparency Activity 24-4. Have students answer the questions. Discuss student responses.

Motivating Activity

Refer students to those parts of the Constitution that deal with impeachment. (*Article I, Sections 2 and 3, Article II, Section 4*) For what reasons may a President be impeached? (*conviction of treason, bribery, or other high crimes and misdemeanors*) Ask students if they can identify the only President who was ever impeached. (*Andrew Johnson*) Point out that Nixon was close to being impeached when he resigned. **L2**

Vocabulary Precheck

Ask students to define each of the "Key Terms." Have a volunteer consult the dictionary for any unfamiliar words. **L1, LEP**

ABCNEWS
INTERACTIVE™

VIDEODISC

Powers of the President

Side Two, Chapter 23
Title: *Watergate Scandal*
Subject: Montage of news reports about the scandal

TEACH
Guided Practice

History Remind students that unlike Kennedy and Johnson, Nixon had been more concerned with foreign affairs than with domestic issues. **L2**

Visualizing
istory Jeb Magruder, a Nixon aide, later said that "the cover-up, thus, was immediate and automatic. No one ever considered that there would not be a cover-up."
Answer to Caption: the principle that the President does not have to provide information to other branches of the government

---

VIDEODISC

Powers of the President

Side Two, Chapter 24
Title: *Presidential Denials*
Subject: Nixon denies involvement in Watergate

Side 2, Chapter 25
Title: *Watergate Committee Hearings*
Subject: Montage of statements

of which was illegally received. Some campaign contributions were used to finance "dirty tricks" against the Democrats.

The Watergate Break-in

A group of CREEP employees were caught "bugging" the offices of the Democratic National Committee in the Watergate building in Washington, D.C. Although the President's press secretary dismissed the break-in as a "third-rate burglary," this seemingly insignificant incident had serious consequences for the President.

Rumors began to circulate that the President himself had ordered the Watergate break-in. Stories were published in the *Washington Post* and other newspapers that linked key members of the White House staff and CREEP to the break-in. It was reported that key Nixon advisers had paid the Watergate burglars almost $1 million in "hush money" to plead guilty and say nothing else at their trials. To quiet the rumors, the President ordered his attorney general to appoint a special prosecutor, Harvard law professor Archibald Cox, to investigate the case.

The Investigation

At the same time, a special Senate committee began to hold televised hearings on the break-in and other abuses alleged to have been committed during the campaign of 1972. Starting in May 1973, millions of Americans watched in fascination as a parade of witnesses testified about illegal activities carried out by the White House staff and by CREEP. Perhaps the most startling discovery was that the President tape-recorded most of the conversations he had in the Oval Office.

Following these revelations, federal grand juries indicted members of the Nixon administration for their illegal activities, including the unauthorized wiretapping, burglaries, illegal campaign contributions, and the bribing of witnesses. Eventually 25 people connected with the administration—including former Attorney General John Mitchell and two of Nixon's closest White House aides, H. R. Haldeman and John D. Erlichman—were convicted and served prison terms for Watergate-related crimes.

■ The President Answers

Month after month President Nixon continued to deny any involvement in Watergate. Claiming **executive privilege,** or the principle that the President does not have to give information to other branches of the government, Nixon refused to turn over the White House tapes to the special prosecutor. In October 1973, he offered to provide written summaries of the tapes.

Visualizing **istory** ▲ WATERGATE The Watergate hearings led to criminal charges against several top White House aides, including H. R. Haldeman (left) and Jeb Stuart Magruder (speaking at hearing). President Nixon disavowed knowledge of the break-in. *What is executive privilege?*

Cultural Perspectives

African Americans and Politics President Nixon's landslide victory over George McGovern in the 1972 election occurred despite the fact that some 86 percent of the African American vote went to McGovern. However, African Americans did achieve some electoral successes—their number in Congress increased from 12 to 15, and Barbara Jordan of Houston, Texas, and Andrew Young of Atlanta, Georgia, became the first African Americans elected to Congress from the South since Reconstruction.

The Saturday Night Massacre

When the special prosecutor insisted on having the tapes, Nixon ordered the attorney general to remove Cox. Both the attorney general and his top assistant resigned rather than carry out the President's order. Finally Nixon found a Justice Department official who was willing to fire Cox. The dismissal of the special prosecutor became known as the "Saturday Night Massacre," and it provoked a wave of public protest as well as the first serious calls for Nixon's impeachment.

Agnew Resigns

October 1973 proved to be a disastrous time for Richard Nixon for other reasons as well. His Vice President, Spiro Agnew, was forced to resign in disgrace. A grand jury found that Agnew, while governor of Maryland, had taken bribes from contractors who did business with the state. It was further revealed that Agnew continued to receive such payments while he was Vice President. Nixon nominated Gerald Ford, the Republican leader of the House of Representatives, as the new Vice President.

Nixon Proclaims Innocence

In an effort to quiet public outrage over the Saturday Night Massacre, Nixon appointed another special prosecutor in November 1973. In April 1974, the President released written transcripts of 47 tape-recorded conversations. Even though the transcripts had been heavily edited, many believed the tapes indicated the President

• •

Footnotes to History

Impeachment in American History

The House of Representatives has voted articles of impeachment against 15 officials. Twelve of those impeached were federal judges. The others are Senator William Blount of Tennessee in 1797, President Andrew Johnson in 1868, and Secretary of War William Belknap in 1876. The Senate has convicted 7 of the impeached judges.

▲ **President Nixon leaves the White House**

had indeed been involved in covering up the Watergate scandal. Nevertheless, the President still continued to proclaim his innocence:

> “ *If read with an open and fair mind and read together with the record of actions I took, these transcripts will show that what I have stated since the beginning to be the truth . . . my actions were directed toward finding the facts and seeing that justice was done, fairly and according to the law.* ”

In July the Supreme Court ruled that the President had to turn over the tapes themselves, not just their transcripts. A month later Nixon complied and handed over the tapes. One tape provided direct evidence that on June 23, 1972, only six days after the Watergate break-in, the President had arranged a cover-up. With this news, even the President's strongest supporters conceded that there was sufficient evidence to

VIDEODISC

Powers of the Congress

Side One, Chapter 39
Title: *Impeachment*
Subject: The process of impeachment; specifically deals with President Richard Nixon

Independent Practice

Expressing Opinions Ask students to answer the following question in a brief essay: Did the Watergate scandal, ending in the first resignation by an American President, prove that the system works, or that we need a new system? Explain your answer. **L2**

📁 Assign Guided Reading Activity 24-4.

📁 Assign Primary and Secondary Source Readings, pp. 68–69: "Watergate Is Linked to the White House."

VIDEODISC

Powers of the President

Side Two, Chapter 26
Title: *House Judiciary Committee*
Subject: Committee votes articles of impeachment

Critical Thinking Activity

Expressing an Opinion Tell students that government officials, such as state governors and the President, can grant reprieves and pardons to individuals convicted of offenses except in impeachment cases. A pardon releases the individual from any punishment due for the crime committed, but it does not free the person from any implied guilt. President Ford's pardon of Richard Nixon was one of the most controversial pardons in American history. Ask students: If you had been President, would you have pardoned President Nixon? Why or why not? **L1**

support impeachment. They advised Nixon that it seemed certain the House would impeach him and that the Senate would find him guilty. On August 8, 1974, Nixon announced on national television that he would resign. He also expressed hope that his departure would begin the process of healing the country.

Ford Becomes President

The next day Gerald Ford was sworn in as the thirty-eighth President. President Ford appointed Nelson Rockefeller, former governor of New York, as his Vice President, making them the first unelected presidential team in the nation's history.

At first, President Ford inspired public confidence. He assured a joint session of Congress that his administration would be free of "illegal tappings, eavesdropping, buggings, or break-ins." The new President seemed to be a decent, candid, and trustworthy man.

A month after entering office, however, Ford damaged his public image by granting Richard Nixon an unconditional pardon for all crimes he committed or may have committed while in office. Ford insisted that he was acting not out of sympathy for Nixon, but in the public interest. He wanted to avoid the publicity and national division that a trial would create. Nevertheless, the pardon aroused fierce and widespread criticism of the new President.

Congress Reasserts Its Authority

When he took office, Gerald Ford promised to adopt a policy of "communication, conciliation, compromise, and cooperation" with Congress. He expected good relations with Congress, since he had served for 25 years as a representative and almost a decade as House Republican leader. However, the President and Congress were often at odds because Ford was a conservative, and liberal Democrats controlled both houses of Congress. In addition, the new President confronted a Congress that was determined to reassert its authority over what some critics called the "imperial presidency."

Congress Attacks Executive Privilege

To counter the trend toward greater presidential power and curb future abuses, Congress passed a series of laws. In the last year of the Nixon administration, as Watergate weakened the President, Congress attempted to regain some of its power. In November 1973, it passed the War Powers Act in spite of President Nixon's veto. This law required that the President report to Congress within 48 hours after sending combat troops abroad or after engaging in any military action. Unless Congress approved his action, the President had to withdraw all troops within 60 days. After the Watergate crisis, Congress passed the Congressional Budget and Impoundment Control Act of 1974, which allowed Congress to force the President to spend any appropriations that he attempted to **impound,** or withhold, unless he could justify his action to both houses.

Quarrels Over the Economy

One of the biggest problems facing President Ford and Congress was the economic recession. To Ford, inflation and the nation's dependence on foreign oil were the greatest threats to recovery. The Democratic Congress was more alarmed by the highest rates of unemployment and the lowest levels of productivity since the Great Depression of the 1930s.

Like Nixon, President Ford wanted to cut spending on social welfare programs and adopt an energy program. He favored **deregulation,** or removing price controls, of gas and oil. This would cause a rise in prices so people would use less. Increased profits would go toward helping companies find alternate forms of energy. Congress, however, did not cooperate. Ford, in turn, prevented the enactment of liberal Democratic legislation by the use of the veto power.

Ford's Foreign Policy

At first, Congress allowed the President greater leeway in foreign policy than it had to past officeholders. Ford met with leaders of NATO and the Warsaw Pact to sign the

Helsinki Accords in August 1975. Under the terms of the accords, the parties recognized the borders of the countries of Eastern Europe and committed themselves to respect and protect the human rights of their citizens.

Soon, however, in foreign policy, as in domestic affairs, Ford came into conflict with the Democratic-controlled Congress. In 1975 Congress refused President Ford's request for additional funds to aid South Vietnam and Cambodia in their continuing civil wars. As a result, the Cambodian government surrendered to the repressive Khmer Rouge forces on April 17. Twelve days later the North Vietnamese and the Vietcong overran Saigon and forced the government of South Vietnam to surrender. Communist regimes were now in control everywhere in Indochina except Thailand, which remained an ally.

■ The Bicentennial

Despite difficulties with Congress, President Ford headed for Boston to participate in the opening ceremonies of the Bicentennial, celebrating the nation's 200th birthday. As July 4, 1976, approached, most people in the United States caught the bicentennial spirit. Cities, towns, and villages held parades and concerts and displayed fireworks. A procession of Conestoga wagons traveled to Valley Forge, Pennsylvania, and eighteenth-century sailing ships from many countries majestically sailed into New York Harbor on the Fourth of July.

 **Visualizing History**

▲ THE NATION'S BICENTENNIAL In 1976 Americans were anxious to put the tragedy of the Vietnam War and the Watergate affair behind them. A bicentennial spirit swept the nation as millions participated in parades, fireworks displays, and other activities. *Who was the nation's President during this time?*

As the Bicentennial ended, the nation felt a new sense of hopefulness. It knew that the constitutional system had curbed the abuses of the imperial presidency. The people of the United States were proud of achievements such as the space program, and they began to regain their sense of confidence.

Section 4 ★ Review

Checking for Understanding

1. **Identify** George McGovern, CREEP, Archibald Cox, Gerald Ford, War Powers Act, Helsinki Accords.

2. **Define** executive privilege, impound, deregulation.

3. **Explain** why President Nixon resigned.

4. **Summarize** actions Congress took to reassert its authority.

Critical Thinking

5. **Interpreting Viewpoints** Explain why many Americans, although dismayed by the Watergate scandal, felt proud of the way their government functioned during the crisis.

ACTIVITY

6. Write a poem of two stanzas. In the first stanza, describe Bicentennial America. In the second, describe America today.

Reteach

Have students write an editorial on congressional reassertion of power after the Watergate scandal. Have them share their editorials.

📁 Have students complete Reteaching Activity 24-4.

Enrich

Have students collect newspaper articles or present a book report on the Watergate affair. A suggested reading is Robert Woodward and Carl Bernstein's *The Final Days*. Reports should include an analysis of Nixon's behavior at the end of this crisis.

📁 Have students complete Enrichment Activity 24.

📁 Assign Geography in History Activity 24.

CLOSE

Tell students that the 1970s have often been called the "years of trials." Ask them if they think this is an accurate description of this period and why. Discuss student answers.

Visualizing History Americans celebrated the anniversary of the birth of their country in 1976. In 1986 the country celebrated the one-hundredth anniversary of the placing of the Statue of Liberty in New York Harbor.
Answer to Caption: Gerald Ford

Answers to SECTION 4 REVIEW

1. George McGovern, 739; CREEP, 739; Archibald Cox, 740; Gerald Ford, 741; War Powers Act, 742; Helsinki Accords, 743
2. All vocabulary words are defined in the Glossary.
3. He was faced with probable impeachment and conviction for his role in the cover-up.
4. passed the War Powers Act and the Congressional Budget and Impoundment Control Act, refused to go along with proposals to cut social spending or adopt energy plan
5. Despite the scandal many Americans were glad that their system of checks and balances worked to force Nixon's resignation and check the executive branch's power.
6. Poems should focus on comparing the eras.

743

GLENCOE
TECHNOLOGY

VIDEODISC

Use the MindJogger Videoquiz to review students' knowledge.

MindJogger Videoquiz

Chapter 24
Disc 3, Side B

Available in VHS.

Using Vocabulary
Terms should be used correctly.

Reviewing Facts
1. mixed idealism with realism
2. Area Redevelopment Act, Housing Act of 1961, increased funding for NASA; defeat of proposals for a new cabinet department and a health insurance
3. Office of Economic Opportunity, Medicare Act, Immigration Act of 1965, Civil Rights Act of 1964
4. Growing inflation led to fewer exports.
5. The federal government's role in the economy was reduced, and many of its tasks were turned over to state and local governments.
6. Watergate break-in, appointment of a special prosecutor, Senate hearings, indictments of administration officials, Saturday Night Massacre, release of June 23, 1972, tape transcript

Using Vocabulary

Each of the terms below has significance for the concept of presidential power. Use each of these terms in a sentence, describing how it is related to this concept.

mandate   executive privilege
pragmatist   impound
consensus

Reviewing Facts

1. **Describe** Kennedy's presidential style.
2. **State** two legislative victories and two legislative setbacks for Kennedy.
3. **Identify** four achievements of the Johnson administration.
4. **Describe** why there was a decrease in United States dominance of world markets.
5. **Explain** the significance of Nixon's new federalism.
6. **Chart** the sequence of events that led to Nixon's resignation.

Understanding Concepts

Domestic Policy

1. Examine the Kennedy and Johnson presidencies and describe how an election mandate affected each man's ability to govern.
2. Explain the importance of political consensus to President Johnson.

Presidential Power

3. What function did secrecy serve in the Nixon presidency? Why did some Americans and members of Congress resent this tactic?
4. When President Nixon resigned over Watergate, some nations expressed astonishment that Americans would force their highest leader to step down over a "relatively small offense." Is it important for our nation to hold politicians accountable for their actions? Explain.

Critical Thinking

1. **Comparing and Contrasting** Explain how Kennedy and Johnson differed in their relationships with Congress.
2. **Drawing Conclusions** What are the lessons of the Watergate scandal? Would you agree that our system of government was vindicated by this affair? What long-term repercussions do you think Watergate had on Americans' views of government and politicians?
3. **Analyzing Fine Art** Study the painting that appears on this page, then answer the questions that follow.
   a. What do you think the artist is expressing in this painting?
   b. How does the artist lead your eye around the composition?
   c. Do you like this painting? Why or why not?

Understanding Concepts
1. Kennedy lack of a clear mandate prevented passage of domestic program. Johnson won a clear mandate and under his leadership through consensus, Congress passed many important laws.
2. With skilled bargaining and compromise, Johnson took over the responsibilities of the presidency with firmness and strength.
3. Nixon used secrecy to control foreign policy. This tactic caused resentment among those who disagreed with his policies.
4. Answers will vary. Americans pride themselves on an egalitarian system of government in which all members are equally accountable.

History and Geography

Reforms in the 1960s and 1970s

1. **Human/Environment Interaction** What was the purpose of urban renewal?

2. **Region** What geographic areas' problems was the War on Poverty formed to combat?

3. **Movement** How did quota reform affect levels of immigration to the United States?

4. **Human/Environment Interaction** What percentage of the nation's energy needs did America's coal reserves supply?

Interdisciplinary Activity: Government

Cooperative Learning

You will work in small groups to investigate testimony before the Senate subcommittee on Watergate. Each group member should select a different witness to research. Use the actual transcripts of the hearings to discover the process the committee really went through. Then meet together and discuss your findings with the class.

Practicing Skills

Drawing Conclusions

Study the map on this page, then answer the questions that follow.

1. Who were the candidates in the 1968 election?

2. Speculate on why Wallace made his best showing in Southern states.

3. Compare this map with the election map on page 724. In both elections, the popular votes are relatively close, but the electoral votes are not so close. Draw conclusions why this was so.

4. Based on this map alone, what conclusions can you draw about the strength of the Democratic party at the national level?

5. What conclusions can you draw about the strength of the Republican party at the national level?

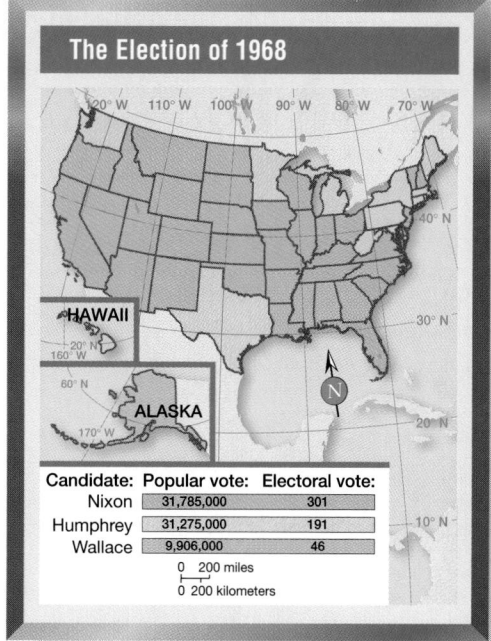

The Election of 1968

Candidate:	Popular vote:	Electoral vote:
Nixon	31,785,000	301
Humphrey	31,275,000	191
Wallace	9,906,000	46

0   200 miles
0   200 kilometers

6. Are the following statements valid conclusions?

- Richard Nixon owed his victory to strong support in the Far West and from New England.

- George Wallace received his strongest support from Midwestern voters.

Writing ABOUT History

Using Your Journal

Review your journal notes about corruption in the government as evidenced by the Watergate scandal. Write a paragraph describing how public awareness of that corruption affected people's views during later scandals in government. To answer, you may have to do extra research.

2. Appalachia and the Deep South
3. It increased immigration from Asia and Latin America.
4. less than 20 percent

Cooperative Learning

You might encourage students to present their findings in a documentary in which students explain the process used by the Senate subcommittee.

Practicing Skills

1. Nixon, Humphrey, and Wallace
2. Wallace was best known in the South.
3. The margin is larger in the electoral vote because usually all electoral votes of a state go to the winning candidate.
4. It had a weak following.
5. It had a strong following.
6. no, no

Writing ABOUT History

Using Your Journal

Students should mention that people were deeply discouraged with government officials as a result of the Watergate scandal. Many hoped that new leaders would restore their confidence.

Critical Thinking

1. A coalition of Southern Democrats prevented Kennedy from getting much of his domestic program passed. Johnson was more comfortable with members of Congress and continued that relationship as President.

2. Answers include abuse of power and the importance of our checks-and-balances system. One repercussion is cynicism.

3. **a.** Artist is expressing his or her ideas about the U.S.

b. Students should note that the flag helps the viewer focus on the open area.

c. Answers will vary.

History and Geography

1. to improve neighborhoods in inner cities

Chapter Bonus Test Question

Ask: Give examples of Great Society legislation that makes a difference in your life or the lives of people in your community. (*Possible answers include the Office of Economic Opportunity, the Elementary and Secondary Education Act, and Medicare.*)

Daily Lesson Objectives	Teacher Classroom Resources	Multimedia
SECTION 1 **Crisis of Confidence** **1 Day** pp. 748–753 1. State reasons for the American public's crisis of confidence. 2. Explain how moral principles directed President Carter's domestic and foreign policy.	Reproducible Lesson Plan 25-1 *Guided Reading Activity 25-1 Concept Mapping Activities 25-A, 25-B *Vocabulary Activity 25 Primary and Secondary Source Readings, pp. 70–71 Workbook Activity 25-1 Reteaching Activity 25-1 *Section Quiz 25-1	Section Focus Transparency 25-1 Chapter Concepts Transparencies 25-A, 25-B Testmaker Vocabulary PuzzleMaker MindJogger Videoquiz Powers of the President Focus on Government The Presidents: A Picture History of Our Nation
SECTION 2 **A Conservative Shift** **1 Day** pp. 754–760 1. Explain the conservative shift in Americans' political convictions in the late 1970s and early 1980s. 2. Describe President Reagan's economic recovery plan, which included cutting taxes and reducing spending. 3. Describe Reagan's foreign policy regarding the Soviet Union.	Reproducible Lesson Plan 25-2 *Guided Reading Activity 25-2 Cooperative Learning Activity 25 Critical Thinking Skills Activity 25 Linking Past and Present Activity 25 Political Cartoons in American History Activity 28 Chapter Skills Activity 25 Workbook Activity 25-2 Reteaching Activity 25-2 *Section Quiz 25-2	Section Focus Transparency 25-2 Skills Transparency 25 Testmaker Communism and the Cold War The Presidents: A Picture History of Our Nation
SECTION 3 **A New Presidency** **1 Day** pp. 762–768 1. Explain how the spread of democracy led to the formation of a new world order. 2. Describe America's role in the post–cold war world. 3. Discuss the reasons for discord between the legislative and executive branches of government under Bush.	Reproducible Lesson Plan 25-3 *Guided Reading Activity 25-3 Outline Map Resource Book, p. 34 Primary and Secondary Source Readings, pp. 73–74 Chapter Map Activity 25 Workbook Activity 25-3 Geography in History Activity 25 Enrichment Activity 25 Reteaching Activity 25-3 *Section Quiz 25-3	Section Focus Transparency 25-3 Map Transparency 25 Testmaker Communism and the Cold War Lessons of War The Presidents: A Picture History of Our Nation
CHAPTER REVIEW AND EVALUATION **1 Day**	Chapter 25 Test, Forms A and B Spanish Chapter 25 Summary Performance Assessment Activity 25	MindJogger Videoquiz Student Self-Test & Review Software *Chapter 25 Audiocassette Activity and Test

*Also available in Spanish

 OUT OF TIME? If time does not permit teaching the entire chapter, use the Chapter 25 Summary on pages 800–801 and the Chapter 25 audiocassette (English and Spanish) to point out the main ideas of the chapter.

A complete, 1-page lesson plan is provided for each section in the *Reproducible Lesson Plan* booklet.

Key to Ability Levels

Teaching strategies have been coded for varying learning styles and abilities.

L1 Basic activities for all students

L2 Average activities for average to above-average students

L3 Challenging activities for above-average students

LEP Limited English Proficiency activities

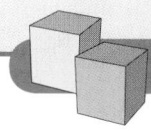

Block Schedule

Block scheduling differs from traditional class scheduling in the amount of time allotted to each period. The extended time frame provided by block scheduling affords you the opportunity to implement a greater number of research-oriented and activity-intense projects to motivate and involve your students. Activities that are particularly suited to use within the block scheduling framework are identified throughout this unit by the following designation:

✔ Performance Assessment Activity

Tracing Major Events Divide the class into small groups and ask each to construct a time line of the major events that shaped American life between 1976 and 1992. The events a group selects can be of national or global significance. Suggest that students use almanacs as well as other sources to research events and compile lists. Then have each group conduct a brainstorming session to put together its final list of events and create the time line. Each group should also write a paragraph defending the choices it made. Encourage groups to share their time lines with the class.

POSSIBLE RUBRIC FEATURES
* Content Information
* Organization
* Evaluation of Evidence
* Written and Oral Communication Skills
* Critical Thinking Skills
* Collaborative Skills

📁 For additional activities, see Performance Assessment Strategies and Activities.

T E A C H E R ' S   C O R N E R

NATIONAL
GEOGRAPHIC
SOCIETY

INDEX TO NATIONAL GEOGRAPHIC MAGAZINE

The following articles may be used for research relating to this chapter:

* "The Brain," by Joel L. Swerdlow, June 1995.
* "Water—The Middle East's Critical Resource," by Priit J. Vesilind, May 1993.
* "Russia: Playing by New Rules," by Mike Edwards, March 1993.
* "Who are the Palestinians?" by Tad Szulc, June 1992.
* "Persian Gulf Pollution: Assessing the Damage One Year Later," by Sylvia A. Earle, February 1992.

* "After the Storm," by Thomas Y. Canby, August 1991.
* "East Europe's Dark Dawn," by Jon Thompson, June 1991.
* "Mother Russia on a New Course," by Mike Edwards, February 1991.
* "Berlin's Ode to Joy," by Priit J. Vesilind, April 1990.
* "The Persian Gulf—Living in Harm's Way," by Thomas J. Abercrombie, May 1988.

NATIONAL GEOGRAPHIC SOCIETY PRODUCTS AVAILABLE FROM GLENCOE

To order the following products for use with this chapter, contact your local Glencoe sales representative or call Glencoe at 1-800-334-7344:

* *The Presidents: A Picture History of Our Nation* (CD-ROM)
* *GTV: A Geographic Perspective on American History* (Videodisc)

* *GTV: The American People: Fabric of a Nation* (Videodisc)

ADDITIONAL NATIONAL GEOGRAPHIC SOCIETY PRODUCTS

To order the following products for use with this chapter, call National Geographic Society at 1-800-368-2728:

* *The Soviet World in Transition* (Filmstrip)
* *The Changing Faces of Communism Series: Poland* (Video)
* *The Rise and Fall of the Soviet Union* (Video)

* *Russia: After the U.S.S.R.* (Video)
* *1945–1989: The Cold War* (Video)

Recording Journal Notes

To get students started, suggest that they use as headings these conservative policies: reduction in taxes, reduction in government spending, higher defense spending.

Linking Across
T I M E

A child during the Great Depression, Jimmy Carter had vivid memories of President Roosevelt's fireside chats. Carter decided to adopt similar methods to promote his programs. He made television addresses from the White House residence rather than the formal setting of the Oval Office.

CHAPTER 25
★★

Search for Solutions
1976–1992

▶ **YELLOW RIBBON TREE TIE**

Setting the Scene

Focus

Despite success in foreign affairs, Jimmy Carter rapidly lost the people's confidence. In the next election, they turned to the conservative Ronald Reagan to restore their confidence. During his administration, the economy recovered and relations with the Soviet Union improved. But Reagan left a mixed legacy, and problems with the economy were passed on to his successor, George Bush, who also had to redefine America's role in world affairs.

Concepts to Understand

★ How **political ideology** shaped events and policies
★ How **leadership** altered the world's political landscape

Read to Discover...

★ what important changes took place in the Soviet Union and Eastern Europe in the late 1980s and early 1990s.

Journal Notes

Why do you think so many Americans were ready for the conservative shift initiated by Ronald Reagan in the 1980s? Note details about it in your journal as you read the chapter.

CULTURAL	• **1979** *Inflation reaches unprecedented rates*	• **1980** *United States boycotts Moscow Olympics* • **1983** *Sally Ride is first American woman in space*
	1975	**1980**
POLITICAL	• **1978** *Camp David Accords are signed* • **1979** *Iran seizes 52 American hostages*	• **1981** *Sandra Day O'Connor is first woman named to Supreme Court* • **1983** *Reagan announces Strategic Defense Initiative*

✚ **EXTRA CREDIT PROJECT**

Analyzing Foreign Relations Refer interested students to a world map. Ask them to trace the map and label the countries or regions mentioned in this chapter. Then have them select one of the countries or regions and research the relationship between their selection and the United States. Their reports should include the political, economic, and geographical implications of the relationship. **L2**

Three Flags
by Jasper Johns, 1958

The paintings of American artist Jasper Johns typically featured two-dimensional objects of everyday life as subjects. Johns, for example, painted pictures that consisted entirely of flags, maps, numbers, and letters of the alphabet.

◀ UNITED STATES SOLDIERS, ACTION DURING THE GULF WAR

- **1986** *Space shuttle* Challenger *explodes*
- **1989** *Bicentennial of the Constitution*
- **1990** *Detroit Pistons win National Basketball Association championship*

1985	1990

- **1986** *Iran-contra scandal*
- **1987** *Reagan and Gorbachev sign nuclear arms reduction treaty*
- **1991** *Persian Gulf War begins*
- **1991** *The Soviet Union collapses*

✓ Performance Assessment

Creating a Public Service Announcement Point out that by the 1970s most immigrants came from Asia, Latin America, and the Caribbean. Yet no matter when they arrived, immigrants faced many of the same problems: finding a job, locating a place to live, learning a new language, and becoming accustomed to a new way of life. Organize the students into groups to prepare a television public service announcement. The ad should offer practical advice to newcomers. Encourage the groups to translate their announcements into at least one of the languages spoken by immigrants in the community. **L2** 📦

📁 Use Performance Assessment Activity 25 as an additional assessment technique.

CHAPTER 25 CONCEPTS

Concept Mapping Activity

On the chalkboard, reproduce the following generalization and concepts map, and have students copy it in their notebooks.

> Two very different leaders, Carter and Reagan, faced the challenge to create a new national mood despite economic uncertainties and disillusionment.

Political Ideology	Leadership

History
AND
ART

In addition to Johns, Andy Warhol, Roy Lichtenstein, and Claes Oldenburg were artists who monumentalized everyday objects.

📁 To reinforce the two chapter concepts, use Concept Mapping Activities 25-A and 25-B.

🕹 📁 Use Chapter Concepts Transparencies 25-A, 25-B.

ABCNEWS
INTERACTIVE™

💿 VIDEODISC

Powers of the President

‖‖‖‖‖‖‖‖‖‖‖‖‖‖

Side Two, Chapter 10
Title: *Manager of the Economy*
Subject: The President's role as manager of the economy

FOCUS

Bellringer

Before taking roll, project Section Focus Transparency 25-1 or hand out Section Focus Transparency Activity 25-1. Have students answer the questions.

Motivating Activity

Tell students that in the mid-1970s many Americans resented presidential authority. Because of the Vietnam War and the Watergate scandal, a lot of people believed that an "imperial presidency" had developed. President Carter tried to develop a more informal approach to government, a style sometimes characterized as "Jacksonian." Ask students: What do you think this means? (*"man of the people" or "folksy" manner*) **L1**

Vocabulary Precheck

Ask students to define each of the "Key Terms." Have a volunteer consult the dictionary for any unfamiliar words. **L1, LEP**

Use the Vocabulary PuzzleMaker Software to create a crossword puzzle. **L1**

Assign Vocabulary Activity 25.

Crisis of Confidence

Setting the Scene

Focus

Americans felt a deep sense of pride and patriotism as they celebrated the Bicentennial in 1976. These feelings, however, could not erase the painful memories of two of the most disillusioning events in United States history—the Vietnam War and the Watergate scandal. Americans were ready for new leadership to bolster the national mood and solve the difficult problems that loomed ahead.

Objectives

After studying this section, you should be able to

★ state reasons for the American public's crisis of confidence.

★ explain how moral principles directed President Carter's domestic and foreign policy.

Key Terms

cartel, double-digit inflation, pork-barrel legislation

◀ HOSTAGE TERRY ANDERSON AFTER HIS RELEASE

At the time of its Bicentennial in 1976, the United States was faced with the grim prospect of diminishing vital natural resources. One result was that the nation was no longer self-sufficient in its production of energy. By then, the United States was importing more than half of its oil. Competition from Japan, Germany, and other countries threatened America's giant automobile and steel industries. With rising inflation and unemployment, the lifestyles of many Americans were critically affected.

There were equally serious problems in foreign affairs. Political turmoil in economically developing nations upset global stability. The Soviet Union pursued an increasingly aggressive foreign policy as the nuclear arms race continued. As the United States began its third century, the American people wondered if the government was capable of meeting these challenges.

Election of 1976

Soon after Gerald Ford became President in 1974, he began to campaign for his election in 1976. The public regarded Ford as a warm, easygoing man of high integrity, but had doubts about his intellectual capabilities and competence as a leader. As a result, conservatives in the Republican party rallied behind Ronald Reagan, the former governor of California. Ford survived the challenge and won the Republican nomination, but only by a few votes.

The Democratic presidential primaries were crowded with candidates including several who were nationally known. One, however, was a political outsider. James Earl "Jimmy" Carter, Jr., a former governor of Georgia, had no previous experience in the federal government. He toured the nation meeting voters face to face. Carter made a virtue of this inexperience:

Classroom Resources for SECTION 1

Blackline Masters:
- Reproducible Lesson Plan 25-1
- Guided Reading Activity 25-1
- Vocabulary Activity 25

- Primary and Secondary Source Readings, pp. 70–71
- Reteaching Activity 25-1
- Section Quiz 25-1

Transparencies:
- Section Focus Transparency 25-1

Multimedia:
- Testmaker
- Vocabulary PuzzleMaker

- MindJogger Videoquiz
- Powers of the President
- Focus on Government
- The Presidents: A Picture History of Our Nation

> *The people of this country want a fresh face, not one associated with a long series of mistakes at the White House and Capitol Hill.*

To almost everyone's surprise, Carter won many of the primaries and secured the Democratic nomination for President. This was partly because his informal, down-home style appealed to Americans tired of the "imperial presidency."

During the presidential campaign, Jimmy Carter vowed to restore people's faith in the federal government by making it more open and efficient. He promised major new programs for energy development, tax reform, welfare reform, and national medical care. Conservatives liked him because he promised to balance the budget. Liberals supported him because he insisted he would not let unemployment rise as a means of lowering inflation.

Although the vote was close, Carter won the election. He took 51 percent of the popular vote and 297 electoral votes to Ford's 48 percent and 241 electoral votes. Carter achieved his victory by combining the support of the old Democratic coalition of the industrial Northeast and the Solid South

(except for Virginia). For the first time since 1848, a candidate from the Deep South had been elected President. To a great extent, Carter owed his margin of victory to African American Southern voters.

■ Energy and Economic Shocks

President Carter believed that America's most serious domestic problem was its increasing dependence on oil as an energy source. Experts warned that world supplies of oil, a nonrenewable resource, would soon be exhausted. The oil-producing countries belonged to a **cartel,** an association of nations promoting its economic interests, the Organization of Petroleum Exporting Countries (OPEC). They set prices at ever-higher levels. Rising oil prices added substantially to the price of consumer goods.

Carter's Energy Program

To address the problem, Carter proposed a national energy program. He persuaded Congress to create a Department of Energy. In order to conserve oil, he promoted the

 ▲ AN INFORMAL PRESIDENCY Both Jimmy Carter and his wife Rosalyn lived a relatively simple life. Both came from close-knit families that stressed hard work, dedication, and religion. *What electoral group helped Carter win the 1976 election?*

CHAPTER 25 Search for Solutions: 1976–1992   **749**

TEACH
Guided Practice

Drama Organize students into small groups to write a scene—set in the 1970s—involving conversations among an American housewife, a manager of an automobile factory, a young unemployed worker, a college student, and a newspaper reporter. Each person should state reasons—energy crisis, foreign competition, rising inflation and unemployment, social and economic inequality—for losing confidence in the nation's future. Have each group dramatize its dialogues. **L1, LEP**

Visualizing **H**istory After the inaugural ceremony, Carter and his family walked up Pennsylvania Avenue from the Capitol to the White House instead of riding in the traditional limousine. This gesture symbolized Carter's desire to create a more informal presidency. **Answer to Caption:** African Americans

 NATIONAL GEOGRAPHIC SOCIETY

 CD-ROM

The Presidents: A Picture History of Our Nation

Have students select President Carter from the main menu and the category GAME. Suggest students learn more about Carter by playing the presidential game with a partner.

Independent Practice

Speech Writing Have students assume the role of President Carter's chief speechwriter in 1979. Ask them to write a political speech in which they outline Carter's foreign policy accomplishments and justify his failures. Ask volunteers to read their speeches to the class. **L3**

📁 Assign Guided Reading Activity 25-1.

Linking Across TIME

The United States has done little to develop alternative energy sources, evidenced by continued dependence on Middle East oil. Americans have made a certain amount of progress nevertheless, as shown by recent developments in nuclear and solar energy, more fuel-efficient cars, and better building materials.

Using Charts

Answer: 1974, 1979, 1980

Chart Skills Practice
Why is "NA" indicated in the No Lead column for the year 1973? *(Nonleaded gasoline was not available to the public in 1973.)*

Gasoline Consumption and Prices

Year	Consumption (billions of gallons)	Reg.	Prem.	No lead
1973	110.5	40	45	NA
1974	106.3	53	57	55
1975	109.0	57	61	60
1976	115.7	59	64	61
1977	119.6	62	67	66
1978	125.1	63	69	67
1979	122.1	86	92	90
1980	115.0	119	128	125

Source: *Statistical Abstract of the United States, 1981*

Chart Study Gasoline prices increased steadily beginning in 1973. *In what years did prices affect consumption?*

---

use of coal and such renewable energy sources as solar energy. The President wanted Americans to join together in a moral crusade against rising consumption:

> ❝ [The nation's] decision about energy will test the character of the American people and the ability of the President and Congress to govern this nation. This difficult decision will be the 'moral equivalent of war'— except that we will be uniting our efforts to build and not to destroy. ❞

The President asked all Americans to make personal sacrifices to reduce their energy consumption. Because the sacrifices he asked people to make were voluntary, however, the public was confused about the seriousness of the crisis. When Carter later proposed stronger methods of restricting consumption, such as a 10 percent tax on all imported oil and emergency authority to impose gasoline rationing, Congress rejected them. Carter did, however, convince Congress to lift controls on domestic oil production and to impose a "windfall profits" tax on the oil companies' huge earnings.

Double-digit Inflation

Sharp rises in the price of oil and gasoline contributed to **double-digit inflation,** or a rise in the general level of prices of 10 percent or more. By 1980 it cost more than $200 to purchase the same goods that $100 would have bought only 10 years earlier. At the same time, the Federal Reserve Board raised interest rates to all-time highs in an effort to discourage borrowing and bring the economy under control. These policies helped reduce inflation but caused a severe business recession.

■ Governmental Disunity

Even though the Democrats held the presidency and had a majority in both houses of Congress, there was a lack of unity between the two branches of government. This was largely because Carter was unwilling to play politics. For example, in 1977 he announced that he would veto appropriation bills for a series of costly dams, canals, and other water projects. Passing such **pork-barrel legislation,** or bills that benefit only a small part of the country, was a common practice. Carter's move saved the nation millions of dollars, but it cost him valuable support.

Carter's inability to sell his political position on important issues puzzled many people. He followed a cautious middle course, promising to reduce government spending while endorsing expensive social programs. The President would not "choose up sides," as newspaper columnist James Reston observed. "Confronted with a series of ambiguous questions, he simply refused to give simple answers." As a result, the public became confused about Carter's goals. By 1979 his popular support had fallen dramatically.

■ Morality in Foreign Policy

In contrast to his leadership in domestic policy, President Carter's foreign policy was clearly defined. Carter denounced past

---

Creating a News Script Organize students into small groups to develop scripts for a newsmagazine program on one of the major events, issues, or policies of the Carter administration. Suggest that the groups use the following structure for their programs: a statement on the subject of the program, a brief report providing background detail on the subject, and a discussion involving a moderator and at least two people with differing views on the subject. Have groups perform their scripts for the rest of the class. **L2**

American foreign policy as "lacking moral principle." A man of strong religious beliefs, Carter argued that instead of relying on military and economic might, the United States must try to be "right and honest and truthful and decent" in its dealings with other nations.

The Panama Canal

Carter demonstrated his new policy over the Panama Canal, which the United States had controlled since 1903. In 1978 he won Senate ratification of the Panama Canal treaties, which transferred control of the canal from the United States to Panama by the end of the century. This action removed a major symbol of United States interventionist policy and signaled a new approach to Latin American relations.

Respect for Human Rights

In his dealings with other nations, Carter expressed a "clear-cut preference for those societies which share with us an abiding respect for human rights." His administration cut off military and economic support to several Latin American governments considered dictatorial and repressive. Carter also strongly condemned the Soviet Union for imprisoning people who protested government policies and for not allowing more of its Jewish citizens to emigrate.

Tension Over Afghanistan

Tension between the United States and the Soviet Union heightened when Soviet troops invaded Afghanistan late in 1979. In keeping with Carter's noninterventionist policy, the United States refrained from sending troops to the area. Instead, the President imposed an embargo on the sale of grain to the Soviet Union and called for a boycott of the 1980 Summer Olympic Games to be held in Moscow.

■ The Troubled Middle East

Carter's greatest foreign policy triumph and his greatest failure involved the Middle East. Since its early history, the region had been troubled by deep political and religious conflicts. Carter acknowledged that:

Visualizing History

▲ AGREEMENT AT CAMP DAVID President Carter meets with Egyptian President Anwar el-Sadat (left) and Israeli Prime Minister Menachem Begin (right) to sign the Camp David Peace Accords. *What was the goal of the agreement?*

FACT or FICTION?
Unlike previous Presidents, Jimmy Carter worked without a chief of staff during the first two years of his presidency.

FACT: Instead, he had several different aides report to him. But this approach proved cumbersome and chaotic and, in part, contributed to his indecisive image and his difficulties with Congress. For the final two years of his term, he returned to the traditional organizational system.

Did You Know?

A graduate of the Naval Academy at Annapolis, Jimmy Carter served as an electrical engineer on battleships and submarines. His love of engineering dated from his boyhood when, while watching mechanics repairing his father's farm machinery, he would try to figure out how things worked.

Visualizing History The Camp David Accords were bitterly opposed by some of the other Arab states. Some Arab states, however, refused either to condemn or support Sadat. **Answer to Caption:** to establish peace in the Middle East

---

Critical Thinking Activity

Classifying Information Tell students that interest groups are made up of people who support a common goal and seek to influence government policies. Interest groups have brought their concerns to the notice of public officials since colonial times. Today, they can be classified into a number of categories—labor, business, farm, professional, special population, and public interest, to name a few. Ask students to provide examples of interest groups that would fall into these categories. Upon completion of this task, have them compare their lists. **L3**

ABCNEWS
INTERACTIVE™

VIDEODISC
Powers of the President

Side Two, Chapter 6
Title: *Roles of the President*
Subject: Former
President Carter discusses
the extraconstitutional
roles of the President

GLENCOE
TECHNOLOGY

VIDEODISC
Focus on Government

Side 3, Chapter 48
Title: *Making
Connections: From
Governor to President*
Subject: The career
preparation of several
American Presidents

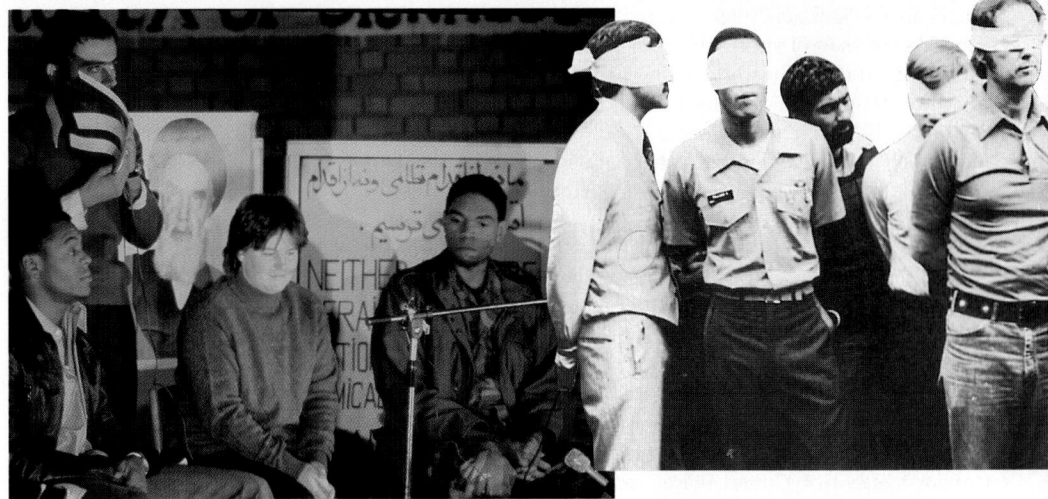

▲ HOSTAGE CRISIS In November 1979 Iranian radicals seized more than 50 Americans as hostages. President Carter condemned the action as "an act of terrorism outside the boundaries of international law." *What actions did Carter take to resolve the crisis?*

> " *[The Middle East] has long been
> a textbook for pessimism, a
> demonstration that diplomatic
> ingenuity was no match for
> intractable human conflicts.* "

*may be a land of human rich-
ness and fulfillment, rather than
a land of bitterness and
continued conflict.* "

The Camp David Accords

Despite this view, President Carter made a bold move to negotiate a peace treaty between Egypt and Israel, nations that had been bitter enemies for 30 years. In 1978 Carter brought Egypt's President Anwar el-Sadat and Israel's Prime Minister Menachem Begin together at Camp David, the presidential retreat in Maryland. The leaders talked for 14 days. More than once the discussions broke down, but Carter persisted until the leaders reached an agreement on September 17, 1978. In front of a joint session of Congress, with Sadat and Begin in the gallery, Carter announced:

> " *This is the first time that an
> Arab and an Israeli leader have
> signed a comprehensive frame-
> work for peace. It contains the
> seeds of a time when the Middle
> East, with all its vast potential,*

The Camp David Accords, which were formally signed in 1979, established peace between Egypt and Israel. Most of the other Arab nations expressed strong opposition to the treaty because they felt Egypt should not have acted alone. Also, the issue of the Israeli-occupied territories inhabited by Palestinians was yet to be solved. Still, an important first step toward peace in the Middle East had been taken.

Crisis With Iran

This success, however, could not make up for Carter's inability to resolve the crisis with Iran in 1979. The United States had long supported the Shah of Iran. Iran served as a major supplier of oil and as a reliable buffer against Soviet expansion in the Middle East. Yet many Iranians had grown unhappy with the Shah's rule. The Shah had brought Western technology and reform to his people with immense revenues from oil, but these changes had only widened the gap between the wealthy and the extremely poor.

Cultural Perspectives

Carter and African Americans Jimmy Carter was a representative of the "New South," a society that would be based on racial harmony rather than conflict and prejudice. Both as governor of Georgia and as President, Carter appointed African Americans to positions of importance, and his belief in racial equality seemed to be a deeply held conviction. As Andrew Young, Carter's ambassador to the United Nations, noted, "Blacks have a kind of radar about white folks and, somewhere along the line, Jimmy passed the test."

Some Islamic leaders objected to the Western social reforms and customs that had been introduced into Iran, claiming that they ran contrary to their religious traditions. Huge protests forced the Shah to flee in 1979, and an Islamic republic replaced the monarchy.

The new regime, headed by the religious leader Ayatollah Ruholla Khomeini (koh•MAY•nee), viewed the United States with deep distrust because of its ties with the Shah. Anti-American feelings were so strong that on November 4, 1979, militants stormed the American embassy in Tehran, the Iranian capital, and took hostage more than 50 Americans. The militants threatened to kill the hostages or try them as spies.

Negotiations for the freedom of the hostages were unsuccessful. As pressure mounted to secure their release, Carter felt he had no choice but to launch a military rescue. One morning in April 1980, Americans awoke to the shocking news that a mission to rescue the hostages had failed. Eight members of the rescue team had died in a helicopter crash in Iran. Despite this setback, Carter persisted in his diplomatic efforts to free the hostages.

■ Election of 1980

The hostage crisis became a key issue in Carter's bid for reelection. Carter fought off a strong challenge from Senator Edward Kennedy of Massachusetts for the Democratic nomination. As Election Day grew near, however, the American people became increasingly impatient with the situation in Iran.

The Republicans chose former California governor Ronald Reagan as their candidate. Reagan's chief opponents in the primaries were two moderate Republicans, former United Nations Ambassador George Bush and Illinois Representative John Anderson. After his nomination, Reagan picked Bush as his running mate.

The Republicans adopted a conservative platform calling for reductions in taxes and government spending in order to restore prosperity. The party did endorse higher defense spending to strengthen the role of the United States in world affairs.

Throughout the campaign, Reagan hammered at Carter's lack of leadership and the nation's weak economy. He promised voters economic growth and development. On Election Day, Reagan claimed victory with 51 percent of the popular vote and 489 electoral votes. Carter won 41 percent, with 49 electoral votes. John Anderson and other candidates of minor parties split the rest of the vote. The conservative tide that elected Reagan resulted in a Republican Senate and reduced the Democratic House of Representatives.

President Carter's failure to obtain release of the hostages sealed his defeat. Only after Ronald Reagan was sworn in on January 20, 1981, did Iran release the Americans, ending their 444 days in captivity.

Section 1 ★ Review

Checking for Understanding

1. **Identify** OPEC, Anwar el-Sadat, Menachem Begin, Camp David Accords, Shah of Iran, Ayatollah Ruhollah Khomeini, John Anderson.

2. **Define** cartel, double-digit inflation, pork-barrel legislation.

3. **List** three features of Carter's energy program.

4. **Summarize** President Carter's successes and failures in negotiations with nations in the Middle East.

Critical Thinking

5. **Evaluating Leaders** Explain why Carter's unwillingness to play politics eroded his support in Congress.

ACTIVITY

6. Divide a sheet of paper into two vertical columns. Label one column "Successes," and the other "Failures." List each of President Carter's domestic and foreign policy efforts in the appropriate column.

ASSESS

Check Understanding
Assign Section 1 Review as homework or an in-class activity.

Evaluate
Assign Section Quiz 25-1 or use the Testmaker to create a customized quiz.

Reteach
Have students complete Reteaching Activity 25-1.

Enrich
Ask students to conduct an energy survey for their families for one day. They should note the electrical appliances used and the time it takes to use them. Have students write a statement summarizing why a national energy policy is important in their lives.

Assign Primary and Secondary Source Readings, pp. 70–71: "A National Malaise."

CLOSE
Tell students that President Carter called the U.S. government the most "wasteful bureaucracy that human beings ever created." Did President Carter contribute to this wastefulness? If so, how?

Answers to SECTION 1 REVIEW

1. OPEC, 749; Anwar el-Sadat, 752; Begin, 752; Camp David Accords, 752; Shah of Iran, 752; Khomeini, 753; Anderson, 753

2. All vocabulary words are defined in the Glossary.

3. created a Department of Energy, lifted controls on domestic oil production, imposed a windfall tax on oil profits

4. Successes: mediated talks between Sadat and Begin, Camp David Peace Accords. Failures: inability to resolve crisis in Iran and to obtain release of American hostages.

5. Carter refused to support pork-barrel legislation, thus costing him support in Congress.

6. Ask students to provide a rationale for their classifications.

753

★★

A Conservative Shift

FOCUS

Bellringer

Before taking roll, project Section Focus Transparency 25-2 or hand out Section Focus Transparency Activity 25-2. Have students answer the questions. Discuss student responses.

Motivating Activity

Present the following excerpt from a Carter campaign speech made at a town meeting in 1980:

"[T]he Republican party now is sharply different from what the Democratic party is. And I might add parenthetically that the Republican party is sharply different under Reagan from what it was under Gerald Ford and Presidents all the way back to Eisenhower."

Ask: What point do you think Carter was trying to make by comparing Reagan to earlier Republican Presidents? *(that Reagan was more radical and conservative than earlier Republicans.)* **L1**

Vocabulary Precheck

Ask students to define each of the "Key Terms." Have a volunteer consult the dictionary for any unfamiliar words. **L1, LEP**

Setting the Scene

Section Focus

Despite the hope they had felt in 1976, Americans became increasingly dissatisfied with the government during Carter's administration. Angered over economic conditions, the energy crisis, and the President's inability to free the hostages, the people turned to a new leader to restore their confidence. The voters were not only reacting against Carter, however, but giving voice to a growing conservative movement that rejected the liberalism of the 1960s and demanded changes in the way the government met challenges at home and abroad.

◀ REPUBLICAN PARTY SYMBOL

Objectives

After studying this section, you should be able to

★ explain the conservative shift in Americans' political convictions in the late 1970s and early 1980s.

★ describe President Reagan's economic recovery plan, which included cutting taxes and reducing spending.

★ describe Reagan's foreign policy regarding the Soviet Union.

Key Terms

supply-side economics, federal deficit, glasnost, perestroika, privatized

Reagan's election indicated a significant conservative shift in Americans' political convictions. In addition to support from traditionally conservative groups such as fundamentalist Christians and antifeminists, many groups that had historically voted Democratic broke with their party and supported Reagan. These included former liberals, blue-collar workers, ethnic voters, and Southerners, who became known as "Reagan Democrats." The 69-year-old Reagan also attracted many older voters.

As a whole, the Reagan conservatives believed that the federal government should withdraw from most areas of domestic life.

They were against liberal social programs and government restrictions on business. In foreign policy, they favored a strong military to stand against communism.

■ Reagan's Economic Program

President Reagan acted quickly to limit the size of the federal government. His first act as President was to place a freeze on the hiring of federal employees. At the same time, he began to ease government controls on many business activities. He set up a task force headed by Vice President Bush to

754   UNIT 7 Redefining America: 1954–Present

Classroom Resources for SECTION 2

Blackline Masters:
- Reproducible Lesson Plan 25-2
- Guided Reading Activity 25-2
- Cooperative Learning Activity 25
- Critical Thinking Skills Activity 25
- Linking Past and Present Activity 25

- Political Cartoons in American History Activity 28
- Chapter Skills Activity 25
- Workbook Activity 25-2
- Reteaching Activity 25-2
- Section Quiz 25-2

Transparencies:
- Section Focus Transparency 25-2
- Skills Transparency 25

Multimedia:
- Testmaker
- Communism and the Cold War
- The Presidents: A Picture History of Our Nation

review federal regulations. As President, Reagan moved to fulfill his campaign promise to get the economy going again. In February 1981, he told Americans:

> *Since 1960 our government has spent $5.1 trillion. Our debt has grown to $648 billion. Prices have exploded by 178 percent. . . . [We] know we must act and act now. We must not be timid. . . .*

To take care of the problem, Reagan proposed a new economic program, which came to be called "Reaganomics."

Cutting Taxes

The first part of the President's program was to make deep cuts in federal taxes. He predicted that income tax reductions would increase consumer spending and would also encourage investments, especially by the wealthy. Similarly, cuts in corporate taxes would allow companies to expand production and hire more workers. Reagan's beliefs were based on an economic theory called **supply-side economics,** which claimed that the economy could best be stimulated by increasing the supply of goods rather than the demand.

Reducing Government Spending

The second part of Reagan's program was to reduce government spending by ending federal job-training programs and cutting back the amount of federal money going into Medicare, food stamps, and education. Critics predicted that Reagan's proposal would cause great suffering for the economically disadvantaged. Reagan denied this, claiming that there would always be a "safety net" of government aid for truly needy Americans.

■ Results of Reaganomics

Although the President faced opposition to his proposals, he had personal qualities that helped to promote his position: a great ability to communicate with his audience and a sense of humor. In March 1981, when he was shot and seriously wounded, the

Visualizing History

▲ ASSASSINATION ATTEMPT In March 1981 President Reagan survived an attempt on his life outside a Washington hotel. His press secretary, a police officer, and a Secret Service agent were also wounded. *What was Reagan's chief concern when he took office?*

TEACH
Guided Practice

Political Science Write the word *conservative* on the chalkboard. Tell students that Ronald Reagan was considered a conservative. Ask students to define in their own words what this term means in its political sense and to include what economic policies conservatives believe in. *(a person who supports traditional views, reductions in taxes and government spending)*
L1, LEP

Visualizing History Twenty-five-year-old John Hinckley, a drifter, fired six shots from a small handgun at Reagan as he emerged from a hotel in Washington, D.C., on March 30, 1981. President Reagan's press secretary, James Brady, was seriously wounded in the incident.
Answer to Caption: to institute a new economic program to cut spending

NATIONAL GEOGRAPHIC SOCIETY

  CD-ROM

The Presidents: A Picture History of Our Nation

Have students view "Ronald Reagan" and use the information to write a brief biography to include in their portfolios.

Special Needs Activity

Study Strategy To understand and evaluate this section, which describes the reawakening of "conservative" feelings in this country, several political ideologies must be understood. Have students write in their notebooks the words *Conservative, Moderate,* and *Liberal* as headings of three columns. Using the categories Social Policy, Foreign Policy, and Economic Policy, see what information can be gained about each heading from their reading of the chapter. Have students work in groups to research the information not included. Discuss their findings. **L1, LEP**

Independent Practice

Interviewing Have students conduct interviews with older relatives on how their lives changed during the Reagan years. Ask them to share the results of their interviews with the class. **L2**

📁 Assign Guided Reading Activity 25-2.

Visualizing  **History** George Bush, Ronald Reagan's running mate in 1980 and 1984, had been in public life for 30 years. He served two terms in the House of Representatives and later became ambassador to the United Nations, director of the CIA, and chairman of the Republican National Committee. **Answer to Caption:** Walter Mondale and Geraldine Ferraro

Did You Know?

A major advantage that Ronald Reagan had in the 1984 election was television. A former actor, Reagan was completely at home in front of the camera. Walter Mondale, on the other hand, came across as awkward and uncomfortable on the screen. After the election Mondale noted, "I never warmed up to television and television never warmed up to me."

Visualizing  **History** ▲ A POPULAR PRESIDENT Some observers noted that President Reagan's strong victories in the 1980 and 1984 elections were due to his personal appeal as well as to growing public support for his conservative policies. *Who were the Democratic candidates in 1984?*

President's aides visited him in the hospital. They assured him that the business of government was continuing as usual. "What makes you think I'd be happy about that?" Reagan quipped.

With his great popularity and shrewd handling of Congress, Reagan soon got much of his economic program passed. The final bill included $39 billion in tax cuts and a 25 percent cut in income taxes. The results of Reaganomics, however, were not quite what the President had hoped. Spending cuts, together with high interest rates, brought inflation down, but at first the cure was painful.

Recession

In 1982 a severe economic recession occurred. Business bankruptcies, factory closings, and farm foreclosures increased at alarming rates. By the end of the year, more than 11 million Americans—10 percent of the workforce—were jobless. Blaming President Reagan's economic programs for the recession, the Democrats won back many seats in the congressional elections.

Recovery

By 1983, however, the economy began to turn around. The Federal Reserve Board lowered interest rates, making it easier for businesses and individuals to borrow money. The inflation rate dropped just as the 25-percent cut in income taxes was putting more money into the hands of consumers. Feeling new confidence in the economy, Americans made purchases they had put off during the recession. Sales of every type of goods and service shot upward, and industries hired back workers who had been laid off during the recession. By the end of Reagan's second term in 1988, unemployment had dropped to 5.5 percent—the lowest in 14 years.

To hail the recovery, President Reagan went before Congress in 1984, saying:

❝ *. . . America is back—standing tall, looking to the '80s with courage, confidence, and hope. . . . Send away the hand-wringers and doubting Thomases.* ❞

Cooperative Learning Activity

Evaluating Policies Have students reread the definition of supply-side economics on this page. Then divide the class into three groups and ask group members to work together to write letters to President Reagan on the impact of his economic policies. One group should represent business owners; another should represent workers in manufacturing industries; and the third should represent people on fixed incomes, such as senior citizens or welfare recipients. Have groups select representatives to read their letters to the rest of the class. **L2** 📦

📁 For additional practice, assign Cooperative Learning Activity 25.

The Federal Debt Increases

Although Reagan promised to balance the budget, the federal debt greatly increased during his first term. He cut taxes, which meant the government received less revenue. In addition, Congress, now controlled by the Democrats, refused to make the deeper cuts in social programs that Reagan requested. On top of that, Reagan himself increased government spending in certain areas, especially defense. The result was the most unbalanced budget in American history.

By 1984 the **federal deficit,** or the difference between the amount of money the government took in and what it spent, was nearly $200 billion a year. When the government spends more money than it collects, it has to borrow to make up the difference. The more the government borrows, the more interest it owes on its debts. In 1984 the interest alone on the federal debt amounted to $153.8 billion, an increase of more than $55 billion from Reagan's first year in office.

■ Election of 1984

Despite the federal deficit, Reagan was still popular, and the economy had made a healthy recovery. These factors made Reagan a formidable candidate for President in the 1984 election. To run against him, the Democrats nominated a traditional liberal, former Vice President Walter Mondale. Mondale created a precedent by choosing Representative Geraldine Ferraro of New York to run as his Vice President. She was the first woman candidate from a major party to run for this office.

Mondale claimed that Reagan's tax and budget cuts benefited only the wealthy. Reagan countered that his economic program had aided all Americans by sharply reducing inflation. To cut the deficit, Mondale proposed raising taxes, always an unpopular political step. Reagan, however, continued to oppose any increases and insisted that economic expansion and deeper cuts in government spending would reduce the deficit.

In November Americans gave the President an overwhelming vote of confidence. Winning 59 percent of the popular vote, he captured 49 states and took 525 electoral votes to Mondale's 13. Reagan won the biggest electoral margin in history.

■ A Conservative Court

With this tremendous mandate, Reagan began his second term confident in his policies. One of his priorities was to appoint conservative justices to the Supreme Court and the lower federal courts. In 1981, the President had appointed Sandra Day O'Connor, the first woman to serve on the Court. In 1986 Reagan selected Antonin Scalia, and a year later he chose Anthony M. Kennedy.

With Reagan's appointees in place, the Supreme Court began to hand down the kind of conservative rulings for which Reagan had hoped. For example, one decision cut back affirmative action programs that had benefited minorities.

■ Strengthening America's Defenses

President Reagan strongly supported America's space program, both as a means of restoring the nation's self-confidence and as a means of strengthening its defenses. Americans took pride in their successes in space exploration, and the launch of reusable space shuttles marked a new era in the space program.

Support for SDI

Reagan had a special interest in the military aspects of the space program. In 1983 he announced a new research project to create a shield that would intercept and destroy nuclear ballistic missiles. It was called the Strategic Defense Initiative (SDI), nicknamed "Star Wars." Opponents feared that SDI would stimulate an intensified nuclear competition between the United States and the Soviet Union. Reagan and the project's supporters, however, believed SDI would improve chances of nuclear disarmament.

Assign Workbook Activity 25-2.

A 1990 magazine interview reported Geraldine Ferraro's belief that, by running for Vice President in 1984, she would make it easier for future women candidates. Said Ferraro in the same interview, "We have a real shot at having a woman President in this . . . decade." Ferraro advised women who aspire to the office to work hard and take risks. To gain the right experience, Ferraro believes that a woman should first be a U.S. senator or a state governor.

NATIONAL GEOGRAPHIC SOCIETY

 CD-ROM

The Presidents: A Picture History of Our Nation

Ask interested students to research information on women candidates for President. Have them present their findings to the rest of the class.

Sidelight: Reagan's Nickname

Throughout his time in office, President Reagan's enormous popularity never wavered. All the trials and tribulations of his administration—economic setbacks, foreign policy mishaps, and rumors of scandal and wrongdoing—made little more than a dent in his standing with the American public. Because neither bad news nor personal mistakes seemed to "stick" to him, opponents named Reagan the *Teflon President*—after the nonstick coating applied to cooking utensils.

Visualizing  **History** The twenty-fifth shuttle flight was the first to have a "civilian observer" aboard. Christa McAuliffe, a teacher from Concord, New Hampshire, was the finalist in a nationwide search for the best example of an American teacher. She was to have taught lessons and provided demonstrations from space that would be beamed live back to Earth. **Answer to Caption:** reusable spacecraft

CURRICULUM CONNECTION

Political Science The superpowers have been holding summit meetings—the 1987 meeting was the sixteenth—since World War II. The results of these meetings have been inconclusive. However, as former President Richard Nixon noted, "when each superpower has the means to destroy . . . the world . . . summit meetings have become essential if peace is to be preserved."

Military Buildup

In addition to Star Wars, Reagan also promoted a military buildup, including new bombers, submarines, and missiles and better training for ground troops. Other aspects of his defense program included placing new nuclear missiles in Europe, basing intercontinental missiles in Western states, and developing expensive new B-2 "stealth" bombers. Stealth bombers are military aircraft designed so that radar cannot easily detect them.

The Cost of Defense

Aside from Star Wars, Reagan's military buildup cost $1 trillion. This caused a sharp rise in the federal deficit. As the deficit increased, a greater share of tax revenues went to pay the interest on the national debt. This left less money available for new programs in education, the environment, and public housing.

Congress responded in 1985 by passing the Gramm-Rudman Act, which put greater pressure on Congress and the President to reach agreement on reducing the budget. If they were unable to reduce the annual deficit to certain limits, this legislation set up automatic, across-the-board federal spending cuts.

Reagan, however, still refused to increase income taxes. He was able to maintain this position only because in 1986 a great drop in oil prices occurred. Fear of inflation lessened as interest rates dropped. Nevertheless, by 1988 the national debt had reached $2.3 trillion.

■ Improved Relations with the Soviet Union

Reagan's desire for a strong defense was based on his belief that the Soviet Union, which he called an "evil empire," was a serious threat to the United States. He aimed to contain and counter communism throughout the world, and he followed this policy until relations with the Soviet Union suddenly began to improve.

When Mikhail Gorbachev (GAWR•buh•CHAWF) became Soviet premier, his country's economy, which was highly centralized under the control of the Communist party, was on the verge of collapse. For decades,

 **Visualizing History** ▲ THE CHALLENGER DISASTER On January 28, 1986, the space shuttle *Challenger* exploded in space, killing all seven astronauts on board. The tragedy temporarily halted the space program. *What innovation had the shuttle introduced?*

Sidelight: "Trickle-Down" Presidents

Political opponents slightingly compared Ronald Reagan to Calvin Coolidge, pointing out the similarity between Reaganomics and Coolidge's "trickle-down" economic policies. They also noted that Reagan, like Coolidge, seemed rather detached from the process of government. Far from being insulted, Reagan reveled in the comparison. He hung Coolidge's portrait in a prominent place in the White House. He also regularly quoted Coolidge's philosophy on business and government.

Linking Past and Present

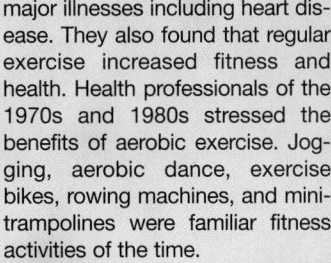

Physical Fitness

Ronald Reagan was one of the oldest Presidents and one of the fittest. He kept trim by riding horses and chopping wood. Thanks in part to Reagan's example, interest in physical fitness bloomed.

Then

The Benefits of Exercise

Tracking individuals over many years, scientists studied the effect of exercise on the body. They concluded that physical inactivity is a significant factor in the development of several major illnesses including heart disease. They also found that regular exercise increased fitness and health. Health professionals of the 1970s and 1980s stressed the benefits of aerobic exercise. Jogging, aerobic dance, exercise bikes, rowing machines, and mini-trampolines were familiar fitness activities of the time.

Now

A Healthy Trend

The fitness boom of the 1980s continued in the mid-1990s. Walking and jogging trails and bicycle paths were developed in neighborhoods all over the country. About 70 million Americans made exercise a part of their regular schedule.

In one year, about 300,000 Americans took part in middle-distance triathlons, three-part races in which they biked for 25 miles, ran 6.2 miles, and swam 1 mile. In that same year, about 250,000 Americans ran in marathons, which are 26.2 miles long.

---

the party had focused on building up the Soviet Union's position as a superpower and neglected the needs of the people. As a result, farms and factories underproduced and the standard of living was low. The centralized communist system of government was also showing serious strain. The people had no voice and had grown very apathetic in the face of total party control.

Gorbachev Sets New Policy

To save his country and party, Gorbachev set some new policies. First, he introduced **glasnost,** meaning "openness." This policy gave people the right to speak freely—and, Gorbachev hoped, in support of his reforms. Then Gorbachev began **perestroika,** a restructuring of the economy and the government. Instead of party officials deciding everything from Moscow, local farm and factory managers now had the power to make some decisions. The nation's businesses were **privatized,** or transferred from government to private ownership. To lessen

the party's control of government, Gorbachev scheduled the first elections in 70 years in which the people had a real choice.

Gorbachev Makes an Astounding Offer

Gorbachev knew that if the arms race could be halted, it would free people and money to produce consumer goods in the Soviet Union. Peace would also allow him to concentrate all his energies on domestic reforms, and could lead to trade agreements and economic aid from the West. So, Gorbachev made the United States an astounding offer, announcing that the Soviet Union would reduce its nuclear weapons.

Reagan and Gorbachev Hold Summit Meeting

When Reagan and Gorbachev met at Reykjavík, Iceland, in 1986, the two leaders tried but could not come to an agreement on the issue of the Strategic Defense Initiative.

Critical Thinking Activity

Verifying Opinions Present this view of Ronald Reagan from his former chief of staff, Donald T. Regan:

"Like [Franklin D.] Roosevelt, Reagan changed the political landscape of the United States—and the way in which Americans saw themselves and their country—in a fundamental and probably permanent way."

Ask students to verify this opinion with facts from the text. Then have them state whether or not they agree with this assessment of Reagan and give reasons for their answers. **L3**

☞ For additional practice, assign Critical Thinking Skills Activity 25.

Linking Past and Present

According to a recent survey, only 36 percent of school-age children in the United States have daily physical education classes. Fewer than half of all children get enough exercise to develop healthy hearts and lungs. Ask students what they do to keep physically fit.

☞ Assign Linking Past and Present Activity 25.

Food of the Times

Along with the growing interest in physical fitness came a new concern for healthy eating. In the 1950s "meat and potatoes" were the standard dinner in the United States. By the 1970s and 1980s Americans were eating more turkey, chicken, and fish and less beef. They were also eating more fruits and vegetables.

ABCNEWS INTERACTIVE™

 VIDEODISC

Communism and the Cold War

Side Two, Chapter 21

Title: *Changing Images*

Subject: Changes in American perceptions of the Soviet Union

ASSESS

ASSESS

Check Understanding

Assign Section 2 Review as homework or an in-class activity.

Evaluate

☑ ▭ Assign Section Quiz 25-2 or use the Test-maker to create a customized quiz.

Reteach

▭ Have students complete Reteaching Activity 25-2.

Enrich

▭ Assign Political Cartoons in American History Activity 28.

Have students create an editorial cartoon to illustrate a significant event during President Reagan's first term in office. Suggest that students display their cartoons on the bulletin board.

CLOSE

Point out that President Reagan reduced federal aid on many housing, education, and health programs. Ask students to discuss how this policy affected life in the United States.

Reagan insisted on pursuing it, and Gorbachev opposed it. When they met again a year later at Washington, D.C., however, they signed a treaty calling for the removal of all intermediate-range nuclear weapons from Europe. This was the first agreement that eliminated an entire class of nuclear weapons. Unbelievably, the cold war was slowly coming to an end.

Along with agreeing to limit nuclear weapons, Gorbachev took other surprising steps that affected international relations. Admitting that the Soviet Union's intervention in Afghanistan had been "morally wrong," he withdrew Soviet troops. He also released political prisoners and allowed freer emigration of Soviet Jews.

■ A Hands-Off Presidency

Although Reagan was a strong leader when it came to establishing public policy, he adopted a "hands-off" attitude toward the day-to-day operations of the presidency. This attitude led to scandals that would tarnish Reagan's final years in office, though he remained popular.

A Master of Delegation

Reagan gave far greater responsibilities to his staff than any other recent President had. The President's detachment allowed his subordinates to function independently. Some acted for financial gain. Others made policy on their own.

The Iran-Contra Scandal

The worst fiasco to hit the Reagan administration was the Iran-contra scandal of 1986. Several of the President's national security aides, including John Poindexter, Robert McFarland, and Lieutenant Colonel Oliver North, had schemed to sell weapons to the Iranians to win the release of American hostages in the Middle East. Then they had diverted the profits from these arms sales to the *contras,* Nicaraguan guerrillas who were fighting to topple the Sandanista government ruling the nation. This was a violation of a congressional ban on such financing.

Critics charged that an undercover foreign policy was being carried out against the express will of Congress. Defenders maintained that the executive branch was forced to take these measures because of congressional interference with the President's authority to conduct foreign policy. A special commission was set up to study the Iran-contra case. Although the commission cleared the President of direct blame, it found fault with Reagan for allowing aides to make policy decisions without his knowledge.

The Iran-contra scandal helped the Democrats win back a Senate majority in 1986. The election produced a divided government—with the presidency held by the Republican party and control of Congress held by the Democrats. Democratic majorities in Congress acted as a brake on the Reagan administration.

Section 2 ★ Review

Checking for Understanding

1. **Identify** Reaganomics, Walter Mondale, Geraldine Ferraro, Sandra Day O'Connor, Gramm-Rudman Act, Strategic Defense Initiative (SDI), Mikhail Gorbachev, Lieutenant Colonel Oliver North, *contras.*

2. **Define** supply-side economics, federal deficit, glasnost, perestroika, privatized.

3. **List** three measures Reagan took to restore the economy.

Critical Thinking

4. **Evaluating Policies** Evaluate whether technology such as the SDI will help prevent nuclear war.

ACTIVITY

5. List in order the three leadership qualities you think are most important to the success of the President. Write an explanation for your reasoning.

Answers to SECTION 2 REVIEW

1. Reaganomics, 755; Walter Mondale, 757; Geraldine Ferraro, 757; Sandra Day O'Connor, 757; Gramm-Rudman Act, 758; Strategic Defense Initiative (SDI), 757; Mikhail Gorbachev, 758; Lieutenant Colonel Oliver North, 760; *contras,* 760

2. All vocabulary words are defined in the Glossary.

3. cut income taxes, cut corporate taxes, reduced federal spending

4. Answers will vary. Supporters will argue that SDI would prevent nuclear attacks due to United States invulnerability and ability to retaliate. Opponents will argue that the system was not feasible and would escalate the arms race into space.

5. Students should present valid reasoning in support of their position.

Reading a Bar Graph

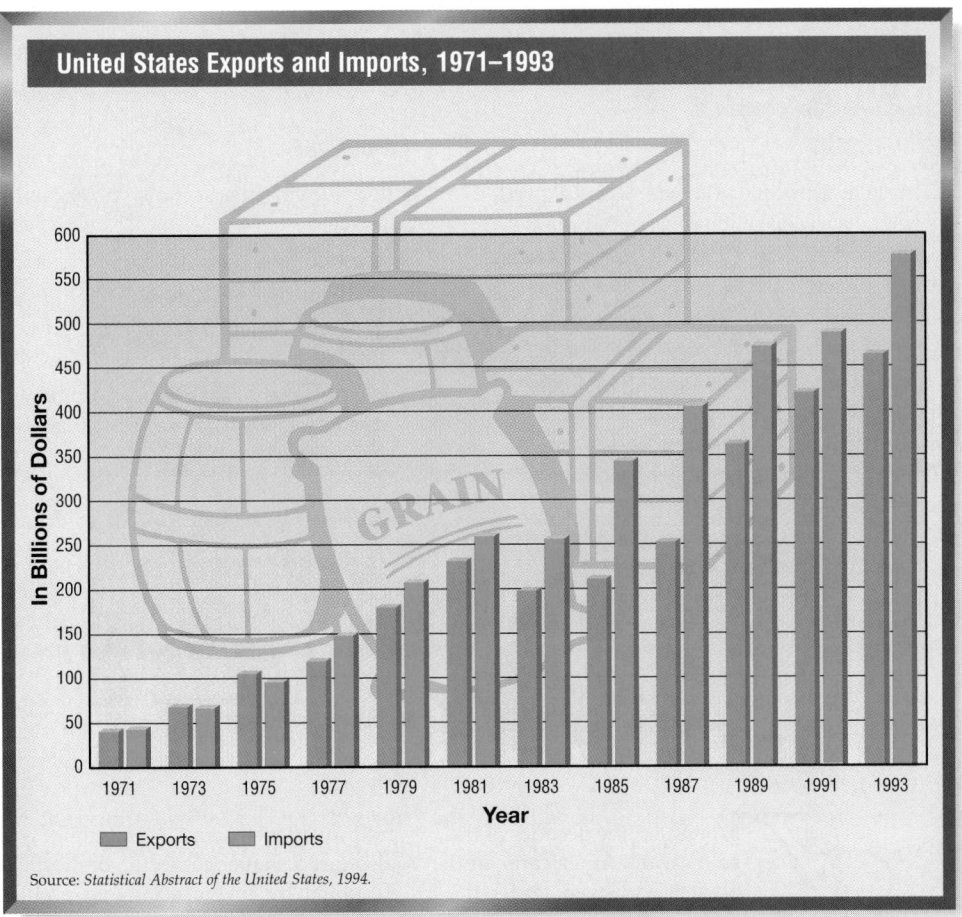

United States Exports and Imports, 1971–1993

In Billions of Dollars (vertical axis: 0, 50, 100, 150, 200, 250, 300, 350, 400, 450, 500, 550, 600)

Year (horizontal axis: 1971, 1973, 1975, 1977, 1979, 1981, 1983, 1985, 1987, 1989, 1991, 1993)

■ Exports   ■ Imports

Source: *Statistical Abstract of the United States, 1994.*

Learning the Skill

Like line graphs, bar graphs are used to compare facts involving numbers. Bars, or columns, of different lengths are used to represent quantities or totals. Some bar graphs show changes over time much like line graphs. Bar graphs can also be used to compare quantities during the same time period. Like line graphs, bar graphs have horizontal and vertical axes that describe the information presented in the graph. Study the graph and answer the questions that follow.

Practicing the Skill

1. What information is presented in the graph? What period is covered?
2. Analyze the trends for both exports and imports from 1971 to 1993.

APPLYING THE SKILL

3. Review the subsection on page 757 entitled "Election of 1984." Create bar graphs that depict the candidates' popular vote percentages and electoral vote totals.

761

BUILDING SKILLS

TEACH

Have students refer to the graph on page 761. Ask them what the graph shows. Tell them that for much of the 1990s, the United States has had a surplus in its balance of trade. An ever-increasing percentage of the economy has been exposed to foreign competition—from 7 percent in the 1960s to more than 70 percent in the 1980s.

 Project Skills Transparency 25 and have students complete Skills Transparency Activity 25.

Use Chapter Skills Activity 25 to reinforce students' understanding of the skill.

CURRICULUM CONNECTION

Economics The main factors in the dramatic growth of the trade deficit in the 1980s were the rising cost of imported oil and the dollar's rising value against foreign currencies. Imports, such as cars and electronics, as a result were less expensive.

Answers to Practicing the Skill

1. the value of exports and imports; 1971–1993
2. In general, the dollar amount of both exports and imports grew during the time period.
3. Bar graphs should show Mondale with 41 percent of the popular vote and 13 electoral votes and Reagan with 59 percent of the popular vote and 525 electoral votes.

FOCUS

Bellringer

 Before taking roll, project Section Focus Transparency 25-3 or hand out Section Focus Transparency Activity 25-3. Have students answer the questions.

Motivating Activity

Write the phrase *New World Order* on the chalkboard and ask students to express in writing what it means to them. *(the new system of international relations in the post–cold war world)* **L2**

Vocabulary Precheck

Ask students to define each of the "Key Terms." Have a volunteer consult the dictionary for any unfamiliar words. **L1, LEP**

NATIONAL GEOGRAPHIC SOCIETY

CD-ROM

The Presidents: A Picture History of Our Nation

Have students research George Bush's experience in foreign affairs. Ask them to identify how the positions he held would be helpful in the presidency.

★★★★★★★★★★★★★★★★★★★★★★★★★★★★★★★★★★

A New Presidency

Setting the Scene

Section Focus

Despite his difficulties, Reagan was still popular when he left office. Promising to continue Reagan's policies, Vice President George Bush won a resounding victory in 1988. In foreign affairs, Bush acted decisively to meet the challenges of what he called "a new world order" and tried to forge a different path for America in the post-cold war world. Domestically, however, many felt his leadership lacked direction, and problems with the economy continued to plague society.

ROAD SIGN IN KUWAIT

Objectives

After studying this section, you should be able to

★ explain how the spread of democracy led to the formation of a new world order.

★ describe America's role in the post-cold war world.

★ discuss the reasons for discord between the legislative and executive branches of government under Bush.

Key Terms

coup d'état, drawdown, user tax, junk bond, underemployed

Throughout the decades of the cold war, Americans and Soviets had lived under the threat of nuclear war as each side built mighty arsenals and viewed almost all disputes around the world in terms of the East-West struggle. Then, with almost surprising suddenness, democratic movements erupted throughout the Soviet Union's Eastern European satellites. Popular demands for political, social, and economic reform toppled one communist government after another. Eventually, even the Soviet Union itself split into independent republics.

Without a Soviet adversary, the United States was the only superpower left. It faced the critical challenge of establishing a new role in world affairs, which was tested when

Iraq invaded Kuwait. Meanwhile, America also faced challenges in the domestic arena. Troubled by severe economic problems, a divided government tried to work toward a solution.

■ Election of 1988

In the election of 1988, there was tough competition for both the Republican and Democratic presidential nominations. In the end, the Republicans selected Vice President George Bush. The final Democratic contenders were the Reverend Jesse Jackson and Massachusetts Governor Michael Dukakis. Jackson, who appealed to a "rainbow coalition" of minorities and reformers,

---

Classroom Resources for SECTION 3

Blackline Masters:
- Reproducible Lesson Plan 25-3
- Guided Reading Activity 25-3
- Outline Map Resource Book, p. 34
- Primary and Secondary Source Readings, pp. 73–74

- Chapter Map Activity 25
- Geography in History Activity 25
- Enrichment Activity 25
- Workbook Activity 25-3
- Reteaching Activity 25-3
- Section Quiz 25-3

Transparencies:
- Section Focus Transparency 25-3
- Map Transparency 25

Multimedia:
- Testmaker
- Communism and the Cold War
- Lessons of War
- The Presidents: A Picture History of Our Nation

picked up support along the way and ran a much stronger race than expected. Dukakis, however, won the nomination.

Early in the race, Dukakis led Bush in the public polls. Then Bush's campaign team unleashed a string of negative television advertisements that portrayed the liberal Dukakis as unpatriotic and soft on criminals. Dukakis, however, failed to respond strongly to these charges. As a result, Dukakis lost his lead to Bush. Slick television commercials seemed to replace debating real issues.

Saying, "Read my lips," the Vice President pledged not to raise taxes. Bush also promised the nation that if elected he would follow Reagan's economic policies. On Election Day he won a resounding victory, taking 40 of the 50 states, with 49 million popular votes and 426 electoral votes. Dukakis had 42 million popular votes and 112 electoral votes.

■ A Tidal Wave of Change

George Bush came to the presidency with a great deal of experience in foreign policy.

In addition to being Vice President, he had been ambassador to the United Nations, ambassador to China, and director of the CIA. This training served Bush well, for he was immediately confronted with a tidal wave of change around the world.

Change in Eastern Europe

Gorbachev's new policies in the Soviet Union triggered demands for change in Eastern Europe. In 1989 the people of the satellite nations of Poland, Hungary, Czechoslovakia, Bulgaria, Romania, and East Germany overthrew their communist rulers and forced democratic elections. When the East German government fell, crowds tore down the Berlin Wall that had divided Germany and symbolized the "iron curtain" that separated Eastern Europe and Western Europe.

The end of the cold war allowed some countries to renew and rethink relationships. In October 1990, East Germany and West Germany reunited. As Western European nations took steps toward political and economic union, Eastern Europe sought to

Visualizing History

▲ THE BARRIER FALLS In November 1989 the Berlin Wall, which had separated the two Germanys since 1961, was opened. On the first weekend after the wall was opened, 3 million visitors crossed from East Berlin to visit West Berlin. *What had the Berlin Wall symbolized?*

TEACH
Guided Practice

Language Arts Have students summarize the major ideas in Section 3 by writing a sentence that expresses the main idea of each subhead. Ask them to share their summaries with the class. **L1**

Visualizing
History In November 1989, the Berlin Wall was torn down. In October 1991, East and West Germany were reunified into a single, democratic country. **Answer to Caption:** the separation of Eastern and Western Europe

ABCNEWS
INTERACTIVE™

 VIDEODISC

Communism and the Cold War

Side One, Chapter 22
Title: *Collapse of European Communism*
Subject: Events leading to rapid political change

Side One, Chapter 23
Title: *Fall of the Wall*
Subject: Fall of the Berlin Wall

Cultural Perspectives

The African American Vote In 1988, as in 1976, the African American vote was vital to the success of the Democratic party. It did not help the Democrats win the election, although African Americans voted for Democrats over Republicans by a 10-to-1 ratio. Even had 10 percent more African Americans than whites voted, the number still would not have pushed Michael Dukakis past George Bush's winning margin of 7 million votes. The African American vote was most effective in 1988 in helping Jesse Jackson come closer to winning the presidential nomination than any African American before him.

Independent Practice

Making a Map Provide an outline map, and ask students to label the nations of Europe and the Commonwealth of Independent States. **L1, LEP**

 Provide the map from the Outline Map Resource Book, p. 34.

 Assign Guided Reading Activity 25-3.

Teaching American Portraits

In 1995, many people urged Powell to run as a candidate for President in 1996. After much deliberation Powell decided that the time was not right to run for political office. Discuss with students the advantages and disadvantages of having a President with a strong military background.

VIDEODISC

Communism and the Cold War

Side One, Chapter 21

Title: *A New Soviet Union: Communist Rule Ends*

Subject: The end of the Soviet Union

forge new ties with them—especially economic ones. In July 1991, the Warsaw Pact between Eastern Europe and the Soviet Union was terminated. This left the future of NATO, which was also a military alliance, in doubt.

The Collapse of the Soviet Union

The loss of Eastern Europe was only the beginning. Despite Gorbachev's efforts to save his country, the Soviet Union itself collapsed. Glasnost and perestroika had unleashed two forces that would bring it down. One was the people's demand for democracy. The other was the desire of different ethnic groups for self-rule; the Soviet Union had been organized without regard for ethnic boundaries. As rumblings for independence began, Gorbachev even dispatched troops to preserve the Soviet Union.

The catalyst came in August 1991 when a group of hard-line Communists attempted a **coup d'état,** or a sudden revolt, and proclaimed an old-style communist government. The plotters arrested Gorbachev and ordered troops to Moscow. They failed, however, to take into account Boris Yeltsin, the recently elected president of the Russian Republic. Appearing before crowds gathered in front of the Russian parliament building, Yeltsin condemned the coup and called for the people's help. To protect him, tens of thousands of Moscow's citizens stood guard unarmed, ready to face down an expected attack. The soldiers refused to carry out orders, and the coup collapsed. Gorbachev was back in office, but Yeltsin now held the real power.

Both men knew that the Communist party had been behind the coup. Soon, Gorbachev stepped down as general secretary and abolished the party. Without communism holding the Soviet state together, the country itself shattered. Republic after republic declared its independence.

On December 25, 1991, Gorbachev formally resigned as Soviet president, saying, "We are living in a new world." His resignation marked the end of what was left of the Soviet Union. By this time, 11 of the 15 former republics had organized a loose union called the Commonwealth of Independent States (CIS).

AMERICAN PORTRAITS

Colin Powell
1937–

Born in New York of Jamaican immigrants, Colin Powell grew up in Harlem and the South Bronx. He recounts in his 1995 autobiography *My American Journey* that his "inability to stick to anything became a source of concern to my parents." Only after he enrolled in his college's Reserve Officers Training Corps (ROTC), did he find a focus: "I put the uniform on and looked in the mirror. I liked what I saw. . . . I felt distinctive."

An infantry officer in the Vietnam War, he was decorated for bravery. In the 1970s, Powell began to rise up the chain of command, receiving ever more important military and political appointments. Then, in 1988, he was named Chairman of the Joint Chiefs of Staff, the first African American to hold the office.

Military experts consider Powell a talented officer with tremendous organizational and leadership qualities. Some even called his management of Operations Desert Shield and Desert Storm "masterful." Powell retired in 1993 as Chairman of the Joint Chiefs of Staff, leaving open the possibility of a political career.

Critical Thinking Activity

Identifying Alternatives Since the first communist government had been established in Russia in 1917, the economy of the former Soviet Union had been strictly controlled. Gorbachev's main objective under *perestroika* was to reform the economic system, not scrap it. In the Russian Republic, Yeltsin moved more boldly. He set up a 500-day plan to legalize private property, abolish government subsidies, lift price controls, and institutionalize private banks and a stock market. Ask students to analyze whether they think such a massive undertaking should proceed at a moderate pace or quickly. **L3**

Troubles in the New States

All the former Soviet and communist bloc states faced serious economic troubles. In trying to set up capitalist economies, the new governments began lifting state controls on economies already in decline. So production fell, prices rose, and unemployment spread. People suffered from shortages of fuel, food, medicine, and housing.

Another problem was ethnic rivalry. Without tight communist control there was a rise of nationalism, and old hatreds surfaced. These hatreds led to the outbreak of bloody civil wars in many states. The worst was in what was formerly Yugoslavia.

Although Western nations, including the United States, quickly recognized the new countries, they were uncertain what kind of aid to send. Some people wanted to send cash to help support the new democracies. Others feared even a non-communist Russia might someday threaten world security and favored increasing trade and sending advisers, along with food and medicine. For the most part the United States government followed the latter course.

Part of the reason the United States was concerned about Russia was that it had most of the former Soviet Union's nuclear weapons. In 1992, Bush and Yeltsin met at Camp David and agreed to drastic reductions. Afterward, the President declared that the meeting marked "a new relationship based on trust, based on a commitment to economic and political freedom."

■ The Persian Gulf War

Meanwhile, the Persian Gulf War gave President Bush an opportunity to further define America's role in the post-cold war world. On August 2, 1990, Iraq's president, Saddam Hussein, sent invasion forces into Kuwait, its oil-rich neighbor. To punish this aggression, Bush froze $20 billion of Iraqi money in American banks and banned imports of Iraqi oil. The United Nations demanded that Saddam Hussein withdraw his forces and called for countries throughout the world to halt all trade with Iraq. But Iraqi troops remained in Kuwait.

Operation Desert Shield

Bush, with assistance from 25 nations around the world, assembled a huge military coalition he called "Operation Desert Shield." The United Nations then authorized military action to restore Kuwait's independence. The coalition waited for 6 months, however, hoping that diplomacy and the threat of force would prevent a war.

Operation Desert Storm

Finally, Bush initiated Operation Desert Storm. He ordered massive air strikes against Iraq on January 16, 1991, rejecting calls for further delay:

Visualizing **History**

▲ THE PERSIAN GULF WAR In January 1991 the United States launched a massive air and missile assault on Iraq after Iraq refused to withdraw from Kuwait. *Why had Iraq invaded Kuwait?*

ABCNEWS INTERACTIVE™

VIDEODISC

Lessons of War

Side Two, Chapter 7
Title: *Who Fights Wars?*
Subject: Thoughts from soldiers who fought in the Persian Gulf conflict

📁 Assign Primary and Secondary Source Readings, pp. 73–74: "Working Together to Discover a New Future."

Visualizing **History** War with Iran left Iraq's economy near collapse. Saddam Hussein needed a strategy for boosting oil revenues and for redirecting the blame for Iraq's worsening economy. He claimed that Kuwait was a historic part of Iraq and that Kuwait had unfairly drilled Iraqi oil. **Answer to Caption:** to gain control of its oil

CURRICULUM CONNECTION

Science and Technology
Computer technology has been adapted for many purposes, including guidance systems for weapons. The Tomahawk cruise missile, for example, uses a number of computerized guidance systems.

Cooperative Learning Activity

Creating a Time Capsule Organize students into groups of three and tell them their task is to create a time capsule that will inform people of the future how ineffective the communist economic system was. Suggest that students search for photographs or other forms of illustration; written materials such as books, pamphlets, or slogans; or artifacts that illustrate some aspect of communism. Have students display the materials they locate. Then ask the class as a whole to select the best materials for inclusion in the time capsule. **L2** 📦

Did You Know?

Of the 2 million individuals serving in the United States armed forces in 1990, about 11 percent were women. Women made up 7 percent of U.S. sailors, 35 percent of administrators, and 10 percent of military officers. Although women were barred from combat units, they flew helicopters carrying troops and supplies, worked as mechanics on tanks and trucks, and also worked as paratroopers and ship navigators.

 **Visualizing History**

▲ **COMING HOME** American military personnel return after taking part in Operation Desert Storm. Coalition forces took part in the military action after diplomatic efforts failed. *Who was the military leader of the operation?*

> ❝ *The world could wait no longer. ... While the world waited, Saddam Hussein met every overture of peace with open contempt. While the world prayed for peace, Saddam Hussein prepared for war.* ❞

After a month of bombing, General Norman Schwarzkopf led a lightning-swift ground assault. Just 100 hours later, Allied forces had crushed the Iraqi army and freed the Kuwaiti people. "Kuwait is liberated," Bush announced. "America and the world have kept their word."

■ Rethinking America's Military Role

The Persian Gulf War caused people in the United States to begin rethinking America's military role in the world. Some leaders felt the United States should scale down its military. They pointed out that the source of a country's power in the new world order promised to be its economy rather than its military. Examples of just such a change were evident by the emergence of Germany and Japan. So, as the federal deficits skyrocketed, Bush called for cuts in defense spending, and Congress made even greater reductions. The Pentagon planned a **drawdown** that would bring troops home from overseas bases in Europe and Asia.

Other experts, however, warned that the United States should maintain a strong military—and that the cost would be worth it. They pointed out that Cuba, North Korea, Vietnam, and the People's Republic of China remained communist nations. Although China had shown some signs of change by instituting various free-market programs, its Communist party leaders had massacred pro-democracy demonstrators at Beijing's Tiananmen Square in 1989.

■ Divided Government

Whereas President Bush acted decisively in foreign affairs, he was accused of wavering leadership at home. Part of the problem was that the government was divided again, with the presidency held by one

Sidelight: What's in a Name?

Iraqi leader Saddam Hussein liked to be called by his first name. For, when pronounced correctly, with the emphasis on the second syllable, *Saddam* means "leader," "learned one," or "he who confronts"—exactly how he wanted to be viewed. During the Persian Gulf Crisis, President Bush insisted on pronouncing the name with the emphasis on the first syllable. Pronounced this way, Saddam means "a boy who fixes or cleans shoes"—a grave insult in many Arab countries. Whether or not this was a conscious act by Bush, it did sum up the way he felt about his adversary.

party and Congress controlled by the other. During the Bush administration, this hindered the process of government.

Bush and Congress in Gridlock

Congress ignored or drastically changed many of the President's proposals. The President, in turn, vetoed many bills, knowing that the Democrats generally lacked the two-thirds vote needed to override his vetoes. The executive and legislative branches of the government quickly became gridlocked over such issues as reforming campaign financing, improving public education, recharging the economy, reducing the federal deficit, and balancing the budget.

Taxation Issues

When the federal deficit rose to a record level of $300 billion, Bush realized he would have to increase revenues. To do so, however, he was forced to break his campaign pledge of "no new taxes." In 1992, after weeks of negotiations with Democratic congressional leaders, Bush agreed to raise some taxes. Among these were gasoline, tobacco, and other **user taxes,** or taxes on products used by consumers. The President also agreed to make deep cuts in Medicare and military spending. Although this plan was defeated by conservative Republicans, the President and congressional leaders finally hammered out a compromise bill.

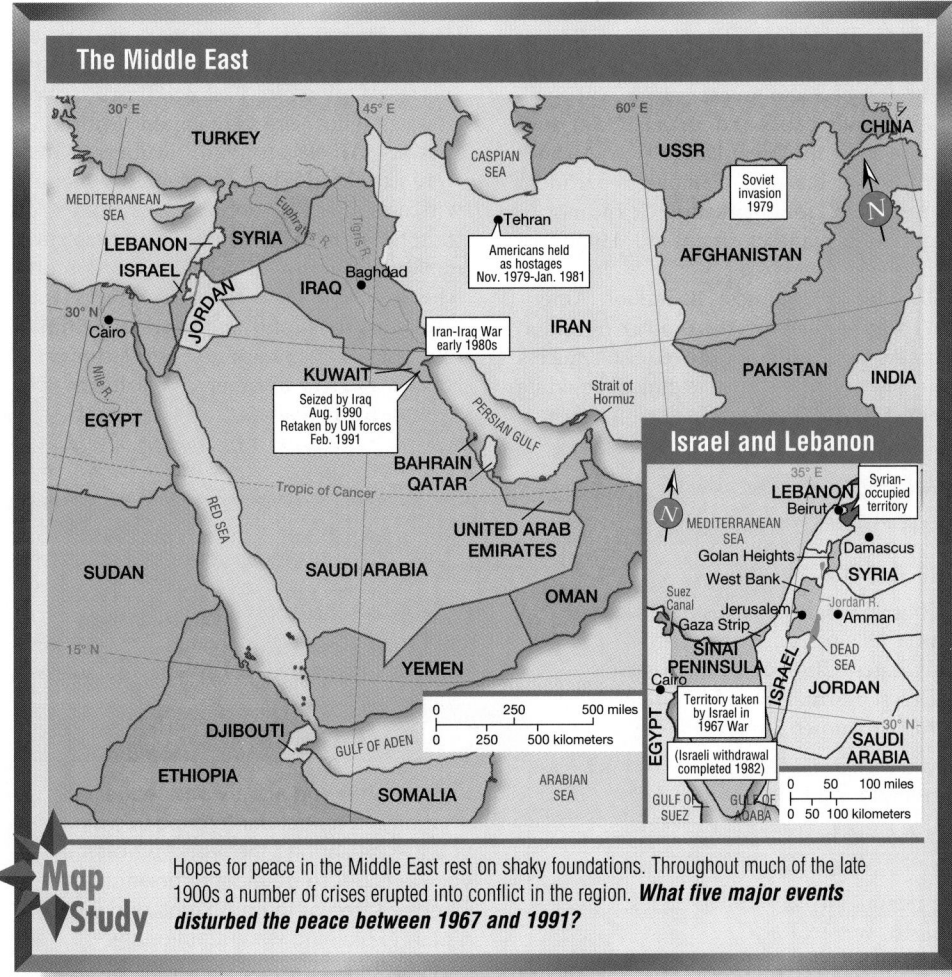

The Middle East

Israel and Lebanon

Map Study

Hopes for peace in the Middle East rest on shaky foundations. Throughout much of the late 1900s a number of crises erupted into conflict in the region. *What five major events disturbed the peace between 1967 and 1991?*

Linking Across TIME

Some political observers have suggested that the way George Bush viewed the Persian Gulf Crisis was deeply influenced by an incident from his high school graduation ceremony in 1940. In the commencement speech, former Secretary of State Henry Lewis Stimson said that, even though the world was at war and civilization was under attack, it was a time of great opportunity, because people had the chance to choose between good and evil.

Map Study *Using Maps*

Answer: 1967 war between Israel and Arab states; Americans taken hostage in Iran in 1979; Soviet invasion of Afghanistan in 1979; Iran-Iraq War, 1980–1988; Iraqi invasion of Kuwait in 1990

Map Skills Practice

Ask students why the United States considers the Persian Gulf an area of great strategic importance. *(It is the waterway through which much of the world's supply of oil must travel.)*

For additional map practice, assign Chapter Map Activity 25.

Assign Map Transparency Activity 25.

Sidelight: Computers

Computer technology has been adapted for many purposes, including guidance systems for weapons. The Tomahawk cruise missile, for example, uses a number of computerized guidance systems. During flight, a scanner matches the landscape to coordinates programmed before the launch and, as the missile approaches the target, a camera matches a picture of the target to data in the memory. Traveling at 550 miles an hour, the missile can hit a target as small as a door from 1,500 miles.

ASSESS

Check Understanding

Assign Section 3 Review as homework or an in-class activity.

Evaluate

Assign Section Quiz 25-3 or use the Test-maker to create a customized quiz.

Reteach

Have students complete Reteaching Activity 25-3.

Assign Workbook Activity 25-3.

Enrich

Have students complete Enrichment Activity 25.

Assign Geography in History Activity 25.

CLOSE

Discuss with students what they think are two of the greatest accomplishments and two of the most serious failures of the Bush administration.

■ Economic Woes in the Early 1990s

During the Bush administration, the economy grew more slowly than at any time since the end of World War II. Among other factors, sharply rising oil prices following Iraq's invasion of Kuwait threw America into a recession that persisted longer than expected.

The long recession was partly caused by consumer and corporate debts incurred during the Reagan era. Deregulation had allowed banks and savings and loans (S&Ls) to lend money more freely. Corporations funded mergers with **junk bonds,** or high-risk bonds that offer high yields.

Consumers ran up large debts on credit cards and home mortgages. The federal government, too, spent far more than it received. These debts limited the ability of consumers, corporations, and the government to spend and invest.

As a result, banks and S&Ls failed at rates unseen since the Great Depression. Airlines went out of business. Famous department stores filed for bankruptcy. Industries announced plant closings and layoffs of workers.

By mid-1992, almost 10 million Americans were unemployed. Another 6 million workers were **underemployed.** This means that these people held part-time jobs while looking for full-time work.

The Problem of Homelessness in America

As unemployment rose, people migrated from one state to another in search of jobs, and some found themselves homeless. Homeless people included battered women, runaway children, alcoholics, drug abusers, deinstitutionalized mental patients, and people lacking family support. Homelessness reflected rising rents, lower wages for unskilled workers, and the urgent need for low-cost housing. Estimates of the number of homeless people in America ranged as high as 3 million.

The Los Angeles Riots

The recession, poverty, and homelessness hit particularly hard at African Americans, Hispanics, and other minorities living in inner cities. Racial tensions ignited after four white police officers in Los Angeles who were videotaped beating an African American man, Rodney King, were acquitted. The city erupted violently with acts of arson, looting, and rioting that claimed more lives than had the 1965 riots in Watts. Conservatives blamed the Los Angeles riots on welfare programs that weakened the family and individual initiative. Liberals blamed the government's general neglect of inner cities during the Reagan-Bush years.

Section 3 ★ Review

Checking for Understanding

1. **Identify** George Bush, Jesse Jackson, Michael Dukakis, Boris Yeltsin, Commonwealth of Independent States (CIS), Saddam Hussein, Operation Desert Storm, General Norman Schwarzkopf, Tiananmen Square.

2. **Define** coup d'état, drawdown, user tax, junk bond, underemployed.

3. **Describe** changes in Eastern Europe that resulted from breaking free of the Soviet Union.

4. **Discuss** the reason why the United States resorted to force against Iraq.

Critical Thinking

5. **Identifying Alternatives**   In your opinion, should Presidents concentrate more on domestic issues or on foreign policy? Explain your answer.

ACTIVITY

6. Imagine that you are a world leader attending a global conference in which you are presenting the world problems you consider to be most important. Choose three of the problems and write a plan explaining what solutions you would offer.

Answers to SECTION 3 REVIEW

1. George Bush, 762; Jesse Jackson, 762; Michael Dukakis, 762–763; Boris Yeltsin, 764; Commonwealth of Independent States (CIS), 764; Saddam Hussein, 765; Operation Desert Storm, 765; General Norman Schwarzkopf, 766; Tiananmen Square, 766

2. All vocabulary words are defined in the Glossary.

3. Changes included: tearing down of the Berlin Wall; reuniting of East and West Germany; termination of Warsaw Pact; lifting of state controls on economies; rise in nationalism.

4. Iraq had refused President Bush's warnings, attempts at negotiation, economic pressure, and threat of warfare.

5. Answers will vary but students should present logical arguments to defend their positions.

6. Solutions should be plausible and address the problem adequately.

As the Brain Grows Older

Life expectancy in the United States increased dramatically in the twentieth century. In the early 1900s, most people died before the age of 50. By the year 2000, the average life expectancy will be 80 years for women and 76 for men. Even more significant is the fact that by 2000, 13 percent of all Americans will be 65 years of age or older. By 2025, one-fourth the population will be over age 65.

The aging population has prompted scientists to study the changes that occur in the brain with age. What these studies show is that the brain loses little functioning during most of the adult years. After age 65, deterioration in memory, spatial skills, and reasoning begins. What is most noticeable in the over-65 population, however, is the greater variation in brain function between individuals. That is, some people show only slight mental decline, while others show very noticeable losses. Alzheimer's disease, a

▲ SENIOR CITIZENS HIKING

condition that limits brain functioning, especially in memory, language, reasoning, and spatial abilities, afflicts millions of older adults in this country.

Research in the 1990s has centered on ways that older individuals can maintain or regain their intellectual strength. Just as diet and exercise have been shown to have a direct impact on physical fitness, researchers hope to identify educational, nutritional, and medical breakthroughs that can build mental fitness.

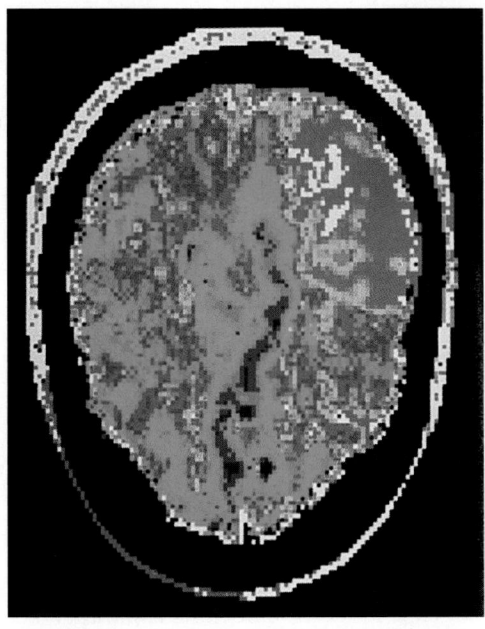

▲ BRAIN SCAN

Making the Science Connection

1. How does brain functioning change with age?

2. Describe two educational or nutritional factors that could be studied in relation to brain function.

Linking Past and Present

3. Why are declines in brain function and diseases such as Alzheimer's of particular significance at this time?

ACTIVITY

4. Research and write a report showing medical progress during the past 25 years on Alzheimer's disease.

CONNECTIONS
History AND SCIENCE

TEACH

In the United States alone, 4 million people are afflicted with Alzheimer's disease. Identified by a German doctor named Alois Alzheimer in 1906, the disease has baffled experts, and its causes have been subject to much conjecture. Some think that aluminum brings on symptoms. Others believe that head injuries could lead to the disease. Other possible causes include a chemical imbalance in the brain, the presence of a virus at birth, and a gene defect.

Did You Know?

Former President Reagan was diagnosed with Alzheimer's disease in 1994.

CURRICULUM CONNECTION

Health Americans' chances of staying alive longer have improved markedly over the last four decades thanks to refinements in the transplanting of organs and microsurgery—the use of high-powered lenses and laser beams in the operating room. A space-age diagnostic tool, the nuclear magnetic resonating scanner, or NRM, uses a combination of radio waves and magnets to detect diseases.

Answers to Making the Connection

1. The brain loses few of its functions during most of the adult years. After age 65, deterioration in memory, spatial skills, and reasoning begins.

2. Educational factors could include the amount of schooling an individual completes or the kinds of intellectual stimulation as one ages. Nutritional factors could include kinds of foods eaten or vitamin supplements taken.

3. A major reason is that people are living longer.

4. Reports should show evidence of research and be organized chronologically.

CHAPTER 25 ★ REVIEW

GLENCOE
TECHNOLOGY

 **VIDEODISC**

Use the MindJogger Videoquiz to review students' knowledge.

MindJogger Videoquiz

Chapter 25
Disc 3, Side B

Available in VHS.

Using Vocabulary

Carter—double-digit inflation, pork-barrel legislation; Reagan—supply-side economics, glasnost, federal deficit, perestroika; Bush—coup d'état, user taxes, drawdown, junk bond, underemployed

Reviewing Facts

1. Americans were interested in a political "outsider" after the scandal.
2. emphasized honesty, nonintervention, and selective support based on human rights
3. Reagan was optimistic, charismatic, and an effective communicator who stressed unifying themes.
4. Gorbachev introduced glasnost and perestroika and took steps to end the cold war.
5. economic crises, relaxation of price controls led to rising prices, low productivity
6. The United States took charge of restoring Kuwait's independence and initiated the assault against Iraq.

Using Vocabulary

On a separate sheet of paper, write three headings: *Carter, Reagan, Bush.* Classify each of the following terms under the Presidents to which they are related. Some terms belong in more than one category.

double-digit inflation	pork-barrel legislation
supply-side economics	federal deficit
glasnost	perestroika
coup d'état	drawdown
user taxes	junk bond
	underemployed

Reviewing Facts

1. **Explain** how Carter's election was partly a result of Watergate.
2. **Summarize** Carter's foreign policy philosophy.
3. **Describe** why Ronald Reagan appealed to the American people.
4. **Discuss** how Mikhail Gorbachev tried to save the Communist party and the Soviet Union.
5. **Describe** the problems faced by the former Soviet and communist bloc states.
6. **Explain** how the problems between Kuwait and Iraq helped define America's new role in world affairs.
7. **Discuss** the reason for Bush's decision to break his campaign promise and raise taxes.

Understanding Concepts

Political Ideology

1. Analyze how the image of the President may have affected popular support during the Carter and Reagan administrations.

Leadership

2. How does the role of the United States government in the economy during the 1980s and 1990s compare to its role during the early 1900s?

Critical Thinking

1. **Assessing Programs** The United States has had difficulty implementing an energy policy. Evaluate Carter's energy program. Explain why it was only partially successful.
2. **Analyzing Media** Television in the 1990s has exposed Americans to an unprecedented amount of news and information.
   a. In what ways does television benefit society?
   b. Do you think the overall effect of television is a positive one or a negative one? Explain.
   c. What role do you think public opinion polls should play in the political process? Explain.
   d. Do you consider television or newspapers a more reliable source of news? Explain.

History and Geography

The Middle East

Use the map on page 767 and information from Chapter 25 to help you answer these questions.

1. **Location** In what city were Americans held hostage?
2. **Region** What body of water separates Saudi Arabia from Sudan?
3. **Place** Why did Iraq invade Kuwait?
4. **Location** What nations border Afghanistan?

---

7. to increase revenues and reduce the federal deficit

Understanding Concepts

1. Answers will vary. Carter's lack of unifying themes made him seem indecisive to many Americans.

Conversely, Reagan was a master at articulating broad themes that unified Americans.

2. Answers will vary but should include that the government takes a much more active role today.

Critical Thinking

1. Answers will vary. Few Americans seem willing to pay the price for a strong policy. Carter found this out when he met strong opposition to his program, which called for sacrifices.

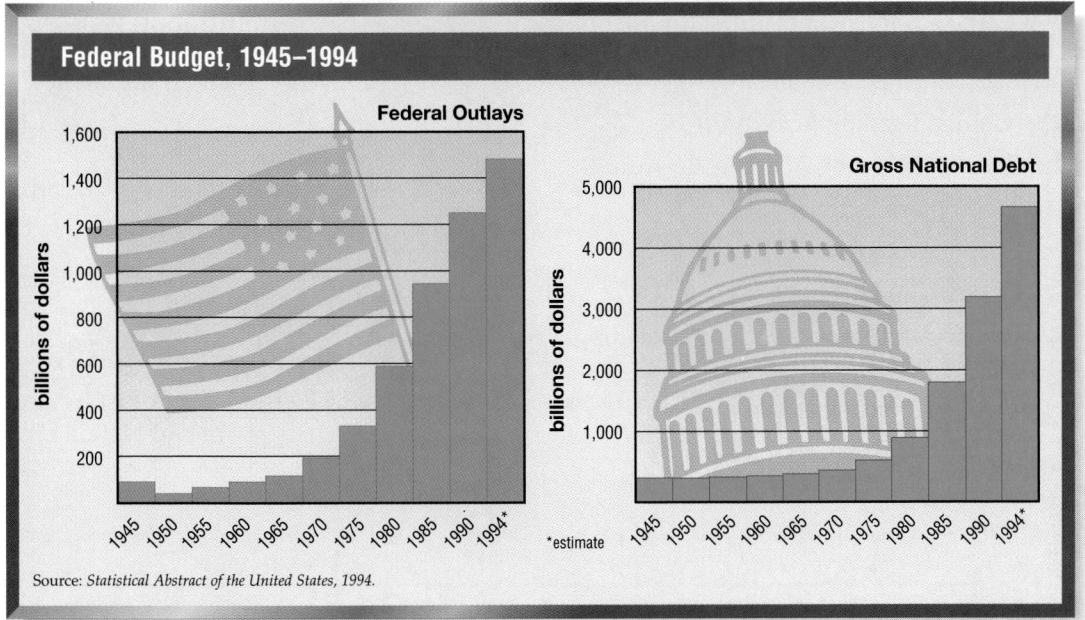

Federal Budget, 1945–1994

Federal Outlays

Gross National Debt

Source: *Statistical Abstract of the United States, 1994.*

Cooperative Learning ## Interdisciplinary Activity: Economics

Organize into four groups to research and analyze the two ways to reduce the federal deficit. Two groups will research and present arguments for and against raising taxes. The other two groups will research and present arguments for and against reduced government spending. You will have one class period to prepare. Select a representative from your group to report your arguments to the class. The members of the class should evaluate the arguments and decide which method would be best.

Practicing Skills

Reading a Bar Graph

Study the bar graphs on this page, then answer the questions that follow.

1. What do the two graphs show?
2. When did federal outlays surpass $400 billion?
3. When did the gross national debt surpass $1 trillion?

4. Why do you suppose federal outlays declined between 1945 and 1950?
5. Describe the trends shown in each graph.

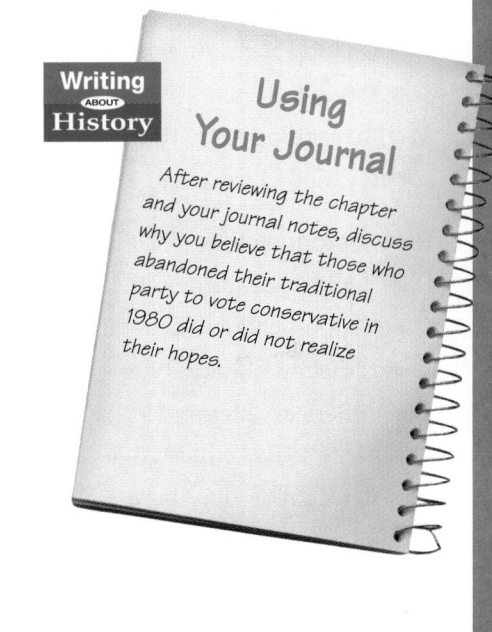

Writing About History Using Your Journal

After reviewing the chapter and your journal notes, discuss why you believe that those who abandoned their traditional party to vote conservative in 1980 did or did not realize their hopes.

which they present their arguments. Then have the other class members decide on the best method.

Practicing Skills

1. the federal outlays and the gross national debt
2. by 1980
3. by 1985
4. It was the period immediately following the war.
5. Federal outlays have increased steadily just as the gross national debt has risen.

Writing About History Using Your Journal

Students may base their views on whether conservative philosophies of low taxes and reduced federal spending have been realized.

Chapter Bonus Test Question

Ask students: Explain the effect of one of the following events.
1. Americans taken hostage in Iran. *(possible answer: key issue in Carter's reelection campaign)*
2. A special commission investigates the Iran-Contra scandal. *(possible answers: Democrats win back a Senate majority in 1986; put a brake on Reagan's programs)*
3. The Soviet Union collapses. *(possible answers: uncertain about how to aid the new countries of the CIS; concern about nuclear weapons in the hands of newly independent states)*

2. **a.** provides coverage of important issues around the world; increases awareness and knowledge about other cultures
b. Answers will vary but students should support their opinions.
c. Answers will vary. Some students might indicate

that public opinion polls should be an integral part of the political process. Others might indicate that polls should have nothing to do with the political process.

History and Geography
1. Tehran

2. Red Sea
3. Hussein invaded Kuwait because it was rich in oil.
4. USSR, Iran, Pakistan, China

Cooperative Learning
You might ask representatives from each group to participate in a panel discussion in

Daily Lesson Objectives	Teacher Classroom Resources	Multimedia
SECTION 1 **Reinventing Government** **1 Day** pp. 774–779 1. Explain why many Americans demanded a change in government in 1992. 2. Explain how gridlock between Congress and the President affected the process of government. 3. Discuss why criticism of the Clinton administration led to Republican control of Congress.	Reproducible Lesson Plan 26-1 *Guided Reading Activity 26-1 Concept Mapping Activities 26-A, 26-B *Vocabulary Activity 26 Chapter Map Activity 26 Critical Thinking Skills Activity 26 Primary and Secondary Source Readings, pp. 75–76 Workbook Activity 26-1 Reteaching Activity 26-1 *Section Quiz 26-1	Section Focus Transparency 26-1 Chapter Concepts Transparencies 26-A, 26-B Map Transparency 26 Testmaker Vocabulary PuzzleMaker MindJogger Videoquiz The Presidents: A Picture History of Our Nation
SECTION 2 **America in a Changing World** **1 Day** pp. 780–785 1. Describe the development of Clinton's foreign policy in the new world order. 2. Explain what key role the United States played in bringing about major breakthroughs between old enemies.	Reproducible Lesson Plan 26-2 *Guided Reading Activity 26-2 Cooperative Learning Activity 26 Political Cartoons in American History Activity 29 American Portrait 72 Geography in History Activity 26 Chapter Skills Activity 26 Workbook Activity 26-2 Reteaching Activity 26-2 *Section Quiz 26-2	Section Focus Transparency 26-2 Skills Transparency 26 Testmaker The Presidents: A Picture History of Our Nation
SECTION 3 **Challenges and Opportunities** **1 Day** pp. 787–792 1. Identify the challenges facing the United States in the 1990s. 2. Describe some of the proposed solutions to these challenges.	Reproducible Lesson Plan 26-3 *Guided Reading Activity 26-3 Linking Past and Present Activity 26 Enrichment Activity 26 American Literary Heritage, p. 49 Workbook Activity 26-3 Reteaching Activity 26-3 *Section Quiz 26-3	Section Focus Transparency 26-3 U.S. History & Art Transparency 28 Testmaker GTV: A Geographic Perspective on American History Powers of the Congress Focus on Government
CHAPTER REVIEW AND EVALUATION **1 Day**	Chapter 26 Test, Forms A and B Spanish Chapter 26 Summary Performance Assessment Activity 26	MindJogger Videoquiz Student Self-Test & Review Software *Chapter 26 Audiocassette Activity and Test

*Also available in Spanish

 OUT OF TIME? If time does not permit teaching the entire chapter, use the Chapter 26 Summary on pages 800–801 and the Chapter 26 audiocassette (English and Spanish) to point out the main ideas of the chapter.

A complete, 1-page lesson plan is provided for each section in the *Reproducible Lesson Plan* booklet.

Key to Ability Levels

Teaching strategies have been coded for varying learning styles and abilities.

L1 Basic activities for all students

L2 Average activities for average to above-average students

L3 Challenging activities for above-average students

LEP Limited English Proficiency activities

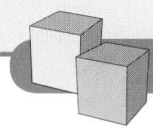

Block Schedule

Block scheduling differs from traditional class scheduling in the amount of time allotted to each period. The extended time frame provided by block scheduling affords you the opportunity to implement a greater number of research-oriented and activity-intense projects to motivate and involve your students. Activities that are particularly suited to use within the block scheduling framework are identified throughout this unit by the following designation:

✔ Performance Assessment Activity

Looking Ahead Divide the class into small groups. Have each prepare a list of the 10 most critical issues Americans face as they approach the year 2000. Ask groups to conduct a survey to determine if other Americans share their views. Suggest that each group compile an unbiased and comprehensive questionnaire for its survey. Based on the results of their survey, invite each group to present its 5 most critical issues to the class. Then have students compare and contrast the various lists. Which issues seem to be most important to teenagers? Which issues are most significant to adults in the community?

POSSIBLE RUBRIC FEATURES

- Research Skills
- Content Information
- Organization
- Written and Oral Communication Skills
- Critical Thinking Skills
- Creativity

📂 For additional activities, see Performance Assessment Strategies and Activities.

TEACHER'S CORNER

NATIONAL GEOGRAPHIC SOCIETY

INDEX TO NATIONAL GEOGRAPHIC MAGAZINE

The following articles may be used for research relating to this chapter:

- "Diminishing Returns," by Michael Parfit, November 1995.
- "Hawaii's Vanishing Species," by Elizabeth Royte, September 1995.
- "Israel's Galilee," by Don Belt, June 1995.
- "New Views of the Holy Land," by Richard Cleave, June 1995.
- "Earth Day: 25 Years Old," by Frank Graham, Jr., April 1995.
- "The Endangered Species Act," by Douglas H. Chadwick, March 1995.

- "The Everglades: Dying for Help," by Alan Mairson, April 1994.
- "Great Flood of '93," by Alan Mairson, January 1994.
- "Tragedy Stalks the Horn of Africa," by Robert Caputo, August 1993.
- "Who Are the Palestinians?" by Tad Szulc, June 1992.
- "Yugoslavia: A House Much Divided," by Kenneth C. Danforth, August 1990.

NATIONAL GEOGRAPHIC SOCIETY PRODUCTS AVAILABLE FROM GLENCOE

To order the following products for use with this chapter, contact your local Glencoe sales representative or call Glencoe at 1-800-334-7344:

- *The Presidents: A Picture History of Our Nation* (CD-ROM)
- *GTV: A Geographic Perspective on American History* (Videodisc)

- *GTV: The American People: Fabric of a Nation* (Videodisc)

ADDITIONAL NATIONAL GEOGRAPHIC SOCIETY PRODUCTS

To order the following products for use with this chapter, call National Geographic Society at 1-800-368-2728:

- *Branches of Government Series* (Video)
- *Democratic Government Series: The United States* (Video)
- *Nations of the World Series: Israel* (Video)

- *Jerusalem: Within These Walls* (Video)
- *Hawaii: Strangers in Paradise* (Video)
- *Energy: The Problems and the Future* (Video)

BEGINNING THE CHAPTER

GLENCOE TECHNOLOGY

VIDEODISC

Use the Chapter 26 MindJogger Videoquiz to preview the content of this chapter.

MindJogger Videoquiz

Chapter 26
Disc 3, Side B

 Available in VHS.

Recording Journal Notes

Suggest that students organize their notes under such headings as education, work opportunities, housing, health care, societal attitudes, and so forth.

Linking Across TIME

The last decade of the twentieth century marked the anniversary of Columbus's first voyage to the Americas. It was less a time of celebration than one of reflection on what the voyage meant to the American people. Many insisted that the nation recognize the effects of that event on the inhabitants of the Americas. Others wanted to commemorate the courage and daring of the voyagers.

CHAPTER 26
★★★

Toward a New Century
1992–Present

► **HAITIAN REFUGEE BOAT**

Setting the Scene

Focus

As 1992 dawned, the cold war had ended and a new world order was emerging. Instead of being sharply divided by the East-West conflict, nations were becoming more integrated, and their leaders were acquiring a more global outlook. As the United States struggled to define its role in this new world, urgent concerns at home threatened changes in government. Despite attempts by political leaders to be more responsive to the needs of the American people, voter dissatisfaction continued to grow.

Concepts to Understand

★ What **changes** occurred in government as a result of Clinton's election

★ How Americans were dealing with the **challenges** they faced

Read to Discover ...

★ how Clinton's policies—both domestic and foreign—affected Americans.

★ what challenges face the American government and people in the future.

Journal Notes

What do you think it would be like to be an immigrant from another country coming to the United States during the 1990s? Note details about it in your journal as you read the chapter.

CULTURAL	• Eric Clapton's "Unplugged" wins Grammy award	• Americorps helps student education • Projections show Hispanics as largest minority by 2010
	1992	**1993**
POLITICAL	• Bill Clinton is elected President • Yugoslav Federation breaks up	• Israel and PLO negotiate peace with American help • Congress approves NAFTA

➕ **EXTRA CREDIT PROJECT**

Congress and the President Congress and Presidents have often engaged in tugs of war over the powers of the executive and legislative branches, even though the Constitution spells out these powers. Suggest that interested students research examples of conflict between the two branches. Have them present their findings to the class and discuss how and why conflicts arise and how these conflicts reflect both the strengths and weaknesses of each branch.

L2

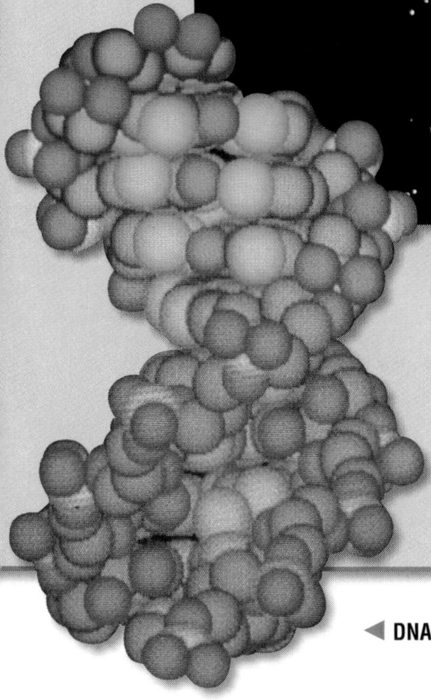

Concept Mapping Activity

On the chalkboard, reproduce the following generalization and concepts map, and have students copy it in their notebooks.

Americans face the future with confidence in their democratic institutions to meet the challenges of a changing society and the demands of global interdependence.

Changes

Challenges

☞ To reinforce the two chapter concepts, use Concept Mapping Activities 26-A and 26-B.

 ☞ Use Chapter Concepts Transparencies 26-A, 26-B.

History AND ART

Use the image to prompt discussion of space exploration. Ask students to consider both the benefits and the risks.

 NATIONAL GEOGRAPHIC SOCIETY

VIDEODISC

GTV: A Geographic Perspective on American History

Side 4, Chapter 14
Title: *You've Grown Accustomed to My Face*
Subject: Information Age

History AND ART

Earth
by David Lawrence, 1994

New technology has opened new avenues for artists. Computer-manipulated art combines actual photography and computer art to create a new image.

◀ **DNA**, COMPUTER MODEL

- *Scientists estimate 1 million Americans have HIV*
- *Internet revolutionizes communications*
- *Myrlie Evers-Williams leads NAACP*

1994	1995

- *Israel and Jordan, assisted by United States, sign peace treaty*
- *Republicans sweep midterm elections*
- *President Clinton authorizes $20 billion in loans and loan guarantees to Mexico*

✔ Performance Assessment

Have students work cooperatively to develop a questionnaire on the greatest challenges facing the world in the twenty-first century. Organize the students into three teams and assign each team the task of administering the questionnaire to one of the following groups: students in other classes, school faculty, adults in the community. Teams should collate results and present them. Representatives from each team should then combine results into a report on the five greatest challenges facing the world today. Display the report on the bulletin board.

L1

☞ Use Performance Assessment Activity 26 as an additional assessment technique.

FOCUS

Bellringer

Before taking roll, project Section Focus Transparency 26-1 or hand out Section Focus Transparency Activity 26-1. Have students answer the questions.

Motivating Activity

Have students give examples of the ways the federal government affects their everyday lives. *(taxes on some items, regulation of food products, air and water quality, prescription drugs, automobiles, and so forth)* Ask them if they agree or disagree with the idea that the federal government is too large. Point out that Section 1 explores reasons many Americans in the 1990s were dissatisfied with the federal government. **L1**

Vocabulary Precheck

Ask students to define each of the "Key Terms." Have a volunteer consult the dictionary for any unfamiliar words. **L1, LEP**

Use the Vocabulary PuzzleMaker for Chapter 26 to create a crossword puzzle. **L1**

Assign Vocabulary Activity 26.

★★★

Reinventing Government

Setting the Scene

Section Focus

Candidate Bill Clinton and his running mate, Al Gore, promised "to redesign, to reinvent, to reinvigorate the entire national government" by making it more efficient and responsive to the needs of the American people. As time passed, however, citizens expressed growing dissatisfaction. In 1994 Republicans won control of both houses of Congress.

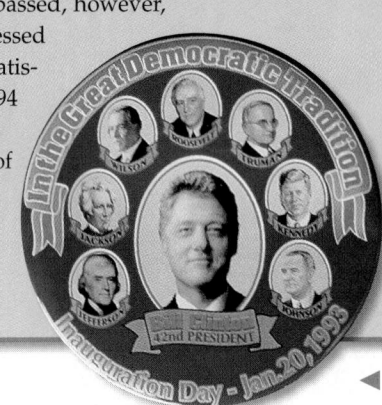

◄ MEMORIAL BUTTON, INAUGURATION DAY 1993

Objectives

After studying this section, you should be able to

★ explain why many Americans demanded a change in government in 1992.

★ explain how gridlock between Congress and the President affected the process of government.

★ discuss why criticism of the Clinton administration increased and led to Republican control of Congress.

Key Terms

incumbent, filibuster, downsizing, line-item veto, appropriations bill

---

At the beginning of the twentieth century, progressives had worked to strengthen and enlarge the small federal government. Their purpose in moving toward this objective was to equip government to handle the social and economic problems caused by industrialization. Toward the end of the century, government had grown so large that more Americans worked in local, state, and national government than in the manufacturing industries.

Many Americans believed government had grown too large, that it taxed too heavily and spent too much. Leaders from both major political parties promised to renovate government and make it more responsive to the needs of the people.

■ Demands for Change

As the election of 1992 approached, many people in the United States expressed demands for change in government. Public opinion had turned against Washington, D.C., "insiders" and **incumbents,** or people currently holding office. Voters blamed incumbents for the recession, the federal deficit, and government gridlock.

Government Scandals

Scandals deepened Americans' anger at incumbents. Revelations that some members of the House of Representatives had bounced checks repeatedly at the House bank outraged many citizens. They asked

---

Classroom Resources for SECTION 1

Blackline Masters:
- Reproducible Lesson Plan 26-1
- Guided Reading Activity 26-1
- Vocabulary Activity 26
- Chapter Map Activity 26
- Critical Thinking Skills Activity 26

- Primary and Secondary Source Readings, pp. 75–76
- Workbook Activity 26-1
- Reteaching Activity 26-1
- Section Quiz 26-1

Transparencies:
- Section Focus Transparency 26-1
- Map Transparency 26

Multimedia:
- Testmaker
- Vocabulary PuzzleMaker
- MindJogger Videoquiz
- The Presidents: A Picture History of Our Nation

▲ HILL AND THOMAS The Senate delayed the confirmation of Clarence Thomas to the Supreme Court when University of Oklahoma law professor Anita Hill accused Thomas of sexual misconduct. *What was the outcome of the confirmation hearing?*

how these officials could manage the nation's economy when they bungled their personal finances. Further angered when members of Congress voted to raise their own salaries, many political leaders and citizens took action. Ultimately, the movement led to the ratification in 1992 of the Twenty-seventh Amendment to the Constitution. This amendment prohibited any congressional pay raise from taking effect until after the following election, thus giving the voters a chance to act.

Another uproar followed President Bush's nomination of Clarence Thomas to the Supreme Court in 1991. One of Thomas's former coworkers, law professor Anita Hill, testified before the Senate Judiciary Committee that Thomas had sexually harassed her. Thomas strongly denied the charge.

The Senate narrowly confirmed Thomas to the Supreme Court, but many Americans were angry. Noting the absence of any women on the Senate Judiciary Committee and seeing that only 2 of the 100 senators were women, they argued that "2 percent is not enough." Building on the rising discon-

tent, more women ran for political office. As "outsiders" in politics, women candidates drew support from both women and men who demanded change.

The Race for President

After victory in the Persian Gulf War, President Bush's reelection seemed assured. Several Democrats declined to run against him. The lengthening recession, however, raised new doubts about his leadership and encouraged challengers to enter the race.

After a short struggle during the primaries, Bush received his party's nomination. He told voters that having set the world in order during his first term, he intended to begin rebuilding the nation. Blaming the Democrats' long control of Congress for gridlock, Bush called for the election of a Republican Congress.

Among the leading Democratic candidates for President was Governor Bill Clinton of Arkansas. Early in the campaign, the press raised questions about Clinton's character and his failure to serve in the armed forces during the Vietnam War. Yet Clinton emerged

Critical Thinking Activity

Making Judgments Early Presidents were able to oversee all the daily activities of the executive office and still have time for leisurely pursuits. Today the President's schedule is packed with meetings, reports, decisions, and ceremonial duties. With all this activity, a President may not have time to keep abreast of the everyday decisions of hundreds of executive agencies and offices. Ask students what part, if any, of the President's responsibilities should be delegated to another person or agency. Have students explain their responses. **L2**

TEACH
Guided Practice

Summarizing Write this outline of Section 1 on the chalkboard.
I. Reinventing Government
  A. Demands for Change
  B. A New Democrat
  C. Government Gridlock Persists
  D. The 1994 Congressional Elections

Direct students to write short summaries of the material presented in each section. Invite volunteers to read their summaries to the class. Suggest any necessary changes.
L1, LEP

Visualizing
History Ask students if they think the vote on the confirmation of Clarence Thomas to the Supreme Court might have turned out differently had there been more women in the Senate.
Answer to Caption: Clarence Thomas was confirmed.

CD-ROM
The Presidents: A Picture History of Our Nation

Suggest interested students select Political Parties from the main menu and the subcategory THIRD PARTIES. Have students identify national elections in which third-party candidates had a significant impact.

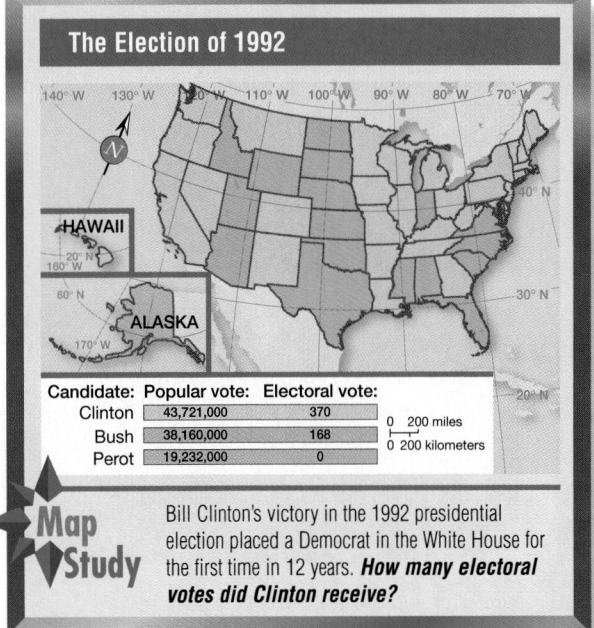

The Election of 1992

Candidate:	Popular vote:	Electoral vote:
Clinton	43,721,000	370
Bush	38,160,000	168
Perot	19,232,000	0

Map Study Bill Clinton's victory in the 1992 presidential election placed a Democrat in the White House for the first time in 12 years. *How many electoral votes did Clinton receive?*

as the leading contender after victories in the South and in Illinois and New York, and he won the nomination.

Texas billionaire H. Ross Perot fashioned a strong third-party challenge. Perot had promised to run if volunteers could collect enough petitions to place his name on all 50 state ballots. The outpouring of volunteers expressed demand for change as well as unhappiness with the two major parties.

A sign in Clinton's campaign headquarters read, "It's the economy, stupid." This blunt message was a strong reminder that, no matter what other topics might be debated, the recession was the number-one issue. Clinton painted the recession as the President's most glaring failure and made a campaign promise to revive the economy.

Election of 1992

About 104 million Americans—the largest number of people ever to go to the polls—voted in the presidential election of 1992. Clinton received 43 percent of the popular vote, while Bush captured 38 percent and Perot 19 percent. Clinton received less than a majority because of Perot's strong

showing, the highest for any third-party candidate since 1912.

Although Republicans gained seats in the House of Representatives for the first time since 1984, the Democrats retained control of both houses of Congress. Voters defeated 24 incumbents in House races and 3 running for reelection to the Senate.

Even more significantly, voters elected a record number of women and minority candidates. Twenty-four new women members were elected to the House, and four won Senate seats. Jay Kim was the first Korean American and Nydia Velazquez the first Puerto Rican woman in the House of Representatives. Carol Moseley Braun of Illinois was the first African American woman senator, while Ben Nighthorse Campbell was the first Native American in the Senate in more than 60 years.

A New Democrat

President Clinton identified himself as a "New Democrat" who represented the moderate wing of the party. Only 46 years old, Clinton was a complex person who, at times, presented different images to different people. He embraced middle-class values, playing music, jogging, and exhibiting a taste for fast foods.

Yet Clinton had graduated from such elite institutions as Georgetown University and the Yale Law School and had attended Oxford University as a Rhodes scholar. Reflecting a tension between these two facets of his personality, Clinton changed positions on a number of issues. Critics complained that these shifts showed that Clinton was a pragmatic politician and compromiser rather than a committed leader.

Taxes

One of the more dramatic shifts concerned a middle-class tax cut. As a candidate, Clinton had called for a tax cut along with new spending to stimulate the economy. Soon after he took office, Clinton learned that the federal deficit would be even bigger than estimated. As a result, Clinton concluded that reducing the deficit would put the government in a stronger position to respond to future economic problems. He abandoned plans for the tax cut and instead supported tax increases to raise more revenue.

Congress passed the deficit reduction plan but then defeated the Clinton administration's $16 billion spending plan that had been intended to stimulate the economy. Opponents of the spending plan had successfully argued that increasing spending while trying to cut the deficit sent a mixed message to Americans.

An Anticrime Program

President Clinton moved quickly to deal with the problem of crime, focusing largely on prevention. The administration's crime bill gave grants to cities and states to hire a total of 100,000 new police officers. The program also contained a "3 strikes and you're out" policy that mandated life imprisonment for those convicted of 3 major felonies.

In addition, the crime bill banned many types of assault (military-style) weapons, and the Brady Law established a waiting period for the purchase of handguns. This waiting period gave authorities a chance to determine whether the buyer had a criminal record. As part of the anticrime package, Congress approved money for such programs as midnight basketball leagues that would keep young people occupied during high-crime hours.

Dealing With the Bureaucracy

The President and Vice President Al Gore planned ways to redesign the national government. They called for greater and more efficient use of computer technology to sustain services with fewer workers, and they launched a National Performance Review to examine each government agency. The purpose of the review was to eliminate outdated and unnecessary functions and to shrink the bureaucracy to create a government that "works better and costs less."

■ Gridlock Continues

With Democratic majorities in both houses of Congress, the President hoped at last to end government gridlock. After an initial "honeymoon," however, during which Congress passed some legislation formerly vetoed by Presidents Reagan and Bush, gridlock reappeared.

Ruth Bader Ginsburg
1933–

★★★★★★★★★★★ AMERICAN PORTRAITS

On August 10, 1993, Ruth Bader Ginsburg was sworn in as the 107th justice of the United States Supreme Court. The second woman ever to serve on the Court, Justice Ginsburg attended law school at a time when women often suffered discrimination. Ginsburg experienced discrimination firsthand when, in 1960, Supreme Court Justice Frankfurter refused to hire her as his law clerk because she was a woman. Having a keen sense of fairness, Ginsburg successfully argued against a number of laws that treated men and women differently, even when the laws gave women favorable treatment.

When Ginsburg became a judge on the United States Court of Appeals, she carefully thought out her decisions just as she had carefully prepared her cases when she was a lawyer. Largely because of those decisions, the Senate approved her appointment to the Supreme Court.

Teaching American Portraits

Point out that women are becoming more influential at all levels of government. The gender barrier was broken in the Supreme Court when President Ronald Reagan appointed Sandra Day O'Connor to the bench, opening the way for Bill Clinton's appointment of Ruth Bader Ginsberg. Ask students what benefits they think women might gain from having two female justices on the Court. (*Answers will vary but may include that the two may bring a different perspective to issues of special interest for women, such as abortion, that could come before the Court.*) **L1**

GLENCOE
TECHNOLOGY

 VIDEODISC

Focus on Government

Side 1, Chapter 17
Title: *Interest Groups*
Subject: Profile of Lead or Leave, a grassroots interest group started by two young activists

Sidelight: The Supreme Court

Unlike jurors who decide cases in the lower courts, justices of the Supreme Court have not been representative of the general population in social class, background, gender, or ethnic group. They have come from upper socioeconomic levels. Only two African American justices have been appointed, Thurgood Marshall and Clarence Thomas, and only two women, Sandra Day O'Connor and Ruth Bader Ginsberg.

Visualizing
History President Clinton asked Vice President Al Gore to investigate ways of redesigning and streamlining government.
Answer to Caption: encouraged greater use of computer technology, launched a National Performance Review of government agencies to eliminate outdated functions and shrink the bureaucracy

ASSESS

Check Understanding

Assign Section 1 Review as homework or an in-class activity.

Evaluate

🖰 ☞ Assign Section Quiz 26-1 or use the Testmaker to create a customized quiz.

Reteach

Ask students to outline the major conflicts between the Clinton presidency and the Congress. Have them write a paragraph or two on how they think such conflicts could have been avoided.

☞ Have students complete Reteaching Activity 26-1.

☞ Assign Workbook Activity 26-1.

Visualizing
History

▲ CLINTON AND GORE From the beginning, the Clinton administration worked to streamline government. *What plans did the administration put in place for redesigning the government?*

Gridlock remained a problem partly because Democrats had split into two camps on some issues. Democrats who favored smaller government were uncomfortable with many of Clinton's proposals. They considered ways to cut back some social programs and many environmental and regulatory provisions.

The Republicans, however, remained united in their opposition to most administration programs. In the Senate, Republicans used delaying tactics to block passage of certain bills. The main weapon they used was the **filibuster.** To filibuster means to keep talking for hours until a majority of the Senate either abandons the bill or agrees to modify its most controversial provisions.

■ The Clinton Health Plan

A central goal for the administration was to set up a system of health care to provide for the 15 percent of Americans with no insurance. The President named his spouse, Hillary Rodham Clinton, an experienced attorney, to lead a task force that would recommend changes in the health-care system. When completed, the Clinton plan guaranteed basic health benefits to all Americans.

The plan required employers to shoulder much of the burden for health insurance for their employees. As a result, the plan was opposed by small-business owners who feared that they could not afford it.

The insurance industry, which stood to lose revenue, was also opposed. This industry sponsored a series of television commercials featuring a fictitious couple who worried what impact the Clinton health plan would have on their lives. The majority of Americans already had medical insurance. As a result, the commercials encouraged people to worry that universal health care might increase their costs and reduce the quality of care they were currently receiving in order to pay for the uninsured.

The Republicans also challenged the Clinton health-care plan, deriding it as too big, complicated, and costly. After viewing a chart representing the Republican view of the administration's program, Clinton's White House chief of staff said:

❝ *It looks more like a New York subway system, and I don't think it represents our health-care plan at all.* ❞

Soon the Democrats, too, deserted the President's plan and proposed a variety of alternatives. None of their plans, however, attracted enough support to be passed into law. Conservative radio talk-show hosts attacked the Clinton health-care plan and criticized the President and his wife, causing Clinton's popularity to dwindle.

■ Criticism Increases

Accusations against his personal morals and financial ethics also hurt the President. A key issue was the Whitewater scandal. Clinton had invested in Whitewater, an Arkansas land development project that had gone bankrupt. Soon, Republicans demanded a congressional investigation.

Many middle-class Americans who still felt insecure economically also criticized the President. Early in Clinton's term the economy improved as unemployment fell,

---

Critical Thinking Activity

Forming an Opinion Have students review the system of checks and balances set up by the Constitution. Ask them to summarize the powers of the Congress and the powers of the President and form an opinion answering the following questions: Do you think the executive branch has become too powerful? Do you think the Congress has become too powerful? Have students explain their answers to the class. **L1**

☞ For additional practice, assign Critical Thinking Skills Activity 26.

inflation remained low, and the federal deficit declined. Many people, however, continued to worry about losing their jobs.

Many men over the age of 50 had lost their jobs because of cutbacks in the defense industry and by corporate **downsizing,** the process by which companies seek to achieve savings by reducing the number of midlevel employees. Many of those who lost their jobs found it hard to locate new employment at comparable salaries. Some had to resort to part-time or temporary jobs with less security, lower income, and no benefits.

The 1994 Congressional Elections

Mounting criticism of the Clinton administration was reflected in the results of the 1994 congressional elections. Before the elections, President Clinton had called on voters to keep Democrats in the majority. Instead, Americans turned control of both the House and Senate over to the Republicans for the first time in 40 years. Every Republican incumbent running for reelection won. Prominent Democrats lost, including House Speaker Tom Foley, who had served in Congress for 30 years.

A key to the Republican victories was their "Contract with America" that proposed lower taxes, stronger restrictions on immigration, tougher anti-crime laws, limits on congressional terms, a balanced budget, and the **line-item veto.** This kind of veto would

allow the President to veto particular items in an appropriations bill without having to veto the entire bill. An **appropriations bill** sets aside money for a specific purpose. The new Republican speaker of the House, Newt Gingrich of Georgia, blamed New Deal and Great Society programs for creating a culture of poverty and violence. Condemning the growth of large government, Gingrich vowed to "erase the slate and start over."

 ▲ THE 100 DAYS Speaker Newt Gingrich (above) and other House Republican leaders promised that they would bring 10 significant measures to a vote within the first 100 days of the session. Most of the measures were passed. Only term limits and the balanced-budget amendment stalled. *What is the line-item veto?*

CHAPTER 26 Toward a New Century: 1992–Present   **779**

Section 1 ★ Review

Checking for Understanding

1. **Identify** Clarence Thomas, H. Ross Perot, Carol Moseley Braun, Hillary Rodham Clinton, Newt Gingrich, Contract with America.

2. **Define** incumbent, filibuster, downsizing, line-item veto, appropriations bill.

3. **List** two reasons for the anti-incumbent mood in the United States during the early 1990s.

4. **Explain** why President Clinton called himself a "New Democrat."

Critical Thinking

5. **Identifying Alternatives** In your opinion, should President Clinton have shifted his political position on key issues, such as the deficit, once he took office? Explain your answer.

ACTIVITY

6. Imagine you are a member of Congress. Write a one-page paper identifying two bills you would introduce. Discuss your choices.

Visualizing
Ⓗistory As speaker of the house, Gingrich led a movement to eradicate public programs that he felt cost the taxpayers too much money. **Answer to Caption:** allows the President to veto particular items in an appropriations bill

Enrich

Suggest students research a past instance in which a President has come into conflict with a Congress dominated by the opposition party. Ask them to analyze the conflict and tell how it was resolved.

🗀 Assign Primary and Secondary Source Readings, pp. 75–76: "Forty Years of Nonsense."

CLOSE

Have students summarize the issues that caused voter dissatisfaction with government. Have them speculate on how the Contract With America might overcome this dissatisfaction.

Answers to SECTION 1 REVIEW

1. Clarence Thomas, 775; H. Ross Perot, 776; Carol Moseley Braun, 776; Hillary Rodham Clinton, 778; Newt Gingrich, 779; Contract With America, 779
2. All vocabulary words are defined in the Glossary.
3. blamed for recession, deficit, and gridlock; voters were angry at behavior

4. He said he represented the moderate wing of the Democratic party.
5. Some may say he should have stuck to his positions and been more aggressive in dealing with opposition; others may say he had to compromise in order to get anything done.
6. Students should provide explanations for making the choices they did.

SECTION 2

★★

America in a Changing World

Setting the Scene

Section Focus

For more than 40 years, the struggle to contain communism determined United States foreign policy and defined America's role in the world. When the Soviet Union dissolved in 1991, the world changed, and America's role changed with it. The United States government now had to consider each country and issue separately.

Objectives

After studying this section, you should be able to

★ describe the development of Clinton's foreign policy in the new world order.

★ explain what key role the United States played in bringing about major breakthroughs between old enemies.

Key Terms

multinational state, genocide, ethnic cleansing, global economy, trade deficit, creditor nation, debtor nation

◀ TRAVEL PASSPORT

The struggle between communism and democracy was virtually over. Yet, throughout the world bloody wars erupted over ethnic hatreds, political boundaries, and religious views.

■ Foreign Policy

In his first year in office, President Clinton began to develop a different direction in foreign policy, stating that the United States should seek to enlarge the global community of market-oriented democracies. Clinton generally sought to achieve his goals through diplomacy or by using economic pressures. Whenever the prospect of using military force arose, however, the President tried to work through the United Nations.

Civil War in Somalia

One of the first crises to confront the Clinton administration was civil war in the east African nation of Somalia. While warring factions battled for power, Somalian civilians were dying of hunger by the thousands. When Clinton took office in 1993, more than 28,000 American troops were already in this war-torn land, having been ordered there by President Bush in 1992 to lead a United Nations mission. The force served to protect deliveries of food to the starving Somalians.

Fierce fighting, however, obstructed the task, and the longer American troops remained in Somalia, the more they were drawn into the conflict. When television cameras recorded the body of an American soldier being dragged through the streets,

780   UNIT 7 Redefining America: 1954–Present

public opinion in the United States, which had favored the Somalia mission, changed. Under fierce criticism for not providing adequate protection for American soldiers, the President set a deadline for withdrawal of all United States troops. In February 1995 American marines returned to ensure safe passage out of Somalia for the remaining American personnel.

Bloodshed in the Balkans

Uneasiness over Somalia made the United States hesitate over involving itself either militarily or via other means in conflict in the Balkans. After World War II had ended, Yugoslavia had been created as a **multinational state,** or a nation with many different ethnic groups. Six republics were part of the new nation—Croatia, Slovenia, Bosnia-Herzegovina, Serbia, Montenegro, and Macedonia.

Although each republic had a dominant ethnic group, the populations were mixed. Dividing the people were centuries-old differences based not only on the ethnic group to which they belonged but on religion and territorial claims as well.

War Begins

In 1991 the republics of Slovenia, Croatia, Bosnia-Herzegovina, and Macedonia declared their independence. They did so after Serbia, the largest of the former republics, refused to agree to a looser confederation that would give the other republics greater autonomy. Under its leader Slobodan Milosevic, Serbia began waging war against the breakaway states.

The most violent fighting occurred in Bosnia-Herzegovina, where Bosnian Serbs wanted to retain ties with Serbia. Bosnian Serb forces followed a policy of **genocide**— the systematic destruction of an ethnic, political, or cultural group—of the Muslims and Croats. The Serbs also engaged in what is known as **ethnic cleansing,** in this case, the expulsion of Bosnian Muslims and other non-Serbs from areas under Bosnian Serb control. As a result of the war, about 300,000 people died and 2.7 million lost their homes.

 ▲ SOMALIA By late 1992 anarchy ruled the east African nation of Somalia, plagued by a civil war for more than 3 years. Gangs of rival clans battled for power while civilians starved. American troops served to protect food deliveries to the people. *Why did public opinion about the mission in Somalia change?*

Exploring Options

The United States and western Europe were unable to decide how to reduce the suffering of the besieged people. Initial steps included the UN instituting an arms embargo against all the former Yugoslav states, placing trade sanctions on Serbia, and sending a peacekeeping force into Bosnia.

Throughout the conflict, the United States also tried to persuade its NATO allies to stage air strikes against Bosnian Serb military sites. NATO jets, acting under the authority of the United Nations, attacked several military targets in November 1994. In retaliation, Bosnian Serbs kidnapped 165 United Nations peacekeepers and offered to exchange them for NATO flight plans.

Then, in a sudden and surprising move, Bosnian Serb leader Radovan Karadzic (RAH•doh•vahn ka•RAH•dzihk) requested the diplomatic services of former United States President Jimmy Carter. Carter managed to arrange a shaky truce that turned increasingly fragile as warfare erupted again in early 1995.

TEACH
Guided Practice

Evaluating Display a wall map of the world. Invite volunteers to locate places around the globe where trouble erupted during the first years of the Clinton presidency. Ask students to write a report explaining which conflict they think was the most serious in terms of United States's political and economic interests. Have students present their reports to the class for discussion. **L2**

Did You Know?

Former President Jimmy Carter has established the Carter Center in Atlanta, Georgia. It is committed to helping solve problems of poverty, public health, and human rights on a global scale. Among its achievements is a dramatic reduction in the incidence of river blindness, a disease that afflicts some 11 million people in economically developing nations.

Visualizing History
Discuss with students how the United States came to be involved in conflicts such as the one in Somalia. **Answer to Caption:** TV cameras recorded an American soldier being dragged through the streets.

Cooperative Learning Activity

Writing a Feature Article Form students into four groups. Assign one of the following topics to each group: Civil War in Somalia, Bloodshed in the Balkans, Unrest in Haiti, Moves Toward Peace in the Middle East. Ask each group to write a feature article evaluating the policies of the Clinton administration in these areas. Each article should define the policy and assess its success. What problems still remain? What speculations can be made about the future in these areas? Have groups share their articles and discuss the strengths and weaknesses of Clinton's foreign policy. **L3**

☞ For additional practice, assign Cooperative Learning Activity 26.

Visualizing
Ⓗistory

▲ REFUGEES In the 1990s poor conditions in Cuba and Haiti swelled the
flow of "boat people" seeking refuge in the United States. ***For what other***
reason did many Haitians leave their homeland?

NATO Responds

When a Bosnian Serb mortar attack killed
39 citizens of Sarajevo and wounded 88
more, NATO responded in force. In a massive bombing campaign—the largest mission in the alliance's history—NATO
aircraft flew more than 500 attacks on Serb
targets in a two-day period in September
1995. The air campaign played an important
part in forcing the combatants back to the
negotiating table.

The Geneva talks ran into new stumbling
blocks, but at the same time offered some
reasons for optimism. Bosnia, Croatia, and
Yugoslavia—acting for the Bosnian Serbs—
reached an agreement that affirmed
Bosnia's territorial integrity but provided
for an independent separate Bosnian Serb
state within its boundaries. American
diplomat Richard Holbrooke heralded
the talks as "an important milestone in
the search for peace." Further negotiations to try to close the gap between the
warring sides hinged on key issues such as
implementing a truce, setting the proportions of the territorial divisions, and providing equitable treatment for Muslim
Croatians.

Conflict in Chechnya

At the start of the 1990s, relations
between the former parts of the Soviet
Union were being radically redefined as
demands for self-rule grew. By the mid-
1990s, tensions were rising in the Russian
Federation. The north Caucasus republic of
Chechnya attempted to secede from the
Federation. Russian leader Boris Yeltsin sent
forces into Chechnya both to bring the
republic back into the Federation and as a
warning against secession to the other Russian republics.

Soon after the invasion, Yeltsin noted,
"Everything will be settled soon on the
Chechen issue. I am in strict control."
Events, however, contradicted Yeltsin's confidence. Vastly outnumbered Chechen
forces held off the Russians' superior firepower. Russian looting, torture, and indiscriminate bombing drew sharp criticism
from human rights leaders. The Russian
government acknowledged only that isolated instances of rights violations had
occurred. After the capital city of Grozny
fell, Chechen forces vowed to take to the
mountains south of the capital and continue
the war from there.

Sidelight: Chechnya

The 1.3 million people of this oil-rich, mostly
Muslim area in Russia's North Caucasus region
make up less than 1 percent of the population of
the Russian Federation. Chechnya under
President Jokhar Dudayev declared its independence in 1991.

Unrest in Haiti

Closer to home, unrest in the Caribbean nation of Haiti posed difficult challenges for the United States. In December 1990, a Roman Catholic priest, Jean-Bertrand Aristide (ah•ree•STEED), had won the presidency of Haiti in the country's first fully democratic elections. In September 1991, however, the Haitian military, headed by Lieutenant General Raoul Cédras (SAY•drahs), overthrew Aristide. The new rulers of Haiti used violence—even murder—to put down opposition, causing thousands of Haitians to flee for their lives to the United States in flimsy boats.

Clinton and the Haitian Refugees

During the presidential campaign, Clinton had criticized the Bush administration's policy of sending Haitians rescued at sea back to their homeland rather than offering them asylum in the United States. Once he took office, however, Clinton also sought to stem the tide of Haitian refugees to the United States. The President accepted the argument of Gulf Coast governors that their states could not absorb large numbers of new and very poor refugees.

Attempts to Restore Democracy

To try to topple the Haitian military government and restore democracy, the UN used economic pressure, imposing an embargo of oil and arms in October 1993 and of all trade seven months later. The United Nations also called for an end to all financial aid to Haiti, which was desperately poor. As a result, in June 1994 Clinton banned all financial transactions between the United States and Haiti. Despite this growing pressure, Haiti's rulers retained their tight grip on the country.

Opting for stronger measures, the United Nations authorized the United States to lead an invasion to drive the military rulers out of Haiti. General Cédras commented, "I am the pin in Haiti's hand grenade—if pulled an explosion will occur." On September 18, 1994, the eve of the planned invasion, President Clinton sent former President Jimmy Carter to negotiate with Haiti's military

rulers. The threat of an invasion persuaded the generals to step down peacefully. The next day, 2,000 American troops met no resistance when they landed in Haiti. Joined by soldiers from other countries, they provided stability for the return of President Aristide on October 15, 1994. In February 1995 Carter returned to Haiti to help implement plans for new elections.

■ Moves Toward Peace in the Middle East

Although bloody wars seemed to be raging all over the post-cold war world, there were also breakthroughs as old enemies moved toward peace. The United States played an important role in several peace efforts in the Middle East.

Israeli-PLO Agreement

Of all the conflicts in the Middle East, the Arab-Israeli conflict had been the most enduring and difficult. When Israel was created from British-occupied Palestine in 1948, Palestinian Arabs had been forced to move to the West Bank of the Jordan River. This area soon came under the control of Jordan, however. In 1964, some of these displaced people formed the Palestine Liberation Organization (PLO) to work toward an independent Arab Palestine.

Then in 1967 Israeli troops seized the Gaza Strip from Egypt and Jordanian territory west of the River Jordan, including Jordan's part of the city of Jerusalem. In 1987, after 20 years of smoldering rage, the Palestinians in both areas began an uprising. Finally, in October 1991 the United States, under President Bush, succeeded in getting the two sides to begin peace talks. By the time Clinton took office, however, hostilities had disrupted them.

Although Clinton devoted much of his first year in office to domestic issues, he put together a Middle East policy team and resumed the peace process. Over the next eight months, talks proceeded erratically, breaking down frequently. Then on September 13, 1993, Israeli Prime Minister Yitzhak Rabin (EE•tsahk rah•BEEN) and Palestine

📁 Assign Workbook Activity 26-2.

Linking Across **T I M E**

Since its emergence as a major industrial power, the United States has usually exported more goods to other nations than it has imported. However, in the 1970s, oil prices rose and the United States imported more oil. The balance of trade shifted, with the United States importing more goods than it exported. This shift was accompanied by the growing economies of Western Europe and Japan, which competed with American companies that wanted to sell their products overseas. In the 1990s the balance was beginning to shift again in favor of the United States.

NATIONAL GEOGRAPHIC SOCIETY

CD-ROM
The Presidents: A Picture History of Our Nation

Suggest students select The Presidency from the main menu and the subcategory PRESIDENTIAL POWERS. Have students list the powers of the President as the nation's chief diplomat.

Sidelight: League of Arab States

The League of Arab States was created in 1945. Among the members are Egypt, Iraq, Jordan, Kuwait, Lebanon, Libya, the Palestine Liberation Organization, Saudi Arabia, Somalia, and Syria. Goals of the organization include promoting economic and political cooperation and mediating disputes among the Arab states. The league also represents Arab states in certain international negotiations.

Visualizing
(H)istory The Palestine Liberation Organization was forced in 1964 to press for an independent Palestinian homeland.
Answer to Caption:
It would grant self-rule to most of the 1 million Palestinians in the West Bank. Israel promised to withdraw troops and close the offices of its military government in the West Bank.

Did You Know?

While many former Communist nations were altering their political and economic fabric in the late 1980s and early 1990s, the People's Republic of China resisted democratic reforms. Leaders of China said they would institute some capitalist-style economic reforms, but they ruled out any Western-style political changes.

Visualizing
(H)istory

▲ **A NEW ACCORD** PLO leader Yasir Arafat, seated right, and Israeli Prime Minister Yitzhak Rabin, seated left, sign the September 1995 agreement in the East Room of the White House. President Clinton, King Hussein of Jordan, third from right, and Egyptian President Mubarak, second from right, viewed the signing. ***What were the terms of the agreement?***

Liberation Organization leader Yasir Arafat (YAH•suhr AIR•uh•FAHT) reached an agreement. The PLO recognized Israel's right to exist, and Israel recognized the PLO as the representative of the Palestinians. In addition, both parties agreed on a framework for limited Palestinian self-rule in the Gaza Strip and the West Bank.

A New Agreement

Almost exactly two years later, Israel's cabinet approved an agreement with the

• •

Footnotes to History

The West Bank *The West Bank* refers to lands west of the Jordan River between Israel and Jordan. The area, which encompasses 2,200 square miles, includes many places of religious and cultural importance for Jews, Christians, and Muslims. Under British rule in the early 1900s, the West Bank was seized by Jordan in 1948. Israel secured the area during the 1967 Mideast War and placed it under military occupation. In December 1987 Palestinians launched work stoppages and demonstrations called the *intifada* to focus world attention on the plight of the Palestinians and to bring international pressure to deal with their conditions.

PLO that would grant self-rule to most of the 1 million Palestinians in the West Bank. Under the new agreement, Israel promised to withdraw troops and close the offices of its military government in the West Bank. The transfer of power faced opposition from Jewish settlers in the West Bank as well as Islamic people opposed to the Israel-PLO peace process.

Then on November 4, 1995, Yitzhak Rabin was shot and killed by an Israeli student at a peace rally in Tel Aviv. The assassination was the first of an Israeli political leader. Acting prime minister Shimon Peres pledged that he would continue Rabin's efforts "with full sails, with full force."

Peace Between Israel and Jordan

President Clinton also had helped work out a peace agreement between Israel and Jordan. In July 1994, Prime Minister Rabin and Jordan's King Hussein signed a historic peace treaty officially ending the state of war that had existed between their countries for nearly half a century. The treaty also had other objectives. It set up a framework for cooperation in such areas as environmental protection, tourism, and trade. The

Cooperative Learning Activity

Assessing Policy Organize the class into seven groups. Assign one of the following areas to each group: South Africa, China, Japan, Western Europe, Eastern Europe, Latin America, and the Middle East. Have each group present a report on American policy today toward its assigned area. Have each student from each group take on a specific task such as obtaining resources, researching, writing, and presenting. Have the spokesperson for each group present a five-minute report, then open the topic for class discussion. **L2** 🗂

two former adversaries stated that they supported a "just, lasting, and comprehensive peace between Israel and its neighbors."

■ America in a Global Economy

Innovations in technology and economics have transformed national and regional economies into a **global economy,** an economic world without strict borders where products, personnel, money, and resources intertwine. Wide-ranging developments in transportation and communications have made international trade a booming business and an economic driving force in today's world. Part of this pattern is the growth of multinational corporations, companies that produce and market goods in a number of different countries.

The United States had long based its economic prosperity on selling its industrial and agricultural goods abroad. By the 1970s, however, the United States was losing its economic dominance as more and more nations strengthened their own industries and trade. America experienced **trade deficits,** purchasing more from foreign nations than they sold in foreign markets. By the early 1970s, the United States had changed from a **creditor nation,** or a lending nation, to a **debtor nation,** or a borrowing one.

The United States reacted to its declining economic position by working to become more competitive in the global marketplace. In recent years, many American multinational companies have become globalized corporations, meaning that they operate throughout the world and not just in specific foreign areas.

The government also pursued ways to strengthen America's economic position in the global marketplace. Just weeks before Clinton took office, the United States, Canada, and Mexico had signed the North American Free Trade Agreement (NAFTA), which lifted all tariffs, making North America the world's largest free trade area.

The agreement offered American manufacturers an opportunity to open factories in Mexico, where wages were lower. At the same time, Mexican and Canadian markets would be more open to American products and services. Critics of the agreement argued, however, that workers would be displaced when nations agree on trade pacts that lower barriers to trade. Congress approved the treaty in November 1993, after an almost year-long battle.

During the 1990s, the American trade record was mixed. The United States achieved trading surpluses with most nations. The nation's trade deficit, however, reached a record $11.43 billion in May 1995. Export growth in merchandise and a $300 million decrease in auto imports were counterbalanced in part by crude oil imports, which increased to their highest level in more than 4 years.

ASSESS
Check Understanding
Assign Section 2 Review as homework or an in-class activity.

Evaluate
⊙ 🗁 Assign Section Quiz 26-2 or use the Testmaker to create a customized quiz.

Reteach
Ask students to summarize the strengths and weaknesses of Clinton's domestic programs and foreign policy initiatives.

🗁 Have students complete Reteaching Activity 26-2.

Enrich
🗁 Assign Political Cartoons in American History Activity 29.

🗁 Assign American Portrait 72: Steven Jobs.

🗁 Assign Geography in History Activity 26.

CLOSE
Discuss with students the impact on American society of the major domestic programs the Clinton administration was able to pass.

Section 2 ★ Review

Checking for Understanding

1. **Identify** Jean-Bertrand Aristide, Raoul Cédras, Palestine Liberation Organization (PLO), Yitzhak Rabin, Yasir Arafat, North American Free Trade Agreement (NAFTA).

2. **Define** multinational state, genocide, ethnic cleansing, global economy, trade deficit, creditor nation, debtor nation.

3. **Explain** why President Clinton found it difficult to decide when and how to intervene in another nation's affairs.

Critical Thinking

4. **Making Judgments** Weigh the pros and cons of American companies' moving factories to foreign countries to take advantage of lower wages there.

ACTIVITY

5. Create a chart titled "World Trouble Spots in the 1990s." Include the countries and regions discussed in Section 2. Use the following headings: "Country or Region," "Location," "Conflicts," and "Resolutions."

Answers to SECTION 2 REVIEW

1. Jean-Bertrand Aristide, 782; Raoul Cédras, 782; Palestine Liberation Organization (PLO), 784; Yitzhak Rabin, 784; Yasir Arafat, 784; North American Free Trade Agreement (NAFTA), 785

2. All vocabulary words are defined in the Glossary.

3. conflicted over whether to use diplomacy to resolve issues or military force

4. Answers will vary. Pro: American workers are overpaid, American companies cannot compete in world markets; Con: move has displaced thousands of U.S. workers.

5. Student charts should include items under each category.

BUILDING SKILLS
Social Studies Skills

TEACH

Tell students that you can draw conclusions about a topic by studying a bar graph. Using information from the graphs, ask students to write a statement about the position of U.S. multinational corporations in the global economy. **L2**

Did You Know?

Multinational corporations are not a new idea. They began to develop around the turn of the century. By 1969 the combined sales of foreign subsidiaries of U.S companies were larger than the gross national product of France or Britain.

 Project Skills Transparency 26 and have students complete Skills Transparency Activity 26.

Use Chapter Skills Activity 26 to reinforce students' understanding of the skill.

CURRICULUM CONNECTION

Economics The profit motivation of multinationals becomes clear when one examines the reasons that a firm goes multinational. Most firms develop into multinational corporations to take advantage of lower production and labor costs, to gain control over raw materials they need, and to avoid international tariffs.

Interpreting Statistics

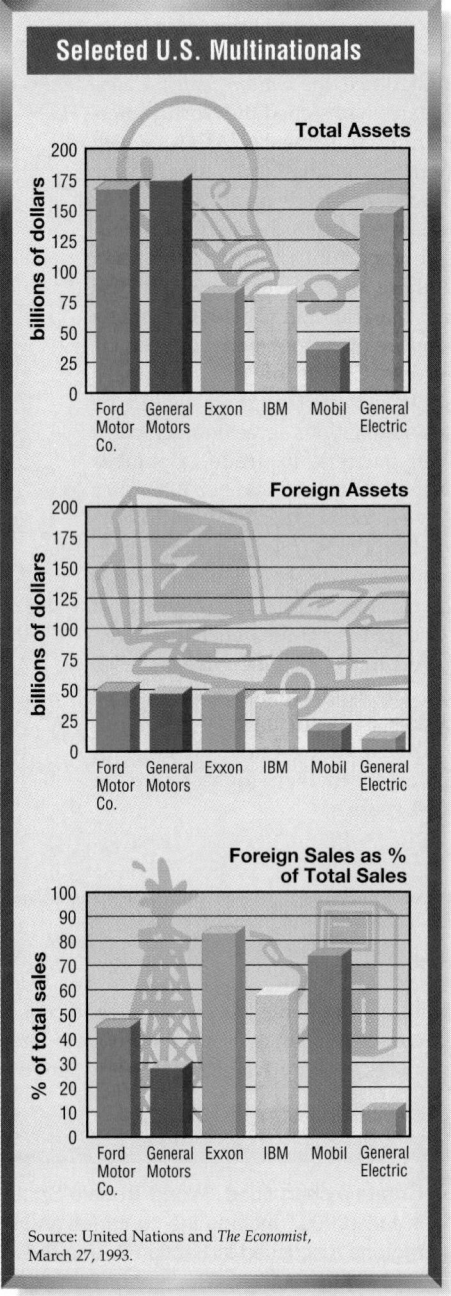

Source: United Nations and *The Economist*, March 27, 1993.

786

Often presented in graphs and tables, statistics, or numerical data, need to be carefully examined to determine their real significance. The ability to interpret statistics allows us to understand probable effects and make predictions.

Learning the Skill

Use the following steps to help you interpret statistical information.

- **Scan** the graphs, reading the title and labels to get an idea of what is being shown.
- **Check** the graphs for unfamiliar terms. When you find one, look up the term in your book's glossary or in a dictionary.
- **Examine** the statistics, looking for increases and decreases, similarities and differences.
- **Determine** the conclusions you can draw from the statistics.

Use these guidelines to help you interpret the statistics on the graphs on this page. Then answer the questions that follow.

Practicing the Skill

1. What subject do all these graphs deal with?
2. What do the graphs' keys tell you?
3. What do the labels on the horizontal axes tell you?
4. Which company has the greatest total assets?
5. How are assets and sales related?
6. Which companies sell more of their products nationally than internationally?

APPLYING THE SKILL

7. List five household items you use. Visit three stores that have these items. Price the items by store and brand and organize your data into five separate graphs. Summarize your findings in a one-page report.

Answers to Practicing the Skill

1. U.S. multinational corporations
2. for two of the graphs, total assets and foreign assets in billions of dollars; for one, foreign sales as a percentage of total sales
3. the companies that the different colored bars represent
4. General Motors
5. Sales are a part of a company's assets.
6. Ford Motor Company, General Motors, and General Electric
7. Students should present complete data. Summaries should be cogent and follow logically from the data.

★★

Challenges and Opportunities

LESSON PLAN
SECTION 3, 787–792

Setting the Scene

Section Focus

Even though the threat of the cold war was over and America was taking its place in the new world order, other challenges faced the United States. Worry about their children's future and the challenges facing the nation during the 1990s troubled many Americans.

◀ **AIDS** RIBBON

Objectives

After studying this section, you should be able to

★ identify the challenges facing the United States in the 1990s.

★ describe some of the proposed solutions to these challenges.

Key Terms

fiscal year, continuing resolution, acid rain, wetland, crack cocaine, illegal alien

FOCUS

Bellringer

Before taking roll, project Section Focus Transparency 26-3 or hand out Section Focus Transparency Activity 26-3. Have students answer the questions.

Motivating Activity

Have students complete the following statements:
"The biggest challenge facing Americans today is . . . ."
"The greatest opportunity we have is . . . ."
After students have explained their choices, lead a discussion that focuses on the criteria they used to decide. Tell students that in this section they will study some of the challenges and opportunities that face the United States today. **L1**

Vocabulary Precheck

Ask students to define each of the "Key Terms." Have a volunteer consult the dictionary for any unfamiliar words. **L1, LEP**

*A*s Americans made their way through the 1990s, they wrestled with a large number of economic and social problems. Some problems were of relatively recent origin, while others were long in the making. All defied easy solutions.

■ Political Issues

American political leaders faced several key issues during the mid-1990s. Included were balancing the budget, cutting the growth of social programs, and toughening standards for welfare and other issues.

Medical Coverage

Much of the debate concerned two medical programs established in 1965. Medicare provides health care for people 65 years of age and over. Medicaid provides health insurance for the needy who could not otherwise afford care.

Lawmakers agreed that changes were needed to guarantee Medicare's existence into the twenty-first century. Republicans and Democrats differed, however, on how to keep the program solvent. Republican leaders proposed $270 billion in cuts in order to balance the budget by 2002. Senate Democrats presented a plan that would save about $90 billion. President Clinton presented his own Medicare blueprint that would trim a total of $124 billion as part of a plan to balance the budget by 2005.

Republicans backed a proposal to reduce projected Medicaid spending over a seven-year span by nearly a third. The federal government would provide the states fixed amounts of money each year, and the states would be free to lay out their own Medicaid programs. President Clinton countered with a proposal that would continue to guarantee

---

Classroom Resources for SECTION 3

Blackline Masters:
- Reproducible Lesson Plan 26-3
- Guided Reading Activity 26-3
- Linking Past and Present Activity 26
- Enrichment Activity 26

- American Literary Heritage, p. 49
- Workbook Activity 26-3
- Reteaching Activity 26-3
- Section Quiz 26-3

Transparencies:
- Section Focus Transparency 26-3
- U.S. History & Art Transparency 28

Multimedia:
- Testmaker
- GTV: A Geographic Perspective on American History
- Powers of the Congress
- Focus on Government

TEACH
Guided Practice

Analyzing Issues Lead a class discussion on the patterns of twentieth-century immigration. Review the traditional "push-pull" factors that influence immigration, such as economic forces, war, and religious persecution. Then ask students to write a brief answer to the following question: What issues do you think have arisen because of the most recent wave of immigration? **L1**

CURRICULUM CONNECTION

Demographics In an article in the 1990 January-February *Futurist*, forecasters made predictions about the future of the United States. Among the predictions: the nation's population will peak at about 302 million by the year 2040; the nation will need to care for about 5 million AIDS patients by 2000.

NATIONAL GEOGRAPHIC SOCIETY

 VIDEODISC

GTV: A Geographic Perspective on American History

Side 4, Chapter 12

Title: *What Goes Around, Comes Around*

Subject: Modern life: an environmental statement

---

care to certain groups of needy Americans and curb costs by limiting annual growth in federal spending per beneficiary.

Government Response

Both Democratic and Republican leaders called for reforming the welfare system, but they had different reasons. Some sought reform because of the cost to the government and to decrease the deficit. Others argued that the system had to change because it created a "culture of poverty" in which the poor were trapped by their dependence on welfare.

In June 1994, Clinton proposed a sweeping reform plan. It offered increased education and training for welfare recipients and set a two-year limit on benefits. After this limit expired, most recipients would have to go to work. The President's plan also called for a crackdown on "deadbeat parents" by using the Internal Revenue Service to collect overdue child support. The Clinton plan, however, stalled in Congress.

Some members of Congress offered different ideas. Speaker of the House Newt Gingrich argued that the government should cut public assistance and emphasized that it was up to the poor to find work. Gingrich also advocated relying on private charities instead of the federal government to rescue the most impoverished.

Welfare

In September 1995 Senate Republicans rejected the House version of welfare reform. Senate Majority Leader Robert Dole

•••••••••••••••••••••••••••••

Footnotes to History

Medicare and the Elderly Reports indicate that by the year 2002 Medicare's hospital trust fund will run out of money. What caused the depletion? One reason is that elderly Americans are living longer because of improved medical science and the access to health care that Medicare provides. In addition, the number of retirees continues to grow in comparison to the number of workers. There were 5.6 workers for every retiree in 1965. By 1995 the ratio of workers to retirees was 3.3 to 1. Estimates indicate that by 2035 the ratio will be 2 to 1.

of Kansas calmed Republican moderates and Democrats with a number of concessions, including more money for child care. The new plan, which provided for a stronger role in welfare to the states, gained President Clinton's support. Implementation of the plan would bring to an end 60 years of federal responsibility for welfare.

The Budget

Yet questions remained on the sweeping changes envisioned for Medicare, Medicaid, and welfare reform because of disputes over appropriations. In order to predict and control revenue and spending for each year, the federal government uses a budget. The federal budget operates in a **fiscal year**—a 12-month accounting period that extends from October 1 of one year to September 30 of the next. Without appropriations for the fiscal year, the government faces the prospects of shutting down.

When it missed the 1996 fiscal deadline, Congress passed a **continuing resolution** giving agencies spending authority over a limited period. Despite this temporary measure to keep the government funded, other decisions loomed. The government's authority to borrow money reached the $4.9 trillion debt ceiling in October. If Congress refuses to raise the ceiling, the government could be forced to default on its bonds. Some House Republicans pledged to use the debt ceiling as a bargaining point to gain President Clinton's support for their budget bill. Speaker Newt Gingrich, however, admitted difficulty in controlling his own party and noted that any budget deal with the White House would require weeks to work out the details.

Looking to 1996

With the 1996 presidential election still more than a year away, several Republican leaders had announced their candidacy. The group included Dole, Senator Phil Gramm of Texas, former education secretary and Tennessee governor Lamar Alexander, and political analyst Pat Buchanan. Dole was the early front-runner for the nomination with Gramm establishing himself as a strong contender. Clinton supporters worked to guarantee the

---

Special Needs Activity

Study Strategy Ask students to think of one specific skill or strategy in these activities that helped them to learn the material in the text. Have them demonstrate the use of this skill or strategy to a classmate using the material in this section. Ask them to consider these questions: What learning procedures continue to be difficult? How can you overcome problems created by your distinct learning style? What effect does the teacher's instructional style have on your learning? Finally, have students complete this sentence: I learn best when I . . . . **L1, LEP**

Linking Past and Present

Third Parties

The Republican and Democratic parties dominate the two-party system, yet the United States has a long history of other political parties that have risen to challenge the major parties.

Then

Voices for Change

The Republican party was itself a third party in 1856; just four years later, it captured the White House.

At the turn of the century, the Populists seriously threatened

◀ **PROGRESSIVE PARTY CARTOON**

the two-party monopoly. The Populist party had an impact on politics and government far beyond its showing in national elections. Most importantly, minor parties have served as vehicles for reform by taking clear-cut stands on controversial issues and proposing bold and original solutions. Other significant third parties include the Free Soil party (1848-1852), the Know Nothings (1856), the Progressive party (1912-1948), and the American Independent party (1968-1972).

Now

The Independence Party

In 1995, business leader and 1992 presidential candidate H.

UNITED WE STAND, AMERICA

Ross Perot formed a third political party—the Independence party.

The Independence party focused on several key issues, including reforming congressional campaign practices, passing a balanced budget amendment, and abolishing the electoral college. Perot contended that his party was for the majority of Americans "who don't feel represented by either the Republicans or the Democrats."

President's renomination and to install organizations and plan strategies for each state—even before the Republicans selected their nominee.

Clouding the political picture were new developments. One was Ross Perot's announcement of the new Independence party. Surveys indicated that Perot had the support of about 20 percent of voters—roughly the same support he received in 1992. Some analysts contended that Perot supporters faced a huge challenge in getting the party on state ballots in all the states. Others countered that it could be done. "In the last 15 years, five people [John Anderson, Ed Clark, Lenora Fulani, Andre Marrou, and Perot himself] have gotten on the ballot in all 50 states and the District of Columbia."

Many Americans held out hope that former Army chief of staff Colin Powell would announce his candidacy. Powell himself seemed to rule out a run as an independent candidate: "It [is] the most difficult way to

do it. The financial aspects to it, the lack of a structure, the lack of an organization. . . ."

Some Republicans worked on a draft Powell movement after polls indicated that Powell would make a better showing against Clinton than the other GOP candidates. Other party members felt that a Dole-Powell ticket might prove unbeatable. Some Republicans, however, contended that a Powell candidacy would undermine the party's agenda, citing Powell's support for abortion rights, affirmative action, and gun registration.

Social Issues

Seeking to help students who had left school before graduation, such programs as Boston's City Year and New York's City Volunteer Corps launched volunteer programs to provide them with job skills. Volunteers received scholarships in return for performing community services such as assisting disabled children.

CHAPTER 26 Toward a New Century: 1992–Present **789**

Independent Practice

Research Have students research an important public health issue in their community. Suggest they collect articles from newspapers and other sources for a period of two weeks. Then have them write a report detailing the issue and possible solutions for presentation to their town or city council. **L3**

📁 Assign Guided Reading Activity 26-3.

Linking Past and Present

Tell students that after announcing the formation of the Independence party, Perot and his followers prepared to register the party in 50 states. To register the party Perot had to abide by the requirements of individual states. In California, for example, the new party needed 890,064 signatures in support of the party. The name of the party would have to be changed in some states, where the Independence party name was already taken. Ask students why a third-party candidate for President would appeal to some people in the United States. **L1**

📁 For additional practice, assign Linking Past and Present Activity 26.

Sidelight: Family Incomes

Median household income for American families decreased between 1989 and 1992. For all households the median income dropped from $31,750 in 1989 to $31,203 in 1990, to $30,126 in 1991. During this period the income for white households fell from $33,398 to $31,569; for African American households from $19,862 to $18,807; for Hispanic-origin households from $24,078 to $22,691, and for Asian and Pacific Islander households from $39,654 to $36,449.

Historically Asian Americans have experienced considerable discrimination. Therefore they have tended to live together for protection and self-help. Although Asian American political gains have not been as dramatic as those of other minority groups, that may soon change. One writer noted, "As younger Americanized (and American-born) Asians enter their adult years, they are likely to become more involved in politics."

Visualizing History ▲ THE MILLION MAN MARCH In October 1995 African American men met in Washington to acknowledge renewed commitment to self-help and family responsibility. A part of the demonstration was devoted to launching a nationwide voter registration drive to help chart government policy. *What Clinton administration programs were aimed at students?*

In addition, at President Clinton's urging, Congress set up Americorps in 1993. This program employed students as resources to deal with the country's most pressing issues. Volunteers received a salary and, after completing their service, scholarships to continue their education. By bringing young people of different economic, racial, and ethnic backgrounds to work together in a common effort, the program helped break down barriers of mistrust and promote a strong sense of community responsibility.

The Environment

Threats to the environment also troubled Americans in the last decade of the twentieth century. The battle continued between those who wanted to preserve natural wilderness unchanged and those who favored greater development of natural resources. Concern about the environment heightened after a 1989 tanker accident off the coast of Alaska caused one of the biggest oil spills in history.

One of the more controversial issues concerned **acid rain,** rain made by acidic gases given off when oil, gas, or coal burn. Environmentalists contended that acid rain kills fish, damages crops, and strips forests, and they called for stricter regulations to prevent it. Developers, on the other hand, warned that more regulations meant higher costs for companies that burn fossil fuels, forcing them either to find other energy sources or to

install pollution-control devices. Accepting either option, they argued, would send costs spiraling upward and lead to loss of jobs.

The President took steps to prevent further loss of America's **wetlands,** or land or areas such as tidal flats or swamps that contain much soil moisture. He also stopped developers from building in areas that would affect migrating birds and other wildlife. In return, the government eased federal restrictions on other land in which developers were interested.

The Clinton administration also pushed for other measures to protect the environment. Some of the new measures reduced solid and toxic wastes as well as air and water pollution. Others reduced American use of substances that destroy the ozone layer of the atmosphere.

Risks to Health

In the 1990s, there were increasing risks to the health of the American people. Diseases such as AIDS (*A*cquired *i*mmune *d*eficiency *s*yndrome) killed thousands in the United States. Drug addiction also wreaked havoc and caused many to demand action from the federal government.

The Spread of AIDS

During the 1980s and 1990s, AIDS spread rapidly throughout the United States. By the mid-1990s, AIDS was the third leading

Cooperative Learning Activity

Finding Solutions The issues addressed in Section 3 unite the world in that they create common concerns, goals, and needs. Point out that students will be involved in the search for solutions to these issues in their adult years. Hold a roundtable discussion on an issue selected by the class. Then organize the class into a number of committees to investigate various aspects of the issue. Have groups report their findings to the class. Ask students to suggest ways in which they as adults would attempt to resolve these issues. **L3**

cause of death among Americans aged 25 to 44. From 1981 through June 1994, more than 400,000 AIDS cases were diagnosed in the United States. During the early 1990s, there were 20,000 deaths a year and estimates placed the number of Americans infected with HIV (which in many cases leads to AIDS) at 1 million.

Responding to these alarming statistics and the growing demand for action, the federal government launched programs to educate Americans about the dangers of AIDS. It encouraged voluntary behavioral changes that would reduce the spread of the disease. President Clinton appointed a federal AIDS policy coordinator. Acting on his proposals, Congress increased the funding for AIDS research and fully funded the Ryan White Care Act, providing $275 million to cities for AIDS treatment.

Drug Abuse

In the 1990s, drug abuse continued to spread. For a while, the "Just Say No" campaign begun in the 1980s during the Reagan administration seemed to be working to limit drug use among children.

Between 1991 and 1995, however, marijuana use among high school students nearly doubled. In a 1994 study, 8 percent of eighth graders, 16 percent of tenth graders, and 20 percent of twelfth graders said they had smoked "pot" during the previous 30 days. Joseph Califano, Jr., a former cabinet member and head of Columbia University's Center on Addiction and Substance Abuse, said:

> ❝ . . . [T]he most frightening thing is that smoking marijuana is clearly a steppingstone to more serious problems. Children who smoke pot are 85 times more likely to use cocaine. ❞

Cocaine use was also on the rise. **Crack cocaine,** a form of the drug that comes in smokable chunks, proved to be extremely potent and able to cause addiction very quickly. Using cocaine while pregnant can cause addiction in a newborn baby, and hospital reports indicated that more and more newborns were testing positive for cocaine.

These children, sometimes called "crack babies," often suffered serious and lasting health and behavioral problems.

The Clinton administration also launched a war against the sale and use of illegal drugs, focusing on lowering the demand for drugs. As part of his crime program, the President proposed "drug courts" that would order hard-core abusers to undergo treatment. Republican leaders in Congress, however, disagreed with Clinton's prevention measures. They viewed supply as the principal problem and advocated a continuing emphasis on stopping drug smuggling from South America and on prosecuting drug dealers.

■ The Issue of Immigration

Economic and political ills around the world brought a new tide of immigration to the United States during the 1990s. Roughly a fifth of the nation's 22.6 million foreign-born residents arrived between 1990 and 1995. Although some Americans called for accepting the immigrants, others expressed alarm. Traditionally known as a "nation of immigrants," the United States was beginning to slam its doors.

Many of the new immigrants were refugees from such places as the former Soviet Union, eastern Europe, Vietnam, Cuba, and Haiti fleeing from political repression and economic hardships in their homelands. Some newcomers were **illegal aliens,** people who enter a country without a legal permit. Many illegal immigrants were from Mexico. Total legal immigration surpassed 1 million a year during the late 1980s, the highest number since the early 1900s. About 50,000 immigrants a year were allowed in from the former Soviet Union alone.

Illegal Aliens

Threatened by the distasteful choice of losing jobs and services or paying higher taxes, many Americans directed their anger at immigrants. The issue took on an even more emotional tone in states with large concentrations of illegal immigrants such as Florida, Texas, and California. For example, California's governor Pete Wilson blamed much of

Food of the Times

Like earlier immigrants, newcomers from Asia, Africa, the Caribbean, Mexico, and Latin America have introduced other Americans to a variety of new foods and dishes. Many have tasted these foods for the first time in the scores of ethnic restaurants spread across the nation.

GLENCOE
TECHNOLOGY

 VIDEODISC

Focus on Government

Side 1, Chapter 9

Title: *Citizenship in the United States*

Subject: Introduction to the requirements for citizenship, the naturalization process, and the responsibilities of citizenship

ABCNEWS
INTERACTIVE™

 VIDEODISC

Powers of the Congress

Side Two, Chapter 49

Title: *Becoming a U.S. Citizen*

Subject: Swearing in a new group of American citizens

Critical Thinking Activity

Making Predictions Remind students of the questions they should ask when making predictions about the outcome of an event or issue: What related prior conditions existed? What caused these conditions? What was the event or issue supposed to accomplish? Based on the answers to the previous questions, what will happen as a result of the event or issue? Have students apply this procedure to make predictions about how the great diversity in our nation may affect society in the future. **L2**

ASSESS
Check Understanding
Assign Section 3 Review as homework or an in-class activity.

Evaluate
Assign Section Quiz 26-3 or use the Testmaker to create a customized quiz.

Reteach
Ask students to outline the major challenges described under each section heading. Then have them outline solutions they would propose for each challenge.

Have students complete Reteaching Activity 26-3.

Assign Workbook Activity 26-3.

Enrich
Suggest the students investigate the cultural diversity of their own community. They might identify foods, holidays, customs, street names, and so forth. Have them report their findings to the class.

Assign Enrichment Activity 26.

CLOSE
Discuss with students whether they think the federal government should concentrate more on domestic issues or on foreign affairs.

the state's economic problems on the costs of providing state services for these immigrants. Wilson argued, "We can no longer allow compassion to overrule reason."

New Laws

In November 1994 California voters approved Proposition 187, which banned illegal aliens from using schools, nonemergency medical care, and other social services. Although critics sought to test the law's constitutionality, its passage indicates deep concern. Proposition 187 also stirred anger among legal immigrants, who reacted strongly to what they considered ethnic prejudice.

Because the largest number of illegal immigrants crossed the border from Mexico, the United States sought ways to bolster the Mexican economy. Leaders and analysts expected the flow of immigration from Mexico to the United States would decrease as economic conditions there improved. During the Clinton administration, Congress also approved spending $1.2 billion over 3 years to strengthen patrols along the border with Mexico.

Along with objecting to the presence of illegal aliens, some Americans proposed to change the treatment of legal immigrants by limiting their access to welfare benefits. Even though immigrants used these benefits less often than American citizens, the number of legal immigrants was rising. This growth in population increased costs for the government.

■ Search for Equal Rights

One group that asserted itself dramatically during the 1990s were Americans with disabilities. Part of this story began in 1962 on the day James Meredith became the first African American to enter the University of Mississippi. That same day Ed Roberts, a paraplegic in a wheelchair, entered the University of California. Like Meredith, Roberts had gone to court to win the right to attend college. While Meredith's story went out over the news wires, Roberts's story was largely overlooked.

Even after winning the right to attend school, Roberts found dormitories and classroom buildings almost impossible to enter. To overcome the barriers to their education, Roberts and a group of friends started the Physically Disabled Students' Program to help disabled students get to class and locate accessible apartments.

In 1990 Congress passed the Americans with Disabilities Act. This law prohibited discrimination against the more than 40 million Americans who had physical, hearing, or visual impairments. Television news correspondent John Hockenberry, who himself uses a wheelchair, noted that the struggle for rights in America was a very old story that people with disabilities were just beginning to go through. "Our struggle for inclusion in this society," he noted, "is a test of whether American society truly wants diversity and freedom for all."

Section 3 ★ Review

Checking for Understanding

1. **Identify** Americorps, AIDS, Ryan White Care Act, drug court, Proposition 187, Ed Roberts.

2. **Define** fiscal year, continuing resolution, acid rain, wetland, crack cocaine, illegal alien.

3. **Describe** how the United States tried in the early 1990s to stop illegal immigration.

4. **Cite** factors that have affected the increase of poverty in the United States.

Critical Thinking

5. **Evaluating Tactics** Do you think the government's efforts in the war on drugs should be focused on stopping the supply of drugs from other countries or on reducing demand?

ACTIVITY

6. Design a poster that illustrates one of the issues mentioned in this section. Make the focus of the poster why young Americans should be concerned.

Answers to SECTION 3 REVIEW

1. Americorps, 790; AIDS, 790; Ryan White Care Act, 791; drug court, 791; Proposition 187, 792; Ed Roberts, 792

2. All vocabulary words are defined in the Glossary.

3. California banned illegal aliens from many social services. Federal government attempted to bolster Mexico's economy so that Mexicans would not emigrate.

4. lacked education to enter the job market; industry declined, hitting hardest workers who lacked technological skills

5. Students may note that past efforts to stop drugs have largely failed. Most may argue that reducing the demand through preventive programs and education is the best answer.

6. Posters should focus on significant issues.

Environmental Issues of the Twenty-First Century

The industrialized world has purchased prosperity at the expense of the environment. The conflict between economic growth and environmental protection may well become the central issue of the twenty-first century.

The disappearing ozone layer—part of the upper atmosphere—is linked to the widespread use of chlorofluorocarbons (CFCs), commonly found in such products as aerosols and foam packaging. Ozone depletion may cause an increase in skin cancer. Another concern is global warming caused by high levels of carbon dioxide and other gases that trap heat from the sun in the atmosphere and cause a greenhouse effect. The destruction of rain forests, which absorb carbon dioxide and release oxygen, compounds the problem. Many scientists believe that global warming could cause polar ice caps to melt, raising ocean levels and flooding coastal cities.

Disposal of wastes, especially toxic and nuclear materials, will also be a continuing issue. The United States alone produces 40 million tons of toxic wastes annually.

▲ EFFECTS OF ACID RAIN

▲ SCIENTISTS TAKING WATER SAMPLES, ARCTIC RESEARCH PROJECT

Making the Geography Connection

1. What is the cause of global warming?

2. How do you think future technology will affect environmental problems?

ACTIVITY

3. Prepare a set of 10 questions to use as a survey. Ask 10 adults and 10 students to answer questions about environmental concerns such as "What do you consider the most pressing environmental issue?" Write a one-page report summarizing the results of the survey.

793

CONNECTIONS
History AND GEOGRAPHY

TEACH

Point out that scientists estimate the greenhouse effect will cause a 2 to 7 degrees Fahrenheit (1 to 4 degrees Celsius) rise in average temperatures in the next 75 years. This is way beyond the range of normal temperature change. Ask students to discuss the impact this warming will have on agriculture. **L1**

 CURRICULUM CONNECTION

Environmental Studies
Some scientists say that although global warming may have little effect at the equator, it will have enormous consequences at the poles. If the polar ice caps begin to melt, sea levels will rise. As a result much of Florida would be flooded.

GLENCOE TECHNOLOGY

 VIDEODISC

Focus on Government

Side 3, Chapter 58
Title: *Our Interdependent World*

Subject: The challenges of international cooperation in protecting the environment

Answers to Making the Connection

1. accumulation of carbon dioxide and other gases in the atmosphere; these gases trap heat from sun

2. Technological developments are largely responsible for today's environmental problems. However, new technology helps scientists understand and combat environmental problems.

3. Summaries should follow from the surveys.

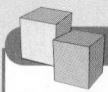

Block Schedule

Team Teaching This selection from *Hunger of Memory* can be presented in a team teaching context in conjunction with English or Language Arts.

Historical Setting

Although the United States remains a unique blend of ethnic, religious, and cultural diversity, immigrants do possess one common thread: Most must adopt a new language. Despite the obvious values of a bilingual upbringing, such an existence poses challenges.

Background

An autobiography is the narrative of a person's life, as written by that particular individual. Most autobiographies possess a chronological narrative; most are psychological in nature. Autobiographies run the gamut from the historical to the kiss-and-tell. Most, however, are similar in emphasis. Analysis, subjectivity, and self-examination are prominent.

About Rodriguez's Work

Born to blue-collar Mexican immigrants, Richard Rodriguez was reared in Sacramento, California. In what he calls "an accident of geography," he attended a Catholic grade school whose students were primarily well-to-do Caucasians. It was there that he embarked on his long journey toward assimilation.

▲ RICHARD RODRIGUEZ

Hispanic Americans cherish their heritage, and many speak only Spanish among their friends and family. However, most of their children's teachers speak only English. As a result, Hispanic students often find school confusing and humiliating. Richard Rodriguez describes his struggle to become "educated" in his autobiography, *Hunger of Memory*.

Read to Discover

Analyze how the author's attitude toward books changes. What difficulties did the author face? How was a yearning to read more complicated, more adult materials expressed by Rodriguez?

Reader's Dictionary

fellowship	companionship
bookish	fond of books or reading

Hunger of Memory (excerpts)

From an early age I knew that my mother and father could read and write both Spanish and English. . . . For both my parents, however, reading was something done out of necessity and as quickly as possible. . . . Their reading consisted of work manuals, prayer books, newspapers, recipes. . . .

. . . I privately wondered: What was the connection between reading and learning? Did one learn something only by reading it? . . . [A sign said:] CONSIDER BOOKS YOUR BEST FRIENDS. Friends? Reading was, at best, only a chore. I needed to look up whole paragraphs of words in a dictionary. Lines of type were dizzying, the eye having to move slowly across the page, then down, and across. . . . What bothered me most, however, was the isolation reading required. To console myself for the loneliness I'd feel when I read, I tried reading in a very soft voice. Until: "Who is doing all that talking to his neighbor?" Shortly after, remedial reading classes were arranged for me with a very old nun.

At the end of each school day, for nearly six months, I would meet with her in the tiny room that served as the school's library. . . . Most of the time we took turns. I began with my elementary text. Sentences of astonishing simplicity seemed to me lifeless and drab: "The boys ran from the rain. . . . She wanted to sing. . . . The kite rose in the blue." Then the old nun would read from her favorite books, usually biographies of early American presidents. Playfully she ran through complex sentences, calling the words alive with her voice, making it seem that the author somehow was speaking directly to me. I smiled just to listen to her. I sat

---

Cultural Perspectives

Hispanic Literature Two other autobiographical works by Hispanic authors have gained acclaim since their publications. One such book is Ernesto Galarza's *Barrio Boy* (1971). Born in Mexico, Galarza emigrated to Sacramento's barrio. *Barrio Boy* is the story of his assimilation. Other works by Galarza include *Zoo Risa* and *Merchants of Labor*. Gary Soto, a professor of Chicano Studies at the University of California at Berkeley, wrote a collection of essays, *Living Up the Street*. Like Galarza's work, it depicts a boyhood in the barrio. Soto's work earned the American Book Award in 1985.

there and sensed for the very first time some possibility of fellowship between a reader and a writer, a communication. . . .

I entered high school having read hundreds of books. My habit of reading made me a confident speaker and writer of English. Reading also enabled me to sense something of the shape, the major concerns, of Western thought. . . . In these various ways books brought me academic success as I hoped that they would. But I was not a good reader. Merely bookish, I lacked a point of view when I read. Rather, I read in order to acquire a point of view. I vacuumed books for epigrams, scraps of information, ideas, themes—anything to fill the hollow within me and make me feel educated. . . .

. . . One day I came across a newspaper article about the retirement of an English professor at a nearby state college. The article was accompanied by a list of the "hundred most important books of Western Civilization." "More than anything else in my life," the professor told the reporter with finality, "these books have made me all that I am." . . . I clipped out the list and kept it for the several months it took me to read all of the titles. Most books, of course, I barely understood. While reading Plato's *Republic,* for instance, I needed to keep looking at the book's jacket comments to remind myself what the text was about. Nevertheless . . . I looked at every word of the text. And by the time I reached the last word, relieved, I convinced myself that I had read *The Republic.* In a ceremony of pride, I solemnly crossed Plato off my list.

▲ *THE LIBRARY* BY JACOB LAWRENCE, 1960

Responding to Literature

1. How did the writer's attitude toward reading change over time?

2. What benefits from reading do you think the writer especially appreciated because he was Hispanic American?

3. Why do you think Rodriguez's parents viewed books differently from his teachers?

ACTIVITY

4. Think about a book that has had a strong influence on you. Write a one-page report explaining the power and fascination the book holds.

Developing Student Understanding

Encourage bilingual students to share some of the difficulties they have encountered in speaking different languages at home and at school. If there are no bilingual students in the class, ask students to speculate why speaking different languages at different times might prove challenging.

Other Works by Richard Rodriguez

While a graduate student at the University of California at Berkeley, Rodriguez published essays in *The Columbia Forum* (1973) and *The American Scholar* (1974). He later published essays in *College English* (1978) and *Change* (1978). These essays, first published in scholarly journals and then refined and transformed, became the basis for this autobiography.

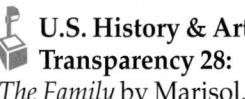

History and the Humanities

🏛 **U.S. History & Art Transparency 28:** *The Family* by Marisol.

📁 **American Literary Heritage, p. 49:** "AmeRícan" by Tato Laviera.

Answers to Responding to Literature

1. At first he found reading a chore, but eventually he learned to read for pleasure.
2. He writes that his "habit of reading made me a confident speaker and writer of English."
3. Like many Hispanic Americans, his parents probably spoke and thought in Spanish, so reading in English was a chore for them. However, the teacher's first language was English, so reading was a pleasure.
4. Students should explain clearly why the books have exerted strong influence.

CHAPTER 26 ★ REVIEW

GLENCOE
TECHNOLOGY

VIDEODISC

Use the MindJogger Videoquiz to review students' knowledge.

MindJogger Videoquiz

Chapter 26
Disc 3, Side B

Available in VHS.

Using Vocabulary

Articles will vary but should use all the vocabulary terms correctly.

Reviewing Facts

1. Liberals believe that government should be active and compassionate; conservatives believe in government restraint and more individual initiative.

2. needed a strong economy to improve conditions internally and to play a strong world role

3. gave grants to cities and states to hire more police, increased prison sentences, banned assault weapons

4. Some splits occurred within the Democratic party over the role of government.

5. initial resistance to sending in troops; the government supported the UN and tried to persuade allies to help

6. felt he had to enforce the order to stem the flood of Haitian refugees

7. beginnings of democracy restored in Haiti;

796

Using Vocabulary

Assume that you are a magazine reporter covering the state of the economy during the Clinton administration. Write an article detailing your findings using the following vocabulary words.

> downsizing
> global economy
> trade deficit
> creditor nation
> debtor nation

Reviewing Facts

1. **Discuss** the differences between liberal and conservative approaches to government.

2. **Explain** why Clinton charged that the economic recession was the Bush administration's most glaring failure.

3. **Describe** President Clinton's crime program, including its overall focus.

4. **Explain** why gridlock in Congress reappeared despite the fact that the Democrats controlled the presidency and held majorities in both the House and the Senate.

5. **Summarize** the United States's reaction to the war in Bosnia.

6. **Describe** why President Clinton decided to turn back Haitian refugees instead of granting them asylum after he had criticized Bush for doing the same thing.

7. **Describe** the positive breakthroughs in world affairs in which the United States played a part.

8. **Summarize** how America became more competitive in order to take its place in the new world order.

Understanding Concepts

Changes

1. Why did Americans demand that politicians "reinvent government," and how did Clinton proceed to carry out this charge?

Challenges

2. What challenges do the American people face in the future, and what are some possible solutions to them?

Critical Thinking

1. **Synthesizing Information** Were any of the problems the United States faced in the last decade of the twentieth century truly new? Explain your answer.

2. **Analyzing Art** The personal computer has become a common tool in homes, schools, and offices. In addition, the computer has revolutionized graphic, illustrated, and animated art. Study the art on this page and answer the questions that follow.

   a. Does the computer extend the creative capacity of artists? Explain.

   b. What do you think the artist is trying to say in this work?

   c. What title would you give it?

peace accords established between Israel and the PLO and between Israel and Jordan

8. U.S. signed agreements to break down trade barriers while industry downsized to become more efficient.

Understanding Concepts

1. Voters blamed incumbents for the recession, the trade deficit, government gridlock, and scandals. Clinton proposed a deficit-reduction act and developed an anticrime program.

2. Poverty, crime and violence, the environment, drugs, health care, and immigration are among the challenges to be faced. Answers should be reasonable and backed up with facts and evidence.

History and Geography

Global Issues

1. **Location** Why was Chechnya the site of much conflict?

2. **Location** Where is the West Bank?

3. **Human/Environment Interaction** Why do some developers call for more lenient environmental regulations?

4. **Human/Environment Interaction** What are two factors that caused increased immigration to the United States during the 1990s?

Cooperative Learning ## Interdisciplinary Activity: Environmental Studies

Many community recycling centers depend on volunteers to help unload cars, sort materials, or bundle newspapers. Work in groups of three to find out how you can participate in your community's recycling program. Share your information about the programs with the class in the form of a poster or leaflet. Post the information around the school to encourage students to volunteer.

Practicing Skills

Interpreting Statistics

Use the table on this page to answer the following questions.

1. What are the three parts of the table?

2. Summarize the changes in the total workforce.

3. How many males were in the workforce in 1993? How many females?

4. Did earnings for female workers compared to earnings for male workers rise or drop between 1983 and 1993? Explain.

5. In order for the percentage of women and minorities in the labor force to increase, what group's percentage must decrease? Is this happening?

6. Are minorities and women achieving equality of earnings in the workplace?

The Labor Force, 1983–1993				
	1983	1985	1990	1993
Total workforce (in thousands)	70,976	77,002	85,082	85,211
Percentage of total workforce				
Male	59.6	59.2	57.6	56.8
Female	40.4	40.8	42.4	43.2
White	87.0	86.3	85.4	85.0
Black	10.4	10.9	11.3	11.4
of Hispanic origin	NA	NA	8.2	8.3
Ratio of weekly median earnings				
Females to Males	66.7	68.2	71.8	76.8
Blacks to Whites	81.8	78.0	77.0	77.4
Hispanics to Whites	NA	NA	71.9	70.0

Source: *Statistical Abstract of the United States*, 1994.

7. How do the percentages of minorities in the workforce compare with the percentages of those minorities in the population? Analyze the graph on page 693 to help you answer this question.

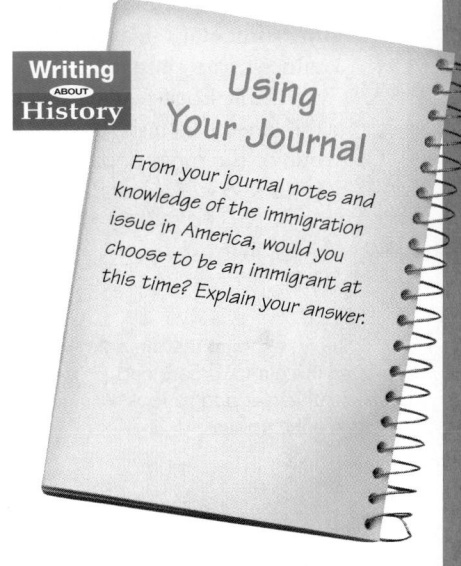

Writing ABOUT History **Using Your Journal**

From your journal notes and knowledge of the immigration issue in America, would you choose to be an immigrant at this time? Explain your answer.

students to make eye-catching posters.

Practicing Skills

1. total workforce, percentage of workforce by sex and certain races and groups, ratio of weekly earnings

2. The workforce has increased between 1983 and 1993.

3. 48.4 million; 36. 8 million

4. rise; from 66.7 in 1983 to 76.8 in 1993

5. percentages of males and whites must decrease; yes

6. Compared with males, females are increasing their earnings; compared with whites, minorities are making very small gains or losing ground.

7. Percentages of African Americans and Hispanics in the workforce are still less than their percentages of the total population.

Writing ABOUT History **Using Your Journal**

Responses will vary, but students should cite details about immigrants and immigration to support their opinions.

? Chapter Bonus Test Question

Ask students: Why is it important for the United States to be part of a new world order? (*Economically and politically the United States is strongly influenced by global events and must be a part of international interdependence.*)

Critical Thinking

1. Answers will vary. Students should provide support for their answers.

2. **a.** Answers will vary, but students should support their position.
   b. Technology is overtaking us.
   c. Answers will vary but may emphasize Earth and the future of the planet.

History and Geography

1. Chechnya wanted to secede from the Russian Federation.

2. on the west bank of the Jordan River

3. Stricter regulations meant higher costs.

4. economic and political ills

Cooperative Learning

Students might contact their community's city or village hall to obtain information about the community's recycling program. Encourage

Rock music was the first form of popular music in the United States to appeal specifically to teenagers. For many it symbolized rebellion against an older generation devoted to the smooth pop songs of the 1940s and early 1950s. Young people were not only attracted by the strong beat and pulsing sounds of rock 'n' roll, they also had enough money to buy records in quantity in this affluent era, and thus be reckoned with as serious consumers.

More About...
Rock Musicals

Rock did not have much impact on Broadway shows until the late 1960s. The first big hit was *Hair* (1967). It was followed by *Tommy* (1968) and *Jesus Christ Superstar* (1971). Another popular musical, *Grease* (1972), spoofed high school life in the rock 'n' roll era of the 1950s.

Cultural Kaleidoscope

The World of Music

ROCKING INTO THE FUTURE

Rock and roll music has been one of the most popular forms of musical expression in the twentieth century. It began as a mixture of styles, borrowing elements from rhythm and blues and country music as well as the popular ballads of the 1950s. Today's rock musicians show the willingness to explore new boundaries. In pushing for new sounds, they have made use of synthesizers and electronic sounds, classical instrumentation, and Latin and African phrasings and rhythms. Rock performers in the late 1900s have created one of the most popular and unique postwar arts.

▲ In the late 1970s and early 1980s, Janet Jackson was best known as the sister of Michael Jackson and for her appearances in televised situation comedies. Her musical albums *Rhythm Nation* and *Janet* pushed her to the top echelon of rock performers.

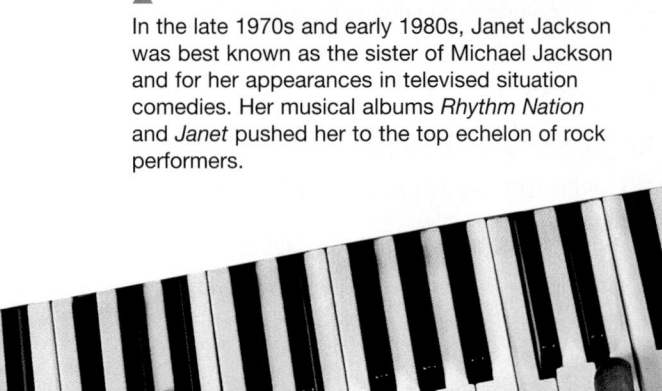

► Such keyboard instruments as the piano, organ, and synthesizer add to rock's eclectic appeal.

Cooperative Learning Activity

Pioneers of Rock Divide the class into five groups. Assign each one a pioneering figure from the early days of rock: Elvis Presley, Bill Haley, Chuck Berry, Buddy Holly, or the Beatles. Have each group research its topic and report to the class. **L2**

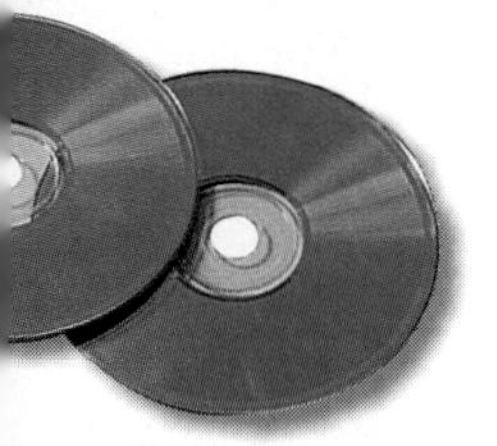

Innovations ranging from the jukebox to the compact disc have helped the popular appeal of rock and roll.

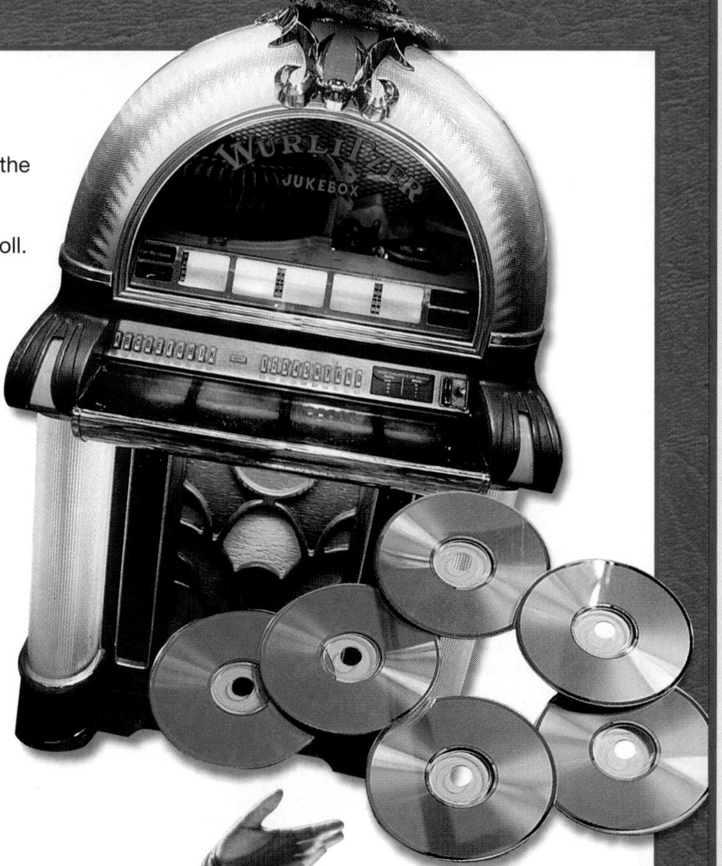

Whitney Houston's billowy soprano voice made "I Will Always Love You" one of the top-selling singles of the 1990s.

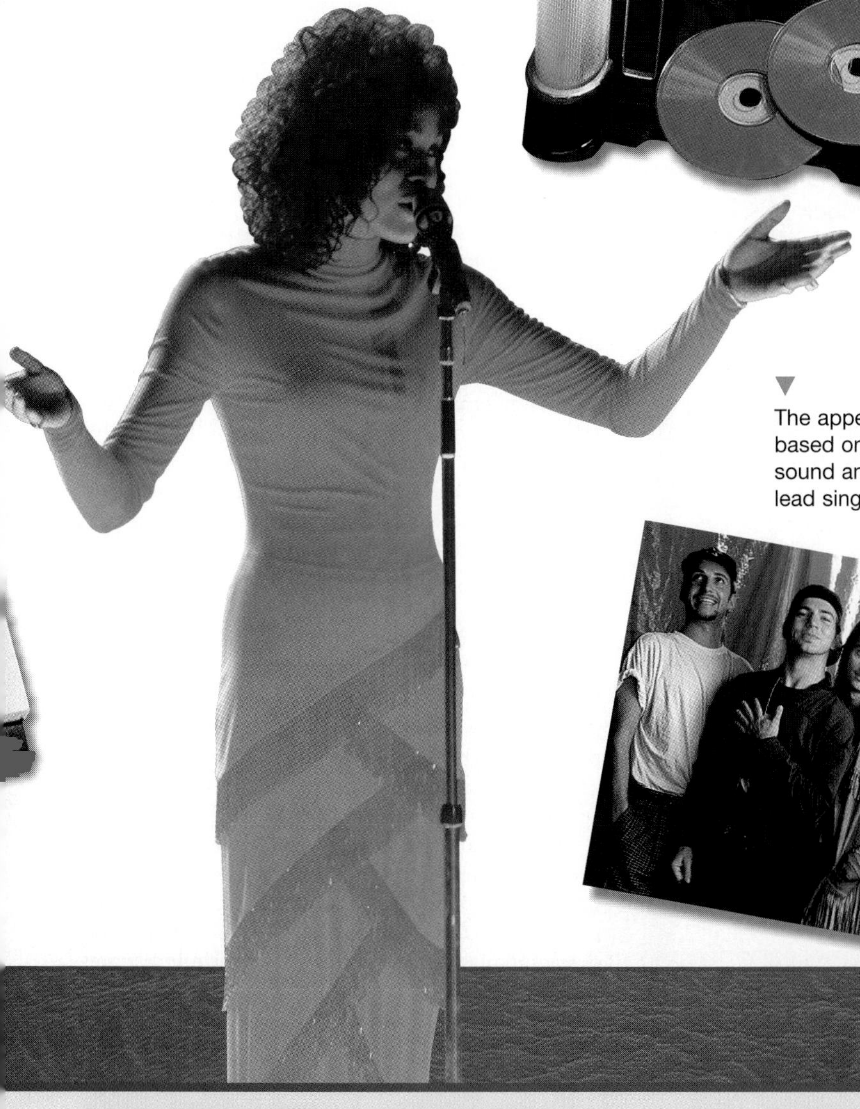

The appeal of Seattle's Pearl Jam is based on the group's hard-rocking sound and the expressive vocals of lead singer Eddie Vedder.

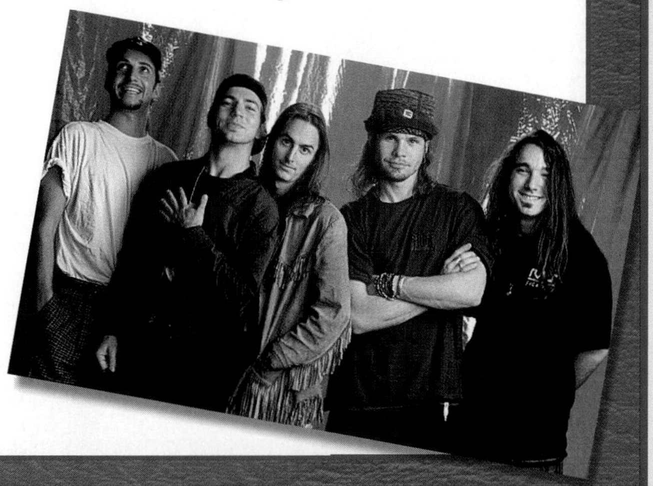

Cultural Kaleidoscope

Portfolio Project

Have students clip articles from newspapers or periodicals about rock performers in the news. In each case they should (a) note who the story is about, and (b) summarize the main idea of the article. **L1**

History and the Humanities

American Music: Cultural Traditions

Early Rock and Roll: "Rocket 88" by Jackie Brenston & his Delta Kings (2:46); "Rock Around the Clock" by Bill Haley & the Comets (2:12)
Soul Music: "I Heard It Through the Grapevine" by Marvin Gaye (3:16)
Modern Rock: "Crossfire" by Stevie Ray Vaughan and Double Trouble (4:11)

Flashcards

Use American History Flashcards to reinforce students' knowledge of places and events in American history.

The Historian's Craft

Many social historians are interested in how popular music reflects the spirit of the times. Throughout this century, titles and lyrics have told a story of their own: the jaunty "Over There" from World War I, the sad "Brother, Can You Spare a Dime?" from the Depression years, and the spirited "Praise the Lord and Pass the Ammunition" from World War II. Rock music, too, has mirrored its times. While Bob Dylan's "Blowin' in the Wind" symbolized the socially conscious 1960s, Michael Jackson's "Thriller" typified the excitement and technical sophistication of 1980s rock videos.

Exploring Unit Themes

The Unit Digest may be used to teach unit coverage when time is limited, to review unit content, or to relate the content of one unit to that of another.

■ Chapter 22

Have students construct a time line showing the major events in the struggle for civil rights.

■ Chapter 23

Ask students to write a one-page essay on the topic "Was the United States right to pull out of Vietnam?"

■ Chapter 24

Ask: How successfully did Presidents Kennedy, Johnson, and Nixon deal with domestic problems?

■ Chapter 25

Ask: What kinds of responsibilities does the United States have to preserve world peace?

Causes and Effects

Have students write a short article that describes the move toward equality since the mid-1950s. Students should use the information in the chart for their articles.

Chapter 22

The Civil Rights Era

In the 1950s many African Americans renewed their fight for full equality and an end to segregation and discrimination. Their efforts were aided by the Supreme Court's decision in *Brown* v. *Board of Education* that stated separation by race was inherently unequal. A quiet pioneer of the civil rights movement was Rosa Parks, who in 1955 refused to give her seat on a Montgomery bus to a white man. Dr. Martin Luther King, Jr., emerged as a very powerful and inspiring leader for nonviolent protest against unjust segregation laws.

Inspired by the energy of civil rights leaders, women and other minority groups began to work for change in their own right.

The Move Toward Equality

CAUSES

- 1955 Rosa Parks is arrested
- 1955 Montgomery bus boycott
- 1957 Conflict at Little Rock
- 1957 SCLC is organized
- 1960 Students stage sit-ins
- 1963 March on Washington

• Toward Equality

EFFECTS

- 1962 James Meredith enters University of Mississippi
- 1967 Thurgood Marshall appointed to Supreme Court
- 1968 Shirley Chisholm elected to House
- 1972 Barbara Jordan and Andrew Young are first Southern African Americans elected to House since 1901

Chapter 23

The Vietnam Era

In April 1965 President Johnson decided to engage American troops in combat. Unable to end the war quickly, the United States found itself increasingly drawn into the conflict.

In January 1968 North Vietnam staged the Tet offensive. Though it was turned back, Americans began to question whether or not the war could be won. When Johnson decided not to run for reelection, Republican Richard Nixon, campaigning on the promise to "bring the nation together," was elected President.

Nixon expanded the war into neighboring Cambodia and Laos to stop enemy lines of supply. This effort failed while antiwar protests increased. Finally, Nixon opted for "Vietnamization," the withdrawal of American troops and replacing them with Vietnamese soldiers.

Chapter 24

Camelot to Watergate

After narrowly winning the 1960 election, President Kennedy wanted to stimulate the economy and to improve life for the poor, but he was assassinated before many of his goals could be realized.

Vowing to continue the work of John Kennedy, President Johnson set out to implement his domestic program known as the Great Society—a blueprint for the elimination of poverty and discrimination in America. As the United States

Cooperative Learning Activity

Analyzing Policies Organize students into groups. Tell students that President Bush suggested that the United States victory in the Gulf War had helped the nation "liberate itself from old ghosts and doubts." Have the groups analyze Bush's point of view by asking: To which old ghosts and doubts was the President referring? How did victory in the Gulf "liberate" the nation from these ghosts and doubts? Given recent developments at home and in the Middle East, do you think Bush was correct? Have the groups present their positions. **L2** 🗃

was drawn more into the Vietnam War, however, Johnson's attention focused on foreign affairs.

President Nixon came to the White House with the hope of bringing America together.

However, throughout his second term, evidence surfaced linking high officials in his administration to a campaign of illegal activity. Finally, transcripts of secret White House tapes proved that Nixon had attempted a cover-up. Faced with impeachment, the President resigned and was succeeded by Gerald Ford.

Chapter 25

Search for Solutions

After Vietnam and Watergate, Americans wanted a change in leadership. Outsider Jimmy Carter barely defeated Gerald Ford in the 1976 election. Carter displayed bold initiative in foreign policy. His greatest triumph was negotiation of a peace treaty between Israel and Egypt. His greatest failure was his inability to secure the release of American hostages in Iran.

Republican Ronald Reagan quickly began to lower taxes and reduce government spending on social programs. Reagan fought communism vigorously, especially in Latin America where he rallied support for *contra* rebels in Nicaragua. Reagan's overwhelming victory in his 1984 re-election bid demonstrated strong support for his policies.

Reagan began his second term intent on keeping the United States strong. The military buildup added to social spending sent the federal deficit soaring. In foreign affairs changing conditions in the Soviet Union eased strained relations with the United States.

The late 1980s and early 1990s were years of astonishing change. One communist government after another toppled, until even the Soviet Union split into independent republics. When Iraq invaded Kuwait in 1990, President Bush acted decisively. When Iraq refused to meet a deadline for withdrawal, United States-led forces launched a devastating series of attacks on Iraqi defenses.

Chapter 26

Toward a New Century

After 12 years of Republican rule, voters elected Democrat Bill Clinton President in 1992.

American society faced pressing problems at home and abroad. Environmentalists struggled with opponents who favored greater use of natural resources. Public health issues, such as the AIDS epidemic and drug abuse, continued to take their toll. Migration patterns to the United States changed. Immigration from Europe decreased, and immigration from Latin America and Asia increased.

The American people and government and business leaders pondered ways to deal with the federal deficit and other economic and social problems that troubled the nation. The end of the cold war changed the United States's role in international affairs. Nations and international organizations searched for ways to work cooperatively.

Understanding Unit Themes

1. **Civil Rights and Liberties** How have the goals of the civil rights movement evolved?

2. **Conflict and Cooperation** What events since World War II helped create a spirit of cooperation between the United States and the Soviet Union? Which events represented low points in their relationship?

3. **Cultural Diversity** How have immigration and increased global interdependence contributed to a more culturally diverse American society?

4. **United States's Role in World Affairs** Why has the United States's relationship with other countries become more interdependent since World War II?

■ **Chapter 26**

In the past, the United States has been called a "melting pot" because of its cultural pluralism. Recently, however, people have revised the metaphor, calling the nation a "cultural quilt." Ask students to discuss which of the two metaphors they feel is more appropriate.

 Student Self-Test Software allows students to test their understanding of historical concepts in this unit.

🎧 Have students listen to the Chapter Digests on the audiocassettes.

Use the **Testmaker** to create a customized test for Unit 7.

GLENCOE TECHNOLOGY

VIDEODISC

Use the MindJogger Videoquiz to review students' knowledge.

MindJogger Videoquiz

 Chapter 22
Disc 3, Side A

 Chapter 23
Disc 3, Side B

 Chapter 24
Disc 3, Side B

 Chapter 25
Disc 3, Side B

 Chapter 26
Disc 3, Side B

 Available in VHS.

Answers to Understanding Unit Themes

1. Goals have evolved from changing laws to preventing discrimination to gaining economic and social status and power.

2. Cooperation: Nuclear Test Ban Treaty, détente, SALT, Gorbachev, glasnost, summit meetings. Low points: Cuban missile crisis, Vietnam War, Berlin Wall, Middle East wars, war in Nicaragua, Soviet invasion of Afghanistan

3. Recent immigration is increasingly from Latin America and Asia. Global interdependence has forced Americans to increase their knowledge of other cultures.

4. The U.S. has become increasingly dependent on trade with other nations. Foreign investment in the U.S. has increased; U.S. investment abroad has increased.

Appendix Contents

Atlas Key

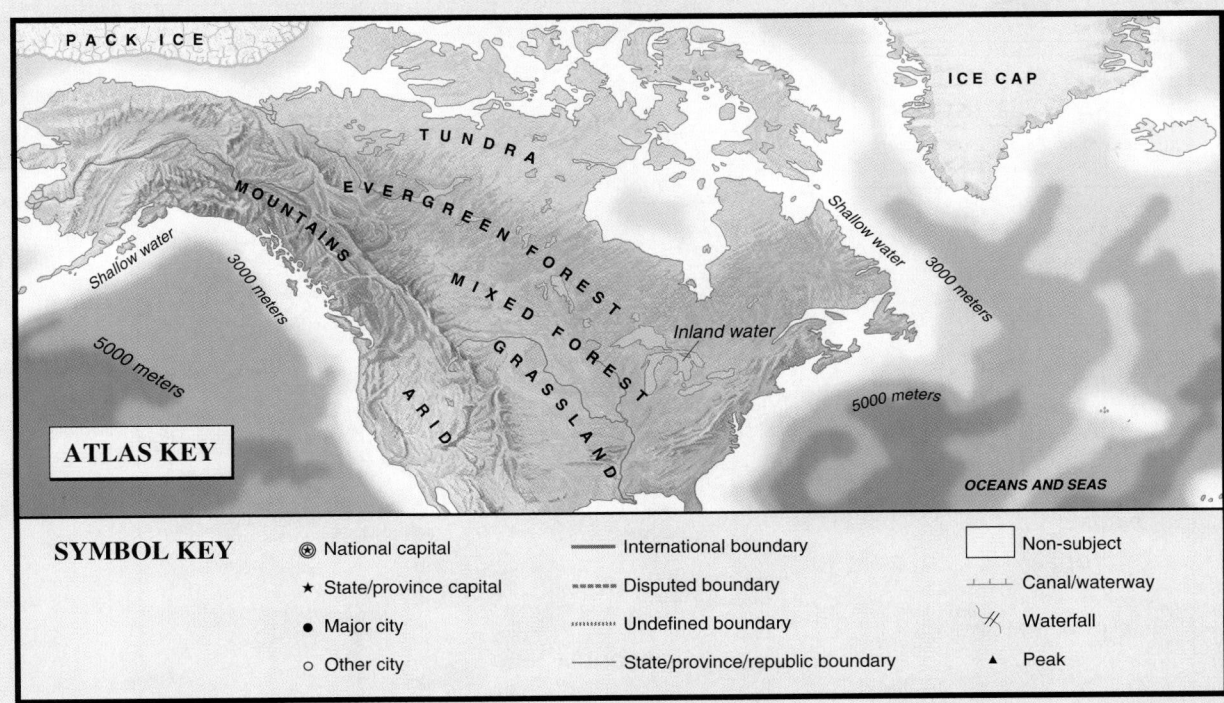

PACK ICE

ICE CAP

TUNDRA

EVERGREEN FOREST

MOUNTAINS

Shallow water

Shallow water

3000 meters

3000 meters

MIXED FOREST

Inland water

5000 meters

ARID

GRASSLAND

5000 meters

OCEANS AND SEAS

ATLAS KEY

SYMBOL KEY

- ⊛ National capital
- ★ State/province capital
- ● Major city
- ○ Other city

- —— International boundary
- ------ Disputed boundary
- ········· Undefined boundary
- —— State/province/republic boundary

- ▢ Non-subject
- ⊥⊥⊥ Canal/waterway
- ⊬ Waterfall
- ▲ Peak

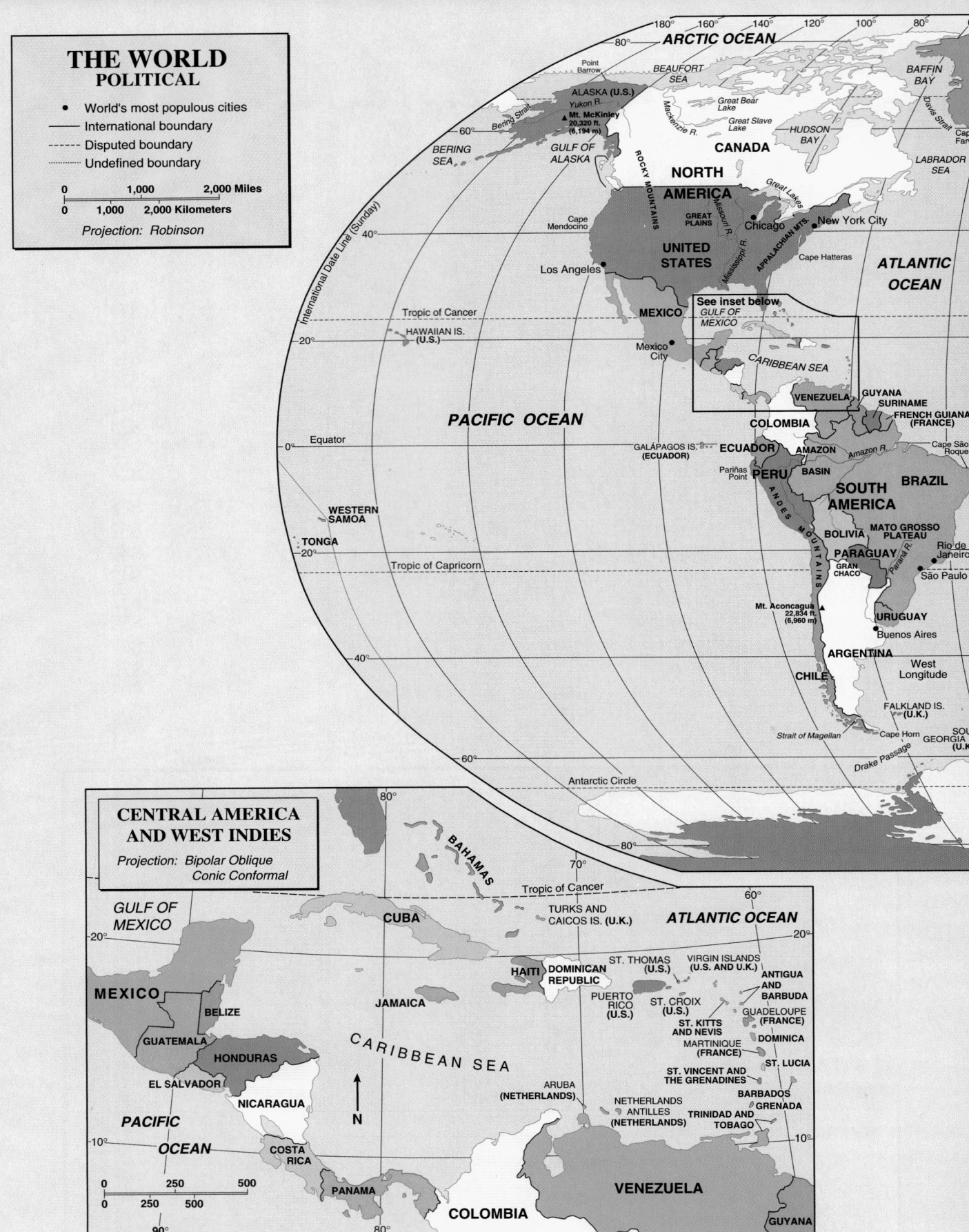

THE WORLD
POLITICAL

- • World's most populous cities
- —— International boundary
- ---- Disputed boundary
- ········ Undefined boundary

| 0 | 1,000 | 2,000 Miles |
| 0 | 1,000 | 2,000 Kilometers |

Projection: Robinson

ARCTIC OCEAN

BEAUFORT SEA

BAFFIN BAY

Point Barrow

ALASKA (U.S.)
Yukon R.
▲ Mt. McKinley
20,320 ft.
(6,194 m)

Great Bear Lake

Great Slave Lake

Mackenzie R.

Davis Strait

Cape Farvel

Bering Strait

BERING SEA

GULF OF ALASKA

CANADA

HUDSON BAY

LABRADOR SEA

NORTH AMERICA

ROCKY MOUNTAINS

GREAT PLAINS

Missouri R.

Great Lakes

Cape Mendocino

UNITED STATES

Mississippi R.

Chicago

APPALACHIAN MTS.

New York City

ATLANTIC OCEAN

Los Angeles

Cape Hatteras

International Date Line (Sunday)

Tropic of Cancer

MEXICO

See inset below
GULF OF MEXICO

HAWAIIAN IS.
(U.S.)

Mexico City

CARIBBEAN SEA

GUYANA
SURINAME
FRENCH GUIANA
(FRANCE)

VENEZUELA

PACIFIC OCEAN

COLOMBIA

Equator

GALÁPAGOS IS.
(ECUADOR)

ECUADOR
AMAZON

Amazon R.

Cape São Roque

Pariñas Point

PERU

BASIN

SOUTH AMERICA

BRAZIL

WESTERN SAMOA

ANDES MOUNTAINS

BOLIVIA

MATO GROSSO PLATEAU

TONGA

Rio de Janeiro

Tropic of Capricorn

PARAGUAY
GRAN CHACO

Paraná R.

São Paulo

Mt. Aconcagua
22,834 ft.
(6,960 m)

URUGUAY

Buenos Aires

ARGENTINA

West Longitude

CHILE

FALKLAND IS.
(U.K.)

Strait of Magellan

Cape Horn

SOUTH GEORGIA IS.
(U.K.)

Drake Passage

Antarctic Circle

CENTRAL AMERICA AND WEST INDIES

*Projection: Bipolar Oblique
Conic Conformal*

GULF OF MEXICO

BAHAMAS

CUBA

TURKS AND CAICOS IS. (U.K.)

ATLANTIC OCEAN

Tropic of Cancer

MEXICO

BELIZE

GUATEMALA

HONDURAS

EL SALVADOR

NICARAGUA

JAMAICA

HAITI

DOMINICAN REPUBLIC

ST. THOMAS (U.S.)

VIRGIN ISLANDS (U.S. AND U.K.)

ANTIGUA AND BARBUDA

PUERTO RICO (U.S.)

ST. CROIX (U.S.)

GUADELOUPE (FRANCE)

ST. KITTS AND NEVIS

DOMINICA

MARTINIQUE (FRANCE)

ST. LUCIA

CARIBBEAN SEA

ST. VINCENT AND THE GRENADINES

PACIFIC OCEAN

ARUBA (NETHERLANDS)

NETHERLANDS ANTILLES (NETHERLANDS)

BARBADOS

GRENADA

TRINIDAD AND TOBAGO

COSTA RICA

N

| 0 | 250 | 500 |
| 0 | 250 | 500 |

PANAMA

VENEZUELA

COLOMBIA

GUYANA

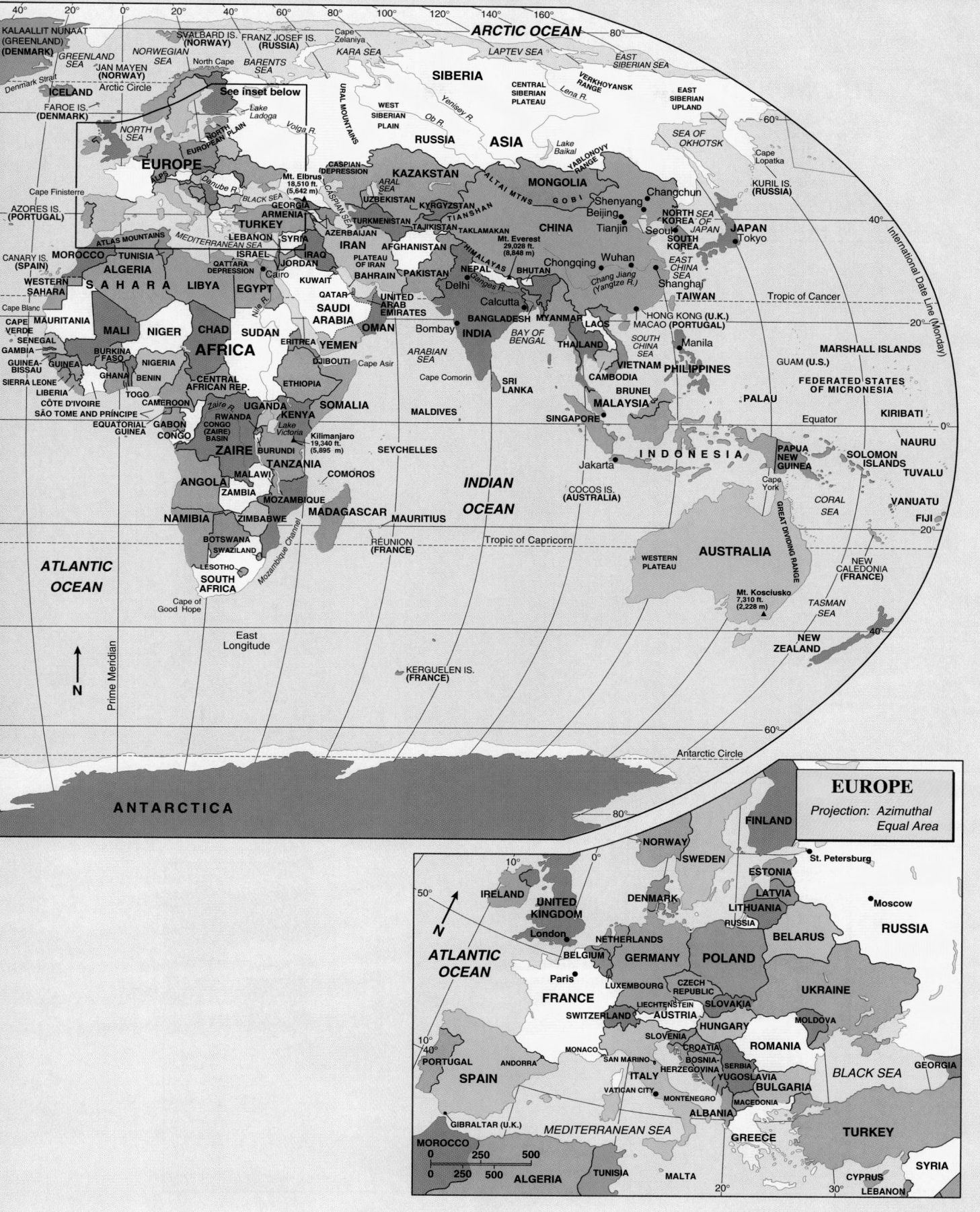

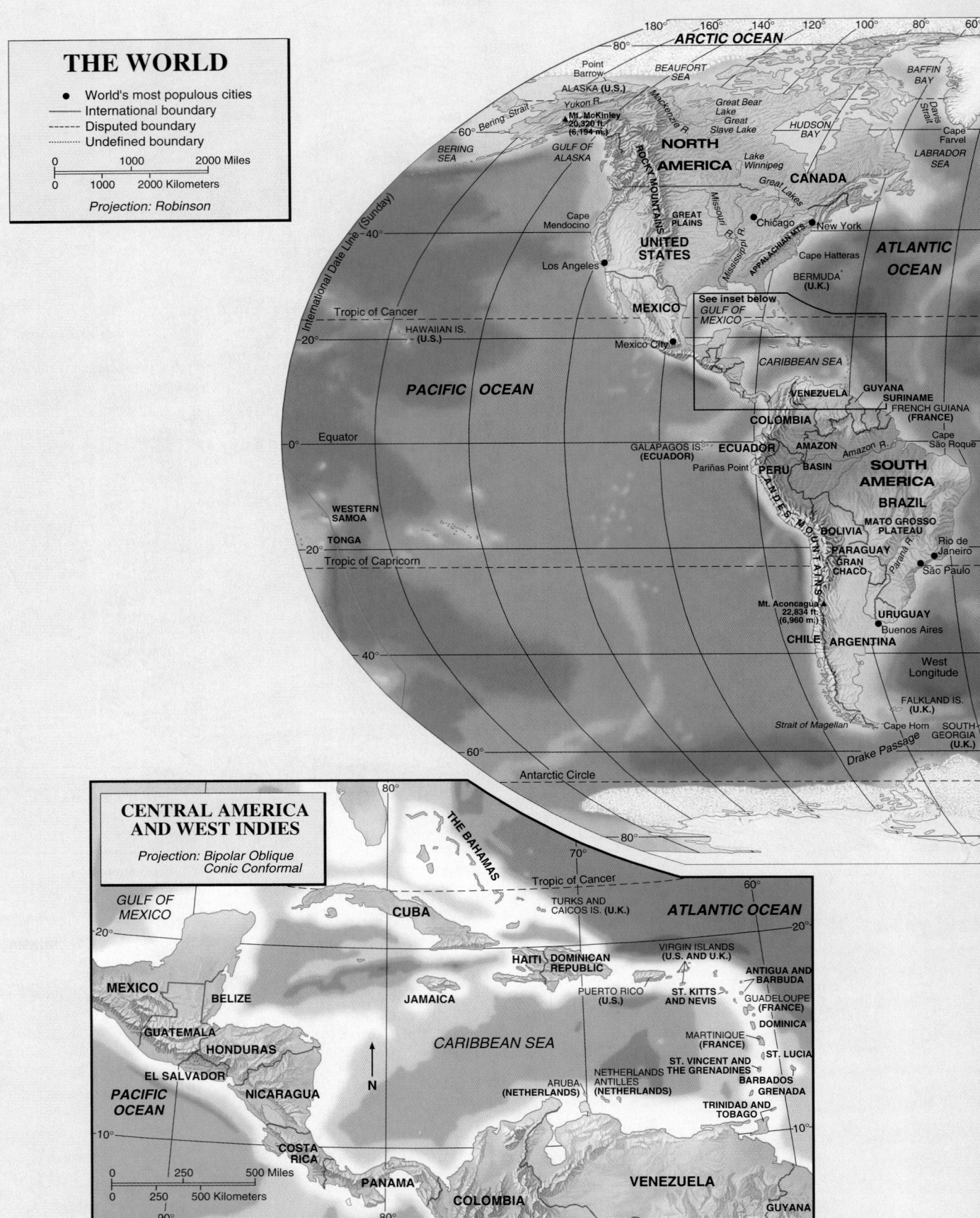

THE WORLD

- ● World's most populous cities
- —— International boundary
- --- Disputed boundary
- ······· Undefined boundary

0   1000   2000 Miles

0   1000   2000 Kilometers

Projection: Robinson

ARCTIC OCEAN

180° 160° 140° 120° 100° 80° 60°

Point Barrow
BEAUFORT SEA
BAFFIN BAY
ALASKA (U.S.)
Yukon R.
Mt. McKinley 20,320 ft. (6,194 m.)
Great Bear Lake
Great Slave Lake
Mackenzie R.
Davis Strait
Cape Farvel
Bering Strait
BERING SEA
GULF OF ALASKA
NORTH AMERICA
HUDSON BAY
CANADA
LABRADOR SEA
ROCKY MOUNTAINS
Lake Winnipeg
Great Lakes
Missouri R.
Mississippi R.
Appalachian Mts.
Cape Mendocino
GREAT PLAINS
Chicago
New York
UNITED STATES
ATLANTIC OCEAN
Cape Hatteras
Los Angeles
BERMUDA (U.K.)
International Date Line (Sunday)
Tropic of Cancer
HAWAIIAN IS. (U.S.)
MEXICO
See inset below
GULF OF MEXICO
Mexico City
CARIBBEAN SEA
PACIFIC OCEAN
VENEZUELA
GUYANA
SURINAME
FRENCH GUIANA (FRANCE)
COLOMBIA
Equator
GALÁPAGOS IS. (ECUADOR)
ECUADOR
AMAZON
Amazon R.
Cape São Roque
Pariñas Point
PERU
BASIN
SOUTH AMERICA
WESTERN SAMOA
BRAZIL
MATO GROSSO PLATEAU
TONGA
ANDES MOUNTAINS
BOLIVIA
Tropic of Capricorn
PARAGUAY
GRAN CHACO
Rio de Janeiro
Paraná R.
São Paulo
Mt. Aconcagua 22,834 ft. (6,960 m.)
URUGUAY
Buenos Aires
CHILE
ARGENTINA
West Longitude
FALKLAND IS. (U.K.)
Strait of Magellan
Cape Horn
SOUTH GEORGIA (U.K.)
Drake Passage
Antarctic Circle

CENTRAL AMERICA AND WEST INDIES

Projection: Bipolar Oblique Conic Conformal

GULF OF MEXICO
THE BAHAMAS
80°
70°
Tropic of Cancer
60°
TURKS AND CAICOS IS. (U.K.)
ATLANTIC OCEAN
20°
CUBA
20°
MEXICO
HAITI
DOMINICAN REPUBLIC
VIRGIN ISLANDS (U.S. AND U.K.)
ANTIGUA AND BARBUDA
BELIZE
JAMAICA
PUERTO RICO (U.S.)
ST. KITTS AND NEVIS
GUADELOUPE (FRANCE)
GUATEMALA
DOMINICA
HONDURAS
CARIBBEAN SEA
MARTINIQUE (FRANCE)
ST. LUCIA
EL SALVADOR
N
ST. VINCENT AND THE GRENADINES
BARBADOS
PACIFIC OCEAN
NICARAGUA
ARUBA (NETHERLANDS)
NETHERLANDS ANTILLES (NETHERLANDS)
GRENADA
TRINIDAD AND TOBAGO
10°
10°
COSTA RICA
0   250   500 Miles
0   250   500 Kilometers
PANAMA
VENEZUELA
90°
80°
COLOMBIA
GUYANA

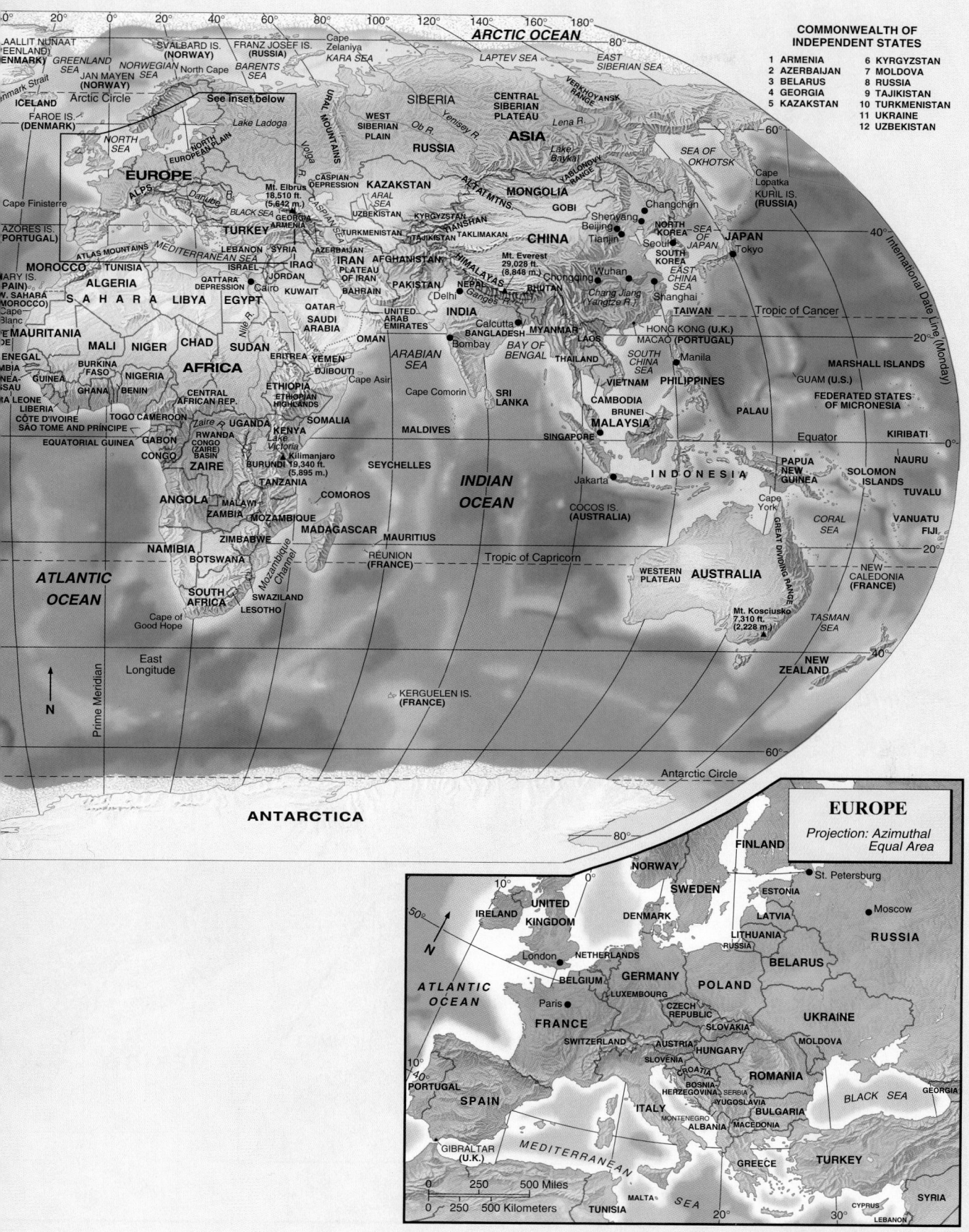

ARCTIC OCEAN

COMMONWEALTH OF
INDEPENDENT STATES

1 ARMENIA   6 KYRGYZSTAN
2 AZERBAIJAN   7 MOLDOVA
3 BELARUS   8 RUSSIA
4 GEORGIA   9 TAJIKISTAN
5 KAZAKSTAN   10 TURKMENISTAN
                  11 UKRAINE
                  12 UZBEKISTAN

SIBERIA

RUSSIA

ASIA

MONGOLIA

CHINA

JAPAN

Mt. Everest
29,028 ft.
(8,848 m.)

INDIA

AFRICA

INDIAN
OCEAN

ATLANTIC
OCEAN

AUSTRALIA

Mt. Kosciusko
7,310 ft.
(2,228 m.)

NEW
ZEALAND

ANTARCTICA

EUROPE

Projection: Azimuthal
Equal Area

FINLAND

NORWAY   SWEDEN   St. Petersburg

IRELAND   DENMARK   ESTONIA
UNITED   LATVIA   Moscow
KINGDOM   LITHUANIA   RUSSIA

                                                 BELARUS

London NETHERLANDS
ATLANTIC BELGIUM GERMANY POLAND
OCEAN
        Paris LUXEMBOURG   UKRAINE
FRANCE   CZECH
              REPUBLIC SLOVAKIA   MOLDOVA
        SWITZERLAND AUSTRIA HUNGARY
              SLOVENIA   ROMANIA
PORTUGAL   CROATIA
SPAIN   BOSNIA   BLACK SEA   GEORGIA
                   HERZEGOVINA SERBIA
                   ITALY MONTENEGRO BULGARIA
                        ALBANIA MACEDONIA
        GIBRALTAR
        (U.K.)   GREECE   TURKEY

MEDITERRANEAN

MALTA   SEA

TUNISIA   CYPRUS   SYRIA
                                                 LEBANON

0   250   500 Miles
0   250   500 Kilometers

Atlas **807**

Seattle

Olympia

WASHINGTON

Portland
Columbia River

Salem

OREGON

IDAHO

Helena
MONTANA

NORTH DAKOTA
Bismarck

Boise

SOUTH DAKOTA
Pierre

Snake River

WYOMING

Missouri

Great Salt Lake

NEBRASKA

Salt Lake City

Cheyenne

North Platte River

Carson City

NEVADA

UTAH

South Platte River

Sacramento

Denver

San Francisco
Oakland
San Jose

CALIFORNIA

COLORADO

KANSAS

Arkansas River

Las Vegas

Colorado River

Los Angeles
San Bernardino

Long Beach

San Diego

ARIZONA

Phoenix

Santa Fe

NEW MEXICO

Rio Grande

PACIFIC OCEAN

OKLAHOMA

Oklahoma City

Red River

Tucson

GULF OF CALIFORNIA

160°   155°   180°   170°   70°   160°   150°

HAWAII
Honolulu

PACIFIC OCEAN

20°   20°

Arctic Circle

Bering Strait

Yukon River

Fort Wo

TEXAS

Austin

Rio Grande

San Antonio

0   100 Miles
0   100 Kilometers

160°   155°

BERING SEA

ALASKA

CANADA

60°

MEXICO

0   250   500 Miles
0   250   500 Kilometers

GULF OF ALASKA

Juneau

130°

CANADA

MINNESOTA

MAINE
★ Augusta

Montpelier • N.H.
VT. ★ Concord
Boston •
Albany MASS.
Rochester Syracuse ★ Hartford Providence •
• • Buffalo NEW YORK CONN. Bridgeport •
R.I.

Lake Superior
Lake Huron
MICHIGAN
Lake Michigan
Grand Rapids Lansing •
• Milwaukee • Detroit
Madison ★

WISCONSIN
Minneapolis • St. Paul ★★
Mississippi River

IOWA
Omaha • Des Moines ★
Lincoln •

ILLINOIS
Springfield ★
Chicago •
Gary • Hammond

Toledo Cleveland •
Akron • Youngstown • Harrisburg ★
Canton • Pittsburgh •

PENNSYLVANIA
Newark • New York
N.J.
Trenton ★
Philadelphia •
Camden

OHIO
Columbus ★
Dayton •
Indianapolis ★
Cincinnati •
INDIANA
Ohio River
Frankfort ★
Louisville •

WEST VIRGINIA
Charleston •

MD.
Baltimore •
Annapolis ★
Washington
D.C.

DEL.
Dover ★

ATLANTIC OCEAN

Topeka ★
Kansas City • • Kansas City
Jefferson City ★
St. Louis •
East St. Louis

MISSOURI

KENTUCKY

VIRGINIA
Richmond ★
Newport News •
Norfolk •

Raleigh ★

Tulsa •

ARKANSAS
Little Rock ★

Memphis •
Mississippi River
Tennessee R.
Nashville ★

TENNESSEE

NORTH CAROLINA

Columbia ★
SOUTH CAROLINA

Dallas •

Birmingham •
ALABAMA
Montgomery ★

Atlanta ★
GEORGIA

Charleston •

LOUISIANA
Baton Rouge ★
Houston •
New Orleans •
Jackson ★
MISSISSIPPI

Jacksonville •

Tallahassee ★
FLORIDA
Orlando •

GULF OF MEXICO

Tampa •
St. Petersburg •

N

Miami •

THE BAHAMAS

CUBA

UNITED STATES

⊛ National capital
★ State capital
• Major city
━━ International boundary
── State boundary

0   150   300 Miles
0   150   300 Kilometers

Projection: Albers Equal Area

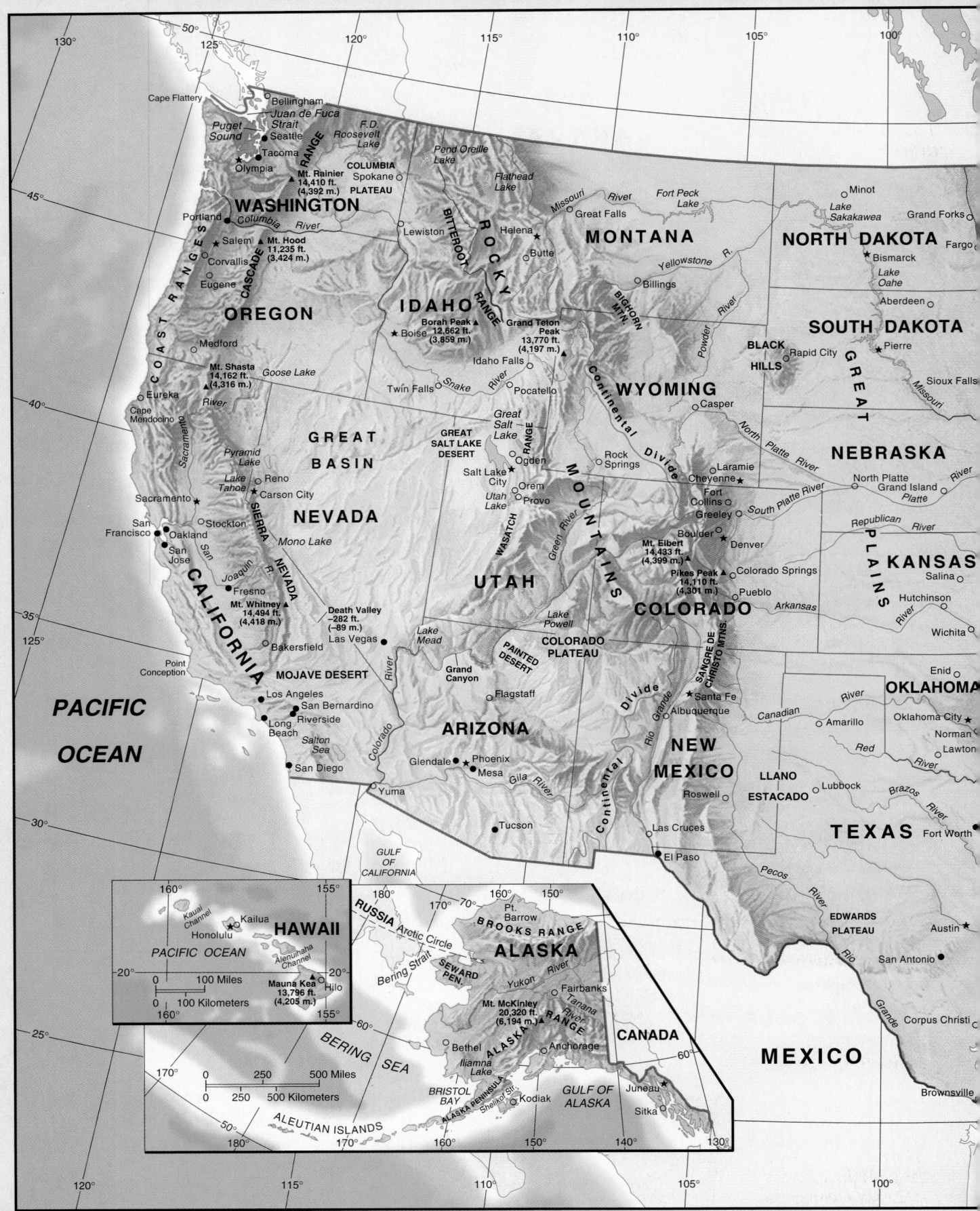

PACIFIC OCEAN

PACIFIC OCEAN

130° 125° 120° 115° 110° 105° 100°

Cape Flattery
Bellingham
Juan de Fuca Strait
Puget Sound
Seattle
Tacoma
Olympia
Mt. Rainier 14,410 ft. (4,392 m.)
Spokane
F.D. Roosevelt Lake
Pend Oreille Lake
COLUMBIA PLATEAU
Flathead Lake
Missouri River
Great Falls
Fort Peck Lake
Minot
Lake Sakakawea
Grand Forks

WASHINGTON
Portland
Columbia River
Salem
Corvallis
Eugene
Mt. Hood 11,235 ft. (3,424 m.)
CASCADE RANGE
Lewiston
BITTERROOT
Helena
Butte
ROCKY
MONTANA
Yellowstone R.
Billings
NORTH DAKOTA
Bismarck
Lake Oahe
Fargo
Aberdeen

OREGON
Medford
Mt. Shasta 14,162 ft. (4,316 m.)
Goose Lake
IDAHO
Borah Peak 12,662 ft. (3,859 m.)
Boise
RANGE
Grand Teton Peak 13,770 ft. (4,197 m.)
Idaho Falls
BIGHORN MTN.
SOUTH DAKOTA
Pierre
BLACK HILLS
Rapid City
GREAT

COAST RANGES
Eureka
Cape Mendocino
Sacramento River
GREAT BASIN
Twin Falls
Snake River
Pocatello
Great Salt Lake
Continental Divide
WYOMING
Casper
North Platte River
NEBRASKA
Sioux Falls
Missouri River

Pyramid Lake
Lake Tahoe
Reno
Carson City
GREAT SALT LAKE DESERT
Salt Lake City
Ogden
RANGE
Rock Springs
Laramie
Cheyenne
Fort Collins
Greeley
North Platte
Grand Island
Platte
South Platte River
KANSAS
Salina

Sacramento
San Francisco
Oakland
San Jose
Stockton
SIERRA NEVADA
Mono Lake
NEVADA
Fresno
San Joaquin R.
CALIFORNIA
UTAH
Utah Lake
Orem
Provo
WASATCH
Green River
MOUNTAINS
Mt. Elbert 14,433 ft. (4,399 m.)
Pikes Peak 14,110 ft. (4,301 m.)
Boulder
Denver
Colorado Springs
Pueblo
COLORADO
Arkansas River
PLAINS
Hutchinson
Wichita

Mt. Whitney 14,494 ft. (4,418 m.)
Death Valley −282 ft. (−89 m.)
Lake Mead
Las Vegas
Bakersfield
MOJAVE DESERT
Lake Powell
Colorado River
COLORADO PLATEAU
PAINTED DESERT
Continental Divide

Point Conception
Los Angeles
San Bernardino
Riverside
Long Beach
Salton Sea
San Diego
Grand Canyon
Flagstaff
ARIZONA
NEW MEXICO
Santa Fe
Albuquerque
Rio Grande
Canadian River
OKLAHOMA
Amarillo
Oklahoma City
Norman
Lawton
Red River

PACIFIC OCEAN

Yuma
GULF OF CALIFORNIA
Glendale
Phoenix
Mesa
Gila River
Tucson
Roswell
Las Cruces
El Paso
LLANO ESTACADO
Lubbock
Pecos River
Brazos River
TEXAS
Fort Worth

HAWAII
160° 155°
Kauai Channel
Kailua
Honolulu
PACIFIC OCEAN
Alenuihaha Channel
Mauna Kea 13,796 ft. (4,205 m.)
Hilo
20°
0 100 Miles
0 100 Kilometers

RUSSIA
Arctic Circle
Pt. Barrow
BROOKS RANGE
180° 170° 160° 150°
70°
SEWARD PEN.
Bering Strait
ALASKA
Yukon River
Fairbanks
Tanana
Mt. McKinley 20,320 ft. (6,194 m.)
ALASKA RANGE
CANADA
60°

EDWARDS PLATEAU
Austin
Rio Grande
San Antonio

BERING SEA
Bethel
Iliamna Lake
Bristol Bay
ALASKA PENINSULA
Shelikof Str.
Kodiak
Anchorage
GULF OF ALASKA
Juneau
Sitka
CANADA

60°
MEXICO
Corpus Christi
Brownsville

ALEUTIAN ISLANDS
0 250 500 Miles
0 250 500 Kilometers

120° 115° 110° 105° 100°

CANADA

Lake of the Woods
Red Lake
Lake Superior
MINNESOTA
Duluth
Minneapolis ★ St. Paul
Rochester
MICHIGAN
WISCONSIN
Green Bay
Appleton
Lake Michigan
Lake Huron
Milwaukee
Madison ★ Racine
Dubuque
Rockford
IOWA
Cedar Rapids
Davenport
Des Moines
Council Bluffs
Lincoln
Sioux City
Omaha
Chicago
Aurora
Joliet
Gary
Hammond
South Bend
Grand Rapids
Flint
Lansing
Detroit
Ann Arbor
Toledo
Fort Wayne
ILLINOIS
LOWLAND
Peoria
CENTRAL
Springfield
Decatur
INDIANA
Muncie
Indianapolis ★
Dayton
Cincinnati
OHIO
Columbus ★
Parkersburg
Akron
Canton
Cleveland
Youngstown
Wheeling
Ohio River
Lake Erie
Erie
Niagara Falls
Buffalo
Lake Ontario
Rochester
Syracuse
Utica
Binghamton
NEW YORK
Albany ★
Worcester
Springfield
Hartford ★
New Haven
Susquehanna River
PENNSYLVANIA
Harrisburg ★
Pittsburgh
Philadelphia
Allentown
Newark
Trenton ★
New York
Yonkers
N.J.
Camden
Wilmington
Dover ★
DELAWARE BAY
DEL.
MD.
Baltimore
Annapolis ★
Washington
Arlington
D.C.
WEST VIRGINIA
Charleston ★
Huntington
Frankfort ★
Lexington
Louisville
Evansville
KENTUCKY
Owensboro
Cumberland River
Tennessee River
APPALACHIAN MOUNTAINS
Roanoke
VIRGINIA
Richmond ★
Newport News
Norfolk
CHESAPEAKE BAY
Roanoke River
Durham
Raleigh ★
Greensboro
Winston-Salem
Mt. Mitchell 6,684 ft. (2,037 m.)
NORTH CAROLINA
Charlotte
Cape Hatteras
ATLANTIC OCEAN
MAINE
Moosehead Lake
Bangor
Mt. Washington 6,288 ft. (1,905 m.)
Augusta ★
Lewiston
Portland
Lake Champlain
Burlington
Montpelier ★
N.H.
VT.
Concord ★
Manchester
ADIRONDACK MTNS.
Hudson R.
Boston ★
MASS.
Cape Cod
Providence ★
R.I.
CONN.
St. Lawrence River

Kansas City
Topeka ★
Lawrence
Kansas City
Jefferson City ★
Independence
Harry S. Truman Res.
St. Louis
East St. Louis
MISSOURI
Springfield
Wabash R.
OZARK PLATEAU
Tulsa
R.S. Kerr Res.
ARKANSAS
Fort Smith
Lake Eufaula
North Little Rock
Little Rock ★
Hot Springs
Pine Bluff
Memphis
Nashville ★
Knoxville
Chattanooga
Huntsville
TENNESSEE
Tennessee R.
Cumberland R.
PLATEAU
Greenville
Spartanburg
Greenville
Columbia ★
SOUTH CAROLINA
Charleston

Lake Texoma
Dallas
Shreveport
LOUISIANA
Toledo Bend Res.
Sam Rayburn Reservoir
MISSISSIPPI
Meridian
Jackson ★
Hattiesburg
Greenville
Birmingham
Tuscaloosa
Montgomery ★
ALABAMA
GEORGIA
Columbus
Augusta
Macon
Atlanta ★
Albany
Savannah
Mississippi River
Baton Rouge ★
Lake Pontchartrain
Biloxi
Pensacola
Mobile
Lake Charles
Lafayette
New Orleans
Houston
GULF OF MEXICO
COASTAL PLAIN
Tallahassee ★
FLORIDA
Jacksonville
Orlando
Cape Canaveral
Tampa
St. Petersburg
Lake Okeechobee
Palm Beach
Miami Beach
Miami
Cape Sable
Key West
Straits of Florida
THE BAHAMAS
CUBA

★ N

UNITED STATES

⊛ National capital
★ State capital
● Major city
⟋⟋ International boundary
— State boundary

0   150   300 Miles
0   150   300 Kilometers

Projection: Albers Equal Area

95° 90° 85° 80° 75° 70° 65°
45° 65° 40° 70° 35° 30° 25°

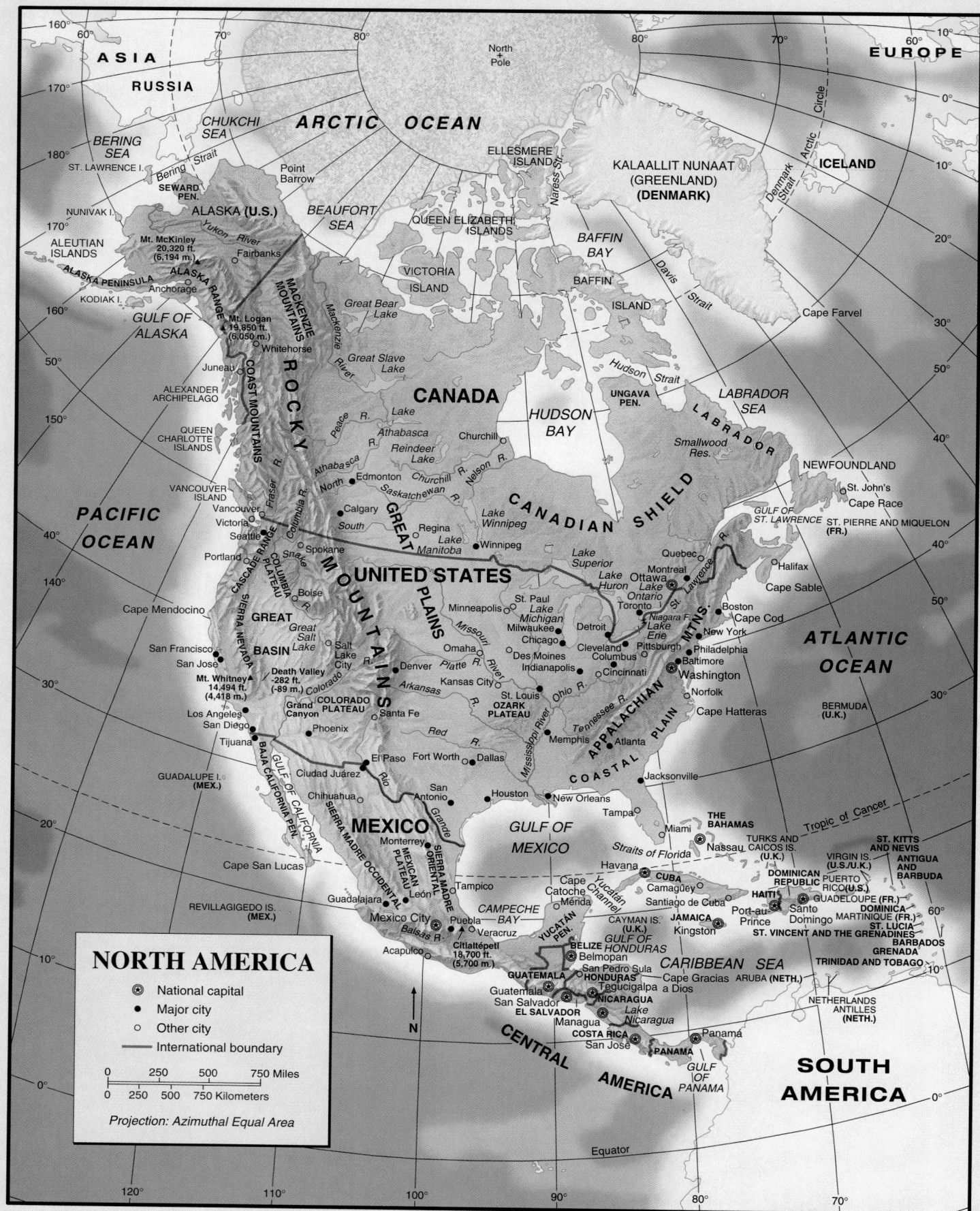

NORTH AMERICA

- ◎ National capital
- ● Major city
- ○ Other city
- —— International boundary

0 | 250 | 500 | 750 Miles
0 | 250 | 500 | 750 Kilometers

Projection: Azimuthal Equal Area

LATIN AMERICA

- ⊛ National capital
- ● Major city
- ○ Other city
- —— International boundary

0 ___ 500 ___ 1000 Miles
0 ___ 500 ___ 1000 Kilometers

Projection: Miller Cylindrical

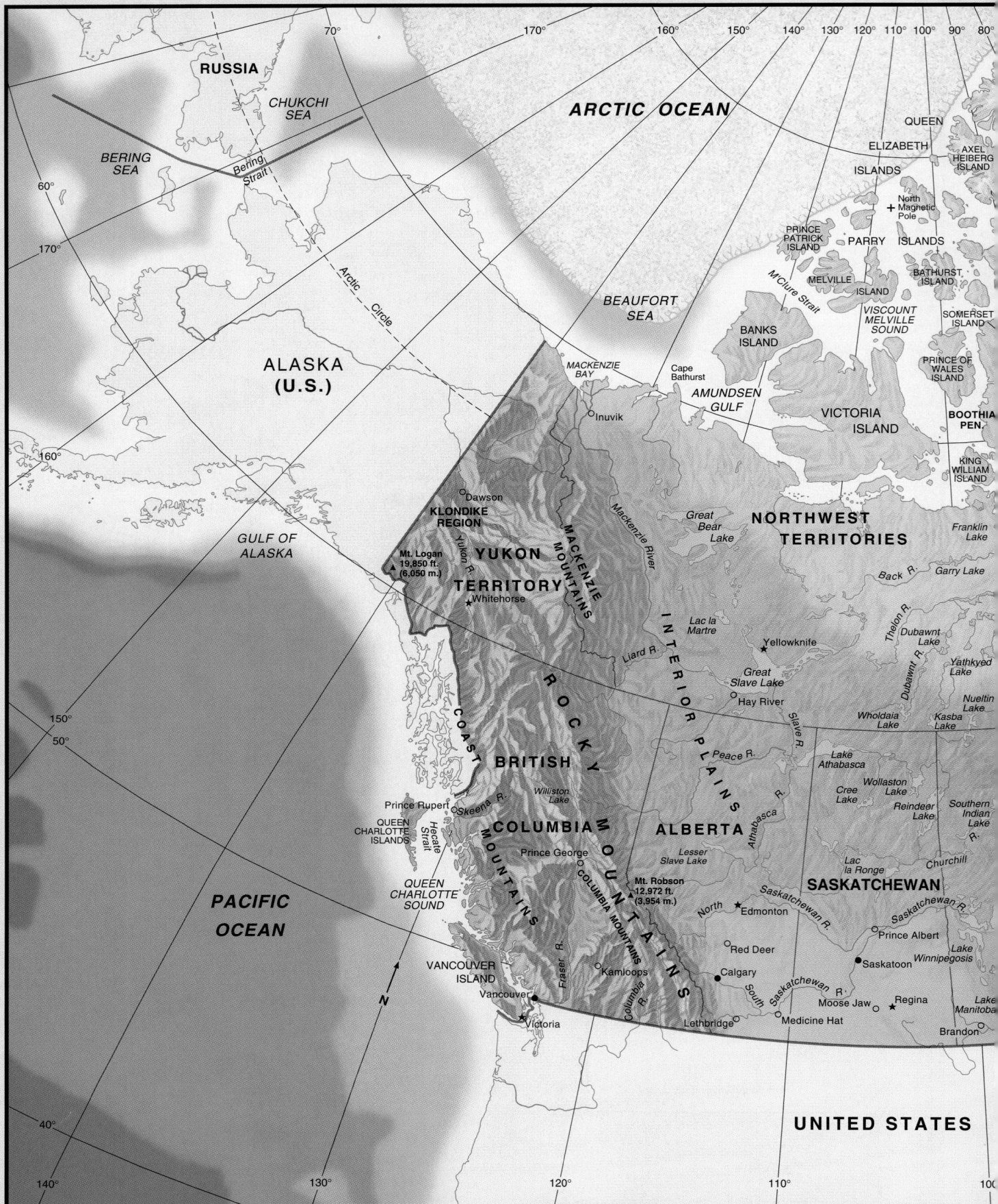

RUSSIA

CHUKCHI
SEA

BERING
SEA

Bering
Strait

ARCTIC OCEAN

QUEEN
ELIZABETH
ISLANDS

AXEL
HEIBERG
ISLAND

North
Magnetic
Pole

PRINCE
PATRICK
ISLAND

PARRY   ISLANDS

BATHURST
ISLAND

MELVILLE
ISLAND

VISCOUNT
MELVILLE
SOUND

SOMERSET
ISLAND

BEAUFORT
SEA

MACKENZIE
BAY

Cape
Bathurst

BANKS
ISLAND

AMUNDSEN
GULF

PRINCE OF
WALES
ISLAND

BOOTHIA
PEN.

ALASKA
(U.S.)

Arctic   Circle

Inuvik

VICTORIA
ISLAND

KING
WILLIAM
ISLAND

GULF OF
ALASKA

Dawson

KLONDIKE
REGION

Mt. Logan
19,850 ft.
(6,050 m.)

Yukon R.

YUKON

TERRITORY

Whitehorse

MACKENZIE
MOUNTAINS

Mackenzie River

Great
Bear
Lake

NORTHWEST
TERRITORIES

Franklin
Lake

Back R.

Garry Lake

Lac la
Martre

Yellowknife

Thelon R.

Dubawnt
Lake

Liard R.

INTERIOR

Great
Slave Lake

Hay River

Slave R.

Yathkyed
Lake

Wholdaia
Lake

Kasba
Lake

Nueltin
Lake

PACIFIC

OCEAN

COAST

R O C K Y

BRITISH

PLAINS

Peace R.

Lake
Athabasca

Cree
Lake

Wollaston
Lake

Reindeer
Lake

Southern
Indian
Lake

Williston
Lake

M O U N T A I N S

Prince Rupert

Skeena R.

QUEEN
CHARLOTTE
ISLANDS

Hecate
Strait

COLUMBIA

ALBERTA

Athabasca R.

Lac
la Ronge

Churchill

QUEEN
CHARLOTTE
SOUND

MOUNTAINS

Prince George

Mt. Robson
12,972 ft.
(3,954 m.)

COLUMBIA MOUNTAINS

Lesser
Slave Lake

SASKATCHEWAN

Saskatchewan R.

Prince Albert

Saskatchewan R.

VANCOUVER
ISLAND

Fraser R.

Columbia R.

Kamloops

Red Deer

Edmonton

North

Saskatchewan R.

Saskatoon

Lake
Winnipegosis

N

Vancouver

Victoria

Calgary

South

Saskatchewan   R.

Moose Jaw

Regina

Lake
Manitoba

Lethbridge

Medicine Hat

Brandon

UNITED STATES

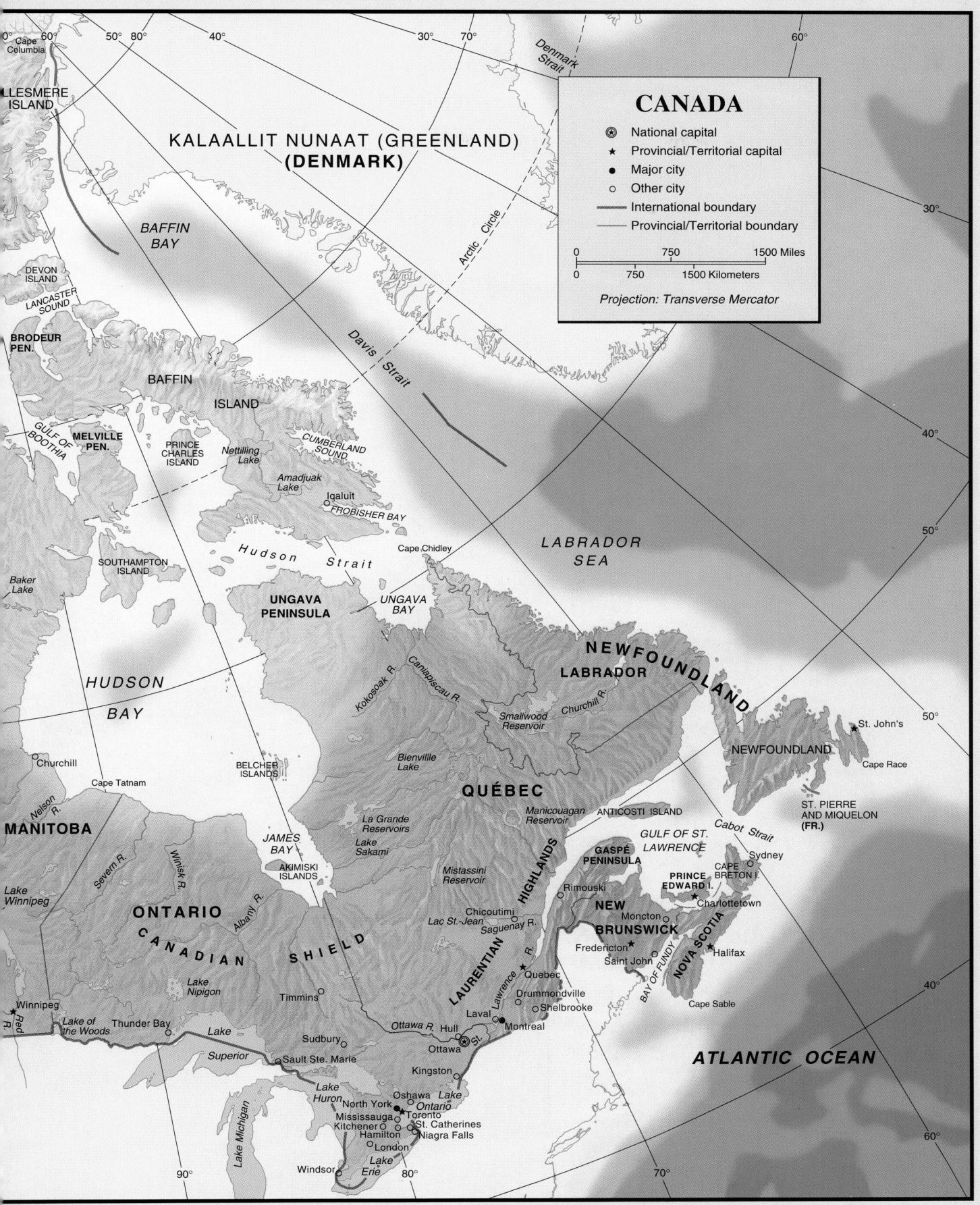

CANADA

- ⊛ National capital
- ★ Provincial/Territorial capital
- ● Major city
- ○ Other city
- ▬▬ International boundary
- ─── Provincial/Territorial boundary

| 0 | 750 | 1500 Miles |
| 0 | 750 | 1500 Kilometers |

Projection: Transverse Mercator

KALAALLIT NUNAAT (GREENLAND)
(DENMARK)

LLESMERE ISLAND

Cape Columbia

BAFFIN BAY

DEVON ISLAND

LANCASTER SOUND

BRODEUR PEN.

BAFFIN ISLAND

Denmark Strait

Arctic Circle

Davis Strait

GULF OF BOOTHIA

MELVILLE PEN.

PRINCE CHARLES ISLAND

Nettilling Lake

CUMBERLAND SOUND

Amadjuak Lake

Iqaluit
FROBISHER BAY

LABRADOR SEA

Hudson Strait

SOUTHAMPTON ISLAND

Baker Lake

UNGAVA PENINSULA

UNGAVA BAY

Cape Chidley

NEWFOUNDLAND
LABRADOR

HUDSON BAY

Churchill

Cape Tatnam

BELCHER ISLANDS

Kokosoak R.

Caniapiscau R.

Smallwood Reservoir

Churchill R.

NEWFOUNDLAND

St. John's

Cape Race

MANITOBA

Nelson R.

Bienville Lake

QUÉBEC

Manicouagan Reservoir

ANTICOSTI ISLAND

ST. PIERRE AND MIQUELON (FR.)

JAMES BAY

La Grande Reservoirs

Lake Sakami

GASPÉ PENINSULA

GULF OF ST. LAWRENCE

Cabot Strait

Sydney

CAPE BRETON I.

AKIMISKI ISLANDS

Mistassini Reservoir

HIGHLANDS

PRINCE EDWARD I.

Charlottetown

Lake Winnipeg

ONTARIO

Severn R.

Winisk R.

Albany R.

Lake Nipigon

CANADIAN SHIELD

Chicoutimi
Lac St.-Jean
Saguenay R.

Rimouski

NEW BRUNSWICK

Moncton

NOVA SCOTIA

Fredericton

Halifax

Timmins

LAURENTIAN

St. Lawrence R.

Quebec

Saint John

BAY OF FUNDY

Winnipeg
Red R.

Lake of the Woods

Thunder Bay

Lake Superior

Sudbury

Sault Ste. Marie

Ottawa R. Hull

Laval
Montreal

Drummondville
Shelbrooke

Cape Sable

ATLANTIC OCEAN

Ottawa

Kingston

Lake Huron

Lake Michigan

Oshawa Lake Ontario

North York
Mississauga Toronto
Kitchener St. Catherines
Hamilton Niagra Falls
London

Windsor

Lake Erie

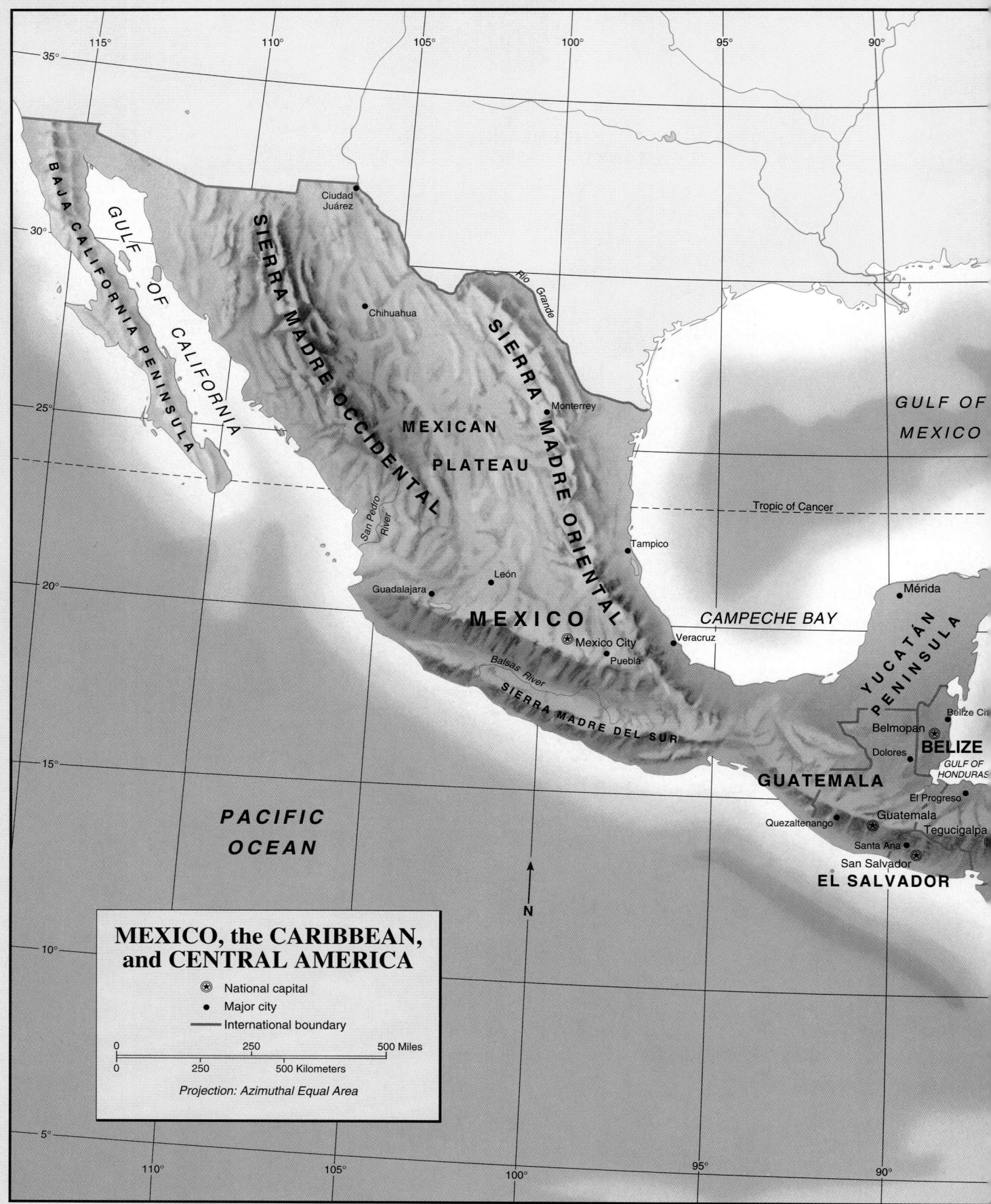

115°   110°   105°   100°   95°   90°

35°

30°   Ciudad
       Juárez

BAJA CALIFORNIA PENINSULA

GULF OF CALIFORNIA

SIERRA MADRE OCCIDENTAL

Chihuahua

Río Grande

SIERRA MADRE ORIENTAL

25°   Monterrey   GULF OF
                     MEXICO

MEXICAN

PLATEAU

San Pedro River   Tropic of Cancer

Tampico

León   CAMPECHE BAY   Mérida

20°   Guadalajara   MÉRIDA

MEXICO   Mexico City   Veracruz   YUCATÁN PENINSULA

Balsas River   Puebla

SIERRA MADRE DEL SUR   Belize City

Belmopan   BELIZE

Dolores   GULF OF
           HONDURAS

15°   GUATEMALA

El Progreso

PACIFIC   Quezaltenango   Guatemala   Tegucigalpa

OCEAN   Santa Ana

San Salvador

EL SALVADOR

N

10°

MEXICO, the CARIBBEAN,
and CENTRAL AMERICA

⊛ National capital
• Major city
— International boundary

0   250   500 Miles
0   250   500 Kilometers

Projection: Azimuthal Equal Area

5°

110°   105°   100°   95°   90°

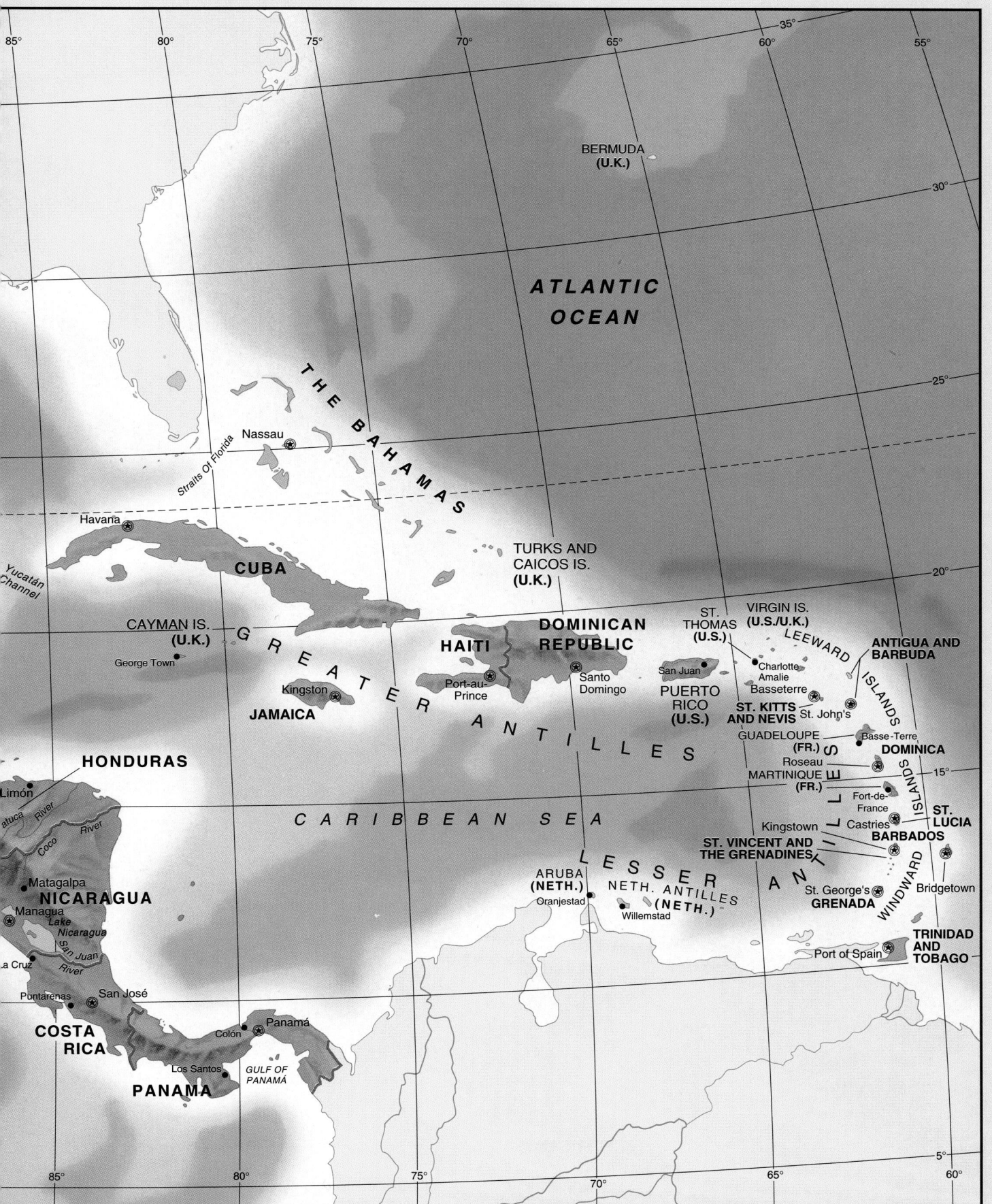

ATLANTIC
OCEAN

BERMUDA
(U.K.)

THE BAHAMAS

Straits Of Florida

Nassau

Yucatán
Channel

Havana

CUBA

TURKS AND
CAICOS IS.
(U.K.)

CAYMAN IS.
(U.K.)

George Town

GREATER ANTILLES

HAITI

DOMINICAN
REPUBLIC

Port-au-
Prince

Santo
Domingo

ST.
THOMAS
(U.S.)

VIRGIN IS.
(U.S./U.K.)

LEEWARD

ISLANDS

ANTIGUA AND
BARBUDA

Kingston

JAMAICA

San Juan

PUERTO
RICO
(U.S.)

Charlotte
Amalie

Basseterre

ST. KITTS
AND NEVIS

St. John's

GUADELOUPE
(FR.)

Basse-Terre

DOMINICA

Roseau

MARTINIQUE
(FR.)

HONDURAS

Limón

atuca
River

Coco
River

CARIBBEAN SEA

LESSER ANTILLES

Fort-de-
France

ST.
LUCIA

Castries

Kingstown

BARBADOS

ST. VINCENT AND
THE GRENADINES

WINDWARD
ISLANDS

Matagalpa

NICARAGUA

Managua
Lake
Nicaragua

San Juan
River

La Cruz

Puntarenas

San José

COSTA
RICA

Colón

Panamá

Los Santos

GULF OF
PANAMÁ

PANAMA

ARUBA
(NETH.)

Oranjestad

NETH. ANTILLES
(NETH.)

Willemstad

St. George's

GRENADA

Bridgetown

Port of Spain

TRINIDAD
AND
TOBAGO

EUROPE

- ⊛ National capital
- ● Major city
- ○ Other city
- ▬▬ International boundary
- ── Republic boundary
- ⊣⊢ Canal

| 0 | 100 | 200 | 300 Miles |
| 0 | 100 | 200 | 300 Kilometers |

Projection: Azimuthal Equal Area

ICELAND
Reykjavik

Arctic Circle

NORWEGIAN SEA

SCANDINAVIAN HIGHLANDS

Trondheim

FAROE IS. (DEN.)

NORWAY

Prime Meridian

GULF OF BOTHNIA

SHETLAND IS. (U.K.)

Bergen
Goldhöpiggen 8,097 ft. (2,468 m.)

ÅLAND I.

SWEDEN

OUTER HEBRIDES IS.
Cape Wrath
ORKNEY ISLANDS

Oslo
Lake Vänem
Uppsala

HIIUMAA I.
SAAREMAA I.
GOTLAND I.

NORTHERN IRELAND (U.K.)
SCOTLAND
Glasgow
Edinburgh

NORTH SEA

Skagerrak

Göteborg
Stockholm

ÖLAND I.

Belfast
PENNINE RANGE
UNITED KINGDOM

Kattegat
JUTLAND
Copenhagen
DENMARK
Malmö
BALTIC SEA

Dublin
IRELAND
Cork
ISLE OF MAN
IRISH SEA
Manchester
Liverpool
Leeds
Sheffield
ENGLAND

Lake Vättern

Odense
BORNHOLM I.

RUSSIA
Gdańsk
NORTH

Cape Clear
St. George's Channel
WALES
Cardiff
Bristol
Birmingham
London

Kiel Canal
Rostock
Szczecin
POLAND

ATLANTIC OCEAN

English Channel
Strait of Dover
NETHERLANDS
Amsterdam
The Hague
Rotterdam
Mittelland Canal
Hamburg
Elbe R.
Bremen
Hannover
Berlin
Magdeburg
Poznań
Warsaw
Łódź
Vistula

GUERNSEY I. (U.K.)
JERSEY I. (U.K.)
BRETON PEN.
Le Havre
Seine River
Antwerp
BELGIUM
Brussels
Liège
LUXEMBOURG
Essen
Dortmund
Cologne
Bonn
GERMANY
Leipzig
Dresden
Chemnitz
Wrocław

Paris
Marne R.
Luxembourg
Frankfurt
Marne-Rhine Canal
Rhine R.
CZECH REPUBLIC
Prague
Brno
Ostrava
Katowic
Krak

Nantes
Loire
FRANCE
Stuttgart
Strasbourg
Danube River
Munich
Bodensee
Linz
Vienna
Bratislava
Miskolc
SLOVAKI

Bordeaux
BAY OF BISCAY
Cape Finisterre
CANTABRIAN MTNS
Lyon
Mt. Blanc 15,771 ft. (4,807 m.)
Lausanne
Geneva
L. Geneva
Zürich
Bern
SWITZERLAND
LIECHTENSTEIN
Valduz
Innsbruck
AUSTRIA
Salzburg
Graz
Budapest
HUNGARY
L. Balaton
Pécs
Tisza R.

Bilbao
PYRENEES
Mt. Rosa 12,203 ft. (4,634 m.)
ALPS
Milan
Turin
PO VALLEY
Po R.
Venice
Genoa
Ljubljana
SLOVENIA
Zagreb
Novi Sad
CROATIA
Sava R.
Belgrade

Porto
Valladolid
Duero River
Ebro River
Toulouse
Midi
Montpellier
Nice
Monaco
MONACO
Bologna
DINARIC ALPS
Split
BOSNIA-HERZEGOVINA
Sarajevo

PORTUGAL
Tagus River
IBERIAN
Zaragoza
Madrid
Aneto Peak 11,168 ft. (3,404 m.)
ANDORRA
Andorra la Vella
Marseille
GULF OF LION
Florence
SAN MARINO
San Marino
APENNINES
ADRIATIC SEA
MONTENEGRO

Lisbon
Setúbal
Guadiana River
PENINSULA
Barcelona
CORSICA (FR.)
VATICAN CITY
Rome
ITALY
MACEDONIA
Tiranë

Cape St. Vincent
SIERRA MORENA
SPAIN
Seville
Valencia
Murcia
BALEARIC IS. (SP.)
Palma
SARDINIA (IT.)
Naples
Bari
ALBANIA

Málaga
Granada
MEDITERRANEAN
TYRRHENIAN SEA
G. OF TARANTO

Strait of Gibraltar
GIBRALTAR (U.K.)
Cagliari
Strait of Sicily
Palermo
SICILY
Catania
IONIAN SEA
KEFALLINIA I.

AFRICA
PANTELLERIA (IT.)
MALTA
Valletta
SEA

N

818   Atlas

North Cape

30°   40°   70°   50°

BARENTS
SEA

Murmansk

KOLA
PENINSULA

TIMAN RIDGE

Pechora R.

URAL MOUNTAINS

60°

WHITE
SEA

Arkhangel'sk

White Sea-
Baltic
Waterway

N. Dvina River

Vychegda River

Mt. Konzhakovskiy
5,147 ft.
(1,569 m.)

Kama R.

ASIA

FINLAND

Lake
Onega

Sukhona River

Perm

70°

Tampere

Lake
Saimaa

Turku

Espoo

Helsinki

Lake
Ladoga

Volga-Baltic
Waterway

St. Petersburg

Rybinsk
Reservoir

Kama River

Kuybyshev
Reservoir

Ufa

50°

GULF OF FINLAND

Kazan

Yaroslavl

ESTONIA

Tallinn

Chudskoye
Lake

Nizhniy
Novgorod

Volga-Baltic
Waterway

Samara

Orenburg

GULF
OF
RIGA

LATVIA

Riga

Dvina R.

BALTIC
PLAIN

EUROPEAN PLAIN

Volga River

Moscow

River

VOLGA UPLAND

Volga River

Ural River

LITHUANIA

Kaunas

Vilnius

Oka

Tula

RUSSIA

Smolensk

Minsk

CENTRAL RUSSIAN UPLAND

Saratov

Volgograd
Reservoir

KAZAKSTAN

BELARUS

Don R.

Voronezh

River

ARAL
SEA

Pripet River

Desna R.

Kursk

Volgograd

Volga River

DEPRESSION

Kiev

Kremenchug
Reservoir

Kharkov

Lugansk

Tsimlyansk
Reservoir

Astrakhan

CASPIAN

UKRAINE

Lvov

DNEIPER UPLAND

Dniester R.

Dnepropetrovsk

Krivoy Rog

Donetsk

Don River

Rostov

Delta of
the Volga

Volga River

40°

CARPATHIAN MTNS.

Debrecen

MOLDOVA

Prut River

Chisinau

DNEIPER
LOWLAND

Dnieper River

Kakhovka
Res.

SEA
OF
AZOV

CRIMEA

Krasnodar

Grozny

CASPIAN SEA

60°

Cluj-Napoca

Odessa

ROMANIA

Timişoara

Braşov

Mt. Elbrus
18,510 ft.
(5,642 m.)

CAUCASUS MTNS.

WALLACHIA
PLAIN

Bucharest

River

Constanta

BLACK   SEA

Danube

SERBIA

Ruse

Niš

BULGARIA

Varna

Sofia

Burgas

40°

Skopje

Plovdiv

Musala Peak
9,536 ft.
(2,926 m.)

PENINSULA   TURKEY

Salonika

Bosporus

BALKAN

Larissa

AEGEAN
SEA

Dardanelles

SEA OF
MARMARA

GREECE

ASIA

30°

Patras

Athens

Piraeus

PELOPONESE
PEN.

CRETE (GR.)

RHODES

30°

Iráklion

30°   40°   50°

Atlas   **819**

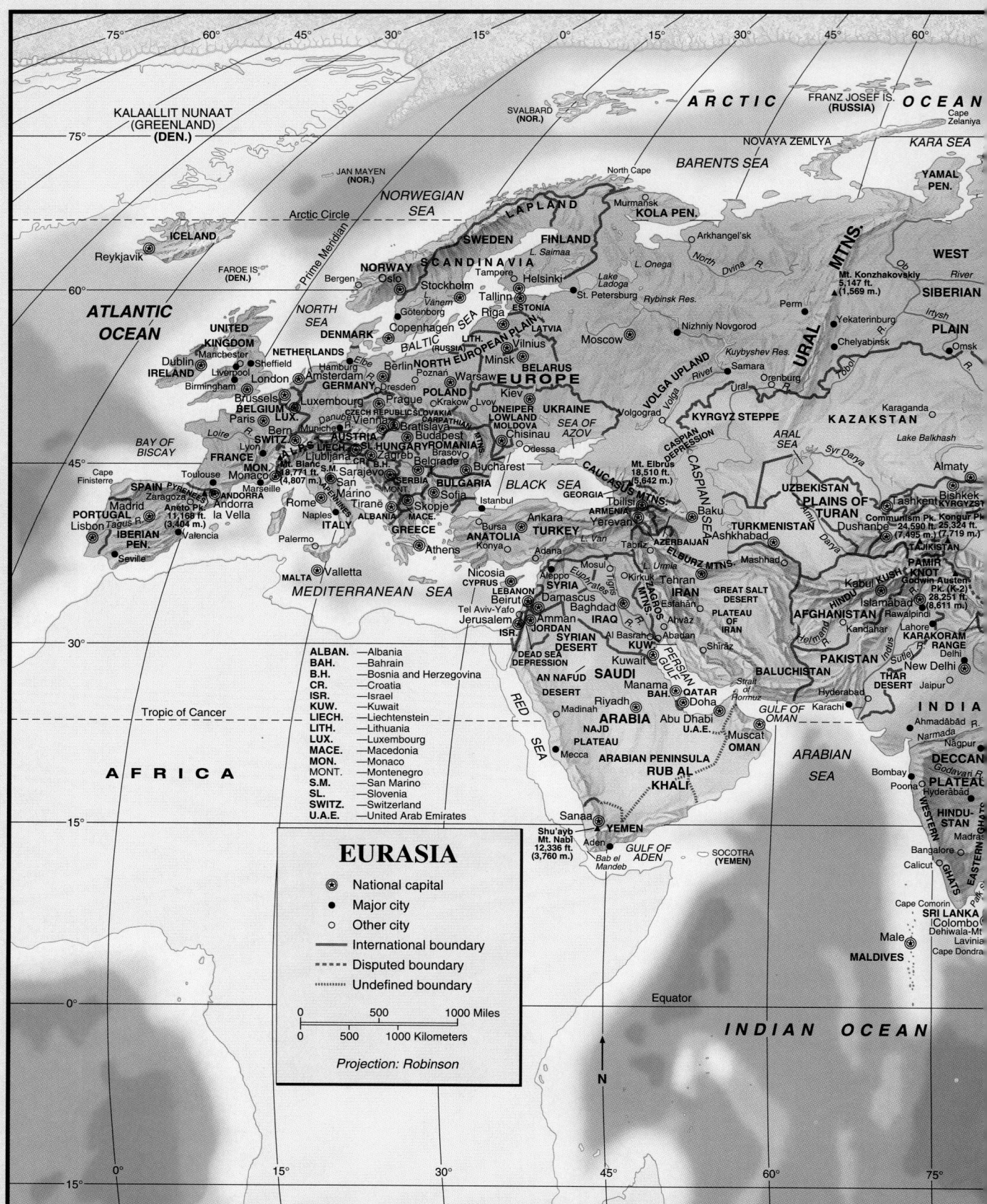

EURASIA

- ✵ National capital
- ● Major city
- ○ Other city
- —— International boundary
- ····· Disputed boundary
- ········· Undefined boundary

ALBAN.	—Albania
BAH.	—Bahrain
B.H.	—Bosnia and Herzegovina
CR.	—Croatia
ISR.	—Israel
KUW.	—Kuwait
LIECH.	—Liechtenstein
LITH.	—Lithuania
LUX.	—Luxembourg
MACE.	—Macedonia
MON.	—Monaco
MONT.	—Montenegro
S.M.	—San Marino
SL.	—Slovenia
SWITZ.	—Switzerland
U.A.E.	—United Arab Emirates

0   500   1000 Miles
0   500   1000 Kilometers

Projection: Robinson

N

90°   105°   120°   135°   150°   165°   180°   165°   150°   135°

SEVERNAYA ZEMLYA

TAYMYR PEN.   LAPTEV SEA   NEW SIBERIAN ISLANDS   EAST SIBERIAN SEA   75°

WRANGEL ISLAND

Noril'sk

CENTRAL SIBERIAN

PLATEAU   VERKHOYANSK RANGE   KOLYMA PLAIN   CHUKOTSK PEN.

Yenisey   LENA PLATEAU   Kolyma   Anadyr R.   Cape Navarin

Lower   Tunguska   R.   Lena   River   Yakutsk   KOLYMA RANGE   60°

RUSSIA   SIBERIA   Magadan   BERING SEA

Angara   Mt. Klyuchevsk 15,584 ft. (4,750 m.)

Krasnoyarsk   Bratsk Res.   STANOVOY RANGE   SEA OF OKHOTSK   KAMCHATKA PEN.   KOMANDORSKIY IS.

Novosibirsk   YABLONOVY RANGE   Cape Lopatka
Novosibirsk Res.   Lake Baykal   Komsomol'sk

Semipalatinsk   SAYAN MTNS.   Amur   La Pérouse Strait   KURIL ISLANDS   45°
Lake Zaysan   Khabarovsk

ALTAI MTNS.   MONGOLIA   Ulaanbaatar   DA HINGGAN LING   NORTHEAST (MANCHURIAN) PLAIN   Songhua   Jiang   L. Khanka   Sapporo

DZUNGARIAN BASIN   Ürümqi   MONGOLIAN PLATEAU   GOBI   Harbin   Vladivostok

TIANSHAN   TURFAN DEPRESSION   Changchun   SEA OF JAPAN

ASIA   Tarim   Shenyang   Anshan   JAPAN

TAKLIMAKAN   CHINA   Huang   Beijing   N. KOREA

KUNLUN SHAN   BAYAN HAR SHAN   Wei   He   Tianjin   NORTH CHINA PLAIN   Pyongyang   Inchon   Seoul   Kawasaki   Tokyo

HIMALAYAS   He   YELLOW SEA   S. KOREA   Kyōto   Yokohama
Annapurns Pk   Xi'an   Taegu   Osaka
26,502 ft.   PLATEAU OF   Kitakyūshū
(8,078 m.)   XIZANG   Nanjing
Mt. Everest   Lhasa   L. Tai   Shanghai
29,028 ft.   Chengdu   Hangzhou   EAST CHINA SEA   PACIFIC   30°
(8,848 m.)   Mt. Kangchenjunga
NEPAL   28,208 ft. (8,598 m.)   Chang   L. Poyang   Nanchang
Kathmandu   Thimphu   YUNGUI   Changsha   Fuzhou   OCEAN
Vārānasi   BHUTAN   PLATEAU   Guiyang   RYUKYU IS.
GANGES   Brahmaputra R.   Taipei
PLAIN   BANGLADESH   Kunming   Xi   Jiang   Guangzhou   TAIWAN
Ganges   Dhaka   Formosa Strait   Kaoheiung
Calcutta   Khulna   Macao   Victoria   Tropic of Cancer

BAY OF   Chittagong   MYANMAR   Hanoi   HONG KONG (U.K.)   Luzon Strait
BENGAL   Mandalay   ANNAMESE CORD.   Haiphong   MACAO (PORT.)   Cape Engaño   PHILIPPINE SEA   15°
Chiang   Mai   LAOS   LUZON
Bassein   Vientiane   Savannakhet   SOUTH   Quezon City
Preparis   Yangon   KHORAT PLATEAU   Da Nang   CHINA   Manila
Channel   THAILAND   Ubon   INDOCHINA   MINDORO   PHILIPPINES
ANDAMAN IS. (IND.)   Ratchathani   VIETNAM   Cebu
Thonburi   CAMBODIA   SEA
ANDAMAN   Krung Thep   Tonle Sap   PALAWAN   MINDANAO
SEA   (Bangkok)   Phnom Penh   Davao
CEYLON   Ho Chi Minh City   SEA   Point Tinaca
NICOBAR IS. (IND.)   MALAY PEN.   Bandar Seri Begawan   SULU ARCH. (PHIL.)
George Town   BRUNEI
Ipoh   Medan   Kuala Lumpur   BORNEO HIGHLANDS   HALMAHERA
Strait of Malacca   MALAYSIA   Equator   0°
SUMATRA   Singapore   BORNEO   Cape d'Urville
SINGAPORE   Pontianak   Jayapura
Jambi   CELEBES   Jaya Pk. 16,499 ft. (5,029 m.)
BARISAN MTNS.   Palembang   Banjarmasin   NEW GUINEA
JAVA SEA   Ujung Pandang   BANDA SEA
Sunda Str.   Jakarta   Semarang   INDONESIA   15°
Bandung   Surabaya   JAVA

90°   105°   120°   135°   150°   165°

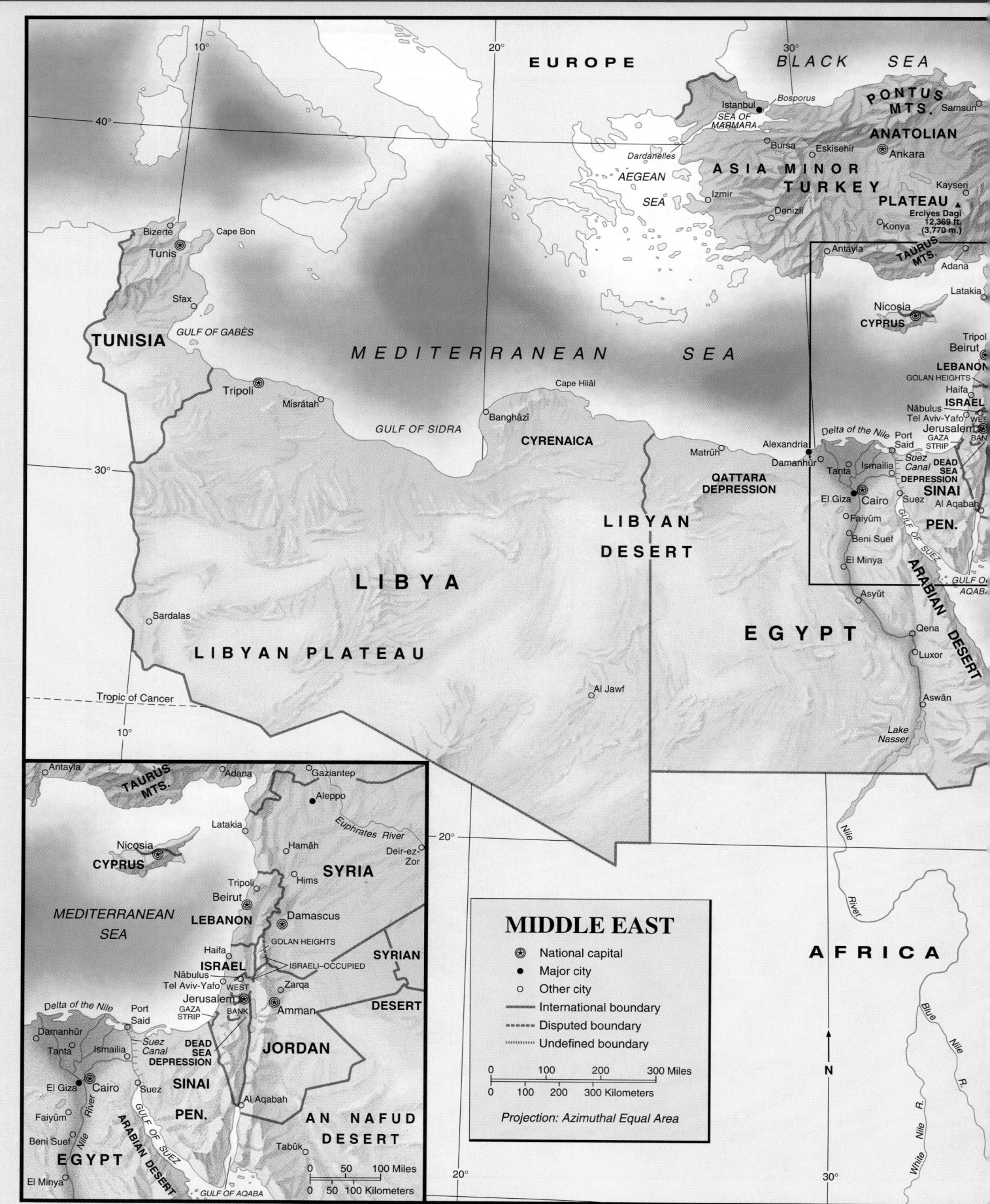

EUROPE

BLACK SEA

PONTUS MTS.

Samsun

Istanbul
Bosporus

SEA OF MARMARA

Dardanelles

Bursa   Eskisehir

ANATOLIAN

Ankara

ASIA MINOR

TURKEY

AEGEAN SEA

Izmir

Kayseri

Denizli

PLATEAU   Erciyes Dagi ▲
            12,369 ft.
            (3,770 m.)

Konya

Antayla

TAURUS MTS.

Adana

Latakia

Nicosia

CYPRUS

Tripol
Beirut

LEBANON

GOLAN HEIGHTS
Haifa

Nābulus   ISRAEL
Tel Aviv-Yafo
            Jerusalem WES
            GAZA   BAN
            STRIP

DEAD SEA DEPRESSION

SINAI PEN.

Al Aqabah

GULF OF AQABA

Bizerte   Cape Bon

Tunis

TUNISIA

Sfax

GULF OF GABÈS

MEDITERRANEAN   SEA

Cape Hilāl

Tripoli

Misrātah

GULF OF SIDRA

Banghāzī

CYRENAICA

Matrûh

Alexandria

Delta of the Nile

Port Said

Damanhūr   Tanta   Ismailia

Suez Canal

El Giza Cairo

Faiyûm   Suez

Beni Suef

El Minya

LIBYAN DESERT

QATTARA DEPRESSION

ARABIAN DESERT

GULF OF SUEZ

LIBYA

Sardalas

LIBYAN PLATEAU

EGYPT

Asyût

Qena

Luxor

Tropic of Cancer

Al Jawf

Aswân

Lake Nasser

Nile River

AFRICA

Nile River

Blue Nile R.

White Nile R.

Antayla

TAURUS MTS.

Adana

Gaziantep

Aleppo

Latakia

Nicosia

CYPRUS

Euphrates River

Hamāh

Deir-ez-Zor

SYRIA

Tripoli   Hims

Beirut

LEBANON

Damascus

Haifa

GOLAN HEIGHTS

ISRAELI-OCCUPIED

SYRIAN

MEDITERRANEAN SEA

ISRAEL

Nābulus
Tel Aviv-Yafo   WEST
            Zarqa

Jerusalem   BANK
GAZA   Amman
STRIP

DESERT

Delta of the Nile

Port Said

Damanhūr

Tanta   Ismailia

Suez Canal

DEAD SEA DEPRESSION

JORDAN

El Giza Cairo

Faiyûm   Suez

SINAI PEN.

Al Aqabah

Beni Suef

EGYPT

ARABIAN DESERT

GULF OF SUEZ

AN NAFUD DESERT

El Minya

Tabûk

GULF OF AQABA

0   50   100 Miles
0   50   100 Kilometers

MIDDLE EAST

⊛ National capital
● Major city
○ Other city
— International boundary
---- Disputed boundary
······ Undefined boundary

0   100   200   300 Miles
0   100   200   300 Kilometers

Projection: Azimuthal Equal Area

N

10°   20°   30°

40°

30°

20°

10°

20°

30°

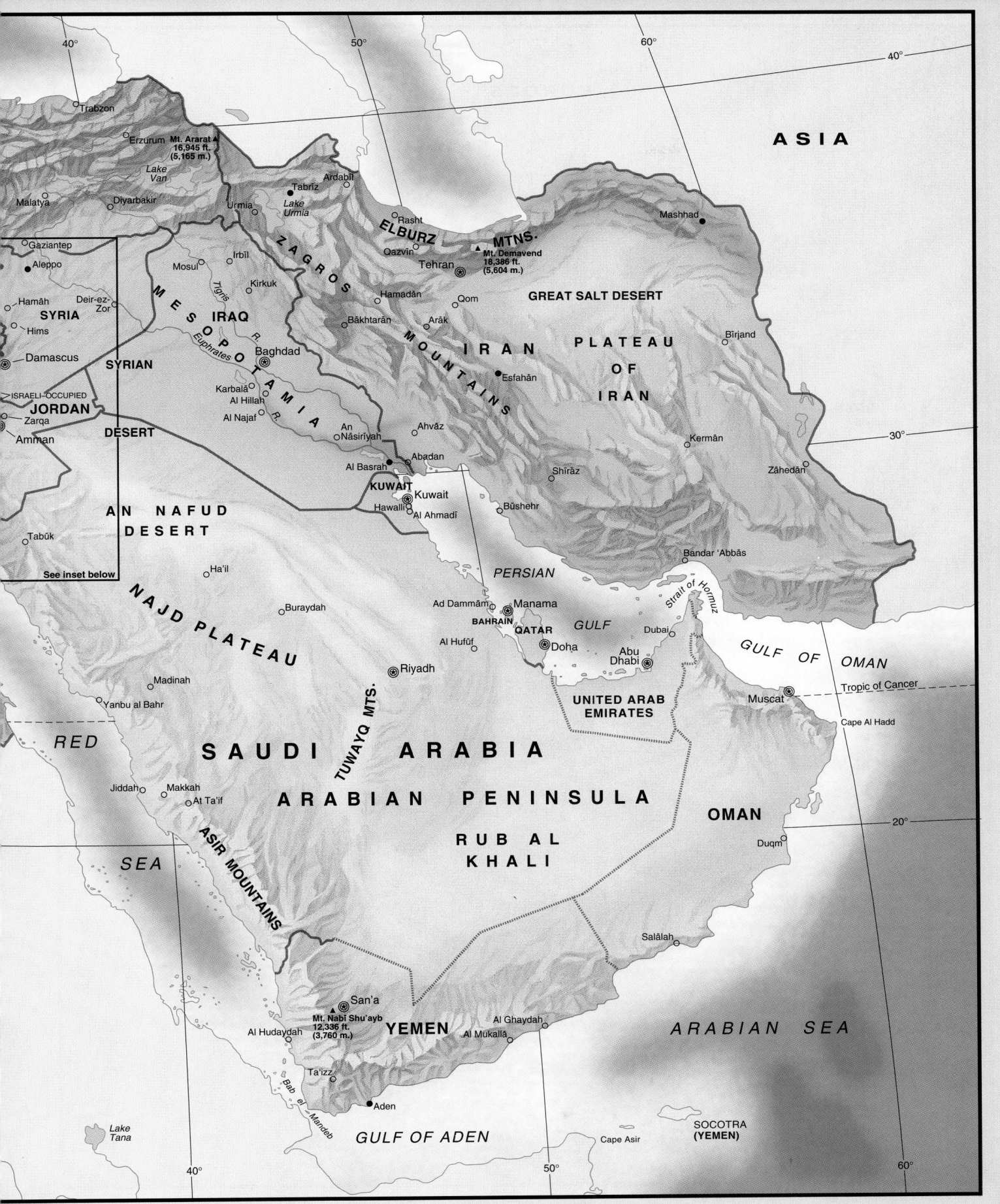

ASIA

Trabzon
Erzurum
Mt. Ararat ▲
16,945 ft.
(5,165 m.)
Lake
Van
Malatya
Diyarbakir
Gaziantep
Aleppo
Hamâh
Deir-ez-
Zor
SYRIA
Hims
Damascus
ISRAELI-OCCUPIED
JORDAN
Zarqa
Amman
SYRIAN
DESERT
Tabûk
AN NAFUD
DESERT
See inset below

Ardabîl
Tabrîz
Lake
Urmia
Urmia
Rasht
ELBURZ
MTNS.
Mt. Demavend
18,386 ft.
(5,604 m.)
Qazvîn
Tehran
Mashhad
Mosul
Irbîl
Kirkuk
Hamadân
Qom
GREAT SALT DESERT
Bâkhtarân
Arâk
Bîrjand
Baghdad
Esfahân
PLATEAU
OF
IRAN
Karbalâ
Al Hillah
Al Najaf
Ahvâz
Kermân
An
Nâsirîyah
Shîrâz
Zâhedân
Abadan
Al Basrah
KUWAIT
Kuwait
Hawalli
Al Ahmadî
Bûshehr
Bandar 'Abbâs
PERSIAN
Ha'il
Ad Dammâm
Manama
BAHRAIN
GULF
Dubai
GULF OF OMAN
Buraydah
QATAR
Al Hufûf
Doha
Abu
Dhabi
Muscat
Tropic of Cancer
Madinah
Riyadh
UNITED ARAB
EMIRATES
Cape Al Hadd
Yanbu al Bahr
NAJD PLATEAU
RED
SAUDI ARABIA
ARABIAN PENINSULA
OMAN
Jiddah
Makkah
At Ta'if
RUB AL
KHALI
Duqm
SEA
ASIR MOUNTAINS
Salâlah
Mt. Nabî Shu'ayb
12,336 ft.
(3,760 m.)
San'a
Al Ghaydah
ARABIAN SEA
Al Hudaydah
YEMEN
Al Mukallâ
Ta'izz
Lake
Tana
Bab
el
Mandeb
Aden
SOCOTRA
(YEMEN)
GULF OF ADEN
Cape Asir

MESOPOTAMIA
IRAQ
ZAGROS MOUNTAINS
IRAN
Tigris
Euphrates
TUWAYQ MTS.
Strait of Hormuz

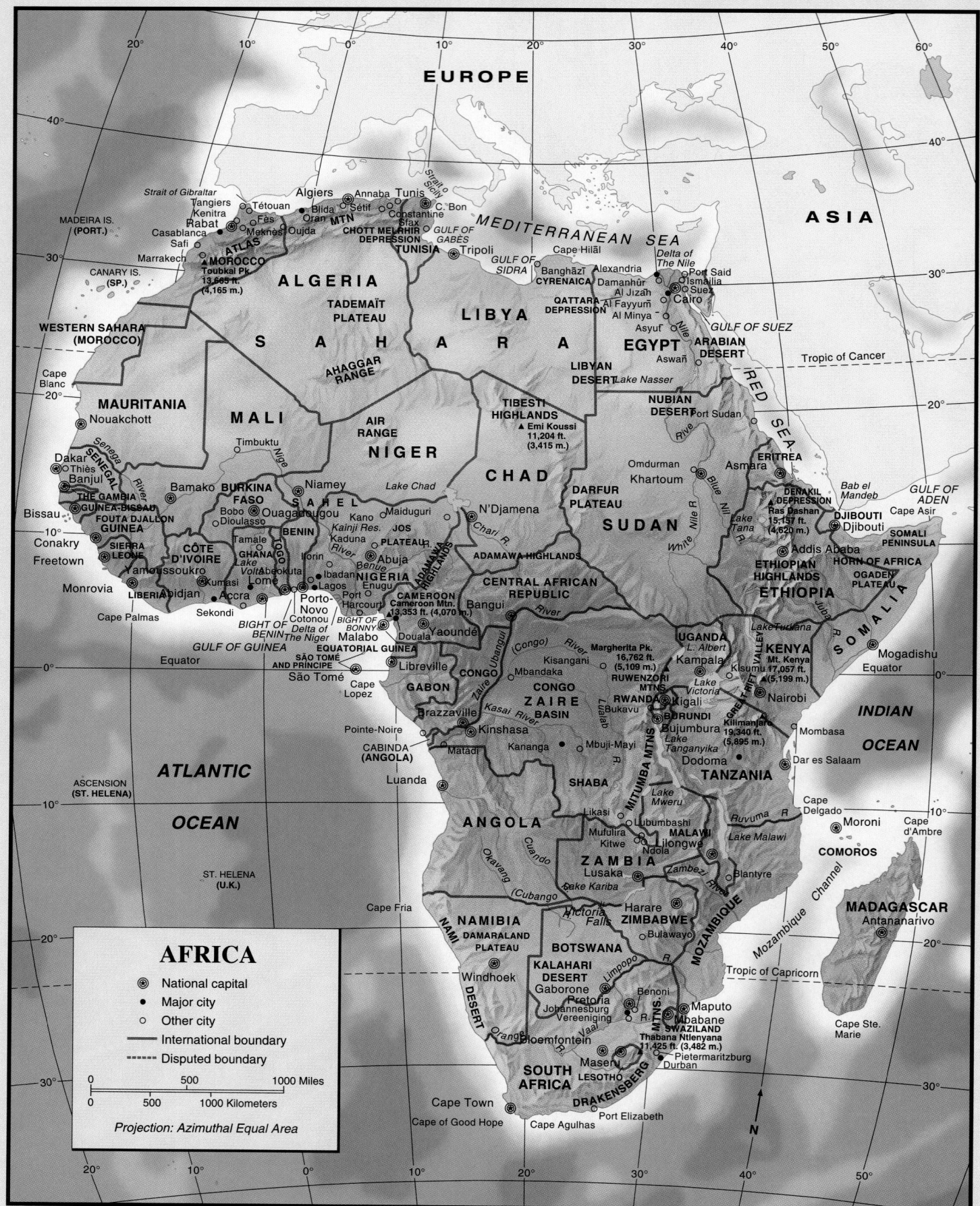

AFRICA

- ⊛ National capital
- ● Major city
- ○ Other city
- —— International boundary
- ------ Disputed boundary

0   500   1000 Miles
0   500   1000 Kilometers

Projection: Azimuthal Equal Area

MAINLAND SOUTHEAST ASIA

◉ National capital
● Major city
○ Other city
— International boundary

| 0 | 200 | 400 Miles |
| 0 | 200 | 400 Kilometers |

Projection: Mercator

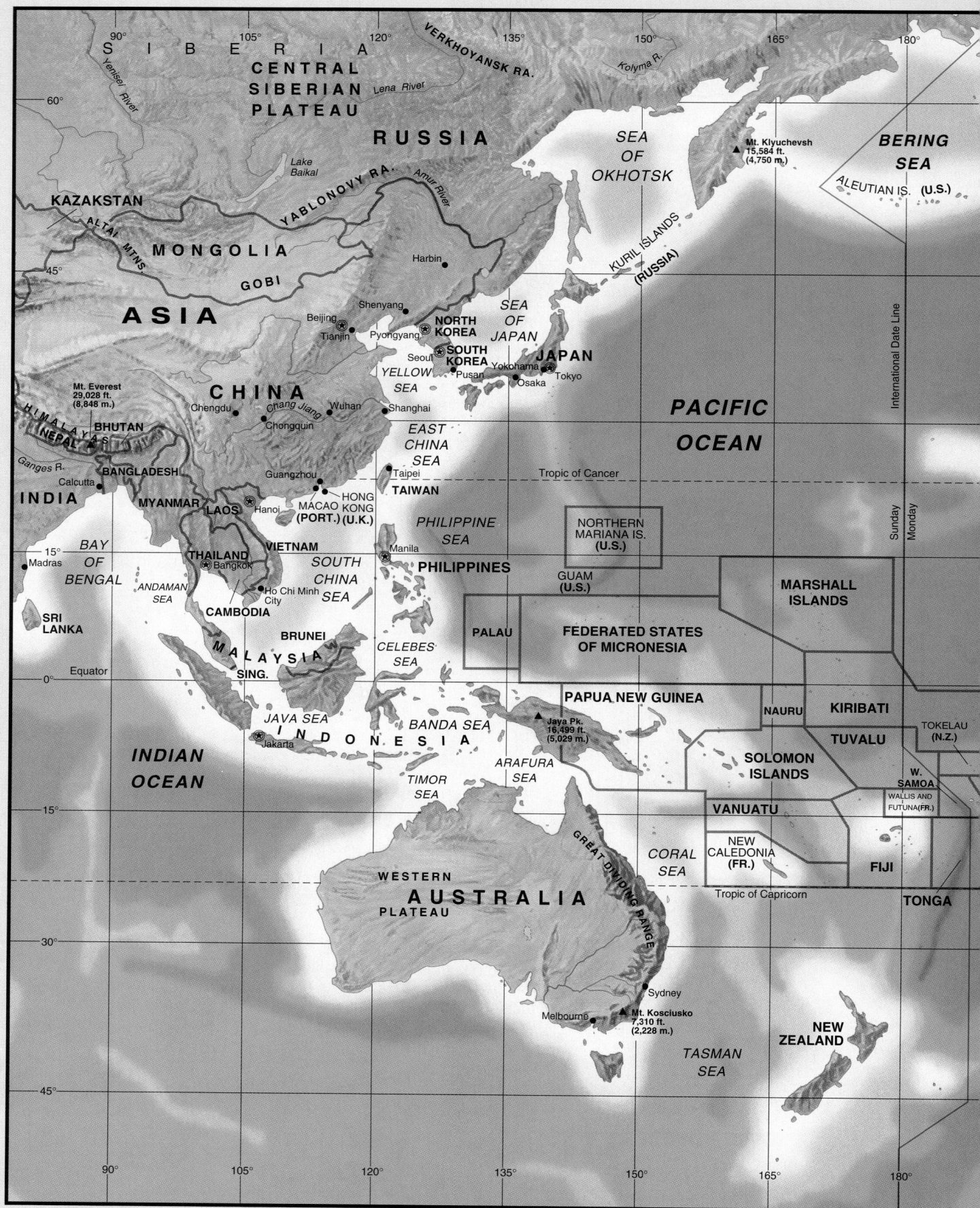

S I B E R I A

CENTRAL
SIBERIAN
PLATEAU

90°   105°   VERKHOYANSK RA.   135°   150°   165°   180°

Yenisei River   60°   Lena River   Kolyma R.   BERING SEA

RUSSIA   SEA OF OKHOTSK   Mt. Klyuchevsh 15,584 ft. (4,750 m.)

KAZAKSTAN   ALTAI MTNS   45°   Amur River   ALEUTIAN IS. (U.S.)

MONGOLIA   YABLONOVY RA.   KURIL ISLANDS (RUSSIA)

Lake Baikal   Harbin   GOBI

ASIA   Beijing   Shenyang   SEA OF JAPAN

Tianjin   Pyongyang   NORTH KOREA   JAPAN   International Date Line

Mt. Everest 29,028 ft. (8,848 m.)   Seoul   SOUTH KOREA   Yokohama   Tokyo   PACIFIC OCEAN

CHINA   Chengdu   Chang Jiang   Wuhan   YELLOW SEA   Pusan   Osaka

HIMALAYAS   Chongquin   Shanghai   EAST CHINA SEA

NEPAL   BHUTAN   Ganges R.   Sunday   Monday

BANGLADESH   Guangzhou   Taipei   Tropic of Cancer

Calcutta   TAIWAN

INDIA   MYANMAR   LAOS   Hanoi   MACAO (PORT.)   HONG KONG (U.K.)

BAY OF BENGAL   15°   VIETNAM   PHILIPPINE SEA   NORTHERN MARIANA IS. (U.S.)

Madras   THAILAND   Bangkok   SOUTH CHINA SEA   Manila   PHILIPPINES   GUAM (U.S.)   MARSHALL ISLANDS

ANDAMAN SEA   Ho Chi Minh City   PALAU   FEDERATED STATES OF MICRONESIA

SRI LANKA   CAMBODIA   CELEBES SEA

BRUNEI

MALAYSIA   NAURU   KIRIBATI

SING.   Equator   0°   PAPUA NEW GUINEA   TOKELAU (N.Z.)

JAVA SEA   INDONESIA   BANDA SEA   Jaya Pk. 16,499 ft. (5,029 m.)   TUVALU

Jakarta   SOLOMON ISLANDS   W. SAMOA   WALLIS AND FUTUNA (FR.)

INDIAN OCEAN   ARAFURA SEA   VANUATU   15°

TIMOR SEA   NEW CALEDONIA (FR.)   FIJI

GREAT DIVIDING RANGE   CORAL SEA

WESTERN   Tropic of Capricorn   TONGA

AUSTRALIA   PLATEAU   30°

Sydney

Melbourne   Mt. Kosciusko 7,310 ft. (2,228 m.)   NEW ZEALAND

TASMAN SEA   45°

90°   105°   120°   135°   150°   165°   180°

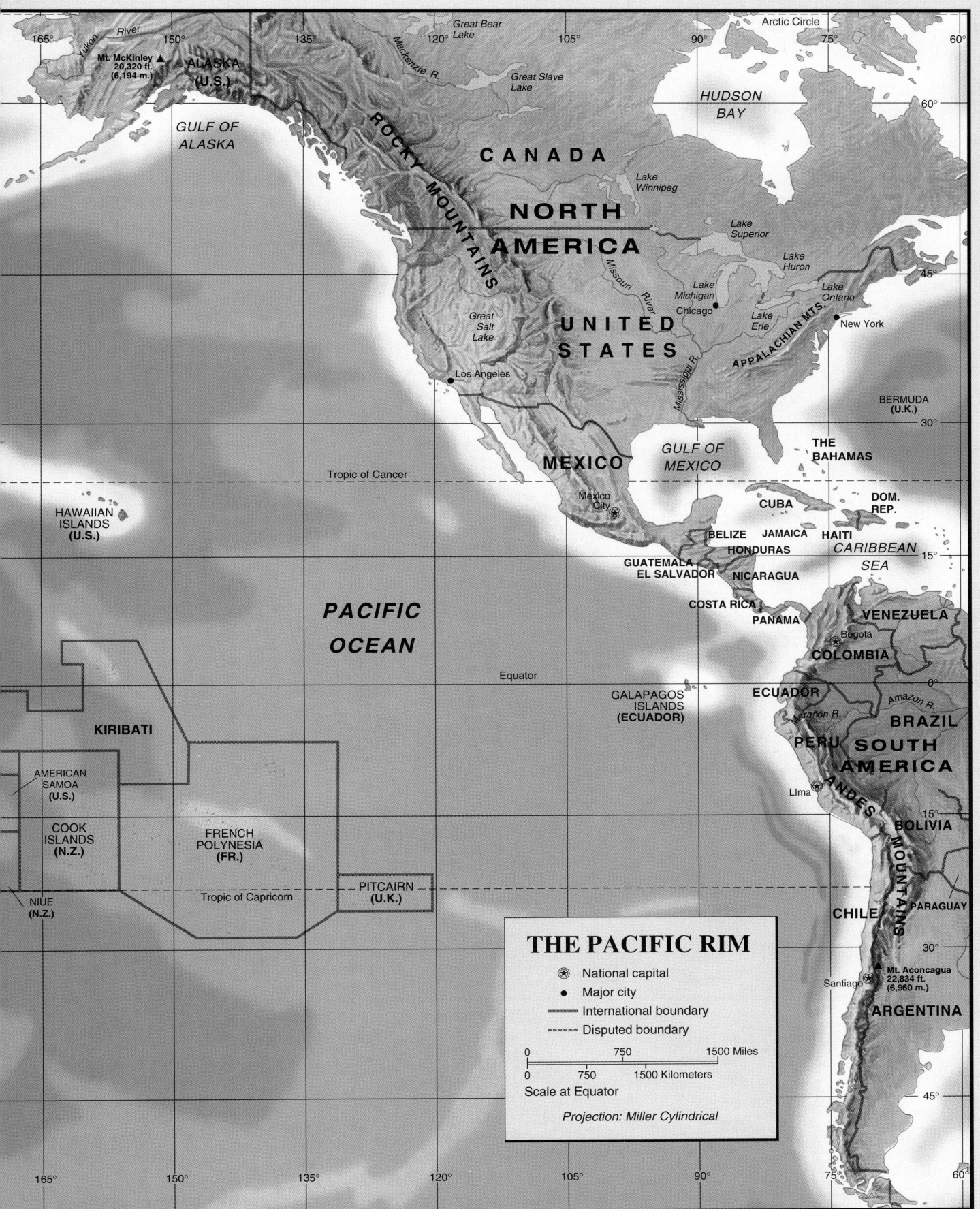

THE PACIFIC RIM

⊛ National capital

● Major city

—— International boundary

┄┄┄ Disputed boundary

0	750	1500 Miles
0	750	1500 Kilometers

Scale at Equator

Projection: Miller Cylindrical

Atlas   827

United States Databank

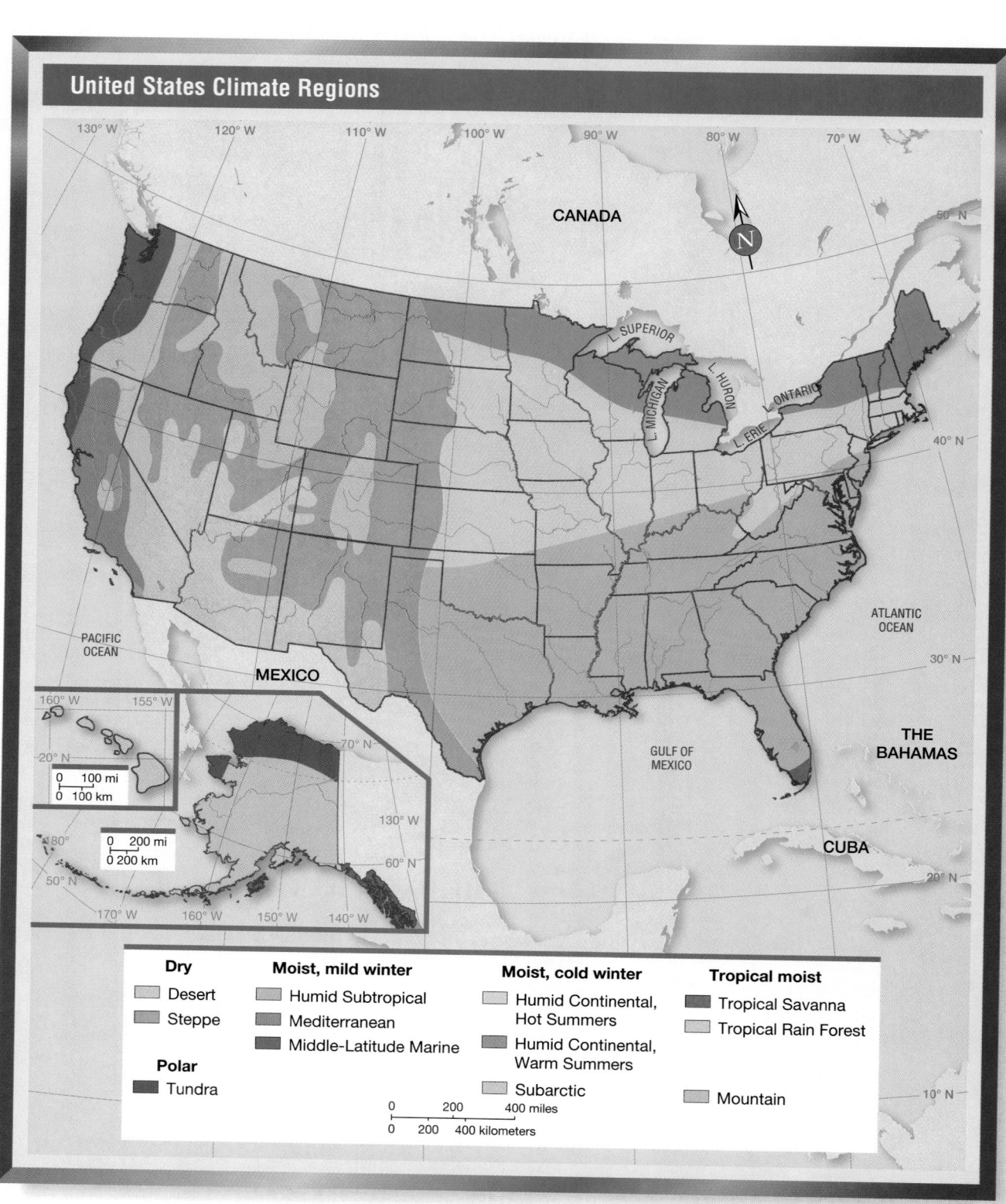

United States Climate Regions

CANADA

L. SUPERIOR
L. HURON
L. MICHIGAN
L. ERIE
ONTARIO

PACIFIC OCEAN

MEXICO

GULF OF MEXICO

ATLANTIC OCEAN

THE BAHAMAS

CUBA

Dry
- Desert
- Steppe

Polar
- Tundra

Moist, mild winter
- Humid Subtropical
- Mediterranean
- Middle-Latitude Marine

Moist, cold winter
- Humid Continental, Hot Summers
- Humid Continental, Warm Summers
- Subarctic

Tropical moist
- Tropical Savanna
- Tropical Rain Forest

- Mountain

0   100 mi
0   100 km

0   200 mi
0   200 km

0   200   400 miles
0   200   400 kilometers

Population of the United States

Year	Population			Year	Population		
1790	3,929,214	4.5	–	1900	76,212,168	21.5	21.0
1800	5,308,483	6.1	35.1	1910	92,228,496	26.0	21.0
1810	7,239,881	4.3	36.4	1920	106,021,537	29.9	15.0
1820	9,638,453	5.5	33.1	1930	123,202,624	34.7	16.2
1830	12,866,020	7.4	33.5	1940	132,164,569	37.2	7.3
1840	17,069,453	9.8	32.7	1950	151,325,798	42.6	14.5
1850	23,191,876	7.9	35.9	1960	179,323,175	50.6	18.5
1860	31,443,321	10.6	35.6	1970	203,302,031	57.5	13.4
1870	38,558,371	10.9	22.6	1980	226,542,203	64.0	11.4
1880	50,189,209	14.2	30.2	1990	248,709,873	70.3	9.8
1890	62,979,766	17.8	25.5				

Key:

☐ Population per square mile of land

☐ Percentage increase over preceding census

Source: U.S. Department of the Census; *Statistical Abstract of the United States,* 1994.

Population Distribution by Age

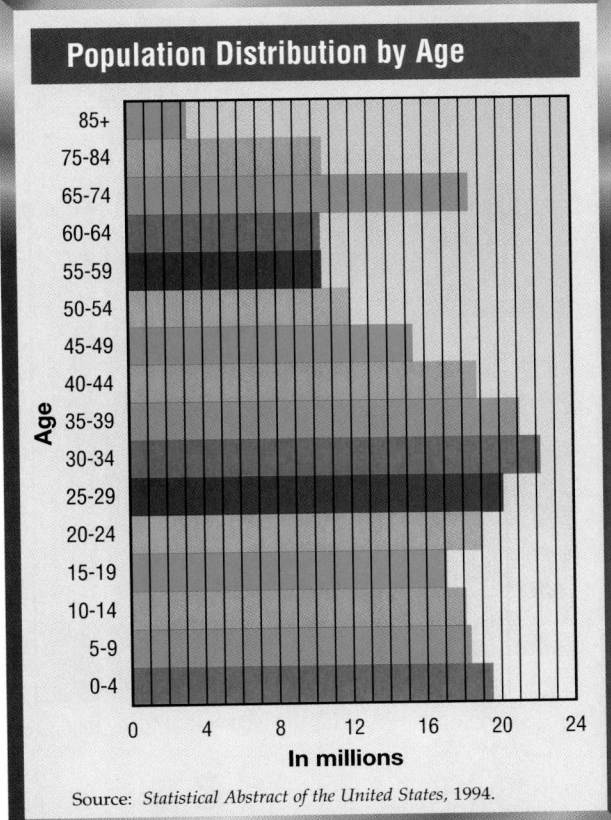

Source: *Statistical Abstract of the United States,* 1994.

Major Religions in the United States

Roman Catholic Church	58,267
Southern Baptist Convention	15,232
United Methodist Church	8,785
National Baptist Convention	3,500
Muslims	6,000
Jews	5,981
Evangelical Lutheran Church	5,245
Church of Jesus Christ of Latter-Day Saints (Mormon)	4,336
Church of God in Christ (Pentecostal)	3,710
Presbyterian Church (U.S.A.)	3,778
National Baptist Convention of America	3,500
Lutheran Church (Missouri Synod)	2,607
Episcopal Church	2,472
African Methodist Episcopal Church	3,500
Assemblies of God	2,235
Greek Orthodox Archdiocese of North and South America	1,950
United Church of Christ	1,584
Churches of Christ	1,690
American Baptist Churches in the U.S.A.	1,528
African Methodist Episcopal Zion Church	1,200
Christian Churches and Churches of Christ	1,071
Christian Church (Disciples of Christ)	1,023
Orthodox Church in America	1,030

In thousands

Source: *Statistical Abstract of the United States,* 1994; *Time* magazine (November 19, 1990).

Political Parties in Power

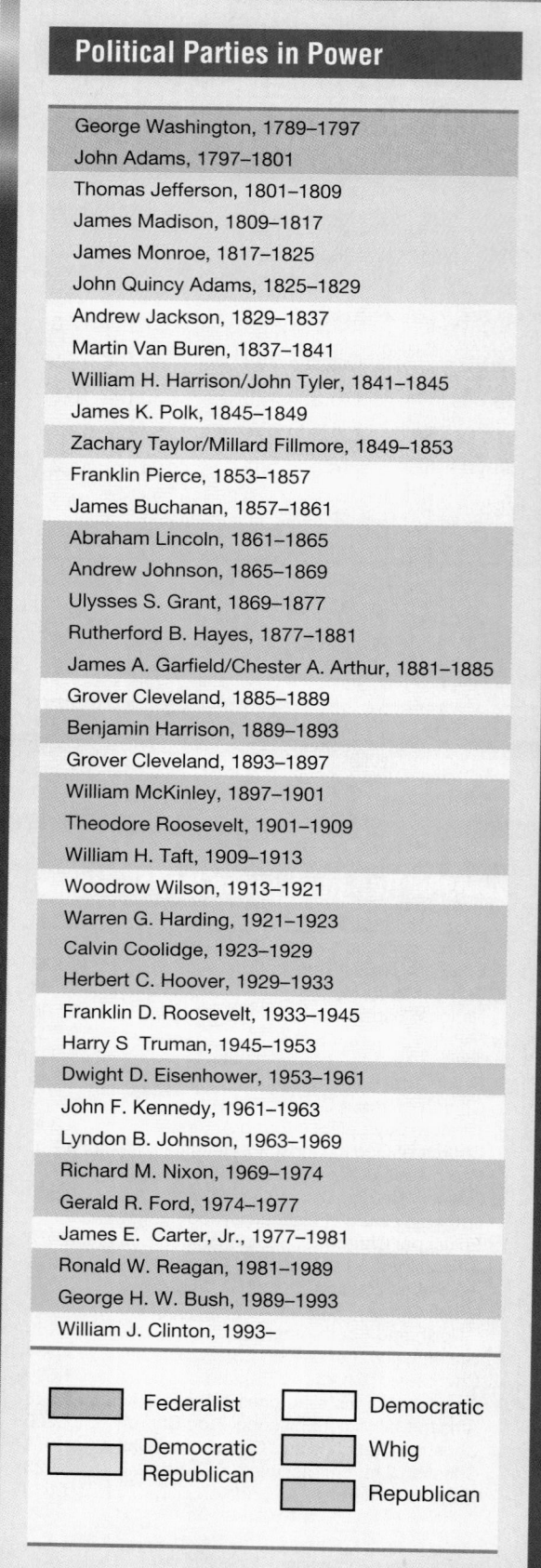

George Washington, 1789–1797
John Adams, 1797–1801
Thomas Jefferson, 1801–1809
James Madison, 1809–1817
James Monroe, 1817–1825
John Quincy Adams, 1825–1829
Andrew Jackson, 1829–1837
Martin Van Buren, 1837–1841
William H. Harrison/John Tyler, 1841–1845
James K. Polk, 1845–1849
Zachary Taylor/Millard Fillmore, 1849–1853
Franklin Pierce, 1853–1857
James Buchanan, 1857–1861
Abraham Lincoln, 1861–1865
Andrew Johnson, 1865–1869
Ulysses S. Grant, 1869–1877
Rutherford B. Hayes, 1877–1881
James A. Garfield/Chester A. Arthur, 1881–1885
Grover Cleveland, 1885–1889
Benjamin Harrison, 1889–1893
Grover Cleveland, 1893–1897
William McKinley, 1897–1901
Theodore Roosevelt, 1901–1909
William H. Taft, 1909–1913
Woodrow Wilson, 1913–1921
Warren G. Harding, 1921–1923
Calvin Coolidge, 1923–1929
Herbert C. Hoover, 1929–1933
Franklin D. Roosevelt, 1933–1945
Harry S Truman, 1945–1953
Dwight D. Eisenhower, 1953–1961
John F. Kennedy, 1961–1963
Lyndon B. Johnson, 1963–1969
Richard M. Nixon, 1969–1974
Gerald R. Ford, 1974–1977
James E. Carter, Jr., 1977–1981
Ronald W. Reagan, 1981–1989
George H. W. Bush, 1989–1993
William J. Clinton, 1993–

Federalist
Democratic
Democratic Republican
Whig
Republican

Graduation Rates

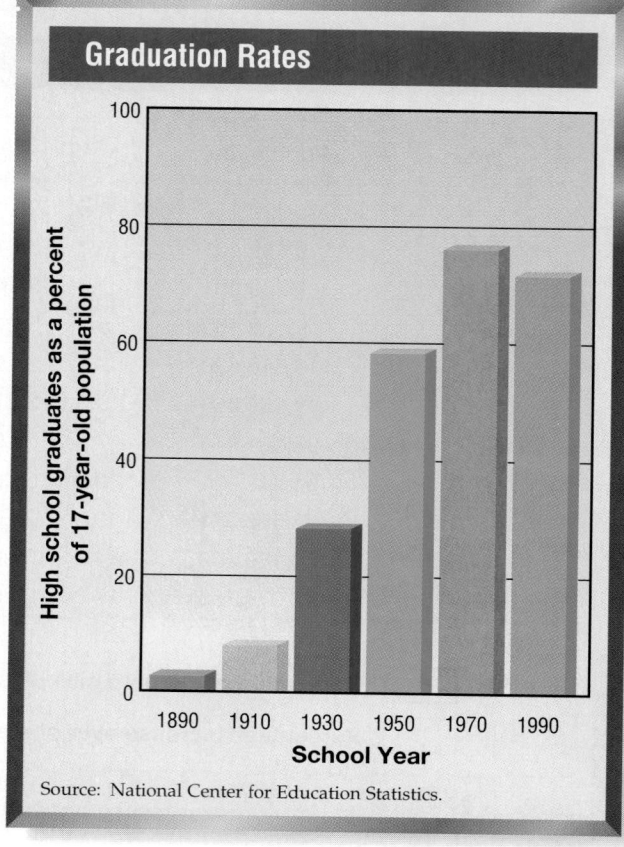

Source: National Center for Education Statistics.

Life Expectancy

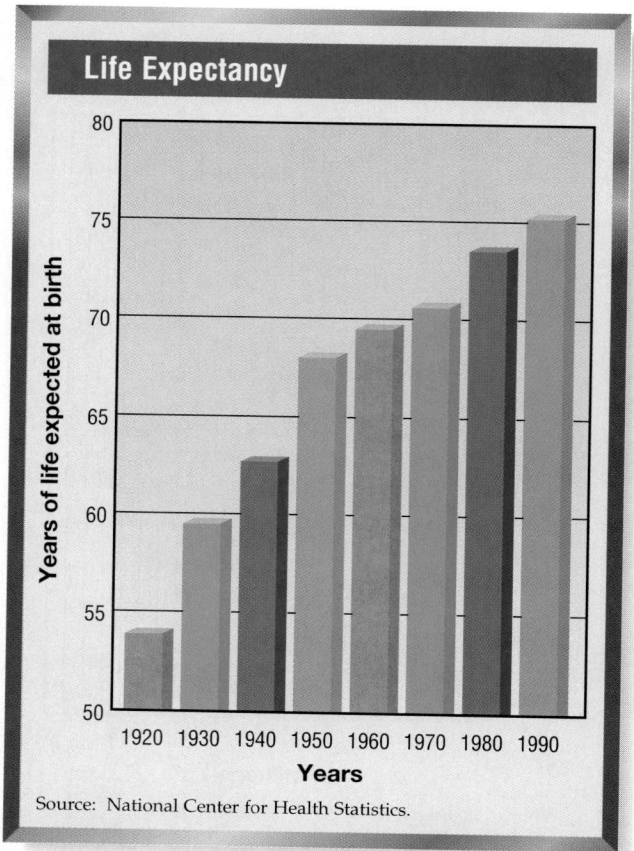

Source: National Center for Health Statistics.

The United States

STATE*	YEAR ADMITTED	POPULATION (1990)	LAND AREA (sq mi)	CAPITAL	LARGEST CITY	HOUSE REP. (1990)**
1. Delaware	1787	666,168	1,954	Dover	Wilmington	1
2. Pennsylvania	1787	11,881,643	44,819	Harrisburg	Philadelphia	21
3. New Jersey	1787	7,730,188	7,418	Trenton	Newark	13
4. Georgia	1788	6,478,216	57,918	Atlanta	Atlanta	11
5. Connecticut	1788	3,287,116	4,845	Hartford	Bridgeport	6
6. Massachusetts	1788	6,016,425	7,838	Boston	Boston	10
7. Maryland	1788	4,781,468	9,774	Annapolis	Baltimore	8
8. South Carolina	1788	3,486,703	30,111	Columbia	Columbia	6
9. New Hampshire	1788	1,109,252	8,969	Concord	Manchester	2
10. Virginia	1788	6,187,358	39,597	Richmond	Virginia Beach	11
11. New York	1788	17,990,455	47,223	Albany	New York	31
12. North Carolina	1789	6,628,637	48,718	Raleigh	Charlotte	12
13. Rhode Island	1790	1,003,464	1,045	Providence	Providence	2
14. Vermont	1791	562,758	9,249	Montpelier	Burlington	1
15. Kentucky	1792	3,685,296	39,732	Frankfort	Louisville	6
16. Tennessee	1796	4,877,185	41,219	Nashville	Memphis	9
17. Ohio	1803	10,847,115	40,952	Columbus	Columbus	19
18. Louisiana	1812	4,219,973	43,566	Baton Rouge	New Orleans	7
19. Indiana	1816	5,544,159	35,870	Indianapolis	Indianapolis	10
20. Mississippi	1817	2,573,216	46,913	Jackson	Jackson	5
21. Illinois	1818	11,430,602	55,593	Springfield	Chicago	20
22. Alabama	1819	4,040,587	50,750	Montgomery	Birmingham	7
23. Maine	1820	1,227,928	30,864	Augusta	Portland	2
24. Missouri	1821	5,117,073	68,898	Jefferson City	Kansas City	9
25. Arkansas	1836	2,350,725	52,075	Little Rock	Little Rock	4
26. Michigan	1837	9,295,297	56,809	Lansing	Detroit	16
27. Florida	1845	12,937,926	53,997	Tallahassee	Jacksonville	23
28. Texas	1845	16,986,510	261,194	Austin	Houston	30
29. Iowa	1846	2,776,755	55,874	Des Moines	Des Moines	5
30. Wisconsin	1848	4,891,769	54,313	Madison	Milwaukee	9
31. California	1850	29,760,021	155,973	Sacramento	Los Angeles	52
32. Minnesota	1858	4,375,099	79,616	St. Paul	Minneapolis	8
33. Oregon	1859	2,853,733	96,002	Salem	Portland	5
34. Kansas	1861	2,477,574	81,823	Topeka	Wichita	4
35. West Virginia	1863	1,793,477	24,086	Charleston	Charleston	3
36. Nevada	1864	1,201,833	109,805	Carson City	Las Vegas	2
37. Nebraska	1867	1,578,385,	76,877	Lincoln	Omaha	3
38. Colorado	1876	3,294,394	103,729	Denver	Denver	6
39. North Dakota	1889	638,800	68,994	Bismarck	Fargo	1
40. South Dakota	1889	696,004	75,897	Pierre	Sioux Falls	1
41. Montana	1889	799,065	145,556	Helena	Billings	1
42. Washington	1889	4,887,941	66,581	Olympia	Seattle	9
43. Idaho	1890	1,006,749	82,750	Boise	Boise	2
44. Wyoming	1890	455,975	97,104	Cheyenne	Cheyenne	1
45. Utah	1896	1,727,784	82,168	Salt Lake City	Salt Lake City	3
46. Oklahoma	1907	3,145,585	68,678	Oklahoma City	Oklahoma City	6
47. New Mexico	1912	1,515,069	121,364	Sante Fe	Albuquerque	3
48. Arizona	1912	3,665,228	113,642	Phoenix	Phoenix	6
49. Alaska	1959	550,043	570,373	Juneau	Anchorage	1
50. Hawaii	1959	1,108,229	6,423	Honolulu	Honolulu	2
District of Columbia (Washington, D.C.)	–	606,900	61	–	–	–
United States of America	–	248,709,873	3,536,341	Washington, D.C.	New York	435

* Numbers denote the order in which states were admitted.
** Number of members in House of Representatives

Presidents of the United States

★ ★ ★ ★ ★ ★ ★ ★ ★ ★ ★ ★ ★ ★ ★ ★ ★

** The Republican party during this period developed into today's Democratic party. Today's Republican party originated in 1854.

George Washington

1789–1797

Born: 1732
Died: 1799
Born in: Virginia
Elected from: Virginia
Age when elected: 56
Occupations: Planter, Soldier
Party: None
Vice President: John Adams

John Adams

1797–1801

Born: 1735
Died: 1826
Born in: Massachusetts
Elected from: Massachusetts
Age when elected: 61
Occupations: Teacher, Lawyer
Party: Federalist
Vice President: Thomas Jefferson

Thomas Jefferson

1801–1809

Born: 1743
Died: 1826
Born in: Virginia
Elected from: Virginia
Age when elected: 57
Occupations: Planter, Lawyer
Party: Republican**
Vice Presidents: Aaron Burr, George Clinton

James Madison

1809–1817

Born: 1751
Died: 1836
Born in: Virginia
Elected from: Virginia
Age when elected: 57
Occupation: Planter
Party: Republican**
Vice Presidents: George Clinton, Elbridge Gerry

James Monroe

1817–1825

Born: 1758
Died: 1831
Born in: Virginia
Elected from: Virginia
Age when elected: 58
Occupation: Lawyer
Party: Republican**
Vice President: Daniel D. Tompkins

John Quincy Adams

6

1825–1829

Born: 1767
Died: 1848
Born in: Massachusetts
Elected from: Massachusetts
Age when elected: 57
Occupation: Lawyer
Party: Republican**
Vice President: John C. Calhoun

Andrew Jackson

7

1829–1837

Born: 1767
Died: 1845
Born in: South Carolina
Elected from: Tennessee
Age when elected: 61
Occupations: Lawyer, Soldier
Party: Democratic
Vice Presidents: John C.
Calhoun, Martin Van Buren

Martin Van Buren

8

1837–1841

Born: 1782
Died: 1862
Born in: New York
Elected from: New York
Age when elected: 54
Occupation: Lawyer
Party: Democratic
Vice President: Richard M.
Johnson

William H. Harrison

9

1841

Born: 1773
Died: 1841
Born in: Virginia
Elected from: Ohio
Age when elected: 67
Occupations: Soldier, Planter
Party: Whig
Vice President: John Tyler

John Tyler

10

1841–1845

Born: 1790
Died: 1862
Born in: Virginia
Elected as V.P. from: Virginia
Succeeded Harrison
Age when became President: 51
Occupation: Lawyer
Party: Whig
Vice President: None

James K. Polk

11

1845–1849

Born: 1795
Died: 1849
Born in: North Carolina
Elected from: Tennessee
Age when elected: 49
Occupation: Lawyer
Party: Democratic
Vice President: George M. Dallas

Zachary Taylor

12

1849–1850

Born: 1784
Died: 1850
Born in: Virginia
Elected from: Louisiana
Age when elected: 63
Occupation: Soldier
Party: Whig
Vice President: Millard Fillmore

Millard Fillmore

13

1850–1853

Born: 1800
Died: 1874
Born in: New York
Elected as V.P. from: New York
Succeeded Taylor
Age when became President: 50
Occupation: Lawyer
Party: Whig
Vice President: None

Franklin Pierce

14

1853–1857

Born: 1804
Died: 1869
Born in: New Hampshire
Elected from: New Hampshire
Age when elected: 47
Occupation: Lawyer
Party: Democratic
Vice President: William R. King

James Buchanan

15

1857–1861

Born: 1791
Died: 1868
Born in: Pennsylvania
Elected from: Pennsylvania
Age when elected: 65
Occupation: Lawyer
Party: Democratic
Vice President: John C.
Breckinridge

Abraham Lincoln

16

1861–1865

Born: 1809
Died: 1865
Born in: Kentucky
Elected from: Illinois
Age when elected: 51
Occupation: Lawyer
Party: Republican
Vice Presidents: Hannibal
Hamlin, Andrew Johnson

Presidents

Andrew Johnson

17

1865–1869

Born: 1808
Died: 1875
Born in: North Carolina
Elected as V.P. from: Tennessee
Age when became President: 56
Succeeded Lincoln
Occupation: Tailor
Party: Republican
Vice President: None

Ulysses S. Grant

18

1869–1877

Born: 1822
Died: 1885
Born in: Ohio
Elected from: Illinois
Age when elected: 46
Occupations: Farmer, Soldier
Party: Republican
Vice Presidents: Schuyler Colfax, Henry Wilson

Rutherford B. Hayes

19

1877–1881

Born: 1822
Died: 1893
Born in: Ohio
Elected from: Ohio
Age when elected: 54
Occupation: Lawyer
Party: Republican
Vice President: William A. Wheeler

James A. Garfield

20

1881

Born: 1831
Died: 1881
Born in: Ohio
Elected from: Ohio
Age when elected: 49
Occupations: Laborer, Professor
Party: Republican
Vice President: Chester A. Arthur

Chester A. Arthur

21

1881–1885

Born: 1830
Died: 1886
Born in: Vermont
Elected as V.P. from: New York
Succeeded Garfield
Age when became President: 50
Occupations: Teacher, Lawyer
Party: Republican
Vice President: None

Grover Cleveland

22 **24**

1885–89, 1893–97

Born: 1837
Died: 1908
Born in: New Jersey
Elected from: New York
Age when elected: 47; 55
Occupation: Lawyer
Party: Democratic
Vice Presidents: Thomas A. Hendricks, Adlai E. Stevenson

Benjamin Harrison

23

1889–1893

Born: 1833
Died: 1901
Born in: Ohio
Elected from: Indiana
Age when elected: 55
Occupation: Lawyer
Party: Republican
Vice President: Levi P. Morton

William McKinley

25

1897–1901

Born: 1843
Died: 1901
Born in: Ohio
Elected from: Ohio
Age when elected: 53
Occupations: Teacher, Lawyer
Party: Republican
Vice Presidents: Garret Hobart, Theodore Roosevelt

Theodore Roosevelt

26

1901–1909

Born: 1858
Died: 1919
Born in: New York
Elected as V.P. from: New York
Succeeded McKinley
Age when became President: 42
Occupations: Historian, Rancher
Party: Republican
Vice President: Charles W. Fairbanks

William H. Taft

27

1909–1913

Born: 1857
Died: 1930
Born in: Ohio
Elected from: Ohio
Age when elected: 51
Occupation: Lawyer
Party: Republican
Vice President: James S. Sherman

Woodrow Wilson

28

1913–1921

Born: 1856
Died: 1924
Born in: Virginia
Elected from: New Jersey
Age when elected: 55
Occupation: College Professor
Party: Democratic
Vice President: Thomas R.
  Marshall

Warren G. Harding

29

1921–1923

Born: 1865
Died: 1923
Born in: Ohio
Elected from: Ohio
Age when elected: 55
Occupations: Newspaper Editor,
  Publisher
Party: Republican
Vice President: Calvin Coolidge

Calvin Coolidge

30

1923–1929

Born: 1872
Died: 1933
Born in: Vermont
Elected as V.P. from: Massachusetts
Succeeded Harding
Age when became President: 51
Occupation: Lawyer
Party: Republican
Vice President: Charles G. Dawes

Herbert C. Hoover

31

1929–1933

Born: 1874
Died: 1964
Born in: Iowa
Elected from: California
Age when elected: 54
Occupation: Engineer
Party: Republican
Vice President: Charles Curtis

Franklin D. Roosevelt

32

1933–1945

Born: 1882
Died: 1945
Born in: New York
Elected from: New York
Age when elected: 50
Occupation: Lawyer
Party: Democratic
Vice Presidents: John N. Garner,
  Henry A. Wallace, Harry S Truman

Presidents

Harry S Truman

33

1945–1953

Born: 1884
Died: 1972
Born in: Missouri
Elected as V.P. from: Missouri
Succeeded Roosevelt
Age when became President: 60
Occupations: Clerk, Farmer
Party: Democratic
Vice President: Alben W. Barkley

Dwight D. Eisenhower

34

1953–1961

Born: 1890
Died: 1969
Born in: Texas
Elected from: New York
Age when elected: 62
Occupation: Soldier
Party: Republican
Vice President: Richard M. Nixon

John F. Kennedy

35

1961–1963

Born: 1917
Died: 1963
Born in: Massachusetts
Elected from: Massachusetts
Age when elected: 43
Occupations: Author, Reporter
Party: Democratic
Vice President: Lyndon B. Johnson

Lyndon B. Johnson

36

1963–1969

Born: 1908
Died: 1973
Born in: Texas
Elected as V.P. from: Texas
Succeeded Kennedy
Age when became President: 55
Occupation: Teacher
Party: Democratic
Vice President: Hubert H. Humphrey

Richard M. Nixon

37

1969–1974

Born: 1913
Died: 1994
Born in: California
Elected from: New York
Age when elected: 55
Occupation: Lawyer
Party: Republican
Vice Presidents: Spiro T. Agnew,
Gerald R. Ford

Gerald R. Ford

38

1974–1977

Born: 1913
Born in: Nebraska
Appointed by Nixon as V.P. upon Agnew's resignation; assumed presidency upon Nixon's resignation
Age when became President: 61
Occupation: Lawyer
Party: Republican
Vice President: Nelson A. Rockefeller

James E. Carter, Jr.

39

1977–1981

Born: 1924
Born in: Georgia
Elected from: Georgia
Age when elected: 52
Occupations: Business, Farmer
Party: Democratic
Vice President: Walter F. Mondale

Ronald W. Reagan

40

1981–1989

Born: 1911
Born in: Illinois
Elected from: California
Age when elected: 69
Occupations: Actor, Lecturer
Party: Republican
Vice President: George H.W. Bush

George H.W. Bush

41

1989–1993

Born: 1924
Born in: Massachusetts
Elected from: Texas
Age when elected: 64
Occupation: Business
Party: Republican
Vice President: J. Danforth Quayle

William J. Clinton

42

1993–

Born: 1946
Born in: Arkansas
Elected from: Arkansas
Age when elected: 46
Occupation: Lawyer
Party: Democratic
Vice President: Albert Gore, Jr.

The American Flag

For Americans, the flag has always had a special meaning. It is a symbol of our nation's freedom and democracy.

The Flag of 1795

The flag of the United States symbolizes the nation's unity and independence. In addition, the flag stands for the hopes and ideas of the American people. Throughout its history, the American flag has undergone numerous changes. The flag of 1795 had 15 stripes, as well as 15 stars, to represent the 15 states.

Rules and Customs

Over the years, Americans have developed rules and customs concerning the use and display of the flag. One of the most important things every American should remember is to treat the flag with respect:

★ The flag should be raised and lowered by hand and displayed only from sunrise to sunset. On special occasions, it may be displayed at night.

★ The flag may be displayed on all days, weather permitting, particularly on national and state holidays and on historic and special occasions.

★ No flag should be flown above the American flag or to the right of it at the same height.

★ The flag may be flown at half-mast to mourn the death of public officials.

★ The flag should never touch the ground or floor beneath it.

★ The flag may be flown upside down only to signal distress.

★ When the flag becomes old and tattered, it should be destroyed by burning. According to an approved custom, the Union is first cut from the flag; and then the two pieces, which no longer form a flag, are burned.

The American Flag

Did You Know?

★ The first official American flag, the Continental or Grand Union flag, was displayed on January 1, 1776.

★ The American flag is said to have been nicknamed "Old Glory" by William Driver, a Massachusetts sea captain.

★ The Stars and Stripes first flew around the world on the ship *Columbia of Boston* on its voyage from September 1787 to August 1790.

★ The flag was unfurled at the North Pole for the first time on April 6, 1909, by naval officer and Arctic explorer Robert Peary.

★ The flag was planted on the moon on July 20, 1969, after astronauts Neil Armstrong and Edwin Aldrin, Jr., piloted the lunar module *Eagle* to a landing on the moon's surface.

The Magna Carta

The Magna Carta, signed by King John in 1215, marked a decisive step forward in the development of constitutional government in England. Later, it became a model for colonists who carried the Magna Carta's guarantees of legal and political rights to America.

1. That the English church shall be free, and shall have her rights entire, and her liberties inviolate; . . .

2. We also have granted to all the freemen of our kingdom, for us and for our heirs forever, all the underwritten liberties, to be had and holden by them and their heirs, of us and our heirs forever. . . .

39. No freeman shall be taken or imprisoned, or diseased, or outlawed, or banished, or in any way destroyed, nor will we pass upon him, nor will we send upon him, unless by the lawful judgment of his peers, or by the law of the land.

40. We will sell to no man, we will not deny to any man, either justice or right.

41. All merchants shall have safe and secure conduct to go out of, and to come into, England, and to stay there and to pass as well by land as by water, for buying and selling by the ancient and allowed customs, without any unjust tolls, except in time of war, or when they are of any nation at war with us. . . .

42. It shall be lawful, for the time to come, for any one to go out of our kingdom and return safely and securely by land or by water, saving his allegiance to us (unless in time of war, by some short space, for the common benefit of the realm).

60. All the aforesaid customs and liberties, which we have granted to be holden in our kingdom, as much as it belongs to us, all people of our kingdom, as well clergy as laity, shall observe, as far as they are concerned, towards their dependents.

63. . . . It is also sworn, as well on our part as on the part of the barons, that all the things aforesaid shall be observed in good faith, and without evil duplicity. Given under our hand, in the presence of the witnesses above named, and many others, in the meadow called Runnymede, between Windsor and Staines, the 15th day of June, in the 17th year of our reign.

The Mayflower Compact

On November 21, 1620, 41 colonists aboard the Mayflower drafted this agreement. The Mayflower Compact was the first plan of self-government ever put in force in the English colonies.

In ye name of God Amen. We whose names are underwritten, the loyall subjects of our dread soveraigne Lord King James, by ye grace of God, of Great Britaine, Franc, & Ireland king, defender of ye faith, &c. Haveing undertaken, for ye glorie of God, and advancemente of ye Christian faith and honour of our king & countrie, a voyage to plant ye first colonie in ye Northerne parts of Virginia, doe by these presents solemnly & mutualy in ye presence of God, and one of another, covenant, & combine ourselves togeather into a Civill body politick; for our better ordering, & preservation & furtherance of ye ends aforesaid; and by vertue hereof to enacte, constitute, and frame such just & equall Lawes, ordinances, Acts, constitutions, & offices, from time to time, as shall be thought most meete & convenient for ye generall good of ye colonie: unto which we promise all due submission and obedience. In witnes whereof we have hereunder subscribed our names at Cap-Codd ye -11- of November, in ye year of ye raigne of our soveraigne Lord King James of England, France, & Ireland ye eighteenth, and of Scotland ye fiftie fourth. Ano Dom. 1620.

The Star-Spangled Banner

During the British bombardment of Fort McHenry during the War of 1812, a young Baltimore lawyer named Francis Scott Key was inspired to write the words to "The Star-Spangled Banner." Although it became popular immediately, it was not until 1931 that Congress officially declared "The Star-Spangled Banner" as our national anthem.

O! say can you see, by the dawn's early light,
What so proudly we hail'd at the twilight's last gleaming,
Whose broad stripes and bright stars through the perilous fight,
O'er the ramparts we watched, were so gallantly streaming?
And the Rockets' red glare, the Bombs bursting in air,
Gave proof through the night that our Flag was still there;
O! say, does that star-spangled banner yet wave
O'er the Land of the free and the home of the brave!

On the shore, dimly seen through the mists of the deep,
Where the foe's haughty host in dread silence reposes,
What is that, which the breeze o'er the towering steep,
As it fitfully blows, half conceals, half discloses?
Now it catches the gleam of the morning's first beam,
In full glory reflected, now shines on the stream.
'Tis the star-spangled banner; O! long may it wave
O'er the land of the free and the home of the brave.

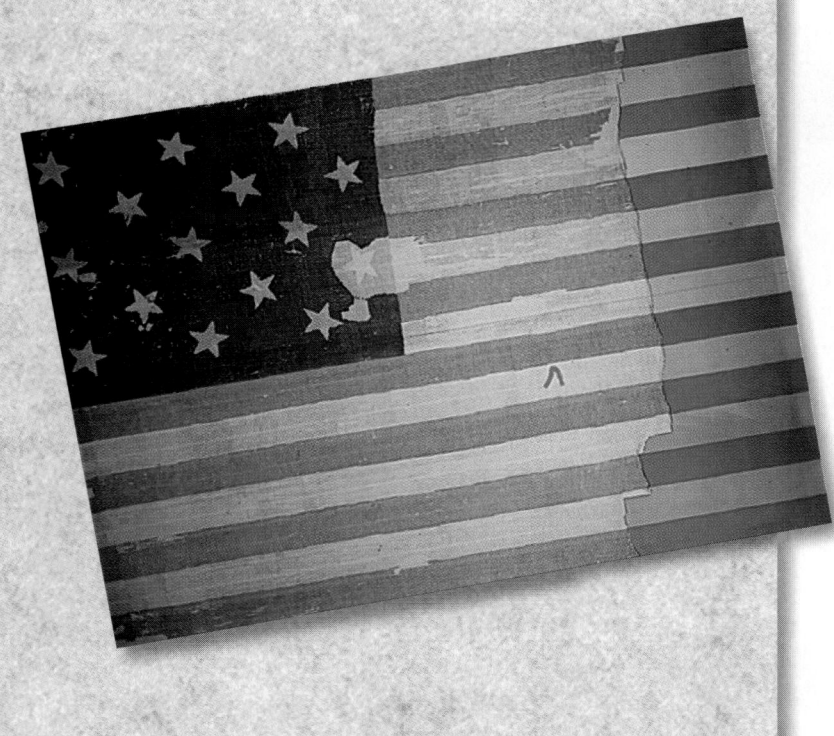

The Monroe Doctrine

In an 1823 address to Congress, President James Monroe proclaimed what has become known as the Monroe Doctrine. The doctrine was designed to end European influence in the Western Hemisphere. In addition, it showed the world the American spirit of strength and unity, and became a cornerstone of United States foreign policy.

. . . With the existing colonies or dependencies of any European power we have not interfered and shall not interfere. But with the governments who have declared their independence and maintained it, and whose independence we have, on great consideration and on just principles, acknowledged, we could not view any interposition for the purpose of oppressing them, or controlling in any other manner their destiny, by any European power in any other light than as the manifestation of any unfriendly disposition toward the United States. . . .

Our policy in regard to Europe, which was adopted at an early stage of the wars which have so long agitated that quarter of the globe, nevertheless remains the same, which is not to interfere in the internal concerns of any of its powers; to consider the government de facto as the legitimate government for us; to cultivate friendly relations with it, and to preserve those relations by a frank, firm, and manly policy, meeting in all instances the just claims of every power, submitting to injuries from none. . . .

Memorial and Protest of the Cherokee Nation

While Native Americans were being forced from their homeland, Cherokee leaders put their protest before the United States Senate. Their call for justice went unheard.

It cannot be concealed that the situation of the Cherokees is peculiarly distressing. In adverting to that situation it is not done to arouse, at this late day, a useless sympathy, but only as matter of history, and from necessity in giving a fair and impartial illustration of their difficulties. It is well known to those who have paid any attention to their history for the last five years, that they have been contending for the faithful execution of treaties between their nation and the United States, and that their distresses have not been mitigated; their efforts seem to have increased their difficulties. It remains for them to seek an adjustment by treaty, and an equitable acknowledgement of their rights and claims, so far as circumstances will permit.

For this purpose, this delegation has been deputed, as the proper organ of the Cherokee people, to settle, by treaty, their difficulties; and they wish, in sincerity, to have them settled, for the good, peace, and harmony of the whole nation.

The Seneca Falls Declaration

One of the first documents to express the desire for equal rights for women is the Declaration of Sentiments and Resolutions, issued in 1848 at the Seneca Falls Convention in New York. Led by Lucretia Mott and Elizabeth Cady Stanton, the delegates adopted a set of resolutions that called for woman suffrage and opportunities in employment and education. Excerpts from the Declaration follow.

When, in the course of human events, it becomes necessary for one portion of the family of man to assume among the people of the earth a position different from that which they have hitherto occupied, but one to which the laws of nature and of nature's God entitle them, a decent respect to the opinions of mankind requires that they should declare the causes that impel them to such a course.

We hold these truths to be self-evident: that all men and women are created equal; that they are endowed by their Creator with certain inalienable rights; that among these are life, liberty, and the pursuit of happiness; that to secure these rights governments are instituted, deriving their just powers from the consent of the governed. Whenever any form of government becomes destructive of these ends, it is the right of those who suffer from it to refuse allegiance to it, and to insist upon the institution of a new government, laying its foundation on such principles, and organizing its powers in such form, as to them shall seem most likely to effect their safety and happiness. Prudence, indeed, will dictate that governments long established should not be changed for light and transient causes; . . . But when a long train of abuses and usurpations, pursuing invariably the same object, evinces a design to reduce them under absolute despotism, it is their duty to throw off such government and to provide new guards for their future security. . . .

The history of mankind is a history of repeated injuries and usurpations on the part of man toward woman, having in direct object the establishment of an absolute tyranny over her. To prove this, let facts be submitted to a candid world. . . .

Now, in view of the entire disfranchisement of one-half the people of this country, their social and religious degradation, in view of the unjust laws above mentioned, and because women do feel themselves aggrieved, oppressed, and fraudulently deprived of their most sacred rights, we insist that they have immediate admission to all the rights and privileges which belong to them as citizens of the United States. . . .

The Emancipation Proclamation

On January 1, 1863, President Abraham Lincoln issued the Emancipation Proclamation, which freed all slaves in states under Confederate control. The Proclamation was a significant step toward the Thirteenth Amendment (1865) that ended slavery in all of the United States.

Whereas on the 22d day of September, A.D. 1862, a proclamation was issued by the President of the United States, containing among other things, the following, to wit: That on the 1st day of January, in the year of our Lord 1863, all persons held as slaves within any state or designated part of a state, the people whereof shall then be in rebellion against the United States, shall be then, thenceforward, and forever free; and the executive government of the United States, including the military and naval authority thereof, will recognize and maintain the freedom of such persons and will do no act or acts to repress such persons, or any of them, in any efforts they may make for their actual freedom.

That the executive will, on the 1st day of January aforesaid, by proclamation, designate the states and parts of states, if any, in which the people thereof, respectively, shall then be in rebellion against the United States; and the fact that any state or the people thereof shall on that day be in good faith represented in the Congress of the United States by members chosen thereto at elections wherein a majority of the qualified voters of such states shall have participated shall, in the absence of strong counter-vailing testimony, be deemed conclusive evidence that such state and the people thereof are not then in rebellion against the United States. . . .

And, by virtue of the power and for the purpose aforesaid, I do order and declare that all persons held as slaves within said designated states and parts of states are, and henceforward shall be, free; and that the executive government of the United States, including the military and naval authorities thereof, will recognize and maintain the freedom of said persons.

And I hereby enjoin upon the people so declared to be free to abstain from all violence, unless in necessary self-defense; and I recommend to them that, in all cases when allowed, they labor faithfully for reasonable wages.

And I further declare and make known that such persons of suitable condition will be received into the armed service of the United States to garrison forts, positions, stations, and other places, and to man vessels of all sorts in said service. . . .

Documents

The Gettysburg Address

On November 19, 1863, President Abraham Lincoln gave a short speech at the dedication of a national cemetery on the battlefield of Gettysburg. His simple yet eloquent words expressed his hopes for a nation divided by civil war.

Four score and seven years ago our fathers brought forth on this continent a new nation, conceived in liberty, and dedicated to the proposition that all men are created equal.

Now we are engaged in a great civil war, testing whether that nation or any nation so conceived and so dedicated can long endure. We are met on a great battlefield of that war. We have come to dedicate a portion of that field as a final resting place for those who here gave their lives that that nation might live. It is altogether fitting and proper that we should do this.

But, in a larger sense, we can not dedicate—we can not consecrate—we can not hallow—this ground. The brave men, living and dead, who struggled here have consecrated it far beyond our poor power to add or detract. The world will little note nor long remember what we say here, but it can never forget what they did here. It is for us, the living, rather, to be dedicated here to the unfinished work which they who fought here have thus far so nobly advanced.

It is rather for us to be here dedicated to the great task remaining before us—that from these honored dead we take increased devotion to that cause for which they gave the last full measure of devotion; that we here highly resolve that these dead shall not have died in vain; that this nation, under God, shall have a new birth of freedom; and that government of the people, by the people, and for the people, shall not perish from the earth.

I Will Fight No More

In 1877 the Nez Perce Indians fought the government's attempt to move them to a smaller reservation. After a remarkable attempt to escape to Canada, Chief Joseph realized that resistance was hopeless and advised his people to surrender.

Tell General Howard I know his heart. What he told me before I have in my heart. I am tired of fighting. Our chiefs are killed. Looking Glass is dead. It is the young men who say yes or no. He who led the young men is dead. It is cold and we have no blankets. The little children are freezing to death. My people, some of them have run away to the hills and have no blankets, no food; no one knows where they are—perhaps freezing to death. I want to have time to look for my children and see how many I can find. Maybe I shall find them among the dead. Hear me my chiefs. I am tired; my heart is sick and sad. From where the sun now stands, I will fight no more forever.

The Pledge of Allegiance

In 1892 the nation celebrated the 400th anniversary of Columbus's landing in America. In connection with this celebration, Francis Bellamy, a magazine editor, wrote and published the Pledge of Allegiance. The words "under God" were added by Congress in 1954 at the urging of President Dwight D. Eisenhower.

I pledge allegiance to the Flag of the United States of America and to the Republic for which it stands, one Nation under God, indivisible, with liberty and justice for all.

The Fourteen Points

On January 8, 1918, President Woodrow Wilson went before Congress to offer a statement of aims called the Fourteen Points. Wilson's plan called for freedom of the seas in peace and war, an end to secret alliances, and equal trading rights for all countries. The excerpt that follows is taken from the President's message.

. . . We entered this war because violations of right had occurred which touched us to the quick and made the life of our own people impossible unless they were corrected and the world secured once for all against their recurrence. What we demand in this war, therefore, is nothing peculiar to ourselves. It is that the world be made fit and safe to live in; and particularly that it be made safe for every peace-loving nation which, like our own, wishes to live its own life, determine its own institutions, be assured of justice and fair dealings by the other peoples of the world, as against force and selfish aggression. All the peoples of the world are in effect partners in this interest, and for our own part we see very clearly that unless justice be done to others it will not be done to us.

The program of the world's peace, therefore, is our program, and that program, the only possible program, as we see it, is this:

I. Open covenants of peace, openly arrived at, after which there shall be no private international understandings of any kind, but diplomacy shall proceed always frankly and in the public view.

II. Absolute freedom of navigation upon the seas, outside territorial waters, alike in peace and in war, except as the seas may be closed in whole or in part by international action for the enforcement of international covenants.

III. The removal, so far as possible, of all economic barriers and the establishment of an equality of trade conditions among all the nations consenting to the peace and associating themselves for its maintenance.

IV. Adequate guarantees given and taken that national armaments will be reduced to the lowest point consistent with domestic safety.

V. Free, open-minded, and absolutely impartial adjustment of all colonial claims, based upon a strict observance of the principle that in determining all such questions of sovereignty the interests of the population concerned must have equal weight with the equitable claims of the Government whose title is to be determined. . . .

XIV. A general association of nations must be formed under specific covenants for the purpose of affording mutual guarantees of political independence and territorial integrity to great and small states alike. . . .

Brown v. Board of Education

On May 17, 1954, the Supreme Court ruled in Brown *v.* Board of Education *that racial segregation in public schools was unconstitutional. This decision provided the legal basis for court challenges to segregation in every aspect of American life.*

The plaintiffs contend that segregated public schools are not "equal" and cannot be made "equal," and that hence they are deprived of the equal protection of the laws. Because of the obvious importance of the question presented, the Court took jurisdiction. . . .

Our decision . . . cannot turn on merely a comparison of these tangible factors in the Negro and white schools involved in each of the cases. We must look instead to the effect of segregation itself on public education.

In approaching this problem, we cannot turn the clock back to 1868 when the Amendment was adopted, or even to 1896 when *Plessy v. Ferguson* was written. We must consider public education in the light of its full development and its present place in American life throughout the nation. Only in this way can it be determined if segregation in public schools deprives these plaintiffs of the equal protection of the laws.

Today, education is perhaps the most important function of state and local governments. Compulsory school attendance laws and the great expenditures for education both demonstrate our recognition of the importance of education to our democratic society. . . . In these days, it is doubtful that any child may reasonably be expected to succeed in life if he is denied the opportunity of an education. Such an opportunity, where the state has undertaken to provide it, is a right which must be made available to all on equal terms.

We come then to the question presented: Does segregation of children in public schools solely on the basis of race, even though the physical facilities and other "tangible" factors may be equal, deprive the children of the minority group of equal educational opportunities? We believe that it does.

. . . .We conclude that in the field of public education the doctrine of "separate but equal" has no place. Separate educational facilities are inherently unequal. Therefore, we hold that the plaintiffs and others similarly situated for whom the actions have been brought are, by reason of the segregation complained of, deprived of the equal protection of the laws guaranteed by the Fourteenth Amendment. . . .

I Have a Dream

On August 28, 1963, while Congress debated wide-ranging civil rights legislation, Martin Luther King, Jr., led more than 200,000 people on a march on Washington, D.C. On the steps of the Lincoln Memorial he gave a stirring speech in which he eloquently spoke of his dreams for African Americans and for the United States. Excerpts of the speech follow.

. . . There are those who are asking the devotees of civil rights, "When will you be satisfied?"

We can never be satisfied as long as the Negro is the victim of the unspeakable horrors of police brutality. . . .We cannot be satisfied as long as the Negro's basic mobility is from a smaller ghetto to a larger one. We can never be satisfied as long as a Negro in Mississippi cannot vote and a Negro in New York believes he has nothing for which to vote. . . .

I say to you today, my friends, that in spite of the difficulties and frustrations of the moment I still have a dream. It is a dream deeply rooted in the American dream.

I have a dream that one day this nation will rise up and live out the true meaning of its creed, "We hold these truths to be self-evident, that all men are created equal."

I have a dream that one day on the red hills of Georgia the sons of former slaves and the sons of former slaveowners will be able to sit down together at the table of brotherhood.

I have a dream that one day even the state of Mississippi, a desert state sweltering with the heat of injustice and oppression, will be transformed into an oasis of freedom and justice.

I have a dream that my four little children will one day live in a nation where they will not be judged by the color of their skin, but by the content of their character. . . .

. . . When we let freedom ring, when we let it ring from every village and every hamlet, from every state and every city, we will be able to speed up that day when all of God's children, black men and white men, Jews and Gentiles, Protestants and Catholics, will be able to join hands and sing in the words of the old Negro spiritual: "Free at last! Free at last! Thank God Almighty, we are free at last!"

Documents

Gazetteer

★ ★

The gazetteer is a geographical dictionary that lists political divisions, natural features, and other places and locations. Following each entry is a description, its latitude and longitude, and a page reference that indicates where each entry may be found in this text.

A

Afghanistan country in south central Asia (33°N/63°E) 767

Africa continent of the Eastern Hemisphere south of the Mediterranean Sea and adjoining Asia on its northeastern border (10°N/22°E) 16

Alabama state in the southeastern United States; 22nd state to enter the Union (32°45'N/87°30'W) 144

Alaska state located in northwestern North America; territory purchased from Russia in 1867 (64°N/150°W) 382

Albany capital of New York; site where Albany Congress proposed first formal plan to unite the 13 colonies (40°45'N/73°45'W) 183

Allegheny River river in western Pennsylvania uniting with the Monongahela River at Pittsburgh to form the Ohio River (40°N/82°W) 44

Andes Mountains mountain system extending along western coast of South America (13°S/75°W) 10

Antarctica continent located around the South Pole (80°15'S/127°E) 16

Antietam Civil War battle site in western Maryland (39°45'N/77°30'W) 193

Appalachian Mountains chief mountain system in eastern North America extending from Quebec and New Brunswick to central Alabama (37°N/82°W) 24

Appomattox Court House site in central Virginia where Confederate forces surrendered ending the Civil War (37°N/77°W) 209

Arctic Ocean ocean in the northernmost part of the world (85°N/170°E) 10

Arizona state in the southwestern United States; 48th state to enter the Union (34°N/113°W) 177

Arkansas state in the south central United States; acquired as part of Louisiana Purchase (34°45'N/93°45'W) 144

Asia continent of the Eastern Hemisphere forming a single landmass with Europe (50°N/100°E) 16

Atlanta capital of Georgia located in the northwest central part of the state (33°45'N/84°30'W) 183

Atlantic Ocean ocean separating North and South America from Europe and Africa (5°S/25°W) 10

B

Baltimore city on the Chesapeake Bay in central Maryland (39°15'N/76°45'W) 24

Barbary Coast north coast of Africa between Morocco and Tunisia (36°45'N/3°E) 129

Baton Rouge capital of Louisiana located on the Mississippi River in the southeastern part of the state (30°30'N/91°15'W) 55

Bay of Pigs site of 1961 invasion of Cuba by U.S.-trained Cuban exiles (22°N/79°W) 696

Beijing capital of China located in the northeastern part of the country (40°N/116°30'E) 391

Berlin city in east central Germany; former national capital divided into sectors after World War II; city reunited in 1989 (52°31'N/13°30'E) 591

Black Hills mountains in southwestern South Dakota; site of conflict between the Sioux and white settlers during 1870s (44°15'N/103°45'W) 250

Boston capital of Massachusetts located in the eastern part of the state; founded by English Puritans in 1630 (42°15'N/71°W) 24

C

California state in the western United States; attracted thousands of miners during gold rush of 1849 (38°15'N/121°15'W) 10

Cambodia country in Southeast Asia bordering Gulf of Siam; official name Democratic Kampuchea (12°N/105°E) 705

Canada country in northern North America (50°N/100°W) 156

Charleston city in South Carolina on the Atlantic coast; original name Charles Town (32°45'N/80°W) 54

Château-Thierry World War I battle site in France (49°N/3°15'E) 465

Chautauqua Lake lake in western New York State (42°15'N/79°45'W) 331

Chesapeake Bay inlet of the Atlantic Ocean in Virginia and Maryland (37°N/76°W) 51

Chicago largest city in Illinois; located in northeastern part of the state along Lake Michigan (41°45'N/87°30'W) 183

China country in eastern Asia; mainland (People's Republic of China) under communist control since 1949 (36°45'N/93°E) 12

Chisholm Trail pioneer cattle trail from Texas to Kansas (34°N/98°W) 250

Cincinnati city in southern Ohio on the Ohio River; grew as result of increasing steamship traffic during the mid-1800s (39°15'N/84°30'W) 65

Colorado state in the western United States (39°30'N/107°W) 177

Columbia River river flowing through southwest Canada and northwestern United States into the Pacific Ocean (46°15'N/124°W) 120

Concord village northwest of Boston, Massachusetts; site of early battle of the American Revolution on April 19, 1775 (42°N/71°W) 73

Connecticut state in the northeastern United States; one of the original 13 states (41°45'N/73°15'W) 24

Cuba country in the West Indies, North America (22°N/79°W) 377

Czechoslovakia former country in central Europe; now two countries, the Czech Republic and Slovakia (49°30'N/16°E) 474

D

Delaware state in the northeastern United States; one of the original 13 states (38°45'N/75°30'W) 24

Detroit city in southeastern Michigan; site of significant battles during the French and Indian War and the War of 1812; center of automobile industry (42°15'N/82°15'W) 65

dust bowl area of the Great Plains where the drought of the 1930s turned the soil to wind-borne dust (37°N/98°W) 555

E

England division of the United Kingdom of Great Britain and Northern Ireland (56°30'N/1°45'W) 16

Erie Canal waterway connecting the Hudson River with Lake Erie through New York State (43°N/76°W) 144

Erie, Lake one of the Great Lakes between Canada and the United States (42°15'N/81°30'W) 19

Europe continent of the northern part of the Eastern Hemisphere between Asia and the Atlantic Ocean (50°N/15°E) 16

F

Florida state in the southeastern United States (30°30'N/84°45'W) 19

Fort Duquesne French fort on the site of Pittsburgh, Pennsylvania (40°30'N/80°W) 44

Fort Sumter Union fort during the Civil War located on island near Charleston, South Carolina; site of first military engagement of Civil War (32°45'N/80°W) 190

France country in western Europe (49°45'N/0°45'E) 16

Fredericksburg city and Civil War battle site in northeast Virginia (38°15'N/77°30'W) 194

Freeport city in northern Illinois; site of 1858 Lincoln-Douglas debate (42°15'N/89°30'W) 186

G

Galveston city on the Gulf of Mexico coast in Texas; created nation's first commission form of city government (29°15'N/95°W) 404

Georgia state in the southeastern United States (32°45'N/83°45'W) 24

Germany country in central Europe; divided after World War II into East Germany and West Germany; unified in 1989 (50°N/10°E) 461

Gettysburg city and Civil War battle site in south central Pennsylvania; site where Lincoln delivered the Gettysburg Address (39°45'N/77°15'W) 194

Great Basin interior drainage area in Nevada (40°15'N/117°15'W) 174

Great Britain commonwealth comprising England, Scotland, and Wales (56°30'N/1°45'W) 42

Great Lakes chain of five lakes, Superior, Erie, Michigan, Ontario, and Huron, in central North America (45°N/87°W) 19

Great Plains flat grassland in the central United States (45°N/104°W) 174

Great Salt Lake lake in northern Utah with no outlet and strongly saline waters (41°15'N/112°45'W) 120

Greece country in southeastern Europe (39°N/21°30'E) 474

Guadalcanal island in the Solomons east of Australia (9°45'S/158°45'E) 654

Guam United States possession in the western Pacific Ocean (14°N/143°15'E) 382

H

Harlem northern section of Manhattan in New York City; cultural center of African Americans in the early and mid-1900s (40°45'N/74°W) 506

Harpers Ferry town in northern West Virginia on the Potomac River (39°15'N/77°45'W) 186

Hartford capital of Connecticut located on the Connecticut River in the central part of the state (41°45'N/72°45'W) 127

Hawaii state in the United States located in the Pacific Ocean (20°N/157°W) 382

Hiroshima city in southern Japan; site of first military use of atomic bomb, August 6, 1945 (34°15'N/132°30'E) 594

Hispaniola island in the West Indies in North America, where Haiti and the Dominican Republic are located (17°30'N/73°15'W) 19

Hong Kong British colony along the southern coast of China in Asia (21°45'N/115°E) 382

Hudson Bay large bay in northern Canada (60°N/86°W) 43

Hudson River river flowing through New York State into the Atlantic Ocean at New York City (52°45'N/74°W) 44

Huron, Lake one of the Great Lakes between the United States and Canada in North America (45°15'N/82°45'W) 19

I

Idaho state in the northwestern United States; ranks among top states in silver production (44°N/115°15'W) 250

Illinois state in the north central United States; one of the states formed in the Northwest Territory (40°30'N/90°45'W) 144

Indian Territory land reserved by the United States government for Native Americans, now the state of Oklahoma (36°N/98°15'W) 156

Indiana state in the north central United States; one of the states formed in the Northwest Territory (39°45'N/86°45'W) 144

Indochina region in Southeast Asia (17°15'N/105°15'E) 651

Iowa state in the north central United States acquired as part of the Louisiana Purchase (42°N/94°15'W) 177

Iran country of the Middle East in southwestern Asia (31°15'N/53°30'E) 474

Iraq country of the Middle East in southwestern Asia (32°N/42°30'E) 655

Israel country of the Middle East in southwestern Asia along the Mediterranean Sea (32°45'N/34°E) 655

Italy country in southern Europe along the Mediterranean Sea (44°N/11°15'E) 461

J

Jamestown first permanent English settlement in North America; located in southeastern Virginia (37°15'N/76°45'W) 23

Japan island country in eastern Asia (36°30'N/133°30'E) 382

K

Kansas state in the central United States; fighting over slavery issue in 1850s gave territory the name "Bleeding Kansas" (38°30'N/98°45'W) 177

Kentucky state in the south central United States; border state that sided with the Union during the Civil War (37°30'N/87°30'W) 126

Kings Mountain Revolutionary War battle site in northern South Carolina (35°15'N/81°15'W) 54

Korea peninsula in eastern Asia between China, Russia, and the Sea of Japan, on which are located the countries of North Korea and South Korea (38°15'N/127°30'E) 594

Kuwait country of the Middle East in southwestern Asia between Iraq and Saudi Arabia (29°N/47°45'E) 474

L

Lexington Revolutionary War battle site in eastern Massachusetts; site of first clash between colonists and British, April 19, 1775 (42°26'N/71°13'W) 73

Little Rock capital of Arkansas located in the center of the state; site of 1957 conflict over public school integration (34°45'N/92°15'W) 183

London capital of United Kingdom located in the southeastern part of England (51°30'N/0°15'W) 585

Los Angeles city along the Pacific coast in southern California; industrial, financial, and trade center of western United States (34°N/118°15'W) 250

Louisiana state in the south central United States (30°45'N/92°45'W) 126

Louisiana Territory region of west central United States between the Mississippi River and the Rocky Mountains purchased from France in 1803 (40°N/95°W) 120

M

Maine state in the northeastern United States; 23rd state to enter the Union (45°30'N/69°45'W) 24

Maryland state in the eastern United States; one of the original 13 states (39°15'N/76°30'W) 24

Massachusetts state in the northeastern United States; one of the original 13 states (42°15'N/72°30'W) 24

Mediterranean Sea sea between Europe and Africa (36°15'N/13°30'E) 39

Mexico country in North America south of the United States (23°45'N/104°W) 174

Mexico, Gulf of gulf south of the United States and east of Mexico in North America (25°15'N/93°45'W) 16

Michigan state in the north central United States; one of the states formed in the Northwest Territory (45°N/85°W) 177

Michigan, Lake one of the five Great Lakes located in the north central United States (43°15'N/87°15'W) 19

Midway Islands United States possession in the central Pacific Ocean; site of Battle of Midway, June 1942 (28°N/177°W) 382

Milwaukee city in eastern Wisconsin along Lake Michigan (43°N/88°W) 300

Minnesota state in the north central United States; fur trade, good soil, and lumber attracted early settlers (46°15'N/96°15'W) 177

Mississippi state in the southeastern United States; became English territory after French and Indian War (32°30'N/89°45'W) 144

Mississippi River river flowing through the United States from Minnesota to the Gulf of Mexico; explored by French in 1600s (29°N/89°W) 19

Missouri state in the south central United States; petition for statehood resulted in sectional conflict and the Missouri Compromise (40°45'N/93°W) 144

Missouri River river flowing through the United States from the Rocky Mountains to the Mississippi River near St. Louis (38°45'N/90°15'W) 19

Montana state in the northwestern United States; cattle industry grew during 1850s (47°15'N/111°45'W) 177

Montgomery capital of Alabama located in the central part of the state; site of 1955 bus boycott to protest segregation (32°30'N/86°15'W) 183

Montreal city on the St. Lawrence River in southern Quebec, Canada (45°30'N/73°30'W) 19

Moscow capital of former Soviet Union and capital of Russia (55°45'N/37°30'E) 590

N

Nashville capital of Tennessee located in the north central part of the state (36°15'N/86°45'W) 183

Natchez city in western Mississippi along the Mississippi River (31°30'N/91°15'W) 144

National Road road from Baltimore, Maryland, to Vandalia, Illinois (40°N/81°30'W) 142

Nebraska state in the central United States (41°45'N/101°30'W) 177

Netherlands country in northwestern Europe (53°N/4°E) 16

Nevada state in the western United States (39°30'N/117°W) 177

New Amsterdam town founded on Manhattan Island by Dutch settlers in 1625; renamed New York by British settlers (40°45'N/74°W) 21

New Hampshire state in the northeastern United States; one of the original 13 states (44°N/71°45'W) 24

New Jersey state in the northeastern United States; one of the original 13 states (40°30'N/74°45'W) 24

New Mexico state in the southwestern United States; ceded to the United States by Mexico in 1848 (34°30'N/107°15'W) 177

New Orleans city in southern Louisiana in the Mississippi Delta (30°N/90°W) 120

New York state in the northeastern United States; one of the original 13 states (42°45'N/78°W) 24

New York City city in southeastern New York State at the mouth of the Hudson River; largest city in the United States (40°45'N/74°W) 24

Nicaragua country in Central America (12°45'N/86°15'W) 388

Normandy region along French coast and site of D-Day invasion, June 6, 1944 (48°N/2°W) 592

North America continent in the northern part of the Western Hemisphere between the Atlantic and Pacific oceans (45°N/100°W) 16

North Carolina state in the southeastern United States; one of the original 13 states (35°45'N/81°30'W) 24

North Dakota state in the north central United States; Congress created Dakota Territory in 1861 (47°15'N/102°W) 177

Northwest Territory territorial division north of the Ohio River and east of the Mississippi River (47°30'N/87°30'W) 65

O

Oberlin college and town in northern Ohio (41°15'N/82°15'W) 330

Ohio state in the north central United States; first state in the Northwest Territory (40°30'N/83°15'W) 126

Ohio River river flowing from Allegheny and Monongahela rivers in western Pennsylvania into the Mississippi River (39°N/85°W) 19

Ohio Valley valley of the Ohio River, which flows from Pennsylvania to the Mississippi River at Cairo, Illinois (37°30'N/88°W) 65

Oklahoma state in the south central United States; Five Civilized Tribes moved to territory 1830–1842 (36°N/98°15'W) 177

Ontario, Lake one of the five Great Lakes between Canada and the United States (43°30'N/79°W) 19

Oregon state in the northwestern United States; adopted woman suffrage in 1912 (43°45'N/123°45'W) 177

Oregon Trail pioneer trail from Independence, Missouri, to the Oregon Territory (42°30'N/110°W) 170

P

Pacific Ocean world's largest ocean located between Asia and the Americas (0°/175°W) 10

Panama country in the southern part of Central America, occupying the Isthmus of Panama (8°N/81°W) 393

Panama Canal canal built across the Isthmus of Panama through Panama to connect the Caribbean Sea and the Pacific Ocean (9°15'N/79°45'W) 393

Pearl Harbor naval base at Honolulu, Hawaii; site of 1941 Japanese attack, leading to United States entry into World War II (21°21'N/157°57'W) 594

Pennsylvania state in the northeastern United States (41°N/78°15'W) 24

Persian Gulf gulf in southwestern Asia between Iran and the Arabian Peninsula (27°45'N/50°30'E) 767

Philadelphia city in eastern Pennsylvania on the Delaware River; Declaration of Independence and the Constitution both adopted in city's Independence Hall (40°N/75°W) 24

Philippines island country in southeast Asia (14°30'N/125°E) 377

Pittsburgh city in western Pennsylvania; one of the great steelmaking centers of the world (40°30'N/80°W) 144

Plymouth town in eastern Massachusetts; first successful English colony in New England (42°N/70°45'W) 25

Promontory Point site in Utah where the first transcontinental railroad was completed (41°45'N/112°15'W) 270

Providence capital of Rhode Island; site of first English settlement in Rhode Island (41°45'N/71°30'W) 183

Puerto Rico United States possession in the West Indies (18°15'N/66°45'W) 19

Pullman company town south of Chicago; site of 1894 railroad strike (41°45'N/87°30'W) 291

Q

Quebec city in Canada, capital of Quebec Province, on the St. Lawrence River; first settlement in New France (46°45'N/71°15'W) 19

R

Raleigh capital of North Carolina located in the north central part of the state (35°45'N/78°45'W) 209

Rhode Island state in the northeastern United States; one of the original 13 states (41°30'N/71°45'W) 24

Richmond capital of Virginia located in the central part of the state; capital of the Confederacy during the Civil War (37°30'N/77°30'W) 209

Rio Grande river between the United States and Mexico in North America; forms the boundary between Texas and Mexico (26°N/97°30'W) 19

Roanoke island off the coast of present-day North Carolina that was site of early British colonizing efforts (35°N/75°39'W) 23

Rocky Mountains mountain range in western United States and Canada in North America (50°N/114°W) 120

Russia name of republic; former empire of eastern Europe and northern Asia coinciding with Soviet Union (60°30'N/64°E) 146

S

Sacramento capital of California located in the north central part of the state (38°30'N/121°30'W) 250

St. Augustine city in northeastern Florida on the Atlantic coast; oldest permanent existing European settlement in North America, founded in 1565 (30°N/81°15'W) 19

St. Lawrence River river flowing from Lake Ontario, between Canada and the United States, through Canada to the Atlantic Ocean (48°N/65°15'W) 19

St. Louis city in eastern Missouri on the Mississippi River (38°45'N/90°15'W) 65

St. Mihiel World War I battle site in France (49°N/5°30'E) 465

Salt Lake City capital of Utah; founded by Mormons in 1847 (40°45'N/111°45'W) 250

San Antonio city in south central Texas (29°30'N/98°30'W) 172

San Francisco city in northern California on the Pacific coast (37°45'N/122°30'W) 250

Santa Fe capital of New Mexico located in the north central part of the state (35°45'N/106°W) 250

Saratoga Revolutionary War battle site in the Hudson Valley of eastern New York State (43°N/73°51'W) 51

Savannah city in eastern Georgia (32°N/81°W) 24

Sea Islands group of islands off the coast of Georgia and South Carolina (31°15'N/81°W) 216

Seneca Falls town in New York State; site of woman's rights convention in 1848 (43°N/77°W) 161

Sierra Nevada mountain range in eastern California (39°N/120°W) 250

South Africa country in southern Africa (28°S/24°45'E) 465

South America continent in the southern part of the Western Hemisphere lying between the Atlantic and Pacific oceans (15°S/60°W) 16

South Carolina state in the southeastern United States; one of the original 13 states (34°15'N/81°15'W) 24

South Dakota state in the north central United States; acquired through the Louisiana Purchase (44°15'N/102°W) 177

Soviet Union former country in northern Europe and Asia (60°30'N/64°E) 579

Spain country in southwestern Europe (40°15'N/4°30'W) 16

Stalingrad city in the former Soviet Union on the Volga River; present name Volgograd (48°45'N/42°15'E) 591

Suez Canal canal built between the Mediterranean Sea and the Red Sea through northeastern Egypt (31°N/32°15'E) 665

Superior, Lake one of the five Great Lakes between Canada and the United States in North America (47°45'N/89°15'W) 19

T

Tampa city in west central Florida (28°N/82°30'W) 270

Tennessee state in the south central United States; first state readmitted to the Union after the Civil War (35°45'N/88°W) 126

Tennessee Valley valley of the Tennessee River, which flows from the Appalachian Mountains to the Ohio River (35°30'N/88°15'W) 553

Tenochtitlán Aztec capital on the site of present-day Mexico City (19°30'N/99°15'W) 10

Texas state in the south central United States; Mexican colony that became an independent republic before joining the United States (31°N/101°W) 177

Tokyo capital of Japan located on the eastern coast of Honshu Island (35°45'N/139°45'E) 594

Toronto city in Canada on Lake Ontario; capital of the province of Ontario (43°45'N/79°30'W) 183

Trenton capital of New Jersey located on the Delaware River; site of Revolutionary War battle in December 1776 (40°15'N/74°45'W) 51

U

Union of Soviet Socialist Republics *See* Soviet Union.

United Kingdom country in northwestern Europe made up of England, Scotland, Wales, and Northern Ireland (56°30'N/1°45'W) 470

United States country in central North America; fourth largest country in the world in both area and population (38°N/110°W) 177

Utah state in the western United States; settled by Mormons in 1840s (39°30'N/112°45'W) 177

V

Valley Forge Revolutionary War winter camp northwest of Philadelphia (40°N/75°30'W) 51

Veracruz city in eastern Mexico on the Gulf of Mexico coast (19°15'N/96°W) 174

Vermont state in the northeastern United States; 14th state to enter the Union (43°45'N/72°45'W) 177

Vicksburg city and Civil War battle site in western Mississippi on the Mississippi River (32°21'N/90°52'W) 195

Vietnam country in southeastern Asia (16°N/108°E) 707

Virginia state in the eastern United States; colony in which first permanent English settlement in the Americas was established (37°N/78°W) 24

W

Wall Street street in New York City at the center of the financial district (40°45'N/74°W) 307

Washington state in the northwestern United States; territory reached by Lewis and Clark in 1805 (47°30'N/121°15'W) 177

Washington, D.C. capital of the United States located on the Potomac River; coinciding with the District of Columbia (38°53'N/77°02'W) 126

West Virginia state in the east central United States (39°N/80°45'W) 177

Wisconsin state in the north central United States; passed first state unemployment compensation act, 1932 (44°30'N/91°W) 144

Wounded Knee site of battle between settlers and Native Americans in southern South Dakota in 1890 and of Native American movement protest in 1973 (43°26'N/102°30'W) 250

Wyoming state in the western United States; territory provided women the right to vote, 1869 (42°45'N/108°30'W) 250

Y

Yorktown town in southeastern Virginia and site of final battle of Revolutionary War (37°15'N/76°30'W) 54

Z

Zaire country in central Africa (1°S/22°15'E) 698

Glossary

★ ★

A

abolitionist 1800s reformer who worked to end slavery (p. 161)

agribusiness large farming operation that includes the cultivation, processing, storage, and distribution of farm products (p. 641)

amendment alteration to the Constitution (p. 71)

amnesty act of a government by which pardon is granted to an individual or groups of persons (p. 217)

anarchism a belief in no direct government authority over society (p. 303)

anarchist one who opposes all forms of government (p. 388)

antebellum customs, manners, and institutions that existed before the Civil War (p. 331)

appeasement policy of compromising or giving in to demands in an attempt to avoid trouble and maintain peace (p. 581)

appropriations bill draft of a law setting aside funds for a specific use (p. 779)

arbitration hearing and resolution of a disagreement between two parties through an impartial third party (pp. 296, 372)

armistice temporary suspension of hostilities between opponents (p. 467)

armory place or building where arms and military equipment are stored (p. 512)

assimilation process of one group or culture absorbing another (p. 683)

automation technique of operating a machine, manufacturing process, or system that will do a job formerly performed by humans (p. 644)

B

balance of payments difference between the value of a nation's imports and its exports; also known as balance of trade (p. 736)

bicameral political system based on two legislative chambers (p. 62)

bilingualism ability to speak two languages (p. 690)

blacklist record kept by companies of employees or former employees who are disapproved of or are to be punished or boycotted (p. 292)

black nationalism belief of militant blacks who advocate separatism from whites and forming self-governing black communities (p. 682)

black power mobilizing economic and political power of African Americans to improve their condition (p. 683)

blitzkrieg war conducted with great speed or force (p. 584)

blockade to close off something (p. 191)

bounty money paid to recruit soldiers for military service; payment to encourage an action (p. 198)

boycott refusal to buy goods or have dealings with a country or other entity, usually to express disapproval or force acceptance of certain conditions (p. 45)

buffer area designed to separate and serve as a protective barrier; neutral area separating conflicting forces (p. 612)

business cycle sequence of economic activity, usually consisting of recession, recovery, growth, and decline (p. 292)

busing transportation of children to a school outside their residential area to establish racial integration in that school (p. 686)

C

cabinet a group of advisers to the President (p. 107)

cartel an association of nations promoting its economic interests (p. 749)

closed shop system where all workers in a particular industry are required to be union members or employer agrees to hire only union members (p. 148)

coalition alliance, combination, or union of parties, people, or states formed for a specific action or purpose (p. 560)

collective bargaining negotiation between organized workers and management to reach an agreement on wages, hours, and working conditions (p. 293)

collective security an agreement to provide for common defense (p. 615)

commodity economic good; product of agriculture; article of commerce (p. 260)

commonwealth self-governing political unit of independent states associated in a common allegiance (p. 26)

commune group of people living together with collective ownership and use of property, often having shared goals, philosophies, and ways of life; large cooperative farms (p. 711)

communism system of government in which the Communist party controls the political, economic, cultural, and social life of the people; economic system in which society as a whole, represented by the Communist party, owns all means of production, distribution, and exchange of goods (p. 610)

company town village built and run by a company where workers are required to live (p. 291)

confederation nonbinding political alliance of independent countries, states, or groups (pp. 9, 63)

congregation body of church members; people meeting for worship and religious instruction (p. 26)

conquistador Spanish adventurer in sixteenth-century Americas (p. 17)

conscientious objector person who refuses to perform military service or to bear arms on the grounds of moral or religious principles or beliefs (p. 709)

conscription compulsory enrollment of people for military service (p. 190)

consensus general agreement; judgment arrived at by most of those concerned; group solidarity in sentiment and belief (p. 728)

conservation the planned management of natural resources to prevent destruction or neglect (p. 424)

conspicuous consumption lavish spending for show (p. 356)

constitution plan of government in America; basic principles and laws of a nation, state, or social group that determine the powers and duties of the government and guarantee certain rights to its people (p. 26)

containment policy of preventing the expansion of a hostile power; post-World War II foreign policy stating the United States would hold Soviet influence within its existing limits (p. 612)

contraband goods or merchandise whose importation, exportation, or possession is forbidden (p. 459)

cooperative enterprise or organization owned by and operated for the benefit of those using its services (p. 342)

corollary proposition added to another as a natural consequence or effect (p. 389)

corporation form of business consisting of a group of people authorized by law to act as a single person and having an identity that survives its incorporators (p. 274)

cotton gin a machine that cleans the seeds from cotton fibers (p. 149)

counterculture a culture with values and mores that run contrary to those of established society (p. 711)

coup d'état a sudden revolt against an existing government (p. 764)

covenant formal and binding agreement between two or more parties (p. 474)

covert secret or undercover; not openly shown or engaged in (p. 652)

craft union labor union in which all members practice the same occupation or skill (p. 562)

credibility gap lack of trust stemming from difference between official government statements and practices (p. 700)

creditor nation a nation that lends money (p. 785)

D

dark horse political candidate unexpectedly nominated, usually as a compromise between groups (p. 173)

debtor nation a country that owes money (p. 785)

defense perimeter boundary of military protection (p. 620)

deficit spending government practice of borrowing money in order to spend more money than is received from taxes (p. 552)

deflation economic condition in which the volume of available money or credit decreases, resulting in the decline of the price of goods and services (p. 345)

deport remove from a country an alien presence (p. 477)

depression economic condition marked by an extended and severe decline in production and sales, and a severe increase in unemployment (p. 66)

deregulation act of removing restrictions and regulations (p. 742)

détente relaxation of cold war tensions between the United States and the Soviet Union that began in the early 1970s (p. 714)

direct primary election in which nominations of candidates for office are made by voters (p. 406)

direct tax one paid directly to the government rather than being included in the price of goods; a tax collected directly from the person on whom the tax burden is expected to fall (p. 45)

disenfranchise having had the legal right to vote taken away (p. 221)

dole money or goods given as charity; grant of government funds to the unemployed (p. 552)

domestic market market composed of buyers and sellers within a nation (p. 495)

double-digit inflation a rise in the general level of prices of 10 percent or more (p. 750)

downsizing to reduce operations or number of employees (p. 779)

drawdown the use of soldiers stationed in Europe and Asia during the Persian Gulf War (p. 766)

E

economies of scale ability of large businesses to operate more cheaply and efficiently than smaller ones, resulting in lower per-unit costs for the products of large companies (p. 269)

emancipation freeing of enslaved persons; act or process of freeing from restraint, control, or the power of another; freedom from bondage (p. 62)

encomienda system of rewarding conquistadors with tracts of land, including the right to tax and demand labor from Native Americans who lived on the land (p. 19)

entrepreneur person who organizes, manages, and assumes the risks of a business or enterprise (p. 267)

enumerated powers those mentioned specifically one after another in the Constitution (p. 111)

escalation increase in extent, volume, number, amount, intensity, or scope (p. 704)

ethnic cleansing expulsion or extermination of a group from a country (p. 781)

ethnic group groups of people who share the same culture, religion, and customs (p. 569)

excise tax one paid by a manufacturer and passed on to those who buy the product; a tax on the manufacture, sale, or consumption of a product within a country (p. 109)

executive privilege principle that the executive branch of government is exempt from disclosing information when such disclosure would adversely affect the functions and decision-making processes of the presidency or national security (p. 740)

expatriate person who leaves his or her native country to live elsewhere (p. 332)

expedition a journey with a specific purpose (p. 119)

F

fascism system of government that is strongly nationalistic and allows private ownership of property while controlling general economic policies; government characterized by racism and militarism; a repressive one-party dictatorship (p. 581)

favorite son presidential candidate supported by the delegates of the candidate's native state at a national political convention (p. 152)

featherbedding requiring of an employer under a union rule or safety statute to hire more employees than are needed (p. 624)

federal deficit difference between the amount of money a government took in and what it spent (p. 757)

federalism system of government in which power is distributed between national and state governments (p. 70)

federalized brought under federal government jurisdiction (p. 674)

feminist person who acts on behalf of women's rights (p. 688)

feudalism a system in which powerful leaders gave land to nobles in return for pledges of loyalty and service (p. 11)

filibuster the use of delaying tactics to prevent action in a legislative assembly (p. 778)

fireside chat the name used to describe how former President Franklin D. Roosevelt talked to people by radio (p. 547)

forage to live off the land (p. 204)

foreclosure legal procedure for reclaiming a piece of property when the owner is unable to keep up the mortgage payments (p. 554)

free-trader one that practices or advocates trade without taxes or tariffs (p. 327)

frigate medium-sized warship smaller than a destroyer; used for escort and patrol duties (p. 127)

G

genocide deliberate and systematic destruction of a group (p. 781)

gentry the upper class of England (p. 29)

glasnost a Russian word for the policy of openness begun by former Soviet President Gorbachev encouraging free expression and an end to party censorship (p. 759)

global economy economic interdependence among countries of the world (p. 785)

gold standard monetary system in which a nation's currency is based on the value of gold (p. 346)

graft acquisition of money or power in dishonest or questionable ways while in public office (p. 316)

greenback paper money that was not backed by gold or silver; legal-tender notes issued by the United States government (p. 199)

guerrilla soldier who barrages the enemy with surprise attacks, harassment, sabotage, and other non-traditional warfare (p. 612)

H

habeas corpus legal principle that requires that people who are arrested be brought to court to show why they should be held; writ inquiring into the lawfulness of retaining a person who is imprisoned or detained in custody (p. 199)

Glossary

holding company one that gains control of other companies by buying their stock (p. 277)

Holocaust systematic mass murder of 12 million European civilians, especially Jews, by Nazis during World War II (p. 593)

horizontal integration joining together of businesses that are engaged in similar business activities or processes (p. 277)

I

impeach to bring charges of a crime against a federal or state public official with the intent of removing the official from office (pp. 75, 223)

imperialism act of creating an empire by dominating other nations (p. 370)

implied powers those suggested but not directly stated in the Constitution (p. 112)

impound to refuse to spend congressionally allocated funds; to seize and hold in the custody of the law (p. 742)

impressment form of military and naval conscription, usually by force, practiced by Britain and other European countries (p. 121)

income tax tax on the net income of an individual or business (p. 431)

incumbent current officeholder (p. 774)

indemnity security or protection against hurt, loss, or damage; exemption from incurred penalties or liabilities (p. 391)

indentured servant person who agreed to work for an employer in colonial America for a specified time in exchange for passage to America (p. 24)

industrial union union that represents every worker in a single industry regardless of his or her job (pp. 298, 562)

inflation decline in money's value when more money is printed, resulting in increased prices of goods and services (p. 345)

inheritance tax tax on an inheritance that an heir must pay to receive the inheritance (p. 433)

initiative procedure enabling citizens to propose a bill by petitioning with a specific number of signatures from registered voters (p. 406)

injunction court order requiring an individual or company to do something or to prohibit a given action; used frequently to stop strikes (p. 299)

installment buying system of paying for goods at regular intervals, usually with interest added to the balance (p. 516)

interlocking directorate system under which the same people serve on the boards of directors of several firms within the same industry (p. 442)

internal improvements roads, canals, and other transportation needs inside a nation's boundaries (p. 140)

isolationism policy or belief that a nation should limit its alliances and involvement in international political and economic affairs (p. 370)

J

joint resolution a resolution passed by both houses of Congress requiring only a simple majority vote (p. 173)

joint-stock company form of business organization; pooled funds of many investors or stockholders who can independently sell their shares of the company (p. 14)

judicial review Supreme Court's power to review all congressional acts and executive actions and reject those it considers unconstitutional (pp. 77, 118)

junk bond high-risk bond that offers a high return to compensate for the high risk of default (p. 768)

jurisdictional strike one resulting from a dispute between unions over which union should represent the workers in a company or industry (p. 624)

K

kickback payback of a sum received from increased fees because of a confidential agreement or act of coercion (p. 317)

L

laissez-faire government doctrine of noninterference in business practices and in the economic affairs of individuals; literally, "let do" (p. 118)

lame duck elected official who continues to hold office during the period between the election and the inauguration of a successor (p. 533)

lend-lease transfer of goods and services to an ally (p. 587)

line-item veto power to veto a single part of a bill (p. 779)

line of demarcation north-south line of longitude through the Atlantic Ocean dividing lands in the Americas claimed by Spain and Portugal (p. 17)

literacy test tests to show if immigrants could read (p. 413)

lobbyist person who promotes or secures the passage of legislation by influencing public officials (p. 319)

lockout closed factory or place of employment caused by a strike; withholding of employment by an employer (p. 293)

long drive cattle run in which a large herd is moved across great distances to a railhead where they are shipped to market (p. 250)

Loyalist American colonist who supported the British government; one who is or remains loyal to a political cause, party, or government (p. 49)

M

mandate clear expression of the wishes of voters, as shown in election results (pp. 220, 723)

martial law form of military rule that suspends Bill of Rights guarantees; law administered by the military in an emergency situation when civilian law-enforcement agencies are not able to maintain order (p. 199)

maverick unbranded range animal or cattle; a motherless calf (p. 249)

mercantilism the theory that a state's power depended on its wealth (p. 20)

mercenary paid soldier hired for service in the army of a foreign country; one that serves merely for wages (p. 52)

merchandising buying and selling of goods in a business for a profit (p. 309)

meridian line of longitude; a great circle on the surface of the earth passing through the poles (p. 258)

mestizo person in the Spanish colonies born of Spanish and Native American parents (p. 19)

militia group of civilians declared by law to be called to military service and trained as soldiers to fight in emergencies (p. 43)

minutemen a group of armed men who were ready to fight the English at a moment's notice (p. 47)

moratorium official authorization to suspend payments, as with a debt; officially authorized period of waiting (p. 523)

multinational state nation with many different ethnic groups (p. 781)

N

nationalism feeling of loyalty and devotion to one's country; honoring that nation above all others and promoting its culture and interests rather than those of other nations (p. 140)

neutrality refusal to take sides (p. 375)

new federalism Richard Nixon's policy of economic partnership between the federal and state governments whereby states and municipalities received less federal funding (p. 737)

nomadic frequent roaming from place to place without a fixed pattern of movement, usually following a food source (p. 242)

nonviolent resistance objection or demonstration to gain political ends without use of violence (p. 672)

northwest passage water route to Asia through North America sought by European explorers (p. 20)

nullification state declaration of a federal law to be invalid (p. 116)

O

on margin method of buying stock with a small cash down payment and the rest borrowed from a stockbroker. Stockbroker holds shares of stock as collateral for the loan; borrower repays broker from stock resale profits (p. 515)

open shop employment practice in which eligibility is not determined by union membership (p. 487)

P

partitioned divided into two or more territorial units having separate political status (p. 390)

Patriot American colonist who favored separation before and during the Revolutionary War (p. 49)

patronage practice of elected officials to make appointments to unelected government positions for political advantage or repayment of favors (p. 323)

perestroika a Russian word for "restructuring"; former Soviet President Gorbachev's name for his economic policy, which favors less government intervention and more private initiative (p. 759)

philanthropy actions to promote human welfare and benefit society (p. 283)

platform declaration of the principles and policies adopted by a political party or candidate (p. 184)

pocket veto indirect rejection of a legislative bill by the President by retaining the bill unsigned until after Congress adjourns (p. 155)

pogrom organized massacres of unarmed people, especially Jews (p. 302)

political machine party organization in big cities that holds power by controlling votes, courts, and police (p. 317)

pooling illegal agreements among individual railroads to divide the total volume of freight among their lines and to keep rates high (p. 342)

popular sovereignty principle that the settlers within a federal territory have the power to decide the legality of slavery within that territory (p. 176)

Glossary

pork-barrel legislation the money that Congress appropriates for local federal projects (p. 750)

post-war disillusionment period after a war in which the populace is disenchanted (p. 504)

pragmatism belief that government actions should meet the needs of society; practical approach to problems and affairs (p. 400)

pragmatist one who searches for practical solutions to problems (p. 724)

presidential succession the order in which others fill the office of President (p. 637)

price-cutting reduction of prices to a level designed to cripple competition (p. 442)

privateer armed private ship commissioned by the government to attack ships of an enemy (p. 127)

privatize transfer state-owned factories and other property to private ownership (p. 759)

propaganda information, not always true, designed to help or harm a cause (p. 49)

proprietor individual who received legal and exclusive right to American colonial land from the king of England and who was expected to administer the land according to English laws (p. 24)

protectionist one who advocates government protection for domestic producers and manufacturers through restrictions on imports (p. 327)

protective tariff high tax on imports intended to protect domestic products from foreign competition rather than to yield revenue (p. 108)

protectorate country that is technically independent, but whose government and economy are controlled by a stronger power; the nation or region controlled by a stronger nation (p. 385)

public land land belonging to the national government and therefore to the people (p. 64)

pump priming government money invested in the economy to stimulate a self-sustaining economic recovery (p. 552)

purge large-scale forced removal of officials who show signs of disloyalty to their superiors (p. 611)

R

racism belief that a particular race is superior to others (p. 682)

ratification to officially approve a proposal (p. 70)

reactionary government government characterized by ultraconservative policies (p. 700)

real wages income adjusted to compensate for reduced earning power due to inflation (p. 290)

realism European-influenced literary movement that strove for accurate representation of nature or real life without idealization (p. 331)

rebate discount in the form of a refund or part of a payment for a product or service (p. 279)

recall removal of an elected official by voters in a special election (p. 406)

recession downturn in the nation's economy marked by reduced economic activity (p. 564)

reciprocity mutual lowering by nations of tariff barriers; recognition by one of two countries of the validity of privileges granted by the other (p. 372)

rediscount small fee charged to a member bank by the Federal Reserve Bank upon acceptance of a business's promissory note (p. 440)

referendum process by which people can vote directly on a proposed law (p. 406)

reparation payments made by nations defeated in war as a penalty for damages caused to other countries (p. 485)

republic a government in which the power is held by the people, who then elect representatives to act for them (p. 49)

revenue sharing plan to share or divide income (p. 737)

revenue tariff low tax on imports intended to provide income for the government rather than protection of domestic products from foreign competition (p. 108)

rider unrelated amendment attached to a bill under legislative consideration (p. 323)

S

salutary neglect policy of noninterference by a governing nation in order to produce a beneficial effect (p. 42)

satellite nations East European nations politically and economically under Soviet domination; country dominated or controlled by another more powerful country (p. 611)

scab nonunion replacement workers during a strike or union members who refuse to strike and continue working (p. 293)

scrip money that can be redeemed only at a company store (p. 291)

search-and-destroy strategy military tactic used to force an enemy into open combat (p. 705)

secession formal withdrawal from an organization (p. 187)

securities stocks, bonds, and other financial instruments traded on a stock exchange (p. 514)

segregation enforced separation of racial groups in schooling, housing, and other public areas (p. 227)

separation of powers the division of power among the legislative, executive, and judicial branches of government (p. 76)

sexism prejudice or discrimination based on gender (p. 689)

sharecropper agricultural worker who cultivates part of another person's land, receives supplies and equipment from the landowner and, in return, gives the landowner part of the harvest (p. 213)

shogun one of a line of military governors ruling Japan until the revolution of 1867–1868; Japanese commander in chief (p. 13)

shuttle diplomacy negotiations carried out by an intermediary who shuttles back and forth between the disputants (p. 717)

sit-in occupying seats or sitting on the floor of an establishment as a nonviolent means of protest (p. 676)

social contract agreement among individuals forming an organized society that defines and limits the rights and duties of each (p. 50)

social Darwinism sociological theory that states only the fittest survive social competition and experience social advancement (p. 282)

social gospel application by religious organizations of Christian principles to social problems (p. 399)

socialism economic system in which government partly owns and controls production and distribution of goods produced (p. 164)

speculator a person who buys bonds, stocks, or land to sell at a profit when the price later goes up (p. 64)

speculation risky business venture involving buying or selling in the hope of making a large, quick profit (p. 514)

sphere of influence area in China during the late 1800s where trade was controlled by a foreign power (p. 390)

spoils system practice of dismissing government job holders affiliated with a defeated party and replacing them with supporters of the winning party (p. 155)

stagflation persistent inflation combined with static consumer demand and relatively high rate of unemployment (p. 736)

student deferment official postponement of military service (p. 709)

subversive person working secretly, attempting to overthrow or undermine a government or political system (p. 627)

summit diplomatic meeting of the superpowers; conference of highest level government officials (p. 714)

supply-side economics an economic theory that claims that the economy can best be stimulated by increasing the supply of goods rather than the demand (p. 755)

T

teach-in lecture, debate, and discussion on controversial topic (p. 710)

technological unemployment jobs lost as the result of machines doing the jobs formerly accomplished by humans (p. 487)

tenant farmer agricultural worker who rents and farms land from another person and pays the rent either in cash or with a portion of the crop (p. 213)

textile fabric, especially woven or knitted; cloth (p. 147)

third party political party operating in addition to two other major parties in a nation or state normally characterized by a two-party system (p. 347)

toll fee charged for a privilege such as the use of a means of transportation (p. 142)

totalitarian type of government controlled by a single person or party; suppressing freedom and controlling every aspect of life (p. 581)

township local unit of government within a county (p. 320)

trade deficit economic condition in which the value of a nation's imports is more than the value of its exports (p. 785)

treason attempt to overthrow the government of the state to which the offender owes allegiance (p. 49)

trust combination of companies to gain control of an industry and reduce competition (p. 277)

turnpike road barricaded by spiked poles where travelers stop to pay a fee to use the road (p. 142)

U

ultimatum a demand that would have serious consequences if ignored (p. 145)

underemployed having less than full-time, regular, or adequate employment (p. 768)

unicameral legislature consisting of a single chamber (p. 63)

urban renewal construction program to replace or restore a city or urban area (p. 725)

user tax a tax on goods or services used by consumers (p. 767)

V

vaudeville stage entertainment consisting of various acts (p. 252)

vertical integration joining together of businesses that are involved in different but related activities or processes (p. 277)

Glossary

veto action by which an executive rejects a bill submitted by a legislature; to refuse to approve (p. 62)

victory gardens gardens for raising one's own vegetables, especially during wartime (p. 470)

vigilance committee organization of citizens who take the law into their own hands for their protection (p. 252)

W

ward division of a city for representative, electoral, or administrative purposes (p. 318)

war of national liberation conflict with goal of freeing one nation from the control of another (p. 702)

welfare capitalism system of benefit programs offered to workers by employers intended to reduce the appeal of unions (p. 488)

"Western" novel, story, or Hollywood motion picture depicting life in the western United States during the latter half of the nineteenth century (p. 253)

wildcat strike work stoppage initiated by a group of workers without formal union approval or in violation of a contract (p. 601)

Y

yellow journalism type of newspaper reporting in the late 1890s that featured sensational headlines and stories (p. 333)

Glossary

Spanish Glossary

★ ★

A

abolitionist/abolicionista reformista del siglo XIX que luchó por la supresión de la esclavitud (p. 161)

agribusiness/negocio agrario operación agrícola grande que incluye cultivo, procesamiento, almacenamiento y distribución de productos agrícolas (p. 641)

amendment/enmienda alteración de la Constitución (p. 71)

amnesty/amnistía acto de un gobierno que otorga el perdón a un individuo o grupo de personas (p. 217)

anarchism/anarquismo la creencia en la ausencia de autoridad directa del gobierno sobre la sociedad (p. 303)

anarchist/anarquista persona que se opone a cualquier forma de gobierno (p. 388)

antebellum/antebellum costumbres, hábitos e instituciones que existieron antes de la Guerra de Secesión (p. 331)

appeasement/apaciguamiento política de compromiso o aceptación de exigencias con el propósito de evitar problemas y mantener la paz (p. 581)

appropriations bill/proyecto de ley de asignaciones proyecto de ley que destina fondos a un uso específico (p. 779)

arbitration/arbitraje audiencia y resolución de un desacuerdo entre dos partes a través de una tercera parte imparcial (pp. 296, 372)

armistice/armisticio suspensión temporal de hostilidades entre adversarios (p. 467)

armory/armería lugar o edificio donde se almacenan armas y equipos militares (p. 512)

assimilation/asimilación proceso en el que un grupo o cultura absorbe a otro (p. 683)

automation/automatización técnica de operación de máquinas, procesamiento industrial o sistema que realiza un trabajo previamente efectuado por seres humanos (p. 644)

B

balance of payments/balanza de pagos diferencia entre el valor de las importaciones y las exportaciones de una nación; también conocida como balanza comercial (p. 736)

bicameral/bicameral sistema político basado en dos cámaras legislativas (p. 62)

bilingualism/bilingualismo capacidad de expresarse en dos idiomas (p. 690)

black list/lista negra registro mantenido por las compañías de los empleados o antiguos empleados con los que se está en desacuerdo o se propone castigar o boicotear (p. 292)

black nationalism/nacionalismo negro creencia de los militantes negros que favorece la separación de los blancos y la formación de comunidades negras con gobierno propio (p. 682)

black power/poder negro la movilización del poder económico y político de los afroamericanos para mejorar sus condiciones de vida (p. 683)

blitzkrieg/blitzkrieg guerra relámpago que se caracteriza por su gran rapidez o fuerza (p. 584)

blockade/bloqueo aislar algo (p. 191)

bounty/recompensa dinero pagado por reclutar soldados para servicios militares; pago para alentar una acción (p. 198)

boycott/boicot rechazo a comprar productos o efectuar negociaciones con un país u otra entidad, usualmente para expresar desacuerdo o forzar la aceptación de ciertas condiciones (p. 45)

buffer/zona de amortiguación área destinada a separar y servir como una barrera protectora; área neutral que separa fuerzas en conflicto (p. 612)

business cycle/ciclo económico secuencia de actividad económica compuesta usualmente de recesión, recuperación, crecimiento y declinación (p. 292)

busing/traslado escolar obligatorio transportación de niños a una escuela fuera de su área residencial para establecer la integración racial en dicha escuela (p. 686)

C

cabinet/gabinete un grupo de asesores del presidente (p. 107)

cartel/cartel grupo de vendedores o productores que obran conjuntamente para subir los precios al restringir la disponibilidad de un producto (p. 749)

closed shop/taller sindicalizado sistema en el que a todos los trabajadores de una industria en particular se les exige ser miembros de un sindicato o cuando el patrón acuerda contratar sólo a miembros sindicales. (p. 148)

coalition/coalición alianza, combinación o unión de partidos, pueblos o estados que se forma para una acción o propósito específico (p. 560)

Spanish Glossary

collective bargaining/convenio colectivo negociación entre trabajadores organizados y la administración para lograr un acuerdo sobre salarios, condiciones y horas de trabajo (p. 293)

collective security/seguridad colectiva un acuerdo para garantizar la defensa común (p. 615)

commodity/mercancía bien económico; producto agrícola; artículo comercial (p. 260)

commonwealth/mancomunidad unidad política con gobierno propio de estados independientes asociados en una lealtad común (p. 26)

commune/comuna grupo de personas que viven juntas con propiedad y uso colectivos de los bienes, compartiendo a menudo metas, filosofías y formas de vida; granjas cooperativas extensas (p. 711)

communism/comunismo sistema de gobierno en el cual el partido Comunista controla la vida política, económica, cultural y social de la población; sistema económico en el cual la sociedad como un todo y representada por el partido Comunista, controla todos los medios de producción, distribución e intercambio de bienes (p. 610)

company town/pueblo de la compañía poblado construido y administrado por una compañía en el que los trabajadores están obligados a vivir (p. 291)

confederation/confederación alianza política voluntaria de países, estados o grupos independientes (pp. 9, 63)

congregation/congregación el cuerpo de miembros de una iglesia; reunión de personas para instrucción religiosa y rendir culto (p. 26)

conquistador/conquistador aventurero español del siglo XVI en el continente americano (p. 17)

conscientious objector/objector de conciencia persona que se niega a cumplir servicio militar o a portar armas debido a principios o creencias morales o religiosos (p. 709)

conscription/reclutamiento enrolamiento obligatorio de personas en las fuerzas militares (p. 190)

consensus/consenso acuerdo general; juicio al que han llegado la mayoría de los interesados; solidaridad de grupo en sentimientos y creencias (p. 728)

conservation/conservación administración planeada de los recursos naturales para prevenir su destrucción o abandono (p. 424)

conspicuous comsumption/consumo conspicuo gastos exagerados para llamar la atención (p. 356)

constitution/constitución plan de gobierno de Norteamérica; principios y leyes fundamentales de una nación, estado o grupo social que determina los poderes y deberes del gobierno y garantiza determinados derechos a su pueblo (p. 26)

containment/contención política de prevención de la expansión de una potencia hostil; política exterior después de la Segunda Guerra Mundial que establecía que los Estados Unidos contendrían la influencia soviética dentro de sus límites existentes (p. 612)

contraband/contrabando bienes o mercancías cuya importación, exportación o posesión está prohibida (p. 459)

cooperative/cooperativa organización o empresa que pertenece y es operada para el el beneficio de áquellos que usan sus servicios (p. 342)

corollary/corolario proposición que se añade a otra como una consecuencia o efecto natural (p. 389)

corporation/corporación forma de negocio consistente en un grupo de personas autorizadas por las leyes para actuar como una entidad única que sobrevive a los que la crearon (p. 274)

cotton gin/desmotadora de algodón máquina que elimina las semillas de las fibras del algodón (p. 149)

counterculture/contracultura conjunto de valores y costumbres opuesto al establecido por la sociedad (p. 711)

coup d'état/golpe de estado el derrocamiento repentino de un gobeirno por parte de gente con autoridad, en violación deliberada de las leyes (p. 764)

covenant/convenio acuerdo formal y obligatorio entre dos o más partes (p. 474)

covert/encubierto secreto o disfrazado; que no se muestra o compromete abiertamente (p. 652)

craft union/sindicato de oficio sindicato laboral en el cual todos sus miembros practican la misma ocupación o especialidad (p. 562)

credibility gap/falta de credibilidad ausencia de confianza debida a la diferencia entre las declaraciones oficiales del gobierno y los procedimientos en la realidad (p. 700)

creditor nation/nación acreedora una nación que presta dinero (p. 785)

D

dark horse/candidato sorpresivo candidato político inesperadamente nominado usualmente debido a un compromiso entre grupos (p. 173)

debtor nation/nación deudora un país que debe dinero (p. 785)

defense perimeter/perímetro defensivo línea fronteriza que delimita un área protegida militarmente (p. 620)

deficit spending/gastos deficitarios procedimiento gubernamental de pedir prestado dinero con el propósito de gastar más dinero del que recauda en impuestos (p. 552)

deflation/deflación situación económica en la cual disminuye el volumen de dinero o crédito disponibles lo que produce una caída en los precios de los productos y servicios (p. 345)

deported/deportado sacar de un país una presencia extranjera es ilegal (p. 477)

depression/depresión situación económica caracterizada por una declinación amplia y profunda de la producción y las ventas mientras aumenta drásticamente el desempleo (p. 66)

deregulation/derogación de regulaciones ley aboliendo restricciones y regulaciones (p. 742)

détente/coexistencia pacífica relajamiento de las tensiones de la Guerra Fría entre los Estados Unidos y la Unión Soviética que se inició a principios de la década de 1970 (p. 714)

direct primary/primarias directas elecciones en las que las nominaciones de los candidatos a cargos oficiales se efectúan por los votantes (p. 406)

direct tax/impuesto directo tributo que se paga directamente al gobierno en vez de ser incluido en el precio de los bienes; un impuesto recaudado directamente de la persona sobre la que recae la carga impositiva (p. 45)

disenfranchised/privación del derecho de sufragio pérdida del derecho legal al voto (p. 221)

dole/subsidio dinero o artículos ofrecidos como donación caritativa; subvención de fondos del gobierno para el desempleo (p. 552)

domestic market/mercado interno mercado compuesto de compradores y vendedores del país (p. 495)

downsizing/reducción disminución de las operaciones o del número de trabajadores (p. 779)

E

economics of scale/economía de escala capacidad de los grandes negocios de funcionar de forma más económica y eficiente que los pequeños, lo que resulta en menor costo por unidad de los productos de las grandes compañías (p. 269)

emancipation/emancipación liberación de una persona esclavizada; acto o proceso de liberar de las restricciones, control o dominio de otro; libre de servidumbre (p. 62)

encomienda/encomienda sistema de recompensar a los conquistadores con tierras, incluyendo el derecho a imponer impuestos y exigir trabajo de los indígenas americanos que las habitaban (p. 19)

entrepreneur/empresario persona que organiza, administra y asume los riesgos de un negocio o empresa (p. 267)

enumerated powers/poderes específicos áquellos mencionados explícitamente, uno detrás del otro, en la Constitución (p. 111)

escalation/escalada aumento en amplitud, volumen, número, cantidad, intensidad o alcance (p. 704)

ethnic cleansing/limpieza étnica expulsión o exterminio de un grupo de un país (p. 781)

ethnic group/grupo étnico población que comparte la misma cultura, religión y costumbres (p. 569)

excise tax/impuesto sobre consumos tributo pagado por el fabricante y que es añadido a áquellos que compran el producto; un impuesto sobre la fabricación, venta o consumo de un producto dentro de un país (p. 109)

executive privilege/privilegio ejecutivo principio de que la rama ejecutiva del gobierno está exenta de suministrar información cuando dicha revelación afectaría adversamente las funciones y el proceso de toma de decisiones del presidente o la seguridad nacional (p. 740)

expatriate/expatriado persona que abandona su país nativo para vivir en otro lugar (p. 332)

expedition/expedición viaje con un propósito específico (p. 119)

F

fascism/fascismo sistema de gobierno que es profundamente nacionalista y permite la posesión privada de propiedades mientras controla la política económica en general; gobierno caracterizado por el racismo y militarismo; una dictadura represiva de un partido (p. 581)

favorite son/hijo favorito candidato presidencial apoyado por los delegados de su estado de origen en una convención política nacional (p. 152)

featherbedding/featherbedding solicitar de un patrón bajo una regulación sindical o estatuto de seguridad que contrate más empleados que los necesarios (p. 624)

federal deficit/déficit del presupuesto federal exceso de gastos federales sobre la recaudación de impuestos e ingresos (p. 757)

federalism/federalismo sistema de gobierno en el cual el poder está distribuido entre el gobierno nacional y los gobiernos estatales (p. 70)

federalized/federalizado llevado bajo la jurisdicción del gobierno federal (p. 674)

feminist/feminista persona que actúa en beneficio de los derechos de la mujer (p. 688)

feudalism/feudalismo sistema en el cual poderosos líderes otorgan tierras a los nobles a cambio de un juramento de lealtad y servicios (p. 11)

filibuster/obstruccionismo el uso de tácticas dilatorias para mantener inactiva una asamblea legislativa (p. 778)

fireside chat/charla al calor del hogar nombre usado para describir cómo el antiguo presidente Franklin

D. Roosevelt se dirigía a la población por la radio (p. 547)

forage/forrajear vivir de la tierra (p. 204)

foreclosure/juicio hipotecario procedimiento legal para reclamar parte de una propiedad cuando el dueño no puede estar al día en los pagos de la hipoteca (p. 554)

free-trader/librecambista alguien que practica o defiende el comercio sin impuestos ni aranceles (p. 327)

frigate/fragata navío de guerra de tamaño medio que es menor que un destructor; se utiliza como escolta y en labores de patrullaje (p. 127)

G

genocide/genocidio exterminio deliberado y sistemático de un grupo (p. 781)

gentry/nobleza la clase superior de Inglaterra (p. 29)

glasnost/glasnost término que se refiere a la política soviética de franqueza y libertad de espresión bajo Mikhail Gorbachev (p. 759)

global economy/economía global interdependencia económica entre los países del mundo (p. 785)

gold standard/patrón oro sistema monetario en el cual la moneda circulante de una nación está respaldada por el valor del oro (p. 346)

graft/soborno adquisición de dinero o poder en forma deshonesta o cuestionable mientras se ocupa un cargo público (p. 316)

greenback/nota de banco papel moneda que no estaba respaldado por oro o plata; notas de curso legal emitidas por el gobierno de los Estados Unidos (p. 199)

guerrilla/guerrilla soldado que combate al enemigo con ataques de sorpresa, acosos, sabotajes y otras formas no tradiciones de guerra (p. 612)

H

habeas corpus/hábeas corpus principio legal que exige que una persona que sea arrestada debe ser llevada ante una corte para saber la causa de su arresto; orden judicial que solicita una investigación sobre la legalidad de retener una persona que ha sido encarcelada o se halla baja custodia (p. 199)

holding company/compañía de holding firma que obtiene el control de otras compañías mediante la compra de sus acciones (p. 277)

Holocaust/Holocausto asesinato masivo y sistemático de 12 millones de civiles europeos, especialmente judíos, llevado a cabo por los nazis durante la Segunda Guerra Mundial (p. 593)

horizontal integration/integración horizontal la unión de negocios dedicados a las mismas actividades o procesos comerciales (p. 277)

I

impeach/impugnar presentar acusaciones de un delito contra un funcionario público federal o estatal con el propósito de destituir al funcionario de su cargo (pp. 75, 223)

imperialism/imperialismo acción de crear un imperio mediante el dominio sobre otras naciones (p. 370)

implied powers/poderes implícitos áquellos sugeridos pero no expresamente enunciados en la Constitución (p. 112)

impound/embargar negarse a gastar fondos congresionales asignados; confiscar y retener bajo la custodia de la ley (p. 742)

impressment/reclutamiento forzoso forma de enrolamiento militar y naval, usualmente por la fuerza, empleado por Inglaterra y otras naciones europeas (p. 121)

income tax/impuesto sobre la renta impuesto sobre el ingreso neto de un individuo o negocio (p. 431)

imcumbent/titular funcionario ejerciendo el cargo (p. 744)

indemnity/indemnidad seguridad o protección contra lesiones, pérdida o daños; exención de penalidades u obligaciones (p. 391)

indentured servant/sirviente bajo contrato persona que acuerda trabajar para un patrón en Norteamérica colonial por un tiempo específico a cambio de la travesía a Norteamérica (p. 24)

industrial union/sindicato industrial sindicato que representa cada trabajador en una industria en particular sin importar su oficio (pp. 298, 562)

inflation/inflación descenso del valor del dinero cuando se emite más moneda circulante, lo que resulta en un aumento de los precios y servicios (p. 345)

inheritance tax/impuesto sobre la herencia gravamen sobre la herencia que el heredero debe pagar para recibirla (p. 433)

initiative/iniciativa procedimiento que permite a los ciudadanos proponer un proyecto de ley mediante una petición con un número específico de firmas de votantes inscritos (p. 406)

injunction/interdicción orden de la corte que exige que un individuo o compañía realice una acción o le prohibe que la realice; aplicada frecuentemente para detener huelgas (p. 299)

installment buying/comprar a plazos sistema de pagar por bienes a intervalos regulares, usualmente con un interés añadido al balance (p. 516)

interlocking directorate/directivas interrelacionadas sistema bajo el cual las mismas personas forman las juntas de directores de varias firmas de la misma industria (p. 442)

internal improvements/adelantos internos caminos, canales y otras necesidades de transportación dentro de las fronteras de una nación (p. 140)

isolationism/aislacionismo política o creencia de que una nación debe limitar sus alianzas y compromisos en los asuntos políticos y económicos internacionales (p. 370)

J

joint resolution/resolución conjunta una resolución aprobada por ambas cámaras del Congreso que requiere solamente una mayoría simple de votos (p. 173)

joint-stock company/sociedad en comandita por acciones forma de organización comercial; reúne fondos de muchos inversionistas o dueños de acciones que pueden independientemente vender sus participaciones en la compañía (p. 14)

judicial review/revisión judicial potestad de la Corte Suprema para revisar todas las actas congresionales y acciones ejecutivas y rechazar áquellas que considere inconstitucionales (pp. 77, 118)

junk bond/bono especulativo bono de corporación generalmente considerado por debajo del grado mediano o especulativo, que paga grandes ganancias para compensar los grandes riesgos de incumplimiento (p. 768)

jurisdictional strike/huelga jurisdiccional la que resulta de una disputa entre sindicatos sobre qué sindicato debe representar a los trabajadores en una compañía o industria (p. 624)

K

kickback/gratificación devolución de una suma recibida de honorarios aumentados debido a un acuerdo confidencial o un acto de coacción (p. 317)

L

laissez-faire/laissez faire doctrina de gobierno de no interferir en los procedimientos comerciales y en los asuntos económicos de los individuos; literalmente significa del francés "dejar hacer" (p. 118)

lame duck/titular no reelegido funcionario electo que continúa en el cargo durante el período comprendido entre las elecciones y la toma de posesión de un sucesor (p. 533)

lend-lease/préstamo-arrendamiento transferencia de bienes y servicios a un aliado (p. 587)

line-item veto/veto selectivo poder para vetar una parte de un proyecto de ley (p. 779)

line of demarcation/línea de demarcación línea de longitud Norte-Sur a través del océano Atlántico que dividió las tierras en las Américas reclamadas por España y Portugal (p. 17)

literacy test/prueba de alfabetización exámenes para comprobar si los inmigrantes sabían leer (p. 413)

lobbyist/cabildero persona que promueve o asegura la aprobación de legislación mediante su influencia sobre los funcionarios públicos (p. 319)

lockout/cierre patronal clausura de una fábrica o centro laboral debida a una huelga; negativa de empleo de un patrón (p. 293)

long drive/arriería traslado de ganado a grandes distancias hasta el ferrocarril, donde es transportado al mercado (p. 250)

Loyalist/lealista colonos norteamericanos que apoyaban el gobierno inglés; alguien que es leal o permanece fiel a una causa política, partido o gobierno (p. 49)

M

mandate/mandato clara expresión del deseo de los votantes tal como se muestra en los resultados de las elecciones (pp. 220, 723)

martial law/ley marcial forma de gobierno militar que suspende las garantías de la Declaración de Derechos; ley administrada por las autoridades civiles en una situación de emergencia cuando las instituciones civiles de aplicación de las leyes no son capaces de mantener el orden (p. 199)

maverick/maverick animal de bosque o ganado sin marcar; un ternero huérfano (p. 249)

mercantilism/mercantilismo teoría de que el poder de un estado depende de su riqueza (p. 20)

mercenary/mercenario soldado a sueldo cuyos servicios se contrataron por el ejército de una nación extranjera; alguien que realiza sus labores solamente por el pago (p. 52)

merchandising/comerciar compra y venta de bienes en un negocio con el propósito de obtener ganancias (p. 309)

meridian/meridiano medida de longitud; un gran círculo alrededor de la superficie de la Tierra que pasa a través de los polos (p. 258)

mestizo/mestizo persona en las colonias españolas nacida de padres español e indígena americano (p. 19)

militia/milicia grupo de civiles autorizados por la ley a ser llamados al servicio militar y entrenados como soldados para combatir en una emergencia (p. 43)

moratorium/moratoria autorización oficial para suspender pagos, como en el caso de deudas; período de espera autorizado oficialmente (p. 523)

multinational state/estado multinacional nación con diferentes y numerosos grupos étnicos (p. 781)

N

nationalism/nacionalismo sentimiento de lealtad y devoción a la patria, honrando esa nación por encima de las demás y promoviendo su cultura e intereses en vez de los de otros países (p. 140)

neutrality/neutralidad negativa a unirse a un bando (p. 375)

new federalism/nuevo federalismo política de Richard Nixon de asociación económica entre el gobierno federal y los gobiernos estatales en la que los estados y municipalidades recibían menos fondos federales (p. 737)

nomadic/nómada traslado frecuente de lugar a lugar sin un patrón fijo de destino, usualmente siguiendo una fuente de alimentos (p. 242)

nonviolent resistance/resistencia pacífica protesta o demostración para lograr fines políticos sin uso de la violencia (p. 672)

northwest passage/paso al noroeste ruta marina a Asia a través de América del Norte que fue buscada por los exploradores europeos (p. 20)

nullification/anulación declaración estatal que considera inválida una ley federal (p. 116)

O

on margin/al margen método de comprar acciones con un pago inicial en efectivo pequeño y un préstamo a un corredor de bolsa para cubrir el balance. El corredor retiene una parte de las acciones como colateral del préstamo; el prestatario reembolsa al corredor con las ganancias producto de la reventa de las acciones (p. 515)

open shop/taller no sindicalizado procedimiento de empleo en el cual la elegibilidad no es determinada por la membresía en un sindicato (p. 487)

P

partitioned/subdividido dividido en dos o más unidades territoriales con identidades políticas separadas (p. 390)

Patriot/Patriota colono norteamericano que favorecía la separación durante la Guerra de Independencia (p. 49)

patronage/patronazgo procedimiento de los funcionarios oficiales electos de ofrecer nombramientos en cargos gubernamentales para ventaja política o como recompensa por favores recibidos (p. 323)

perestroika/perestroika reestructuramiento fundamental de la economía soviética; política introducida por Mikhail Gorbachev (p. 759)

philanthropy/filantropía actividades para promover el bienestar de los seres humanos para beneficio de la sociedad (p. 283)

platform/plataforma declaración de la política y principios adoptados por un partido o candidato político (p. 184)

pocket veto/veto de bolsillo rechazo indirecto de un proyecto de ley legislativo por el presidente mediante la retención del proyecto sin firmar hasta el receso del Congreso (p. 155)

pogrom/pogrom masacres organizadas de población desarmada, especialmente judíos (p. 302)

political machine/maquinaria política organización de partido en las grandes ciudades que sustenta su poder mediante el control de votaciones, tribunales y policía (p. 317)

pooling/pooling acuerdos ilegales entre compañías ferrocarrileras individuales para dividir el volumen total de flete entre sus ferrovías y mantener precios elevados (p. 342)

popular sovereignty/soberanía popular principio de que los colonizadores de un territorio federal tienen el poder para determinar la legalidad de la esclavitud dentro de ese territorio (p. 176)

post-war disillusionment/desencanto de posguerra período posterior a una guerra en el que la población está desengañada (p. 504)

pragmatism/pragmatismo creencia de que las acciones gubernamentales deben resolver las necesidades sociales; enfrentamiento práctico de problemas y asuntos (p. 400)

presidential succession/sucesión presidencial el orden en que es ocupado el cargo de presidente (p. 634)

price-cutting/reducción de precios rebaja de precios hasta un nivel establecido para anular la competencia (p. 442)

privateer/corsario embarcación privada armada que era comisionada por el gobierno para atacar los barcos enemigos (p. 127)

privatize/privatizar conversión de factorías y otras propiedades del gobierno a propiedad privada (p. 759)

propaganda/propaganda comunicaciones, verdaderas o falsas, basadas en una selección cuidadosa y la manipulación de datos, con la intención de influir en los pensamientos o emociones de un grupo, y cambiar su comportamiento (p. 49)

proprietor/propietario persona que recibía del rey de Inglaterra el derecho legal y exclusivo sobre tierras coloniales en América y de quien se esperaba que administrara las tierras de acuerdo a las leyes inglesas (p. 24)

protectionist/proteccionista alguien que aboga por la protección gubernamental de productores y fabricantes domésticos mediante restricciones sobre las importaciones (p. 327)

protective tariff/arancel proteccionista impuesto elevado sobre importaciones con el objetivo más bien de proteger los productos domésticos de la competencia extranjera y no para recaudar fondos (p. 108)

protectorate/protectorado país que es técnicamente independiente pero cuyos gobierno y economía son controlados por una potencia mayor; la nación o región dominada por una potencia mayor (p. 385)

public land/tierra pública terrenos pertenecientes a un gobierno nacional y, por tanto, al pueblo (p. 64)

pump priming/inyección monetaria dinero gubernamental invertido en la economía para estimular una autorecuperación económica (p. 552)

purge/purga destitución obligatoria en gran escala de funcionarios que muestran señales de deslealtad hacia sus superiores (p. 611)

R

racism/racismo creencia de que una raza en particular es superior a las demás (p. 682)

reactinary government/gobierno reaccionario gobierno que se caracteriza por su política ultraconservadora (p. 700)

real wages/salario real ingreso ajustado para compensar el poder adquisitivo reducido debido a la inflación (p. 290)

realism/realismo movimiento literario de influencia europea que pretende una representación fiel de la naturaleza o de la vida real sin idealización (p. 331)

rebate/devolución descuento en forma de un reembolso de dinero o rebaja en los pagos de un producto o servicio (p. 279)

recall/elección revocatoria destitución de un funcionario electo por los votantes en elecciones especiales (p. 406)

recession/recesión retroceso en la economía de un país caracterizado por la reducción de sus actividades económicas (p. 564)

reciprocity/reciprocidad descenso mutuo de las barreras arancelarias entre las naciones; reconocimiento

de uno de dos países de la validez de privilegios otorgados por el otro (p. 372)

rediscount/redescuento honorario pequeño que el Banco de la Reserva Federal cobra a un banco miembro al aceptar el pagaré de un negocio (p. 440)

referendum/referéndum proceso mediante el cual el pueblo puede votar directamente sobre una ley propuesta (p. 406)

reparation/indemnización pagos hechos por las naciones derrotadas en una guerra como castigo por los daños causados a otros países (p. 485)

republic/república gobierno en el cual el poder descansa en los ciudadanos que votan para que otras personas los representen (p. 49)

revenue sharing/repartición de ingresos plan para compartir o dividir ingresos (p. 737)

revenue tariff/arancel sobre ingresos impuesto aduanal pequeño sobre importaciones con el propósito más bien de recaudar fondos para el gobierno y no para proteger productos domésticos de la competencia extranjera (p. 108)

rider/adición marginal enmienda no relacionada a un proyecto de ley bajo consideración legislativa (p. 323)

S

salutary neglect/negligencia saludable política de no interferencia de una nación gobernante con el objetivo de producir un efecto beneficioso (p. 42)

satellite nation/nación satélite naciones de Europa oriental bajo la dominación política y económica de la Unión Soviética; país controlado o dominado por otro más poderoso (p. 611)

scab/rompehuelga trabajadores sustitutos no sindicalizados durante una huelga o miembros del sindicato que se niegan a declararse en huelga y continúan trabajando (p. 293)

scrip/vale dinero que sólo puede ser usado en una tienda de la compañía (p. 291)

search-and-destroy strategy/estrategia de búsqueda y destrucción táctica militar empleada para forzar al enemigo a un combate abierto (p. 705)

secession/secesión retiro formal de una organización (p. 187)

securities/valores acciones, bonos y otros instrumentos financieros objetos de transacciones en un mercado financiero (p. 514)

segregation/segregación establecimiento de la separación de grupos raciales en escuelas, edificios de vivienda y otras áreas públicas (p. 227)

separation of powers/separación de poderes principio del gobierno estadounidense por el cual el poder se divide en tres ramas: ejecutiva, legislativa y judicial, y cada una verifique lo que efectúen las otras dos (p. 76)

sexism/sexismo prejuicio o discriminación basada en la identidad sexual (p. 689)

sharecropper/aparceros trabajadores agrícolas que cultivaban parte de la tierra de otra persona, recibían abastecimientos y equipos del dueño y en cambio le entregaban a éste parte de la cosecha (p. 213)

shogun/shogun perteneciente a la dinastía de gobernantes militares que controló Japón hasta la revolución de 1867-1868; comandante en jefe japonés (p. 13)

shuttle diplomacy/diplomacia viajera negociaciones efectuadas por un intermediario que viaja frecuentemente entre los contendientes (p. 717)

sit-in/huelga de brazos caídos ocupar asientos o permanecer sentados en el piso de un establecimiento como forma de protesta (p. 676)

social contract/contrato social acuerdo entre individuos para formar una sociedad organizada que define y limita los derechos y deberes de cada cual (p. 50)

social Darwinism/darwinismo social teoría sociológica que afirma que sólo los mejores adaptados sobreviven la competencia social y experimentan adelantos sociales (p. 282)

social gospel/evangelio social aplicación por organizaciones religiosas de los principios cristianos a los problemas sociales (p. 399)

socialism/socialismo sistema económico en el cual el gobierno es dueño en parte y controla la producción y distribución de los bienes que se producen (p. 164)

speculation/especulación empresa comercial riesgosa basada en compra o venta con la intención de obtener grandes ganancias de forma rápida (p. 64)

sphere of influence/esfera de influencia área en China a finales del siglo XIX donde el comercio era controlado por una potencia extranjera (p. 390)

spoils system/sistema de acaparamiento procedimiento de destituir a los trabajadores en cargos gubernamentales afiliados al partido derrotado por los partidarios del partido vencedor (p. 155)

stagflation/recesión con inflación inflación persistente combinada con una demanda de consumo estancada y una tasa relativamente alta de desempleo (p. 736)

student deferment/aplazamiento estudiantil posposición del servicio militar (p. 709)

subversives/subversivos personas que trabajan en secreto con la intención de derrocar o debilitar un gobierno o sistema político (p. 627)

summit/conferencia cumbre encuentro diplomático de las superpotencias; conferencia de funcionarios gubernamentales de alto nivel (p. 714)

supply-side economics/economía de oferta política económica diseñada para aumentar la oferta global o para desplazar la curva de oferta global hacia la derecha (p. 755)

T

teach-in/teach-in conferencia, debate y discusión de temas polémicos (p. 710)

technological unemployment/desempleo tecnológico empleos perdidos como resultado de maquinarias efectuando labores anteriormente realizadas por seres humanos (p. 487)

tenant farmer/agricultor arrendatario trabajador agrícola que arrendaba y cultivaba la tierra de otra persona y pagaba el arrendamiento con dinero o con una parte de la cosecha (p. 213)

textile/textil tela, especialmente tejida o de punto; paños (p. 147)

third party/tercer partido partido político menor funcionando aparte de otros dos grandes partidos en una nación o estado que se caracteriza normalmente por us sistema bipartidista (p. 347)

toll/peaje precio que se cobra por el uso de un medio de transportación (p. 142)

totalitarian/totalitario tipo de gobierno controlado por una persona o partido; supresión de la libertad y control de cada aspecto de la vida (p. 581)

township/municipalidad unidad local de gobierno dentro de un condado (p. 320)

trade deficit/déficit comercial situación económica en la cual el valor de las importaciones de una nación es mayor que el valor de sus exportaciones (p. 785)

treason/traición intento de derrocar el gobierno del estado al que la persona le debe lealtad (p. 49)

trust/trust combinación de compañías para obtener el control de una industria y reducir la competencia (p. 277)

turnpike/carretera de peaje vía cerrada con una barrera donde los viajeros se detienen a pagar un precio para poder usarla (p. 142)

U

ultimatum/ultimátum una exigencia que traerá graves consecuencias si es ignorada (p. 145)

unicameral/unicameral legislatura compuesta de una sola cámara (p. 63)

urban renewal/renovación urbana programa de construcción para reemplazar o restaurar una ciudad o un área urbana (p. 725)

V

vaudeville/vodevil entretenimiento que consiste en varios actos representados en un escenario (p. 252)

vertical integration/integración vertical unión de negocios que desarrollan diferentes, aunque relacionadas, actividades o procesos (p. 277)

veto/veto acción por la cual un ejecutivo rechaza un proyecto de ley sometido por una legislatura; negativa a aprobar (p. 62)

victory gardens/jardines de la victoria jardines donde se cosechan los vegetales propios, especialmente durante tiempos de guerra (p. 470)

vigilance committee/comité de vigilancia organización de ciudadanos que toma la ley en sus propias manos para su protección (p. 252)

W

ward/barriada electoral división de una ciudad con propósitos representativos, electorales o administrativos (p. 318)

war of national liberation/guerra de liberación nacional conflicto con el propósito de liberar una nación del control de otra (p. 702)

welfare capitalism/capitalismo de bienestar sistema de programas benéficos ofrecido a los trabajadores por los empresarios con el objetivo de reducir el atractivo de los sindicatos (p. 488)

"Western"/"Oeste" novela, narración o película de Hollywood que representa la vida en el Oeste de los Estados Unidos durante la segunda mitad del siglo XIX (p. 253)

wetland/tierras pantanosas terrenos o áreas que contienen mucha humedad (p. 789)

wildcat strike/huelga ilegal suspensión del trabajo iniciada por un grupo de trabajadores sin la aprobación formal del sindicato o en violación de un contrato (p. 601)

Y

yellow journalism/prensa amarilla tipo de reportaje periodístico a finales de la década de 1890 que presentaba titulares e historias sensacionalistas (p. 333)

Spanish Glossary

Italicized page numbers refer to illustrations. Preceding the page number, abbreviations refer to a map (m), chart (c), photograph or other picture (p), graph (g), cartoon (crt), or painting (ptg). Quoted material is referenced with the abbreviation (q) before the appropriate page number.

A

B

F

K

Index

N

Index

Index

Q

R

S

Index

W

Index

X

Y

Z

Acknowledgments

★ ★

36 "Constitution of the Five Nations," from William N. Fenton, ed., *Parker on the Iroquois*, Copyright © 1868 by Syracuse University Press; used by permission. **37** "Navajo Song of the Rain Chant," from Nataline Curtis, ed., *The Indians' Book*, Harper and Brothers, 1907; used by permission. **123** Southgate letter from James A. Henretta, et al, *America's History*, Chicago: Dorsey Press, 1987. **254** From Mark Twain, *Roughing It*. Berkeley: University of California Press, 1972. **386** From *Official Proceedings of the Democratic National Convention. . . . 1890*, reprinted in *The Annals of America*, vol. 12. Chicago: Encyclopaedia Britannica, 1968. **402** From Theodore Dreiser, *Sister Carrie*. New York: W.W. Norton, Critical Ed., 1970. **498** "Recuerdo" by Edna St. Vincent Millay, From *Collected Poems*, Harper & Row, Copyright © 1922, 1950 by Edna St. Vincent Millay. Reprinted by permission of Elizabeth Barnett, Literary Executor. **499** "Dream Boogie," reprinted by permission of Harold Ober Associates, Inc. Copyright © 1932, 1951 by Langston Hughes, Copyright renewed 1979 by George Houston Bass. **572** From John Steinbeck, *The Grapes of Wrath*, Copyright © 1939, renewed © 1967 by John Steinbeck. Used by permission of Viking Penguin, a division of Penguin Books USA, Inc. **605** Ota excerpt from *"The Good War": An Oral History of World War Two* by Studs Terkel. Copyright © 1984. Reprint by permission of Pantheon Books, a division of Random House. **794** From *Hunger of Memory* by Richard Rodriguez. Copyright © 1981 by Richard Rodriguez. Reprinted by permission of David R. Godine, Publisher. **852** "I Have a Dream" copyright © 1963 by Martin Luther King, Jr. Used by permission, Joan Daves Agency.

Photo Credits

★ ★

Archive; **345** Library of Congress; **346** North Wind Picture Archive; **347** Frank & Maria-Therese Wood/The Picture Bank; **348** Bettmann Archive; **349** FPG International; **351** From THE DEPRESSION YEARS AS PHOTOGRAPHED BY ARTHUR ROTHSTEIN, Dover Publications, Inc.; **352** National Portrait Gallery, Smithsonian Institution, Art Resource, NY; **353** (l) National Portrait Gallery, Smithsonian Institution/Art Resource, NY, (r) Frank & Maria-Therese Wood/The Picture Bank; **354** Courtesy Metropolitan Life Insurance Company; **355** (l) Archive Photos, (r) William Johnson/Stock Boston; **357** Frank & Maria-Therese Wood/The Picture Bank; **358** (l) The Metropolitan Museum of Art, New York. Gift of Edith Minturn Phelps Stokes (Mrs. I.N. Phelps Stokes), 1938, (r) Frank & Maria-Therese Wood/The Picture Bank; **360** (t) Steve Smith/H. Armstrong Roberts, (bl) M. Roessler/H. Armstrong Roberts, (br) file photo; **361** (t) The Auschutz Collection, Denver, CO, (bl) Bob Mullenix, (br) KS Studios; **362** (t) Courtesy AT&T, (b) Pictorial History Research; **363** (tl) Collection of Picture Research Consultants Inc., (tr) Library of Congress, (bl) Frank & Maria-Therese Wood/The Picture Bank; **364** (l) David Diaz Guerrero/Collection of Roddy Moore, (r) Los Angeles County Museum of Art, Los Angeles County Fund, CLIFF DWELLERS by George Bellows; **365** (tl) Library of Congress, (tr) Mark Burnett, (bl) Boltin Picture Library; **366** (t) file photo, (bl) Brown Brothers, (br) David Austen/Stock Boston; **367** (t) SEF/Art Resource, NY, (cl) Giraudon/Art Resource, NY, (cr,bl) Bettmann Archive, (br) Courtesy Ford Motor Company; **368** Mark Sexton/Peabody Essex Museum; **369** (t) Courtesy U. S. Naval Academy Museum, (b) Bettmann Archive; **370** Courtesy Hawaii Visitor's Bureau; **371** Bettmann Archive; **372** (l) file photo, (r) Johnny Johnson; **374** North Wind Picture Archives; **375** Collection of David J. and Janice L. Frent; **376** (l) The Chicago Historical Society, (r) file photo; **378** Brown Brothers; **379 380** Bettmann Archive; **381** National Archives; **382** Bettmann Archive; **383** (l) Smithsonian Institution, (r) Kenji Kerins; **385** California Museum of Photography; **386** Library of Congress; **387** Smithsonian Institution; **389** Bettmann Archive; **390** Superstock; **392** National Guard Bureau; **394** Boltin Picture Library; **395** (t) The Lone Tenement, by George Bellows. Chester Dale Collection ©1995 Board of Trustees, National Gallery of Art, Washington, (b) Larry Hamill; **396** Courtesy Labor Archives and Research Center, San Francisco State University; **398** (l) Charles Phelps Cushing/H. Armstrong Roberts, (r) Bettmann Archive; **399** Culver Pictures; **401 402** Brown Brothers; **403** FPG International; **404** Nebraska State Historical Society; **406** (l) Superstock, (r) Schlesinger Library, Radcliffe College; **408** (l) Library of Congress, (r) UPI/Bettmann; **409** (l) Mark Burnett/Central Ohio Council of

B S A, (r) Joseph DiChello; **411** Courtesy, American Jewish Historical Society, Waltham, MA; **412** Smithsonian Institution; **413** (l) Chicago Historical Society, (r) Lewis Hine/International Museum of Photography at George Eastman House; **414** (l) courtesy of the NAACP, (r) Library of Congress; **415** Bettmann Archive; **416** H. Armstrong Roberts; **417** Library of Congress; **418** North Wind Picture Archives; **419** Theodore Roosevelt Collection, Harvard College Library; **420** Courtesy of AT&T; **421** (t) file photo, (b) National Baseball Library; **422** Devaney Stock Photos; **423 424** Brown Brothers; **425** (l) Craig Kramer, (r) Paul Nesbit; **427** Lloyd Lemmermann; **428** Theodore Roosevelt Collection, Harvard College Library by permission of the Houghton Library, Harvard University; **429** file photo; **430** (l) Culver Pictures, (r) Geoff Butler; **432** Theodore Roosevelt Collection/ The Houghton Library-Harvard University; **433** (t) file photo, (b) Library of Congress; **434** Library of Congress; **437** Smithsonian Institution; **438** (l) The New York Historical Society, (r) Smithsonian Institution; **439** (l) file photo, (r) Tim Courlas Photography; **442** National Portrait Gallery, Smithsonian Institution/Art Resource, NY; **444** H. Armstrong Roberts; **446** (tr) Henry Ford Museum, (c) W. H. Clark/H. Armstrong Roberts, (bl) H. Armstrong Roberts, (br) Brown Brothers; **447** (tl,b) H. Armstrong Roberts, (tr) Culver Pictures; **449** (t) Lloyd Lemmermann, (b) Library of Congress; **450** (l) file photo, (c) National Museum of American Art, Washington, DC/Art Resource, NY, (r) Collection of Picture Research Consultants, Inc.; **451** (l) Collection of Colonel Stuart S. Corning, photo ©Rob Huntley/Lightstream, (r) National Archives; **452** (t) SEF/Art Resource, NY, (c) United Nations, (bl) Franklin D. Roosevelt Library, (br) Museum of the City of New York; **453** (t) file photo, (b) H. Armstrong Roberts; **454** Bettmann Archive; **455** (tl) Library of Congress, (tr) Allies Day, May 1917 by Childe Hassam. Gift of Ethelyn McKinney in memory of her brother, Glenn Ford McKinney, ©1995 Board of Trustee, National Gallery of Art, Washington, (bl) Library of Congress; **456** Bettmann Archive; **457** UPI/Bettmann; **458** Bettmann Archive; **459** Archive Photos; **460 462** Bettmann Archive; **463** (l) UPI/Bettmann, (r) file photo; **464** (l) National Archives, (r) Bettmann Archive; **466** (l) Library of Congress, (r) Superstock; **467** Collection of Colonel Stuart S. Corning. Photo by Rob Huntley/Lightstream; **468** Library of Congress; **469** Bettmann Archive; **470** American Red Cross, Washington, DC; **471** Archive Photos; **472** Library of Congress; **473 474** Collection of Colonel Stuart S. Corning. Photo by Rob Huntley/Lightstream; **475** National Portrait Gallery, Smithsonian Institution/Art Resource, NY; **476** Bettmann Archive; **477** file photo; **479** UPI/Bettmann; **480** Museo Nacional de Arte Moderno, Mexico City; **482** Private collection, photo by Rob Huntley/Lightstream; **483** (t)

Thomas Hart Benton "City Activities with Dance Hall" from America Today, 1930. Distemper and egg tempera with oil glaze on gessoed linen. Size: 92x134" Collection, The Equitable Life Assurance Society of the United States. Photo 1988 by Dorothy Zeidman, (b) ©1992 Jan White Brantley. Courtesy Louisiana Jazz Club Collection, Louisiana State Museum; **484 485 487** Bettmann Archive; **489** (t) UPI/Bettmann, (b) Bettmann Archive; **490** Collection of David J. and Janice L. Frent; **491 492** file photo; **493** Archive Photos; **495** (l) Ford Motor Company, (r) Collection of Colonel Stuart S. Corning. Photo by Rob Huntley/ Lightstream; **496** (l) National Museum of American Art, Smithsonian Institution, Washington, DC/Art Resource, NY, (r) Bettmann Archive; **497** Superstock; **498** (l) Brown Brothers, (r) National Museum of American Art, Washington, DC/Art Resource, NY, (b) Bettmann Archive; **499** National Museum of American Art, Washington, DC/Art Resource, NY; **500** Smithsonian Institution; **501** (l) Bettmann Archive, (r) Archive Photos; **502** Everett Collection, Inc.; **503** (l) Matt Meadows, (r) Studiohio; **504 505 506** Bettmann Archive; **507** The Howard University Gallery of Art, Washington, D.C.; **508** National Portrait Gallery, Smithsonian Institution/Art Resource, NY; **510** Smithsonian Institution; **511** (t) National Museum of American Art, Washington, DC/Art Resource, NY, (b) Courtesy Department of the Treasury, Bureau of Alcohol, Tobacco and Firearms; **512** Bettmann Archive; **513** (l) Gerald Peters Gallery, New York, (r) Courtesy Department of the Treasury, Bureau of Alcohol, Tobacco and Firearms; **514** UPI/Bettmann; **516** Arthur Beck/Photo Researchers; **518** (l) Culver Pictures, (r) UPI/Bettmann; **519** George Meany Memorial Archives; **521** Dallas Museum of Art; **522** UPI/Bettmann; **523** Library of Congress; **525** National Portrait Gallery, Washington, DC/Art Resource, NY; **526** file photo; **527** (l) Bettmann Archive, (r) Culver Pictures; **528** file photo; **529** The Oakland Museum; **530** UPI/Bettmann; **531** Collection of the Whitney Museum of American Art Purchase; **532** Franklin D. Roosevelt Library; **533** UPI/Bettmann; **534** Library of Congress; **536** (t) Archive Photos/Jon Leifert, (c) Aaron Haupt Photography, (bl) Superstock, (br) Popperfoto/Archive Photo; **537** (t) Aaron Haupt Photography, (cl) Archive Photos, (cr,b) Bettmann Archive; **539** (t) UPI/Bettmann, (b) Collection of Colonel Stuart S. Corning. Photo by Rob Huntley/ Lightstream; **540** (l) U. S. Army, (r) Warren Motts Photographic Center, (b) Library of Congress; **541** (t) Library of Congress, (b) Bettmann Archive; **542** (tr) Hugo Jaeger/Life Magazine ©Time Warner, Inc, (c) UPI, (br) Franklin D. Roosevelt Library; **543** (tl) Bettmann Archive, (tr) Topham Picture Source/The Image Works, (b) United Nations; **544** Aaron Haupt Photography; **545** (tl,bl) Library of Congress, (r) The But-